EARLIEST TENNESSEE LAND RECORDS

&

EARLIEST TENNESSEE LAND HISTORY

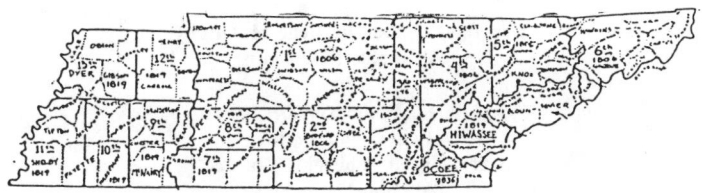

IRENE M. GRIFFEY

CERTIFIED GENEALOGIST

CLEARFIELD

Printed for
Clearfield Company, Inc. by
Genealogical Publishing Co., Inc.
Baltimore, Maryland
2000

International Standard Book Number: 0-8063-5041-5

Made in the United States of America

TABLE OF CONTENTS

CREDITS

My sincere thanks go to Ann Evans Alley, archivist with The Tennessee State Library and Archives. Without her inspiration, consistent prodding, and constant reminders, this work of ten years would never have been completed.

Thanks also go to Jill Hastings-Johnson, archivist of Montgomery County, Tennessee, for help in many different ways.

Thanks also to all those other people who helped in so many ways.

INTRODUCTION

The land is where "IT" is. The "IT," of course, represents the history of our state and our ancestors. We have moved the soil around a bit, built a few skyscrapers here and there, and dammed up the streams; but the soil is still the same soil our ancestors trudged across, always in search of better land. Historians and genealogists alike have resisted the legalese in land records and missed the most accurate story of our ancestors. As areas became heavily populated, the value of land increased. Settlers were able to sell their land for enough to purchase twice that amount on the frontier. Thus, following the movement of our ancestors leads to a study in migration, geography, economics, and history. It is true that many of the first purchasers were land speculators, but they divided larger tracts into smaller tracts and went back to their home community to find purchasers.

The unfortunate transfer of governmental ownership, from North Carolina to the United States South of the River Ohio (a territory) and then to Tennessee, has added much to the confusion. However, when one simply understands the cession act as a mere deed transferring ownership, understanding becomes clearer. Only the unsurveyed and vacant land was transferred from one governmental entity to another. Each cession act included the same restriction—that the North Carolina Revolutionary Continental soldier's promise of land must be satisfied. That was the problem. No one could say how much land would be needed to "pay off" the soldiers should the military reservation not be sufficient. This "pay off" had to be made to prevent litigation between North Carolina and its citizenry. So, the title transferred to the United States contained this restriction. Since the North Carolina restriction had not been completed, it was necessary that the "pay off" clause be included in the transfer to Tennessee.

This land history has been an attempt to clear up some of the confusion of the Tennessee land records with the hope that they can be restored to their proper status in research. The legal complication caused the inclusion of hundreds of footnotes so that the reader can refer to the law for verification and complete understanding. Just as we understand today's laws, which affect our day-to-day life, our ancestors understood the laws affecting their lives. They were familiar with the land laws of their day; to anticipate their actions, we, too, must be familiar with these same laws.

Having been involved with the land all of my adult life, this work has been a labor of love. It is hoped that the information included will be of benefit to the reader.

The colonies, and those states formed from the colonies, pioneered the transfer of land from the government to the individual. The thirteen original colonies together with Kentucky, Maine, Tennessee, Texas, Vermont and later Hawaii and West Virginia became known as the state land states in which the land was surveyed in metes (distances) and bounds (boundary lines) after the individual had selected it. The federal government benefited from the states' earlier experiences of overlapping boundary lines. When it began disposal of its land with the Land Ordinance of 1785—a comparatively late date—a system was incorporated requiring the land to be surveyed in townships and ranges prior to it being offered for sale. This is called the rectangular survey system. Those states having federal lands for sale became known as the public land states. The popular terms "public land" and "state land" are now used to distinguish between land owned and granted by the federal government and that owned and granted by private states.[1] In state land states tracts were surveyed only after selection, therefore the two land granting methods differ greatly. Understanding Tennessee land requires an understanding of both survey practices because portions of the land that are now Tennessee, were controlled at different times by the state land states of North Carolina and Tennessee, as well as the public land federal government. The two very different methods of surveying controlled the remaining steps in the land granting or patenting process.

[1]E. Wade Hone, *Land & Property Research in the United States* (Salt Lake City: Ancestry, Inc.., 1997), pages 59 & 102. State land states are: Connecticut, Delaware, Georgia, Hawaii, Kentucky, Maine, Maryland, Massachusetts, New Hampshire, New Jersey, New York, North Carolina, Pennsylvania, Rhode Island, South Carolina, Tennessee, Texas, Vermont, Virginia, West Virginia. Public land states are: Alabama, Alaska, Arizona, Arkansas, California, Colorado, Florida, Idaho, Illinois, Indiana, Iowa, Kansas, Louisiana, Michigan, Minnesota, Mississippi, Missouri, Montana, Nebraska, Nevada, New Mexico, North Dakota, Ohio, Oklahoma, Oregon, South Dakota, Utah, Washington, Wisconsin, Wyoming.

PUBLIC LAND GRANTING SYSTEM

The Northwest Ordinance of 1785 was instituted by the federal government and included the following provisions:[2]

- The land should be purchased from the Indians prior to settlement
- Land should be surveyed and laid out in townships and sections (rectangular survey system based on meridians and base lines) before settlement
- The first tracts surveyed should be drawn by lot for military bounties that had been promised earlier
- Remaining tracts should then be offered for sale at public auction in township and section units
- Certain lands should be set aside for educational purposes
- Absolute (or fee simple) title should be transferred with all lands

The land was surveyed into townships (six mile squares) using division lines called meridian and base lines. Each township was then divided into thirty-six numbered sections of six hundred and forty acres or one square mile each. The sections were numbered according to their distance and direction from the meridian and base lines. The land was then offered for sale to the individual in sections or fractional sections.

The portions of the Northwest Ordinance of 1785 most important to the study of Tennessee land when it fell under the control of the federal

[2]Val D. Greenwood, *The Researcher's Guide to American Genealogy*, 3rd edition (Baltimore: Genealogical Publishing Company, Inc., 2000), pages 375-397.

- That the land should be purchased from the Indians prior to settlement
- That lands should be reserved for educational purposes

Prior to North Carolina's ceding or deeding of the land to the United States in 1789, neither of these policies was followed completely in Tennessee.

EARLY DISPOSAL OF TENNESSEE LAND

Because North Carolina needed money with which to finance rapidly accumulating expenses for the Revolutionary War, land offices were opened to raise funds from the sale of the vacant and unappropriated land—vacant land which had not been granted by the crown. Settlement, at that time, was limited to the northeastern corner of Tennessee.

Transferring title for Tennessee land from the government to the individual is different from that of any other state, but once the basic terminology and record keeping system has been mastered, research can easily fall into place. It can be complex and confusing if one tries to interpret the records separate and apart from a thorough knowledge of Tennessee history, or tries to use the systems of other states as a guide. Closely associated with the land granting system from 1770 to 1836 was acquisition of the land from the Indians which occurred in patchwork fashion over the entire state. This, together with the area at various times coming under the control of North Carolina, Territory of the United States South of the River Ohio, and finally the State of Tennessee, contributes greatly to the confusion and requires an accurate understanding of each government's land policies. It is hoped this paper will aid in clearing some of the confusion.

Some have theorized that because of a giant land fraud, in which some of the highest officials of the state were involved, the records are not credible. There were high officials who obtained land fraudulently, but the methods they used affected only a few of the official records, although it did result in a loss of revenue for North Carolina. It is true that when some of the criminals knew they had been discovered they tried to destroy some of the records.[3] But the most important records had already been placed in the official land office of North Carolina, where they were exceptionally well preserved. They are now preserved by the North Carolina Archives. These records have been microfilmed and the films are available in several research centers.[4] An exact inventory of the records held by each repository is not given, since the inventory changes as new records are acquired and an accurate list today might not suffice at a later date.

The loss suffered by North Carolina was caused by some crooks obtaining land at a lesser price than they were entitled and some citizens being cheated out of land to which they were entitled. But the fraud had little effect on the official records. With the exception of the mountainous land surveyed with very primitive tools, the courts have settled any question of title. It was the author's good fortune to spend many hours in the land office of North Carolina before it was dismantled and the records microfilmed. There is no substitute for time spent in examining the records retained in the same manner in which they were created.

When the citizens of Tennessee realized they had no records for their most prized procession, the land, they arranged with North Carolina

[3]Legislation required the surveys to be made in the order of the recording of the entries in the entry books. Some of the fraudulent practices included leaving blanks between entries so that favorites could be placed ahead of other people. Currently, the only land in Tennessee which cannot be traced to the grants appears to be that in the mountainous area where exact surveying with primitive instruments was impossible.

[4]All the records are available in the North Carolina State Archives; microfilm copies of the warrants and surveys are in the Tennessee State Library & Archives, together with John Overton's hand copied transcripts of the entry books and grant books. Many of the records, including microfilms of the North Carolina land grant books are available in the Family History Library, Salt Lake City, Utah.

to send agents there to make copies of those records pertaining to Tennessee. John Overton and his associates, appointed by the Tennessee Legislature, performed a mammoth job in the North Carolina land office by searching for and hand copying those records applicable to Tennessee thus reconstructing the Tennessee land office.[5] The land office in North Carolina had recorded the grants pertaining to Tennessee in the same books as other North Carolina land. So, it was by the search and copy method that the Overton team extracted and copied the Tennessee grants. The most damaging culprit to these reconstructed records kept in Tennessee has been neglect and mismanagement. The official Tennessee land office was moved several times before finding a permanent resting place in the Tennessee State Library and Archives. It is supposed that some records were lost or misplaced during these moves, but the office itself appears to have been kept intact for some time before it was finally dismantled and microfilmed by persons who failed to realize the importance of retaining as nearly as possible the order in which the records originated.

North Carolina, the parent of Tennessee, granted most of the land in the present state of Tennessee. Nearly all of the land warrants were issued by North Carolina. Although the area was controlled at different times by three different governments, North Carolina controlled the transfer of the land to the individual well into the 1800s and it is their records with which we are most concerned.[6]

The earliest land offices applicable to Tennessee were:

- The Washington and Sullivan County land offices
- The John Armstrong office, also called the Hillsboro office
- The military office operated by Martin Armstrong and situated in Nashville, Tennessee

WASHINGTON AND SULLIVAN COUNTY LAND OFFICES

Washington County was formed, and a land office opened there in the present state of Tennessee in 1777. When first formed, the boundaries of Washington County reached west to the Mississippi. For approximately two years, until the formation of Sullivan County in 1779, Washington County covered the entire state of Tennessee. These counties were formed for the disposal of North Carolina frontier land. At that time, only a very small portion of this area had been cleared of Indian title and settlement was confined to the extreme northeast corner of Tennessee.[7] The boundaries of Washington County when formed were as follows:

Beginning at the most northwesterly part of the county of Wilkes on the Virginia Line; thence running with the Line of Wilkes County, to a point thirty six miles south of the Virginia Line; thence due west, to the ridge of the great Iron Mountain which heretofore divided the hunting grounds of the Overhill Cherokees, from those

---

[5]"An Act concerning the agent from this State and the State of North Carolina," 8 November 1803, George Roulstone, compiler, *Acts Passed at the First Session of the State of Tennessee* (Knoxville: George Roulstone, 1803), chapters 81 & 82.

[6]See footnote 4 for location of North Carolina original and microfilms of the land records in Tennessee.

[7]See the Appendix for a detailed description of applicable Indian treaties. Those treaties signed before 1785 were: (1) Treaty of Lochabar, 1770. Between Virginia and the Cherokees, the treaty conveyed lands in Virginia, West Virginia, Kentucky, and a small strip of the upper Watauga Valley in Tennessee. It marks the first settlements on the north banks of the Holston. (2) Transylvania Purchase, 1775. Richard Henderson & Company purchased from the Cherokees all the lands lying between the Kentucky, Ohio, and Cumberland Rivers and extending eastward along the north bank of the Holston to a point where it intersects the Virginia line. (3) Avery's Treaty, 1777. Between the Cherokees and Virginia and North Carolina, this treaty confirmed the Watauga cessions made in 1775.

of the middle settlements and valley; thence running a southwesterly course, along the said ridge, to the Unacoy Mountain, where the trading path crosses the same from the valley to the Overhills; thence south with the line of this state, adjoining the state of South Carolina; thence due west to the great river Mississippi; thence up the said river the courses thereof, to a point due west from the beginning; thence due east with the line of this state to the beginning; and it is hereby declared, that all that part of this state comprehended with the lines aforesaid shall from henceforth be and remain the county of Washington, and shall be, and is hereby declared to be part of the district of Salisbury. [8]

Sullivan County was formed from Washington County with dividing boundaries as follows:

. . . a line beginning at the steep rock; thence running along the dividing ridge that divides the waters of the Great Kanawee and Tennessee, to the head of Indian Creek; thence along the ridge that divides the waters of Holstein and Watauga, to the mouth of Watauga; thence a direct line, to the highest part of the Chimney Top Mountain, at the Indian boundary; and all that part of said county of Washington which lies northwardly of said dividing line, shall be erected into a new and distinct county, by the name of Sullivan county; and that

[8]"An Act for erecting the District of Washington into a County by the name of Washington County" November 1777, Walter Clark, editor, *The State Records of North Carolina*, 26 Vols. (Goldsboro, North Carolina: Nash Brothers, 1907), 24: 141-142, chapter 31.

all that other part of said county which lies southwardly of said dividing line, shall continue and remain a distinct county, by the name of Washington. [9]

An entry taker was assigned to each land office as it was opened. Guidelines were legislated for the keeping of the records by the entry taker. John Carter was appointed entry taker of Washington County and entries were accepted for land lying both west and east of the boundary of the treaty of Long Island. [10] It was not difficult to ignore the Indians' right of possession since they were actively assisting the British at the time.

The 1777 land office legislation set the price and provided for the sale of land to any citizen, or person willing to become a citizen, of North Carolina. The land office entry taker was authorized to administer the oath of allegiance as prescribed by the law of North Carolina. Men in military service of either North Carolina or the United States were exempt from the oath. The purchaser was offered six hundred forty acres of land for himself, one hundred acres for his wife, and one hundred acres for each of his children at the rate of two pounds ten shillings per hundred acres, plus fees of the entry taker and surveyor. More than this amount could be purchased at the rate of five pounds per hundred acres.

[9]"An Act for dividing the County of Washington for securing the rights of such persons in the County of Washington as lie between the river Holstein and the line lately run by the Commissioners of this State and the State of Virginia, as the dividing line between the said States; and for dividing the said County of Washington into two distinct Counties, and for other purposes . . . ." October 1779, Clark, *State Records of North Carolina*, 24: 300-302, chapter 29.

[10]Treaty of Long Island, also known as Avery's Treaty. "...Beginning on the Kentucky line, running thence to the Holston at the mouth of Cloud's Creek; thence to the highest point of the Highrock or Chimneytop mountain; thence to the Nolichucky at the mouth of Camp Creek; thence a south east course to the top of the ridge of the great Iron mountain." This line is also known as Brown's line. William Robertson Garrett and Albert Virgil Goodpasture, *History of Tennessee, Its People and Its Institutions* (Nashville: Brandon Printing Co., 1900), page 131.

Limitations were set at one thousand acres for land that lay between the lines of land already surveyed or six hundred forty acres where the land was bounded in any part by vacant lands.[11] Relatively small tracts were purchased at this time.

Both the county offices and the office of John Armstrong were closed by the North Carolina legislative act of May 25, 1784, and they were never reopened.[12] Thomas Jefferson, United States secretary of state, in his report to Congress on 8 November 1791, listed the acreage sold from these offices as:[13]

- Washington County entries issued

Entries & grants issued	746,362.50 acres
Leaving void (probably located beyond the Indian boundary)	214,549.75 acres
	531,812.75 acres

- Sullivan County entries issued

Entries & grants issued	240,524 acres
Leaving many void or lapsed	173,332 acres
	67,192 acres

Many of these entries, estimated as being located west of the Indian boundary line known as Brown's Line, were presented to the courts for trial and were declared void because the land was not

open for entry.[14]

THE HILLSBORO OR THE JOHN ARMSTRONG OFFICE

By the legislative act of January 1781,[15] it was directed that all purchases made for the use of the public by the state should be paid for in specie, in certificates, or in circulating currency according to the par of exchange at the time of payment.[16] By the legislative Act of April 1782,[17] *indented certificates* were issued to the officers and soldiers of the Continental Line, to make good the losses sustained by them from the depreciation of the paper currency and other causes. For the purpose of redeeming these certificates and discharging the arrears due to the army, the legislative act of April 1783[18] was passed for establishing a

---

[11]"An Act for establishing Offices for receiving Entries of Claims for Lands in the several Counties within this State, for ascertaining the Method of obtaining Titles to the same, and for other Purposes therein mentioned," November 1777, Clark, *State Records of North Carolina*, 24:43-48, chapter 1.

[12]"An Act to Prevent Doubts as to the Rights of Sovereignty and Jurisdiction in and Over the Territory Lying West of the Apalacian Mountains, for Shutting the Land Office, and for Indemnifying John Armstrong, Esq., Entry-Taker, Against Vexatious Suits for His Conduct in office," 1784, Clark, *State Records of North Carolina*, 24:398-401, chapter 7.

[13]Clarence Edwin Carter, compiler, *The Territorial Papers of the United States* Volume 4 (Washington: Government Printing Office, 1936), pages 85-100.

[14]*Jackson v. Honeycut*, William Frierson Cooper, *Tennessee Reports of Cases Argued and Determined in the Highest Courts of Law and Equity of the State of Tennessee* Volume I (St. Louis: Soule, Thomas, and Winsor, 1870), pages 25-32; *Cobb's heirs v. Conway's heirs*, John Haywood, *Supreme Court of Errors and Appeals for the State of Tennessee 1816-1817*, Volume 3 (Louisville: Fetter Law Book Company, 1909), pages 21-22. *Proffitt v. Williams*, George S. Yerger, *Reports of Cases Argued and Determined in the Supreme Court of Tennessee* Volume I (Columbia, Missouri: E. W. Stephens Publishing Company, 1912), pages 89-92; *Preston v. Brownder*, B. R. Curtis, *Reports or Decisions in The Supreme Court of The United States* Volume 3 (Boston: Little, Brown and Company, 1864), pages 485-489.

[15]"An Act for appointing District Auditors for the settlement of Public Claims . . ." September 1780, Clark, *State Records of North Carolina*, 24: 373-375, chapter 3.

[16]James Iredell, *Laws of the State of North Carolina* (Edenton: Hodge & Wills, MDCCXCI), page 412.

[17]"An Act for the relief of the Officers and Soldiers in the Continental line, and for other purposes therein mentioned," April 1782, Clark, *State Records of North Carolina*, 24: 419-422, chapter 3.

[18]"An Act for opening the Land Office for the redemption of specie and other certificates, and discharging the arrears due the army," April 1783, Clark, *State Records of North Carolina*, 24: 478-482, chapter 2.

land office. This office was opened at Hillsboro and John Armstrong was elected entry taker of that office. [19]

Since the Cherokee Indians had assisted the British in the close of the Revolutionary War, North Carolina no longer felt obligated to honor the Cherokee Indians' claim to the land and the entire western area (the present state of Tennessee) was opened for sale, except:

- A reservation where the Indians actually lived and which was bounded on the south by the southern boundary of the state, and on the north, west, and east by the Tennessee, Holston, French Broad, and Big Pigeon rivers

- The military reservation, which had been laid off in northern Middle Tennessee

- The great island in the Holston River [20]

Any citizen of the state was authorized to make entry in this office for any quantity of land, not exceeding five thousand acres, payable at the rate of ten pounds per hundred acres in *specie or specie certificates or certificates for currency*, valued by the scale of depreciation. [21] The holder of these certificates was not obligated to purchase land but could redeem the certificates for *specie.* [22] John Haywood in his *Civil and*

[19]"An Act for emitting One Hundred Thousand Pounds in Paper Currency, for the purposes of government for seventeen hundred and eighty three, for the redemption of paper currency now in circulation, and advancing to the Continental officers and soldiers part of their pay and subsistence, and for levying a tax, and appropriating the confiscated property for the redemption of the money now to be emitted," April 1783, Clark, *State Records of North Carolina*, 24: 475-478, chapter 1.

[20]"An Act for opening the Land Office for the redemption of specie . . . ," April 1783, *State Records of North Carolina*, 24:475-478, chapter 2.

[21]Ibid.

[22]"An Act for levying a Money and Specific Provisions Tax for the year One Thousand Seven Hundred and Eighty One . . ." June 1781, Clark, *State Records of North*

Political History of the State of Tennessee says:

"These certificates were issued by Boards of Auditors appointed by public authority for services performed, and articles impressed or furnished in the time of the Revolutionary War were made payable in specie . . . vast numbers of persons crowded to the office, and were so clamorous and disorderly that no business could be done in the office till the 23d, before which time they agreed to settle by lot the order in which their locations should be presented to be entered in the entry takers book. By the 25th of May, 1784, vast quantities of land were entered, and certificates to a very large amount had been paid into the public offices. [23]

It should be noted that drawing by lot was to determine the order in which the land would be surveyed and not location of the land itself, the location having already been selected by the enterer.

This office was closed May 25, 1784 in anticipation of a proposed cession of land from North Carolina to the United States, which when made was not accepted; nevertheless, this land office, as well as the county offices, never opened again. All entries made after May 25, 1784 except those made by the commissioners, who surveyed the boundary lines of the military reservation, and their attendants, the surveyors, guards, chain carriers, etc. were declared void. [24]

Carolina, 24:390-394, chapter 3.

[23]John Haywood, *The Civil and Political History of the State of Tennessee From Its Earliest Settlement Up to the Year 1796* (Glendale, California: The Arthur H. Clark Co., 1915), page 122.

[24]"An Act to Prevent Doubts as to the Rights of Sovereignty and Jurisdiction in and

In 1788 holders of John Armstrong grants west of Cumberland Mountain, which had not been registered, were allowed to register them in the county in which the holder lived. Those who owned land westward of Cumberland Mountain and not residing in the county where the land lay were allowed to register them in Hawkins County.[25] This act was extended in 1790 for two years[26] and probably later.

THE MILITARY OFFICE, ALSO CALLED MARTIN ARMSTRONG OFFICE

The military land office was opened in Nashville, Tennessee, the center of the military district, with Martin Armstrong, surveyor general.

Absalom Tatum, Isaac Shelby, and Anthony Bledsoe were appointed commissioners to superintend the laying off of the military reservation in one or more tracts. The particular boundaries of the tract were left to the discretion of the commissioners. In the winter of 1782-1783, there is indication that they designated a tract bounded on the south by the southern boundary of the state, on the north by a line parallel to this line and fifty-five miles distant, on the west by the Mississippi, and on the east by the meridian of the intersection of Elk River and the southern boundary of the state.[27] But it appears this tract was not satisfactory to

the military officers and at their request, the North Carolina Legislature, by the Act of April 1783, chapter 3, section 7, "for the prevention of disputes", passed legislation that a tract should be surveyed for that purpose as follows:

> Beginning on the Virginia line, where the Cumberland River intersects the same, thence south fifty-five miles, thence west to the Tennessee River, thence down the Tennessee to the Virginia line, thence with said Virginia line, east to the beginning.

Section 7 of chapter 19, passed in 1784, reads:

> In case it should happen that there is not a sufficient quantity of tillable land within the boundaries laid off for the officers and soldiers of the continental line of this State, the deficiency shall, and is hereby directed to be made upon any unappropriated lands within the limits of this State.[28]

There was much litigation over whether the troops were confined to the military reservation. Judge Whyte contended that the military claims were liens upon all the unappropriated land of the state. He thought that the Acts of 1780, 1782, and 1783 did not confine those claims to the military reservation. He thought those claims were entitled only to the same right of removal as other claims. The whole court decided that by the second legislative session of 1784, this right of removal extended beyond the reservation to any vacant land. They also decided a military claimant could remove his warrant, if he had entered land already

Over the Territory Lying West of the Apalacian (sic) Mountains for Shutting the Land Office, and for Indemnifying John Armstrong, Esq., Entry-Taker, Against Vexatious Suits for His Conduct in office," 1784, Clark, State Records of North Carolina, 24:563-564, chapter 12.

[25]"An Act for Relief of Persons Who Have Suffered or May Suffer by Their Grants, Deeds and Mesne [intermediate] Conveyances Not Being Proved and Registered . . . ," November 1788, Clark, State Records of North Carolina, 24:967-968, chapter 24.

[26]"An Act to Continue in Force an Act Passed at Fayetteville, in the Year One Thousand Seven Hundred and Eighty-eight . . . ," November 1790, Clark, State Records of North Carolina, 24: 80, chapter 17.

[27]Haywood, Cooper, 269-272. This publication contains John Overton's Volumes I & II Tennessee Reports.

Hughlet, Cooper, The Civil and Political History of Tennessee, page 124; Bickerstaff v. Tennessee Reports.

[28]"An Act to empower the County Surveyors to make surveys and returns . . . ," April 1784, Clark, State Records of North Carolina, 24:570-571, chapter 19.

- Make entry in the military land office for land based on service in the Continental Line of North Carolina[33]

- Make entry and purchase land in the John Armstrong office in Hillsboro[34]

- Make entry based on military service performed for the protection of Davidson County[35]

- Make entry based on services rendered in laying off the military reservation[36]

* Petition the North Carolina Legislature for special legislative grants[37]

- Make entry based on settlements made on vacant and unoccupied lands:
    a. Within the military reservation[38]
    b. South of the French Broad and Holston Rivers[39]

---

appropriated, to some other land when the tillable lands had been exhausted in the military district. They decided that the surveyor general of the district where his location was made was the exclusive judge of the right of the claimant to make the location.[29] In other cases, a contrary opinion was expressed.[30] There was no question relative to moving a warrant when the good, tillable land within the reservation was exhausted.

In addition to the officers and soldiers of the Continental Line, other persons allowed to enter land in the military reservation were:[31]

- The commissioners who laid off the reservation—Anthony Bledsoe, Absalom Tatum, and Isaac Shelby, the surveyors, guard, and others who accompanied the commissioners on that duty

- Those persons who were then settled on Cumberland River and had a right of pre-emption, and whose claims were reserved to them

Within all these land offices there were seven methods by which citizens could acquire title to land in Tennessee:

- Make entry and purchase land in the county entry taker's office[32]

---

[33]"An Act for the relief of the Officers and Soldiers . . . ," April 1782, Clark, *State Records of North Carolina*, 24:419-422, chapter 3.

[34]"An Act for opening the Land Office for the redemption of specie and other certificates, and discharging the arrears due the army . . . ." April 1783, Clark, *State Records of North Carolina*, 24:478-482, chapter 2.

[35]"An Act for Raising Troops for the Protection of the Inhabitants of Davidson County," November 1786, Clark, *State Records of North Carolina*, 24:783-786, chapter 1.

[36]"An Act intituled An Act for the relief of the Officers and Soldiers . . . ," April 1782, Clark, *State Records of North Carolina*, 24:482-485, chapter 3.

[37]"An Act to vest certain lands in fee simple in Richard Henderson and others . . . ," 1783, Clark, *State Records of North Carolina*, 24:530-531, chapter 38.

[38]"An Act for the relief of the Officers and Soldiers in the Continental line, and for other purposes therein mentioned . . . ," April 1782, Clark, *State Records of North Carolina*, 24:419-422, chapter 3.

[39]"An Act for the Purpose of Ceding to the United States of America Certain

---

[29]*Overton's Lessee v. Campbell*, John Haywood, *Supreme Court of Errors and Appeals for the State of Tennessee* Vol. 5 (Louisville: Fetter Law Book Co., 1908), pages 165-224; *Catron's Lessee v. Lowry*, 5 Haywood, page 165; *Pinson & Harkins v. Ivey*, 1 Yerger, 297-360.

[30]*Goodloe v. Wilson*, Cooper, 59-67; *Lydia v. Pucket*, Cooper, 335-339.

[31]"An Act to Amend an Act intituled "An Act for the relief of the Officers and Soldiers . . . " April 1784, Clark, *State Records of North Carolina*, 24:566-568, chapter 15.

[32]"An Act for opening the Land Office for the redemption of specie and other certificates, and discharging the arrears due to the army . . . ," April 1783, Clark, *State Records of North Carolina*, 24:566-568, chapter 2.

THE PRE-EMPTORS IN DAVIDSON COUNTY, TENNESSEE

The inhabitants of Davidson County, with whom the Commissioners negotiated, and who had settled upon the land by June 1, 1780, made petition for their pre-emptions. These persons were named as follows:

John Cockrill, Ann Cockrill, formerly the widow Ann Johnston, Robert Espy, John Buchannan, Cornelius Ruddle, James Mulkerin, James Todd, Isaac Johnston, John Gibson, Francis Armstrong, John Kennedy, Sen., Mark Roberson, William Ellis, James Thompson, James Shaw, James Franklin, Henry Howdyshall, Pierce Castillo, Morris Shean, William Logan, David Hood, John White, Peter Looney, William Collins, Jonas Menifiee, Capt. Daniel Williams, John Evans, Andrew Thomson, Casper Mansco, George Freeland, Daniel Johnston, Edward Swanson, Andrew Kellow, Francis Hodge, John Mulkerin, James Freeland, John Tucker, James Foster, Amos Heaton, Dennis Condry, Frederick Stump, Russell Gower, Andrew Erwin, Thomas Prater, Isaac Lindsey, Moses Winters, James Harris, John Browne, Lewis Crane, John Montgomery, Stephen Ray, Daniel Hogan, Thomas Spencer, Humphrey Hogan, Haydon Wells, Henry Ramsey, John Barrow, Jno. Thomas, Wm. Stuart, Saml. Walker, David Rounsevall, Arthur MacAdoe, Jas. McAdoe, Henry Turner, Saml. Burton, John Dunham, Ephraim Pratt and James Robertson, each and every one of them, receive a grant of six hundred and forty acres of land, including their pre-emptions, without being required to pay any price to

the State for the same. And the Committee are further of opinion that the Heirs or devisees of Zachriah White, Alexander Buchannan, James Leper, James Harrod, Alexander Thomson, David Maxwell, Robert Lucas, Timothy Tirrell, William Hood, Edward Carvin, William Nicley, James Shanklin, Samuel Morrow, George Kennedy, John Robertson, Abel Gower, Sen., Abel Gower, Jun., Nicholas Trammell, Philip Mason, James Turpin, Nathan Turpin, Jacob Stump, Nicholas Gentry, William Cooper, Jacob Jones, James Mayfield, William Green, William Johnston, Samuel Scott, George Aspie, William Leighton, John Evans, John Crutchfield, Joseph Hay, John Searcey, Isaac Lucas, Patrick Quigley, Jacob Stull, Joseph Milligam, Abram Jones, David Fane, Benjamin Porter, Edward Larimore, William Gausney, Jonathan Jennings, David Gowin, Jesse Bialston, Joseph Renfrew, Philip Coonrod, William Gausnay, John Bernard, John Lumsden, John Gilkey, Solomon Phelps, James John, Thomas Harney, Alexander Allerson, John Blackamore, James Fowler, John McMuntry, John Shockley, John Galloway and Isaac Lavaour, who were killed in the settlement and defense of the said County of Davidson, receive grants for the same number of acres in the same manner, and on the same terms and conditions as the former.[40]

The committee decided that those who arrived at the Cumberland settlement from different places soon after the date prescribed by law for obtaining pre-emptions and those who were there before the expiration

---

Western Lands Therein Described . . . .", November 1789, Clark, *State Records of North Carolina*, 24:4-6, chapter 2.

[40]Clark, *State Records of North Carolina*, 19:572 & 573.

date, but were under age, were also eligible for free grants of six hundred forty acres. This was conditional upon their having stayed there continuously since their arrival and had been assisting in defending the country. They were allowed the liberty of laying their pre-emptions wherever they could find vacant lands. They were required to place their entries with the entry officer of Davidson County and were required to pay the usual office fees. The names of these were as follows:

Christopher Gais, Sen., Christopher Gais, Jun., Jonathan Gais, Kasper Bocker, Richard Breeze, Francis Cocke, Mark Nobles, John Kitts, Isaac Mayfield, Samuel Hollis, Isaac Rounsevall, Enias Thomas, Joshua Thomas, Caleb Winters, John Buchannan, Sen., John Kennedy, Sen., John Kennedy, Jun., John Castello, Robert Thomson, and Swanson Williams.[41]

PROCESS FOR OBTAINING A GRANT OF TENNESSEE LAND

The land granting process itself involved the completion of six consecutive legislated steps. Each step will be discussed separately.

- Location
- Entry
- Warrant or Warrant of Survey
- Survey
- Plat
- Grant or Patent

LOCATION

In Tennessee, a state land state, the first step in the land granting process was for either the person acquiring the land, or his agent, to actually go upon the premises and make a preliminary description of the desired boundaries and estimated acreage. The land was surveyed **after** selection rather than before.[42] Few of the larger land speculators, who obtained many thousands of acres of land, actually came to the area. They engaged the services of agents who were trained with a special talent for selecting the very best land. The landowner paid the agent for this service with a portion of the land selected. This compensation method resulted in the agent himself becoming a land speculator and insured that he would select the very best land possible since he would receive a portion of that same land for himself.

To obtain land in the military reservation, the officer or soldier applied to the secretary of state, verified his military service, and received a warrant of survey for such quantity of land within the reservation as he was entitled. This warrant was directed to Martin Armstrong, the surveyor of the reservation.[43] Neither the North Carolina Land Act of 1715,[44] nor the Act of 1783,[45] required a record or entry to be made of the locations in a book. However, the courts decreed that the title was vested in the applicant from the date the endorsement of the location was made on

---

[41]Ibid.

[42]"An Act for establishing Offices, for receiving Entries of Claims for Lands in the several Counties within this State, for ascertaining the Method of obtaining Titles . . . ," November 1777, Clark, *State Records of North Carolina*, 24:42-44, chapter 1.

[43]"An Act to amend an Act, intituled An Act for the relief of the Officers and Soldiers of the Continental Line . . . ," April 1783, Clark, *State Records of North Carolina*, 24:482-485, chapter 3.

[44]"An Act to regulate divers abuses in taking up of lands, and to ascertain the Method to be Observed, from Henceforth, in taking up & Surveying Lands," 1715, Clark, *State Records of North Carolina*, 23:42-44, chapter 33.

[45]"An Act to amend an Act, intituled An Act for the relief of the Officers and Soldiers of the Continental Line . . . ," April 1783, Clark, *State Records of North Carolina*, 24:482-485, chapter 3.

the warrant of survey. This was done so as to exclude any subsequent appropriation of the land.[46] Legislation of April 1784 corrected this error and specified the entry taker should keep "a proper book" in which to enter all locations and provided the following example to pattern and rule his book.[47] The military entry book was not opened until the fall of 1784.[48] After the legislative Act of 1784, these locations were entered in the book without any regard to their respective dates. The result was those claimants who made earlier locations and deposited them first with the surveyor might not be entered first in the entry book.

Persons Name	No. of Warrant	Quantity of Acres	When Located	Description

This was the same format as had been legislated for the entry takers in the county offices, as well as in the John Armstrong office. After the particular location of the vacant land desired was selected, the enterer presented to the entry taker a writing, afterwards called a *location*, setting forth:[49]

- Where, or the name of the county, in which the land was situated
- The name of the water courses, mountains, and remarkable places nearest the land
- The name of the water courses, lakes, ponds, and remarkable places as within the land
- Specify the natural boundaries and lines of other persons, which divided it from other lands

ENTRY

The entry was a very important part of the land granting process because it showed the earliest date the grant was intended to be obtained--in other words, first in line for the choicest selections.

The entry taker accepted the location presented to him, endorsed it on the back with the name of the claimant, the estimated number of acres in the desired tract of land, and the date and time of his receiving it. The entry taker entered a copy of the contents of the location in a "well bound" book, ruled with large margins into equal spaces, copied one location and its endorsement in each space, and consecutively numbered the entries in the margin. The format used was the same as that used in the military land office (see above example). When this registration was completed, the *location* became an *entry*. The process was then suspended for three months to allow any adverse claimants adequate time to make known their claims for the same land and to prosecute a *caveat*[50] against the enterer. If an additional claimant appeared within the time limit, the entry taker noted his claim in the margin of the book opposite the claim in dispute and referred the matter to the county court in the county where the land lay. It was the responsibility of the court to determine definitely what part of the land in controversy belonged to the caveator, and distinguish it from other parts of the tract.[51] This explains why there were so many land cases litigated

---

[46] *Lester & Polk v. Craig,* Cooke 482-489.

[47] "An Act to amend an Act, intituled An Act for the relief of the Officers and Soldiers of the Continental line . . . ," April 1784, Clark, *State Records of North Carolina,* 24:566-568, chapter 15.

[48] *Lester & Polk v. Craig,* Cooke, 488.

[49] "An Act for establishing Offices, for receiving Entries of Claims for Lands in the several Counties . . . ," November 1777, Clark, *State Records of North Carolina,* 24:44, chapter 1; "An Act for opening the Land Office for the redemption of specie and other certificates and discharging the arrears due to the army," April 1783, Clark, *State Records of North Carolina,* 24:478-482, chapter 1.

[50] A caveat was a warning made by someone who was claiming the same land.

[51] "An Act for establishing Offices, for receiving Entries of Claims for Lands in the several Counties . . . ," November 1777, Clark, *State Records of North Carolina,* 24:44, chapter 1; "An Act for opening the Land Office for the redemption of specie and other

within the courts. Many times it was impossible to tell which lands had been entered and which had not.

When the disputed claim was referred to the county court by the entry taker, the sheriff summoned "a good and lawful jury" to decide the question. This jury was called a *jury view*. A notice of ten days was given to the parties involved, after which time the jury actually went upon the premises in dispute, and decided the question. The person who claimed an earlier entry was required to post a bond of fifty pounds payable to the adverse party. If the prosecutor failed in his prosecution, he was required to pay all costs and damages for having caused the delay. The decision was presented to the rightful party who then entered it with the entry taker. The entry taker gave him an order of survey (warrant of survey). The money of the losing contestant was refunded except for the fees to the entry taker. The decision of the court was final. [52] Later, an appeal to the superior court was allowed. [53]

If an applicant made entry for land previously entered, he was allowed to remove his entry to another location. In doing so, he was not required to make another entry, but retained his place in line in the entry book. This is why so many entries in the entry books are marked "removed to another location."

SOME COURT DECISIONS APPLICABLE TO ENTRIES

Because there was so much litigation to establishing the earliest claimant, some of these decisions are included. Legal definitions in

brackets are from *Black's Law Dictionary*. [54]

The court held that a location would take effect from the time it was deposited with the surveyor, and not from its place in the book, [55] and that the Act of 1784 required the location to be entered in a book not for the purpose of creating a right to the land but so that other locators would avoid the land. The entry was accepted as taking effect from the date of the endorsement of the location on the warrant. [56]

But, the court refused to admit the warrant of survey and location endorsed as evidence to show the beginning of the plaintiff's title, as well as explain an erasure on the entry book. [57]

Other cases decided that the book of entries was a record, and that word of mouth evidence was not admissible to show an alteration or erasure, or that an entry was put on the record after the date expressed in the record itself. [58]

In chancery, an entry was not set aside in favor of a younger entry, merely because it had an earlier date than the warrant upon which it was based. In the absence of proof of fraud, the assigning of something out of its proper place was considered by accident. [59]

By decision of the court, an entry to some purposes was considered as giving a *legal right* [right by law], and to some purposes, an *equitable right* [right by fairness, justice and right dealing] to the land. As a subject

---

certificates and discharging the arrears due to the army," April 1783, Clark, *State Records of North Carolina*, 24:478–482, chapter 1.

[52]"An Act to amend an Act, intituled An Act for establishing offices for receiving entries . . . ," October 1779, Clark, *State Records of North Carolina*, 24:270–271, chapter 4.

[53]*Murfree v. Leeper*, Cooper, 1-2.

[54]Henry Campbell Black, *Black's Law Dictionary*, Sixth Edition (St. Paul, Minnesota: West Publishing Co., 1990), passim.

[55]*Graham v. Dudley*, Cooke, 353-6.

[56]*Lester & Polk v. Craig's Lessee*, Cooke, 482-9.

[57]*Goodloe v. Wilson*, Cooper, 59-67.

[58]*Kerr's Lessee v. Porter*, Cooper, 14-15; *Reid's Lessee v. Dodson*, Cooper, 402.

[59]*Trousdale & Nichols v. Campbell & Phillips*, 5 Haywood 5, 101-104.

of taxation, generally, it was a legal right, and also a legal right for the purpose of satisfying creditors' executions.[60]

Entries were bought and sold and several court contests were brought relative to the degree of title being transferred. The purchaser of a sale acquired whatever title the seller had at the time of the sale. If, after the sale, the debtor having possession of the plat and certificate of survey obtained a grant in his own name from the register, he would hold the legal title as trustee for the purchaser.[61]

In the case of ordinary sales of entries, every person involved in acquiring an entry was presumed to know the facts—whether the land had or had not been granted by the state. This was a matter of public record, and by exercising ordinary diligence, the facts could be ascertained before the parties entered into a contract. Therefore, the person who bought an entry from the owner was required to abide by what the seller held, as in the case of the purchase of any other equity. If there had been a previous sale of the same article, the prior purchaser was the owner. Where equities were equal, priority determined the right.[62]

In those suits where the right of the title came into question, an entry carried the legal right, and was superior to the grant, over the older grant based on a later entry. In that case, it constituted a purely legal title. An entry made before a grant was considered at law as an inchoate [barely begun] legal right generally. After the grant it was considered evidence of

[60]Terrell v. Murray, George S. Yerger, Reports of Cases Argued and Determined in the Supreme Court of Tennessee Volume 2 (Louisville: Fetter Law Co., 1906), 384-390.

[61]Bumpus v. Gregory, George S. Yerger, Reports of Cases Argued and Determined in the Supreme Court of Tennessee Volume 8 (Columbia, Missouri: E. W. Stephens Publishing Co., 1912), 46-56.

[62]Craig v. Leiper, 2 Yerger, 193-199.

legal title in the case of an older entry and younger grant over a younger entry and an older grant.[63]

Neither party was allowed to produce the warrant of survey as evidence in an action to restore possession of property to the person entitled to it. Nor were they allowed to show priority of title, or to show a discrepancy between the entry and warrant.[64]

A party was not allowed to show that the entry had been abandoned, and the land left vacant for a time. Had that been allowed, it might possibly have been a ground for applying to a court of equity—the ground being that such an abandonment would be a kind of declaration to the world that they might enter the land without fear of interruption from the enterer.[65]

WARRANT OR WARRANT OF SURVEY

The warrant or warrant of survey differed slightly in each of the different land offices. In the John Armstrong office and the county land offices, the warrant was verification that the purchase price and fees had been paid. Thus, it was authorization for the survey of the desired land to be made.[66]

[63]Terrell v. Murray, 2 Yerger, 384-390.

[64]Trousdale & Campbell, George S. Yerger, Reports of Cases Argued and Determined in the Supreme Court of Tennessee Volume 3 (Columbia, Missouri: E. W. Stephens Publishing Co., 1912), pages 160-167.

[66]Malone's Lessee v. Deboe, John Haywood, Supreme Court of Errors and Appeals for the State of Tennessee Volume 4 (Louisville: Fetter Law Book Co., 1908), 259-264.

[66]"An Act for establishing Offices, for receiving Entries of Claims for Lands in the several Counties within this State, for obtaining Titles to the same, and for other Purposes therein mentioned . . . ," 1777, Clark, State Records of North Carolina, 24:44-45, chapter 1; and "An Act for opening the Land Office for the redemption of specie and other certificates, and discharging the arrears due to the army . . . ," 1783, Clark, State Records of North Carolina, 24:478-482, chapter 2.

In the military office, the warrant of survey was verification that the person to whom the warrant was issued was entitled to have the specified acreage surveyed. If the land was in the military reservation and had escheated to the state, the entry taker delivered the warrant of survey to the University of North Carolina to whom the land had been given by the Act of 1789.[67] The land escheated to the state when the soldier died without heirs. If the soldier died leaving heirs, the warrant was issued to persons claiming to be his heirs. Or, if it was supposed an assignment had been made when none had, the warrant was issued to the supposed assignees. In all these cases, the person to whom the warrant had been issued was considered as a trustee to the soldier, the true claimant. The issuance of the warrant and the adjudication preceding such issuance decided nothing conclusively except the quantity of land to which the officer or soldier was entitled. Though issued to the University, it did not conclusively decide there had been an escheat. If issued to heirs, it did not decide that the persons claiming were truly the heirs of the officer or soldier. If issued to the assignee, it did not decide conclusively whether the warrant had been in fact assigned, or if assigned, whether *bona fide*, secretly, fraudulently, with or without consideration. Neither the secretary nor those who, by the Act of 1819, were substituted for him held any other judicial power than simply to decide that the applicant for the warrant was entitled to have it for a specific quantity of land. What relation the applicants' obtaining the warrant might place him in as to other persons was not believed to have been intended to be settled by the secretary of state or by the commissioners, since no other person appeared before him or them but

[67]"An Act for Raising a Fund for Erecting the Buildings and for the Support of the University of North Carolina," November 1789, Clark, *State Records of North Carolina*, 25:24-25, chapter 21; "An Act to amend an Act intituled, An Act for the relief of the Officers and Soldiers . . . ," April 1783, Clark, *State Records of North Carolina*, 24:482-485, chapter 3.

the applicant.[68] In many instances, this resulted in people unlawfully obtaining the land, particularly the largest land speculators who understood how the system worked and made fraudulent claims.

The North Carolina secretary of state issued the military land warrants and continued to do so until 1819, when a commission was created for that purpose. This commission consisted of the governor, treasurer, and comptroller, and was authorized to hear and determine all applications for military land warrants. Their direction in writing, or the direction in writing of a majority of them, was necessary. The authority for the secretary to issue a warrant was for such quantity of land as each applicant was entitled.[69]

REMOVAL OF WARRANTS

At first the ideal was that military warrants should be confined to the military district. Later when there was not sufficient tillable land to fulfill the acreage of the warrant in one tract, removal of the warrant was permitted, and it appears no restriction was placed on whether or not removal was confined to the military district.

By the North Carolina Act of April 1778, chapter 3, section 2, it was provided that where the quantity of land surveyed fell short of the entry, the county entry taker was required to refund to the enterer the exact deficiency between the entry and the actual survey, which was noted on the survey.

By the Act of April 1784, chapter 14, section 7, in case of an entry of land previously granted, or entered and located, the surveyor was directed to survey the quantity on any vacant lands in the state, in which the enterer or his agent might locate or describe.

[68]*Pinson & Harkins v. Ivey*, William Frierson Cooper, *Reports of Cases in the Supreme Court of Tennessee*, Volume 6 (Missouri: Columbia, 1912), 268-325.

[69]*Nelson v Allen*, 1 Yerger, 340-341.

By the Act of October 1784, chapter 19, section 6, if any person had located his entry on land previously located, he or his assignee was allowed to remove his warrant to any other land not previously located. The new location was to be surveyed, and the survey returned as in other cases.

By the Act of 1786, chapter 20, section 7, surveys of removed warrants were confirmed.

By the Cession Act of 1789, chapter 3, section 1, *condition 1*, entries made in the office of John Armstrong on lands previously located were to be removed to any lands not specially located. The clauses of the Act of 1784 (cited above) are general and not confined to any particular kind of claims.[70]

SURVEY

The survey was the legal description of the land describing its natural boundaries running east, west, north, and south. Legislation specified that it be an "exact square or oblong with the length not exceeding double the breadth" unless that interfered with lands already granted or surveyed. The value of a tract of land sometimes depended upon the streams within it. Laws were passed to prohibit individuals from monopolizing the water supply. Complete control of a stream could result in an unhealthy control over the community. If the land bounded on a navigable river, the water was to form one side of the survey only—the breadth along the water was not to exceed one-fourth part of the distance back from the water.[71] The surveyor was expected to proceed in his surveys according to the number and date of the respective entries. The

first enterers were to have preference to all others in surveying and obtaining grants. When the bounds of two or more entries joined or intersected each other, they were to be surveyed in sequence, the eldest first.[72] It appears, perhaps, that some surveys were being made without actually going onto the lands for the Act of April 1784, chapter 14, section 7, specified that every survey was to be made on the lands entered, and as near as could be agreeable to the location thereof.

It is included in the preamble to the Act of 1786[73] that the intent of the Act of 1783 was for the first enterers of the vacant and unappropriated lands, if specially located, to have preference to all others in surveying and obtaining grants. By the Act of 1787,[74] surveyors were required to survey all entries of land according to the priority of such entry, paying due respect to the number of each warrant. If the surveyor had not been restricted in this manner as to the priority of performing the survey, he could be influenced into surveying for a person with a later entry, adversely affecting a second enterer, who had actually entered the land first. This was the most fraudulently used method and it was done to be certain that favorites were able to obtain the best land. They simply left some blank spaces so some locations, which should have been entered later, could be inserted before others.

The surveyor prepared a legal description of the boundaries of the land indicating the beginning, angles, distances, marks, and water courses, and "other remarkable places" which the lines of the land

[70] *Sevier & Anderson's Lessee v. Hill*, Cooper, 29; *Polk's Lessee v Hill, Wendel and others*, Cooper, 155.

[71] "An Act for establishing Offices, for receiving Entries of Claims for Lands . . . ," November 1777, Clark, *State Records of North Carolina*, 24:43–48, chapter 1.

[72] "An Act to amend An Act entitled, An Act to amend an Act for establishing Offices for receiving entries . . . ," January 1779, Clark, *State Records of North Carolina*, 24:214-216, chapter 6.

[73] "An Act to Prevent the Obtaining of Grants for Lands lying in the Western Parts of this State . . . ," November 1786, chapter 20, Clark, *State Records of North Carolina*, 24:811-812, chapter 20.

[74] "An Act to amend the several Acts of Assembly...further time to Surveyors . . . ," November 1787, Clark, *State Records of North Carolina*, 24:912, chapter 23.

crossed, and the quantity of acres in the tract. In actually marking the survey, the surveyor used persons to carry the thirty-three foot measuring chain. A person, called a marker, was used to mark the measurements. The surveyor administered an oath to the chain carriers and marker to measure "justly and right lines." The person for whom the survey was being made paid their fees. Every survey was required to have lines running east, west, north, and south either in a square or oblong.[75]

Warrants directed to the surveyor of the Military Reservation were returned to the office of the North Carolina secretary, after the surveying was completed.[76]

PERTINENT COURT DECISIONS APPLICABLE TO SURVEYING

The sequence in which entries were made but not followed was one of the biggest problems involved in the surveying process. There was much litigation involving the order in which the surveyor surveyed the land. Therefore, some of the more important decisions handed down through the courts are included here.

The courts held that if the surveyor failed to do his duty in surveying the oldest entry first, the claim of the oldest entry should nevertheless be in no worse situation than if the surveyor had done his duty. This was based upon the universally accepted principle of equity that what ought to have been done should be considered as done from that time.[77]

The court decided the intent of the legislature was that surveys should not interfere or run into each other, although in avoiding it, the

surveyor sometimes was obliged, in some measure, to depart from the directions of the entry.[78]

The survey of a younger entry before an older one did not affect the right of the latter. Every man was assumed to know that if there was an older entry, the younger must be put aside until the older was surveyed. Then if any land was left, the younger entry took it, and if there was not enough left for his entry, the law allowed him to locate elsewhere.[79]

In making his survey, the surveyor was bound to regard the natural boundaries and lines of prior entries and grants. He was to survey every tract as nearly as he could. He adhered according to the calls of the entry as accurately as possible. Although a survey might have been made differently, if the calls were complied with, the enterer who had no control over the surveyor was not prejudiced.[80]

When an improvement such as a cabin, spring, sinkhole, hill, buffalo wallow, etc., was named in the entry, the survey might include it in any part of its bounds—either in the center, on one side, in one corner, or in any one of the four corners of a square or oblong. If a subsequent entry calling for a former entry was surveyed first, the survey should steer clear of every part which the former entry might legally include. The survey could be made in any shape the law allowed. If not so surveyed and the first entry was afterwards surveyed according to law, and included part of the land included in the first survey, the younger enterer could not impeach the survey of the elder.[81]

[75] "An Act for establishing Offices, for receiving Entries of Claims for Lands in the several Counties . . . ," November 1777, Clark, State Records of North Carolina, 24:43-48, chapter 1.

[76] "An Act for opening the Land Office for the redemption of specie . . . ," April 1783, Clark, State Records of North Carolina, 24:478-482, chapter 2.

[77] Murfree v. Logan, Cooper, 220-229.

[78] Kerr's Lessee v. Porter, Cooper, 353-361.

[79] Barnet v. Russell, Cooper, 10-19; Kendrick v. Dallum, Cooke 220-238; Cooper, 489-508; Kendrick v. Dallum, Cooke, 211-213.

[80] Carter & Stubblefield v. Ward, Cooper, 340-341; Hoggat v. McCrory & Gillaspie, Cooper, 8-12. These cases overrule Douglass v. Harrison & Baldwin, Cooper, 172-173.

[81] Wilson v. Kilcannon & Brice, 4 Haywood, 182-187.

When an improvement was named, it was the controlling call. The party was entitled to have his entry so surveyed as to include it, even though it involved the necessity of abandoning the beginning.[82]

The courts uniformly decided that the elder enterer was not obliged to point out in his entry the manner in which the survey should be made, so as to give notice to the subsequent enterers. Angular distance in making the survey was secured by statute. The legislature had so ordered, and the younger enterer had no right to complain. *Ita lex scripta est* [so the law is written]. The law was to be obeyed notwithstanding the apparent rigor of its application. In surveying an entry to include a spring, the survey could include it in any part. So, also, was an entry calling for a beginning without naming a course. Both entries were good and could be surveyed, in a square or oblong or adjoining other surveys already made in any manner so that the calls were complied with.[83]

If an entry called to include a particular spot, the law did not presume the enterer intended for the surveyor to place it in any given point in the survey. The option was intended for the surveyor to place it in any part he might think proper. So, if an entry began at a certain special point, without specifying any course, a survey in any direction from that point would be good.[84]

The courts decreed that a survey ought to be made so as to include within its bounds a spring or other object, which the entry directed to be included. If this could not be done without a small deviation from other calls, that deviation could be made so far as was indispensable to the accomplishment of the purpose. This is implied in the entry as strongly as if expressed, and whatever is inevitably implied is a part of it. Thus, where

the entry was six hundred forty acres on Little Harpeth River, to begin "one quarter of a mile above improvement of the enterer, and half a mile on the east side of the river, and running west and south for quantity, to include his improvement and spring," the surveyor should go a quarter of a mile up the creek. He must then go half a mile east of the creek and then run west so as to lay the tract on both sides of the creek. If a survey to the cardinal points from the termination of the first line would exclude the spring, he was required to find a point from which a survey to the cardinal points would include it.[85]

The result to be deduced from these decisions is, if the locative call was contained within any part of the survey, the entry was special, though it was at one corner. A tract of land was protected from future acquirers much larger than necessary for the satisfaction of the claim.[86]

Where adjacent entries called for the same beginning, the one to run east and north for quantity, the other east and south, the elder could not, unless compelled by the interference of older claims, be surveyed so as to interfere with the younger.[87]

A special entry was to be surveyed in a square or oblong if the calls of the entry were such that a section was to be included which diverged from a square or oblong; then the survey must be made in a square or oblong, after including the section.[88]

By adopting the square figure for his entry, the enterer renounced all

---

[82] *Stubblefield's Lessee v. Short*, 4 Haywood, 265-271.

[83] *Philips v. Robertson*, Cooper, 416.

[84] Ibid.

[85] *White v. Crockett*, John Haywood, *Supreme Court of Errors and Appeals for the State of Tennessee 1816-1817*, Volume 3 (Louisville: Fetter Law Book Co. 1909), 183-9; *White v. Crockett*, 3 Haywood, 234-236.

[86] *McMillan v. Claxton*, 4 Haywood, 174-279; *Smith v. Craig*, Cooper, 287-302; *Napier's Lessee v. Simpson*, Cooper, 448-452. In *Shepherd v. Bailey*, Cooke, pages 369-373, the federal court, McNairy presiding, rejected this idea.

[87] *Craddock's Lessee v. Stalcut*, Cooper, 351-353.

[88] *Sappington v. Hill*, 4 Haywood, 120-121.

the land, which would not be included by a square beginning at the corner called for in his entry, as well as that which would be included by an oblong as by any other figure.[89]

If the entry did not direct how the survey should be made, it was left to the discretion of the surveyor to make it in a square or oblong, so as to include the objects called for. In such case, the surveyor acted for the government independently of the claimant.[90]

When older claims interfered, the surveyor was authorized, or rather constrained, to depart from the oblong or square figure, and to bound his survey on old lines, until he got the desired quantity.[91]

An enterer had a right to the quantity of land called for in his entry, unless he was restricted by older claims, natural boundaries, or the calls of his location or if he were restricted by older claims south and west and by a lake on the east, so as to place him upon the lands north for his quantity. If there was nothing in his entry restraining him from going north, it was the duty of the surveyor to extend his line north so as to obtain the quantity called for. This, of course, was true if the land was vacant in that direction when the entry was made, and especially if the entry called for running north for quantity. A settlement on the land by an occupant subsequent to such an entry was no impediment to the survey, and the surveyor, notwithstanding such occupancy, might be compelled by mandamus [we command] to make the survey.[92]

By the Act of 1801, chapter 3, section 4, if in surveying an entry made on a warrant, it appeared there was not enough land to fill such warrant, the surveyor should give a certificate to the owner or his agent. The certificate would state the quantity so deficient, expressing the number of the warrant, and to whom granted, with the several assignees. The certificate was legal evidence to the entry taker to authorize the holder to enter the land. On such entry, the surveyor should survey and return plats as on other warrants.

The surveyor could disregard an inconsistent call, if the land was surveyed according to a consistent construction of the whole entry. Thus, when the entry called to lie *south* of the beginning, and be *bounded* at the same time by a certain line, and yet to run it with the line would make the land lie *north* of the beginning, and the next call, in that case, ran into a prior survey—the surveyor could drop the call, *with the line*, and run the lines south and west, so as to include the objects called for. The *quantity* also was a controlling call, and would justify the surveyor in deviating from the square or oblong figure, so as to get it by including all the vacant land left by older surveys legally made. The Act did not require the survey be made in the square or oblong figure where land already granted or surveyed prevented it. The surveyor was not required to *certify a deficiency* until the adjacent vacant lands had been included. The certificate when made had a very different effect from a plat and certificate of survey returned to the office as the foundation of a grant. The person for whose benefit it was made could either use it or not at his pleasure. He could, notwithstanding this certificate, proceed to survey his entry, including all the land legally within it or which was vacant and not claimed by other conflicting entries, and procure a grant for the same. But if he did not remove his warrant and use the certificate and if the land which he might have entered was entered by another, equity would not take it from the enterer and give it to the party who might have included it at first, but who did not. This was true, even though he was misled by the certificate to believe that he was bound by it to abandon the land which

[89]Ibid.

[90]*Kendrick v. Dallum*, Cooper, 220-234, 238.

[91]*Kerr v. Porter*, Cooper, 353-362.

[92]*Caldwell v. Watson*, West H. Humphreys, *Reports of Cases Argued and Determined in the Supreme Court of Tennessee*, Volume 6 (Nashville: E. E. M'Kennie & Co, 1846), pages 498-500.

he might have entered, unless the surveyor purposely deceived him, and entered the land himself."[93]

It was not the essence of a grant that a survey should have preceded it if the land was described in the grant so that it could be identified. If its boundaries could be ascertained, it ought to hold the land, though no survey was ever made in fact. The surveyor was the officer of the government. The grantee was forced to trust him and had no power over him. The laws prescribed the duties of the surveyor, and if he certified that he had performed those duties, he could not either willingly or by compulsion contradict his certificate to the prejudice of the grantee.[94]

A survey was not essential to the validity of a grant. However, the laws directing the mode of appropriating land and prescribing the requisites to pass the title from the state to the individual required a survey to be made. It especially designated the land to be comprehended in the grant and in all cases, the law presumed an actual survey was made where a grant issued. On trials in ejectment [action for recovery of land], the grant was conclusive evidence of it. It could not, therefore, be averred [in pleading, to declare or assert], in such a case, that there had been no actual survey. This has been an established principle in making out land titles, recognized by many decisions in the supreme court, and not to be contradicted. The reasoning of the judges, upon this point, was that the law gave credence to the acts of public officers if done in the due course of the execution of their duties. The emanation [that which flows or comes forth from something] of a grant, which was the completion of title, was the highest evidence of the regular execution of all the prerequisites to its own execution. Evidence, in its own

[83]Shute v. Buchanan, 3 Haywood, 206-209.

[84]Smith v. Buchanan, Cooper, 305-307; Rucker v. Vaughan, Jacob Peck, Reports of Cases Argued and Adjudged in the Supreme Court of Errors and Appeals of the State of Tennessee, Volume 1 (Louisville: Fetter Law Book Co., 1909), 272-273.

nature, established it as being a public record, importing absolute verity [truthfulness], and sanctioned by the great seal of the state, admitted no averment, plea, or proof to the contrary. These principles were applicable in all trials in ejectment [action for recovery of land] and in all cases when the grant came in collaterally to be used as evidence.[95]

Such was the authority of a survey, that when the boundaries of land have been ascertained by one, the courts could not, in a dispute between man and man, know that there was more land in the tract than the original surveyor had returned upon oath. Moreover, when on the plat originally annexed to a grant, the surveyor certified that there was a certain quantity the law implied that there was no more. The law did not authorize that another surveyor be called to disprove what the original officer had returned upon oath. The surveyor was an officer of government and grants made by an officer of government, in whose acts the citizens were commanded by the fundamental principles of society to place confidence. The citizen was not expected to know more of the matter than the position of the boundaries assigned to his possessions by the government through its officer.[96] Nor could the original surveyor himself be called on to invalidate his own act. His plat, being of record, must be conclusive.[97]

A survey, in the first instance, was not proven at all unless it was returned into the office of the secretary. For, before that, it might have been lost, the principal surveyor might not have approved it, it might have been withdrawn and suppressed because of incorrectness, a wrong representation or description, or wrong locality. And besides all this, if a survey could be established by word of mouth, it might have been placed

[95]Garner & Dickson v. Norris's lease, 1 Yerger, 62-66.

[96]Hickman v. Tait, Cooke, 460-463.

[97]Davidson v. Shelton, Cooper,1-2; Sevier & Anderson v. Hill, Cooper, 23-26; Davidson v. Shelton, Cooper, 74.

here, there, anywhere. Its lines might be made and marked improperly and for fraudulent purposes. Corners might be made also and established by the most deceptive testimony to the ruin of those who were in a situation to be affected by misrepresentation. Therefore, if a survey was made for any purpose but was not returned according to law, it was of no estoppel [that party is prevented by his own acts from claiming a right to estoppel of other party who was entitled to rely on such conduct and has acted accordingly] either of the person for, or of whose land it was made, nor of any other person. If others bound themselves upon such survey, they were in the same circumstances as when they ran into an adjacent entry in inviolable [safe from trespass or assault] character of a survey as a record. Yet, if in making it, a mistake was made, the surveyor had a right and it was his duty to correct his survey, and discard a part where he had included too much. The fact that he had done so may be shown by oral evidence.[98]

The surveyor acquired rights by causing his own lands to be surveyed adjoining the survey in which the error existed. After that, he could not correct his mistakes.[99]

Every reasonable effort should have been made to defend the surveyor's acts. If, however, it appeared that the surveyor had obviously departed from the calls of the entry, or surveyed contrary to the law, his acts could be voided by those injured to the extent of such departure.[100]

PLAT

The plat is an actual drawing to scale of the boundary lines of the land, indicating the place of beginning and pertinent monuments such as

[98]*Bishop v. Arnold*, Peck, 366.

[99]*Blakemore v. Chambless*, Cooper, 3-6; *Sullivan v. Brown*, Cooper, 6-8.

[100]*Blount v. Ramsey*, Cooke, 489-493.

trees, etc. The surveyor made two copies of the boundary lines of the tract. The secretary of state retained one copy of the plat and filed it in the land office, the other was annexed to the grant when it was issued.[101]

The surveyor was given a period of eighteen months after receiving the warrant to return the survey and plat to the secretary of state. In some instances it must have been tempting to omit actually carrying the chain around the boundaries, especially when the Indians were actively pursuing the "land stealers," as they called them. The survey could not be made without chain carriers, who were "sworn the truth to tell."

It must be remembered that after he performed the field work, the surveyor's work still was not finished. The surveyor had very primitive tools including poor quality paper and ink with which to prepare the plat and survey. Drawing of the plat to scale by hand must have been a task of great magnitude since it was required that two identical copies be drawn. After the plat and survey were prepared, the surveyor or his deputy signed the survey and listed the chain carriers, who were sworn to actually measure the land surveyed in a "justly manner." The chain carriers are listed on the plat.[102] Usually family or neighbors of the claimant were chain carriers and marker.

GRANT

A grant was the certificate that actually passed title from the government to the individual. The secretary of state made out all grants for the signature of the governor. When the governor signed the grant, title passed from the government to the individual.[103] After the governor

[101]"An Act for establishing Offices, for receiving Entries...," November 1777, Clark, *State Records of North Carolina*, 24:46, chapter 1; "An Act for opening the Land Office . . . ," April 1783, Clark, *State Records of North Carolina*, 24:478-482, chapter 2.

[102]Ibid. Chain Carriers are not listed on the grant.

[103]*Phillips & Campbell's Lessee v. Erwin*, Cooper, 235; *Reid's Lessee v. Dodson*, Cooper, 401-402.

signed the grant, it was then countersigned by the secretary of state and recorded in a grant book kept in his office for that purpose. Legislation required the grant to be recorded in the office of the register, in the county where the land lay, within twelve months from its issue.[104]

There were different type grants as follows:

- Purchase grants
- Military grants
- Pre-emption grants
- Commissioners grants
- Service grants for surveyors, markers, guards and hunters
- Legislative grants

PURCHASE GRANTS

Purchase grants could be obtained by paying the legislated price per acre. They were obtained from the county offices and the Hillsboro office, also called the John Armstrong office, as follows:[106]

- County offices - the price was 2 pounds, 10 shillings per 100 acres limited to 640 acres for the head of household, 100 acres for his wife, and 100 acres for each of his children. Additional acreage was priced at 5 pounds per 100 acres

- John Armstrong office - the price was 10 pounds per 100 acres,

[104]"An Act for establishing Offices, for receiving Entries of Claims . . . ," November 1777,"Clark, *State Records of North Carolina*, 24:43-48, chapter 1.

[105]Ibid; "An Act for opening the Land Office . . . ," April 1783, Clark, *State Records of North Carolina*, 24:478-482, chapter 2.

[106]"An Act for establishing Offices, for receiving Entries of Claims . . . ," November 1777, Clark, *State Records of North Carolina*, 24:43-46, chapter 1.

payable in specie or specie certificates. Specie was hard money and very scarce. Specie certificates were given for the purchase of provisions during the Revolutionary War and could be redeemed only in the John Armstrong office

MILITARY GRANTS

Military grants were issued to fulfill promises for payment of military service in the Revolutionary War, and in Evans' Battalion, a militia unit furnishing protection from Indians for the Davidson County settlers. The North Carolina militia did not receive bounty land. The acreage obtained was legislated in proportion to military rank and length of service. The heirs of the officer or soldier received the lands to which the officer or soldier was entitled, in case of his death in military service. The amounts of land due each soldier according to his rank was as follows:[107]

- To each private   640 acres
- To each non-commissioned officer   1,000 acres
- To each subaltern   2,500 acres
- To each captain   3,840 acres
- To each major   4,800 acres
- To each lieutenant colonel   5,760 acres
- To each lieutenant colonel commandant   7,200 acres
- To each colonel   7,200 acres
- To each brigadier general   12,000 acres
- To each chaplain   7,200 acres
- To each surgeon   4,800 acres
- To each surgeon's mate   2,500 acres

If a soldier fell in defense of the country, his heirs or assigns were

[107]"An Act for the relief of the Officers and Soldiers . . . ," April 1782, Clark, *State Records of North Carolina*, 24:419-422, chapter 3.

entitled to receive the same quantity of land as the deceased would have been entitled to receive, had he served during the entire war. If the soldier or officer received wounds or bodily infirmity and was rendered unfit for service, he received the same quantity of land as if he had served during the entire war.[108] If no heir came forward for the grant, it was made to the North Carolina University.

PRE-EMPTION GRANTS

A pre-emption was a right, granted by the government to the actual settler to the exclusion of all other persons, to purchase a portion of the land he had settled upon or cultivated.[109] This only meant that he was given first choice to purchase it. All pre-emption grants were not free. Squatters always moved into unsettled areas first, anticipating being able to obtain that particular land at a lesser price. In many instances pre-emption rights were allowed and pre-emption grants were provided for in most of the land offices. It was the best way to prevent rioting among large groups of squatters, who were securely, although illegally, settled upon their illegally claimed premises. Pre-emption grants were issued to settlers in compensation for their services in defending the Middle Tennessee area from the Indians.[110] After each Indian treaty by which additional land was obtained, pre-emption rights were granted those squatters who were illegally settled there on the date specified by legislation. The first squatters to receive pre-emption rights were those settled along the Cumberland River in Middle Tennessee. Their names can be found in another section of this work.

[108] Ibid.

[109] Henry Campbell Black, *Black's Law Dictionary* (St. Paul, Minn: West Publishing Company, 1990), 1178.

[110] "An Act for the relief of the Officers and Soldiers in the Continental line . . . April 1782," Clark, *State Records of North Carolina*, 24:417-422, chapter 3.

SURVEYOR GRANTS

Surveyor grants were also called service rights and were issued to surveyors and their assistants in compensation for their services in surveying the land. The person, whose land was being surveyed, paid the surveyor for his services. The surveyor was an officer of the government whose duties were legislated by the government. He was paid by the person for whom the survey was being made, usually in a portion of the land being surveyed, since land was more plentiful than hard cash. He could correct his mistakes if they were discovered before other lands adjoining the survey in which the error existed were surveyed.[111] Martin Armstrong, as surveyor general of the military district, was allowed to lay off for himself within the military district a quantity of land equal to the amount of his fees, rating the land at ten pounds per hundred acres.[112] He engaged many deputies who actually performed the work for him. These deputies were also paid with a portion of the land they surveyed. This explains why so many service grants were issued to both Martin Armstrong and his deputies.

COMMISSIONER GRANTS

Commissioners were appointed by the North Carolina legislature and sent into middle Tennessee to lay off a reservation in which the North Carolina bounty land grants would be located. The commissioners, and their entourage of assistants, sent to superintend the laying off of boundaries for the military reservation were allowed service grants within the military reservation. The three commissioners appointed were Absalom Tatum, Isaac Shelby, and Anthony Bledsoe.

[111] See *Blakemore v. Chambles*, Cooper, 3-6; *Sullivan v. Brown*, Cooper, 6-8.

[112] "An Act to amend an Act, intituled, An Act for the relief of the Officers and Soldiers in the Continental line . . . ." April 1782, Clark, *State Records of North Carolina*, 24:482-485, chapter 3.

They were allowed three surveyors, and the *usual* number of chain carriers and markers, and such a number of hunters, not exceeding six, as might be necessary to supply the group with provisions.[113] In compensation, land was allotted to each of these as follows:

- To each surveyor   2,500 acres
- To each chain carrier   640 acres
- To each marker   640 acres
- To each hunter   640 acres
- To each private of the guard   320 acres
- To each officer of the guard [in proportion to his military pay][114]

The commissioners, surveyors, guards, and others who laid off the military reservation were required in 1783 to enter their lands with the entry taker of Davidson County, who was ordered to receive their claims and grant them warrants without any purchase money.[115] They had erroneously entered their land with the Cumberland River pre-emptors. Later, in April 1784, they were authorized to make their entries in the office of John Armstrong,[116] which meant they were allowed to place them anywhere in the state they chose, except the Indian reservation in the extreme southeast corner of the State.

---

[113]"An Act for the relief of the Officers and Soldiers . . . ," April 1782, Clark, *State Records of North Carolina*, 24:419-422, chapter 3.

[114]Ibid.

[115]An Act to amend an Act, intituled, An Act for the relief of the Officers and Soldiers . . . April 1783," Clark, *State Records of North Carolina*, 24: 482-485, chapter 3.

[116]"An Act to Prevent Doubts as to the Rights of Sovereignty and Jurisdiction . . . West of the Apalachian Mountains . . . ," April 1784, Clark, *State Records of North Carolina*, 24:563-564, chapter 12.

EVANS' BATTALION

Because of the frequent, hostile attacks committed by the Indians against the settlers in Davidson County on the Cumberland River, the North Carolina legislature, in November 1786, authorized the enlistment of two hundred and one men to be sent there to protect the settlers. The men were formed into three companies, each consisting of sixty-seven men, one captain, one lieutenant, one ensign, and four sergeants under the command of one major. Their term of service was two years. They met at Clinch Mountain and cut and cleared a road into the Cumberland settlements. Land grants were promised for a portion of their pay. Every private was allowed 400 acres of land to be laid off and allotted west of the Cumberland Mountain, in full satisfaction of the half pay of his first year. The same was granted in proportion for the time he served over and above one year. The commanding officer was allotted 2,000 acres for one half of the first year of service and one-half of the pay due him for the time he served over and above service for one year.[117]

LEGISLATIVE GRANTS

Legislative grants were issued to individuals in exchange for their special and unusual services. Special legislation awarded grants to the following people:

- Richard Henderson & Co.   200,000 acres
- Alexander Martin   2,000 acres
- David Wilson   2,000 acres
- Nathaniel Greene   25,000 acres

---

[117]"An Act for Raising Troops for the Protection of the Inhabitants of Davidson County," November 1786, Clark, *State Records of North Carolina*, 24:783-786, chapter 1; Haywood, *Civil and Political History of Tennessee*, 229.

Richard Henderson

Richard Henderson, Thomas Hart, John Williams, William Johnston, James Hogg, David Hart, Leonard Henly Bullock, Nathaniel Hart, John Luttrel, Landon Carter, and Robert Lucas were co-owners of The Transylvania Company. On 17 March 1775, they concluded a treaty with the Cherokee Indians, called the Sycamore Shoals Treaty. In paying the Cherokee Indians about $50,000 in goods, they obtained title from them for lands lying between the Kentucky, Ohio, and Cumberland Rivers. This line extended eastward along the north bank of the Holston River to the point where it intersected the Virginia line; it ran thence westwardly along that line to the western boundary of the Lochabar Purchase, and north along that boundary to its intersection with Powell Mountain. The treaty embraced two deeds known as the "Path Deed" and the "Great Grant." The main portion of the land was in Kentucky, with a small portion in Virginia, and a portion in Tennessee. Neither North Carolina nor Virginia admitted the legality of this purchase; however, both states allowed the purchase to extinguish the claims of the Cherokees.[118] In compensation for the land, Virginia granted The Transylvania Company 190,000 acres of land. The North Carolina Legislature, in 1783, granted to The Transylvania Company 190,000 acres and to Landon Carter, son of John Carter, and to Robert Lucas, who was killed in defense of Davidson County, 10,000 acres each, making the total of 200,000 acres, located in Powell's Valley in East Tennessee.[119]

Legislative Grants to Alexander Martin and David Wilson

The North Carolina Legislature granted to Alexander Martin and

---

[118]William Robertson Garrett and Albert Virgil Goodpasture, *History of Tennessee, Its People and Its Institutions* (Nashville, TN: Brandon Printing Co., 1900), 131; "An Act to vest certain lands in fee simple in Richard Henderson and others, March 1775," Clark, *State Records of North Carolina*, 24:530, chapter 38.

[119]Ibid.

David Wilson 2,000 acres each to be located within the military reservation.[120] Martin made his entry on the 13th of October 1783, ten or fifteen miles from the boundary of the military reservation. Because it was not within the reservation it was considered invalid, but the courts held it to be legal.[121] The exact location of David Wilson's 2,000 acres has not been determined.

General Nathaniel Greene

Major General Greene was allotted 25,000 acres of land by North Carolina.[122] The commissioners surveyed his land when they surveyed the land for the military reservation, but it was located just outside the southern boundary of the military reservation.[123]

FEES

Fees were specifically set for the officials handling the various procedures of completing the grants, as follows:[124]

- Entry taker, appointed by the county court   16 shillings
- Surveyors for up to 300 acres surveyed   30 shillings

---

[120]"An Act to amend an Act intituled An Act for the relief of the Officers and Soldiers of the Continental line . . . ," April 1783, Clark, *State Records of North Carolina*, 24:482-485, chapter 3.

[121]*Henderson's Lessee v. Long*, Cooke, 128-130.

[122]"An Act for the relief of the Officers and Soldiers in the Continental line . . . ," April 1782, Clark, *State Records of North Carolina*, 24:419-422, chapter 3.

[123]"An Act to describe the Lands granted to Major General Nathaniel Greene . . . ," April 1784, Clark, *State Records of North Carolina*, 24:569-570, chapter 18.

[124]"An Act for establishing Offices, for receiving Entries of Claims . . . ," November 1777, Clark, *State Records of North Carolina*, 24:43-48, chapter 1.

- Surveyors for each 100 acres over 300 acres   3 shillings
- Secretary of State for the "great seal"   3 shillings

It was the responsibility of the entry taker to pay over to the public treasury all the money he had received for entries on the first day of April and October of every year. He received two per cent for his risk in carrying the money to the office of the secretary of state and carrying the completed grants from the office of the secretary of state back to his office and delivering them to the rightful owners.[125] In 1778 legislation allowed three months after the date of receiving the entry before the money was required to be turned into the treasury.[126]

Each official was sworn "to well and impartially perform the several duties of his respective office" and was required to provide a bond. The entry taker and the surveyor were required to furnish a two thousand pound bond, promising to pay into the public treasury all monies they collected in their office. The bond was made payable to the governor, whose responsibility it was to make restitution to any injured parties. Provision was enacted for failure of the entry taker or surveyor to perform his duties, resulting in the loss of his job and a fine of five hundred pounds. If the entry taker made entry for land purchased in his own name, record to that effect was supposed to be made in the entry book in the proper place.[127]

Acceptable purchase money for the land was Continental bills of credit and the dollar bills issued at the Congress held at Hillsboro and Halifax.[128]

PERTINENT COURT CASES PERTAINING TO GRANTS

The registration of a grant in the land office was not essential to its existence. It was the business of the secretary to register the grant before delivering it to the owner; but the owner was not in fault and was not penalized by the omission of this duty. If the clerk certified that the grant had been registered in the office of the secretary, and not by the secretary himself, it was still good."[129]

By Act of October 1779, chapter 4, section 4, in case of the death of any enterer of land before the making out of the grant, his heirs or assignees would have a fee simple interest in the premises, although the grant was made in the name of the decedent.

By North Carolina Act of 1715, chapter 29, section 6, lands taken up for a deceased person, were granted in the name of his heir at law. However, this did not bar any dowry, tenant by the curtesy, or devisee that might claim under the deceased. If an entry was made in a man's lifetime and removed after his death, it could be re-entered in the office of the surveyor general. The Act of 1806, chapter 1, sections 7 & 10, made this entry compatible with the meaning of the Act of 1779."[130]

It was not mandatory that an actual survey should have preceded the grant. If the land was so described in the grant that it could be identified, and its boundaries ascertained, although no survey was ever made, it *ought* to hold the land. The land could be identified by other means than the survey. For instance, if the grant itself contained such calls as would enable the grantee, by reasonable means, to locate it to a certain tract of

---

[125]Ibid.

[126]"An Act to amend an Act, intituled 'An Act for establishing Offices for receiving Entries . . . ,'" April 1778, Clark, *State Records of North Carolina*, 24:159-160, chapter 3.

[127]"An Act for establishing Offices, for receiving Entries . . . ," November 1777, Clark, *State Records of North Carolina*, 24:43-48, chapter 1.

[128]Ibid.

[129]*Ayres v. Stewart*, Cooper, 221-222.

[130]*Dougherty v. Edmiston*, Cooke, 134-136.

land, it was all that was necessary. The survey, rather than the grant, was the mode pointed out by law as most convenient to designate boundaries. But, the surveyor was the officer of the government and the grantee was forced to trust him and had no power over him. The laws prescribing the office of the surveyor were his guide. If the surveyor certified that he did survey the land and a grant had been issued for that survey, the grantee was entitled to the same benefit under the grant as if it had been issued upon the actual survey. The surveyor could not be forced to contradict his own certificate by compulsion nor could he voluntarily do so.[131]

A grant was good if it described the land by its natural features, such as water courses, mountains, lakes, etc., or if it was described by artificial monuments, such as lines and corners of other surveys. If an actual survey of the tract itself was made, to which a plat and certificate was annexed, then it also was considered to be good. But, if the beginning of the survey or plat was a tree marked in a certain manner, and that tree did not accompany the call with a description, which would enable the beginning to be identified, it could not be made good by extraneous evidence derived from other circumstances.[132]

By section 10 of the Act of 1777, chapter 1, one of the plats made out by the surveyor had to accompany the warrant and be filed in the land office. The other had to be annexed to the grant. But the plat annexed to the grant was not an essential part of the grant. If it were referred to, it was for the purpose of explanation and not to destroy its validity.[133]

If doubt in regard to a boundary arose from the calls of a grant or doubt to the entry upon which the grant was based, the plat and certificate of survey could be referred to, to remove the doubt.[134]

A plat attached to a grant made out by the surveyor, as his duty required him to do, and what he said he did, was admissible evidence of what was the intention of the state through its officer, as to location of the land, even when there were different calls on the face of the grant.[135]

The issuance of a grant from the state refers to possession of the specific land in the grant. It actually transfers that possession, as well as the right and title, to the grantee, as effectually and as completely to all intents and purposes as if livery of seizin had been made. Livery of seizin was a common law ceremony for transferring possession of lands by a seller to a buyer. It occurred when both parties went together upon the land, and there a twig, clod, key or other symbol was delivered in the name of the whole from the seller to the buyer. In the form of state grants, the Acts of the Assembly authorizing the issuance of grants intended that an absolute estate in fee simple passed from the state to the buyer or grantee. This gave the grantee a perfect right and possession, without actual entry. It, therefore, attached to the grantee all the legal remedies incident to such estate as the state had held. It was not to be doubted that the legislature had the power to give a perfect title and possession by the grant without actual entry. It also was not to be doubted that they intended to and did just that. "No livery of seizin" said the court, "is necessary to perfect a title by letters patent." A grantee in such case took by matter of record, and the law determined a grant a matter of record, and it was generally known as such in the neighborhood. It is the union of the right and seizin that constitutes a

---

[131] Smith v. Buchannon, Cooper, 305-308.

[132] Rutledge v. Buchanan, Cooke, 363-365.

[133] Polk's Lessee v. Hill, Windel and others, Cooper,153. In Reid's lessee v. Dodson, Cooper, 402-403, the court declined giving a decided opinion upon this point.

[134] Dallum v. Breckenridge, Cooke, 152-158; Patton v. Carothers, Cooke, 148-149.

[135] Childress v. Holland, 3 Haywood, 274-287; 2 Haywood, 208.

perfect title.[136]

A grant was a public record, evidenced by the great seal of the state, for it could not issue before it was recorded. The act of recording was one of the essentials necessary to constitute it a grant. Being a record, it carried absolute truth. And, as such, it could not receive a trial by witnesses, jury, or otherwise, but only by itself. Records signify in themselves such uncontrollable credit and truth that there could be no declaration or positive assertion of proof to the contrary. A state grant or patent, therefore, was conclusive evidence of its contents. The state passed its title to the lands contained in the description of the grant. All previous requisites existed that were necessary to authorize it to be a complete and lawful act and which were material to it, such, for example, as would have been examinable and controvertible upon *caveat*. If there were no entry or location to base it upon, this was a material and impeachable fact and would have been grounds for an application to the governor for a suspension of the issuance of the grant until after an investigation was completed.[137] If such a defect existed and the grant had been issued it was conclusive evidence at law of the existence of the entry, and also of its validity.[138]

Ever since the case of Polk's Lessee versus Windel & others, it has been held that entries and grants are void, and may be resisted in a trial in ejectment, whenever there is lack of property in the grantor, or lack of power in the officers appointed by the government to receive the entries or issue the grants. Thus, an entry of an island in the Tennessee River in

the office of the entry taker of Ocoee District, and a grant founded on such entry, when the island constituted part of Hiwassee District and not of Ocoee District, is void, because the entry taker had no authority to receive the entry, nor the register and governor to issue the grant founded upon it.[139]

If a grant was absolutely void for matter apparent on its face, or for matter that could be collected from inspection of the grant, and from the records of the country, taken together, then it could be impeached when exhibited in evidence, either in ejectment or any other action, and held *void*. But if the matter objected to in a grant was not of the nature that it could be known to all men, then it was only in avoidance being dehors [without] the grant, such as frauds in the previous steps required, compliance with particular forms, etc. before issuance. These, and others of a like nature, could be shown only in a suit brought for the purpose of impeaching the grant.[140]

The English referred to the United States grants as assertive land grants for land to which there could be no inquiry into the consideration. An assertive grant could not be defeated by any extrinsic or outside testimony. The court could not inquire whether the prerequisites were compiled or not, but all of them are presumed to have been observed by the officers, who held the duty of performing them.[141]

There are but a few excepted cases in which we can go beyond the grant for the purpose of voiding it. And when forgery is recognized as

---

[136]*Peeler v. Norris*, 4 Yerger, 331, 343-344.

[137]"An Act for opening the Land Office for the redemption of specie and other certificates, and discharging the arrears due to the army ...," 1783, Clark, *State Records of North Carolina*, 24:478-482, chapter 2, section 21.

[138]*Overton's Lessee v. Campbell & Lackey*, 5 Haywood, 188-190. Per Judge Whyte.

---

[139]*Crutchfield v. Hammock*, 4 Humphrey, 203-205.

[140]*Campbell & Lackey*, 5 Haywood, 196-202; *Smith's Lessee v. Winton*, Cooper, 230-233. For the general causes, for which grants are *void or voidable ab initio* [from the beginning] see 5 Haywood, 215-216 and *Smith's Lessee v. Winton*, Cooper, 230-233. And on all these points, see Roane's opinion in the same case, by whom the result is briefly stated.

[141]*Sevier & Anderson v. Hill*, 2 Overton 23-29; *Polk's Lessee v. Hill, Windel & others*, Cooper, 118-163 & 433-436; *Craig v. Vance*, Cooper, 182-183.

one, it is that technical offence; it cannot be inferred from the fact that different warrants are to be found in the office of the secretary of the same number.[142]

The lands given to Evans' Battalion were to lay west of the Cumberland Mountain. Nevertheless, a grant issued to one of those claimants for land east of the mountains was neither void nor voidable except by the state.[143]

Where a grant was believed to have been issued for services performed by Martin Armstrong in surveying the military reservation, it was held that it could not be shown by a earlier enterer, and that at the date of the grant, he had not performed services to the value of the land granted.[144]

In short, there was no exception to the generality of the rule that extrinsic evidence of every kind is inadmissible to impeach a grant. The exception, known alone to the land law of Tennessee, that an older entry could be given in evidence, at law, to show that the state had already parted from the land previous to the issuance of the grant.[145]

And this exception was probably allowed because, by the Acts of 1786, chapter 10, section 1, and 1787, chapter 23, section 1, grants obtained on younger entries to the prejudice of older ones are declared void, and so it was thought as a result, that such a grant would be no obstacle to a grantee claiming under an older entry, even in a court of law, and that a resort to a process for repealing the void grant was unnecessary.[146]

[142]*Polk's Lessee v. Hill, Windel & others*, Cooper, 433-436.

[143]*Winton v. Rogers*, Cooper, 185-187.

[144]*Kerr v. Porter*, Cooper, 15-16.

[145]*Polk v. Windel*, Cooper, 433-436.

[146]Ibid.

A grant called to begin on a "Post Oak," on Reed's line a former survey of 640 acres" but there never had been a survey in the neighborhood in the name of Reed. There had been one of the same surveyor, in the name of Reed, and it appeared that the grant to Reed, and the one in question, both called to lay on the same creek and to include the same trace, so the court held that a presumption arose that Reed's tract was intended. The court held that nothing less than proof that Reed actually had a "former survey in the neighborhood" would overthrow this presumption. In Ramsey's grant, his line and a chain of hills were called for, when Ramsey had no line nor was there any chain of hills. But, as there were other circumstances from which the intention of the grantor could be ascertained, the grant was adjudged good. So, if there were uncertainty as to which line of Reed's survey the tract in question was to adjoin without interfering with it, and if it could not adjoin that survey on any other than the second line, the court held that it was intended to adjoin it on the second line. It was uncertain at what point on the second line the tract in question was to begin, yet it was to begin on a post oak on the second line. There was a post oak at the end of the first and beginning of the second line, and there was no other post oak, much less a marked one, shown to exist on the second line. Nevertheless, a grant might be lost for uncertainty, if there are means by which its plaintiff must show a marked boundary, or some proof from which its boundaries can be defined. A title to land cannot exist without boundaries. The plaintiff must show a marked boundary, or some proof from which a boundary can be ascertained, before he can say to the defendant, though he be *an actual possessor*, "I have a better right to possess this particular piece of land than you have."[147]

In order to establish the boundaries of a tract of land, it is not absolutely necessary that some corner or marked line be proved to exist.

[147]*White's Lessee v. Hembree*, Cooper, 529-535.

If it is proved to have existed, or any monument, corner, or marks from which the boundaries called for in the grant or deed can be ascertained, it was sufficient, and particularly so, against a possessor who has no title.[148]

Before processioning by public authority was provided for by the Act of 1806, chapter 1, section 21, a remarking by the grantee privately, made bona fide and in reasonable conformity with the calls of the grant, was held to be evidence of the original survey. It was binding upon the state and the grantee. A survey thus made by the grantee, beginning sixteen poles west of the point called for as the beginning in the grant, binds the state and subsequent appropriators of the land.[149]

RELATION OF GRANTS IN CASE OF CONFLICT OF ENTRY

The claimant furnished the entry taker with a description of the land to be purchased by him. From this, the entry-taker was to transcribe this writing in his record of entries, in the order of time in which it was received, and number it accordingly. With the warrant or order of survey, the claimant would deliver to the surveyor a copy of the entry with its proper number, so that he could proceed in his surveys according to the number and date of the respective entries. In reciting in the preamble of the Act of 1786, chapter 20, it was the intent of the act of 1783, chapter 2, that the first enterer of vacant and unappropriated land, if specially located, should have preference over all others in surveying and obtaining grants for it. It provided that an enterer of land already entered should be prevented from obtaining a grant on it to the prejudice of the first enterer. The Act of 1787, chapter 23, section 1, provided that all entries of land should be surveyed according to the priority of entry. The surveyor should pay due respect to the number of each warrant, and

[148]*White's Lessee v. Hembree*, Cooper, 533-534.

[149]*Garner & Dickson v Norris's Lessee*, 1 Yerger, 62-69.

declare that grants thereafter otherwise obtained should be void. In all these provisions, the legislature had the intent to avoid a *conflict of entries*, and to secure to the first enterer or purchaser the first survey and a perfect title.[150]

In North Carolina, in conformity with these provisions of the law, it was the general practice for the claimants or their agents to attend and show the land to the surveyor. Deputies, well acquainted with the lines of previous surveys, were assigned to particular districts, and were able to avoid interferences.[151]

But, in Tennessee, because of the unknown, unsettled, and wilderness state of the country, as well as the absence of claimants, it was not in the power of surveyors to proceed according to priority of entry. If deputies, not well acquainted with the lines of previous surveys, had been assigned to particular districts, interferences could not generally have been avoided.[152]

In few cases of entries made in the wilderness could the surveyor expect to find the land entered without being shown it. For him to make search for it alone was too difficult and dangerous. Hence, in general, surveys were not made until owners or agents the settlement of the country, these owners being out of the area, and having attended to show the land. And, in the early periods of no agents, innumerable younger entries were surveyed before older ones. This caused many interferences to take place, and the younger enterers obtained the oldest grants.[153]

[150]*Murfree v. Logan*, Cooper, 220-229; *Kerr's Lessee v. Porter*, Cooper, 353-361.

[151]*Phillips v. Robertson*, Cooper, 405.

[152]Ibid.

[153]Cooper, 12-13, *note*; *Phillips v. Robertson*, Cooper, 405.

At first, the elder enterer sought relief in equity, by a bill to divest the title out of the grantee and vest it in himself. The ground of this relief was not knowledge, but notice of the prior entry in the defendant. The only medium through which the grantee could be shown to have had this notice was the prior entry itself, as transcribed in the book of entries, a public record accessible to every citizen.[154]

It is plain that the intent of the first locator could not indicate to a subsequent locator the land meant to be appropriated. So, the intent of the claimant was to appeal to the conscience of the subsequent locator with unfairness, should he be tempted to appropriate the same land afterwards. Personal notice to a subsequent enterer that an entry included the land was not the notice that the law prescribed. It directed an *entry* of the location in a public record for that purpose, which is the same thing as to say, in effect, "you shall give notice in writing."[155] Hence, it was held, that the entry must give notice on its face of the land appropriated by it.[156]

Whether an entry gave that notice or not, it could not be made better or worse by oral proof of what the enterer intended, and extrinsic evidence to add to or alter an entry was inadmissible.[157]

Verbal evidence was admissible to demonstrate that the features or name of a particular spot claimed, corresponded with, and fulfilled the calls of the entry. The notice, which an entry must give on its face of the spot appropriated, was not notice to that precise and technical certainty that nothing short of a recorded survey could create. Such a degree of certainty was unattainable in the unexplored and dangerous situation of the country at that time. To give notice, all that was required by the legislature was that the entry should, in some part of it, contain a reference to some place, natural object, artificial mark, or to some thing, or to several of these, which, either singularly or together, could be ascertained with reasonable ease by those acquainted in the neighborhood.[158]

In other words, an entry should carry, on the face of it, notice to the common understanding of men acquainted in the neighborhood of the land, or of some call or object therein, so that other enterers might know when they were within its area.[159]

In the technical language of the land law, a prior entry would be held as notice to a subsequent enterer that the land in question had been previously entered. This would enable a court of equity, if he had obtained the first grant, to divest him of the title, on the ground of notice. The entry was styled a *special* entry and an entry, which would not be such notice, was denominated *vague*.[160]

As early as 1798-9, our courts permitted the party having the eldest entry to give it as evidence, and held that he should stand in the same situation at law, as if his grant had been issued on the day he made his entry. In other words, the entry was to be considered as evidence of a sale for a valuable consideration, passing the fee to the enterer. The date of the entry held as proof conclusive that the sale evidenced by the entry

[154] 1 Haywood, 107, 135, 259, 375, 456, 498, *as cited by* Overton in *Reid v. Buford*, Cooper, 419, *decided in* 1809; *Anderson v. Cannon*, Cooke, 27-39, in 1811; *Winchester v. Gleaves*, 3 Haywood, 213, in 1817; *Hickman v. Gaither*, 2 Yerger, 202, in 1828; *Brown v. McCan*, 5 Haywood, 124-127, in 1818.

[155] *Winchester v. Gleaves*, 3 Haywood, 213-215; *Mitchel v. Barry*, 4 Haywood, 136-143.

[156] Ibid.

[157] Ibid; *Reid's Lessee v. Dodson*, Cooper, 396, 408-413.

[158] *Barnet's Lessee v. Russell and others*, Cooper, 10-21.

[159] *Kendrick v. Dallum*, Cooke, 230; *Murfree v. Logan*, Cooper, 220-229; *McMillan v. Claxton*, 4 Haywood, 274-279.

[160] *Wallen v. Campbell*, Cooper, 320-322.

had been fairly conducted and legally consummated.[161]

At first, this doctrine was sustained in argument by supposing that the Acts of 1786, chapter 20 and 1787, chapter 23, section 1, authorized the entry to be given in evidence in ejectment.[162] But it was soon observed that these acts were merely declaratory of the meaning of the Acts of 1777, chapter 1 and 1783, chapter 2, which themselves denote nothing less than that the first enterer shall be the grantee, on the ground of his being from the date of the entry, a purchaser of the land by actual payment of the prescribed consideration into the state treasury through the medium of the entry taker.[163] Whatever was the origin of the practice, it has been firmly established in our courts for a long period of years.[164]

And, from the beginning, the administration of the rule was attended at law with the same qualifications, which naturally attached to its administration in equity. Accordingly, it was held that in a contest between the prior grant founded on a later entry and a later grant founded on a prior entry, in order to set aside the elder grant, such entry must have been special.[165]

In every case, therefore, where the priority of the entry was relied upon to set aside an elder grant, the entry was closely scrutinized, and its claims to be regarded as special enough to advertise the subsequent enterer of its locality, questioned. The courts were compelled, as a matter of course, to lay down general rules of construction applicable to

[161]*Wilson v. Kilkannon, Cooper, 202-207; Kendricks v. Dallum, Cooper, 427-428; Anderson v. Cannon, Cooke, 27-36.*

[162]*Hoggatt v. McCrory & Gillespie, Cooper, 9-12.*

[163]*Reid's Lessee v. Buford, Cooper, 413-421; Anderson v. Cannon, Cooke, 27-36.*

[164]Cooke, page 32; Cooper, 419-420.

[165]*Simms'' Lessee v. Dickson, Cooke, 137-141.*

---

entries, and to define what the requisite specialty was.

An entry, as we have seen, must set forth where, or the county in which the land intended to be appropriated lay, mountains, and remarkable places nearest the land, the water courses, lakes, ponds, and remarkable places within the land, and its boundaries, natural and artificial.

It is plain, that specifying the county or other district of country or stream in, or on which the land was situated would be very indefinite, when the counties were so large as Washington, Sullivan, Green and Davidson, the only counties established as early as 1783.

By pointing out the water courses, mountains, and remarkable places nearest to the land, the subsequent locator would be led to its neighborhood. If the entry specified one or more water courses, lakes, ponds, or remarkable places within the land, this lead directly to the locality. It would have been made by designating what mountains, streams, or earlier surveys, if any, it was bounded on or by.

By pointing out a place of beginning a certain course and distance, or by the meanders of a stream, the different boundaries or "calls" of an entry were divided by the courts into two classes and described as follows:

1. The calls for the *county, or other district of country*, a valley for example, in which the land lay, and the calls for the *water courses, mountains and remarkable places* nearest the land, were designated *directory calls*—because they pointed out, not the land itself, but the vicinity of the land and the *direction* in which it was to be sought.

2. The calls for water courses, lakes, ponds and remarkable places *within* the land, and the calls for its boundaries, were termed *locative* calls, because they

located to a certain spot, or designated the very land intended to be appropriated.

If the calls were for land lying—

- On the south side of Cumberland river
- On the third big creek above Stones river
- About two miles from the mouth of said creek
- Including an improvement at a spring
- And a tree marked at the spring W. O.

If it was clear that there was but one spring on the specified creek about two miles from its mouth, at which there was an improvement, the entry must have failed for uncertainty as to the place intended, but for the last call, which alone distinguishes the spring from all others in the neighborhood. The four first calls are *directory*, the last *locative*.[166]

So, when the calls were for 274 acres of land—

1. In Sumner County
2. In the waters of Rocky Creek
3. Adjoining a tract entered by M. S. on the west running west and south for quantity

Here, the first and second calls are *directory*, the third *locative*.[167]

Again, where the entry was of two thousand acres of land,

1. On the waters of the Harpeth
2. About two miles south of the military lines
3. To include the Buffalo lick

Here the two first calls were held to be *directory*, the third *special or locative*.[168]

In short, the calls in every entry easily divide themselves into these two kinds as will be seen.[169]

If an entry contained no other than directory calls, as for example, if it called to lie in the woods, in the state, in the county, in a valley, or on a certain river etc., it would fail, because it could not be fixed to any particular spot.[170]

If an entry contained both classes of calls, still the entry would fail, if the locative call or calls were equally applicable to a *multitude* of things. Thus, *"on the south side of Duck river"* is a good call to *direct* to the part of the country where the land lay. *"On Lytle's creek"* is still nearer to the place. But, *beginning at a tree marked S. D., and running up the creek so as to include a tree marked A. B."* gives no clue to the identical tree, unless the creek on which it stands was so short as to make it not unreasonable to require subsequent locators to search for it.[171] Hence it is established in general that, in general, a call for a tree, or even for a

---

[166]*Barnett's Lessee v. Russel and others*, Cooper,10-21.

[167]*McMillan v. Claxton*, 4 Haywood, 274-279.

[168]*Kendrick and others v. Dallum*, Cooper, 489-498; Cooke, 220-238.

[169]*Burns v. Greaves*, Cooke, 75, 83-87; *Henderson v. Long*, Cooke,128-130; *Dallum v. Breckenridge*, Cooke,152-158; *Baird & Kennedy v. Trimble's Lessee*, Cooke, 282, 287-289; *Anderson v. Weakley*, Cooke, 410, 411; *Blount v. Ramsey*, Cooke, 489-493; *Murfree v. Logan*, Cooper, 220-229, and many others.

[170]*Wallen v. Campbell*, Cooper, 320-322.

[171]*Dallum v. Breckenridge*, Cooke, 152-158; *Wallen v. Campbell*, Cooper, 320-322.

tree marked in a particular manner, is not good.[172]

So, if the locative call is applicable to *two* places indifferently, the entry is void, for an entry is never to be so construed as to enable the enterer to hold at more than one place.[173] For example, if the locative call is "*adjoining an entry made by A. for B.*" and there is more than one such entry, the entry is *void*, and is not curable by testimony."[174]

But all calls of an entry are to be taken together, and an ambiguity produced by extraneous testimony may be removed by some other call in the entry itself. Thus, if the locative call is equally applicable, taken by itself, to two objects, the one meant by the locator may be shown by another call of the entry. For example, if the locative call is for the 12 mile tree on the continental line, and there are two 12 mile trees, one east, the other west of Mount Pisgah, the call, "*including Hardin's creek*" will ascertain which tree was meant, if there was a creek of that name near one of the trees and not at the other, and this, even though the creek was called by some Hardin's and by others Carter's creek.[175]

If the call was for twenty-seven chains north of a certain fork of a certain *trace*, and eighteen poles east of a certain fork of a named creek, and there were two such places, the one meant by the locator would be well designated by a call for a tree marked in a certain manner, if the tree that was actually marked be found at one of them. For then, there was but one place that answers *all* the calls.[176]

If there was *incompatibility or repugnancy* in the calls of an entry, it might nevertheless have been good, if the disagreement was not between calls of the same class. Thus, incompatibility or repugnancy between the *directory* and *locative* calls would not defeat an entry. For example, if the directory called to *lie on a certain river*, and the locative call *was to adjoin a certain tract* already granted or surveyed, and the river and the tract are ten miles apart, so that both cannot be complied with, the entry would be good if the locative call was sufficiently special, because it will prevail over the directory call, and the latter will be rejected as surplus.[177]

Upon this principle an entry was sustained, which called for land "on Little Harpeth, beginning above Absalom Tatum's line" etc. though Tatum's tract was on West Harpeth. For Tatum's tract would be *locative*, and the call for the river, would be *directory*, being inconsistent to the locative call, would be rejected, and yet there was no doubt as to the place intended to be appropriated.[178]

If a directory call is *impossible*, the entry will still be good, if the locative call is so special as to fix the spot intended. Thus, when the same person made two entries in succession on the entry book, and in the first called for land lying on a certain creek, and in the second, called for land adjoining the above on the upper side, and running up the creek for quantity, the latter entry was held good. The directory call for running up the creek was impossible because the first entry included all the land on both sides of the creek to the head of it. For the locative call, to *adjoin the first tract on the upper side*, precisely ascertained the land intended to be taken.[179]

Among calls of the same class, directory or locative, those for natural

---

[172]Ibid.

[173]*Reid's Lessee v. Dodson*, Cooper, 396, 403-413.

[174]*Mitchell v. Barry*, 4 Haywood, 136-143.

[175]*Baird & Kennedy v. Trimble*, Cooke, 282, 287-289.

[176]*Nell v. Ezel*, 4 Haywood, 162-165.

[177]*Reid's Lessee v. Dodson*, Cooper, 410-413.

[178]*Graham v. Dulley*, Cooke, 353-356.

[179]*Phillips v. Robertson*, Cooper, 399-423.

objects prevailed over those for artificial marks, rivers, creeks, branches, springs, etc., and over letters on trees, lines of others etc. [180]

But locative calls, though they were for artificial objects or marks will always prevail over directory call though they were for natural objects. Thus, calls for course and distance, which in all cases are locative calls, prevailed over calls for natural objects, when these are only directory. [181]

In the first of these cases, the land was described as lying on the *south* side of Cumberland River, but when surveyed according to course and distance, it was found to lie on both sides of the river. Nevertheless, the court held that the course and distance, being locative calls, controlled the call for south side of the river, which was only directory.

In the second case, the land were to lay on *both* sides of a certain creek, but the special boundaries called for, according to course and distance, placed it all on the same side of the creek. Here again the calls for course and distance prevailed over the calls for natural objects. [182]

It was not sufficient that there were locative calls in an entry. To support it, those calls, or at least some one of them, must be so specially set forth as to enable the surveyor, or a majority of those acquainted in the neighborhood, to find the land. Otherwise, it is no notice to a subsequent enterer of the previous appropriation of any particular spot. If such a person obtained a grant for a tract already granted to a younger enterer, he could not pretend that his grant should relate to the date of that entry, and that he should be regarded as having been the first purchaser by that entry, of that tract, since the entry does not describe that tract or any other. [183]

---

[180] *Weakley's Lessee v. Wilson & Simmons*, Cooper, 370-378.

[181] *Roberts v. Cunningham*, M. & Y., 67-73; *Wright v. Mabry*, 1 Yerger, 55-57.

[182] Ibid.

[183] *Barnet's Lessee v. Russell and others*, Cooper, 19-21; *Kendrick v. Dallum*, Cooper, 489, 508; Cooke, 230; *Burns v. Greaves*, Cooke, 75, 83-87; *Simm's Lessee v.*

From these cases it will be seen that if the locative calls or some one of them can, without extraordinary trouble, be identified by means of the description given in the entry of the object or objects which constitute such call or calls, the entry will be regarded as valid. The party ejected, having had a younger grant than his adversary for the land mentioned in the entry, may read the entry, and his grant will be held to relate to it, just as if it had been issued on the date of the entry, if his adversary entry is of later date.

Locative calls were specially set forth when the following questions could be answered in the affirmative:

1. Are the objects called for in the entry on the ground?
2. Can the place be known by the objects called for, when seen by a subsequent locator?
3. Can it be found by means of the description in the entry, by reasonable inquiry of those who have been there before the entry was made?

This excludes the necessity for *universal or general knowledge* of the objects called for, throughout the world, or state, or district, or country, or captains' company, or neighborhood of the place. For if no such knowledge existed, the entry might yet have been good, if the objects called for in the entry were known to a party of men, or to the greater part of them, or to the survivors of them, who were there before the entry, when the country was a wilderness. These men could have been a small locating, or hunting or trapping party, which went into the wilderness before any settlement began to be formed around the place entered, or

---

Dickson, Cooke, 137-140; *Dallum v. Breckenridge*, Cooke, 152-158; *Kendrick v. Dallum*, Cooke, 230; *Henderson v. Long*, Cooke, 128-130; *Murfree v. Logan*, Cooper, 220-229; *Smith v. Craig*, Cooper, 287-302; *Wallen v. Campbell*, Cooper, 320-322; *Philips v. Robertson*, Cooper, 399-423; *Mitchel v. Barry*, 4 Haywood, 136-143; *McMillan v. Claxton*, 4 Haywood, 274-279.

near it. In this way all the first locations were made, and none of them could stand against later and more precise appropriations, if *general notoriety* of the objects called for were necessary to make them good.[184]

But an entry might also be good so as to hold the land against an elder grant founded on a younger entry. If the entry gave no other description of the land but to designate the beginning on some object *within* it by a name it might be good. In that case the specified object or objects must have acquired *general notoriety* by the names ascribed to them in the entry. Upon no other principle could the entry in *Goodloe's heirs v. Wilson* have sustained, where the locative call was *"to include the Buffaloe lick."* For there is no other description given of the lick, the locative call, but its name, and if not known generally by that name, but by some other or by none, the entry would not give notice of the land intended to be entered.[185]

So where an entry described the watercourse on which the land lay as the *"First big fork on the west side of Yellow Creek"* to make the entry good, the fork called for must have been known as the *first big fork.* This would not have been sufficient when the majority of persons acquainted with it called it by another name.[186]

In the case of *Simms' Lessee v. Dickson,*[187] in which the entry called for land lying on the north side of Duck River, on the first creek above *Spring* Creek, beginning on the river, three quarters of a mile below the mouth of said creek" &c., the place of beginning could not be found except by means of the notoriety of *Spring* Creek, and if the creek so

[184]*Rogers v. Burton & others,* Peck,106-118.

[185]*Goodloe's Heirs v. Wilson,* Cooper, 59-67.

[186]*Weakley v. Wilson,* Cooper, 377-378.

[187]*Simms' Lessee v. Dickson,* Cooke, 137-141.

designated had been known by another name, the entry would have failed.

And if the locative call became notorious by the name given it in the entry, before the inception of the conflicting claim, that was held sufficient, though it was not at the date of the entry.[188]

But where the *notoriety* of the locative call was relied upon instead of a *special description* of it, it must be not a neighborhood, but an identified spot which was notorious by the name given it in the entry to authorize an enterer to call for it, or to adjoin it. Although it was notorious previous to the entry that a particular person had a claim in a given neighborhood previous to the entry calling to adjoin, that would not sufficiently identify the subsequent entry calling to adjoin it, unless the claim had been fixed to some well defined spot previous to such subsequent entry.[189] If the locative call was notorious by two names, a designation of it in the entry by either was sufficient.[190]

A grant could not be held to relate to the date of an entry *unless* it appeared upon its face, or by the plat and certificate of survey attached to it, to have been founded on such entry. Thus, a grant to one man could not be held to relate to the date of entry made in the name of another, unless the grant on its face recite that entry as the basis of it, or the plat and certificate of survey attached to the grant showed it.[191]

The only relation established in North Carolina and Tennessee between a grant and any initiatory act of appropriation, to overreach the

[188]*Simms v. Wilson,* Cooke, 140-141; *Baird & Kennedy v. Trimble's Lessee,* Cooke, 282-289; *Winchester v. Gleaves,* 3 Haywood, 213-219; *Thompson v. Garrison,* 5 Haywood, 257; *Talbot v. McGavock,* 1 Yerger, 262-271.

[189]*Graham v. Dudley,* Cooke, 353-356; *Craig v. Polk & Miller,* 3 Yerger, 248-257.

[190]*Baird & Kennedy v. Trimble's Lessee,* Cooke, 252-259.

[191]*Patton & Erwin v. Carothers,* Cooke, 148-149.

elder grant and confer a better title, was the relation between the younger grant and the elder legal entry. Our courts have never conceded to the elder survey from the beginning of our system.[192]

NORTH CAROLINA'S CESSION OF LAND TO THE UNITED STATES

Just one year after the opening of the John Armstrong office, North Carolina passed an act to cede to the United States all the territory of the state west of the Allegheny Mountains. This closed the John Armstrong office and voided all entries made after May 25, 1784, except entries of lands allowed the commissioners, agents, and surveyors who extended the line of the military reservation, and the guards, hunters, chain carriers, and markers, who attended the commissioners.[193] This cession was repealed by an act passed at the October session, 1784, but the land office was never reopened.[194]

In December 1789, another act was passed to cede to the United States, all the western territory of the state as a common fund for the payment of the debt of the states, according to their respective proportions. By the terms of this act, **the lands were to remain subject to all *bona fide* claims of every description, which had been derived before the cession, from the laws of North Carolina. The United** States, by an act of Congress passed on April 2, 1790, accepted this cession, and Tennessee became The Territory of the United States South of the River Ohio.[195]

To understand the early Tennessee land records from this point, it is of utmost importance that the political, financial, and legal situation of each of the three governments involved be thoroughly understood.

In the vernacular of the real estate profession, it could be said that North Carolina made an offer to the United States and the United States accepted their offer. After the offer was accepted, then the deed was executed transferring the title held by North Carolina to the United States. You see, it is the title to the land and not the land itself that transfers. Also it is important to remember at this point that only the degree of title held by the grantor—whether it be an *estate in fee simple* [complete ownership] or one of lesser ownership such as a *life estate, leasehold estate*, etc can be passed to the grantee. It is also important to remember that within a deed there can be *restrictive covenants running with and restricting the use of the land.*[196]

These are the **terms** on which North Carolina offered to **deed the title to the United States. These are the terms on which Tennessee accepted and was legally required to follow when title to the land was** received.

On March 3, 1791, Congress requested President Washington to provide before their next session an estimate of the quantity and situation of the lands not claimed by the Indians nor claimed by any of the citizens of the United States. The President referred this request to Secretary of

---

[192]*Donnegan v. Taylor*, 6 Humphrey, 501-504; *Trousdale & Nichol v. Campbell*, 3 Yerger, 160-167 and 5 Haywood,101-104; *White v. Crockett*, 3 Haywood,183-188; *Terrell v. Murray*, 2 Yerger, 384-390; 5 Haywood, 190.

[193]"An Act Ceding to the Congress of the United States Certain Western Lands Therein Described and Authorizing the Delegates from this State in Congress to execute a Deed or Deeds for the **same** . . . ," April 1784, Clark, *State Records of North Carolina*, 24:561-562, chapter 11.

[194]"An Act to Repeal an Act of the Last General Assembly, Intituled An Act Ceding to the Congress of the United States Certain Western Lands . . . ," 1784, Clark, *State Records of North Carolina*, 24:678-679, chapter 16.

[195]Clarence Edwin Carter, compiler and editor, *The Territorial Papers Of The United States* Volume IV (Washington: Government Printing Office, 1936), 13-17.

[196]The compiler/author held a Tennessee Real Estate Brokers License for 35 years and these thoughts are from the experience in dealing with land titles, deeds, etc, in the real estate profession.

State Thomas Jefferson who made his report on November 8, 1791.[197] This was an impossible job for the Territory South of the River Ohio, since North Carolina—a state land state—had not surveyed the land prior to its being granted to individuals. The next best approach was to provide information on the completed land grants as well as those grants not completed but upon which the granting process had begun.

The report, which Mr. Jefferson had obtained from North Carolina Governor James Glasgow, was as follows:[198]

1. That the entries in Washington County—Carter's office—amounted to 746,362 ½ acres had been made for 214,549 3/4 acres of which grants had issued. Of the remaining 531,812 3/4 acres a considerable proportion was declared void by the laws of the state, that is the lands lay west of Brown's Line or were over the Indian boundary line.[199]

2. That entries in Sullivan County amounting to 240,624 acres had been made, for 173,332 acres of which grants had issued, Of the remaining entries many were over Brown's Line and void, or void for some other reason.

3. That within the military reservation grants had been issued for 1,239,498 acres and warrants for 1,549,726 acres, making a total of 2,789,224 acres.

4. That the entries made in the John Armstrong office were not yet entirely known nor would be until December 20, 1792, the last day given for completing them. The total certificates which had been paid for the warrants issued before May 20, 1790 was 373,649 pounds, 6 shillings, 5 denarius at the rate of 10 pounds per hundred acres. This indicated that warrants had issued for 3,736,493 acres, of which grants had been issued for 1,762,660 acres and which were located in Greene and Hawkins Counties, and partly in the country from there to the Mississippi. It was also known that there were some outstanding warrants, which had not yet been paid for.

5. That the locations of the lands granted to Evans' Battalion, the guard sent to protect the citizens of Davidson County, had not been made.

6. That of the lands intended to compensate services rendered in laying off of the military reservation, there had been granted:
   a. to the surveyor general for his fees 30,203 acres.
   b. to the commissioners Shelby, Bledsoe and Tatum, and also to their guards, chain carriers, markers, and hunters, who attended them 35,932 acres.

7. That legislative grants to particular persons had been issued:
   a. To Richard Henderson and his associates, 200,000 acres
   b. Alexander Martin 2,000 acres
   c. To David Wilson 2,000 acres
   d. To General Greene 25,000 acres

[197]Walter Lowrie and Matthew St. Clark Clarke, eds., *American State Papers, Public Land*, Volume I (Washington, D. C.: Gales and Seaton, 1832-1834), 476; U. S. Congress, *1st Statutes at Large*, 225.

[198]Lowrie and Clarke, *ASP*, Volume 1:17-18.

[199]Brown's line was the Indian boundary in Washington County over which the citizens were forbidden to settle.

completed, as well as all of the bounty land promises to the soldiers of the North Carolina Continental Line. If the military reservation proved insufficient to fulfill the bounty land warrants, North Carolina had reserved the privilege of satisfying them in areas outside the military reservation. This need manifested itself very early in the land granting process.

In its typical, methodical fashion, the first action taken by Congress was to ask for an assessment of what lands would be available after all the North Carolina restrictive clauses in the cession deed had been fulfilled. This was impossible to estimate in a metes and bounds state in which the total available acreage had never been determined. The only possible solution was to obtain a list of all the grants that had been issued, together with all those which were in the process of completion and existed in entries, warrants or surveys. These were constantly changing ownership simply by an endorsement upon the back of the documents. This list was made but does not appear to have provided in any way the land that would be available to the United States for sale. **The United States was legally bound by the North Carolina cession deed and held title only to the vacant and unappropriated land remaining after the North Carolina cession deed restrictive clauses had been fulfilled. And these restrictive clauses were not being rapidly terminated.**

The United States recognized the Indian rights to the land, and immediately placed "off limits" those lands within Tennessee which had not been obtained by treaty. The area was not encumbered by Indian title at the date of acceptance by the United States was very small indeed. Only the area of Washington & Sullivan Counties and most of the military reservation in northern middle Tennessee had been cleared of Indian title. The people were suffering because they were not allowed to claim and occupy the land they had paid for and for which, in many instances, they already held fee simple title from North Carolina.

It is important to understand these situations because many have

In February 1796, the territory prepared its constitution and in the following June was admitted to the Union as the State of Tennessee. Documents of the new state, which were assumed to be compatible with the Constitution of the United States were:

a. The Bill of Rights
b. The Constitution of North Carolina
c. The Cession Act
d. The ordinance for the government

It seems appropriate at this time to analyze the Tennessee land situation as it was applicable to all three entities—United States, North Carolina, and Tennessee:

THE UNITED STATES

At the time of the land crisis in Tennessee, the United States could be described as a novice in the land business for they were only beginning to dispose of their own public lands. The United States passed legislation governing the sale of the public land in 1785 known as the Ordinance of 1785. It was a slow start and took an enormous amount of time since legislation required the land to be surveyed before its sale. Public land office activity did not begin until 1797 when western lands were sold from an office in New York City. A land office in Philadelphia followed in 1800. By 1805, there were two land offices which had been opened in Ohio and the Mississippi Territories.[200]

The restrictions North Carolina included in the cession deed had to be fulfilled before the United States could know if any vacant and unappropriated land in Tennessee would be left. The restrictions required all of the outstanding North Carolina entries and warrants to be

[200]E. Wade Hone, *Land & Property Research in the United States*, page 101.

was a legal obligation that North Carolina fulfill the promises made to its Continental Line—promises of land in lieu of payment for their placing their lives on the line, so to speak. Failure to complete these obligations in a court of law would have brought about insolvency of the state. North Carolina citizens were those suffering from inability to obtain their land.

The Tennessee Legislature became impatient with the stagnant land situation and decided to take matters into their own hands. In January 1799, they passed a land law[202] designed to cover the land with another set of entries, threatening the grants already issued. Later, realizing that this would create a real land conflict with North Carolina, the plan was abandoned. In the meantime North Carolina, suspicious of Tennessee began to exercise the right reserved in the cession deed. North Carolina proceeded to confirm and make good all lawful grants and entries made, and warrants and grants issued, by the state of North Carolina, for lands lying within the limits of the Tennessee, and authorized the secretary and governor to perfect or complete into titles to all lawful [outstanding] entries and warrants.[203]

In order to prevent this from happening, the Tennessee legislature passed legislation prohibiting surveying, entering or marking the land for the purpose of obtaining titles from North Carolina, with a penalty of $5,000, payable to the informer and recoverable in any court of Tennessee. Any grant issued by North Carolina upon such claims, was

[202] "An Act for Establishing Offices for Receiving Entries of Claims for All Vacant Lands Within the Several Counties in the State and Ascertaining the Method of Obtaining Title to the Same. . . ."January 1799,George Roulstone, compiler, *Acts Passed at the Second Session of the Fourth General Assembly of the State of Tennessee, 1799* (Knoxville: Routstone & Wilson, printer, 1799), chapter 24.

[203] "An Act to confirm and make good all lawful grants and entries made, and warrants and grants issued by the state of North Carolina, for lands lying within the limits of the state, and to authorize the secretary and governor of the same to perfect titles to all lawful entries and warrants that are not yet perfected. . . ." 21 September 1801, *Acts Passed at the First Session of the Fourth General Assembly of the State of Tennessee* (Knoxville: George Roulstone, printer, 1801), chapter 1.

criticized the United States for the delay. The United States was not idle during this time but was busy clearing the land of Indian title. From April 2, 1790, the date of the cession acceptance, until April 18,1806, the date of the compact between North Carolina, Tennessee and the United States, Congress negotiated the following land treaties:[201]

• Treaty of Holston or Blount's Treaty	July 2, 1791
• First Treaty of Tellico	October 2, 1798
• Chickasaw Cession	July 23, 1805

Other pertinent land treaties later negotiated by Congress were:

• Chickasaw Old Fields	September 11, 1807
• Cherokee Agency	July 18, 1817
• Chickasaw (West Tennessee)	October 19. 1818
• Calhoun's Treaty, Cherokee	February 27, 1819
• Chickasaw	October 20, 1832
• Cherokee	December 29, 1835

NORTH CAROLINA AND TENNESSEE

North Carolina and Tennessee wanted the same conclusion to bring about completion of land titles and occupation of the land but as daughter and parent states, they sometimes were at odds with each other. North Carolina continued to complete titles and issue new military warrants into the 1790s, a process which appeared most inadequate by a government far from the area of action. However, North Carolina was **legally obligated** to complete into grants those entries, warrants, and surveys for which she had accepted money in payment. In addition, there

[201] J. W. Powell, *Bureau of Ethnology* 18th Annual Report (Washington: Government Printing Office, 1899), passim. All treaty information is from this source. Only those treaties which cleared the Indian title are listed.

made inadmissible as evidence in any of the courts of Tennessee.[204]

At the same session, in order to bring about a more peaceable solution, the governor was empowered to appoint an agent to go to North Carolina to request that state to pass an act transferring to Tennessee the right claimed by North Carolina to complete into grants those land entries made prior to the cession deed to the United States.[205]

This had not been done when the legislature again met in 1803. At that time, John Overton was appointed to go to North Carolina to obtain the desired legislation.[206] He obtained the passage of the North Carolina act in November 1803, which was accepted and ratified by the legislature of Tennessee on August 4, 1804.[207] This act gave Tennessee full right and authority to issue grants and perfect titles to all claims of land lying in Tennessee in the same manner as North Carolina possessed by the Cession Act, except that North Carolina reserved the exclusive right to continue issuing military warrants. **Tennessee was to issue no grant but such as North Carolina might have lawfully issued.**[208] This compact could not take effect, however, until agreed to by the United States who still held title under the Cession Act. This compact was agreed upon April 18, 1806, by an act to authorize the State of

Tennessee to issue grants and perfect titles to certain lands therein described, and to settle the claims to the vacant and unappropriated lands within the same.[209]

PROVISIONS OF THE COMPACT

The first section of this legislative act, approved by the three governments, was to define the limits of the vacant and unappropriated land as protection of the United States' rights to the excess land, after all North Carolina obligations were complete. A division line was marked separating the western one third of Tennessee from the other two thirds. This line was called the *Congressional Reservation Line* and began at the place where the eastern or main branch of Elk River intersects the boundary of the state, thence due north to the northern or main branch of Duck River; thence down the waters of Duck River to the military boundary line, thence with said line west to the Tennessee River, thence down the Tennessee to the northern boundary of the state.

Tennessee surrendered all rights to the land south and west of this line, and also agreed to United States' property being exempt from taxes while it remained the property of the United States and for five years afterwards. In exchange, the United States agreed to cede to Tennessee their claim and title to the vacant lands north and east of this line.

North Carolina and the United States gave Tennessee full power to issue grants and perfect titles to those lands north and east of the congressional reservation line, under the following conditions:

- All entries, rights of location and warrants of survey, and all interfering locations, removable by the cession Act of North

---

[204]Ibid., chapter 1, section 7.

[205]Ibid, chapter 4, section 14.

[206]"An Act for the appointment of an agent on the part of this state to go to the legislature of the state of North Carolina for the purpose of finally settling and adjusting the landed business between the two states, and for other purposes," 19 September 1803, (Knoxville: George Roulstone, printer, 1803), chapter 82.

[207]"An Act to ratify and act for the appointment of an agent on the part of this state to go to the legislature of the state of north Carolina for the purpose of finally settling and adjusting the landed business between the two states, and for other purposes," 4 August 1804 (Knoxville: George Roulstone, printer, 1804), chapter 14.

[208]*Bass v. Dinwiddie*, Cooke, 130-133; *Carson v. Gordon*, Cooke, 149-152.

[209]"An Act to authorize the state of Tennessee to issue grants and perfect title to certain lands therein described, and to settle the claims to the vacant and unappropriated lands within the same . . . ," 18 April 1806, Richard Peters, ed., *The Public Statutes at Large of the United States of America*, Volume II (Boston: Charles C. Little and James Brown, 1845), 381-383.

- if the territory ceded to Tennessee should not contain a sufficient quantity of land fit for cultivation in which to perfect all existing legal claims charged thereon by the conditions of the cession act, the United States would provide for them out of the lands west and south of the congressional line. The land west of the Tennessee River had not been ceded to Tennessee at this time.

The surrender of the land east and south of the congressional reservation line was accepted by Tennessee September 5, 1806,[212] and Tennessee had the power—which had been coveted for so long—to decide what were the *bona fide* claims to lands within the limits of the state, which had originated before the date of the cession by North Carolina to the United States on February 25, 1790, and the power to provide for their satisfaction.

The legislative act of 1806, chapter 1,[213] amended by the act of

Carolina, which were not actually located within the limits reserved to the United States at the date of the cession—February 25, 1790, and all interfering grants, which had been located east and north of the above line, should be located, and the titles perfected within the territory ceded to Tennessee

- Tennessee should appropriate 100,000 acres within the bounds assigned to the Indians by the North Carolina Act of 1783,[210] to the use of two colleges to be established by the state, one in east, and one in west Tennessee

- 1,000 acres within the same limits be set aside for academies

- 640 acres in each six miles square in the ceded territory, where existing claims would allow of it, for the use of schools for the instruction of children forever

- The people south of French Broad and Holston, and west of Big Pigeon Rivers, should be secured in their rights of pre-emption and occupancy

- No person, until authorized by Tennessee, would locate any warrant, issued by North Carolina, within the limits reserved to

- the Cherokees by the Act of 1783, chapter 2, section 5[211]

thence up the middle of the Tenasee and Holston to the middle of French Broad, thence up the middle of French Broad river (which lines are not to include and island or islands in the said river) to the mouth of Big Pidgeon river, thence up the same to the head thereof, thence along the dividing ridge between the waters of Pidgeon river and Tuckasejah river, to the Southern boundary of this State; and that the lands contained within the aforesaid bounds shall be, and are hereby reserved unto the said Cherokee Indians and their nation for ever, anything herein to the contrary, notwithstanding."

[212]"An Act to ratify and confirm an act of the Congress of the United States of America, entitled, 'An act to authorize the state of Tennessee to issue grants and perfect titles to certain lands therein described, and to settle the claims to the vacant and unappropriated lands within the same,'" 18 April 1806, Elizabeth Roulstone, compiler, *Acts Passed at the First Session of the Sixth General Assembly of the State of Tennessee*, (Knoxville: J. B. Hood, printer, 1806), chapter 10.

[213]"An Act directing the division of the state into convenient districts, for the appointment of principal surveyors thereof, and for ascertaining the bona fide claims against the same, agreeable to an act of congress passed the eighteenth day of April, One Thousand Eight Hundred and Six entitled ' An act to authorize the State of Tennessee to issue grants and perfect titles to certain lands therein described, and to settle the claims to the vacant and unappropriated lands within the same.'" April 1806, Elizabeth Roulstone, *compiler, Acts*

[210]"An Act for Opening the Land Office for the redemption of specie . . . ." April 1783, Clark, *State Records of North Carolina*, 24:478–482, chapter 3.

[211]"An Act for Opening the Land Office for the redemption of specie . . . ."April 1783, Clark, *State Records of North Carolina*, 24:478–482, chapter 2. Section 5 reads: "And be it further enacted, by the authority aforesaid, that the Cherokee Indians shall have and enjoy all that tract of land bounded as follows, to wit: Beginning on the Tenasee where the southern boundary of this State intersects the same, nearest to the Chickamawga towns,

1807, chapter 2,[214] a method of ascertaining the *bona fide* claims to lands in Tennessee, which had arisen under the laws of North Carolina, was set in motion. **After this system had been in operation for nearly twelve years, it was determined that the North Carolina claims were not to be satisfied without resorting to the area south and west of the congressional reservation line.** On April 4, 1818, Congress passed an act supplementary to the act of 1806, which gave Tennessee authority to issue grants and complete titles on the land west and south of the congressional line, in the same manner as had been done east and north of that line. This law provided that this would be done on the following:[215]

- On all special entries and locations made pursuant to the laws of North Carolina before the date of the cession, which lay west and south of the congressional reservation line

- On all warrants of survey, interfering entries and locations, which might be removed by the cession act

- On all interfering grants or warrants and certificates, issued in consequence of such interference

Passed at the First Session of the Sixth General Assembly of the State of Tennessee (Knoxville: J. B. Hood, printer, 1806), chapter 1.

The same disposal practice could now be performed on the land west and south of the congressional reservation line, as was done by the laws of Tennessee for lands east and north of that line. [216]

Tennessee accepted this Act of Congress and applied the same system of adjudication to the country south and west of the reservation line as to the north and east of it. [217]

On February 18, 1841, by legislative act, Congress gave power to Tennessee to act as agent for the United States to sell the remaining vacant and unappropriated land south and west of the congressional reservation line, on the following condition:

- That the holders of North Carolina land warrants might locate them on lands not previously located on, or claimed as occupant preemptions, within one year from the time fixed by Tennessee for carrying this act into effect; and if default was made of such location within that year, the warrants might be satisfied by the payment of twelve and one half cents per acre, out of the proceeds of the sale; the warrant holder was restricted to produce the warrant for payment within two years, or be forever barred from presenting it.

Those persons entitled by the laws of Tennessee to rights of occupancy and preemption, should have a preference of entry or purchase for not exceeding two hundred acres at twelve and one-half

---

[214]"An Act to amend an act, entitled, 'An act directing the division of the State into convenient districts for the appointment of principal surveyors thereof, and for ascertaining the *bona fide* claims against the same, agreeable to an act of Congress, passed the eighteenth day of April, one thousand eight hundred and six entitled 'An Act to authorize the State of Tennessee to issue grants and perfect titles to certain lands therein described, and to settle the claims to the vacant and unappropriated lands within the same, 'and to point out the mode hereafter to be pursued in ascertaining the unsatisfied claims, and in perfecting titles on the same," 26 September 1807, *Acts Passed at the First Assembly of the State of Tennessee, 1808* (Knoxville: William Moore, printer, 1808), chapter 2.

[215]"An Act supplementary to the act, entitled 'An Act supplementary to authorize the state of Tennessee to issue grants and perfect titles to certain lands therein described, and to settle the claims to the vacant and unappropriated land within the same . . . " 4 April 1818, chapter XXV, 15th Congress, 1st session, Richard Peters, editor, *The Public Statutes at Large of the United States of America*, 8 Volumes (Boston: Charles C. Little and James Brown, 1846), 3:416.

[216]"An Act . . . to authorize the state of Tennessee to issue grants and perfect titles to certain lands therein described . . . , 4 April 1818, 15th Congress, 1st session.

[217]"An act making provision for the adjucation (sic) of North Carolina land claims, and for satisfying the same, by an appropriation of the vacant soil south and west of the congressional reservation line, and for other purposes . . . " 1819, *Acts of a Public or General Nature Passed At First Session of the Thirteen Assembly of The State of Tennessee* (Nashville: G. A. & A. C. Sublett, printers, 1819), chapter 1.

cents per acre.

The proceeds of the residue were to be annually accounted for and paid over by Tennessee to the United States. This agreement was accepted by Tennessee by the Act of 1841, by which provisions were made for performing the duties assumed by them.[218]

Finally, on August 7, 1846 the United States surrendered to Tennessee on all their right and title to all the lands south and west of the congressional reservation line, which remained unappropriated. The United States released and transferred to Tennessee the proceeds of such lands as had been sold under the act of 1841, but not paid for nor deposited subject to the order of the United States.[219]

The lands released to Tennessee and the proceeds obtained from them were to remain subject to all the same claims, encumbrances, and liabilities, in relation to North Carolina land warrants, or other claims of North Carolina, as if the lands still remained in the hands of the United States.

PERFECTING NORTH CAROLINA IN THE AREA NORTH AND EAST OF THE CONGRESSIONAL RESERVATION LINE

After the cession deed, North Carolina had no power to sell an acre of land within the ceded territory. No new right could be acquired to land under the laws of North Carolina. Tennessee had the right to perfect the remaining incomplete titles only.[220] And as to perfecting titles, the Cession Act left things precisely as they were before its passage.[221]

The compact between North Carolina and Tennessee, with the consent of the United States in 1806, gave Tennessee the right to perfect titles to the lands within the limits designated, including the greatest part of the State. Until this arrangement, Tennessee had no right to make title to an acre of soil within the state limits, and was assumed were void.[222]

In perfecting or completing titles under the compact of 1806, Tennessee acted only by the power delegated by North Carolina; grants issued under this authority did not come from Tennessee's consequently those acts passed in 1799 and 1801[223] in which power sovereign power but from that of North Carolina. Therefore, where one party who had been ejected claimed land under a grant issued by North Carolina and the other party claimed under a grant issued by Tennessee, it was considered that both grants came from the same state. In a contested suit, it was not transferable from the state to the federal courts.[224]

---

[218] An Act to carry into effect an act of Congress, passed and approved the 18th day of February, 1841, authorizing the State of Tennessee to perfect titles to the vacant and unappropriated lands South and West of the Congressional reservation line in this State, 1841," *Acts Passed At The First Session of the Twenty-Fourth General Assembly of the State of Tennessee 1841-1842*, (Murfreesborough: D. Cameron & Co., printers, 1842), chapter 34.

[219] "An Act to surrender to the State of Tennessee all Title the United States have to Lands in Tennessee, south and west of the Line commonly called the Congressional Reservation Line, and to release to said State the Proceeds of such of said Lands as may have been sold by the State of Tennessee, as the Agent of the United States," 7 August 1846, chapter 92, 29th Congress, 1st session, George Minot, editor, *Statutes at Large and Treaties of the United States of America* (Boston: Charles C. Little and James Brown, 1851), 9:66-67.

[220] *Polk's Lessee v. Hill, Windel & Others*, Cooper,160.

[221] *Polk's Lessee v. Hill, Windel & Others*, Cooper, 157.

[222] *Miller's Lessee v. Holt*, Cooper, 243-245.

[223] "An Act for Establishing Offices for Receiving Entries of Claims for All Vacant Lands Within the Several Counties in the State and Ascertaining the Method of Obtaining Title to the same," January, 1799, George Roulstone, compiler, *Acts Passed at the Second Session of the Fourth General Assembly of the State of Tennessee, 1799* (Knoxville: Roulstone & Wilson, 1799), chapter 24; "An Act to confirm and make good all lawful grants and entries made, and warrants and grants issued by the state of North Carolina, for lands lying within the limits of the state, and to authorize the secretary and governor of the same to perfect titles to all lawful entries and warrants that are not yet perfected," 21 September 1801, *Acts Passed at the First Session of the Fourth General Assembly of the State of Tennessee* (Knoxville: George Roulstone, printer, 1801), chapter 2, section 7.

[224] *Thompson v. Kendrick and McQuary v. Kendrick*, 5 Haywood, 113-117.

The Tennessee legislature had no absolute right under the Cession Act to legislate the disposition of Tennessee vacant soil. Claim to make good the warrants originating under the laws of North Carolina was transmitted to Tennessee only for that purpose. [225]

ADJUDICATION OF CLAIMS

Since the claims that Tennessee could satisfy were specified to be *bona fide* claims which had begun under the laws of North Carolina, before February 25, 1790, it was necessary for Tennessee to adopt some method of determining which claims were *bona fide*.

Legislation was passed for this purpose in 1806 and 1807. [226] The first of these acts in 1806 [227] divided that part of the state, which lay north and east of the congressional reservation into six surveyors' districts. A map, drawn by Fred Smoot, together with district boundary lines, can be found in the Appendix. This system was patterned after the federal method of surveying in township and range. It was found not to be practical, because, with patchwork surveys already made, it was virtually impossible to survey using a true township and range method. A surveyor was appointed for each district. Instructions for the surveyors were as follows:

- To divide his district into sections six miles squares by lines running to the cardinal points [north, east, south, west]
- To connect every survey in his district upon which a grant had been issued with some sectional line, if practicable
- To cause locations founded upon *bona fide* warrants legally issued, and so described as to be ascertained with certainty, to be surveyed
- To conform, in making his surveys, to the laws in force and use at the passing of the Cession Act, and to the special calls of the warrant

Commissions were created by legislative act of 1807, [228] one for east Tennessee and one for west Tennessee (now middle Tennessee). Each commission consisted of a single commissioner. The two commissions were established **for the purpose of judging and ascertaining the validity of all warrants within the state of Tennessee. This responsibility had been given to Tennessee by the Cession Acts of North Carolina and United States Congress. The right to accept new entries or issue new warrants was not given Tennessee at this time.** The claims that were to be satisfied were described and classified as follows:

- Entries made in the office of John Armstrong, Carter or Adair,

---

[225]*Townsend v. Shipp's heirs*, Cooke, 302-303.

[226]"An Act directing the division of the state into convenient districts, for the appointment of principal surveyors thereof, and for ascertaining the bona fide claims against the same, agreeable to an act of congress passed the eighteenth day of April, one thousand eight hundred and six entitled, 'An Act to authorize the State of Tennessee to issue grants and perfect titles to certain lands therein described, and to settle the claims to the vacant and unappropriated lands within the same.'" Elizabeth Roulstone, *Acts Passed at the Second Session of the Sixth General Assembly of the State of Tennessee*, 1806, (Knoxville: J. B. Wood, printer, 1806), chapter 1; "An Act to amend an act, entitled, 'An act directing the division of the state into convenient districts; for the appointment of principal surveyors thereof, and for ascertaining the *bona fide* claims against the same, agreeable to an act of Congress, passed the eighteenth day of April, one thousand eight hundred and six, entitled 'An act to authorize the State of Tennessee to issue grants and perfect titled to certain lands therein described, and to settle the claims to the vacant and unappropriated lands within the same, and to point out the mode hereafter to be pursued in ascertaining the unsatisfied claims, and in perfecting titles on the same . . . ." 26 September 1807, *Acts Passed at the First Assembly of the State of Tennessee, 1808* (Knoxville: William Moore, printer, 1808), chapter 2.

[227]Ibid.

[228]Ibid.

the purchase money on which were paid, but no warrants issued

- Entries made in the John Armstrong office on which no warrants had issued because the entire purchase money had not been paid

- Entries in the entry books of Samuel Barton, entry taker of the pre-emption and guard rights in Davidson County, on which no warrants had been issued or grants obtained

- Warrants, purporting to have been issued on entries in the John Armstrong office, in all other respects regular except they had not been signed by the entry taker

- Warrants issued on entries in the office of John Armstrong, Carter or Adair, and by any means lost or mislaid so as not to be found

- Warrants issued upon entries made in any office established by the laws of North Carolina, not actually located west and south of the congressional reservation line, on or before the 25th of February 1790. [Note: This was only for warrants east and north of the congressional reservation line and did not include **any west and south** of the congressional reservation line.]

- Warrants on any of the above offices on which no grants had been issued by North Carolina

- Warrants (or duplicates) obtained from the office of the North Carolina secretary of state for military services, on which no grants had been issued by North Carolina

- Warrants obtained from the office of the secretary of state of North Carolina for services performed as a commissioner, surveyor, or other person, who accompanied the commissioners appointed to lay off the lands for the continental officers and soldiers

- Warrants obtained from the office of the secretary of state of North Carolina for service under the Act of North Carolina, entitled, "An Act for raising troops for the protection of Davidson

County"

- Warrants obtained from the North Carolina land office for pre-emption rights

- A file obtained from the North Carolina land office marked No. 29, of military warrants, &c, accompanied with plats and certificates of survey, examined and copied by John Overton, upon which it was believed no grants had been issued—**provided said surveys were made East and North of the Congressional Reservation Line**

- Warrants issued under the **voided Tennessee Act of 1801, chapter 1,** upon North Carolina grants for lands, whereon there were older and better titles

- Grants issued by North Carolina on good and valid warrants for lands taken by the interference of a grant of better title, issued by North Carolina for the same, or any part of the land

- Grants issued by North Carolina on good and valid warrants for land, the locality of which could not be ascertained on account of the vagueness of the calls of the surveyor, or from the calls or corners of the survey being lost or destroyed, or on account of the surveyor and chain carriers being dead

- Grants from North Carolina for lands south of French Broad and Holston or Tennessee, and west of Big Pigeon River, or east and north of the congressional reservation line, on good and valid warrants, where the lands had been actually paid for, and the price not refunded, or the claim not satisfied by a grant of other lands, not within said district

It should be noted that **no new warrants were to be issued by Tennessee at this time, and the authorization to the commissioner was to judge only those documents already issued by North Carolina initiating the granting of lands by that state.** The documents to be used by the commissioners to determine the validity of the claims presented to them were the following:

- A copy of the John Armstrong entry book, as transcribed by John Overton, agent to North Carolina, with the account and abstract, including the appendix made in the entry book by John Overton

- The books made by John Overton, which contained copies of Carter warrants on which grants had issued

- The book procured from the office of the secretary of state of the United States, which contains reports of the lands entered in Sullivan and Washington counties[229]

- The book which contains copies of the entries made in Hardin's office, transcribed by Samuel Love[230]

- The book which contained copies of the entries made in the entry taker's office of Sullivan County

- A book furnished the commissioners of East Tennessee, by John Adair, the correctness of which he had sworn to before Josiah Nichol, Esq.

- The book transcribed by John Overton, sgent to North Carolina, which contains copies of the military warrants, issued by the State of North Carolina

- The entry book of the entry taker of Davidson County, put into the hands of Nathan Ewing, and then in the hands of the commissioners of west Tennessee (now middle Tennessee)

- The abstract formed by John Overton, the late agent to North Carolina, relative to the claims of the troops raised for the protection of Davidson County, or a copy taken from them or

[229]*Polk's Leesee v. Windel and Others*, Cooper, page 435.

[230]Samuel Love was an assistant to John Overton in copying the North Carolina records.

either of them, in case it should become necessary

- And all other transcripts, documents, and records taken by John Overton or copies thereof if necessary

The above list of evidence was not to be viewed by the commissioners as conclusive evidence. In addition, they might use information derived from other documents obtained from the secretary of state of North Carolina, which could be evidence of their correctness or incorrectness.

During the process of determining their validity, the claims lost their locality, except in some particular cases where special entries had been made. Their characteristic names became military, John Armstrong, Evans' Battalion, county warrants, pre-emption, commissioner, guard and service rights. Any significance to their previous location disappeared and all became equal having the same principles and the same rights. The vacant, disposable land was assigned as a common fund from which the commissioners' decisions were to be satisfied. The division into districts with separate district offices and officers was for the purpose of facilitating the satisfaction of the claims and the completion of the title.[231]

The commissioners did not decide between two or more claimants of a warrant, which had a right to it, but in the case where a warrant was judged valid, they delivered it to the person, or his representative, who filed it for adjudication.[232] If a certificate was issued to a person who was

[231]*Armstreet Stubblefield Lessee v. William Short*, 5 Haywood 266.

[232]"An Act to amend an act, entitled 'An act directing the division of the State into convenient districts; for the appointment of principal surveyors thereof, and for ascertaining the bona fide claims against the same, agreeable to an act of Congress, passed the eighteenth day of April, one thousand eight hundred and six, entitled, 'An Act to authorize the State of Tennessee to issue grants and perfect titles to certain lands therein described, and to settle the claims to the vacant & unappropriated lands within the same.'" September 1807, *Acts Passed at the First Assembly of the State of Tennessee, 1808* (Knoxville: William Moore, printer, 1808), chapter 2 section 13.

not the real owner of the title, the true owner was authorized to sue for and recover the value of the certificate from the person to whom the certificate was issued.[233]

By a resolution passed in 1832, the legislature designated certain grants, belonging to the area south of French Broad and Holston or Tennessee, and west of Big Pigeon River, or east and north of the congressional line, as valid. These were on good and valid warrants, where the lands had been actually paid for, and the price not refunded or the claim not satisfied by a grant of other lands, not within the above district. The legislature directed the Tennessee secretary of state to issue certificates to the person entitled to the grant. Under this resolution, the secretary of state could not be forced to issue a certificate or warrant unless the grant was shown to have not been made on a valid warrant. The following guidelines were declared upon which the claimant could show he was entitled to a certificate from the secretary of state.[234]

- That no duplicate warrant had issued
- That the warrant was good and valid
- That it had been lost or mislaid
- That it had never been adjudicated
- That no other grant had issued on it

Specific spots of land designated by a North Carolina entry or location, and not taken by a prior entry or location, were to be surveyed for the person having a duplicate or certificate warrant.[235] Entries made

prior to 1806 were to be surveyed according to the entries' boundary lines.[236]

After receiving a warrant from the board of commissioners, a claimant produced it to the surveyor of the district where the land lay. The location on which the warrant was issued, specified the water courses, mountains or other prominent places nearest the land, its natural boundaries and the lines of adjoining land owners, if any, which separated it from other lands. The surveyor performed the survey immediately or if two persons entered the same location at the same time, lots were used to determine **priority of entry.** Entry was then made in an entry book kept for that purpose. The claimant might make two or more entries on the same warrant as long as they were made with the same surveyor and in the same district.[237]

New entries on the same warrant were allowed in cases where all or

[233]Ibid.

[234]*Dunlap v. Smith,* Yerger 4, pages 509-528.

[235]An Act Directing the Division of the state into convenient districts, for the appointment of principal surveyors thereof, and for ascertaining the bona fide claims against the same, agreeable to an act of congress passed the eighteenth day of April, one thousand eight hundred and six, entitled, 'An act to authorize the State of Tennessee to issue grants

and perfect titles to certain lands therein described, and to settle the claim to the vacant and unappropriated lands within the same.'" Elizabeth Roulstone, *Acts Passed at the Second Session of the Sixth General Assembly of the State of Tennessee,* (Knoxville: J. B. Wood, printer, 1806), chapter 1.

[236]An Act to amend an act, entitled 'An act directing the division of the state into convenient districts; for the appointment of principal surveyors thereof, and for ascertaining the *bona fide* claims against the same, agreeable to an act of Congress, passed the eighteenth day of April, one thousand eight hundred and six, entitled 'An act to authorize the State of Tennessee to issue grants and perfect titled to certain lands therein described, and to settle the claims to the vacant and unappropriated lands within the same,' and to point out the mode hereafter to be pursued in ascertaining the unsatisfied claims, and in perfecting titles on the same;" An Act to amend an act, entitled ' An act directing the division of the State into convenient districts; for the appointment of principal surveyors thereof, and for ascertaining the bona fide claims against the same, agreeable to an act of Congress, passed the eighteenth day of April, one thousand eight hundred and six, entitled, ' An Act to authorize the State of Tennessee to issue grants and perfect titles to certain lands therein described, and to settle the claims to the vacant & unappropriated lands within the same,'" September 1807, *Acts Passed at the First Assembly of the State of Tennessee, 1808* (Knoxville: William Moore, printer, 1808). chapter 2.

[237]Ibid.

part of the land entered was taken by a prior claim. Also, new entries were allowed when it was determined there was not enough vacant land as would take to satisfy, when it was determined all or part of the land was taken by a prior claim. Where it was determined there was not enough land available for the quantity of land needed to satisfy the warrant, new entries could be made. The new entry was required to be made in the same surveyor's office, however.[238] As soon as possible after receiving the location the surveyor surveyed the land described by the separate acts of 1777, 1806 and 1807.[239]

The legislative acts of 1806 and 1807 directed the surveys to be made as soon after delivered to the surveyor as practicable. The surveyor was required to run and to have every line marked either by the claimant or by some other person at the expense of the claimant. The claimant was required to attend the surveyor while he was surveying the land.[240] When entries joined each other or were for the same land, the surveys were to be made according to the priority of entry, unless the claimant refused to call on the surveyor to have his prior entry surveyed within a term of twelve days after the time when the survey was to be made.[241]

Surveys were to be made by the lawful surveyor within one year

from the passage of the act of November 12, 1813. The enterers were required to make application within six months from that date to the surveyor. Minors were allowed twelve months after they reached the age of twenty-one to make their surveys. Lands entered by persons who failed to have their surveys made as specified by this law were considered to be vacant and could be entered by any person.[242]

By 1815, entries were required to be surveyed within one year after the entry date. It was made the duty of the surveyor, upon request by the claimant or his agent, to appoint a day not more than six weeks after such request for making the survey and on that date to proceed with the survey until finished.[243]

If any survey contained more than one tenth over the quantity called for, the excess was declared vacant and deemed vacant. No surveyor was to survey more than five thousand acres in one tract. The surveyor was to make a plat and certificate of each survey containing a correct number of acres, the county and district in which the land lay, the kind of warrant or certificate it was founded upon, the courses and distances of the boundaries, and the names whose former lines had joined the land surveyed. Within three months after the surveyor completed the survey, the surveyor recorded the plat and certificate at full length in a bound book kept for that purpose. He then delivered a copy to the person for whom the survey was made.[244]

---

238 Ibid.

239 *Bickerstaff v. Hughlett*, Cooper, 272.

240 An Act to amend an act, entitled ' An act directing the division of the State into convenient districts; for the appointment of principal surveyors thereof, and for ascertaining the bona fide claims against the same, agreeable to an act of Congress, passed the eighteenth day of April, one thousand eight hundred and six, entitled, ' An Act to authorize the State of Tennessee to issue grants and perfect titles to certain lands therein described, and to settle the claims to the vacant & unappropriated lands within the same," 26 September 1807, *Acts Passed at the First Assembly of the State of Tennessee, 1808* (Knoxville: William Moore, printer, 1808), chapter 2.

241 Ibid.

242 "An act to prescribe the duties of the different surveyors in this state in particular cases, November 12, 1813," *Acts Passed at the First Session by the Tenth General Assembly of the State of Tennessee, 21 September 1813* (Nashville: T. G. Bradford, 1813), chapter 84.

243 An Act to amend an act entitled 'Act to prescribe the duties of the different surveyors in this state,'" 12November 1813, *Acts Passed at the First Session of the Eleventh General Assembly of the State of Tennessee* (Nashville: T. G. Bradford, printer, 1815), chapter 174.

244 An Act to amend an act, entitled 'An act directing the division of the state into convenient districts; for the appointment of principal surveyors thereof, and for ascertaining

Any other claimant could, at any point, prevent the party who had caused the survey to be made from obtaining a grant by filing in the surveyors office within three months after the receipt of the plat and certificate and by filing a caveat in the county court clerk's office where the land lay. The clerk entered the caveat in a book and issued summons directed to the sheriff in the county where the defendant lived. The caveat stated the reason it was being issued and required the defendant to appear on the first day of the next succeeding court and defend his right to the land. The court then proceeded, without pleadings in writing, to impanel a jury and give judgment. Either party could appeal to the superior court. A copy of the judgment of the county or superior court was delivered to the office of the principal surveyor. The judgment in the caveat was conclusive of the right between the parties.[245]

The claimant delivered his plat and certificate of survey to the register of the appropriate land office, who made out a grant to the party having the right to the land. If a grant was issued to an heir or assignee of an original claimant, the pertinent circumstances were recited in the grant. The register issued a grant to an assignee only if the assignment was upon the plat and certificate and had been proven by two witnesses in open court in the county where the land lay.[246]

After the 1818 purchase of the land west of the Tennessee River, presently known as West Tennessee, the same system of adjudication was adopted by legislative act of 1819. In general it followed the same provisions for adjudication as that legislated for the area of land north and east of the congressional reservation line.[247] There were, however, a few differences.

In order to enable the district surveyors to ascertain which lands had actually been granted by North Carolina and to determine the vacant residue, old grantees were required to procession or resurvey their lands and define their boundary lines by the first day of October 1820. If they failed to do so, the surveyors caused it to be done, so that new entries could be made in conformity with the boundaries of the old grants. The court ruled that the grantee might take the land processioned, if he

---

the *bona fide* claims against the same, agreeable to an act of Congress, passed the eighteenth day of April, one thousand eight hundred and six, entitled An act to authorize the State of Tennessee to issue grants and perfect title to certain lands therein described, and to settle the claims to the vacant and unappropriated lands within the same,' and to point out the mode hereafter to be pursued in ascertaining the unsatisfied claims, and in perfecting titles on the same," 26 September 1807, *Acts Passed at the First Assembly of the State of Tennessee, 1808* (Knoxville: William Moore, printer, 1808), chapter 2.

245"An Act directing the division of the state into convenient districts, for the appointment of principal surveyors thereof, and for ascertaining the bona fide claims against the same, agreeable to an act of Congress passed the eighteenth day of April, one thousand eight hundred and six entitled,' An act to authorize the State of Tennessee to issue grants and perfect titles to certain lands therein described, and to settle the claims to the vacant and unappropriated lands within the same . . . ' 1806, Elizabeth Roulstone, *Acts Passed at the Second Session of the Sixth General Assembly of the State of Tennessee 1806* (Knoxville: J. B. Hood, Printer, 1806), chapter 1; "An Act to amend an act entitled, 'An act directing the division of the State into convenient districts; for the appointment of principal surveyors thereof, and for ascertaining the bona fide claims against the same, agreeable to an act of Congress, passed the eighteenth day of April, one thousand eight hundred and six, entitled, 'An act to authorize the State of Tennessee to issue grants and perfect titles to certain lands therein described, and to settle the claims to the vacant & unappropriated lands within the same,' and to point out the mode hereafter to be pursued in ascertaining the unsatisfied claims, and in perfecting titles on the same, September 1807,'" *Acts Passed at the First Session of the Seventh General Assembly of the State of Tennessee, 1808* (Knoxville: William Moore, printer, 1808), chapter 2. *Peeler & Campbell v. Norris*, 4 Yerger, 326-331.

246 "An Act to amend an act, entitled , 'An act directing the division of the state into convenient districts; for the appointment of principal surveyors thereof, and for ascertaining the *bona fide* claims against the same, agreeable to an act of Congress, passed the eighteenth day of April, one thousand eight hundred and six, entitled An act to authorize the State of Tennessee to issue grants and perfect titled to certain lands therein described, and to settle the claims to the vacant and unappropriated lands within the same, and to point out the mode hereafter to be pursued in ascertaining the unsatisfied claims, and in perfecting titles on the same" *Acts passed at the First Session of the Seventh General Assembly of the State of Tennessee* (Knoxville: William Moore, Printer, 1808), chapter 2.

247"An Act making provision for the adjudication of North Carolina land claims, and for satisfying the name, by an appropriation of the vacant soil south and west of the congressional reservation line, and for other purposes," 1819, *Acts of a Public or General Nature Passed at The First Session of the Thirteen General Assembly of The State of Tennessee* (Nashville: George Wilson, Printer, 1819), chapter 1.

pleased, and no other person could interfere with him but he was not bound to accept an erroneous survey on the part of the state.[248]

The same rules of surveying required in the area north and east of the congressional reservation line were applied to the area south and west of the congressional reservation line.

The lands south and west of the congressional reservation line belonged to the United States. Any one settled upon them had no title or right to them and were considered trespassers. The Tennessee legislature had no power to grant any right of possession to these lands. But, to keep down strife among the citizens residing upon these lands, it was provided that when one man turned another out of actual possession, or held him out, he might be restored by the writ of forcible entry, and this, without regard to the right of the soil. But no right to the land itself could be gained or lost by contracts between these trespassers.[249]

But as soon as Congress relinquished those lands to Tennessee, and Tennessee became vested with the title, the occupant laws previously enacted were applied to those who had complied with their provisions. Settlers upon the land were trespassers until their pre-emptions were granted them.[250]

In 1801 Tennessee legislated plans for surveying and entering land in Tennessee, regardless of the cession deed of North Carolina. The courts declared this act to be void and it was repealed. The 1806 provision was made for enterers under this law to be given a preference for six months from the time of opening the land office to enter the same warrant on the same piece of ground. The land office was opened on the

first Monday of August 1807. Of course, this was conditioned on the warrant being judged valid by the commissioners.[251]

By 1807 this preference was not to extend where another person had settled on and was in actual possession of the land entered before and at the time of making entry in the county entry takers office. Every person, his heirs, or assigns who had made entry under the act of 1801 on a warrant adjudged valid by the commissioners was allowed two years to make his entry for the same piece of ground. The entry was to be made in the office of the surveyor of the district where the land lay. Enterers of service rights as assignees of Martin Armstrong and his deputies in the military land office and enterers in the same office on warrants previously adjudged invalid were given a preference of two years to enter the same piece of land under any valid warrant.[252]

The office was supposed to be opened on the August 3, 1807, but it appears that no entries, except occupancy claims, were made until August 5, 1807.[253]

Any person settled upon and in actual possession of vacant and unappropriated land before May 1, 1806 was entitled to 200 acres. He had a preference of entering the land within three months after the first Monday in June 1807, upon any valid warrant, provided his improvement was included in the center of a square.[254] Circumstances before that day

[248] *Sheppard v. Johnson*, 2 Humphrey, 285-298.

[249] *Gillespie v. Wood & Douglass*, 4 Humphrey, 437-438; *Barnhart v. Neisler*, 6 Humphrey, 493-495.

[250] *Knox v. Thomas*, 5 Humphrey, 473-575; *Brown v. Massey*, 3 Humphrey, 470-472.

[251] "An Act Directing the Division of the state into convenient districts, for the appointment of principal surveyors thereof, and for ascertaining the bona fide claims against the same, agreeable to an act of congress passed the eighteenth day of April, one thousand eight hundred and six, entitled, 'An act to authorize the State of Tennessee to issue grants and perfect titles to certain lands therein described, and to settle the claim to the vacant and unappropriated lands within the same,'" Elizabeth Roulstone, *Acts Passed at the Second Session of the Sixth General Assembly of the State of Tennessee*, (Knoxville: J. B. Wood, printer, 1806), chapter 1, sections 37 & 38.

[252] *Anderson v. Weakley*, Cooke, 410-413.

[253] *Bass v. Dinwiddie*, Cooke, 130.

[254] "An Act Directing the Division of the state into convenient districts, for the

were not considered. All the occupants were trespassers upon the lands until their possessions were legalized. **This was done to prevent the confusion that might arise from removing the settlers or permitting others to acquire a title to that land and the settler to be ejected from his possessions.** The person with the entry made on the earliest number was allowed the preference if the same land was being claimed by more than one settler. Judge Whyte was of the opinion that possession by a son, servant, or agent was a sufficient possession to entitle the party to make an entry. Judge Roane thought the preference belonged to the person in possession. Both agreed that if that person were a minor son, his father might be considered his assignee and enter the land for him.[255] In another court case, the court held that possession by a purchaser from the enterer would be sufficient and so was possession by tenant.[256]

An improvement was supposed to be in the center of the occupancy. If the improvements of two occupants were only one hundred yards apart, and the survey of one included his two hundred acres in the opposite direction from the improvement of the other, the other could not object if that improvement was not included in the center.[257]

It was stipulated in the compact between Tennessee and North Carolina that no preference would be given to the citizens of Tennessee over the citizens claiming under North Carolina in entering and obtaining titles to lands. No occupancy or possession would give a preference to one in such a way as to take away the right of any person then claiming by entry, grant, or otherwise under North Carolina. The court held that the preference given by the act of 1806 to occupant claims over claims under North Carolina was void because Tennessee had exceeded her power. The full federal court agreed.[258] In another case Judge McNairy, sitting alone, was of the opinion that Tennessee had a right to pass the occupant law of 1807. Both cases were decided at the same term.[259]

Under the act of 1807, if a person had made an actual settlement and seated himself on vacant and ungranted land and was in possession on September 12, 1807, he was given a term of two years to make entry. The term was two years from December 3, 1807. The entry could not exceed three hundred acres, nor be less than one hundred, unless prevented by interfering claims--to include his improvement. The occupant had to obtain a valid warrant or certificate from the board of commissioners, which he presented to the surveyor. The surveyor had nine months from December 3, 1807 to make the survey. The surveyor also was required to enter in his book the warrant or certificate to be applied to each survey, which he returned to the registers office who issued the grant.[260] Any assignments were required to be written upon

appointment of principal surveyors thereof, and for ascertaining the bona fide claims against the same, agreeable to an act of congress passed the eighteenth day of April, one thousand eight hundred and six, entitled, 'An act to authorize the State of Tennessee to issue grants and perfect titles to certain lands therein described, and to settle the claim to the vacant and unappropriated lands within the same,' . . . ," 1806, Elizabeth Roulstone, *Acts Passed at the Second Session of the Sixth General Assembly of the State of Tennessee, 1806* (Knoxville: J. B. Wood, printer, 1806), chapter 3.

255 *Morris v. Gilliam*, 3 Haywood, 165-173.

256 *Cooke v. Shute*, Cooke, 67-75; *Smith v. Kain*, Cooper, 196-198.

257 *Morris v. Gilliam*, 3 Haywood, 165-173.

258 *Bass v. Dinwiddie*, Cooke, 130-133.

259 *Cason v. Gordon*, Cooke, 149-152.

260 "An Act to amend an act, entitled 'An act directing the division of the state into convenient districts; for the appointment of principal surveyors thereof, and for ascertaining the *bona fide* claims against the same, agreeable to an act of Congress, passed the eighteenth day of April, one thousand eight hundred and six, entitled 'An act to authorize the State of Tennessee to issue grants and perfect titled to certain lands therein described, and to settle the claims to the vacant and unappropriated lands within the same, and to point out the mode hereafter to be pursued in ascertaining the unsatisfied claims, and in perfecting titles on the same,'" 1807, *Acts passed at the First Session of the Seventh General Assembly of the State of Tennessee*, 1808 (Knoxville: William Moore, state printer, 1808), chapter 2.

the plat and certificate, when proved in open court by two credible witnesses or acknowledged by the assignor, to which was attached the clerks certificate.[261]

The surveyor had the responsibility to ascertain that the person claiming the survey had made an actual settlement and was seated on the land in possession on September 12, 1807.[262] If the surveyor included more or less land in his survey than the quantity specified in the law, he could amend his survey by adding or reducing the quantity so as to correspond with the law. This amendment could be made even after the limit of nine months. The correction could especially be made where the plat and certificate had not been returned to the office of the secretary.[263] If an occupancy grant was assigned, it was required that the claim was assigned for the total acreage. When presented to the register of the land office, it was his responsibility to decide the assignee.[264]

Under the act of 1809, occupancy grants were allowed those persons who had settled and were in possession of the land on January 1, 1809. They were allowed twelve months from the date of the act to have the land surveyed, including his improvements, if it were not less than one hundred acres or more than three hundred acres. The survey was delivered to the land office register where the grant was issued the grant.[265]

---

[261] Ibid.

[262] Clinton v. McClain, 3 Haywood, 288-294; Carson v. Gordon, Cooke, 149-152.

[263] Campbell v. Seahorn, Cooper, 195-196.

[264] Clinton v. McClain, 3 Haywood, 288-299.

[265] An act for extending further indulgence to occupants, " 1809, Acts passed at the Second Session of the Seventh General Assembly of the State of Tennessee (Knoxville: John B. Hood, 1809) chapter 12.

The occupancy law of 1807 allowed the occupant preference of entry, for not exceeding three hundred acres nor less than one hundred acres. By the act of 1809, the restriction of less than one hundred acres was omitted.[266]

Under the occupancy act of 1819, a person proposing to obtain land through the right of occupancy, was required to produce to the surveyor the deposition of two respectable people taken in the county where they resided. A deposition from a justice of the peace of that county was required specifying that the deponents were acquainted with the spot or piece of ground entered or to be entered. The justice also was required to depose that the land was within the district of that surveyor and that the enterer resided on the same spot or piece of land on September 1, 1819. He was also required to state that he believed the land proposed to be entered to be ungranted and unappropriated. Upon this proof, the surveyor was to permit the person producing it to make an entry for one hundred sixty acres in a square or oblong, including his improvement.[267]

Under the occupancy act of 1823, every person in actual possession of any vacant and unappropriated land, north and east of the reservation line and north of Tennessee River, except the Hiwassee District, had a preference of priority of entry for three months after the opening of the office to make an entry. It was required that the entry be not less than fifty acres nor more than one hundred sixty acres, so as to include his improvements in as near a square or oblong as possible.[268]

---

[266] Henderson v. Robertson & Blackman, Cooke, 207-211.

[267] "An Act making provision for the adjudication of North Carolina land claims, and for satisfying the same, by an appropriation of the vacant soil south and west of the congressional reservation line, and for other purposes . . . , " 1819, Acts of a Public or General Nature, Passed at the First Session of the Thirteenth General Assembly, 1819 (Nashville: George Wilson, Printer, 1819), chapter 1.

[268] An Act to establish Offices for receiving Entries for the vacant Lands in this state, lying north and east of the Congressional reservation line, and north of Tennessee River . . . , " 1823, Acts Passed at the First Session of the Fifteenth General Assembly of the

Provision was made for interference between occupants or between the owners of small tracts, or between an occupant and the owners of a small tract, in the appropriation of the vacant land adjoining them. The surveyor could appoint two disinterested persons, who chose a third, and the three persons went upon the land in dispute and divided it between the claimants.[272]

By the occupancy act of 1829, the provisions of the Act of 1827 were re-enacted and applied to persons under the name of resident occupants upon vacant and unappropriated land south and west of the reservation line December 30, 1829.[273]

Under the act of 1837, persons who were bona fide resident occupant settlers before November 11, 1837, upon vacant and unappropriated land south and west of the congressional reservation line and north of Winchester's line,[274] were allowed to include their improvements and land not exceeding two hundred acres. The land was surveyed by the county surveyor or deputy and represented on the plan of the county by the entry-taker. By section 11 of this Act, they or their assignees who had three years peaceable possession were protected in their rights of occupancy. The county offices were required to remain open from January 1, 1838 to January 1, 1839 for them to make entry, etc.[275]

By 1842, all persons entitled to any of the vacant and unappropriated

Under the occupancy act of 1825, those persons who were settled on the land on November 25, 1825, were considered bona fide resident occupants, and also those who should be such before May 1, 1826.[269]

Under the act of 1826 persons who had settled and were actually residing upon any vacant and unappropriated land south and west of the congressional reservation line on or before the first day of May 1826, were entitled to not more than two hundred acres nor less than twenty-five acres unless confined by lines of lands already appropriated. The land was to be surveyed in a square or oblong not more than twice as long as broad.[270]

Under the occupancy act of 1827, persons who had settled and were actually residing upon vacant and unappropriated land south and west of the congressional reservation line, at or before the passage of the act of November 28, 1827, were allowed any quantity not more than two hundred acres nor less than twenty-five acres, unless confined by lands already appropriated. The survey was to be made in a square or oblong not more than twice as long as broad, and to include their improvements.[271]

---

[272]Ibid.

[273]"An Act for the relief of the Occupants south and west of the Congressional reservation line, and for other purposes," 30 December 1829, Allen A. Hall & Frederick S. Heiskell, Acts Passed at the First Session of the Eighteenth General Assembly of the State of Tennessee, 1829 (Nashville: Republican & Gazette, 1829), chapter 22.

[274]Winchester's line was a narrow strip of land extending along the southern border of West Tennessee joining Mississippi.

[275]Chester v. Hubbard, 2 Humphrey, 354-360.

[269]State of Tennessee, 1823 (Murfreesborough: J. Norvell, G. A. & A. C. Sublett, printers,1823), chapter 49.

[269]"An Act, to settle the claims of North Carolina for the benefit of the occupants of the Western District . . . " 1825, Acts Passed at the Regular Session of the Sixteenth General Assembly of the State of Tennessee 1826 (Knoxville: Heiskell & Brown, 1826), chapter 39; Reese v. Crockett, Yerger 8, pages129-133.

[270]"An Act, to further provide for the occupants south and west of the Congressional reservation line," 20 November 1826, Acts Passed at the Extra Session of the Sixteenth General Assembly of the State of Tennessee, 1826 (Knoxville: Heiskell & Brown, 1827), chapter 6.

[271]"An Act directing the mode of surveying and granting occupant entries, and extending the rights of occupancy," November 28, 1827, Acts passed at the Stated Session of the Seventeenth General Assembly of the State of Tennessee, 1827 (Nashville: Hall & Fitzgerald and Heiskell & Brown, 1827), chapter 29.

lands south and west of the congressional reservation line, as occupant or pre-emption rights, were given the preference and priority of entry for the whole term of four years from the opening of the land office to exercise their right. The act of July 1, 1843 provided that at any time within four years a person could enter the claim or any part of it by paying to the entry taker twelve and one-half cents per acre.[276]

The owner of more than two hundred acres of granted land was not entitled to an extension of entry. The law for that was intended for such persons as owned less than two hundred acres, to enable them to make up their tracts to two hundred acres.[277]

SOUTH OF THE FRENCH BROAD & HOLSTON RIVERS

Rights of property owners south of the French Broad and Holston Rivers were protected by the first Constitution. These lands were sold with purchase price payment by the installment plan. The first law governing the sale of this land was in 1805.[278] A register and surveyor were not appointed until 1806.[279] The citizens living in this area petitioned

for and received relief for payment of various installments. Acts granting this relief extended from 1805 until 1879.[280]

HIWASSEE DISTRICT

The Hiwassee District was opened for sale in 1819.[281] The amount of land available to purchasers was limited to 640 acres per individual. The price of this land was two dollars per acre with terms available.

The township and range system was followed in disposal of the land in this area.

THE OCOEE DISTRICT

The Ocoee District in the extreme southeast corner of the state was opened for sale in 1836.[282] This area was made a separate district. The township and range system was followed in the surveying of it.[283] Sale of this land continued well into the 1879's.

---

[276] An act to carry into effect an act of Congress, passed and approved the 18th day of February, 1841, authorizing the State of Tennessee to perfect titles to the vacant and unappropriated lands South and West of the Congressional reservation line in this State," 11 January 1842, *Acts Passed at The First Session of the Twenty-Fourth General Assembly of The State of Tennessee, 1842* (Murfreesborough: D. Cameron & Co., printers, 1842), chapter 34, section 5.

[277] *Lacy v. Anderson*, 6 Humphrey, 495-498.

[278] "An act directing the mode of ascertaining the bounds of improvement and occupant claims south of the rivers French Broad and Holston, between the rivers Big Pigeon and Tennessee, and authorizing the plats of such improvement, when filed, to be evidence when bounds of such improvement may come in question," 28 October 1805, *Acts Passed at the First Session of The Sixth General Assembly of The State of Tennessee, 16 September 1805* (Knoxville: John B. Hood and Co., 1805), chapter 72, sections 5 & 6

[279] "An Act for the appointment of a register of the land office, and providing for the sale of the lands south of Holston and French Broad, agreeably to the Constitution of this State, and the provisions of the act of Congress therein referred to," 6 September 1806,

Elizabeth Roulstone, *Acts Passed at the Second Session of the Sixth General Assembly of the State of Tennessee 1806* (Knoxville: J. B. Hood, printer, 1806), chapter 2.

[280] "An Act to amend an act passed September 12, 1806, entitled, 'An Act for the appointment of a Register of the land office, and providing for the sale of the land south of Holston and French Broad, agreeable tot he Constitution of this State, and the provisions of act of Congress therein referred to,'" 31 March 1879, *Public Acts of the State of Tennessee passed by the Forty-first General Assembly* (Nashville: The American Book & Job Printing Office, 1879), chapter 252.

[281] "An Act to dispose of the lands lying between the rivers Hiwassee and Tennessee, and north of Little Tennessee River," 15 November 1819, *Acts Passed at The First Session of the Thirteenth General Assembly of The State of Tennessee 1819* (Nashville: George Wilson, printer, 1819) chapter 59.

[282] "An act to provide for the survey of the lands ceded to the United States by the Cherokee nation of Indians within the State of Tennessee, by the treaty of the 23rd day of May 1836," 18 October 1836, *Public Acts Passed at Called Session of the Twenty-First General Assembly of The State of Tennessee* (Nashville: S. Nye and Co., printers, 1836), chapter 2.

[283] Ibid.

The act of 1837, was passed to dispose of lands in the Ocoee District. For three months from November 1, 1838 at seven dollars and fifty cents per acre, these lands were subject to entry by occupants exclusively for three months from November 1, 1838 at seven dollars and fifty cents per acre. This was then extended at three month intervals for a lower price until the price became one cent per acre.[284] In this same session Chapter 196 was passed in which the entry taker was directed to designate before the first Monday of November 1838, two half townships from which the money collected would be paid over to the trustees of East Tennessee College and Nashville University in equal proportions. This was conditioned upon their agreeing to receive that amount in full satisfaction of claims held by those institutions against that state.[285]

Any person who was in actual possession and residing upon vacant and unappropriated land in Ocoee District November 20, 1837, or his rightful assignee, was for three months after November 5, 1838, entitled to a preference for one hundred sixty acres of land. The tract was required to include his improvements and dwelling house, provided it could be surveyed by beginning at one corner of a quarter section and run with the lines there. No person was entitled to more than one quarter section and occupancy or preference under this act.[286]

By 1839, any person, or his assignee, in possession of a vacant and unappropriated quarter or fractional quarter section of land in the Ocoee District was entitled after November 28, 1839 to a preference under the

---

[284] "An Act to dispose of the Lands in the Ocoee District," 20 November 1837, *Acts Passed at The First Session of the Twenty-Second General Assembly of the State of Tennessee* (Nashville: S. Nye & Co, printers to the State, 1838) chapter 2.

[285] *State v. Nashville University, 4 Humphrey,* 157-168.

[286] "An Act to dispose of the Lands in the Ocoee District," 20 November 1837, *Acts Passed at The First Session of the Twenty-Second General Assembly of the State of Tennessee* (Nashville: S. Nye & Co, printers, 1838), chapter 2, section 5.

specifications prescribed by the act of 1837. The right of entering forty or eighty acres of a quarter section was given in the same manner.[287]

If the occupant did not enter the land sell his right of entry, he was entitled—before he was compelled to surrender possession—to demand compensation for his improvements from any person who would make an entry for it.[288]

The courts decreed that section 2 of the act of 1839, chapter 8, dispensed with the requirement that the improvement of an occupancy should be included in his entry in cases where less than a quarter section was entered. The courts also decreed that an occupant might enter a part of his quarter section at one time, and another part at a later date. If he permitted another person to enter that part of his entry, which included his improvement, it would not prevent him from entering the residue himself at a later date.[289]

By 1840, any person not already owning two hundred acres of land, who became the owner by deed, grant, entry or occupant reservation of a less quantity than two hundred acres, could enlarge the same to any quantity not exceeding two hundred acres. This was allowed as long as it did not interfere with any occupant settler.[290]

TITLES TO LAND IN TENNESSEE ISSUED BY VIRGINIA AND KENTUCKY

The boundary line between North Carolina (presently Tennessee) and Virginia (presently Kentucky) was the parallel of thirty-six degrees

[287] Ibid.

[288] *Harvey v. Jones, 3 Humphrey,* 157-162.

[289] *Davis v. Broomfield, 3 Humphrey,* 174-177.

[290] "An Act for the benefit of the occupant settlers south and west of the Congressional Reservation line ...," 1840 (Nashville: J. Geo. Harris, printer, 1840), chapter 62.

thirty minutes. Commissioners from both states attempted to survey and mark that line in 1779-1780. In an effort to avoid disputes between the citizens of each state, the commissioners agreed upon a beginning and ran the line westward for about forty miles. Then they disagreed. The Virginia commissioners extended the line to the Tennessee River, but the North Carolina commissioners ran another two miles north for about half that distance. The first of these lines is known as Walker's Line, the other as Henderson's Line. Virginia claimed the right to grant titles to Walker's Line and North Carolina to Henderson's Line. North Carolina later confirmed Walker's Line, but not until December 11, 1790, after the cession to the United States.

Virginia and Tennessee appointed commissioners, who came to an agreement on December 8, 1802, and ran a due west line for the boundary between the states. Tennessee confirmed this agreement[291] which provided that all claims or title derived from the government of Virginia to lands that by the adjustment of the line fell within the State of Tennessee, should remain secure to the owners as if derived from the government of North Carolina or Tennessee.[292]

In 1819, Kentucky caused a line to be run by Alexander and Munsell as the boundary between the two states, running the parallel of thirty-six degrees thirty minutes was found to be considerably south of Walker's line. This brought the dispute to a crisis and made it necessary for both States to act decisively. Consequently, they referred the matter to commissioners and gave them full power to settle it.[293] The commissioners agreed on February 2, 1820 to make Walker's line the boundary from the southeastern corner of Kentucky to the Tennessee River, and Alexander and Munsell's line from the Tennessee River to the Mississippi. Claims to land west the of Tennessee River and north of Alexander and Munsell's line derived from North Carolina or Tennessee or from Virginia or Kentucky south of that line were declared null and void.[294]

Claims to land east of the Tennessee River, between Walker's line and the latitude of thirty-six degrees thirty minutes, derived from Virginia, in consideration of military services, were considered as rightfully granted and the claimants were allowed to enter upon the land or assert their rights in the courts of justice without prejudice by lapse of time.[295]

In the space between Walker's Line and the latitude of thirty-six degrees thirty minutes from the southeastern corner of Kentucky to Cumberland River near the mouth of Obed's River, private rights already granted by Virginia, North Carolina, Kentucky, or Tennessee were considered as rightfully emanating from none of those states. Claims, which had not been completed, were to be completed into grants by the states of Kentucky or Tennessee according to their origin. The validity of conflicting claims were tested by the laws of the state from which they emanated.[296]

---

[291]"An Act for confirming the boundary line between this state and the state of Virginia, as settled and designated by certain commissioners; and for appropriating certain monies therein mentioned," November 3, 1803, *Acts Passed at the First Session of the Fifth General Assembly of the State of Tennessee* (Knoxville: George Roulstone, printer, 1803), chapter 58.

[292]Ibid.

[293]"An Act to adjust the boundary line between this state and the state of Kentucky," 23 November 1819, *Acts of a Public or General Nature Passed at The First Session of the Thirteenth General Assembly of The State of Tennessee* (Nashville: George Wilson, Printer, 1819), chapter 67.

[294]"Convention Entered into by the Commissioners of the States of Tennessee and Kentucky, Concerning the Boundary Line between the Same, on the 2d Day of February, 1820," John Haywood, *The Civil and Political History of the State of Tennessee from its Earliest Settlement up to the Year 1796* (Glendale, California: The Arthur H. Clark Co., 1915), Appendix page 499-504.

[295]Ibid.

[296]Ibid.

A grant issued by Virginia for land in the territory between Walker's and Henderson's lines could not be read in evidence in Tennessee courts, unless authenticated under the seal of the state, or according to the Act of Congress of 1804, chapter 58.[297]

By legislative act of 1903, chapter 416, the State of Tennessee legislated a disclaimer from making any further granting of the land as follows:

. . . if the State owns any lands, which have never been granted, they should not be given away by the State, but should be sold at their actual value, and the proceeds turned into the school funds . . . .

. . . if the State does not own any lands, it should not be a party to the fraudulently granting of said lands.

Therefore, . . . all laws and parts of laws authorizing land grants in this State be, and the same are hereby repealed.[298]

---

[297] *Richards v. Hicks & Campbell*, Cooper, 207-208.

[298] *Acts of the State of Tennessee Passed by the Fifty-Third General Assembly* (Nashville, Tennessee: Foster and Webb, Printers), pages 1203-1204.

NORTH CAROLINA JOHN ARMSTRONG GRANT- JOHN BUCHANAN - LAND GRANT SUPPORTING PAPERS

John Buchanan was a hunter in the guard for the commissioners when they laid off the boundaries for the military district. He spent his time hunting for wild game while the surveyors, chain carriers and markers measured the land. It was necessary for the commissioners to have a guard of one hundred men to protect them from the Indians. They were allowed six hunters, and John Buchanan was one. For this job John Buchanan was given 500 acres. He selected this land on Duck River. At that time, 24 January 1787, Greene County extended to the Mississippi River and included all of Middle Tennessee except Davidson County, which was also the Military Bounty Land Reservation. Since it was selected outside the Military Reservation, it had to be entered in John Armstrong's Office. The warrant and survey is contained in the Middle Tennessee section of warrants and surveys.

The warrant is copied as follows:

"State of North Carolina No. 38

John Armstrong entry officer of the claims for the western lands,

To: the surveyor of Greene County

You are hereby required to lay of and survey for John Bohannon a hunter in the guard to ascertain the bounds of the land allotted the officers & soldiers of the continental line of this state enters 500 acres of land lying on big hunting creek as north fork of Elk river including the first main fork below where a large war trace crosses said creek

Observing the directions of the act of assembly in such case made and provided for running out lands. Two just and fair plans thereof, you are to transmit to the secretary's office with this warrant, in the time limited by law. Given under my hand at Hillsborough, the 24th day of Jany Anno. Dom. 1787."

[Signed:] John Armstrong

State of North-Carolina. *№38*

JOHN ARMSTRONG entry officer of claims for the western lands.

To the *surveyor of Green County*

You are hereby required to lay of and survey for

John Bohannon a hunter in the guard to ascertain the bounds of the land alloted the officers & soldiers of the continental line of this state enters 500 acres of land lying on big hunting creek as north fork of Elk river including the first main fork below where a large war trace crosses said creek

Observing the directions of the act of assembly in such case made and provided for running out lands. Two just and fair plans thereof, you are to transmit to the secretary's office with this warrant, in the time limited by law.

Given under my hand at Hillsborough, the ___ *day of* ___ ___ *Anno. Dom. 178* ___

Jno. Armstrong

Warrant

No. 269
TENNESSEE

County *Rutherford, then Jno*

Name *Buchannon, John*

Acres *500*

Grant No. *114*

Issued *27 Apr. 1793*

Warrant No. *81*   Entry No. *38*

Entered *24 Jany 1787*

Book No. *81*   Page No. *32*

Location *Duck River &c*

Jacket

In 1784 (N. C. chapter 14) the western portion of North Carolina (presently Tennessee), except the military reservation and Washington and Sullivan Counties, was divided into three sections and surveyors were appointed for each section. The section of Greene County and Cumberland Mountain was known as the eastern district. The section between Cumberland Mountain and Tennessee River was known as the middle district and the section between the Tennessee and Mississippi Rivers was known as the Western District.

This plat was in the middle district of The Territory of the United States South of the River Ohio, since the date was after 1790 (the date of the cession Act of North Carolina). There is an error on the plat itself — the number of acres written on the plat should be 500 instead of 5000. The plat is drawn to a scale of forty chains to an inch.

It reads as follows:

"Territory of the River Ohio
Middle District

By Virtue of a Warrant from the Entry taker of the State of No. Carolina No. 38 Dated January the twenty fourth day One thousand Seven hundred & Eighty seven, I have surveyed for John Buckhannon a hunter in the guard to ascertain the bounds of the land Allotted for the Officers & Soldiers of the Continental line of the State of North Carolina five hundred Acres of land lying on the South side of Duck River on the East waters of Lytles Creek Beginning at a white Oak Alexander Brackenredges and David Looneys North East Corner and James Browns South East Corner runs east sixty two chains fifty links to an Elm thence South Eighty Chains to an Ash thence West Sixty two Chains fifty links to a Stake on said Brackenriges and Looneys line then with there line North Eighty chains to the Begining.   Given under my hand November 30, 1792."

[Signed:] R. Weakley, D[eputy] S[urveyor]

David Justice)
           &   )   S[worn] C[hain] C[arriers]
Charles Reese)

NORTH CAROLINA JOHN ARMSTRONG GRANT - LAND GRANT SUPPORTING PAPERS - COL. ANTHONY BLEDSOE'S HEIRS

Col. Anthony Bledsoe was killed by the Indians in 1788. His heirs, Anthony, Isaac, Abraham, and Henry Bledsoe, completed the paper work necessary to receive the 3,000 acres of land. Col. Bledsoe was eligible to receive land as a commissioner for laying off the lands of the North Carolina Continental Line. Col. Anthony Bledsoe, himself, made entry for the 3,000 acres and received entry number 7 from John Armstrong on January 4, 1786.

The warrant was as follows:

"No. 7. State of North Carolina

John Armstrong, entry officer of claims for the western Lands,

To the Surveyor of the Middle District

You are hereby required to lay off and survey for Anthony Bledsoe, one of the Commissioners for laying off the lands granted the Contl. Line of this State, three thousand acres of land lying on the North side of Duck River, on Walnut Creek, beginning on the creek about two miles & one half from the mouth & running down the creek for quantity.

Observing the direction of the Act of assembly in such case made and provided for running out lands. Two just and fair plans thereof, you are to transmit to the secretary's office this warrant, in the time limited by law.

Given under my hand at Hillsboro, the fourth day of January Anno. Dom., 1786.

[Signed:] Jno. Armstrong

The survey is the description of the bounds (boundaries, both natural and artificial, such as streams, etc.). The metes (measurements of length such as inches, feet, yards, and rods), and monuments (natural such as landmarks—tree or river, or artificial such as a road or fence.)

In 1784 the western portion of North Carolina (presently Tennessee), except the military reservation, Washington, and Sullivan Counties were divided into three sections. A surveyor was appointed for each section. The section of Greene County and Cumberland mountain was known as the eastern district. The section between Cumberland Mountain and Tennessee River was known as the middle district. The section between the Tennessee and Mississippi Rivers was known as the western district. The plat for the Bledsoes was in the middle district of the District of The Territory South of the River Ohio.

The plat reads:

"Done by a scale of two hundred poles to the inch. Isaac Bledsoe & Joseph Lefna, Chain Carriers.

Middle District   July 15, 1792

Agreeable to the inclosed Warrant No. 7, I have surveyed for Thomas Bledsoe, Anthony Bledsoe, Isaac Bledsoe, Abraham Bledsoe, and Henry Bledsoe, heirs of Coll. Anthony Bledsoe, deceased, three thousand acres of land lying on the East fork of Obids river including Isaac Bledsoe Senr's hunting camp at a Spring. Beginning two hundred and forty poles up the Branch at a Ash tree, thence south eight hundred poles to a stack thence eight hundred poles to a stack thence east six hundred poles to a steak, thence north eight hundred poles to a steak, thence six hundred poles to the Beginning. Surveyed by

David Wilson, D[eputy] S[urveyor]"

Plat and Survey

Back of Plat & Survey

NORTH CAROLINA MILITARY GRANT - PRIVATE JOHN THOMASSON LAND GRANT SUPPORTING PAPERS

John Thomasson served in the North Carolina Continental Line as a private for which he received a 640 acre grant in the North Carolina military district. In order to receive a military land grant, the veteran first had to prove his service and receive a warrant from the North Carolina secretary of state. None of the certificates issued for military service have survived. The secretary of state or his deputy (in this case Deputy W. Williams) presented him with a warrant to Martin Armstrong, Surveyor of the military district.

This warrant was taken by either the veteran or his agent to the western land where the 640 acres were selected. The veteran or his agent then made entry with Martin Armstrong, which should be listed in the entry book.

Martin Armstrong directed one of his deputies—in this case R. Weakley–to survey and prepare two copies of the plat and survey to be sent to

North Carolina. One copy of the plat and survey was attached to the grant when it was issued, and the other became a part of the secretary of state's land office. The grant was issued and returned to the veteran. The final step in the process, which took about 18 months, was for the veteran to have his grant recorded in the county where the land lay.

No. 574

County ___

Name Thomasson, John

Acres 640

Grant No. 340

Issued 15" Sept 1787 Entry No. ___

Warrant No. 640

Entered ___

Book No. 63 Page No. 131

Location West Jacket
R.d. River

Jacket or Shuck

Warrant

The shuck for File No. 374 shows that John Thomasson's grant was issued September 15, 1787 as no. 340, and was recorded by the secretary of state in Grant Book 63, page 131. It was located on the West Fork of Red River.

The warrant reads:

"No. 649. State of North Carolina. The Honble James G. Glasgow, Esq., Secretary of State - To Colo. Martin Armstrong. Greetings. You are hereby required to lay off and Survey for John Thomasson, private - in the line of this State Six hundred and forty acres of land within the limits of the land reserved by Law for the Officers and Soldiers of the Continental Line in this State - Observing the directions of the Act of Assembly in such case made and provided for running out lands, two just and fair plans thereof with a Certificate to Each annexed, you are to Transmit to my Office within the Time limited by Law. Given under my hand at Hillsboro the 23rd day of April 1784.

[Signed:] W. Williams D[eputy] Sec[retary]."

The plat was drawn on a scale of forty chains to an inch and the survey made on October 22, 1785.

The survey reads as follows:

"State of North Carolina, Davidson County. By virtue of a Military Warrant No. 649 Located August the Thirteenth day One Thousand seven hundred and Eighty-four. I have surveyed for John Thomasson six hundred and forty acres of Land lying On the West fork of Red River. Beginning at a Beach on the bank of the river on John Harrys line and Runs with his line south fifty six chains sixty links to a large poplar and dogwood, then West One Hundred Thirteen chains Twenty links to a white oak and dogwood, thence North fifty six chains sixty links to a stake, thence East One hundred thirteen chains Twenty links to the Beginning.

[Signed:] Ro. Weakley, D[eputy] Sur[veyor]."

The SCC [sworn chain carriers] were: John Bell and William Nash, who signed the plat and survey. The chain carriers are not named on the warrant or grant - only on the plat and survey.

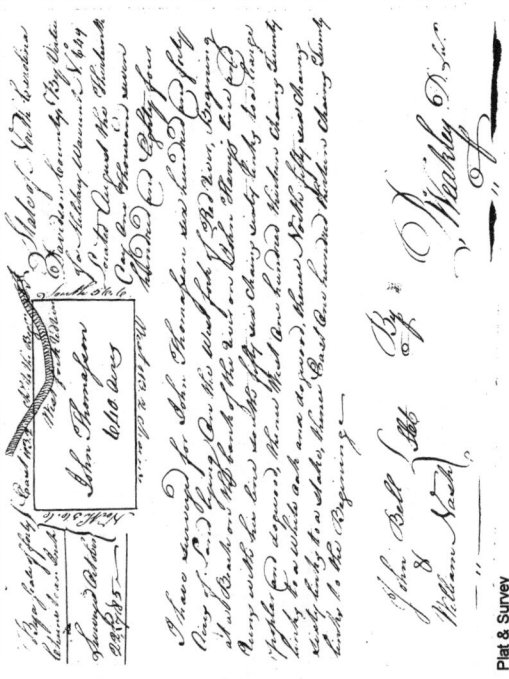

Plat & Survey

NORTH CAROLINA PRE-EMPTION GRANT - HAYDON WELLS - LAND GRANT SUPPORTING PAPERS

Haydon Wells received a 640 acre - pre-emption grant for having been the head of a family settled on land within the boundaries of North Carolina's military reservation when the commissioners measured the boundary lines for the reservation. It was required that he be living on the land before the first day of June 1780. A pre-emption meant that he was eligible to become the first owner of that particular land. The right to have the pre-emption grant was prescribed by North Carolina law. His entry can be found in Irene Griffey's *The Pre-emptors: Middle Tennessee's First Settlers* (Clarksville, TN: Priv. Pub., 1989), page 2. It reads as follows: "Haden Wells obtained a pre emp of 640 acres of Land Lying on McAdow's Creek on the North side of Cumberland river about one mile above the mouth of said Creek including a tree at the head of a Spring marked thus HW and an old Indian Town in the fork between the River and Creek aforesd."

This File No. 1147 provides the information pertaining to this pre-emption grant, which is recorded in the North Carolina Grant Book No. 66, page 180. The grant was for 640 acres of land and was numbered 124. The land was entered on January 24, 1784, and the grant was issued on April 17, 1786.

The warrant was issued by Samuel Barton, entry taker for Davidson County, North Carolina (now Tennessee), the county in which the land was located. The warrant gave the surveyor authority to survey the land

The warrant reads: "State of North Carolina, Davidson County, To the Surveyor of sd County, Greetings:

These are to direct you to Measure, Lay off and survey a pre-emption of 640 acres of Land for Haydon Wells lying on the McAdows Creek on the No. Side of Cumberland river about one mile above the Mouth of sd Creek including a tree at a Spring mark'd thus HW and an old Indian town in the forks between the river and creek aforesaid--as per ent[ry] No. 172 dated Jany. 24th 1784 - and for so doing this shall Be your Warrant Given under my hand the 24th day of April 1784. [Signed:] Saml. Barton E[try] T[aker]"

Jacket or Shuck

No. 1147
County Davidson
Name Wells Haydon
Acres 640
Grant No. 124
Issued Feby 17 1786
Warrant No. 172   Entry No. 172
Entered 24 Jan 1784
Book No. 66   Page No. 180
Location Beginning on McAdows Cr on the No. side of Cumberland river about one mile above the mouth of sd Creek

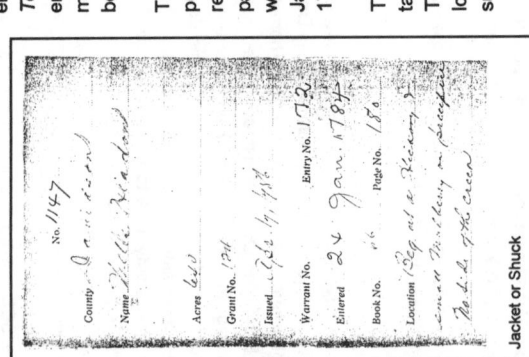

Warrant

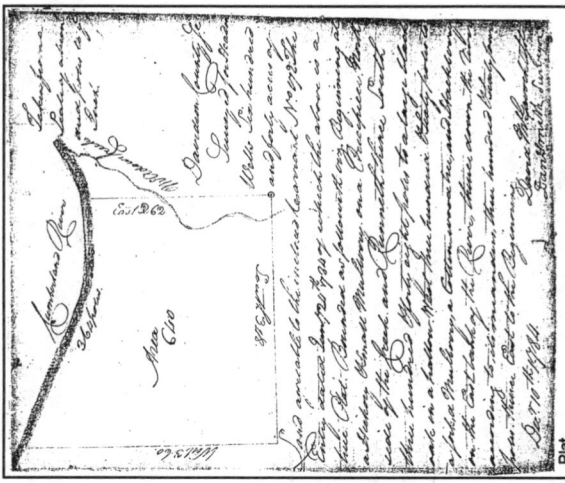

Plat

This plat was drawn on a scale of one hundred chains to an inch, and surveyed on December 10, 1784.

The survey reads as follows:

"Davidson County, &C

Surveyed for Headon Wells Six Hundred and forty acres of Land agreeable to the inclosed Warrant No. 172. The Entry dated Jany 14th 1784 of which the above is a true Plat. Bounded as followeth viz, Beginning at a Hickory & Small Mulberry on a Precipice North side of the Creek and Runneth thence South three hundred & forty eight poles to a large black oak in a hollow, West three hundred & Sixty poles to a fork, a Mulberry, a Cottonwood tree, and Hackberry on the East bank of the River, thence down the river according to its meanders, three hundred & Sixty four poles, thence East to the Beginning.

[Signed:] David McGavock
        Daniel Smith, Surveyor

Decr. 10th 1784"

NORTH CAROLINA ASSIGNEE GRANT - GEORGE NEVILLE - LAND GRANT SUPPORTING PAPERS

George Neville purchased the right of William Loggins for a pre-emption grant before it was entered by William Loggins. To have been eligible for a pre-emption grant, William Loggins had to have been settled on the land within the boundaries of North Carolina's Military Reservation when the commissioners measured the boundary lines for the reservation. It was required that he be living on the land before the first day of June 1780. A pre-emption meant that he was eligible to become the first owner of that particular land. The right to have the pre-emption grant was prescribed by North Carolina law.

The entry can be found in Irene Griffey's, *The Pre-emptors: Middle Tennessee's First Settlers* (Clarksville, TN: Priv. Pub., 1989), page 19 as follows: "No. 200. George Neville assee [assignee] of William Groggins obtained a pre emption of 640 acres of land Lying at the mouth of a little Creek that heads up against Richland Creek which runs into big Harpeth it being the first Creek below the mouth of Little Harpath, begin'g at the mouth of sd Creek running up the Creek on the lower side to include a spring and improvement marked on a tree S M for Compliment." Thus, William Loggins sold his right to the land to George Nevill before the warrant was issued."

The warrant reads as follows: "State of No. Carolina, Davidson County.

To the Surveyor of sd County Greeting.

These are to Direct you to Lay off and Survey a preempt of 640 Acres of land for George Neville assee [assignee] of William Logins - Lying at the Mouth of a Little Creek that heads up against Richland Creek Which runs into Big Harpeth, It being the Creek Below the Mouth of Little harpeth Beginning At the mouth of sd Creek Running Up the Creek on Both sides for to include the Spring and Impt. [improvement] Mark'd S. M. -- Assee Entry No. 438 May 12th 1784 -- and for so doing This shall Be Your Warrant given und. [under] My hand this 22d day of July 1784. [Signed:] Saml. Barton, E[ntry] T[aker]"

Warrant

No. 1247 TENNESSEE
County Davidson
Name Neville George
Acres 640
Grant No. 262
Issued July 13, 1788
Warrant No. 438
Entered 12 May 1784
Book No. 66 Page No. 129
Location Beg the mouth
of the Little Creek below
Little Harpeth

Jacket or Shuck

The plat was drawn to a scale of two hundred poles to an inch, and included the river. It can be located today using a topographical map.

The survey reads as follows:
"Davidson County &c
September 11th 1785

Surveyed for George Neville Six hundred & forty acres of land agreeable to the inclosed Warrant No. 438 (the entry dated May 12th 1784 of which the above is a true plat bounded as follows:

Beginning at the mouth of the first Creek below Little Harpeth running West one hundred & sixty four poles to an Ash & Black Oak on the North bank of Big Harpeth - thence North three hundred & twenty Poles to two Hickorys - thence East three hundred & twenty-one Poles to a Stake - thence South three hundred & thirty-eight Poles to an Ash & Beech - thence West forty Poles to a white Walnut on the bank of the aforesaid Creek - thence down said Creek according to its several Courses on a Conditional Line with Thomas Molloy one hundred & thirty-eight Poles to the beginning.

[Signed] Thos. Molloy, Dep[uty] Surveyor
Danl. Smith, Surveyor

William Herrington)
) C[hain] C[arriers]"
      &   )
John Phipps   )

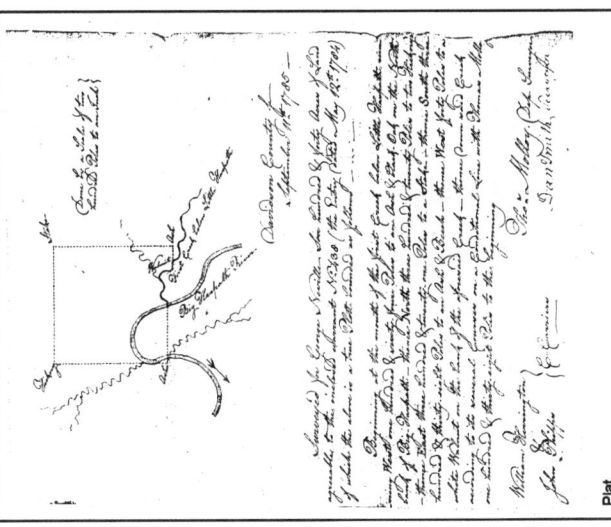

Plat

NORTH CAROLINA MILITARY LAND GRANT - NICHOLAS LONG ASSIGNEE OF KEDAR COPELAND

Kedar Copeland, a soldier in the Continental Line of North Carolina, proved his military service to the North Carolina secretary of state and received a warrant listed as #9 for 640 acres of land. After receiving this warrant he sold the land to Nicholas Long and the plat and survey were made in the name of Nicholas Long, as shown in the following copies:

```
MILITARY WARRANT ——— TENNESSEE
            No. 358

County    Jefferson
Name   Long & Nicholas
    assignee of Kedar Copeland
Acres      640
Grant No.  2203
Issued   30 May 1793
Warrant No.   9     Entry No.
Entered  15 Oct 1783
Book No.   81    Page No.   169
Location   Big Pidgeon Creek
Jacket or Shuck
```

State of North Carolina   No. 9
The Honorable James Glasgow Esquire
Secretary of State

To Colonel Martin Armstrong, Greetings
You are hereby required to lay off and Survey for Kedar Copeland, a Soldier in the line of the State Six hundred and forty acres of Land within the limits of the land reserved by law for the Officers and Soldiers.

Observing the directions of the Act of Assembly in such case made and provided for running out Lands. Two just and fair plans (plats) thereof with a certificate to each annexed. You are to transmit to my office within the time limited by law.

Given under my hand at Hillsboro this 15th day of October Anno Dom. 1783.

/s/ J. Glasgow

Warrant

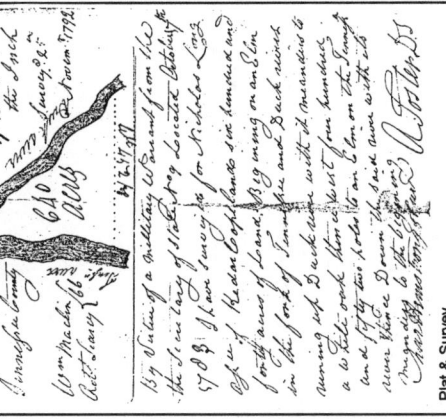

Plat & Survey

Outside of Warrant

Mero District, Tennessee County
Platted by a scale of 200 poles to the Inch.
Surveyed 25th November 1792

Wm. Maclin)
)   C[hain] C[arriers]
Robt. Searcy)

By virtue of a Military Warrant from the Secretary of State No. 9 located October 7, 1783 I have surveyed for Nicholas Long assee of Kedar Copeland six hundred and forty acres of land. Beginning on an Elm in the fork of Tennessee and Duck river running up Duck river with its meanders to a white oak thence West four hundred and fifty two poles to an Elm on the Tennessee river thence Down the said river with its meanders to the beginning.

Martin Armstrong, Sur[veyor]
A. Foster, D[eputy] S[urveyor]

Note: When the land was surveyed the boundaries of Tennessee County reached to the Tennessee River. The area had been ceded to the United States in 1790 and thus was within Mero District. It can be seen that grants continued to be made by North Carolina.

How To Use Earliest Tennessee Land Records

Following is the index or finding aid used by the North Carolina Land Office in locating the records necessary for issuing a land grant for land in Tennessee. These records are often referred to as the loose papers or miscellaneous papers of the land office. Actually they are the entries, warrants, plats, and surveys authorizing the issuance of a grant.

The records refer to a file number used to find the envelope, called the shuck, which contained these papers. This file number was a superficial number assigned to the shuck and had no purpose in the granting process.

An explanation of the arrangement of the information is necessary for clarity in interpreting the records, and is given on the spreadsheet in the order of its appearance on the shucks.

The North Carolina Archives has microfilmed the contents of these shucks and placed the originals in storage. The official North Carolina Land Office has been closed. Information contained on the shuck and appearing on these pages is the information necessary for the North Carolina State Archives or Tennessee State Library & Archives to locate the desired information.

Few works are without errors and this is no exception. The errors that may be found on these spreadsheets may be as follows:

- Those made by the humans generating the records
- Those made by the humans transcribing the records, which we hope are few—in some instances accurate deciphering was impossible
- Some shucks were empty, the contents having been lost or taken by a selfish researcher, who believed a private family collection, rather than a public archives, is a more appropriate place for the documents
- In some instances the land office officials tampered with the records and grants were issued to the wrong people.

It was the compiler's good fortune to visit the North Carolina Land Office several times before it was dismantled. There is no substitute for this knowledge. Using the records in the same environment in which they were created aided greatly in reconstructing exactly how the system worked.

Claimant: The claimant is the person to whom the grant or patent was issued.

File #: The file number is the number assigned to each shuck to aid in finding the desired records. The shucks containing the records were arranged in the land office by name of the county in which the land lay at the time of issuing the grant, and then by the file number.

Assignee: The assignee in some instances was the person from whom the grant was obtained. In other instances it was the person to whom the grant was assigned. Spreadsheet space did not permit distinguishing between the two.

County: The county listed was the county in which the land lay at that time. The boundaries of the county may not have been the same as the boundaries of that county today. The pedigree or history of that particular county, can be very useful in locating the land being granted.

Acres: The number of acres in that grant.

Grant #: The grant number is the number assigned to that particular grant. It should be noted that each land office used its own sequence of numbers, which resulted in the same grant number being assigned to several grants. But, each of these numbers was issued from a different land office, and each for a different type grant. Never was more than one grant issued from the same land office with the same grant number. It appears when a grant number is preceded with a zero, that grant was not actually issued. This can be ascertained from the lack of book and page number where the grant should have been recorded.

Grant Date: The grant date is the date the grant was actually issued and may be useful in identifying the applicable land office from which it issued.

Entry #: The entry number was assigned to each entry made in the applicable land office. Each land office used its own sequence of numbers, which resulted in the same entry numbers for entries made in different land offices. A study of the land offices may be helpful in reconciling this conflicting information. In some land offices, the entry number served as the warrant number also and, in that case, the number for each was the same.

Entry Date: The entry date was the date the locator actually made location of the land. This date is useful in determining the applicable land office, as well as the actual date the land was located. It documents the claimant's first intent to claim that particular land.

Book and Page: After the grant was issued, it was recorded in a grant book. This book and page number refers to the official grant book in which the grant was recorded. This book is now in the North Carolina Archives. **The numbers do not match the copies of the grant books contained in the Tennessee State Library & Archives.** The grant books in the Tennessee State Library & Archives are those copied in the early 1800s by John Overton to be used in Tennessee. They were extracted from grant books containing grants for both North Carolina and Tennessee.

Location by Stream Name: The most desirable land was located along streams or the waters of those streams. Locating the stream can be useful in determining the county in which the land is today. Additional research in county deed records can provide additional information.

Military: Indicates a grant **based** on military service in the Revolutionary War. The claimant may not have performed the military service but may have obtained the warrant from someone who did. The grant will list both the person entitled to the grant, as well as the assignee. Only those who served the required time in the North Carolina Continental Line were eligible to receive land in North Carolina Military Reservation, which was located in north, central Tennessee. The papers are filed under the named of the recipient of the grant or the last assignee, who may or may not have been the person eligible for the grant. Thus, the land grant will be indexed in county deed books under the name of the last recipient or assignee and not under the name of the person who performed the military service.

Claimant:	File #:	Assignee:	County:	Acres:	Grant:	Grant Date:	Entry:	Entry Date:	Bk:	Pg:	Location by Stream Name:	Military:
Aaronvine, John	1068		Washington	250	1018	27 Nov 1792	2612	13 Aug 1780	80	181	Stone Creek	
Aaronwine, John	450		Sullivan	600	329	10 Nov 1784	346	24 Mar 1780	69	187	N/S Holston River	
Abbott, John	498	Bradley, James	Davidson	428	470	15 Sep 1787	1427	1 Mar 1786	63	171	Second Creek	
Abbott, Isaac	321	Hays, Rachel	Tennessee	640	2038	20 May 1793	2340	29 Sep 1785	81	133	N/S Cumberland River	yes
Abbott, Jonathan	799	Davis, Joshua	Sumner	640	2260	20 May 1793	2404	19 Nov 1792	81	183	Caney Fork Creek	yes
Abbott, Waddington	545	Douglass, William	Sumner	640	1748	29 Aug 1793	1955	22 Dec 1792	81	66	S/S Cumberland River	yes
Aberrion, John	021	Armstrong & Donelson	Middle Dist	640			1914					yes
Abims [Abrams], Joseph	1048	Blount, John Gray	Sumner	640	2527	8 Dec 1795	2495	30 Apr 1795	88	280	S/S Big Harpeth River	yes
Abuck, John	125	Bonds, Wright	Tennessee	640	327	23 Feb 1793	1580	22 Feb 1785	76	327	N/S Cumberland River	yes
Accuff, John	142		Hawkins	100	176	26 Dec 1791	400	18 Apr 1780	75	174	Headwaters Sinking Cr.	
Acinclash, Duncan	787	Phillips, Mann	Sumner	640	2246	20 May 1793	2259	30 Nov 1792	81	180	Waters of Dixons Cr.	yes
Ackinclass, Absalom	220	Boyd, John	Sumner	274	1125	26 Nov 1789	3529	19 Apr 1788	74	141	S/S Cumberland River	yes
Ackinclass, John	016	Bowman, William	Sumner	640			2496	12 Mar 1787			Both sides Cooks Branch	yes
Acock, Moses	40	Mountflorence, J. C.	Sumner	640	872	17 Jun 1789	1480	17 May 1788	63	303	N/S Cumberland River	yes
Acock, Robert	867	Shannon, Samuel	Davidson	228	881	17 jan 1789	1482	22 Dec 1785	63	305	Waters of Whites Creek	yes
Acock, William	41	Mountflorence, J. C.	Sumner	640	873	17 Jan 1789	1481	17 May 1788	63	303	On waters of Red River	yes
Acuff, Timothy	23		Sullivan	386	34	23 Oct 1782	1694	21 Sep 1779	43	253	Beg at a white oak	
Adair, David	077		Eastern District	250	102	9 Feb 1781	738	9 Feb 1781	75	178	Waters of Whites Creek	
Adair, David	1083		Hawkins	200	369	4 Jul 1797			91	592	In the Grassey valley	
Adair, David	439		Hawkins	250	371	29 Jul 1793	584	8 Feb 1790	80	269	N side of Clinch River &c	
Adair, James	1082		Hawkins	100	368	4 Jul ----			91	591	N side of Clinch river	
Adair, James	207		Hawkins	120	194	26 Dec 1791	172	9 Apr 1790	77	311	Headspring Roseberrys Cr.	
Adair, James	364		Eastern District	200	280	26 Feb 1796	57		88	466	In the Grassey Valley	
Adair, James	534		Eastern District	400	407	29 Jul 1793	295	28 Jun 1780	80	279	N/S Holston Grassey Valley	
Adair, James Ass.	883		Hawkins	400	143	4 Feb 1795			84	143	On N side of Clinch River	
Adair, James, Ass	345	Wheeler, Sam	Eastern District	274	2611	7 Mar 1796			88	332	N/S Clinch on Cole Creek	
Adair, James, Ass.	291		Eastern District	100	152	4 Feb 1795			84	148	On S side of Clinch river	
Adair, James, Ass.	344		Eastern District	274	2610	7 Mar 1796			88	331	On N side of Clinch River	
Adair, John	03		Knox	640			460	24 Apr 1780			In the Grassey Valley	
Adair, John	05		Green	200			102	26 Feb 1778				
Adair, John	111		Eastern District	640	100	17 Nov 1790	423	17 Apr 1780	76	176	Both sides of Whites Creek of Holstein	
Adair, John	127		Eastern District	640	137	15 Jul 1793	1667	3 Feb 1780	76	495	N W side of the river Clinch	
Adair, John	192		Hawkins	200	125	16 Nov 1790	515	28 Sep 1780	77	192	On Whites Creek	
Adair, John	202 (207)		Hawkins	200	189	26 Dec 1791	1900	7 Oct 1779	77	310	On the N side of Holston River	
Adair, John	27		Eastern District	300	27	11 Jul 1788	172	19 Feb 1780	67	351	On the N side of Beaverdam Creek	
Adair, John	28		Eastern District	640	28	11 Jul 1788	8	8 Feb 1780	67	351	On the head of Whites Creek	
Adair, John	29		Eastern District	400	29	11 Jul 1788			67	351	On bull run of Clinch River &c	
Adair, John	31		Eastern District	300	31	11 Jul 1788	506	28 Apr 1780	67	352	On the s side of the Beaverdam Creek	
Adair, John	313		Sullivan	200 [?]	449	20 Sep 1787	134	9 Feb 1780	65	442	N/S Holstein River	
Adair, John	413		Eastern District	15	336	24 Jun 1793			90	195	Dry fork of Buffalo Creek	
Adair, John	442		Hawkins	300	320	29 Jul 1793			80	192	On the S fork of the Second Creek &c	
Adair, John	521		Hawkins	150	394	29 Jul 1793	2076	3 Feb 1780	80	275	Including the fork of Whites Creek	
Adair, John	526		Hawkins	300	399	29 Jul 1793	591	7 Jun 1780	80	277	On both sides of Beaverdam Creek	
Adair, John	527		Hawkins	200	400	29 Jul 1793	463	24 Apr 1780	80	277	On first creek that fall into Clinch River	
Adair, John	539		Hawkins	640	412	29 Jul 1793	593	7 Jun 1780	80	280	On both sides of Beaverdam Creek	

Claimant:	File #:	Assignee:	County:	Acres:	Grant:	Grant Date:	Entry:	Entry Date:	Bk:	Pg:	Location by Stream Name:	Military:
Adair, John	540		Hawkins	400	413	29 Jul 1793	1028	20 oct 1779	80	280	N side of Clinch River &c	
Adair, John	545		Hawkins	200	418	29 Jul 1793			80	282	On both sides of Beaverdam Creek	
Adair, John	549		Hawkins	300	422	29 Jul 1793	595	7 Jun 1780	80	283	N side of Clinch River &c	
Adair, John	567		Hawkins	1280	441	29 Jul 1793			80	287	S/S Clinch River	
Adair, John	84		Sullivan	400 (420	95	23 oct 1782	1736-1737	27 Sep 1779	43	283	On the N side of Holston River &c	
Adair, John	876		Hawkins	200	646	6 Feb 1795	833	26 Aug 1782	84	134	In the Grassey Valley	
Adair, John, Ass	333		Eastern District	100	254	8 Dec 1795			883	273	In the Grassey Valley	
Adair, John, Sr.	441		Hawkins	50	319	24 Jun 1793	183 (783)	27 Apr 1780	80	192	In the Grassey Valley	
Adair, Mary	357		Hawkins	500	350	8 Mar 1793			78	485	On N side of Tennessee River	
Adam, Jas & Clinton	1453		Sumner	640	472	19 Sep 1800	466	31 May 1784	109	272	On E fork of Bledsoe's Creek	
Adam, John	40		Sullivan	292	51	23 Oct 1782	1818	6 Oct 1779	43	262	Beg at two white oaks	
Adams, Arthur	2231	Ore, James	Davidson	274	2592	7 Mar 1796			88	322	On N side of Holston River	yes
Adams, Elisha	793		Sumner	50	725	2 Dec 1796	538	29 Apr 1781	91	278	Including where he lives.	
Adams, Howell	4	Neville, George	Montgomery	323	3379	1 Dec 1801	173				On the middle fork of Barton's Creek	
Adams, Jacob	1271	McKinney, Ro.	Sumner	640	2999	10 Apr 1797	936	12 Jan 1797	90	293	S side Cumberland River	yes
Adams, Jas. Jr	1406	Curry, John	Sumner	640	3337	6 Dec 1797	3746	25 Oct 1797	97	54	On waters of Big Barrow	yes
Adams, John	020	Buckanon, John	Sumner	640			2631	10 Nov 1790			On Jinning fork Round Lick Creek	yes
Adams, John	1220		Washington	22-1/2	1165	18 Aug 1795	2916	28 Aug 1795	87	503	On waters of great Limestone	
Adams, John	414		Washington	188	406	13 Oct 1783	805	28 Dec 1778	52	268	On the S side of great Limestone Creek	
Adams, Simson	255		Hawkins	100	243	Mar 1792	110	26 Feb 1778	77	333	On the head of Lyons Creek	
Adamson, Enos	04		Hawkins	100							S side of Holston River	
Adare, David	271		Sullivan	200	410	9 Aug 1787	2215	13 Nov 17779	61	429	Incl. the plantation the said Adare lives	
Adcock, Edward	1391	Morrow, John	Sumner	640	3317	6 Dec 1797	1045	25 Oct 1796	97	41	On the head of the 1st big branch	yes
Adcock, George	036	Blair, Thos.	Not given	640			967	20 Mar 1788			S side of Cumberland River	yes
Adcock, Joshua	728	McKadon, William	Davidson	274	701	11 Jul 1788	438	14 Sep 1778	63	247	S side of Red River	yes
Adcock, Leonard	111		Washington	100	279	24 Oct 1782	393	14 Sep 1778	44	287	W branch of limestone fork &c	
Adcock, Leonard	72		Washington	130	240	23 Oct 1782	493	7 Oct 1778	44	266	On Limestone fork of Lick Creek	
Adcock, Leonard	87		Washington	300	255	23 Oct 1782	392	14 Sep 1778	44	274	E branch of Lick Creek	
Addleman, John	328		Tennessee	274	2077	20 May 1793	1103	12 Oct 1792 (surv.)	81	143	On an E fork of Yellow Creek	
Adel, William	98		Washington	239	266	23 Oct 1782			44	281	Including the spring of Shepmans Fork	
Adjuton, John	1231	Sanders, William	Sumner	1000	2502	12 Nov 1795	1622	21 Jan 1786	89	420	Lying on Big Barren	yes
Adkins, Benjamin	2008	Blount, John Gray & Thom	Davidson	208	1953	20 may 1793	1489	21 Feb 1786	81	113	On both sides of Otter Creek	yes
Adkins, David	270		Davidson	640	256	7 Mar 1786	658		63	93	South side of Cumberland River	yes
Adkison, Michael	2314	Sanders, James	Davidson	640	2503	12 Nov 1795	1650		89	420	On Second Creek	yes
Affadavit as to Entries	064		Sullivan									
Agee, Anthony	607		Sullivan	548	562	26 Dec 1791	89	8 Feb 1780	77	307	On the S side of Reedy Creek	
Aicuff, Timothy	193	Evans, Richard	Davidson	640	178	7 Mar 1786	1223		63	67	Bet Stewarts and Forming Creeks	yes
Aims, Thomas	285	Glasgow, James	Davidson	640	271	24 Jan 1787	1154	19 mar 1785	63	99	S side of Red river	yes
Ake, Joseph	161		Hawkins	188	94	16 Nov 1790	426	7 Jun 1784	77	183	On the N side of Holston River &c	
Akers, Elizabeth	1382		Green	200	1237	27 Jan 1793	1280	13 Mar 1779	79	508	On waters of Nolichuckey	
Alberson, Joseph	453		Middle District	1250	392	17 Dec 1794	2581	25 May 1784	84	257	On main fork of Elk River	
Albright, James	534	Hadley, James	Sumner	640	1728	20 May 1793	2828	10 Mar 1788	81	60	On waters of Collins River	yes
Albritton, Henry	420	Cobb, Jesse	Tennessee	640	2466	31 Dec 1793	1325	3 Nov 1784	81	432	On main W fork of Guesses Creek	yes
Alden, Roger, Geo & Jas.	1548		Green	640	1308	7 Jul 1794	900	25 Oct 1783	81	623	On N side of French Broad River	
Alden, Roger, Geo & Jas	1549		Green	640	1309	7 Jul 1794	599	10 Sep 1792	81	624	On Sinking fork of Copelands Creek	

Claimant:	File #:	Assignee:	County:	Acres:	Grant:	Grant Date:	Entry:	Entry Date:	Bk:	Pg:	Location by Stream Name:	Military:
Alderson, Simon	2002 [?]		Davidson	1000	2270	20 May 1793	2071		81	185	On waters of W fork of Stones River	yes
Aldridge, William	216	McMahan, Daniel	Davidson	228	202	7 Mar 1786	685		63	75	On waters of Big Harpeth River	yes
Alexander, Andrew	27		Smith	1000	393	31 Mar 1804	1993	30 Apr 1784	118	328	On waters of Roaring river	
Alexander, Andrew	28		Smith	1000	394	31 Mar 1804	1993	20 Apr 1804	118	329	On waters of Roaring River	
Alexander, Cameron	8	Molloy, Thomas	Montgomery	491	2983	30 Dec 1796	3636				S side of Cumberland River	yes
Alexander, Ebenezer	1649		Davidson	640	300	17 Nov 1790	49		76	181	On Hurricane Creek of Stones River	
Alexander, Ebenezer	1865	Matthews, W.	Davidson	640	1599	27 Apr 1793	2437		81	17	On S side of Cumberland River	yes
Alexander, Ebenezer	41		Middle District	3000	43	10 Jul 1788	2081	6 May 1784	67	426	On Alexanders Creek &c	
Alexander, Ezekiel	346		Middle District	1000	294	6 Dec 1794	1817	23 Apr 1784	84	109	On N side of Duck River	
Alexander, Geo.	772	Wesley, John	Sumner	274	2224	20 May 1793	3237	1 Aug 1792	81	174	On S side of Cumberland River	
Alexander, Geo.	773	Hays, Samuel	Sumner	640	2225	20 May 1793	2266	1 Aug 1792	81	174	On S side of Cumberland River	yes
Alexander, George	1688		Green	100	1364	27 Nov 1795	1014	26 Feb 1778	89	287	On N side of Noleychuckey River	
Alexander, George	2146	Brukinds, John	Davidson	640	2440	31 Mar 1794	3236		81	423	On waters of W Harpeth	yes
Alexander, George	314		Middle District	2000	290	17 Dec 1794	2080	6 May 1784	88	332	N side of North fork of Duck River	
Alexander, George	893	Bruskins, George	Sumner	274	2439	31 Dec 1793	2262	19 Dec 1792	81	423	On waters of E fork of Goose Creek	yes
Alexander, George	97		Middle District	1000	99	10 Jul 1788	1820	23 Apr 1784	67	458	Lying on the W/S of Alexanders Creek	
Alexander, James	1571		Green	225	1317	5 Jan 1795			83	161	On Dumplin Creek	
Alexander, Jas. & George	118		Eastern District	600	151	29 Jul 1793	646	28 Oct 1783	76	480	On Emeries River	
Alexander, John	482		Washington	100	667	15 Jul 1786	2399	15 Feb 1780	59	355	Joining Andrew Martins survey	
Alexander, John	483		Washington	50	668	1 Nov 1786	2914	28 Aug 1781	60	441	Beg upon his old line &c	
Alexander, John McKnitt	21		Western District	3660	21	10 Jul 1788	1010	29 Oct 1783	67	288	On the N fork of Looshatcher rRiver	
Alexander, Joseph	1528	Thompson, Jason	Davidson	640	1085	26 Nov 1789	3441		74	123	On E waters of Spring Creek	yes
Alexander, Joseph	1597		Green	70	1339	22 Feb 1795	271	Dec 1788	83	439	S side of Dumplin Creek	
Alexander, Matthew	308		Middle District	1000	284	17 Dec 1794	1821	23 Apr 1784	83	330	On Spring Creek &c	
Alexander, Nathaniel	86		Davidson	1000	72	14 Mar 1786	781		63	29	North side of Tennessee River	
Alexander, Reuben	1316	Hinds, John	Sumner	640	3116	14 Sep 1797	4393	10 May 1797	90	410	On the waters of Big Barren	yes
Alexander, Robert	412		Middle District	1000	351	17 Dec 1794	2281	24 May 1784	84	229	On waters of Harpeth River	yes
Alexander, Robert	451		Middle District	2000	390	17 Dec 1794	2082	6 May 1784	84	256	On S side of Duck River	
Alexander, Robert	858	Walker, Aaron	Sumner	274	2364	20 May 1793	3030	18 nov 1782	81	205	On Deans Lick Creek	yes
Alexander, Robert, Ass	664		Sumner	274	1984	20 May 1793	2982	18 Nov 1792	81	120	On main E fork of Bledsoe's Creek	yes
Alexander, Robt.	665	Nash, Jos.	Sumner	640	1985	20 May 1793	3206	18 Nov 1792	81	120	Ridge--hdwtrs Bledsoes & Trammels Cr.	yes
Alexander, Robt.	786	Brooks, Robt.	Sumner	428	2243	20 May 1793	2984	18 Nov 1792	81	129	On a branch above Defeated Creek	yes
Alexander, Stephen	443		Middle District	716	382	17 Dec 1794	1803	23 apr 1784	84	252	In Wilsons valley	
Alexander, Thomas	1335	Hickman, Thomas	Sumner	640	3135	14 Sep 1797	4394	3 Jun 1797	81	417	On Salt Lick Fork of Big Barren	yes
Alexander, William	11		Smith	200	3400	15 Dec 1802		21 Aug 1800	110	277	On waters of Disons Creek	
Alexander, William	18		Knox	800	313	9 Jan 1802			114	390	On Poplar Creek	
Alexander, William	1886		Davidson	2560	1644	27 Apr 1793	189		81	88	On South side of Stones River	yes
Alexander, William	19		Knox	200	314	9 Jan 1802			114	390	On waters of Poplar Creek	
Alexander, William	355		Sumner	200	1460	4 Jan 1792	3585	21 Oct 1791	77	366	On both sides of the Wartrace Creek	
Alexander, William	845		Sumner	200	2348	20 May 1793	3582	27 Oct 1792	81	201	On Middle fork of Goose Fork	yes
Alexander, William	847	Wilson, David	Sumner	168	2350	20 May 1793	3584	27 Oct 1792	81	202	On N side of Cumberland River	yes
Alexander, William	854		Sumner	200	2359	20 May 1793	3583	27 Oct 1792	81	204	On Wartrace Creek	yes
Alford, John	11	Fenner, Richard	Tennessee	640	1159	26 Nov 1789	2165	12 Sep 1785	74	158	On N side of Cumberland River	yes
Alford, William	01	Reasons, Thomas	Tennessee	640			1069	31 May 1784			On rite hand fk 1st large crk of TN River	
Alford, William	02	Mitchell, John	Tennessee	640			775	1 May 1784			On 4th large cr emptying into Tenn. River	

Claimant:	File #:	Assignee:	County:	Acres:	Grant:	Grant Date:	Entry:	Entry Date:	Bk:	Pg:	Location by Stream Name:	Military:
Alford, William	03	Alford, William	Tennessee	640			1442	20 Nov 1784			Rite /sic/ hand fork of the 1st large creek	Yes
Alford, Wm.	03	Howel, John	Tennessee	640			1442	20 Nov 1784			On rite hand fork of the 1st large creek	

Claimant:	File #:	Assignee:	County:	Acres:	Grant:	Grant Date:	Entry:	Entry Date:	Bk:	Pg:	Location by Stream Name:	Military:
Alford, Wm.	04	Butts, Wm.	Tennessee	640	622	15 Sep 1787	773	1 May 1784	63	221	4th large creek emptying into Tenn River	
Allen, Alexander	649	Nich.Moore heir	Davidson	640	2136						E side of Sulphur Fork	yes
Allen, Archibald, Ass	333		Tennessee	640	2103	20 May 1793	2049	26 Aug 1785	81	150	On 2nd large fk on W side of Yellow Cr.	
Allen, Benjamin	959		Green	100	873	17 Nov 1790	2806	1 Mar 1781	76	129	N/S of French Broad River on Atkins Cr	
Allen, Charles	2121	Bowman, Robert	Davidson	1695	2402	7 Jan 1793	24		81	392	On S side of Cumberland River	yes
Allen, Daniel	631		Sullivan	75	579	27 Jun 1793	1393	24 May 1779	80	374	Beg at Nath. Clark's corner &c	
Allen, Daniel	718		Sullivan	64	663	4 Dec 1794	190	21 Feb 1780	84	167	Beg at a poplar & white oak	
Allen, George	532	Jerem Brantley hrs.	Davidson	640	504	15 Sep 1787	2047		63	182	West side of the Wartrace Creek	yes
Allen, James	0929	Payton, Ephraim	Sumner	640			1534		81	637	On Dixon's Creek	yes
Allen, Jesse	1491	Smith, Daniel	Davidson	220	1044	27 Nov 1789	3227	9 Dec 1785	74	46	On S side of Cumberland River	yes
Allen, John	118	Smith, William	Davidson	640	104	17 Mar 1786	377		63	42	E fork of Buffaloe Creek	yes
Allen, John	1761		Green	200	1438	2 Dec 1797	152	16 Feb 1780	96	16	Both sides of Lick waters of Nolichuckey	
Allen, John	1940	Allen, Thomas heir	Davidson	1940	1761	20 May 1793	1827		81	69	On Duck River beg at an ash	yes
Allen, John	2222	Allen, Thomas Adm. Of	Davidson	2560	2524	8 Dec 1795	432		88	278	On S W side of Big Harpeth River	yes
Allen, John	36	Bonner, Jno.&Jas.	Davidson	1600	387	8 Sep 1785					On head of W branches of Spring Creek	yes
Allen, John	4		Green	150	367	15 Apr 1793					N side of French Broad River	
Allen, John	507		Green	300	509	20 Sep 1787	1475	26 Mar 1785	65	525	On the S side of Holston Riv on a branch	
Allen, Mary	376	Peter Furney hr.	Davidson	640	348	15 Sep 1787	2123		63	131	South side of Big Harpeth	yes
Allen, Peggy	513	Lawless, Matt.	Davidson	640	485	15 Sep 1787	2059		63	176	On North side of Sulphur Fork	yes
Allen, Robert	1361		Washington	50	1278	30 Jun 1797	2636	7 Sep 1780	92	56	Waters of Big Limestone	
Allen, Samuel	536	Jno.Jones heirs	Davidson	640	508	15 Sep 1787	2162		63	183	On head of Gilbeesons Creek	yes
Allen, Samuel	536	Jones, John	Davidson	640	508	15 Sep 1787	2162		63	183	On head of Gilbeesons /sic/ Creek	yes
Allen, Sarah	019 [?]	Leavvin, Jno.	Montgomery	640			2157		63	117	Piney fork of Little West fork of Red River	yes
Allen, Thomas	328	Fenner, Richard	Davidson	640	314	28 Jun 1787	2163	11 Mar 1797	63		On waters of Sulphur Fork	yes
Allen, Walter	76		Davidson	912	62	14 Mar 1786	433		63	25	South side of Cumberland River	yes
Allen, William	206	Marshall, John	Sumner	640	1111	26 Nov 1789	2269		74	134	Beg. at an ash	yes
Allen, William	327	Groves, Wm.	Tennessee	640	2076	20 May 1793	2126	9 Sep 1785	81	143	On 1st large fork on W side of Yellow Cr	yes
Alientharpe, John	2295	Green, Burwell	Davidson	640	2772	9 Sep 1796	1851	29 Mar 1779	88	523	On Deer Creek	yes
Alleson, Francis	103		Washington	100	271	24 Oct 1782	1311	2 Oct 1778	44	283	Joining John Allison Senr	
Alleson, John	551		Washington	640	816	11 Jul 1788	468	2 Oct 1778	64	334	On Clarks branch	
Alleson, Robert	774		Washington	100	588	10 Nov 1784	818	25 Dec 1778	69	135	On N side of Wataugha River	
Allhead, Vernon	1530	Cannon, Minos	Davidson	640	1087	26 Nov 1789	2105		74	124	On the waters of Mill creek	yes
Alligood, Henry	1666	Robertson, James	Davidson	640	1589	23 Feb 1783	1350		76	307	On the waters of Little Harpeth	yes
Allin, Sarah	242	Socoroons,Jno.hrs.	Tennessee	640	1596	27 Apr 1793	2157	9 Sep 1785	81	16	On both sides of Cumberland River	
Allison William, heir to Alex	1558		Davidson	640	293	24 Nov 1790	220	20 Jan 1784	74	240	On middle fork of Station Camp Creek	yes
Allison, Andrew	1452		Sumner	640	3367	5 Dec 1800	253	26 Oct 1783	108	320	On both sides of Goose Creek	
Allison, Charles	1362		Washington	140	1279	30 Jun 1797	2518	4 Apr 1780	92	57	On a branch of Big Limestone	
Allison, Charles	301		Washington	400	168	24 Oct 1782	3563	2 Feb 1779	47	81	On a Miry branch	
Allison, David	01	Sheppar, John	Sumner	1714			3750	8 Jan 1795			On head waters of Flinns Creek	yes
Allison, David	03		Hawkins	640			598	7 Jun 1778				
Allison, David	097		Not given	640				13 Sep 1796				
Allison, David	1426		Green	260	1238	27 Nov 1792	130	7 Jun 1784	85 (80)	166	On N/S Nolichucky River on Richland Cr	yes
Allison, David	2220	Sheppard, Jno.	Davidson	1714	2522	8 Dec 1795		7 Jun 1784	88	277	On head waters of Flinns Creek	yes
Allison, David	555	Steed, Jesse	Sumner	357	1774	20 May 1793	549	7 Oct 1791	81	72	On first creek below Obids River	yes
Allison, David	6		Davidson	640	4	20 Dec 1791			62	306		

Claimant:	File #:	Assignee:	County:	Acres:	Grant:	Grant Date:	Entry:	Entry Date:	Bk:	Pg:	Location by Stream Name:	Military:
Allison, David	938		Hawkins	5000	720	8 Dec 1795	1513	20 Feb 1784	88	276	Beg at a small post oak	
Allison, David, Ass.	933		Hawkins	28,800 [	715	5 Dec 1795	45 wts [sic]		88	268	On both sides of Clinch River	
Allison, Ewing	1302		Green	200	1152	12 Jan 1793	1349	20 Apr 1779	78	396	N side of French Broad River	
Allison, James	105		Green	222	63	1 Nov 1786	1877	7 Jun 1784	59	424	On Dumpling Creek	
Allison, James	1095		Washington	150	1045	27 Nov 1792	538	26 Oct 1778	80	203	On the waters of Cherokee Creek	
Allison, James	1671		Green	100	1376	20 Jul 1796	2842	25 May 1780	88	490	Joining lines with Joseph Brown	
Allison, James	656		Washington	100	750	26 oct 1786	2804	9 Jan 1780	66	34	On the waters of Big Limestone &c	
Allison, James	965		Green	200	879	17 Nov 1790	812	29 Oct 1783	76	131	On Dumplin Creek	
Allison, John	412	Wilkes, Francis	Davidson	228	384	15 Sep 1787	1091		63	143	On N boundary of his other claim	yes
Allison, John	423	Farrow, Wm.	Davidson	228	395	15 Sep 1787	1090		63	147	North side of Cumberland River	yes
Allison, John	463		Washington	200	455	13 Oct 1783	980	2 Jan 1779	52	291	On the N side of Watauga River	
Allison, John	566		Washington	400	831	11 Jul 1788	469	2 Oct 1778	64	336	On Clarks branch	
Allison, John	575		Washington	100 (191	840	11 Jul 1788	396	17 Sep 1778	64	338	On the waters of Big Limestone &c	
Allison, Robert	167		Washington	150	135	23 Oct 1782	470	2 Oct 1778	47	16	N side of Watauga River	
Allison, Robert	41		Washington	200	331	24 Oct 1782	2324	2 Dec 1779	43	311	On Middle Creek &c	
Allison, Thomas	93		Middle District	4000	95	10 Jul 1788	451	25 Oct 1783	67	456	On Flat Creek	
Almond, Joshua	664	Alexander, Robert	Sumner	274	1984	20 May 1793	2982	18 Nov 1792	81	120	On Main E fork of Bledsoes Creek	yes
Alston, John McCoy	344	Yeates, John	Tennessee	640	2150	20 May 1793	22	17 Oct 1783	81	161	On Red River, beg at the bank	
Alston, John McCoy	430	Armstrong, M.	Tennessee	30	160	9 Jan 1794			81	442	On Red River	
Alston, John McCoy	431	Armstrong, M.	Tennessee	30	161	9 Jan 1794		12 Jun 1792	81	442	On waters of Red River	
Alston, John McCoy	509	Gillobe, Isaac	Davidson	640	481	15 Sep 1787	1066		63	174	Lying on Red River	yes
Alston, William	107		Western District	2000	107	10 Jul 1788	561	27 Oct 1783	67	322	On the S side of Looshatcher	
Alston, William	424		Western District	1000	418	8 Dec 1795	2647	25 May 1784	89	323	On waters of S fork of Obion River	
Alston, William	425		Western District	1000	419	8 Dec 1795	2646	25 May 1784	89	323	On waters of S fork of Obion River	
Amacher [sic]	47	Indian Lands	Tennessee	640	12			8 Sep 1819			Beg at a small hickory & chestnut tree	
Ambrose, David	897		Davidson	1000	913	18 May 1789	890		63	315	On Sycamore Creek	yes
Ames, Thomas	1		tennessee	200	22	29 Feb 1788			70	29	On the N side of Holstein River	
Ames, Thomas	147		Hawkins	200	181	26 Dec 1791	222	26 May 1778	75	176	In Carters Valley	
Ames, Thomas	355		Sullivan	100	234	10 Nov 1784	241	1 Mar 1780	69	157	Lying on both sides of Big Creek	
Amies, Thomas	73		Eastern District	73	68	27 Nov 1789	701	25 Sep 1780	74	33	On N side of Holstein River	
Amis [Avery?], Thomas	1144	Harris, Edward	Sumner [?]	640	2651	4 Jun 1796	1889	1 Jun 1795	88	351	Joining Harris survey	yes
Amis, James	1432	Wilburn, Daniel	Sumner	640	3307	6 Dec 1797	1948	20 Jul 1796	98	179	About 3 miles E of the pond lick	yes
Amis, John	180	Glasgow, John	Tennessee	640	1459	4 Jan 1792	1153	11 Aug 1784	77	366	On both sides of Yellow Creek	yes
Amis, Thomas	121		Hawkins	640	155				75	166	In Carters Valley	
Amis, Thomas	312		Sullivan	150	463	23 Aug 1788	1788	9 Oct 1779	64	359	On the N side of Holstein River &c	
Amis, Thos	05		Hawkins	200			888	25 Dec 1783			N side of Holston River	
Amiss, Thomas	72		Eastern District	100	67	27 Nov 1789	799	13 Jun 1781	74	33	On S side of Holstein River	
Amus, James	0124	Welbern, Daniel	Sumner	640			1948	20 Jul 1796			On both sides Pond Lick Creek	yes
Anderson, Barnabas	22		Giles	486	53	15 Jul 1812	1474	1 Aug 1779	126	448	Lying on Big Creek	
Anderson, Benjamin	437		Green	600	439	20 Sep 1787	136	7 Jun 1789	65	499	Lying on the Roaring Fork of Lick Creek	
Anderson, Charles	341	Marley, Robert	Davidson	640	326	1 Aug 1787	2106		63	121	Beg at a white oak & ash	yes
Anderson, Daniel	1444		Green	100	1254	27 Nov 1792	99	16 May 1789	80	172	On the waters of Edwards Branch	
Anderson, Daniel	1533	Lanier, Robt.hrs.	Davidson	640	1090	26 Nov 1789	2205		74	126	On S side of Cumberland River	yes
Anderson, Daniel	216	Reed, Stephen	Sumner	640	1121	26 Nov 1789	2230	23 Mar 1789	74	439	On N side of Cumberland River	yes
Anderson, Daniel	38	Lee, Hardy	Tennessee	640	1222	10 Dec 1790	2935	30 Sep 1785	74	339	On N side of Cumberland River	yes

Claimant:	File #:	Assignee:	County:	Acres:	Grant:	Grant Date:	Entry:	Entry Date:	Bk:	Pg:	Location by Stream Name:	Military:
Anderson, Daniel	38	Yearby, Jno. hrs.	Sumner	640	868	11 Jan 1789	2898	5 Jun 1788	63	302	On waters of Red River	yes
Anderson, Daniel	46	Troublefield, Benj.	Tennessee	640	1238	10 Dec 1790	2888	30 Sep 1785	74	344	On N side of Cumberland River	
Anderson, Daniel	48	Fenner, Wm.	Tennessee	640	1247	10 Dec 1790	2806	30 Sep 1785	74	347	On N side of Cumberland River	
Anderson, Daniel	64	Wyhan, Wm.	Tennessee	640	1301	10 Dec 1790	3486	26 Feb 1786	74	366	On N side of Cumberland River	yes
Anderson, Daniel	826	Whitakers, Jos.hrs.	Davidson	640	829	17 Jan 1789	2894		63	292	On waters of Caney Fork	yes
Anderson, Daniel	831	Norwood, Wm.	Davidson	640	834	17 Jan 1789	3369		63	293	On waters of Caney Fork	yes
Anderson, Daniel	835	Weatherington, Jess	Davidson	640	838	17 Jan 1789	2891		63	294	On N side of Cumberland River	yes
Anderson, Daniel	836	Tolar, Danl.	Davidson	640	839	17 Jan 1789	1383		63	294	On North side of Cumberland River	yes
Anderson, Daniel	848	Pipkin, Willis hrs.	Davidson	640	853	17 Jan 1789	2872		63	298	On N side of Cumberland River	yes
Anderson, Daniel	853	Williamson, Job hrs	Davidson	640	860	17 Jan 1789	2897		63	300	On waters of Caney Fork	yes
Anderson, Daniel	916	Brewer, Benj.hrs.	Davidson	640	932	18 May 1789	3488		63	320	On N side of Cumberland River	yes
Anderson, Danl	51	Johnston, Archib.	Tennessee	640	1256	10 Dec 1790	2854	30 Sep 1785	74	351	On N side of Cumberland River	
Anderson, Danl	62	Cobb, Wm.	Tennessee	640	1296	10 Dec 170	2909	30 Sep 1785	74	364	On N side of Cumberland River	
Anderson, Danl	73	O'Barr, Michael	Tennessee	640	1317	10 Dec 1790	1658	15 Jun 1790	74	371	On S side of Cumberland River	
Anderson, Danl, Ass	70		Tennessee	640	1310	10 Dec 1790	2884	30 Sep 1785	74	369	On N side of Cumberland River	
Anderson, George, heirs of	020		Sullivan	250			191	21 Feb 1780			On Reedy Creek	
Anderson, James	018		Sullivan	150			1741	27 Sep 1779				
Anderson, James	1014	Ray, Archib.	Davidson	640	1031	18 May 1789	1060	8 Jan 1779	63	344	On Smiths Fork	yes
Anderson, James	1618		Green	200	1330	5 Dec 1794	470	3 Oct 1778	84	157	On waters of Lick Creek	
Anderson, James	18		Hawkins	200	14	23 Aug 1788	1690	17 Jun 1782	67	434	On the Meadow Fork of Big Creek	
Anderson, James	20		Hawkins	100	17	23 Aug 1788	503	28 Apr 1780	67	435	On Meadow Fork of Big Creek	
Anderson, James	575		Sullivan	250	573	29 Jul 1793	76	8 Feb 1780	76	472	Upon a branch of Fall Creek	
Anderson, James	576		Sullivan	25	574	29 Jul 1793	1823	7 Oct 1779	76	472	N side of Holstein River	
Anderson, James	592		Sullivan	166	590	29 Jul 1793	2036,.2013	24 & 27 Oct 1779	76	476	Beg at the S side of Reedy Creek &c	
Anderson, Jno & Wm. Shell.	486		Sullivan	630 [sic]	497	18 May 1789	49	8 Feb 1780	71	10	Incl. plantation Anderson & Shellum live	
Anderson, John	017		Sullivan	65			372	29 Mar 1780			Beg at Joshua Taylor's corner	
Anderson, John	019		Sullivan	40			3736	13 oct 1796				
Anderson, John	026	Ford, James	Montgomery	640			1555		81	114	On the waters of Sulphur Fork	yes
Anderson, John	2013	Blount, Jno.Gray &Thos.	Davidson	640	1960	20 May 1793	3736				On S W side of Harpeth &c	yes
Anderson, John	2298	Nash, William	Davidson	640	2776	9 Sep 1796	1176		88	525	On E side of Stones River	yes
Anderson, John	292	Cobb, Jesse	Tennessee	640	1922	20 May 1793	2543	24 Aug 1792 (Sur	8 [?]	105	On both sides of 2nd large creek &c	yes
Anderson, John	555		Washington	99	820	11 Jun 1788	754	24 Apr 1780	64	335	Waters of Big Limestone	
Anderson, John	640		Hawkins	697	492	27 Jun 1793	49	23 June 1784	80	359	On one of the head springs of Flat Cr	
Anderson, John	762		Sullivan	54	693	20 Jul 1796	14	8 Feb 1780	91	80	Beg at a chestnut tree	
Anderson, John	802		Sullivan	65	745	17 Nov 1797	540	Feb 1780	94	148	Waters of Reedy Creek	
Anderson, John	945	Hardcock, Isham	Davidson	1000	961	18 May 1789	3707	29 Aug 1792	63	327	On waters of Caney Fork	yes
Anderson, Matt.	02		Sumner	182							On waters of Drakes Creek	yes
Anderson, Matthew	2075	Seal, Frances	Davidson	182	2222	20 may 1793	590		81	174	On the waters of Drakes Creek	yes
Anderson, Matthew	398		Sumner	501	409	27 Jun 1793	406	23 Aug 1784	80	344	Bet the W and Middle forks &c	yes
Anderson, Meeds [?]	1294	Hendricks, Joseph	Sumner	400	199	8 Jun 1797	1446		90	320	On the old Cumberland road	yes
Anderson, Robert	1612		Green	300	14\324	5 Dec 1794	543	21 Jun 1779	84	153	On waters of Chume [?] Camp Creek	
Anderson, Stewart	073		Sullivan	50	600	27 Jun 1793		11 Apr 1791 (Dated)	80	384	Lying in Territory South of the River Ohio	
Anderson, Stewart	652		Sullivan	50		27 Jul 1793					On the W fork of Reedy Creek	
Anderson, Thomas	1067		Washington	150	1017	27 Nov 1792	2538	10 Apr 1780	80	181	On Little Doe River	
Anderson, William	1277	Barry, Redmond Dillon	Sumner	425	3036	8 Jun 1797	4040	29 Mar 1797	90	313	On one of the head branches &c	yes

Claimant:	File #:	Assignee:	County:	Acres:	Grant:	Entry:	Grant Date:	Entry Date:	Bk:	Pg:	Location by Stream Name:	Military:
Anderson, William	157	Rearden, Jeremiah	Davidson	174	143	746	14 Mar 1786		63	55	E side of Harpeth River	yes
Anderson, William	30	Sanders, James	Sumner	640	787	523	11 Jul 1788	8 Jul 1784	63	276	Beg at the N bank of Cumberland River	yes
Anderson, William	394		Sullivan	200	273	1741	10 Nov 1784	29 Feb 1780	69	168	Beg. at a white oak & ash	
Anderson, William	420		Sullivan	250	299	1740	10 Nov 1784	27 Sep 1779	69	176	On N side of Holstein River	
Anderson, William	457		Middle District	731	396	1274	17 Dec 1794	23 Dec 1783	84	259	On N side of Tennessee	
Anderson, William	693		Sullivan	400	641	1740	9 Jul 1794	27 Sep 1779	81	635	Including said Andersons plantation	
Anderson, William	81		Hawkins	400	54	1740	27 Nov 1789	27 Sep 1779	74	41	On Caney Creek	
Andrews, James	1373	Ray, Archibald	Sumner	640	3228	1705	17 Nov 1797	24 Feb 1787	94	166	On N branches of Smiths Fork	yes
Andrews, John	322	Blount, Jno.Gray & Thos.	Tennessee	640	2054	1742	20 May 1793	22 Apr 1785	81	138	On S side of Cumberland River	yes
Andrews, John Cole	0138	Donelson, Stockley	Sumner	2560				13 Jan 1795			N E side of Obeys River	yes
Andrews, Nathan	243	Boayd [sic], John	Sumner	274	1148	3528	26 Nov 1789	19 Apr 1788	74	153	On S side of Cumberland River	yes
Andrews, Richard	548		Davidson	2200	520	111	15 Sep 1787		63	187	On first large or running into Cumberland	yes
Andrews, Thomas	636	Phillips, Mann	Davidson	640	609	2258	15 Sep 1787		63	217	On S side of Big Barren River	yes
Andrews, Watson	1036	Easton, James	Sumner	640	2698	3962	27 Mar 1796	11 May 1795	88	255	On waters of Caney Fork	yes
Angel, Thomas	1269	Donelson, John	Sumner	274	2920	88	19 Feb 1797	13 Aug 1796	90	248	Both sides of a branch &c	yes
Angel, Thomas	30	Blount, John	Davidson	224	16		14 Mar 1786		63	7	On Big Harpeth River	yes
Anglen, Benjamin	335	Barton, Samuel	Sumner	640	1642	3111	23 Feb 1793	7 Oct 1792	76	333	On Bartons Creek	yes
Anglin, Cornelius	2285	Tyner, Lewis	Davidson	640	2767	440	20 Jul 1796		88	464	On a large creek of Tennessee	yes
Ansley, William	85		Green	640	43	345	1 Nov 1786	7 Jun 1784	59	404	On the neck known by the name of ?	
Anthony, Abraham	915		Washington	200	892	1435	17 Nov 1790	15 Oct 1785	76	141	S side of Noleychuckey River &c	
Anthony, Abraham	942		Washington	200	919	235	17 Nov 1790	15 Oct 1789	76	150	On E fork Of Cherokee Creek	
Anthony, James	2000	Wilson, David	Davidson	640	1941	1003	20 May 1793		81	110	On E fork of Harpeth River	yes
Anthony, James	2457		Davidson	640	465	2829	19 Dec 1799		103	446	W fork of Stones River	
Anthony, Jonathan	1439		Sumner	640	465	254	19 Dec 1799	9 Feb 1784	103	446	W fork of Stones River	
Anthony, Jonathan	2458		Davidson	640	466	256	19 Dec 1799	9 Feb 1784	103	447	S side of Cumberland River	
Anthony, William	374		Sullivan	500	253	836	10 Nov 1784	29 Dec 1778	69	163	Beg at Thomas Harris's pine tree	
Appleton, John	791	McNees, John	Davidson	1000	794	3530	23 Aug 1788	12 Mar 1788	63	278	On waters of Duck Spring Creek	yes
Applewhite, Abraham	199	Hart, Anthony	Sumner	640	1104	2483	26 Nov 1789	12 Mar 1788	74	131	On W side of Caney Fork River	yes
Applewhite, Jesse	020	Armstrong & Donelson	Middle District	640								yes
Applewhite, John	358	Gamble, Edmond	Sumner	640	1480	2482	4 Jan 1792	6 May 1791	77	371	On the head of Drakes Creek	yes
Archer, Baker	148	Murphree, Hardy	Davidson	640	134	126	14 Mar 1786		63	52	On waters of Wolf Creek	yes
Archer, Baker, heir of Jesse	225		Davidson	640	211	2899	7 Mar 1786		63	78	On Haw Creek	yes
Archer, Demsey	017	Brehon, James Gloster	Sumner	640	211	126	7 Mar 1786	5 Jun 1788	63	78	On waters of Red River	yes
Archer, Jesse	225	Archer, Baker hr of Jesse	Davidson	640	240	215	7 Mar 1786		63	88	On Haw Creek	yes
Archer, Leticia heiress	254		Davidson	640	1490	2364	4 Jan 1792	24 Jul 1791	77	373	S side of Cumberland River	yes
Archer, Thomas	201	Haston, Daniel	Tennessee	2640	1001	125	18 May 1789		63	336	S side of Cumberland River	yes
Archer,Demsey	984a	Brehon, James Gloster	Sumner	640	295	1822	6 Dec 1794	23 Apr 1784	83	389	On waters of Red River	yes
Archibald, Robert	332		Middle District	1500	410	783	27 Jun 1797	4 Feb 1786	80	344	In Willsons Valley	yes
Arington, Charles	399		Sumner	640	103	1921	10 Nov 1790	12 Aug 1785	74	389	On the S side of Cumberland River	
Armstrong & Bradford	1630		Davidson	200	65	1903	18 May 1789		71	223	Beg at the corner of Public survey	
Armstrong & Crutcher	190	Roper, Richard	Sumner	228	761	1894		5 Jan 1785			On the waters of Station Camp Creek	yes
Armstrong & Daugherty	015		Green	1000				24 Apr 1784	66	530	On the N W side of Clinch River	
Armstrong & Daugherty	720		Green	1000	763	1899	11 Jul 1788	5 Jan 1785	66	531	Both sides Mountain Creek of Clinch River	
Armstrong & Daugherty	722		Green	800	764	1918	11 Jul 1788	5 Jan 1785	66	531	On N W side of Clinch Rtv below Lick Cr	

Claimant:	File #:	Assignee:	County:	Acres:	Grant:	Grant Date:	Entry:	Entry Date:	Bk:	Pg:	Location by Stream Name:	Military:
Armstrong & Daugherty	724		Green	1000	765	11 Jul 1788	1896	5 Jan 1785	66	531	On Mountain Creek &c	
Armstrong & Daugherty	725		Green	1000	766	11 Jul 1788	1890	5 Jan 1785	66	532	On Rivets Creek of Clinch River	
Armstrong & Daugherty	726		Green	900	767	11 Jul 1788	1901	24 Apr 1784	66	532	N/S Tennessee at Junction of 2nd Creek	
Armstrong & Daugherty	727		Green	300	768	11 Jul 1788	1925	5 Jan 1784	66	532	On S side of Clinch River	
Armstrong & Daugherty	728		Green	1000	769	11 Jul 1788	1895	5 Jan 1784	66	533	On the SoEt [sic] side of Clinch River	
Armstrong & Daugherty	729		Green	1000	770	11 Jul 1788	1893	5 Jan 1785	66	533	1st cr emptying into Holston above Tenn	
Armstrong & Daugherty	731		Green	500	772	11 Jul 1788	1906	11 Jul 1788	66	533	On S E side of Clinch Riv on the Lick Cr	
Armstrong & Daugherty	737		Green	1000	778	11 Jul 1788	1891	5 Jan 1785	66	535	On hd branches of a small sinking creek	
Armstrong & Daugherty	738		Green	1000	779	11 Jul 1788	1888	5 Jan 1785	66	535	On both sides of Beaverdam Creek &c	
Armstrong & Daugherty	739		Green	1000	780	11 Jul 1788	1097	5 Jan 1785	66	536	On N/S of Holston River on a branch	
Armstrong & Daugherty	745		Green	500	786	11 Jul1788	1917	5 Jan 1785	66	537	On S E side of Clinch Riv on Lick Branch	
Armstrong & Daugherty	747		Green	1000	788	11 Jul 1788	1889	5 Jan 1785	66	538	Adj former surv on small cr of Holston Riv	
Armstrong & Daugherty	748		Green	1400	789	11 Jul 1788	1910	5 Jan 1785	66	538	Adj their former survey at a large spring	
Armstrong & Daugherty	749		Green	1000	790	11 Jul 1788	1886	5 Jan 1785	66	538	Joining their former survey &c	
Armstrong & Donelson	015	Whitaker,Jos.hrs	Middle District	640			2963					
Armstrong & Donelson	016	Jefferson,Joel hrs	Middle District	640			2933					
Armstrong & Donelson	017	Fuller,Garnet hrs	Middle District	640			2915					
Armstrong & Donelson	018	Watson,Wm.hrs.	Middle District	640			2893					
Armstrong & Donelson	019	Sheppard,Val.hrs	Middle District	640			2960					
Armstrong & Donelson	020	Applewhite, Jesse	Middle District	640			2829					
Armstrong & Donelson	021	Aberrion, Jno.hrs	Middle District	640			1914					
Armstrong & Donelson	023	Wyne, Jno.hrs.	Middle District	640			2965					
Armstrong & Donelson	024	Truebeck,Geo.hrs	Middle District	640			2974					
Armstrong & Donelson	025	Brantley,Marma.hrs	Middle District	640			2484					
Armstrong & Donelson	03	Williams, Solomon	Middle District	640			1395					
Armstrong & Donelson	031	Hinton, Jno.hrs	Middle District	640			2929					
Armstrong & Donelson	041	Morris, Benj.hrs	Middle District	640			1476					
Armstrong & Donelson	11		Hawkins	500	7	23 Aug 1788			67	431	On N/S Tenn Riv below mouth of Clinch	
Armstrong & Donelson	52		Eastern District	1000	49	18 May 1789	956	29 Oct 1783	72	260	On N/S Holston River on Second Creek	
Armstrong & Donelson	53		Eastern District	640	50	18 May 1789	353	24 Mar 1780	72	260	On S/S of Clinch River in Hinds Valley	
Armstrong & Donelson	56		Eastern District	200	53	18 May 1789	789	14 Feb 1781	72	261	On the N/S of Clinch River in Bald Valley	
Armstrong & Donelson	58		Eastern District	400	55	18 May 1789	433	19 Apr 1780	72	262	On Beaverdam Creek	
Armstrong & Donelson	944	Whitaker, Josiah	Sumner	640	2468	21 Feb 1795			83	426	E side of W Fork of Obeys River &c	
Armstrong & Donelson	994	Watson, Wm.	Sumner	640	2476	21 Feb 1795			84	326	On E side of W fork of Obeys River	yes
Armstrong & Ewing	1019		Sumner	100	212	27 Feb 1796		26 Aug 1792	88	167	On waters of S Fork of Red River	
Armstrong & Gubbins	1583		Davidson	500	1244	10 Dec 1790	1331		74	346	On waters of Richland Creek	
Armstrong & Houston	1045		Green	200	1272	29 Jul 1793	32	26 Feb 1778	76	493	S side of Holston River	
Armstrong & Johnston	642		Tennessee	278	209	27 Feb 1796		10 Mar 1792	88	165	On waters of the Sulphur Fork	
Armstrong & Thos.Johnston	439		Tennessee	200	206	27 Feb 1786	42	29 Dec 1791	88	164	On waters of Millers Creek	
Armstrong & Thos.Johnston	440		Tennessee	50	207	27 Feb 1796	41	21 Aug 1792	88	164	On the waters of Sulphur fFork	
Armstrong & Thos.Johnston	443		Tennessee	100	210	27 Feb 1796	46	12 May 1790 (date	88	166	On waters of Millers Creek	
Armstrong & Thos.Johnston	444		Tennessee	160	211	27 Feb 1796	40	9 Dec 1791	88	166	On Calebs Creek	
Armstrong, Andrew, Jessop	239	Andrew,Jessop	Sumner	640	1144	26 Nov 1789	2807	7 Oct 780	74	151	On head of Drakes Creek	yes
Armstrong, Andrew	246	Floyd,Augustine	Sumner	640	1151	26 Nov 1789	2451	7 Oct 1789	74	154	On head of Drakes Creek	yes
Armstrong, Andrew	334	Flower, Chas.hrs	Davidson	640	320	28 Jun 1787	2182		63	119	West Fork of Goose Creek	yes

Claimant:	File #:	Assignee:	County:	Acres:	Grant:	Grant Date:	Entry:	Entry Date:	Bk:	Pg:	Location by Stream Name:	Military:
Armstrong, Andrew	335	Harrison, Jona. hrs	Davidson	1000	321	28 May 1787	2127		63	119	On one of the branches of Sulphur Fork	yes
Armstrong, Andrew	39	Zealott, Shadrach	Sumner	640	870	17 Jan 1789	3394	19 May 1788	63	302	On first fork of Big Barren	yes
Armstrong, Andrew	640		Washington	300	734	26 Oct 1786	769	24 Dec 1778	66	284	On the S side of Noleychuckey River	
Armstrong, Andrew	825	Tate, Thomas	Davidson	640	828	17 Jan 1789	3384		63	292	On N side of Red River	yes
Armstrong, Andrew	830	Hair, David hrs	Davidson	640	833	17 Jan 1789	3466		63	293	On N side of Cumberland River	yes
Armstrong, Andrew	832		Davidson	1286	835	17 Jan 1789	337		63	293	On North side of Cumberland River	yes
Armstrong, Andrew	850	Langford, Peter	Davidson	640	855	17 Jan 1789	2206		63	298	N boundary Robt Nelsons Sugar Camp	yes
Armstrong, Andrew	857	Conner, Chris. hrs	Davidson	640	866	17 Jan 1789	1701		63	301	On North side of Red River	yes
Armstrong, Col. Martin	1455		Davidson	1000	56	18 May 1789	1093		71	221	On the Long branch of Drake Creek	
Armstrong, Edward	176		Middle District	500	186	20 Dec 1791	2655	25 May 1784	75	231	On both sides of Duck River	
Armstrong, Francis	1044		Davidson	640	18	17 Apr 1786	164	21 Jan 1784	66	40	Beg Honey Locust Wt Fork of Richland Cr	
Armstrong, Henry Joab	2382	Barry, Redmond D.	Davidson	640	3164	14 Sep 1797	4241		90	427	Branches of Stones River on Suggs Cr	yes
Armstrong, James	1041	Mills, Wm.	Hawkins	280	2959	22 Feb 1797			90	234	Waters of Caney Creek	
Armstrong, James	245		Hawkins	500	233	20 Dec 1791			77	324	On the S E side of Clinch River &c	
Armstrong, James	318		Green	300	320	20 Sep 1787	2586	5 Jul 1780	65	464	On waters of the Dry Fork of Lick Creek	
Armstrong, James	49		Davidson	7200	35	14 Mar 1786	84		63	14	On waters of Stones River	yes
Armstrong, James	6		Green	500	539	29 Jun 1781					To a beech on the river	
Armstrong, James	727		Hawkins	100	547	12 Jun 1794	347	24 Mar 1780	82	170	On the N side of Holston River	
Armstrong, Jno hr of Rich.	022		Middle District	327			859				On S/S N fk Woolf, Muddy, or Black River	
Armstrong, Jno.	110		Green (Orange)	5000	552	27 Oct 1783	851					
Armstrong, John	02	Moslanders,Abel hrs	Middle District	2560			1561					
Armstrong, John	027	Boyce, Jesse hrs	Middle District	228								
Armstrong, John	1		Middle District	250	146	18 May 1789	48	20 Jun 1787			N Fork of Duck River	
Armstrong, John	115		Middle District	5000	117	10 Jul 1788	558	27 Oct 1783	67	466	On Richland Creek	
Armstrong, John	1471	Craddocks,Jno.	Davidson	3840	1047	7 Apr 1790	530		71	262	On the N side of Cumberland River	yes
Armstrong, John	71		Davidson	570	57	14 Mar 1786	17		63	24	On Officers & Soldiers South Boundary	yes
Armstrong, John	966	White, Richard	Sumner	327	2429	22 Feb 1795			84	311	On N side of W fork of Obeys River	yes
Armstrong, John	989	Bryar, Jesse	Sumner	228	2471	21 Feb 1795		23 Dec 1778	84	323	On E side of W fork of Obeys River	yes
Armstrong, Lanthy	189		Washington	300	57	23 Oct 1782	743		47	27	On waters of Big Limestone	
Armstrong, M & S.Donelson	940	Hinton, John hrs	Sumner	640	2464	21 Feb 1795	738	24 Mar 1785	83	424	E side of W Fork of Obeys River &c	
Armstrong, M. & A.Crutcher	07		Not given	500							Beg at a sweet gum	
Armstrong, M. & Daugherty	721		Green	1000	762	11 Jul 1788	1898	5 Jan 1785	66	530	Adj his former survey of 1000 acres &c	
Armstrong, M. & Daugherty	730		Green	320	771	10 Jul 1788	1915	11 Jul 1788	66	533	On the 1st creek &c	
Armstrong, M. & Daugherty	732		Green	700	773 (713)	11 Jul 1788	1904	24 Apr 1784	66	534	On bald or emptying into Clinch Riv SE side	
Armstrong, M. & Daugherty	733		Green	1000	774	10 Jul 1788	1902	24 Apr 1784	66	534	Near the Pilot Knob &c	
Armstrong, M. & Daugherty	735		Green	1000	776	11 Jul 1788	1905	11 Jul 1788	66	535	On both sides of the S E Fork of Lick	
Armstrong, M. & Daugherty	736		Green	320	777	11 Jul 1788	1916	11 Jul 1788	66	535	On the S E side of Clinch River &c	
Armstrong, M. & Daugherty	740		Green	800	781	11 Jul 1788	1908	5 Jan 1785	66	536	Adjoining their former survey 320 acres	
Armstrong, M. & Daugherty	741		Green	1000	782	11 Jul 1788	1909	5 Jan 1785	66	536	On Whites Cr the Wt Fk of No br Holston	
Armstrong, M. & Daugherty	742		Green	1200	783	11 Jul 1788	1912	5 Jan 1785	66	536	Adjoining their former survey 1500 acres	
Armstrong, M. & Daugherty	743		Green	1000	784	11 Jul 1788	1907	11 Jul 1788	66	537 [?]	On sm cr emptying into Holston on N side	
Armstrong, M. & Daugherty	744		Green	1000	785	11 Jul 1788	1914	11 Jul 1788	66	537	On Reeds Creek called by Brooks & Co.	
Armstrong, M. & Daugherty	746		Green	1000	787	11 Jul 1788	1887	11 Jul 1788	66	529	Adj a former survey of 1500 acres	
Armstrong, M. & Dav Shelby	975	Gorley,Ayeres hrs	Sumner	640	2439	22 Feb 1795	1814	12 Aug 1785	84	316	On N side of Cumberland River	yes
Armstrong, M. & Dougherty	719		Green	150	760	11 Jul 1788	1913	5 Jan 1785	66	530	At lge spring running across Indian path	

Earliest Tennessee Land Records

Claimant:	File #:	Assignee:	County:	Acres:	Grant:	Grant Date:	Entry:	Entry Date:	Bk:	Pg:	Location by Stream Name:	Military:
Armstrong, M. & S. Donelson	50		Eastern District	1000	47	18 May 1789	1220		72	259	Incl place where the Canoe man (?) &c	
Armstrong, M. & S. Donelson	54		Eastern District	400	51	18 May 1789	482	7 Jun 1780	72	261	S/S Clinch Riv on N/S W fk Bald Valley Vr	
Armstrong, M. & S. Donelson	55		Eastern District	2000	52	18 May 1789	1666	25 Jun 1784	72	261	On N side of Tennessee River &c	
Armstrong, M. & S. Donelson	58		Eastern District	400	55	18 May 1789	433	19 Apr 1780	72	262	On Beaverdam Creek	
Armstrong, M. & S. Donelson	59		Eastern District	600	56	18 May 1789	934	29 Oct 1783	72	262	On the N side of Tennessee River &c	
Armstrong, M. & S. Donelson	60		Eastern District	1000	57	18 May 1789	1073	30 Oct 1783	72	263	On the N side of Tennessee River &c	
Armstrong, M. & S. Donelson	61		Eastern District	600	58	18 May 1789	3551	24 Mar 1780	72	263	On Camp Cr waters of Outstons [sic] Riv	
Armstrong, M. & S. Donelson	621		Eastern District	640	59	18 May 1789	354	24 Mar 1780	72	263	On N side of Tennessee River	
Armstrong, M. & S. Donelson	63		Eastern District	600	60	18 May 1789	357	24 Mar 1780	72	264	In Bald Valley	
Armstrong, M. & S. Donelson	64		Eastern District	600	61	18 May 1789	1080	3 Oct 1783	72	264	On Beaverdam Vreek &c	
Armstrong, M. & S. Donelson	66		Eastern District	640	63	18 May 1789	356	24 Mar 1780	72	265	On N side of Clinch River in Bald Valley	
Armstrong, M. & S. Donelson	67		Eastern District	1000	64	18 May 1789	961	30 Oct 1783	72	265	On the N side of Holston River	
Armstrong, M. & S. Donelson	68		Eastern District	1000	65	18 May 1789	1074	30 Oct 1783	72	266	On the N side of Tennessee River &c	
Armstrong, M. & S. Donelson	792		Green	500	597	23 Jul 1788			68	261	On N side of Tennessee River &c	
Armstrong, M. & S. Donelson	934	Williams, Solomon	Sumner	640	2458	21 Feb 1795			83	421	E side of W Fork of Obeys River &c	yes
Armstrong, M. & S. Donelson	943	Truebuck, Geo.	Sumner	640	2467	21 Feb 1795			83	425	E side of W Fork of Obeys River	
Armstrong, M. & S. Donelson	958	Fulks, Garret hrs.	Sumner	640	2421	21 Feb 1795			84	307	On E side of W Fork of Obeys River	yes
Armstrong, M. & S. Donelson	959	Morris, Benj. Hrs	Sumner	640	2422	21 Feb 1795			84	307	On E side of W Fork of Obeys River	yes
Armstrong, M. & S. Donelson	961	Poe, John hrs.	Sumner	640	2424	21 Feb 1795			84	398	On E side of W Fork of Obeys River	yes
Armstrong, M. & S. Donelson	963	Brantley, Marm.hrs	Sumner	640	2426	22 Feb 1795			84	309	On E side of W Fork of Obeys River	yes
Armstrong, M. & S. Donelson	984	Jefferson, Joel	Sumner	640	2449	21 Feb 1795			84	321	On E side of W Fork of Obeys River	yes
Armstrong, M. & S. Donelson	991	Harrell, Holland hrs	Sumner	640	2473	22 Feb 1795			84	324	On E side of W Fork of Obeys River	yes
Armstrong, M. & S. Donelson	992	Wyne, John hrs	Sumner	640	2474	21 Feb 1795			84	325	On E side of W Fork of Obeys River	yes
Armstrong, M. & S. Donelson	993	A(M)errian, John	Sumner	640	2575	21 Feb 1795			84	325	On E side of W Fork of Obeys River	yes
Armstrong, M. & S. Donelson	996	Applewhite, Jess.hrs	Sumner	640	2479	21 Feb 1795			84	327	On E side of W Fork of Obeys River	yes
Armstrong, M.	441		Tennessee	100	208	27 Feb 1796	43		88	165	N side of Spring Creek	
Armstrong, Martin	01		Davidson	1280			383	27 Oct 1784			N side of Cumberland River	
Armstrong, Martin	01		Green	300	46		1324	18 May 1789			Plumb Meadow ork of Beaverdam creek	
Armstrong, Martin	02		Green	200	66		1328	18 May 1789			On Beaverdam Creek	
Armstrong, Martin	03		Green	400	54		1330	18 may 1789			On Beaverdam Creek	
Armstrong, Martin	03		Middle District	5000			2840 [?]	28 Mar 1784				
Armstrong, Martin	06		Not given	640			1141	8 Nov 1785			N side of Cumberland River	
Armstrong, Martin	08		Not given	306			679	5 Mar 1785			N side of Cumberland River	
Armstrong, Martin	09		Not given	400				31 Mar 1783 [?]			N side of Cumberland River	
Armstrong, Martin	1027		Davidson	640	175	8 Dec 1787			64	315	N/S Cumberland riv at mouth of Red River	
Armstrong, Martin	1183		Sumner	1000	286	6 Jun 1796		14 Jul 1792	88	381	On S side of Cumberland River	
Armstrong, Martin	121		Western District	5000	121	10 Jul 1788			67	327	On a S branch of a Riv running into Miss.	
Armstrong, Martin	123		Middle District	5000	125	10 Jul 1788	1107	30 Oct 1783	67	470	On Richland Creek	
Armstrong, Martin	1430		Davidson	400	47	8 Oct 1787			68	159	N/S of Cumberland Riv on the N Cross Cr	
Armstrong, Martin	1431		Davidson	274	48	274	627		68	159	Both sides of muddy fk a br of Sinking Cr	
Armstrong, Martin	1432		Davidson	425	49	8 Oct 1787			68	159	Lying on the S side of Cumberland River	
Armstrong, Martin	1433		Davidson	306	50	8 Oct 1787			68	160	Joining James Shaws preemption	
Armstrong, Martin	1434		Davidson	640	51	8 Oct 1787	1144		68	160	On small cr on the N/S of Cumberland Riv	
Armstrong, Martin	1435		Davidson	640	52	8 Oct 1787	584		68	160	On both side of Red River	
Armstrong, Martin	1472	Messer, Benj.	Davidson	274	1048	27 Nov 1789	575		71	282	On the E waters of Cedar Lick	yes

Claimant:	File #:	Assignee:	County:	Acres:	Grant:	Grant Date:	Entry:	Entry Date:	Bk:	Pg:	Location by Stream Name:	Military:
Armstrong, Martin	1473	Cash, John	Davidson	640	1049	27 Nov 1789	1671		71	283	On the S side of Cumberland River	yes
Armstrong, Martin	1476		Davidson	400	79	27 Nov 1789			71	284	on the N side of Cumberland River	
Armstrong, Martin	159		Middle District	5000	159	10 Dec 1790			74	377	On E fork of Richland Creek	
Armstrong, Martin	162		Western District	5000	162	10 Jul 1788			67	359	On S Fork of N Fork of Forked Deer River	
Armstrong, Martin	164		Western District	5000	164	10 Jul 1788			67	360	On Forked Deer river &c	
Armstrong, Martin	29		Western District	5000	29	10 Jul 1788			67	291	On head of a branch of Richland Creek	
Armstrong, Martin	30		Middle District	3000	32	10 Jul 1788	1116	30 Oct 1783	67	421	On the S side of Duck River &c	
Armstrong, Martin	366		Davidson	3840	1	16 Feb 1786			63	1 (inter)	On both sides of Sugar Creek	
Armstrong, Martin	377	Padgett, Thos. Hrs	Davidson	640	349	15 Sep 1787	1298		63	132	On Strugeon Creek	yes
Armstrong, Martin	38		Western District	5000	38	10 Jul 1788			67	294	On the Obion River &c	
Armstrong, Martin	399		Western District	5000	323	14 Dec 1793	797	29 Oct 1783	82	145	On the waters of Miss &c	
Armstrong, Martin	400		Western District	5000	324	14 Dec 1793	796	29 Oct 1783	82	145	On waters of Mississippi &c	
Armstrong, Martin	454	Ryan, Cornelius	Davidson	640	426	15 Sep 1787	389		63	157	S side of Richland	yes
Armstrong, Martin	467	Harris, Peter	Davidson	1000	439	15 Sep 1787	1657		63	161	S side of Cumberland River	yes
Armstrong, Martin	49		Eastern District	300	46	18 May 1789			72	259	On plumb meadow Fork of Beaverdam Cr	
Armstrong, Martin	508	Smith, John	Davidson	640	480	15 Sep 1787	571		63	174	S side of Cumberland	yes
Armstrong, Martin	514	Rothwell, David hrs	Davidson	640	486	15 Sep 1787	279		63	176	On head waters of Marrowbone Creek	yes
Armstrong, Martin	552		Tennessee	235	357	10 Apr 1797	55	31 Dec 1796	90	282	W side of Harpeth River	
Armstrong, Martin	57		Eastern District	400	54	18 May 1789			72	262	On Beaverdam Creek	
Armstrong, Martin	580	Douglass, John	Davidson	640	552	15 Sep 1787	566		63	198	On both sides of E Fork of Yellow Creek	yes
Armstrong, Martin	68		Western District	5000	68	10 Jul 1788			67	307	On waters of Reelfoot & Grove Creek	
Armstrong, Martin	69		Eastern District	200	66	18 May 1789			72	266	On Beaverdam Creek &c	
Armstrong, Martin	7		Davidson	3840	1	16 Feb 1786			63	1	On both sides of Sugar Creek	
Armstrong, Martin	70		Middle District	5000	72	10 Jul 1788	1196	3 Nov 1783	67	445	On the N side of Elk River &c	
Armstrong, Martin	734		Green	1000	775	11 Jul 1788	1892	11 Jul 1788	66	534	In the Beaverdam Valley &c	
Armstrong, Martin	871	Rice, John	Davidson	168	54	25 Apr 1789			63	306	Beg at a red oak	yes
Armstrong, Martin	879	Bryant, Thos.	Sumner	595	2398	7 Jan 1794	328	13 Mar 1788	81	391	On S side of Cumberland River	yes
Armstrong, Martin	88		Middle District	2000	90	10 Jul 1788	1117	30 Oct 1783	67	454	On the S side of Duck River &c	
Armstrong, Martin	885		Sumner	3840	140	7 Jan 1794		1 Nov 1792	81	397	On Obeys River	
Armstrong, Martin	95		Middle District	5000	97	10 Jul 1788	1106	30 Oct 1783	67	457	Lying on Richland Creek	
Armstrong, Martin	96		Western District	5000	96	10 Jul 1788	793	29 Oct 1783	67	318	Lying on the Obion River &c	
Armstrong, Martin & [blank]	12		Hawkins	640	8	23 Aug 1788			67	431	On the N side of Tennessee River &c	
Armstrong, Martin & Anthony	1587	Croucher, Anto.hrs	Davidson	2560	1255	10 Dec 1790	345		74	350	On waters of White Creek	yes
Armstrong, Martin & Anthony	1463		Davidson	500	67	18 May 1789			71	224	On S/S Cumberland River at a sweet gum	
Armstrong, Martin & Anthony	455	Ford, John	Davidson	2560	427	15 Sep 1787	298		63	158	On Thompsons Creek	
Armstrong, Martin, Jr.	1475		Davidson	640	78	27 Nov 1789			71	283	On the S side of Cumberland River	
Armstrong, Martin, Jr.	27		Western District	500	128	2 [sic]	27	10 Jul 1788	67	290	On the Forked Deer River &c	
Armstrong, Martin, Sr.	126		Middle District	250	128	10 Jul 1788	16	10 Jan 1780	67	471	Lying on Weakleys Creek	
Armstrong, Martin, Sr.	66		Middle District	250	68	10 Jul 1788	14	10 Jan 1786	67	443	On head waters of Weakleys Creek &c	
Armstrong, Mary etal	140		Eastern District	2000	106	6 Sep 1791	1228	25 Sep 1785	77	224	On the N side of Tennessee River	
Armstrong, Richard	128	Isley, Saml. Hrs.	Tennessee	640	1634	23 Feb 1793	2808	30 Sep 1785	76	329	On the waters of Wells Creek	
Armstrong, Robert	145		Green	400	615	23 Aug 1788	289	7 Jun 1784	64	346	On the S of Holston River	
Armstrong, Robert	753		Washington	300	567	10 Nov 1784	662	7 Dec 1778	69	129	On E branch of Little Limestone Creek	
Armstrong, Robert	9		Green	300	72	1 Nov 1786	60	1 Nov 1786	58	433	On the S side of Nollihuckie River	
Armstrong, Thomas	178	Fowler, Absolom	Davidson	640	164	7 Mar 1786	86	14 Jan 1785	63	62	Joining James Armstrongs' 7200 acres	yes

Claimant:	File #:	Assignee:	County:	Acres:	Grant:	Grant Date:	Entry:	Entry Date:	Bk:	Pg:	Location by Stream Name:	Military:
Armstrong, Thomas	550	George Walker & S. Lewis	Sumner	640	1764	20 May 1793	2164	16 Jul 1792	81	70	On Drakes Creek	yes
Armstrong, Thomas	62		Davidson	3840	48	14 Mar 1786	81		63	20	On main West Fork of Stones River	yes
Armstrong, Thomas & James	1026	Wms. Jas. heir of Herb.	Davidson	1000		15 Sep 1787	862		63	347	On South side of Cumberland River	yes
Armstrong, Thos. Templeton	141		Middle District	3000	143	10 Jul 1788	1115	20 Oct 1783	67	477	On the waters of Elk River &c	
Armstrong, Thos. Templeton	26		Middle District	2000	28	10 Jul 1788	1114	30 Oct 1783	67	420	On the waters of Elk River &c	
Armstrong, William	161		Sullivan	240	168	10 Oct 1783	234	26 Feb 1780	53	145	On N side of Holston River	
Armstrong, William	172		Hawkins	50	105	16 Nov 1790	235	26 Feb 1780	77	186	In Gravelly at hd of Wt Fk of Renfrows Cr	
Armstrong, William	182		Hawkins	100	115	16 Nov 1790	90	8 Feb 1780	77	189	In Gravelly Valley	
Armstrong, William	39		Davidson	3840	25	14 Mar 1786	62		63	11	South side of Cumberland River	yes
Armstrong, William, Sr.	724		Hawkins	200	544	12 Jun 1794	1882	12 Feb 1780	82	169	On N side of Clinch River &c	
Armrong, John	46	Dobbins, Wm.	Eastern District	250	146	18 May 1789			72	257	On the N Fork of Duck River	
Arnett, Jacob	773		Hawkins	300	613	12 Jul 1794	1313	29 Mar 1779	82	216	On Buffelow Creek	
Arnold, David	021	Darden [?], John	Sumner	274			3115	25 Nov 1783		353	S side of Cumberland River	yes
Arnold, James	154	Wenoah, Jno.	Tennessee	640	1408	20 Dec 1791			77	169	On W side of Pine River	
Arnold, James	720		Sullivan	100	665	4 Dec 1794	436	19 Apr 1780	84	138	Beg at a birch	
Arnold, John	785		Washington	100	599	10 Nov 1784	2552	24 May 1783	69	264	On E fork of Cobbs Creek	
Armstrong & Donelson	65		Eastern District	640	62	18 May 1789	429	19 Apr 1780	72	557	On Beaverdam Creek &c	
Arrield, William	195		Eastern District	100	167	23 Apr 1794	267		81	185	On Spring Fork of Sycamore Creek	
Arth, Adam & F. Mayberry	173		Eastern District	640	128	24 Jun 1793	991	4 Jan 1779	80	420	On S side of Clinch River	
Arthur, Stephen	1343	Barbour, Richard	Sumner	640	3143	14 Sep 1797	3851	31 Aug 1795	90	349	S side of Caney Fork	yes
Arthuston, Saml.	1225		Green	100	1075	12 Jan 1793			78	200	On S side of Noleychuckey River	
Artist, John	841	Baryer, George Henry	Sumner	274	2343	20 May 1793	3204	27 Oct 1792	81	435	Bet. Little Cedar Creek &c	yes
Arwinne, Jno & Hatchett	21		Hawkins	640	17	23 Aug 1788	1609	13 Sep 1779	67		Cumberland valley on Cainey Fk Clear Cr	
Ash, Stephen heirs	044	Hughlett, William	Middle District	640			2830			455		
Ashart, William	286		Green	123	288	20 Sep 1787	1299	24 Nov 1785	65	381	At the Rocky Spring of Hineses branch	
Ashburn, Martin	456		Eastern District	500	309	13 Apr 1801	1096	24 Jun 1794	112	382	S side of Holston River	
Ashburn, Martin	457		Eastern District	800	310	13 Apr 1801	1096	24 Jun 1784	112	382	S side of Holston River	
Ashburn, Martin	458		Eastern District	200	311	13 Apr 1801	1096	24 Jun 1784	76	321	S E side of Clinch River	
Ashe, Charles	1684	Robertson, James Randolp	Davidson	640	1618	23 Feb 1793	1355		90	311	On Big Harpeth River	yes
Ashe, Daniel	1330		Washington	200	1254	6 Jun 1797	2568	26 May 1780	63	94	S side of Powells River	
Ashe, John Baptist	271		Davidson	4457	257	14 Mar 1786	496			11	N side of Tennessee River	yes
Ashe, Samuel	41		Davidson	1508	27	14 Mar 1786	693		63	27	Both sides of E & W Fk of Thompsons Cr	yes
Ashe, Samuel	80		Davidson	2560	66	14 Mar 1786	594		63	179	On Wolf Creek	yes
Asher, John	1061		Washington	89	1011	27 Nov 1792	1116	14 Jan 1779	80	229	On both sides of Watauga River	
Asher, Mary	1034		Hawkins	640	797	1 Mar 1797	654		90	484	S side of Holston River	
Asher, William	1000		Green	123	1827 [?]	29 Jul 1793	1299	1 Jan 1784	76	9	On Haines branch of Bent Creek	
Asher, William	807		Green	600	801	17 Nov 1788	172	22 Oct 1783	70	131	In Cane valley waters of Bent Creek	
Ashers, Charles	683	Doneison, John	Sumner	1000	2029	20 May 1793	3330	14 Jul 1791	81	450	On S side of Cumberland River	yes
Ashmore, James	26		Green	300	89	1 Nov 1786	242	7 Jun 1784	58	441	On Lick Creek	
Ashmore, James	122		Green	300	138	1 Nov 1786	573	1 Nov 1784	59	338	On both sides of Lick Creek	
Asker, Charles	576		Washington	300	841	11 Jul 1788	1099	18 Oct 1787	64	220	Lying on both sides of Watauga River	
Asker, Charles	867		Washington	300	851	18 May 1789	1099	17 May 1779	72	183	Beg at a stake &c	
Askew, Jesse	797	Sheppard, William	Sumner	640	2258	20 May 1793	2827	24 Nov 1792	81	212	On waters of Hickmans Creek	yes
Askew, Wm.	1261	Biggett, Jesse	Sumner	640	2937	1 Mar 1797	1747	22 Mar 1796	90	342	Waters of Fifth Creek	yes
Askin, William	1577	Shannon, Samuel	Davidson	640	1231	10 Dec 1790	2630		74		On waters of Stones River	yes

Claimant:	File #:	Assignee:	County:	Acres:	Grant:	Grant Date:	Entry:	Entry Date:	Bk:	Pg:	Location by Stream Name:	Military:
Asobron, William John	210	Reed, Jesse	Sumner	640	1115	26 Nov 1789	3501	12 Mar 1788	74	136	On W side of Caney Fork River	yes
Aspley, John	162	Davis, Thomas	Davidson	640	148	14 Mar 1786	471		63	56	On both sides of Blue Creek	yes
Assembly, Resolution of	01										Congressional Reservation Passed 1818	
Astin, John	1151		Washington	100	1109	17 Jul 1794	2484	10 Mar 1780	81	614	Beg at a stake	
Atkins, Joseph	400		Middle District	3000	339	17 Dec 1794	2617	25 May 1784	84	223	On waters of Duck River	
Atkinson, Benjamin	639		Green	680	314 [?]	11 Jul 1788	1049	23 Jun 1784	66	454	On Clinch River at the mouth of a creek	
Atkinson, Charleton	666	Johnston, Ben. hrs	Tennessee	640	3335	6 Dec 1797	3859		97	53	Adjoining Hugh Williamson S boundary	
Atkinson, Nathan	632		Green	1000	673	11 Jul 1788	585	25 Jun 1784	66	451	On the headwaters of Bull Run &c	
Atkinson, Nathan	633		Green	400	674	11 Jul 1788	873	25 Jun 1784	66	451	On both sides of the N Fork of Bull Run	
Atkinson, Nathan	649		Green	400	690	11 Jul 1788	1874	23 Jun 1784	66	457	On head N Fk of Bull Run -- into Clinch	
Atkinson, Nathan	653		Green	300	694	11 Jul 1788	1876	23 Jun 1784	66	458	Bet. Mountain & Clinch River on Flat Creek	
Atkinson, Nathan	664		Green	300	705	11 Jul 1788	1048	25 Jun 1784	66	462	On Clinch River &c	
Atkinson, Nathan	673		Green	300	714	11 Jul 1788	1877	23 Jun 1784	66	464	Lying on Flat Creek &c	
Atkinson, Nathan	674		Green	400	715	11 Jul 1788	1875	23 Jun 1784	66	465	Chiefly on W side of Flat Creek &c	
Attogan [O'Hagen], Charles	2422	Espic, William	Davidson	500		23 Apr 1796			92	93	Deed Wm Espie; indexed O'Hagen	
Atway, Hardy	512	Isbell, Thomas	Davidson	640		15 Sep 1787	2781		63	175	On S side of Big Barren	yes
Ausgood, Thomas	3	Jones, David	Robertson	640	2927	19 Feb 1797	3909	13 Aug 1796			On waters of Red River	yes
Ausley, William	51		Green	640	114	1 Nov 1786	347	7 Jun 1784	81	475	On the N side of Nollichuckie River	
Austin, John	1151		Washington	100	1109	17 Jul 1794	2484	10 Mar 1780	81	614	Beg at a stake	
Austin, John	1157		Washington	250	1115	7 Jul 1794	2878	2 Jul 1781	81	615	Beg at McNabb's corner	
Austin, Thomas	2440	H. Tatum & Henry Wiggins	Davidson	640	3282	6 Dec 1797	4156		98	162	On the waters of Overalls Creek	yes
Autry, James	046	Redmon Dillonberry [sic]	Sumner	640			4226	14 Oct 1797			On head of main Middle Fork &c	yes
Avent, James	674		Sumner	228	2005	20 May 1793	95	7 Oct 1791	81	125	On S side of Cumberland River	yes
Averall, William	2141	Halsted, Jollef	Davidson	160	2418	7 Jan 1794	995		81	405	On N side of Cumberland River	yes
Avery, Estridge	2139	Mulherrin [sic], James	Davidson	640	2415	7 Jan 1794	3299		81	404	On S side of Cumberland River &c	yes
Avery, Estridge	926	Mulkerin [sic], James	Davidson	640	942	18 May 1789			63	323	On Hickman's Creek	yes
Avery, James	1178	Harris, Edward	Sumner	640	2663	4 Jun 1796	1312	1 Jun 1795	88	362	Joining said Harris survey	yes
Avery, Waighstill	3		Carter	250	1307	4 Dec 1801			114	86	Beg at a poplar	
Avery, Waighstill	481		Washington	130	472	10 Nov 1784	314	24 Aug 1778	55	9	Upon the head branches of Doe River	
Avery, Waighstill	482		Washington	100	473	10 Nov 1784	313	24 Aug 1778	55	9	Both sides Doe Riv.--Surry Co. NC	
Avery, Waighstill	483		Washington	180	474	10 Nov 1784	315	24 Aug 1783	55	10	Upon the Roaring Fork of Doe River	
Axadale, James	309		Green	300	311	20 Sep 1787			65	462	On Little Chuckey	
Babb, Philip	519		Green	100	521	20 Sep 1787			65	529	On the S branch of Lick Creek	
Babb, Phillip	1243		Green	100	1093	12 Jan 1793	1869	6 Oct 1779	78	360	On a branch of Lick Creek	
Babb, Phillip	991		Green	100	1218	29 Jul 1793	1212	15 Dec 1779	76	483	On the waters of Stocktons Creek	
Babb, Phillip	06		Green	94			2292	27 Nov 1779			On the waters of Stocktons Creek	
Back, Water	50		Tennessee	640	34			8 Sep 1819			Bl Ok Ool-lah-not-less SW corner	
Backhonham, John	231	Reed, Jesse	Sumner	640	1136	24 Nov 1789	2633	12 Mar 1788	74	147	On waters of Hickman's Creek	yes
Bacon, Isaac	1318		Washington	45	345	19 Feb 1797			90	255	S fork of Boone Creek	
Bacon, Isaac	1336		Washington	200	1260	8 Jun 1797	2861	23 May 1781	90	329	Waters of Sinking Creek	
Bacon, Michael	1329		Green	200	1071	24 Dec 1792	149	22 Oct 1783	78	428	Beg at a chestnut etc	
Bacon, Michael	1555		Green	200	1227	12 Jun 1794			82	182	Beg at a Red oak &c	
Badwell, Zadock	302	Dixon, Joseph	Tennessee	1000	1992	20 May 1793	2593	30 Sep 1785	81	122	On E Fork of Bartons Creek	yes
Bag or Sapsucker	51		Tennessee	640	7			3 Aug 1819			Beg at plum bush; Indian Lands	
Bagbey, Matthias	1384	Barton, Samuel	Sumner	640	3251	24 Nov 1797	3946	20 Mar 1797	97	34	Bet Spring Creek & Bartons Creek	yes

Earliest Tennessee Land Records

Claimant:	File #:	Assignee:	County:	Acres:	Grant:	Grant Date:	Entry:	Entry Date:	Bk:	Pg:	Location by Stream Name:	Military:
Bagley, Isaac	1133	Harris, Edward	Sumner	640	2639	4 Jun 1796	1807	1 Jun 1795	88	347	Joining a survey of sd Harris	yes
Bags, Jno	568		Green	100	248	20 Sep 1787		9 Oct 1778	66	156	On the Et side of Little Chuckey	
Bags, Jno.	22		Green	100	165	20 Sep 1787	248	22 Oct 1783			E side of Little Chuckey	
Bagwell, Frederick	862	W. Wykoff & L. Clark	Davidson	640	876	17 Jan 1789	2110		63	304	Abt 2 or 3 mi S of Cumberland Riv	yes
Bagworth, Jesse	937	Blount, Reading	Davidson	640	953	18 May 1789	2559		63	325	On the first creek	yes
Bailes, Barnabus	1015	Pettie, John	Davidson	228	1032	18 May 1789	1821		63	344	On E Fork of Whites Creek	yes
Bailey, Benjamin	52		Davidson	3840	38	14 Mar 1786	552		63	16	North side of Cumberland River	yes
Bailey, Charles	475	Taylor, James	Sumner	640	1641	27 Apr 1793	810	5 Jun 1784	81	27	Both sides of Sulphur Fork of Red River	yes
Bailey, Claudius	351		Green	320	353	20 Sep 1787	1251	24 Oct 1763	65	473	A S branch of Lick Creek & Lick Cr [sic]	
Bailey, Cottrell	514		Washington	100	777	16 Aug 1787			64	145	Beg at a beach on Robt Taylor's line	
Bailey, Etheldred	1009	Mulherrin, James	Davidson	640	1026	18 May 1789			63	343	On Hickmans Creek	yes
Bailey, Etheldred	2140	Mulherrin, James	Davidson	640	2416	7 Jan 1794	3329		81	405	On Stones River	yes
Bailey, John	24	Dickson, Edward	Tennessee	640	1187	30 Nov 1790	241	25 Oct 1783	74	317	On S side of Cumberland River	yes
Bailey, John	475		Sullivan	383	354	10 Nov 1784	783	26 Dec 1778	69	197	On S side of Holstein River	
Bailey, Lewis	2113	Blount,Jno.G.& Thos.	Davidson	228	2371	20 May 1793	1133		81	206	On W side of Harpeth River	yes
Bailey, Macon	745	Hart, Anthony	Davidson	640	718	11 Jul 1788	3416		63	252	On N waters of Sycamore Creek	yes
Bailey, Morris	023	Donelson, S.	Tennessee	640			3420	31 Jan 1786			S side of Cumberland River	yes
Bailey, Morris	863	Hart, Anthony	Davidson	640	877	17 Jan 1789	3420		63	304	On W Fork of Spring Creek	yes
Bailey, Reuben	1101		Washington	291	1051	27 Nov 1792	838	29 Dec 1778	80	2(3)05	On the S side of Nolichuckey River	
Bailey, Robert	1056	King, William	Sumner	640	2533	10 Dec 1795	1584	8 Aug 1795	88	290	Joining an entry of Robert King's	yes
Bailey, Robert	18	Johnson, William	Robertson	640	2932		1584	25 Jul 1796			On waters of Red River	yes
Bailey, Robert	44		Washington	100	334	24 Oct 1782	593	10 Nov 1778	43	312	On the waters of Cherokee Creek	
Bailey, Robert	736		Washington	307	550	10 Nov 1784	1030	6 Jan 1779	69	123	On both sides of Cherokee Creek	
Bailey, Sarah	616		Sullivan	200	566	5 Jun 1793	1687	9 Oct 1779	80	158	On the N side of Eatons ridge	
Bailey, Thomas	158	Medlin (?) Elisha	Tennessee	640	1415	20 Dec 1791	1437	19 Nov 1784	77 (97)	355	On both sides of Pine River	
Bailey, Thomas	279	Brittain, Phillip	Tennessee	274	1864	20 May 1793	972	21 May 1784	81	92	On a small creek on W side of Piney River	
Bailey, Thomas	774		Green	320	579	11 Sep 1788	1013	1 Jan 1779	68	253	On the waters of Little Gap Creek	
Bailey, William	1489	Donelson, John	Davidson	640	1202	20 Nov 1790	3246		73	279	On S side of Cumberland	yes
Bailey, William	591		Hawkins	200	465	29 Jul 1793	428	19 Apr 1780	80	293	On S side of Holsten River on Buck Creek	
Bailey, William	765		Hawkins	640	605	12 Jul1794	2351	16 Dec 1779	82	213	On the N side of Clinch River &c	
Bailey, William Henry	060	Mebane, Chs.	Middle District	640			3757					yes
Bailey, Wm.	7	Wm Bailey Pvt Cont Line	Smith	360	3362	18 Oct 1800	4054	7 Jul 1800	108	132	On the head of Dixons Lick Creek	yes
Baileys, William	105		Sullivan	175	116	23 Oct 1782	1873	6 Oct 1779	43	293	On the waters of Holston River &c	yes
Baird, Joseph	2344	Malloy, Thomas	Davidson	640	2989	10 Apr 1797	3943		90	289	On Harpeth River	yes
Baker (Barker), Thomas	209		Washington	100	77	23 Oct 1782	860	30 Dec 1778	47	37	N side of Nolachuckey River	
Baker, Amos	1881	Bond, John	Davidson	640	1627	27 Apr 1793	1581		81	24	On head branches of Stones Creek	yes
Baker, Charles	035	Willoughby, Solom	not given	640			2784	6 Jul 1786			S side Cumberland	
Baker, Charles	176	Willoughby, Solomon	Tennessee	640	1453	20 Dec 1791			77	364	On the S side of the Cumberland River	
Baker, Charles	2046	Matthews, John	Davidson	274	2069	20 May 1793	3036		81	141	On a small branch of Gaspers Creek	yes
Baker, Elisha	1320		Green	300	1170	12 Jan 1793	364	23 Oct 1785	78	406	On Long Creek	
Baker, Elisha	1324		Green	200	1174	12 Jan 1793	832	26 Aug 1781	78	409	On N side of French Broad River	
Baker, Elisha	502		Green	640	504	20 Sep 1787	248	22 Oct 1782	65	523	On the N side of Holstein River	
Baker, Francis	952		Washington	100	929	17 Nov 1790	2439	28 Feb 1780	76	154	Beg at a large hickory &c	
Baker, James	1058		Hawkins	100	767	21 Jan 1797	1635	21 Jan 1780	91	114	S side of Holsten River	
Baker, John	09	Devonshire, Joshua	Tennessee	640		19 Dec 1792	3403	19 Dec 1792			S side of Cumberland River	

Claimant:	File #:	Assignee:	County:	Acres:	Grant:	Grant Date:	Entry:	Entry Date:	Bk:	Pg:	Location by Stream Name:	Military:
Baker, John	118		Tennessee	640	1619	23 Feb 1793	717	29 Apr 1794	76	321	S Side of Cumberland River &c	
Baker, John	221	McAndrews, Andrew	Sumner	640	1126	26 Nov 1789	3402	2 Jun 1788	74	142	On N side of Cumberland River	yes
Baker, John	240	Nelson, Collins	Sumner	640	1145	26 Nov 1789	3404	14 Jun 1788	74	151	On N side of Cumberland River	yes
Baker, John	637	Thomas, Zeb	Sumner	640	1926	10 May 1793	3405	19 Nov 1792	81	106	On the W side of Caney Fork	yes
Baker, John	644	Jacobs, Ambrose	Sumner	640	1935	20 May 1793	3406	19 Nov 1792	81	108	On W side of Caney Fork	yes
Baker, John	742	Hargrove, Wm.	Sumner	1000	2137	20 May 1793	3565	15 Aug 1792	81	158	On W side of Caney Fork	yes
Baker, John	776	Bush, Aaron	Sumner	640	2229	20 May 1793	3407	19 Nov 1792	81	175	On W side of Caney Fork	yes
Baker, John	809	Gray, Andrew	Sumner	640	2276	20 May 1793	3410	19 Nov 1792	81	186	Beg at a sycamore	yes
Baker, John	832	Lath, Alner(?)	Sumner	640	2318	20 May 1793	3413	19 Nov 1792	81	195	Beg at a white oak & beach	yes
Baker, John, Capt Cont line	1449		Sumner	1462	3358	17 Sep 1800			108	128	On waters of Round Lick Creek	yes
Baker, Jonathan	571	Sanford, Samuel	Sumner	640	1808	20 May 1793	2367	6 Aug 1792	81	81	On head of a branch &c	yes
Baker, Joseph	109	Robertson, Charles	Tennessee	640	1581	23 Feb 1793	1035	26 May 1784	76	303	On the 1st big creek &c	yes
Baker, Joshua	1744	Armstrong, M.	Davidson	8	109	20 Dec 1791			77	380	N/S Cumberland Riv at mouth of Bull Run	
Baker, Obediah	05		West District	1000			1518	20 Feb 1784			S side of Tennessee River	
Baker, Obediah	865	Trust, Steph.	Sumner	640	2377	20 May 1793	509	10 Sep 1788	81	207	On Smiths Fork	yes
Baker, Peter	1719	McCulloh, Benjamin	Davidson	640	1387	20 Dec 1791	2499		77	348	On Knob Creek of Duck River	yes
Baker, Samuel	1013		Green	100	1240	29 Jul 1793	583	7 Nov 1778	76	486	Waters of Horn or S/S of Nolychucka Riv	
Baker, Simon	788	Davis, Joshua	Sumner	640	2247	20 May 1793	2405	19 Nov 1792	81	180	On the Caney Fork	
Balch, Amos	1099		Green	200	942	26 Sep 1791	80	16 Nov 1788	77	258	On N side of French Broad River	
Balch, Amos	138		Green	400	120	1 Nov 1786	239	7 Jun 1784	60	452	Upon Long Creek	
Balch, Amos	21		Middle District	1000	23	10 Jul 1788	1919	24 Apr 1784	67	417	On N side of Duck River &c	
Balch, Hezekiah	33		Green	250	96	1 Nov 1786	133	7 Jun 1784	58	457	On a branch of Richland Creek	
Balch, John	49		Green	200	112	1 Nov 1786	240	7 Jun 1784	58	473	On the N side of French Broad River	
Balck, Hezekiah	22		Middle District	1000	24	10 Jul 1788	2126	10 Mar 1784	67	418	On the N side of Tennessee River &c	
Baldridge, James	638		Green	5000	679	11 Jul 1788	461	22 Oct 1787	66	453	In fork of Big Pigeon & French Broad Riv	
Baldwin, Jesse	203		Hawkins	640	190	26 Dec 1791	903	7 Jun 1784	77	310	Situate in the Dry Valley	
Baldwin, Jesse	745		Washington	578	585	7 Jul 1794	517	27 Oct 1783	82	205	On the waters of Lost Creek	
Bales, Thomas	92		Washington	640	260	23 Oct 1782	460	30 Sep 1778	44	277	Beg at a black oak & hickory	
Balew, Thos.	712	Harrison, Robt.	Sumner	640	2093	20 May 1793	2657	9 Sep 1792	81	147	On Dishas Creek	yes
Bailey, John	1		Washington	150	1707	24 Sep 1779					On Stewarts Creek	
Bailey, John	327		Sullivan	150	467	10 Jul 1788			67	480	On Stewarts branch &c	
Balis, Samuel	1281		Washington	300	1219	4 Dec 1795	2293	27 Sep 1779	89	335	On waters of Little Limestone	
Balis, Samuel	1282		Washington	74	1220	4 Dec 1795	2794	27 Feb 1781(?)	89	335	On waters of Little Limestone	
Ball, Amos	1303		Washington	100	1189	4 Dec 1795	2349	11 Dec 1779	89	430	On Little Doe River	
Ballard, Burwell	015	Breher, James Gloster	Tennessee	640			3334	7 Jan 1786			S side of Cumberland	yes
Ballard, Drury	379	Hays, Robert	Sumner	640	1560	14 Jan 1793	2838	9 Apr 1788	79	271	On both sides of S Fork of Smiths Fork	yes
Ballard, James	721	Sheppard, Nancy	Davidson	640	694	11 Jul 1788	1350		63	244	On waters of Sycamore	yes
Ballard, Jethro	011	Blount, John Gray	Tennessee	640			2594	30 Sep 1785			S side of Spring Creek	yes
Ballard, Joab	045	Glasgow, James	Davidson	640			448	10 Jan 1785			S side of Red River	yes
Ballard, Joab	304	Braky, Andrew	Davidson	640	290	3 May 1787			63	108	S side of Red River	yes
Ballard, Kedar	384		West District	3840	2461	31 Dec 1793			81	430	About 8 miles from the Missippia [sic]	
Ballard, Kedar	765		Sumner	3846	2184	20 May 1793	1560	30 Nov 1792	81	167	On waters of Caney Fork beg at an ash	yes
Ballard, Peter	97	Person, Thomas	Tennessee	640	1379	20 Dec 1791	2166	12 Sep 1785	75	504	On both sides of Bushes meat house	yes
Ballenger, James	327		Green	95	329	20 Sep 1787	161	20 Jul 1784	65	466	On Pigeon Creek	
Ballenger, Moses	15		Hawkins	300	11	23 Aug 1788			67	432	On the N side of Holston River	

Claimant:	File #:	Assignee:	County:	Acres:	Grant:	Grant Date:	Entry:	Entry Date:	Bk:	Pg:	Location by Stream Name:	Military:
Ballentine, Maltine	38	Hunt, James	Robertson	640	3060	24 Dec 1796	3753	24 Dec 1796			W waters of Spring Creek	yes
Balmore, John	1761	Hays, Robert	Davidson	640	1540	14 Jan 1793	1749		79	267	On waters of W Harpeth	yes
Baloote, Peter	60 (7)		Davidson	3840	46	14 Mar 1786	265		63	19	On both sides of Duck River	yes
Batrip, James	223	Marshall, John	Sumner	640	1128	26 Nov 1789	2270	9 Feb 1787	74	143	On waters of Caney Fork	yes
Bandy, James	2387	Searcy, Robert	Davidson	640	3170	14 Sep 1797	4003		90	430	E side of S Harpeth	yes
Banks, Richard	565	Blackface, William	Tennessee	640	3001	10 Apr 1797	4252		90	293	N side of Cumberland River	yes
Banks, Robt	1273	Banks, Gilbert	Sumner	182	3015	10 Apr 1797	3904	22 Nov 1796	90	299	On the Caney Fork	yes
Banks, Thomas	98		Sullivan	479	109	23 Oct 1782	414	14 Apr 1780	43	290	Beg at 3 chestnut trees	
Banner, Joseph	875	Saunders, Susannah	Sumner (7)	640	2392	7 Jan 1793	1739	19 Sep 1792	81	389	On waters of Obeys River	yes
Barber, James	2025	McCulloh, Benjamin	Davidson	640	2031	20 May 1793	3332		81	132	On waters of Duck River	
Barber, Joshua	2048	Long, Nicholas	Davidson	274	2080	20 May 1793	2287		81	144	On Marrowbone Creek	yes
Barbey, John	448	Ivey, David	Davidson	274	420	15 Sep 1787	821		63	155	S side of Cumberland River	yes
Barbour, Richard	1314	Terrell, Nimrod	Sumner	1000	3144	14 Sep 1797	4758	27 Feb 1797	90	420	On Flat Creek	yes
Barbour, Richard	1325	Harrison, Wm.	Sumner	1097	3147	14 Sep 1797	4096	8 Dec 1796	90	421	On Pipe Creek	yes
Barbour, Richard	1343	Arthur, Stephen hrs	Sumner	640	3143	14 Sep 1797	3851	31 Aug 1795	90	420	S side of Caney Fork	yes
Barbour, Richard	430	Lippencut, Wm.	East District	640	3145	14 Sep 1797	4185		90	421	Beg & cornering on two hickorys	
Barbour, Richard	431	Davis, Frederick	East District	365	3146	14 Sep 1797	4186		90	421	On Spring Creek	
Barclay, George	690		Washington	100	504	10 Nov 1784	1501	7 Aug 1779	69	106	On a branch of Limestone	
Barclay, George	692		Washington	100	506	10 Nov 1784	572	4 Nov 1778	69	107	Upon a branch of Cherokee	
Barco, John	24	Noble, Mark	Robertson	274	2385		4188	17 Jul 1800			On Brush Creek	yes
Barden, John	1353		Green	250	1199	23 Feb 1793	1649	19 Sep 1792	78	441	On S side of Noley Chuckey River	
Barfield, Marmaduke	403	Glasgow, James	Tennessee	640	2405	20 Dec 1793	446	15 Feb 1784	81	420	On main E Fork of Buds Creek	yes
Barfield, Wm, heir of Stephen	404		Tennessee	640	2408	14 Dec 1793	447	15 Feb 1784	81	421	On waters of Yellow Creek	
Bargineer, John	328	Boyd, John	Sumner	228	1614	23 Feb 1793	65	20 Dec 1785	76	319	W side of Drakes Creek	yes
Barker, Elias	296	McCulloh, Benjamin	Tennessee	640	1969	20 May 1793	2079	1 Sep 1785	81	116	On S side of Cumberland River	yes
Barker, Levi	307	Rice, John	Davidson	640	293	13 Jun 1787	1088		63	109	On the fork of Cumberland & Red River	yes
Barker, Lewis	034	Griffis, Saml.	Robertson	400				10 Jan 1794			W of the Cumberland Mts	
Barker, Lewis	652	Griffis, Saml.	Tennessee	400	203	3 Nov 1797			94	130	W of the Cumberland Mountain	
Barker, Nicholas	1717	McCulloh, Benjamin	Davidson	640	1385	20 Dec 1791	2498		77	347	On Knob Creek of Duck River	yes
Barker, Samuel	9	Fenner, Richard	Tennessee	640	1157	26 Nov 1789	2167	12 Sep 1785	74	157	On N side of Cumberland River	yes
Barker, Thomas	209		Washington	100	77	23 Oct 1782	860	30 Dec 1778	47	37	N side of Nolachuckey iver	
Barker, Thomas	511	Howard, Solomon	Davidson	220	483	15 Sep 1787	714	20 Sep 1787	63	175	On S Fork of Red River	yes
Barkins, John	19		Green	100	414		59				On the head of clear Creek	
Barkley, George	973		Washington	144	950	17 Nov 1790	1269	8 Sep 1783	76	161	Beg at a forked chestnut	
Barksdell, Cleavers	29		Washington	320	319	24 Oct 1782	689	16 Dec 1778	43	306	On the N side of Watauga River &c	
Barlow, George	343	Marley, Robert	Davidson	640	328	1 Aug 1787	2109		63	122	On waters of Spring Creek	yes
Barnatt, John	207		Sullivan	600	214	10 Oct 1783	446	28 Sep 1778	53	164	On Bush Creek	
Barnes, Henry	1397	Lewis, Joshua hrs	Sumner	640	3324	6 Dec 1797	4247	17 Jun 1797	97	46	Waters of Round Lick Creek	yes
Barnes, Hezekiah	1437	McCamon, Isaac	Sumner	357	3352	12 Dec 1797	5009	27 Nov 1797	98	185	On both sides of Larkins Creek	yes
Barnes, Hezekiah	203		Tennessee	357	1493 (24	4 Jan 1792	1574	22 Feb 1785	77	374	S side of Cumberland River &c	
Barnes, John	24		Green	640	15	30 Jun 1787					W side of Little River	
Barnes, John	396		Davidson	640	368	15 Sep 1787	650		63	138	S side Cumberland River	yes
Barnes, Moses	496	Barton, Samuel	Sumner	640	1664	20 May 1793	3646	5 Dec 1789	81	45	On Bartons Creek	yes
Barnes, Thomas	1908	Robertson, James	Davidson	640	1667	20 May 1793	752		81	45	On S branches of Big Harpeth River	yes
Barnes, William	2078	Geo. Walker & Seth Lewis	Davidson	640	2238	20 May 1793	1256		81	178	On S side of Cumberland River	yes

Claimant:	File #:	Assignee:	County:	Acres:	Grant:	Grant Date:	Entry:	Entry Date:	Bk:	Pg:	Location by Stream Name:	Military:
Barnes, William	751	Dickson, Joseph	Davidson	640	724	11 Jul 1788	2833		63	254	E of Capt Vance's claim	yes
Barnet, James	280	Benton, Jesse	Tennessee	274	1865	20 May 1793	3128	16 Dec 1785	81	93	On S side of Cumberland River &c	yes
Barnet, Michael	347		Hawkins	200	341	8 Mar 1793			78	480	On S Fork of Clear Creek	
Barnet, Mickel	23		Green	200	341			6 Dec 1792			On S Fork of Clear Creek	
Barnet, Robert	1772	Garrison, Stephen	Davidson	640	1558	14 Jan 1791	610		79	271	On waters of West Harpeth	yes
Barnet, Robert	467	Pervin, John hrs	Sumner	640	1624	27 Apr 1793	3677	17 Feb 1790	81	23	On S side of Cumberland River	yes
Barnet, Sion	380	Borin, John	Tennessee	320	2334	20 May 1793	1173	26 Aug 1784	81	198	On Cranks Branch	yes
Barnhart, Conrod	1488		Green	200	1251	12 Jul 1794	2531	10 Apr 1780	81	579	On S side of Nolichuckey River	
Barren, Willis	1213	Mattock, Nicholas	Sumner	427	2492	26 Sep 1795	1426	19 Sep 1785	89	103	Lying near 2 miles W of a large spring	yes
Barret, John	44		Eastern District	150	70	7 Apr 1790	683	1 Sep 1780	71	278	S/S of Holston River & on Doctors Creek	
Barret, John	046	Hughlett, William	Middle District	640			2794					yes
Barrett, Thos Jr. heir of Wm.	505		Davidson	3840	477	15 Sep 1787	578		63	173	On or abt 6 mi below 1st Timbered Island	yes
Barrett, William	112		Eastern District	188	101	17 Nov 1790	356	19 May 1780	76	176	S side of Clinch River &c	
Barrett, William Jr.	505		Davidson	3840	477	15 Sep 1787	578		63	173	On or abt 6 mi below 1st Timbered Island	
Barron, James	684		Washington	100	498	10 Nov 1784	3588	17 Jul 1780	69	104	On the Falling Rock &c	
Barron, James	911		Washington	50	888	17 Nov 1790	2606	13 Aug 1780	76	140	Including a big spring	
Barron, James	951		Washington	75	928	17 Nov 1790	2832	1 Apr 1781	76	153	On the Dividing Ridge	
Barron, John	847		Washington	150	661	10 Nov 1784	2590	17 Jul 1780	69	155	On waters of Sinking creek	
Barron, Joseph	02		Washington	200			875	31 Dec 1778			On drains of Sinking Creek	
Barron, Joseph	941		Washington	134 (130	918	17 Nov 1790	850	30 Dec 1778	76	150	On N fork of Sinking Creek &c	
Barron, Joseph, Senr	678		Washington	50	492	10 Nov 1784	2590	7 Jul 1780	69	101	Above Ezekial Smiths road	
Barron, Sherrod	890	Davis, Arch.	Sumner	640	2406	20 Jan 1794	2732	4 Mar 1786	81	420	On or that Joseph Thomas was killed on	yes
Barron, William	1366		Washington	100	1281	17 Nov 1797	1185	4 Feb 1779	94	141	On the head of Morgan Murrays Branch	
Barron, William	669		Washington	100	483	10 Nov 1784	2589	17 Jul 1780	69	98	On head of the Meadow Fork	
Barrow, Betsy	306	Parker, Isom hrs.	Sumner	640	1375	20 Apr 1791	2756	20 Nov 1790	74	396	On E side of Jennings Fork	yes
Barrow, Henry	1638	Pursley, John hrs	Davidson	640	1373	20 Apr 1791	2755		74	395	On S side of Cumberland River	yes
Barrow, Henry	901	Wiggins, Carter	Sumner	640	2457	31 Dec 1793	2785	8 Mar 1786	81	429	On Buffaloe Creek	yes
Barrow, James	305	Stone, John hrs	Sumner	640	1374	20 Apr 1791	2771	20 Nov 1790	74	396	On E side of Jennings Fork	yes
Barrow, James	807	Fort, Elias	Sumner	357	2274	20 May 1793	3573		81	185	On waters of Smiths Fork	yes
Barrow, James	902	Hammon, Tiston	Sumner	640	2458	31 Dec 1793	2727	27 Jun 1788	81	429	On a small E Fork of Smiths	yes
Barrow, John	1439	Moore, Saml.	Davidson	320	85	10 Jul 1788	388	5 Apr 1784	68	230	Lying on the N side of Cumberland River	yes
Barrow, Matthew	307	Underwood,Jas.hrs	Sumner	640	1376	20 Apr 1791	2779	20 Nov 1790	74	396	On W side of Jennings Fork	yes
Barrow, Sherrod	1637	Hansel, Charles	Davidson	640	1372	20 Apr 1791	2725		74	395	On S side of Cumberland River	yes
Barrow, Sherrod	304	Purcell, Barnet	Sumner	640	1371	20 Apr 1791	2754	20 Nov 1790	74	394	On waters of Collins River	yes
Barrow, Sherrod	891	James, Truman	Sumner	640	2407	20 Jan 1794	2739	2 Mar 1786	81	420	On E side of the Caney Fork	yes
Barry, Redmon D.	1350	Bradley, Nimrod	Sumner	640	3162	14 Sep 1797	4283	20 Feb 1797	90	427	Waters of Falling Creek	yes
Barry, Redmon D.	1354	Dodd, Thomas	Sumner	640	2777	10 Oct 1796	3903	12 Aug 1796	91	22	Waters of Martins Creek	yes
Barry, Redmon D.	1355		Sumner	640	2778	10 Oct 1796	2860	12 Aug 1796	91	23	On Martin's Creek	yes
Barry, Redmon Dillen	022	Johnson, Ptolemy	Sumner	640			4416	14 Oct 1797			E waters of Middle fork Drakes Creek	yes
Barry, Redmon Dillen	024	Shaw, Harmon	Sumner	640			4335	19 Sep 1797			On waters of Mackersfield Creek	· yes
Barry, Redmon Dillen	028	Ham, John	Sumner	640			4408	14 Oct 1797			On Caney Fork of W Fork of Drakes Creek	yes
Barry, Redmon Dillen	029	Hughes, Bartley	Sumner	640			4389	14 Oct 1797			On dividing ridge &c	yes
Barry, Redmon Dillen	030	Hood, Archibald	Sumner	640			4462	18 Sep 1797			On waters of middle fork Drakes Creek	yes
Barry, Redmon Dillen	031	Oggden, Dempsey	Sumner	640			4410	14 Oct 1797			Headwaters of Middle Fork of Drakes Cree	yes
Barry, Redmon Dillen	032	Ogleby, Nehemiah	Sumner	640			4417	14 Oct 1797			On head of Middle Fork of Drakes Creek	yes

Claimant:	File #:	Assignee:	County:	Acres:	Grant:	Grant Date:	Entry:	Entry Date:	Bk:	Pg:	Location by Stream Name:	Military:
Barry, Redmon Dillen	033	Owen, John	Sumner	640			4469	1 Sep 1797			On dividing ridge &c	yes
Barry, Redmon Dillen	034	Phelps, Jesse	Sumner	1000			4470	14 Oct 1797			On W branches of Trammels Creek	yes
Barry, Redmon Dillen	035	Reynolds, Silvester	Sumner	640			4391	22 Sep 1797			On dividing ridge &c	yes
Barry, Redmon Dillen	036	Yarby, Joseph	Sumner	274			4475	6 Sep 1797			On waters of N Fork of Red River	yes
Barry, Redmon Dillen	038	Start, Henry	Sumner	640			4472	14 Oct 1797			On waters Middle Fork of Drakes Creek	yes
Barry, Redmon Dillen	039	Malone, Jacob	Sumner	640			4390	14 Oct 1797			Waters of Middle Fork of Drakes Creek	yes
Barry, Redmon Dillen	040	Letchmore, Watson	Sumner	640			4414	14 Oct 1797			On dividing ridge &c	yes
Barry, Redmon Dillen	041	Minters, John	Sumner	640			4334	14 Oct 1797			On headwaters W Fork of Drakes Creek	yes
Barry, Redmon Dillen	042	Nowland, Jesse	Sumner	640			4466	19 Sep 1797			On head branches Sulphur Lick Fork &c	yes
Barry, Redmon Dillen	043	Nicholson, Isaac	Sumner	640			4464	19 Sep 1797			On head waters of Maxels Fork &c	
Barry, Redmon Dillen	046		Sumner	640			4226	14 Oct 1797			On head of Main Middle Fork of Drakes Cr	
Barry, Redmon Dillen	047	Dillon, Thos.	Sumner	1000			4460	14 Oct 1797			Head branches of W Fork Drakes Creek	yes
Barry, Redmon Dillen	048	Garner, Gregory	Sumner	1000			4204	11 Apr 1797			E side E Fork Stones River	yes
Barry, Redmon Dillen	049	Bayler, John	Sumner	640			4205	13 June 1797			E side of E fk Stones Creek	yes
Barry, Redmon Dillen	050	Seasenver, John	Sumner	640			4215	28 Oct 1797			E side E Fork Stones River	yes
Barry, Redmon Dillen	051	Campbell, Andrew	Sumner	640			4406	6 Sep 1797			Waters of W Fork of Drakes Creek	yes
Barry, Redmon Dillen	052	Conner, Wm.	Sumner	640			4182	14 Oct 1797			Head of W branches of Middle Fork &c	yes
Barry, Redmon Dillen	053		Sumner	640			4405	19 Sep 1797			On Rainey Fork &c	yes
Barry, Redmon Dillen	054		Sumner	640			4459	14 Oct 1797			Headwaters Middle Fork of Drakes Creek	
Barry, Redmon Dillen	055	Faulkner, Francis	Sumner	640			4461	6 Sep 1797			Waters S Fork Red River	yes
Barry, Redmon Dillen	056	Earpe, John	Sumner	228			4524	14 Oct 1797			Headwaters first big creek &c	yes
Barry, Redmon Dillen	057	Derden, Joseph	Sumner	640			4411	19 Sep 1797			W Fork of Red River	yes
Barry, Redmon Dillen	1287	Mahon, James	Sumner	640	3046	8 Jun 1797	4062	29 Mar 1797	90	316	On 32 Mile Creek	yes
Barry, Redmon Dillen	1352	Nicholas, Richard	Sumner	640	3167	14 Sep 1797	4245	20 Feb 1797	90	429	On the Falling Creek	yes
Barry, Redmon Dillen	23	Wilson, Whitfield	Sumner & Robe	100	4112	6 Sep 1797					On ___ [sic] fork of Red River	yes
Barry, Redmon Dillen	2389	Williams, Daniel	Davidson	640	3177	14 Sep 1797	4005		90	432	On S Harpeth	yes
Barry, Redmon Dillen	44	Greer, John Gee	Sumner	640	4336	14 Oct 1797					Head branches of W Fork Drakes Creek	yes
Barry, Redmon Dillon	1277	Anderson, Wm.	Sumner	425	3036	8 Jun 1797	4040	29 Mar 1797	90	313	On one of the head branches of Salt Lick	yes
Barry, Redmon Dillon	1278	Hoggard, Wm.	Sumner	228	3037	8 Jun 1797	1924	7 Apr 1797	90	313	Waters of West Fork of Peytons Creek	yes
Barry, Redmon Dillon	1279	Lawton, Leonard	Sumner	640	3038	8 Jun 1797	4057	29 Mar 1797	90	313	On Spring Creek	yes
Barry, Redmon Dillon	1280	Wharton, James	Sumner	640	3039	8 Jun 1797	4044	20 Mar 1797	90	314	Both sides of the road	yes
Barry, Redmon Dillon	1281	Lucas, Matthew	Sumner	640	3040	8 Jun 1797	1056	29 Mar 1797	90	314	On Turkey Creek	yes
Barry, Redmon Dillon	1282	Lewis, Thos.	Sumner	640	3041	8 Jun 1797	4055	29 Mar 1797	90	314	On waters of 32 Mile Creek	yes
Barry, Redmon Dillon	1283	Monk, Isaac. hrs.	Sumner	640	3042	8 Jun 1797	4061	29 Mar 1797	90	315	On 32 Mile Creek	yes
Barry, Redmon Dillon	1284	Saunders, Thos.hrs	Sumner	640	3043	8 Jun 1797	4063	29 Mar 1797	90	315	Including fks of Turkey & Spring Creeks	yes
Barry, Redmon Dillon	1285	Miridith,Benj.hrs	Sumner	640	3044	8 Jun 1797	4036	29 Mar 1797	90	316	On Doe Creek	yes
Barry, Redmon Dillon	1286	Whood, Wm. Hrs	Sumner	640	3045	8 Jun 1797	4045	29 Mar 1797	90	316	Where Cumberland road takes mountain	yes
Barry, Redmon Dillon	1288	B(P)illips, Thos.	Sumner	425	3047	8 Jun 1797	4041	29 Mar 1797	90	317	Joins an entry of his own	yes
Barry, Redmond D.	1351		Sumner	274	3163	14 Sep 1797	4217	20 Feb 1797	90	427	On a branch of Falling Creek	yes
Barry, Redmond D.	2382	Armstong, Henry Joab	Davidson	640	3164	14 Sep 1797	4241		90	427	Branches of Stones River & Suggs Creek	yes
Barry, Redmond D.	2384	Gilbert,Abraham.hrs	Davidson	640	3166	14 Se 1777 (si	4242		90	428	On Eastern branches of Stones River	yes
Barry, Redmond D.	2385	Ouse, Jonathan.hrs	Davidson	640	3168	14 Sep 1797	4243		90	428	Branches of Suggs Creek & Stones River	yes
Barry, Redmond, D.	2363	Odum,Dickerson.hrs	Davidson	640	3165	14 Sep 1797	4244		90	428	On Eastern branches of Stones River	yes
Bartee, John	1910	Gillaspie, Wm.	Davidson	1000	1672	20 May 1793	1137	20 May 1793	81	47	On both sides of Big Harpeth River	yes
Bartee, John	700		Sumner	640	2072	20 May 1793			81	142	On a fork of Roaring River	

Claimant:	File #:	Assignee:	County:	Acres:	Grant:	Grant Date:	Entry:	Entry Date:	Bk:	Pg:	Location by Stream Name:	Military:
Bartholowmew, John	241	Mountflorence & Fenner	Sumner	228	1148	26 Nov 1789	1599	11 Jun 1789	74	152	Bet. Middle Fork &c	yes
Bartin, Samuel	1839		Davidson	640	337	27 Nov 1792	630	3 Dec 1784	81	5	On S Side Cumberland River	
Bartles, John	1517	McDowell, Joseph	Davidson	640	1074	26 Oct 1789	2045		74	117	On E side of Mill Creek	yes
Bartlett & Pearce	302		Eastern District	700	211	22 Feb 1795	174	19 Feb 1780	84	287	On S side of Holston River	
Bartlett, Joseph	226		Hawkins	50	213	26 Dec 1791			77	318	On S side of Holston River	
Barton, Gabriel, Ass.	1396		Sumner	440	3323	6 Dec 1797	3782	4 May 1797	97	45	On Round Lick Creek	yes
Barton, Joseph	3	Marshall,Emanuel hrs	Wilson	640	389	12 Dec 1801	3389		114	92	On waters of Round Lick Creek	
Barton, Saml	134	Howell, John hrs.	Tennessee	640	1644	23 Feb 1793	2651	30 Sep 1785	76	334	S side of Cumberland River &c	
Barton, Saml	1440	Mannifee, Jones	Davidson	320	86	10 Jul 1788	773	21 Feb 1785	68	231	Lying on the waters of Big Harper [sic]	
Barton, Samuel	352	Jones, Stephen	Sumner	640	1439	20 Dec 1791	2654	9 Nov 1790	77	361	On E waters of Cedar Creek	yes
Barton, Samuel	03	Ross, Nicholas	Sumner	640			4574	20 Mar 1797			Cocker Cr Aaron Parsons & Wm. Meeks	yes
Barton, Samuel	032	Jones, Stephen	Davidson	640			3654	14 Dec 1795			E side of Stones River	
Barton, Samuel	04	Butts, Peter	Sumner	640			4575	20 Mar 1797			On waters of Cedar Creek	yes
Barton, Samuel	05	McCollister, James	Sumner	640			1158				On E side of Bartons Creek	yes
Barton, Samuel	06	Arman, Pain	Sumner	640			3666	5 Dec 1789			Bet. head of Round Lick & Cedar Creek	yes
Barton, Samuel	07	Pain, John	Sumner	640			3665	19 Dec 1789			On Jennings Fork Round Lick Creek	yes
Barton, Samuel	1086		Davidson	640	60	17 Apr 1786	646	5 Jan 1785	66	54	On the head of Browns Creek	
Barton, Samuel	1144		Davidson	640	121	17 Apr 1786	60	5 Jan 1784	66	179	On Wt fk of Browns Cr beg honey locust	
Barton, Samuel	1206	Pooram, John	Sumner	400	162	26 Mar 1795		20 Mar 1792	89	91	On Bartons Creek	yes
Barton, Samuel	1208	Jordon, River	Sumner	400	164	26 Mar 1795		20 Mar 1792	89	92	On Bartons Creek	yes
Barton, Samuel	1209	Campbell, Chas.	Sumner	400	166	26 Mar 1795		18 Nov 1792	89	93	On head of W Fork of Bartons Creek	yes
Barton, Samuel	1210	Jordon, River	Sumner	400	167	26 Mar 1795		5 Dec 1792	89	93	On S side of Cumberland River	yes
Barton, Samuel	1211		Sumner	400	168	26 Mar 1795		10 Nov 1792	89	94	On Bartons Creek beg at an iron wood	yes
Barton, Samuel	1212	Poor--(?), John	Sumner	400	169	26 Mar 1795		10 Nov 1792	89	94	On Bartons Creek	yes
Barton, Samuel	1279		Davidson	640	244	10 Jul 1788	295	16 Feb 1784	66	423	On Knife Cr that empties into Cumberland	
Barton, Samuel	1382		Sumner	1000	203	6 Dec 1797			97	32	S side of Cumberland River	yes
Barton, Samuel	1384	Bagley, Matthias hrs.	Sumner	640	3251	24 Nov 1797	3946	20 Mar 1797	97	34	Bet Spring Creek & Bartons Creek	yes
Barton, Samuel	1427	Crunch(?) John Watts	Sumner	1000	3301	6 Dec 1797	4438	20 Jun 1797	98	175	On waters of Round Lick Creek	yes
Barton, Samuel	1428	Roberts, Thos. W.	Sumner	640	3302	6 Dec 1797	4663	20 Jun 1797	98	176	On the waters of Round Lick Creek	yes
Barton, Samuel	1687	Bates(Boles ?), Matt	Davidson	640	1643	23 Feb 1793	3131		76	333	S/S of Cumberland Riv on head of Mill Cr	yes
Barton, Samuel	1742	Armstrong, M.	Davidson	100	105	4 Jan 1792	765	3 Se 1785	77	379	On the head waters of Hays Creek	
Barton, Samuel	1847		Davidson	640	347	27 Nov 1792	716	26 Apr 1785	81	8	On head waters of Hays Creek	
Barton, Samuel	1913	Hooks, Wm. Hrs	Davidson	640	1686	20 Dec 1793	2731	7 Oct 1792	81	50	On head waters of Mill Creek	yes
Barton, Samuel	335	Angels, Benj.	Sumner	640	1642	23 Feb 1793	3111	18 Nov 1792	76	333	On Bartons Creek	yes
Barton, Samuel	336	Howell, John	Sumner	274	1645	23 Feb 1793	1939	18 Nov 1792	76	334	On Bartons Creek near the head	yes
Barton, Samuel	337	Bradish(?) Wm.	Sumner	320	113	23 Feb 1793	837	8 Dec 1792	76	248	On Bartons Creek	
Barton, Samuel	376	Rodes, Lewis	Sumner	640	1556	14 Jan 1793	2952	19 Dec 1789	79	270	Near head waters of Jining Fork &c	yes
Barton, Samuel	481		Sumner	640	117	27 Apr 1793	765	3 Se 1785	81	33	On W Fork of Bartons Creek	
Barton, Samuel	496	Barnes, Moses	Summner	640	1664	20 May 1793	3646	5 Dec 1789	81	45	On waters of Bartons Creek	yes
Barton, Samuel	497		Summner	640	1665	20 May 1793	1565	18 Nov 1792	81	45	On head waters of Mill Creek	yes
Barton, Samuel	499	Beaks, Ignatious hrs	Sumner	640	1668	20 May 1793	3444	18 Nov 1792	81	46	On Bartons Creek	yes
Barton, Samuel	507	McKinsey, Hugh	Sumner	640	1670	20 May 1793	1717	19 Nov 1792	81	46	On Bartons Creek	yes
Barton, Samuel	513	Hooks, Wm. Hrs	Sumner	640	1690	20 May 1793			81	51	On E side of Bartons Creek	yes
Barton, Samuel	528		Sumner	640	1721	20 May 1793	2231	18 May 1793	81	58	On waters of Bartons Creek	yes
Barton, Samuel	531	Duffey, John	Sumner	640	1725	20 May 1793	745	18 Nov 1792	81	59	On the waters of Bartons Creek	yes

Earliest Tennessee Land Records

Claimant:	File #:	Assignee:	County:	Acres:	Grant:	Grant Date:	Entry:	Entry Date:	Bk:	Pg:	Location by Stream Name:	Military:
Barton, Samuel	581	Reynolds, Wm. Hrs	Tennessee	640	3028	10 Apr 1797	1033		90	304	N side of Cumberland River	
Barton, Samuel	593	Farmer, Peter hrs	Tennessee	1000	3063	19 Jul 1797	3594		90	375	Waters of Little West Fork	
Barton, Samuel	8	Ramsey, Henry	Sumner	640	3668	28 Nov 1789					Bet. head of Round Lick br & Cedar Creek	yes
Barton, Samuel	99		Middle District	500	101	10 Jul 1788	713	28 Oct 1783	67	459	On the N side of Duck River &c	
Barton, Samuel.	293	Sear(?), Jas.	Sumner	640	1311	10 Dec 1790	3653	28 Nov 1789	74	369	Beg at a white oak	yes
Barton, Samuel.	299	Carter, Jos	Sumner	640	1356	10 Dec 1790	3649	24 Apr 1790	74	384	On waters of Cedar Creek	yes
Barton, Samuel.	339	Thos., Thos (?)	Sumner	640	1390	20 Dec 1791	1952	21 May 1791	77	348	On E waters of Cedar Creek	yes
Barton, Samuel.	349	Hering, Burrell	Sumner	640	1433	20 Dec 1791	3660	21 May 1791	77	359	On E waters of Cedar Creek	yes
Barton, Samuel.	387		Sumner	640	358	26 Jun 1793	430	7 May 1787	80	319	On S/S of Cumberland River	
Barton, Samuel.	1779		Davidson	640	557	26 Jun 1793	821	14 Sep 1792	80	318	Lying in the ceded territory	
Barton, Samuel.	1781		Davidson	640	361	26 Jun 1793	814	1 Mar 1792	80	320	On headwaters of Mill Creek	
Barton, Thomas	563		Sullivan	100	566	17 Nov 1790	229	25 Feb 1780	76	193	On the waters of Holstein River	
Barton, Thomas	786		Sullivan	85	718	2 Dec 1796	580	1 Jun 1780	91	275	Joining tract where sd Barton lives	
Bartons, James McAnge*	3	Barton, Robert, P of A	Tennessee			19 Oct 1786 (dated)			69	211	S side of Cumberland River	
Baryer, Geo. Henry	841		Sumner	274	2343	20 May 1793	3204	27 Oct 1792	81	200	Bet. Little Cedar Cr & Round Lick Creek	yes
Baryer, George Henry	850	Clark, Osborn	Sumner	503	2353	20 May 1793	3079	27 Oct 1792	81	202	Bet. Spring Cr & head of Little Cedar Cr	yes
Basco, Lemon	267	Laurence, Adam	Sumner	640	1230	10 Dec 1790	606	31 Dec 1784	74	341	On S side of Cumberland River	yes
Basdel, Jacob	398	Sheppard, Benj.	Davidson	640	370	15 Sep 1787	2332		63	139	N side Cumberland River	yes
Baskins, John	382		Washington	173	374	13 Oct 1783	1232	23 Feb 1779	52	252	On the onion branch &c	
Baskins, John	412		Green	100	414	20 Sep 1787			65	492	On the head of Clear Creek	
Bass [or Brass?], Moses	2028	McCulloh, Benjamin	Davidson	640	2039	20 May 1793	3221		81	134	On N side of Cumberland River	yes
Bass, Britain	09		Sumner	640			3244				No plat	yes
Bass, Drury	708	Whitehead, William	Sumner	243	2088	20 May 1793	820	21 Nov 1792	81	146	On Spring Creek	yes
Bass, Esau	1992	Whitfield, Bryant	Davidson	274	1911	20 May 1793	1531		81	103	On E side of Stones River	yes
Bass, Jonathan	214	Reed, Jesse	Sumner	640	1119	26 Nov 1789	3419	12 Mar 1788	74	138	On headwaters of Collins River	yes
Batchelor, George	852	Mountflorence, Jas.	Davidson	640	858	17 Jan 1789	1870		63	299	On S side of Cumberland River	yes
Bateman, Navey	668	Coonurod [sic], Nicholas	Sumner	640	1988	20 May 1793	3445	2 Nov 1786	81	121	On Cedar Creek &c	yes
Bateman, William	602	Stewart, Duncan	Tennessee	1000	3104	14 Sep 1797	4441	22 Dec 1796	90	404	S side of Cumberland River &c	yes
Bates [or Boles], Matthias	1687	Barton, Samuel	Davidson	640	1643	23 Feb 1793	3131		76	333	S side of Cumberland River	yes
Bates, Hezekiah	154		Hawkins	100	330	29 Jul 1793			76	466	Cocker Cr Aaron Parsons & Wm. Meeks	
Bates, Luke	604	Felts, Archibald	Sumner	640	1854	20 May 1793	495	12 Sep 1792	81	90	On the W Fork of Drakes Creek	yes
Bates, Simon	480	Price, Jonathan	Tennessee	228	2763	20 Jul 1796	1644		88	462	On Beaverdam Creek	yes
Bates, Thomas	92		Washington	640	260	23 Oct 1782	460	30 Sep 1778	44	277	Beg at a black oak & hickory	
Batey, Wallis	238		Hawkins	200	225	26 Dec 1791	110	8 Feb 1780	77	322	Lying joining John Longs survey	
Batey, Walter	340		Sullivan	230 (200	460	10 Jul 1788			67	486	On road bet Thos Taylors & John Looneys	
Batts, Sampson	392	Sheppard, Benjamin	Davidson	640	364	15 Sep 1787	2320	1 Nov 1794	63	137	On both sides E Fork of Drakes Creek	yes
Batts, Simon	012	Price, Jonathan	Robertson	228			1694				On Beaverdam Creek	yes
Baulwin, John	491		Green	200	493	20 Sep 1787	929	29 Oct 1783	65	57(1)6	On the dry fork of Lick Creek	
Baxley, John	1242		Sumner	640	2841	21 Jan 1797	1039	19 Aug 1796	90	45	On Martins Creek	
Baxter, Samuel	988	Sheppard, William	Davidson	1000	1005	18 May 1789	267		63	337	On N side of Cumberland River	yes
Baxter, Thomas	2097	Williams, Sampson	Davidson	640	2317	20 May 1793	2410	14 Mar 1789	81	194	On Mill Creek & Stewarts Creek	yes
Bay, Andrew	300		Sumner	357	1359	10 Dec 1790	812	11 Jul 1791	74	385	On S side of Cumberland River	yes
Bay, Andy. Ass.	2165		Davidson	40	178	9 Jan 1794				448	On waters of Whites Creek	
Bayler, John	049	Dellenberry, Redmond	Sumner	640			4205	13 Jun 1797			E side E Fork of Stones River	yes
Bayles [Boyle?], Samuel	706		Washington	300	520	10 Nov 1784	2345	10 Dec 1779	69	112	Beg at Thomas Brummicks entry	

Claimant:	File #:	Assignee:	County:	Acres:	Grant:	Grant Date:	Entry:	Entry Date:	Bk:	Pg:	Location by Stream Name:	Military:
Bayles, Daniel	749		Washington	100	563	10 Nov 1784	1194	8 Feb 1779	69	128	On a fork &c	
Bayles, Hezekiah	03		Washington	100		12 Jul 1794	1471	15 Jul 1779			On Cherokee Creek	
Bayles, Hezekiah	791		Hawkins	100	691	11 Aug 1789	2479	10 Mar 1780	82	224	On the waters of Bever Creek	
Bayles, John	856		Washington	150	865	11 Aug 1789	713	19 Dec 1778	71	32	At the N Fork of Cherokee Creek	
Bayles, John	857		Washington	50	866	11 Aug 1789	1508	10 Aug 1779	71	32	Joining a survey of his own	
Bayles, Samuel	628		Washington	74	722	26 Oct 1786	3004	19 Jun 1784	66	22	Beg at 2 marked red oaks	
Bayley, Claudius	567		Green	100	247	20 Sep 1787	124	29 Nov 1784	66	156	On br of Lick Cr where sd Bailey lives	
Bayley, Claudius	570		Green	300	250	20 Sep 1787	2306	27 Nov 1779	66	157	On the waters of Lick Creek &c	
Bayley, Claudius	588		Green	200	269	20 Sep 1787	2305	23 Nov 1779	66	163	On the S branch of Lick Creek	
Bayley, John	2409	McConnell, Robert	Davidson	640	3202	14 Sep 1797	4689		92	5	W side of S Harpeth	
Bayly, Carr	515		Sullivan	89	531	26 Nov 1789	759	13 Feb 1781	73	45	On both sides of Holston River	
Bazemore, Robert	931	Blount, Reading	Sumner	640	2455	22 Feb 1795	2558	30 Sep 1789	83	419	On the main fork of Obeys River	yes
Beach, Robert	841	Brock, Joseph	Davidson	640	846	17 Jan 1789	3443		63	296	On N side of Cumberland River	yes
Beach, Robert	9	Donelson, Stockley	Robertson	640	2820	12 Jan 1797	3443	13 Aug 1796	76		On waters of Red River	yes
Beaird, Hugh	1022		Green	100	1249	29 Jul 1793	1560	31 Aug 1796	76	488	On Deep Creek N/S of French Broad Riv	
Beaird, Isaac Shelby	652		Hawkins	300	522	May 1794	2271	23 Nov 1779	81	555	Beg at an elm beech & white walnut	
Beaird, John	1435		Green	300	1246	27 Nov 1792	2201	12 Nov 1779	80	169	N/S of Holston Riv on a branch of Flat Cr	
Beaird, Jos	189	Morris, Jas., hrs	Eastern District	640	1660	15 Jul 1793	3777		81	44	Beg at two buckeyes	
Beaird, Jos.	188		Eastern District	640	1659	15 Jul 1793			81	43	Beg at a walnut	
Beaird, Jos. & Wm. Terrell	260		Eastern District	1000	207	28 Feb 1795	1024	29 Oct 1783	83	365	N side of Clinch River	
Beaird, Jos. & Wm. Terrell	261	Edwards, Robert	Eastern District	320	209	3 Feb 1795	3825		83	381	S side of Clinch River	
Beaird, Joseph	185	Rush, Wm. Hrs.	Eastern District	640	1656	15 Jul 1793	2761		81	43	Beg at two beech trees	
Beaird, Joseph	187	English, Jos. Hrs.	Eastern District	640	1658	15 (25) Jul 179	1317		81	43	Beg at a large ash	
Beaird, Joseph	206		Eastern District	100	178	May 1794	115	8 Feb 1780	81	560	1st bot. Abv mouth of Big Buffaloe	
Beaird, Joseph	207		Eastern District	340	179	May 1794	114	9 Mar 1780	81	560	On N W side of Clinch River	
Beaird, Joseph	487		Hawkins	1000	359	29 Jul 1793			80	266	S side of Clinch River on Williams Creek	
Beaird, Joseph	617		Hawkins	200	313	15 Jul 1793	763, 739	12 Feb 1781	80	300	On Clair Fork of Flat Creek	
Beaird, Joseph	622		Hawkins	1500	319	15 Jul 1793	175		80	301	On S fork of Big Buffelow Creek	
Beaird, Joseph	626		Hawkins	640	323	15 Jul 1793	2272	19 Feb 1780	80	302	N W/S Clinch Riv at bunch of Sycamores	
Beaird, Joseph	647		Hawkins	340	517	May 1794	2270	23 Nov 1779	81	553	N side of Clinch River	
Beaird, Joseph	649		Hawkins	400	519	May 1794	219	23 Nov 1790	81	554	On head of Whites Creek	
Beaird, Joseph	650		Hawkins	400	520	May 1794	839	14 Jul 1781	81	554	On N side of Clinch River	
Beaird, Joseph	653		Hawkins	100	523	May 1794	682	12 Jan 1784	81	555	On head of Joseph Brooks branch	
Beaird, Joseph	654		Hawkins	400	524	May 1794		1 Sep 1780	81	555	On N side of Holston River	
Beaird, Joseph	656	Modlin, Ezekial	Hawkins	640	2482	23 May 1794	3781		81	556	N side of Clinch River	
Beaird, William	627		Hawkins	170	324	15 Jul 1793	1940		80	302	On W Fork of Flat Creek	
Beak, Robt & Wm. McL(?)	154		Middle District	1000	150	27 Nov 1789	1939	29 Apr 1784	74	43	On N side of Duck River	yes
Beaks, Ignatious	499	Barton, Samuel	Sumner	640	1668	20 May 1793	3444		81	46	On Bartons Creek	
Bealer, John	012		Sullivan	428			1606	13 Sep 1779			On waters of Beaver Creek	
Bealer, Joseph	323		Sullivan	248	459	28 Nov 1787	1649	17 Sep 1779	67	220	On waters of Beaver Creek	
Bealer, Willery	85		Sullivan	150	96	23 Oct 1782	1620	17 Sep 1779	43	284	On N side of Holston River	
Beall [Bealer?], Geo.	82		Sullivan	258	93	23 Oct 1782	1376		43	282	On waters of Beaver Creek &c	
Bealor, Jacob	920		Washington	200	897	17 Nov 1790		6 Sep 1779	76	143	On Stoney Creek	
Bean, Edward [Edmon?]	205	Shaffer, Richard	Sumner	640	1110	26 Nov 1789	3446	12 Mar 1788	74	134	On W side of Caney Fork River	yes
Bean, George	011		Green	400			1964	19 Oct 1779			S side of Little Chuckey	

Claimant:	File #:	Assignee:	County:	Acres:	Grant:	Grant Date:	Entry:	Entry Date:	Bk:	Pg:	Location by Stream Name:	Military:
Bean, Henry	675	King, Robert	Hawkins	640	2385	12 [?] Jul 1794	399	6 Jan 1787	81	601	In a valley &c	yes
Bean, Jesse	698		Green	2000	739	11 Jul 1788	3822		66	473	German Cr below 1st fork of sd Creek	
Bean, Jesse	939	Cameron, Alexr.	Green	320	2509	20 Nov 1795			88	281	On N side of Holston River	
Bean, John	1093		Washington	153	1043	27 Nov 1792	1540	28 Aug 1779	80	202	On the dreams of Nob Creek	
Bean, John	922		Hawkins	1000	731	27 Feb 1796	1229	22 Feb 1779	88	234	On waters of Clinch River	
Bean, Robert	250		Hawkins	640	238	26 Dec 1791	75	26 Sep 1778	77	326	On N side of Holston River &c	
Bean, Robert	397	Coonrod, Nicholas	Tennessee	226	2420	7 Jan 1794	3448	2 Feb 1786	81	406	On Millers Creek	yes
Bean, William	0470		Hawkins	250	342	29 Jul 1793	1937	11 Oct 1778	80	261 [?]	N/S of Holston R & S/S W fk German Cr	
Bean, William	511	King, Robert	Middle District	640	2691	6 Jun 1796	3447		88	366	On N side of Spring Creek	yes
Bean, William	6		Hawkins	200			2311	23 Nov 1779			N side of Clinch River	
Bean, William	965		Washington	180	942	17 Nov 1790	600	23 Mar 1779	76	158	N side of Boons Creek	
Beane, Wm.,. Sr.	974		Washington	400	951	17 Nov 1790	722	23 Mar 1779	76	162	Beg at a poplar &c	
Beane, William	07		Hawkins	200			2312	23 Nov 1779			S side of Clinch River	
Bear, Jesse	763	Lanier, James	Davidson	640	736	11 Jul 1788	3449		63	259	On main Salt Lick Fork	yes
Beard, Andrew	870		Washington	200	854	18 May 1789	256	2 Sep 1785	72	221	Bet at a white oak &c	
Beard, David	411		Sumner	640	422	27 June 1793	732	30 May 1785	80	348	On a fork of Red River	
Beard, Hugh	1152		Green	300	995	26 Dec 1791	1035	29 Oct 1783	77	280	On waters of William Enerys River	
Beard, Hugh	1544		Green	150	1304	17 Jul 1794	2101	31 Oct 1779	81	610	On N side of French Broad River	
Beard, Hugh	804		Washington	150	618	10 Nov 1784	2430	23 Jan 1790	69	143	Beg at a stake	
Beard, James	673	Nelson, Robert	Davidson	640	3230	8 Dec 1787	2975		63	229	On E side of Big Harpeth	yes
Beard, John	01		Hawkins	400			130	26 Feb 1778			On head of West Fork of Flat Creek	
Beard, John	011		Sullivan	100			632	6 Jan 1780			N side of Holson River	
Beard, John	047		Hawkins	1000							N side of Holston River	
Beard, John	083		Washington	100			1762	1 Oct 1779			N side of Holston River	
Beard, John	09		Hawkins	120			1425	21 Jun 1784			N side of Holstein River	
Beard, John	1163		Washington	400	1006	26 Dec 1791			77	284	On Wt side of Flat Creek	
Beard, John	242 (243)		Green	100	199	20 Sep 1787	632	6 Jun 1780	65	430	On N side of Holston River &c	
Beard, John	429		Green	400	431	20 Sep 1787	1333	25 Jun 1784	65	497	On N/S of French Broad Riv on Deep Cr	
Beard, John	8		Hawkins	360	1012	29 oct 1783					Adjoining place Beard now lives on	
Beard, John Lewis	241	Kidwell, Elijah	Davidson	640	227	7 Mar 1786	601		63	83	On Harpeth River	yes
Beard, John Lewis	242	Manyr, John hrs	Davidson	640	228	7 Mar 1780	749		63	84	On Harpeth River	yes
Beard, John, Ass	911		Hawkins	100 (400	243	27 Feb 1796	1155	31 Jan 1779	88	181	On head of West Fork of Flatt Creek	
Beard, Jos. & Thos. Jackson	623		Eastern District	640	320	15 Jul 1793			80	301	S/S of Clinch Riv above Hendersons line	
Beard, Jos. & Wm. Terrell	262		Eastern District	640	210	3 Feb 1795	565	16 May 1780	83	381	On Bull Run	
Beard, Joseph	03		Eastern District	400							On Beaverdam Creek	
Beard, Joseph	099		Washington	640			1780	2 Oct 1779				
Beard, Joseph	119		Eastern District	100	152	29 Jul 1793			76	481	S/S of Clinch Riv E side of Williams Creek	
Beard, Joseph	128		Eastern District	1000	138	15 Jul 1793	1281	24 Dec 1783	76	495	S side of Clinch River	
Beard, Joseph	129		Eastern District	640	139	15 Jul 1793		2 Oct 1779	76	495	On waters of Clinch on Bull Run	
Beard, Joseph	130		Eastern District	640	140	15 Jul 1793	1617	14 Sep 1779	76	495	N side of Clinch River	
Beard, Joseph	132		Eastern District	375	142	15 Jul 1793	1940	25 Jun 1784	76	496	On waters of Clinch River &c	
Beard, Joseph	133		Eastern District	640	143	15 Jul 1793	2865	29 May 1781	76	496	On waters of Clinch River on Bull Run	
Beard, Joseph	134		Eastern District	500	144	15 Jul 1793	1294	25 Jun 1784	76	496	On waters of N Fork of Bull Run	
Beard, Joseph	135		Eastern District	200	145	15 Jul 1793	1490	27 Jul 1789 [?]	76	497	Waters of Holston R. on W Fork of Flat Cr.	
Beard, Joseph	280		Eastern District	1000	215	12 Jan 1795	2481	25 May 1784	84	46	On N side of Clinch River	

Claimant:	File #:	Assignee:	County:	Acres:	Grant:	Grant Date:	Entry:	Entry Date:	Bk:	Pg:	Location by Stream Name:	Military:
Beard, Joseph	331		Eastern District	200	251	2 Dec 1779	940	7 Jan 1779	88	272	On Beaver Creek	
Beard, Joseph	388		Eastern District	290 (200	228	11 May 1795	942	7 Jan 1779	89	117	On head of Beaver Creek	
Beard, Joseph	616		Hawkins	300	312	15 Jul 1793	801	18 Feb 1782	80	300	On S side of Clinch River	
Beard, Lewis	1356	Gray, Henry	Sumner	1000	2779	16 Oct 1796	3738	10 Nov 1795	91	23	N side of Cumberland River	yes
Beard, Lewis	2366	Smith, James	Davidson	640	3081	19 Jul 1797	3737		90	383	On Leepers Fork of Harpeth	yes
Beard, Saml	1276		Green	100	1126	12 Jan 1793	1512	10 Aug 1779	78	381	S side of Horse Creek	
Beasley, John	40	Gloster, Thomas	Tennessee	357	1227	10 Dec 1790	3145	16 Dec 1785	74	340	On S side of Cumberland River	yes
Beates, John	2172	Williams, Willoughby	Davidson	640	2493	1 Apr 1794	1746		81	452	On waters of Stones River	yes
Beatey, William	56		Washington	115	346	24 Oct 1782	697	18 Dec 1778	43	317	On waters of Lick Creek &c	
Beaty, Alexander	1757		Green	80	1434	17 Nov 1797	229	10 Mar 1780	94	145	Waters of Lick Creek	
Beaty, David	2359	Armstrong, M.	Davidson	50	381	19 Jul 1797	40		90	368	Waters of Browns Creek	
Beaty, Walter	728		Hawkins	216	548	12 Jun 1794	1837	6 Oct 1790	82	170	Joining plantation where sd Beaty lives	
Beaty, William	1		Grainger	250	200	4 Jul 1797	2	10 Jan 1786			On waters of Richland Creek	
Beaty, William	438		Eastern District	250	200	4 Jul 1797			91	596	Waters of Richland Creek	
Beaty, William	805		Sullivan	250	748	17 Nov 1797	1873	7 Oct 1779	94	150	N side of Holstein River	
Beaver Toter	48		Tennessee	640	18			8 Sep 1819			Br of first or above Comet town house	
Beaver, John	661	Bushnell, E. & Dobbs	Davidson	1000	634	15 Sep 1787			63	225	On waters of Stones Creek	yes
Beavers, John	228	Marshall, John	Sumner	640	1133	26 Nov 1789	1608	21 Jan 1786	74	145	On Main S Fork of Big Barren River	yes
Beavers, John	098	Marshall, John	Sumner	640			1609	9 Feb 1787			On a fork of Caney Fork	yes
Beck, George	2187	Wootson, David	Davidson	1000	2443	22 Feb 1795	1695	1 Jan 1780	84	318	On both sides of Duck River	yes
Beck, Katherine	1674		Green	300	1379	20 Jul 1796	310		88	491	N of French Broad River	
Beck, William	140	Pierson, Samuel	Davidson	640	126	14 Mar 1786	513	8 Jan 1779	63	49	S side of Cumberland River	yes
Beck, William	255	Row, George	Davidson	640	241	7 Mar 1786	514	2 Jul 1785	63	88	At a poplar & dogwood	yes
Beck, William	27		Tennessee	1096	1190	30 Nov 1790	1103	9 Jun 1784	74	318	On both sides of upper fk of Bartons Cr	
Beel (Bell), Robert	1572	Brown, James	Davidson	640	1215	10 Dec 1790	1424		74	336	On waters of Mill Creek	yes
Beell, William	1441		Green	400	1251	27 Nov 1792	1493	7 Jun 1784	85(0)	171	N side of French Broad Riv on Clay Creek	
Beelar, Jacob	522		Sullivan	75	538	26 Nov 1789	310	13 Nov 1780	73	48	On waters of Sinking Creek	
Beelor, Daniel	765		Sullivan	110	696	20 Jul 1796	372	29 Mar 1780	91	81	Beg at David Worleys corner	
Beeman, Francis	564	Gilmore, Charles	Davidson	640	536	15 Sep 1787	1987	8 Jan 1779	63	193	On N side of Cumberland River	yes
Been, Jesse	705		Washington	500	519	10 Nov 1784	1061		69	111	Including his improvements	
Been, John	084		Washington	200			2644	2 Jul 1785			Beg at a pine & post oak	
Been, John	716		Washington	637	530	10 Nov 1784	1119	21 Jan 1779	69	115	On both sides Wataugha River	
Been, John, Sr.	1174		Washington	200	1132	7 Jul 1794			81	620	On Fall branch of Horse Creek	
Been, Robert	61		Washington	440	229	23 Oct 1782	160	14 Mar 1778	44	259	On a branch of Lick Creek	
Beeton, John	763		Sullivan	200	694	20 Jul 1796	518	28 Apr 1780	91	81	Beg at two white oaks	
Before, Andrew	1250		Green	300	1100	12 Jan 1793	4	24 Feb 1778	78	364	Joining 640 acres granted Alex Campbell	
Belar, John	317		Sullivan	260 (266	453	28 Nov 1787	1652		67	217	On waters of Beaver Creek	
Belar, John	320		Sullivan	300	456	28 Nov 1787	3474	17 Jan 1779	67	218	On the waters of Beaver Creek	
Belberry, Nathaniel	462		Sumner	228	1606	27 Apr 1793	2832	1 Dec 1792	81	19	On a small fork of Sulphur fork of Red Rive	yes
Belch, James	1501	Clark, William	Davidson	640	1058	26 Nov 1789	117		74	106	On N side of Cumberland River	yes
Beler, Joseph	587		Sullivan	100	585	29 Jul 1793		8 Feb 1780	76	475	On the waters of Bear Creek &c	
Bell (Beel), Robert	460		Middle District	1150	399	17 Dec 1794	2247	22 May 1784	84	261	On Rains Creek	
Bell, Elias	335	Gordon, George	Eastern District	640	2510	20 Nov 1795	1583		88	282	On N side of Clinch River	yes
Bell, George	1045		Davidson	640	19	17 Apr 1786	434	10 May 1784	66	40	Beg at Red River at Josephs corner	
Bell, James	704		Washington	200	518	10 Nov 1784	4942	8 Oct 1778	69	111	On Cherokee Creek	

Earliest Tennessee Land Records

Claimant:	File #:	Assignee:	Acres:	Grant:	Grant Date:	Entry:	Entry Date:	Bk:	Pg:	Location by Stream Name:	Military:
Bell, John	1356		100	1273	19 Oct 1797	1110	18 May 1779	92	49	On head drafts of Brush Creek	
Bell, John	913		100	890	17 Nov 1790	845	30 Dec 1778	76	151	On N fork of Sinking Creek	
Bell, Robert	1604	Jackson, James	228	1327	16 Dec 1790	1928		74	374	On waters of Mill Creek	yes
Bell, Robert	1944		2560	1772	20 May 1793	20		81	72	On S side of Cumberland Riv on Jones Cr	yes
Bell, William	162		2000	172	20 Dec 1791	200	19 Mar 1785	75	224	On headwaters of Big Harper River	
Bell, William	163		1000	173	20 Dec 1791	199	18 Mar 1785	75	225	On waters of Willson Creek	
Bell, William	888		150	820	Sep 1790	820	12 May 1784	74	280	On N side of French Broad River	
Bell, William	904		640	1067	Jul 1792	1067	24 Feb 1778	74	446	On both sides of Pigeon River	
Bell, William	921		50	898	17 Nov 1790	2475	10 Mar 1780	76	143	On waters of Big Limestone	
Bell, William, Ass.	687		50	190	17 Jul 1794		Martin Armstrong	81	605	On S side of Holston River	
Bellers, Chas.	1023	King, Robt & Jno Thompso	274	2953	1 Mar 1797	4482		90	219	On Caney Valley Creek	yes
Belwood, Samuel	1889	Oneill, Thomas	640	1571	25 May 1793	2986	9 Aug 1819	81	30	On N side of Holston	yes
Ben, John	49		640	29						On Cainey Fork of Tuckasedge River	
Bennett, William	733	McCrory, Thomas	640	706	11 Jul 1788	2111		63	248	On S waters of Big Harpeth	yes
Bennet, Joel	243	Curtis, George	357	1619	27 Apr 1793	1570	22 Feb 1785	81	22	On N side of Cumberland River	yes
Bennet, William	868	Jones, Ambrose	640	883	17 Jan 1789	1507	12 Apr 1788	63	305	On E side of Cedar Creek	yes
Bennett, Henry	466	Hays, Robert	640	2594	7 Mar 1796	2837	30 Sep 1785	88	323	Beg at a red oak	yes
Bennett, John	1104		300	947	26 Dec 1791	201	7 Jan 1784	77	261	On a branch of Richland Creek	
Bennett, Nehemiah	693	Sheppard, Nancy	640	666	8 Dec 1787	1496		63	236	On a small creek &c	yes
Bennett, Solomon	1670	Robertson, James	640	1594	23 Feb 1973	2706		76	309	On Warpath River &c	yes
Bennett, Stephen	434		150	313	10 Nov 1784	713	12 Dec 1781	69	181	On Flat branch of Horse Creek	
Bennett, William	410	Blair, John	640	387	15 Sep 1787	2108		63	143	E fork of Spring Creek	yes
Bennite, Moses	532	Tatum, Howell	304	1726	20 May 1793	1744	7 Jun 1792	81	60	On N side of Cumberland River	yes
Benson, Bailey	1050	King, William	640	2535	10 Dec 1795	504	8 Aug 1795	88	291	On Salt River	yes
Benson, John	291	Fenner, Richard	640	277	22 Mar 1787	2171		63	101	S Side of Cumberland River	yes
Bentford, James	329	Williams, Willoughby	640	2391	3 Feb 1795	2704		83	387	W side of W Fork of Obeys River	yes
Bentley, Isaac	308	McCulloh, Benjamin	640	2009	20 May 1793	2078	1 Sep 1785	81	126	On N side of Cumberland River	yes
Bentley, John	246	Nelson, John & Alex	640	1630	27 Apr 1793	1884	11 Jul 1785	81	24	On N side of Cumberland River	yes
Benton, Jesse	237	Gooch, Jas.	640	340	27 Nov 1792	107	15 Apr 1784	81	6	N side of Cumberland River SR	
Benton, Jesse	280	Barnet. Jas.	274	1865	20 May 1793	3128	16 Dec 1785	81	93	On S side of Cumberland River &c	
Benton, Jesse, dec'd	616	Mickelray, John	274	1881	20 May 1793	3129	19 Dec 1792	81	96	On Otter Fork of Bledsoe's Creek	yes
Benton, Julian	574	Smith, Abraham	640	3021	10 Apr 1797	3639		90	302	N side of Cumberland River	yes
Benton, Kedar	690	Davis, Joshua	228	2045	20 May 1793	2354	29 Nov 1792	81	135	To join an entry of his own	yes
Benton, Robert, Ass.	1		5000	2	14 Jul 1812			126	426	Lying & being on Big Creek	
Benton, Solomon	2421	Irwin, Joseph	640	3225	19 Oct 1797	2561		92	92	Waters of South Harpeth	yes
Benton, William	585	Sanford, Samuel	640	1824	20 May 1793	2369	6 Aug 1792	81	84	On W Fork of Roaring River	yes
Berkley, William	563	Donahoe, John	640	1786	20 May 1793	2987	9 Jun 1792	81	75	Beg at a white oak in Spencers line	yes
Bernard, Walter hr of Jno.	1851		588	352	27 Nov 1792	210	30 Jan 1784	81	10	Beg at an elm & box elder	
Berry, David, Ass.	1001		400	157	17 Dec 1794		11 Dec 1792	84	333	On both sides of a small fork &c	yes
Berry, Francis	279		10	418	9 Aug 1787	443	22 Apr 1780	61	437	On both sides of Sinking Creek	
Berry, Francis	687	Hays, Patty Thompson	640	2041	20 May 1793	2337	29 Oct 1792	81	134	On Thompsons Creek	
Berry, Hugh	1233		200	1083	12 Jan 1793	1108	13 Jan 1779	78	354	On N side of French Broad River	yes
Berry, James	1110		300	830	15 Sep 1797	228	24 Feb 1780	94	137	On Powells Valley	
Berry, James	1117		100	837	16 Sep 1797	631	25 Nov 1788	94	140	Both sides of Powell River	
Berry, James	2		200	1299	10 Jun 1799	2204	22 Nov 1779	101	347	Powells Valley near Cumberland Gap	

Claimant:	File #:	Assignee:	County:	Acres:	Grant:	Grant Date:	Entry:	Entry Date:	Bk:	Pg:	Location by Stream Name:	Military:
Berry, James	294		Hawkins	221	257	24 Dec 1792	1923	11 Oct 1779	78	446	On N side of Clinch River	
Berry, James	99		Tennessee	640	1514	10 Apr 1792	789	3 Apr 1784	75	506	S side of Cumberland River	
Berry, Jas & Fr. Mayberry	172		Eastern District	640	127	24 Jun 1793	1661	17 Sep 1779	80	185	N side of Clinch River	
Berry, Jas.	297		Hawkins	200	260	24 Dec 1791	1863	7 Oct 1779	78	447	On N side of Holston River	
Berry, Jas. & Harry Brown	1127		Hawkins	640	846	2 Nov 1797	126	9 Feb 1780	96	5	Both sides of Lanhans Creek	
Berry, John	45	Hughlett, William	Middle District	640			2793					yes
Berry, John	952	Pasmore, David	Davidson	1000	969	18 May 1789	361		63	329	On head of a small creek	yes
Berry, John heirs	45	Hughlett, William	Middle District	640	2793							
Berry, Thomas	575		Davidson	429	547	15 Sep 1787	74		63	196	On N Fork of Main Harpeth	
Berry, Thomas	665	Conner, John	Davidson	274	638	15 Nov 1787	1397		63	226	On small creek empties into N/S Tenn Riv	yes
Berry, Thomas	666	Morgan, Wm.	Davidson	274	639	15 Nov 1787	1398		63	227	On small creek empties into Tenn River	yes
Berry, Thomas	667	McAfee, Azariah	Davidson	640	640	15 Nov 1787	1112		63	227	On small creek empties into Tenn River	yes
Berry, William	200		Washington	200	68	23 Oct 1782	623	24 Nov 1778	47	32	Head draft of Mill Fork &c	
Berry, William	376		Washington	25	368	10 Oct 1783	2688	18 Dec 1780	52	250	On the waters of Mill Fork &c	
Berry, William	409		Washington	150	401	13 Oct 1783	2468	10 Mar 1780	52	266	On the head of Sinking Creek	
Berry, William	472		Washington	150	464	13 Oct 1783	2467	10 Mar 1780	52	295	On the head of Sinking Creek	
Berry, William	95		Washington	200	263	23 Oct 1782	1502	5 Jun 1780	44	279	On head waters of Mill Fork &c	
Besell, Elisha	591	Reed, Jesse	Davidson	640	563	15 Sep 1787	2003		63	202	S side of Big Barren rRiver	yes
Best, John	1010	Shaw, William	Davidson	640	1027	18 May 1789	3442		63	343	On N side of Cumberland River	yes
Betts, Jonathan	379	Sheppard, Benjamin	Davidson	640	351	15 Sep 1787	2309		63	132	W side of E fork of Drakes Creek	yes
Betts, Wm.	034	Hicks, Howell	Montgomery	274			1277				On Saline Creek	
Betts, Wm.	577	Cantrell, John	Tennessee	640	3024	10 Apr 1797	3930		90	303	On Barnetts Creek	yes
Bevearis, John	098	Marshall, John	Sumner	640			1609	9 Feb 1787			On a fork of Caney Fork	
Bewley, Anthony	1402		Green	100	1214	27 Nov 1792	2874	29 Jun 1781	80	155	On N side of Nolachucky River	yes
Bewley, Anthony	765		Washington	100	579	10 Nov 1784	2874	29 Jun 1781	69	132	Incl place where Uriah Aker now lives	
Bibble, David	1320	McConnel, Robert	Sumner	1000	3120	14 Sep 1797	4476	15 May 1797	90	411	Joining an entry &c	yes
Bibby, Edmond	1096	Easten, James	Sumner	640	2587	7 Mar 1796	3928	22 Jul 1795	88	320	On E side of large fork of Caney Fork	yes
Biffle, Adam	42		Sullivan	154	53	23 Oct 1782	1592	29 Jul 1779	43	263	On S side of Holston River	
Bigby, James	053	Dillenbery, Redmond [sic]	Sumner	640			4405	19 Sep 1797			On Rainny Fk of W Fork of Drakes Creek	yes
Biggett, Jesse	1261	Askew, William	Sumner	640	2937	1 Mar 1797	1747	22 Mar 1796	90	212	Waters of Fifth Creek	yes
Biggs, John	1237		Green	200	1087	12 Jan 1793			78	350	On waters of Long Creek	
Biggs, Nathaniel	2398	Hays, Robert	Davidson	640	2795	20 Dec 1796	2790		91	470	E side of Stones River	yes
Biggs, Robert	012		Green	300			1410	20 Oct 1785			The Sinking Fork of Long Creek	
Biggs, Robert	512		Green	300	574 (514)	20 Sep 1787	1348	6 Apr 1795	65	527	On Sinking Fork of Long Creek	
Biggs, Robert	539	Williams, Etheldred	Middle District	640	2963	2 Mar 1797	3941		90	257	On S ward path	yes
Biggs, Robert	962		Green	200	876	17 Nov 1790	1244	7 Jun 1784	76	130	Bet the Cedar Cr & Sinking Fk of Long Cr	
Bigham, John	158		Middle District	3200	159	6 Dec 1790	2071	5 May 1784	74	245	On Richland Creek	
Bigham, William	370		Green	100	372	20 Sep 1787	2847	12 May 1781	65	478	On S side of Nolachuckey River	
Bigham, William	399		Washington	600	391	13 Oct 1783	491	7 Oct 1778	52	261	On S side of Nolichuckey River	
Bigham, William	598		Green	500	555	20 Sep 1787	379	7 Jun 1784	66	248	N/S of French Broad on head of Clark Cr	
Bigworth, Stephen	027	Donelson, Stockley	Robertson	640			2559	13 Aug 1796			On waters of Red River	yes
Bilingsley, John	1262		Washington	300	1200	4 Dec 1795	1439	11 Jun 1779	89	325	Beg at a post oak	
Bilinsly, John	1285		Washington	290	1223	4 Dec 1795	1328	4 Jan 1779	89	337	Beg on 3 red oaks	
Billego, John	212	Reed, Jesse	Sumner	640	1117	26 Nov 1789	3417	12 Mar 1788	74	137	On W side of Caney Fork	yes
Billingsbee, John	013		Sullivan	75			541	29 Apr 1780			Beg at a post oak saplin in the Barrens	

Claimant:	File #:	Assignee:	County:	Acres:	Grant:	Grant Date:	Entry:	Entry Date:	Bk:	Pg:	Location by Stream Name:	Military:
Billingsbee, John	700		Sullivan	30	645	5 Dec 1794	541	29 Apr 1794	84	158	Beg at a double white oak	
Billingsbee, Samuel	255		Sullivan	100	3942	9 Aug 1787	1793	3 Aug 1779	61	413	Joining John Clark &c	
Billingsbee, Samuel	286		Sullivan	100	425	9 Aug 1787	532	29 Apr 1780	61	444	Beg at Charles Robersons corner	
Billips, John	631		Davidson	274	603	15 Sep 1787	116		63	215	E side of Stones River	yes
Billups, Thomas	1288	Barry, Redmond Dillon	Sumner	425	3047	8 Jun 1797	4041	29 mar 1797	90	317	Joins an Entry of his own	yes
Bineham, Hodge, heirs of	619		Sumner	640	1891	20 May 1793	3210	10 Dec 1792	81	98	On an E branch of Goose Creek	yes
Binion, John	768	Bledsoe, Isaac	Davidson	640	741	11 Jul 1788	520		63	260	On N side of Cumberland River	yes
Birch, John	626	Stewart, Charles	Tennessee	640	3190	14 Sep 1797	568		90	438	S side of Cumberland River	yes
Bird, Amos	10		Hawkins	1000	2462	25 May 1784					N side of Holston River	
Bird, Amos	268		Green	500	225	20 Sep 1787	1898	7 Oct 1779	65	440	On N side of Tennessee River	
Bird, Amos	27		Green	400	90	1 Nov 1786	190	22 Oct 1783	58	451	On the N side of Chuckey River	
Bird, Amos	307		Washington	300	174	24 Oct 1792	24	26 Feb 1778	47	84	N side of Nolachuckey River	
Bird, John	1255		Green	175	1105	12 Jan 1793	2100	23 Aug 1792	78	366	Beg at a hickory & white oak	
Bird, John	988		Green	100	1215	29 Jul 1793			76	482	N side of French Broad River	
Bird, Jonathan	361		Washington	200	353	13 Oct 1783	221	17 Dec 1778	52	244	On Penson Branch	
Bird, Jonathan	850		Washington	200	664	10 Nov 1784	349	3 Sep 1778	69	156	Bet. Sandeford Kesiahs & Walter Karr	
Bird, Joseph	1056		Green	300	899	26 Dec 1791	191	20 Sep 1787	77	242	On S side of Nolachucky River &c	
Bird, Joseph	531		Green	300	533	20 Sep 1787	818	7 Jun 1784	65	533	On Oven Creek	
Bird, Joseph	84		Eastern District	500	109	26 Dec 1791	338	23 Oct 1783	75	181	E side of Little Pigeon River	
Birdwell, George	1801		Davidson	640	374	26 Jun 1793	591		80	332	Beg I mile above Heatons Station	
Birdwell, Joseph	586		Hawkins	200	460	29 Jul 1793	237	28 Feb 1780	80	291	On W Fork of Rockey Spring branch	
Bishop (Bushop), Colden	2151	Spellce,_ rebell [?]	Davidson	640	2464	31 Dec 1793	2796		81	431	On waters of Whites Creek	yes
Bishop (Bushop), William	1675	Sheppard, Wm & Jas	Davidson	640	1600	23 Feb 1793	2795		76	312	On both sides of S Harpeth River	yes
Bishop, Joseph	1132		Washington	50	1090	12 Jul 1794	2027	15 Aug 1793	81	566	Beg at a red oak	
Biss, Silas	379	Blount, John Gray & Thom	Tennessee	640	2331	20 May 1793	2792	30 Sep 1785	81	198	On S side of Cumberland River &c	
Bizzell, David hr.	160	Bizzell, David hr.Enos	Davidson	640	146	14 Mar 1786	120		63	56	On both sides of Barton Creek	yes
Bizzle, Enos	160	Bizzell, David hr.Enoch	Davidson	640	146	14 Mar 1786	120		63	56	On both sides of Bartons Creek	yes
Black (Balch), Hezekiah	1260		Green	150	1110	12 Jan 1793	2974	28 Oct 1779	78	370	On E side of Richland Creek	
Black, Anthony	337		Tennessee	640	2124	20 May 1793	3068	30 Nov 1785	81	155	On S side of Cumberland River	
Black, James	1263		Green	207	1113	12 Jan 1793			78	372	On a branch of Lick Creek	
Black, James	575		Hawkins	100	449	29 Jul 1793	1470	15 Jul 1779	80	289	N side of Holston River	
Black, John	459		Sumner	640	1600	27 Apr 1793	1468	8 Aug 1792	81	17	On S side of Cumberland River	yes
Black, Martin	617	Ward, George	Tennessee	274	3179	14 Sep 1797	3976	23 Nov 1796	90	433	S side of Cumberland River	yes
Black, Peter	84	Robertson, Elijah	Davidson	640	817	20 Nov 1788	3300		63	287	On waters of Caney Fork	yes
Black, William	1247		Green	150	1097	12 Jan 1793	1264	6 Mar 1779	78	362	S side of Nolichuckey River	
Black, William	162		Green	300	632	23 Aug 1788	858	7 Jun 1784	64	352	On Clear Creek	
Black, William	197		Green	640	154	20 Sep 1787	752	20 Oct 1783	65	415	On N/S of Tenn Riv in Cumberland Valley	
Black, William	270		Green	640	227	20 Sep 1787	680	7 Jun 1784	65	441	On N side of Clinch River &c	
Black, William	357		Middle District	1500	296	17 Dec 1794	1808	23 Apr 1784	84	205	In Wilsons Valley	
Black, William	562		Sullivan	190	545	17 Nov 1790	143,-764	28 Mar 1781	76	193	N side of Holston River	
Blackborn, Randolph	56	Blount, John Gray	Tennessee	640	1274	10 Dec 1790	2497	30 Sep 1785	74	357	On N side of Cumberland River	
Blackburn, Archibald	1335		Washington	160	1259	8 Jun 1797	966	9 Nov 1784	90	328	N side of Nolachuckey River	
Blackburn, Archibald	387		Green	400	389	20 Sep 1787	362	7 Jun 1784	65	482	S/S Little Nolechucky & on Little Lick Cr	
Blackburn, Jno.	584		Green	400	265	20 Sep 1787	80	7 Dec 1784	66	162	On Long Creek &c	
Blackburn, John	1294		Green	360	1144	12 Jan 1793	387	11 Sep 1778	78	390	On headwaters of Carsons Creek	

Earliest Tennessee Land Records

Claimant:	File #:	Assignee:	County:	Acres:	Grant:	Grant Date:	Entry:	Entry Date:	Bk:	Pg:	Location by Stream Name:	Military:
Blackburn, Robert	159		Eastern District	500	129	14 Jan 1793	1045	7 Jan 1779	79	289	At the head of Town Creek	
Blackburn, Robert	333		Washington	229	200	24 Oct 1782	661	8 Dec 1778	49	226	On S side of Little Limestone Creek	
Blackburn, Robert	47		Washington	200 (150	337	24 Oct 1782	341	2 Sep 1778	43	314	On Horse Camp Creek &c	
Blackburn, Robert	586		Green	200	267	20 Sep 1787	78	21 Oct 1785	66	163	Richland or on N/S of Nolichuckey River	
Blackburn, Thomas	914		Green	200	828	17 Nov 1790	33	26 Feb 1778	76	114	Waters of Nolechuckey on Camp Creek	
Blackface, William	2348	Rothwell, William	Davidson	640	3003	10 Apr 1797			90	294	On Harpeth River	yes
Blackface, William	566	Minshaw, Mica. Heirs	Tennessee	640	3002	10 Apr 1797	3641		90	294	S side of Cumberland River	
Blackface, William	568	Turner, And. Heirs	Tennessee	640	3005	10 Apr 1797	4397		90	295	S side of Cumberland River	
Blackface, Wm.	565	Banks, Richard hrs.	Tennessee	640	3001	10 Apr 1797	4252		90	293	N side of Cumberland River	
Blackface, Wm.	567	Hamond, Ed heirs	Tennessee	640	3004	10 Apr 1797	1759		90	295	N side of Cumberland River	
Blackledge, Richard	126		Western District	2000	126	10 Jul 1788	1163	31 Oct 1783	67	329	On Cane Creek	
Blackledge, Richard	61 (?)		Western District	3000	61	10 Jul 1788	1162	31 Oct 1780	67	304	On Wolf River &c	
Blackley, Robert	439		Washington	100	431	13 Oct 1783	2741	20 Jan 1780	52	280	On the waters of Big Limestone	
Blackley, Robert	478		Washington	100	270 [?]	13 Oct 1783	2740	20 Jan 1781	52	298	On waters of Big Limestone	
Blackley, Robert	927		Washington	200	904	17 Nov 1790	1424	5 Jun 1779	76	145	Joining land Wm Rickey sold Blackley	
Blackmore, Aaron	785	McKissack, Daniel	Sumner	640	2242	20 May 1793	3252	18 Nov 1792	81	179	On S side of Cumberland River	yes
Blackmore, Geo. D.	1010	Armstrong, M.	Sumner	80	175	26 Mar 1795			86	378	About 3 miles from Bledsoes Lick	
Blackmore, Geo.D. & Jno.Pay	783	Lytle, Arch.	Sumner	640	2240	20 May 1790	1718		81	178	On S side of Cumberland River	yes
Blackmore, George	068	Douglass, Elmore	Sumner	320			743	14 Jun 1785			On Winchester Fork	yes
Blackmore, John	1087		Davidson	640	61	17 Apr 1786	492	19 Jun 1784	66	55	N/S of Cumberland Riv above mo Dry Creek	
Blackmore, John	424		Sumner	640	435	27 Jun 1793	672	28 Jan 1785	80	353	On E fork of Station camp Creek	
Blackmore, John, Ass	320		Sumner	640	313	17 Nov 1790	493	19 Jun 1784	76	185	On Rocky Creek &c	
Blackmore, Mary, Ass	423		Sumner	640	434	27 Jun 1793	674	29 Jan 1785	80	352	On middle fork of Station Camp Creek	
Blackwell, Ann	723		Hawkins	200	543	12 Jun 1794			82	168	On N side of Holston River &c	
Blair, Alex	20		Green	200	406	20 Sep 1787	586	4 Oct 1784			N side of Holston River	
Blair, Alexander	1012		Hawkins	150	334	29 Dec 1796		???	90	194	On the Big Branch, M.Armstrobg	
Blair, Alexander	168		Hawkins	150	101	16 Nov 1790	1782	9 Oct 1780	77	185	Joining the plantation he now lives on	
Blair, Alexander	404		Green	200	406	20 Sep 1787	273	22 Oct 1783	65	486	On S side of Holston River	
Blair, Alexander	515		Hawkins	200	388	29 Jul 1793	442	25 Oct 1783	80	274	On S side of Holston River	
Blair, Catherine	220		Eastern District	1000	163	30 Dec 1793	2375	25 May 1784	82	145	On the Main Fork of Wolf River	
Blair, James	1027		Hawkins	100	790	22 Feb 1797	324	17 May 1780	90	225	Waters of Horse Valley Creek	
Blair, James	1044		Hawkins	250	808	8 Jun 1797	48	8 Feb 1780	90	324	N side of Holston River	
Blair, James	11		Hawkins	200	858	17 Nov 1790	1738	17 Apr 1784			On waters & west side of Poor Valley Cr	
Blair, James	1140		Green	200	983	26 Dec 1791	263	7 Mar 1780	77	276	Joining his former survey	
Blair, James	1965	Watkins, Walter	Davidson	274	1838	20 May 1793	3508		81	87	On waters of Mill Creek	yes
Blair, James	2032	Harris, Gilbert	Davidson	640	2044	20 May 1793	3512		81	135	On headwaters of Mill Creek	yes
Blair, James	304		Hawkins	300	269	24 Dec 1792	271	22 Oct 1783	78	450	On N side of Holston River	
Blair, James	306		Hawkins	200	271	24 Dec 1792	977	29 Oct 1793	78	451	On N side of Holston River	
Blair, James	333		Green	100	335	20 Sep 1787	987	8 Sep 1785	65	468	On N side of Holston River &c	
Blair, James	339		Green	200	341	20 Sep 1787			65	469	Abt 5 mi below end of Clinch Mountain	
Blair, James	487		Sullivan	300	498	18 May 1789	526, 354	5 May 1779	71	10	On N side of Holston River &c	
Blair, James	544		Hawkins	300	417	29 Jul 1793			80	281	On N side of Cumberland Mountain	
Blair, James	565		Hawkins	100	439	27 July 1793	737	6 Oct 1781	80	287	N/S Holston Riv joining two of his surveys	
Blair, James	777		Hawkins	150	617	12 Jul 1794	55	8 Feb 1780	82	218	On waters Clear Fork of Cumberland &c	
Blair, James	879		Green	200	829	27 Nov 1789	2295	27 Nov 1779	74	36	On N side of Holstein River	

Claimant:	File #:	Assignee:	County:	Acres:	Grant:	Grant Date:	Entry:	Entry Date:	Bk:	Pg:	Location by Stream Name:	Military:
Blair, James	944		Green	200	858	11 Nov 1790	992	20 Sep 1787	76	124	On waters & west side of Poor Valley Cr	
Blair, James, Jr.	5		Middle District	300	683	9 Dec 1778					N side of the Cumberland Mtns	
Blair, James, Senr	1010	Armstrong, M.	Hawkins	100	330	29 Dec 1796			90	191	Joining Wm. Owens & Wm. Pattersons	
Blair, Jno.	616		Green	1000	657	11 Jul 1788	1477 & 147	8 May 1787	66	446	On Brimstone Cr the waters of Wolf Riv	
Blair, John	1002		Green	100	1229	29 Jul 1793	2833	1 Apr 1781	76	484	N side of Holston River	
Blair, John	111		Green	500	484		1491	19 Feb 1784			On Main Fork of Woolf River	
Blair, John	1352		Green	300	1198	23 Feb 1793	1681	16 Nov 1785	78	440	On Beaverdam Creek	
Blair, John	1360		Washington	100	1277	30 Jun 1797	2488	10 Mar 1780	92	56	Waters of Big Limestone	
Blair, John	1493	Ridden, John	Green	400	1256	12 Jul 1794	822	26 Jul 1781	81	580	On N side of Clinch River	
Blair, John	1615		Davidson	640	1343	10 Dec 1790	696		74	360	On waters of Stones River	yes
Blair, John	384		Green	100	386	20 Sep 1787	1002	29 Oct 1783	65	482	Abt 2 miles below Poor Valley Creek	
Blair, John	386		Hawkins	100 (150	507	27 Jan 1793	308	8 Feb 1780	79	493	On N side of Holston River	
Blair, John	410	Bennett, William	Davidson	640	387	15 Sep 1787	2108		63	143	E fork of Spring Creek	yes
Blair, John	410		Washington	150	402	13 Oct 1783	1519	13 Aug 1779	52	266	On waters of Big Limestone	
Blair, John	416	Pettigrew, Hara (?)	Davidson	1000	388	15 Sep 1787	2022		63	145	On waters of Spring Creek	yes
Blair, John	474		Hawkins	200	346	29 Jul 1793		15...1779 (sic)	80	262	On Powell's River on the S side	
Blair, John	528		Hawkins	200	401	29 Jul 1793	1687	21 Sep 1779	80	277	Below Blairs Gap on the Holston River	
Blair, John	610		Hawkins	500	484	29 Jun 1793			80	296	On Main Fork of Wolf River	
Blair, John	742		Hawkins	150	582	7 Jul 1794	1773	1 Oct 1779	82	204	N side of Holston River &c	
Blair, John	749		Hawkins	220	589	7 Jul 1794	90	7 Jun 1784	82	206	N side of Holston River &c	
Blair, Samuel	2238		Davidson	400	179	6 Jun 1796			88	336	On waters of Stones River	
Blair, Thomas	1507	Adcock, George	Davidson	640	1064	26 Nov 1789			74	111	On S side of Cumberland River	yes
Blair, Thomas	36		not given	640	967	20 Mar 1788					S side of Cumberland River	
Blake, John	065	Donohoe, Thomas	Sumner	1000			1873	10 Apr 1797			S branches of Many Fork Creek	yes
Blake, William	068	Donoho, (sic) Thomas	Sumner	1000			1873	10 Apr 1797			S branches of Many Fork Creek	yes
Blamer, John	2436	Tatum, Howell	Davidson	540	3278	6 Dec 1797	3041		98	158	On waters of Arrington Creek	yes
Blanchard, John	1738	Walton, William	Davidson	640	1501	4 Jan 1792	3693		77	376	W side of Kaspers Creek	yes
Blaning, John	1883	Cloud, Joseph	Davidson	228	1629	27 Apr 1793			81	26	On S branches of Stones Creek	yes
Blanset, Frederick	22	Rice, John	Sumner	640	779	11 Jul 1788	1930	21 Sep 1787	63	273	On waters of Caney Fork	yes
Blanshet, Robert	792	Davis, Joshua	Sumner	640	2252	20 May 1793	2362	19 Nov 1792	81	181	On E side of Caney Fork	yes
Blanton, John	421		Sumner	600	300	10 Nov 1784	1720	25 Sep 1779	69	176	On N side of Holston River	
Blanton, John	518		Sullivan	114	534	26 Nov 1789	330	22 Mar 1780	73	46	On N side of Holston River	
Bledsoe, Ant.	324	White, Thos.	Sumner	225	1575	23 Feb 1793			76	301	On the Otter fork of Bledsoes Creek	yes
Bledsoe, Anthony	010	White, Jacob Jr.	Sumner	274			276	19 Dec 1792			On Otter Fork of Bledsoes Creek	yes
Bledsoe, Anthony	1368		Davidson	6280	51	8 Oct 1787	42108109		68	142	On both sides Bledsoe Creek	
Bledsoe, Anthony	248		Sullivan	400	387	9 Aug 1787	210	8 May 1778	61	406	On N side of Holston &c	
Bledsoe, Anthony	252		Sullivan	500	391	9 Aug 1787	106,-671	8 Feb 1780	61	410	On N side of Holston River	
Bledsoe, Anthony	329	Stedman, Geo.	Sumner	640	1617	23 Feb 1793	3024	18 Nov 1792	76	320	On a W branch of Middle Fk of Goose Cr	yes
Bledsoe, Anthony	415		Sumner	640	426	27 Jun 1793	110	15 Jan 1784	80	350	On S side of Cumberland	
Bledsoe, Anthony	482	Estis, Abraham	Sumner	320	118	27 Apr 1793	535	19 Jul 1784	81	33	On S side of Cumberland River	yes
Bledsoe, Anthony	497		Sullivan	600	508	18 May 1789	2079	28 Oct 1779	71	15	Including his old plantation &c	
Bledsoe, Anthony	498		Sullivan	300	509	18 May 1789	2081	29 Oct 1779	71	15	Joining Steels lines &c	
Bledsoe, Anthony	499		Sullivan	300	510	18 May 1789	2078	28 Oct 1779	71	16	On main road bet hd of Holston & Long Is.	
Bledsoe, Anthony	502	Peter, Daniel	Sumner	274	1673	20 May 1793	3018	30 Nov 1792	81	47	Waters of Middle Fk of Station Camp Cr	yes
Bledsoe, Anthony	670	Steedmore, Peter	Sumner	640	1997	20 May 1793	3026	18 Nov 1792	81	123	On E Fork of Joes Creek	yes

Claimant:	File #:	Assignee:	County:	Acres:	Grant:	Grant Date:	Entry:	Entry Date:	Bk:	Pg:	Location by Stream Name:	Military:
Bledsoe, Anthony	675	Dean, Starling	Sumner	640	2006	20 May 1793	2017	30 Nov 1792	81	126	On W side of E Fork of Goose Creek	yes
Bledsoe, Anthony	704	Logan, James	Sumner	365	2083	20 May 1793	1052	8 Jul 1785	81	145	On Tramels Creek	yes
Bledsoe, Anthony	835	Lamore, Lewis	Sumner	274	2321	20 May 1793	3012	18 Nov 1792	81	195	On Bledsoe Creek	yes
Bledsoe, Anthony H.	701	Jacobs, Abraham	Sumner	640	2073	20 May 1793	2183	20 Mar 1786	81	142	On the Round Lick Creek	yes
Bledsoe, Isaac	011	Obarr, Daniel	Sumner	457			1408	2 Aug 1785			At mouth of Bledsoes Creek	yes
Bledsoe, Isaac	012	Searcy & Bristow	Sumner	228			882	2 Aug 1785			N side of Cumberland River	
Bledsoe, Isaac	1180		Davidson	640	157	17 Apr 1786	5	5 jan 1784	66	188	Bledsoes Cr at elm at NW cor Public Surv	
Bledsoe, Isaac	1225	Terrell, Obidiah	Davidson	640	189	10 Jul 1788	57	5 Jan 1784	66	409	Bounded by Anthony Bledsoe on Wt etc.	
Bledsoe, Isaac	1333		Davidson	1196	19	18 Aug 187	56	5 Jan 1784	68	128	In fk bet Bledsoes Cr & Bledsoes Lick	
Bledsoe, Isaac	218	Harris, Thompson	Sumner	640	1123	26 Nov 1789	1203		74	140	Beg on E side of Bledsoes Creek	yes
Bledsoe, Isaac	566	Taylor, John	Sumner	640	1799	20 May 1793	3631	10 Apr 1789	81	79	On waters of Bledsoes Creek	yes
Bledsoe, Isaac	614	Michael———	Sumner	640	1873	20 May 1793	1719	27 Jul 1786	81	94	On N side of Cumberland River &c	yes
Bledsoe, Isaac	647	Heakes(?), Robt.	Sumner	228	1943	20 May 1793	346	31 Jul 1792	81	110	On N side of Cumberland River	
Bledsoe, Isaac	669	Searcy, Ruben	Sumner	228	1993	20 May 1793			81	122	On N side of Cumberland River	yes
Bledsoe, Isaac	721	Harris, Sherwood	Sumner	228	2105	20 May 1793	1712	31 Jul 1792	81	150	On S side of Cumberland River	yes
Bledsoe, Isaac	760	McCall, Archibald	Sumner	640	2173	20 May 1793	1010	31 Jul 1792	81	166	On N side of Cumberland River	yes
Bledsoe, Isaac,	768	Binion, John	Davidson	640	741	11 Jul 1788	520		63	260	On North side of Cumberland River	yes
Bledsoe, Isaac, Ass.	1199		Davidson	320	71	8 Oct 1787	59	5 Jan 1784	66	223	Bledsoes cr at S E cor of Preemption	
Bledsoe, Jacob	798	heir of Aaron (?)	Sumner	6409	2259	20 May 1793	1353	30 Nov 1792	81	183	Head small branch desc. into Goose Cr	
Bledsoe, Thos, Issac & Jno.	266	Bledsoe, Abram & Henry	Middle District	3000	113	27 Apr 1793	7	4 Jan 1786	81	32	On E Fork of Obids Fiver	
Blevins, William	244		Sullivan	312	383	9 Aug 1787	508	16 Oct 1778	61	402	On N side of Holston River	
Blevins, William	775		Sullivan	200	707	17 Nov 1796	1599	12 Sep 1779	91	86	On top of Iron Mountain	
Blevins, Williams	326		Sullivan	1120	466	10 Jul 1788	941,-942,-2	2 Jan 1779	67	479	On N side of Holston River	
Blevins, Williams	775a		Sullivan	92	706	17 Nov 1796	940	2 Jan 1779	91	86	S side of Holston River	
Blithe, James	500		Washington	150	763	16 Aug 1787	2607	5 Aug 1780	64	140	On Kendricks Creek &c	
Blough, Benjamin	2055	McCulloh, Benjamin	Davidson	640	2145	20 May 1793	1991		81	159	On waters of Stones River	yes
Blount, Benjamin Hodges	230		Davidson	640	216	7 Mar 1786	618			80	S E cor Nathaniel Lawrences Survey	yes
Blount, Frederick	617		Davidson	640	589	15 Sep 1787	531		63	210	On Sulphur Fork of Red River	yes
Blount, Jacob	278		West District	5000	304	25 Apr 1789	1253	24 Jun 1784	70	262	On S side of Big Hatcher River	
Blount, John	30	Angel, Thomas	Davidson	224	16	14 Mar 1786			63	7	On Big Harpeth River	yes
Blount, John G & Thomas	037	Rogers, Elisha	not given	640			1548	14 Jun 1792			On Harpeth River	
Blount, John G & Thomas	093		not given	5000			1665	16 Apr 1784				
Blount, John G & Thomas	14		Sumner	1000	23		2382	— —1790			No plat	yes
Blount, John G.	89	Craig, John	Tennessee	640	1353	10 Dec 1790	2502	30 Sep 1785	74	363	On N side of Cumberland River	
Blount, John Gray	011	Ballards, Jethro hrs	Tennessee	640			2594	30 Sep 1785			S side Spring Creek	
Blount, John Gray	012	Bladsby, Joel	Tennessee	1000			2597	30 Sep 1785			On a draft of Spring Creek	
Blount, John Gray	013	Bromer, John	Tennessee	1000			2598	30 Sep 1785			N side Red River	
Blount, John Gray	013	McNees, John	Sumner	3840				10 Jun 1795			S side Cumberland River	yes
Blount, John Gray	07	Steadman, Tobias hrs	Tennessee	640			2817	30 Sep 1785			S side Red River	
Blount, John Gray	08	McDaniel, Allen hrs	Tennessee	640			2533	30 Sep 1785			S side Spring Creek	
Blount, John Gray	1034	McNeese, John	Sumner	3840	2571	7 Mar 1796			88	191	On waters of Caney Fork	yes
Blount, John Gray	1035	Dillan, Benj.	Sumner	2560	2572	7 Mar 1793	3829	5 Jun 1795	88	191	On waters of Caney Fork	yes
Blount, John Gray	1048	Abims, Joseph	Sumner	640	2527	8 Dec 1795	2495	30 Apr 1795	88	280	On S W side of Bigg Harpeth River	yes
Blount, John Gray	1237	Dillon, Benj.	Sumner	2560	2572	7 Mar 1796			89	531	On waters of the Caney Fork	yes
Blount, John Gray	1243	Hance, Job	Sumner	640	2842	21 Jan 1797	4291	14 Dec 1796	90	45	On Camp Creek	yes

Claimant:	File #:	Assignee:	County:	Acres:	Grant:	Grant Date:	Entry:	Entry Date:	Bk:	Pg:	Location by Stream Name:	Military:
Blount, John Gray	1244	McGound, Thomas	Sumner	640	2843	21 Jan 1797	4249	13 Dec 1793	90	46		yes
Blount, John Gray	1247	Young, Robert Jr.	Sumner	640	2852	21 Jan 1797	4292	14 Dec 1796	90	50	On Camp Creek	yes
Blount, John Gray	1250	Province, John	Sumner	640	2854	21 Jan 1797	4293	14 Dec 1793	90	51	On Camp Creek	
Blount, John Gray	151	Dugald, John	Tennessee	640	1404	20 Dec 1791	2509	30 Sep 1785	77	353	On S side of Spring Creek	
Blount, John Gray	1947	Dunkinson, John	Davidson	640	1780	20 May 1793	2504		81	74	On Middle Fork of Jones's Creek	yes
Blount, John Gray	265		Western District	1000	265	10 Jul 1788	2312	25 May 1784	67	406	On waters of Reelfoot River &c	
Blount, John Gray	37	Hennes, Benbury	Tennessee	640	1219	10 Dec 1790	2517	30 Sep 1785	74	338	On N side of Cumberland River	
Blount, John Gray	44	McDaniel, Jno.	Tennessee	640	1235	10 Dec 1790	2532	30 Sep 1785	74	343	On N side of Cumberland River	
Blount, John Gray	440	Patton, John	Davidson	7200	412	15 Sep 1787	354		63	153	On E Fork of Third Big Creek	yes
Blount, John Gray	45	Williams, Thos.	Tennessee	640	1236	10 Dec 1790	2825	30 Sep 1785	74	343	On N side of Cumberland River	
Blount, John Gray	56	Blackburn, Randolph	Tennessee	640	1274	10 Dec 1790	2497	30 Sep 1785	74	357	On N side of Cumberland River	
Blount, John Gray	592	Brickles, Thos.	Tennessee	1000	3062	19 Jul 1797	395		90	375	Headwaters of Half Pone Creek	
Blount, John Gray	667	Dawson, Levi	Tennessee	2125	3338	6 Dec 1797	1377	11 Nov 1784	97	55	On S side of Cumberland River	
Blount, John Gray & Thomas	084		not given	5000			1660	16 Apr 1784				
Blount, John Gray & Thomas	090		not given	5000			854	29 Oct 1783				
Blount, John Gray & Thomas	168		Western District	1000	168	10 Jul 1788	2305	25 May 1784	67	362	Lying on waters of Obion River	
Blount, John Gray & Thomas	169		Western District	1000	169	10 Jul 1788	2482	25 May 01784	67	362	Lying on S fork of Obion River	
Blount, John Gray & Thomas	170		West District	1000	170	10 Jul 1788	2492	25 May 1784	67	363	On waters of Obion River &c	
Blount, John Gray & Thomas	171		Western District	1000	171	10 Jul 1788	2304	25 May 1784	67	363	On waters of Reelfoot River	
Blount, John Gray & Thomas	172		Western District	1000	472	10 Jul 1788	1152	31 Oct 1783	67	364	On waters of Rutherford Fk of Obion Riv	
Blount, John Gray & Thomas	173		Western District	1000	173	10 Jul 1788	2429	25 May 1784	67	364	On S Fork of Obion River	
Blount, John Gray & Thomas	174		Western District	1000	174	10 Jul 1788	2383	25 May 1784	67	364	On S side of Obion River	
Blount, John Gray & Thomas	175		Western District	1000	175	10 Jul 1788	2452	25 May 1784	67	365	On waters of Obion River	
Blount, John Gray & Thomas	176		Western District	1000	176	10 Jul 1788	2476	25 May 1784	67	365	On S Fork of Obion River	
Blount, John Gray & Thomas	177		Western District	1000	177	10 Jul 1788	2460	25 May 1784	67	366	On both sides of Looshatcher River	
Blount, John Gray & Thomas	178		Western District	1000	178	10 Jul 1788	2456	25 May 1784	67	366	On both sides of Looshatcher River &c	
Blount, John Gray & Thomas	179		Western District	1000	179	10 Jul 1788	2449	25 May 1784	67	366	On S side of Looshatcher River &c	
Blount, John Gray & Thomas	180		Western District	1000	180	10 Jul 1788	2314	25 May 1784	67	367	On waters of Reelfoot River	
Blount, John Gray & Thomas	181		Western District	1000	181	10 Jul 1788	2464	25 May 1784	67	367	On S side Looshatcher &c	
Blount, John Gray & Thomas	182		Western District	1000	182	10 Jul 1788	2483	25 May 1784	67	368	On head of S Fork of Indian Creek &c	
Blount, John Gray & Thomas	183		Eastern District	1000	160	27 Jun 1793	2428		80	368	On N side of Holston River	
Blount, John Gray & Thomas	183		Western District	1000	183	10 Jul 1788	2434	25 May 1784	67	368	On S fork of Obion River &c	
Blount, John Gray & Thomas	184		Western District	1000	184	10 Jul 1788	2318	25 May 1784	67	369	On waters of Reelfoot River &c	
Blount, John Gray & Thomas	185		Western District	1000	185	10 Jul 1788	2494	25 May 1784	67	369	On S branch of Indian Creek &c	
Blount, John Gray & Thomas	186		Western District	1000	186	10 Jul 1788	2466	25 May 1784	67	370	On waters of Obion River	
Blount, John Gray & Thomas	187		Western District	1000	187	10 Jul 1788	2400	25 May 1784	67	370	On S Fork of Obion River	
Blount, John Gray & Thomas	188		Western District	1000	188	10 Jul 1788	2311	25 May 1784	67	370	On Grave Creek	
Blount, John Gray & Thomas	189		Western District	1000	189	10 Jul 1788	2448	25 May 1784	67	371	On W side of N Fork of Obion River	
Blount, John Gray & Thomas	190		Western District	1000	190	10 Jul 1788	2480	25 May 1784	67	371	On both sides of Looshatcher River &c	
Blount, John Gray & Thomas	191		Western District	1000	191	10 Jul 1788	2398	25 May 1784	67	372	On S side of Obion River &c	
Blount, John Gray & Thomas	192		Western District	1000	192	10 Jul 1788	2488	25 May 1784	67	372	On S Fork of Indian Creek	
Blount, John Gray & Thomas	193		Western District	1000	193	10 Jul 1788	2427	24 May 1784	67	373	On S side of Obion River &c	
Blount, John Gray & Thomas	194		Western District	1000	194	10 Jul 1788	2394	25 May 1784	67	373	On S fork of Obion River &c	
Blount, John Gray & Thomas	195		Western District	1000	195	10 Jul 1788	2484	25 May 1784	67	394	On both sides of Looshatcher River &c	
Blount, John Gray & Thomas	196		Western District	1000	196	10 Jul 1788	2385	25 May 1784	67	374	On both sides of Obion River &c	

Claimant:	File #:	Assignee:	County:	Acres:	Grant:	Grant Date:	Entry:	Entry Date:	Bk:	Pg:	Location by Stream Name:	Military:
Blount, John Gray & Thomas	197		Western District	1000	197	10 Jul 1788	2491	25 May 1784	67	375	On a creek running into Indian Creek	
Blount, John Gray & Thomas	1976	Meeks, Robt.	Davidson	274	1878	20 May 1793	524		81	96	On Harpeth River	yes
Blount, John Gray & Thomas	198		Western District	1000	198	10 Jul 1788	2376	25 May 1784	67	375	On S Fork of Obion River &c	
Blount, John Gray & Thomas	1980	Carpenter, William	Davidson	185	1885	20 May 1793	3264		81	97	N/S of Big Harpety River beg a beach & el	yes
Blount, John Gray & Thomas	199		Western District	1000	199	10 Jul 1788	2450	25 May 1784	67	375	On S side of Looshatcher River	
Blount, John Gray & Thomas	1996		Davidson	640	1933	20 May 1793	946		81	108	On waters of Leapers Creek	yes
Blount, John Gray & Thomas	1998	Parish, Henry	Davidson	274	1937	20 May 1793	1552		81	109	S W/S Big Harpeth & on W Fk Trunbuls Cr	yes
Blount, John Gray & Thomas	200		Western District	1000	200	10 Jul 1788	2457	25 May 1784	67	376	On S side of Looshatcher River	
Blount, John Gray & Thomas	2001	Wills, James	Davidson	640	1942	20 May 1793	2823		81	110	On S W side of Big Harpeth	yes
Blount, John Gray & Thomas	2008	Adkins, Benjamin	Davidson	308	1953	20 May 1793	1489	21 Feb 1786	81	113	On both sides of Otter Creek	yes
Blount, John Gray & Thomas	201		Western District	1000	201	10 Jul 1788	2395	25 May 1784	67	376	On S fork of Obion River &c	
Blount, John Gray & Thomas	2013	Anderson, John	Davidson	640	1960	20 May 1793	2485	25 May 1785	81	114	On S W side of Harpeth on Jones Creek	yes
Blount, John Gray & Thomas	202		Western District	1000	2020	10 Jul 1788	1546	14 Jan 1786	67	377	On S Fork of Indian Creek &c	
Blount, John Gray & Thomas	2021	Crow, William	Davidson	640	1999	20 May 1793	2317	25 May 1784	81	124	On Big Harpeth River	yes
Blount, John Gray & Thomas	203		Western District	1000	203	10 Jul 1788	1544		67	377	On waters of Reelfoot &c	
Blount, John Gray & Thomas	2030	Broadstree, James	Davidson	640	1998	20 May 1793	2511		81	124	On West Fork of Stones River	yes
Blount, John Gray & Thomas	2031	Dill, George	Davidson	640	2043	20 May 1793	2516		81	135	On S side of Cumberland River	yes
Blount, John Gray & Thomas	2039		Davidson	640	2055	20 May 1793	2306		81	138	On S side of Big Harpeth	yes
Blount, John Gray & Thomas	204		Western District	1000	204	10 Jul 1788	2447	25 May 1784	67	378	On waters of Reelfoot River	
Blount, John Gray & Thomas	205		Western District	1000	205	10 Jul 1788	1303	25 May 1784	67	378	On N side of Obion River &c	
Blount, John Gray & Thomas	2058	Collins, Joseph	Davidson	274	2160	20 May 1793	2489		81	163	On S W side of Big Harpeth	yes
Blount, John Gray & Thomas	206		Western District	1000	206	10 Jul 1788	2515	25 May 1784	67	379	On S Fork of Indian Creek	
Blount, John Gray & Thomas	2066	Guist, Thomas	Davidson	640	2204	20 May 1793	2493		81	169	On S side of Harpeth River	yes
Blount, John Gray & Thomas	207		Western District	1000	207	10 Jul 1788	2430	25 May 1784	67	379	On waters of Indian Creek	
Blount, John Gray & Thomas	208		Western District	1000	208	10 Jul 1788	2475	25 May 1784	67	381	On both sides of cr running into Indian Cr	
Blount, John Gray & Thomas	209		Western District	1000	209	10 Jul 1788	2307	25 May 1784	67	380	On S fork of Obion River &c	
Blount, John Gray & Thomas	210		Western District	1000	210	10 Jul 1788		25 May 1784	67	381	On waters of Reelfoot River	
Blount, John Gray & Thomas	2103	Byrd, Moses	Davidson	274	2332	20 May 1793	1302		81	198	On S side of Harpeth River	yes
Blount, John Gray & Thomas	2104	Rogers, Elisha	Davidson	640	2333	20 May 1793			81	198	On Harpeth River	yes
Blount, John Gray & Thomas	2106	Darden, John	Davidson	640	2337	20 May 1793	1545		81	199	On Big Harpeth River	yes
Blount, John Gray & Thomas	2107	Gardner, Geo. Hrs.	Davidson	640	2344	20 May 1793			81	201	On S W side of Big Harpeth	yes
Blount, John Gray & Thomas	211		Western District	1000	211	10 Jul 1788	2472	25 May 1784	67	382	S side of S Fork of Obion River	
Blount, John Gray & Thomas	2113	Bailey, Lewis	Davidson	226	2371	20 May 1793	1133		81	206	On W side of Harpeth River	yes
Blount, John Gray & Thomas	214		Western District	1000	214	10 Jul 1788	2310	25 May 1784	67	382	On Grove Creek &c	
Blount, John Gray & Thomas	215		Western District	1000	215	10 Jul 1788	2505	25 May 1784	67	383	On waters of Reelfoot River	
Blount, John Gray & Thomas	216		Western District	1000	216	10 Jul 1788	2390	25 May 1784	67	383	On both sides of S Fork of Obion River	
Blount, John Gray & Thomas	217		Western District	1000	217	10 Jul 1788	2478	25 May 1784	67	384	On the Obion River &c	
Blount, John Gray & Thomas	218		Western District	1000	218	10 Jul 1788	2399	25 May 1784	67	384	On both sides of Spring Creek	
Blount, John Gray & Thomas	219		Western District	1000	219	10 Jul 1788	2487	25 May 1784	67	385	On Looshatcher near head of sd River	
Blount, John Gray & Thomas	220		Western District	1000	220	10 Jul 1788	2396	25 May 1784	67	385	On S fork of Obion River	
Blount, John Gray & Thomas	221		Western District	1000	221	10 Jul 1788	2313	25 May 1784	67	386	On waters of Reelfoot River &c	
Blount, John Gray & Thomas	222		Western District	3000	222	10 Jul 1788	1150	31 Oct 1783	67	386	on waters of — &c [sic]	
Blount, John Gray & Thomas	223		Sumner	1000	223	10 Jul 1788	2453	25 May 1784	67	386	S fork of Obion River	
Blount, John Gray & Thomas	224		Western District	1000	224	10 Jul 1788	2451	25 May 1784	67	387	On both sides of Looshatcher River	
Blount, John Gray & Thomas	225		Western District	1000	225	10 Jul 1788	2467	25 May 1784	67	387	On both sides of Looshatcher River	

Earliest Tennessee Land Records

Claimant	File #	Assignee	County	Acres	Grant	Grant Date	Entry	Entry Date	Bk	Pg	Location by Stream Name	Military
Blount, John Gray & Thomas	226		Western District	1000	226	10 Jul 1788	2319	25 May 1784	67	388	On waters of Indian Creek	
Blount, John Gray & Thomas	227		Western District	2000	227	10 Jul 1788	1153	31 Oct 1783	67	388	On the Obion River &c	
Blount, John Gray & Thomas	228		Western District	1000	228	10 Jul 1788	2479	25 May 1784	67	389	On waters of Reelfoot River &c	
Blount, John Gray & Thomas	229		Western District	1000	229	10 Jul 1788	2303	25 May 1784	67	389	On waters of Reelfoot River &c	
Blount, John Gray & Thomas	230		Western District	1000	230	10 Jul 1788	2459	24 May 1784	67	390	On the Lick Fork of Obion River	
Blount, John Gray & Thomas	231		Western District	1000	231	10 Jul 1778	2449	25 May 1784	67	390	On both sides of Lick Fork of Obion River	
Blount, John Gray & Thomas	232		Western District	5000	232	10 Jul 1788	1145	31 Oct 1783	67	391	On both sides of Obion River &c	
Blount, John Gray & Thomas	233		Western District	1000	233	10 Jul 1788	2377	25 May 1784	67	391	On S fork of Obion River	
Blount, John Gray & Thomas	234		Western District	3000	234	10 Jul 1788	1157	31 Oct 1783	67	392	On Rutherfords Fork of Obion River	
Blount, John Gray & Thomas	235		Western District	1000	235	10 Jul 1788	2318	25 May 1784	67	392	On heads of Grove Creek & Spring Creek	
Blount, John Gray & Thomas	236		Western District	1000	236	10 Jul 1788	2397	25 May 1784	67	393	On S side of Obion River &c	
Blount, John Gray & Thomas	237		Western District	2000	237	10 Jul 1788	1160	31 Oct 1783	67	393	Waters of Rutherfords Fork of Obion Riv	
Blount, John Gray & Thomas	238		Western District	1000	238	10 Jul 1788	2378	25 May 1784	67	394	On S Fork of Obion River	
Blount, John Gray & Thomas	239		Western District	1000	239	10 Jul 1788	2490	25 May 1784	67	394	On head of Looshatcher River	
Blount, John Gray & Thomas	240		Western District	1000	240	10 Jul 1788	2473	25 May 1784	67	395	On S side of Obion River	
Blount, John Gray & Thomas	241		Western District	1000	241	10 Jul 1788	2379	25 May 1784	67	395	On S Fork of Obion River	
Blount, John Gray & Thomas	242		Western District	1000	242	10 Jul 1788	2463	25 May 1784	67	395	On S side of Looshatcher River	
Blount, John Gray & Thomas	243		Western District	1000	243	10 Jul 1788	2320	25 May 1784	67	396	On waters of ReelfoodRiver	
Blount, John Gray & Thomas	243		Middle District	2000	216	27 Jun 1793	1678	20 Dec 1789	80	360	On both sides of South Fork of Duck River	
Blount, John Gray & Thomas	244		Western District	1000	244	10 Jul 1788	2445	25 May 1784	67	396	On waters of Obion River	
Blount, John Gray & Thomas	244		Middle District	5000	217	27 Jun 1793	1668		80	360	On both sides of Middle Fork of Duck River	
Blount, John Gray & Thomas	245		Western District	1000	245	10 Jul 1788	2440	25 May 1784	67	397	On S side of Looshatcher River &c	
Blount, John Gray & Thomas	245		Middle District	5000	218	27 Jun 1793	1147		80	360	On both sides of South Fork of Duck River	
Blount, John Gray & Thomas	246		Middle District	2000	246	10 Jul 1788	1665	31 Oct 1783	67	397	On both sides War Trace Fork of Duck Riv	
Blount, John Gray & Thomas	246		Middle District	5000	219	27 Jun 1793	1151		80	361	On waters of N Fork of Forked Deer River	
Blount, John Gray & Thomas	247		Western District	1000	247	10 Jul 1788	1661	31 Oct 1783	67	398	On both sides of Obion River &c	
Blount, John Gray & Thomas	247		Middle District	5000	220	27 Jun 1793	2438		80	361	On both sides of Middle Fork of Duck River	
Blount, John Gray & Thomas	248		Western District	1000	248	10 Jul 1788	1670	25 May 1784	67	398	On a S branch of Indian Creek	
Blount, John Gray & Thomas	248		Middle District	5000	221	27 Jun 1793	2380		80	362	on both sides of Middle fork of Duck River &c	
Blount, John Gray & Thomas	249		Western District	1000	249	10 Jul 1788	1677	25 May 1784	67	398	On N side of S Fork of Obion River	
Blount, John Gray & Thomas	249		Middle District	5000	222	27 Jun 1793	2465		80	362	On both sides of the War Trace &c	
Blount, John Gray & Thomas	250		Western District	1000	250	10 Jul 1788	1667	25 May 1784	67	399	On waters of Obion River	
Blount, John Gray & Thomas	250		Middle District	5000	223	27 Jun 1793	2309		80	362	On both sides of South Fork of Duck River	
Blount, John Gray & Thomas	251		Western District	1000	251	10 Jul 1788	1671	25 May 1784	67	399	On waters of Obion River	
Blount, John Gray & Thomas	251		Middle District	5000	224	27 Jun 1793	1155		80	363	On both sides of Middle Fork of Duck River &c	
Blount, John Gray & Thomas	252		Western District	1000	252	10 Jul 1788	1660	31 Oct 1783	67	400	On waters of Rutherfords Fk of Obion Riv	
Blount, John Gray & Thomas	252		Middle District	5000	225	27 Jun 1793	2495		80	363	On both sides of Duck River	
Blount, John Gray & Thomas	253		Western District	1000	253	10 Jul 1788	1662	25 May 1784	67	400	On waters of Indian Creek	
Blount, John Gray & Thomas	253		Middle District	2000	226	27 Jun 1793	1158		80	364	On head branches of Overalls Fork	
Blount, John Gray & Thomas	254		Western District	1000	254	10 Jul 1788	1140	31 Oct 1783	67	401	On waters of Rutherfords Fork &c	
Blount, John Gray & Thomas	255		Western District	3000	255	10 Jul 1788	1154	31 Oct 1783	67	401	On the waters of ----- &c [sic]	
Blount, John Gray & Thomas	256		Western District	1000	256	10 Jul 1788	1672	31 Oct 1783	67	402	On waters of Rutherfords Fork &c	
Blount, John Gray & Thomas	256		Middle District	5000	228	27 Jun 1793	2431	25 May 1784	80	264	On the main W Fork of Stones River	
Blount, John Gray & Thomas	257		Western District	1000	257	10 Jul 1788	1659		67	402	On S Fork of Obion River	
Blount, John Gray & Thomas	257		Middle District	5000	229	27 Jun 1793			80	365	On both sides of South Fork of Duck River &c	

Claimant:	File #:	Assignee:	County:	Acres:	Grant:	Grant Date:	Entry:	Entry Date:	Bk:	Pg:	Location by Stream Name:	Military:
Blount, John Gray & Thomas	257		Middle District	5000	227	27 Jun 1793	1664	27 Jun 1793	80	364	On both sides of Main Fork of Stones Riv	
Blount, John Gray & Thomas	258		Western District	1000	258	10 Jul 1788	2323	25 May 1784	67	403	On Lick Fork of Obion River	
Blount, John Gray & Thomas	258		Middle District	5000	230	27 Jun 1793	1658		80	365	On both sides of S Fork of Duck River	
Blount, John Gray & Thomas	259		Western District	1000	259	10 Jul 1788	2302 [?]	25 May 1784	67	403	On waters of Reelfoot River	
Blount, John Gray & Thomas	259		Middle District	5000	231	27 Jun 1793	1675		80	365	On both sides of South Fork of Duck River	
Blount, John Gray & Thomas	260		Western District	1000	260	10 Jul 1788	2392	25 May 1784	67	403	On S fork of Obion River &c	
Blount, John Gray & Thomas	260		Middle District	5000	232	27 Jun 1793	1669		80	366	On both sides of Middle Fork of Duck Riv	
Blount, John Gray & Thomas	261		Western District	1000	261	10 Jul 1788	1761	31 Oct 1783	67	404		
Blount, John Gray & Thomas	261		Middle District	5000	233	27 Jun 1793	1656		80	366	On both sides of South Fork of Duck River	
Blount, John Gray & Thomas	262		Western District	1000	262	10 Jul 1788	2470	25 May 1784	67	404	On N waters of Obion River &c	
Blount, John Gray & Thomas	262		Middle District	5000	234	27 Jun 1793	1676		80	367	On both sides of the War Trace &c	
Blount, John Gray & Thomas	263		Western District	1000	263	10 Jul 1788	2308	25 May 1784	67	405	On waters of Obion River	
Blount, John Gray & Thomas	263		Middle District	5000	235	27 Jun 1793	1657		80	367	On both sides of Main Fork of Duck River	
Blount, John Gray & Thomas	264		Western District	1000	264	10 Jul 1788	2384	25 May 1784	67	405	On waters of Obion River	
Blount, John Gray & Thomas	266		Western District	1000	266	10 Jul 1788	2515	25 May 1784	67	406	On Grove Creek	
Blount, John Gray & Thomas	267		Western District	1000	267	10 Jul 1788	1156	31 Oct 1783	67	407	On Rutherfords Fork of Obion River	
Blount, John Gray & Thomas	268		Western District	2000	268	10 Jul 1788	1159	31 Oct 1783	67	407	On waters of N Fork of Forked Deed River	
Blount, John Gray & Thomas	276	Dupont, Joseph	Tennessee	640	1856	20 May 1793	2507	30 Sep 1785	81	91	On Johnson Creek	
Blount, John Gray & Thomas	32	Lanier, James	Davidson	2560	18	14 Mar 1786	475	14 Mar 1786	63	8	On waters of Harpeth River	yes
Blount, John Gray & Thomas	322	Andrews, John	Tennessee	640	2054	20 May 1793	1742	22 Apr 1485	81	138	On S side of Cumberland River	
Blount, John Gray & Thomas	327		Western District	1000	327	18 May 1789	2393	25 May 1784	72	272	N side of North Fork of Obrian [sic] River	
Blount, John Gray & Thomas	328		Western District	1000	328	18 May 1789	2468	25 May 1784	72	273	On N side of N Fork of Obion River	
Blount, John Gray & thomas	33	Capps, William	Davidson	640	19	14 Mar 1786	476	14 Mar 1786	63	8	E side of Tennessee River	yes
Blount, John Gray & thomas	377	Dosher, Chris	Tennessee	640	2329	20 May 1793	2508	30 Sep 1785	81	197	On S side of Cumberland River	
Blount, John Gray & Thomas	378	Lewis, Wm.	Tennessee	640	2330	20 May 1793	3136	14 Dec 1785	81	197	On S side of Cumberland River	
Blount, John Gray & Thomas	378		Western District	5000	342	17 Nov 1790	976	29 Oct 1783	76	167	S side Big Hatcher River	
Blount, John Gray & Thomas	379	Biggs, Silas	Tennessee	640	2331	20 May 1793	2792	20 Sep 1785	81	198	On S/S of Cumberland Riv E/S Bartons Cr	
Blount, John Gray & Thomas	381	Dupont, Jesse	Tennessee	640	2338	20 May 1793	2503	30 Sep 1785	81	199	On S side of Cumberland River	
Blount, John Gray & Thomas	618	Parish, Nicholas	Sumner	274	1883	20 May 1793	1550	4 Jun 1792	81	97	On Jonas Creek waters of Harpeth	yes
Blount, John Gray & Thomas	646		Hawkins	95,000	517	26 Apr 1794	849-85	1783-1784	81	553	On S E side of Clinch River	
Blount, John Gray & Thomas			Western District	1000	211	10 Jul 1788	2471	25 May 1784	67	381	On S side of Reelfoot River &c	
Blount, John Gray, Ass.	06		Tennessee	640			2824	30 Sep 1785			S side of Spring Creek	
Blount, Reading	028	Hardy, John hrs	Middle District	640			2043					
Blount, Reading	029	Coons, Thos. Hrs.	Middle District	640			2115					
Blount, Reading	030	Hannock, Samuel hrs	Middle District	640			2654					
Blount, Reading	032	Wallace, Brown hrs.	Middle District	640			2553					
Blount, Reading	033	Peraythe, Jos hrs.	Middle District	640			2150					
Blount, Reading	1520	Willis, Jacob	Davidson	640	1077	26 No 1789	2556		74	118	On S waters of Persons Creek	yes
Blount, Reading	2221	Williams, James	Davidson	274	2523	8 Dec 1795	1629		88	278	On S W side of Bigg Harpeth River	yes
Blount, Reading	28		Davidson	4800	14	1 (?) Mar 1786	261 (264)		63	7	On waters of Stones River	yes
Blount, Reading	431	Rymore, Nathan hr. Dan	Davison	640	403	15 Sep 1787			63	150	On S branches of Sycamore Creek	yes
Blount, Reading	432	Oglesby, Timothy	Davidson	640	404	15 Sep 1787			63	150	N side of Cumberland River	yes
Blount, Reading	433	Harrison, Dan hr Henry	Davidson	640	405	15 Sep 1787			63	150	S branches of Sycamore Creek	yes
Blount, Reading	434	Rever, James	Davidson	640	406	15 Sep 1787	2152		63	151	North branches of Marrowbone Creek	yes
Blount, Reading	435	Smith, Absolom	Davidson	640	407	15 Sep 1787	2545		63	151	On S branches of Sycamore Creek	yes

Claimant:	File #:	Assignee:	County:	Acres:	Grant:	Grant Date:	Entry:	Entry Date:	Bk:	Pg:	Location by Stream Name:	Military:
Blount, Reading	436	Tallafarrow,Jas hr Ric	Davidson	640	408	15 Sep 1787			63	151	On ridge bet. Sycamore & Marrowbone	yes
Blount, Reading	437	Shaffer, Geo hr Henry	Davidson	640	409	15 Sep 1787			63	152	N side of Cumberland River	yes
Blount, Reading	439	Welch,Geo.hr of Wm.	Davidson	640	410	15 Sep 1787			63	152	South branches of Sycamore Creek	yes
Blount, Reading	439	Wood,Geo.hr of Solomon	Davidson	640	411	15 Sep 1787	2555		63	152	Lower Road leads ft Nashville to Red Riv	yes
Blount, Reading	707	Miller, James heirs	Davidson	640	680	8 Dec 1787	2146		63	240	Head waters of Long Fork Sycamore Cr	yes
Blount, Reading	708 (707)	Strand,Lewis hr Jno.	Davidson	640	681	8 Dec 1787			63	240	On Sycamore Creek	yes
Blount, Reading	711	Williams, John	Sumner	274	2092	20 May 1793	1634	22 Aug 1785	81	147	On N side of Cumberland River	yes
Blount, Reading	827	Simons, Peter	Sumner	640	2306	20 May 1793	1637	22 Aug 1785	81	192	On both sides of Wartrace Creek	yes
Blount, Reading	898	Murdock, Nathaniel	Davidson	640	914	18 May 1789			63	316	On N branch of E Fork of Stone River	yes
Blount, Reading	899	Thompson, George	Davidson	640	915	18 May 1789	2551		63	316	On N side of Cumberland River	yes
Blount, Reading	900	Wolf, Abra	Davidson	640	916	18 May 1789	2045		63	316	On head branches of E Fork of Stones Riv	
Blount, Reading	931	Basamore(?), Robt.	Sumner	640	2455	22 Feb 1795	2558	30 Sep 1789	83	419	On the main fork of Obeys River	yes
Blount, Reading	936	Richards, Clement	Davidson	640	952	18 May 1789	2154		63	325	On waters of Caney Fork	yes
Blount, Reading	937	Bagwell, Jesse	Davidson	640	953	18 May 1789	3559		63	325	On the first creek???	yes
Blount, Reading	937	Church, Christo. Hrs.	Sumner	640	2461	22 Feb 1795	3256	23 Dec 1785	83	422	On the main fork of Obeys River &c	yes
Blount, Reading	938	Burden, Tim, hr of Jacob	Davidson	640	954	18 May 1789	2560		63	325	On waters of Caney Fork	yes
Blount, Reading	939	Willoughby, Nathan	Davidson	640	955	18 May 1789	2039		63	325	On E waters of Halfpone Creek	yes
Blount, Reading	940	Thurst, Edward	Davidson	640	956	18 May 1789	2552		63	326	On E Fork of Stones River	yes
Blount, Reading	945	Wallace, Bunn	Sumner	640	2469	22 Feb 1795			83	426	On main fork of Obeys River &c	yes
Blount, Reading	955	Whimer, Carter hrs	Sumner	640	2418	22 Feb 1795	2554	30 Sep 1785	84	305	On main fork of Obeys River	yes
Blount, Reading	967	Hardy, John hrs.	Sumner	640	2430	22 Feb 1795			84	311	On main fork of Obeys River	yes
Blount, Reading	968	Bowler, James hrs.	Sumner	640	2431	22 Feb 1795	2113	9 Sep 1785	84	312	On main fork of Obion River	yes
Blount, Reading	971	Peasy, Joseph	Sumner	640	2435	22 Feb 1795			84	314	On main fork of Obeys River	yes
Blount, Reading	976	Basmore(?),Michl hrs	Sumner [?]	640	2440	22 Feb 1795	2557	30 Sep 1785	84	316	On main fork of Obeys River	yes
Blount, Reading	979	Tripp, John hrs	Sumner	640	2444	22 Feb 1795	2550	30 Sep 1785	84	318	On main fork of Obeys River	yes
Blount, Reading	982	Himnock, Saml. Hrs.	Sumner	640	2447	22 Feb 1795			84	320	On main fork of Obeys River	yes
Blount, Reading	987	Siver, Jos. Hrs.	Sumner	640	2452	22 Feb 1795	2546	30 Sep 1792	84	322	On main fork of Obeys River	yes
Blount, Reading, Ass.	974		Sumner	640	2438	22 Feb 1795			84	315	On main fork of Obeys River	yes
Blount, Thomas	1978		Davidson	274	1880	20 May 1793	619	21 Mar 1792	81	96	S side of Big Harpeth on Turnbulls Creek	yes
Blount, Thomas	655	Lytle, William	Sumner	853	1966	20 May 1793	274	26 Nov 1784	81	116	On S side of Cumberland River	yes
Blount, Thos.	05	Warwick, Shadrack	Tennessee	640			1474	26 Nov 1784			Right hd fk 1st large cr empties in TN Riv	
Blount, Thos.	010	Ellison, Peter	Tennessee	640			1354	6 Nov 1784			Right hd fk 1st large cr empties in TN Riv	
Blount, Thos.	1950	Howard, Benjamin	Davidson	274	1789	20 <au 1793	1553		81	76	On Poplar Cr a small branch of S Harpeth	yes
Blount, William	29	Rolston, Isaac	Davidson	1240	15	14 Mar 1786	977		63	7	North side of Tenesee River	yes
Blount, William	291	Hooks, Ephraim	Sumner	228	1299	10 Dec 1790	1307	30 Apr 1785	74	365	Beg at a sugar tree	yes
Blount, William	31	Ralston, Robert	Davidson	1097	17	14 Mar 1786	1004		63	8	On waters of Harpeth River	yes
Blount, William	479		Green	5000	481	20 Sep 1787	427	23 Oct 1783	65	512	William Emeris Riv on N side of Clinch Riv	
Blount, Wm. & Jas. White	136		Eastern District	210	102	6 Sep 1791	64		77	222	On N side of Holston River on Second Cr	
Blythe, James	185		Sullivan	275	192	10 Oct 1783	1807	6 Oct 1779	53	155	On Fall Creek	
Blythe, James	186		Sullivan	264	193	10 Oct 1783	672	19 Jul 1781	53	155	On Fall Creek	
Blythe, James	682		Washington	198	496	10 Nov 1784	526	23 Oct 1778	69	103	On a branch of Kendricks Creek	
Blythe, James	778		Washington	100	592	10 Nov 1784	2692	19 Nov 1780	69	136	On the rich valley &c	yes
Blythe, James	837		Washington	100	651	10 Nov 1784	287	1 Aug 1778	69	152	On head of Kendricks Creek	yes
Blythe, Joseph	84		Davidson	4800	70	14 Mar 1786	196		63	28	On head branches of W Harpeth River	yes
Boaz, Edmund	477		Green	60	479	20 Sep 1787	1300	1 Jan 1784	65	511	On West Fork of Dodson's Creek &c	

Earliest Tennessee Land Records

Claimant:	File #:	Assignee:	County:	Acres:	Grant:	Grant Date:	Entry:	Entry Date:	Bk:	Pg:	Location by Stream Name:	Military:
Boddie, Elijah	371		Middle District	2500	310	17 Dec 1794	1923	16 Apr 1784	84	211	On main fork of Elk River	
Boddy, James	139		Green	400	121	6 Nov 1786	170	22 Oct 1783	60	453	On Bent Creek	
Bodie, Elijah	410		Middle District	2500	349	17 Dec 1794	1924	26 Apr 1784	84	228	On main fork of Elk River	
Bodsby, Joel	012		Tennessee	1000			2597	30 Sep 1785			On a draft of Spring Creek	yes
Boeder, Michael	510		Green	250	512	20 Sep 17	859	12 Dec 1778	62	526	On the S side of Nolachuckey River	
Bogart, Henry	1167		Washington	100	1125	7 Jul 1794	635	25 Nov 1778	81	618	On Wautauga River	
Bogart, Samuel	1146		Washington	128	1104	12 Jul 1794	2504	10 Apr1780	81	570	Joining lands of Francis McFalls &c	
Boggess, Bennet, Ass	1583		Green	50	130	4 Feb 1795			83	402	On Lick Creek	
Boggs, Ezekial	723		Sumner	274	2107	20 May 1793	1208	31 Jul 1792	81	151	Beg at a poplar & white oak	yes
Boggs, John	594		Sumner	274	1836	20 May 1793	1007	20 Aug 1785	81	87	on Bledsoes Creek beg at an elm	yes
Bogle, Joseph	232		Green	236	189	20 Sep 1787	186	7 Jun 1784	65	427	Little Chuckey at mouth of Delaneys Cr	
Bohannan, William	32		Hawkins	500	64	7 Apr 1790	426	19 Apr 1780	71	286	On waters of Flatt Creek	
Boliston, William	1188		Green	200	1031	26 Dec 1791	363	23 Oct 1783	77	293	On N side of French Broad River	
Bolic, John	484	McCoy, Andn.	Tennessee	480	193	20 Jul 1796	12	14 Apr 1792	88	473	W of Cumberland Mountain	yes
Bolice, John	079		not given	480							no plat	
Boling, Andrew, heirs of	1868		Davidson	640	1605	27 Apr 1793	286		81	19	On S side of Richland Creek	yes
Bolton, Thomas	2443	Tatum & Wiggins	Davidson	640	3285	6 Dec 1797	4160		98	164	On waters of Overalls Cr of Stones River	yes
Boman, Esaiah [?]	899		Green	400	830	Sep 1790	860	29 Oct 1783	74	293	On N side of Tennessee River	yes
Bond, Avery	985		Green	400	1212	29 Jul 1793	1409		76	469	Both sides of Little Chuckie	
Bond, Charles	054	Dillenberry, Redmon	Sumner	640			4459	14 Oct 1797			Head waters Middle Fork of Drakes Creek	yes
Bond, Elisha	154	Ross, James	Davidson	224	140	14 Mar 1786	28	54	63	54	On Sinking Creek	yes
Bond, George	16		Sullivan	412	27	23 Oct 1782	336	24 Mar 1780	43	250	In Carters Valley	
Bond, James	312	Ewing, Alexander	Sumner	224	1525	10 Apr 1792	1628	27 Jun 1788	75	509	On Smiths Fork a branch of Cain River	yes
Bond, James	885	Ford, John	Davidson	640	899	17 Jan 1789	927		63	311	On N side of Cumberland River	yes
Bond, John	1015		Washington	50	964	14 Jan 1793	1681	20 Nov 1792	79	275	Beg at 2 white oaks	
Bond, John	1018		Washington	150	967	14 Jan 1793	852	20 Nov 1792	79	275	Beg at a double white oak	
Bond, John	120	Nucum, Aron hrs	Davidson	640	1622	23 Feb 1793	1835	14 Jun 1785	76	323	Abt 5 miles from mouth of Red River	yes
Bond, John	1866	Harris, Richard	Davidson	640	1601	27 Apr 1793	1592		81	18	On head of S branches of Stones Creek	yes
Bond, John	1870	Sherwood, Edward	Davidson	640	1608	27 Apr 1793	1681		81	19	On head branches of Stones Creek	yes
Bond, John	1881	Baker, Amos hrs	Davidson	640	1627	27 Apr 1793	1681		81	24	On head branches of Stones Creek	yes
Bond, John	750	Sykes, Samson	Sumner	640	2153	20 May 1793	945	3 Mar 1790	81	161	On waters of Round Lick Creek	yes
Bonds, William	2232	Robeson [sic], James	Davidson	640	2595	7 Mar 1796	1336		88	324	On S Harpeth	yes
Bonds, Wright	125	Abuck, John hrs.	Tennessee	640	327	23 Feb 1793	1580	22 Feb 1785	76	327	N side of Cumberland River	yes
Bonner, James	285	Ewell(?), Stephen	Sumner	523	1283	10 Dec 1790	1125	23 Mar 1789	74	360	On Peytons Creek	yes
Bonner, Jas	283	West, Levi	Sumner	428	1280	10 Dec 1790			74	359	On head waters of Goose Creek	yes
Bonner, John	759	Chapman, Samuel	Sumner	3292	2172	20 May 1793	880	13 Sep 1785	81	166	On S side of Cumberland River	yes
Bonner, John & James	015	Porter, Joshua	Sumner	640			1825	13 Sep 1785			N side of Cumberland River	yes
Bonner, John & James	036		Davidson	1600			387	8 Sep 1785			On head of W branches of Spring Creek	yes
Bonner, John & James	413	Porter, Wm.	Tennessee	640	2445	31 Dec 1793	1823	11 Jun 1785	81	425	On waters of Sycamore	
Bonner, John & James	522	Diggs, Anthony	Davidson	1097	494	15 Sep 1787	1124		63	179	N side of Cumberland River	yes
Bonner, John & James	606	Moye(?), George	Davidson	228	578	15 Sep 1787	380		63	207	S side of Cumberland River	yes
Bonner, John & James	629	Ekols, Wm.	Davidson	738	601	15 Sep 1787	1237		63	214	N side of Cumberland River	yes
Bonner, John & James	698	Harrison, Thos.	Sumner	274	2070	20 May 1793	382	22 Aug 1785	81	142	On S side of Cumberland River	yes
Bonner, John & James	734		Sumner	640	2121	20 May 1793	463	14 Apr 1792	81	154	On/near head one of E br of Roaring Riv	yes
Bonner, John & James	771	Bullock, Drury	Sumner	640	2219	20 May 1793	463	1 Dec 1792	81	173	On ridge bet poplar grove or & rush or	yes

Claimant:	File #:	Assignee:	County:	Acres:	Grant:	Grant Date:	Entry:	Entry Date:	Bk:	Pg:	Location by Stream Name:	Military:
Bonner, John & James, Ass.	35	Greer, Andrew	Sumner	640	2162	20 May 1793	1453	14 Apr 1792	81	163	Dividing ridge bet hd Big Barren & Cumb.	yes
Bonner, William	059	Robertson, James	Montgomery	1000	3244	20 Nov 1797	4769				W side of Harpeth	yes
Boon, David			Davidson	640			2632	3 Dec 1792			On Hollises Fork &c	yes
Boon, Elisha	337	Ross, William	Davidson	640	322	28 Ki; 1787			63	120	First large cr comes into Cumberland Riv	yes
Boon, Solomon	1125		Washington	100	1084	12 Jul 1794	2135	5 Nov 1779	81	563	Upon Little Doe River	
Boone, Aaron	374	Lancaster, John	Tennessee	640	2289	20 May 1793	1994	16 Aug 1785	81	189	On N side of Cumberland River	yes
Boone, Jacob heirs	925	Hughlett, William	Davidson	640	941	18 May 1789	2831		63	322	On the waters of Sulphur Fork	Yes
Boone, James	1498	Mountflorence, James C.	Davidson	640	1055	26 Nov 1789	1493	2 Sep 1779	74	104	On N side of Cumberland River	yes
Boran, James	04		Washington	225			1572	2 Sep 1779			On waters of S Fork of Cherokee Creek	
Boren, Bazel	037	Johnson, Thos.	Robertson	50				14 Jun 1796			Beg at a hickory	
Boren, Bazel	448	Grant, Squire	Tennessee	50	232	27 Feb 1796		7 Mar 1785	88	176	On Sulphur fork of Red River	
Boren, Bazel			Robertson	50	309						On Sulphur Fork of Red River	
Boren, Bazil	475	Armstrong, M.	Tennessee	50	209	20 Jul 1796		23 Apr 1789, Surv	88	443	On Sulphur Fork of Red River	
Boren, Stephen	488	Elliot, John	Tennessee	480	157	26 Mar 1795	157 [sic]	26 Mar 1795 [sic]	89	88	On the Wartrace Creek	
Boren, William	474	Armstrong, M.	Tennessee	100	308	20 Jul 1796			88	443	On Dry Branch Lick	
Boren, Wm.	30	Grant, Squire	Robertson	100	308			2 Mar 1786			On Dry Branch Lick	
Borin, John	380	Barnet, Sion	Tennessee	320	2334	20 May 1793	1173	26 Aug 1784	81	198	On Cranks Creek	
Borin, John	427	Armstrong, M.	Tennessee	50	157	9 Jan 1794		10 Sep 1794	81	441	On waters of Sulphur Fork &c	
Borough, Joel	056	John Rice &c	not given	1000			1668	20 Sep 1788			N side of Cumberland River	yes
Bosley, James	011		not given	103			749	31 Mar 1785			Near the Stone Lick	
Bosley, James	013		not given	21			846	17 Jun 1785			S side of Cumberland River	
Bosley, James	014		not given	34			845	18 Jun 1785			S side of Cumberland River	
Bosley, James	015		not given	107			850	15 Apr 1785			Joining etc on French Lick Branch	
Bosley, James	016		not given	139				12 May 1785			S side of Cumberland River	
Bosley, James	10	Armstrong, M.	Davidson	71	4	16 Feb 1786			63	2	S side of Cumberland River	
Bosley, James	11	Armstrong, M.	Davidson	107	5	16 Feb 1786			63	3	Joining John Cockerills & Peter Turneys	
Bosley, James	1214		Davidson	640	178	10 Jul 1788	14	26 Dec 1783	66	367	Wal & ash on Commrs line-- Dentons Lick	
Bosley, James	1229		Davidson	640	193	10 Jul 1788	43	31 Dec 1783	66	410	Beg at a small ash	
Bosley, James	1270		Davidson	640	235	10 Jul 1788	7	26 Dec 1783	66	420	Wh oak & bl oak George Freelands SW cor	
Bosley, James	13	Armstrong, M.	Davidson	139	7	16 Feb 1786			63	4	S side of Cumberland River	
Bosley, James	1320	Gower, Russell	Davidson	320	6	18 Aug 1787	8	26 Dec 1783	68	122	West boundary Jas Robertson preemption	
Bosley, James	14	Armstrong, M.	Davidson	34	8	16 Feb 1786			63	4	S side of Cumberland River	
Bosley, James	1746	Armstrong, M.	Davidson	75	112	20 Dec 1791			77	380	S side of Cumberland River	
Bosley, James	20 (70)	Rigsby, Frederick	Davidson	274	6	16 Feb 1786	751	29 Jan 1791	63	3	S side of Cumberland River	
Bosley, James	369	Armstrong, M.	Davidson	21	4	16 Feb 1786			63	2	S side of Cumberland River	
Bosley, James	370	Armstrong, M.	Davidson	107	5	16 Feb 1786			63	3	Jno Cockereille & Peter Turneys preempt	
Bosley, James	372	Armstrong, M.	Davidson	139	7	16 Feb 1786	63		63	4	S side of Cumberland River	
Bosley, James	373	Armstrong, M.	Davidson	34	8	16 Feb 1786			63	4	S side of Cumberland River	
Bosley, James	4		Davidson	640	2	20 Dec 1791			62	297	Including Dentons Lick Beg at a red oak	
Bosley, James Robert	1678	Cahoon, Joseph	Davidson	640	1603	23 Feb 1793	2413		76	314	On West Harpeth	yes
Bosmore, Michael	976	Blount, Reading	Sumner	640	2440	22 Feb 1795	2557	30 Sep 1785	84	316	On main fork of Obeys River	yes
Bosten, Andrew	2337	Malloy, Thomas	Davidson	228	2981	10 Apr 1797	1859		90	286	On Overalls Creek	yes
Bosten, Jacob	1524		Davidson	228	1081	26 Nov 1789	1858		74	121	On headwaters of Whites Creek	yes
Bostian, Andrew	1016		Davidson	228	1035or31	18 May 1792	1859		63	344	E waters of Main E Fork of Stones River	yes
Bostian, Jacob	1909	Hains, Phillip	Davidson	640	1671	20 May 1793	1714		81	46	First large cr comes into Cumberland Riv	yes

Earliest Tennessee Land Records

Claimant:	File #:	Assignee:	County:	Acres:	Grant:	Grant Date:	Entry:	Entry Date:	Bk:	Pg:	Location by Stream Name:	Military:
Bounds, Jesse	1040		Washington	200	990	14 Jan 1793	250	6 Oct 1792	79	282	Beg at a stake & stone	
Bounds, Jesse	1516		Green	640	1277	12 Jul 1794	205	22 Oct 1783	81	587	On Roaring Fork	
Bowden, Hampton	1539	Gilmour, Charles	Davidson	640	1096	26 Nov 1789	3418		74	129	On N side of Cumberland River	yes
Bowen, Henry	12		Hawkins	200	533	27 Jan 1793	985	29 Oct 1783	79	502	On Richland Creek	
Bowen, John	0104		Washington	200			1949	10 Oct 1779			In Carters Valley	
Bowen, John, heir of Moses	1382		Davidson	320	65	8 Oct 1787	326	2 Mar 1784	68	147	On Stewarts Cr a branch of Stones Cr	
Bowen, Stephen	198	Hicks, Daniel	Tennessee	428	1484	4 Jan 1792	239	25 Oct 1783	77	372	S side of Cumberland River &c	yes
Bowen, William	1132		Davidson	640	109	17 Apr 1786	627	20 Nov 1784	66	176	Thompsons Cr 2 hick Wt br of large cr	
Bowen, William	1376		Davidson	320	59	8 Oct 1787	325	2 Mar 1784	68	145	Stewarts Creek a branch of Stones cr	
Bowen, William	1818		Davidson	640	391	26 Jun 1793	570	12 Aug 1784	80	338	On S side of Cumberland River	
Bowen, Wm.	1438	Shane, Morris	Davidson	320	84	10 Jul 1788	196	28 Jan 1784	68	230	N/S Cumberland Riv at mouth of Kaspers Cr	
Bowers, Giles	111	Owens, Christopher	Davidson	640	97	14 Mar 1786	477		63	39	S side of Big Harpeth River	
Bowers, John	1289		Green	200	1139	12 Jan 1793			78	387	On a branch of Lick Creek	
Bowers, John	1408		Green	200	1220	27 Nov 1792	2561	15 May 1780	80	161	On a branch of Lick Creek	
Bowers, John	570		Davidson	228	542	15 Sep 1787	94		63	195	On waters of Sulphur Fork of Red River	yes
Bowers, Kesia	1151		Green	100	994	26 Dec 1791	1503	10 Aug 1779	77	279	On Wt side of Lick Creek	
Bowler, James	968	Blount, Reading	Sumner	640	2431	22 Feb 1795	2113	9 Sep 1785	84	312	On main fork of Obeys River	yes
Bowman, Charles	975	Brehon, James G.	Davidson	1000	992	18 May 1789	3331		63	334	On N side of Cumberland River	yes
Bowman, Jacob	1213		Green	100	1057	-- Nat 1792	2006	22 Oct 1779	77	403	N side of the Nolachuckey River	
Bowman, Jesse	2083	McCulloh, Benjamin	Davidson	640	2281	20 May 1793	2834		81	187	On waters of Lepers Lick Creek	yes
Bowman, John	1474		Green	200	1238	12 Jul 1781	2751	16 Jan 1781	81	574	On S side of Nolichuckey River	
Bowman, John	693	Shores, Jacob	Sumner	640	2056	20 May 1793	3602	4 Jun 1791	81	138	On S side of Cumberland River	yes
Bowman, Peter	1021		Washington	100	971	14 Jan 1793	2141	12 Oct 1792	79	276	Beg at 2 post oaks	
Bowman, Robert	1500	Mountflorence, James C.	Davidson	640	1057	26 Nov 1789	3035		74	106	On N side of Cumberland River	yes
Bowman, Robert	2121	Allen, Charles	Davidson	1695	2402	7 Jan 1793	84		81	392	On S side Cumberland River	yes
Bowman, Sparling	1272		Green	100	1122	12 Jan 1793	26	3 Jan 1784	78	378	Beg at two small white oaks	
Bowman, Sparling	1164		Green	300	1007	26 Dec 1791	2330	4 Dec 1779	77	284	S/SNolachuckey river on Camp Creek	
Bowman, William	14	Slade, Nathaniel	Sumner	640	771	11 Jul 1788	254	22 Jan 1789	63	270	On S side of N fork of Red River	yes
Bowman, William	16	Ackinclass, John	Sumner	640	2496	12 Mar 1787					On both sides of Cooks Branch	yes
Bowman, William	234	Callahan, John	Davidson	640	220	7 Mar 1786	877		63	81	On waters of Stones River	yes
Bowman, William	24	McDugald, Archibald	Sumner	640	781	11 Jul 1788	2530	1 Mar 1787	63	274	On both sides of Long Branch &c	yes
Bowman, William	25	Simms, Drury	Sumner	640	782	11 Jul 1788	2818	23 Mar 1787	63	274	On N side of N Fork of Red River	yes
Bowman, William	26	Donstan, James	Sumner	640	783	11 Jul 1788	2506		63	274	Bet the N & M fork of Red River	yes
Bowman, William	5	Vanderfield, Wm.	Sumner	640	762	11 Jul 1788	282	29 Dec 1786	63	267	On both sides of N Fork of Red River	yes
Bowman, William	6		Sumner	640	763	11 Jul 1788			63	268	On N side of N fork of Red River	yes
Bowman, William	761	Morrow, Samuel	Davidson	640	734	11 Jul 1788	2531		63	258	W & N/S land William Harrison lives on	yes
Bowmans, Cornelius	36		Washington	100	326	24 Oct 1782	869	31 Dec 1778	43	309	On N side of Wattauga River	
Box, Edward	611		Washington	60	705	26 Oct 1786	1135	25 Jan 1779	66	13	Beg at a marked white oak	
Box, Joseph	15		Green	200	1249	12 Jul 179-	98	20 Feb 1793			Buffaloe branch of Pidgeon Creek	
Box, Michael	615		Green	150	656	11 Jul 1788	1260	7 Jun 1784	66	445	S/S Nolichuckey Riv both sides Camp Cr	
Box, Robert	468		Washington	100	460	13 Oct 1783	724	21 Dec 1778	52	293	On camp Creek	
Box, Robt	17		Green	300	435	20 Sep 1788	332	23 Oct 1783			On Meadow Creek	
Boxley, John	1246	Donelson, Stockley	Sumner	640	2850	21 Jan 1797	1039	13 Aug 1796	90	49	Waters of Martins Creek	
Boxley, Joseph	294	Terrell, William	Eastern District	640	2399	1 Feb 1795			84	150	On S side of Clinch River	yes
Boy, Robert	436		Green	300	438	20 Sep 1787			65	498	On Meadow Creek &c	

Earliest Tennessee Land Records

Claimant:	File #:	Assignee:	County:	Acres:	Grant:	Grant Date:	Entry:	Entry Date:	Bk:	Pg:	Location by Stream Name:	Military:
Boyan, Richard	1143	Harris, Edward	Sumner	640	2649	4 Jun 1796	1400	1 Jun 1795	88	350	Joining Harris survey	yes
Boycars [?], Henry	359		Western District	5000	344	26 Dec 1791	1680	16 Apr 1784	75	182	On Reelfoot River	
Boyce, Jesse	027	Armstrong, John	Middle District	228			1561					yes
Boyce, Seth	1054	King, William	Sumner	640	2531	10 Dec 1795	1333	8 Aug 1795	88	289	On a creek called Lick Creek	yes
Boyd, Adam	169		Davidson	7200	155	14 Mar 1786	247		63	59	N side of Cumberland River	yes
Boyd, Adam	92		Western District	5000	92	10 Jul 1788	1226	6 Nov 1783	67	316	On S side of the Forked Deer River &c	
Boyd, Andrew	1047		Davidson	640	21	17 Apr 1786	704	9 Apr 1785	66	41	Lying on water of the Rocky Creek	
Boyd, Andrew	1249		Davidson	644	214	10 Jul 1788	236	5 Feb 1784	66	415	Head of Browns Cr beg at a red oak	
Boyd, Andrew	215	Wilson, George	Sumner	640	1120	26 Nov 1789	3387	18 Mar 1789	74	139	On S side of Cumberland River	yes
Boyd, Andrew	432		Sumner	640	443	27 Jun 1793	746	20 Jun 1785	80	355	On Deshas Fork of Bledsoes Creek	yes
Boyd, Andrew & Jno.Hacket	433		Middle District	2000	372	17 Dec 1794	1634	12 Apr 1784	84	239	On S side of Duck River	
Boyd, Andrew & Jno.Hacket	466		Middle District	3740	405	17 Dec 1794	1635	12 Apr 1784	84	264	On S side of Elk River	
Boyd, Francis	4	Johnson, William	Robertson	640	2933	19 Feb 1797	3072	25 Jul 1796			Beg at a hickory	yes
Boyd, James	783		Sullivan	84	715	2 Dec 1796	441,-117,-4	Apr & Feb 1780	91	273	Beg at a red oak _aller [?] Kings corner	
Boyd, John	1214	Chano(?), David	Sumner	228	2494	26 Sep 1795	1319	3 Jan 1786	89	104	On N side of Cumberland River	yes
Boyd, John	127	Melbom, David	Tennessee	274	1633	23 Feb 1793	518	20 Apr 1784	76	328	On Wells Creek	
Boyd, John	1405	Duroy, Timothy	Sumner	228	3336	6 Dec 1797	4738	3 May 1797	97	54	On waters of Cedar Creek	yes
Boyd, John	1855	Kirkpatrick, John	Davidson	476	1580	27 Apr 1793	1382		81	12	On waters of Harpeth	yes
Boyd, John	220	Ackenclass, Absalom	Sumner	274	1125	26 Nov 1789	3529	19 Apr 1788	74	141	On S side of Cumberland River	yes
Boyd, John	243	Andrews, Nathan	Sumner	274	1148	26 Nov 1789	3528	19 Apr 1788	74	153	On S side of Cumberland River	yes
Boyd, John	328	Baringer, John	Sumner	228	1614	23 Feb 1793	65	20 Dec 1785	76	319	W side of Drakes Creek	yes
Boyd, John	375	Gains, Geoffrey	Davidson	640	347	15 Sep 1787	737		63	131	On a branch of Spring Creek	
Boyd, John, Jr.	1378	Johnson, Arthur	Sumner	640	3240	24 Nov 1797	4093	14 Apr 1797	94	173	Waters of Smiths Fork	yes
Boyd, John, Jr.	1379	Hedspeth, Steph	Sumner	640	3241	24 Nov 1797	4084	14 Apr 1797	94	173	On waters of Smiths Fork	yes
Boyd, John, Jr.	399	McDillon, Jos.	Tennessee	230	2426	31 Dec 1793			81	408	On Maccadoo Creek	
Boyd, John, Senr	2012	McDelton, Joseph	Davidson	20	1959	24 May 1793	3542		81	114	Part of 274 but bounded by the river	yes
Boyd, John, Sr	1380	McKenney, Danl.	Sumner	640	3242	24 Nov 1797	4102	14 Apr 1797	94	174	Waters of Smiths Fork	yes
Boyd, Robt	517	Southerland, John	Sumner	274	1695	20 May 1793	210	11 Sep 1792	81	52	On waters of Drakes Creek	yes
Boyd, Robt & Wm. Logan	1088		Green	600	931	26 Dec 1791	1615	2 Apr 1784	77	253	On N side of Nolachuckey	
Boyer, Thomas	855	Donald, William	Sumner	228	2360	20 May 1793	3296	24 Jun 1789	81	204	On waters of Drakes Creek	yes
Boyer, Thomas	865	Tuton, William	Davidson	640	879	17 Jan 1789	3491		63	304	On N side of Cumberland River	
Boyles, Daniel	1349		Washington	200	1266	19 Oct 1797	522	19 Oct 1778	92	44	Waters of Brush Creek	
Boyles, Hezekiah	760		Washington	100	574	10 Nov 1784	1193	8 Feb 1779	69	131	Upon W side of Cherokee Creek	
Boyles, John	1345		Washington	70	1261	10 Jul 1797	2566	30 May 1780	91	602	Beg at Moses Brooks line	
Boyles, John	1348		Washington	100	1265	19 Oct 1797	2565	20 May 1780	92	44	Beg at Moses Brooks entry	
Boyles, John	432		Western District	5000	431	17 Feb 1801	423	25 Oct 1783	112	343	On S fork of Obion River	
Boyles, Reuben	728		Washington	200	542	10 Nov 1784	1351	3 May 1779	69	119	On a drain of Browns Branch	
Boyles, Samuel	628		Washington	74	722	26 Oct 1786	3004	19 Jun 1784	66	22	Beg on two marked red oaks	
Boyles, Samuel	706		Washington	300	520	10 Nov 1784	2345	10 Dec 1779	69	112	Beg at Thomas Brummicks entry	
Boyne, John	608	Gorham, James C.	Tennessee	274	3152	14 Sep 1797	4529		90	423	Waters of Little West Fork of Red River	yes
Brabble, John, heir of James	625		Sumner	640	1902	20 May 1793	1257		81	101	On Roaring River	yes
Braboy, Jacob	336		Tennessee	228	2122	20 May 1793	1304	2 Nov 1784	81	155	On W side of Milners [?] Creek	
Bracken, Joseph	2335	Malloy, Thos	Davidson	640	2979	10 Apr 1797	3164		90	285	S side of Cumberland River	yes
Bracken, Matthew	1727	McCulloh, Benjamin	Davidson	640	1442	20 Dec 1791	2500		77	361	On Knob Creek of Duck River	yes
Bradcutt, Richard	603		Washington	165	697	26 Oct 1786	1500	22 Sep 1781	66	10	On Caney Fork &c	

Claimant:	File #:	Assignee:	County:	Acres:	Grant:	Grant Date:	Entry:	Entry Date:	Bk:	Pg:	Location by Stream Name:	Military:
Bradley, Edward	1848		Davidson	584	348	27 Nov 1792	370	23 Mar 1784	81	8	On W side of Stones River	
Bradley, Geo.	605		Davidson	3840	577	15 Sep 1787	323		63	206	Lying on S side of Cumberland	yes
Bradley, James	433		Green	400	435	20 Sep 1787			65	498	On S side of Holston River	
Bradley, James	461	Warren, S. heirs	Davidson	640	433	15 Sep 1787	2103		63	159	On second or a branch of Stones River	yes
Bradley, James	493	Savage, Micajah	Davidson	220	465	15 Sep 1787	2291		63	169	On head of Cranes Creek	yes
Bradley, James	498	Abbett, John	Davidson	428	470	15 Sep 1787	1427	1 Mar 1786	63	171	On waters of Second Creek	yes
Bradley, James	683		Davidson	274	656	8 Dec 1789	691		63	232	On E Fork of White Creek	yes
Bradley, James	93		Davidson	1280	79	14 Mar 1786	741		63	32	S side of Cumberland River	yes
Bradley, John	0107	Phillips, Phil & Michael	Sumner	640		3 Mar 1787	2172				West fork of Drakes Creek	yes
Bradley, Nimrod	1350	Barry, Redmond D.	Sumner	640	3162	14 Sep 1797	4283	20 Feb 1797	90	427	Waters of Falling Creek	yes
Bradley, Robert	152		Davidson	640	138	14 Mar 1786	642		63	53	On Camp Creek	yes
Bradley, Sampson	569	Sheppard, Benjamin	Sumner	640	1806	20 May 1793	2326	30 Nov 1792	81	81	On waters of Dixons Creek	yes
Bradley, Sion	850		Hawkins	100	675	22 Feb 1795	392	22 Mar 1780	83	433	N side of Bays Mountain &c	
Bradley, Walter	165		Middle District	640	175	20 Dec 1791			75	225	On head waters of Big Harper River	
Bradley, Zion	2340	Malloy, Thomas	Davidson	220	2984	10 Apr 1797	3963		90	287	On Pigeon Creek	
Bradly, Abraham	235		Washington	640	103	23 Oct 1782	642	6 Sep 1779	47	50	On head of Cedar Creek	yes
Brady, James	18		Green	400	435	20 Sep 1787	309	23 Oct 1783			S side of Holston River	
Bradon, Alexander	1409	Weston, Aquilla	Sumner	1000	3341	6 Dec 1797	4683	8 May 1797	97	57	On waters of Big Barren	yes
Bradshaw, Ephraim	627	Stewart, Charles	Tennessee	640	3191	14 Sep 1797	3860		90	439	Headwaters of Johnstons Creek	yes
Bradshaw, Hugh	448		Sumner	640	353	27 Nov 1792	454	20 May 1784	81	10	On N side of Cumberland River	yes
Bradshaw, James	17	McConnon & Balch	Middle District	5000	19	10 Jul 1788	1785	23 Apr 1784	67	415	On S side of Duck River &c	
Bradshaw, John	1069		Green	475	938	26 Dec 1791			77	257	On waters of Dumplin Creek	
Bradshaw, John	13		Green	475	939		906	20 Jan 1786			On waters of Dumplin	
Bradshaw, John	1593		Green	200	1335	22 Feb 1795	324	22 Jun 1778	83	437	Above head of Dumplin Creek	
Bradshaw, John	19	Saunders, Edward	Robertson	640	3014		1506	11 Nov 1796			On waters of Sulphur Fork of Red River	yes
Bradshaw, John	492		Green	200	494	20 Sep 1787	824	18 Feb 1785	65	516	On head of Dumplin Creek	
Bradshaw, William	13		Maury	1000	29	14 Jul 1812	2102	30 Nov 1812	126	438	On S side Duck River	
Bradsher, John	1955	Harget, Frederick	Davidson	640	1796	20 May 1793	1126	16 Mar 1781	81	78	On S fork of E Fork of Stones River	yes
Brady, John	334		Hawkins	100	328	8 Mar 1793	756	3 May 1780	78	473	On S side of Copper ridge	
Bragg, David	27		Sullivan	270	38	23 Oct 1782	580	5 Sep 1780	43	256	On Walkers Fork &c	
Bragg, Joseph	206		Sullivan	200	213	10 Oct 1783	687		53	164	On S side of Walkers Fork	
Brahon, John Gloster	17	Archer, Jac & Demcey	Sumner	640	2899	5 Jun 1788					On waters of Red River	yes
Braiden, Charles	1588	McilyKida, John	Davidson	1000	1259	10 Dec 1790	1235		74	352	On waters of Spring Creek	yes
Brakey, Andrew	304	Ballard, Joab	Davidson	640	290	3 May 1787			63	108	S side of Red River	yes
Braley, Walter	201		Middle District	640	188	20 Dec 1791			78	330	On headwaters of Big Harpeth River	
Braley, Walter	202		Middle District	640	189	20 Dec 1791			78	330	On head waters of Big Harper River	
Braley, Walter	203		Middle District	640	190	20 Dec 1791			78	331	On head waters of Big Harper River	
Braley, Walter	92		Middle District	3000	94	10 Jul 1788	1792	23 Apr 1784	67	456	On head waters of E Fork of Spring Cr	
Branch, Job	697	Ramsey, Allen	Sumner	350	2067	20 May 1793	1436	11 Jun 1791	81	141	On S side of Cumberland River	yes
Branch, John	943		Green	5000	857	17 Nov 1790	1468	7 Feb 1784	76	124	On waters of Duck River	
Branch, William	941		Green	5000	855	17 Nov 1790	1467	7 Feb 1784	76	123	On waters of Duck River	
Brand, Joseph			Hawkins	400	346	8 Mar 1793	446	14 Dec 1787	78	482	On N side of Clinch River	
Brandon, James	171		Middle District	640	181	20 Dec 1791	1		75	228	On Spring Creek	
Brandon, James	172		Middle District	400	182	20 Dec 1791			75	228	On E Fork of Spring Creek	
Brandon, James	82		Middle District	1000	84	10 Jul 1788	1649	30 Nov 1784	67	451	On both forks of Spring Creek	

Earliest Tennessee Land Records

Claimant:	File #:	Assignee:	County:	Acres:	Grant:	Grant Date:	Entry:	Entry Date:	Bk:	Pg:	Location by Stream Name:	Military:
Brandon, James	89		Middle District	2000	91	10 Jul 1788	1653	16 Apr 1784	67	454	On both sides of N Fork of Duck River	
Brandon, Jenatt [?]	706		Sullivan	100 (50)	651	5 Dec 1794	804	14 Jun 1781	84	161	On waters of Horse Creek	
Brandon, Thomas	424		Washington	150	416	13 Oct 1783	2463	11 Mar 1780	52	273	Headwaters of Mill Fork of Big Limestone	
Brandon, William	169		Middle District	640	179	20 Dec 1791			75	227	On head waters of Big Harper River	
Brandon, William	177		Middle District	640	187	20 Dec 1791			75	231	On waters of Flat Creek	
Brandon, William, Jr.	164		Middle District	640	174	20 Dec 1791			75	225	On waters of Cany Spring Creek	
Brandon, Wm.	869	Fluellen, Isaac	Sumner	640	2385	1 Jan 1794	3431	19 Sep 1792	81	386	Beg at a large sycamore &c	yes
Braner, Joseph	184	Thompson, Jason	Tennessee	640	1464	4 Jan 1792	2348	20 Jul 1791	77	367	S side of Cumberland River	yes
Branks, Robert	1328	Hollis, Henry	Davidson	320	14	18 Aug 1787	508	5 Jul 1784	68	126	S/S Cumberland riv & W side of Stones Riv	
Brannon, James	094	Lytle, Archalbald	Sumner	1000			1467	23 Jun 1788			S side of Cumberland River	
Brannon, Thomas	418		Washington	50	410	13 Oct 1783	2700	20 Dec 1780	52	270	On the Mill Fork &c	
Brannon, Thomas	660		Washington	400	474	10 Nov 1784	2692	19 Dec 1780	69	95	On waters of Roaring Fork	
Brannor, Michael	350	Toton, William	Davidson	274	335	29 Aug 1787	1636		63	124	On Caney Fork River	yes
Brantley, Charles	524		Green	150	526	20 Sep 1787	324	7 Jun 1784	65	531	On N side of Holston River	
Brantley, Jeremiah	532	Allen, George	Davidson	640	504	15 Sep 1787	2047		63	182	W side of War Trace Creek	yes
Brantley, Marmaduke	025	Armstrong & Donelson	Middle District	640			2484					yes
Branton, Brittain	2429	Wells, Lewis	Davidson	640	3325	6 Dec 1797	1582		97	47	On a branch of Stones River	yes
Branton, Levi	2439	Tatum, H & Wiggin	Davidson	640	3281	6 Dec 1797	4265		98	161	Waters of Overalls Creek of Stones River	yes
Braselton, Isaac	584		Hawkins	100	458	29 Jul 179	2191 (2171	8 Nov 1779	80	291	S side of Holston River	
Braswell, Richd	01415	Carver, Robt & Wm.	not given					dtd 16 May 1759 [	18	432		yes
Bray, Cornelious	558	Burgess, William	Sumner	320	1777	20 May 1793	356	19 Dec 1792	81	73	On a W branch of Goose Creek	yes
Brayboy, John	019	Brewer, Sterling	Sumner	640								yes
Brayboy, John	021	Mann, John	Montgomery	600			4572	27 Mar 1797			On Williams Creek	yes
Breakey, Andrew	302	Smith, John	Davidson	640	288	3 May 1787			63	107	On waters of Sulphur Fork	yes
Breaky, Andrew	303	Mayo, Gardner	Davidson	428	289	3 May 1787	1324		63	108	On Gilkersons Creek	yes
Breaky, Andrew	305	Cherry, Jess hr of Jno.	Davidson	640	291	3 May 1787	1156		63	109	S side of Sulphur	yes
Breckenridge & Looney	226		Middle District	5000	206	27 Nov 1792	498	25 Oct 1783	80	209	Lying on the S side of Duck River &c	
Breckon, James G.	1578	Ballard, Burwell	Davidson	640	1232	10 Dec 1790			74	342	On S side of Cumberland River	
Breckon, James G.	59	Stokes, Peter	Tennessee	640	1286	10 Dec 1790	3379	7 Jan 1786	74	361	On S side of Cumberland River	
Breckon, James G.	90	Simmons, Joshua	Tennessee	640	1355	10 Dec 1790	2879	30 Sep 1785	74	384	On S side of Cumberland River	
Breckon, Jas. G.	41	Jenkins, Josiah	Tennessee	640	1233	10 Dec 1790	2853	30 Sep 1785	74	342	On S side of Cumberland River	
Breckon, Jas. G.	41	Wilder, Randall	Tennessee	1000	1228	10 Dec 1790	2895	30 Sep 1785	74	341	On S side of Cumberland River	
Breckon, Jas. G.	43	Lowell, Jas.	Tennessee	640	1234	10 Dec 1790	2877	30 Sep 1785	74	343	On N side of Cumberland River	
Breed, Avery	05		Washington	200			863	31 Aug 1779			On Little Chuckey	
Breeding, Jas	300		Hawkins	300	263	24 Dec 1791	311	16 Mar 1780	98 [?]	449	On S side of Holston River	
Breeley, William	907	Glasgow, James	Davidson	640	923	18 May 1789	1318		63	318	On waters of Ceader Lick Creek	
Brehon, James G.	18	Sparkman, Wm. Hrs	Tennessee	640	1166	26 Nov 1793	2880	30 Sep 1785	74	162	OP waters of Sulphur Fork	yes
Brehon, James G.	2465	Butler, Nathan hrs	Davidson	640	3399	10 Dec 1802	3492	1 Mar 1791	110	277	On head of Nelsons Creek	yes
Brehon, James G.	935 (938	Stratin, Joab	Davidson	640	951	18 May 1789	3498		63	324	On waters of Mulherins Creek	yes
Brehon, James G.	981	Venters, Arthur	Davidson	640	998	18 May 1789			63	336	On N side of Cumberland River	yes
Brehon, James G.	982	Skipton, Andrew hrs	Davidson	640	999	18 May 1789	2882		63	336	Beg SE corner David Henry's preemption	yes
Brehon, James G.	987	Turner, Absalom hrs	Davidson	640	1004	18 May 1789	2887		63	337	S boundary of James C. Mountflorence	yes
Brehon, James Gloster	984	Archer, Demsey hrs.	Sumner	640	1001	18 May 1789	125		63	336	On waters of Red River	yes
Brehon, James Gloster	985	Weatheritngton, Jac hrs	Davidson	640	1002	18 May 1789	2892		63	337	On waters of Red River	yes
Brehon, James Gloster	986	Stone, John hrs	Davidson	640	1003	18 May 1789	2881		63	337	On N side of Cumberland River	yes

Earliest Tennessee Land Records

Claimant:	File #:	Assignee:	County:	Acres:	Grant:	Grant Date:	Entry:	Entry Date:	Bk:	Pg:	Location by Stream Name:	Military:
Brehow, James G.	934	Johnston, Wm.	Davidson	640	950	18 May 1789	3388		63	324	On the Caney Fork	yes
Brehow, James G.	975	Bowman, Chas hrs	Davidson	1000	992	18 May 1789	3331		63	334	On N side of Cumberland River	yes
Breker, James Glouster	015	Ballard, Burwell hrs	Tennessee	640			3334	7 Jan 1786			S side of Cumberland	
Brekon, James	919	Joyner, Thomas	Davidson	2560	935	18 May 1789	3551		63	321	On S side of Cumberland River	yes
Brekon, James G	1724	Butler, Nathan	Davidson	640	1421	20 Dec 1791			77	356	On the head of Nelson Creek	
Brekon, Jas.	88	Lee, Timothy	Tennessee	640	1352	10 Dec 1790	2934	30 Sep 1785	74	383	On S side of Cumberland River	
Brekon, Jas. G.	63	Valentine, Silas	Tennessee	640	1297	10 Dec 1790	2889	30 Jul 1790	74	364	On S side of Cumberland River	
Bremby, Austin	302		Green	100	304	20 Sep 1787	1031	6 Jan 1779	65	460	On a branch of Nolechuckey River	
Brenaman, Melcher	578	Stone, Sylvanus hrs	Tennessee	640	3025	10 Apr 1797	3938		90	303	N side of Cumberland River	
Breselton, Wm. J.	13		Hawkins	155	509	27 Jan 1793	582	27 Oct 1783			S/S Holston river on draft of Loos Creek	
Brevard, Alexander	274		Davidson	3840	260	14 Mar 1786	761		63	95	N side of Tennessee River	yes
Brevard, Joseph	278		Davidson	2560	264	14 Mar 1786	762		63	96	N side of Tennessee River	yes
Brewer, Benjamin	916	Anderson, Daniel	Davidson	640	932	18 May 1789	3488		63	320	On N side of Cumberland River	yes
Brewer, George & Thelford	468	Wood, Charles	Sumner	1000	1625	27 Apr 1793	31	24 Jan 1786	81	23	On head of a creek of Stones River	yes
Brewer, Henry	547	Douglass, William	Sumner	360	1751	29 Aug 1793	199		81	67	On W fork of Bartons Creek	yes
Brewer, Reese	077	Fowler, David	Sumner	320			4526	21 Jun 1797			Waters of White Oak Creek	yes
Brewer, Sterling	018	Davis, David	Sumner	640			4333	15 Apr 1797			E side of Stones River	yes
Brewer, Sterling	1296	Rowan, Abraham J.	Sumner	1000	3058	19 Jul 1797	4477	27 Apr 1797	90	373	Waters of Big Barren	yes
Brewer, Sterling	1305	McRae, Reuben hrs.	Sumner	1000	3077	19 Jul 1797	4294	27 Apr 1797	90	381	Waters of Big Barren	yes
Brewington, Benjamin	893	Ewing, Alexander	Davidson	640	909	17 Jan 1789			63	314	On both sides of Smith's Fork	yes
Briant, William	811	Hays, Robert	Sumner	640	2278	20 May 1793	2406	19 Nov 1792	81	186	On the Caney Fork	yes
Brickel, Nathaniel	942	Robt King & Jas. Cooper	Hawkins	640	2692	6 Jun 1796	3964		88	367	On Stone Fork Valley	yes
Brickell, James	1721	Jones, Josiah	Davidson	1000	1393	20 Dec 1791	720		77	349	S boundary of General Sumner's survey	yes
Brickell, James	191	Pulley, James hrs.	Davidson	278	177	7 Mar 1786	705		63	66	On waters of Richland Creek	yes
Bricklea, Thomas	592	Blount, John Gray	Tennessee	1000	3062	19 Jul 1797	395		90	375	Headwaters of Halfpone Creek	yes
Bridges, Benjamin	605		Sumner	274	1855	20 May 1793	822	28 Jun 1788	81	91	On N side of Smiths Fork	yes
Brigam, David	1372		Davidson	320	55	8 Oct 1787	184	16 Jan 1784	68	143	On Station Camp Creek	
Brigam, James	764		Sullivan	100	695	20 Jul 1796	90	8 Feb 1780	91	81	Joining land said Brigham [sic] lives on	
Brigance, Wm.	1220	Armstrong, M.	Sumner	50	193	27 Aug 1795			89	409	Waters of W Fork of Station Camp Creek	
Brickell, James	1222	Armstrong, M.	Sumner	50	195	27 Aug 1795			89	410	On W fork of Station Camp Creek	
Brigance, Wm.	392	Armstrong, M.	Sumner	50	130	29 Aug 1793			80	324	On E fork of Station Camp Creek	
Briggs, William	2451	Wheaton & Tisdale	Davidson	640	3295	6 Dec 1797	2317	21 Sep 1779	98	171	Bet. Marrowbone & Sycamore Creeks	yes
Brigham, James	014		Sullivan	340			1697	23 Apr 1781				
Brigham, James	015		Sullivan	150			775	23 Apr 1781				
Brigham, James	134		Sullivan	600	147	23 Oct 1782	1697.-775,-	23 Apr 1781	43	329	On the S Fork of Muddy Creek	
Brigham, James	321		Sullivan	470	457	28 Nov 1787		23 Apr 1781	67	219	Beg white oak & buckeye 2 hickorys	
Brigham, James	53		Hawkins	300 (340	38	18 May 1789	1697	21 Sep 1779	72	251	On the N side of Clinch River &c	
Bright, Simon	983	Hutchings, Edward	Davidson	1000	1000	18 May 1789	2786		63	336	On N side of Cumberland River	yes
Brigman, William	394		Sumner	50	140	29 Aug 1793			80	328	On E Fork of Station Camp Creek	
Brigriance, William	715	Gibson, Fuller	Sumner	228	2097	20 May 1793	1692	24 Oct 1792	81	148	Waters of W Fork of Station Camp Creek	yes
Brimer, Benjamin	1144		Washington	300	1102	12 Jul 1794	2712	7 Jan 1794	81	570	On Browns Branch	
Brinkley, Josiah	2420	Erwin, Joseph	Davidson	640	3224	19 Oct 1797	2563		92	91	W side of South Harpeth	
Brister, James	736		Sumner	228	2128	20 May 1793	348	3 Dec 1783	81	156	On N fork of Red River	yes
Bristoe, Charles	1314	McConnel, Robert	Sumner	1000	3114	14 Sep 1797	4688	5 May 1797	90	409	Including forks of Puncheon Camp Creek	yes
Bristoe, James	348		Hawkins	200	342	8 Mar 1793	837	28 Oct 1778	78	480	On waters of Beaver Creek	yes

Earliest Tennessee Land Records

Claimant:	File #:	Assignee:	County:	Acres:	Grant:	Grant Date:	Entry:	Entry Date:	Bk:	Pg:	Location by Stream Name:	Military:
Briston, James	268	Harris, Goldman	Sumner	228	1237	10 Dec 1790	1410	23 Mar 1787	74	344	Near head of E Fork of Goose Creek	yes
Bristow, James	688	Woodliffee, George	Sumner	640	2042	31 Jul 1793	1200	31 Jul 1792	81	134	On S side of Cumberland River	yes
Bristow, John	1095		Hawkins	100	388	19 Jul 1797			91	618	N side of Clinch River	
Bristow, John	1115		Hawkins	100	835	15 Sep 1790 [? 631		19 Feb 1780	94	139	S side of Clinch River	
Bristow, Phllemon	012	Bledsoe, Isaac	Sumner	228			882	2 Aug 1785			N side of Cumberland River	yes
Bristow, Wm. Jr	388		Hawkins	155	509	27 Jan 1793	1259	2 Mar 1779	79	494	On S side of Holston River	
Brittain, Abraham	557		Sullivan	100	540	17 Nov 1790	2370	6 Aug 1792	76	191	Beg at a linn Saplin &c	
Brittain, Hardy	591	Sanford, Samuel	Sumner	640	1833	20 May 1793	971	26 Nov 1792	81	86	On the dividing ridge &c	yes
Brittain, James	568		Sumner	274	1803	20 May 1793			81	80	On waters of Caney Fork	yes
Brittain, Joseph	1117		Washington	190	1076	12 Jul 1794			81	561	Beg on a hickory	
Brittnall, James	556	Wright, Stephen	Sumner	274	1775	20 May 1793	767	4 Jul 1786	81	73	On head waters of Drakes Cr & Red River	
Britton, Daniel	1079		Green	200	922	26 Dec 1791	2906	28 Aug 1781	77	249	Branch of Lick Creek called Roaring Fork	
Britt, John	756		Hawkins	250	596	12 Jul 1794	2246	22 Nov 1779	82	209	On S side of Holston River	
Britt, Sherrard	332	Mountflorence, James Cole	Davidson	640	319	28 Jun 1787	2169		63	119	S side of Sulphur Fork	yes
Brittain, Abraham, Jr.	828		Sullivan	100	771	17 Nov 1797	459	24 Apr 1780	94	163	Beg at an ash & Chestnut oak	
Brittain, Philip	279	Bailey, Thomas	Tennessee	274	1862	20 May 1793	972	21 May 1784	81	92	On a small creek &c	yes
Brittain, Richard	776		Sullivan	484	708	17 Nov 1793	144-1641	1 Feb 1780	91	87	On Abbotts branch	
Brittle, Benjamin	1774	Hays, Robert	Davidson	640	1562	14 Jan 1793	1748		79	272	On N branches of Stones River	yes
Brizner, Henry, heirs of	1878		Davidson	640	1622	27 Apr 1793	280		81	23	On Nelsons Creek	yes
Broadbent, Richard	2237	Harget, Frederick	Davidson	640	2608	7 Mar 1796	1337		88	330	On Murpheys Fork of Harpeth River	yes
Broadstreet, James	2020	Blount, Jno G. & Thos.	Davidson	640	1998	20 May 1793	1544		81	124	On W fork of Stones River	yes
Brock, George	1087		Green	200	930	26 Dec 1791			77	252	On fork of Holstein River &c	
Brock, George	16		Green	211	261	20 Sep 1787	295	23 Oct 1783			On N side of Nolichuckey River	
Brock, George	580		Green	211	261	20 Sep 1787	68	12 May 1784	66	161	On N side of Nolichucky River	
Brock, James	368		Hawkins	150	302	14 Jan 1793			79	291	On South Fork of Swan Pond	
Brock, James	987		Davidson	200	736	9 Sep 1796	6	11 Sep 1783	88	517	On the Swan Pond Creek	
Brock, Joseph	1407	Armstrong, M.	Davidson	640	24	8 Oct 1787	562		68	154	On S side of Red River	
Brock, Joseph	1410	Armstrong, M.	Davidson	640	27	8 Oct 1787	1046		68	155	Situate the S side Red River	
Brock, Joseph	35	Collins, Brittain hrs.	Sumner	640	859	17 Jan 1789	3337	1 May 1788	63	299	On waters of Red River	yes
Brock, Joseph	36	Hart, Joseph heirs	Sumner	640	861	17 Jan 1789	3358	17 May 1788	63	300	On waters of Red River	yes
Brock, Joseph	748	Zutson, John hrs.	Davidson	640	721	11 Jul 1788	2702		63	253	On Pearsons Creek	yes
Brock, Joseph	823	Simpson, Dred	Davidson	640	826	17 Jan 1789	3482		63	291	On N side of Cumberland River	yes
Brock, Joseph	824	James, Charles hrs	Davidson	640	827	17 Jan 1789	3469		63	291	On N side of Cumberland River	yes
Brock, Joseph	829	Holland, Charles hrs	Davidson	640	832	17 Jan 1789			63	293	On N side of Cumberland River	yes
Brock, Joseph	834	Cat–ch, John hrs.	Davidson	640	837	17 Jan 1789	3450		63	294	On N side of Cumberland River	yes
Brock, Joseph	838	Harrington, James	Davidson	640	841	17 Jan 1789	3351		63	295	On waters of Suphur Fork	yes
Brock, Joseph	839	Flanagan, Geo. Heirs	Davidson	640	842	17 Jan 1789	3346		63	295	On N side of Cumberland River	yes
Brock, Joseph	841	Beach, Robert heirs	Davidson	640	840	17 Jan 1789	3443		63	296	On N side of Cumberland River	yes
Brock, Joseph	842	Carter, George hrs.	Davidson	640	847	17 Jan 1789	3339		63	296	On N side of Cumberland River	yes
Brock, Joseph	845	Hanver, James hrs.	Davidson	640	850	17 Jan 1789	3352		63	297	On N side of Cumberland River	yes
Brock, Joseph	856	Vicory, John	Davidson	640	864	17 Jan 1789	521		63	301	On N side of Cumberland River	yes
Brock, Joseph	858	Gafford, William	Davidson	640	867	17 Jan 1789	3349		63	301	On N side of Cumberland	yes
Brock, Moses	95	Dennis, William	not given	640	3355	7 Apr 1800	935	29 Nov 1785			On the Beaverdam Creek	yes
Brols, Mathias &Woodhite	75		Washington	150	243	23 Oct 1782	466	2 Oct 1778	44	268		
	612		Washington	200	706	26 Oct 1786	1567	31 Aug 1779	66	14	Joining Francis Hugh's former survey	

Claimant:	File #:	Assignee:	County:	Acres:	Grant:	Grant Date:	Entry:	Entry Date:	Blk:	Pg:	Location by Stream Name:	Military:
Broils, Mathias &Woodhite	674		Washington	200	488	10 Nov 1784	920	1 Jan 1779	69	100	On S side of Nolachucka River	
Brokens, Thomas	749	Farmer, Thomas	Davidson	640	722	11 Jul 1788	879		63	254	On head of Caleb Winters Creek	yes
Brook, Zedikiah	1325	McConnel, Robert	Sumner	640	3125	14 Sep 1797	3951	6 May 1797	90	413	Waters of Big Barren	yes
Brooks, Asa	492	Sharp, Anthony	Sumner	1000	1654	20 May 1793	2107	10 Oct 1785	81	42	On N side of Cumberland River	yes
Brooks, Chris Wm, hr of Geo.	104		Davidson	1000	90	14 Mar 1786	312		63	37	S side of Cumberland River	yes
Brooks, Daniel	538	Tatum, Howell	Sumner	640	1735	20 May 1793	2564	5 Oct 1786	81	62	On N side of Cumberland River	yes
Brooks, Ebenezer	1251		Davidson	640	216	10 Jul 1788	437	12 May 1784	66	415		
Brooks, Ebenezer	1802		Davidson	640	375	26 Jun 1793	436	12 May 1784	80	332	On W Fork of Harpeth	
Brooks, George	104		Davidson	1000	90	14 Mar 1786	312		63	37	S side of Cumberland River	yes
Brooks, George	358		Sullivan	200	237	10 Nov 1784			69	158	On S/North [?] side of Holstein River	
Brooks, Giles	1873	Love, Thomas	Davidson	640	1613	27 Apr 1793	3415		81	21	On waters of West Fork of Stones River	yes
Brooks, Jas & Jas Woods	297		Middle District	640	257	7 Jul 1794	472	25 Apr 1780	82	202	On both sides of Obeys River	
Brooks, Jas & Jas Woods	299		Middle District	640	259	7 Jul 1794	470	25 Apr 1780	82	202	On a branch of Wolf River	
Brooks, Jas. & Jas Woods	295		Middle District	300	255	7 Jul 1794	471	25 Apr 1780	82	201	On both sides of Obeys River	
Brooks, John	2	Dabney, John	Wilson	228	3388		3801	15 Jul 1800	114	92	On waters of Jennings Fork	
Brooks, Matthew	1337		Sumner	640	3137	14 Sep 1797	4158	5 May 1797	90	418	Waters of E Fork of Big Barren Creek	yes
Brooks, Matthew	1338	Onsley, Thomas	Sumner	640	3138	14 Sep 1797	4170	6 May 1797	90	418	E Fork of Big Barren	yes
Brooks, Robert	786	Alexander, Robert	Sumner	421 (428	2243	20 May 1793	2984	18 Nov 1792	81	179	On a branch above the Defeated Creek	yes
Brooks, Stephen	889	Mosland, John	Davidson	640	905	17 Jan 1789	3515		63	313	On waters of Stones River	yes
Brooks, Stephen	894	Gloughn, William	Davidson	640	910	17 Jan 1789	2917		63	314	On E side of Stones River	yes
Brooks, Stephen	895	Goodman, Sm.	Davidson	640	911	17 Jan 1789			63	315	On first creek above Stones Lick Creek	yes
Brooks, Thomas	108	Haddock, Andrew	Davidson	429	94	14 Mar 1786	311		63	38	Joining Nathaniel Dickersons	yes
Brooks, Thomas	197		Hawkins	400	130	16 Nov 1790	370	28 Mar 1780	77	193	Joining plantation Robt Ko_[?] now lives on	
Brooks, Thomas	426		Hawkins	200	315	5 Jun 1793	659	20 Jul 1780	80	158	N side of Holston River &c	
Broom, Mason	1939	Jesse Cobb & Ezekial Smit	Davidson	224	1760	29 Aug 1793	1127		81	69	On N side of Cumberland River	yes
Broomfield, Moses	846	Fenner, Richard	Davidson	640	851	17 Jan 1789	2170		63	297	On N side of Cumberland River	yes
Broomfield, Robert	67		Davidson	1000	53	14 Mar 1786	780		63	22	N Fork of Buffaloe Creek	
Broshere, Robert Samuel	270		Sullivan	300	409	9 Aug 1787	1997	21 Oct 1779	61	428	On N side of Holston River &c	
Browenen, John	013	Blount, John Gray	Tennessee	1000			2598	30 Sep 1785			N side of Red River	yes
Browk, Moses	75		Washington	150	243	23 Oct 1782	466	2 Oct 1778	44	268	Middle br of waters of Cheroke Creek	
Brown, Alexander	294		Green	300	296	20 Sep 1787	1481	19 Feb 1784	65	457	On S side of Holston	
Brown, Benjamin	171	Brown, Lewis hr.	Davidson	640	157	7 Mar 1786	873		63	60	On waters of Station Camp Creek	yes
Brown, Benjamin	618		Sullivan	200	567	27 Nov 1792	692	21 Nov 1778	80	208	On the Beaver Dam Fork	
Brown, Benjamin	751		Sullivan	400	727	5 Apr 1797	1596	12 Sep 1779	90	276	Beg at a pine tree	
Brown, Benjamin	752		Sullivan	100	728	5 Apr 1797	2329	4 Dec 1779	90	277	On Beaverdam Creek	
Brown, Benjamin	753		Sullivan	100	729	5 Apr 1797	1166	1 Feb 1779	90	277	Waters of Beaver Dam Creek	
Brown, Charles	084	Dupree, Meal hrs	Davidson	640			4693	7 Aug 1797			On Harpeth River	
Brown, Chas.	034	Dupree, Meal	Davidson	640			4693	7 Aug 1797			On Harpeth River	
Brown, Claiborne	421	Reardon, Jeremiah	Eastern District	200	2950	1 Mar 1797	4509		90	218	In a row of Knobs	
Brown, David	623		Green	200	664	11 Jul 1788	200	22 Oct 1783	66	448	Lying on cane branch &c	
Brown, David	682	McRory, John	Davidson	640	655	8 Dec 1787	1267		63	232	On S waters of Big Harpeth	yes
Brown, David	837		Green	150	818	13 Feb 1791	90	25 Apr 1789	73	375	On Sinking Fork of Long Creek	
Brown, Frederick	078	White, John	Davidson	640			2042	24 Jan 1791			On waters of Little Harpeth	yes
Brown, George	1071		Washington	300	1021	27 Nov 1792	2113	2 Nov 1779	80	182	On Campbells Creek	
Brown, George	789		Sullivan	400	721	2 Dec 1796	622,_507	Jun & Apr 1780	91	276	On Beaverdam Creek	

Claimant:	File #:	Assignee:	County:	Acres:	Grant:	Grant Date:	Entry:	Entry Date:	Bk:	Pg:	Location by Stream Name:	Military:
Brown, George	849		Green	100	830	13 Feb 1791	2521	23 May 1787	73	378	Knobbs above head Sinking Fk of Long Cr	
Brown, Haggard, & Mayfield	1999	Peter, Jan—(?)	Davidson	640	1939	20 May 1793	2345		81	109	On waters of Mill Creek	yes
Brown, Henry	412		Hawkins	200	533	27 Jan 1793			79	502	On Richland Creek	
Brown, Hugh	990		Green	100	1217	29 Jul 1793	1537	24 Aug 1779	76	483	N/S French Broad River inc a Sinking Spring	
Brown, Hugh & House	1143		Green	200	980	26 Dec 1791	1039	8 Jan 1779	77	277	On the waters of Lick Cr on Greasey Cr	
Brown, Isaac	1488	Thompson, Jason	Davidson	640	1201	16 Mar 1791	3678		73	278	On Mill Creek & Stones River	yes
Brown, Jacob	1045		Washington	640	995	14 Jan 1793	1267	7 Jul 1779	79	284	Beg at a marked white oak	
Brown, Jacob	1202		Washington	200	1156	3 Feb 1795	2704	20 Dec 1780	83	389	N side of Nolechuckey	
Brown, Jacob	527		Washington	640	790	16 Aug 1787	652	22 Apr 1779	64	149	Beg at a black oak &c	
Brown, James	1105		Washington	225	1055	27 Nov 1792			80	206	On S fork of Cherokee Creek	
Brown, James	138	Morris, William	Davidson	640	124	14 Mar 1786	1065		63	48	On a small creek on S side Sulphur Fork	yes
Brown, James	142		Middle District	3980	1	15 Apr 1798	47	25 Oct 1783	68	163	Lying on Lytles Creek &c	
Brown, James	1572	Bell, Robert	Davidson	640	1215	10 Dec 1790	1424		74	336	On waters of Mill Creek	yes
Brown, James	274	Hargett, Frederick	Tennessee	274	1831	20 May 1793	1461	25 Nov 1784	81	86	On S side of Cumberland River	yes
Brown, James	277	Ward, Elijah	Sumner	640	1269	10 Dec 1790			74	355	On N side of Cumberland River	yes
Brown, James	315		Middle District	450	291	17 Dec 1794	1554	26 Mar 1784	83	333	N side of Tennessee &c	
Brown, James	318		Middle District	635	294	17 Dec 1794	2243	22 Mar 1784	83	334	N side of Tennessee &c	
Brown, James	385		Hawkins	200	506	27 Jan 1793	155	15 Feb 1780	79	493	On N side of Holston River	
Brown, James	415		Middle District	500	354	17 Dec 1794	1270	23 Dec 1783	84	231	On Swan River	
Brown, James	434		Middle District	1000	373	17 Dec 1794	1269	23 Dec 1783	84	249	On N side of Tennessee River	
Brown, James heirs	398	Meres, John	Tennessee	274	2424	31 Dec 1793	823	11 May 1784	81	407	On Pine River	
Brown, Jennings	288	Malloy, Thomas	Sumner	228	1293	10 Dec 1790	1690		74	363	On N side of Cumberland River	yes
Brown, Jesse	777	Mountflorence, James Cole	Davidson	1000	750	11 Jul 1788	2112		63	263	On E side of W Fork of Station Camp Cr	yes
Brown, Jno.	1156		Davidson	640	133	17 Apr 1786	253	7 Feb 1784	66	182	S/S Cumberland riv & Wt Fk of Mill Cr	
Brown, John	1		Carter (Washing	400	1303	29 Oct 1801			111	103	Upon Fitzgerrells Branch	
Brown, John	116		Western District	4000	116	10 Jul 1788	493	25 Oct 1793	67	325	both sides of S fk of Forked Deer River	
Brown, John	1321		Washington	225	1242	5 Apr 1797	103	26 Feb 1778	90	278	Beg at a cherry tree	
Brown, John	1379		Washington	200	1304	28 Sep 1801	634	25 Nov 1778	111	67	Upon Garland Mill Creek	
Brown, John	1380		Washington	400	1303	29 Oct 1801	633	-- Apr 1779	111	103	Upon Fitzgerrells Branch	
Brown, John	1603	Copeland, Richard	Davidson	223	1319	10 Dec 1790	103		74	372	On S side of Cumberland River	yes
Brown, John	1836		Davidson	640	330	27 Nov 1792	498		81	4	On waters of Mills Creek & Stones River	
Brown, John	1929	Frazier, Simon	Davidson	274	1740	20 May 1793	1940		81	63	On Otter Creek waters of Harpeth	yes
Brown, John	2157	Armstrong, Martin	Davidson	60	166	9 Jan 1794			81	444	On Auter Creek waters of Harpeth	
Brown, John	269		Western District	1000	269	29 Nov 1788	2193	14 May 1784	70	27	On waters of Big Hatcher on N side	yes
Brown, John	271		Western District	1000	271	29 Nov 1788	2192	14 May 1784	70	28	On waters of Big Hatcher on N side	yes
Brown, John	278	Hammonds, John	Sumner	640	1270	10 Dec 1790	2049	26 Aug 1785	74	355	On S side of Cumberland River	yes
Brown, John	333	Allen, Archibald	Tennessee	640	2103	20 May 1793			81	150	On 2nd large fork &c	yes
Brown, John	453	Christee, John	Sumner	350	1584	27 Apr 1793	44	6 Dec 1789	81	13	On a creek of Stones River	yes
Brown, John	47	McDowell, Joseph	Davidson	1737	33	14 Mar 1786	800		63	13	On Pleasant Creek	
Brown, John	472	Hern, Drury	Sumner	228	1636	27 Apr 1793	69	6 Dec 1789	81	26	Adjoining the said Browns tract	yes
Brown, John	92		Hawkins	200	250	-- Jul 1792	1012	20 Oct 1779	74	444	Beg at a red oak	
Brown, John & John Davis	1942	Pervice, James	Davidson	640	1793	20 May 1793	2813		81	70	S W/S Harpeth River on Turn Bull's Creek	yes
Brown, John [Ass?]	244		Sumner	640	1149	26 Nov 1789	2813	19 Apr 1788	74	153	On S side of Cumberland River	yes
Brown, John, Ass.	2158		Davidson	100	167	9 Jan 1794		20 Feb 1792	81	444	On Otter Creek waters of Harpeth	yes
Brown, John, heir of Clement	705		Sumner	640	2084	20 May 1793	788	21 Nov 1784	81	145	On Drakes Creek	yes

Claimant:	File #:	Assignee:	County:	Acres:	Grant:	Grant Date:	Entry:	Entry Date:	Bk:	Pg:	Location by Stream Name:	Military:
Brown, Joseph	08		Green	200			2118	4 Apr 1780			Beg at a black oak	
Brown, Joseph	085		Washington	200			2703	20 Dec 1780			Beg at a white oak	
Brown, Joseph	1211		Washington	100	1155	4 Feb 1795			84	108	Beg at a white oak	
Brown, Joseph	1334		Washington	130	1258	8 Jun 1797	1796	5 Oct 1779	90	328	Waters of Big Limestone	
Brown, Joseph	1429		Green	200	1241	27 Nov 1792			80	167	On N side of French Broad River &c	
Brown, Joseph	1667		Green	200	1372	27 Feb 1793			88	488	Beg a black oak	
Brown, Joseph	206		Washington	459	74	23 Oct 1782	541	28 Oct 1778	47	35	N side of Noneychuckey River	
Brown, Joseph	462		Middle District	640	401	17 Dec 1794	2242	22 May 1782	84	262	On N side of Tennessee	
Brown, Joseph	7		Green	200	346			3 Sep 1778			On waters of Nolachuckey	
Brown, Joseph	814		Washington	200	628	10 Nov 1784	1348	30 Apr 1779	69	146	On head of Gipsons Branch	
Brown, Joseph	819		Washington	200	633	10 Nov 1784	391	12 Sep 1778	69	47	On waters of Nolechuckee River	
Brown, Joseph	905		Washington	150	882	17 Nov 1790	2794	20 Feb 1781	76	138	On waters of Cherokee Creek	
Brown, Joseph	918		Green	100	832	17 Nov 1790	2446	28 Feb 1780	76	115	On French Broad River	
Brown, Joseph	919		Green	200	833	17 Nov 1790	2489	10 Mar 1780	76	116	Nolichuckey on Puncheon Camp Creek	
Brown, Joseph & Harry	953		Green	250	867	17 Nov 1790	867 [sic]	12 Oct 1779	76	127	Beg a hickory on Hugh Browns line	
Brown, Joseph & Miller	1363		Washington	100	1280	30 Jun 1797	2635	7 Sep 1780	92	57	Waters of Big Limestone	
Brown, Lewis, heir of Benj.	171		Davidson	640	157	7 Mar 1786	873		63	60	On waters of Station Camp Creek	yes
Brown, Morgan	1		not given	150	342							
Brown, Morgan	553	Armstrong, M.	Tennessee	100	359	10 Aug 1797	401	12 Dec 1796	90	282	S side of Cumberland River	
Brown, Morgan, heirs of	563		Tennessee	640	2998	10 Apr 1797	3943		90	292	S side of Cumberland River	
Brown, Morgan, Ass.	543		Tennessee	150	342	19 Feb 1797			90	253	S side of Cumberland	
Brown, Peter	1268		Washington	300	1206	4 Dec 1795	410	21 Sep 1778	89	327	On a branch of Boons Creek	
Brown, Peter	1283		Washington	200	1221	4 Dec 1795	1581	11 Sep 1779	89	336	On Boons Creek	
Brown, Peter	492		Washington	200	755	16 Aug 1787	1581	2 Sep 1786	64	137	On Boons Creek &c	
Brown, Peter	521		Washington	300	784	16 Aug 1787	410	4 Sep 1786	64	147	On Boons Creek &c	
Brown, Robert	1536		Green	100	1296	17 Jul 1794	2713	4 Jan 1781	81	608	On N side of Holston River	
Brown, Thomas	014		Tennessee	640			931	19 May 1784			S side Cumberland	
Brown, Thomas	1228		Davidson	640	192	10 Jul 1788	401	9 Nov 1784	66	410	Ash, sugar tr Francis Hodges Et bound.	
Brown, Thomas	18		Washington	200	308	24 Oct 1782	927	15 May 1779	43	300	On W fork of Mill Creek	
Brown, Thomas	270		Western District	1000	270	29 Nov 1788	2191	14 May 1784	70	28	On waters of Big Hatcher on N side	
Brown, Thomas	272		Western District	1000	272	29 Nov 1788	2190	14 May 1784	70	29	On waters of Big Hatcher River on N side	
Brown, Thomas	317		Washington	200	184	24 Oct 1782	532	26 Oct 1778	49	219	On W fork of Morrisons Mill Creek	
Brown, Thomas	402		Greenn	200	404	20 Sep 1787	2569	26 May 1780	65	406	On Browns Creek	
Brown, Thomas	403		Green	300	405	20 Sep 1787	949	18 Feb 1786	65	486	On N side of Holston River	
Brown, Thomas	843		Green	250	824	13 Feb 1791	104	16 May 1785	73	376	Lying at head of Sinking Fork of Long Cr	
Brown, William	1986	Smith, Oliver	Davidson	274	1893	20 May 1793	3717		81	99	On S side of S Harpeth	yes
Brown, William	214		Hawkins	250	201	26 Dec 1791	1854	7 Oct 1779	77	314	On a creek known by name of Rentfrows	
Brown, William	2152	Kelley, Thomas	Davidson	274	2471	31 Dec 1793	984		81	433	On Whites Creek	yes
Brown, William	222		Hawkins	400	209	26 Dec 1791	1482	7 Apr 1787	77	316	On S side of Holston River &c	
Brown, William	374		Middle District	500	3131	17 Dec 1794	1553	26 Mar 1784	81	212	On a fork of Buffalo River	
Brown, William	53		Washington	100	801	16 Aug 1787	2984	18 Mar 1786	64	152	Beg at 3 marked white oaks &c	
Brownan, William	1007	Buckanan, John	Davidson	640	1024	18 May 1789	3241		63	342	On waters of Barlows Creek	yes
Brownee, Samuel	1067	S. Donelson & R. King	Sumner	640	2544	10 Dec 1795	3242		88	295	Including the place &c	yes
Browner, John	10	Nelson, Robert	Montgomery	60	3232	17 Nov 1797	3531	20 Jul 1797			N side of Cumberland River	yes
Browners, John	655	Nelson, Robert	Tennessee	60	3232	14 Nov 1797	2531	15 Feb 1786	94	169	N side of Cumberland River	yes

Claimant:	File #:	Assignee:	Acres:	County:	Grant:	Grant Date:	Entry:	Entry Date:	Bk:	Pg:	Location by Stream Name:	Military:
Brownguary, Gasper	1763	Hays, Robert	640	Davidson	1542	14 Jan 1793	2595	12 Mar 1788	79	267	On E branches of Stones River	yes
Browning, Baker	232	Reed, Jesse	640	Sumner	1137	26 Nov 1789	3421		74	147	On W side of Caney Fork River	yes
Brownum, David	605	Gorham, James C.	640	Tennessee	3149	14 Sep 1797	4201		90	422	Waters of W Fork of Red River	yes
Broyle, Micheals	871		100	Washington	855	18 May 1789	2583	30 Jun 1780	72	222	Beg at two may poles &c	
Broyles, Lewis	1542		450 (420	Green	1302	17 Jul 1794	2460	9 Mar 1780	81	609	On waters of Horse Creek	
Broyles, Surus	583		28	Washington	678	26 Oct 1786	2929	24 Mar 1784	66	1	Beg at a white tree &c	
Bruce, George	1089	Donelson S.	640	Sumner	2580	7 Mar 1796	3905	8 Aug 1792	88	316	On W side of W Fork of Obeys River	yes
Brukins, John	2146	Alexander, George	640	Davidson	2440	31 Mar 1794	3236		81	423	On waters of W Harpeth	yes
Brumley, Augustin	1157		100	Green	1000	26 Dec 1791	2384	28 Nov 1779	77	281	On N/S of Chuckey River joining sd river	
Brumley, Augustus	686		200	Green	727	11 Jul 1788	311	2 Sep 1773	66	468	On N side of Nolichuckey River &c	
Brumley, Barnt	1437		200	Green	1247	27 Nov 1792	2346	11 Dec 1779	80	170 (27	Richland Cr Beg at a double box oak	
Brumley, John	1159		40	Green	1002	26 Dec 1790	2882	22 Jan 1781	77	282		
Brumley, Thomas	497		100	Green	499	20 Sep 1787	207	3 Feb 1785	65	518	On Little Sinking Creek	
Brumley, William	1860	Nash, William	640	Davidson	1588	27 Apr 1793			81	14	On S side of Cumberland River	yes
Brummet [?], Thomas	529		200	Washington	792	16 Aug 1787	2382	27 Jan 1786	64	150	Beg at a small poplar &c	yes
Brunfield, Peter	2408	McConnell, Peter	228	Davidson	3201	14 Sep 1797	4080		92	4	E of S Harpeth	yes
Brunk, Christopher	666		200	Washington	480	10 Nov 1784	317	2 Sep 1778	69	97	On E branch of Limestone	
Brunk, Christopher	670		100	Washington	484	10 Nov 1784	580	7 Nov 1778	69	98	Joining a tract of land &c	
Brunk, Christopher	718		250	Washington	532	10 Nov 1784	2410	10 Apr 1780	69	116	Near head of Weavers Spring Branch	
Brunt, John	1060	S. Donelson & R. King	640	Sumner	2537	10 Dec 1798	3266	24 Dec 1785 (date	88	292	On both sides of a creek	yes
Bruskins, John	893	Alexander, George	274	Sumner	2439	31 Dec 1793	2262	19 Dec 1792	81	423	On waters of E Fork of Goose Creek	yes
Bryant, Bryant	340		400	Green	342	20 Sep 1787	224	7 Jun 1784	65	470	On both sides of Lick Creek	
Bryant, Demsey	1241	Tyrrell, William	1000	Sumner	2840	21 Jan 1797	893	11 Apr 1796	90	44	S side of Cumberland River	yes
Bryant, Edward	4		50	not given	350	1 Mar 1797	4597	6 Jun 1791			S side of Cumberland	
Bryant, Edward	534		50	Tennessee	350	1 Mar 1797			90	224	S side of Cumberland River	
Bryant, James	458	Elliott, James	274	Davidson	430	15 Sep 1787	453	15 Sep 1787	63	159	South side of Cumberland River	yes
Bryant, James	810		200	Green	811	11 Aug 1789	431	25 Oct 1783	71	33	On a branch of Copelins Creek	
Bryant, James	880		400	Green	817	24 Nov 1790	1534	12 Mar 1784	74	231	On waters of French Broad River	
Bryant, John	1505	Lash, Christian	640	Davidson	1062	26 Nov 1789	2788		74	109	On N side of Cumberland River	yes
Bryant, John	520	Tayloe, John	430	Davidson	492	15 Sep 1787	225		63	178	N side Cumberland River	yes
Bryant, Morgan	746	Simmons, John	274	Davidson	719	11 Jul 1788	1557		63	253	On Beaverdam Creek	yes
Bryant, William	1177		200	Green	1020	26 Dec 1791	1417	29 may 1779	77	288	On a fork of Little Chuckey	
Bryant, William	244	Murphree, Hardy	274	Davidson	230	7 Mar 1786	734		63	84	On headwaters of Long Fork of Sycamore	yes
Bryant, William	592		110	Washington	686	26 Oct 1786	1237	24 Feb 1779	66	5	Beg at a white oak &c	
Bryant, William	768		500	Green	573	23 Aug 1788	43	24 Oct 1783	68	250	Lying on N side of French Broad River	
Bryant, Ambrose	206	Holderness, William	640	Davidson	192	7 Mar 1786	308		63	71	On waters of Goose Creek	yes
Bryant, Morgan	018		100	not given				9 Jun 1785			Sulphur fork of Red River	
Bryant, Morgan	1550	Armstrong, M.	100	Davidson	90	26 Nov 1789	2173		74	171	On Sulphur Fork of Red River	yes
Bryant, Obed	2002	Buckanan, John	640	Davidson	1945	20 May 1793	2766		81	111	On Harpeth River	yes
Bryant, Peter	1230		300	Green	1080	12 Jan 1793	328	8 Feb 1781	78	351	On French Broad River	yes
Bryant, Thomas	879	Armstrong, Martin	595	Sumner	2398	7 Jan 1794		13 mar 1788	81	391	On S side of Cumberland River	yes
Bryant, Ward N_hie [?]	160		640	Sullivan	167	10 Oct 1783	1625		53	145	On Holston River	
Bryant, William	12	Montgomery, Michael	640	Sumner	769	11 Jul 1788	2629	25 may 1794	63	270	On waters of Collins River	yes
Bryle, Jacob	010		200	Green							W side of Horse Creek	
Bryle, James	1317		200	Green	1167	12 Jan 1793	933	10 May 1791	78	404	Beg at a white oak	

Claimant	File #	Assignee	County	Acres	Grant	Grant Date	Entry	Entry Date	Bk	Pg	Location by Stream Name	Military
Bryle, Jane	1309		Green	200	1159	12 Jan 1793	2607	27 Dec 1790	78	399	Beg at a white oak	
Bryle, Michael	1504		Green	100	1265	12 Jul 1794	766	24 Aug 1787	81	583	Beg at a stake	
Bryles, Michael	1472		Green	100	1236 (12	12 Jul 1794	2456	29 Aug 1784	81	574	Beg at a stake	
Bryner, William	687	McCraw, Samuel	Davidson	640	660	8 Dec 1787	2789		63	233	On head drafts of Sycamore	yes
Bryson, Hugh	603		Green	200	560	20 Sep 1787	32	9 Nov 1784	66	249	Richland Cr Beg at a double box oak	
Buchanan, Alexander	1030		Davidson	640	84	17 Apr 1787	28	29 Dec 1783	65	412	On N side of Cumberland River	
Buchanan, John	019	Hart, John	Sumner	640			1334	5 Nov 1790			On Jennings Fork &c	
Buchanan, John	1013	Richards, John heirs	Davidson	640	1030	18 May 1789	1981		63	343	On Stones River	yes
Buchanan, John	1563	Hutchins, James	Davidson	640	1185	30 Nov 1790	1095		74	316	On waters of Mill Creek	yes
Buchanan, John	1566	Garner, Nathan	Davidson	640	1199	30 Nov 1790	2722		74	32	On waters of Stones River	yes
Buchanan, John	1956	Rollins, James	Davidson	640	1797	20 May 1793	1654		81	78	On S road bet big & Little Harpeth	yes
Buchanan, John	2034	McDuel, Willis	Davidson	640	2047	20 May 1793	2573		81	136	On waters of Mill Creek	yes
Buchanan, John	2037	Haycraft, Mark	Davidson	640	2052	20 May 1793	1104		81	137	On S side of Cumberland River	yes
Buchanan, John	2079	Mabbey, Wm.	Davidson	640	2244	20 May 1793	2064		81	179	On Mill Creek	yes
Buchanan, John	2126	Armstrong, M.	Davidson	53	145	7 Jan 1794			81	399	Beg at a sugar tree	
Buchanan, John	2277	Sowell, Lewis	Davidson	640	2754	20 Jul 1796	1031		88	460	On waters of Hurricane Creek	yes
Buchanan, John	2278	Ross, John heirs	Davidson	640	2758	30 Jul 1796	2051		88	460	Waters of Hurricane Cr beg at an ash	yes
Buchanan, John	2279	Manson, John	Davidson	640	2759	20 Jul 1796	2529		88	461	On Hurricane Cr beg at a dogwood	yes
Buchanan, John	405	Lewis, Joshua	Davidson	640	377	15 Sep 1787	1773		63	141	On Stones River	yes
Buchanan, John	928	Wyatte, Ephraim	Davidson	640	944	18 May 1789	2479		63	323	On Cedar Lick Creek	
Buchanan, John, Ass.	2203		Davidson	600	220	27 Feb 1796		21 Dec 1792	88	171	On S side of Cumberland River	
Buchanan, John, heir of Alex.	1849		Davidson	640	349	27 Nov 1792	27	12 Aug 1784	81	9	On N side of Cumberland River	
Buchanan, John, Junr	1029		Davidson	640	83	17 Apr 1786	452	18 May 1784	65	412	Lying in Mill Creek	
Buchanan, Samuel	1206		Davidson	320	78	8 Oct 1787	74	10 Jan 1784	66	225	Head of Whites Branch beg at a hickory	
Buchannan, Robert	305		Middle District	640	281	17 Dec 1794	2020	3 May 1784	83	328	S side of Elk River	
Buchanon, David	361		Middle District	640	300	17 Dec 1794	2045	3 May 1784	84	207	On N side of Elk River	
Buchanon, John	1569	Armstrong, M.	Davidson	200	95	30 Nov 1790			74	323	On W side of Mill Creek	
Buchanon, Robert	360		Middle District	1280	319	17 Dec 1794	2041	3 May 1784	84	214	On W side of Little River	
Buck, William	2004	Overton, John	Davidson	640	1948	20 May 1793	2102		81	111	W/S of West Fork of Big Harpeth River	yes
Buckanan, Jas & John Duffie	498		Middle District	2000	298	26 Sep 1795	1268	10 Jul 1784	86	528	On S side of Cumberland River	
Buckanan, John	1007	Browman, Wm.	Davidson	640	1024	18 May 1789	3241		63	342	On waters of Barlows Creek	yes
Buckanan, John	1564		Davidson	28	926	30 Nov 1790		7 Nov 1789	74	317	On waters of Little Harper	
Buckanan, John	1905	Lea, James	Davidson	640	144	27 Apr 1793	817	1 Sep 1792	81	39	On waters of Stones River	
Buckanan, John	2002	Bryant, Obed	Davidson	640	1945	20 May 1793	2173		81	111	On Harpeth waters	yes
Buckanan, John	2125		Davidson	550	144	7 Jan 1794	34		81	398	On S waters of Harpeth	
Buckanan, John	2177		Davidson	640	454	27 Nov 1793			81	499	On N side of Cumberland River	
Buckanan, Samuel	339	Armstrong, M.	Davidson	400	324	1 Aug 1787		5 Dec 1785	63	121	West waters of Stones River	
Buckanen, John	2276	Corben, Francis hrs	Davidson	640	2756	20 Jul 1796	1316		88	459	On waters of Hurricane Creek	yes
Buckannan, Jno & W.Terrell	2253		Davidson	180	311	20 Jul 1796		9 Jun 1796	88	444	On waters of Mill Creek	
Buckannan, John	1549	Armstrong, M.	Davidson	138	89	26 Nov 1789		15 Nov 1788	74	171	On waters of Mill Creek	
Buckannan, Moses & Sam'l.	436		Middle District	1800	375	17 Dec 1794	2029	3 May 1784	84	249	On E fork of Little River	
Buckannon, John	1561	Harris, Abraham	Davidson	640	1183	30 Nov 1790	2730		74	315	On head waters of Noel [?] Creek	yes
Buckanon & Edmondson	423		Middle District	2000	362	17 Dec 1794	2028	3 May 1784	84	235	On N side of Elk River	
Buckanon, Archibald	1479		Davidson	640	283	26 Nov 1789	533	11 Jan 1784	73	256	W/S Stones Riv inc pl called clover bottom	
Buckanon, Benjamin	779	Sheppard, William	Sumner	640	2233	20 May 1793	2791	24 Nov 1792	81	176	On waters of Hickmans Creek	yes

Claimant:	File #:	Assignee:	County:	Acres:	Grant:	Grant Date:	Entry:	Entry Date:	Bk:	Pg:	Location by Stream Name:	Military:
Buckanon, David	424		Middle District	1000(19	363	17 Dec 1794	2030	3 May 1787	84	235	On N side of Elk River	
Buckanon, John	020	Adams, John	Sumner	640			2631	10 Nov 1790			On Jennings Fork &c	yes
Buckanon, John	1750		Davidson	320	108	20 Dec 1791	771		77	383	On waters of Stones River	
Buckanon, John	267		Middle District	500	114	27 Apr 1793	38	24 Jan 1787	81	32	On S side of Duck River	
Buckhanan, Ezekial	519		Washington	150	782	16 Aug 1787	2383	27 Feb 1779	64	146	On waters of Little Limestone	
Buckhannon, John	149	Thompson, Thomas	Davidson	640	135	14 Mar 1786	817		63	52	On waters of Mill Creek	yes
Buckhanon, John	1424		Davidson	200	41	8 Oct 1787			68	158	On West side of Stones Creek	
Buckingham, Thomas	1112		Green	600	955	26 Dec 1791	776	28 Oct 1783	77	265	On the S side of French Broad River	
Buckingham, William	75	O'Bryan, Lawrence	Tennessee	640	1320	10 Dec 1790	1798	4 May 1785	74	372	On Brush Creek	yes
Buckle, Thomas	1768	Coffee, Henry	Davidson	640	1551	14 Jan 1793	2836		79	269	On waters of Mill Creek	yes
Buckman, Samuel	338	Carter, Anthony heirs	Davidson	640	323	1 Aug 1787	1755		63	120	Beg at a honey Locust	yes
Buckner, Michael	629	Whitaker, John	Sumner	640	1912	30 May 1793	3248	19 Jul 1788	81	103	On waters of E Fork of Stones River	yes
Buckner, William	554		Sullivan	300	537	17 Nov 1790	1976	15 Oct 1779	76	190	W side of Baleys entry &c	
Bud, Samuel	674	Wine(?), James	Davidson	640	647		3409		63	229	On West side of Millers Creek	yes
Bud, Samuel	681	Sumner, Jacob hrs	Davidson	640	654	8 Dec 1787	2958		63	232	On ridge bet Milners & Brush Creeks	yes
Bud, Samuel	715	Nichlet, John hrs	Davidson	640	6888	8 Sept 1787	2617		63	242	W side of Milner's Creek	yes
Budd, Samuel, Ass.	25		Davidson	3840	11	16 Feb 1786	729		63	5	On both sides of Lick or Budd Creek	yes
Buds, Samuel	100	Kenady, Anthony	Tennessee	640	1516	10 Apr 1792	3408	29 Jan 1786	75	506	On S side of Cumberland River	
Buel, Ambrose	810	Moran, John hrs	Sumner	1000	2277	20 May 1793	2078	24 Nov 1792	81	186	On S side of Cumberland River	yes
Buffington, Samuel	627	Smith, Thomas	Sumner	1000	1908	20 May 1793	2596	23 Sep 1785	81	102	On Caney Fork River	yes
Bugg, John	1039		Green	110	1266	29 Jul 1793			76	491	N side of Noleychuckey River &c	
Bulingsbee, John	705		Sullivan	15	651	5 Dec 1794	541	29 Apr 1780	84	61	Beg at Loyd Ford's corner	
Bulingsbee, John	707		Sullivan	75	652	5 Dec 1794	541	29 Apr 1780	84	162	Beg at Pickings corner	
Bull, John	1418		Green	55	1230	27 Nov 1792	1384	21 May 1779	80	164	In Bull Gap of Beays Mountain	
Bullar, Isaac	1295		Green	200	1145	12 Jan 1793	1305	27 Mar 1779	78	391	On N side of Lick Creek	
Bullar, Isaac	335		Washington	200	202	23 Oct 1782	388	12 Sep 1778	49	227	On the N side of Noleychuckey River	
Bullar, John	567		Washington	100	832	11 Jul 1788	2592	15 Jan 1785	64	337	Joining Thomas McCullochs line	
Bullar, John	83		Washington	400	251	23 Oct 1782	739	23 Dec 1778	44	272	On Grimes Branch	
Bullar, Joseph	208		Washington	200	76	23 Oct 1782	239	17 Oct 1778	47	36	On Little Limestone Creek	
Bullar, Joseph	239		Washington	640	107	23 Oct 1782	240	22 Jun 1778	47	52	N side of Nolachuckey	
Bullar, Joseph	298		Washington	150	165	24 Oct 1782	390	12 Sep 1778	47	80	On a small creek &c	
Bullar, Joseph	876		Washington	150	860	18 May 1789	390	12 Sep 1788	72	223	On a small creek &c	
Bullar, Isaac	1482		Green	340	1245	12 Jul 1794	15	25 Feb 1778	81	577	Upon the side of Lick Creek	
Bullard, Isaac	472		Green	640	474	20 Sep 1787	97	21 Jul 1785	65	509	On Lick Creek	
Bullard, Isaac	832		Green	100	818	19 Nov 1790	389	11 Sep 1778	73	275	N/S of Lick Creek on Swan Camp Creek	
Bullard, John	014		Hawkins	345			2187	12 Nov 1779			S side of Holston River	
Bullard, Joseph	141		Green	200	611	23 Aug 1788	1306	27 Mar 1779	64	345	On head of Loss Creek &c	
Bullard, Joseph	201		Green	400	158	20 Sep 1787	1431	3 Dec 1785	65	416	On a branch of Lick Creek	
Bullard, Joseph	202		Green	3000	159	20 Sep 1787	390	7 Jun 1784	65	417	On S/S of Holston River on Loss Creek	
Bullard, Joseph	203		Green	1000	160	20 Sep 1787	516	7 Jun 1784	65	417	On Beaverdam Creek	
Bullard, Joseph	214		Green	100	171	20 Sep 1787	1885	24 Apr 1784	65	421	On S side of Holston River	
Bullard, Joseph	249		Green	400	206	20 Sep 1787	840	29 Oct 1783	65	432	On S side of Holston River inc an island	
Bullard, Joseph	257		Green	140	214	20 Sep 1787		4 Nov 1783	65	435	On N side of Lick Creek	
Bullard, Joseph	269		Green	400	226	20 Sep 1787	1484	1784 [?]	65	440	On Beaverdam Creek	
Bullard, Joseph	601		Green	600	558	20 Sep 1787			66	248	On Lick Creek &c	

Earliest Tennessee Land Records

Claimant:	File #:	Assignee:	County:	Acres:	Grant:	Grant Date:	Entry:	Entry Date:	Bk:	Pg:	Location by Stream Name:	Military:
Bullard, Joseph	658		Washington	150	806	20 Sep 1787	390		66	159	On a branch &c	
Bullard, Joseph	75		Hawkins	300	75	19 Nov 1790	1546	26 May 1785	73	273	On S side of Holstein River	
Bullard, Joseph	76		Hawkins	80	76	19 Nov 1790	1979	15 Oct 1779	73	274	On S/S of Holston River on Beaver Creek	
Bullard, Joseph	77		Hawkins	150	77	19 Nov 1790	943	25 Jun 1784	73	274	S/S Holston riv on a cr called Buffaloe Cr	
Bullard, Joseph	78		Hawkins	100	78	19 Nov 1790	2583	30 Jun 1780	73	274	On S side of Holston River &c	
Bullard, Joseph	783		Green	100	588	23 Aug 1788	1454	20 Sep 1787	68	257	Lying on Little Sinking Creek	
Bullard, Joseph	787		Green	250	592	23 Aug 1788	1453	2 Feb 1784	68	259	On waters of Loss Creek	
Bullard, Joseph	793		Green	400	598	23 Aug 1788	112	20 Sep 1787	68	261	Lying on S side of Holstein River &c	
Bullard, Joseph	794		Green	100	599	23 Aug 1788	1533	21 Aug 1779	68	261	Lying on S side of Holstein River	
Bullard, Joseph	833		Green	200	819	19 Nov 1790	288	23 Aug 1788	73	276	On S side of Holstein River	
Bullard, Joseph	834		Green	500	820	19 Nov 1790	1547	18 Feb 1788	73	276	On S side of Holstein River &c	
Bullard, Joseph	835		Green	400	821	19 Nov 1790	1430	24 Jan 1784	73	277	On S side of Holstein River &c	
Bullard, Waker	324	Williams, Willoughby	Middle District	640	2386	3 Feb 1795	2709		83	385	W side of W Fork of Obeys River	yes
Bullin, Michael	136		Davidson	640	122	14 Mar 1786	648		63	48	On Camp Creek	yes
Bullingsbee [?], John	698		Sullivan	24	643	5 Dec 1794			84	158	Beg at a pine	
Bullock, Drury	734	Bonner, John & Jas.	Sumner	640	2121	20 May 1793	463	14 Apr 1792	81	154	On or near head of one of E branches	yes
Bullock, Drury	771	Bonner, John & Jas.	Sumner	640	2219	20 May 1793	463	1 Dec 1792	81	173	On ridge bet Poplar Grove Creek &c	yes
Bullock, John	075	Tyrrell, William	Davidson	228			461	27 May 1796			On waters of Duck	yes
Bullock, Lemuel	2272	Casey, John	Davidson	1000	2750	20 Jul 1796	3965		88	457	On a large creek of Tenn River	yes
Bullock, Richard	588		Washington	100	682	26 Oct 1786	2542	24 Apr 1780	66	3	On the N spring of Dinham's Fork &c	
Bulworth, James	075	Williams, Willoughby	Middle District	640			2705				Beg at a pine &c	yes
Bun, John	987		Washington	200	872	16 Nov 1790	325		77	182	Beg at a pine &c	
Bunch, James	643		Green	200	684	11 Jul 1788	325	21 Sep 1787	66	455	On the N side of Holstein River &c	
Bunch, John	720		Hawkins	200	540	12 Jun 1793	272	17 Mar 1780	82	167	On the head of Bunches Camp Creek	
Bunch, John & Isaac Cloud	425		Hawkins	640	314	5 Jun 1793	370	22 Oct 1783	80	157	W side of Holston	
Bunch, John & Thos. King	1026		Hawkins	200	789	22 Feb 1797	1072	28 Mar 1780	90	205 [?]	S side of Richland Creek	
Buncomb, Edward	469	Thos. Buncomb hrs.	Davidson	7200	441	15 Sep 1787		12 Feb 1780	63	162	West side of Richland Creek	yes
Buncomb, Thos, hr of Edward	469		Davidson	7200	441	15 Sep 1787			63	162	West side of Richland Creek	yes
Bunday, Simon	283		Washington	50	150	23 Oct 1782	1911	12 Feb 1780	47	73	On the draft of Gap Creek	
Bunnington, William	1522	Thompson, John	Davidson	640	1079	26 Nov 1789	2407		74	119	On E waters of Mill Creek	yes
Buntcot, Joseph	1131		Washington	200	1089	12 Jul 1794			81	565	Beg at a white oak	
Bunton, Andrew	470		Washington	450	462	13 Oct 1783	730	21 Dec 1778	56	294	On the Lwell (?) Fork of Holston	
Bunton, James	325	Williams, Willoughby	Middle District	640	2387	3 Feb 1795	2708		83	385	W side of W Fork of Obeys River &c	yes
Burass, Elijah & Farlar Evans	1384		Washington	150	1310	10 Dec 1803	2396	10 Jan 1780	118	117	On waters of Indian Creek	
Burden, Archabald	827	Tuton, William	Davidson	640	830	17 Jan 1793	3494		63	292	On N side of Cumberland River	yes
Burden, Jacob	938	Blount, Reading	Davidson	640	954	18 May 1789	2560		63	325	On waters of Caney Fork	yes
Burden, James	2423	Nelson, Robert	Davidson	510	3230	17 Nov 1797			94	167	S side of Big Harpeth	yes
Burden, Jarrett	1063		Washington	100	1013	27 Nov 1797	1346	23 Apr 1779	80	180	Bet. the lines of David Mattocks &c	yes
Burden, Thomas	2413	McConnel, Robert	Davidson	640	3206	14 Sep 1797	4577		92	6	W side of S Harpeth	yes
Burdwell, George	162		Sullivan	27	169	10 Oct 1783	255	1 Mar 1780	53	146	On S side of Holstein River	
Burdwell, George	460		Sullivan	100	339	10 Nov 1784	225	22 Feb 1780	69	191	On N side of Holstein River	
Burdwell, George	681		Sullivan	118	629	9 Jul 1794	416	14 Apr 1780	81	631	On N side of Holstein River	
Burdwell, George	721		Sullivan	32	666	5 Dec 1794	255	3 Mar 1780	84	169	Beg at a hickory	
Burdwell, George	830		Sullivan	375	773	17 Nov 1797	570	22 May 1780	94	164	On Kindricks Creek	
Burdwell, Robert	568		Sullivan	200	551	17 Nov 1790	750	23 Dec 1778	76	196	On Clear Creek &c	

Claimant:	File #:	Assignee:	County:	Acres:	Grant:	Grant Date:	Entry:	Entry Date:	Bk:	Pg:	Location by Stream Name:	Military:
Burdwell, Robert	684		Sullivan	60	632	9 Jul 1794	719	26 Dec 1780	81	632	On one of the branches of Clear Creek	yes
Burges, Wm.	552	Sanderlin, Levi(?)	Sumner	228	1768	20 May 1793	3020	20 Dec 1792	81	75	On W Fork of Goose Creek	yes
Burgess, Absolem	105		Davidson	1000	91	14 Mar 1786	982		63	37	South side of Cumberland River	
Burgess, George	703	Selby Harney & A. Bledsoe	Sumner	274	2082	20 May 1793	3208	18 Nov 1792	81	145	On Bledsoes Creek	
Burgess, Philip	110		Davidson	640	96	14 Mar 1786	643		63	39	On Camp Creek	yes
Burgess, Wm.	558	Bray, Cornelius	Sumner	320	1777	20 May 1793	356	19 Dec 1792	81	73	On a W branch of Goose Creek	yes
Burgess, Wm.	761	Mains (sic)	Sumner	274	2174	20 May 1793	3209	19 Dec 1792	81	166	On E branch of Middle fk Goose Creek	yes
Burgess, Wm.	764	Gallop, Isaac	Sumner	320	2182	20 May 1793	3016	19 Dec 1792	81	166	Middle Fk of West Fk of Goose Creek	yes
Burgiss, Thomas	420		Sumner	640	431	27 Jun 1793	827	22 Nov 1792	80	351	On a small S fork &c	
Burk, Abraham	601	Hart, Anthony	Davidson	640	573	15 Sep 1787	2707		63	205	S side of Big Barren River	
Burk, John	726		Sullivan	100	671	22 Feb 1795			84	290	On S side of Holston River	
Burke, Charles	621	Wikoff & Clark	Davidson	640	593	15 Sep 1787	1947		63	212	N side of Cumberland River	yes
Burke, William	481		Sullivan	640	491	17 Nov 1788	258	6 Mar 1780	70	10	On Buffelow Creek	
Burke, William	484		Sullivan	640	494	17 Nov 1788	257	6 Mar 1780	70	12	On Buffelow Creek	
Burke, William	664		Sullivan	92	612	12 Jul 1794	598		81	598	On Kindreds Creek	
Burleson, Aaron	82		Washington	200	250	23 Oct 1782	571	4 Nov 1778	44	272	On waters of Lick Creek	
Burlisson, Aaron, Jr.	392		Washington	100	384	13 Oct 1783	572	24 Mar 1779	52	257	On Aron Pensons Creek	
Burn, Andrew	87	Hays, John	Tennessee	640	1351	10 Dec 1790	2562	30 Sep 1785	74	382	On S side of Cumberland River	yes
Burnes, Barnabas	1949 [?]	Wilson, John	Davidson	640	1787	20 May 1793	1358		81	73	On Yellow Creek	yes
Burnes, Jas	268	Bowlen, Saml.	Tennessee	640	1742	20 May 1793	3250	24 Dec 1785	81	64	On waters of Red River	
Burnett, John heirs	046	Hughlett, William	Middle District	640			2794					
Burnham, Isaac	2320	Tyrrell, Wm. & Wm. Lytle	Davidson	640	2853	21 Jan 1797	1194		90	51	On waters of W. Harpeth	yes
Burnham, Isaac	595		Sumner	640	1837	20 May 1793	1001	8 Jul 1785	81	87	On the middle fork of Drakes Creek	yes
Burns, Isum	10	Fenner, Richard	Tennessee	640	1158	26 Nov 1789	2168	12 Sep 1785	74	158	On N side of Cumberland River	yes
Burns, John heirs	174		Davidson	640	160	17 Mar 1786	599		63	61	S side of Red River	yes
Burns, Wm., Hr of John	174		Davidson	640	160	17 Mar 1786	599		63	61	S side of Red River	yes
Burnsides, David	1859	Kirkpatrick, Michael	Davidson	360	1586	27 Apr 1793	222		81	14	On waters of Big Harpeth	yes
Burrington, Demsey	369	Hickman, Edwin	Tennessee	274	2256	20 May 1793	2268	30 Sep 1785	81	185	Joining N boundary &c	yes
Burton, Jacob	1514	Douglass, Edward	Davidson	228	1071	26 Nov 1789	1696		74	115	On waters of W Fork of Camp Creek	yes
Burton, John	57	Murphree, Hardy	Davidson	1168	43	14 Mar 1786	172		63	18	S side of Cumberland River	yes
Burton, Robert	322	Johnston, Briton hrs	Davidson	640	308	13 Jun 1787	1145		63	115	On a branch of Smiths Creek	yes
Burton, Robert, Ass	1		Maury	5000	1	14 Jul 1812			126	425	On S side of Duck River	
Bush, Aaron	776	Baker, John	Sumner	640	2229	20 May 1793	3407	19 Nov 1792	81	175	W side of Caney Fork	yes
Bush, John	574		Davidson	914	546	15 Sep 1787	216		63	196	On waters of Stewarts Creek	yes
Bush, Phillip	1149		Davidson	640	126	17 Apr 1786	465		66	181	On Sulphur Fork of Red River	
Bush, William	2464		Davidson	640	473	19 Sep 1800	556		109	272	On S side of Cumberland River	
Bush, William	42		Davidson	2560	28	14 Mar 1786	175		63	12	Both sides of E Fork of Thompsons Creek	yes
Bushneal, Eus. & Wm Dobbin	037	Rollen, Henry	Davidson	1000			1673	12 Aug 1785			S side of Cumberland	
Bushneal, Eus. & Wm Dobbin	652	Gwinn, Jacob heirs	Davidson	640	625	15 Sep 1787	1686		63	222	On waters of Stewarts Creek	yes
Bushneal, Eus. & Wm Dobbin	659	Simmons, Allason	Davidson	1000	632	15 Sep 1787	1660		63	224	On waters of Stones River	yes
Bushnell, Eusebrus	651	Jacobs, Daniel	Davidson	1000	624	15 Sep 1787	1674		63	222	On waters of Stones River	yes
Bushnell, Eusebrus	847	Goodwin, Peter	Davidson	640	852	17 Jan 1789	1670		63	298	On South side of Cumberland	yes
Bushnell, Eusebrus & Dobbin	650	Williford, Joseph	Davidson	640	623	15 Sep 1787	1667		63	221	On waters of Stones River	yes
Bushnell, Eusebrus & Dobbin	653	Davis, Wm. Heirs	Davidson	640	626	15 Sep 1787	1685		63	222	On Moses Shelbys West boundary line	yes
Bushnell, Eusebrus & Dobbin	654	Ward, John	Davidson	1000	627	15 Sep 1787			63	223	Both sides of main W Fork of Stones River	yes

Claimant:	File #:	Assignee:	County:	Acres:	Grant:	Grant Date:	Entry:	Entry Date:	Bk:	Pg:	Location by Stream Name:	Military:
Bushnell, Eusebrus & Dobbin	655	Lyles, Benjamin	Davidson	640	628	15 Sep 1787	1672		63	223	On S side of Cumberland River	yes
Bushnell, Eusebrus & Dobbin	656	Woods, Capt. Matt.	Davidson	1640 (16	629	15 Sep 1787	572		63	223	On main E Fork of Stones River	yes
Bushnell, Eusebrus & Dobbin	657	Cole, Henry	Davidson	1000	630	15 Sep 1787	1665		63	224	On waters of Stones River	yes
Bushnell, Eusebrus & Dobbin	658	Hill, Isaac	Davidson	228	631	15 Sep 1787	1689		63	224	On waters of Stones River	yes
Bushnell, Eusebrus & Dobbin	660	Hayse, William	Davidson	1000	633	15 Sep 1787			63	225	On South side of Cumberland	yes
Bushnell, Eusebrus & Dobbin	661	Beaver, John	Davidson	1000	634	15 Sep 1787			63	225	On waters of Stones Creek	yes
Bushnell, Eusebrus & Dobbin	662	Dykes, John	Davidson	640	635	15 Sep 1787	1682		63	225	On South side of Cumberland	yes
Bushnell, Eusebrus & Dobbin	663	Dickey, Jacob hrs	Davidson	640	636 (630)	15 Sep 1787	1683		63	226	On S side of Cumberland River	yes
Butler, Edward	671	Hays, Robert	Davidson	1000	644	15 Nov 1787	1666		63	228	On Bizzells Salleen	yes
Butler, Elisha	502		Washington	200	765	16 Aug 1787	2435	24 Feb 1780	64	141	Joining Richard Coxes line &c	
Butler, Isaac	259		Davidson	228	245	7 Mar 1786	139		63	90	Beg at the mouth of McAdoes Creek	yes
Butler, John	176		Davidson	228	162	7 Mar 1786	125		63	61	On waters of Stones River	yes
Butler, McL.	1205		Washington	180	1159	5 Dec 1794			83	417	On the waters of Big Limestone	
Butler, Nathan	2465	Brehan, James G.	Davidson	640	3399	10 Dec 1802	3492	1 Mar 1791	110	277	On head of Nelsons Creek	yes
Butts, Archibald	031	Campbell, Laughlan	Davidson	1000			634	31 Jul 1784			N side of Cumberland	yes
Butts, Archibald	281		Davidson	1000	267	7 Mar 1786	401		63	97	North side of Cumberland and Red River	yes
Butts, Peter	04	Barton, Samuel	Sumner	640			4575	20 Mar 1797			On waters of Cedar Creek	yes
Butts, William	04	Alford, William	Tennessee	640			773	1 May 1784			On the 4th large creek &c	
Buxton, William	125	Tear [?], William	Davidson	640	111	7 Mar 1786	652		63	44	South side of Cumberland River	yes
Buxton, William	346	Gold, Davis heirs	Davidson	640	331	28 Jul 1787	2918	16 Aug 1785	63	123	On headwaters of Station Camp Creek	yes
Buxton, William	347	Lilly, Sarah hr of John	Davidson	640	332	28 Jul 1787	2743		63	123	North side of Cumberland River	yes
Buzby, Thomas	044		Hawkins	200			1412	25 May 1779			On the Short Fork of Panther Creek	
Buzby, Thomas	1005		Green	200	1232	29 Jul 1793			76	485	On the Short Fork of Panther Creek	
Byanom, Drury	273	Fort, Elias	Tennessee	1000	1795	20 May 1793	436	9 Feb 1784	81	78	On S side of Cumberland River	yes
Byarin, Ebenezer	336		Hawkins	100	330	8 Mar 1793	1208	13 Feb 1779	78	474	Adjoining his said corner	
Bykin, Thomas	491	Nelson, Robert	Tennessee	640	2488	26 Sep 1795	1995	16 Aug 1785	89	101	On N side of Red River	yes
Byler, Abraham	1246		Washington	100	1218	27 Feb 1796	2325	8 Nov 1795	88	507	Beg on a black oak	
Byler, Abraham	1250		Washington	640	1222	20 Jul 1796	1722	20 Sep 1792	88	509	On waters of Rones Creek	
Byler, Abraham	1329		Washington	200	1253	6 Jun 1797	196	5 Feb 1793	90	310	S side of Rones Creek	
Byler, Abraham	27		Giles	200	58	23 Apr 1813	1283	16 Mar 1779	127	331	On Dry Fork of Wakeleys Creek	
Byler, Abraham	29		Maury	100	48	15 Jul 1812	2471	10 Mar 1780	126	446	Lying on a small branch	
Byler, Abraham	29		Giles	150	61	23 Apr 1813	2044	27 Oct 1779	127	332	On Dry Fork of Wakelies Creek	
Byler, Abraham	31		Maury	200	50	15 Jul 1812	2106	30 Oct 1779	126	446	Lying on Catheys Creek	
Byler, Abraham	32		Maury	250	59	23 Apr 1813	1934	15 Oct 1779	127	331	A small branch waters of Bigtomibigby [sic]	
Byler, Abraham, Ass	26		Maury	200	45	15 Jul 1812	1082	8 Jan 1788	126	445	Beg on Big Swan Creek	
Byler, Abraham, Ass.	27		Maury	200	46	15 Jul 1812	2470	10 Mar 1780	126	445	Lying on Big Swan	
Byler, Abraham, Ass.	28		Maury	100	47	10 Jul 1812	1081	6 Jan 1778	126	445	On W Fork of Cathays Creek	
Byler, Abraham, Ass.	30		Maury	100	49	15 Jul 1812	2631	1 Sep 1780	126	446	N of Dry Fork	
Byler, Jacob	25		Giles	100	56	23 Apr 1813	2039	27 Oct 1779	127	330	On dry branch of Weaklies Creek	
Byler, Jacob	30		Giles	300	63	21 Dec 1815	1358	6 May 1779	130	99	On a branch of Dry Creek	
Byler, Jacob	31		Giles	300	64	21 Dec 1815	213	14 May 1778	130	100	On Richland Creek	
Bylers, Abraham	28		Giles	100	60	23 Apr 1813	1192	8 Feb 1779	127	331	On waters of Big Creek	
Byleston, William	1479		Green	200	1242	12 Jul 1794	2377	10 Aug 1784	81	576	Beg at a stake	
Bylestone, Wm.	1318		Green	175	1168	12 Jan 1793	1291	7 Jul 1779	78	331	Beg at a red oak	
Byran, Ebenezer	131		Green	200	35	11 Jul 1788	1334	12 Jan 1784			On the waters of Beaverdam Creek	

Claimant:	File #:	Assignee:	County:	Acres:	Grant:	Grant Date:	Entry:	Entry Date:	Bk:	Pg:	Location by Stream Name:	Military:
Byrd, Amos	1280		Green	300	1130	12 Jan 1793	155	22 Oct 1783	78	383	N side of Nolichuckey River	
Byrd, Amos	14		Green	400	90		126	18 May 1783			N side of Chuckey River	
Byrd, Jno.	682		Green	100	723	11 Jul 1788	719	20 Feb 1787	66	467	N side of the French Broad River &c	
Byrd, Moses	2103	Blount, John Gray & Thom	Davidson	274	2332	20 May 1793	1302		81	198	On S side of Harpeth River	yes
Byrd, Richard	687		Green	200	728	11 Jul 1788	1787	2 oct 1779	66	469	On S side of Holston River	
Byrn, James	503	English, John	Sumner	640	1674	20 May 1793	858	22 Mar 1786	81	47	On E Fork of Bledsoes Creek	yes
Byrnes, James	1903	Drake, Benj.	Davidson	640	140	27 Apr 1793	157	17 Jan 1784	81	38	On Leepers Fork of Harpeth	
Byrns, James	1370		Davidson	320	530	8 Oct 1787	55	14 Dec 1784	68	143	Branch left hand fork of Kaspers Creek	
Byron, Ebenezer	406		Green	300	408	20 Sep 1787			65	487	On the head waters of Little Chuckey	
Byrum, Abernezer [sic]	128		Washington	200	296	24 Oct 1762	1207	13 Feb 1779	44	296	On a small branch &c	
Byrum, Ebenezer	296		Middle District	699 (691	256	7 Jul 1794	1749	21 Apr 1784	82	201	On the S side of Cumberland Mountain	yes
Byrum, Ebenezer	365		Eastern District	300	281	26 Feb 1796	1327	25 Jan 1781	88	466	On both sides of Beaver Creek	
Byrum, Ebenezer	39		Eastern District	400	39	11 Jul 1788	1326	12 Jan 1784	67	355	On Beaverdam Creek	
Byrum, Ebenezer	41		Eastern District	400	41	11 Jul 1788	1331	12 Jan 1784	67	356	On Beaverdam Creek beg at a white oak	
Byrum, Ebenezer	42		Eastern District	400	42	11 Jul 1788	1336	24 Jun 1787	67	356	West of Beaverdam Cr Beg at a red oak	
Byrum, Lawrence	608		Sumner	228	1863	20 May 1793	202	24 Oct 1783	81	92	On Red River adjoining Thos. White	yes
Cabatt, Moses	359		Sullivan	50	238	10 Nov 1764	613	15 Jun 1780	69	158	On S side of Holstein River	
Cabbert, Richard	921	Nash, William	Davidson	640	936	18 May 1789			63	321	E Fork First Creek above Stones Lick Cree	yes
Caffery, Barnard	862		Washington	100	846	23 Feb 1793	2462	30 Mar 1780	76	218	On Lick Creek	
Caffery, Jno.	1165		Davidson	640	142	17 Apr 1786	284	14 Feb 1784	66	184	Both side of Stones Cr a br of Stones Riv	
Cage, William	1386		Green	200	1241	27 Jan 1793	2778	15 Mar 1783	79	510	On S side of Clinch River	
Cage, William	435		Sumner	400	320	27 Nov 1792	221	30 Jan 1784	81	1	Beg at a hickory & mulberry	
Cage, William	455		Middle District	1800	394	17 Dec 1794	1753	22 Apr 1784	84	258	Between Harpeth & Duck River	
Cage, Wm.	1024	Armstrong, M.	Sumner	228	244	27 Feb 1796			88	181	Adjoining Richd Hogans West boundary	
Cahoon, Joseph	1678	Bosley, Jas. Robertson	Davidson	640	1603	23 Feb 1793	2413		76	314	On W Harpeth	yes
Cain, James	1458		Davidson	100	59	18 May 1789	2991	2 Oct 1786	71	221	On the waters of Sulphur Fork	
Cain, James	80		Sullivan	260	91	23 Oct 1763	72	8 Feb 1780	43	281	On both sides of Big Creek	
Calcett, Moses	566		Sullivan	326	549	17 Nov 1790	728		76	195	S side of Holstein River	
Caldwell, Alexander	48		Eastern District	400	45	18 May 1789	1029	6 Jan 1779	72	258	On Beaverdam Creek &c	
Caldwell, benoni	993		Hawkins	50	703	12 Nov 1795	700	25 Oct 1780	89	144	On N side of Holston River	
Caldwell, John	021		Sullivan	498			1772	24 Feb 1780			N side of Clinch River	
Caldwell, John	201		Hawkins	100	189	26 Dec 1791	788	27 May 1781	77	309	On S/S Clinch Riv below Lone Mountain	
Caldwell, John	417		Green	498	419	20 Sep 1787			65	493	On the N side of Clinch in Bald Valley	
Caldwell, Lemuel	810	Robertson, Elijah	Davidson	640	813	20 Nov 1788	3304		63	286	On waters of Caney Fork	yes
Caldwell, Thomas	030		Green	200			310	16 Mar 1780			Both sides of Callwells Creek	
Caldwell, Thomas	101		Eastern District	200	90	17 Nov 1790	6748	12 Aug 1780	76	173	N side of Clinch Mtn &c	
Caldwell, Thomas	111		Sullivan	347	122	23 Oct 1782	1860	7 Oct 1779	43	296	On the N side of Holstein River &c	
Caldwell, Thomas	395		Sullivan	400	274	10 Nov 1784	1856	7 Oct 1779	69	169	On Caldwell Creek	
Caldwell, Thomas	439		Sullivan	220	318	10 Nov 1784	300	10 Mar 1780	69	182	On N side of Holstein River	
Caldwell, William	796	Robertson, Elijah	Davidson	640	799	20 Nov 1788	3303		63	280	On waters of Caney Fork	yes
Caler, Frederick	274		Sullivan	640	413	9 Aug 1787	928	1 Jan 1779	61	432	On the S side of Holston River	
Calf, Robert	577		Davidson	274	549	15 Sep 1787	621		63	197	On third creek below the Cross Creek	
Calison, James	05		Knox	640			128	26 Feb 1779			At the head of Buffalow Hollow	yes
Callahan, Charles	1624		Green	100	1345	22 Feb 1795	1891	Dec 1789	84	328	On Dumplin Creek	
Callahan, John	754		Washington	400	568	10 Nov 1784	684	9 Dec 1778	69	129	Upon Nobb Creek	

Earliest Tennessee Land Records

Claimant:	File #:	Assignee:	County:	Acres:	Grant:	Grant Date:	Entry:	Entry Date:	Bk:	Pg:	Location by Stream Name:	Military:
Calloway, John heirs of	403		Sumner	640	414	27 Jun 1793	745	20 Jun 1785	80	346	On the E fork of Middle Fk of Goose Cr	
Callenden, Thomas	63		Davidson	3840	49	14 Mar 1786	871		63	20	N side of Cumberland River	yes
Calleyhaw, Cornelius	017		Tennessee	274			620	22 Apr 1784			S side of Cumberland River	
Callison, James	1190		Green	600	1033	26 Dec 1791	957	5 Nov 1786	77	294	On S side of Holstein River	
Callison, William	155	Smith, Oliver	Tennessee	640	1409	20 Dec 1791	2640	30 Sep 1785	77	353	On both sides of Pine River	yes
Callom, John	44		Green	100	107	1 Nov 1786	1743	21 Apr 1784	58	468	On the waters of Dumplin Creek	
Calloway, Richard	06	Carter, Jno & Landon	Washington	640								
Calsay, Hugh	1266		Green	200	116	12 Jan 1793	627		78	374	On N side of French Broad River	
Calshan [?], Robert	612		Davidson	640	584	15 Sep 1787	627		63	209	On Meat Camp or Bartons Creek	yes
Calvert, Alexander	531		Sullivan	100	534	13 Feb 1791	311	14 Mar 1780	73	381	Beg at said Calverts old corner	
Calvert, Jane	1459		Green	300	1219	27 Nov 1793	132	26 Aug 1791	81	508	Beg at a stake	
Calvet, Moses	626		Sullivan	100	574	27 Jun 1793	1580	10 Sep 1779	80	372	On Sinking Cr waters of Holstein River	
Calvit, Rodrick	022		Sullivan	400			1100	9 Jan 1779			On S side of Holston River	
Calvit, William	64		Sullivan	600	75	23 Oct 1782	52	8 Feb 1780	43	275	On the N side of Holston River	
Calwell, Joseph	894		Green	400	825	Sep 1790	827	29 Oct 1783	74	291	On Crooked Creek	
Calwell, Robert	547		Green	300	549	20 Sep 1787	345	2 Sep 1778	65	541	S/S Nolichuckey Riv mouth of Camp Creek	
Cambell, Geo & R. Elliott	301		Middle District	400	261	7 Jul 1794	99	7 Oct 1779	82	203	On N side of Ohio River &c	
Cameron, Abel	1299	Hickman, Thomas	Sumner	640	3068	19 Jul 1797	4590	6 Apr 1797	90	377	S side of Cumberland	yes
Cameron, Alexander	239	Malloy, Thomas	Tennessee	491	2983	10 Apr 1797			90	286	S side of Cumberland River	yes
Cameron, Alexander	939	Bean, Jesse	Hawkins	320	2509	20 Nov 1795	3822		88	281	On N side of Holston River	yes
Cameron, Elizabeth	1756		Green	216	1433	17 Nov 1797			94	145	Beg on Andrew Englishes line	
Cameron, James	034		Green	200			1406	17 Jan 1784			On the E side of Cove Creek	
Cameron, James	678		Green	200	719	11 Jul 1788	1433	11 Apr 1780	66	466	on S/S Nolichuckey Riv & on E/S Cove Cr	
Cameron, Sampson	1315	McConnel, Robert	Sumner	640	3115	14 Sep 1797	4589	6 May 1797	90	409	To incl the fks of Puncheon Camp Creek	yes
Campbell, Abraham	1378		Washington	160	1303	10 Sep 1801	581	7 Nov 1778	111	49	On waters of Big Limestone	
Campbell, Adly	287		Middle District	640	243	12 Jun 1794			82	181	On the Clear Fork of Cumberland River	
Campbell, Alexander	175		Washington	224	43	23 Oct 1782	340	1 Sep 1779	47	19	E side of Big Limestone Creek	
Campbell, Alexander	180		Washington	100	48	23 Oct 1782	579	7 Nov 1778	47	22	On both sides great Limestone Creek	
Campbell, Alexander	195		Washington	207	63	23 Oct 1782	357	5 Sep 1778	47	30	On Little Limestone	
Campbell, Alexander	764		Washington	200	578	10 Nov 1784	1476	19 Jul 1779	69	132	On Big Limestone	
Campbell, Andrew	051	Dillenberry, Redmond	Sumner	640			4406	6 Sep 1797			Waters of W Fork of Drakes Creek	yes
Campbell, Arthur	314		Sullivan	600	450	28 Nov 1787			67	215	On the Holston River	
Campbell, Arthur	316		Sullivan	640	452	28 Nov 1787			67	216	On a large creek that empties into Clinch &c	
Campbell, Arthur	661		Hawkins	625	566	12 Jul 1794	1	8 Feb 1788	81	592	On Indians Creek	
Campbell, Charles	1209	Barton, Samuel	Sumner	400	166	26 Mar 1795		18 Nov 1792	89	93	On head of W Fork of Bartons Creek	yes
Campbell, Charles	1211	Barton, Samuel	Sumner	400	168	26 Mar 1795		10 Nov 1792	89	94	On Bartons Creek &c	yes
Campbell, Charles	404		Sullivan	140	283	10 Nov 1784	374	29 Mar 1780	69	171	On N side of Holstin River	
Campbell, Chas.	1057		Davidson	640	31	17 Apr 1786	426	1 May 1784	66	45	Lying on Station Camp Creek	
Campbell, Daniel	535	Hickman, Edwin	Davidson	640	507	15 Sep 1787	1700		63	183	N side of Cumberland River	yes
Campbell, Daniel, heirs of	464		Sumner	640	1612	27 Apr 1793	1856	1 Apr 1788	81	20	On Smiths Fork of Caney Fork	yes
Campbell, David	224		Washington	143	92	23 Oct 1782	574	6 Nov 1778	47	44	E side of Mirey Branch	
Campbell, David	43		Eastern District	500	43	11 Jul 1788			67	356	On Turkey Creek &c	
Campbell, David	434		Washington	200	426	13 Oct 1789	178	7 Nov 1778	52	278	On the Reedy Fork of Sinking Creek	
Campbell, David	464		Washington	200	456	13 Oct 1782	575	2 Nov 1779	52	292	On the head of Stones Creek	
Campbell, David	56		Green	640	14	1 Nov 1786	575		59	375	On waters of Nolachuckey River	

Earliest Tennessee Land Records

Claimant:	File #:	Assignee:	County:	Acres:	Grant:	Grant Date:	Entry:	Entry Date:	Bk:	Pg:	Location by Stream Name:	Military:
Campbell, David	583		Hawkins	640	457	29 Jul 1793		12 Mar 1784	80	291	On the E fork of Turkey Creek	
Campbell, David	59		Green	270	17	1 Nov 1786		21 Oct 1783	59	378	Upon Flat Creek	
Campbell, David	60		Green	600	18	1 Nov 1786	69	21 Oct 1783	59	379	Beg at a stake on John Beards line	
Campbell, Demps, heir of Sol.	491		Davidson	640	463	15 Sep 1787	778	15 Sep 1787 [sic]	63	168	About 3 miles N of Cumberland River	yes
Campbell, Henry	325	Robertson, Elijah	Sumner	640	1576	23 Feb 1793	3335	28 Jun 1788	76	301	On Cold Creek &c	yes
Campbell, James	1066		Washington	100	1016	27 Nov 1792	583	6 Nov 1778	80	181	On Doe River & the Lorrel Fork	
Campbell, James	110	Robertson, James	Tennessee	640	1590	23 Feb 1793	1274	28 Oct 1784	76	307	S side of Cumberland River	yes
Campbell, James	221		Middle District	100	201	27 Nov 1792	2563	25 May 1784	80	208	On the S side of Duck River	
Campbell, James	228		Middle District	100	208	1 Jan 1793	2582	25 May 1784	80	210	Situate on the S side of Duck River	
Campbell, James	235		Middle District	100	215	1 Jan 1793	2584	25 May 1784	80	213	On S side of Duck River	
Campbell, James	37		Green	600	873	17 Nov 1790	378	23 Oct 1783			S side of Holston River	
Campbell, James	442		Sullivan	365	321	10 Nov 1784	321 [sic]	17 Mar 1780	69	183	In Carters Valley	
Campbell, James	589		Sullivan	100	587	29 Jul 1793	1893	7 Oct 1779	76	475	N side of HolstonRriver	
Campbell, James	706		Hawkins	200	526	12 Jun 1794	609	7 June 1780	82	162	On a branch of Indian Creek	
Campbell, James	79		Davidson	2075	65	14 Mar 1786	367		63	26	Beg at a white oak & dogwood	yes
Campbell, James	835		Washington	168	649	10 Nov 1790	581	7 Nov 1778	69	151	On Dunhams Spring Branch	
Campbell, James	896		Washington	600	873	17 Nov 1790			76	135	N side of Holston &c	
Campbell, Jas.	487	Howard, Thos.	Sumner	320	131	27 Apr 1793	840	12 Dec 1792	81	36	On S side of Cumberland River	yes
Campbell, Jeremiah	1097		Washington	94	1047	27 Nov 1792	582	6 Nov 1778	80	204	On Doe River	
Campbell, John	016		Hawkins	130			2325	4 Dec 1779			S side of Holston River	
Campbell, John	100		Davidson	2560	86	14 Mar 1786	41		63	35	South side of Cumberland River	yes
Campbell, John	385		Green	300	387	20 Sep 1787	313	7 Jun 1784	65	482	On the S side of Holston River	
Campbell, Joseph	1147		Hawkins	225	865	20 Aug 1800	312	23 Oct 1783	108	107	On N side of Holston River	
Campbell, Laughlin	031	Betts, Archibald	Davidson	1000			634	31 Jul 1784			N side of Cumberland	
Campbell, Patrick	644	Stewart, Duncan	Tennessee	428	3218	14 Sep 1797	91		92	13	S side of Cumberland River	
Campbell, Patrick	846	Gillespie, William	Sumner	1900	2349	20 May 1793	3581	27 Oct 1792	81	202	On Cumberland River	yes
Campbell, Robert	1457		Davidson	50	58	18 May 1789	2169	11 Feb 1786	71	221	Moulders trace a br of Sapling Lick Fork	
Campbell, Robert	1709		Green	640	1424	8 Jun 1797	108	21 Oct 1783	90	320	N side of Nolachuckey River	
Campbell, Robert	196		Washington	400	64	23 Oct 1782	576	6 Nov 1778	47	30	On a branch of Big Limestone Creek	
Campbell, Robert	309		Sullivan	130	448	9 Aug 1787	321	17 Mar 1780	61	467	In Carters Valley	
Campbell, Robert	316		Washington	600	183	24 Oct 1782	577	6 Nov 1778	49	219	On Little Sinking Creek	
Campbell, Robert	419		Sullivan	130	298	10 Nov 1784	1711	24 Sep 1779	69	176	In Carters Valley	
Campbell, Thomas	500		Davidson	274	472	15 Sep 1787	994		63	171	N side of Cumberland River	yes
Campbell, William	1252		Washington	200	1224	27 Feb 1796	2509	31 Mar 1780	88	509	Carters Valley Carmacks&Thos Gibbeons	
Campbell, William	14		Washington	100	304	24 Oct 1782	1227	22 Feb 1779	43	299	On the N side of Sinking Creek &c	
Campbell, William	155		Hawkins	200	88	16 Nov 1790	1813	6 Oct 1779	77	181	On the E Fork of Spring Creek	
Campbell, William	193	Sullivan, Michael	Tennessee	640	1473	4 Jan 1792	795	4 May 1784	77	369	S side of Cumberland River	yes
Campbell, William	435		Hawkins	50	313	24 Jun 1793	558	6 May 1780	80	190	Holston on a fork of Spring Creek	
Campbell, William	446		Hawkins	100	324	24 Jun 1793	827	28 Jul 1781	80	194	S/S Holston Riv head of E Prong Spring Cr	
Campbell, William	457		Hawkins	150	336	24 Jun 1793	833	26 Aug 1781	80	197	On the W Fork of Spring Creek	
Campbell, William	545		Washington	254	810	11 Jul 1788	229	26 May 1778	64	333	On the Cedar Branch &c	
Campbell, Wm.	975		Green	150	889	17 Nov 1790	1812	6 Oct 1779	76	134	On the E Fork of Spring Creek	
Campbell, Wm.	338		Hawkins	400	332	8 Mar 1793	2503	27 Mar 1780	78	475	In Beaver Creek Valley	
Campbell, Zachariah	1376		Washington	100	1291	9 Dec 1797	2711	22 Mar 1779	96	14	S side of Watauga River	
Campbell, Michael &P Phillips	1697	McKinns, Timothy	Davidson	640	1658	23 Feb 1793	3390		76	339	On the waters of Stones River	yes

Earliest Tennessee Land Records

Claimant:	File #:	Assignee:	County:	Acres:	Grant:	Grant Date:	Entry:	Entry Date:	Bk:	Pg:	Location by Stream Name:	Military:
Campble, David	38		Green	640	14	1 Nov 1786	110	27 Apr 1785	63	218	On the waters of Nolachuckey River	
Campin, James	640		Davidson	2560	613		334				On South side of Cumberland River	yes
Canady, John (or Jacob)	283		Eastern District	200	208	5 Jan 1795	1963	10 Oct 1779	84	56	On N side of Holston River	
Canbon, James	423	Donelson, S. & John Latha	Eastern District	275	2955	1 Mar 1797	4483		90	220	Beg at a Black oak & Post oak	yes
Canbrill [sic], Stephen	1304		Davidson	640	269	10 Jul 1788	316	28 Feb 1784	66	431	Beg at a tree marked W & W	
Candler, Joseph	796	Hickman, Edwin	Sumner	640	2257	20 May 1793	2333	29 Oct 1792	81	182	On Lick Creek	yes
Cane, Richard	699		Sullivan	66	644	5 Dec 1794			84	158	Beg at Alex Catwell [sic] corner	
Cane, William	949	Whitsett, John	Davidson	640	966	18 May 1789			63	328	On both sides of Smiths Fork	yes
Cannady, David	1098	Easten, James	Sumner	640	2589	7 Mar 1796	3929	22 Jul 1795	88	321	On E side of a large fork of Caney Fork	yes
Cannon, Edward	2241	Stewart, Duncan	Davidson	640	2668	6 Jun 1796	3863		88	364	On S side of Harpeth River	yes
Cannon, Lewis	19		Tennessee	1584	1167	26 Nov 1789	1217	22 Sep 1784	74	162	On N side of Cumberland River	
Cannon, Minos	1530	Alhead, Vernon hrs.	Davidson	640	1087	26 Nov 1789	2105		74	124	Mill cr, nr ridge bet sd cr & Stones Riv	yes
Cannon, Sampson	681	Beard, Joseph	Hawkins	474	2392	17 Jul 1794	3536		81	603	On N side of Clinch River	yes
Cannon, Thomas	016	Clark, Lardner, Esq.	Tennessee	640			2174	12 Sep 1785			S side of Cumberland River	yes
Cannon, Thomas	857		Green	100	837	13 Feb 1791			73	382	On Sinking Fork of Long Creek	
Cantrell (Cottrell?), John	1071		Hawkins	200	758	2 Dec 1796	1791	2 Oct 1779	91	270	In Pinchin Camp Valley	
Cantrell, John	577	Betts, William	Tennessee	640	3024	10 Apr 1797	3930		90	303	On Barnetts Creek	yes
Cantrell, Stephen	1003	Weaver, M.	Davidson	274	1020	18 May 1789			63	341	On head branches of Second Creek	yes
Cantrell, Stephen	1402	Johnston, John	Sumner	228	3332	6 Dec 1797	4141	6 Feb 1797	97	51	Waters of Manshoes & Madisons Creek	yes
Cantrell, Stephen	510	Britton, George	Davidson	640	482	15 Sep 1787	351		63	175	On Sulphur Fork of Red River	yes
Cantril, Stephen	1381		Davidson	640	64	8 Oct 1787	203	29 Jan 1785	68	147	On Stewarts Cr a branch of Stones River	
Cantwell, Stephen	942	Mcileway, John hr of	Davidson	1000	958	18 May 1789			63	326	On North side of Cumberland River	yes
Capehart, John	2171	Williams, Willoughby	Davidson	640	2492	1 Apr 1794	2840		81	452	On waters of Stones River	yes
Caper, Robert	1595		Davidson	1000	1284	10 Dec 1790			74	360	On W Fork of Jones Creek	
Capps, Demsey	124	Riding, Robert	Tennessee	274	1630	23 Feb 1793	3273	26 Dec 1785	76	327	Bet. Grice & Yellow Creek	
Capps, James	822	Wycoff, W. & L. Clark	Davidson	1000	825	17 jan 1789	2117		63	291	On S side of Cumberland River	yes
Capps, William	33	Blount, John Gray & Thom	Davidson	640	19	14 Mar 1786	476		63	8	E side of Tennessee River	yes
Caps, Oliver	1419	Hadley, Joshua	Sumner	228	3274	6 Dec 1797	4550	8 May 1797	98	156	On headwaters of Cedar Creek	yes
Caps, Thomas	1368		Washington	100	1283	17 Nov 1797	2711	2 Jan 1781	94	142	On headwaters of Wolf Branch	
Capton, John	1674	Greer, Alex. & J. Robertson	Davidson	640	1599	23 Feb 1793	2798		76	312	On the head waters of S Harpeth River	yes
Card, Joseph	2229	Harget, Frederick	Davidson	640	2590	7 Mar 1796	1332	19 Dec 1792	88	321	On E Fork of Turnbulls Creek	yes
Carder, Godfrey	086		Washington	570			939	2 Jan 1779			N side of Watauga River	
Carder, Godfrey	166		Washington	500	34	23 Oct 1782			47	15	N side of Watauga River	
Caree, John	461	Donelson, S. & Wm. Tyrrell	Tennessee	2560	2555	7 Mar 1796	11		88	308	On W branch of Sulphur ork	yes
Carey, William	1093	Easten, James	Sumner	640	2584	7 Mar 1796	3855	22 Jul 1795	88	318	E/S of large fk of the Caney Fork	yes
Carleton, John	2269	Coghlin, James	Davidson	640	2747	20 Jul 1796	3153		88	456	On a large creek of Tennessee Creek	
Carlisle, James	249		Sullivan	200	388	9 Aug 1787	755	14 Mar 1781	61	407	On S side of Holston River	
Carlisle, James	98		Hawkins	342	132	18 Dec 1791	2177	9 Nov 1779	75	154	On Roseberrys Creek	
Carlock, George	770	Scott, James	Sumner	182	2218	20 May 1793	3698	19 Dec 1792	81	173	On S side of Cumberland River	yes
Carlton, John	1022	Drake, Jonathan	Davidson	640	1040	18 May 1789	3153		63	346	On Raccoon Creek	yes
Carmach, Cornelius	55		Hawkins	298	40	23 Apr 1794	1902	8 Oct 1779	72	252	N/S Holson Riv on both sides of [?] cr	
Carmack, John	661		Sullivan	500	608	23 Apr 1794	2093	26 Oct 1779	81	556	On both sides of Sinking Creek	
Carleton, John	42		Hawkins	295	27	18 May 1789	290	10 Mar 1780	72	247	In Carters valley on the N/S of Big Creek	
Carmack, Cornelius	44		Hawkins	400	29	18 May 1789	1894	6 Oct 1779	72	248	Carters Valley Carmacks&Thos Gibbeons	
Carmack, John	642		Hawkins	640	511	23 Apr 1794	222	22 Feb 1780	81	552	In Powells Valley	

Earliest Tennessee Land Records

Claimant:	File #:	Assignee:	County:	Acres:	Grant:	Grant Date:	Entry:	Entry Date:	Bk:	Pg:	Location by Stream Name:	Military:
Carmack, John, Senr.	57		Hawkins	156	42	18 May 1789	2094	26 Oct 1779	72	253	N/S Holsons rv on both sides of Big Cr	
Carmack, Joseph	036	Hobbs, Joel	Robertson	640			2925	13 Aug 1796			On Elk Fork of Red River	
Carmady, James	336	Peters, Thomas	Eastern District	640	2511	20 Nov 1795	2114		88	282	On N side of Clinch River	yes
Carmichael, James	855		Washington	450	864	11 Aug 1789	666	8 Dec 1778	71	32	On both sides of Horse Pasture Branch	
Carnahan, Andrew	706		Davidson	640	679	8 Dec 1787	1265		63	239	On waters of Big Harpeth	yes
Carnahan, Dennis	1416	Hadley, Joshua	Sumner	228	3271	6 Dec 1797	4546	21 Jun 1797	98	154	On the waters of Spring Creek	yes
Carnes, John	469		Sullivan	400	348	10 Nov 1784	464	24 Apr 1780	69	195	On N Fork of Holstein River	
Carnes, Joseph	1053		Hawkins	300	763	21 Jan 1797	2185	12 Nov 1779	91	112	On Lyons Creek	
Carnes, Joseph	1430		Green	400	1242	27 Nov 1792	2952	27 Oct 1779	80	168	On the waters of French Broad Rlv &c	
Carney, Andrew	085	Hickman, Thomas	Sumner	640			4587	6 Apr 1797			On waters of Main E Fork &c	yes
Carney, Thomas	543		Washington	300	808	11 Jul 1788	2663	14 Nov 1780	64	333	On the S side of Watauga River	
Carney, Thomas	561		Washington	320	826	11 Jul 1788	1553	27 Aug 1779	64	336	On Wautaugah	
Carothers, John	167		Sullivan	220	174	10 Oct 1783	438	21 Apr 1780	53	147	On the N side of Holston iver	
Carpenter, Job	43	Tuton, William	Sumner	640	882	17 Jan 1789	3493	5 Jun 1788	63	305	On N side of Red River	yes
Carpenter, William	1980	Blount, John Gray & Thom	Davidson	185	1885	20 May 1793	3264		81	97	On N side of Big Harpeth &c	yes
Carr, Abner	346	Kerkendall, Matthew	Sumner	428	1426	20 Dec 1791	3455	25 Oct 1786	77	358	On Middle Fork of Red River	yes
Carr, Jane	478		Sullivan	460	357	10 Nov 1784	767	2 Apr 1781	69	199	Beg at a white oak	
Carr, Patrick	08		Sullivan	200			1653	17 Sep 1779				
Carr, Patrick	368		Washington	200	360	11 Oct 1783	2923	10 Sep 1780	52	247	On the head of Sinking Creek	
Carr, Patrick	675		Sullivan	144	623	9 Jul 1794	160	11 Feb 1780	81	629	On a branch of Whitetop Creek	
Carr, William	287	Mountflorence, Jas. C.	Sumner	1000	1290	10 Dec 1790	3391	12 Jun 1787	74	362	On N side of Cumberland River	
Carraway, Thomas	719	Sheppard, Nancy	Davidson	640	692	11 Jul 1788	1865		63	244	On waters of Caspers Creek	yes
Carrick, Samuel C.	117		Eastern District	100	150	29 Jul 1793	2678	11 Dec 1780	76	480	N side of Holston River	
Carrick, Samuel C.	124		Eastern District	50	157	29 Jul 1793	2680	11 Dec 1780	76	482	N side of Holston River &c	
Carrick, Zachariah	589	Nelson, Robert	Tennessee	1000	3057	19 Jul 1797	4402		90	372	Main head of a South Fork	yes
Carrick, Samuel	359		Eastern District	274	276	20 Jul 1796	1488	19 Feb 1784	88	435	On N side of Holston River	
Carrier, John	296	Phillips, P. & M. Campbell	Sumner	640	1316	10 Dec 1790	2366	23 Jun 1788	74	371	On Round Lick Creek	yes
Carigen, Godfrey	560		Washington	300	825	11 Jul 1788	560	30 Oct 1778	64	335	On Buck Creek	
Cariger, Godfrey	708		Green	2000	749	11 Jul 1788	1131	30 Oct 1783	66	477	On Richland Creek beg at a stake	
Carringer, Michael	1251		Washington	50	1223	27 Feb 1796	2001	22 Oct 1779	88	509	On waters of Watagah River	
Carrol, Daniel	229	Marshall, John	Sumner	228	1134	26 Nov 1789	1601	21 Sep 1787	74	146	On Manskers Trace	yes
Carrol, William	2044	Sheppard, Nancy	Davidson	640	2064	20 May 1793	1754		81	140	2nd cr that the boundary line crosses	yes
Carroll, Douglas	1614	Hill, Bennett	Davidson	428	1342	12 Jul 1794	136		74	379	On N Cross Creek	yes
Carroll, Harwell	488	Marshall, John	Davidson	640	460	15 Sep 1787	1605		63	167	On Maney Fork Creek	yes
Carrom, James	785	Hickman, Thomas	Davidson	640	758	11 Jul 1788	2638		63	266	On 1st creek &c	yes
Caruthers, Andrew, Ass	310		Eastern District	200	178	26 Mar 1795	5		86	379	In the Grassey Valley	
Caruthers, Jonathan	1148		Washington	148	1106	12 Jul 1794	2547	25 Apr 1780	81	571	Joining to lands of John Young &c	
Carry, Shadrack	21		Maury	274	39	14 Jul 1812	187	29 Nov 1809	126	442	On both sides of Casheys Creek	
Carsiner, Jacob	1133		Washington	100	1091	12 Jul 1794	2380	27 Nov 1779	81	566	Beg at a red oak	
Carsiner, Jacob (Joseph)	1119		Washington	200	1078	12 Jul 1794	2533	10 Apr 1780	81	561	Beg at a small white oak	
Carson, Charles	1169		Washington	30	1127	7 Jul 1794	2658	26 Sep 1780	81	619	On Wautauga River	
Carson, David	426		Middle District	1280	365	17 Dec 1794	2036	3 May 1784	84	236	On N side of Elk River	
Carson, James	035	O'Neal, Matthew	Davidson	640			2536	29 Oct 1787			On both sides of Stones Cr.	
Carson, James	2049	O'Neal, Matthias	Davidson	640	2115	20 May 1793	2536		81	153	On both sides of Stones Creek	yes
Carson, John	1676	Sheppard, Wm. & J. Rober	Davidson	640	1601	23 Feb 1793	2797		76	313	S/S Harpeth River below Fletcher's Lick	yes

Claimant:	File #:	Assignee:	County:	Acres:	Grant:	Entry:	Grant Date:	Entry Date:	Bk:	Pg:	Location by Stream Name:	Military:
Carson, Moses	295		Green	200	297	2484	20 Sep 1787	10 Mar 1780	65	457	On the waters of Lick Creek	
Carson, Moses	438		Green	100	440	2220	20 Sep 1787	16 Nov 1779	65	499	On the waters of Lick Creek	
Carson, Moses	525		Washington	50	788	1333	16 Aug 1787	8 Apr 1779	64	148	On a water of Big Limestone	
Carson, Robert	488		Washington	100	673	3001	1 Nov 1786	26 Mar 1784	60	446	Beg upon a red oak	
Carson, Robert	563		Washington	100	828	353	11 Jul 1788	4 Sep 1778	64	336	Upon waters of Big Limestone	
Carson, Robert	838		Green	200	819	1542	13 Feb 1791	7 Mar 1784	73	375	On waters of French Broad	
Carson, Samuel	1596		Green	100	1338		22 Feb 1795	19 Feb 1780	83	438	N side of French Broad River	
Carson, William	1580		Green	200	1331	2704	4 Feb 1795	20 Dec 1780	83	399	On the Sinking Fork of Long Creek	
Carter, Abraham	345		Green	275	347	256	20 Sep 1787	23 Oct 1783	65	471	On Lick Creek	
Carter, Benjamin	1168		Green	100	1011		26 Dec 1791		77	285	On the Roaring Fork of Lick Creek	
Carter, Benjamin	85		Davidson	3840	71	694	14 Mar 1786		63	29	On both sides Carter Creek	yes
Carter, Caleb	305		Eastern District	200	214	463	22 Feb 1795	2 Apr 1780	84	289	On S side of Holstons River	
Carter, Caleb	537		Green	500	539	255	20 Sep 1787	22 oct 1783	65	536	On Lick Creek	
Carter, Charles	1207	McLaughlin, Neill	Sumner	400	163		26 Mar 1795	1 Nov 1792	89	91	On Bledsoes Lick Creek	yes
Carter, Daniel	296		Green	400	298	253	20 Sep 1787	7 Jun 1784	65	458	On both sides of Lick Creek	
Carter, David	1932	Dean, James	Davidson	640	1749	1698	29 Aug 1793		81	66	On the Big & Little Harpeth	yes
Carter, Emanuel	1143		Washington	360	1101	663	12 Jul 1794	8 Dec 1778	81	569	Beg at a black oak & dogwood	
Carter, George	2282	Gilston, David	Davidson	700	2764	3339	20 Jul 1796		88	463	On Leepers Fork of Harpeth River	yes
Carter, George	842	Brook, Joseph	Davidson	640	847	3339	17 Jan 1789		63	296	On N side of Cumberland River	yes
Carter, Giles	253		Davidson	274	239	872	7 Mar 1786		63	88	On both sides of Madisons Creek	
Carter, Henry	332	Fenner, Richard	Davidson	640	318	2178	28 Jun 1787		63	118	S side of Cumberland River &c	yes
Carter, Humphrey	2310	Kilgore, Thomas	Davidson	640	2511	978	27 Aug 1795		89	41	Bet Red River & Sulphur Fork	yes
Carter, Isaac	2449	Wheaton, Daniel	Davidson	640	3292	4325	6 Dec 1797		98	169	On the W Fork of Sams Creek	yes
Carter, Jacob	313		Green	200	315	342	20 Sep 1787	7 Jun 1784	65	463	On the Roaring Fork of Lick Creek	
Carter, John	02		Carter	Depositions								
Carter, John	112		Western District	1000	112	596	10 Jul 1788	27 Oct 1783	67	324	In the fork of the Forked Deer River	
Carter, John	228		Washington	640	96	603	23 Oct 1782	23 Nov 1778	47	46	On Watauga River	
Carter, John	307		Green	100	309	1457	20 Sep 1787	2 Feb 1784	65	461	On the Roaring Fork of Lick Creek	
Carter, John	39		Green	100	309	261	20 Sep 1787	8 Nov 1784			On the Roaring Fork of Lick Creek	
Carter, John	487		Washington	300	672	604	1 Nov 1786	15 Jun 1786	60	445	Beg at 2 white oaks &c	
Carter, John	673	Sullivant, Lucas	Hawkins	228	2382	3727	12 Jul 1794		81	600	On N side of Clinch River	yes
Carter, John	820		Washington	400	634	2457	10 Nov 1784	28 Feb 1780	69	147	On S side of Linn Mountain	
Carter, John	865		Green	100	815	73	27 Nov 1789	12 May 1784	74	18	On a fork of Gists Creek	
Carter, John	970		Washington	300	947	76	17 Nov 1790		76	160	Beg at 2 white oaks &c	
Carter, John & John McAnulty	605		Middle District (	3000	375	1610	20 Aug 1800	2 Apr 1784	108	107	On Eagle Creek	
Carter, John, Jr.	344		Green	250	346	257	20 Sep 1787	23 Oct 1783	65	471	On Lick Creek & the Dry Fork	
Carter, Joseph	299	Barton, Samuel	Sumner	640	1356	3649	10 Dec 1790	24 Apr 1790	74	384	On waters of Cedar Creek	yes
Carter, Joseph	515		Green	250	517	55	20 Sep 1787	21 Oct 1783	65	528	Lying on Grassy Creek	
Carter, Joseph, Jr.	1387		Green	200	1242	1325 (?)	27 Jan 1793	3 Apr 1779	79	510	Joining Joe Caters [sic] Senr land	
Carter, Landon	093		Washington	200		260-2769		1778-1781				
Carter, Landon	1138		Washington	100	1096	2329	12 Jul 1794	4 Dec 1779	81	568	On the drafts of Stoney Creek	
Carter, Landon	1140		Washington	276 (376	1098	2769-260	12 Jul 1794	1781 & 1778	81	568	Beg at a stooping chesnut	
Carter, Landon	1221		Washington	640	1166	178	27 Aug 1795	19 Mar 1778	87	514	On waters of Stoney Creek	
Carter, Landon	1222		Washington	640	1167	200	27 Aug 1795	22 Oct 1779	87	514	On N side of Iron Mountain	
Carter, Landon	1223		Washington	200	1168	2493	27 Aug 1795	11 Mar 1780	87	515	Joining to E of Martin Shoulters entry	

Claimant:	File #:	Assignee:	County:	Acres:	Grant:	Grant Date:	Entry:	Entry Date:	Bk:	Pg:	Location by Stream Name:	Military:
Carter, Landon	1224		Washington	640	1169	27 Aug 1795	413	17 Sep 1778	87	516	On waters of Watauga	
Carter, Landon	1225		Washington	100	1170	27 Aug 1795	2456	7 Mar 1780	87	517	On waters of Wataga River	
Carter, Landon	1226		Washington	300	1171	27 Aug 1795	264	23 Jul 1778	87	517	Beg at 2 white oaks	
Carter, Landon	1227		Washington	640	1172	27 Aug 1795	1416	1 Jun 1779	87	518	On waters of N side of Wataga	
Carter, Landon	1228		Washington	250	1173	27 Aug 1795	2298	27 Nov 1779	87	518	Beg at a double white oak	
Carter, Landon	1229		Washington	600	1172 (?)	27 Aug 1795	262	22 Jul 1778	87	519	On waters of Watauga	
Carter, Landon	1230		Washington	600	1175	27 Aug 1795	1975	19 Oct 1779	87	520	On S side of the Linn Mountain	
Carter, Landon	1231		Washington	200	1176	27 Aug 1795	2494	11 Mar 1780	87	320	Where the path &c	
Carter, Landon	1232		Washington	640	1177	27 Aug 1795	1156	1 Feb 1779	87	521	On waters of Watauga & Doe Rivers	
Carter, Landon	1233		Washington	480	1178	27 Aug 1795	619	23 Nov 1778	87	521	On waters of Watauga	
Carter, Landon	1238		Washington	640	1210	20 Jul 1796	965	2 Jan 1779	88	504	On both sides of Stoney Creek	
Carter, Landon	1254		Washington	1140	1226	4 Feb 1796	796 & 552	30 Oct 1779	88	510	On N of Wataugh River	
Carter, Landon	1261		Washington	100	1199	4 Dec 1795	2910	28 Aug 1781	89	324	Beg on a black oak	
Carter, Landon	1332		Green	50	1178	23 Feb 1793	1160	1 Feb 1779	78	430	Large cr supposed to be waters of Duck Riv	
Carter, Landon	1333		Green	640	1179	23 Feb 1793	81	26 Feb 1778	78	430	On Elk River	
Carter, Landon	1334		Green	150	1180	23 Feb 1793	1282	16 Mar 1779	78	431	On waters of Elk River	
Carter, Landon	1335		Green	400	1181	23 Feb 1793	50	26 Feb 1778	78	432	Large cr supposed be waters Duck River	
Carter, Landon	1336		Green	150	1182	23 Feb 1793	938	1 Jan 1779	78	432	On waters of Elk River	
Carter, Landon	1337		Green	150	1183	23 Feb 1793	316	2 Feb 1778	78	433	On waters of Elk River	
Carter, Landon	1338		Green	640	1184	23 Feb 1793	82	26 Feb 1778	78	433	On a branch of Stones River	
Carter, Landon	1339		Green	640 (600	1185	23 Feb 1793	1185 [sic]	4 Jan 1793	78	434	On Duck River &c	
Carter, Landon	1340		Green	150	1186	23 Feb 1793	1176	1 Feb 1779	78	434	Nr trace leads fr Nashville to Chicamauga	
Carter, Landon	1341		Green	300	1187	23 Feb 1793	599	21 Nov 1778 [?]	78	435	Including a walnut bottom	
Carter, Landon	1342		Green	200	1188	23 Feb 1793	316	2 Sep 1778	78	435	On waters of Elk River	
Carter, Landon	1343		Green	200	1189	23 Feb 1793	925	1 Jan 1779	78	430	Creek supposed to be waters of Elk River	
Carter, Landon	1344		Green	200	1190	23 Feb 1793	1319	31 Mar 1779	78	436	On waters of Elk River	
Carter, Landon	1345		Green	200	1191	23 Feb 1793	1498	4 Aug 1779	78	437	Joining lower side survey of sd Carters	
Carter, Landon	1346		Green	200 (220	1192	23 Feb 1793	1142	27 Jan 1779	78	437	On waters of Elk River	
Carter, Landon	1367		Washington	640	1283	17 Nov 1797	1664	18 Sep 1779	95	141	Beg at an oak	
Carter, Landon	1447 [?]		Green	640	1257	27 Nov 1792	82	24 Feb 1778	80	173	On Burds Creek inc the cedar spring	
Carter, Landon	1484		Green	150	1247	12 Jul 1794	193	6 Apr 1778	81	577	On waters of Elk River	
Carter, Landon	1492		Green	640	1255	12 Jul 1794	1098	9 Jan 1779	81	580	On S side of Holston River	
Carter, Landon	1502		Green	640	1263	12 Jul 1794	138	29 Feb 1778	81	583	On S side of Holston River	
Carter, Landon	1682	Clinton, John	Davidson	228	1611	23 Feb 1793	422		76	317	On South Harpeth River	yes
Carter, Landon	182		Middle District	1280	164	17 Nov 1790			76	178	W side of Cumberland Mountain &c	
Carter, Landon	310		Western District	500	309	18 May 1789	943	2 Jan 1779	72	258	On Harris's Fork of Obion River	
Carter, Landon	311		Western District	200	311	18 May 1789	961	2 Jan 1779	72	267	On N side of N Fork of Obion River	
Carter, Landon	312		Western District	300	312	18 May 1789	953	2 Jan 1779	72	267	On N side of N Fork of Obion River	
Carter, Landon	313		Western District	500	313	18 May 1789	954	2 Jan 1779	72	267	On both sides of Harrie's Fork &c	
Carter, Landon	314		Western District	300	314	18 May 1789	952	2 Jan 1779	72	268	On E side of Harris's Fork &c	
Carter, Landon	315		Western District	200	315	18 May 1789	957	2 Jan 1779	72	268	On the N side of N Fork of Obion River	
Carter, Landon	316		Western District	300	316	18 May 1789	947	2 Jan 1779	72	268	On the N side of Harris's Fork &c	
Carter, Landon	317		Western District	400	317	18 May 1789	1007	4 Jan 1779	72	269	On the N side of N fork of Obion River	
Carter, Landon	318		Western District	640	318	18 May 1789	955	2 Jan 1779	72	269	On a branch of Harris's Fork &c	
Carter, Landon	319		Western District	400	319	18 May 1789	999	4 Jan 1779	72	269	On waters of Harrie's Fork	

Claimant:	File #:	Assignee:	County:	Acres:	Grant:	Grant Date:	Entry:	Entry Date:	Bk:	Pg:	Location by Stream Name:	Military:
Carter, Landon	320		Western District	300	320	18 May 1789	759	23 Dec 1778	72	270	On the Long Fork	
Carter, Landon	321		Western District	600	321	18 May 1789	956	2 Jan 1779	72	270	On Harris's Fork &c	
Carter, Landon	322		Western District	640	322	18 May 1789	997	4 Jan 1779	72	270	On E side of Harris's Fork &c	
Carter, Landon	323		Western District	640	323	18 May 1789	993	2 Jan 1779	72	271	On Harris's Fork &c	
Carter, Landon	324		Western District	300	324	18 May 1789	2893	2 Jun 1782	72	271	On the N side of N Fork of Obion River	
Carter, Landon	325		Western District	500	325	18 May 1789	954 (945)	20 Feb 1785	72	271	On E side of Harris's Fork &c	
Carter, Landon	326		Western District	640	326	18 May 1789	956	2 Jan 1779	72	272	On both sides of Harris's Fork	
Carter, Landon	38		Hawkins	640	23	18 May 1789	2119	3 May 1783	72	245	N/S Tennessee Riv & North Fork of Deep Riv	
Carter, Landon	45		Hawkins	640	30	18 May 1789			72	248	On S/S of Clinch Riv on Gap Creek Valley	
Carter, Landon	47		Eastern District	640	310	18 May 1789			72	258	On Harris' Fork of Obran River	
Carter, Landon	48		Hawkins	640	33	18 May 1789	2500	10 Mar 1780	72	249	On S side of Clinch River on Gap Creek	
Carter, Landon	516		Washington	150	779	16 Aug 1787	2381	27 Dec 1779	64	145	North easterly side of the Big Ridge	
Carter, Landon	70		Eastern District	640	72	16 Nov 1790	2563	30 May 1780	73	396	On N side of Tennessee River &c	
Carter, Landon	71		Eastern District	600	73	16 Nov 1790			73	396	On N/S Tenn riv on E Fork of Big Creek	
Carter, Landon	771		Hawkins	500	611	12 Jul 1794	183	19 Mar 1778	82	215	N/S Holston Riv & both/S of mo. Richland	
Carter, Landon	772		Hawkins	500	612	12 Jul 1794	184	19 Mar 1778	82	216	N/S Holston both sides Richland Cr join #183	
Carter, Landon	992		Washington	300	964	26 Dec 1791	2398	15 Jan 1780	77	297	Joining 2 other surveys	
Carter, Landon	993		Washington	200	965	26 Dec 1791	667	8 Nov 1778	77	297	On Stoney Creek	
Carter, Landon	994		Washington	100	966	26 Dec 1791	424	23 Sep 1778	77	297	Joining his survey &c	
Carter, Landon	995		Washington	200	967	26 Dec 1791	669	8 Dec 1778	77	298	On Stoney Creek	
Carter, Landon	996		Washington	280	968	26 Dec 1791	609	23 Nov 1778	77	298	Joining a survey &c	
Carter, Landon	997		Washington	640	969	26 Dec 1791	608	23 Nov 1778	77	299	On Stoney Creek &c	
Carter, Landon	998		Washington	300	970	26 Dec 1791	2397	15 Jan 1780	77	299	On Stoney Creek	
Carter, Langdon	027		Green	640			2015	25 Oct 1779			S side of Clinch River	
Carter, Levi	1383		Green	175	1238	27 Jan 1793	1429	27 jan 1784	79	508	On both sides of Lick Creek	
Carter, Nathan	1367		Green	200	1222	27 Jan 1793	1362	10 May 1779	79	504	On waters of Nolachuckey	
Carter, Robert	229	Murphree, Hardy	Davidson	228	215	7 Mar 1786	736		63	79	On both sides E Fk of Station Camp Cr	yes
Carter, Samuel	1152	Harris, Edward	Davidson	640	2657	4 Jun 1796	3845		88	353	Joining sd Harris survey	yes
Carthy,Geo&Wm.Campbell	1814		Davidson	640	387	26 Jun 1793	774	22 Nov 1785	80	337	On the S side of Cumberland River	
Cartwright, Joseph	551		Davidson	640	525	15 Sep 1787	831		63	189	North side of Cumberland River	yes
Cartwright, Robert	1215		Davidson	640	179	10 Jul 1788	279	13 Feb 1784	66	367	On S side of public land of Gaspers Lick	
Cartwright, Robert	1726	Lewellen, Thomas	Davidson	224	1437	20 Dec 1791	405		77	360	On the waters of Dry Creek	yes
Cartwright, Robert	753		Sumner	640	2157	20 May 1793	830	23 Jun 1792	81	162	Waters of an E branch of Roaring River	yes
Cartwright, Robert	855	Ferrell, enoch	Davidson	366	863	17 Jan 1787	21		63	300	On waters of Station Camp Creek	yes
Cartwright, Thomas	609		Sumner	640	1864	20 May 1793	837	23 Jun 1792	81	92 [?]	On waters of an E br of Roaring River	yes
Caruther, Samuel	662		Sullivan	100	610	12 Jul 1794	122	9 Feb 1780	81	598	Beg at a white oak near Holston River	
Carveat, Alexander	2362	L--den, John hrs of	Davidson	640	461	19 Jul 1797	591	23 Aug 1784	90	371	On Heaton Stations Creek	
Carvin, William	1152		Davidson	640	129	17 Apr 1786	427	5 May 1784	66	181	On the N side of Cumberland River	
Cary, James	1358		Davidson	480	41	8 Oct 1787	98	14 Jan 1784	68	138	On Rockey Creek	
Casbol, Robert	2296	Lomack, William	Davidson	274	2774	10 Sep 1796	3205		88	524	On W side of Stones river	yes
Caseleman, Benj	340	Phillips, John	Sumner	640	1400	20 Dec 1791	181	26 Jun 1788	77	351	S side of Cumberland River	
Casey, James	831		Green	300	814	18 Apr 1790	290	23 Oct 1783	73	260	On the N side of Lick Creek	
Casey, John	2271	McCulloch, Alex	Davidson	640	2749	20 Jul 1796	556		88	457	On a large creek of the Tennessee river	yes
Casey, John	2272	Bullock, Lemuel hrs of	Davidson	1000	2750	20 Jul 1796	3965		88	457	On a large creek of Tennessee River	yes
Cash, James	515		Washington	500	778	16 Aug 1787	827	29 Dec 1778	64	145	On Little Lime Stone	

Claimant:	File #:	Assignee:	County:	Acres:	Grant:	Grant Date:	Entry:	Entry Date:	Bk:	Pg:	Location by Stream Name:	Military:
Cash, James	907		Washington	100	884	17 Nov 1790	1481	25 Jul 1779	76	139	On the waters of Cherokee Creek	
Cash, John	1473	Armstrong, Martin	Davidson	640	1049	27 Nov 1789	1671		71	283	On S side of Cumberland River	yes
Cash, William	02		Davidson	100							S side of Cumberland River	
Casleman, Benm.	942	Cole, Burwell	Sumner	640	2466	22 Jul 1795	2636	21 Dec 1792	83	425	On the Caney Fork	yes
Casner, Jacob	1269		Washington	180	1207	4 Dec 1795	2703	20 Dec 1780	89	328	Beg at 2 white oaks	
Casner, Jacob	1270		Washington	150	1208	4 Dec 1795	2532	10 Apr 1780	89	329	Joining Thomas Brummit	
Cason, William	089	James, Daniel	Sumner	640			522	3 Jan 1786			N side of Cumberland River	yes
Cason, William	892	James, Daniel	Davidson	640	908	17 Jan 1789			63	313	On N side of Cumberland river	yes
Casselman, Andrew, Ass.	334	Stobbotle, James	Sumner	640	1636	23 Feb 1793	3525	3 Dec 1792	76	330	On the North boundary	yes
Casselman, Jacob	286	McKeel, Joshua	Sumner	640	1287	10 Dec 1790	3471	26 Jun 1788	74	361	On waters of Bartons Creek	yes
Cassilman, Benj.	269	Cloyd, John	Sumner	640	1251	10 Dec 1790	2641	14 Apr 1790	74	348	Near head waters of Cedar Creek	yes
Casson, William	931		Washington	200	908	17 Nov 1790	1097	9 Jan 1779	76	147	On N fork of Sinking Creek	
Casteel, John, Senr	306		Green	311-1/4	1373	7 Jun 1784	65	461			On Punchin Camp Creek	
Casteele, Jacob	186		Tennessee	640	1466	4 Jan 1792	3288	28 Dec 1785	77	368	S side of Cumberland River	
Castendre, Metre [sic]	965	Donelson, Stokley	Davidson	640	982	18 May 1789	207		63	332	On second creek above Bradleys Lick	yes
Castle, Thomas	507	Sheppard, William	Davidson	274	479	15 Sep 1787	1855		63	174	N side of Cumberland River	
Castleman, Andrew	1897		Davidson	320	123	27 Apr 1793	601	11 Oct 1784	81	34	On N side of Cumberland River	
Castleman, Andrew	2246		Davidson	150	295	20 Jul 1796		21 Feb 1789	88	438	On waters of Mill Creek	
Castleman, Andrew, Ass	2248		Davidson	249	299	20 Jul 1796		27 Jan 1789	88	439	On waters of Cedar Lick Creek	
Castleman, Jacob	604	Price, William	Davidson	640	576	15 Sep 1787	951	24 Jan 1784	63	206	S side of Cumberland River	yes
Castleman, Jacob heirs	1823		Davidson	512	396	26 Jun 1793	207	24 Jan 1784	80	341	The waters of Cumberland & Stones Cr	
Castleman, Jacob heirs	1846		Davidson	523	346	27 Nov 1792	207	29 Jan 1784	81	8	Waters of Cumberland & Stones Creeks	
Casun, Charles	848		Washington	300	662	10 Nov 1784	1107	13 Jan 1778	69	155	On waters of Watauga River	
Caswell, Martin	127		Green	640	4	15 Jul 1786	477	28 Oct 1783	60	246	On N side of Nolachuckey	
Caswell, Richard	024		Sullivan	640			449	28 Sep 1778			On both sides Beech Creek	
Caswell, Richard	137		Washington	400	5	22 Oct 1782	452	28 Sep 1778	47	1	On head branches of Boons Creek	
Caswell, Richard	138		Washington	600	6	22 Oct 1782	442	28 Sep 1778	47	1	On head branches of Lick Creek	
Caswell, Richard	139		Washington	640	7	22 Oct 1782	440	28 Sep 1778	47	2	On waters of Biglimestone	
Caswell, Richard	140		Washington	640	8	22 Oct 1782	437	28 Sep 1778	47	2	Inc head spring &c	
Caswell, Richard	141		Washington	640	9	22 Oct 1782	441	28 Sep 1778	47	3	Inc the Big Pond Spring	
Caswell, Richard	142		Washington	640	10	22 Oct 1782			47	4	On head of Walnut Valley	
Caswell, Richard	3		Sullivan	640	14	22 Oct 1782	451	28 Sep 1778	43	243	On both sides of Bush Creek	
Caswell, Richard	4		Sullivan	640	15	22 Oct 1782			43	243	On both sides of Bush Creek	
Caswell, William	120		Sullivan	640	132	24 Oct 1782			43	320	On both sides of Beech Creek &c	
Caswell, William	143		Washington	400	11	22 Oct 1782	412	21 Sep 1778	47	4	On both sides of Boons Creek	
Caswell, William	144		Washington	300	12	22 Oct 1782	411	21 Sep 1778	47	5	On E branch of Biglimestone	
Caswell, William, heir of Wm.	647	Hudler, John	Davidson	640	620	15 Sep 1787	481		63	220	On N side of Joseph Blocks entry	yes
Caswell, Wm	669	Hudler, Lemuel	Tennessee	274	3343	6 Dec 1797			97	59	On Red River	
Caswell, Wm hr Wm.	647	Hudler, John	Davidson	640	620	15 Sep 1787	483		63	220	On N side of Joseph Brock's entry	Yes
Caswell, Wm.	025		Sullivan	640			448	28 Aug 1781			On both sides of Beach Creek	
Caswell, Wm.	026		Sullivan	640			445				On S side of Beech Creek	
Caswell, Wm.	07		Sullivan	640			450				On both sides of Buck Creek	
Caswell, Wm.	210	Hudler, Jos.	Tennessee	640	1500	4 Jan 1792	480	9 June 1779	77	375	S side of Cumberland River &c	
Caswell, Wm.	5		Sullivan	640	16	22 Oct 1782		9 Mar 1784	43	244	On the S side of Buck Creek	
Caswell, Wm.	6		Sullivan	640	17	22 Oct 1782			43	245	On both sides of Bush Creek	

Claimant:	File #:	Assignee:	County:	Acres:	Grant:	Grant Date:	Entry:	Entry Date:	Bk:	Pg:	Location by Stream Name:	Military:
Caswell, Richard Wm. Heir	646	Willcock, David	Davidson	640	619	15 Sep 1787	479		63	220	On N boundary of his other survey	yes
Caswell, Richard Wm. Heir	76		Green	357-1/2	34	1 Nov 1786	396 (warran	25 Oct 1783	59	395	Inc the Island in French Broad River	
Cate, William	1388		Green	250	1243	27 Jan 1793	97	3 Feb 1781	79	510	Beg at a pine	
Cates, Joshua	23	Huse, Samuel	not given	640			4307					yes
Cates, Mathew	189	Thompson, Robert	Davidson	274	175	7 Mar 1786	1011		63	66	W side of Big Harpeth River	yes
Cates, Zechariah	1	Fulkison, Abraham	Robertson	640			1465	17 Sep 1786			On waters of Red River	yes
Cathey, George	93		Western District	1130	93	10 Jul 1788	1570	1 Apr 1784	67	317	On waters of Rutherfords Ford &c	
Cathey, George Sr	131		Middle District	3000	133	10 Jul 1788	1568	1 Apr 1784	67	473	Lying on N side of Duck River	
Cathey, Richd	1000	Weaver, Wm.	Davidson	640	1017	18 May 1789	1734		63	340	On E fork of Stones River	yes
Cathey, William	1011	Garrett, Wm. Heirs	Davidson	640	1028	18 May 1789	1645		63	343	On N branch of E fork of Stones River	yes
Cathey, William	121		Middle District	4000	123	10 Jul 1788	649		67	469	Lying on S side of Duck River	
Cathey, William	1921	Deal, John	Davidson	640 (380	1716	20 May 1793	1082	28 Apr 1783	81	57	On S side of Cumberland River	
Catheys, George Sr.	105		Middle District	2500	107	10 Jul 1788	1578	1 Apr 1784	67	462	On S side of Duck River &c	
Cator, John	382	Sheppard, Benjamin	Davidson	640	354	15 Sep 1787	2323		63	133	E fork of Drakes Creek	yes
Catral, John	594		Sullivan	136	592	29 Jul 1793	195	21 Feb 1780	76	476	Beg at Henry Gochers &c	
Catron, Peter	1134		Davidson	640	111	17 Apr 1786	583	18 Aug 1784	66	177	Wt Fk of Mill Cr-Jonathan Drakes Et bound	
Catron, Philip	1040		Davidson	640	14	17 Apr 1786	584	18 Aug 1784	66	38	On Et waters of Wt Fork of Mill Creek	
Cavanaugh, Hugh	368		Green	100	370	20 Sep 1787	1447	21 Jun 1779	65	478	On Dunhams branch	
Cavanaugh, Hugh	509		Green	100	511	20 Sep 1787	1458	22 Jun 1779	65	525	On Dunhams branch	
Cavatt, Alexander	178		Washington	348	46	23 Oct 1782	627	24 Nov 1778	47	21	On Holston River	
Cavatt, Alexander	1899		Davidson	480	133	27 Apr 1793	532	17 Jul 1784	81	37	On N side of Cumberland River	
Cavatt, Moses	278		Sullivan	63	417	9 Aug 1787	716	20 Dec 1780	61	436	On the fall branch of Horse Creek	
Cavatt, Moses	44		Sullivan	50	55	23 Oct 1782	613	15 Jun 1780	43	264	On S side of Holston River	
Cave, Wm.	032		Green	39			472	24 Sep 1786			S side of Holston River	
Cavell, Alexander	163		Sullivan	94	170	10 Oct 1783	1792	3 Oct 1779	53	146	On N side of Holston River	
Cavenor, Timothy	1173	Harris, Edward	Sumner	640	2678	4 Jun 1796	2993	1 Jun 1795	88	360	Joining sd Harris	yes
Cavett, Richard	1231		Davidson	640	195	10 Jul 1788	355	12 Mar 1784	66	411	On Middle Fk of Red Riv Beg on N/S sd cr	
Cavit, Moses	125		Washington	200	293	24 Oct 1782	350	4 Sep 1778	44	295		
Chadwick, Benjamin	2217	Glasgow, James	Davidson	640	2547	19 Oct 1795			88	186	On waters of Stones River	yes
Chamberlain, Andrew	77		Green	3750	35	1 Nov 1786	393	8 Apr 1786	59	396	N side of Holston River	
Chamberlain, Hannah	257		Eastern District	1000	204	1 Jan 1795			83	245	S/S of Holston Riv on Chamberlain Br	
Chamberlain, Henry	326	Williams, Willoughby	Middle District	640	2388	3 Feb 1795	2711		83	386	W side of W fk of Obeys River	yes
Chamberlain, Jacob	620		Washington	200	714	26 Oct 1786	798	23 Dec 1778	66	18	On the waters of Wataugah River	
Chamberlain, Jeremiah	16		Green	1000	79	1 Nov 1786	474	25 Oct 1783	58	440	On N side of Holstein River	
Chamberlain, Jeremiah	19		Green	400	82	1 Nov 1786	1250	22 Nov 1783	58	443	Beg at a black oak	
Chamberlain, Jeremiah	223		Green	640	180	20 Sep 1787	297	23 Oct 1783	65	424	On N side of Holsten River	
Chamberlain, Jeremiah etal	212		Middle District	1000	198	14 Jan 1793	2171	13 May 1784	79	286	On E side of Tennessee River	
Chamberlain, Nehemiah	803		Washington	200	617	10 Nov 1784	1369	11 May 1779	69	143	On head of John Riches Branch	
Chamberlain, Nenian	18		Green	500	81	1 Nov 1786	515	27 Oct 1784	58	442	On N side of Holstein River	
Chamberlain, Ninian	1424		Green	200	1236	27 Nov 1792	1369	11 May 1779	80	166	On waters of Long Creek	
Chamberlain, Ninian	484		Washington	135-1/2	669	1 Nov 1786	2453	29 Feb 1780	60	442	Beg at 2 Chestnuts	
Chamberlain, Ninian, Ass	1527		Green	310	2390	12 Jul 1794	3271	24 Dec 1785	81	602	On waters of Long Creek	
Chambers, Alexander	691		Washington	62	505	10 Nov 1784	2447	28 Feb 1780	69	106	Bounded by Joshua Green &c	
Chambers, Daniel	1654		Davidson	640	305	17 Nov 1796	558	28 Jul 1784	76	183	On S fk of Whites Creek	
Chambers, Daniel	1806		Davidson	640	379	26 Jun 1793	557	28 Jul 1784	80	335	On Stewarts Creek	

Claimant:	File #:	Assignee:	County:	Acres:	Grant:	Grant Date:	Entry:	Entry Date:	Bk:	Pg:	Location by Stream Name:	Military:
Chambers, Mark	028		Green	400	313			17 Mar 1780			N side of Holston River	
Chambers, Mark	100		Eastern District	150	89	17 Nov 1790	1842	7 Oct 1779	76	172	N side of Hastine Creek	
Chambers, Mark	103		Eastern District	150	92	17 Nov 1790	1929	15 Oct 1779	76	173	On Terrells Creek	
Chambers, Mark	136		Sullivan	400	149	23 Oct 1782	313	10 Mar 1780	43	330	N side of Holston River	
Chambers, Mark	504		Hawkins	100	376	29 Jul 1793	1534	21 Aug 1779	80	271	Bet John Groves & Robt Prices lines	
Chambers, Mark	640		Hawkins	100	509	23 Apr 1794	161	4 Oct 1791	81	552	On S side of Holston River	
Chambers, Mark	96		Eastern District	140	85	17 Nov 1790	15	25 Feb 1778	76	171	S/S Holstein River on Terrells Cr	
Chambless, Joel	1459		Sumner	228	1742	20 Dec 1800	5127	3 May 1800	112	282	On head of first big branch	yes
Chance, David	1214	Bayd, John	Sumner	228	2494	26 Sep 1795	1319	3 Jan 1786	89	104	On N side of Cumberland River	yes
Chance, Philemon	382	Cobb, Jesse	Tennessee	274	233	20 May 1793	1129	28 Jul 1784	81	200	On Red River	yes
Chapman, Abner	225		Green	400	182	20 Sep 1787	1241	7 Jun 1784	65	425	On S side of Powells River	
Chapman, Abner	226		Green	640	183	20 Sep 1787	1240	22 Oct 1787	65	425	Waters of Russels Cr & Powells R	
Chapman, Abner	469		Green	640	471	20 Sep 1787			65	508	On White Horn Creek	
Chapman, Abner	911		Green	400	825	17 Nov 1790	1239	20 Sep 1787	76	113	On waters of Clinch River	
Chapman, John	098		Washington	300			1443	17 Jun 1779				
Chapman, Samuel	759	Bonner, John	Sumner	3292	2172	20 May 1793	880	13 Sep 1785	81	166	On S side of Cumberland River	yes
Chapman, Thomas	306		Eastern District	3000	215	22 Feb 1795	1443		84	289	Inc the fork of Big Creek	
Chapman, Thomas	417		Eastern District	400	289	8 Jan 1797	1941	29 Oct 1784	90	209	In the Grasey Valley	
Chapman, Thomas	630		Washington	200	724	26 Oct 1786	1315	30 Mar 1779	66	23	Inc a large spring &c	
Chapman, Thomas	648		Washington	56	744	26 Oct 1786	2598	4 Aug 1780	66	31	On Big Limestone &c	
Chapman, Thomas	712		Green	200	753	11 Jul 1788	2782	22 Feb 1781	66	479	N/S Holstin R on Wt Fork of Platt Cr	
Chapman, Thos	648		Washington	50	742	26 Oct 1786	2598	4 Aug 1780	66	31	On Big Limestone	
Chappell, Edward	055	O'Neill, Thomas	not given	640			2635	5 Oct 1792			N side of Tenecy(sic) River	yes
Charlescraft, James	056	McCall, Alex	Middle District	288			1576					yes
Charter, Anthony	338	Buckanan, Samuel	Davidson	640	323	1 Aug 1787	1755		63	120	Beg at a honey locust	yes
Charter, James	79		Washington	138	247	28 Oct 1782	1295	23 Mar 1779	44	270	On Little Limestone	
Chastain, John	117		Sullivan	400	129	23 Oct 1782	2307	27 Nov 1779	43	319	On a little creek of Horse Creek	
Chastian, James	205		Sullivan	300	212	10 Oct 1783	2344	10 Dec 1779	53	164	On Indian Camp Creek	
Cheason, Joshua	1679	Tatum, Howell	Davidson	224	1606	23 Feb 1793	1640		76	315	N side of Cumberland River &c	yes
Cheek, James	400		Hawkins	200	521	27 Jan 1793	1584	12 Sep 1779	79	498	On S side of Holston River	
Cheek, Jesse	05		not given	100	409	29 Nov 1797					Both sides of Kentucky River [sic]	
Cheek, Jesse	1133		Hawkins	100	409	29 Nov 1797			96	18	Both sides of Kentucky road	
Cheek, Jesse	476		Green	595	478	20 Sep 1787	116	21 Oct 1783	65	510	On the head of Fall Creek &c	
Cheek, John	2	Cheek, William	Robertson	640	3368	16 Dec 1800	3623	15 Jul 1800	112	159	On Powells Br waters of Red River	
Cheeney, John	200	Johnston, William	Davidson	428	186	7 Mar 1786	983		63	69	On Red River	yes
Cherney, Robert	114	Guice, Christopher	Davidson	640	100	14 Mar 1780	451		63	40	On Guices Creek	yes
Cherokee Indians	052		Indian lands					20 Aug 1824				
Cherry, Job	331	Fenner, Richard	Davidson	640	317	28 Jan 1787	2179		63	118	S side of Cumberland River	yes
Cherry, John	305	Breakey, Andrew	Davidson	640	291	3 May 1787	1156		63	109	S side of Red River	yes
Cherry, Jonathan	891	Sugg, Aquilla	Davidson	640	907	17 Jan 1789	2446		63	313	On 2nd creek above Stewarts Cr	yes
Cherry, Willis	1	Hicks, James	Wilson	228	3386	12 Dec 1801	5117	19 Aug 1800	114	91	On waters of Bartons Creek	
Chesnut, Joseph	1129	Harris, Edward	Sumner	640	2635	4 Jun 1796	2996	1 Jun 1795	88	346	Joining sd Harris survey	yes
Chescolm, John	875		Green	600	825	27 Nov 1789	825	30 Jun 1787	74	23	Beg at three red oaks	
Chester, David	188	Spencer, Thomas	Davidson	1000	174	7 Mar 1786	70		63	65	N side of Cumberland River	yes
Chester, Robert	2102	Sheppard, Nancy	Davidson	640	2327	20 May 1793	1495		81	197	On waters of Duck River	yes

Claimant:	File #:	Assignee:	Acres:	Grant:	Grant Date:	Entry:	Entry Date:	Bk:	Pg:	Location by Stream Name:	Military:
Child, Francis	613		3000	392	24 Nov 1803	695	28 Oct 1783	117	362	On Richland Creek	
Child, Francis	91		3840	77	14 Mar 1786	34		63	32	On the Cane Fork	yes
Childers, John	368		5000	374	20 Dec 1791	1511	20 Feb 1784	75	221	On S side of Tennessee River	
Childers, John	370		5000	376	20 Dec 1791	1510	20 Feb 1784	75	222	On S side of Tennessee River	
Childers, John	371		2000	377	20 Dec 1791	1512	20 Feb 1784	75	222	On 3rd crabove mouth of Duck R	
Childers, John	571	Keagey, John	640	3009	10 Apr 1797	3931		90	297	N side of Cumberland River	yes
Childers, John	670		600	575	12 Jul 1794	486	25 Oct 1783	81	595	On N side of Tennessee River	
Childers, Robert	704	Lenear, James	640	677	8 Dec 1787	3338		63	239	On Brush Creek	yes
Chiseling, John	96		90	264	23 Oct 1782	15	21 Feb 1778	44	280	Beg on 2 hickorys &c	
Chisholm, Elijah	02		200				7 Jul 1797			On Straights [sic] Creek	
Chisholm, Elijah	05		1000				no date				
Chisholm, Elijah	027		90			1001	4 Jan 1779			N side of Holston River	
Chishum, Elijah	962		640	732	20 Jul 1796	359	24 Mar 1780	88	431	On N side of Clinch	
Chishum, Elijah	963		640	733	20 Jul 1796	2274	24 Nov 1779	88	433	On N side of Clinch River	
Chisolm, Elijah	332		150	253	2 Dec 1795	2698	19 Dec 1780	88	272	On N side of Clinch River	
Chisolm, Elijah	334		200	255	8 Dec 1795	139	30 Oct 1781	88	273	On N side of Clinch River	
Chisolm, Elijah	775		284	615	12 Jul 1794	71	21 Sep 1792	82	217	On the S side of Holston River &c	
Chisolm, James	015		3 surveys		28 Jan 1796						
Chisom, Elijah	198		150	170	23 Apr 1794	261	13 May 1780	81	558	On Spring Fork of Sycamore Creek	
Chisom, James	196		150	168	23 Apr 1794	1637	5 Oct 1791	81	557	On Spring Fk of Sycamore Creek	
Chison, Isom & others	291		100	268	23 Feb 1793	1878	26 Mar 1785	78	444	On N side of Holston River	
Chissum, Elijah	210		100	197	26 Dec 1791	741	12 Feb 1781	77	312	On N side of Holston River	
Chisum, Ignatius	2275	Donelson, John	274	2754	20 Jul 1796	3953		88	459	On waters of Stones Creek	yes
Chisun, Elijah	04		100	741	12 Feb 1781					N side of Clinch River	
Choate, Christopher	832		200 (250	646	10 Nov 1784	1249	27 Feb 1779	69	151	On S Fork of Kendricks Creek	
Chooke, Christopher	697		150	511	10 Nov 1784	2780	21 Feb 1781	69	109	On N fork of Sinking Creek	
Choate, Christopher	775		300	589	10 Nov 1784	851	30 Dec 1778	69	135	On waters of Kendricks Creek	
Chote, Austin	1112		150	1067	27 Jun 1793	2608	13 Aug 1780	60	392	On waters of Kendricks Creek	
Chote, Benjamin	614		100	768	26 Oct 1786	2617	19 Aug 1780	66	15	On waters of Kendricks Creek	
Chote, Christopher	501		150	764	16 Aug 1787	2779	21 Feb 1781	64	140	Beg at a corner white oak &c	
Chote, Christopher	510		140	773	16 Aug 1787	2781	21 Feb 1781 [?]	64	143	Beg at a hickory saplin	
Chrisham, Elijah	241		250	380	9 Aug 1787	71	26 Feb 1778	61	399	On S side of Holston River	
Chrisham, Elijah	400		220	279	10 Nov 1784	564 [?]	16 May 1780	69	170	On S side of Holstin River	
Chrisoling (Chisolmy), John	96		90	264	23 Oct 1782	15	21 Feb 1778	44	280	2 hickorys & a large white oak	
Chrisolm, John	312		200	626	10 Nov 1784	2602	1 Aug 1780	69	145	On head spring &c	
Christer, John	453	Brown, John	350	1584	27 Apr 1793	44	6 Dec 1789	81	13	On a creek of Stones River	yes
Christian, Gilbert	14		250	25	23 Oct 1782	1871	6 Oct 1779	43	249	On N side of Holston River	
Christian, Gilbert	179		450	161	17 Nov 1790	1870	6 Oct 1779	76	177	On a branch of Mill Creek &c	
Christian, Gilbert	191		1280	205	29 Jul 1793	447 & 462	Apr 1780	76	478	S side of Cumberland River &c	
Christian, Gilbert	660		600	609	27 Nov 1793			81	500	On N side of Holston	
Christian, James	194	Drake, Jonathan	640	180	7 Mar 1786	143		63	67	2 Lyn trees bank Cumberland R	yes
Christian, Lewis	107		100	141	26 Dec 1791			75	159	On S side of Holson River	
Christian, Lewis	939		250	853	17 Nov 1790	130	27 Jun 1780	76	122	On Lick Fork of Bent Creek	
Christian, William	1298	Hickman, Thomas	640	3067	19 Jul 1797	4588	6 Apr 1796	90	377	S side of Cumberland River	yes
Christian, Thos.&Josh English	473		200	475	20 Sep 1787	264	22 Oct 1783	65	509	Clay Liick Cr br of French Broad R	

Claimant:	File #:	Assignee:	County:	Acres:	Grant:	Grant Date:	Entry:	Entry Date:	Bk:	Pg:	Location by Stream Name:	Military:
Christmas, John	201	Hogan, Humphrey	Davidson	640	187	7 Mar 1786	50		63	70	On both sides of Sulphur Fork	yes
Church, Christopher	0106	Payton, Thomas	Sumner	640			3256	19 Dec 1787			On both sides Jinnings Creek	yes
Church, Christopher	937	Blount, Reading	Sumner	640	2461	22 Feb 1795	3256	23 Dec 1785	83	422	On main fk of Obeys River &c	yes
Church, William	249		Tennessee	228	1640	27 Apr 1793	1306	2 Nov 1784	81	27	On N side of Spring Creek	
Churchell, Samuel	490		Sumner	1000	1652	29 Jul 1793	1469	31 Jan 1792	81	41	On first South Fork &c	yes
Clark & Wycoff	757	Howell, Daniel	Davidson	640	730	11 Jul 1788	1980		63	257	On N side of Cumberland River	Yes
Clark & Wykoff	1422	Armstrong, Martin	Davidson	228	39	28 Oct 1787			68	157	On E Fork of Blooming Grove	
Clark, Abraham	192	Donelson, S., Robt Wood	Eastern District	640	2380	8 Apr 1794	1597		81	439	Lying bet 1st & 2nd creeks	yes
Clark, Abraham	578	Williams, Eliza	Middle District	640	2785	20 Dec 1796	1597		91	321	On Cain Creek	yes
Clark, Benjamin	601	Stewart, Duncan	Tennessee	640	3103	14 Sep 1797	4435		90	403	S side of Cumberland River &c	yes
Clark, Downham [?]	109		Western District	5000	109	10 Jul 1788	780	29 Oct 1783	67	323	On Obion River at high water mark	
Clark, Henry	556		Sullivan	200	539	17 Nov 1790	1226	22 Feb 1779	76	191	On a branch of Kendricks Creek	
Clark, Henry	95		Western District	5000	95	10 Jul 1788	781	29 Oct 1783	67	318	On S side of Obion River &c	
Clark, Isaac	378		Sumner	640	1559	14 Jan 1793	896	8 Aug 1792	79	271	On Jinings Fork of Round Lick Creek	yes
Clark, James	284		Tennessee	428	1877	20 May 1793	2072	31 Aug 1785	81	95	S/S of Cumberland on Johnstons Ct.	
Clark, James & William	350	Robeson, Edward	Tennessee	640	2177	20 May 1793	3687	27 Jun 1789	81	167	On the Elk Fork of Red River	
Clark, John	504		Washington	100	767	16 Aug 1787	2987	27 Sep 1783	64	141	Beg at a marked ash	
Clark, John	806		Washington	37.50	620	10 Nov 1784	1777	1 Oct 1779	69	144	On Clarks Branch	
Clark, John	853		Washington	640	844	17 Nov 1788	217	25 May 1778	70	11	Beg at a white oak	
Clark, Josiah	2095	Sheppard, Nancy	Davidson	640	2313	20 May 1793	2088		81	194	On W Fork of Bledsoes Creek	yes
Clark, Lardner	010		not given	320				Martin Armstrong			On a fork of Wells Creek	
Clark, Lardner	016	Cannon, Thos. Hrs.	Tennessee	640			2174	12 Sep 1785			S side of Cumberland River	
Clark, Lardner	018		Davidson	228							On waters of Richland Dreek	
Clark, Lardner	038	Guthrop, John	not given	640			1384	7 Oct 1789			S side of Cumberland River	
Clark, Lardner	106	Jones, Thomas	Davidson	228	92	14 Mar 1786	1232		63	37	On both sides of a branch	
Clark, Lardner	1112		Davidson	640	89	17 Apr 1786	77	10 Jan 1784	66	172	White oak at a Sinking Spring	
Clark, Lardner	114	Smithwick, Jos.	Tennessee	640	1609	23 Feb 1793	2163	26 Aug 1785	76	317	On Wells Creek	
Clark, Lardner	1150		Davidson	640	127	17 Apr 1786	513	6 Jul 1784	66	181	Sugar tr Green Hills Wt boundary	
Clark, Lardner	1374		Davidson	320	57	8 Oct 1787	81	12 Jan 1784	68	144	On the E fork of Mill Creek	
Clark, Lardner	1387	Armstrong, M.	Davidson	500 (560	4	8 Oct 1787	937	31 Apr 1785	68	150	Lying on Indian Creek	
Clark, Lardner	1398	Armstrong, M.	Davidson	640	15	8 Oct 1787	498	10 Dec 1784	68	152	On N side of Cumberland	
Clark, Lardner	1405		Davidson	96	22	8 Oct 1787	993	16 May 1785	68	154	On W Fork of Mill Creek	
Clark, Lardner	1409	Armstrong, M.	Davidson	200	26	8 Oct 1787	1387	19 Sep 1785	68	155	S/S Cumberl below mo of Stones R	
Clark, Lardner	1462		Davidson	150	64	18 May 1789	1595	26 Nov 1785	71	223	White oak on bank of Stones River	
Clark, Lardner	1548	Armstrong, M.	Davidson	228	88	26 Nov 1789			74	170	On waters of Mill Creek	
Clark, Lardner	1574	Patterson, Hardy	Davidson	640	1217	10 Dec 1790	1659		74	337	On big Harpeth River	yes
Clark, Lardner	1601	Parker, Jeptha	Davidson	1000	1306	10 Dec 1790	87		74	367	On waters of Harrian Creek	yes
Clark, Lardner	1680	Huddleston, Wm. Hrs	Davidson	640	1608	23 Feb 1793			76	316	On waters of Richland Creek	yes
Clark, Lardner	1681	Ramsey, Mills	Davidson	640	1610	23 Feb 1793	2956		76	317	N side of W Harpeth River	yes
Clark, Lardner	182	Liskow, Thomas	Davidson	640	168	7 Mar 1786	816		63	63	In the fork of Mill Creek	yes
Clark, Lardner	2305	Jackson, Job	Davidson	640	2499	18 Nov 1795	2572		89	136	On a branch of the first Big Creek	yes
Clark, Lardner	240	Duglas, Wm.	Tennessee	1000	1583	27 Nov 1793	72	21 — 1783	81	13	Fork bet Red River & Sulphur Fork	
Clark, Lardner	262	Martin, Robert	Davidson	428	248	7 Mar 1786	1209		63	91	On waters of Stones River	yes
Clark, Lardner	289	Ganthrop, John	Sumner	640	1294	10 Dec 1790			74	363	On S side Cumberland River	yes
Clark, Lardner	391	Armstrong, M.	Sumner	228	129	29 Aug 1793			80	323	On waters of Richland Creek	yes

Claimant:	File #:	Assignee:	County:	Acres:	Grant:	Grant Date:	Entry:	Entry Date:	Bk:	Pg:	Location by Stream Name:	Military:
Clark, Lardner	454	Armstrong, M.	Tennessee	320	249	27 Feb 1796	1190		88	184	On a fork of Wills Creek	
Clark, Lardner	613	Faddis, Andrew hrs	Davidson	640	585	15 Sep 1787	1190		63	209	First small cr on N/S Cumberland R	yes
Clark, Lardner	668	Fetner,Geo.hr.Henry	Davidson	1000	641	15 Nov 1787	2605		63	227	Bizzells Salleen joining Jno Harvey	yes
Clark, Lardner	669	Lewis, Charles	Davidson	640	642	15 Nov 1787	1835		63	228	On waters of the Salleen	yes
Clark, Lardner	670	Styron, Samuel	Davidson	640	643	15 Nov 1787	1578		63	228	On the Salleen	yes
Clark, Lardner	675	Holf—?, Mordice	Davidson	640	648	8 Dec 1787	1661		63	230	On waters of Hurricane Creek	yes
Clark, Lardner	820	Robertson, Jesse	Davidson	1000	823	17 Jan 1789	844		63	290	On waters of W Harpeth River	yes
Clark, Lardner & Wm. Wykoff	1267		Davidson	640	232	10 Jul 1788	777	2 Dec 1785	66	419	Beg Thos Fains So Wt corner	
Clark, Lardner & Wycoff	119	Farmer, William	Davidson	228	105	7 Mar 1786	413		63	42	N side of Cumberland River	yes
Clark, Nathaniel	028		Sullivan	175			1391	24 May 1779			On Kendricks Creek	
Clark, Nathaniel	092		Washington	450			414	22 Sep 1778			On Kendricks Creek	
Clark, Nathaniel	176		Sullivan	164	183	10 Oct 1783	1390	24 May 1779	53	150	On Stewarts branch	
Clark, Nathaniel	177		Sullivan	83	184	10 Oct 1783	1392	24 May 1779	53	151	George Russells corner white oak	
Clark, Niel	612	Stewart, Duncan	Tennessee	640	2161(7)	14 Sep 1797	1365	9 Nov 1784	90	426	N side of Cumberland	yes
Clark, Ozbum	850	Baryer, George Henry	Sumner	503	2353	20 May 1793	3079	27 Oct 1792	81	202	Bet Spring Creek	yes
Clark, Robert	934		Green	200	848	17 Nov 1790	1233	7 Nov 1783	76	121	Fork of French Broad & Big Pidgeon	
Clark, Thos.	23	Armstrong, M.	Tennessee	128	80	26 Nov 1789		26 May 1789	74	167	On N side of Red River	
Clark, Vachel	543	Hean(?), Geo.	Sumner	640	1746	29 Aug 1793	3393		81	65	On W fork of Bartons Creek	
Clark, William	1124		Hawkins	100	843	2 Nov 1797	58	8 Feb 1780	96	3	On waters of Buck Creek	yes
Clark, William	1601	Belch, James hrs	Davidson	640	1058	26 Nov 1789	139		74	106	On N side of Cumberland River	yes
Clark, William	372		Green	180	374	20 Sep 1787	291	21 Oct 1783	65	479	On the river ridge &c	
Clark, William	587		Washington	100	681	26 Oct 1788	770	24 Dec 1778	66	3	On S side of Noleychuckey River	
Clark, William	678	Phillips, Mark hrs	Davidson	640	651	8 Dec 1787	1785		63	231	On Middle Fork of Red River	yes
Clark, William	947		Sumner	340 (357	2480	22 Feb 1795	1843	23 Mar 1789	83	427	Bet Goose Cr & Big Barren River	yes
Clarke, Henry	123		Washington	300	291	24 Oct 1782	745	23 Dec 1778	44	294	On both sides of Kindricks Creek	
Clarke, Thomas	43		Davidson	2560	29	14 Mar 1786	77		63	12	S side of Cumberland River	yes
Clarke, Thomas	603		Davidson	7200	575	15 Sep 1787	259		63	206	On S side of Cumberland River	yes
Clay, Jeremiah	245	Haywood, John	Sumner	1000	1150	26 Nov 1789	3112	10 Mar 1788	74	154	On both sides of Caney Fork	yes
Clayton, Leward	951	Lindsay, Isaac	Sumner	400	154	1 Dec 1794		14 Apr 1792	83	478	Beg at Wm. Dillard's lower corner	yes
Clendening, James	1170		Davidson	640	147	17 Apr 1786	211	30 Jan 1784	66	185	Sinking Cr on N side of Cumberland	
Clendening, James	1445		Davidson	320	91	10 Jul 1788	758	20 Aug 1783	68	233	Lying on N side of Cumberland River	
Clendening, John	03		Davidson	429			857	12 May 1786			On head of Browns Creek	
Clendening, John	772		Davidson	2560	745	11 Jul 1788	805		63	262	On S side of Big Harpeth River	yes
Clendining, John, Ass.	946		Davidson	429	962	18 May 1789			63	327	At head of Browns Creek	yes
Clever, John, heir of Jacob	1454		Davidson	620	700	28 Nov 1788	1006		70	22	On N side of Tennessee River	yes
Click, Matthias	678		Sullivan	133	626	9 Jul 1794	652	15 Jul 1780	81	630	On S side of North Fork	
Clifton, Absolem	972	Galloway, James	Sumner	640	2436	22 Feb 1795	1704	19 Nov 1792	84	314	On Caney Fork	yes
Clifton, Daniel	0134	Hamilton, Thomas	Sumner	640			1208	18 Jun 1792			On waters of Red River	yes
Clifton, Richard	1187	Donelson, Stockley	Sumner	640	2709	20 Jul 1796	1262	8 Jun 1796	88	444	On both sides of Pond Lick Creek	yes
Clike, Peter	602		Sullivan	150	557	26 Dec 1791	551	29 Apr 1780	77	305	Beg at a chestnut &c	
Clinton, Archibald	1453		Sumner	640	472	19 Sep 1800	486	31 May 1784	109	272	On E fork of Bledsoe's Creek	
Clinton, John	1682	Carter, Landon	Davidson	228	1611	23 Feb 1793	422 (122)		76	317	On S Harpeth River	yes
Cloud, Isaac	1148		Hawkins	640	870	16 Dec 1802	88	21 Oct 1783	110	275	On N side of Holston River	
Cloud, Isaac	1153		Hawkins	640	869	19 Dec 1801			114	86	On N side of Holston River	
Cloud, Jason	306		Sullivan	300	445	9 Aug 1787	93	8 Feb 1780	61	464	In Carters Valley	

Claimant:	File #:	Assignee:	County:	Acres:	Grant:	Grant Date:	Entry:	Entry Date:	Bk:	Pg:	Location by Stream Name:	Military:
Cloud, Jason	348		Sullivan	200	488	10 Jul 1788	800	13 Jul 1781	67	490	On the S side of Holeson River	
Cloud, Jason	430		Green	640	432	20 Sep 1787	87	21 Oct 1783	65	497	Lying on S side of Holston River &c	
Cloud, Joseph	107		Sullivan	300	118	23 Oct 1782	481	5 Oct 177.. [sic]	43	294	On S side of Holston River &c	
Cloud, Joseph	1150		Hawkins	150	867	27 Jun 1801	820	14 Jul 1781	111	16	In the Hicory Cove	
Cloud, Joseph	1883	Blaning, Peter hr John	Davidson	640	1629	27 Apr 1793			81	26	On S branches of Stones Creek	yes
Cloud, Joseph	383		Hawkins	150	504	27 Jan 1793	820	14 Jul 1781	79	492	Joining the tract Cloud now lives on	
Cloud, Peter	172	Johnston, Daniel	Davidson	274	158	7 Mar 1786	735		63	60	On Harpeth Creek	yes
Cloud, William	424		Green	640	426	20 Sep 1787	92	21 Oct 1783	65	495	On N side of Holston River &c	
Cloud, William	478		Green	640	480	20 Sep 1787	86	21 Oct 1783	65	511	On Poor Valley Cr on N/S of Holston	
Cloud, Wm., Isaac, Jason	446		Eastern District	1200	300	27 Nov 1797	514	25 Jun 1784	96	17	Tenn Riv above the mouth of Clinch	
Clower, William	0110	Robertson, Michael	Sumner	640			1857	1 Apr 1788			S side of Cumberland River	yes
Cloyd, John	269	Cassilman, Benjamin	Sumner	640	1251	10 Dec 1790	2641	14 Apr 1790	74	348	Near head waters of Cedar Creek	yes
Clubb, Tho	065		Tennessee	640	8			9 Sep 1819			On S branch of Sugartown Fork &c	
Cluck, Matthias	708		Sullivan	46	653	5 Dec 1974	379	3 Apr 1780	84	162	Near the survey he now lives on	
Clyer, James	838	Willson, James	Sumner	640 (633	2336	20 May 1793	3669	6 Oct 1789	81	199	On waters of Station Camp reek	yes
Coalston, James	252		Davidson	274	238	7 Mar 1786	722		63	87	N side of Cumberland River	yes
Coart, John	081	Totewind, Winder hrs	Davidson	640			1102	7 Sep 1796			On Harpeth River	
Cobb & Caswell	0100		Washington					24 Feb 1778			Entries & affidavit	
Cobb, Anthony	913	Mulherin, James	Davidson	640	929	18 May 1789			63	319	On waters of Caney Fork	yes
Cobb, Benjamin	571		Washington	600	836	11 Jul 1788	277	31 Jul 1778	64	337	On Knobb Creek	
Cobb, Ethelread	1312		Washington	40	193	29 Dec 1796			90	193	N side of Watauga River	
Cobb, Ethelread	1313		Washington	50.	333	29 Dec 1796			90	193	On a branch of Lick Creek	
Cobb, Jesse	0141	Jones, Wm. Hr of Jno.	Sumner	640			1486	12 Jan 1785			Road bet Bledsoe Lick to Holston	yes
Cobb, Jesse	085	Jones, Wm.	Davidson	389			1487	8 Jan 1785			On Browns Creek	
Cobb, Jesse	1097		Hawkins	200	390	19 Jul 1797		Martin Armstrong	91	619	S side of Clinch River	
Cobb, Jesse	1994	Jones, William	Davidson	389	1920	20 May 1793			81	105	On Brown Creek	yes
Cobb, Jesse	1995	Gray, Samuel	Davidson	640	1931	20 May 1793	109		81	107	On W/S of Stones River	yes
Cobb, Jesse	2009	Stradley, James	Davidson	640	1955	20 May 1793	1128		81	113	On waters of Stones River	yes
Cobb, Jesse	291	Stafford, Josiah	Tennessee	274	1921	20 May 1793	1483		81	105	On both sides of Red River	
Cobb, Jesse	292	Anderson, John	Tennessee	640	1922	20 May 1793	1176	24 Aug 1792	81	105	2nd large cr running into Tenn River	
Cobb, Jesse	293	Rogers, Joseph	Tennessee	640	1946	20 May 1793	1175	28 Aug 1784	81	111	2nd large creek running into Tenn R	
Cobb, Jesse	303	Warren, Wm.	Tennessee	228	1994	20 May 1793	1161	28 Aug 1784	81	123	On both sides of Red River	
Cobb, Jesse	382	Chase, Philemon	Tennessee	274	2339	20 May 1793	1129	28 Jul 1784	81	200	On Red River	
Cobb, Jesse	383	Cooper, Nath.	Tennessee	228	2340	20 May 1793	1234	8 Oct 1744	81	200	On both sides of Red River	
Cobb, Jesse	414	Rayford, John	Tennessee	640	2448	31 Dec 1793	1236	16 Oct 1784	81	426	On S side of Cumberland River	
Cobb, Jesse	419	Hale, Josiah	Tennessee	640	2465	31 Dec 1793	1203	26 Sep 1784	81	431	Main head of E Fk of Gueses Creek	
Cobb, Jesse	420	Albritton, Henry	Tennessee	640	2466	31 Dec 1793	1325	3 Nov 1784	81	432	On main W fork of Gueses Creek	
Cobb, Jesse	421	Ryans, Mary	Tennessee	640	2467	31 Dec 1793	1279	28 Oct 1784	81	432	Head br of Main W Fk of Gueses Cr	
Cobb, Jesse	422	Hopkins, Jonathan	Tennessee	1000	2468	31 Dec 1793	1564	21 Feb 1785	81	432	Both main forks of Gueses Creek	
Cobb, Jesse	423	Shelke, Lewis	Tennessee	640	2469	31 Dec 1793	1174	28 Aug 1784	81	433	On main E fork of Gueses Creek	
Cobb, Jesse	640	Jones, Wm.	Sumner	640	1929	20 May 1793			81	107	Road from Bledsoes Lick to Holston	
Cobb, Jesse	667	Taylor, Jeffrey	Sumner	640	1987	20 May 1793	1119	30 Nov 1792	81	121	On Cedar Creek	yes
Cobb, Jesse	672	Wears, John	Sumner	640	2003	20 May 1793			81	125	On waters of Jinings Fork	yes
Cobb, Thomas	691	Lane, Thomas	Davidson	274	664	8 Dec 1787	1261		63	235	On Brush Creek	yes
Cobb, Jesse & Ezekial Smith	1939	Broom, Mason	Davidson	224	1760	29 Aug 1793	1127		81	69	N/S Cumberland both sides Sulphur Cr	yes

Earliest Tennessee Land Records

Claimant:	File #:	Assignee:	County:	Acres:	Grant:	Grant Date:	Entry:	Entry Date:	Bk:	Pg:	Location by Stream Name:	Military:
Cobb, Jos	048	McDaniel, I., Cobb, & P. Du	Hawkins	640	822	19 Jul 1797	3841	26 Feb 1778	91	615	ON Blairs Creek	yes
Cobb, Jos, J Smith,Wm Payn	1093		Hawkins	640			111				On waters of Richland Creek	
Cobb, Joseph	017		Hawkins	160							N side of Clinch River	
Cobb, Joseph	018		Hawkins	274							N side of river knobs	
Cobb, Joseph	1008		Hawkins	100	325	29 Dec 1796		Martin Armstrong	90	189	N side of Holston River	
Cobb, Joseph	1009		Hawkins	40	327	29 Dec 1796		Martin Armstrong	90	190	N side of Clinch Mountain	
Cobb, Joseph	1024		Hawkins	640	823	19 Jul 1797	112	26 Feb 1778	91	615	S side of Clinch River	
Cobb, Joseph	1097		Hawkins	200	390	19 Jul 1797		Martin Armstrong	91	619	N side of Clinch Mountain	
Cobb, Joseph	1098		Hawkins	200	391	19 Jul 1797		Martin Armstrong	91	619	N side of Clinch Mountain	
Cobb, Joseph	1099		Hawkins	100	392	19 Jul 1797		Martin Armstrong	91	620	Joining of Daniel Robesons survey	
Cobb, Joseph	1100		Hawkins	50	393	19 Jul 1797		Martin Armstrong	91	620	N side of Holston River	
Cobb, Joseph	1101		Hawkins	63	394	19 Jul 1797		Martin Armstrong	91	621	N side of Clinch River	
Cobb, Joseph	1105		Hawkins	300	825	12 Aug 1797	2196	12 Nov 1779	91	624	N side of Clinch Mountain	
Cobb, Joseph	411		Eastern District	200	324	29 Dec 1796		Martin Armstrong	90	188	On a branch of Richland Creek	
Cobb, Joseph	412		Eastern District	100	326	19 Dec 1796		Martin Armstrong	90	189	S side of Rich Land Creek	
Cobb, Joseph	412 (a)		Eastern District	50	328	29 Dec 1796		Martin Armstrong	90	191	N side river inc Sycamore Creek	
Cobb, Joseph	444		Eastern District	100	400	19 Jul 1797		Martin Armstrong	91	624	N side of Holston River	
Cobb, Joseph	758		Hawkins	200	598	12 Jul 1794	472	25 Apr 1780	82	210	In the Poor Valley &c	
Cobb, Peter	327	Mountflorence, J. C. & Fen	Davidson	640	313	28 Jun 1787	2175		63	116	S side of Cumberland River	yes
Cobb, Pharaoh	673		Washington	200	487	10 Nov 1784	2392	3 Jan 1780	69	99	Beg at Wm. Cobb's corner	
Cobb, Pharaoh	559		Washington	300	824	11 Jul 1788	567	2 Nov 1778	64	335	On E Fork of Knobb Creek	
Cobb, Pharaoh	573		Washington	640	838	11 Jul 1788	566	2 Nov 1778	64	338	On E fork of Knobb Creek	
Cobb, Pharough	1002		Washington	200	974	26 Dec 1791	2393	3 Jan 1780	77	300	Joining to his other survey &c	
Cobb, Shadrack	1515	Drake, Benjamin	Davidson	640	1072	26 Nov 1789	1922	24 Feb 1778	74	115	On N side of Cumberland River	yes
Cobb, Stephen	913		Green	640	827	17 Nov 1790	5	8 Jan 1779	76	114	On Nolachuckey River	
Cobb, William	0107		Washington	640			1052				Beg at a large poplar	
Cobb, William	62	Anderson, Daniel	Tennessee	640	1296	10 Dec 1790	2909	30 Sep 1785	74	364	On N side of Cumberland River	yes
Cobb, William & Joseph	338		Eastern District	640	231	20 Nov 1795	1284	24 Dec 1783	88	283	On N side of Clinch River	yes
Cobb, William & Joseph	337		Eastern District	640	230	20 Nov 1795	1287	24 Jan 1783	88	283	On N side of Clinch River	yes
Cobb, William & Joseph	940		Hawkins	320	698	20 Nov 1795	1283	7 Jun 1784	88	284	On N side of Clinch River	
Cobb, Wm.	081	Hunneycut, A.	Washington	260			1358	3 Nov 1792			E fork of Knob Creek	
Cobb, Zebulon	558	Malloy, Thomas	Tennessee	640	2992	10 Apr 1797	2841		90	290	S side of Cumberland River	
Cobbs, Anthony	2138	Mulherrin, James	Davidson	640	2414	7 Jan 1794	3305		81	404	On S side of Cumberland River	
Cochran, Wm.	31	Cochran, Jas. Hrs	Tennessee	640	1195	30 Nov 1790	2753	30 Sep 1785	74	320	On S side of Cumberland River	
Cock, Peter	656		Sullivan	300	604	5 Jun 1793			81	338	On Cainey Creek	
Cock, William	1704	King, John	Davidson	640	320	23 Feb 1793	631	18 Dec 1784	76	344	In oeded territory on Harpeth River	
Cock, William	595		Sullivan	400	593	29 Jul 1793	2040, 2041	27 Oct 1779	76	477	N side of Holston River	
Cock, William	615		Sullivan	1330	568	14 Jan 1793	1136	2 Jan 1779	79	292	On N side of Holston River	
Cockarell, John., Ass	2155		Davidson	138	155	9 Jan 1794		16 Jan 1789	81	440	On E side of Mill Creek	
Cockburn, John	281	Phillips, Philip & M. Campb	Sumner	640	1277	10 Dec 1790	3451	4 Mar 1790	74	358	On waters of Bartons Creek	yes
Cocke, Aaron	542	White, Thomas	Sumner	640	1744	20 May 1793	2639	25 Apr 1787	81	65	On waters of E fork of Goose Creek	yes
Cocke, Peter	386		Sullivan	250	265	10 Nov 1784	304	5 Aug 1778	69	160	On S side of Holstein River	yes
Cocke, Peter	405		Sullivan	300	284	10 Nov 1784	303	5 Aug 1778	69	171	On Buck Creek	
Cocke, Peter	431		Sullivan	300	310	10 Nov 1784	989	4 Jan 1779	69	180	On Caney Creek	
Cocke, Richard	124		Washington	199	292	24 Oct 1782	867	30 Dec 1779	44	294	Inc. a spring	

Claimant:	File #:	Assignee:	County:	Acres:	Grant:	Grant Date:	Entry:	Entry Date:	Bk:	Pg:	Location by Stream Name:	Military:
Cooke, Thomas, Ass.	316		Sumner	640	309	17 Nov 1790	700		76	184	On waters of Bledsoes Creek	
Cooke, William	111		Middle District	5000	113	10 Jul 1788	530	27 Oct 1783	67	464	On N side of Duck River &c	
Cooke, William	288		Green	470	290	20 Sep 1787	163	14 Mar 1778	65	455	Russells Cr waters of Powells R	
Cooke, William	292		Hawkins	400	255	24 Dec 1792	58	8 Feb 1780	78	445	On the Poor Creek	
Cooke, William	468		Green	320	470	20 Sep 1787	1003	4 Jan 1779	65	507	Cedar branch of Russells Creek	
Cooke, William	470		Green	400	472	20 Sep 1787	1021	14 Oct 1786	65	508	On a branch of Russells Creek &c	
Cooke, William	496		Green	200	498	20 Sep 1787	2494	12 Oct 1786	65	518	Waters of Clinch River in valley &c	
Cooke, William	624		Green	640	665	11 Jul 1788	328	23 Oct 1782	66	448	Richland Cr inc his own improvement	
Cooke, William	652		Green	300	693	11 Jul 1788	952	5 Jun 1786	66	458	On N side of Holstein River &c	
Cooke, William	695		Hawkins	400	497	16 Dec 1793	67	8 Feb 1780	82	99	S side of Clinch River &c	
Cooke, William	696		Green	300	737	11 Jul 1783	356	22 Oct 1783	66	472	N/S of Holston Riv upon Richland Cr	
Cooke, William	696		Hawkins	400	498	16 Dec 1793	1924	15 Oct 1779	82	100	On waters of Clinch River &c	
Cooke, William	697		Hawkins	400	499	16 Dec 1793	1926	15 Oct 1779	82	100	On S side of Clinch River &c	
Cooke, William	705		Green	200	746	11 Jul 1788	1994	19 Oct 1779	66	476	S/S of Richland Cr beg at a hickory	
Cooke, Wm	035		Green	640	665		328	17 Jan 1787			On Richland Creek	
Cooke, Wm.	147		Eastern District	400	117	24 Dec 1792	59	8 Feb 1780	78	452	1st big cr that Campbells line crosses	
Cooke, Wm.	148		Eastern District	400	118	24 Dec 1792	66	8 Feb 1780	78	453	On S side of Clinch River	
Cooke,Wm & David Stuart	574		Green	400	254	20 Sep 1787	381	30 Mar 1786	66	158	Waters of Clinch River & War Creek	
Cookon, John	422	Nichols, John	Davidson	640	394	15 Sep 1787	2565	Guard right	63	141	On waters of Sulphur Fork	yes
Cooker, William, Ass.	308		Eastern District	400	161	17 Dec 1794		Guard right	84	335	On S side of Holston River	
Cookon, John	259		Sullivan	170	398	9 Aug 1787	743	12 Feb 1781	61	417	On S side of Reedy Creek &c	
Cockran, John	029	Lee, James	Tennessee	228		4 May 1784	192	4 May 1784			N side of Cumberland River	yes
Cockran, John	83		Sullivan	250	94	23 Oct 1782	113,-184	8 & 21 Feb 1780	43	283	On N side of Holston River &c	
Cockran, William	28		Tennessee	640	1192	30 Nov 1790	2528	30 Sep 1785	74	319	On S side of Cumberland River	
Cockran, William	29		Tennessee	640	1193	30 Nov 1790	2736	30 Sep 1785	74	319	S of Cumberland River	
Cockran, William	30		Tennessee	640	1194	30 Nov 1790	2749	30 Sep 1785	74	320	On S side of Cumberland River	
Cockran, Wm hr of James	31		Tennessee	640	1195	30 Nov 1790	2753	30 Sep 1785	74	320	S side of Cumberland River	
Cockreel, John, Ass	2166		Davidson	420	182	9 Jan 1794		16 Jan 1789	81	449	On E side of Stones River	
Cockrell, Jno	1172		Davidson	640	149	17 Apr 1786	113	15 Jan 1784	66	186	Head of some So br of Little Harpeth	
Cockrell, Jno.	1171		Davidson	640	148	17 Apr 1786	13	26 Dec 1783	66	186	Beg at an ash marked R	
Cockrell, Jno.	1194		Davidson	640	171	17 Apr 1786	83	12 Jan 1784	66	191	On waters of E Fork of Mill Creek	
Cockrell, John	234	Castleton, Pearce	Tennessee	640	448	27 Jun 1793	825	20 Dec 1792	80	357	N side of Cumberland River &c	
Coffery, John	06	Halley, John	Robertson	640	3000	10 Apr 1797	3844	13 Jan 1796			On head spring of Clear Branch	
Coffey, John	2303	Thompson, Laurence	Davidson	1806	2491	26 Sep 1795	2836		89	103	On E Fork of Stones River	yes
Coffey, John	564	Holley, John heirs	Tennessee	640	3000	10 Apr 1797	790		90	293	On head springs of clear branch	
Coffey, Nimrod	1414	Tyrrell, Wm.	Sumner	228	3269	6 Dec 1797	398	22 Jun 1797	98	153	On waters of Spring Creek	yes
Coffey, Cheslie	07	Carter, Landon	Washington	300				16 May 1781			On head spring of Clear Branch	
Coffey, Henry	1768	Buckle, Thomas	Davidson	640	1551	14 Jan 1793	222	7 Jun 1784	79	269	On waters of Mill Creek	yes
Coffey, John	2088	Thompson, Laurence	Davidson	1806	2291	20 May 1793	1069	8 Jan 1779	81	189	On E Fork of Stones River	yes
Coffield, Benjamin	477	Terrell, William	Tennessee	1607	2739	20 Jul 1796	398		88	452	On headwaters of Half Pone Creek	yes
Coffield, Gresham	045		Robertson	50				30 Sep 1796			On Brush Creek	
Coffman, Andrew	301		Green	200	303	20 Sep 1787	222	7 Jun 1784	65	459	On W side of Lick Creek	
Coffman, David	1685		Green	200	1362	18 Nov 1795	1069	8 Jan 1779	89	140	On Lick Fork of Bent Creek	
Coffman, David	276		Green	200	278	20 Sep 1787	331	23 Sep 1787	65	452	On S side of Lick Creek	
Coghlin, James	2268	Percy, Francis	Davidson	1000	2746	20 Jul 1796			88	455	On a large fork of Tennessee River	yes

Earliest Tennessee Land Records

Claimant:	File #:	Assignee:	County:	Acres:	Grant:	Grant Date:	Entry:	Entry Date:	Bk:	Pg:	Location by Stream Name:	Military:
Coghlin, James	2269	Carleton, John hrs	Davidson	640	2747	20 Jul 1796	3153		88	456	A large creek of Tennessee River	yes
Coghlin, James	2270	Gafford, Wm. Hrs	Davidson	640	2748	20 Jul 1796			88	456	A large creek of Tennessee River	yes
Coil, Robert	217		Hawkins	150	204	26 Dec 1791	221	22 Feb 1780	77	315	On N side of Holstons River &c	
Coil, Robert	295		Hawkins	400	258	24 Dec 1792	86	8 Feb 1780	78	446	On N side of Holston River	
Coil, Robert	296		Hawkins	200	259	24 Dec 1792	98	8 Feb 1780	78	447	Lying in the hickory cove	
Coil, Robt	52		Hawkins	199	37	18 May 1789	363	27 Mar 1780	72	251	Head branches of Caney Creek	
Coile, Robert	278		Green	100	280	20 Sep 1787	327	7 Jun 1787 [?]	65	453	N/S Holston River below Clouds Cr	
Coile, Robert	449		Green	50	451	20 Sep 1787	974	29 Oct 1783	65	502	On N side of Holston River &c	
Coile, Robert	494		Green	100	496	20 Sep 1787	973	29 Oct 1783	65	517	S/S Holston mouth of Clouds Creek	
Coile, Robert	518		Green	250	520	20 Sep 1787	12	21 Oct 1783	65	529	On N side of Holston River	
Coit, Farwell	493	Collins, Matt	Sumner	640	1661	23 Aug 1793	3590	7 Jun 1788	81	44	On a branch of New River	yes
Coit, Farwell	494	Speight, Jas.	Sumner	640	1662	23 Aug 1793	3769	27 Oct 1793	81	44	On waters of Cumberland	yes
Coke, Philip	156		Davidson	640	142	14 Mar 1786	647		63	54	On Camp Creek	yes
Colbert, Laurence	843	Hart, Anthony	Davidson	640	848	17 Jan 1789	3422		63	297	On the dividing ridge &c	yes
Colbert, Richard	920	Nash, William	Davidson	640	936	18 May 1789			63	321	On E Fork of First Creek &c	yes
Colbey, John	2377	Stewart, Duncan	Davidson	640	3098	14 Sep 1797	4151		90	400	On S Harpeth River	yes
Colbreth, Alexander	398		Green	50	400	20 Sep 1787	2830	28 Mar 1781	65	485	On Sinking Creek	
Colby, Absalon	380	Sheppard, Benjamin	Davidson	640	352	15 Sep 1787	2306		63	133	On both sides of Large Creek	yes
Colden, Phillip	1504	Williams, Sampson	Davidson	428	1061	26 Nov 1789	3424		74	108	On N side of Cumberland River	yes
Coldwell, Bennoni	415		Hawkins	50	303	27 Nov 1792	337	24 Oct 1780	80	148	N/S Holston joining John Lowney	
Coldwell, James	158		Hawkins	63	91	16 Nov 1790	645	11 Jul 1780	77	182	In Carters Valley	
Coldwell, Thomas	109		Eastern District	200	98	17 Nov 1790	710	31 Aug 1780	76	175	N/S Holston both sides Caldwell Cr	
Coldwell, Thomas	45		Eastern District	400	71	7 Apr 1790	1860	6 Oct 1779	71	278	S/S Clinch River on a sinking branch	
Coldwell, Thomas	514		Green	400	516	20 Sep 1787	309	16 Mar 1780	65	527	On N side of Holston River &c	
Coldwell, Thomas	606		Hawkins	250	480	29 Jul 1793	2259	22 Nov 1779	80	296	On Forth Fork of Buck Creek	
Coldwell, Thomas	70		Hawkins	200	70	26 Nov 1789	1857	6 Oct 1779	73	1	S/S Holston River & on Buck Creek	
Coldwell, Thos (?)	537		Hawkins	300	410	29 Jul 1793	1828	3 Feb 1779	80	279	In Hannes Valley	
Cole, Burwell	942	Casleman, Benjamin	Sumner	640	2466	22 Jul 1795	2636	21 Dec 1792	83	425	On Caney Fork	yes
Cole, Edward	425	Nichols, John	Davidson	640	397	15 Sep 1787			63	148	N side of Cumberland River	yes
Cole, George	913	Smith, John	Sumner	274	2482	31 Dec 1793	672	25 Nov 1789	81	437	On Round Lick Creek	yes
Cole, Henry	657	Bushnell, E. & Wm. Dobbin	Davidson	1000	630	15 Sep 1787	1665		63	224	On waters of Stones River	yes
Cole, James	696	Sheppard, Nancy	Sumner	640	2066	20 May 1793	2087	29 Oct 1792	81	141	On W fork of Roaring River	yes
Cole, Jesse	150	Taylor, Thomas	Davidson	640	136	14 Mar 1786	1210		63	52	E side of W Fork of Harpeth River	yes
Cole, Joseph	118		Sullivan	50	130	23 Oct 1782	1952	12 Oct 1779	43	219 (31	Beg at a white oak &c	
Cole, Joseph	540		Sullivan	72	517	27 Nov 1789	1953	19 Oct 1779	74	28	On Linvil Creek	
Cole, Joseph	702		Sullivan	200	647	5 Dec 1794	1078	8 Jan 1779	84	159	Beg at two walnuts on a hill	
Cole, Joseph, Sr.	538		Sullivan	363	515	27 Nov 1789			74	27	On Beaver Creek	
Cole, Martin	409	Nichols, John	Davidson	1000	381	15 Sep 1787	90		63	142	On waters of Station Camp Creek	yes
Cole, Pemple, William [sic - ?	145	Johnston, John	Tennessee	1500	1396	20 Dec 1791	246	25 Oct 1783	77	350	On E fork of Pine River	yes
Cole, Phillip	031		Green	40		24 Oct 1794					On the delight of Luke Creek	
Cole, Solomon	29		Sullivan	200	40	23 Oct 1782	1079	8 Feb 1779	43	257	On Lindal Creek	
Cole, Solomon	525		Sullivan	386	341 (541)	26 Nov 1779	1702	22 Sep 1779	73	50	On both sides of Beaver Creek	
Cole, Thomas	23	Looney, David	Sumner	350 (357	780	11 Jul 1788	455	21 Sep 1787	63	273	On waters of Caney Fork	yes
Cole, William	445		Davidson	224	417	15 Sep 1787	678		63	154	On N side of Sulphur Cork	yes
Coleman, Benjamin	1874		Davidson	3840	1014	27 Apr 1793	266		81	21	On S W side of Big Harpeth	yes

Earliest Tennessee Land Records

Claimant:	File #:	Assignee:	County:	Acres:	Grant:	Grant Date:	Entry:	Entry Date:	Bk:	Pg:	Location by Stream Name:	Military:
Coleman, John	950		Green	1000	864	17 Nov 1790	2576	25 May 1784	76	126	Small Cr West Fk of Stones River	
Coleman, Spelby	186		Sumner	640	199	10 Jul 1788	206	29 Jan 1784	66	411	Beg at a small tree &c	yes
Coleman, Spilley	602	Toney, Anthony	Sumner	640	1852	20 May 1793	57	8 Jul 1785	81	90	On Second Creek &c	
Coleman, William	620		Green	150	661	11 Jul 1788	18	7 Jun 1784	66	447	On No Et side of Big Pigeon River	
Coles, Joseph	310		Sullivan	400	461	8 Dec 1787			64	312	On Beaver Creek	
Coleston, Henry	2407		Davidson	274	2805	26 Dec 1796	183		91	476	S side of Cumberland River	yes
Collahan, John	234	Bowman, William	Davidson	640	220	7 Mar 1786	877		63	81	On waters of Stones River	yes
Collet, John	2414	McConnel, Robert	Davidson	640	3207	14 Sep 1797	4691		91	7	On S Harpeth River	yes
Collette, Isaac	1277		Green	640	1127	12 Jan 1793	147	10 Mar 1778	78	381	S side Nolichuckey	
Collier, John & John Ryan	1740		Green	20	1391	2 Dec 1796	538	29 Apr 1781	91	273	Beg at a Spanish oak	
Collier, William	621		Green	130	662	11 Jul 1788	183	7 Jan 1784	66	447	Lying below Andrew Leepers &c	
Collins, Benjamin	345	Payton, Ephraim	Sumner	289	1412	20 Dec 1791	1537	9 Dec 1785	77	354	On Paytons Creek	yes
Collins, Brittain	35	Brock, Joseph	Sumner	640	859	17 Jan 1789	3337	1 May 1788	63	299	On waters of Red River	yes
Collins, Burwell	1155	Harris, Edward	Sumner	640	2660	4 Jun 1796	1134	1 Jun 1795	88	354	Joining said Harris survey	yes
Collins, Dillard	1154	Harris, Edward	Sumner	640	2659	4 Jun 1796	1135	1 Jul 1795	88	354	Joining said Harris survey	yes
Collins, George	968	Donelson, Stokley	Davidson		985	18 May 1789			63	333	On N Fork of Smiths Fork	yes
Collins, John	610		Davidson	274	582	15 Sep 1787	999		63	208	On Moores Creek	yes
Collins, John	914	West, Eli	Davidson	428	930	18 May 1789	679		63	320	On S side of Cumberland River	yes
Collins, Joseph	2058	Blount, JnoGray & Thos	Davidson	274	2160	20 May 1793	1303		81	163	On S W side of Big Harpeth	
Collins, Josiah	735	Nichols, John	Davidson	640	708	11 Jul 1788	2566		63	249	On the head of a branch	yes
Collins, Matthew	493	Coit, Farwell	Sumner	640	1661	23 Aug 1793	3590	7 Jun 1788	81	44	On a branch of New River	yes
Collins, Samuel	326	Mountflorence & Fenner	Davidson	640	312	28 Jun 1787	2176		63	116	N side of Cumberland River	yes
Collins, William	349		Tennessee	640	2171	20 May 1793	687	26 Apr 1784	81	166	On S side of Cumberland River	
Collins, William	557	Gise, Jonathan	Davidson	640	529	15 Sep 1787	604		63	190	S side of Cumberland River	yes
Collinsworth, William	1069		Davidson	640	43	17 Apr 1786	315	28 Feb 1784	66	49	Lying on Little Harpeth	
Collinsworth, William	1265		Davidson	640	230	10 Jul 1788	124	15 Jan 1784	66	419	On Browns Creek &c	
Collinsworth, William	1289		Davidson	640	254	10 Jul 1788	448	12 May 1784	66	426	On the Main Harpeth &c	
Collinsworth, Wm.	1200		Davidson	640	72	8 Oct 1787	410	19 Apr 1784	66	223	N branch of Little Harpeth &c	
Collison, James	380		Western District	640	381	29 Jul 1793			76	479	At the head of Buffolow Hollow &c	
Colpoh, Henry	446		Sullivan	750	325	10 Nov 1784	796,-1274	1779 and 1781	69	185	On the Blew Spring	
Colpoh, Henry	97		Sullivan	100	108	23 Oct 1782	678	24 Aug 1780	43	289	On S side of Holston River &c	
Colquehoon, James	750		Hawkins	640	590	12 Jul 1793	1668	7 Sep 1779	82	207	On N side of Holston River	
Colson, Isaac	592	Walls, Daniel (?)	Davidson	640	564	15 Sep 1787	2591		63	202	On N side of Cumberland River	yes
Cotter, John	46		Sullivan	200	57	23 Oct 1782	1885	6 Oct 1779	43	265	Fork bet. Holston & N Fork	
Cotter, Levi	583		Davidson	640	555	15 Sep 1787	902		63	199	On waters of Goose Creek	
Cotton, Thomas	737	Hafler, Thomas	Sumner	640	2130	20 May 1793	3257	9 Aug 1792	81	156	On both sides of Jining Creek	yes
Coltrain, Abraham, heirs of	283		Tennessee	640	1874	20 May 1793	3070	30 Nov 1785	81	95	On waters between War trace &c	yes
Colvin, John	1091	Easton, James	Sumner	640	2582	7 Mar 1796	3840	22 Jul 1795	88	317	E side of Large Fork of Caney Fork	yes
Colvin, Obed	739	Hart, Anthony	Davidson	640	712	11 Jul 1788	3423		63	250	On N side of Holston River	yes
Colwell, John	294	Fort, Elias	Sumner	389	1312	10 Dec 1790	1114	23 Mar 1789	74	369	On N side of Cumberland River	yes
Colyer, Charles	1042		Washington	640	992	14 Jan 1793	331	2 Sep 1778	79	283	In the Limestone Cove	
Colyer, William	898		Washington	200	875	17 Nov 1790	2669	19 Nov 1779	76	136	On Bumpus Creek &c	
Colyer, William	919		Washington	150	896	17 Nov 1790	1554	29 Aug 1779	76	143	In Bumpus Cove	
Colyer, William	981		Washington	200	958	17 Nov 1790	620	27 Oct 1783	76	165	Both sides of Noleychuckey &c	
Coman, James	1290	Swearingham,Zan hrs	Sumner	640	3049	8 Jun 1797	4181	5 Apr 1797	90	318	On a branch or small creek	yes

Earliest Tennessee Land Records

Claimant:	File #:	Assignee:	County:	Acres:	Grant:	Grant Date:	Entry:	Entry Date:	Bk:	Pg:	Location by Stream Name:	Military:
Coman, James	2357	Gilkey, Saml.	Davidson	640	3035	10 Apr 1797	4607		90	307	On a fork of the Caney Fork	yes
Coman, Jas.	1291	Wright, Stephen hrs	Sumner	640	3050	8 Jun 1797	4236	5 Apr 1797	90	318	On the ridge bet Flynns & Doe Creek	yes
Coman, Jas.	1292	Wright, Stephen	Sumner	640	3051	8 Jun 1797	4208	5 Apr 1797	90	318	Inc a spring	yes
Combs, William	041	Sitgreaves, Joseph	Tennessee	640			2642	30 Sep 1785			On the waters of Bartons Creek	yes
Comer, James	775		Green	500	580	23 Aug 1788	969	29 Oct 1783	68	253	S/S Clinch River above Island Fork	
Comers, James	1699	Phillips, Phillip & M. Camp	Davidson	428	1660	23 Feb 1793	106		76	340	Abt 3 miles from black foxes camp	yes
Comon, James	534	White, Jacob	Middle District	1000	2934	22 Feb 1797	4666		90	238	On a fork of Caney Fork	yes
Comon, James	535	East, Sampson hrs	Middle District	640	2935	22 Feb 1797	597 [?]		90	238	Both sides of Muirs Fork	yes
Comon, James	540	Galders, Geo. Hrs	Middle District	640	2964	2 Mar 1797	4603		90	257	Waters of Calf Killers Creek	yes
Comon, James	541	Foster, William hrs.	Middle District	640	2965	2 Mar 1767	4601		90	258	N of the Cumberland Mountain	yes
Comon, James	542	Gogan, John hrs.	Middle District	640	2966	2 Mar 1767	4604		90	258	Beg near S W corner Gap Survey	yes
Comon, James	543	Cale, Geo. C. heirs	Middle District	640	2967	2 Mar 1797	4602		90	259	S side of Caney Fork	yes
Condray, James	957		Washington	200	934	17 Nov 1790	1906	8 Oct 1779	76	155	On a branch of Lick Creek &c	
Condron, William	1150		Washington	160	1108	17 Jul 1794	2539	10 Apr 1780	81	613	Adjoining Michael Woods land	
Condry, Richard	824		Washington	100	638	10 Nov 1784	1465	28 Jun 1779	69	148	On the Christians War road	
Conley, Jno.	643		Middle District	55	737	26 Oct 1786	2867	28 May 1781	66	29	Beg at a white oak &c	
Con-naugh-ty	053		Tennessee	640	6			3 Aug 1819			N bank Oconolufto River	
Conner, Christopher	857	Armstrong, Andrew	Davidson	640	866	17 Jan 1789	1701		63	301	On N side of Red River	yes
Conner, Davy	1668	Robertson, James	Davidson	640	1592	23 Feb 1753	1016		76	308	On Harpeth River &c	yes
Conner, James	154		Green	500	624	23 Aug 1788	711	28 Oct 1783	64	349	On S side Clinch River &c	
Conner, James	250		Green	1000	207	20 Sep 1787	1526	7 Mar 1784	65	433	On N side of Clinch River &c	
Conner, James	599		Middle District	1000	364	9 Dec 1797	2235	22 May 1784	96	10	On Swift Creek &c	
Conner, James	600		Middle District	640	365	9 Dec 1797	2240	22 May 1780	96	10	On Swift Creek	
Conner, John	665	Berry, Thomas	Davidson	274	638	15 Nov 1797	1397		63	226	On a small creek &c	yes
Conner, Tarrance	1133		Green	300	976	26 Dec 1791	241	24 Jun 1778	77	275	On S side of Holstein River	
Conner, William	052	Dillenberry, Redmon	Sumner	640			4182	14 Oct 1797			On head of W branches	yes
Connor, James	598		Middle District	1000	363	9 Dec 1797	2230	22 May 1784	96	9	On Swift Creek	
Conrad, Nocholas, Ass	941		Sumner	213	2465	22 Feb 1795	1340	14 Sep 1785	83	424	S side of Cumberland River	yes
Connod, Nicholas	1259		Davidson	640	224	10 Jul 1788	577	13 Aug 1784	66	417	On S side of Cumberland	
Connod, Nicholas	1294		Davidson	640	259	10 Jul 1788	576	13 Aug 1784	66	428	On So side of Cumberland River	
Connod, Nicholas	2186	Rowland, James	Davidson	274	2433	22 Feb 1795	3251		84	313	Sulphur Fork of Red River	yes
Connod, Nicholas	371	Phelps, Garret	Tennessee	640	2264	20 May 1793	3564	24 Oct 1787	81	184	On head branch of Buds Creek	
Connod, Nicholas	400	Dawson, Isaac	Tennessee	274	2427	31 Dec 1793			81	408	Bet Millers Creek & Brushey Creek	
Conway, Henry	179		Green	300	649	11 Jul 1793			64	358	On N side of French Broad River	
Conway, Henry	180		Middle District	640	162	17 Nov 1790	16	24 Feb 1778	76	177(?)	Joining place called the barrens &c	
Conway, Henry	40		Green	600	103	1 Nov 1786	306	30 Jul 1784	58	464	Upon N side of Nolihuckie River	
Conway, Joseph	679	McCafferty, James	Tennessee	640	3402	17 May 1803	1450	22 Jul 1785	110	319	Little West Fork of Red River	yes
Conway, Joseph	929		Green	200	843	17 Nov 1790	1065	30 Oct 1783	76	119	S side of Nolachuckey River &c	
Conway, Joseph	970		Green	70	884	17 Nov 1790	60	12 May 1784	76	132	S side of Nolichuckey River	
Conway, William	140		Green	600	122	1 Nov 1786	232	26 Mar 1785	60	454	On N side of Nolichuckey River	
Conway, William	964		Green	25	878	17 Nov 1790	1472	20 Jun 1787	76	130	N side of Nolachuckey River	
Cook, Frederick	2266	Terrell, William	Davidson	640	2742	20 Jul 1796	3066		88	454	On N side of Cumberland River	yes
Cook, George	1233		Davidson	640	197	10 Jul 1788	611	27 Oct 1784	66	411	N/S Red Riv white oak & huckleberry	
Cook, Jonah	1961	Sanford, Samuel	Davidson	640	1816	20 May 1793	2371		81	83	On waters of W Harpeth	yes
Cook, Richard	1466	Woolam(?), Stephen	Sumner	540	3384	12 Dec 1801	654	7 Mar 1801	114	90	Beg at an ash	yes

Claimant:	File #:	Assignee:	County:	Acres:	Grant:	Grant Date:	Entry:	Entry Date:	Bk:	Pg:	Location by Stream Name:	Military:
Cook, Richard	658	Faybourne, Joel	Tennessee	640	3235	24 Nov 1797	925	19 May 1784	94	170	Waters of Wells Creek	
Cook, Richard [?]	1374	Hays, Thos.	Sumner	274	3236	24 Nov 1797	1197	20 Aug 1785	94	171	N side of Cumberland River	yes
Cook, Sanders	615		Sumner	640	1875	20 May 1793	836	23 Jun 1788	81	95	Headwaters Mansooes trace Creek	yes
Cook, William	1302		Davidson	640	267	10 Jul 1788	198	28 Jan 1784	66	430	On N side of Cumberland River &c	
Cook, Wm.	279		Hawkins	400	290	14 Jan 1793	1297	7 Jun 1784	78	342	On S side of Holston River	
Cooke, Isaac	465	Davis, Joshua	Davidson	640	437	15 Sep 1793	2412		63	161	On fifth creek after Red River	
Cooke, Joseph	766		Sullivan	100	697	20 Jul 1796	49,436	Apr & Feb 1780	91	82	Waters of Reedy Creek	
Cooke, Richard	1375	Smith, Wm.	Sumner	1000	3237	24 Nov 1797	1375	13 Jul 1797	94	171	On W Fork of Drakes Creek	yes
Cooke, Richard	1376	Harrold, Jno. Heirs	Sumner	1000	3238	24 Nov 1797	4066	13 Aug 1797	94	172	Bet two Creeks	yes
Cooley, Gabriel	0142		Sumner	640	3371-72	29 Apr 1801	16	21 Aug 1800			W fk of Drake Creek	yes
Cooley, Gabriel, heirs of	1461		Sumner	240	3371	29 Apr 1801			112	388	On Main Middle Fork of Baron	yes
Cooley, Gabriel, heirs of	1462		Sumner	400	3372	29 Apr 1801			112	388	W Fork of Drakes Creek	yes
Cooley, Samuel	92	Mountflorence, Jas C.	Davidson	1428	78	14 Mar 1786	397		63	32	On both sides of Red River	yes
Coon, Conrad	2474	Harris, Ed	Dav.&Robertson	228	3411	10 Feb 1804			118	300	Both sides of Sycamore Creek	
Coon, Conrad	8	White, David	Dav.&Robertson	228	3411	10 Feb 1804	1123		118	300	On both sides of Sycamore Creek	
Coonrod, Nicholas	668	Hay, David	Sumner	640	1988	20 May 1793	3445	2 Nov 1786	81	121	On Cedar Creek &c	yes
Coonrad, Nicholas	397	Bean(?), Robert	Tennessee	226	2420	7 Jan 1794	3448	2 Feb 1786	81	406	On Millers Creek	
Coonrod, Nicholas	1478		Davidson	640	282	26 Nov 1789	26	27 Dec 1783	73	255	On S side of Cumberland River	
Coonrod, Nicholas	526	Holland, William	Davidson	640	498	15 Sep 1787	715	17 Mar 1784	63	180	N side of Cumberland River	yes
Coons, Michael	856		Green	640	841	13 Feb 1791	1545	17 Mar 1784	73	381	On waters of French Broad	
Cooper, Abraham	1159		Washington	200	1117	7 Jul 1794	688	10 Dec 1778	81	616	On waters of Buffaloe Creek	
Cooper, Henry	1396	Barton, Gabriel	Sumner	440	3023	6 Dec 1797	3782	4 May 1797	97	45	On Round Lick Creek	yes
Cooper, James	029		Green	400			322	17 Mar 1780				
Cooper, James	114		Hawkins	250	148				75	163	On N side of Holson River	
Cooper, James	185		Middle District	640	167	17 Nov 1790	1670	17 Apr 1779	76	179	On Coopers Creek	
Cooper, James	186		Middle District	600	168	17 Nov 1790	2350	11 Dec 1779	76	179	On Cowpen Creek &c	
Cooper, James	240		Sullivan	1218	379	9 Aug 1787	497-498	3 May 1783	61	398	In Carters Valley	
Cooper, James	294		Sullivan	380	433	9 Aug 1787	322	17 Mar 1783	61	452	On N side of Holstons River &c	
Cooper, James	375		Sullivan	300	254	10 Nov 1784	499	27 Apr 1780	69	163	In Stanleys Valley	
Cooper, James	433		Sullivan	163	312	10 Nov 1784	2237	22 Nov 1779	69	180	In Carters Valley	
Cooper, John	178		Middle District	400	160	17 Nov 1790	1872	7 Oct 1779	76	177	Both sides of Cowpen Creek	
Cooper, John	462		Sullivan	180	341	10 Nov 1784	1234	8 Oct 1784	69	191	On N side of Holstein River	
Cooper, Nathaniel	383	Cobb, Jesse	Tennessee	228	2340	20 May 1793	2086		81	200	On both sides of Red River	yes
Cooper, Nathaniel	695	Sheppard, Nancy	Davidson	640	668	8 Dec 1787	636		63	236	On N side of Tennessee River	yes
Cooper, Peavance	805		Washington	300	619	10 Nov 1784	1438	25 Nov 1778	69	144	On Watauga River	
Cooper, Robert	1180		Washington	400	1138	7 Jul 1794	1731	11 Jun 1779	81	622	Beg at 3 chesnut trees	
Cooper, Robert, Ass.	458		Sumner	274	1597	27 Apr 1793	1558	27 Nov 1792	81	17	On S bank of Cedar Lick Creek	yes
Cooper, Samuel	857	Wilson, David	Sumner	274	2362	20 May 1793	2117	27 Oct 1792	81	204	On S side of Cumberland River	yes
Cooper, Solomon	329	Fenner, Richard	Davidson	640	315	28 Jun 1787	2117	2 Feb 1780	63	117	On waters of Moneyfork Creek	yes
Cooper,Jas & N Henderson	714		Hawkins	640	534	12 Jun 1794	1600	12 Sep 1779	82	165	Head N Fork of Sycamore Creek	
Cooper,Jas & N Henderson	722		Hawkins	640	542	12 Jun 1794	1620	24 May 1784	82	168	On N side of Wallings Ridge	
Coor, James	100		Western District	1000	100	10 Jul 1788	2515	24 May 1784	67	320	On waters of the North Fork &c	yes
Coor, James	101		Western District	1000	101	10 Jul 1783	2514	25 May 1784	67	320	On waters of North Fork &c	yes
Coor, James	72		Western District	1000	72	10 Jul 1788	2512	25 May 1784	67	308	On waters of Obion River &c	yes
Coor, James	85		Western District	1000	85	10 Jul 1788	2513	25 May 1784	67	313	On waters of Obion River &c	

Claimant:	File #:	Assignee:	County:	Acres:	Grant:	Grant Date:	Entry:	Entry Date:	Bk:	Pg:	Location by Stream Name:	Military:
Coor, James	87		Western District	1000	87	10 Jul 1788	2516	25 May 1784	67	314	On waters of N Fork &c	
Coor, James (or Thomas)	102		Western District	1000	102	10 Jul 1788	2520	25 May 1784	67	321	On N waters of the North Fork &c	
Coor, James (or Thomas)	103		Western District	1000	103	10 Jul 1788	2521	25 May 1784	67	321	N waters North Fork of Forked Deer	
Coor, James (or Thomas)	104		Western District	1000	104	10 Jul 1788	2519	25 May 1784	67	321	Waters of North Fork of Forked Deer	
Coor, James (or Thomas)	105		Western District	1000	105	10 Jul 1788	2517	25 May 1784	67	322	On waters of N Fork of Forked Deer River	
Cooten, James	99		Western District	1000	99	10 Jul 1788	2518	25 May 1784	67	319	On waters of North Fork &c	
Cooten, James	335		Tennessee	853	2120	20 May 1793	319	27 Nov 1783	81	154	On the waters of Red River	
Copelain, Joseph	503		Sullivan	200	521	7 Apr 1790	154	16 Feb 1780	71	279	On N side of Holeson River	
Copelain, Joseph	504		Sullivan	300	522	7 Apr 1790	342	24 Mar 1788	71	279	N side of Holston River	
Copeland, David	421		Green	200	423	20 Sep 1787	370	7 Jun 1784	65	494	S/S Holston N E Fork of Turkey Cr	
Copeland, David	471		Green	200	473	20 Sep 1787	810	29 Oct 1783	65	508	S/S Holston Riv on Ceader Creek	
Copeland, David	498		Green	300	500	20 Sep 1787	676	29 Oct 1783	65	518	On S side of Holston River &c	
Copeland, James	451		Sullivan	300	330	10 Nov 1784	341	24 Mar 1780	69	187	On N side of Holstein River	
Copeland, Joab	2338	Malloy, Thomas	Davidson	640	2982	10 Apr 1797	1040		90	286	On Harpeth River	yes
Copeland, John	033		Green	25	2688	16 Oct 1796					On waters of Sinking Creek	
Copeland, John	709	Jamison, William	Sumner	1000	2089	20 May 1793	1169	20 Aug 1783	81	147	On waters of W Fork Goose Creek	yes
Copeland, Joseph	025		Green	640			499	27 Oct 1783			S side of French Broad River	
Copeland, Joseph	117	Mayfield, Sutterline	Davidson	640	103	7 Mar 1786	783		63	41	On Mill Creek	yes
Copeland, Kedar	358	Long, Nicholas	Tennessee	640	2203	20 May 1793	9	15 Oct 1783	81	169	Beg on an elm	yes
Copeland, Repley	039	Devers, John	Davidson	274			71	13 Apr 1790			N side of Cumberland River	yes
Copeland, Richard	1603	Brown, John	Davidson	228	1319	10 Dec 1790	103		74	372	On S side of Cumberland River	yes
Copenhafer, Thomas	0101	Duplicate Warrants	Washington	320 & 300			2270-71					
Copenhafer, Thomas	1821		Sullivan	960	189	10 Oct 1783	2269-70	22 & 23 Nov 1779	53	153	On N side of Holston River	
Copiad, Wm.	333		Davidson	200	327	8 Mar 1793	1326	4 Apr 1779	78	473	NW side of Clinch River	
Coplan, William	284		Sullivan	150	423	9 Aug 1787	407	10 Apr 1780	61	442	On N side of Holston River	
Copland, Wm.	323		Hawkins	200	327	8 Mar 1793	1326	4 Apr 1779	78	473	On N W side of Clinch River	
Copland, Wm.	329		Hawkins	200	323	8 Mar 1793	1261	2 Mar 1779	78	471	In Beaver Creek Valley	
Copland, Wm.	330		Hawkins	200	324	8 Mar 1793	349	3 Sep 1778	78	471	On S side of Clinch River	
Copland, Wm.	331		Hawkins	200	325	8 Mar 1793	1354	5 May 1779	78	472	On S E side of Clinch River	
Copland, Wm.	332		Hawkins	300	326	8 Mar 1793	1495	29 Jul 1779	78	472	On S E side of Clinch River	
Coplin, David	706		Green	300	747	11 Jul 1788	19	2 Dec 1783	66	474	On N side of Nolichuckey River &c	
Coppage, James	281		Middle District	250	248	12 Jul 1794			81	599	On Buffalo River	
Coppedge, James, Ass	338		Middle District	250	165	12 Dec 1794			83	440	On Buffalo River	
Coppedge, Jas.	0132		Green	250	248	12 Jul 1794					On Buffc(sic) River	
Corben, Francis	2276	Buckanan, John	Davidson	640	2756	20 Jul 1796	1316	24 Jan 1787	88	459	On waters of Harricane Creek	yes
Corbeth, Jno.	590		Green	200	271	20 Sep 1787	863	7 Jun 1784	66	164	On Blue Spring Branch	
Corbin, Arthur	2094		Davidson	274	2312	20 May 1793	3159		81	193	On Harpeth River	yes
Corbin, Arthur	840	Wilson, David	Sumner	274	2342	20 May 1793	3238	21 Oct 1791	81	200	On waters of Paytons Creek	yes
Corbin, Francis	1357	Hickman, Thomas	Sumner	640	2783	11 Dec 1796	1316	28 Oct 1796	91	296	N side of Cumberland River	yes
Corbin, James	193	Donelson, Stockley	Eastern District	640	2381	8 Mar 1794	1315		81	439	On N side of Clinch River	yes
Corbin, James	577	Williams, Eliza	Middle District	640	2784	20 Dec 1796	1315		91	321	In a valley known as Calf Killers	yes
Corbin, Richard	1300	Hickman, Thomas	Sumner	640	3070	19 Jul 1797	4591	6 Apr 1797	90	378	S side of Cumberland River	yes
Corbitt, John	29		Green	100	92	1 Nov 1786	862	29 Oct 1783	58	453	Beg upon an oak	
Corderey, John	783	Dange(?), Jacob	Davidson	274	756	11 Jul 1788	415		63	265	On the Sulphur Fork of Red River	yes
Corkin, George	030		Sullivan	40			161	17 Feb [sic]			Joining land he now lives on	

Claimant:	File #:	Assignee:	County:	Acres:	Grant:	Grant Date:	Entry:	Entry Date:	Bk:	Pg:	Location by Stream Name:	Military:
Cormack, John	2080	Pearson, James	Davidson	640	2265	20 May 1793	3038		81	184	On Cripple Creek	yes
Corne, Thomas	029	Blount, Reading	Middle District	640			2115					yes
Cornelius, Elijah	426	Phillips, Isaac	Tennessee	640	2486	31 Dec 1793	2713	30 Sep 1785	81	438	Beg at a ceader bluff	yes
Conyer, Stephen	031	Dorris, Joseph	Robertson	357			3784	4 Feb 1796			On Sulphur Fork of Red River	yes
Cosby, James	1115		Green	1000	958	26 Dec 1791	1208	4 Jan 1784	77	266	On S side of French Broad River	
Cosby, James	1128		Green	640	971	26 Dec 1791	448	25 Oct 1783	77	271	On S side of French Broad River	
Cosby, James & Sam Givins	261		Green	2000	218	20 Sep 1787	4596		65	437	On N side of Tennessee River &c	
Cosman [?], James	2356	Epsom, John hrs	Davidson	640	3034	10 Apr 1797			90	307	Both sides of Muirs Fork	
Coston, Henry	1372	Harden, Moses	Sumner	640	3227	17 Nov 1797	3772	25 Oct 1796	94	166	Waters of Drakes Creek	yes
Coswey [?], Joseph	1494		Davidson	640	1051	26 Nov 1789	1450		74	102	Div ridge Hdwtrs Gaspers & Cane Cr	yes
Cotanich, John	834	Brock, Joseph	Davidson	640	837	17 Jan 1789	3450		63	294	On N side of Cumberland River	yes
Cotanich, Peter	1540	Thompson, Jason	Davidson	640	1097	26 Nov 1789	3454		74	130	On E waters of Mill Creek	yes
Cotes, Benjamin	1922	Robertson, James	Davidson	365	1718	20 May 1793	3058		81	58	On E side of Harpeth River	yes
Cothran, John	2224	Lee, James	Davidson	228	2514	8 Dec 1795			88	287	On waters of Sycamore	yes
Cotter, James	590		Hawkins	400	464	29 Jul 1793	306	6 Aug 1778	80	292	N side of Holston River &c	
Cotter, John	163		Hawkins	200	96	16 Nov 1790	744	12 Feb 1781	77	184	Inc the Lick Spring	
Cotter, John	460		Hawkins	200	332	29 Jul 1793	1804	6 Oct 1779	80	258	Inc the Stone Lick	
Cotter, John	556		Hawkins	100	429	29 Jul 1793	1259	2 Mar 1779	80	284	N side of the Holston River	
Cotter, Stephen	840		Green	100	821	13 Feb 1791	2022	10 Oct 1780	73	375	Head of Horse Camp Cr of Lick Cr	
Cotton, Ephraim	2093	Sheppard, Nancy	Davidson	640	2311	20 May 1793	1752		81	193	On the head of Jinings Creek	yes
Cotton, Samuel; Legatee	1691		Green	1000	1367	27 Nov 1795			89	288	On S side of Noleychuckey River	
Cotton, Samuel; Legatee	393		Eastern District	1000	235	27 Nov 1795			89	291	The N side of Clinch River	
Cotton, Thomas	2313	Smith, Joseph hrs	Davidson	640	2512	7 Aug 1795			89	415	On waters of Stones River	yes
Cotton, Thomas	260	Smith, James	Davidson	640	246	7 Mar 1786	723		63	90	S side of Cumberland River	yes
Cottrell, John	1071		Hawkins	200	758	2 Dec 1796	1791	2 Oct 1779	91	270	In Puncheon Camp Valley	
Couch, George	1215		Green	100	1215	May 1792	44	10 Mar 1791	77	404	Gap Bays Mountain on Big Gap Cr	
Coulter, John	125		Hawkins	400	159	26 Nov 1789	1884	6 Oct 1779	75	167	On N bank of Holson River	
Council, James	170	Council(?), Arthur	Tennessee	3840	1435	20 Dec 1791	1149	11 Aug 1784	77	360	On both sides of Duck River &c	
Counts, Nicholas	1015		Hawkins	127	759	26 Dec 1796	5	26 Feb 1778	90	202	Waters of Richland Creek	
Courts, Nicholas	036		Green	200	607	12 Jul 1794	1811	12 Jul 1794			On Richland Creek	
Courts, Nicholas	767		Hawkins	200	607	12 Jul 1794			82	214	On Richland Creek	
Covenan, Benjamin	387	Sheppard, Benjamin	Davidson	640	359	15 Sep 1787	2335	20 Aug 1785	63	135	On both sides W Fork of Drake Cr	yes
Coving, Isham, heirs of	995		Sumner	640	2477	22 Feb 1795	1429		84	326	On N side of Cumberland River	yes
Covington, John	781	Harrington, Henry Wm.	Sumner	2560	2236	20 May 1793	1828	30 Nov 1792	81	177	On the ridge bet Bledsoe's Creek &c	yes
Covinton, John	1050	Hadley, Joshua	Sumner	400	177	2 Dec 1795			88	285	On N side of Cumberland River	yes
Cowan, Absolm	086	Hickman, Thomas	Sumner	640			2447	4 Jun 1796			S side of Cumberland River	yes
Cowan, Andrew, Ass.	1619		Green	400	154	22 Feb 1795		23 Aug 1779	84	280	On S side of French Broad River	
Cowan, James	2173	Williams, Willoughby	Davidson	640	2494	1 Apr 1794	2839		81	452	On waters of Stones River	yes
Cowan, John	80		Eastern District	640	105	26 Dec 1791			75	179	On N side of Tennessee River	
Cowan, William	895		Green	250	826	Sep 1790	544	3 May 1790	74	291	On S side of Little River	
Coward, James	150		Washington	360 (260	18	23 Oct 1782	757	23 Dec 1778	47	8	S fork of Boons Creek	
Coward, Peter	882	Ford, John	Davidson	640	896	17 Jan 1789	1467	10 Nov 1784	63	310	On N side of Cumberland River	yes
Coward, Zacharias	839		Washington	100	653	10 Nov 1784	2839		69	152	On N side of Big Limestone Creek	
Cowen, John	1705		Green	280	142	19 Feb 1797	965	20 Apr 1784	90	244	An island in French Broad River	
Cowen, Joseph	2437	Tatum, Howell	Davidson	220	3279	6 Dec 1797	3637		98	160	On waters of Overalls Creek	yes

Earliest Tennessee Land Records

Claimant:	File #:	Assignee:	County:	Acres:	Grant:	Grant Date:	Entry:	Entry Date:	Bk:	Pg:	Location by Stream Name:	Military:
Cowen, Robert	646		Washington	200	740	26 Oct 1786	2998	6 Feb 1784	66	30	On the S side of Nolichuckey River	
Cowen, Robert	755		Washington	300	569	10 Nov 1784	723	21 Dec 1778	69	129	Beg at a poplar &c	
Cowen, Robert	90		Sullivan	100	101	21 Oct 1782	1642	16 Sep 1779	43	286	On N side of Holston River	
Cox, Abraham	251		Sullivan	307	390	9 Aug 1787	776	25 Dec 1778	61	409	On S side of Holstons River	
Cox, Benjamin	594		Green	140	551	20 Sep 1787	615	27 Oct 1783	66	247	N/S Nobs. bet Holstein & Fr Broad	
Cox, Charles	1575	Johnson, Thomas	Davidson	228	1224	10 Dec 1790	3452		74	339	On waters of Cripple Creek	yes
Cox, Edward	031		Sullivan	230			281	9 Mar 1780			Beg at 2 Spanish oaks	
Cox, Edward	1079		Davidson	640	53	17 Apr 1786	152	17 Jan 1784	66	52	On head E Fork of Station Camp Cr	
Cox, Edward	1202		Davidson	640	74	8 Oct 1787	151	17 Jan 1784	66	224	Lying on E branches of Mill Creek	
Cox, Edward	1215	Phillips, Mann	Sumner	640	2496	26 Sep 1795	1243	8 Aug 1795	89	105	On both sides of Pond Lick	yes
Cox, Edward	1898		Davidson	800	129	27 Apr 1793	148	16 Jan 1784	81	36	On waters of Stewarts Creek	
Cox, Edward	438		Sullivan	292	317	10 Nov 1784	281	9 Mar 1780	69	182	On N side of Holston River	
Cox, Edward	79		Western District	1000	79	10 Jul 1788	1926	26 Apr 1784	67	311	On the waters of the North Fork &c	
Cox, Ephraim	522		Green	400	524	20 Sep 1787	276	19 Nov 1783	65	530	Beg upon a stake	
Cox, Jacob	032		Sullivan	200			753	23 Dec 1778			On head of Horse Creek	
Cox, Jacob	1038		Hawkins	570	787	22 Feb 1797	102,-105	8 Feb 1780	90	232	Both sides the N fork of Holston R	
Cox, Jacob	461		Sullivan	200	340	10 Nov 1784			69	191	On head of Horse Creek	
Cox, James	05		Eastern District	300			2768	22 Mar 1783			On Bear Creek	
Cox, James	1144		Green	173	987	26 Dec 1791	565	21 Jan 1784	77	277	At a cedar on S side of Nolachuckey River	
Cox, James	1170		Green	35	1013	26 Dec 1791	1305	4 Jan 1784	77	286	In an island on Nolachuckey River	
Cox, James	958		Washington	90	935	17 Nov 1790	2652	26 Sep 1780	76	156	Beg at a white oak on Scotts line	
Cox, Jeremiah, Jr.	722		Sullivan	84	667	5 Dec 1794	190	21 Feb 1780	84	170	Beg at two poplars	
Cox, Jesse	434		Hawkins	100	312	24 Jun 1793	2787	24 Feb 1781	80	190	On Sinking Spring	
Cox, John	1413	Armstrong, M.	Davidson	100	30	8 Oct 1787	868	23 Apr 1785	68	155	On the W side of Whites Creek	
Cox, John	275		Sullivan	400	414	9 Aug 1787	413	12 Apr 1780	61	433	On the N side of Holston River	
Cox, John	511		Sullivan	100	527	26 Nov 1789	291	9 Mar 1780	73	43	N side of Holston River	
Cox, John Jr	62		Sullivan	220	73	23 Oct 1782	1057	7 Jan 1779	43	274	On the N side of Holston River	
Cox, John Jr	774		Hawkins	200	614	12 Jul 1794	97	10 Oct 1782	82	217	On S side of Holston River &c	
Cox, John Sr	033		Sullivan	346			1019	5 Jan 1779			On Holson River	
Cox, Matthew	1551		Green	100	1216	30 Dec 1793	1216 [sic]	25 Aug 1793	82	144	On Roaring fork of Lick Creek	
Cox, Phenix	038	Duffy, Peter	Davidson	640			763	16 Aug 1784			On waters of Marrowbone	
Cox, Samuel	511		Green	500	513	20 Sep 1787	843	29 Oct 1783	65	526	On S side of Holston River	
Cox, Solomon	019		Hawkins	100			181	21 Feb 1780			In the Indian Hollow	
Cox, Solomon	966		Green	250	880	17 Nov 1790	676	16 Oct 1780	76	131	S/S Holston River waters Long Cr	
Cox, Thomas	1209		Davidson	640	81	8 Oct 1787	149	16 Jan 1784	66	226	Beg at two white oaks &c	
Cox, Thomas	1360		Davidson	320	43	8 Oct 1787	150	17 Jan 1784	68	139	Joining his service right	
Cox, Thomas	2120	Newman, Anthony	Davidson	640	2396	7 Jan 1794	1549	20 Feb 1790	81	390	The waters of Roaring River	yes
Cox, Thomas	47	Tatum, Howell	Tennessee	274	1239	10 Dec 1790	1244	20 Feb 1790	74	344	On S side of Cumberland River	yes
Cox, Thos.	349		Hawkins	300	343	8 Mar 1793	468	24 Apr 1780	78	481	On S side of Clinch River	
Cox, Thos. & Wm. Hawkins	24		Eastern District	500	24	11 Jul 1788			67	349	On N side of Clinch River &c	
Cox, William	020		Hawkins	400			1877	6 Oct 1779			N E fork of Bull Run	
Cox, William	738		Davidson	228	711	11 Jul 1788	2023	11 Jul 1788	63	250	On head of Millers Creek	
Cox, William	844		Green	140	825	13 Feb 1791	2405	19 Jan 1780	73	376	On Sinking Cr waters of Nolichuckey	yes
Cox, William	846		Washington	500	660	10 Nov 1784	690	16 Dec 1778	69	154	On S fork of Boons Creek	
Cox, William, Senr	641		Hawkins	100	510	23 Apr 1794	115	8 Feb 1780	81	552	On S side of Holston River	

Claimant:	File #:	Assignee:	County:	Acres:	Grant:	Grant Date:	Entry:	Entry Date:	Bk:	Pg:	Location by Stream Name:	Military:
Cox, Wm. & M. Massingell	849		Hawkins	100	674	22 Feb 1795	368	Mar 1780	83	433	S side Holston River on Mossy Cr	
Cox, John	511		Sullivan	100	527	26 Nov 1789	291	9 Mar 1780	73	43	On S side of Holeson River &c	
Coyart, David	241	Whitard, William	Tennessee	274	1590	27 Apr 1793	597	21 Apr 1784	81	15	Both sides of W Fork of Red River	yes
Coyle, Robert	1118		Hawkins	640	838	17 Nov 1797	1033	6 Jan 1779	94	140	On Caney Creek	
Coyle, Robert	1120		Hawkins	640	839	21 Nov 1797	85	8 Feb 1780	96	1	N side of Holston River	
Coyle, Robert	397		Sullivan	400 (321	276	10 Nov 1784	1861	6 Oct 1779	69	169	On N side of Holstein River	
Coyles, Robert	173		Hawkins	111	106	16 Nov 1790	1013	5 Jan 1779	77	187	On Coales Ridge	
Coyles, Robert	178		Hawkins	160	111	16 Nov 1790	1014	5 Jan 1779	77	188	On Caney Creek	
Coyles, Robert	189		Hawkins	400	122	16 Nov 1790	985	4 Jan 1779	77	191	On Caney Creek	
Crab, Richard	2098	Sheppard, Nancy	Davidson	640	2323	20 May 1793	1751		81	196	On E fork of E Fork of Stones River	yes
Crabb, Benjamin	1887	Weakley, Robert	Davidson	428	1640	27 Apr 1793	3126		81	28	On S side of Cumberland River	yes
Crabb, Joseph, Dec'd	448		Eastern District	640	316	15 Dec 1802	6	21 Oct 1783	110	270	On German Creek	
Crabtree, James	05		Davidson	480				14 Apr 1794			Waters of big Harpeth Hays Creek	
Crabtree, James	1101		Davidson	640	75	17 Apr 1786	368	23 Mar 1784	66	59	On S side of Cumberland River	
Crabtree, James	1228	Douglas & Wm. Montgome	Sumner	480	176	27 Aug 1795	729	14 Apr 1792	89	413	On waters of Drakes Creek	yes
Crabtree, James, Ass	421		Sumner	640	432	27 Jun 1793	729	May 1785	80	352	On S side of Cumberland River	
Crabtree, John	1102	Farmer, Thomas	Sumner	640	2603	7 Mar 1796	878		88	328	On S side of Obeys River	yes
Craddock, John	1471	Armstrong, John	Davidson	3840	1047	7 Apr 1790	530		71	282	On N side of Cumberland River	yes
Craddock, John	1526	Dove, William	Davidson	264	1083	26 Nov 1789	3202		74	122	Dry Fork of West Fork of Red River	yes
Craddock, John	1534	Wiggins, Thos. Heirs	Davidson	640	1091	26 Nov 1789	1448		74	126	On N side of Red River	yes
Craddock, John	1537	Roberts, Hardy heirs	Davidson	640	1095	26 Nov 1789	2474		74	129	Waters W Fork of Station Camp Cr	yes
Craddock, Shadrack	1417	Hadley, Joshua	Sumner	228	3272	6 Dec 1797	4547	21 Jun 1797	98	155	Beg @ Samuel Jones S E corner	yes
Crafford, Hugh	034		Sullivan	190			69-488	Feb & Apr 1780			Beg @ red oak & gum Saplin	
Crafford, Hugh	69		Sullivan	227	70	23 Oct 1782	170	19 Feb 1780	43	277	In Stanley Valley	
Crafford, Hugh	907	Kuykendall, Saml.	Sumner	274	2476	31 Dec 1793	3470	2 Jun 1785	81	435	W Fork of Station Camp Cr	yes
Crafford, William	1093		Davidson	640	67	17 Apr 1786	134	16 Jan 1784	66	57	Et Fork of Station Camp Creek	
Crafford, Wm.	105	Hollis, Wm.	Tennessee	640	316	17 Nov 1790	375	1 Jun 1789	76	186	On Red River	
Craft, Michael	190 (191)		Sullivan	92	198	10 Oct 1783	1974	19 Oct 1779	53	157	Joining Stephen Easleys &c	
Craft, Michael	454		Sullivan	100	333	10 Nov 1784	789	26 Dec 1778	69	188	On S side of Hostlein River	
Cragan, Patrick	429		Sullivan	170	308	10 Nov 1784	863	30 Dec 1778	69	179	On Indian Creek	
Craig, Andrew	629		Hawkins	200	491	27 Jun 1793	1695	21 Sep 1779	80	358	On Stock Creek	
Craig, David	22		Maury	3200	40	14 Jul 1812	706	10 Jul 1784	126	443	On both sides of Big Tom Bigby Cr	
Craig, David	52		Green	300	115	1 Nov 1786	213	22 Oct 1784	58	476	N side of French Broad River	
Craig, David	881		Green	640	818	2 Dec 1790	53	21 Oct 1783	74	231	On N bank of French Broad River	
Craig, James	1267		Green	430	1117	12 Jan 1793	286	7 Jun 1784	78	374	On S side of Nolichuckey River	
Craig, John	139		Sullivan	430	152	21 Oct 1782	105	8 Feb 1780	43	332	On N fork of Holstin River	
Craig, John	232		Sullivan	200	371	9 Aug 1787	104	8 Feb 1780	61	390	On N side of Holston River	
Craig, John	2460		Davidson	640	467	23 Jan 1800	375	22 Apr 1784	106	367	On W side of Harpeth River	
Craig, John	89	Blount, John Gray	Tennessee	640	1353	10 Dec 1790	2502	30 Sep 1785	74	383	On N side of Cumberland River	yes
Craig, Lewis	1262		Davidson	640	227	10 Jul 1788	449	14 May 1784	66	418	On N side of Cumberland River	
Craig, Robert	689		Hawkins	400	578	17 Jul 1794	94	26 Feb 1778	81	611	On S side of Holston	
Craige, Archibald, heirs of	1740		Davidson	640	1505	4 Jan 1792			77	377	On S side of Harpeth	
Craiige, Archibald	1194	Donelson, Stockley	Sumner	640	2720	20 Jul 1796	538	8 Jun 1796	88	449	On N Fork of 1st Creek	yes
Craighead, Thomas & others	2183	Trustees, Davidson Acad.	Davidson	240		12 Jun 1794		26 Sep 1786	82	226	On S side of Cumberland River	
Craighead, Thomas Brown	442		Middle District	1280	381	17 Dec 1794	2031	3 May 1784	84	252	Small branch empties into Little Riv	

Earliest Tennessee Land Records

Claimant:	File #:	Assignee:	County:	Acres:	Grant:	Grant Date:	Entry:	Entry Date:	Bk:	Pg:	Location by Stream Name:	Military:
Crain, John	071	McFarling, Jas.	Tennessee	100				26 Mar 1785			N side of Sulphur Fork	
Craven, James	308		Sumner	1280	1512	10 Apr 1792	2296	10 Feb 1787	75	505	On both sides of Smiths Fork	yes
Crawford, David	373		Western District	2000	379	20 Dec 1791	2156	11 May 1784	75	223	S W/S S Fork of Forked Deer River	
Crawford, John	128		Hawkins	150	162	26 Dec 1791	393	7 Apr 1781	75	168	On head branches of Bever Creek	
Crawford, John	230		Hawkins	300	217	26 Dec 1791	1325	12 Jan 1784	77	319	N/S Holston Riv head branch creek	
Crawford, John	359	Weakley, Robert	Davidson	640	343	4 Sep 1787	1753		63	128	W side of Sycamore Creek	yes
Crawford, John	393		Sullivan	100	272	10 Nov 1784	1591	12 Sep 1779	69	168	On Clear Fork of Horse Creek	
Crawford, John	435		Eastern District	400	286	21 Jan 1797	1751	3 Jan 1784	91	121	Waters of Whites Creek	
Crawford, John	445		Washington	638 (640	437	13 Oct 1783	1020	6 Feb 1778	52	283	On Clear Fork of Horse Creek	
Crawford, John	734		Hawkins	200	554	12 Jun 1794	110	10 Jul 1780	82	173	In the Caney Valley	
Crawford, John	94		Eastern District	500	83	17 Nov 1790	505	28 Apr 1780	76	170	On the waters of Whites Creek	
Crawford, John	95		Eastern District	300	84	17 Nov 1790	580	5 Jun 1780	76	171	On waters of Whites Creek	
Crawford, Micajah	593	Crawford, Samuel	Sumner	640	1835	20 May 1793	2372	10 Dec 1792	81	86	On S Fork of Cedar Creek	yes
Crawford, Samuel	136		Hawkins	200	170	26 Dec 1791	98	26 Feb 1778	75	172	On head of Whites Creek	
Crawford, Samuel	817		Washington	300	631	10 Nov 1784	2438	28 Feb 1780	69	147	Beg at a poplar corner	
Crawley, William	961	Donelson, Stokley	Davidson	640	978	18 May 1789			63	331	On S side of Cumberland River	
Creesey, Tho & Wm. Murray	033	Waters, John	Montgomery	1000	3394		5033	13 Oct 1800			On waters of Pleasant Creek	yes
Cresman [?], John	677		Sullivan	200	625	9 Jul 1794	550	29 Apr 1780	81	629	On N side of Holston River	yes
Cresswell, James	418		Hawkins	500	306	27 Nov 1792	697	22 May 1780	80	149	On S side of Holston River	
Cresswell, James	785		Green	50	590	23 Aug 1788	1466	27 Oct 1787	68	258	On S side of Holston River	
Cresswell, James	8		Hawkins	1000	21	23 Aug 1788	962	29 Oct 1783	64	860	Both sides West Fork of Turkey Cr	
Criner, John	69		Hawkins	200 (100	69	26 Nov 1789	1826	6 Oct 1779	73	1	On N side of Holston River &c	
Criner, John	71		Hawkins	400	71	26 Nov 1789	334	23 Oct 1783	73	2	On N side of Holston River &c	
Criner, John	72		Hawkins	400	72	26 Nov 1789	2261	22 Nov 1779	73	2	On Poor Valley Creek	
Criner, John	97		Hawkins	640	131	16 Dec 1791	2358	17 Dec 1779	75	153	On N side of Stock Creek	
Cripo [?], Christian	1283		Davidson	640	248	10 Jul 1788	662	17 Jan 1785	66	424	On Browns Creek &c	
Crisman [?], John	682		Sullivan	100	630	9 Jul 1794	122	9 Feb 1780	81	637	N side of Holston River	
Crisp, William	833	Harney, S. & A. Bledsoe	Sumner	640	2319	20 May 1793	3012	30 Nov 1792	81	195	Waters of Middle Fork of Goose Cr	yes
Croass, Elij. & Moses Looney	784		Sullivan	200	716	2 Dec 1796	1872	6 Oct 1779	91	274	Bet at a hickory & spanish oak	
Crocker, Abraham	727	Kearr, Robert	Davidson	274	700	11 Jul 1788	3426		63	246	On Sulphur Fork of Red River	yes
Crocker, Andrew	817		Sullivan	140 (149	760	17 Nov 1796	270	9 Mar 1780	94	157	Bet at a white oak	
Crocket, John	1431		Green	197	1243	27 Nov 1792	2425	15 Feb 1780	80	168	On waters of Lick Creek	
Crocket, Robert	392		Sullivan	281	271	10 Nov 1782	1879	6 Oct 1779	69	168	On N side of Holstein River	
Crockett, Andrew	106		Eastern District	280	95	17 Nov 1790	1805	6 Oct 1779	76	174	S side of Clinch River	
Crockett, Andrew	1195		Davidson	640	174	17 Apr 1786	474	7 Jun 1784	66	191	On Little Harper [sic] &c	
Crockett, Andrew	1293		Davidson	640	258	10 Jul 1788	475	7 Jun 1784	66	427	On S side of Cumberland River	
Crockett, Andrew	1419	Armstrong, M.	Davidson	106	36	8 Oct 1787		1785 [sic]	68	157	Poplar Wm. Collingsworth's preemp	
Crockett, James	04		Davidson	640			472	7 Jun 1784			On S Fork of Little Harpeth	
Crockett, James	1173		Davidson	640	150	17 Apr 1786	471	7 Jun 1784	66	186	Headwaters Middle Fk Station Camp Cr	
Crockett, James	1834		Davidson	640	324	27 Nov 1792	473	7 Jun 1784	81	3	Beg at a red oak & hickory	
Crockett, Jn.	1136		Davidson	640	113	17 Apr 1786	486	10 Jun 1784	66	177	Waters of Big & Little Harper	
Crockett, John	087		Washington	300			1228	22 Feb 1779			On S side of Main Holston River	
Crockett, John	1206		Green	300	1050	Mar 1792			77	340	On S side of Main Holston Road	
Crockett, John	172		Sullivan	200	179	10 Oct 1783			53	149	On Level Creek	
Crockett, Joseph	528		Sullivan	85	544	26 Nov 1789	2437	27 Feb 1780	73	52	On both sides of Beaver Creek	

Claimant:	File #:	Assignee:	County:	Acres:	Grant:	Grant Date:	Entry:	Entry Date:	Bk:	Pg:	Location by Stream Name:	Military:
Crockett, Joseph	653		Sullivan	80	601	27 Jun 1793	1817	7 Oct 1779	80	384	On a branch of Beaver Creek	
Crockett, Robert	410		Green	100	412	20 Sep 1787	704	19 Dec 1778	65	492	On waters of Lick Creek	
Crockett, Samuel	758		Sullivan	138	737	28 Jul 1797	247	2 Mar 1780	90	386	Beg at a sugar tree	
Crockley, Allen	041	Donelson, Stockley	not given	640			3425	4 Aug 1796			S side of Cumberland River	yes
Crockley, Allen	887	Marson, Samuel	Davidson	640	903	17 Jan 1789	3425		63	312	On the Spring Creek	yes
Croker, Thomas	680	Donelson, S & Joseph Bear	Hawkins	300	2391	12 Jul 1794	3535		81	602	Beg at a stake	yes
Cromlin, Francis	1362	Tatum, H. & Henry Wiggins	Sumner	320	3210	14 Oct 1797	4262	26 Jun 1797	92	8	Waters of W Fork of Goose Creek	yes
Cromwell, Rowlen	2280	Joslin, Daniel	Davidson	274	2760	20 Jul 1796	3534		88	461	On waters of W Harpeth	yes
Cronister, Matthias	1147		Washington	320	1105	12 Jul 1794			81	571	On right hand fork of Cobbs Creek	
Crook, Hilliary	52	Fenner, Richard	Tennessee	640	1257	10 Dec 1790	2501	30 Sep 1785	74	351	On S side of Cumberland River	yes
Crook, William	428	Nichols, John	Davidson	1000	400	15 Sep 1787	2601		63	149	Lying on Spring Creek	yes
Cross, Anthony	2236	Hamilton, William	Davidson	640	2607	7 Mar 1796	2119		88	330	On E side of Stones River	yes
Cross, Elijah	687		Sullivan	390	635	9 Jul 1794	1106	13 Jan 1779	81	633	On waters of Beaver Creek	
Cross, Frederick	769	Hickman, Thomas	Davidson	640	742	11 Jul 1788	2712		63	261	On waters of 1st creek &c	yes
Cross, Henry	026		Green	100	408	21 Sep 1778					On Long Fork of Lick Creek	
Cross, Henry	1064		Green	100	907	26 Dec 1791	407	18 Aug 1790	77	244	On Long Fork of Lick Creek	
Cross, Henry	1679		Green	50	1384	20 Jul 1796	1776	1 Oct 1779	88	493	On waters of Lick Creek	
Cross, Henry	448		Washington	100	440	13 Oct 1783	409	21 Sep 1778	52	285	On Cedar Fork of Lick Creek	
Cross, Henry	993		Green	200	1220	29 Jul 1793	1056	8 Jan 1779	76	483	On Sinking Fork of Lick Creek	
Cross, Joel	1032	Sheppard, John	Sumner	640	2569	8 Mar 1794	2643		88	190	On waters of Obeys River	yes
Cross, Martin	881	Walker, John	Sumner	640	2400	7 Jan 1794	781 [?]	26 Jul 1784	81	392	On S side of Cumberland River	yes
Cross, Randal	045	Hart, Anthony	not given	640			2485	12 Mar 1788			On head waters of a large creek	yes
Cross, Richard	2014	Crince(?), Johnathan	Davidson	640	1961	20 May 1793	1962		81	114	On waters of Mill Creek	yes
Cross, Richard	86		Western District	5000	86	10 Jul 1788	1046	29 Oct 1783	67	314	On N Fork of Looshatcher River	
Cross, Silas	336	Williams, Willoughby	Middle District	640	2395	31 Jan 1795	2710		83	392	W side of West Fork of Obeys River	yes
Crossey, Anthony	2412	McConnell, Robert	Davidson	640	3205	14 Sep 1797	4586		92	6	W/S Harpeth above the Hurricane	yes
Crouch, John	1209		Washington	200	1163	26 Mar 1795	2110	2 Nov 1779	83	443	Beg at a white oak &c	
Crouch, John	1258		Washington	200	1230	10 Sep 1796	406	19 Sep 1778	88	512	On head spring &c	
Crouch, John	1333		Washington	300	1857(125	8 Jun 1797	1536	24 Aug 1779	90	327	On head spring &c	
Crouch, John, Ass	1210		Washington	200	1164	26 Mar 1795	1225	22 Feb 1779	83	445	S side of Sinking Creek	
Crouch, John, Jr.	1370		Washington	300	1285	17 Nov 1797	2199	12 Nov 1779	94	143	On a branch of Boons Creek	
Crouch, Joseph	972		Washington	100	949	17 Nov 1790	2883	1 Aug 1781	76	161	Beg at a birch	
Croutcher, Anthony	1587	Armstrong, Martin	Davidson	2560	1255	10 Dec 1790	345	25 Apr 1780	74	350	On waters of Whites Creek	yes
Crow, Benjamin	1129		Green	200	972	26 Dec 1791	475		77	272	Beg at a small white oak	
Crow, Benjamin	486		Green	300	488	20 Sep 1787	129	17 Sep 1784	65	514	On S side of Nolichuckey River &c	
Crow, Jn	1145		Davidson	640	122	17 Apr 1786	319	28 Feb 1784	66	180	On waters of White Creek &c	
Crow, John	38		Green	300	101	1 Nov 1786	591	20 Nov 1778	58	462	On both sides of Sinking Creek	
Crow, John	79		Green	150	37	1 Nov 1786	2469	10 Mar 1780	59	398	On Sinking Creek	
Crow, Milliford	1422	Hadley, Joshua	Sumner	228	3277	6 Dec 1797	4549	21 Jun 1797	98	158	On waters of Spring Creek	
Crow, William	0114	Scott, Joshua & H. Crawfor	Sumner	228			4714	12 May 1797			E side W Fork &c	yes
Crow, William	2021	Blount, John Grey & Thom	Davidson	640	1999	20 May 1793	1546	14 Jan 1786	81	124	On big Harpeth River	yes
Crowell, Rowland	040	Donelson, John	Davidson	274			3534	10 May 1796			S side of Cumberland River	yes
Crowson, William	699		Green	400	740	11 Jul 1788	21	1 Oct 1783	66	473	Lying on No Et side of Big Pigeon R	
Crozier, Arthur	1319	McConnel, Robert	Sumner	640	3119	14 Sep 1797	4592	6 May 1797	90	411	On Punchin Camp Creek	yes
Cruck, Archibald, heirs of	142		Tennessee	640	1392	20 Dec 1791	1366	9 Nov 1784	77	349	On S side of Red River	yes

Claimant:	File #:	Assignee:	County:	Acres:	Grant:	Grant Date:	Entry:	Entry Date:	Bk:	Pg:	Location by Stream Name:	Military:
Cruder, Jacob	991	Rutherford, Griffith	Davidson	428	1008	18 May 1789	3225		63	338	On E Fk of Stones River	yes
Cruice, Johnston	2014	Cross, Richd	Davidson	640	1961	20 May 1793	1962		81	114	On waters of Mill Creek	yes
Crumley, George	745		Sullivan	110	676	13 Nov 1795	1462	22 Jun 17779	89	277	On both sides of Weavers Creek	
Crumley, George	791		Sullivan	34	723	2 Dec 1796	538	29 Apr 1781	81	277	Beg at a white oak	
Crump, Abraham	899	Harrison, James	Sumner	228	2453	31 Dec 1793	2292	21 Sep 1787	81	427	On Rockey Creek	yes
Crumpler, Raiford	2401	Williams, Davis heirs	Davidson	640	2798	6 Jun 1796	3861		91	471	S W side of Big Harpeth River	yes
Crumstock, Thomas	1401	Armstrong, M.	Davidson	100	18	8 Oct 1787	818		68	153	N side of Cumberland River &c	
Crumstock, Thomas	1428		Davidson	100	45	8 Oct 1787	1207	8 Aug 1785	68	158	Situate on N side of Cumberland R	
Crunch, John Watts	1427	Barton, Samuel	Sumner	1000	3301	6 Dec 1797	4438	20 Jun 1797	98	175	On waters of Round Lick Creek	yes
Crutcher, Anthony	33	Smith, Thomas	Sumner	640	844	17 Jan 1789	303	28 Jul 1784	63	296	On N side of Cumberland River	yes
Crutcher, Anthony	433		Tennessee	100	169	9 Jan 1794		29 Nov 1792	81	445	On waters of Red River	
Crutcher, Arthur	607	Hamilton, John heirs	Davidson	640	579	15 Sep 1787	1845		63	207	N side of Cumberland River	yes
Crutcher, William	2154	Armstrong, Martin	Davidson	100	154	9 Jan 1794			81	440	On White Creek	
Crutcher, Wm.	452	Armstrong, M.	Tennessee	50	240	27 Feb 1796	5	17 Nov 1792	88	180	On N side of Sulphur Fork	
Crutchfield, John, Ass	413		Sumner	640	424	27 Jun 1793	480	8 Jun 1784	80	349	On S side of Cumberland River	
Cubbins, William	013	Duncan, Martin	Robertson	640			1664	30 Dec 1794			Abt mile below John Grimes	yes
Culberson, Joseph	1137		Washington	120	1095	12 Jul 1794	2510	31 Mar 1780	81	567	Beg at a Sycamore	
Culberson, Samuel	309		Washington	400 (450	176	24 Oct 1778	530	23 Oct 1778	47	85	On Indian Creek	
Culberson, Samuel	91		Washington	450	259	23 Oct 1782	549	30 Oct 1778	44	277	On Indian Creek	
Culbeson, Samuel	1172		Washington	100	1130	7 Jul 1794	2513	31 Mar 1780	81	620	Beg on a beech	
Culbison, Samuel	1153		Washington	300	1111	7 Jul 1794	2519	76 Apr 1780	81	614	Beg at a white oak	
Culbreth, Benjamin	1374		Washington	200	1296	14 Dec 1798	2159	5 Jul 1796	97	300	W side of James Lartains Improvem	
Culbreth, Daniel	1373		Washington	100	1295	14 Dec 1798	2414	1 Feb 1780	97	300	Upon the Lorrell Fork.	
Cullenver, Samson	888	Searcy, Bennet	Sumner	640	2428	31 Dec 1793	2994	30 Nov 1792	81	409	Bet Bartons Creek & Stones River	yes
Culliver, James	548	Malloy, Thomas	Tennessee	640	2973	5 Apr 1797	4251		90	275	S side of Cumberland River	yes
Cummings, Hugh	743		Sullivan	90	684	7 Dec 1795	348	24 Mar 1780	89	224	On waters of Beaver Creek	
Cummins, George	1735	Perkins, Adam	Davidson	274	1475	4 Jan 1792	1726		77	370	S/S Cumberland River on Pond Cr	yes
Cummins, George	643	Smithly, Thomas	Sumner	640	1934	20 May 1793	3325		81	108	S/S Cumberland River on Lick Creek	yes
Cummins, John	1008	Gillam, Howell heirs	Davidson	1000	1025	18 May 1789	420		63	342	On N side of Cumberland River	yes
Cummins, Samuel	591		Middle District	5000	333	20 Dec 1796	489	25 Oct 1783	91	423	On Elk River	
Cummins, Samuel	593		Middle District	1000	335	20 Dec 1796	1561	26 Mar 1784	91	424	N side of Tennessee	
Cummins, Samuel, Jr.	592		Middle District	2500	334	20 Dec 1796	1560	26 Mar 1784	91	424	On Elk River	
Cunningham, Christopher	344		Washington	150	211	24 Oct 1782	2429	7 Feb 1780	49	231	On Dry Fork of Horse Creek	
Cunningham, Christopher	45		Washington	590	335	24 Oct 1782	803	23 Dec 1778	43	312	On both sides of Buffalow Creek	
Cunningham, Christopher	816		Washington	240	630	10 Nov 1784	479	5 Oct 1778	69	146	On head of Sinking Creek	
Cunningham, James	537	Hamilton, Thomas	Davidson	640	509	15 Sep 1787	1938		63	184	West side of Caney Fork	
Cunningham, James, Ass	891		Hawkins	130	153	2 Mar 1795		Martin Armstrong	84	279	On E Fork of Whites Creek	yes
Cunningham, Jno	697		Green	100	738	11 Jul 1788	219	22 Oct 1783	66	472	On S side of Nolichuckey River	
Cunningham, Paul	1568		Green	300	1314	6 Jan 1795	364	28 Mar 1780	83	159	S side of Holston River	
Cunningham, Paul	720		Washington	100	534	10 Nov 1784	1210	15 Feb 1779	69	116	Beg at a white oak	
Cunningham, Thomas	391		Hawkins	220	512	27 Jan 1793	981	29 Oct 1783	79	495	On S side of Holston River	
Cunningham, William	1373		Washington	50	1288	23 Nov 1797	2895	20 Aug 1781	96	11	On S Fork &c	
Curganus, Jeremiah	378	Sheppard, Benjamin	Davidson	640	350	15 Sep 1787	2304		63	132	Both sides Middle Fk of Drakes Cr	yes
Curk, William	483	Marshall, John	Davidson	640	455	15 Sep 1787	2271		63	166	On Money Fork Creek	yes
Curles, John	0143	Welburn, Daniel	Sumner	640	3007		1974	16 Sep 1796			S of Cumberland River	yes

Earliest Tennessee Land Records

Claimant:	File #:	Assignee:	County:	Acres:	Grant:	Grant Date:	Entry:	Entry Date:	Bk:	Pg:	Location by Stream Name:	Mil
Curles, Thomas	1716	McCulloh, Benjamin	Davidson	640	1384	20 Dec 1791	1975		77	347	On Knob Creek of Duck River	y
Currin, Elisha	569	Tatum, Barnard	Davidson	640	541	15 Sep 1787	665		63	194	S side of Cumberland River	yt
Currin, Hugh	727	Tatum, Barnard	Sumner	640	2112	20 May 1793	604 [?]	31 Jul 1792	81	152	On S side of Cumberland River	ye
Curry, John	1406	Adams, James	Sumner	640	3337	6 Dec 1797	3746	25 Oct 1797	97	54	On waters of Big Barren	ye!
Curry, John	248	Nelson, Alex	Tennessee	640	1624	27 Apr 1793	1885	15 Aug 1785	81	25	S boundary of Mills Ramseys survey	yes
Curry, Samuel	277		Washington	181	145	23 Oct 1782	223	26 May 1778	47	70	S side of Holston River	
Curry, Samuel	561		Sullivan	200	544	17 Nov 1790	238	22 June 1778	76	192	S fork of Beech Creek	
Curry, Thomas	556	Malloy, Thomas	Tennessee	350	2978	10 Apr 1797	3577	13 Dec 1787	90	284	S side of Cumberland River	yes
Curry, Thompson	025	Verell, William	Robertson	357	3374	29 Sep 1801	4530	21 May 1800			On waters of Sycamore Creek	yes
Curtis, Bartholomew	769		Sumner	185	2216	20 May 1793	3053	10 Dec 1792	81	172	On Peytons Creek	yes
Curtis, George	243	Bennet, Joel	Tennessee	357	1619	27 Apr 1793	1570	22 Feb 1785	81	22	On N side of Cumberland River	
Curtis, Nathaniel	455		Green	150	457	20 Sep 1787	300	23 Oct 1783	65	503	S/S Nolechuckey on Little Lick Creek	
Curtis, Thomas	290	MacCollum, Isaac	Eastern District	224	2397	8 Feb 1795	1703		84	137	On W side of Cumberland Mountain	yes
Cuury, John	1406	Adams, James	Sumner	640	3337	6 Dec 1797	3746	25 Oct 1797	97	54	On waters of Big Barrow	yes
Cuury, Samuel	561		Sullivan	200	544	17 Nov 1790	238	22 Jun 1778	76	192	On S Fork of Beech Creek &c	
Cypell, Robert	081	Snider, Frederick	not given	358			45	13 Mar 1784			On waters of Whites Creek	
Cyprett, Robert	1293	Tyrrell, William	Sumner	640	3053	8 Jun 1797	57	17 Mar 1784	90	319	Both sides of Drakes Creek	yes
Cyprett, Robert	2358	Tyrrell, William	Davidson	358	3052	8 Jun 1797	45		90	319	Waters of Whites Creek	yes
Dabney, Cornelius	1448	Summers, Wm.	Sumner	640	470	26 Aug 1800	569	12 Aug 1784	108	111	On S side of Cumberland River	yes
Dabney, John	2	Brooks, John	Wilson	228	3388		3801	15 Jul 1800	114	92	On waters of Jennings Fork	
Dacra, John	047		Green	200			330	22 Mar 1780			N side of Holston River	
Daffin, John	884	Ford, John	Davidson	640	898	17 Jan 1789	2645		63	311	On N side of Cumberland River	yes
Daget, James	2254	Doneison, Stockley	Davidson	640	2712	20 Jul 1796	1912		88	446	On waters of Stones River	yes
Dagy, Geser [?]	627		Green	200	668	11 Jul 1788	1067	30 Oct 1783	66	449	On S side of French Broad River	
Dailey, Charles	0131	Young, Abraham	Sumner	274			3213	11 Aug 1786			N side of Cumberland River	yes
Dale, James	1064		Washington	50	1014	27 Nov 1792	2504	27 Mar 1780	80	180	Lying on a branch of Big Limestone	
Dale, James	1376		Washington	200	1300	29 Nov 1800	274	29 Jul 1778	109	449	On waters of Big Limestone	
Dale, William	86		Washington	100	254	23 Oct 1782	1483	26 Jul 1779	44	274	Headwaters of Boons Creek	
Dallam [?], Richard	147		Middle District	5000	153	7 Apr 1790	1044	29 Oct 1783	71	290	On S side of Duck River	
Dalley, George	387		Hawkins	150	508	27 Jan 1793	2308	27 Nov 1779	79	493	On Lick Branch of Sinking Creek	
Daly, John & William Henry	799		Hawkins	500	216	20 Oct 1794			83	142	N/S Clinch River & S/S of Hunting Cr	
Dameron, Joseph	1021		Green	200	1248	29 Jul 1793	900	3 Dec 1778	76	288	Beg at a post oak, corner of Hoggs	
Dan, Mallica	999	Gloster, Thomas	Davidson	640	1016	18 May 1789	3098		63	340	On N side of Cumberland River	yes
Dange [?], Enoch	2469	Dange, Zachariah	Davidson	274	3393	25 Oct 1802		30 Dec 1800	115	437	On S side of Cumberland River	yes
Dange, James	2035		Davidson	640	2049	20 May 1793	1247		81	136	On waters of W Harpeth	yes
Dange, James	450		Davidson	428	422	15 Sep 1787	985		63	156	On the first creek	yes
Dange, Peter	878		Sumner	2057	2397	7 Jan 1794	3783	20 Nov 1792	81	391	On Harts Creek	yes
Dange, Richard	397		Davidson	640	369	15 Sep 1787	408		63	138	On N branches of Sycamore	yes
Dange, Zachariah	2469	Dange, Enoch	Davidson	274	3393	25 Oct 1802	1260	30 Dec 1800	115	437	On S side of Cumberland River	yes
Danges, Jacob	783	Corderey, John	Davidson	274	756	11 Jul 1788	415		63	265	On Sulphur Fork of Red River	yes
Daniel, Benjamin	752	Nichols, John	Davidson	640	725	11 Jul 1788	2567		63	255	On N side of Tenners survey	yes
Daniel, Ephraim	2286	Robertson, James	Davidson	640	2760	20 Jul 1796			88	464	On both sides of Big Harpeth River	yes
Daniel, James	1081		Green	700	924	26 Dec 1791	1006	29 Oct 1783	77	250	On S side of Holstein River	yes
Daniel, James	354		Sullivan	163	233	10 Nov 1784	1002	4 Jan 1779	69	157	On N bank of Holston River	
Daniel, Richard	1182		Washington	100	1140	7 Jul 1794	2324	3 Dec 1779	81	623	On N fork of Kendricks Creek	

Earliest Tennessee Land Records

Claimant:	File #:	Assignee:	County:	Acres:	Grant:	Grant Date:	Entry:	Entry Date:	Bk:	Pg:	Location by Stream Name:	Military:
Daniel, Thomas	649	Overton, John	Sumner	1000	1951	20 May 1793	3341	19 Nov 1792	81	112	On the Cedar Lick	yes
Daniel, William	175		Hawkins	150	108	16 Nov 1790	487	26 Apr 1780	77	187	S/S Holeston River on Younces Cr	
Daniel, William	468		Hawkins	300	340	29 Jul 1793			80	260	S/S Holston below mouth Youngs Cr	
Danley, Solomon	2170	Williams, Willoughby	Davidson	640	2491	1 Apr 1794	2845		81	451	On waters of Stones River	yes
Dann, Jeffry	65	Gloster, Thomas	Tennessee	640	1303	10 Dec 1790	3099	8 Dec 1785	74	366	On S side of Sulphur Fork	yes
Darby, Patrick	731	Kincannon, Matthew	Davidson	640	704	11 Jul 1788	2415		63	248	Lying on Second Creek	yes
Darden, John	021	Arnold, David	Sumner	274			3115	25 Nov 1783			S side of Cumberland River	yes
Darden, John	2106	Blount, John Gray & Thom	Davidson	640	2337	20 May 1793	1545		81	199	On Big Harpeth River	yes
Darker, William	714		Sullivan	55	659	4 Dec 1794			84	165	S of the River Ohio	
Darmond, John	165		Green	200	635	23 Aug 1788			64	353	On the N Fork of Emerys River	
Darnel, Henry, heirs of	1		Montgomery	503	3396	15 Nov 1802	27	20 Feb 1801	110	276	On Spring Creek	yes
Darnell, Henry, heirs of	2	Crutcher, James Anthony	Montgomery	1325	3366	2 Dec 1800	27,-1343	18 Jan 1786	112	443		
Darnell, Henry, heirs of	3		Montgomery	163	3377	1 Dec 1801	27	9 Feb 1801	114	87	S side of Cumberland River	
Darnell, Henry, heirs of	3		Robertson	1849	3378	1 Dec 1801			114	87	On S side of Red	
Darnold, Geo. heir of Henry	021		Robertson	1849	3378	1 Dec 1801	27	20 Feb 1801			On S side of Red River	
Darnold, Thomas	630	Hanner, Rody	Sumner	640	1913	20 May 1793	2341	27 Nov 1792	81	103	Waters West Fork Drakes Cr	yes
Darron, Benjamin	482	McCoy, Anan.	Tennessee	480	190	20 Jul 1796	11	14 Apr 1792	88	472	W of Cumberland Mountain	yes
Darrow, Benjamin	483	McCoy, Ananias	Tennessee	400	192	20 Jul 1796		14 Apr 1792	88	473	W of Cumberland Mountain	
Darrow, Benjamin	486	McCoy, Anan.	Tennessee	480	195	20 Jul 1796	10	14 Apr 1792	88	474	W of Cumberland Mountain	yes
Daugharty, Wm& CorMcGuire	1588	Armstrong, Martin	Green	1200	162	22 Feb 1795			83	429	S/S French Broad River	
Daugherty, George	142	Smith, Reuben	Davidson	640	128	14 Mar 1786	424		63	50	E Fork of Buffaloe Creek	yes
Daugherty, George	17		Davidson	4800	3	6 Feb 1786	18		63	2	On both sides Walnut Creek	yes
Daugherty, George	275		Green	400	277	30 Sep 1787	24	21 Oct 1783	65	451	On N side of Nolichuckey	
Daugherty, George	822		Green	20	823	11 Aug 1789	710	28 Oct 1783	71	38	On an island in French Broad River	
Daugherty, George, Ass	351		Eastern District	200	285	6 Jun 1796			88	380	On Dumplin Creek	
Daughterty, Francis	103		Hawkins	300	137	26 Dec 1791			75	157	On S side of Holson River	
Daughterty, George	98		Western District	3000	98	10 Jul 1788	1123	30 Oct 1783	67	319	On Reelfoot River &c	
Daughtry, John	1062	King, William	Sumner	640	2539	10 Dec 1795	505	8 [blank]	88	293	On a creek called Lick Creek	yes
Daughtry, Lewis	69	Hart, Anthony	Tennessee	640	1309	10 Dec 1790	1516	20 Jan 1785	74	368	On N side of Cumberland River	yes
Daughty, Samuel	2115	Donelson, John	Davidson	228	2374	20 May 1793	1822		81	207	On S side of Cumberland River	yes
Davee, John	341	Walker, Moses	Sumner	228	1402	20 Dec 1791	326	22 Oct 1785	77	352	Adjoining Wt Richard Hagens preemp	yes
Davenport, Jos	1877	Lock, Matthew	Davidson	640	1618	27 Apr 1793	2067		81	22	On both sides of S Harpeth	yes
Davey, Gabriel	083		Davidson	5000								
David, Edmund (Edward)	108		Sullivan	160	119	23 Oct 1782	1686	21 Feb 1779	43	295	On the waters of Fall Creek &c	
David, Richard	1374		Green	200	1229	27 Jan 1793	1903	8 Oct 1779	79	506	On waters of Lick Creek	
David, Richard	797		Sullivan	100	732	6 Jul 1797	748	14 Feb 1780	91	601	Plantation where David now lives	
Davidson, Amos	2168	Williams, Willoughby	Davidson	640	2489	1 Apr 1794	2844		81	451	On waters of Stones River	yes
Davidson, Ephraim	118		Western District	2000	118	10 Jul 1788	2153	11 May 1784	67	326	Waters N Fork of Forked Deer River	
Davidson, Ephraim	65		Western District	2000	65	10 Jul 1788	2152	11 May 1784	67	305	Waters o fk of Forked Deer River	
Davidson, Geo. Hr. of Wm.	45		Davidson	5760	31	14 Mar 1786	254		63	13	N side of Tennessee River	
Davidson, George	119		Western District	2500	119	10 Jul 1788	1577	1 Apr 1784	67	326	On the waters of the N Fk &c	
Davidson, George	137		Middle District	1500	139	10 Jul 1788	728	28 Oct 1783	67	476	Lying on N side of Duck River	
Davidson, James	129		Western District	1000	129	10 Jul 1788	1573	1 Apr 1784	67	330	On Rutherfords Fork &c	
Davidson, James	2326	Molloy, Thomas	Davidson	640	2971	5 Apr 1797	3627		90	274	N side of Cumberland River	yes
Davidson, James, heirs of	473		Sumner	640	1637	27 Apr 1793	3605	15 Feb 1791	81	26	Both sides of the War Trace Creek	yes

Earliest Tennessee Land Records

Claimant:	File #:	Assignee:	County:	Acres:	Grant:	Grant Date:	Entry:	Entry Date:	Bk:	Pg:	Location by Stream Name:	Military:
Davidson, Jean [?]	52		Western District	2000	52	10 Jul 1788	725	28 Oct 1783	67	300	On both sides of the Obion River &c	
Davidson, John	1383	McGueston, John	Sumner	640	3250	24 Nov 1797	4644	13 May 1797	97	32	On waters of Cedar Creek	yes
Davidson, Joseph	750		Washington	200	564	10 Nov 1784	2627	1 Sep 1780	69	128	Joining Jesse Been &c	
Davidson, Mary	115		Western District	2000	115	10 Jul 1788	721	28 Oct 1783	67	325	On N side of Obion River &c	
Davidson, Samuel	603		Middle District	640	368	17 Feb 1800	2239	22 May 1784	106	369	On W side of the Main East	
Davidson, Thomas	2019	McCrory, James	Davidson	640	1990	20 May 1793	3570		81	122	On Harpeth waters	yes
Davidson, Thomas	44		Western District	3000	44	10 Jul 1788	634	28 Oct 1783	67	297	On the Obion River &c	
Davidson, William	1186		Green	305	1029	26 Dec 1791	311	23 Oct 1783	77	292	On the S side of Holstein River	
Davidson, William	1434		Green	300	1245 (a)	27 Nov 1792	1459	2 Feb 1784	80	169	N/S Nolichuckey head of Delany Cr	
Davidson, William	375		Middle District	1000	314	17 Dec 1794	1937	29 Apr 1784	84	212	On N side of Duck River	
Davidson, William	45	Davidson, George (heir)	Davidson	5760	31	14 Mar 1786	254		63	13	N side of Tennessee River	yes
Davidson, William	73		Western District	2000	73	10 Jul 1788	1571	1 Apr 1784	67	308	On S side of Rutherfords Fork &c	
Davie, Richard	196	Robertson, James	Davidson	274	182	7 Mar 1786	29		63	68	S side of Cumberland River	yes
Davis, Alexander	048		Green	640			378	31 Mar 1780			On Davies Branch	
Davis, Archibald	468	Lambert, Aaron	Tennessee	274	2601	7 Mar 1796	1399	16 Nov 1784	81	327	On both sides of Pine River	yes
Davis, Archibald	890	Barron, Sherrod	Sumner	640	2406	20 Jan 1794	2732	4 Mar 1786	81	420	On the creek &c	yes
Davis, Bartley	248	Love, Josiah	Sumner	640	1153	26 Nov 1789	1490	12 Jun 1787	74	155	On N Fork of Red River	yes
Davis, Benjamin	2378	Stewart, Duncan	Davidson	640	3100	14 Sep 1797	4233		90	402	On an E Fork of S Harpeth	yes
Davis, Benjamin	559		Sumner	376	1779	20 May 1793	825	21 Dec 1792	81	74	On S side of Cumberland River	yes
Davis, Cyrus	1442	Thornton, Yancey	Sumner	228	3354	7 Apr 1800	1225		106	439	On both sides of Middle Fork	yes
Davis, David	018	Brewer, Sterling	Sumner	640			4333	15 Apr 1797			E side Stones River	yes
Davis, David	221		Hawkins	200	208	26 Dec 1791	1610	13 Sep 1779	77	316	On N side of Holston River	
Davis, David	264		Middle District	250	236	27 Jun 1793		24 Jan 1787	80	367	Waters of W Fork of Stones River	
Davis, David	265		Middle District	250	237	27 Jun 1793	34	24 Jan 1787	80	268	Waters of W Fork of Stones River	
Davis, Edward	049		Green	300			328	18 Mar 1780			N side of Holston River	
Davis, Elisha	122	Ea(?)man, Benjamin	Davidson	274	108	7 Mar 1786	392		63	43	S side of Cumberland River	yes
Davis, Frederick	431	Barbour, Richard	Eastern District	365	3146	14 Sep 1797	4186		90	421	On Spring Creek	yes
Davis, George	1037		Washington	119	897	14 Jan 1793	2803	28 Feb 1781	79	281	On Mill Creek	
Davis, Henry	2355	Wood, William	Davidson	640	3033	10 Apr 1797	3643		90	306	On E Fork of Harpeth River	yes
Davis, Isaac	044		Green	125	401	20 Sep 1787		27 Dec 1785			On waters of Little Gap Creek	
Davis, Isaac	399		Green	125	528	20 Sep 1787	2161	6 Nov 1779	65	485	On branches of Little Gap Creek	
Davis, Isaac	930		Green	100	844	17 Nov 1790	2221	16 Nov 1779	76	119	Up Double Lick Fork of Lick Creek	
Davis, Isaac	994		Green	100	1221	29 Jul 1793			76	483	On waters of Lick Creek	
Davis, James	1393	Kits, Demsey heirs	Sumner	640	3320	6 Dec 1797	3989	17 Jun 1797	97	43	On waters of Cedar Creek	yes
Davis, James	1505		Green	50	1266	12 Jul 1792	2638	17 May 1794	81	584	On N side of Nolichuckey River	
Davis, James	1730	McCulloh, Benjamin	Davidson	640	1445	20 Dec 1791	2080		77	362	On the dividing ridge	yes
Davis, James	708		Washington	50	522	10 Nov 1784	2853	12 May 1781	69	112	Joining another survey &c	
Davis, James	714		Washington	100	528	10 Nov 1784	1230	22 Feb 1779	69	114	On a branch of Little Limestone	
Davis, James	764		Hawkins	200	604	12 Jul 1794	247	2 Mar 1780	82	213	On S side of Holston River	
Davis, James	771	Hickman, Thomas	Davidson	640	744	11 Jul 1788	1791		63	261	On the 1st creek &c	yes
Davis, John	1797		Davidson	60	144	29 Aug 1793			80	330	On S side of Cumberland River	
Davis, John	2290		Davidson	265	312	12 Aug 1796			88	480	On SW side of Big Harpeth River	
Davis, John	2316	Armstrong, M.	Davidson	60	261	6 Jun 1796			88	509	On waters of Browns Creek	
Davis, John	2317		Davidson	265	262	6 June 1796			89	509	On S side of Big Harpeth River	
Davis, John	2396	Armstrong, M.	Davidson	155	322	16 Dec 1796			91	311	N side of Big Harpeth River	

Claimant:	File #:	Assignee:	County:	Acres:	Grant:	Grant Date:	Entry:	Entry Date:	Bk:	Pg:	Location by Stream Name:	Military:
Davis, John	2397	Armstrong, M.	Davidson	40	323	16 Dec 1796	3868		91	311	N/S Big Harpeth River	
Davis, John	2402	Ryal, William	Davidson	640	2799	6 June 1796			91	472	S W side of Big Harpeth River	
Davis, John	533		Washington	100	796	16 Aug 1787	1148	30 Jan 1779	64	151	Beg at a marked white oak	
Davis, John	539		Washington	200	802	16 Aug 1787	964	2 Jan 1779	64	153	Beg at a marked sugar tree	
Davis, John	624		Davidson	3840	596	15 Sep 1787	295		63	213	N side of Cumberland River	yes
Davis, John, Ass	2214		Davidson	250	245	27 Feb 1796			88	182	On both sides of Harpeth River	
Davis, Jonathan	1512	Thompson, Jason	Davidson	640	1069	26 Nov 1789	3458		74	114	Lying on Mill Creek	
Davis, Joseph	831	Givin, Edwin	Sumner	320	2316	20 May 1793	1706	28 Nov 1792	81	194	On waters of Drake's Creek	yes
Davis, Josh.	794	Sanderlin, Isaac	Sumner	640	2254	20 May 1793	2435	29 Oct 1792	81	182	Dividing ridge Big Barren & Cumber.	yes
Davis, Josh.	828	Williams, Zachariah	Sumner	640	2308	20 May 1793	2444	19 Nov 1792	81	193	On the Caney Fork	yes
Davis, Joshua	367	Hasten, Willis	Tennessee	640	2245	20 May 1793	2423	30 Sep 1785	81	179	On N side of Cumberland River	yes
Davis, Joshua	465	Cook, Isaac	Davidson	640	437	15 Sep 1787	2412		63	161	On fifth creek after Red River	yes
Davis, Joshua	530	Harris, George	Davidson	640	502	15 Sep 1787	2355		63	181	On both sides of the third creek	yes
Davis, Joshua	533	Palmer, Jno hr of Jos.	Davidson	640	505	15 Sep 1787			63	182	3rd creek the VA line crosses	yes
Davis, Joshua	534	Worton, Ed	Davidson	640	506	15 Sep 1787	2441		63	183	E/S Caney Fk above mo Collins River	yes
Davis, Joshua	657	Upton, Willie	Sumner	640	1974	20 May 1793	2440	19 Nov 1792	81	118	On Caney Fork beg at a red oak	yes
Davis, Joshua	677	Sage, Edward	Sumner	640	2020	20 May 1793	2437	29 Oct 1792	81	129	On Crabapple Creek	yes
Davis, Joshua	685	Speight, Frances	Sumner	640	2037	20 May 1793	2361	18 Nov 1792	81	133	On the Caney Fork	yes
Davis, Joshua	688	Harrison, John heirs	Davidson	640	661	8 Dec 1787	2421		63	234	On waters of Salleen	yes
Davis, Joshua	689	Wigby, Thomas	Davidson	640	662	8 Dec 1787	2442		63	234	Beg at the SE corner of 1000 acres	yes
Davis, Joshua	690	Benton, Kedar	Sumner	228	2045	20 May 1793	2354	29 Nov 1792	81	135	To join an entry of his own # 2354	yes
Davis, Joshua	691	Jones, Hezekiah	Sumner	228	2048	20 May 1793	2356	29 Nov 1792	81	136	On the waters of Dixons Creek	yes
Davis, Joshua	788	Baker, Simon	Sumner	640	2247	20 May 1793	2405	19 Nov 1792	81	180	On the Caney Fork	yes
Davis, Joshua	791	Harrison, Aug.	Sumner	640	2250	20 May 1793	2422	19 Nov 1792	81	181	On Caney Fork beg at a sugar tree	yes
Davis, Joshua	792	Blan(?), Robt.	Sumner	640	2252	20 May 1793	2362	19 Nov 1792	81	181	On E side of Caney Fork	yes
Davis, Joshua	799	Abbott, Jonathan	Sumner	640	2260	20 May 1793	2404	19 Nov 1792	81	183	On Caney Fork &c	yes
Davis, Joshua	800	Jones, Josiah	Sumner	228	2261	20 May 1793	2359	29 Nov 1792	81	183	On waters of Dixons Creek	yes
Davis, Joshua	814	Guin, Daniel	Sumner	640	2282	20 May 1793	2358	19 Nov 1792	81	187	Beg at a sugar tree	yes
Davis, Joshua	823	Mundine (?), Joshua	Sumner	640	2301	20 May 1793	2427	19 Nov 1792	81	191	On E side of Caney Fork	yes
Davis, Joshua	824	Polson, John	Sumner	228	2303	20 May 1793	2357	30 Nov 1792	81	192	On waters of Dixons Creek	yes
Davis, Leonard	1297	Hickman, Thomas	Davidson	640	3064	19 Jul 1797	4594	6 Apr 1797	90	376	S side of Cumberland River	yes
Davis, Leonard	686	Ewing, Alex.	Davidson	640	659	8 Dec 1787	1005		63	233	On both sides of Big Harpeth River	yes
Davis, Moses	549	Robertson, James	Sumner	640	1759	29 May 1793	3457	4 Jul 1789	81	69	S/S Cumberland waters Spencers Cr	yes
Davis, Nathan	194		Washington	200	62	23 Oct 1782	133	21 Dec 1778	47	29	On head of E branch of Lick Creek	
Davis, Nathan	606		Washington	30 (31)	700	26 Oct 1786	2364	20 Dec 1779	66	11	Beg at 3 marked white oaks &c	
Davis, Nathaniel	1109		Washington	200	1064	27 Jun 1793	1120	21 Jan 1779	80	390	On Lick Creek	
Davis, Nathaniel	1118		Washington	170	1077	12 Jul 1794	2900	23 Aug 1781	81	561	Beg on Mark Mitchels line	
Davis, Nathaniel	1230	Saunders, William	Sumner	640	2501	12 Nov 1795	1813	21 Jan 1786	89	419	On waters of Big Barren River	yes
Davis, Nathaniel	160		Washington	199	28	23 Oct 1782	1121	21 Jan 1779	47	13	On Lick Creek	
Davis, Nathaniel	454		Green	200	456	20 Sep 1787	1120	10 May 1779	65	503	On Lick Creek	
Davis, Nathaniel	477		Sullivan	200	356	10 Nov 1784	1453	21 Jun 1779	69	198	Beg at a hicory & Walnut	
Davis, Nathaniel, Jr.	917		Washington	200	894	17 Nov 1790	1452	21 Jun 1779	76	142	In the fork of Watauga &c	
Davis, Nicholas	1369		Washington	150	1284	17 Nov 1797	699	18 Dec 1778	94	143	Waters of Boons Creek	
Davis, Ralph	608		Green	300	565	20 Sep 1787	134	7 Jan 1784	66	250	Lying on Little Chuckey &c	
	1310	Donelson, Stockley	Sumner	457	3108	14 Sep 1797	4279	12 May 1797	90	405	N side of the Falling Creek	yes

Claimant:	File #:	Assignee:	County:	Acres:	Grant:	Grant Date:	Entry:	Entry Date:	Bk:	Pg:	Location by Stream Name:	Military:
Davis, Robert	452		Washington	50	444	13 Oct 1783	2897	23 Aug 1781	52	286	Beg at a stake	
Davis, Robet [sic]	050		Green	200			1031	7 Jun 1784			On Plumb Creek	
Davis, Samuel	1		Robertson	278	3361	18 Oct 1800	5131	21 May 1800	108	132	On waters of the Sulphur Fork	
Davis, Samuel	1042		Hawkins	200	379	19 Jul 1797		Armstrong Service	90	367	On Holstein River	
Davis, Samuel	506	Sheppard, William	Davidson	357	478	15 Sep 1787	1205		63	173	N side of Cumberland River	yes
Davis, Samuel	626	Norris, Thomas	Davidson	357	598	15 Sep 1787	1463		63	213	E boundary James Browns survey	yes
Davis, Thomas	1254		Green	200	1104	12 Jan 1793	38	20 Sep 1787	78	366	Beg at two post oaks	
Davis, Thomas	162	Aspley, John	Davidson	640	148	14 Mar 1786	471		63	56	On both sides Blue Creek	yes
Davis, Thomas	504		Green	200	506	20 Sep 1787	2885	1 Aug 1781	65	524	S/S of Nolechuckey on Camp Creek	
Davis, Thomas hr. of Jno.	904		Sumner	1000	2470	31 Dec 1793	2068	20 Sep 1792	81	433	On a fork of Obeys River	yes
Davis, Thos.	1174		Davidson	640	151	17 Apr 1786	458	24 May 1784	66	186	On S side of Cumberland River	
Davis, William	211		Tennessee	2468	1502	4 Jan 1792	248	28 Oct 1783	77	376	On both sides of Yellow Creek	
Davis, William	653	Bushnell, E. & Wm. Dobbin	Davidson	640	626	15 Sep 1787	1685		63	222	Moses Shelby's W boundary line	yes
Dews, William	2167	Williams, Willoughby	Davidson	640	2488	1 Apr 1794	2842		81	451	On waters of Stones River	yes
Dawson, Isaac	2242	Williams, Sampson	Davidson	274	2697	6 Jun 1796	1983		88	371	On the dividing ridge	yes
Dawson, Levi	667	Blount, John Gray	Tennessee	2125	3338	6 Dec 1797	1377	11 Nov 1784	97	55	On S side of Cumberland River	yes
Dawson, Matthew	504	Gilmour, Charles	Davidson	640	476	15 Sep 1787	3269		63	173	Joining E boundary of a military Surv.	
Daysert, James	550		Hawkins	640	423	29 Jul 1793	4	8 Feb 1780	80	283	On the N side of Powells River	
Dayton, John	1184	Armstrong, M.	Sumner	86	294	20 Jul 1796			88	437	On a Fork of Drakes Creek	yes
Deaderick, John	2390	Inman, William	Davidson	320	3178	14 Sep 1797	4263		90	433	Waters of West Harpeth River	yes
Deaderick, John	554	Vickery, Henry	Sumner	640	1770	20 May 1793	1963	10 Mar 1792	81	75	On N side of Cumberland River	yes
Deakins, Richard	621		Washington	173	715	26 Oct 1786	1132	25 Jan 1779	66	18	On Noleychuckey River &c	
Deal, Edward	1064	King, William	Sumner	640	2541	10 Dec 1795	441		88	294	On a creek called Lick Creek	yes
Deal, Isaac	9		Smith	640	3397	7 Dec 1802	4346	27 Aug 1800	110	276	On waters of McFarlins Creek	yes
Deal, John	1921	Cathey, William	Davidson	640 (380)	1716	20 May 1793	1082		81	57	On S side of Cumberland River	yes
Deal, Lewis	660	McCulloh, Benjamin	Sumner	640	1979	20 May 1793	2999	16 Nov 1792	81	119	On waters of Bledsoes Creek	yes
Dean, Abraham	1935	Robertson, James	Davidson	640	1755	29 Aug 1793	1891	1 Nov 1780	81	68	On N side of Cumberland River	yes
Dean, Francis	811		Green	50	812	11 Aug 1789	2170	2 Feb 1784	71	33	On n side of French Broad River	
Dean, Francis	983		Green	100	1210	29 Jul 1793	2999		76	468	N side of French Broad River	
Dean, James	1932	Carter, David	Davidson	640	1749	29 Aug 1793	1698		81	66	On the Big & Little Harpeth	yes
Dean, Starling	675	Bledsoe, Anthony	Sumner	640	2006	20 May 1793	2017	30 Nov 1792	81	126	On W side of E Fork of Goose Creek	yes
Dearman, Michael	1351	Barry, Redmond D.	Sumner	274	3163	14 Sep 1797	4217	20 Feb 1797	90	427	On a branch of Falling Creek	yes
Deason, John	236		Tennessee	640	450	27 Jun 1793	834	30 Nov 1792	80	358	Beg at a Honey Locust	
Deaugherty, Robert	197		Sumner	640	291	26 Nov 1789	409	17 Apr 1784	73	259	On S side of Cumberland River	
Deboyce, Nicholas	1346	Stewart, Duncan	Sumner	640	3154	14 Sep 1797	4258	30 May 1797	90	424	On the ridge	yes
Decern, Francis	2119	Kirby, Edmund	Davidson	640	2395	7 Jan 1794	1299		81	390	On both sides of Halfpone Creek	yes
Dedrick, Geo. Michael	2428	Harris, Job	Davidson	640	3318	6 Dec 1797	2923		97	42	Waters of Overalls Creek	yes
Dedrick, Jacob	993	Weakley, Robert	Davidson	640	1010	18 May 1789	2264		63	339	On E Fork of Stones River	yes
Dedwell, Martin	108		Washington	400	276	24 Oct 1782	167	14 Mar 1778	44	286	On Indian Creek	
Deferel, William	2060	Donelson, John & Samuel	Davidson	640	2165	20 May 1793	1185	11 Mar 1795	81	164	Both sides S Fork of Stones Creek	yes
Delaney, A. J.	1038	Easton, James	Sumner	640	2700	27 Mar 1796	3970	22 Feb 1779	88	255	On waters of Caney Fork	yes
Delaney, James	157		Washington	100	25	23 Oct 1782	1217	22 Feb 1779	47	11	On Holleys Creek	
Delaney, James	268		Washington	100	136	23 Oct 1782	1216	22 Feb 1779	47	66	On Cedar Branch	
Delaney, James	281		Green	200	283	20 Sep 1787	204	7 Aug 1784	65	453	On Delaneys Creek	
Delaney, John	1416		Green	100	1228	27 Nov 1792	921	9 Nov 1790	80	163	N/S Nolachuckey waters Sinking Cr	

Claimant:	File #:	Assignee:	County:	Acres:	Grant:	Grant Date:	Entry:	Entry Date:	Bk:	Pg:	Location by Stream Name:	Military:
Delaney, John	740	Hogg, Thomas	Davidson	640	713	11 Jul 1788	3080		63	251	On waters of Sycamore Creek	yes
Delaney, Michael	1149	Harris, Edward	Sumner	640	2655	4 Jun 1796	3838	1 Jun 1795	88	352	Joining a survey of sd Harris	yes
Delaney, William	141		Sullivan	640	154	23 Oct 1782	1266	8 Mar 1779	43	333	On S side of Holston River &c	
Delaney, William	175		Sullivan	100	182	10 Oct 1783	1761	18 Sep 1779	53	150	On N side of Holston River	
Delaney, William	356		Sullivan	56	235	10 Nov 1784	168	17 Feb 1783	69	157	On a small creek	
Delany, John	474		Washington	400	466	13 Oct 1783	453	28 Sep 1778	52	296	On Sinking Creek	
Delay, George	407		Sullivan	100	286	10 Nov 1784	740	12 Feb 1781	65	172	Beg on George Vinunts corner	
Dellaney, John	450		Green	100	452	20 Sep 1787	2404	29 Jan 1780	65	502	On Sinking Creek	
Dem[_?_]rce, Timothy	634		Davidson	1000	607	15 Sep 1787	3278		63	216	N side of Cumberland River	yes
Demcey, David	1927	Weakley, Robert	Davidson	274	1738	20 May 1793	1347		81	63	On S side of Cumberland River	yes
DeMedices, Cosimo	2219		Davidson	1872	2521	8 Dec 1795	3608		88	277	On SW side of Big Harpeth River	yes
Demmet, William	093	Lytle, Archibald	Sumner	640			1707	24 Mar 1787			S side of Cumberland River	yes
Demott, Robert	84		Hawkins	400	76	13 Feb 1791	58	26 Feb 1778	74	284	On head of creek called Woods Cr	
Dennet, William	093	Lytle, Archibald	Sumner	640			1707	24 Mar 1787			S side of Cumberland River	yes
Denney, David	632		Davidson	274	604	15 Sep 1787	457		63	215	Lying on Caleb's Creek	yes
Dennis, William	1443	Carter, John	Sumner (?)	640	3355	7 Apr 1800			106	439	Adj Jonathan Price	
Dennis, Wm.	095	Brock, Jos.	not given	640	3355	7 Apr 1800	935	29 Nov 1785	63	203	On Beaverdam Creek	
Denny, Abraham	594		Davidson	365	566	15 Sep 1787	456		88	465	Lying on Caleb's Creek	yes
Denny, Alexander	1199		Sumner	640	156	20 Jul 1796	851	16 Apr 1795	69	162	On N Fork of Pond Lick Creek	
Densmore, Adam	372		Sullivan	380	251	10 Nov 1784	492	26 Apr 1780	74	142	Beg at a w. oak & b. oak	
Denson, William	222	Marshall, John	Sumner	640	1127	26 Nov 1789	1620	21 Jan 1786	80	372	On both sides of one of head creeks &c	yes
Denton, James	627		Sullivan	100	575	27 Jun 1793	837	22 Sep 1783	80	382	Beg at a white oak saplin	
Denton, James	647		Sullivan	300	595	27 Jun 1793	745	23 Dec 1778	78	400	On head spring of Panthers branch	
Denton, John	1310		Green	600	1160	12 Jan 1793	675	21 Oct 1783	64	136	On Lick Creek	
Denton, Joseph	490		Washington	550	753	16 Aug 1787	584	7 Nov 1778	69	125	Beg at a white oak &c	
Denton, Joseph	740		Washington	335	554	10 Nov 1784	912	30 Dec 1778	66	22	On waters of Brush Creek	
Denton, Samuel	629		Washington	529	723	26 Oct 1786	841	3 May 1779	66	431	Beg at a marked black walnut tree	
Denton, Thomas	1305		Davidson	640	270	10 Jul 1788	308	19 Feb 1784	66	188	Beg at a large white oak & poplar &c	
Denton, Thos.	1184		Davidson	640	161	17 Apr 1786	307	17 Feb 1784	69	148	On the middle fork of Red River &c	
Depreast, Randall	822		Washington	100	636	10 Nov 1784	993	30 Dec 1772			On N side of Watauga River	
Derden, Joseph	057	Dillenberry, Redmon	Sumner	640			4411	19 Sep 1797	77	267	W fork of Red River	yes
Dermond, John	1117		Green	500	960	26 Dec 1791	2060	10 Oct 1780	77	401	On S side of Holston River	
Derring, Reuben	1209		Green	200	1053	May 1792	2178	11 Nov 1779	66	44	N side of Nolichuckey River &c	yes
Desh [?], Robert	1055		Davidson	640	29	17 Apr 1796	386	31 Mar 1784	91	88	On Deshs Fork of Bledsoes Creek	
Devault, Michael	778		Sullivan	50	710	18 Nov 1796	236	28 Feb 1780	81	140	In Sullivan County	
Devenport, Thomas	695	Mauldin, Ambrose	Sumner	274	2062	20 May 1793	3459	9 Aug 1786			On Red River	yes
Dever, Alexr.	063		Sullivan	640			1688	3 Feb 1780			On N side of Holson River	
Dever, James	97		Western District	1000	97	10 Jul 1788	1574	1 Apr 1784	67	319	On Rutherfords Fork &c	
Dever, John	284	Howard, Ed	Sumner	228	1281	10 Dec 1790	203	28 Jun 1784	74	359	Waters Middle Fork Station Camp Cr	yes
Dever, John	458		Sullivan	537	337	10 Nov ---	781	22 Apr 1782	69	190	On N side of Holstin(sic) River	
Devers, John	021	Dillard, Osburn	Tennessee	228			802	6 May 1784			N side of Cumberland River	
Devers, John	039	Copeland, Replay	Davidson	274			71	13 Apr 1790			N side of Cumberland River	
Devining, James	946	Clendening, John	Davidson	429	962	18 May 1789			63	327	At head of Brown's Creek	yes
Devonshire, Joshua	09	Baker, John	Tennessee	640			3403	19 Dec 1792			S side of Cumberland River	yes
Dew, John	302	Rogers, Abraham	Sumner	640	1362	10 Dec 1790	3671	4 Dec 1789	74	386	On both sides of Cainey (sic) Fork	yes

Claimant:	File #:	Assignee:	County:	Acres:	Grant:	Grant Date:	Entry:	Entry Date:	Bk:	Pg:	Location by Stream Name:	Military:
Dewel, Jesse	574	Sanford, Samuel	Sumner	640	1811	20 May 1793	2373	6 Aug 1792	81	82	Lying on creek called Crabapple Creek	yes
Deyarmond, John	757		Washington	300	571	10 Nov 1784		7 Nov 1778	69	130	On S side of Noleychuckey River	
Dial, James	223	Robertson, James	Davidson	274	209	7 Mar 1786	756	31 Dec 1778	63	77	On bent of Cumberland River	yes
Dickens, William	460		Washington	100	452	13 Oct 1783	894		52	290	On Nolechucke River	
Dickerson, Henry	7	Hickman, Thomas	Sumner	274	764	11 Jul 1788	3456	30 Aug 1787	63	268	On waters of Caney Fork	yes
Dickerson, Henry	182	Totevine, William	Tennessee	640	1462	4 Jan 1792	3676	10 Dec 1788	77	367	S side of Cumberland River &c	yes
Dickerson, Jacob, Ass	2251		Davidson	50	302	20 Jul 1796			88	440	On waters of Whites Creek	
Dickerson, Nathaniel	95		Davidson	944	81	14 Mar 1786	63 [sic]		63	33	S side of Cumberland River	yes
Dickey, Jacob	663	Bushnell, E. & W. Dobbins	Davidson	640	636	15 Sep 1787	1683		63	226	On S side of Cumberland	yes
Dickey, Thomas	251	McDaniel, Jane heir of Alex	Davidson	1000	237	7 Mar 1786	1222		63	87	On waters of West Harpeth River	yes
Dickey, Thomas	268	Eiler, Jno. heir of Jos.	Davidson	640	254	7 Mar 1786	1221		63	93	On waters of Stones River	yes
Dickman, Edwin	596	Frazier, John	Davidson	640	568	15 Sep 1787	1646		63	203	S side of Cumberland River	yes
Dickner, David	683	King, Robert	Hawkins	640	2394	17 Jul 1794			81	603	On N side of Wallens Ridge	yes
Dickson, Edward	209	Mott, Daniel	Tennessee	640	1499	4 Jan 1790	3723	23 Nov 1790	77	375	S side of Cumberland River &c	
Dickson, Edward	24	Bailey, John	Tennessee	640	1187	30 Nov 1790	241	25 Oct 1783	74	317	On S side of Cumberland River	
Dickson, Edward, Ass.	213		Tennessee	640	1507	4 Jan 1792			77	377	S side of Cumberland River &c	
Dickson, James	207	Morrow, Thomas	Tennessee	640	1497	4 Jan 1792	3657	10 Dec 1788	77	375	S side of Cumberland River &c	
Dickson, James	214	Pinor, John	Tennessee	640	1509	4 Jan 1792	1913	15 Jul 1785	77	378	S side of Cumberland River &c	
Dickson, James	516		Green	100	518	20 Sep 1787	320	23 Oct 1783	65	528	Lying on N side of Holston River	
Dickson, Jas.	188	Lamb, Gibbs	Tennessee	640	1468	4 Jan 1792	251	25 Oct 1783	77	368	On both sides of Jones Creek	
Dickson, Joel	042	Shacker, Philip	Tennessee	640			1801	11 May 1785			On Little West Fork of Red River	yes
Dickson, John	020	Diller, John heirs	Tennessee	640			3655	10 Dec 1788			Eastern brs upper fk of Bartons Cr	
Dickson, John	163	Wilkins, Elisha	Tennessee	640	1424	20 Dec 1791	1909	15 Jul 1785	77	357	On both sides of Pine River	
Dickson, John	183	Griffin, Jos.	Tennessee	640	1463	4 Jan 1792	3661	10 Dec 1788	77	367	S side of Cumberland River	
Dickson, John	190	Harris, Nathan	Tennessee	640	1470	4 Jan 1792	1915	15 Jul 1785	77	369	S side of Cumberland River	
Dickson, John	191	Marret, Wm.	Tennessee	640	1471	4 Jan 1792	1910	15 Jul 1785	77	369	S side of Cumberland River	
Dickson, John	199	Wilson, Jacob	Tennessee	640	1486	4 Jan 1792	2729	30 Sep 1785	77	372	W side of W Fork of Jones Creek	
Dickson, John	206	Hair, James	Tennessee	640	1496	4 Jan 1792	1905	15 Jul 1785	77	374	S side of Cumberland River &c	
Dickson, John	233		Middle District	1000	213	1 Jan 1793	2110	21 May 1784	80	212	S side of Duck River	
Dickson, John	25		Tennessee	640	1188	30 Nov 1790	74 [sic]	318 [sic]	74	318	On S side of Cumberland River	
Dickson, Joseph	27		Middle District	5000	29	10 Jul 1788	434	25 Oct 1783	67	420	Both sides of N Fork of Duck River	
Dickson, Joseph	751	Barnes, Wm. Heirs	Davidson	640	724	11 Jul 1788	2833		63	254	East of Captain Vances claim	yes
Dickson,Jno & Headon Wells	252	Armstrong, M.	Tennessee	200	125	27 Apr 1793		20 Nov 1792	81	31	On N side of McAdows Creek	
Dickson,Jno & Jas. Russell	32		Tennessee	62	93	30 Nov 1790		22 Sep 1792	74	322	On E branch of Yellow Creek	
Didwell, Martin	338		Washington	100	205	24 Oct 1782	1289	17 Mar 1779	49	228	On Indian Creek	
Delon [?], Thomas	513		Middle District	5000	314	20 Jul 1796	1661	16 Apr 1784	88	429	On waters of Elk River	
Diggs, Anthony	522	Bonner, John & James	Davidson	1097	494	15 Sep 1787	1124		63	179	N side of Cumberland River	yes
Diggs, William	812	Robertson, Elijah	Davidson	640	815	20 Nov 1788	3310		63	287	On waters of Caney Fork	yes
Dilenberry, Redmon	023	Stowbridge, John	Sumner	640			4387	22 Sep 1797			Ridge bet. long creek & Trammels	yes
Dilenberry, Redmon	025	Sherlock, Dempsey	Sumner	640			4474	14 Oct 1797			On E Fork of Main Middle Fork &c	yes
Dilenberry, Redmon	026	Strong, George	Sumner	640			4337				On head of Shaws Creek	yes
Dilenberry, Redmon	037	O'Connor, Sullivan	Sumner	274			4467	19 Sep 1797			On dividing ridge &c	yes
Dill, George	2031	Blount, John Gray & Thom	Davidson	640	2043	20 May 1793	2511		81	135	On S side of Cumberland River	yes
Dillar, John	020	Dickson, John	Tennessee	640	3655	10 Dec 1788					Eastern br upper fork of Bartons Cr	yes
Dillard, John	1911	Robertson, James	Davidson	357	1676	20 May 1793	808		81	48	On Harpeth River	yes

Claimant:	File #:	Assignee:	County:	Acres:	Grant:	Grant Date:	Entry:	Entry Date:	Bk:	Pg:	Location by Stream Name:	Military:
Dillard, Osborn	021	Devers, John	Tennessee	228			802	6 May 1784			N side of Cumberland River	yes
Dillard, Peter	325	Fenner, Richard	Davidson	640	311	28 Jun 1787	2181		63	116	On waters of Second Creek	yes
Dillard, Sampson	805	Fort, Elias	Sumner	640	2272	20 May 1793	3578	9 Sep 1788	81	185	On waters of Smiths Fork	yes
Dillard, Wm.	1023	Armstrong, M.	Sumner	320	230	27 Feb 1796			88	175	On S side of Cumberland River	
Dillard, Wm.	998	Harrison, Patrick	Sumner	400	154	17 Dec 1794			84	332	On a fork of Roaring River	yes
Dillebo, Andrew	2389	Williams, Daniel	Davidson	640	9177	14 Sef 1797	4005		90	432	On S. Harpeth	yes
Dillenberry, Redmon	022	Jourdon, Ptolemy	Sumner	640			4416				E waters E Fork Drakes Cr	yes
Dillenberry, Redmon	024	Shaw, Harmon	Sumner	640			4335	19 Sep 1797			Waters of Mackerofield Cr.	yes
Dillenberry, Redmon	045	Howard, John	Sumner	640			4206	3 Apr 1797			E side E Fork of Stones River	Yes
Dillingham, Redmon	177		Sullivan	940	185	10 Oct 1783	1575-2323	4 Sep 1779	53	151	On Horse Creek	
Dillingham, Vachel	178 (177)		Sullivan	940	185	10 Oct 1783	1575-2323	4 Sep 1779	53	151	On Horse Creek	
Dillingham, Vaugh	212		Washington	149	80	23 Oct 1782	378	9 Sep 1778	47	39	On a branch of Horse Creek	
Dillon, Benjamin	022	Donelson, S. & W. Terrell	Tennessee	2560			3829				On W branches of Sulphur Fork	yes
Dillon, Benjamin	1035	Blount, John Gray	Sumner	2560	2572	7 Mar 1796	3829	5 Jun 1795	88	191	On waters of Caney Fork	yes
Dillon, Thomas	047	Dillenberry, Redmon	Sumner	1000	4460	14 Oct 1796	378				Headbranches W Fork Drakes Cr	yes
Dillon, Thomas	1454	Glasgow, James	Sumner	640	3404	21 June 1803	1320	2 May 1785	110	320	On Dry Fork of Bledsoes Creek	yes
Dillon, Thomas	419		Western District	3000	420	20 Jul 1796	2389 (?)	28 Oct 1783	88	429	On S side of Tennessee River	
Dillon, Thomas	420		Western District	1000	421	20 Jul 1796	2441	25 May 1784	88	430	Below mouth of Duck River	
Dillon, Thomas	47	Dillenberry, Redmon	Sumner	1000	4460	14 Oct 1797					Head branches W Fork Drakes Creek	yes
Dillon, Thomas	512		Middle District	5000	313	20 Jul 1796	449	25 Oct 1783	88	429	Being part of a cove	yes
Dillon, Wm.	058	Witty, James	Sumner	366			66	15 Apr 1791			Joining an entry of John Boyd	
Dillonberry, Redmon	023	Whitfield, Wilson	Sumner	100	4112	6 Sep 1797					On [blank] fork of Red River	yes
Dillonberry, Redmon	028	Haun, John	Sumner	640			4408	14 Oct 1797			On Caney Fork of WF of Drakes Cr.	
Dillonberry, Redmon	029	Hughes, Bartley	Sumner	640			4389	14 Oct 1797			On dividing ridge &c	Yes
Dillonberry, Redmon	030	Hood, Archibald	Sumner	640			4462	18 Sep 1797			Waters of WF of Drakes Cr.	yes
Dillonberry, Redmon	031	Oggden, Demsey	Sumner	640			4410	14 Oct 1797			Headwaters of mid. Fk. Drakes Cr.	yes
Dillonberry, Redmon	032	Ogleby, Nehemiah	Sumner	640			4417	14 Oct 1797			Headwaters of mid. Fk. Drakes Cr.	yes
Dillonberry, Redmon	032	Ogleby, Nehemiah	Sumner	640			4417	14 Oct 1797			Head Middle Fork of Drakes Cr	yes
Dillonberry, Redmon	034	Phelps, Jessee	Sumner	640			4470	14 Oct 1797			W branches of Trammells Cr	yes
Dillonberry, Redmon	035	Reynolds, Sylvestor	Sumner	640			4391	22 Sep 1797			Dividing ridge	yes
Dillonberry, Redmon	036	Yarby, Joseph	Sumner	640			4475	6 Sep 1797			Waters of N fork of Red River	yes
Dillonberry, Redmon	037	O'Connor, Sullivan	Sumner	274			4467	19 Sep 1797			Dividing ridge	yes
Dillonberry, Redmon	038	Short, Hrenry	Sumner	640			4472	14 Oct 1797			Waters middle fork of Drakes Cr	yes
Dillonberry, Redmon	039	Malone, Jacob	Sumner	640			4300	14 Oct 1797			Waters middle fork of Drakes Cr	yes
Dillonberry, Redmon	040	Leidmore, Watson	Sumner	640			4414	14 Oct 1797			Dividing ridge	yes
Dillonberry, Redmon	041	Minters, John	Sumner	640			4334	19 Sep 1797			Headwaters of W fork Drakes Cr	yes
Dillonberry, Redmon	042	Rowland, James	Sumner	640			4466	19 Sep 1797			Head br of Sulphur Lick Fork	yes
Dillonberry, Redmon	043	Middleton, Isaac	Sumner	640			4464	19 Sep 1797			Headwaters of Mussie fork [no cr]	yes
Dillonberry, Redmon	044	Greer, John G.	Sumner	640			4336	14 Oct 1797			Head br of W fork of Drakes Cr/	yes
Dillonberry, Redmon	045	Howard, John	Sumner	640			4206	3 Apr 1797			E/S N fork of Stones River	yes
Dillonberry, Redmon	046		Sumner	640			4226	14 Oct 1797			Head of Main Mid Fork of Drakes Cr	yes
Dillonberry, Redmon	047	Dillon, Thomas	Sumner	1000			4460	14 Oct 1797			Head br of W fork of Drakes Cr	yes
Dillonberry, Redmon	048	Garner, Gregory	Sumner	1000			4204	11 Apr 1797			W/S E fork of Stones River	yes
Dillonberry, Redmon	049	Bayles, John	Sumner	640			4205	13 Jun 1797			E/S E fork of Stones River	yes
Dillonberry, Redmon	050	Boonerver, John	Sumner	640			4215	28 Oct 1797			E/S E fork of Stones River	yes

Claimant:	File #:	Assignee:	County:	Acres:	Grant:	Grant Date:	Entry:	Entry Date:	Bk:	Pg:	Location by Stream Name:	Military:
Dillonberry, Redmon	051	Cambell, Andrew	Sumner	640			4406	6 Sep 1797			Waters W fork of Drakes Cr.	yes
Dillonberry, Redmon	052	Conner, Wm.	Sumner	640			4182	14 Oct 1797			Head of brs of Middle fork	yes
Dillonberry, Redmon	053		Sumner	640			4405	19 Sep 1797			On Rainey Fork &c	yes
Dillonberry, Redmon	054		Sumner	640			4459	14 Oct 1797			Headwaters Middle Fk of Drakes Cr	yes
Dillonberry, Redmon	055		Sumner	640			4461	6 Sep 1797			Waters S fork of Red River	yes
Dillonberry, Redmon	056	Harps, John	Sumner	228			4524	14 Oct 1797			Headwaters of first big creek	yes
Dillonberry, Redmon	057	Darden, Joseph	Sumner	640			4411	19 Sep 1797			W fork of Red River	yes
Dillonberry, Redmon	1249		Sumner	1000	2807	29 Dec 1796			90	52	On head branches of Spring Creek	yes
Dillonberry, Redmon	1287	Mahon, James	Sumner	640	3046	8 Jun 1797	4062	29 Mar 1797	90	316	On 32 Mile Creek	yes
Dillonberry, Redmon	1352	Nicoles, Richard	Sumner	640	3167	14 Sep 1797	4245	20 Feb 1797	90	429	On the Falling Creek	yes
Dillum, James	310	Donelson, John	Sumner	2560	1518	10 Apr 1792	3550	11 Apr 1788	75	507	On both sides N Fork of Smiths Fork	yes
Dilmore, Joseph	3	Smith, Daniel	Sumner	274	760	11 Jul 1788	2998	3 Oct 1787	63	267	Head of E branches of Drakes Cr	yes
Dilway, George	460	Reed, Jesse	Davidson	274	432	15 Sep 1787	3429	15 Sep 1787	63	159	S side of Big Barren River	yes
Diniston, John, Ass.	971		Hawkins	200	743	20 Jul 1796	1206	13 Feb 1779	88	496	On S side of Holston River	yes
Dinton, James	241		Washington	403	109	23 Oct 1782	614	24 Nov 1778	47	53	On Sinking Creek	
Diska, Joseph	1009	Armstrong, M.	Sumner	50	173	26 Mar 1795			86	377	On Trace Fk of Trammels Creek	
Dix, William	247	Hudson, George	Sumner	640	1152	26 Nov 1789	1428	21 Sep 1787	74	155	On waters of Bradleys Lick Creek	yes
Dixon, Benjamin	10		Smith	180	3398	8 Dec 1802	3694	3 may 1800	110	277	Beg at 2 white Walnuts & a Linn	
Dixon, Charles	55		Davidson	2560	41	14 Mar 1786	61		63	17	On both sides W Fork of Goose Cr	yes
Dixon, Charles	954	Gunter, Joel	Davidson	274	971	18 May 1789			63	329	Head brs 1st creek above Bradley Lick Cr	yes
Dixon, Charles, Exec.	564		Sumner	3362	1793	20 May 1793	60	17 Jul 1784	81	77	On N side of Cumberland River	yes
Dixon, Henry	360	Gubbins, William	Davidson	640	344	4 Sep 1787	1802	17 Jul 1784	63	128	S side of Sulphur Fork	yes
Dixon, Henry & Chas.	564		Sumner	3362	1793	20 May 1793	60	17 Jul 1784	81	77	On N side of Cumberland River	yes
Dixon, James, Jr.	107		Eastern District	125	96	17 Nov 1790	125	14 Sep 1779	76	175	Betw Thos Brock & Charles Brantley	
Dixon, Joel	751	Young, John	Sumner	274	2155	20 May 1793	1803	3 Feb 1786	81	162	On a small branch of Drakes Creek	yes
Dixon, John	2006	Womble, Benj.	Davidson	228	1950	20 May 1793	1944		81	112	On E waters of Mill Creek	yes
Dixon, Jos.	302	Bedwell, Zadock	Tennessee	1000	1992	20 May 1793	2593	30 Sep 1785	81	122	On E Fork of Bartons Creek	
Dixon, Thomas	385	Lambert, Aron	Tennessee	640	2381	14 Dec 1793	1341	4 Nov 1784	81	385	On N side of Cumberland River	yes
Dixon, Tighman	2050	Southerland, Wm.	Davidson	640	2125	20 May 1793	1519		81	155	On a branch of Stones River	yes
Dixon, Tighman	2051	Jacobs, Peter	Davidson	640	2126	20 May 1793	1405		81	155	ON S side of Cumberland River	yes
Dixon, Tighman	596	Obarr, Robt.	Sumner	457	1839	20 May 1793	1407	20 Aug 1785	81	87	On N side of Cumberland River	yes
Dixon, Tighman	741	York, Will	Sumner	533	2136	20 May 1793	1402	20 Aug 1782	81	158	Beg on S bank of Cumberland River	yes
Dixon, Tilman	34		Davidson	3840	20	14 Mar 1786	46		63	9	On Dixons Creek	yes
Dixon, Tilman	608		Middle District	3000	381	17 Mar 1801	12	4 Jan 1786	112	363	On Wartrace Fork	yes
Dixon, Tilman	956	Roberts, Vinson	Davidson	308	973	18 May 1789			63	330	On a small fk of Big Harpeth River	yes
Dixon, Tilmon	059	King, James	Sumner	3840							On a creek of Stones River	yes
Dixon, Tilmon	1012		Sumner	640	2582	26 Mar 1795			86	380	On N side of Cumberland River	yes
Dixon, Tilmon	1641	Vaughn, James	Davidson	640	1515	10 Apr 1792	1518		75	500/50	On head of a branch of Syones Cr	yes
Dixon, Tilmon	454	Lott, George	Sumner	640	1587	27 Apr 1793			81	14	On a creek of Stones River	yes
Dixon, Tilmon	478	Jackson, Thos.	Sumner	640	1649	27 Apr 1793	2201	25 Feb 1788	81	29	Adjoining preemption John Donelson	yes
Dixon, Winn	762		Sumner	2560	2175	20 May 1793	48	25 Apr 1785	81	167	Beg at a Sycamore & maple	yes
Doak, Samuel	22		Sullivan	300	33	23 Oct 1782	1899	7 Oct 1779	43	253	On waters of the Reedy Creek	
Doak, Samuel, Ass.	268		Eastern District	150	161	22 Feb 1795		Service right	83	429	S side of Holston River	
Doak, William	222		Green	300	179	22 Sep 1787	2827	27 mar 1781	65	423	On the N side of Holston River &c	
Dobbins, John	1240		Sumner	500	197	21 Nov 1796		12 Sep 1794	90	44	On the waters of Arringtons Fork &c	yes

Claimant:	File #:	Assignee:	County:	Acres:	Grant:	Grant Date:	Entry:	Entry Date:	Bk:	Pg:	Location by Stream Name:	Military:
Dobbins, William	390		Western District	250	391	27 Nov 1793	54	20 Apr 1787	81	504	On waters of Tennessee River	
Dobbins, William	391		Western District	250	392	27 Nov 1793	52		81	504	On S side of Tennessee River	
Dobbins, William	393		Western District	640 (650	394	27 Nov 1793	55 & 56		81	505	On S side of Tennessee River	
Dobbins, William	396		Western District	5000 (50	397	27 Nov 1793	50		81	505	On E side of the Missippia [sic]	
Dobbins, William	516	Hadley, Joshua	Sumner	640	1693	20 May 1793	1048	29 Aug 1792	81	52	On E Fork of Bledsoes Creek	yes
Dobbins, William	747	Gmalian, Abraham	Davidson	640	720	11 Jul 1788	3439		63	253	On head of a small branch	yes
Dobbins, Wm.	924	Armstrong, M.	Sumner	30	182	9 Jan 1794			81	449	Beg at a small red oak	
Dobbins, Wm.	925	Armstrong, M.	Sumner	10	184	9 Jan 1794			81	450	On waters of Arrington Fork	
Dobins, William	145		Middle District	1500	149	11 Aug 1789	49	29 Jun 1787	71	245	On S side of Duck River &c	
Dobson, Elias	07	Johnson, Henry	Robertson	640							On waters of Red River	
Dobson, John	2144	Stump, Christopher	Davidson	274	2423	31 Dec 1793	1679 (7)		81	407	On waters of Whites Creek	yes
Doby, James	933	Mulherin, James	Davidson	640	949	18 May 1789			63	324	On waters of Caney Fork	yes
Dodd, David	1333	Hickman, Thomas	Sumner	1000	3133	14 Sep 1797	4551	6 ----1797	90	417	Waters of E Fork of Big Barren	yes
Dodd, Jesse	419	King, Robert	Eastern District	274	2942	1 Mar 1797	4487		90	214	N side of Holston River	yes
Dodd, Thomas	1354	Barry, Redmond D.	Sumner	640	2777	10 Oct 1796	3903	12 Aug 1796	91	22	Waters of Martins Creek	yes
Dodge, Griffith & D. Stewart	647	Dange, Griffith	Tennessee	1000	3222	14 Sep 1797	407		92	15	On E Fork of Wells Creek	
Dodson, Beitha	1324	McConnel, Robert	Sumner	640	3124	14 Sep 1797	4595	6 May 1797	90	413	Joining his entry	yes
Dodson, Charles	1021	Donelson, S. & Jas. Latha	Hawkins	274	2948	1 Mar 1797	4486		90	217	N side of the great road	yes
Dodson, Elisha	376		Sullivan	200	255	10 Nov 1784	813	26 Jun 1780	69	163	On S side of Holston River	
Dodson, Jesse	1158		Green	300	1001	26 Dec 1791	764	28 Oct 1783	77	282	On n side of Holstein River	
Dodson, Lazarus	523		Sullivan	300	539	26 Nov 1789	681	1 Sep 1780	73	48	On S side of Holeson River &c	
Dodson, Nimrod	4		Eastern District	1000	303	13 Mar 1801	1095	30 Oct 1783	112	359	N side of Lone Mountain	
Dodson, Rawleigh	513		Sullivan	150	529	26 Nov 1789	1383	21 May 1779	73	44	On S side of HolsTon River	
Dodson, Rawleigh, Senr	521		Sullivan	150	537	26 Nov 1789	466	24 Apr 1780	73	47	On S side of Holston River	
Dodson, Thomas	440		Eastern District	100	297	19 Jul 1797	1404	24 May 1779	91	616	N side of Holston River	
Dohearty, George	383		Green	30	385	20 Sep 1787	1380	14 Jan 1784	65	481	Including Island in French Broad Riv &c	
Doherty, Daniel	628		Hawkins	58	490	27 June 1793	835	26 Aug 1781	80	358	On S side of Holston River	
Doherty, Geo.	083		not given	1500			1124	30 Oct 1783				
Doherty, George	110		Western District	3500	110	10 Jul 1788	1125	30 Oct 1783	67	323	On N side of Woolf River &c	
Doherty, George	161		Western District	2000	161	10 Jul 1788	1122	30 Oct 1783	67	359	On W side of Reelfoot River	
Doherty, George	32		Western District	2000	32	10 Jul 1788	1199	3 Nov 1783	67	292	On both sides of Indian Creek &c	
Doherty, George	35		Western District	3000	35	10 Jul 1788	1201	3 Nov 1783	67	293	On Reelfoot River &c	
Doherty, George	50		Middle District	5000	52	10 Jul 1788	1225	6 Nov 1783	67	436	On Richland Creek &c	
Doherty, George	51		Western District	4000	51	10 Jul 1788	1128	28 Oct 1783	67	300	On Reelfoot River &c	
Doherty, George	593		Washington	100	687	26 Oct 1786	2105	31 Oct 1779	66	5	Beg at a marked hickory &c	
Doherty, George	69		Western District	2500	69	10 Jul 1788	1198	3 Nov 1783	67	307	On N side of Looshatcher River &c	
Doherty, George	70		Western District	1000	70	10 Jul 1788	1129	30 Oct 1783	67	307	On the N side of Looshatcher River	
Doherty, George	94		Western District	2500	94	10 Jul 1788	1200	3 Nov 1783	67	317	On N side of Looshatcher River	
Doherty, James	151		Eastern District	500	121	24 Dec 1792	43		78	454	In a small valley N side of Clinch R	
Doherty, Michaells	143		Hawkins	200	177	26 Dec 1791	1993	19 Oct 1779	75	174	On Pattersons Mill Creek	
Doke, William	241		Green	300	198	20 Sep 1787	607	27 Oct 1783	65	430	On S side of Holston River	
Dominas, Domina	313	Rice, John and others	Davidson	1000	299	13 Jun 1787	2602		63	112	On Middle Fork of Drakes Creek	yes
Donahoe, John	563	Berkley, Wm. Heirs	Sumner	640	1786	20 May 1793	2987	9 Jun 1792	81	75	Beg at a white oak in Spencers line	yes
Donahoe, John, Ass.	321		Sumner	640	314	17 Nov 1790	754	4 Aug 1784	76	186	N side of Cumberland River	
Donald, William	855	Boyd, Thos.	Sumner	228	2360	20 May 1793	3296	24 Jun 1789	81	204	On waters of Drakes Creek	yes

Claimant:	File #:	Assignee:	County:	Acres:	Grant:	Grant Date:	Entry:	Entry Date:	Bk:	Pg:	Location by Stream Name:	Military:
Donaldson [sic], Stockley	193		Hawkins	640	126	16 Nov 1790	1097	12 Apr 1787	77	192	On N side of Holston River &c	
Donaldson, John	151	Ryal, Joseph	Davidson	640	137	14 Mar 1786	1074		63	53	On waters of Big Harpeth River	yes
Donaldson, John	1642	McCabe, Peter heirs	Davidson	640	1520	10 Apr 1792	2574		75	508	On S side of Cumberland River	yes
Donaldson, Stockley	437		Sullivan	385	316	10 Nov 1784	984	2 Jan 1779	69	182	On N side of Holstein River	
Donelson & Armstrong	034	Harrell, Holland hrs	Middle District	640			1479					
Donelson & Armstrong	035	Poe, John heirs	Middle District	640			3776					
Donelson & Armstrong	07		Eastern District	640			2499	22 May 1780			N side of Tennessee River	
Donelson & Armstrong	07		Eastern District	640			2499	22 May 1780			N side of Tennessee River	
Donelson & Armstrong	378		Eastern District	5000	229	27 Aug 1795	1668	16 Apr 1784	89	97	Upon Crow Creek, beg at a Sugar tree	
Donelson & Armstrong	385		Eastern District	5000	236	27 Aug 1795	1931	27 Apr 1784	89	99	Upon Crow Creek	
Donelson & Lackey	285		Eastern District	1280	210	4 Feb 1795			84	103	On N side of Tennessee River	
Donelson, Jesse	2261	Donelson, Stockley	Davidson	640	2725	20 Jul 1796	444		88	451	On waters of Stones River	yes
Donelson, Jno.	1238		Davidson	640	203	10 Jul 1788	742	3 Jun 1785	66	412	On the S side of Cumberland River	
Donelson, Jno.	1244		Davidson	640	209	10 Jul 1788	327	3 Mar 1784	66	414	Bet. Cumberland & Stones Rivers &c	
Donelson, Jno. G.	1137		Davidson	640	114	17 Apr 1786	290	16 Feb 1784	66	178	Lying in Big Harpeth River	
Donelson, John	040	Crowell, Rowland	Davidson	274			3534	10 May 1796			S side of Cumberland River	
Donelson, John	060	Simmons, Malia	Sumner	640			1946	8 Jan 1796			N branches of Cedar Lick Creek	yes
Donelson, John	1196	Malloy, John	Sumner	640	2753	20 Jul 1796			88	458	Near mouth of Bradleys Lick Creek	
Donelson, John	1197	Webb, Joshua	Sumner	640	2755	20 Jul 1796	3056	3 Jan 1796	88	459	On both sides of Cedar Lick Creek	yes
Donelson, John	1269	Angel, Thos.	Sumner	274	2920	19 Feb 1797	88	13 Aug 1796	90	248	Both sides branch of Cedar Lick Cr	yes
Donelson, John	1387	Lenoir(?), Chas.	Sumner	640	3312	6 Dec 1797	4640	10 Apr 1797	97	38	On a S branch of Falling Creek	yes
Donelson, John	1388	Ruth, John	Sumner	640	3313	6 Dec 1797	4667	10 Apr 1797	97	39	On a S branch of Falling Creek	yes
Donelson, John	1389	Laughlin, Cornelius	Sumner	640	3314	6 Dec 1797	4635	10 Apr 1797	97	39	On a S branch of Falling Creek	yes
Donelson, John	1489	Bailey, Wm. Heirs	Davidson	640	1202	20 Nov 1790	3246		73	279	On S side of Cumberland	yes
Donelson, John	1492	Carney, Arthur	Davidson	420	1045	27 Nov 1789	1196		74	47	On S side of Cumberland River	yes
Donelson, John	1845		Davidson	640	345	27 Nov 1792	431	7 May 1784	81	7	On left hand fork of Stones Creek	
Donelson, John	1906		Davidson	320	145	27 Apr 1793	812	26 Sep 1791	81	40	On head br left hand fork of Stones Cr	
Donelson, John	1969	Lamb, Nathan	Davidson	640	1847	20 May 1793	2522		81	89	On E of William Stewarts preemption	yes
Donelson, John	1972	Groves, Nicholas	Davidson	640	1859	20 May 1793			81	91	On a small fork of Stones Creek	yes
Donelson, John	2024	Hartley, John	Davidson	640	2026	20 May 1793	1647		81	131	On head of Stones Creek	yes
Donelson, John	2115	Daughty, Samuel	Davidson	228	2374	20 May 1793	1822		81	207	On S side of Cumberland River	yes
Donelson, John	2195	Freeman, Wm. Hrs.	Davidson	640	2485	18 Aug 1795	2847		87	508	On a small fk W side of Big Harpeth	yes
Donelson, John	2273	Smith, Benj.	Davidson	274	2751	20 Jul 1796	1116		88	457	On Stones Creek	yes
Donelson, John	2274	Elkins, Jos. Heirs	Davidson	640	2732	20 Jul 1796	3607		88	458	On both sides of Stones Creek	yes
Donelson, John	2275	Chisum, Ignatius	Davidson	274	2754	20 Jul 1796	3953		88	459	On waters of Stones Creek	yes
Donelson, John	2307	Armstrong, M.	Davidson	100	192	27 Aug 1795		21 Jan 1788	89	409	Lying in Jones Bent	yes
Donelson, John	2325	Templeton, Thos heirs	Davidson	1000	2919	19 Feb 1797	2624		90	248	Both sides of Stones Creek	yes
Donelson, John	2386	Norton, Jeremiah	Davidson	1000	3169	14 Sep 1797	4246		90	429	S side of Falling Creek	yes
Donelson, John	310	Dillum, Jas.	Sumner	2560	1518	10 Apr 1792	3550	11 Apr 1788	75	507	On both sides N Fork of Smiths Fork	yes
Donelson, John	315		Sumner	640	308	17 Nov 1790	573	12 Aug 1784	76	184	Both sides of Spencers Creek	
Donelson, John	600	Bass, Britton	Sumner	640	1848	20 May 1793			81	89	On both sides of Spencers Creek	yes
Donelson, John	681	Mitchell, John	Sumner	640	2027	20 May 1793	3473	10 Feb 1787	81	131	On E Fork of Stones	yes
Donelson, John	682	Gay, Wm.	Sumner	640	2028	20 May 1793	1587	25 Nov 1785	81	131	On both sides of Bradleys Creek	yes
Donelson, John	683	Askers, Chas.	Sumner	1000	2029	20 May 1793	3330	14 Jul 1791	81	131	On S side of Cumberland River	yes
Donelson, John	745	Griffin, Jas.	Sumner	640	2147	20 May 1793	3463	11 Apr 1788	81	160	On both sides of Cedar Lick Creek	yes

Claimant:	File #:	Assignee:	County:	Acres:	Grant:	Grant Date:	Entry:	Entry Date:	Bk:	Pg:	Location by Stream Name:	Military:
Donelson, John	746	Gale, Daniel	Sumner	100	2148	20 May 1793	1710	31 Jan 1792	81	160	On E Fk of Stones River	yes
Donelson, John	755		Green	1500	574	11 Jul 1788	1084	12 Sep 1786	68	217	On N side of Tennessee River	
Donelson, John	917	Armstrong, M.	Sumner	100	156	9 Jan 1794			81	440	On N side of Cumberland River	
Donelson, John & Samuel	966	Freeman, John	Davidson	640	983	18 May 1789			63	332	On both sides of Big Harpeth River	yes
Donelson, John & Samuel	2060	Defnel(?), Wm.	Davidson	640	2165	20 May 1793	1185		81	164	On both sides of S Fk of Stones R	yes
Donelson, John (Survey)	039		not given	11,520							vacant land	
Donelson, John, Ass	2161		Davidson	45	174	9 Jan 1794		22 Sep 1787	81	446	On N side of Cumberland River	
Donelson, John, Ass	2163		Davidson	100	176	9 Jan 1794			81	447	On N branches of Harpeth River	
Donelson, John, Ass	2249		Davidson	100	300	20 Jul 1796		10 Jun 1796	88	440	On waters of Murfrees Ford	
Donelson, John, Sr.	1138		Davidson	640	115	17 Apr 1796	282	14 Feb 1784	66	178	On a branch of Big Harpeth &c	
Donelson, S & Jas. W Lackey	285		Eastern District	1280	210	4 Feb 1795			84	103	On E side of Tennessee River	
Donelson, S. & Alex. Kelly	246		Eastern District	1000	213	30 Oct 1794			83	141	N/S Tennessee R on Nine MileCreek	
Donelson, S. & Chas. McClun	513		Green	1000	386	29 Jul 1793	2325	25 May 1784	80	273	S side of Noleychuckey River	
Donelson, S. & Geo. Gardner	1592		Green	1000	1334	22 Dec 1795			83	436	On Lick Creek	
Donelson, S. & Geo. Gordon	1636		Green	500	1339	27 Aug 1795	1209	10 Apr 1785	87	510	On Potter Creek a fork of Lick Creek	
Donelson, S. & Geo. Gordon	1579		Green	840	1330	4 Feb 1795	124	23 Apr 1790	83	398	N side of Clinch River &c	
Donelson, S. & James King	819		Hawkins	5000	641	27 Jan 1795			83	362	N side of Clinch River &c	
Donelson, S. & James King	820		Hawkins	5000	642	27 Jan 1795			83	363	Joining former entry Donelson & Kings	
Donelson, S. & James Latha	1020	Tilly, Lewis	Hawkins	274	2947	1 Mar 1797	4517		90	216	N side of great road	
Donelson, S. & James Latha	1021	Dodson, Charles	Hawkins	274	2948	1 Mar 1797	4486		90	217	N side of great road runs N 55 E	
Donelson, S. & Jno. Gowan	297		Eastern District	1280	156	22 Feb 1795			84	281	On head of Mossey Creek	
Donelson, S. & Jno. Hackett	1627		Green	5000	1347	22 Feb 1795	1707	16 May 1788	84	330	In Pleasant Garden Valley	
Donelson, S. & Jno. Hackett	252		Green	5000	209	20 Sep 1787	8 warrants	15 Feb 1780	65	433	In Pleasant Garden Valley &c	
Donelson, S. & Jno. Latham	423	Carbar, Jas.	Eastern District	275	2955	1 Mar 1797			90	220	Beg on a Black oak & Post oak	
Donelson, S. & Jno.Chisum	202		Eastern District	1000	174	8 Apr 1794	2388	5 Jan 1785	81	559	On S side of Holston	
Donelson, S. & John Latham	1024	Providford, James	Hawkins	275	2954	1 Mar 1797	4501		90	220	Beg on a white oak & Sugar tree	
Donelson, S. & John Latham	1025	Wren, William	Hawkins	275	2956	1 Mar 1797	4518		90	221	Beg on a stake corner	
Donelson, S. & Jos. Beard	131		Eastern District	400	141	15 Jul 1793	736	16 Feb 1781	76	496	Waters of Bull Run of Clinch river	
Donelson, S. & Jos. Beard	279		Eastern District	1000	214	4 Jan 1795	2477	11 Apr 1790	84	45	On S side Clinch River	
Donelson, S. & Jos. Beard	485		Hawkins	1000	357	29 Jul 1793			80	265	S side of Clinch River on Dry Bluff	
Donelson, S. & Jos. Beard	624		Hawkins	3376	321	15 Jul 1793			80	301	S side of Holston River	
Donelson, S. & Jos. Beard	655		Hawkins	1000	525	May 1794	2394	25 May 1784	81	555	On Buffalow Creek	
Donelson, S. & Jos. Beard	680	Cooper, Thomas	Hawkins	300	2391	12 Jul 1794	3535		81	602	Beg at a stake	
Donelson, S. & Jos. Beard	681	Cannon, Sampson	Hawkins	474	2392	17 Jul 1794	3536		81	603	On N side of Clinch River	
Donelson, S. & Jos. Beard	684	Sevenson, Peter, pt(?)	Hawkins	1000	2395	17 Jul 1794	3545		81	603	On S side of Wallings ridge	
Donelson, S. & Jos. Beard	692		Hawkins	4000	581	17 Jul 1794			81	612	On waters of Flatt creek	
Donelson, S. & Lackey	274		Eastern District	5000	209	4 Jan 1795	1025	29 Oct 1783	84	42	Beg at 2 elms & Sycamore	
Donelson, S. & M. Armstrong	957		Sumner	640	2420	21 Feb 1795			84	306	On E side of W Fork of Obeys river	yes
Donelson, S. & Robt. King	1060	Brevat, John	Sumner	640	2537	10 Dec 1798			88	292	On both sides of a creek	yes
Donelson, S. & Robt. King	1067	Browan(?)	Sumner	640	2544	10 Dec 1795	3242		88	295	Including the great Salt Lick	yes
Donelson, S. & Robt. King	414	Moore, Phillip	Eastern District	1000	2806	28 Dec 1796	2066		90	206	In the Greasey Valley	
Donelson, S. & S. Mitchell	1089	Bruce, George heirs	Sumner	640	2580	7 Mar 1796	3905	8 Aug 1792	88	316	On W side of W Fk of Obeys River	yes
Donelson, S. & S. Pike	062		Sumner	3840			1566	2 Nov 1795			On a fork the Pond Lick Creek	yes
Donelson, S. & Wm. Lewis	1714		Davidson	640	356	29 Jul 1793			76	479	S side of Cumberland River	
Donelson, S. & Wm. Terrel	497		Middle District	40000	289	6 Jan 1795	2297 etc	1793	85	343	On Roaring Spring Creek	

Earliest Tennessee Land Records

Claimant:	File #:	Assignee:	County:	Acres:	Grant:	Grant Date:	Entry:	Entry Date:	Bk:	Pg:	Location by Stream Name:	Military:
Donelson, S. & Wm. Terrell	1501		Green	640	1262	12 Jul 1794			81	582	On E Fork of Grassey Creek	
Donelson, S. & Wm. Terrell	254		Eastern District	1000	207	6 Jan 1795			83	175	In Powell's Valley	
Donelson, S. & Wm. Tyrrell	461	Caree, John	Tennessee	2560	2555	7 Mar 1796	11		88	308	On West branches of Sulphur Fork	
Donelson, S. & Wm. Tyrrell	018	Vance, John	Tennessee	2560			330	27 Nov 1783			On W branches of the Sulphur Fork	
Donelson, S. & Wm. Tyrrell	019		Tennessee	2560							On W branches of Sulphur Fork	
Donelson, S. & Wm. Tyrrell	022		Tennessee	2560			3829				On W branches of the Sulphur Fork	
Donelson, S. & Wm. Tyrrell	06		Davidson	640			321	1 Mar 1784			S side of Cumberland River	
Donelson, S. & Wm. Tyrrell	09		Middle District	5000				no date				
Donelson, S. & Wm. Tyrrell	1073		Sumner	640	2549	7 Mar 1796			88	305	On head branches of Carrs Creek	yes
Donelson, S. & Wm. Tyrrell	1074		Sumner	640	2551	7 Mar 1796			88	306	Joining their survey	yes
Donelson, S. & Wm. Tyrrell	1075	McCoy, James heirs	Sumner	640	2552	7 Mar 1796			88	306	On head branches of Carrs Creek	
Donelson, S. & Wm. Tyrrell	1077		Sumner	640	2554	7 Mar 1796			88	307	Joining their survey	yes
Donelson, S. & Wm. Tyrrell	1078		Sumner	640	2558	7 Mar 1796			88	309	Joining sd Stockleys & Tyrrells survey	yes
Donelson, S. & Wm. Tyrrell	1079		Sumner	640	2559	7 Mar 1796			88	310	Joining their survey	
Donelson, S. & Wm. Tyrrell	1081	Chesson, James	Sumner	640	2562	7 Mar 1796			88	311	On a large fork of Caney Fork	yes
Donelson, S. & Wm. Tyrrell	1082		Sumner	640	2563	7 Mar 1796			88	312	Joining their survey	yes
Donelson, S. & Wm. Tyrrell	1084	Perrey, Wm. Heirs	Sumner	640	2577	7 Mar 1796	2946	2 Nov 1795	88	313	On a branch of Pond Lick Creek	yes
Donelson, S. & Wm. Tyrrell	1086	McMullen, Isaac	Sumner	640	2577	7 Mar 1796	2863	2 Nov 1795	88	315	On head of Pond Lick Creek	yes
Donelson, S. & Wm. Tyrrell	1087	Perry, Wm. Heirs	Sumner	640	2578	7 Mar 1796	2941		88	315	On a branch of the Pond Lick Creek	yes
Donelson, S. & Wm. Tyrrell	11		Eastern District	640	1712	24 Sep 1779					On a branch that runs into Sinking Creek	
Donelson, S. & Wm. Tyrrell	1105		Sumner	640	2609	7 Mar 1796	4 warrants		88	331	Joining sd Donelsons & Tyrrells survey	yes
Donelson, S. & Wm. Tyrrell	1698		Green	20000	1415	8 Jan 1797		22 Dec 1784	90	210	In fk of Holston & French Broad Rivers	
Donelson, S. & Wm. Tyrrell	208		Eastern District	400	194	12 Jul 1794	589		81	595	On N side of Beaverdam Creek	
Donelson, S. & Wm. Tyrrell	2226	McCoy, James	Davidson	640	2550	7 Mar 1796	2461		88	305	On waters of Stones River	yes
Donelson, S. & Wm. Tyrrell	2228	Whitney, James heirs	Davidson	1000	2561	7 Mar 1796	2301		88	311	On waters of Stones River	yes
Donelson, S. & Wm. Tyrrell	232		Eastern District	640	187	12 Jun 1794	2474		82	179	In Hines's Valley	
Donelson, S. & Wm. Tyrrell	252		Western District	5000	205	6 Jan 1795	1659	16 Apr 1784	83	173	N/S Tennessee River opposite an island	
Donelson, S. & Wm. Tyrrell	258		Eastern District	5000	205	27 Jan 1795			83	364	N side of Clinch River &c	
Donelson, S. & Wm. Tyrrell	322		Eastern District	300	262	7 Mar 1796		7 Jun 1780	88	198	On Old Field Branch	
Donelson, S. & Wm. Tyrrell	339		Eastern District	1000	257	7 Mar 1796	2940	25 Mar 1784	88	299	In the Grassey Valley	
Donelson, S. & Wm. Tyrrell	340		Eastern District	1000	258	7 Mar 1796	1674	25 May 1784	88	299	In the Crab Orchard valley	
Donelson, S. & Wm. Tyrrell	341		Eastern District	1000	259	7 Mar 1796	456	25 May 1784	88	300	In the Grassey Valley	
Donelson, S. & Wm. Tyrrell	421		Western District	5000	422	20 Jul 1796		16 Apr 1784	88	430	On N Fork of Obion River	
Donelson, S. & Wm. Tyrrell	462	Robchete(?), Joshua	Tennessee	640	2556	7 Mar 1796			88	308	On W branches of Sulphur Fork	
Donelson, S. & Wm. Tyrrell	463	Newberry, Wm. Heirs	Tennessee	640	2573	7 Mar 1796		30 Sep 1785	88	313	On head branches of Carrs Creek	
Donelson, S. & Wm. Tyrrell	506		Middle District	5000	301	7 Mar 1796			88	302	On waters of Elk River	
Donelson, S. & Wm. Tyrrell	507		Middle District	640	303	7 Mar 1796			88	303	On waters of Caney Fork	
Donelson, S. & Wm. Tyrrell	509		Middle District	3000	305	7 Mar 1796		Jun 1784	88	304	Inc the Crab Orchard	
Donelson, S. & Wm. Tyrrell	596	Kites, Chas.	Tennessee	274	3076	19 Jul 1797	4143	19 Jul 1797	90	381	N side of Cumberland River	yes
Donelson, S. & Wm. Tyrrell	935		Hawkins	1000	717	8 Dec 1795	2480	5 Jan 1785	88	274	On S side of Holston River	
Donelson, S.& Tho.Hutchings	3		Eastern District	3000	3	11 Jul 1788		11 Jul 1788	67	340	On Bluff Creek of Clinch River	
Donelson, S.& Tho.Hutchings	4		Eastern District	1000	4	11 Jul 1788	2866	11 Jul 1788	67	340	N Tenn River above mouth of Clinch	
Donelson, Severn (?) [sic]	06		Eastern District	1200							Lying on Brimstone Creek	
Donelson, Spencer	587		Davidson	428	559	15 Sep 1787	1081	29 May 1781	63	200	On Middle Fork of Red River	yes
Donelson, Srock & W.Tyrrell	1080	Clayton, Miles heirs	Sumner	640	2560	7 Mar 1796			88	310	Joining sd Donelsons & Tyrrells survey	yes

Claimant:	File #:	Assignee:	County:	Acres:	Grant:	Grant Date:	Entry:	Entry Date:	Bk:	Pg:	Location by Stream Name:	Military:
Donelson, Stockley	672	Corbin, Francis	Hawkins	640	2381	12 Jul 1794	792,996	1783	81	599	On Brush Creek	
Donelson, Stockley	1005		Hawkins	7000	781	21 Jan 1797		1783	90	56	S side of Holston River	
Donelson, Stockley	0		Middle & Eastern District	conveyed	no date					Field in Eastern Dist #01	
Donelson, Stockley	01		Eastern & Middle District	conveyed			no date			On Bluff Creek	
Donelson, Stockley	010		Eastern District	1000			29 Jan 1786			Lying on N/s of Clinch in Bald Valley	
Donelson, Stockley	011		Eastern District	640	11	11 Jul 1788			67	344	SW side of Obeys River	yes
Donelson, Stockley	0137	Andrews, John Cole	Sumner	3840				13 Apr 1795			NE side of Obeys River	yes
Donelson, Stockley	0138		Sumner	2560				13 Jan 1795			On waters of Gap Creek	
Donelson, Stockley	0139		Green	5000			7	24 Mar 1780			On waters of Red River	
Donelson, Stockley	014	Garrett, Wm.	Robertson	640			1645	26 Aug 1796			On S side of Duck River	
Donelson, Stockley	014		Middle District	5000			1726	16 Apr 1784			On waters of Red River	
Donelson, Stockley	015	Todd, Josiah	Robertson	640			1590	13 Aug 1796			On waters of Elk Fork of Red River	
Donelson, Stockley	016	Vickery, John	Robertson	640			521	13 Aug 1796			On head of Mossy Branch	
Donelson, Stockley	02	Cowan, John	not given								1st branch of N side of Cumberland	yes
Donelson, Stockley	02		Montgomery	640			2615	13 Feb 1797			On waters of Red River	
Donelson, Stockley	027	Bigworth, Stephen	Robertson	640			2559	13 Aug 1796			
Donelson, Stockley	036		Sullivan	200			749	14 Feb 1781			Waters of Bednagoes Fk of Sycamore	
Donelson, Stockley	039	Gideon, Richard	Robertson	1000			2608	13 Aug 1796			W of the Cumberland Mountains	
Donelson, Stockley	039		Middle District	400							On both sides the Pond Branch	
Donelson, Stockley	040	Gowan, David	Robertson	1000			2609	13 Aug 1796			On waters of Mill Creek	
Donelson, Stockley	040	Nelson, Jesse	not given	640			1314	9 Jun 1796			On Honeycutts Creek	
Donelson, Stockley	040		Sullivan	500			794	10 Jun 1781			On waters of Bush Creek	
Donelson, Stockley	040		Green	640			302	8 Nov 1793			S side of Cumberland River	
Donelson, Stockley	041	Crockley, Allen	not given	640			3425	4 Aug 1796			On waters of Red River	
Donelson, Stockley	041	Henry, Jonathan	Robertson	640			3262	13 Aug 1796			On waters of Red River	
Donelson, Stockley	043	Saunders, Peter	Robertson	640			3158	13 Aug 1796			
Donelson, Stockley	046		Hawkins	200							
Donelson, Stockley	049	Armstrong, M.	Hawkins	400			44	13 Apr 1787			In Sinking Creek Valley	
Donelson, Stockley	05	Wimpsie, Wm.	Jefferson	100							On waters of Red River	
Donelson, Stockley	05		Robertson	640			3044	25 Jul 1796			S side of Cumberland River	
Donelson, Stockley	06		Middle District	1280				24 Apr 1786			On first creek E of Pond Lick Creek	yes
Donelson, Stockley	061	Laine, Thomas	Sumner	640			3095	10 May 1796			W side W Fk Obeys River	yes
Donelson, Stockley	063	Stringer, Simon	Sumner	640			3185	13 Apr 1795			On headwaters of Salt Lick Creek	yes
Donelson, Stockley	064	Meloy, Thomas	Sumner	1000	2616	7 Aug 1796	3443	12 Aug 1796			
Donelson, Stockley	065		Sullivan	100			137	12 Feb 1780			
Donelson, Stockley	066		Sullivan	400			433	19 Apr 1780			
Donelson, Stockley	07		Middle District	10000							On Spring Creek	
Donelson, Stockley	08	James, Chas.	Robertson	640	3469	13 Aug 1796					N side of Tennessee River	
Donelson, Stockley	08		Eastern District	2000				7 Jun 1787			Joining a survey	
Donelson, Stockley	08		Middle District	5000			459	25 Oct 1783			
Donelson, Stockley	088		not given	5000			2099	16 Apr 1784			On waters of Red River	
Donelson, Stockley	09	Beach, Robt.	Robertson	640	2820	12 Jan 1797	3443	12 Aug 1796			Fragments	
Donelson, Stockley	09		Eastern District						67	339	S/S of Clinch River in Hanses Valley	
Donelson, Stockley	1		Eastern District	400	1	11 Jul 1788			67	342	On Bluff Creek of Clinch River	
Donelson, Stockley	10		Eastern District	2000	10	11 Jul 1788						

Claimant:	File #:	Assignee:	County:	Acres:	Grant:	Grant Date:	Entry:	Entry Date:	Bk:	Pg:	Location by Stream Name:	Military:
Donelson, Stockley	10		Hawkins	500	6	23 Aug 1788	732	28 Oct 1783	67	431	Lying on N side of Holston River &c	
Donelson, Stockley	1004		Hawkins	20000	780	21 Jan 1797			90	53	N side of Tennessee River	
Donelson, Stockley	1007		Hawkins	959	783	21 Jan 1797	2994-501	1783-1780	90	57	Betwn Holston Riv & the mo Nolichuckey	
Donelson, Stockley	1076	Rogers, James heirs	Sumner	640	2553	7 Mar 1796	2951	2 Nov 1795	88	307	On head of Pond Lick Creek	yes
Donelson, Stockley	1085	Reed, Joseph heirs	Sumner	640	2575	7 Mar 1796	2948	2 Nov 1795	88	314	On head waters of the Pond Lick Creek	
Donelson, Stockley	11		Sullivan	21	500	22 Oct 1782			43	247	On Honeycutts Creek	
Donelson, Stockley	1186	McDaniel, Alex	Sumner	640	2708	20 Jul 1796	3912	9 May 1796	88	444	On branches of Spencers Creek	yes
Donelson, Stockley	1187	Clifton, Richard heirs	Sumner	640	2709	20 Jul 1796	1262	8 Jun 1796	88	444	On both sides of Pond Lick Creek	yes
Donelson, Stockley	1188	Holloway, John	Sumner	640	2716	20 Jul 1796	2491	10 May 1796	88	445	On first creek E of Pond Lick Creek	yes
Donelson, Stockley	1189	McNutty, John	Sumner	640	2711	20 Jul 1796	3846	19 May 1796	88	445	On Spencers Creek	yes
Donelson, Stockley	1190	Dagget, James	Sumner	640	2713	20 Jul 1796			88	446	On N Fork of First Creek	yes
Donelson, Stockley	1191	Pope, Sam	Sumner	640	2714	20 Jul 1796	3879	8 Jun 1796	88	446	On first creek E of Pond Lick Creek	yes
Donelson, Stockley	1192	Williamson, John	Sumner	640	2717	20 Jul 1796	3880	8 Jun 1790	88	448	N side of first creek E of Pond Lick	yes
Donelson, Stockley	1193	Garris, Stephen	Sumner	640	2719	20 Jul 1796	3154	10 May 1796	88	448	On first creek E of Pond Lick Creek	yes
Donelson, Stockley	1194	Craigie, Arch'd	Sumner	640	2720	20 Jul 1796	538	8 Jun 1796	88	449	On N fork of First Creek	
Donelson, Stockley	12		Eastern District	600	12	11 Jul 1788			67	344	On waters of Bluff Creek	
Donelson, Stockley	1204		Sumner	60400	230	28 Aug 1795			89	82	On S side of Cumberland River	yes
Donelson, Stockley	1238		Sumner	640	2844	12 Jan 1797	3801	7 Aug 1796	90	28	On Martins Creek	yes
Donelson, Stockley	1239	Elmore, Morgan	Sumner	640	2839	12 Jan 1797	3440	Aug 1796	90	40	On Martin's Creek	yes
Donelson, Stockley	1242		Sumner	640	2841	21 Jan 1797	1039	19 Aug 1796	90	45	On Martins Creek	yes
Donelson, Stockley	1245		Sumner	1000	2848	21 Jan 1797			90	48	On headwaters of Salt Lick Creek	yes
Donelson, Stockley	1246	Boxley, John	Sumner	640	2850	21 Jan 1797	1039	13 Aug 1796	90	49	Waters of Martins Creek	yes
Donelson, Stockley	1248		Sumner	640	2855	21 Jan 1797	1455	7 Aug 1796	90	52	Waters of Martin's Creek	yes
Donelson, Stockley	1251		Sumner	1000	2729	21 Jul 1796			90	183	S side of Obeys River	yes
Donelson, Stockley	1252		Sumner	1000	2730	21 Jul 1796			90	183	On head creek that runs into Obeys River	yes
Donelson, Stockley	1254		Sumner	640	2732	21 Jul 1796			90	184	W side of West Fork of Obeys River &c	yes
Donelson, Stockley	1255		Sumner	640	2733	21 Jul 1796			90	185	W side of W Fork of Obeys River	yes
Donelson, Stockley	1256		Sumner	640	2734	21 Jul 1796			90	185	Waters of Cainey Fork of Buffalo River	yes
Donelson, Stockley	1257		Sumner	640	2735	21 Jul 1796			90	186	W side of W Fork of Obeys River	yes
Donelson, Stockley	1258		Sumner	640	2736	21 Jul 1796			90	186	Waters of Caney Fork &c	yes
Donelson, Stockley	1259		Sumner	640	2737	21 Jul 1796			90	187	Waters of Caney Fork & joining entry	yes
Donelson, Stockley	1260	Stillwell, Jer. Heirs	Sumner	640	2738	21 Jul 1795	213	4 Apr 1785	90	187	W side of W Fork of Obeys River &c	yes
Donelson, Stockley	13		Eastern District	1000	13	11 Jul 1788	945	29 Oct 1783	67	345	On E Fork of Bluff Creek	
Donelson, Stockley	1309	Gunter, Samuel	Sumner	205	3107	14 Sep 1797	4280	12 May 1797	90	405	Waters of Spencers Creek	yes
Donelson, Stockley	1310	Davis, Ralph	Sumner	457	3108	14 Sep 1797	4279	12 May 1797	90	405	N side of the Falling Creek	
Donelson, Stockley	14		Eastern District	1200	14	11 Jul 1788			67	345	On E Fork of Bluff Creek	
Donelson, Stockley	14		Hawkins	5000	10	23 Aug 1788			67	432	On N side of Tennessee River &c	
Donelson, Stockley	146		Green	1000	616	23 Aug 1788	1078	27 Dec 1787	64	346	S/S Tennessee Riv in Cumberland Valley	
Donelson, Stockley	146		Middle District	5000	152	7 Apr 1790			71	278	On W side of Richland Creek	
Donelson, Stockley	147		Green	1000	617	23 Aug 1788	958	25 Jul 1785	64	347	On N/S Tenn Riv Pleasant Garden Valley	
Donelson, Stockley	15		Eastern District	640	15	11 Jul 1788	360	24 Mar 1780	67	346	On Whites Creek of Holston River	
Donelson, Stockley	151		Middle District	2000	154	17 Jun 1790	1228	6 Nov 1783	73	95	On S side of Duck River &c	
Donelson, Stockley	152		Middle District	5000	155	17 Jun 1790			73	95	On Richland Creek &c	
Donelson, Stockley	153		Green	600	623	23 Aug 1788	1712	20 May 1783	64	349	On S side of Clinch River	
Donelson, Stockley	155		Green	640	625	23 Aug 1788	1779	4 Jul 1783	64	349	On N side of Clinch River &c	

Claimant:	File #:	Assignee:	County:	Acres:	Grant:	Grant Date:	Entry:	Entry Date:	Bk:	Pg:	Location by Stream Name:	Military:
Donelson, Stockley	157		Green	600	627	23 Aug 1788	933	29 Oct 1783	64	350	On the waters of Flat Creek &c	
Donelson, Stockley	1656		Green	5000	1355	27 Aug 1795	1499	12 Apr 1790	87	527	On N side of Nolechuckey River	
Donelson, Stockley	1657		Green	5000	1356	27 Aug 1795	8 warrants	24 Mar 1780	87	527	On N side of Noleychuckey River &c	
Donelson, Stockley	1658		Green	60400	1357	28 Aug 1795	1357 [sic]	28 Aug 1795 [sic]	87	528	On S side of French Broad River	
Donelson, Stockley	1664		Green	200	284	6 Jan 1796			88	380	Joining David Francis lines	
Donelson, Stockley	1683		Green	5000	1358	28 Aug 1795	257	17 Mar 1780	89	77	N side of Noleychuckey River	
Donelson, Stockley	1684		Green	5000	1359	28 Aug 1795	2359	25 May 1784	89	78	On waters of Noleychuckey River	
Donelson, Stockley	17	Thomas, Jeremiah	Robertson	640	1589	30 Jul 1796					On Sulphur Fk of Red River	
Donelson, Stockley	17		Sullivan	400	28	23 Oct 1782	1991	19 Oct 1779	43	250	On Robertsons Creek	
Donelson, Stockley	1725		Green	1098	1404	21 Jan 1797	449	8 Feb 1780	91	127	Bet French Broad River & Dumplin Creek	
Donelson, Stockley	1726		Green	4360	1405	21 Jan 1797	43	10 Mar 1780	91	128	On Buck Creek	
Donelson, Stockley	1727		Green	5000	1406	21 Jan 1797	5	16 Nov 1793	91	128	Waters of Gap Creek & Beech Creek	
Donelson, Stockley	1728		Green	5000	1407	21 Jan 1797	44	1 Mar 1780	91	129	Joining 500 acres of sd Donelsons &c	
Donelson, Stockley	1729		Green	5000	1408	21 Jan 1797	2321	28 Aug 1795	91	129	Waters of Beech Creek	
Donelson, Stockley	1730		Green	5000	1409	21 Jan 1797	1694	16 Apr 1784	91	130	Joining a survey of sd Donelsons &c	
Donelson, Stockley	1731		Green	640	1410	21 Jan 1797			91	130	Waters of Buck Creek	
Donelson, Stockley	1732		Green	5000	1411	21 Jan 1797	333 &c	15 Feb 1780	91	131	Waters of Bent Cr waters of Holsten Riv	
Donelson, Stockley	1733		Green	500	1412	21 Jan 1797			91	131	On a branch of Tuckathoe Creek	
Donelson, Stockley	1734		Green	500	1413	21 Jan 1797			91	132	On Tuckeyho Creek	
Donelson, Stockley	1735		Green	1000	1414	21 Jan 1797			91	132	Both sides of Long Creek	
Donelson, Stockley	174	Whitfield, Jesse hrs	Hawkins	3000 [?]	107	16 Nov 1790	1075,76,77	30 Oct 1783	77	187	On N side of Clinch River &c	
Donelson, Stockley	1784		Davidson	640	365	26 Jun 1793	724	6 May 1785	80	321	On both sides of Stones Creek	
Donelson, Stockley	18		Sullivan	340	29	23 Oct 1782	752	3 Mar 1780	43	251	On Dodsons Creek &c	
Donelson, Stockley	186		Eastern District	640	1657	15 Jul 1793			81	43	Beg at a stake	
Donelson, Stockley	193	Corbin, James heirs	Eastern District	640	2381	8 Mar 1794	1315		81	439	On n side of Clinch River	
Donelson, Stockley	195		Middle District	1000	357	29 Jul 1793	2433	23 May 1784	76	479	N side of Duck River &c	
Donelson, Stockley	197		Middle District	5000	200	15 Jul 1793			76	493	Both sides of S fork of Duck River	
Donelson, Stockley	199		Middle District	5000	202	15 Jul 1793			76	494	N side of Elk River	
Donelson, Stockley	2		Eastern District	300	2	11 Jul 1788			67	339	On NE side of Bluff Creek	
Donelson, Stockley	203		Eastern District	1000	175	8 Apr 1794			81	559	On the Calney Creek	
Donelson, Stockley	209		Eastern District	640	195	12 Jul 1794	2216	21 May 1784	81	596	In Hinds Valley	
Donelson, Stockley	210		Eastern District	350	196	12 Jul 1794	742	28 Oct 1783	81	596	On S side of Clinch River	
Donelson, Stockley	211		Eastern District	500	197	12 Jul 1794			81	596	On Valley Fork of Big Creek	
Donelson, Stockley	212		Eastern District	200	198	12 Jul 1794	1165	7 Jun 1794	81	596	On N side of Powells River	
Donelson, Stockley	216		Eastern District	5000	104	26 Dec 1791			81	624	On Little Pigeon River, beg on an elm	
Donelson, Stockley	217		Eastern District	5000	105	26 Dec 1791	8		81	624	On Little Pigeon River	
Donelson, Stockley	221		Eastern District	640	164	23 Apr 1794			82	154	On a branch that runs in Sinking Cr	
Donelson, Stockley	2227	Jessop, Isaac heirs	Davidson	640	2557	7 Mar 1796			88	309	On waters of Stones River	yes
Donelson, Stockley	225		Eastern District	400	180	12 Jun 1794	1756	30 Sep 1779	82	176	On N/S of Holston on Roseberry Cr	
Donelson, Stockley	2254	Daget, James	Davidson	640	2712	20 Jul 1796	1912		88	446	On waters of Stones River	yes
Donelson, Stockley	2255	Parker, Hillary heirs	Davidson	640	2715	20 Jul 1796	3807		88	447	N on waters of Stones River	yes
Donelson, Stockley	2256	Mills, Elijah heirs	Davidson	640	2716	20 Jul 1796	1323		88	447	Waters of Stones Riv at a mulberry	yes
Donelson, Stockley	2257	Williamson, John	Davidson	640	2718	20 Jul 1796			88	448	On waters of Mill Creek	yes
Donelson, Stockley	2258	Hughs, Burwell heirs	Davidson	640	2722	20 Jul 1796	2930		88	450	Waters of Hurricane & Harts Spring Cr.	yes
Donelson, Stockley	2259	Myres, Jacob	Davidson	640	2723	20 Jul 1796	1960		88	450	On waters of Stones River	yes

Claimant:	File #:	Assignee:	County:	Acres:	Grant:	Grant Date:	Entry:	Entry Date:	Bk:	Pg:	Location by Stream Name:	Military:
Donelson, Stockley	226		Eastern District	640	181	12 Jun 1794	953		82	177	On N side of Clinch River &c	
Donelson, Stockley	2260	King, Edward	Davidson	640	2724	20 Jul 1796	444		88	451	On waters of Harts Spring Branch	yes
Donelson, Stockley	2261	Donelson, Jesse	Davidson	640	2725	20 Jul 1796	444		88	451	On waters of Stones River	yes
Donelson, Stockley	2262	Hay, Abraham	Davidson	640	2726	20 Jul 1796	448		88	451	On waters of Stones River	yes
Donelson, Stockley	2263	Stringer, Lineage	Davidson	640	2727	20 Jul 1796	3185		88	452	On waters of Stones River	yes
Donelson, Stockley	2264	Smith, Thomas	Davidson	465	2728	20 Jul 1796	1379		88	452	On waters of Leepers Fork	yes
Donelson, Stockley	227		Eastern District	1000	182	12 Jun 1794			82	177	ON Sycamore Creek	
Donelson, Stockley	228		Eastern District	200	183	12 Jun 1794			82	177	Inc the head of Fourth Creek	
Donelson, Stockley	230		Eastern District	300	135	12 Jun 1794	715	14 Feb 1782	82	178	On waters of Fourth Creek	
Donelson, Stockley	231		Eastern District	200	186	12 Jun 1794	794	23 Dec 1778	82	178	On the New road leading to Ky	
Donelson, Stockley	233		Eastern District	640	188	12 Jun 1794			82	179	On N side of Wallings Ridge &c	
Donelson, Stockley	234		Eastern District	250	189	12 Jun 1794	77		82	179	On both sides the Beaverdam	
Donelson, Stockley	236		Eastern District	1000	191	12 Jun 1794			82	180	N/S Wallens ridge head Russells Cr	
Donelson, Stockley	237		Eastern District	350	192	12 Jun 1794	59		82	180	On head of West Fork of Turkey Cr	
Donelson, Stockley	2379	Pratt, James	Davidson	274	3105	14 Sep 1797	4278		90	404	On the Falling Creek	yes
Donelson, Stockley	238		Eastern District	300	193	12 Jun 1794	89	21 Oct 1783	82	181	W Fork of Third Creek	
Donelson, Stockley	2380	McCumber, Humphrey	Davidson	1000	3106	14 Sep 1797	4254		90	405	On the Falling Creek	yes
Donelson, Stockley	2381	Winday, Absolam	Davidson	365	3109	14 Sep 1797	4256		90	406	On a branch of Stones River	yes
Donelson, Stockley	251		Eastern District	100	204	6 Jan 1795			83	173	Between the rivers Holston & Tennessee	
Donelson, Stockley	251		Green	1000	208	20 Sep 1787			65	433	On N side of Tennessee River &c	
Donelson, Stockley	255		Eastern District	600	208	6 Jan 1795	931	28 Nov 1778	83	175	Clinch Mountain on waters of Flat Creek	
Donelson, Stockley	258		Green	400	215	20 Sep 1787	644	28 Nov 1778	65	436	Small valley on S Side of Cumberland Valley	
Donelson, Stockley	263		Green	1000	220	20 Sep 1787	1072	25 Jun 1784	65	438	N/S Tennessee Riv in Cumberland Valley	
Donelson, Stockley	265		Green	600	222	20 Sep 1787	200	21 Feb 1780	65	439	N/S Tennessee Riv in Cumberland valley	
Donelson, Stockley	266		Green	600	223	20 Sep 1787	2987	22 Jul 1785	65	439	Lying on N side of Tennessee River &c	
Donelson, Stockley	27		Hawkins	400	59	7 Apr 1790			71	284	On N side of Holston River	
Donelson, Stockley	277		Eastern District	1000	212	4 Jan 1795			84	44	N side of Clinch River on Cole Creek	
Donelson, Stockley	278		Eastern District	1000	213	4 Jan 1795	2469	25 May 1784	84	45	In Powells Valley	
Donelson, Stockley	28		Hawkins	250	60	7 Apr 1790	301	10 Mar 1780	71	284	On S side of Holston River	
Donelson, Stockley	28		Sullivan	400	39	23 Oct 1782	689	22 Sep 1780	43	256	On Robertsons Creek	
Donelson, Stockley	283	Dugan, Jesse	Middle District	640	2383	12 Jul 1794			81	600	On waters of Cumberland River	yes
Donelson, Stockley	289		Middle District	5000	245	12 Jun 1794			82 [?]	182	On Hardens Creek	
Donelson, Stockley	295		Eastern District	50000	647	1 Jan 1795			84	152	Bet Holston, Tennessee, & Clinch Rivs.	
Donelson, Stockley	327		Eastern District	200	267	7 Mar 1796	628	25 Nov 1778	88	200	On S side of Beaverdam Creek	
Donelson, Stockley	328		Eastern District	200	268	7 Mar 1796	834	1780	88	200	On a branch of Big Creek	
Donelson, Stockley	342		Eastern District	9600	260	7 Mar 1796		12 warrants	88	300	On N side of Holston River	
Donelson, Stockley	343		Eastern District	2000	261	7 Mar 1796	2425	1784	88	301	On waters of Holston River	
Donelson, Stockley	344		Hawkins	600	338	8 Mar 1793	6	8 Feb 1780	78	478	Beg at the mouth of Flat Creek	
Donelson, Stockley	345		Hawkins	3000	339	8 Mar 1793	997	25 Jun 1784	78	479	On S side of Clinch River	
Donelson, Stockley	361		Eastern District	19000	278	20 Jul 1796	1932 &c	4 warrants, 1783	88	436	On N side of Tennessee River	
Donelson, Stockley	368		Eastern District	20000	283	20 Jul 1795			88	531	On N side Tennessee River	
Donelson, Stockley	369		Eastern District	5000	220	28 Aug 1795	4		89	78	Upon Crow Creek	
Donelson, Stockley	370		Eastern District	5000	221	28 Aug 1795	5 warrants	1784	89	79	Upon Crow Creek, beg at a poplar	
Donelson, Stockley	371		Eastern District	5000	222	28 Aug 1795	2454	25 May 1784	89	79	Upon Crow Creek; beg at a black —	
Donelson, Stockley	372		Eastern District	5000	223	28 Aug 1795	1685	16 Apr 1784	89	79	Upon Crow Creek beg at a walnut	

Earliest Tennessee Land Records

Claimant:	File #:	Assignee:	County:	Acres:	Grant:	Grant Date:	Entry:	Entry Date:	Bk:	Pg:	Location by Stream Name:	Military:
Donelson, Stockley	373		Eastern District	5000	224	28 Aug 1795	1831	23 Apr 1784	89	80	On Crow Creek beg at a black walnut	
Donelson, Stockley	377		Eastern District	5000	228	27 Aug 1795	1699	16 Apr 1784	89	96	Upon Crow Creek, beg at a white oak	
Donelson, Stockley	378		Eastern District	5000	229	27 Aug 1795	1668	16 Apr 1784	89	97	On CrowCreek, beg at a sugar tree	
Donelson, Stockley	379		Eastern District	5000	230	27 Aug 1795	1680	16 Apr 1784	89	97	Waters Crow Creek being Survey #3	
Donelson, Stockley	380		Eastern District	5000	231	27 Aug 1795	1687	16 Apr 1784	89	97	Upon Crow Creek beg at a mulberry	
Donelson, Stockley	381		Eastern District	5000	232	27 Aug 1795	1227	25 Jun 1784	89	98	Upon Crow Creek, beg at a black oak	
Donelson, Stockley	382		Eastern District	5000	233	27 Aug 1795		1 May 1784	89	98	Upon waters of Crow Creek &c	
Donelson, Stockley	383		Eastern District	5000	234	27 Aug 1795	790	24 Jun 1784	89	98	Upon Crow Creek, beg at a hickory	
Donelson, Stockley	384		Eastern District	5000	235	27 Aug 1795	1675	Apr 1784	89	99	Upon Crow Creek, beg at 2 poplars	
Donelson, Stockley	385		Eastern District	5000	236	27 Jun 1795	1931	27 Apr 1784	89	99	Upon Crow Creek	
Donelson, Stockley	386		Eastern District	5000	237	27 Aug 1795	2566	27 May 1784	89	100	Waters of Crow Creek, beg at 2 poplars	
Donelson, Stockley	387		Eastern District	5000	238	27 Aug 1795			89	100	Upon Crow Creek, beg at a sweet gum	
Donelson, Stockley	434		Eastern District	300	285				91	121	Both sides of Honeycutts Warpath	
Donelson, Stockley	464	Mardera, James heirs	Tennessee	640	2576	7 Mar 1796	2939	30 Sep 1785	88	314	On branch of Sulphur Fork	
Donelson, Stockley	470		Middle District	5000	297	22 Feb 1795	1687	16 Apr 1784	84	291	About 2 miles above old Indian War Road	
Donelson, Stockley	476	Roberts, John heirs	Tennessee	640	2721	20 Jul 1796	2814	30 Sep 1785	88	449	On waters of Sulphur Fork	
Donelson, Stockley	490		Hawkins	5000	362	29 Jul 1793	1674	12 Apr 1789	80	267	In Powell's Valley on Big Cove Creek	
Donelson, Stockley	491	Jones, Peter	Sumner	640	1653	20 May 1793	1834		81	42	On E side of Stones River	yes
Donelson, Stockley	496		Tennessee	640	2808	12 Jan 1797			90	25	S side of Cumberland River	
Donelson, Stockley	497		Tennessee	640	2809	12 Jan 1797			90	26	S side of Cumberland River	
Donelson, Stockley	498		Tennessee	1000	2810	12 Jan 1797			90	26	On Bedengoes [sic] Fork of Sycamore	
Donelson, Stockley	499		Tennessee	640	2811	12 Jan 1797			90	26	S side of Cumberland River	
Donelson, Stockley	5		Eastern District	640	5	11 Jul 1788			67	341	On both sides of Clinch River &c	
Donelson, Stockley	500		Tennessee	640	2812	12 Jan 1797			90	27	On waters of Red River	
Donelson, Stockley	501		Tennessee	640	2813	12 Jan 1797			90	27	On the waters of Spring Creek	
Donelson, Stockley	502		Tennessee	640	2815	12 Jan 1797			90	28	On head branches of Stergions Creek	
Donelson, Stockley	503		Tennessee	640	2816	12 Jan 1797			90	29	On waters of Red River	
Donelson, Stockley	504		Tennessee	640	2817	12 Jan 1797			90	29	On S side of Cumberland River	
Donelson, Stockley	505		Tennessee	640	2818	12 Jan 1797			90	30	Waters of Elk Fork of Red River	
Donelson, Stockley	506		Tennessee	640	2819	12 Jan 1797			90	30	On waters of Red River	
Donelson, Stockley	507		Tennessee	640	2820	12 Jan 1797			90	31	On waters of Red River	
Donelson, Stockley	508		Middle District	60000	304	7 Mar 1796	13 warrants		88	303	On S side of Cumberland River	
Donelson, Stockley	508		Tennessee	640	2821	12 Jan 1797			90	31	On waters of Red River &c	
Donelson, Stockley	509		Tennessee	640	2822	12 Jan 1797			90	32	On waters of Red River	
Donelson, Stockley	510		Tennessee	640	2823	12 Jan 1797			90	32	On waters of Red River	
Donelson, Stockley	511		Hawkins	600	384	29 Jul 1793	932	25 Jun 1784	80	273	N side of Holston incl the fks of Flat Cr	
Donelson, Stockley	511		Tennessee	640	2824	12 Jan 1797			90	33	On waters of Red River	
Donelson, Stockley	514		Tennessee	1000	2825	12 Jan 1797			90	33	Both sides Pond Branch of Davis Creek	
Donelson, Stockley	515		Tennessee	640	2826	12 Jan 1797			90	34	On waters of Red River	
Donelson, Stockley	516		Tennessee	640	2827	12 Jan 1797			90	34	S side of Cumberland River	
Donelson, Stockley	517		Tennessee	640	2828	12 Jan 1797			90	35	Both sides of Stergion Creek	
Donelson, Stockley	518		Tennessee	640	2029	12 Jan 1797			90	35	On waters of Red River	
Donelson, Stockley	519		Tennessee	640	2830	12 Jan 1797			90	36	S side of Cumberland River	
Donelson, Stockley	520		Tennessee	640	2831	12 Jan 1797			90	36	On waters of Red River	
Donelson, Stockley	521		Tennessee	640	2833	12 Jan 1797			90	37	On Sulphur Fork of Red River	

Claimant:	File #:	Assignee:	County:	Acres:	Grant:	Grant Date:	Entry:	Entry Date:	Bk:	Pg:	Location by Stream Name:	Military:
Donelson, Stockley	522		Hawkins	1000	395	29 Jul 1793	2496	25 May 1784	80	276	S side of Clinch River &c	
Donelson, Stockley	522		Tennessee	640	2833	12 Jan 1797			90	37	On Spring Creek a branch of Red River	
Donelson, Stockley	523		Tennessee	640	2834	12 Jan 1797			90	38	S side of Cumberland River	
Donelson, Stockley	524		Middle District	10240	336	8 Jan 1797	593,-1644,-	1784	90	210	On West Fk of Obeys River &c	
Donelson, Stockley	524		Hawkins	640	397	29 Jul 1793	2426	25 May 1784	80	276	On N side of Clinch & Tennessee River	
Donelson, Stockley	524		Tennessee	640	2835	12 Jan 1797			90	38	Waters of Red River	
Donelson, Stockley	525		Tennessee	640	2836	12 Jan 1797			90	39	On waters of Red River	
Donelson, Stockley	526		Tennessee	640	2837	12 Jan 1797			90	39	S side of Cumberland River	
Donelson, Stockley	527		Tennessee	640	2838	12 Jan 1797			90	40	On waters of Red River	
Donelson, Stockley	544		Middle District	950 (195	343	8 Jul 1797		27 Oct 1783	90	341	On a large creek	
Donelson, Stockley	545		Middle District	1500	344	8 Jun 1797	1127	24 Jun 1784	90	341	On a large creek	
Donelson, Stockley	546		Middle District	5000	345	8 Jun 1797	1070		90	341	On a large creek &c	
Donelson, Stockley	547		Middle District	5000	346	8 Jun 1797	3562	12 Jan 1785	90	346	On a large creek &c	
Donelson, Stockley	548		Middle District	1500	347	8 Jun 1797	2093	6 May 1784	90	342	On a creek	
Donelson, Stockley	549		Middle District	2500	348	8 Jun 1797	2563	25 May 1784	90	342	On a large creek	
Donelson, Stockley	550		Middle District	1000	349	8 Jun 1797	1028	29 Oct 1783	90	343	On a large creek	
Donelson, Stockley	551		Middle District	640	350	8 June 1797	1061	30 Oct 1783	90	343	On a large creek	
Donelson, Stockley	552		Middle District	640	351	8 Jun 1797	1060	25 Jun 1784	90	343	On a large creek &c	
Donelson, Stockley	553		Middle District	500	352	8 Jun 1797	935	25 Oct 1784	90	344	On a large creek	
Donelson, Stockley	554		Middle District	400	353	8 Jun 1797	1485	31 Jul 1787	90	344	On a large creek	
Donelson, Stockley	574		Hawkins	640	448	29 Jul 1793			80	289	N side of Holston River &c	
Donelson, Stockley	58		Hawkins	74.75	43	18 May 1789	367	28 Mar 1780	72	253	On N side of Holson River &c	
Donelson, Stockley	59		Hawkins	300	44	18 May 1789	1687	9 Oct 1779	72	254	On S side of Clinch River	
Donelson, Stockley	594	Magley, Robt heirs	Tennessee	640	3066	19 Jul 1797	2811		90	376	N side of Cumberland River	
Donelson, Stockley	6		Eastern District	640	6	11 Jul 1788		24 Mar 1780	67	341	On waters of Bull Run	
Donelson, Stockley	601		Hawkins	1500	475	29 Jul 1793	2114, 474		80	295	N side of Clinch River &c	
Donelson, Stockley	618		Hawkins	2000	314	15 Jul 1793	2474		80	300	On waters of Clinch on Bull Run	
Donelson, Stockley	625		Hawkins	750	322	15 Jul 1793		10 Mar 1780	80	302	Beg on the S side of Bull Run	
Donelson, Stockley	674	Morris, Richard	Hawkins	250	2383	12 Jul 1794			81	600	In Hind's Valley	
Donelson, Stockley	676	Robertson, Hooker	Hawkins	300	2386	12 Jul 1794	3548		81	601	On S side of Clinch River	
Donelson, Stockley	694		Hawkins	5000	496	16 Dec 1793	1673	14 Feb 1784	82	99	S/S of Clinch Riv on both sides Bull Run	
Donelson, Stockley	7		Eastern District	500	7	11 Jul 1788	1182	31 Oct 1783	67	342	On Beaverdam Cr & Grassy Fork	
Donelson, Stockley	726		Hawkins	640	546	12 Jun 1794	384	10 Sep 1778	82	169	In a valley &c	
Donelson, Stockley	731		Hawkins	100	551	12 Jun 1794	1893	6 Oct 1779	82	171	On the S side of Clinch River &c	
Donelson, Stockley	736		Hawkins	640	556	12 Jun 1794	1071	8 Jan 1779	82	173	On a branch of Flat Creek &c	
Donelson, Stockley	74		Hawkins	5000	74	17 Jun 1790			73	96	On Poplar Creek	
Donelson, Stockley	741		Hawkins	300	560	12 Jun 1794	109	8 Feb 1780	82	175	On Holston River &c	
Donelson, Stockley	750		Green	1000	569	11 Jul 1788	359	24 Mar 1780	68	215	On N side of Tennessee River	
Donelson, Stockley	751		Green	1000	570	11 Jul 1788	2458	5 Jan 1785	68	215	On N side of Clinch River	
Donelson, Stockley	752		Green	640	571	11 Jul 1788			68	216	On N side of Clinch River	
Donelson, Stockley	753		Green	640	572	11 Jul 1788			68	216	On N side of Tennessee River &c	
Donelson, Stockley	762		Green	500	581	11 Jul 1788	583	8 Feb 1780	68	219	On N side of Tennessee River	
Donelson, Stockley	770		Green	2000	575	23 Aug 1788	1717	8 May 1787	68	251	N/S Tennessee Riv in Cumberland Valley	
Donelson, Stockley	78		Eastern District	15000	103	26 Dec 1791			75	178	On S side of French Broad River	
Donelson, Stockley	781		Hawkins	300	621	12 Jul 1794	561	29 Oct 1778	82	220	On S side of Clinch River on Hinds Valley &c	

Claimant:	File #:	Assignee:	County:	Acres:	Grant:	Entry:	Grant Date:	Entry Date:	Bk:	Pg:	Location by Stream Name:	Military:
Donelson, Stockley	786		Green	400	591	1608	23 Aug 1788	13 Sep 1779	68	258	Near the end of Clinch Mountains	
Donelson, Stockley	79		Eastern District	5000	104		26 Dec 1791		75	179	On little Pigeon River	
Donelson, Stockley	8		Eastern District	1000	8		11 Jul 1788		67	342	Bluff Cr Donelsons & Hutchings line	
Donelson, Stockley	8		Sullivan	300	19	703	23 Oct 1782	27 Oct 1780	43	246	On S side of Holstons River &c	
Donelson, Stockley	845		Hawkins	3150 (21	670	1662	21 Feb 1795	16 Apr 1784	83	431	N side of Clinch River &c	
Donelson, Stockley	85		Eastern District	50	Service						Concerning settlement of estate	
Donelson, Stockley	865		Eastern District	400	641		4 Jan 1795		84	47	On N side of Holston River	
Donelson, Stockley	9		Hawkins	2300	5		23 Aug 1788		67	430	On N side of Tenesee [sic] River &c	
Donelson, Stockley	914		Hawkins	200	723	629	7 Mar 1796	25 Nov 1779	88	202	In Hines Valley	
Donelson, Stockley	918		Hawkins	640	727		7 Mar 1796		88	204	On Main Fork of Flat Creek	
Donelson, Stockley	92		Eastern District	640	81	1856 [?]	17 Nov 1790	9 Oct 1779	76	170	On Poplar Creek	
Donelson, Stockley	93		Eastern District	640	82	435	17 Nov 1790	19 Apr 1780	76	170	On Poplar Creek	
Donelson, Stockley	941		Hawkins	640	302	461	7 Mar 1796	24 Apr 1780	88	302	On Main Fork of Flat Creek	
Donelson, Stockley	943	Hodgin, Holder heirs	Davidson	640	959	1830	18 May 1789		63	326	On S side of Cumberland River	yes
Donelson, Stockley	959	Muss, John heirs	Davidson	640	976		18 May 1789		63	331	On a fork of Smiths Creek	
Donelson, Stockley	960	Tuckers, William hrs	Davidson	640	977		18 May 1789		63	331	On both sides of N Fork of Smiths Creek	yes
Donelson, Stockley	961	Crawley, William	Davidson	640	978		18 May 1789		63	331	On S side of Cumberland River	yes
Donelson, Stockley	963	Ingrim, George hrs	Davidson	640	980		18 May 1789		63	332	On both sides of a fork of Smith's Fork	yes
Donelson, Stockley	964	Hammett, John	Davidson	640	981		18 May 1789		63	332	On second creek above Bradleys Lick	yes
Donelson, Stockley	965	Castendree, Metre	Davidson	640	982		18 May 1789		63	332	On 2nd creek above Bradleys Lick	yes
Donelson, Stockley	965		Hawkins	5000	735	795	20 Jul 1796	29 Oct 1783	88	433	On N side of Great Tennessee River	
Donelson, Stockley	967	Gray, Peter heirs	Davidson	640	984		18 May 1789		63	333	On both sides of Smiths Fork	yes
Donelson, Stockley	968	Collins, George heirs	Davidson	640	985		18 May 1789		63	333	On both sides N Fork of Smiths Fork	yes
Donelson, Stockley	989		Green	250	1216		29 Jul 1793		76	483	On a branch of S side of Holston River	
Donelson, Stockley, Ass	350		Eastern District	100	281		6 Jun 1796		88	379	In the Sinking Cave Valley	
Donelson, Stockley, Ass	879		Hawkins	600	139		4 Feb 1795		84	141	On both sides of great wagon road	
Donelson, Stockley, Ass	880		Hawkins	200	140		4 Feb 1795	Martin Armstrong	84	141	Both sides of Peters Spring Branch	
Donelson, Stockley, Ass	881		Hawkins	200	141		4 Feb 1795	Martin Armstrong	84	142	Inc where Jonathan Bird now lives	
Donelson, Stockley, Ass	886		Hawkins	500	146		1 Jan 1795	Martin Armstrong	84	144	On Beaverdam Creek	
Donelson, Stockley, Ass.	017		not given	640		3420		21 Apr 1786			Beg at a stake	
Donelson, Stockley, Ass.	023		Tennessee	640	5		12 Jun 1794	31 Jan 1786	62	310	S side of Cumberland River	
Donelson, Stockley, Ass.	1		Sumner	640			7 Mar 1794				Including Drake's Lick	
Donelson, Stockley, Ass.	1088	Durham, Jachariah hrs	Sumner	1000	2579		21 Jul 1796		88	316	On Little Lick Creek	yes
Donelson, Stockley, Ass.	1253		Sumner	640	2731		6 Jun 1796		90	184	Both sides of Chimauga [sic] path	yes
Donelson, Stockley, Ass.	1663		Green	60	282		8 Apr 1794		88	379	On N side of French Broad River	
Donelson, Stockley, Ass.	201		Eastern District	640	179	1011	12 Jun 1794	4 Jan 1779	81	559	On N side of Holston River	
Donelson, Stockley, Ass.	224		Eastern District	200	1		12 Jul 1794		82	176	On W side of Coxes Creek	
Donelson, Stockley, Ass.	239		Eastern District	400	186		17 Jul 1794		82	227	On N side of Holston River	
Donelson, Stockley, Ass.	686		Hawkins	300					81	604	Beg at a stake	
Donelson, Stockley, Ass.	740		Sullivan	300	683		8 Dec 1795	16 Feb 1782	88	270	On both sides of Beaver Creek	
Donelson, Stockley, Ass.	960		Hawkins	200	283		6 Jun 1796		88	379	On N side of Clinch River	
Donelson, Stokeley	085	Walker, Mary estate	Green	1000	210						On N side of Tennessee River &c	
Donelson, Stokeley	253		Green	1000	210		20 Sep 1787		65	434	On N side of Tennessee River &c	
Donelson, Stokeley	255		Green	1000	212		20 Sep 1787		65	434	On N side of Tennessee River &c	
Donelson, Stokeley	259		Green	200	216	699	20 Sep 1787	20 Sep 1780	65	436	Cumberland Valley on W Fork of Richland Cr	

Claimant:	File #:	Assignee:	County:	Acres:	Grant:	Grant Date:	Entry:	Entry Date:	Bk:	Pg:	Location by Stream Name:	Military:
Donelson, Stokeley	262		Green	400	219	20 Sep 1787	984		65	437	In a small valley &c	
Donelson, Stokeley	437		Sullivan	385	316	10 Nov 1784		2 Jun 1779	69	182	On N side of Holstein River	
Donelson, W.	540	Smart, Thos.	Sumner	640	1740 (a)	20 May 1793	3577	8 Aug 1795	81	64	On both sides of Cedar Lick Creek	yes
Donelson, William	1163		Davidson	640	140	17 Apr 1786	286	11 Feb 1784	66	184	On a branch of Big Harpeth &c	
Donelson, William	1239		Davidson	640	204	10 Jul 1788	620	13 Nov 1784	66	413	In fks betw. Cumberland & Stones River	
Donelson, William	217		Green	250	174	20 Sep 1787	2766	22 Dec 1783	65	421	On Little Sinking Creek	
Donelson, Wood & McCoy	192	Clark, Abraham heirs	Eastern District	640	2380	8 Apr 1794			81	439	Lying bet First & Second creeks	
Donelson,S.& Tho.Hutchings	9		Eastern District	500	9	11 Jul 1788			67	342	On NW side of Clinch River	
Donnahoe, Bartholomew	444		Hawkins	100	322	24 Jun 1793	459	24 Apr 1780	80	193	On creek beg at a Black oak	
Donnal [?], James	407		Middle District	1280	346	17 Dec 1794	2043	3 May 1784	84	227	On S side of Elk River	
Donnelly, James	354	Howard, Isaac	Davidson	274	339	4 Sep 1787	550		63	126	On clear Branch	yes
Donoho, Thomas	065	Blake, John	Sumner	1000	1873	10 Apr 1797				419	S branches of Maney Fork Creek	yes
Donoho, Thomas	1229	Hicks, Reubin	Sumner	1000	2500	12 Nov 1795	1651	1 Mar 1786	89	419	On Second Creek	yes
Donoho, Thomas	87		Davidson	4800	73	14 Mar 1786	194		63	30	N side of Cumberland River	yes
Donohoe, John, Ass	321		Sumner	640	314	17 Nov 1790	754	6 Aug 1784	76	186	N side of Cumberland River	
Donohoe, John, Ass	563	Barkley, Wm. Heirs	Sumner	640	1786	20 May 1793	2987	9 Jun 1792	81	75	Beg white oak in Spencers line	yes
Donohoe, Thomas	066		Sumner	1000	1873	10 Apr 1797					S branches of Many Fork Creek	yes
Donohoe, William	770	Saunders, James	Davidson	640	743	11 Jul 1788	1419		63	261	On Second Creek	yes
Donohoo, Bartholomew	34		Hawkins	100	66	7 Apr 1790	2014	24 Oct 1779	71	286	On S side of Holeson River &c	
Donthin, Elijah	219		Hawkins	640	206	26 Dec 1791	2132	5 Nov 1779	77	315	On Youngs Creek	
Donwoodly, Samuel	780		Green	200	584	23 Aug 1788	72	1 Nov 1786	68	255	On S side of Little Chucky	
Dore, Josiah	386	Thomas, Richard	Sumner	640	1570	4 Feb 1793	2313	30 Nov 1785	79	294	On E fork of Stones River	yes
Dorman, West	233	Reed, Jesse	Sumner	640	1138	26 Nov 1789	3427	12 Mar 1788	74	148	On W side of Caney Fork River	yes
Dorris, Joseph	031	Coryer, Stephen	Robertson	357	3784	4 Feb 1796					On Sulphur Fk of Red River	
Dosher, Christopher	377	Blount, Jno.G. & Thos.	Tennessee	640	2329	20 May 1793	2508	30 Sep 1785	81	197	On S side of Cumberland River	yes
Dotson, Elijah	170		Green	200	640	23 Aug 1788	1543	25 Jun 1784	64	355	N/S Holston opposite Chimney Rock	
Dotson, William	776		Hawkins	345	616	12 Jul 1794			82	218	Beg at a Post oak near a rock	
Dotson, William	860		Washington	100	867	26 Nov 1789	845	30 Dec 1778	71	384	On N Fork of Sinking Creek	
Dotson, William	899		Washington	75	876	17 Nov 1790	2831	7 Apr 1781	76	136	Joining lines w/&c	
Dotson, William	956		Washington	100	933	17 Nov 1790	848	30 Dec 1779	76	155	N side of Sinking Creek &c	
Doty, James	2137	Mulherrin, James	Davidson	640	2412	7 Jan 1794	3306		81	403	On Stones River	yes
Doud, Cornelius	986	McDonald, Colin	Sumner	640	2451	22 Feb 1795			84	322	On Main Fork of Obeys River	yes
Doud, Cornelius, Ass	986	McDonald, Colin hrs	Sumner	986	2451	22 Feb 1795			84	322	On Main Fork of Obeys River	yes
Dougan, James	127		Western District	3000	127	10 Jul 1788	598	27 Oct 1783	67	329	On S side of Obion River &c	
Dougan, John	62		Western District	2165	62	10 Jul 1788	686	28 Oct 1783	67	304	On both sides of the Obion River &c	
Dougherty, George	358		Green	640	360	20 Sep 1787	26	21 Oct 1783	65	475	A large poplar near a large spring	
Dougherty, George	305		Green	300	307	20 Sep 1787	25	13 Aug 1785	65	461	E a Post oak on S/S of the creek	
Dougherty, George	520		Green	100	522	20 Sep 1787	1232	7 Nov 1783	65	529	On N side of Nolichuckey River	
Dougherty, George	98		Eastern District	3000	98	10 Jul 1788	98	30 Oct 1783	67	319	On Reelfoot River &c	
Dougherty, Joseph	1278		Davidson	640	243	10 Jul 1788	485	10 Jun 1784	66	422	On S side of Cumberland River	
Doughlass, Jonathan	456		Sullivan	200	335	10 Nov 1784			69	189	In Carters Valley	
Douglas, Benjamin	1031	Sheppard, John	Sumner	640	2568	8 Mar 1796	2910	15 Aug 1790	88	189	On Obeys River	yes
Douglas, David	1616	Farmer, John	Davidson	640	1344	10 Dec 1790	2512		74	380	On waters of Bartons Creek	yes
Douglas, Ed. & Isaac Bledsoe	1014		Sumner	640	2583	17 Dec 1794			86	382	Beg at a white oak	
Douglas, Ed. & Wm. Montg.	1228	Crabtree, James	Sumner	480	176	27 Aug 1795		14 Apr 1792	89	413	On waters of Drakes Creek	yes

Claimant:	File #:	Assignee:	County:	Acres:	Grant:	Grant Date:	Entry:	Entry Date:	Bk:	Pg:	Location by Stream Name:	Military:
Douglas, Edw.	043		Green	2300	174	27 Aug 1795	527	27 Oct 1783	89	412	N side of Tennessee River	yes
Douglas, Edward	1226	Ellis, Underhill	Sumner	400	856	17 Jan 1789	97		63	299	On N side of Cumberland River	yes
Douglas, Edward	851	Seymore, Wm.	Davidson	274	92	17 Apr 1786	222	30 Jan 1784	66	172	Waters of W Fk of Station Camp Creek	
Douglas, Elmore	1115		Davidson	640	139	17 Apr 1786	215	30 Jan 1784	66	184	On Station Camp Creek	
Douglas, Elmore	1162		Davidson	640	260	10 Jul 1788	223	30 Jan 1784	66	428	On the middle fork of Station Camp	
Douglas, Ezekial	1295		Davidson	640	451	27 Nov 1793	352	11 Mar 1784	81	498	On S side of Cumberland Camp	
Douglas, James	2174	Hays, John	Sumner	274			1263	16 Jul 1786			E waters E fk Station Camp Creek	yes
Douglas, John	069		Green	200	2322	28 Feb 1780					On S side of Holston River	
Douglas, Jonathan	046		Green	250	735	11 Jul 1788	940	15 Jun 1787			On S side of Holston River	
Douglas, Wm.	041	Armstrong, M.	Sumner	24	189	27 Aug 1795					Adjoining land of Wm. Cage	
Douglass, Benjamin	1217	Ross, John	Green	200	685	11 Jul 1788	1539	17 Mar 1784	89	408	Valley-Clinch Mn & Cooper Ridge-War Cr	
Douglass, Edward	644	Burton, Jacob	Davidson	182			3708	23 Mar 1790	66	455	N side Cumberland River	yes
Douglass, Edward	067	Harris, Coburn heirs	Sumner	228	1071	26 Nov 1789	1696		74	115	Waters of West Fork of Station Camp Creek	
Douglass, Edward	1514	Miller, Jacob hr of Jas.	Davidson	640	1699	20 May 1793	884	25 Jan 1791	81	53	On N side of Cumberland River	yes
Douglass, Edward	520	Mills, Jacob	Davidson	640	517	15 Sep 1787			63	186	On waters of Station Camp Creek	yes
Douglass, Edward	545	Blackamore, Geo.	Sumner	400	153	17 Dec 1795		20 Nov 1792	84	331	W of Cumberland Mountain	yes
Douglass, Elmore	997		Sumner	320			743	14 Jun 1785			On Winchesters Fork	yes
Douglass, Elmore	068		Davidson	320	102	10 Nov 1790			74	390	On Winchester Fork	
Douglass, James	1632		Sumner	274	1073	26 Nov 1789			74	116	E waters of E Fork of Station Camp	
Douglass, James	1516	Armstrong, M.	Sumner	236	66	18 May 1789			71	224	On the S side of Cumberland River	
Douglass, John	191	Guttery, Henry	Sumner	640	2512	20 Nov 1795	1425	23 Nov 1789	88	283	Beg at a buckeye	yes
Douglass, John	1049	Armstrong, M.	Davidson	640	552	15 Sep 1787	566		63	198	On both sides E Fk of Yellow Creek	yes
Douglass, John	580		Green	250	820	18 Aug 1789			71	37	On waters of French Broad River	
Douglass, Jonathan	819		Green	200	1250	12 Jul 1794			81	578	ON S side of Holston River	
Douglass, Jonathan	1487		Sullivan	456	377	9 Aug 1787	1891	8 Feb 1780	61	396	On the N side of Holston River	
Douglass, Jonathan	238		Sullivan	200	335	10 Nov 1784			69	189	In Carters Valley	
Douglass, Jonathan	456		Hawkins	500	351	29 Jul 1793	1268	8 Mar 1779	80	263	On Brush Creek	
Douglass, Jonathan	479		Hawkins	400	461	29 Jul 1793	1891		80	292	N side of Holston River &c	
Douglass, Jonathan	587		Green	250	735	11 Jul 1788	2841	7 Nov 1787	66	471	On the S side of Holston River	
Douglass, Jonathan	694		Sullivan	450	83	23 Oct 1782	304	10 Mar 1780	43	278	On N side of Holston River	
Douglass, Jonathan	72		Sullivan	200	88	23 Oct 1782	1073	8 Jan 1779	43	280	Carters Valley &c	
Douglass, Reubin	77	Howell, John heirs	Davidson	640	495	15 Sep 1787	207		63	179	On waters of Station Camp Creek	yes
Douglass, Robert	523		Davidson	2560	89	14 Mar 1786	631		63	36	On Wolf Creek	yes
Douglass, Wm.	103	Armstrong, M.	Sumner	50	190	27 Aug 1795			89	408	Adjoining land of Wm. Cage &c	
Douglass, Wm.	1218	Abbott, Wadington hrs	Sumner	640	1748	29 Aug 1793	1955	22 Dec 1792	81	66	On S side of Cumberland River	yes
Douglass, Wm.	545	Brewer, Henry	Sumner	360	1751	29 Aug 1793	199		81	67	On W Fks of Bartons Creek	yes
Dove, William	547	Craddock, John	Davidson	264	1083	26 Nov 1789	3202		74	122	On Dry Fork of W Fork of Red River	yes
Dowd, Cornelius	1526	McDonald, Colin hrs	Middle District	640			3811					
Dowde, John	036	Williams, Daniel	Davidson	640	1936	20 May 1793	932		81	109	On SW side of Big Harpeth	yes
Dowden, Samuel	1997	Nelson, Robert	Davidson	640	1448	20 Dec 1791	1286		77	363	E side of Harpeth &c	yes
Dowell, James	1732	Hall, David	Sumner	274			598	20 Aug 1785			N side of Cumberland River	yes
Dowell, James	082	Murphey, Archibald	Davidson	274	621	15 Sep 1787	197		63	221	On waters of Drakes Creek	yes
Downdy, Bolin [?]	648	Sheppard, John	Sumner	640	2567	8 Mar 1796	2644	15 Aug 1792	88	189	On waters of Obeys River	yes
Downing, George	1030	Wycoff, William	not given	274			1460	8 Dec 1785			E Fork of N Cross Creek	yes

Claimant:	File #:	Assignee:	County:	Acres:	Grant:	Grant Date:	Entry:	Entry Date:	Bk:	Pg:	Location by Stream Name:	Military:
Downs, Benjamin	809		Sullivan	26	782 (752)	17 Nov 1797	538	23 Apr 1796	94	152	N side of Holston River	
Downs, William	746		Sullivan	100	685	9 Dec 1795	1869	7 Oct 1779	89	394	On waters of Muddy Creek	
Dozers, James	719	Winchester, David	Sumner	640	2101	20 May 1793	3650	7 Jun 1792	81	149	Beg at 2 Cedar trees &c	yes
Drake, Benjamin	1190		Davidson	640	167	17 Apr 1786	64	6 Jan 1784	66	190	N/S Cumberland River & Whites Cr	
Drake, Benjamin	1375		Davidson	320	58	8 Oct 1787	165	23 Jan 1784	68	145	On N side of Cumberland River	
Drake, Benjamin	1515	Cobb, Shadrack hrs	Davidson	640	1072	26 Nov 1789	1922		74	115	On N side of Cumberland River	yes
Drake, Benjamin, Sr.	1482	Robertson, Charles	Davidson	640	286	26 Nov 1789	228	31 Jan 1784	73	257	On the E waters of Whites Creek	
Drake, Cornelius	041		Davidson	640			404	11 Sep 1784			On waters of Little Harpeth	
Drake, Isaac	1253		Davidson	640	218	10 Jul 1788	128	15 Jan 1784	66	416	On waters of Hays Creek	
Drake, Isaac	1456		Davidson	1000	57	18 May 1789			71	221	On Heatons Lick Branch	
Drake, Jno.	1114		Davidson	640	91	17 Apr 1786	63	6 Jan 1784	66	172	N/S of Cumberland River & Whites Creek	yes
Drake, John	1354		Davidson	640	37	8 Oct 1787	264	10 Feb 1784	68	136	On the S side of Cumberland River	
Drake, John	1404	Armstrong, M.	Davidson	26	21	8 Oct 1787	1380	16 Sep 1785	68	154	On West side of Milnear Creek &c	
Drake, Jonathan	1022	Carleton, John hrs	Davidson	640	1040	18 May 1789	3153		63	346	On Raccoon Creek	yes
Drake, Jonathan	1130		Davidson	640	107	17 Apr 1786	34	30 Dec 1783	66	176	Lying on S side of Cumberland River &c	
Drake, Jonathan	1915	Elliott, John hr of Thos	Davidson	640	1696	20 May 1793			81	52	Small cr runs into E Fork of Stones R	yes
Drake, Jonathan	194	Christian, James	Davidson	640	180	7 Mar 1786	143		63	67	2 lyn trees on bank of Cumberland R	yes
Drake, Jonathan	224	Laton, William	Davidson	640	210	7 Mar 1786	608		63	78	N side of Cumberland River	yes
Drake, Jonathan	522	Ellis, Robert	Sumner	640	1701	20 May 1793	3490	26 Nov 1792	81	53	On N side of Cumberland River	yes
Drake, Jonathan	64		Western District	1600	64	10 Jul 1788	1816	23 Apr 1784	67	305	On both sides of the Long Fk &c	
Drake, Jonathan	979	Saunders, Peter hrs	Davidson	640	996	18 May 1789	3158		63	335	On Raccoon Creek	yes
Drake, Jonathan	997	Evans, Joseph hrs	Davidson	640	1014	18 May 1789	3265		63	340	On Halfpone Creek	yes
Drakes, Benjamin	481	Barton, Samuel	Sumner	640	117	27 Apr 1793	765	3 Sep 1785	81	33	On W fk of Bartons Creek	yes
Drakes, Isaac	012		not given	50				12 Nov 1786			On Hatons Lick Branch	
Draper, Jno.	1068		Davidson	640	42	17 Apr 1786	607	19 Oct 1784	66	48	On Bledsoes Creek &c	
Drawhorn, John	2218	Glasgow, James	Davidson	640	2548	19 Oct 1795			88	186	On waters of Stones River	yes
Drew, John	1556	Welch, Thos heirs	Davidson	6040 (sic)	1172	29 Nov 1790	2158		74	233	On N side of Cumberland River	yes
Drew, John	1557	Minceys, Geo heirs	Davidson	640	1173	29 Nov 1790	2145		74	234	On N side of Cumberland River	yes
Drew, John	249	Lewis, Watt heirs	Sumner	640	1174	29 Nov 1790	2135		74	234	On N side Cumberland River	yes
Driskiel, David	222	Hill, Green	Davidson	274	208	7 Mar 1786	1057	23 Mar 1789	63	77	N side of Cumberland River	yes
Driver, Charles	1099	Jackson, A. & S. Donelson	Sumner	640	2599	7 Mar 1796	1793	12 Nov 1795	88	326	Beg at a small white oak	yes
Drummon, Joseph	196	Weakley, Robert	Sumner	640	1052	27 Nov 1789	3428	3 Jun 1786	71	289	On Maddesons Creek	yes
Drury, John	120		Davidson	640	106	7 Mar 1786	867		63	42	On Yellow Creek	
Drury, Morgan	202		Tennessee	640	1491	4 Jan 1792			77	373	On both sides of Yellow Creek &c	
Ducawn [?], James	2015	McCulloh, Benjamin	Davidson	640	1970	20 May 1793	2510		81	117	On Snow Cr waters of Duck River	yes
Dudley, Bennet	801	Robertson, Patsey	Davidson	640	804	20 Nov 1788	3308		63	282	On waters of Caney Fork	yes
Dudley, Guilford	042		Green	5000			1636	30 Nov 1784			On the waters of Duck River	
Dudley, Matthias	798	Robertson, Elijah	Davidson	640	801	20 Nov 1788	174		63	281	On waters of Hickman Creek	yes
Dudley, Thomas	40		Davidson	2560	26	14 Mar 1786			63	11	On Well's Creek	yes
Duff, William	236		Sullivan	200	375	9 Aug 1787	782	26 May 1781	61	394	Lying bet. the land of John Sharpe &c	
Duffield, Thomas	457	Looney, David	Sumner	411	1594	27 Apr 1793	497	26 Jan 1785	81	16	On upper fork of Gooses Creek	yes
Duffney, David	271	Lewis, Seth & Geo. Walker	Tennessee	497	1784	20 May 1793	1184	15 Sep 1784	81	75	On Beaverdam Creek	yes
Duffy, John	531	Barton, Samuel	Sumner	640	1725	20 May 1793	745	18 Nov 1792	81	59	On the waters of Bartons Creek	yes
Duffy, Peter	038	Cox, Phenix	Davidson	640			763	16 Aug 1784	77		On waters of Marrow Bone	yes
Dugald, John	151	Blount, John Gray	Tennessee	640	1404	20 Dec 1791	2509	30 Sep 1785	77	352	On S side of Spring Creek	yes

Claimant:	File #:	Assignee:	County:	Acres:	Grant:	Grant Date:	Entry:	Entry Date:	Bk:	Pg:	Location by Stream Name:	Military:
Dugan, Jesse	283	Donelson, Stockley	Middle District	640	2383	12 Jul 1794	1005	4 Jan 1779	81	600	On waters of Cumberland River	yes
Dugard, William	1083		Washington	200	1034	27 Nov 1792	1160		80	199	On Watauga River &c	
Duggan, Jesse	582	Williams, Eliza	Middle District	640	2789	20 Dec 1796			91	323	Both sides of Caney Fork	yes
Duggard, Mary	524		Washington	226	787	16 Feb 1787		8 Sep 1778	64	148	On both sides of Watauga River &c	
Duggard, William	1050		Washington	150	150	27 Nov 1792	1345	23 Apr 1779	80	176	On the Beaverdam branches	
Duggin, Daniel	222		Sullivan	247	361	9 Aug 1787	1678	18 Sep 1779	61	380	Beg at a forked Chesnut &c	
Duggin, John	1121	Harris, Edward	Sumner	640	2627	4 Jun 1796	2799	1 Jun 1795	88	343	Joining sd Harris survey	yes
Duglas, William	2053	Walker, George	Davidson	640	2139	20 May 1793	1159		81	158	On S side of Cumberland River	yes
Duglass, William	240	Clark, Lardner	Tennessee	1000	1583	27 Nov 1793	72	21 1783	81	13	In fk bet. Red River &c	yes
Duglass, McAllister & Sharp	1030		Green	1000	1257	29 Jul 1793	2422	25 May 1784	76	489	Waters Cumberland Riv on Spring Creek	
Duke, Green	357	Gamble, Edmond	Sumner	640	1479	4 Jan 1792	2486	6 May 1791	77	371	On the head of Drakes Creek	yes
Duke, Hardeman	219	Taylor, Thomas	Sumner	429	1124	26 Nov 1789	1656	9 Apr 1788	74	141	On S side of Cumberland River	yes
Duke, McDaniel & Cobb	048	McCoy, Roger heirs	Hawkins	640			3841					yes
Duke, Plea	048	Duke, Plea. McDaniel, & C	Hawkins	640			3841					yes
Duke, Pleasant	310		Green	200	312	20 Sep 1787	335	13 Sep 1785	65	462	On N side of Holsten River	
Duke, Pleasant	354	Fort, Elias	Green	80	356	20 Sep 1787	1879	13 Aug 1785	65	474	On N side of Holston River	
Duke, Sherod	489	Sanders, William	Davidson	640	461	15 Sep 1787	2272		63	168	S fork of Moneyfork Creek	yes
Dukes, Arthur	330	Fenner, Richard	Davidson	640	316	28 Jun 1787	2180		63	118	On waters of Second Creek	yes
Dukes, Elisha	696	Sheppard, Benjamin	Davidson	1000	669	8 Dec 1787	2318		63	237	On a small creek &c	yes
Dun, James	1194		Washington	43.50	1147	6 Jan 1796	2801	28 Feb 1781	83	176	On waters of Horse Creek	
Dun, William	1246		Green	100	1096	12 Jan 1793	834	21 Oct 1783	78	362	N side of Nolachuckey River	
Dunbar, Dun	271	Fort, Elias	Sumner	688	1253	10 Dec 1790	316	13 Sep 1785	74	249	On N side of Cumberland River	yes
Dunbar, Isaac	813	Robertson, Elijah	Davidson	640	816	20 Nov 1788	3307		63	287	On waters of Caney Fork	yes
Dunbar, John	1107	Harris, Edward	Sumner	640	2613	4 Jun 1796	856	1 Jun 1795	88	337	Joining sd Harris survey	yes
Duncan [Dunken], Lawrence	1372		Washington	100	1287	24 Nov 1797	2918	7 Jan 1795	96	11	Upon the Laurel Fork	
Duncan, Charles	1257		Washington	106	1229	20 Jul 1796			88	512	Joining Cobbs &c	
Duncan, Charles	496		Washington	113	759	16 Aug 1787	2834	27 Mar 1781	64	138	On waters of Knobs Creek	
Duncan, Charles	698		Washington	400	512	10 Nov 1784	657	28 Nov 1778	69	109	On Nobb Creek	
Duncan, Chas., son of Robt	296		Washington	198	163	24 Oct 1782	672	9 Dec 1778	47	79	S Fork of Horse Creek	
Duncan, Elizabeth	1203		Washington	300	1157	5 Dec 1794	1279 & 271	1779 & 1781	83	415	S side of Watagah &c	
Duncan, George	407	Persons, Thomas	Tennessee	228	2433	18 Mar 1794	1542	12 Feb 1785	81	421	On waters of Beaver Creek	yes
Duncan, Jesse	1728	Robertson, Charles	Davidson	274	1443	20 Dec 1791	539		77	361	N side of Cumberland River	yes
Duncan, John	08		Washington	404			14				On Falling Branch of Horse Creek	
Duncan, John	09		Washington	400			14				On Falling branch of Horse Creek	
Duncan, John	1149		Green	302	992	26 Dec 1791	1414	17 Jan 1784	77	279	Forks of Holstein & French Broad R	
Duncan, John	560		Sullivan	400	543	17 Nov 1790			76	192	On the Falling Branch of Horse Creek	
Duncan, John	674		Sullivan	50	622	9 Jul 1794			81	628	On waters of Horse Creek	
Duncan, Joseph	010		Washington	267			670	9 Dec 1778			On Boons Creek	
Duncan, Joseph	011		Washington	175			1334	8 Apr 1779			Joining Duncan's manor plantation	
Duncan, Joseph	1185		Washington	300	1070	30 Dec 1793	670	9 Dec 1778	82	143	On Boons Creek	
Duncan, Joseph	1382		Washington	100	1306	3 Dec 1801	846	30 Dec 1778	114	85	On head of Limestone	
Duncan, Joseph	668		Washington	320	482	10 Nov 1784	678	9 Dec 1788	69	98	On S branch of Boons Creek	
Duncan, Joseph	943		Washington	200	920	3 Apr 1780	385	9 Dec 1788	76	151	Beg at a walnut &c	
Duncan, Lawrence	1057		Washington	100	1007	27 Nov 1792	2557	18 May 1780	80	179	On the Lorell Fork of Doe River	
Duncan, Lawrence	1372		Washington	100	1287	24 Nov 1797	2918	7 Jan 1795	96	11	Upon the Laurel Fork	

Claimant:	File #:	Assignee:	Acres:	County:	Grant:	Grant Date:	Entry:	Entry Date:	Bk:	Pg:	Location by Stream Name:	Military:
Duncan, Martin	013	Cubbins, Wm.	640	Robertson	3056	19 Jul 1797	1664	30 Dec 1794	90	372	Abt a mile below John Grimes	
Duncan, Martin	588	McCubbins, Isaac hrs.	640	Tennessee	754	20 Jul 1796			88	501	Abt a mile below John Grimeses	
Duncan, Michael	982		75	Hawkins	398	19 Jul 1797	216	21 Feb 1780	91	623	On N side of Holston River	
Duncan, Peter	443		100	Eastern District							N side of the river Knobs	
Duncan, Stephen	010		400	Knox							S side of Holston River	
Duncan, Stephen	012		200	Eastern District							S side of Holston River	
Duncan, Stephen	013		640	Eastern District				1795			S side of Holston River	
Duncan, Stephen	014		250	Eastern District				14 Oct 1795			On waters of Abner Witts Creek	
Duncan, Stephen	015		225	Eastern District				15 Oct 1795			S side Holston River	
Duncan, Stephen	016		1000	Eastern District							On waters of New River	
Duncan, Stephen	045		400	Green	273	1636	1636	2 Feb 1780			S side of Holston River	
Duncan, Stephen	051		281	Green	274	20 Jul 1796	1381	21 May 1779	88	200	On S side of Holston River	
Duncan, Stephen	326		640	Eastern District	266	7 Mar 1796	594	7 Jun 1780	90	329	On S side of Holston	
Duncan, Stephen	427		1000	Eastern District	294	8 Jun 1797	105, 357	8 Feb 1780	90	330	E fork of New River	
Duncan, Stephen	428		1000	Eastern District	295	8 Jun 1797	784	3 Oct 1783	88	434	On Bufface Creek	
Duncan, Stephen, Ass.	356		400	Eastern District	273	20 Jul 1796			88	434	On S side of Holston River	
Duncan, Stephen, Ass.	357		281	Eastern District	274	20 Jul 1796			63	167	On S side of Holston River	
Duncan, William	486	Marshall, John	228	Davidson	458	15 Sep 1787	1602	22 Apr 1780	91	276	On Money Fork Creek	yes
Duncan, William	788		20	Sullivan	720	2 Dec 1796	441	29 Aug 1792			On Beaverdam Creek	
Dundelow, Benjamin	096	Mackey, Alexander	640	Sumner			2568				Beg at a white oak &c	yes
Dundels, Hugh	070	Sheppard, John	640	Middle District			2911		76	183		yes
Dungeth, Charles	314		640	Sumner	307	17 Nov 1790	721	4 May 1785	66	30	On E Fk of Spencers Creek	yes
Dungins, Jeremiah	647		200	Washington	741	26 Oct 1786	1343	23 Apr 1779	69	117	On Caney Run &c	
Dungins, Jeremiah	721		400	Washington	535	10 Nov 1784	887	3 Dec 1778	69	122	Inc the plantation &c	
Dungins, Jeremiah	734		397	Washington	548	10 Nov 1784	888	31 Dec 1778	66	191	On both sides Wataugha River	
Dunham, Daniel	1196		640	Davidson	173	17 Apr 1786	122	15 Jan 1784	66	368	Large ash on James Thompson's line	
Dunham, Daniel	1216		640	Davidson	180	10 Jul 1788	120	15 Jan 1784	47	17	Sugar tree & walnut N/S Little Harpeth	
Dunham, Daniel	171		200	Washington	39	23 Oct 1782	91	26 Feb 1778	66	250	E branch of Lick Creek	
Dunham, Henry	606		200	Green	563	20 Sep 1787	214	22 Jul 1785	66	60	On Pegion [sic] Creek &c	
Dunham, Jno.	1103		640	Davidson	77	17 Apr 1786	269	11 Feb 1784	52	250	Near East Fork of Richland Cr	
Dunham, John	378		300	Washington	370	13 Oct 1783	554	30 Oct 1778	59	436	On the waters of Horse Creek	
Dunham, Joseph	117		500	Green	133	1 Nov 1786	184	2 Jul 1784	80	199	N side of Nolachuckie River	
Dunkin, Anthony	1083		152	Washington	1033	27 Nov 1792	847	3 Dec 1778	81	74	On the head of Sinking Creek	
Dunkinson, John	1947	Blount, John Gray	640	Davidson	1780	20 May 1793	2504		83	172	On Middle Fork of Jones Creek	
Dunlap, Ephraim	250		100	Eastern District	203	6 Jan 1795	15	25 Feb 1780	83	169	S of Holston River &c	
Dunlap, Ephraim	813		140	Hawkins	649	6 Jan 1795	15	25 Feb 1778	81	558	Including the Grassey Spring	
Dunlap, Hugh	200		5000	Eastern District	172	8 Apr 1794			88	198	In Cades Cove	
Dunlap, Hugh	323		500	Eastern District	263	7 Mar 1796	302	1 Mar 1780	90 (91)	122	Bet French Broad & Holston Rivers	
Dunlap, Hugh	436		150	Eastern District	287	21 Jan 1797	1745	16 Sep 1779	88	203	N side of Holston River	
Dunlap, Hugh	916		640	Hawkins	725	7 Mar 1796	15	24 Feb 1778	74	16	On waters of Big Creek	
Dunlapp, James	863		300	Green	813	27 Nov 1789	950	2 Jan 1779	80	179	Beg at a white oak	
Dunlop, Ephraim	1059		440	Washington	1009	27 Nov 1792	951	2 Jan 1779	80	182	Beg at a white oak	
Dunlop, Ephraim	1070		200	Washington	1020	27 Nov 1792	988	7 Jun 1794	82	202	On waters of Lorrel Fork of Holston	
Dunlop, Ephraim	298		400	Middle District	258	7 Jun 1794	6	8 Feb 1780	82	203	On S W side of the Clear Fork &c	
Dunlop, Ephraim	300		640	Middle District	260	17 Jul 1794					On Cowpen Creek	

Earliest Tennessee Land Records

Claimant:	File #:	Assignee:	County:	Acres:	Grant:	Grant Date:	Entry:	Entry Date:	Bk:	Pg:	Location by Stream Name:	Military:
Dunlop, Ephraim	302		Middle District	640	262	7 Jul 1794	2	27 May 1780	82	203	On Ball Creek	
Dunlop, Ephraim	519		Hawkins	400	392	29 Jul 1793	988	2 Jan 1779	80	275	On S side of Copper Ridge	
Dunlop, Ephraim	572		Hawkins	640	446	29 Jul 1793	5	8 Feb 1780	80	288	On N side of Wallings Ridge	
Dunlop, Ephraim	579		Hawkins	400	453	29 Jul 1793	15	24 Feb 1778	80	290	On S bank of Holston River	
Dunlop, Ephraim	827		Green	600	808	18 May 1789		18 May 1789	72	244	On the N side of Tennessee River &c	
Dunlop, Ephraim	859		Green	640	839	13 Feb 1791	15	17 Feb 1778	73	385	On the N side of Nolechuckey River	
Dunlop, Ephraim	860		Green	200	840	13 Feb 1791	15	24 Feb 1778	73	385	S/S of Nolechuckey River on Warpath	
Dunlop, Ephraim	874		Green	640	824	27 Nov 1789	808	19 May 1779	74	23	Beg at 2 possimmons [sic]	
Dunlop, Ephraim	984		Washington	640	1061	29 Jul 1793	948	2 Jan 1779	74	477	On Roan Creek	
Dunlop, Hugh	04		Knox	150			560	15 May 1780	76		N side of Holston River	
Dunlop, Hugh & Wm.	1062		Hawkins	600	771	21 Jan 1797	1834	8 Feb 1780	91	116	On the black oak ridge	
Dunlop, James	1047		Green	500	1274	29 Jul 1793	52	25 Feb 1778	76	493	W side of French Broad River	
Dunlop, James	866		Green	640	816	27 Nov 1789	15	7 Jun 1787	74	18	Beg at a black & 2 white oaks	
Dunlop, Thomas	2434	Mann, John	Davidson	640	3263	6 Dec 1797	4139		98	149	Headwaters of Trace Cr of Harpeth	yes
Dunn, Daniel, Jr.	586		Washington	200	680	26 Oct 1786	1365	11 May 1779	66	2	On waters of Wataugah River	
Dunn, Thomas	034	McCullock, Benj.	Tennessee	640			2008	16 Aug 1785			On Red River	yes
Dunnagen, John	1063	King, William	Sumner	640	2540	10 Dec 1795	503		88	293	On a creek called Lick Creek	yes
Dunnick, Peter	163		Davidson	640	149	14 Mar 1786	657		63	57	S side of Cumberland River	yes
Dunnick, Peter	584	Tyrell, Williams	Tennessee	360	3032	10 Apr 1787	3711		90	306	On W Fk of Williams Creek	yes
Dunning, James	057	Robertson, James	not given	357	4200		4200	17 Mar 1797			W fk of Jones Creek	yes
Dunwoody, Samuel	75		Green	300	33	1 Nov 1786	1307	24 May 1779	59	394	ON Delaneys Creek	
Duoster, James	26	Bowman, William	Sumner	640	783	11 Jul 1788	2506		63	274	Bet the N & Middle Fk of Red River	yes
Duoston, Abraham	762	Isbell, Thomas	Davidson	640	735	11 Jul 1788	2505		63	258	S side of Big Barren River	yes
Dupont, Jesse	381	Blount, John Gray & Thom	Tennessee	640	2338	20 May 1793	2503	30 Sep 1785	81	199	On S side of Cumberland River	
Dupont, Joseph	276	Blount, John Gray & Thom	Tennessee	640	1856	20 May 1793	2507	30 Sep 1785	81	91	On Johnsons Creek	yes
Dupreast, Richard	1234	Sanders, Williams	Sumner	640	2507	12 Nov 1795	2297		89	422	On waters of Goose Creek	yes
Dupree, Mial	034	Brown, Charles	Davidson	640			4693	7 Aug 1797			On Harpeth River	yes
Dupree, Mial	084	Brown, Charles	Davidson	640			4693	7 Aug 1797			On Harpeth River	yes
Durham, Nathaniel	466	Sloss, John	Sumner	640	1620	27 Apr 1793	211	10 Sep 1788	81	22	On Smiths Fork of Caney Fork	yes
Duroy, Timothy	1405	Boyd, John, Jr.	Sumner	228	3336	6 Dec 1797	4738	3 May 1797	97	54	On waters of Cedar Creek	yes
Durrum, William	99		Washington	120	267	23 Oct 1782	1251	27 Feb 1779	44	281	On Little Dan River	
Duval, Jacob	608		Sullivan	150	563	26 Dec 1791	549	29 Apr 1780	77	307	On Sleechers Fork &c	
Dye, Hopkins, pt.	092		not given	274			3802					
Dye, Hopkins	092		not given	274			3802					yes
Dyer, Jacob	1577		Green	150	1328	4 Feb 1795	2216	13 Nov 1779	83	397	On waters Little Cr & Little Chuckey	
Dyer, Joel	420	Hyde, Andrew	Eastern District	110	2946	1 Mar 1797	4490		90	216	Joining lines w/ James Armstrong	
Dykes, John	662	Bushnell, E. & Wm. Dobbin	Davidson	640	635	15 Sep 1787	1682		63	225	On S side of Cumberland	yes
Dykes, William	417		Sullivan	640	296	10 Nov 1784	447	28 Sep 1778	69	175	On Back Creek	
Eackart, David	2302	Crabtree, Jos.	Davidson	480	170	26 Mar 1795			89	95	On waters of Big Harpeth	
Eagan, Edward	748		Washington	200	562	10 Nov 1784	2100	31 Oct 1779	69	127	On a branch of Horse Creek	
Eagleton, David	582		Green	500	263	20 Sep 1787	281	22 Oct 1783	66	161	On Little Chuckey beg on the S bank	
Earheart [?], David	011		Davidson	480							On waters of Big Harpeth	
Earl, James, heirs of	070		Sumner	640			1420				Waters Puntchin Camp Creek	
Earley, Thomas	454		Washington	200	446	13 Oct 1783	2372	21 Sep 1787	52	287	On a branch of Buffalow Creek	yes
Earnest, Henry	299		Washington	45	166	24 Oct 1782	695	6 Apr 1782	47	80	N side of Nolachuckey River	

Claimant:	File #:	Assignee:	County:	Acres:	Grant:	Grant Date:	Entry:	Entry Date:	Bk:	Pg:	Location by Stream Name:	Military:
Earnest, Henry	845		Washington	600	659	10 Nov 1784	694	16 Dec 1778	69	154	On S side of Nolechuckee River	
Earpe, John	056	Dillenberry, Redmon	Sumner	228			4524	14 Oct 1797			Head waters 1st big creek &c	yes
Eart, Robert	718		Sumner	297	2100	20 May 1793	784	20 Aug 1785	81	149	On 1st lge br emptying into Bledsoes	
Easley, Stephen	117		Washington	613	285	24 Oct 1782			44	290	On Horse Creek	
Easley, Stephen	192		Sullivan	320	199	10 Oct 1783	1973	15 Oct 1779	53	158	E/S of Survey formerly Geo. Ridleys	
Easley, Stephen	30		Sullivan	500	41	23 Oct 1782	786	26 Dec 1778	43	257	On Horse Creek	
Easley, Stephen	60		Sullivan	300	71	23 Oct 1782	787	26 Dec 1778	43	273	On Horse Creek &c	
Easman, Benjamin	122	Davis, Elisha	Davidson	274	108	7 Mar 1786	392		63	43	S side of Cumberland River	yes
Eason, Joseph, heir of Thos.	038		Middle District	640			3804				Main Fk of Obeys River	
Eason, Joseph, heir of Thos.	977		Sumner	640	2441	22 Feb 1795			84	317	On Main Fork of Obeys River	
Eason, Thomas	561	Lewis, W. T.	Tennessee	640	2996	10 Apr 1797	3615	29 Nov 1788	90	291	On Dry Fk of Spring Creek	yes
East, Sampson	535	Comon, James	Middle District	640	2935	22 Feb 1797	4597		90	238	Both sides of Muirs Fk	yes
Easten, James	1091	Colvin, John heirs	Sumner	640	2582	7 Mar 1796	3840	22 Jul 1795	88	317	On E side of large fk of Caney Fork	yes
Easten, James	1092	Orme, James heirs	Sumner	640	2583	7 Mar 1796	3858	22 Jul 1795	88	318	On E fk of a large fk of Caney Fk	yes
Easten, James	1094	Parnel, Joshua heirs	Sumner	640	2585	7 Mar 1796	2219	22 Jul 1795	88	319	On E side of large fk of Caney Fk	yes
Easten, James	1096	Bibby, Edmond heirs	Sumner	640	2587	7 Mar 1796	3928	22 Jul 1795	88	320	On E side of large fk of Caney Fk	yes
Easten, Jas.	1040	Reed, Watson	Sumner	640	2702	27 Mar 1796	3966	11 Mar 1795	88	256	On waters of Caney Fork	yes
Easten, Jas.	1042	Goodwin, Wm. Heirs	Sumner	640	2704	27 Mar 1796	2920	11 Mar 1795	88	257	On waters of the Caney Fork	yes
Easten, Jas.	1093	Carey, Wm. Heirs	Sumner	640	2584	7 Mar 1796	3855	22 Jul 1795	88	318	On E side of large fk of Caney Fk	yes
Easten, Jas.	1095	Etheridge, Edward hrs	Sumner	640	2586	7 Mar 1796	3847	22 Jul 1795	88	319	On a large fk of Caney Fk	yes
Easter, Moses	347	Wikoff, William	Tennessee	640	2168	20 May 1793	2046	26 Aug 1785	81	165	On N side of Red River	yes
Eastes, Bartlet	1052	Lee, James	Sumner	640	2516	8 Dec 1795	1417	5 Nov 1790	88	288	On Jinning Fork	
Easton, James	071	Whitfield, Jesse	Sumner	640				11 Mar 1795			On waters of Caney Fork	yes
Easton, James	1036	Andrews, Watson	Sumner	640	2698	27 Mar 1796	3962	11 May 1795	88	255	On waters of Caney Fork	yes
Easton, James	1038	Delainey, A. J. hrs	Sumner	640	2700	27 Mar 1796	3910	11 Mar 1795	88	255	On waters of Caney Fork	yes
Easton, James	1039	McAdoe, James hrs	Sumner	640	2701	27 Mar 1796	3968	11 May 1795	88	256	On waters of Caney Fork	yes
Easton, James	1041	Moore, Jno. Davis hrs	Sumner	640	2703	27 Mar 1796	3969	11 May 1795	88	257	On waters of the Caney Fork	yes
Easton, James	1097	Jordon, Jones hrs	Sumner	640	2588	7 Mar 1796	3932	5 Jun 1795	88	320	On S side of Cumberland River	yes
Easton, James	1098	Cannady, Dav.	Sumner	640	2589	7 Mar 1796	3929	22 Jul 1795	88	321	On E side of large fk of Caney Fk	yes
Easton, Jas.	1037	Tyson, Grisham heirs	Sumner	640	2699	27 Mar 1796			88	255	On waters of Caney Fork	yes
Easton, Jas.	1044	McCoy, Dugald heirs	Sumner	640	2706	27 Mar 1796	1716	11 May 1795	88	258	Joining sd Eastens survey	yes
Easton, Jas.	1045	Weaver, John heirs	Sumner	640	2707	27 Mar 1796	1130	30 Nov 1792	88	258	On waters of the Caney Fk	yes
Easton, Jas.	1090	Hicks, Henry heirs	Sumner	640	2581	7 Mar 1796			88	317	On E side of a large fk of Caney Fork	yes
Easton, Jas., Ass.	1043		Sumner	640	2705	27 Mar 1796			88	258	On waters of Caney Fork	yes
Eastwood, John	204	Hart, Anthony	Sumner	640	1109	26 Nov 1789	2448	12 Mar 1788	74	132	On W side of Caney Fork River	yes
Eaton, John	1513	Spear, Seth	Davidson	640	1070	26 Nov 1789	3499		74	114	On N side of Cumberland River	yes
Eaton, John	22		Tennessee	640	1170	26 Nov 1789	3520	8 Feb 1786	74	164	On N side of Cumberland River	
Eaton, Pinkerton	2393	Eaton, Pinkerton	Davidson	4800	2782	10 Dec 1796	353		91	296	Waters of Big Harpeth River	
Eaton, Joseph	213		Green	200	170	20 Sep 1787			65	420	On the Myery Branch	yes
Eatton, Joseph	572		Green	200	252	20 Sep 1787	2764	8 Feb 1781	66	158	N/S Holstein Riv below Sulphur Spring Br	
Eavens, Archer	1156		Washington	160	1114	7 Jul 1794	1350	24 Apr 1779	81	615	Beg at a white oak	
Eavens, John	804 [?]		Hawkins	400	640	6 Jan 1795			83	164	On head of Panther Creek	
Eburn, John	644		Davidson	1640	617	15 Sep 1787	105		63	219	On W Fk of Stones River	yes
Echolds [?], Abner	2026	McCulloh, Benjamin	Davidson	640	2032	20 May 1793	3222		81	132	On N side of Cumberland River	yes
Ecols, William	906	Glasgow, James	Davidson	1000	922	18 May 1789			63	318	On N side of Cumberland River	yes

Earliest Tennessee Land Records

Claimant:	File #:	Assignee:	County:	Acres:	Grant:	Grant Date:	Entry:	Entry Date:	Bk:	Pg:	Location by Stream Name:	Military:
Eden, James	1237		Washington	50	1209	20 Jul 1796	2576	30 May 1780	88	503	On waters of Gap Creek	
Eden, James	554		Washington	100	819	11 Jul 1788	1980	29 Oct 1779	64	335	Valley above big spring on Gap Cr	yes
Edens, John	343	McCulloh, Benjamin	Tennessee	640	2144	20 May 1793	2647	30 Sep 1785	81	159	On S side of Cumberland River	
Edge, John	619	Sutton, Bailey	Tennessee	640	3181	14 Sep 1797	3865	12 Oct 1795	90	434	Waters of Bartons Creek	yes
Edge, Joseph	632	Robertson, James	Tennessee	640	3196	14 Sep 1797	3064	14 Aug 1795	90	441	Near the head of Bartons Creek	yes
Edge, Thomas	600	Stewart, Duncan	Tennessee	640	3102	14 Sep 1797	4433	22 Dec 1796	90	403	S side of Cumberland River	yes
Edger, George	809		Green	300	807	29 Nov 1788	1407	17 Jan 1784	70	31	On the N side of Nolichuckey	
Edger, George	887		Green	400	843	24 Nov 1790	947	29 Oct 1783	74	280	Including the head of Lins Branch	
Edin, James	547		Washington	100	812	11 Jul 1788	2571	3 May 1780	64	334	Joining survey sd Edin now lives on	
Edkins, John	102	Atkinson, Jno & Robt Nelso	Tennessee	358	1522	10 Apr 1792	198	8 May 1784	75	509	On N side of Sycamore	yes
Edmison, Thomas	1154		Davidson	640	131	17 Apr 1786	188	26 Jan 1784	66	182	On the N side of Harpeth River &c	
Edmiston, William	1363		Davidson	320	46	8 Oct 1787	190	26 Jan 1784	68	140	On both sides of Arringtons Creek	
Edmonds, Abel	1664	Robertson, James	Davidson	275	1587	23 Feb 1793	1415		76	306	On the waters of W Harpeth River	
Edmondson, John	381		Middle District	640	320	17 Dec 1794	2042	3 May 1784	84	214	On S side of Elk River	
Edmondson, Mary	869		Green	100	819	27 Nov 1789			74	20	On Little Chuckey	
Edmondson, Robert	377		Middle District	800	316	17 Dec 1794	2018	3 May 1784	84	213	On S side of Elk River	
Edmondson, Robert	463		Middle District	1280	402	17 Dec 1794	2027	3 May 1784	84	262	On N side of Elk River	
Edmondson, Samuel	405		Middle District	1286	344	17 Dec 1794	2037	3 May 1784	84	226	On Main fork of Little River	
Edmondson, Samuel	439		Middle District	2000	378	17 Dec 1794	2034	3 May 1784	84	250	N side of Elk River	
Edmondson, Thos. & Berry	425		Middle District	1600	364	17 Dec 1794	2035	3 May 1784	84	236	On N side of Elk River	
Edmondson, William	364		Middle District	1200	303	17 Dec 1794	2023	3 May 1784	84	208	On S side of Elk River	
Edmondson, William	435		Middle District	1280	374	17 Dec 1794	2025	3 May 1784	84	249	On N side of Elk River	
Edmondson, William	437		Middle District	1280	376	17 Dec 1794	2033	3 May 1784	84	250	On N side of Little River	
Edmondson, William	438		Middle District	2440	377	17 Dec 1794	2032	3 May 1784	84	250	On N side of Elk River	
Edmonson, John, Jr.	406		Middle District	1200	345	17 Dec 1794	2040	30 May 1784	84	226	On S side of Elk River	
Edmonson, Mary & John	052		Green	150			102	30 Jun 1789			On the head of Little Chuckey	
Edmonson, Samuel	378		Middle District	1280	317	17 Dec 1794	2019	3 May 1784	84	213	On S side of Elk River	
Edmonson, Thomas	2463		Davidson	640	470	21 Aug 1800	717	30 Apr 1785	108	108	On waters of Arrington Creek	
Edmunson, Thos.	1576	Weeks, Thos.	Davidson	258	1226	10 Dec 1790	1806		74	340	On W fk of Mill Creek	yes
Edward, Frederick	1158		Davidson	640	135	17 Apr 1786	92	14 Jan 1784	66	183	On Indian Creek &c	
Edwards, David	115	Johnson, S. hr of Richard	Davidson	640	101	14 Mar 1786	699		63	41	On Sycamore Creek	yes
Edwards, David	127	Peace, Jere hr of Thos	Davidson	640	113	7 Mar 1786	700		63	45	On Station Camp Creek	yes
Edwards, David	213	Ray, Eliz. hr of Steph.	Davidson	640	199	7 Mar 1786	701		63	74	On a branch of Sycamore Creek	yes
Edwards, Jesse	834	McCoy, Spence	Sumner	640	2320	20 May 1793	3133	27 Nov 1792	81	195	On N side of Cumberland River	yes
Edwards, Nicholas	363		Sullivan	250	242	10 Nov 1784	278	9 Mar 1780	69	159	In Stanleys Valley	
Edwards, Robert	261	Beaird, J. & Wm. Tyrrell	Eastern District	320	209	3 Feb 1795	3825		83	381	S side of Clinch River	yes
Edwards, Robert	613	Little, Archibald	Sumner	100	1872	20 May 1793	1202	31 Jul 1792	81	94	On waters of Britons Creek	yes
Edwick, Edwd.	1872	Elliott, John	Davidson	640	1611	27 Apr 1793			81	20	On waters of W Fork of Harpeth River	yes
Egnar, Matthias	362	Willson, David & John Dicks	Sumner	640	1503	4 Jan 1792	950	2 Oct 1791	77	376	N side of Cumberland &c	yes
Eigalton, David	367		Hawkins	640	360	8 Mar 1793	2211	12 Nov 1779	78	489	On N side of Tennessee River	
Eiperson, Joseph	91		Hawkins	200	249	Jul 1792	1324	2 Apr 1779	74	443	On Cedar Creek	
Ekart, Robert	718		Sumner	297	2100	20 May 1793	784	20 Aug 1785	81	149	1st large branch empties in Bledsoes Cr	
Ekols, William	629	Bonner, John & James	Davidson	738	601	15 Sep 1787	1237		63	214	N side of Cumberland River	
Eldridge, Wm, heir of Levy	1046		Sumner	640	2525	8 Dec 1795	283	12 Aug 1792	88	279	On main fk of Obeys River	yes
Eliot, William	912		Green	100	826	17 Nov 1790	2091	15 Jun 1784	76	113	Land now property of Mr. Keer	yes

Claimant:	File #:	Assignee:	County:	Acres:	Grant:	Grant Date:	Entry:	Entry Date:	Bk:	Pg:	Location by Stream Name:	Military:
Elkins, Joseph	2274	Donelson, John	Davidson	640	2752	20 Jul 1796	3607		88	458	On both sides of Stones River	yes
Eller, Jacob	527		Sullivan	100	543	26 Nov 1789	1593	29 Jul 1779	73	51	On S side of Holston River	
Eller, Joseph	268	Dickey, Thomas	Davidson	640	254	7 Mar 1786	1221		63	93	On waters of Stones River	yes
Elliot, Frokner [sic]	408		Sumner	640	419	27 Jun 1793	507	6 Jul 1784	80	347	On Roaring River	
Elliot, James	458	Bryan, James	Davidson	274	430	15 Sep 1787	453		63	159	S side of Cumberland River	yes
Elliot, John	1447	Barton, Sam	Davidson	640	93	10 Jul 1788	750	24 Jun 1785	68	233	S/S Cumbert Cedar Cr & Thompson	
Elliot, John	1809		Davidson	640	382	26 Jun 1793	849		80	336	On the waters of Whites Creek	
Elliot, John	1945	Shaw, Robert	Davidson	274	1773	20 May 1793	3295		81	72	On S side of Cumberland River	yes
Elliot, John & Daniel James	1894		Davidson	320	115	27 Apr 1793	847	17 Dec 1792	81	32	On waters of White Creek	
Elliot, John, heirs of	1872	Edwick, Edwd.	Davidson	640	1611	27 Apr 1793		81	20	Waters of W Fork of Harpeth River	yes	
Elliot, John, heirs of	953		Davidson	640	970	18 May 1789	452		63	329	Head of W Fork of Ceader Lick Cr	yes
Elliot, Simon	270	Hoover, Henry	Middle District	400	132	27 Apr 1793	60		81	36	On N waters of Richland Creek	
Elliot, Simon	276		Middle District	400	150	27 Apr 1793	62		81	41	On S side of Duck River	
Elliot, Thomas	1805		Davidson	640	378	26 Jun 1793	306	19 Feb 1784	80	334	On both sides of Stewarts Creek	
Elliot, William	1707		Green	50	344	19 Feb 1797		2 May 1793	90	254	Beg at a stake	
Elliot, William	1798		Davidson	640	371	26 Jun 1793	722	4 May 1785	80	331	On the waters of Harpeth	
Elliot, Falkner & I. Peterson	1341	Davidson, William	Davidson	480	27	18 Aug 1787	334	8 Mar 1784	68	131	On the N side of Red River	
Elliot, Jabez, hr. of R. Grant	2069		Davidson	640	2211	20 May 1793	1329		81	171	On Lick Creek N waters of Duck R	yes
Elliot, James	219	Moore, Joseph	Tennessee	320	107	20 Dec 1791	676	8 Jan 1789	77	382	On Milners Creek	
Elliot, Jno.	1271		Davidson	640	236	10 Jul 1788	518	10 Jul 1784	66	420	On Wt Fk of Red River &c	
Elliot, John	0126	Williams, Samp. & Jno Boy	Sumner	642			1875	7 Jan 1791			N side of Cumberland River	yes
Elliot, John	033	Englin, Henry Cornel.	Davidson	640			440	14 Nov 1785			On W Fk of Ceader Lick Creek	
Elliot, John	1357		Davidson	640	40	8 Oct 1787	159	17 Jan 1784	68	137	Beg at the creek	
Elliot, John	1584	Faulke(?), James	Davidson	640	1245	10 Dec 1790	270		74	346	On W Fork of Stones River	yes
Elliot, John	1598	McVey, John	Davidson	640	1289	10 Dec 1790			74	362	On W Fork of Stones River	yes
Elliot, John	488	Boren, Stephen	Tennessee	480	157	26 Mar 1795	157 [sic]	14 Apr 1792	89	88	On War Trace Creek	yes
Elliot, Joseph	978	Williams, Turner	Davidson	640	995	18 May 1789			63	335	On Smith's Fork of Caney Fork	yes
Elliot, Simon	269	Johnston, Walter	Middle District	700	128	27 Apr 1793	59		81	36	On Richland Creek	
Elliot, Simon	271	Blair, John	Middle District	200	134	27 Apr 1793	61		81	37	On N side of Duck River	
Elliot, Simon	450		Middle District	1000	389	17 Dec 1794	2137		84	256	On Duck River	
Elliot, Thomas	1915	Drake, Jonathan	Davidson	640	1696	20 May 1793	3462	11 May 1784	81	52	A small creek of E Fk of Stones Riv	yes
Elliot, Thos.	017		Eastern District	225							In Knox Co on a branch of Whites Cr	
Elliot, William	347		Sullivan	300	487	10 Jul 1788	2123	4 Nov 17779	67	490	On Reedy Creek &c	
Elliot, William	578		Sullivan	300	576	29 Jul 1793	2123	4 Nov 1779	76	472	Upon Reedy Creek	
Ellis, Charles	19		Giles	200	43	15 Jul 1812	2892	29 Jun 1781	126	444	Lying on Big Creek	
Ellis, Charles	25		Maury	100	44	15 Jul 1812	2877	29 Jun 1781	126	444	On big Swan Creek	
Ellis, Charles, Ass.	23		Maury	100	41	15 Jul 1812	2808	9 Mar 1781	126	443	E side of Dry Fork	
Ellis, Charles, Ass.	24		Maury	200	42	15 Jul 1812	2357	17 Dec 1779	126	443	Lying on a branch of Big Big Boy [sic]	
Ellis, Christopher	1176		Green	100	1019	26 Dec 1791	2328	4 Dec 1779	77	288	Incl plantation where sd Ellis liveth	
Ellis, James	980		Sumner	1000	2445	22 Feb 1795	3270	8 Aug 1792	84	319	On a fork of Obeys River	yes
Ellis, John	1396		Green	400	1208	27 Nov 1792	2599	4 Aug 1780	85 (80)	153	On the Long Fork of Sinking Creek	
Ellis, John	1590		Green	150	1332	22 Feb 1795			83	435	N side of French Broad River	
Ellis, Levi	1224		Sumner	400	172	27 Aug 1795		14 Apr 1792	89	411	On ridge dividing Red River waters	yes
Ellis, Robert	275		Tennessee	274	1844	20 May 1793	2028	26 Aug 1785	81	88	On S side of Cumberland River &c	
Ellis, Robert, Ass.	388		Sumner	640	559	26 Jun 1793	353	11 Mar 1784	80	319	On Spring Creek	

Claimant:	File #:	Assignee:	County:	Acres:	Grant:	Grant Date:	Entry:	Entry Date:	Bk:	Pg:	Location by Stream Name:	Military:
Ellis, Robt.	522	Drake, Jonathan	Sumner	640	1701	20 May 1793	3490	26 Nov 1792	81	53	On N side of Cumberland River	yes
Ellis, Saml	1322		Green	200	1172	12 Jan 1793	372	9 Sep 1778	78	408	In head of Long Fk of Sinking Creek	
Ellis, Underhill	1225		Sumner	400	173	27 Aug 1795		14 Apr 1792	89	412	On ridge that divides Red River	yes
Ellis, Underhill	1226	Douglas, Edward	Sumner	400	174	27 Aug 1795			89	412	On N side of Cumberland River	yes
Ellis, William	1248		Washington	100	1220	27 Feb 1796	2665	14 Nov 1780	88	507	On Boons Creek	
Ellis, William	1249		Washington	100	1221	27 Feb 1796	543	29 Oct 1779	88	508	On the Redey Branch	
Ellison, Ackiss	409	Haywood, John	Tennessee	640	2435	18 Mar 1794	1949	1 Aug 1785	81	422	On S side of Cumberland River	yes
Ellison, John	012		Washington	189			396	17 Sep 1778			E branch of Big Limestone Creek	
Ellison, John	013		Washington	200			736	22 Dec 1778			A branch known as Cedar Branch	
Ellison, Jos.	17	Awell, Jas.	Sumner	274	774	11 Jul 1788			63	271	N branch of Bradleys Lick Creek	yes
Ellison, Joseph	072	Owell, James	Sumner	274			3015	2 Apr 1787			On N branch of Bradleys Lick Creek	yes
Ellison, Peter	010	Blount, Thomas	Tennessee	640			1354	6 Nov 1784			Rite hand fk of 1st large creek &c	yes
Ellison, Robert	304		Washington	290	171	24 Oct 1782	590	9 Nov 1778	47	83	S Fork of Big Limestone	
Ellison, William	110		Washington	195	278	24 Oct 1782	257	20 Jul 1778	44	287	On the Cedar Branch	
Elmore, George	28	Hart, David	Sumner	274	785	11 Jul 1788	776	21 Sep 1787	63	275	On waters of Goose Creek	yes
Elmore, Morgan	1239	Donelson, Stockley	Sumner	640	2839	12 Jan 1797	3440	Aug 1796	90	40	On Martins Creek	yes
Elsey, William	847		Hawkins	300	672	22 Feb 1795	884	15 Dec 1779	83	432	N side of Clinch Mountain	
Embree, Thomas	894		Washington	200	869	13 Feb 1791	2732	16 Jan 1781	74	288	Beg at 2 white oaks	
Embree, Thomas	932		Washington	35	909	17 Nov 1790	2442	28 Feb 1780	76	147	N side of Nolechuckey River	
Emit, James	249		Davidson	1600	235	14 Mar 1786	365		63	86	Both sides of McAdoo Cr	yes
Emmert, George	1344		Washington	170	1248	10 Apr 1797	2097	30 Oct 1779	91	572	N side of Wataugah River	
Emmert, Jacob	1072		Washington	100	1022	27 Nov 1792	2671	19 Nov 1780	80	182	Beg at 3 black oaks &c	
Emmert, Jacob	1342		Washington	640	1246	10 Apr 1797	1669	18 Sep 1779	91	571	S Fork of Doe River	
Emmert, Jacob	1343		Washington	640	1247	10 Apr 1797	2132	5 Nov 1779	91	572	S Fork of Doe River	
Emmoret, George	937		Washington	300	914	17 Nov 1790	1301	25 Mar 1779	76	149	Beg at 2 sweet gums in Sharps line	
Emmory, Stephen	1153	Harris, Edward	Sumner	640	2658	4 Jun 1796	1414	1 Jun 1795	88	353	Join Harris survey	yes
Emory, John	744	Holderness, William	Davidson	640	717	11 Jul 1788	309		63	252	On head of Nelson & Kerns Creek	yes
Empson, John	2356	Cosman, James	Davidson	640	3034	10 Apr 1797	4596		90	307	Both sides of Muirs Fork	yes
Empson, John	911	Sawyer, Willie heir	Sumner	640	2480	31 Dec 1793			81	436	On Harts Creek	yes
Engle, George	1078		Washington	450	1028	27 Nov 1792	794	27 Dec 1778	80	184	On both sides of Watauga River	
Engle, George	1309		Washington	100	1195	4 Dec 1795	869	31 Dec 1778	89	433	On N side of Rones Creek	
Engle, John	1058		Washington	300	1008	27 Nov 1792	2374	25 Dec 1779	80	179	On Cedar Creek	
Englin, Cornelius	033	Elliott, John	Davidson	640		14 Nov 1785	warr#40 [?]				On W Fork of Cedar Lick Creek	yes
English, Andrew	1046		Washington	200	996	14 Jan 1793	1998	22 Oct 1779	79	285	Beg at Jos. Alexander's SW corner	
English, Andrew	1380		Green	35	1235	27 Jan 1793	2003	22 Oct 1779	79	508	On Pyburns Fork of Lick Creek	
English, Andrew	1381		Green	25	1236	27 Jan 1793	2004	22 Oct 1779	79	508	On waters of Lick Creek	
English, Andrew	146		Washington	31.50	14	23 Oct 1782	1458	29 Jun 1779	47	6	On waters of Lick Creek	
English, Andrew	184		Washington	250	52	23 Oct 1782	774	24 Dec 1778	47	24	On Sinking Fork &c	
English, Andrew	320		Washington	50	187	23 Oct 1782	1457	29 Jun 1779	49	220	On the waters of Lick Creek	
English, Andrew	327		Washington	92	194(4)?	24 Oct 1782	1055	8 Jan 1779	49	223	On the S side of Lick Creek	
English, Andrew	393		Hawkins	300	514	27 Jan 1793	2838	19 Apr 1781	79	495	On draught of Third Creek	
English, Andrew	394		Hawkins	150	515	27 Jan 1793	2104	31 Oct 1779	79	496	In the Grassey Valley	
English, Andrew	411		Hawkins	300	532	27 Jan 1793	2837	19 Apr 1781	79	501	In a grassey valley	
English, Andrew	506		Green	200	508	20 Sep 1787			65	524	Upon a water of Lick Creek	
English, Andrew	97		Washington	300	265	23 Oct 1782	230	23 Jun 1779	44	280	On Christians War Path	

Claimant:	File #:	Assignee:	County:	Acres:	Grant:	Grant Date:	Entry:	Entry Date:	Bk:	Pg:	Location by Stream Name:	Military:
English, James	025		Eastern District	640			2317	27 Nov 1779			Knox Co on N/S of Clinch River	
English, James	1029		Washington	280	979	14 Jan 1793	771	24 Dec 1778	79	278	Both sides Limestone Fork of Lick Cr	
English, James	1373		Green	200	1228	27 Jan 1793	2840	19 Apr 1781	79	506	On Long Fork of Lick Creek	
English, James	164		Washington	100	32	23 Oct 1782	282	1 Aug 1778	47	14	A white oak & 2 dogwood saplings	
English, James	172		Washington	200	40	23 Oct 1782	285	1 Aug 1778	47	18	On Limestone Fork of Lick Creek	
English, James	173		Washington	200	41	23 Oct 1782	286	1 Aug 1778	47	18	On Limestone Fork of Lick Creek	
English, James	193		Washington	200	61	23 Oct 1782	284	1 Aug 1778	47	29	Beg at 3 black oaks & a white oak	
English, James	201		Washington	100	69	23 Oct 1782	281	1 Aug 1778	47	33	On both sides of Lick Creek	
English, James	203		Washington	140	71	23 Oct 1782	288	1 Aug 1778	47	34	On Lick Creek	
English, James	589		Washington	100	683	26 Oct 1786	709	19 Dec 1778	66	3	Bet Englishs tract & war path	
English, James	590		Washington	150	684	26 Oct 1786	703	19 Dec 1778	66	4	E/S his mill Limestone Fk of Lyck Cr.	
English, James	655		Washington	100	749	26 Oct 1786	283	1 Aug 1778	66	34	On both sides of the Limestone Fork &c	
English, James	70		Washington	100	238	23 Oct 1782	705	19 Dec 1778	44	265	On waters of Lick Creek	
English, John	1208		Washington	200	1162	5 Dec 1794	1054	8 Jan 1779	83	418	On the Fall Branch &c	
English, John	374		Washington	37.50	366	13 Oct 1783	2745	20 Jan 1781	52	249	On Horse Creek	
English, John	400		Washington	62.50	392	13 Oct 1783	2746	20 Jan 1781	52	261	On Limestone Fork of Lick Creek	
English, John	503	Byrn, James	Sumner	640	1674	20 May 1793	858	22 Mar 1786	81	47	On E Fork of Bledsoes Creek	yes
English, Joseph	187	Beard, Joseph	Eastern District	640	1658	15 Jul 1793	1317		81	43	Beg at a large ash	yes
English, Joseph	912		Washington	160	889	17 Nov 1790	815	29 Dec 1778	76	140	N side of Nolachuckey River	
English, Joshua	025	Fenner, Richard	Tennessee	640			2449	30 Sep 1785			N side of Cumberland River	yes
English, Robert	1298		Washington	300	1184	4 Dec 1795	1323	2 Apr 1779	89	428	On SE side of the creek	
English, William	223		Hawkins	300	210	26 Dec 1791			77	317	On the N side of Holston River &c	
English, William	541		Green	640	543	20 Sep 1787		29 Dec 1778	65	538	On Horse Creek	
Enman, Abednego	118		Washington	200	286	24 Oct 1782	878	31 Dec 1778	44	291	On a branch of Big Limestone	
Enman, Abednego	276		Washington	200	84		877	31 Dec 1778	47	41	N side of Big Limestone Creek	
Enman, Ebednego	118		Washington	200	286	24 Oct 1782	878	31 Dec 1778	44	291	On a branch of Big Limestone	
Enman, Ebednego	191		Washington	200	59	23 Oct 1782	879	31 Dec 1778	47	28	E branch of Big Limestone Creek	
Ennit [?], James	249		Davidson	1600	235	14 Mar 1786	365		63	86	On both sides S fk of McOdees [?] Creek	yes
Entrytakers Certificate	078		Washington									
Eppenson [sic], Joseph	873		Green	100	823	27 Nov 1789	108	12 Jul 1789	74	22	On S side of Chuckey River	
Epperson, Anthony	1339		Washington	150	1232	2 Dec 1796	1563	31 Aug 1779	91	270	Beg @ corner red oak &c	
Epperson, Benj	090		Washington	100			305	10 Mar 1780			Beg at a white oak	
Epperson, Peter	088		Washington	100			305	10 Mar 1780			On waters of Kendricks Creek	
Epperson, Peter	089		Washington	150			2608	13 Aug 1780			On waters of Kendricks Creek	
Ervin, Andrew	1179		Davidson	640	156	17 Apr 17896	129	15 Jan 1784	66	187	On S side of Cumberland River	
Ervin, David	104		Sullivan	440	115	23 Oct 1782	230	25 Feb 1780	43	293	On S side of Holston River &c	
Ervin, George	521		Green	1040	523	20 Sep 1787	537	27 Oct 1783	65	530	Situated on N side of Holston River	
Ervin, Joseph	1221		Davidson	582	394	26 Jun 1793	536	17 Jul 1784	80	340	On Browns Creek	
Erwin, John	80(800)?		Hawkins	400	640	6 Jan 1795			83	164	On land of Panther Creek	
Erwin, Joseph	1829		Davidson	401.50	402	26 Jun 1793	530	17 Jul 1784	80	343	On Browns Creek	
Eshnall [?], Thos.	597		Green	200	554	20 Sep 1787			66	247	Beg at a red oak &c	
Espy, James	1123		Davidson	640	100	17 Apr 1786	145	16 Jan 1784	66	174	N side of Cumberland River	
Espy, James	1168		Davidson	640	145	17 Apr 1786	144	16 Jan 1784	66	185	On the N side of Cumberland River	
Espy, James	1485		Davidson	640	289	26 Nov 1789	216	30 Jan 1784	73	258	On E Fork of Bledsoes Lick Creek	
Espy, James	1552		Davidson	320	98	26 Nov 1789	114	15 Jan 1784	74	172	In a large bent [sic] of the river	

Claimant:	File #:	Assignee:	County:	Acres:	Grant:	Grant Date:	Entry:	Entry Date:	Bk:	Pg:	Location by Stream Name:	Military:
Espy, Robert	419		Middle District	1280	358	17 Dec 1794	1748	21 Apr 1784	84	233	On the Third Creek	
Espy, Robert	437		Sumner	640	322	27 Nov 1792	27	29 Dec 1783	81	2	On W Fork of Espy's Branch	
Essins, Thomas	83	Tatum, Howell	Tennessee	640	1339	10 Dec 1790	1368	9 Nov 1784	74	378	On S side of Cumberland River	yes
Ester, William	353	Howell, John	Sumner	640	1440	20 Dec 1791	2365	25 Nov 1789	77	361	S side of Cumberland River	yes
Estes, John	333		Western District	5000	333	18 May 1789	2144	11 May 1784	72	274	On S side of Big Hatchee River	
Estes, John	334		Western District	5000	334	18 May 1789	2145	11 May 1784	72	275	On both sides of Big Hatcher River	
Estes, John	335		Western District	5000	335	18 May 1789	2143	11 May 1784	72	275	On Big Hatches River &c	
Estis, Abraham	482	Bledsoe, Anthony	Sumner	320	118	27 Apr 1793	5354	19 Jul 1784	81	33	On S side of Cumberland River	yes
Estis, Jno.	1303		Davidson	640	266	10 Jul 1788	349	11 Mar 1784	66	431	Beg at a sycamore &c	
Estridge, Thomas	1918	Roberson, James	Davidson	640	1709	20 May 1793	670		81	55	On both sides of Big Harpeth River	yes
Estridge, Thomas	2057	Laurence, Adam	Davidson	640	2154	20 May 1793	1466		81	161	On S side of Cumberland River	yes
Etheredge, Daniel	1367	Jones, David & D Stewart	Sumner	1000	3216	14 Sep 1797	3283	1 Jun 1797	92	12	On Indian Creek	yes
Etheredge, Edward	1095	Easten, James	Sumner	640	2586	7 Mar 1796	3847	22 Jul 1795	88	319	On large fork of Caney Fork	yes
Etheredge, William	536	Johnson, Henry J.	Tennessee	640	2928	19 Feb 1797	2646	30 Sep 1785	90	2928	Waters of Sulphur Fork	yes
Etherington, Margaret	1017	Taylor, Elijah	Rutherford	274			3549		82	423	On branch of Broad River	
Eu-chu-lac	055		Tennessee	640	36			8 Sep 1819			Water oak & dogwd on Tennessee R	
Eunoch, or Trout	054		Tennessee	640	11			8 Sep 1819			Black oak NW corner near a branch	
Evans, Amos	658		Sullivan	300	606	5 Jun 1793	328	22 Mar 1780	81	339	On waters of Buck Creek	
Evans, Andrew	1051		Green	37	894	26 Dec 1791	1386	13 Apr 1785	77	240	Inc an island in French Broad River	
Evans, Andrew	1268		Green	250	1118	12 Jan 1793	421	21 Oct 1793	78	375	On N side of French Broad River	
Evans, Evan	1189		Green	200	1032	26 Dec 1791	13	21 Oct 1783	77	293	On the N side of Nolachuckey River	
Evans, Evan	430		Sumner	640	441	27 Jun 1793	283	14 Feb 1784	80	355	W side of Cumberland River &c	
Evans, Farlen & Elija Burress	1384		Washington	150	1310	10 Dec 1803	2396	10 Jan 1780	118	117	On waters of Indian Creek	
Evans, James	600		Hawkins	100	474	29 Jul 1793	206	26 May 1778	80	295	S side of Clinch River &c	
Evans, Jeremiah	1235	Sanders, James	Sumner	640	2508	12 Nov 1795	2980	22 Sep 1787	89	422	On the Many Fork Creek	yes
Evans, Jr.	1075		Davidson	640	49	17 Apr 1786	202	29 Jan 1784	66	51	N/S Cumberland both sides Evans Spr.	
Evans, John	148		Hawkins	250	182	26 Dec 1791	1301	1 Jan 1784	75	176	On S side of Holston River	
Evans, John	168		Green	112	638	23 Aug 1788	802	28 Dec 1778	64	354	On N side of Holston River	
Evans, John	413		Hawkins	200	301	27 Nov 1792	677	9 Dec 1778	85 (80)	148	S side of Holston River &c	
Evans, John	414		Hawkins	200	302	27 Nov 1792	156	14 Mar 1778	80	148	S/S of Holston River on Dodsons Cr	
Evans, John	421		Hawkins	150	309	23 Aug 1788	206	7 Mar 1785	80	150	S side of Holston River &c	
Evans, John	802		Green	150	607				68	264	S/S of Holston River	
Evans, Joseph	997	Drake, Jonathan	Davidson	640	1014	18 May 1789	3265	21 Feb 1780	63	340	On Halfpone Creek	yes
Evans, Nathan. & Thos. King	1680		Green	500	1385	20 Jul 1796	216	21 Feb 1780	88	494	On waters of Long Creek	
Evans, Nathaniel	279		Green	600 [?]	281	20 Sep 1787	93	20 May 1785	65	453	On N/S French Broad R on Long Cr	
Evans, Nathaniel	76		Eastern District	600	1111	26 Dec 1791	1230	7 Nov 1783	75	154	On S side of French Broad River	
Evans, Philip	1128	Harris, Edward	Sumner	640	2634	4 Jun 1796	3001	1 Jul 1795	88	345	Joining sd Harris survey	yes
Evans, Richard	1163	Harris, Edward	Sumner	640	2668	4 Jun 1796	3881	1 Jun 1795	88	357	Joining sd Harris survey	yes
Evans, Richard	193	Alcuff, Timothy	Davidson	640	178	7 Mar 1786	1223		63	67	Bet Stewarts & Foaming Creek	yes
Evans, Thomas	531		Davidson	3840	503	15 Sep 1787	564		63	182	On waters of Big Harpeth River	yes
Evans, Thomas	672		Washington	100	486	10 Nov 1784	1398	24 May 1779	69	99	Bet Martin & John Webb's	
Evans, Thomas	870		Sumner	428	2387	31 Dec 1793	1569	12 Dec 1785	81	387	On waters of Station Camp	yes
Evans, Thos.	1636	Gary, Joseph	Davidson	228	370	30 Nov 1790	1572		74	393	On N side of Cumberland River	yes
Evans, William	495	Hart, Anthony	Tennessee	640	2495	26 Sep 1795	2801	30 Sep 1785	89	105	On Wellses Creek	yes
Evans, William	638		Hawkins	100	507	23 Apr 1794	397	8 Apr 1780	81	551	Joining a survey of John Evans	yes

Earliest Tennessee Land Records

Claimant:	File #:	Assignee:	County:	Acres:	Grant:	Grant Date:	Entry:	Entry Date:	Bk:	Pg:	Location by Stream Name:	Military:
Evens, Nathan & Jos.	1300		Green	300	1150	12 Jan 1793	2339		78	395	On waters of French Broad River	
Evens, Waller	233		Hawkins	24	220	26 Dec 1791		11 Jan 1780	77	320	In an Island of Holston River	
Everett, James	1340		Washington	70	1233	13 Dec 1796	1201	10 Feb 1779	91	310	On Sinking Creek	
Everett, Thos.	764	Lanier, James	Davidson	640	737	11 Jul 1788	3461		63	259	On the main salt lick &c	yes
Everit, John	495		Washington	225	758	16 Aug 1787	2648	19 Sep 1780	64	138	Joining lands of John Everit	
Evins, Evin	1057		Green	40	900	26 Dec 1791		12 Jul 1789 [sic]	77	242	On N side of Chuckey River	
Evins, John	1562		Green	150	214	30 Oct 1794			83	141	N side of French Broad River	
Evins, John	215		Hawkins	400	202	26 Dec 1791	1629	16 Sep 1779	77	314	Lying on the Great Road	
Evins, John	227		Hawkins	640	214	26 Dec 1791	1632	6 Sep 1779	77	318	Opposite the head of Panter (?) Cr	
Evins, Jonathan	543		Green	500	545	20 Sep 1787	14	3 Feb 1785	65	539	On Little Sinking Creek	
Eweel, Stephen	285	Bonner, James	Sumner	523	1283	10 Dec 1790	1125	23 Mar 1789	74	360	On Peytons Creek	yes
Ewell, Samuel	1700	Campbell, Michael & P. Phil	Davidson	640	1661	23 Feb 1793	3152		76	341	Beg at a black walnut	yes
Ewell, William	515	Williams, Willoughby	Davidson	404	487	15 Sep 1787	429		63	176	S side of Cumberland River	yes
Ewing, Alexander	312	Bond, Jas.	Sumner	224	1525	10 Apr 1792	1628	27 Jun 1788	75	509	On Smiths Fork &c	yes
Ewing, Alexander	541	Manning, John heirs	Sumner	640	1743	20 May 1793	1513	6 Mar 1788	81	64	On both sides of Cedar Lick Creek	yes
Ewing, Alexander	686	Davis, Leonard	Davidson	640	659	8 Dec 1787	1005		63	233	On both sides Big Harpeth River	yes
Ewing, Alexander	893	Brewington, Benj.	Davidson	640	909	17 Jan 1789			63	314	On both sides of Smiths Fork	yes
Ewing, George	124		Green	487	150	1 Nov 1786	247	1 Nov 1786	59	443	N side of Holston River	
Ewing, Robert	1468		Davidson	50	75	18 May 1789	3064		71	227	On waters of Drakes Creek	
Ewing, Robert	1469		Davidson	50	76	18 May 1789	3046	30 Oct 1786	71	227	On the middle fork of Red River	
Ewing, Robert	1470		Davidson	50	77	18 May 1789	3045	30 Oct 1786	71	228	Waters of middle fork of Red River	
Ewing, Robert	1892	Armstrong, M.	Davidson	100	126	27 Apr 1793		3 Oct 1786	81	31	First main right hand fk of Whites Cr	
Ewing, Robert	2299	Martin, John	Davidson	400	159	26 Mar 1795			89	89	On W of Cumberland Mt	
Ewing, Robert	2300	Martin, John	Davidson	400	161	26 Mar 1795			89	90	On W of Cumberland Mt.	
Ewing, Samuel	1261		Davidson	640	226	10 Jul 1788	611	29 Oct 1784	66	418	On N side of Red River &c	
Ewing, William	1174		Green	300	1017	26 Dec 1791	2258	22 Nov 1779	77	287	On N side of Holstein River &c	
Ewins, Thomas	497		Davidson	640	469	15 Sep 1787	1061		63	170	S side of Cumberland River	yes
Exum, Etheldred	977	Tuton, William	Davidson	640	994	18 May 1789	1899		63	335	On the Caney Fork	yes
Faddis, James	264	Fifer, Caleb	Davidson	640	250	7 Mar 1786	669		63	91	On Pleasant Creek	yes
Faigan, George	1529	McDowell, Joseph	Davidson	640	1086	26 Nov 1789	2031		74	124	On Mill Creek	yes
Fain, John	40		Washington	100	330	24 Oct 1782	109	26 Feb 1778	43	310	On a branch of Cherokee Creek	
Fain, Melchior	2346	Malloy, Thomas	Davidson	640	2991	10 Apr 1797	3634		90	289	On waters of Little Harpeth River	yes
Fain, Nicholas	219		Washington	400	87	23 Oct 1782	298	4 Aug 1778	47	42	On a branch of Little Limestone	
Fain, Nicholas	236		Washington	200	104	23 Oct 1782	158	26 Feb 1778	47	50	On a branch of Little Limestone	
Fain, Samuel	401		Washington	640	393	13 Oct 1783	309	2 Sep 1778	52	262	On W side of Nob Creek	
Fain, Samuel	634		Washington	400	726	26 Oct 1786	251	2 Jul 1778	66	25	On a branch of Little Limestone	
Fain, William	1351		Washington	165 (144	1268	19 Oct 1797	1262	2 Mar 1779	92	45	On head draughts of a branch &c	
Fain, William	1352		Washington	200	1269	19 Oct 1797	2551	2 May 1780	92	46	On head draughts of Knobb Creek	
Fain, William	617		Washington	200	711	26 Oct 1786	2647	10 Sep 1780	66	16	Beg at a marked chesnut	
Faircloth, William	042	Ford, John	not given	640			1559	19 Jul 1785			On first large creek &c	yes
Faircloth, William	537	Williams, Etheldred	Middle District	730	2961	2 Mar 1797	4077		90	256	On a creek known by name of Mill	yes
Faircloth, William	881	Ford, John	Davidson	640	895	17 Jan 1789			63	310	On the 1st large creek &c	yes
Fairfax, Frederick	700	Sheppard, Benjamin	Davidson	1000	673	8 Dec 1787	2307		63	238	On n side of Cumberland River	yes
Fairfax, William	399	Sheppard, Benj.	Davidson	640	371	15 Sep 1787	2310		63	139	On both sides W Fork of Drakes Cr	yes
Faison, James	613	Kemp, Joseph	Tennessee	274	3172	14 Sep 1797	4033	25 Nov 1796	90	430	S side of Cumberland River	yes

Claimant:	File #:	Assignee:	County:	Acres:	Grant:	Grant Date:	Entry:	Entry Date:	Bk:	Pg:	Location by Stream Name:	Military:
Faith, William	786	Fuller, John	Davidson	640	759	11 Jul 1788	3344		63	266	On W side of Samuel Hepleys claim	yes
Faithfull, William	1926	Robertson, James	Davidson	640	1737	20 May 1793	910	3 entry dates	81	63	On Harpeth River	yes
Fammon, Richard	716		Sullivan	394	661	4 Dec 1794	3 warrants		84	166	On N side of Holston River	
Fanner, Thomas	749	Broknes, Thomas	Davidson	640	722	11 Jul 1788	879		63	254	On head of Caleb Winters Creek	yes
Fannon, Thomas	789	McCulloch, Benjamin	Sumner	274	2248	20 May 1793	3002	30 Nov 1792	81	180	On the Defeated Creek	yes
Faragut, George	199		Eastern District	380	171	8 Apr 1794	173	19 Feb 1780	81	558	On 3rd creek in the Grassey Valley	
Farden, Joseph	712	Tramer [?], Phillip	Davidson	640	685	8 Dec 1787	2513		63	241	On Middle Fork of Red River	yes
Farmer, John	1616	Douglas, David	Davidson	640	1344	10 Dec 1790	2512		74	380	On waters of Bartons Creek	yes
Farmer, Peter	593	Barton, Samuel	Tennessee	1000	3063	19 Jul 1797	3594		90	375	Waters of Little West Fork	yes
Farmer, Thomas	1101	Truett, Franklin	Sumner	640	2602	7 Mar 1796	673		88	327	On S side of Obeys River	yes
Farmer, Thomas	1102	Crabtree, John	Sumner	640	2603	7 Mar 1796	878		88	328	On S side of Obeys River	yes
Farmer, Thomas	1103	Teuton, Caleb	Sumner	640	2604	7 Mar 1796			88	328	On N side of Obeys River	yes
Farmer, William	119	Clark, Lardner & Wycoff	Davidson	228	105	7 Mar 1786	413		63	42	N side of Cumberland River	yes
Farns, Thos. Hr. of Jno.	550		Davidson	640	522	15 Sep 1787	629		63	188	First creek below the Cross Creeks	yes
Farnsworth, George	1606		Green	56	1323	4 Feb 1795			84	108	On S side of Nolachucka River	
Farnsworth, Henry	119		Green	655	135	1 Nov 1786	159	22 Oct 1783	59	438	On Richland Creek	
Farnsworth, Henry	587		Green	224	268	20 Sep 1787	96	21 Oct 1783	66	163	Joining Benja Jamisons land	
Farrell, Clement	53	Hamilton, Thomas	Tennessee	640	1258	10 Dec 1790	1054	26 May 1784	74	351	On S side of Cumberland River	yes
Farrow, William	423	Allison, John	Davidson	228	395	15 Sep 1787	1090		63	147	N side of Cumberland River	yes
Faulkner, Francis	055	Dillenberry, Redmon	Sumner	640			4461	6 Sep 1797			Waters of S Fork Red River	yes
Faulkner, Francis	1573		Davidson	428	1216	10 Dec 1790	799		74	336	On S side of Cumberland River	yes
Fauller, Wm.	054		Green	100			1200	6 Apr 1781			On S side of Blair Creek	
Fawn, William	81		Davidson	3840	67	14 Mar 1786	231		63	27	On fork of Elk Creek	yes
Faybourne, Joel	658	Cook, Richard	Tennessee	60	3235	24 Nov 1797	925	19 May 1784	94	170	Waters of Wells Creek	yes
Feary, Jno.	604		Green	121	561	20 Sep 1787			66	249	On S side of Holston River &c	
Felin, Jas. & S. Williams	1468		Sumner	640	475	28 Dec 1802	545	23 Jul 1784	116	334	On N bank of Cumberland River	yes
Fell, Watson	1275	Pendlar, Thos. Heirs	Tennessee	640	3017	10 Apr 1797	3181		90	300	Abt 1-1/2 miles below Dyers Creek	
Feltner, Henry	380		Hawkins	100	501	27 Jan 1793			79	491	Joining the plantation he lives on	
Felts, Archibald	604	Bates, Luke	Sumner	640	1854	20 May 1793	495	12 Sep 1792	81	90	On W Fork of Drakes Creek	yes
Fenner, Richard	048	Howell, Peter	Not given	640								Yes
Fenner, Richard	073	Heel, Joseph	Sumner	640			2101	17 May 1788			N side of Cumberland River	yes
Fenner, Richard	080	Hadley, Joshua	Sumner	640			2914	22 Dec 1792			On waters of Station Camp	yes
Fenner, Richard	10		Tennessee	640	1158	26 Nov 1789	2168	12 Sep 1785	74	158	On N side of Cumberland River	
Fenner, Richard	11	Alford, Jno.	Tennessee	640	1159	26 Nov 1789	2165	12 Sep 1785	74	158	On N side of Cumberland River	
Fenner, Richard	13		Tennessee	640	1161	26 Nov 1789			74	159	On N side of Cumberland River	
Fenner, Richard	288		Davidson	2560	274	22 Mar 1787	399		63	100	On waters of Station Camp	yes
Fenner, Richard	289	Richardson, James hrs.	Davidson	640	275	22 Mar 1787	2542		63	100	On Sulphur Fork of Red River	yes
Fenner, Richard	290	Griffin, Jacob	Davidson	640	276	22 Mar 1787	2096		63	101	S side of Cumberland River	yes
Fenner, Richard	291	Benson(?), John hrs.	Davidson	640	277	22 Mar 1787	2171		63	101	S side of Cumberland River	yes
Fenner, Richard	292	Green, Randel heirs	Davidson	640	278	22 Mar 1787	2095		63	102	S side of Cumberland River	yes
Fenner, Richard	32	Langston, Josiah hrs	Sumner	640	843	17 Jan 1789	2103	17 May 1788	63	295	On N side of Cumberland	yes
Fenner, Richard	325	Dillard, Peter	Davidson	640	311	28 Jun 1787	2181		63	116	On waters of Second Creek	yes
Fenner, Richard	328	Allen, Thomas hrs	Davidson	640	314	28 Jun 1787	2163		63	117	On waters of Sulphur Fork	yes
Fenner, Richard	329	Cooper, Solomon hrs	Davidson	640	315	28 Jun 1787	2117		63	117	On waters of Caney Fork Creek	yes
Fenner, Richard	330	Dukes, Arthur hrs	Davidson	640	316	28 Jun 1787	2180		63	118	On waters of Second Creek	yes

Earliest Tennessee Land Records

Claimant:	File #:	Assignee:	County:	Acres:	Grant:	Grant Date:	Entry:	Entry Date:	Bk:	Pg:	Location by Stream Name:	Military:
Fenner, Richard	331	Cherry, Job heirs	Davidson	640	317	28 Jun 1787	2179		63	118	S side of Cumberland River	yes
Fenner, Richard	332	Carter, Henry hrs	Davidson	640	318	28 Jun 1787	2178		63	118	S/S Cumberland 1st cr below Goose	yes
Fenner, Richard	42	Steel, Joseph hrs	Sumner	640	875	17 Jan 1789	3478 [?]	19 Feb 1788	63	303	On N side of Cumberland River	yes
Fenner, Richard	518	Reyley, John	Davidson	640	490	15 Sep 1787	2540		63	177	On N boundary of Phillips Alston	yes
Fenner, Richard	52		Tennessee	640	1257	10 Dec 1790	2501	30 Sep 1785	74	351	On S side of Cumberland River	
Fenner, Richard	77		Western District	5000	77	11 Jul 1788	2567	25 May 1784	67	310	On mouth of Woolf River	
Fenner, Richard	773	Hickman, Charles hrs	Davidson	640	746	11 Jul 1788			63	262	On N side of Sycamore	yes
Fenner, Richard	780	Fenner, Richard	Davidson	640	753	11 Jul 1788	2190		63	264	On N waters of Sycamore Creek	Yes
Fenner, Richard	780	Hatten, James	Davidson	640	753	11 Jul 1788	2190		63	264	On N waters of Sycamore Creek	yes
Fenner, Richard	837	Glover, Solomon hrs	Sumner	640	840	17 Jan 1789	2185	13 Mar 1788	63	295	On Caney Fork River	yes
Fenner, Richard	846	Broomfield, Moses hrs	Davidson	640	851	17 Jan 1789	2170		63	297	On N side of Cumberland River	yes
Fenner, Richard	9	Parker(?), Saml.	Tennessee	640	1157	26 Nov 1789	2167	12 Sep 1785	74	157	On N side of Cumberland River	
Fenner, Richd	025	English, Joshua	Tnnessee	640			2449	30 Sep 1785			N side of Cumberland River	
Fenner, Richd	860	Zealott, Joshua	Davidson	640	871	17 Jan 1789	3395		63	302	On N side of Cumberland River	yes
Fenner, Robert	52		Middle District	4030	54	10 Jul 1788	2660	25 May 1784	67	437	On S/S Richland Creek of Elk River	
Fenner, Robert	97		Davidson	3840	83	14 Mar 1786	333		63	34	On Blue Creek	yes
Fenner, William	48	Anderson, Daniel	Tennessee	640	1247	10 Dec 1790	2806	30 Sep 1785	74	347	On N side of Cumberland River	yes
Fenners, Robert hr. of Wm.	35		Davidson	2057	21	14 Mar 1786	332		63	9	Both sides Sulphur Fork of Red River	yes
Fenton, John	858		Green	320	838	13 Feb 1791	1303	1 Jan 1784	73	382	On Long Cr waters of Chuckey River	yes
Fenton, Thomas	451	Walton, William	Sumner	640	1573	27 Apr 1793	3259	19 Dec 1787	81	11	On both sides of a fork of Roaring River	yes
Fenwick, Nathaniel	1302	Hickman, Thomas	Sumner	640	3071	19 Jul 1797	4700	6 Apr 1797	90	379	Headwaters of Round Lick Creek	yes
Ferebee, Joseph	64		Davidson	1371	50	14 Mar 1786	675		63	21	On waters of Mill Creek	yes
Ferebee, William	78		Davidson	3062	64	14 Mar 1786	688		63	26	On Beaver Creek	yes
Fergison, John	1275		Washington	200 (284	1213	4 Dec 1795	524	22 Oct 1778	89	331	On waters of Big Limestone	
Fergus, James	89		Davidson	4800	75	14 Mar 1786	742		63	31	On waters of Mill Creek	yes
Ferrel, John	780		Hawkins	100	620	12 Jul 1794	839	12 Jan 1784	82	219	Waters of the West fork of Flat Cr	
Ferrel, Enoch	855	Cartwright, Robert	Davidson	366	863	7 Jan 1787	21		63	300	On waters of Station Camp Creek	yes
Ferrell, James	1884	Herndon, Benjamin	Davidson	274	1889	20 May 1793	42		81	98	On Harpeth River in the first bend	yes
Ferrell, John	273		Green	200	275	20 Sep 1787	83	8 Feb 1780	65	451 (45	On N side of Holston River &c	
Ferrell, William	0133	Armstrong, M.	Sumner	640							On waters of Cedar Creek	yes
Ferrell, William	79	Rice, John	Tennessee	640	1324	10 Dec 1790	1077 [?]	1 Jun 1784	74	373	On N side of Cumberland River	yes
Ferrill, Isaac	037		Sullivan	100	787	27 May 1781					S side of Holston River	
Ferrill, Jacob	319	Rice, John & others	Davidson	640	305	13 June 1787	767	24 Apr 1780	63	114	N side of Tennessee River	yes
Fettner [sic], Henry	038		Sullivan	100			458				Joining plantation he now lives on	
Fifer, Caleb	264	Faddis, Jno hr of James	Davidson	640	250	7 Mar 1786	669		63	91	On Pleasant Creek	
Filigena [?], William	062	Sheppard, John	Middle District	640			2848					yes
Fin, Jno.	717		Green	100	758	11 Jul 1788	120	21 Oct 1783	66	481	S/S Nolichuckey & on Flag Branch	
Fine, John	1041		Washington	150	991	14 Jan 1793	1549	25 Aug 1779	79	282	On N fork of Cherokee Creek	
Fine, Peter	602		Green	200	559	20 Sep 1787	229	27 Jul 1785	66	249	N/S French Broad Riv above mo Clear Cr	
Fine, Vinet	055		Green	200			825	29 Oct 1783			Beg at a white oak tree	
Finley, Abraham	057	Sheppard, John	Middle District	640			2913					yes
Finley, James	021		Hawkins	200			2240	22 Nov 1779				
Finley, James	249		Eastern District	640	237	26 Dec 1791			77	325	Including the plantation he now lives on	
Finley, John	033		Eastern District	100							On waters of New River	
Finly, Abraham	670	Mann, John	Tennessee	640	3257	6 Dec 1797	2913		98	146	On Barretts Creek	yes

Claimant:	File #:	Assignee:	County:	Acres:	Grant:	Grant Date:	Entry:	Entry Date:	Bk:	Pg:	Location by Stream Name:	Military:
Finn, John	0113		Green	200			1403	24 May 1779			N side French Broad River	
Finn, John	431		Green	150	433	20 Sep 1787	1403	24 May 1779	65	497	Waters Lick Cr on John Prices Branch	
Finney, Thomas	0129	Wilson, James	Sumner	274			2002	26 Nov 1792			On waters of Caney Fork	yes
Finney, Thomas	51		Davidson	2560	37	14 Mar 1786	108		63	15	On Richland Creek	yes
Fishback, Jacob	545		Green	400	547	20 Sep 1787	126	19 Feb 1785	65	540	On N side of Nolachuckey	
Fishburn, Phillip	848	Parker, Joseph	Sumner	1000	2351	20 May 1793	1492	27 Oct 1792	81	202	At the head of Flins Creek	yes
Fisher, Archibald	467		Sullivan	300	346	10 Nov 1784	2131	8 Oct 1780	69	194	On N side of Holstein River	
Fisher, Frederick	042	Parker, William	Davidson	640			3140	12 Sep 1790			Ridge hdwts Whites Cr & Marrowbone	yes
Fisher, Joel	316	McCulloh, Benj	Tennessee	640	2017	20 May 1793	2989	30 Sep 1785	81	128	On S side Cumberland River	yes
Fisher, Joshua	1460		Sumner	200	206	17 Mar 1801		10 Aug 1800	112	364	Waters of Rocky Creek	yes
Fisher, Peter	074		Sumner	400				27 Nov 1792			Middle Fork Drakes Creek	yes
Fisher, Peter	075		Sumner	400				27 Nov 1792			Middle Fork Drakes Creek	yes
Fisher, Peter	077		Sumner	400				27 Nov 1792			On waters of Rocky Creek	
Fist, Samuel	430	Nickels, John	Davidson	640	402	15 Sep 1787	1189		63	149	On E side of Caney Fork	yes
Fitzgarold, Garrett	558		Sullivan	40	541	17 Nov 1790	2650	19 Sep 1780	76	191	Joining tract Fitzgarold formerly lived	
Fitzgarrald, Garret	1693		Green	100	1368	9 Dec 1795	762	24 Mar 1781	89	403	On N side of French Broad River	
Fitzgarrald, Garret	1694		Green	100	1369	9 Dec 1795	784	27 May 1781	89	404	N/S French Broad Riv nr lead mines	
Fitzgarrald, Garret	259		Hawkins	400	1038	Mar 1792			77	335	On a branch of Lick Creek	
Fitzgarrald, Garrett	1195		Green	1000	1039	Mar 1792	2443	23 May 1784	77	336	On N side of French Broad River	
Fitzgarrald, Garrett	1196	Swingle, Michael & Jno	Green	350	1040	Mar 1792	1735	17 Apr 1784	77	336	On N side of French Broad River	
Fitzgarrald, Garrett	208		Sullivan	400	215	10 Oct 1783	427	25 Sep 1778	53	165	On Buck Creek	
Fitzgarrald, Garrett	291		Sullivan	100	430	9 Aug 1787	531	29 Apr 1780	61	449	On S side of Holston	
Fitzgarrald, Jarrett	987		Green	640	1214	29 Jul 1793	2398	25 May 1784	76	470	N side of French Broad River	
Fitzgarrold, Garrett	715		Green	400	756 [?]	11 Jul 1788	1538	18 Jan 1787	66	480	On N side of Holston River &c	
Fitzgarrold, Garrett	276		Sullivan	100	615	9 Aug 1787	398	7 Sep 1778	61	434	Beg at Vances corner	
Fitzgarrold, Garrett	532		Sullivan	177	527	13 Feb 1791	529	23 Oct 1778	73	383	On a branch of Holston River &c	
Fitzgerald, Garet	126		Green	150	142	1 Nov 1786	368	23 Oct 1783	59	445	S side of Nolachuckie River	
Fitzgerald, Garret	25		Green	600	88	1 Nov 1786	10	28 Nov 1785	58	449	On N side of French Broad River	
Fitzgerald, Garrett	922		Green	300	836	17 Nov 1790	11	29 Nov 1785	76	117	On waters of French Broad River	
Fitzgereld, Jno. King	614		Green	400	655	11 Jul 1788	326	18 Jan 1787	66	445	On a branch of French Broad River	
Fitzgereld, Garrett	457		Sullivan	200	336	10 Mar 1784	1872	20 May 1779	69	189	Beg at a spanish oak	
Fitzgerrald, Garret	716		Green	300	757	11 Jul 1788	1544	17 Mar 1784	66	480	On Richland Creek &c	
Fitzgerrald, Garret	84		Green	300	42	1 Nov 1786	7	21 Oct 1783	59	403	N side of the French Broad	
Fitzgerrald, Garret	921		Green	640	835	17 Nov 1790	978	29 Oct 1783	76	116	On waters of French Broad River	
Fitzgerreld, Garrett	385		Sullivan	100	264	10 Nov 1784	762	24 Mar 1781	69	166	In the Sugar Tree Valley	
Fitzgerreld, Garrett, Ass.	0133		Green	400	1038	Mar 1792	1538	17 Mar 1784			On a branch of Lick Creek	
Fitzjarrell, Jarret	204		Sullivan	63	211	10 Oct 1783	2440	28 Feb 1780	53	163	On Horse Creek	
Fitzpatrick, Jarret	02		Jefferson	640			5	25 Feb 1778				
Fitzpatrick, John	1126		Hawkins	200	845	2 Nov 1797	175	19 Feb 1780	96	4	Both sides of Powells River	
Flack, James	220		Middle District	290	200	27 Nov 1792	2013	1 May 1784	80	208	On N side of Duck River	
Flanagan, George	839	Brock, Joseph	Davidson	640	842	17 Jan 1789	3346		63	295	On N side of Cumberland River	yes
Flanakin, Samuel	192		Washington	200	60	23 Oct 1782	587	7 Nov 1778	47	28	N side of Nolachuckey River	
Flanery, Daniel	1317	_ork(?), Wm.	Davidson	320	3	18 Aug 1787	419	24 Apr 1784	68	121	On Red River	
Fleming, Joseph	395		Davidson	640	367	15 Sep 1787	636		63	138	N side of Cumberland River	yes
Fleming, Thomas	44	Williams, Sampson	Sumner	640	888	17 Jan 1789	1708		63	308	On Little Fork of Spencers Creek	yes

Earliest Tennessee Land Records

Claimant:	File #:	Assignee:	Acres:	County:	Grant:	Grant Date:	Entry:	Entry Date:	Bk:	Pg:	Location by Stream Name:	Military:
Fleming, Wm.	450	Privet, Rosana	274	Sumner	1572	27 Apr 1793	542	12 Oct 1792	81	10	On N side of Cedar Lick Creek	yes
Fleming, Wm.	622	Rice, John	640	Sumner	1898	20 May 1793	1188	12 Oct 1792	81	100	On S side of Cumberland River	yes
Flesher, Robert	020	Johnson, Henry, Jr.	640	Robertson	2929		1834	13 Aug 1796			On waters of Spring Creek	yes
Fletcher, Aaron	022		30	Hawkins			748	14 Feb 1781			S bank of the Holston River	
Fletcher, Aaron	041		20	Sullivan			748	14 Feb 1781			On S bank of Holston River	
Fletcher, Golden	518		100	Hawkins	391	29 Jul 1793	563	31 Oct 1778	80	275	On S side of Holston River	
Fletcher, Jeremiah	1033	Sheppard, John	640	Sumner	2570	8 Mar 1796	2912	15 Aug 1792	88	190	On Obeys River	yes
Fletcher, John	1135	Harris, Edward	640	Sumner	2641	4 Jun 1796	1992	1 Jun 1795	88	348	Joining sd Harris survey	yes
Fletcher, Joseph	20	Mallet, Theodore	640	Tennessee	1168	26 Nov 1789	3342	7 Jan 1786	74	163	On N side of Cumberland River	yes
Fletcher, Simon	89		100	Eastern District	78	17 Nov 1790	2659	27 Sep 1780	76	169	S side of Holstein River	
Fletcher, Thomas	104		100	Washington	272	24 Oct 1782	559	29 Oct 1778	44	284	Beg on 2 white pines	
Fletcher, Thomas	204		580	Davidson	190	7 Mar 1786	681		63	71	E Fork of Mill Creek	yes
Fletcher, William	566		1000	Davidson	538	15 Sep 1787	986		63	193	S side of Cumberland River	yes
Flewry [?], Henry	738		1000	Sumner	2131	20 May 1793	3580	4 Jun 1791	81	156	Both sides of E Fork of Roaring River	yes
Flimin, Samuel	069	Sugg, Geo. A.	640	Davidson			2802	29 Jun 1791			On headwaters of Marrowbone	yes
Fling, Michael	7	Mountflorence, J. C.	640	Tennessee	1155	26 Nov 1789	2120	9 Sep 1785	74	156	On N side of Sulphur Fork &c	yes
Flipen, Thomas	053		475	Green			211	7 Jun 1784			S side of Holston River	
Flipen, Thomas	140		475	Hawkins	174	26 Dec 1791			75	173	On S side of Holston River	
Flippen, Thomas	220		200	Green	177	20 Sep 1787	1413	17 Jan 1784	65	423	On N side Holston River &c	
Flippen, Thomas	230		200	Green	187	20 Sep 1787	562	27 Oct 1783	65	426	On N side Holston River &c	
Flood, Alexander	732		304	Davidson	705	11 Jul 1788	724		63	248	2 or 3 miles N of Cumberland River	
Flood, Benjamin	170		640	Davidson	156	7 Mar 1786	406		63	59	S side of Cumberland River	yes
Flood, Elisha	2081	McCulloh, Benjamin	640	Davidson	2266	20 May 1793	2013		81	184	On waters of Stones River	yes
Flood, Frederick	092	Lytle, Archibald	640	Sumner			1052	24 Mar 1787			S side of Cumberland River	yes
Flood, Joseph	385	Thomas, Richard	640	Sumner	1569	4 Feb 1793	2321	30 Nov 1792	79	293	On waters of Dixons Creek	yes
Flood, Zachariah	562	Sheppard, Benjamin	640	Davidson	534	15 Sep 1787	2317		63	192	S side of Big Barren River	yes
Flora, Daniel	980		100	Hawkins	752	20 Jul 1796	35	8 Feb 1780	88	501	Joining a survey of Carmacks	
Flord, Augustine	246	Armstrong, Andrew	640	Sumner	1151	26 Nov 1789	2451	7 Oct 1789	74	154	On head of Drakes Creek	yes
Floron, Lazarus	21		274	Davidson	7	16 Feb 1786	988		63	4	On Little Harper	
Flowers, Charles	334	Armstrong, Andrew	640	Davidson	320	28 Jun 1787	2182		63	119	W Fork of Goose Creek	yes
Flowers, David	309		2500	Western District	298	25 Apr 1789	2140	11 May 1784	72	91	On waters of Big Hatcher River &c	yes
Flowers, William	594	Hill, William	274	Middle District	3087	19 Aug 1797	4373		92	2	Middle District on Barron Creek	yes
Flowron [?], Richard	23		274	Davidson	9	16 Feb 1786	989		63	4	S side of Cumberland River	yes
Floyd, Charles	365	Sanders, Williams	640	Davidson	345	15 Sep 1787	1614		63	130	On Money Fk Creek	yes
Floyd, Francis	311	McCulloh, Benjamin	640	Tennessee	2012	20 May 1793	2010	16 Aug 1785	81	127	On S side of Cumberland River	yes
Floyd, Joseph	2101	Sheppard, Nancy	640	Davidson	2326	20 May 1793	1766		81	196	On 2nd Creek &c	yes
Fluellen, Isaac	869	Brandon, William	640	Sumner	2385	1 Jan 1794	3431	19 Sep 1792	81	386	Beg at a large Sycamore	yes
Fogarty, James	595	Wilson, John	274	Davidson	567	15 Sep 1787	204		63	203	N side of Cumberland River	yes
Folk, Christopher	467	Robeson [sic], James	640	Tennessee	2597	7 Mar 1796	1335	3 Nov 1784	88	325	On the Upper West Fk	yes
Folsom, Nathaniel	1072		250	Hawkins	799	10 Apr 1797	2250	22 Nov 1779	91	567	On Rob Camp Creek &c	yes
Folsom, Nathaniel	1073		250	Hawkins	800	10 Apr 1797	2254	22 Nov 1779	91	568	On Powells River	
Folsom, Nathaniel	1074		300	Hawkins	801	10 Apr 1797	2258	22 Nov 1779	91	568	On Powells River	
Folsom, Nathaniel	1075		300	Hawkins	802	10 Apr 1797	2197	12 Nov 1779	91	569	N fork of Clinch River	
Folsom, Nathaniel	1076		300	Hawkins	803	10 Apr 1797	2196	12 Nov 1779	91	569	N fork of Clinch River &c	
Folsom, Nathaniel	1077		300	Hawkins	804	10 Apr 1797	2200	12 Nov 1779	91	569	N Fork of Clinch River &c	

Claimant:	File #:	Assignee:	County:	Acres:	Grant:	Grant Date:	Entry:	Entry Date:	Bk:	Pg:	Location by Stream Name:	Military:
Folsom, Nathaniel	1079		Hawkins	250	806	17 Apr 1797	2251	22 Nov 1779	91	571	On Rob Camp Creek &c	
Forbes, Joseph (or Joshua)	546		Davidson	428	518	15 Sep 1787	674		63	187	On waters of Mill Creek	yes
Ford, Alexander	703		Sullivan	100	648	5 Dec 1794	164	17 Feb 1780	84	160	Beg at a hickory & beech	
Ford, Alexander	806		Sullivan	40	749	17 Nov 1797	14	1 Feb 1780	94	150	N side Holstein River	
Ford, Elias	941	Grant, Ephraim heirs	Davidson	640	957	18 May 1789			63	326	Beg at the N E corner of Suggs tract	yes
Ford, James	026		Montgomery	640			3736	13 Oct 1796			On waters of Sulphur Fork	yes
Ford, John	042	Faircloth, Wm.	not given	640			1559	19 Jul 1785			On 1st large cr S/S Cumberland Riv	
Ford, John	07		Davidson	640			142	29 Mar 1784			On the head of Thomas Creek	
Ford, John	1599	Grimes, Ant hr of And.	Davidson	640	1292	10 Dec 1790	2454		74	363	On waters of Mill Creek	yes
Ford, John	1989	King, Edmund	Davidson	640	1905	20 May 1793	953		81	101	On N/S Cumberland on Parsons Cr	yes
Ford, John	455	Armstrong, M. & A. Crutch	Davidson	2560	427	15 Sep 1787	298		63	158	On Thompsons Creek	yes
Ford, John	463	Griffin, Wm.	Sumner	640	1610	27 Apr 1793	357		81	20	On a fork of Roaring River	yes
Ford, John	47	Phew, Richd	Sumner	640	965	18 May 1789	2217	20 Sep 1788	63	328	On N Fork of Puncheon Camp Creek	yes
Ford, John	619	Hagins, James	Davidson	640	591	15 Sep 1787	898		63	211	On S side of Cumberland	yes
Ford, John	834		Washington	100	648	10 Nov 1784	2681	11 Dec 1780	69	151	On Sinking Creek	
Ford, John	861	Lewis, Jonathan	Davidson	274	874	17 Jan 1789	1642		63	303	On N side of Cumberland	yes
Ford, John	873	Goldsberry, Wm.	Davidson	640	886	17 Jan 1789	1861		63	307	On waters of Battle Ground Creek	yes
Ford, John	881	Faircloth, William	Davidson	640	895	17 Jan 1789			63	310	On 1st large cr on S/S of Cumberland	yes
Ford, John	882	Coward, Peter	Davidson	640	896	17 Jan 1789			63	310	On N side of Cumberland River	yes
Ford, John	883	Middleton, Solomon	Davidson	640	897	17 Jan 1789	921		63	311	On N side of Cumberland River	yes
Ford, John	884	Daffin, John	Davidson	640	898	17 Jan 1789	2645		63	311	On N side of Cumberland River	yes
Ford, John	885	Bond(?), James	Davidson	640	899	17 Jan 1789	927		63	311	On N side of Cumberland River	yes
Ford, John	888	Willis, Wm. Hr of Taylor	Davidson	640	904	17 Jan 1789	3243		63	321	On N side of Cumberland River	yes
Ford, John	974		Washington	178	952	17 Nov 1790	2517	4 Apr 1780	76	162	On head waters of Sinking Creek	
Ford, Loyd	183		Sullivan	371	190	10 Oct 1783	541	29 Apr 1780	53	154	On Sinking Creek	
Ford, Loyd	217		Sullivan	200	224	10 Oct 1783	555	1 May 1780	53	168	On both sides of Cavetts Mill Creek	
Ford, Milton	730		Hawkins	92	550	12 Jun 1794	685	3 Aug 1780	82	171	Joining Ingrams line	
Ford, Mordica [?]	350		Sullivan	100	490	10 Jul 1788 [?]	524	29 Apr 1780	67	492	On Sinking Creek	
Forge, Simon	612	Kerkendall, Jane	Sumner	79.50	1871	20 May 1793	1693	22 Aug 1792	81	94	Beg at a double elm	yes
Ford, Thomas	1736	Perry, John	Davidson	228	1476	4 Jan 1792	1573		77	370	S side of Cumberland River	yes
Ford, Wm.	1293		Green	100	1143	12 Jan 1793	1612	2 Dec 1778	78	190	On a branch of Lick Creek	
Foreman, Jno.	1072		Davidson	640	46	17 Apr 1786	310	20 Feb 1784	66	56 (50)	On Jonathan Drakes No Et corner	
Foreman, Jno.	1108		Davidson	640	85 [?]	17 Apr 1786	309	20 FEb 1784	66	171	Beg at a poplar	
Forges [?], Andrew	67		Sullivan	400	78	23 Oct 1782	96	8 Feb 1780	43	276	On Possen Creek in Stanley Valley	
Forgey, James	417		Hawkins	500	305	27 Nov 1792	1765	1 Oct 1779	80	149	N side of Holston River &c	
Fork, William	483		Sumner	320	124	27 Sep 1793	684	15 Feb 1785	81	35	On first W Fork of Bledsoes Creek	yes
Forne, Thomas	1987		Davidson	640	1894	20 May 1793	628		81	99	On Jones Creek beg at an Ash	yes
Fornes, Thos. Hr. of Wm.	2068		Davidson	640	2207	20 May 1793	661		81	170	On Middle Fork of Jones Creek	yes
Forrest, Matthew	235	Reed, Jesse	Sumner	640	1140	26 Nov 1789	2715	12 Mar 1788	74	149	On W side of Caney Fork River	yes
Fort, Elias	271	Dunbar, Dun(?)	Sumner	688	1253	10 Dec 1790	316	13 Sep 1785	74	349	On N side of Cumberland River	yes
Fort, Elias	273	Byenom, Drury	Tennessee	1000	1795	20 May 1793	436	9 Feb 1784	81	78	On S side of Cumberland River	
Fort, Elias	294	Colwell, John	Sumner	389	1312	10 Dec 1790	1114	23 Mar 1789	74	369	On N side of Cumberland River	yes
Fort, Elias	372	Overton, Edward	Tennessee	640	2271	20 May 1793	1528	2 Feb 1785	81	185	On Buds Creek	
Fort, Elias	805	Dillard, Sampson	Sumner	640	2272	20 May 1793	3578	9 Sep 1788	81	185	On waters of Smiths Fork	yes
Fort, Elias	807	Barrow, Jas.	Sumner	357	2274	20 May 1793	3573		81	185	On waters of Smiths Fork	yes

Claimant:	File #:	Assignee:	County:	Acres:	Grant:	Grant Date:	Entry:	Entry Date:	Bk:	Pg:	Location by Stream Name:	Military:
Fort, Elias	862	Mannin, Tymothy	Sumner	228	2370	20 May 1793	3589	9 Sep 1788	81	206	Joining his other entry	yes
Fort, Josiah	227		Tennessee	320	143	29 Aug 1793	833	20 Jun 1792	80	329	Joining East of Gibson's Guardright	
Fort, Josiah	254	Rule, Andrew	Tennessee	320	122	27 Apr 1793		29 Nov 1792	81	34	Joining E/S Guardright of Wm. Fort	
Fort, Spear	027	Jones, Jas.	Montgomery	640			3733	4 Jun 1796 (located)			In fork of Brush Creek	yes
Fort, Wm.	253	Gibson, John	Tennessee	320	120	27 Apr 1793	496	29 Nov 1792	81	34	On N side of Red River	
Fort, Wm. & Howell Tatum	327	Young, Sion	Sumner	640	1607	23 Feb 1793	320	15 Dec 1792	76	316	On N fork of Red River	yes
Foster, Anthony	024	Price, Thos.	Tennessee	640			1556	14 Feb 1785			N side of Cumberland River	
Foster, Anthony	043	More, Benj.	not given	640			3051	19 Dec 1792			On waters of Stones River	
Foster, Anthony	1008	Armstrong, M.	Sumner	103	172	26 Mar 1795			86	376	On N side of Cumberland River	
Foster, Anthony	107	Moore, B. heirs	Tennessee	640	1577	23 Feb 1793			76	302	On waters of Stones River	
Foster, Anthony	108	Hathcock, Fred.	Tennessee	228	1578	23 Feb 1793	3526	15 Feb 1786	76	302	S side of Cumberland River	
Foster, Anthony	1705	Gibson, Jno.	Davidson	640	321	23 Feb 1793	846	15 Dec 1792	76	344	On E fork of Stones River	
Foster, Anthony	1920	Stallings, Jas. Hrs	Davidson	640	1715	20 May 1793	1743		81	57	On waters of W Harpeth	yes
Foster, Anthony	326	Morris, Jno heirs	Sumner	640	1579	23 Feb 1793	1745	4 Oct 1785	76	303	S side of Cumberland &c	yes
Foster, Anthony	455	Armstrong, M.	Tennessee	100	250	27 Feb 1796		22 — 1792	88	184	On S side of Cumberland River	
Foster, Anthony & Lewis	1657	Smith, H.	Davidson	640	1574	23 Feb 1793	11		76	3000	On waters of Whites Creek	yes
Foster, James	1140		Davidson	640	117	17 Apr 1786	389	5 Apr 1784	66	178	Beg at a dogwood &c	
Foster, Thomas	620	McRee, Samuel	Tennessee	640	3182	14 Sep 1797	3835		90	435	S side of Cumberland River	yes
Foster, William	541	Coman, James	Middle District	640	2965	2 Mar 1767 [sic]	4601		90	258	N of Cumberland Mountain	yes
Foust (Forest), Philip	820		Sullivan	47	763	17 Nov 1797	459	24 Apr 1780	94	159	N side of Holston River	
Foust, John	807		Sullivan	8	750	17 Nov 1797	377	31 Mar 1780	94	151	Waters of Reedy Creek	
Fower, Thomas	324		Green	150	326	20 Sep 1787	2116	14 May 1785	65	466	On Clay Creek	
Fowler, Abraham	673	Mann, John	Tennessee	640	3265	6 Dec 1797	4770		98	151	On head of Barretts Creek	yes
Fowler, Burwell	335	Williams, Willoughby	Middle District	640	2394	31 Jan 1795	2716		83	391	W side of W Fork of Obeys River	yes
Fowler, David	076	Lucas, Ball(?)	Sumner	640			4528	25 Jun 1797			On waters of White Oak Creek	
Fowler, David	077	Brewer, Reese	Sumner	320			4526	21 Jun 1797			Waters of White Oak Creek	yes
Fowler, Frances	656	McCulloh, Benjamin	Sumner	640	1967	20 May 1793	2991	16 Nov 1792	81	116	On waters of Bledsoes Creek	yes
Fowler, John, heir of James	1477		Davidson	640	281	26 Nov 1789	756	1 May 1786	73	255	2nd Cr. eastern branch of Stones R	
Fowler, Joseph	185		Washington	150	53	23 Oct 1782	280	31 Jul 1778	47	25	S side of Lick Creek	
Fowler, Thomas	978		Green	200	1205	29 Jul 1793	871	31 Dec 1779	76	466	On waters of Clay Creek	
Fox, Andrew	1171		Green	300	1014	26 Dec 1791	362	29 Mar 1787	77	286	On the S side of Chuckey River	
Fox, Andrew	1328		Green	92	1070	30 Dec 1792	572	27 May 1780	78	428	On S side of Nolichuckey	
Fox, Francis	713	Kerr, Joseph	Davidson	274	686	8 Dec 1787	498		63	242	On a branch of Big Harpeth River	
Fox, William	575	Sanford, Samuel	Sumner	640	1812	20 May 1793	2374	11 Oct 1792	81	82	On waters of E Fork of Goose Cr	yes
Foys, Patrick	147	Greer, Ann	Tennessee	1000	1398	26 Dec 1791	1140	9 Aug 1784	77	350	On both sides of Duck River	yes
Fraecker, Michael	1594		Green	100	1336	22 Feb 1795	221	9 Jan 1793	83	437	N side of French Broad River	
Fraezer, Samuel	1394		Green	320	1206	27 Nov 1792	2332	4 Dec 1779	80	151	On Sinking Creek	
Fraezer, Samuel	1403		Green	100	1215	27 Nov 1792	2319	27 Nov 1779	80	156	On head of Little Sinking Creek	
Fragments of paper	096		not given									
Francesco, Geo. & A. Foster	1078		Davidson	640	52	17 Apr 1786	45	20 May 1784	66	52	On Red River beg at a sugar tree	
Francesco, George	1052		Davidson	640	26	17 Apr 1786	497	28 Jun 1784	66	43	On S side of Cumberland River	
Francis, John, Ass.	198		Sumner	640	292	26 Nov 1789	380	30 Mar 1784	73	260	On the S side of Cumberland River	
Francisco, John	298		Hawkins	140	261	24 Dec 1792	1994	19 Oct 1779	78	448	On N side of Holston River	
Franklin, James	1098		Davidson	640	72	17 Apr 1786	174	26 Jan 1784	66	58	Lying on Station Camp Creek	
Franklin, Samuel	192		Washington	200	60	23 Oct 1782	587	7 Nov 1778	47	28	N side of Nolachuckey River	

Claimant:	File #:	Assignee:	County:	Acres:	Grant:	Grant Date:	Entry:	Entry Date:	Bk:	Pg:	Location by Stream Name:	Military:
Franks, John	043		Davidson	640	685	8 Dec 1787	660	8 Apr 1791	63	241	N side of Cumberland River	
Franmer [?], Phillip	712	Fardin, Joseph hrs.	Davidson	640			2513				On Middle Fork of Red River	yes
Fraser, Daniel	527		Middle District	400	198	22 Feb 1797			90	234	Waters of Cumberland River	
Frazier, Daniel	1127		Davidson	640	104	17 Apr 1786	390	5 Apr 1784	66	175	On Whites Creek &c	
Frazer, George	1525	Morgan, Griffin hrs	Davidson	640	1082	26 Nov 1789	2467		74	121	On N side of Cumberland River	yes
Frazer, James, Ass.	444		Sumner	640	335	27 Nov 1792	407	16 Apr 1784	81	5	S of the River Ohio	
Frazier, Samuel	1394		Green	1394	1206	27 Mar 1792	2332	4 Dec 1779	80	151	On Sinking Creek	
Frazier, Samuel	1403		Green	100	1215	27 Mar 1792	2319	27 Nov 1779	80	156	On Little Sinking Creek	
Frazier, Alex, Jr.	087		Middle District	3000	1772			23 Apr 1784			On the Middle Fork of Elk River	
Frazier, Hugh	1513		Green	100	1274	12 Jul 1794	894	31 Dec 1792	81	586	On waters of Dumplin Creek	
Frazier, Jeremiah	1132	Harris, Edward	Sumner	640	2638	4 Jun 1796	2649	1 Jun 1795	88	347	Joining sd Harris survey	yes
Frazier, John	1052		Hawkins	100	762	21 Jan 1797	744	12 Feb 1781	91	112	Near 3 miles from Knoxville	
Frazier, John	596	Hickman, Edwin	Davidson	640	568	15 Sep 1787	1646		63	203	S side of Cumberland	
Frazier, Samuel	1521		Green	150	1282	12 Jul 1794	2308	27 Nov 1779	81	589	On W side of Sinking Creek	yes
Frazier, Simon	1929	Brown, John	Davidson	274	1740	20 May 1793	1920		81	63	On Otter Creek waters of Harpeth	yes
Frazier, William	508		Hawkins	400	381	29 Jul 1793	638	25 Nov 1778	80	272	S side of Holston River &c	
Frazor, Daniel	1041		Davidson	640	15	17 Apr 1786	608	19 Oct 1784	66	39	Lying on No side of Cumberland R	
Frazor, James	1286		Davidson	640	251	10 Jul 1788	394	5 Apr 1784	66	425	On Drakes Creek Beg at a black oak	
Frazor, William	1336		Davidson	320	22	18 Aug 1787	391	5 Apr 1784	68	129	On waters of Drakes Creek	
Freames [?], William	768		Washington	100	582	10 Nov 1784	1310	27 Mar 1779	69	133	On a branch of Watauga River	
Freeaker, Michell	0147		Green	100			221	9 Jan 1793			N side French Broad River	
Freel, Edw. & Thos. Jackson	510		Green	640	110	26 Dec 1791	2193	12 Nov 1779	75	182	On N side of Holston River	
Freel, Edward, Ass	1002		Hawkins	274	2498	10 Nov 1795	3802		89	425	On N side of Holston River	
Freeland, George	1067		Davidson	640	41	17 Apr 1786	85	13 Jan 1784	66	48	Line of land laid off for French Lick	yes
Freeland, George	1210		Davidson	320	82	8 Oct 1787	84	13 Jan 1784	66	227	Beg hickory, bank of Cumberland R	
Freele, Edward	453		Hawkins	300	321	24 Jan 1793	587	7 Jun 1787	80	196	On the N side of Holston River &c	
Freeman, David	036	Neilson, John	Tennessee	640			1880	11 Jul 1785			S Fork of the Sileen	
Freeman, John	966	Donelson, John	Davidson	640	983	18 May 1789	64		63	332	On both sides of Big Harpeth River	yes
Freeman, Nathan	443	Hughlet, William	Davidson	640	415	15 Sep 1787	64		63	154	On S side of Cumberland River	yes
Freeman, Richard	92	Harget, Fred	Tennessee	640	1368	30 Nov 1790	1254		74	393	On N side of Cumberland River	yes
Freeman, Sam, pt. Cont. Line	1451		Sumner	640	3363	14 Nov 1800	8	25 Jul 1800	108		On the barren fork of Drakes Creek	yes
Freeman, William	2195	Donelson, John	Davidson	640	2485	18 Aug 1795	2847		87	508	Small fork W side of Big Harpeth	yes
Freleer, John	932	Nichols, John	Davidson	640	948	18 May 1789			63	324	On head of a small creek &c	yes
French, Henry	569		Washington	100	834	11 Jul 1788	2121		64	337	On the waters of Cherokee Creek	
Freysher, Hugh	578	Hickman, Edwin	Davidson	1000	550	15 Sep 1787	2603	25 Aug 1779	63	197	S side of Cumberland	yes
Friley, Martin	639		Hawkins	400	508	23 Apr 1794	1643	16 Sep 1779	81	551	On Flat Creek	
Frost, John	039		Sullivan	60			406	10 Apr 1780			Beg at Rich'd Gammons corner	
Frost, William	1977	Whitfield, Bryan	Davidson	640	1879	20 May 1793	3247		81	96	On head waters of Piney River	yes
Fry, Basel	1205	Shelby, David	Sumner	400	160	26 Mar 1795			89	90	On Middle Fork of Goose Creek	yes
Fryor, Josiah	323	Williams, Willoughby	Middle District	640	2385	3 Feb 1795	1181	29 Nov 1792	83	384	W side of W Fork of Obeys River &c	yes
Fryor, William	076	Williams, Willoughby	not given	228	1180	3 Aug 1789					On Sulphur Fork	yes
Fulcher, James	421	Neilson, Robert	Davidson	640	393	15 Sep 1787	2121		63	146	On Groves Creek	yes
Fulcher, Joel	537	Shelby, David	Sumner	640	1731	20 May 1793	2122	22 Oct 1785	81	61	On W Fork of Station Camp Creek	yes
Fulgham, James	114		Washington	90	282	24 Oct 1782	379	10 Sep 1778	44	289	N side of Nolachuckey River	yes
Fulkerson, Abraham	274		Green	500	276	20 Sep 1787	847	29 Oct 1783	65	451	On N side of French Broad River &c	

Earliest Tennessee Land Records

Claimant:	File #:	Assignee:	Acres:	County:	Grant:	Grant Date:	Entry:	Entry Date:	Bk:	Pg:	Location by Stream Name:	Military:
Fulkerson, Abraham	282		500	Green	284	20 Sep 1787	1533	16 Mar 1784	65	454	On N side of French Broad River &c	
Fulkerson, Abraham	289		500	Green	291	20 Sep 1787	846	29 Oct 1783	65	456	On N side of French Broad River &c	
Fulkerson, Abraham	405		224	Green	407	20 Sep 1787	1536	16 Mar 1784	65	487	On N side of French Broad River	
Fulkerson, Abraham	529		500	Green	534	20 Sep 1787	1535	16 Mar 1784	65	533	On N side of French Broad River	
Fulkerson, Abraham	668		500	Green	709	11 Jul 1788	848	3 Feb 1787	66	463	N/S French Broad waters Dumplin Cr	
Fulkerson, Frederick	1073		200	Green	916	26 Dec 1791	1395	24 May 1779	77	247	On waters of Dumpling Creek	
Fulkerson, John	1173		100	Green	1016	26 Dec 1791	2850	12 May 1781	77	287	Including the Sinking Spring	
Fulkison, Abraham	01	Cates, Zachariah	640	Robertson			1465	17 Sep 1796			On waters of Red River	
Fulks, Garret	017	Armstrong & Donelson	640	Middle District			2915					yes
Fuller, John	786	Faithe, William	640	Davidson	759	11 Jul 1788	3344		63	266	On W side of Samuel Hepleys claim	yes
Fuller, William	304	Hague, John	640	Tennessee	1995	20 May 1793	3345	7 Jan 1786	81	123	On waters of Red River	yes
Fulton, John	199		100	Hawkins	187	6 Dec 1791	1377	21 — 1779	77	309	S side of Holstine River	
Funk, Henry	668	Simpson, Smith	274	Tennessee	3342	6 Dec 1797	3268		97	58	S side of McAdows Creek	
Funkhauser, Christopher	1240		640	Davidson	205	10 Jul 1788	437	10 Mar 1784	66	413	On both sides of Little Harpeth River &c	
Furbe, David	1931	Weakley, Robert	640	Davidson	1745	20 May 1793	2648		81	65	On waters Stones River	yes
Furney, Peter	376	Allen, Mary	640	Davidson	348	15 Sep 1787	2123		63	131	S side of Big Harpeth	yes
Futrell, Isaac	373		100	Sullivan	252	10 Nov 1784			69	162	On S side of Holstein River	
Gabbard, George	903		640	Washington	880	17 Nov 1790	2186	12 Nov 1779	76	137	On Little Doe &c	
Gable, Thomas	1483		150	Green	1246	2 Jul 1794	2730	16 Jan 1781	81	577	On S side of Nolichuckey River	
Gafford, William	2270	Coghlin, James	640	Davidson	2748	20 Jul 1796	3349		88	456	On large creek of Tennessee River	yes
Galley, William	40		300	Eastern District	40	11 Jul 1788	477	25 Apr 1780	67	355	On waters of Beaverdam Creek	
Gainer, Samuel	2473		640	Davidson	3403	31 Dec 1803	325		118	140	On N side of Cumberland River	yes
Gaines, James	510		1000	Middle District	306	7 Mar 1796	634	6 Jul 1780	88	304	On both sides of a fork of Caney Fork	
Gaines, William D.	0123		50	Green			189	21 Feb 1780			On the — of Lick Creek	
Gaines, Anthony	126		640	Davidson	112	7 Mar 1786	131		63	44	Main W Fork of Stones River	yes
Gaines, Geffrey	375	Boyd, John	640	Davidson	347	15 Sep 1787	737		63	131	On a branch of Spring Creek	yes
Gaines, Richard	930		640	Davidson	946	18 May 1789	285		63	323	Waters Wesblock Ceadar Lick Creek	yes
Galbreath, Alex.	1240		400	Green	1090	12 Jan 1793	962	2 Jan 1779	78	358	On Sinking Creek	
Galbreath, Arthur	26		271	Hawkins	58	7 Apr 1790	1890	7 Oct 1779	71	282	On N side of Holson River &c	
Galbreath, Arthur	330		70	Sullivan	470	10 Jul 1788	326	18 Mar 1780	67	481	Lying in Carters Valley	
Galbreath, James	1017		640	Green	1244	29 Jul 1793	1267	8 Mar 1779	76	487	On the draft of Richland Creek	
Galbreath, James	1217		500	Green	1217	May 1792	966	29 Oct 1783	77	405	Noleychuckey mouth of Cove Creek	
Galbreath, James	1218		600	Green	1218	May 1792	2048	25 Oct 1779	77	406	On a branch of Franks Creek	
Galbreath, James	1275		100	Green	1125	12 Jan 1793	9	12 Sep 1783	78	380	On S side of Nolichuckey	
Galbreath, James	262		200	Hawkins	273	14 Jan 1793	2073	3 Dec 1792	78	333	On N side of Holston River	
Galbreath, James	284		200	Hawkins	295	14 Jan 1793	1959	19 Oct 1779	78	344	On N side of Holston River	
Galbreath, James	361		31.50	Green	363	20 Sep 1787	42	7 May 1784	65	476	Beg at a stake	
Galbreath, James, Jr.	272		100	Hawkins	283	14 Jan 1793	2305	27 Nov 1779	78	338	On S side of Holstein River	
Galbreath, Saml	266		100	Hawkins	277	14 Jan 1793	840	30 Dec 1778	78	335	On N side of Holston River	
Galbreath, Saml	307		478	Hawkins	272	24 Dec 1792	1251	2 Nov 1783	78	452	On waters of Turkey Creek	
Galders, George	540	Coman, James	640	Middle District	2964	2 Mar 1797	4603		90	257	Waters of Calf Killers Fork	yes
Gale, Daniel	746	Donelson, John	100	Sumner	2148	20 May 1793	1710	31 Jan 1792	81	160	On the East Fork of Stones River	yes
Gale, George C.	543	Coman, James	640	Middle District	2967	2 Mar 1797	4602		90	259	S side of Caney Fork	yes
Galey, James	160		500	Eastern District	130	14 Jan 1793	2016	10 Oct 1780	79	389	On N side of Holston River	yes
Galey, James	621		200	Hawkins	318	15 Jul 1793	1187	4 Feb 1779	80	301	On the head of Big Creek	

Claimant:	File #:	Assignee:	County:	Acres:	Grant:	Grant Date:	Entry:	Entry Date:	Bk:	Pg:	Location by Stream Name:	Military:
Galleher, James	1126		Washington	150	1085	12 Jul 1794	930	24 May 1788	81	564	On N side of Noleychuckey River	
Gallaspie, George	1446	Golliper	Green	100	1256	27 Nov 1792	373	9 Sep 1778	80	173	On head of McCartneys branch	
Galleher, James	01129		Washington									
Galleher, James	1129		Washington	400	1087	12 Jul 1794	929	1 Jan 1779	81	565	S side of Noleychuckey River	yes
Gallespie, George	1452		Green	100	1262	27 Nov 1792	389	12 Sep 1778	80	175	On McCartneys Creek	
Gallespie, Thomas	87		Green	200	45	1 Nov 1786	371	23 Oct 1783	59	406	Upon Nolachuckie River	yes
Gallespie, Thos.	636		Washington	490	730	26 Oct 1786	219	25 May 1773	66	26	Beg at a marked white oak &c	
Galliher, Thomas	805		Green	600	610	23 Aug 1788	208	22 Oct 1783	68	265	On S side Clinch River	
Galliker, James	1118		Green	800	961	26 Dec 1791	482	26 Apr 1780	77	268	On Gallikers Creek &c	
Galliland, Jno.	701		Green	240	742	11 Jul 1788	1063	10 Feb 1787	66	474	Bet French Broad & fk Big Pigeon	
Gallispie, George	90		Green	200	48	1 Nov 1786			59	409	N side of Lick Creek	
Gallispie, Thomas	485		Washington	150	670	1 Nov 1786	498	9 Oct 1778	60	443	Beg at a white oak &c	
Gallop, Isaac	764	Burgess, William	Sumner	320	2182	20 May 1793	3016	19 Dec 1792	81	166	On Middle Fk of W Fk of Goose Cr	yes
Galloway, Charles	388		Western District	5000	388	27 Nov 1793	2531	25 May 1784	81	503	On waters of Massippia [sic]	
Galloway, Charles	972	Clifton, Absalom hrs	Sumner	640	2436	22 Feb 1795	1704	19 Nov 1792	84	314	On the Caney Fork	yes
Galloway, James	449		Middle District	5000	388	17 Dec 1794	665	28 Oct 1783	84	255	On S side of Duck River	
Galloway, Jno.	(2?)1438		Sumner	640	463	6 Jun 1799	384	30 Mar 1784	101	344	On Dry fk of Bledsoes Cr	
Galloway, John	221	Hays, Robert	Tennessee	1000	1547	14 Jan 1793	1757	23 Apr 1785	79	268	On waters of Red River	yes
Galloway, Richard	389	Sheppard, Benjamin	Davidson	640	361	15 Sep 1787	2322		63	136	W side of E Fk of Drakes Creek	yes
Gambell, Bradley	413		Washington	200	405	13 Oct 1783	637	25 Nov 1778	52	268	On Boons Creek	
Gambell, Moses	976		Washington	400	953	17 Nov 1790	1801	14 Feb 1789	76	163	N side of Watauga River	
Gambill, Bradley	1581	Armstrong, M.	Davidson	64	1242	10 Dec 1790			74	345	Lying on Mill Creek	
Gambill, Bradley	1619	Granston, Geo.	Davidson	640	1350	10 Dec 1790	2514	9 Mar 1780	74	382	On waters of Bartons Creek	yes
Gamble, David	406		Sullivan	280	285	10 Nov 1784	277	9 Mar 1780	69	172	In Stallings Valley	
Gamble, Edmond	357	Duke, Green heirs	Sumner	640	1479	4 Jan 1792	2486	6 May 1791	77	371	On head of Drakes Creek	yes
Gamble, Edmond	358	Applewhite, John hrs	Sumner	640	1480	4 Jan 1792	2482	6 May 1791	77	371	On head of Drakes Creek	yes
Gamble, Edmund	175	McCarty, Florence	Tennessee	822	1452	20 Dec 1791	1172	26 Aug 1784	77	364	On S side of Red River	
Gamble, Edmund	178		Tennessee	1158	1457	20 Dec 1791	600	25 Apr 1784	77	365	On West Fork of Persons Creek	
Gamble, Robert, Sr.	1714		Green	100	1429	8 Jun 1797	9	2 Sep 1782	90	323	On Little Chuckey	
Gambling, James	187	Neville, George	Davidson	350	173	7 Mar 1786	832		63	65	On Red River	yes
Gambril, Bradley, Ass	280		Sumner	640	1273	10 Dec 1790	2460	14 Nov 1789	74	356	On waters of Bartons Creek	yes
Gammon, Richard	193		Sullivan	400	200	10 Oct 1783	406	10 Apr 1780	53	158	On N side of Holstein River	
Gammon, Richard	345		Sullivan	640	485	10 Jul 1788	378	31 Mar 1780	67	489	Branch by name of Deevers Br	
Gammon, Richard	715		Sullivan	60	660	4 Dec 1794	406	10 Apr 1780	84	165	On N side of Holstein River	
Gammon, Richard	716		Sullivan	394	661	4 Dec 1794	3 warrants	3 entry dates	84	166	On N side of Holston River	
Gannon, Robert	789	McCullough, Benjamin	Sumner	274	2248	20 May 1793	3002	30 Nov 1792	81	180	On the Defeated Creek	yes
Gardner, Dempsey	464	Hadley, Joshua	Davidson	274	436	15 Sep 1787	459		63	160	N side of Cumberland River	yes
Gardner, George	2107	Blount, John Gray & Thom	Davidson	640	2344	20 May 1793	1359		81	201	On S W side of Big Harpeth	yes
Gardner, Jacob	443		Sullivan	200	322	10 Nov 1784	1401	24 May 1779	69	184	Bet. Sinking Creek & Dicks Branch	
Gardner, James	274		Hawkins	340	285	14 Jan 1793			78	339	On S side of Holston River	
Gardner, James	418	McCrery, Thomas	Davidson	640	390	15 Sep 1787	1982	1 Sep 1792	63	145	1st br E fr big S road & Big Harper	yes
Gardon, Robert	485	Pirtle, George	Sumner	320	126	27 Apr 1793			81	35	Both sides Middle Fork of Goose Cr	
Garland, Samuel	1062		Washington	150	1012	27 Nov 1792	2031	26 Oct 1779	80	180	On both sides of Roans Creek	yes
Garland, Samuel	1292		Washington	200	1197	12 Nov 1795	2142	6 Nov 1779	89	417	On waters of Stoney Creek	yes
Garland, Samuel	558		Washington	300	823	11 Jul 1788	607	23 Nov 1778	64	335	On the Flagpon Branch &c	

Earliest Tennessee Land Records

Claimant:	File #:	Assignee:	County:	Acres:	Grant:	Grant Date:	Entry:	Entry Date:	Bk:	Pg:	Location by Stream Name:	Military:
Garner, Gregory	048	Dillenberry, Redmon	Sumner	1000			4204	11 Apr 1797			E side E Fork of Stones River	yes
Garner, Nathan	1566	Buchanan, John	Davidson	640	1199	30 Nov 1790	2722		74	321	On waters of Stones River	yes
Garner, Thomas	525	King, Robert	Middle District	640	2943	1 Mar 1797	4605		90	214	Waters of Caney Fork	yes
Garrall, John	502		Davidson	440	474	15 Sep 1787	998		63	172	N side of Cumberland River	yes
Garrett, Jesse	068	Sheppard, John	Middle District	640			2916					yes
Garrett, William	014	Donelson, Stockley	Robertson	640			1645	26 Aug 1796			On waters of Red River	yes
Garrett, William	1011	Cathey, William	Davidson	640	1028	18 May 1789	1645		63	343	On N branch of E Fork of Stones R	yes
Garris, Joshua	327	Williams, Willoughby	Middle District	640	2389	3 Feb 1795	2717		83	386	W side of W Fork of Obeys River &c	yes
Garris, Seth	1175	Harris, Edward	Sumner	640	2680	4 Jun 1796	952	1 Jun 1795	88	361	Joining sd Harris survey	yes
Garris, Stephen	1193	Donelson, Stockley	Sumner	640	2719	20 Jul 1796	3154	10 May 1796	88	448	On 1st creek E of Pond Lick Creek	yes
Garrison, Joseph	243		Hawkins	600	230 (235)	26 Dec 1791	975	29 Oct 1783	77	323	On head of Loos Creek	
Garrison, Stephen	1772	Barnet, Robert	Davidson	640	1558	14 Jan 1791	610		79	271	On waters of W Harpeth	yes
Garrison, William	802	Robertson, Elijah	Davidson	640	805	20 Nov 1788	3312		63	283	On waters of Caney Fork	yes
Garvey, Matthew	2367	Stewart, Duncan	Davidson	640	3088	14 Sep 1797	4000		90	396	E side of S Harpeth River	yes
Garvis, Nicholas, heirs of	078		Sumner	640			3347				No plat	
Gary, George	048	McCall, Alex	Middle District	228			1571 (74)					yes
Gary, Joseph	1636	Evans, Thomas	Davidson	228	1370	30 Nov 1790	1572		74	393	On N side of Cumberland River	yes
Gass, John	343		Green	400	345	20 Sep 1787	466	23 Nov 1784	65	471	On both sides of Lick Creek	
Gass, John	397		Green	200	399	20 Sep 1787	1353	20 Sep 1784	65	485	On waters of Lick Creek	
Gates, Charles	388		Sullivan	200	267	10 Nov 1784	1178	2 Feb 1779	69	167	On waters of Horse Creek	
Gates, Charles, Sr.	179		Sullivan	372	186	10 Oct 1783	736	6 Jan 1781	53	152	On Stewart Branch	
Gates, James	426		Sullivan	150	305	10 Nov 1784	1245	27 Feb 1779	69	178	Beg at Wm. Cornelius corner	
Gates, James	466		Sullivan	150	345	10 Nov 1784	675	21 Aug 1780	69	193	On Kindricks Creek	
Gates, John	383		Sullivan	75	262	10 Nov 1784	1172	1 Feb 1779	69	165	On a branch of Horse Creek	
Gatley (Gillalee), Isaac	509	Alston, John McCoy	Davidson	640	481	15 Sep 1787	1066		63	174	Lying on Red River	yes
Gatlin, John	620	Sheppard, John	Sumner	640	1892	20 May 1793	906	4 Jun 1795	81	98	On S side Cumberland River	yes
Gatlin, John	735	Holliman, Kinchen	Sumner	228	2123	20 May 1793	3568	4 May 1791	81	155	On S side of Cumberland River	yes
Gatling, John	044	Mullin, Wm.	not given	365							Transfer Papers. No plat.	
Gay, James	646	Stewart, Duncan	Tennessee	1000	3221	14 Sep 1797	4442		92	14	N side of Cumberland River	
Gay, William	682	Donelson, John	Sumner	640	2028	20 May 1793	1587	25 Nov 1785	81	131	On both sides of Bradleys Creek	yes
Gaylord, Aaron	561	Sheppard, Benjamin	Davidson	640	533	15 Sep 1787	2303		63	192	Both sides Middle Fork of Drakes Cr	yes
Gaylord, Thomas	1051	Wilkins, Wm., pt(?)	Hawkins	156	3153	14 Sep 1797			90	423	N side of Holston River	
Geddy, John	500		Middle District	5000	307	7 Mar 1796	470	23 Oct 1783	88	196	Both sides of large fork of Obeys R	
Geddy, John	501		Middle District	1280	308	7 Mar 1796	111,-2598	1780,-1783	88	196	On both sides of a creek &c	
Gee, James	2354	Tyrrell, William	Davidson	3840	3031	10 Apr 1797	38	20 Nov 1791	90	306	Waters of Mill Creek & Stewart Cr	yes
Gee, John	877 (?)		Sumner	3840	2394	7 Jan 1794			81	390	On Obey River	yes
Geen (Gann?), Adam	874		Washington	100	858	18 May 1789	1362	28 Jul 1785	72	223	Beg at the end of the 2nd line &c	
Gennings, John	128		Davidson	365	114	7 Mar 1786	828		63	45	S side of Cumberland River	yes
Gentry, Charles	452		Sullivan	500	331	10 Nov 1784	347	3 Sep 1778	69	188	On a branch of Kindricks Creek	
Gentry, Charles	80		Washington	250	248	23 Oct 1782	807	22 Dec 1772	44	270	E branch of Big Limestone Creek	
Gentry, Charles	328		Washington	250	195	24 Oct 1782	936	1 Jan 1779	49	224	On a branch of Big Limestone Creek	
Gentry, Bartlet	1299		Green	100	1149	12 Jan 1793	812	2 May 1779	78	394	Beg at a pine	
Gentry, Charles	1182		Green	400	1025	26 Dec 1791	2	20 Nov 1791	77	290	On N side of French Broad River	
Gentry, Jess	1327		Green	6000	1177	12 Jan 1793	141	21 Oct 1783	78	412	Beg at a black walnut	
Gentry, John	611		Sullivan	240	566	26 Dec 1791	983	2 Jan 1779	77	308	Including part of the plantation &c	

Claimant:	File #:	Assignee:	County:	Acres:	Grant:	Grant Date:	Entry:	Entry Date:	Bk:	Pg:	Location by Stream Name:	Military:
Gentry, Nicholas	1817		Davidson	640	390	26 Jun 1793	243	6 Feb 1784	80	338	Lying on S Fork of Browns Creek	
Gentry, Nicholas	603		Sullivan	200	558	28 Dec 1791	1809	7 Oct 1779	77	305	Including said Gentrys plantation	
Gentry, Robert	319		Green	475	321	20 Sep 1787	210	7 Jun 1784	62	464	On S side of French Broad River	
Gentry, Robert	710		Washington	375	524	10 Nov 1784	810	28 Dec 1778	69	113	On Little Limestone	
George, Britton	510	Cantrell, Stephen	Davidson	640	482	15 Sep 1787	351		63	175	On Sulphur Fork of Red River	yes
George, Edward	169		Green	400	639	23 Aug 1788	2179	17 Feb 1781	64	354	On N side of French Broad River	
George, Edward	851		Green	200	832	13 Feb 1791	1487	23 Aug 1788	73	378	On waters of French Broad	
George, John	737	Robeson, Charles	Davidson	640	710	11 Jul 1788	573		63	250	On head of Calebs Creek	yes
George, Silas	58		Green	150	16	1 Nov 1786	1192	3 Nov 1783	59	377	N side of French Broad River	
George, Thomas	1139	Harris, Edward	Sumner	640	2645	4 Jun 1796	2452	1 Jun 1795	88	349	Joining scd Harris survey	yes
Gerard, Charles	270	Somberland, James	Tennessee	274	1767	20 May 1793	1284	20 Oct 1784	81	71	On S side of Cumberland River &c	
Gerard, Charles	272	Mathews, Joseph	Tennessee	640	1788	20 May 1793	1595	24 Apr 1785	81	76	On S side of Cumberland River	
Gerard, Charles	353	Moore, Moses	Tennessee	640	2181	20 May 1793	3050	26 Nov 1785	81	166	On S side of Cumberland River	
Gerard, Charles	749	Spane, Eps	Sumner	1000	2152	20 May 1793	3560	10 Nov 1789	81	161	On S side of Cumberland River	yes
Gerard, Chas.	757	Spain, Wm.	Sumner	1000	2165	20 May 1793	3562	10 Nov 1789	81	164	On S side of Cumberland River	yes
German, Benjamin	0109	Ray, William	Sumner	365			1166	22 Dec 1792			W side of Caney Fork	yes
Gerrard, Charles	46		Davidson	2560	32	14 Mar 1786	82		63	13	S side of Cumberland River	
Gerrard, Charles	68	Moore, Wm.	Tennessee	640	1307	10 Dec 1790			74	368	On N side of Cumberland River	
Gervis, John	548	Hadley, Joshua	Sumner	640	1753	29 Aug 1793	1044	26 May 1784	81	67	On waters of Station Camp Creek	yes
Gest, Benjamin	234		Washington	400	102	23 Oct 1782	1335	9 Apr 1779	47	49	On waters of Lick Creek	
Gett (Gest?), Joshua	1024		Green	150	1251	29 Jul 1793			76	488	N side of French Broad River &c	
Gibbons, Thomas	399		Sullivan	640	278	10 Nov 1784	22	8 Feb 1780	69	170	On N side of Holstin River	
Gibbons, Thomas	47		Hawkins	300	32	18 May 1789	119	9 Feb 1780	12	249	In Carters Valley &c	
Gibbons, Thomas	61		Hawkins	300	46	18 May 1789	108	9 Feb 1780	72	254	In Carters Valley &c	
Gibbons, Thomas	763		Hawkins	640	603	12 Jul 1794	959	2 Jan 1779	82	212	S side of Clinch River &c	
Gibbons, Thomas	862		Hawkins	100	641	16 Jan 1795	379		84	38	On S side of Clinch River	
Gibbs, Nicholas, Ass.	320		Eastern District	100	257	7 Mar 1796		Service right	88	193	On E fork of Beaverdam Creek	
Gibbs, Raybon	044	Gibbs, Joel	Davidson	640			187	9 Feb 1784			On Elk Creek	
Gibson, Charles	526	King, Robert	Middle District	640	2951	1 Mar 1797	4606		90	218	N of Cumberland Mountain	yes
Gibson, Colin	8	Goodrich, Sol. & S. Wheato	Smith	1000	3365	19 Nov 1800	4439	13 May 1800	109	417	On N side of Cumberland River	
Gibson, Elisha	2447		Davidson	640	3290	6 Dec 1797	4423		98	167	On E side Harpeth River &c	yes
Gibson, Fuller	715	Brignance, William	Sumner	228	2097	20 May 1793	1692	24 Oct 1792	81	148	Waters of W Fork of Station Camp Cr	yes
Gibson, James	0595	Aspey, William	Middle District	1000				6 May 1796 dated				
Gibson, James	444		Green	200	446	20 Sep 1787	446 [sic]	7 Jun 1784	65	500	Lying on head branch of Pigeon Cr	
Gibson, James	842		Green	150	823	13 Feb 1791	62	19 May 1787	73	376	On waters of French Broad	
Gibson, Jas. & Isaac Taylor	0142		Green	640			67	21 Oct 1793			Beg at a stake	
Gibson, Jas. & Isaac Taylor	1023		Green	640	1250	29 Jul 1793			76	488	N side of French Broad	
Gibson, John	54	Trousdale, John	Tennessee	640	1262	10 Dec 1790	2104	2 Sep 1784	74	353	On N side of Cumberland River	yes
Gibson, John	945		Green	200	859	17 Nov 1790	2286	27 Nov 1779	76	124	On head waters West Fork Holly Cr	
Gibson, Jordan	1177		Davidson	640	154	17 Apr 1786	249	8 Feb 1784	66	187	Both sides of Bledsoes Lick Creek	
Gibson, Samuel	556		Green	100	236	20 Sep 1787	1419	5 Jan 1779	66	153	On Wt side of Sinking Creek &c	
Giddy, Thomas	497	Barton, Samuel	Sumner	640	1665	20 May 1793	1565	18 Nov 1792	81	45	On waters of Bartons Creek	yes
Gideon, Richard	039	Donelson, Stockley	Robertson	1000			2608	13 Aug 1796			Waters Bednegoes Fk of Sycamore	yes
Gifford, James	539	Tate, William	Davidson	428	511	15 Sep 1787	3081		63	184	On Red River	yes
Gifford, William	858	Brock, Joseph	Davidson	640	867	17 Jan 1789	3349		63	301	On N side of Cumberland	yes

Claimant:	File #:	Assignee:	County:	Acres:	Grant:	Grant Date:	Entry:	Entry Date:	Bk:	Pg:	Location by Stream Name:	Military:
Gilbert, Abraham	2384	Barry, Redmond D.	Davidson	640	3166	14 Sep 1797	4242		90	428	On Eastern Branches of Stones R	yes
Gilbert, John	253		Sullivan	236	392	9 Aug 1787	2213	13 Nov 1779	61	411	On waters of Beaver Creek	
Gilbert, John	702	Harney, Selby & A. Bledsoe	Sumner	640	2081	20 May 1793	3104	30 Nov 1792	81	144	On N side of Cumberland River	yes
Gilbert, William	108		Middle District	5000	110	10 Jul 1788	542	27 Oct 1783	67	463	On both sides of Mountain [?] Creek	
Gilbreath, William	1232	Sanders, James	Sumner	640	2504	12 Nov 1795	2650	21 Sep 1787	89	421	On Many Fork Creek	yes
Gilbreath, Hugh	290		Hawkins	200	301	14 Jan 1793	1516	1 Nov 1779	78	347	On S side of Holston River	
Gilbreath, James	284		Green	2000	286	20 Sep 1787	685	28 Oct 1783	65	454	On S side of Holstein River	
Gilbreath, James	427		Green	50	429	20 Sep 1787	45	6 May 1784	65	496	On Reedy Fork of Sinking Creek	
Gilbreath, John	923		Green	100	837	17 Nov 1790	9	12 Sep 1783	76	117	On Sinking Creek	
Gilbreath, Thomas	300		Green	640	302	20 Sep 1787	265	7 Jun 1784	65	459	On little Chuckey	
Gilbreath, William	143		Middle District	100(100	2	15 Apr 1795	2263	24 May 1784	68	164	On S side of Duck River &c	
Gilbreath, William	1600		Green	400	1332	27 Apr 1795	132	9 Mar 1778	83	490	On Tilmans Creek	
Gilbreath, William	35		Green	250	98	1 Nov 1786	2173	27 Oct 1784	58	459	Beg on W side of John Trimbles line	
Gilbreath, William	467		Green	200	469	20 Sep 1787	679	28 Oct 1782	65	507	Cub Cr the waters of Holstein River	
Gilbreath, Wm & Jchamberlain	59		Middle District	1000	61	10 Jul 1788	1925	26 Apr 1784	67	440	Lying on S side of Duck River &c	
Giles, Edward	316		Middle District	640	292	17 Dec 1794	1807	23 Apr 1784	83	333	In Wilsons Valley &c	
Gilespie, Thoas. (sic)	356		Hawkins	400	349	8 Mar 1793	2082	29 Oct 1779	78	484	On N side Clinch River	
Gilgore, Chas.	599		Green	300	556	20 Sep 1787	212	7 Jun 1784	66	248	On N side of Nolechuckey River	
Giliam, Charles	014	Richeson, Jesse	Knox	328			1945	20 Apr 1793			S side of Holston River	
Gilkey, Robert	1648		Davidson	640	299	17 Nov 1790	359	12 Mar 1784	76	181	On E Fork of Mill Creek	
Gilkey, Samuel	2357	Coman, James	Davidson	640	3035	10 Apr 1797	4607		90	307	On a fork of the Caney Fork	yes
Gilkison, James	483	Fork, William	Sumner	320	124	27 Apr 1793	684	15 Feb 1785	81	35	On first W Fork of Bledsoes Creek	yes
Gill, Thomas	84		Middle District	1860	86	10 Jul 1788	1071	30 Oct 1783	67	452	On N side of Duck River &c	
Gill, William	304		Middle District	5000	280	6 Dec 1794	468	25 Oct 1783	83	207	Both sides West Fork of Stones R	
Gilahan, John	727		Washington	400	541	10 Nov 1784	458	30 Sep 1778	69	119	Upon head of Thos. Browns Creek	
Gillam, Charles	348	Richardson, Jesse	Eastern District	328	2695	6 Jun 1796			88	368	S side of Holston River	
Gillam, John	119		Hawkins	250	153	26 Dec 1791	23		75	165	On a Cainey Valley	
Gillaspie, George	278	Reason?	Tennessee	274	1860	20 May 1793	252	25 Oct 1783	81	92	On N side of Cumberland River &c	
Gillaspie, George	999		Washington	100	971	26 Dec 1791	1612	13 Sep 1779	77	299	Beg at a small white oak &c	
Gillaspie, James	206		Middle District	3030	192	5 Dec 1792	503	27 Oct 1783	78	457	On S side of Duck River	
Gillaspie, John	1076		Green	50	919	26 Dec 1791	2170	9 Dec 1779	77	248	On McCartneys Branch	
Gillaspie, Robert	1769		Davidson	793	1552	14 Jan 1793	366	24 May 1780	79	270	On main W Fork of Stones River	yes
Gillaspie, Thomas	1004		Washington	200	976	26 Dec 1791	2561	24 May 1780	77	301	On W side of Nolachuckey River	
Gillaspie, Thomas	229		Washington	83	97	23 Oct 1782	498	9 Oct 1778	47	47	S side of Nolachuckey River	
Gillaspie, Thomas	65		Green	200	23	1 Nov 1786	469	25 Oct 1783	59	384	Upon Dumplin Creek	
Gillaspie, Thos.	205		Middle District	1000	191	5 Dec 1792	37	20 Jun 1787	78	457	On waters of Flat Creek	
Gillaspie, William	1910	Bartee, John	Davidson	1000	1672	20 May 1793	1137	31 Jan 1784	81	47	On both sides of big Harpeth River	yes
Gilleland, John	1088		Davidson	640	62	17 Apr 1786	224	31 Jan 1784	66	55	On Thompsons Creek &c	
Gillespey, Thomas	969		Washington	640	946	17 Nov 1790	417	12 Jan 1779	76	159	Beg at 2 white oaks &c	
Gillespey, Thomas	149		Green	300	619	23 Aug 1788			64	347	On S side of Clinch River	
Gillespey, Thomas	172		Green	200	642	23 Aug 1788	1302	27 Mar 1779	64	355	On the Swan Pond &c	
Gillespie, David	1243		Davidson	640	208	10 Jul 1788	714	25 Apr 1785	66	413	On S side of Big Harpeth River	
Gillespie, David	1882	Kirkpatrick, Michael	Davidson	274	1625	27 Apr 1793	161		81	25	On waters of Big Harpeth	yes
Gillespie, George	1014		Washington	200	963	14 Jan 1793	2561	18 May 1781	79	274	On draughts of Big Limestone Creek	
Gillespie, George	106		Washington	300	274	24 Oct 1782	218	20 May 1778	44	285	Near Noleychuckey River	

Claimant:	File #:	Assignee:	County:	Acres:	Grant:	Grant Date:	Entry:	Entry Date:	Bk:	Pg:	Location by Stream Name:	Military:
Gillespie, George	1262		Green	300	1112	12 Jan 1793	1074	18 May 1780	78	371	On the Cedar Branch	
Gillespie, George	14		Green	50	77	1 Nov 1786	2601	5 Aug 1780	58	438	Lying on McCartneys Branch	
Gillespie, George	1415		Green	100	1227	27 Nov 1792	2667	19 Nov 1781	80	163	On McCartneys Creek	
Gillespie, George	1445		Green	50	1255	27 Nov 1792	2601	4 Aug 1780	80	172	N side of Nolichuckey &c	
Gillespie, George	230		Washington	394	98	23 Oct 1782	216	25 May 1778	47	48	N side of Nolachuckey River	
Gillespie, George	62		Green	200	20	1 Nov 1786	18	17 Oct 1783	59	381	N side of Nolichuckie River	
Gillespie, George	89		Washington	211	257	23 Oct 1782	108	26 Feb 1778	44	276	On a branch of Big Limestone	
Gillespie, George	999		Washington	100	971	26 Dec 1791	1612	13 Sep 1779	77	299	Beg at a small white oak &c	
Gillespie, George, Jr.	1224		Green	300	1074	12 Jan 1793	108	26 Feb 1778	78	348	On N side of Noleychuckey River	
Gillespie, James	029	Armstrong, Martin	Eastern District	640								
Gillespie, James	346		Green	150	348	20 Sep 1787	285	22 Oct 1783	65	472	On Lick Creek	
Gillespie, James, Ass.	1610		Green	640	376	4 Feb 1795			84	140	On S side of Little River	
Gillespie, Jas.	861	Ryan, Cornelius	Sumner	640	2368	20 May 1793	955	21 Oct 1791	81	205	N side of Cumberland River &c	yes
Gillespie, John	1076		Green	50	919	26 Dec 1791	2170	9 Nov 1779	77	248	On McCartney Branch	
Gillespie, John	1166		Green	177	1009	26 Dec 1791	2168	9 Nov 1779	77	285	On McCartney Creek	
Gillespie, Thomas	1276		Davidson	640	241	10 Jul 1788	628	20 Nov 1784	66	422	On waters of Stones River &c	
Gillespie, Thomas	13		Green	1000	76	1 Nov 1786	1412	7 Jan 1784	58	437	Beg at a stake	
Gillespie, Thomas	1468		Green	250	1232	12 Jul 1794	1004	4 Jan 1779	81	571	Upon a branch of Swan Pond	
Gillespie, Thomas	535		Washington	150	798	16 Aug 1787	2668	19 Nov 1780	64	151	On Rock House Branch	
Gillespie, Thomas	542		Washington	100	805	16 Aug 1787	2788	24 Feb 1781	64	154	Joining sd Gillespie's survey &c	
Gillespie, Thomas	66		Green	100	24	1 Nov 1786	456	28 Sep 1778	59	385	Upon Dumplin Creek	
Gillespie, Thomas	791		Green	200	596	23 Aug 1788	92	26 Feb 1778	68	260	Lying on N side of Clinch River &c	
Gillespie, William	1062		Davidson	640	36	17 Apr 1786	68	8 Jan 1784	66	46	Ash, shell bark hick. & sm. sugar t.	
Gillespie, Wm.	846	Campbell, Patrick	Sumner	1900	2349	20 May 1793	3581	27 Oct 1792	81	202	On Cumberland River	yes
Gilliam, Charles	348	Richeson, Jesse, pt.	Eastern District	328	2695	6 Jun 1794			88	368	On S side of Holston River	
Gillham, John	1038		Washington	200	988	14 Jan 1793	2686	11 Dec 1780	79	281	On waters of Big Limestone	
Gillihan, John	221		Sullivan	300	228	10 Nov 1784	1175	1 Feb 1779	55	270	On S side of Holstein River	
Gilliland, Jno.	637		Green	66	678	1[?] July 1788	2064	13 Feb 1787	66	453	Fr Broad R an island at War Ford	
Gilliland, Jno.	711		Green	100	752	11 Jul 1788	237	22 Oct 1783	66	478	Joining Gilllands at a white walnut	
Gilliland, Jno.	718		Green	640	759	11 Jul 1788	176	15 Feb 1787	66	481	Sycamore at mouth of Big Pigeon R	
Gilliland, John	967		Washington	200	944	17 Nov 1790	1408	27 Oct 1779	76	159	Beg at 2 white oaks &c	
Gilliland, John	982		Washington	640	1059	29 Jul 1793	237	18 Jun 1778	76	469	On Cherokee Creek	
Gilliland, Ramsey & Stewart	685	Ward & Turnin	Green	200	726	11 Jul 1788	2828	3 Mar 1787	66	468	Head of waters of Fr Broad River	
Gillingham, James	2347	James, Miles hrs.	Davidson	640	2995	10 Apr 1797	3934		90	291	On Harpeth River	yes
Gillingham, James	560		Tennessee	640	2994	10 Apr 1797	3983		90	291	N side Cumberland River	
Gillispie, Geo.	1259		Green	400	1109	12 Jan 1793	1109	31 Dec 1778	78	369	On McCartney Branch	
Gillispie, John	291		Green	450	293	20 Sep 1787	232-250	22 Oct 1783	65	456	On Lick Creek	
Gillispie, Thomas	531		Washington	150	794	16 Aug 1787	756	23 Dec 1778	64	150	On Rock House Branch	
Gillispie, Thomas	78		Middle District	4000	80	10 Jul 1788	508	27 Oct 1783	67	449	Lying on Flatt Creek	
Gillum, Howell	1008	Cummins, John	Davidson	1000	1025	18 May 1789	420		63	342	On N side of Cumberland River	yes
Gilmore, Charles	1518	Watson, Jacob	Davidson	640	1075	26 Nov 1789	3281		74	117	On N side of Cumberland River	yes
Gilmore, Charles	1539	Bowden, Hampton	Davidson	640	1096	26 Nov 1789	3418		74	129	On N side of Cumberland River	yes
Gilmore, Charles	637	Harper/Hayes? Robt hr	Davidson	640	610	15 Sep 1787	2659		63	217	On waters of Stones Creek	yes
Gilmore, Charles	755	Tollock, Arthur	Davidson	640	728	11 Jul 1788	3503		63	256	On N side Cumberland River	yes
Gilmour, Charles	1535	Mansher, George	Davidson	640	1092	26 Nov 1789	3514		74	127	On N side of Cumberland River	yes

Claimant:	File #:	Assignee:	County:	Acres:	Grant:	Grant Date:	Entry:	Entry Date:	Bk:	Pg:	Location by Stream Name:	Military:
Gilmour, Charles	504	Dawson, Matthew	Davidson	640	476	15 Sep 1787	3269		63	173	Joining the E boundary of a military Survey	yes
Gilmoure, Charles	563	Sherrod, Robert	Davidson	640	535	15 Sep 1787	1979		63	192	N side of Cumberland River	yes
Gilmoure, Charles	564	Beeman, Francis hrs	Davidson	640	536	15 Sep 1787	1987		63	193	On N side of Cumberland River	yes
Gilston, David	2282	Carter, George	Davidson	700	2764	20 Jul 1796	3339		88	463	On Leepers Fork of Harpeth River	yes
Gilston, David, heir of Saml	4		Wilson-Sumner	1000	3391	8 Feb 1802	201	8 Oct 1783	114	394	On S side of Cumberland River	
Gimbell, Bradley	413		Washington	200	405	13 Oct 1783	637	25 Nov 1778	52	268	On Boons Creek	
Gin, Jacob	1297		Washington	100	1183	4 Dec 1795	1460	1 Jul 1779	89	427	Waters of Noleychuckey River	
Ginn, David	584	Sanford, Samuel	Sumner	640	1823	20 May 1793	2377	6 Aug 1792	81	84	On head of E branch of Roaring River	yes
Ginn, Henry	412	Nelson, Robert	Tennessee	640	2443	18 Mar 1794	2453	30 Sep 1785	81	424	On both sides of Red River	Yes
Ginnings, Thomas	197		Davidson	365	196	7 Mar 1786	974		63	68	On a branch of Caspers Creek	Yes
Ginnis, George	011	Russell, James	Montgomery	640			1019	14 Aug 1797			On a small fork of Yellow Creek	Yes
Gipson, John	1216		Green	100	1060	May 1792	1200	12 Dec 1778	77	405	On Pidgeon Cr N/S of Noleychuckey River	
Gipson, William	2153	Walker, George	Davidson	640	2472	31 Dec 1793	686		81	434	S/S Cumberland River	Yes
Gise(?), Jonathan	557	Collins, William	Davidson	640	529	15 Sep 1787	604		63	190	S/S of Cumberland River	Yes
Gist, Benjamin	1257		Green	395	1107	12 Jun 1793	1462	2 Feb 1784	78	368	Beg. at a sugar tree & hickory	
Gist, Benjamin	589		Green	400	270	20 Sep 1787	193	22 Oct 1783	66	164	N/S Nolichuckey on Gist Branch	
Gist, John	354		Hawkins	200	347	8 Mar 1793	1226	22 Feb 1779	78	483	Joining a survey of Stockley Donelson	
Gist, Joseph	465		Green	200	467	20 Sep 1787	467	22 Oct 1783	65	506	On Gines? Creek	
Gist, Joshua	114		Green	200	130	1 Nov 1786	145	16 Apr 1785	59	433	N/S French Broad	
Gist, Joshua	13		Hawkins	50	9	23 Aug 1788	1471	19 Oct 1784	67	432	S/S Clinch River	
Gist, Joshua	257		Tennessee	853	1655	20 May 1793	680	26 Apr 1784	81	42	N/S Cumberland River	
Gist, Joshua	39		Green	135	102	1 Nov 1786	1473	25 Jul 1785	58	463	On the waters of Dumplin Creek	
Gist, Joshua	792		Hawkins	300	632	12 Jul 1794	824	26 Jul 1779	82	224	On the road that leads from Knoxville	
Gist, Robert	406	Parsons, Thomas	Tennessee	640	2432	18 Nov 1794	1294	1 Nov 1784	81	421	On a W/branch of Pine River	Yes
Gitt, Edward	831	Davis, Jos.	Sumner	320	2316	20 May 1793	1706	28 Nov 1792	81	194	On waters of Drakes Creek	Yes
Gitt, Jesse	698	Sheppard, Benj.	Davidson	1000	671	8 Dec 1787	2315		63	237	To join John Halley's entry	Yes
Givins, James	1838		Davidson	640	334	27 Nov 1792	792	26 Jan 1787	81	5	On waters of Spencers Creek	
Givins, James & others	138	Chas Carlson & Baker	Eastern Dist	1200	114	6 Sep 1791	77	5 Nov 1783	1216	223	On the waters of Big Sinking Creek	
Glandon, Major	363	Long, Nicholas	Tennessee	1000	2220	20 May 1793	10	15 Oct 1783	81	173	N/S Tennessee River	
Glasgow	0140		Sumner	5000			1205	2 Nov 1783			W/S Wt/FK Obeys River	yes
Glasgow, James	0139		Sumner	5000			1660	16 Apr 1784			W/S Wt/FK Obeys River	Yes
Glasgow, James	015		Washington	640			439	28 Sep 1778			On a branch of Big Limestone	
Glasgow, James	016		Washington	500			519	17 Oct 1778			On waters of Big Limestone	
Glasgow, James	017		Washington	200			334	29 Aug 1778			On N/S Watauga River	
Glasgow, James	018		Washington	640			438	28 Sep 1778			Incl. place where Hunting path...(?)	
Glasgow, James	030	Smith, John	Davidson	640			1115	25 Apr 1785			On the waters of Sulphur Fork	
Glasgow, James	045	Bullard, Joab	Davidson	640			448	10 Jan 1785			S/S Red River	
Glasgow, James	08		Davidson	Letter to								
Glasgow, James	1		Sullivan	477	13	2 Oct 1782			43	242	Beg. at a poplar	
Glasgow, James	1436	Armstrong, M.	Davidson	428 (142	53	8 Oct 1787			68	161	On Goose Creek	
Glasgow, James	1454	Thomas Dillon	Sumner	640	3404	21 June 1803	1320	28 June 1780	110	320	On Dry Fork of Bledsoes Creek	Yes
Glasgow, James	180	Amis, John	Tennessee	640	1459	4 Jan 1792	1153	5 May 1785	77	366	On both sides of Yellow Creek	
Glasgow, James	2		Sullivan	640	13	22 Oct 1782	815	11 Aug 1784	43	242	On waters of Sinking Creek	
Glasgow, James	2147	Wollard, Jesse	Davidson	228	2441	18 Mar 1794	1151	30 June 1781	81	423	On waters of Stoney River	Yes
Glasgow, James	2148	Warren, Ed	Davidson	228	2442	18 Mar 1794	1155		81	424	On waters of Stones River	Yes

Claimant:	File #:	Assignee:	County:	Acres:	Grant:	Grant Date:	Entry:	Entry Date:	Bk:	Pg:	Location by Stream Name:	Military:
Glasgow, James	2217	Chadwick, Benjamin	Davidson	640	2547	19 Oct 1795			88	186	On waters of Stones River	Yes
Glasgow, James	2218	Drahom, John	Davidson	640	2548	19 Oct 1795			88	186	On waters of Stones River	Yes
Glasgow, James	23		Hawkins	5000	55	7 Apr 1789			71	280	N/S Clinch River	
Glasgow, James	39		Hawkins	5000	24	18 May 1789	1508	—19, 1784	72	246	On N/S Clinch River	
Glasgow, James	390		Eastern Dist	1460	232	27 Nov 1795	1515	20 Feb 1784	89	289	N/S Clinch River	
Glasgow, James	391		Eastern Dist	640	233	27 Nov 1795	1798	16 Sep 1779	89	290	N/S Clinch River	
Glasgow, James	401	Stringer, Samuel	Tennessee	521	2403	20 Dec 1793	1107	14 June 1784	81	419	N/S Cumberland River	
Glasgow, James	402	Hodges, Jno.	Tennessee	792	2404	20 Dec 1793	1122	26 Jul 1784	81	419	S/S Cumberland River	
Glasgow, James	403	Banfield, Marmaduke	Tennessee	640	2405	20 Dec 1793	446	15 Feb 1784	81	420	E/Fk of Beeds Creek	
Glasgow, James	445		Hawkins	640	323	24 June 1793	332	2 Sep 1778	80	193	On Holston River beg at a cedar	
Glasgow, James	464		Hawkins	640	336	29 July 1793	332	29 Aug 1778	80	259	N/S Clinch River	
Glasgow, James	472	Lowell, Zadock	Davidson	228	444	15 Sep 1787	1150		63	163	N/Boundary of Major Bartons preemption	Yes
Glasgow, James	588	Webb, Giles	Davidson	640	560	15 Sep 1787	149	201	63	201	S/S Cumberland River	Yes
Glasgow, James	634		Hawkins	1000	144	20 Dec 1793			81	450	In the Walnut Cove	
Glasgow, James	716	Harrison,Fran.hr of Jas	Davidson	640	689	8 Nov 1787	1568		63	243	On Sinking Creek	Yes
Glasgow, James	79		Hawkins	1000	87	16 Nov 1790	58	Guard rights	73	333	W/S of Emeays River	
Glasgow, James	83		Eastern Dist	640	108	26 Dec 1791	1681	18 Feb 1779	75	181	S/S of Holston River	
Glasgow, James	906	Eools, William	Davidson	1000	922	18 May 1789			63	318	On N side Cumberland River	yes
Glasgow, James	907	Breeley, William	Davidson	640	923	18 May 1789	1318		63	318	On waters of Cedar Lick Creek	Yes
Glasgow, James Col.	287	Martin, Thomas	Davidson	228	273	24 Jan 1787	1152		63	100	N/S Cumberland River	Yes
Glasgow, James, Co.	285	Aims, Thomas	Davidson	640	271	24 Jan 1787	1154	19 Mar 1785	63	99	S/S Red River	Yes
Glasgow, James, Col	286		Davidson	640	272	24 Jan 1787	1313		63	99	On the Wartrace Creek	Yes
Glass, Jas & Robt King	946	Nelson, Wm.	Hawkins	250	266	6 Jun 1796	378	M. Armstrong	88	373	On both sides of Powells River	
Glass, John	1450		Green	100	1260	27 Nov 1792	65	12 May 1784	80	174	On the waters of Pigeon Creek	
Glaze, Larence	056		Green	247			22	9 Dec 1783			Beg at a stake	
Glaze, Laurence	1078		Green	247	921	26 Dec 1791	21	3 Dec 1783	77	249	S/S of Chuckey River	
Glaze, Lawrence	999		Green	200	982	26 Dec 1791	312	2 Sep 1778	77	275	S/S of Nolechuckey River	
Glaze, Lawrence	1154		Green	150	997	26 Dec 1791	2593	22 Feb 1780	77	280	On S/S of Nolachuckey River	
Glaze, Samuel	145	Hunt, Memucan	Davidson	1000	131	14 March 1786	860		63	51	W/Fk of Harpeth River	Yes
Gleaves, Michael	09		Davidson	640			378	30 Mar 1784			On both sides of Seader Lick Creek	
Gleaves, Michael	1268	Daun, Jeffrey	Sumner	640	459	1 Mar 1797	378	30 Mar 1784	90	223	S/S of Cumberland River	
Gloster, Thomas	65	Mallica, Dan	Tennessee	640	1303	10 Dec 1790	3099	8 Dec 1785	74	366	S/S Sulphur Fork	
Gloster, Thomas	999		Davidson	640	1016	18 May 1789	3098		63	340	N/S of Cumberland River	Yes
Gloster, Thos	40	Beasley, John	Tennessee	357	1227	10 Dec 1790	3145	16 Dec 1785	74	340	S/S Cumberland River	
Gloughn, William	894	Stephen Brooks	Davidson	640	910	17 Jan 1789	2917		63	314	E/S of Stones River	Yes
Glover, John	1236	James Sanders	Sumner	200	2509	12 Nov. 1795	1603	30 Mar 1786	89	423	N/S Cumberland River	Yes
Glover, Jones	475	John Marshall	Davidson	228	447	15 Sep 1787	2273		63	164	On Station Camp Creek	Yes
Glover, Michael	1646		Davidson	640	297	17 Nov 1790	563	3 Aug 1784	76	180	S/S Cumberland River	
Glover, Samuel	557	Thomas Malloy	Tennessee	1000	2988	10 Apr 1797	3734		90	288	On Yellow Creek	Yes
Glover, Solomon	837	Richard Fenner	Sumner	640	840	17 Jan 1789	2185	13 Mar 1788	63	295	On Caney Fork River	Yes
Gmalier, Abraham	747	William Dobbins	Davidson	640	720	11 Jul 1788	3439		63	253	On head of a small branch	Yes
Goacher, Henry	183		Washington	198	51	23 Oct 1782	1223	22 Feb 1779	47	24	S/S Holston River	
Goar, John	1575		Green	300	1326	4 Feb 1795	174	19 Feb 1780	83	396	On waters of Lick and Bent Creeks	
Goddard, William Sr.	533		Sullivan	95	528	13 Feb 1791	164	17 Feb 1780	73	383	On waters of Reedy Creek	
Godfrey, Clement	5	Edward Harris	Montgomery	274	3410	10 Feb 1802	3598	19 Feb 1801	118	300	On Fk of McAdoo Creek	Yes

Claimant:	File #:	Assignee:	County:	Acres:	Grant:	Grant Date:	Entry:	Entry Date:	Bk:	Pg:	Location by Stream Name:	Military:
Godfrey, Jas. Hr of Anthony	906		Sumner	1000	2474	31 Dec 1793	1709	22 Dec 1792	82	434	On waters of Red River	Yes
Godfrey, William	360		Sumner	274	1489	4 Jan 1792	1270	18 Nov 1791	77	373	N/S Cumberland River	Yes
Goff, Andrew	1250		Davidson	640	215	10 July 1788	659	8 Jan 1785	66	415	On waters of Big Harpeth	
Goforth, William	1063		Green	100	906	26 Dec 1791	2641	8 Sep 1760	77	244	Incl. plantation sd Goforth lives on.	
Goforth, William	341		Green	350	343	20 Sep 1787	28	21 Oct 1783	65	470	On Richland Creek	
Gogun, John	542	James Coman	Middle Dist	640	2966	2 Mar 1797	4604		90	258	Beg near SW corner of Gap Survey	Yes
Going, Thomas	657		Washington	225	751	26 Oct 1786	1468	29 June 1779	66	35	Joining Tiptons' lines	
Golbreath, William	610		Middle Dist	640	383	30 Nov 1801	2265	24 May 1784	114	85	On Buckhannon's Creek	
Gold, David	346	William Buxton	Davidson	640	331	28 Jul 1787	2918		63	123	On headwaters of Station Camp Creek	Yes
Golden, Wm	1145		Hawkins	100	863	24 Dec 1798	95	8 Feb 1780	97	309	Joining lines with Joel Dyer & others	
Goldsberry, William	873	John Ford	Davidson	640	886	17 Jan 1789	1861		63	307	On waters of Battleground Creek	Yes
Goldsmith, Jesse	752	William Pryor	Sumner	640	2156	20 May 1793	3724	8 Feb 1792	81	162	On waters of Middle Fork of Drakes	Yes
Gole, Stephen	816	Elijah Robertson	Davidson	640	819	20 Nov 1788	3311		63	288	On waters of Caney Fork	Yes
Golliper, James	1126		Washington	150	1085	12 July 1794	930	24 May 1788	81	564	N/S Nolechuckey River	
Golliper, James	1129		Washington	400	1087	12 July 1794	929	1 Jan 1779	81	565	S/S Nolichuckey River	
Good, John	131		Sullivan	33	144	23 Oct 1782	2115	4 Nov 1779	43	327	S/S Holston River	
Good, John	1755		Green	50	1432	30 Jan 1797			92	59	Waters of Lick Creek	
Good, John	3	Hayden Wells	Montgomery	228			4717	21 Sep 1797			Beg on the E/boundary of Wm. Shaw	Yes
Good, William	2455	Seebery, Mary hr Alston	Davidson	640	3351	12 Dec 1797	649	13 July 1780	98	185	On Swan Creek near the head	Yes
Good, William	333		Sullivan	200	473	10 July 1788	2301	27 Nov 1779	67	483	Beg at the Sour(?) of the Horse Gap	
Good, William	341		Sullivan	100 (150	481	10 July 1788	1178	2 Feb 1779	67	486	On the head of Lick Branch	
Good, William	349		Sullivan	200	489	10 July 1788	459, 122	Apr & Feb 1780	67	491	On the waters of Horse Creek	
Good, William	795		Sullivan	300	730	6 July 1797			91	600	On Walkers Ford	
Good, William - Heir of	2454	Howell, Frederick	Davidson	640	3350	12 Dec 1797			98	184	On the waters of Harpeth River	Yes
Good, Wm.	022		Robertson	Report of Com. &c								
Good, Wm.	13	Thomas, John	Smith	640	3375	26 Oct 1801	1271	23 Sep 1785	111	97	On E/S Caney Fork River	
Good, Wm.	1444	Webb, John	Sumner	640	3356	6 May 1800	1462	23 Sep 1785	107	367	S/S Cumberland River	Yes
Good, Wm.	909	Thomas, John	Sumner	297	2478	31 Dec 1793	1271	29 July 1792	81	436	On Whites Fork of New River Cancelled.	Yes
Good, Wm.	910	Webb, John	Sumner	640	2479	31 Dec 1793	1462	29 July 1792	81	436	On Whites Cr.of New Riv. Cancelled	Yes
Gooden, Drury	291		Washington	337	158	24 Oct 1782	782	26 Dec 1778	47	77	N/S Watauga River	
Goodin, Benjamin	293		Green	230	295	20 Sep 1787	912	7 June 1784	65	457	On both sides of Gap Creek	
Goodin, Benjamin	335		Green	400	337	20 Sep 1787	249	22 Oct 1783	65	468	On Roaring Fork of Lick Creek	
Goodin, Benjamin	435		Green	120	437	20 Sep 1787	2518	22 Oct 1783	65	498	On the head of Swan Pond Creek	
Goodin, Benjamin	703		Green	600	744	11 July 1788	343	23 Oct 1783	66	475	On A draught of Lick Creek	
Goodin, Benjamin	713		Green	600	754	11 July 1788	333	11 July 1783	66	479	On the waters of Bent Creek	
Goodin, Conrad	291		Sullivan	150	567	29 July 1793	2216	13 Nov 1779	76	470	Incl. the plantation	
Goodin, Enos	386	Sheppard, Benjamin	Davidson	640	358	15 Sep 1787	2328		63	136	S/S Big Barren River	Yes
Goodin, James	464		Green	200	466	20 Sep 1787	1456	7 June 1784	65	506	Both sides of Lick Creek	
Gooding, William	069	Sheppard, John	Not given	640			2921	15 Aug 1792			On Obeys River	Yes
Goodloe, Robert	046	Harris, Elisha	Davidson	640			3052	9 Sep 1786			No. waters of Little Harpeth	
Goodloe, Robert	231		Middle Dist	1500	211	27 Nov 1792	587	27 Oct 1783	80	211	Lying on the S/S of Duck River	
Goodloe, Robert	66		Western Dist	66	66	10 July 1788	1754	22 Apr. 1784	67	305	Lying on Fork of Looshatcher & Woolf Riv.	
Goodloe, Robert	91		Western Dist	3000	91	10 July 1788	572	27 Oct 1783	67	316	On Looshtcher River	
Goodman, Chloe	1596	Goodman, Wm.	Davidson	640	1285	10 Dec 1790	706		74	360	On Big Harpeth River	Yes
Goodman, Christopher, Capt	337		Middle Dist	3840	2396	8 Feb 1795	959		83	392	On Brimstone Creek	Yes

Claimant:	File #:	Assignee:	County:	Acres:	Grant:	Grant Date:	Entry:	Entry Date:	Bk:	Pg:	Location by Stream Name:	Military:
Goodman, John	057		Green	50				13 Aug 1780			On the waters of Lick Creek	
Goodman, Joseph	503		Washington	100	766	16 Aug 1787	1558	29 Aug 1779	64	741	On Sinking Creek	
Goodman, Joseph	817		Hawkins	100	653	6 Jan 1795		3 Apr 1780	83	171	S/S of Clinch River	
Goodman, Tobias	726		Davidson	640	699	11 Jul 1788	3075		63	246	North Branch of Sycamore	Yes
Goodman, William	1596	Goodman, Chloe	Davidson	640	1285	10 Dec 1790	706		74	360	On Big Harpeth River	Yes
Goodman, William	895	Brooks, Stephen	Davidson	640	911	17 Jan 1789			63	315	On 1st Creek above Stones Lick Creek	Yes
Goodman, William, heirs of	250		Tennessee	3840	1650	27 Apr 1793	2972	10 Nov 1783	81	29	S/S Cumberland River	
Goodness, Richard	34	Mountflorence, Jas. C.	Sumner	640	857	17 Jan 1789	2184	10 Mar 1788	63	299	S/S Cumberland River	
Goodrich, Solomon & Sterling	2447	Gipson, Elisha	Davidson	640	3290	6 Dec 1797	4423		98	167	On E/S Harpeth; 1 mi.above narrows	Yes
Goodrich, Solomon P.	675	Wright, Thos heirs	Tennessee	640	3289	6 Dec 1797	4257		98	167	On the waters of Buetts Creek	
Goodrich, Solomon P. &	2446	Wooten, Wm &Simpkins, Jo	Davidson	640	3288	6 Dec 1797	4427		98	166	On Dog Creek of Harpeth River	Yes
Goodrum, Thomas	064	Rowan, William	Davidson	640			3663	17 Mar 1790			Waters of Little Harpeth	Yes
Goodrun, Thomas	063	Rowan, William	Davidson	640			3663	17 Apr 1790			On waters Little Harpeth River	Yes
Goodson, James	1770	Shelby, David	Davidson	640	1553	14 Jan 1793	1756		79	270	On N/S Cumberland	Yes
Goodson, William	2425	White, James L.	Davidson	640	3245	30 Nov 1797	4083		94	176	E/S E/Fk of S. Harpeth	Yes
Goodwin, Christopher, Capt.	337		Middle Dist	3840	2396	8 Feb 1795	959		83	392	On Brimstone Creek	Yes
Goodwin, Joseph	15		Washington	100	305	24 Oct 1782	1558	29 Aug 1779	43	299	Both sides Sinking Creek	
Goodwin, Peter	847	Bushnell & Dobbins	Davidson	640	852	17 Jan 1789	1670		63	298	On S/S Cumberland	Yes
Goodwin, Thomas	198		Green	150	155	20 Sep 1787	1452	26 Mar 1785	65	415	On a draught of Lick Creek	
Goodwin, William	1042	Eaton, James	Sumner	640	2704	27 Mar 1796	2920	11 Mar 1795	88	257	On Waters of Caney Fork	Yes
Gooin (sic), Thomas	484		Green	300	486	20 Sep 1787	250	7 June 1784	65	574	On Lick Creek	
Gorden, Robert	1573		Green	25	1324	4 Feb 1795	2421	20 Aug 1784	83	395	N/S Nolechuckey	
Gorden, Robt & Wm Terrell	1607		Green	250	1323	4 Jan 1795			84	138	S/S Noleychuckey River	
Gorden, Robt & Wm. Terrell	1574		Green	250	1325	4 Feb 1795			83	395	S/S Noleychuckey River	
Gorden, Geo & Jno. Rhea	077		Sullivan	1920			24	15 Jul 1780			On waters of Spring & Wolf Creeks	
Gordon, Geo. & Robt. Young	389		Eastern Dist	150	250	27 Nov 1795	1623	5 Oct 1791	89	148	S/S Black Oak Ridge	
Gordon, Geo. & Robt. Young	406		Eastern Dist	640	248	27 Nov 1795	1735	16 Sep 1779	89	298	In the Grassy Valley	
Gordon, Geo & Robt. Young	400		Eastern Dist	274	242	27 Nov 1795	577	June 1779	89	295	N/S Clinch River	
Gordon, Geo.& Robt. Young	401		Eastern Dist	400	243	27 Nov 1795	1350	12 Jan 1784	89	295	N/S Clinch River	
Gordon, George	1651		Green	900	1350	28 Aug 1795	578, 2012	21 Dec 1784	87	524	Beg at a small post oak	
Gordon, George	072		Washington	720			14-1883	Jul & Dec 1779			Waters of Dumpling Creek	
Gordon, George	1456		Green	219	143	7 Jan 1794	5	3 Dec 1791	81	398	Beg on a black oak	
Gordon, George	1576		Green	200	1327	4 Feb 1795	402	8 Apr 1780	83	396	N/S Noleychuckey River	
Gordon, George	1643		Green	100	1346	27 Aug 1795	179	7 Jan 1778	87	512	N/S Noleychuckey River	
Gordon, George	1648		Green	720	1347	28 Aug 1795			87	523	On waters of Dumplin Creek	
Gordon, George	335	Bell, Elias heirs	Eastern Dist	640	2510	20 Nov 1795			88	282	N/S Clinch River	
Gordon, George	395		Eastern Dist	640	237	27 Nov 1795	1784	16 Sep 1779	89	292	N/S Clinch River	
Gordon, George	396		Eastern Dist	1920	238	27 Nov 1795	1760	1779, 1783	89	292	On N/S Clinch River	
Gordon, George	403		Eastern Dist	640	245	27 Nov 1795	1729	16 Sep 1779	89	290 (29	N/S of Clinch River	
Gordon, George	404		Eastern Dist	1280	246	27 Nov 1795	1727	16 Sep 1779	89	296	N/S Clinch River	
Gordon, George	405		Eastern Dist	1150	247	27 Nov 1795	211	1779, 1783	89	297	N/S Clinch River	
Gordon, George	728		Sullivan	640	673	27 Aug 1795	1742	16 Sep 1779	87	522	On both sides Beaver Creek	
Gordon, Hastin	803	Robertson, Elijah	Davidson	640	806	20 Nov 1788	3313		63	283	On waters of Caney Fork	Yes
Gore, Jonathan	621	Hendry, William	Tennessee	274	3184	14 Sep 1797	4072	3 Dec 1796	90	435	On waters of Saline Creek	
Gorham, J. C.	604	Reiley, Edm. Heirs	Tennessee	640	3148	14 Sep 1797	4348		90	422	N/S Cumberland River	

Claimant:	File #:	Assignee:	County:	Acres:	Grant:	Grant Date:	Entry:	Entry Date:	Bk:	Pg:	Location by Stream Name:	Military:
Gorham, James C	607	Locust, Arthur hrs	Tennessee	640	3151	14 Sep 1797	4064		90	423	Waters W/Fk of Red River	
Gorham, James C.	605	Broman, David hrs	Tennessee	640	3149	14 Sep 1797	4201		90	422	Waters W/Fk Red River	
Gorham, James C.	608	Boyne, Francis hrs.	Tennessee	274	3152	14 Sep 1797	4529		90	423	Waters Little W/Fk Red River	
Gorham, John	606	Locust, Francis hrs	Tennessee	640	3150	19 Sep 1797	4065		90	422	Waters W/Fk Red River	
Gorley, Ayeres	975	M. Armstrong & D.Shelby	Sumner	640	2439	22 Feb 1795	1814	12 Aug 1785	84	316	N/S Cumberland River	Yes
Goslin, Daniel	2280	Cromwell, Rowlen	Davidson	274	2760	20 Jul 1796	3534		88	461	Waters of W. Harpith	Yes
Goss, Jacob	1362		Green	50	1217	27 Jan 1793	2916	28 Aug 1781	79	503	Waters of Lick Creek	
Gough, William	6	Montflorence, Jas. C.	Tennessee	1000	1154	26 Nov 1789	3556	1 Aug 1787	74	150	N/S Cumberland River	Yes
Gourly, Thomas	1290		Washington	41	1205	9 Dec 1795	2982	21 June 1794	89	403	Waters of Little Limestone	
Gowan, David	040	Donelson, Stockley	Robertson	1000		13 Aug 1796	2609	13 Aug 1796			Both sides Pond Branch	Yes
Gowan, William	1046		Davidson	640	20	17 Apr 1786	116	15 Jan 1784	66	40	Et branches of Mill Creek	
Gowen, John	1822		Davidson	640	395	26 June 1793	115	15 Jan 1784	80	340	E/S Mill Creek	
Gower, Alexander	2180		Davidson	50	188	17 July 1794		Nov 1791	81	604	N/S Cumberland River	
Gower, Alexander	2211		Davidson	50	234	27 Feb 1796		24 Nov 1791	88	177	On Bull Run	
Gower, Elijah	1890	Armstrong, M.	Davidson	50	121	27 Apr 1793		6 Sep 1791	81	30	Head of Sulphur Creek	
Gower, Elijah, Elisha & Wm	1298		Davidson	640	263	10 July 1788	614	2 Nov 1784	66	429	Beg sugar tree & beech on Cumberland Riv	
Gower, Robert	2179	Armstrong, M.	Davidson	50	187	17 July 1794		24 Nov 1791	81	604	N/S Cumberland River	
Gower, Robert	2204		Davidson	50	223	27 Feb 1796		24 Nov 1791	88	172	On Bull Run	
Gower, Russell	1418	Hadley, Joshua	Sumner	228	3273	6 Dec 1797	4552	8 May 1797	98	155	Waters of Cedar Creek	yes
Gower, Samuel	02		Middle Dist	50							N/S Cumberland River	
Gower, Samuel	2181		Davidson	50	189	17 July 1794			81	605	N/S Cumberland River	
Grace, James	72	Phillips,P. & Campbell, M.	Tennessee	640	1315	10 Dec 1790	2124	9 Sep 1785	74	370	S/S Cumberland River	Yes
Gragg, Nathan	220		Washington	400	88	23 Oct 1782	913	31 Dec 1778	47	42	In the fork of Holston River	
Gragg, Robert	1296		Green	340	1146	12 Jan 1793	902	31 Dec 1778	782	392	Beg at a post oak	
Gragg, Samuel	1006	Armstrong, M.	Sumner	50	170	26 Mar 1795	1527	14 Aug 1779	86	375	Both sides of Persimon Branch	
Gragg, Samuel	1308		Green	200	1158	12 Jan 1793	27	17 Jan 1783	78	399	On Meadow Creek	
Gragg, Samuel	825		Green	100	806	18 May 1789		23 Apr 1784	72	243	Beg at a pine on S/S of a hill	
Gragg, Thomas	1375		Green	200	1230	27 Jan 1793	1304	8 July 1779	79	506	Beg at a Elm bush	
Gragg, Thomas	1632		Green	500	1335	18 Aug 1795	1024	1 Jan 1782	87	501	Beg at a stake	
Gragg, Thos. & Thos. Potter	1041		Green	640	1268	29 July 1793	2836	9 Apr 1781	76	492	Beg at 2 white oak bushes on a hill	
Graham, James	205		Green	29.25	162	20 Sep 1787	3	10 Aug 1785	65	417	S/S of Nolechuckey River	
Graham, James	762		Washington	100	576	10 Nov 1784	1527	14 Aug 1779	69	131	S/S of Oneon branch	
Graham, John	58		Middle Dist	2000	60	10 July 1788	638	2 Oct 1783	67	440	S/S Duck River	
Graham, Joseph	281	Holbrook, John	Tennessee	640	1866	20 May 1793	1883	11 Jul 1785	81	93	S/S of Cumberland River	
Graham, Joseph	326	Sloan, David	Tennessee	640	2075	20 May 1793	1882	11 July 1785	81	143	On 2nd large fork of W/S of Yellow Creek	
Graham, Joseph (Matilda)	101	Hammond	Tennessee	640	1519	10 Apr 1792	3082	30 Nov 1785	75	507	S/S Cumberland	
Graham, Peter	572	Smith, John	Tennessee	640	3010	10 Apr 1797	3170	19 Dec 1785	90	297	S/S of Cumberland River	Yes
Graham, Samuel	140		Middle Dist	2000	142	10 Jul 1788	1791	23 Apr 1784	67	477	N/S Duck River	
Graham, Thomas	530		Green	200	532	20 Sept 1787	1038	7 June 1784	65	533	Beg at a white oak on a So. Hillside	
Graham, Wm.	1032		Davidson	640	6	17 Apr 1786	102	14 Jan 1784	66	35	Sulphur Fork of Red River	
Graigg, Henry	1297		Green	200	1147	12 Jan 1793	200	6 Apr 1778	78	392	Beg at a large red oak	
Grammer, John	1406	Armstrong, M.	Davidson	40	23	8 Oct 1787	1529	22 Oct 1785	68	154	On Wortraw(?) Creek	
Granaway, James	242		Eastern Dist	350	204	30 Oct 1794			83	136	Bakers Cr.- waters of Tennessee River	
Granberry, John	76		Tennessee	792	1321	10 Dec 1790	112	22 Oct 1783	74	372	S/S Cumberland River	
Grandall, John	312	McCullah, Benjamin	Tennessee	640	2013	20 May 1793	2007	16 Aug 1785	81	127	S/S Cumberland River	Yes

Claimant:	File #:	Assignee:	County:	Acres:	Grant:	Grant Date:	Entry:	Entry Date:	Bk:	Pg:	Location by Stream Name:	Military:
Granston, George	1619	Gambill, Bradley	Davidson	640	1350	10 Dec 1790	2514	8 Feb 1780	74	382	Waters of Bartons Creek	Yes
Grant, Alexander	243		Sullivan	200	382	9 Aug 1787	77		61	401	N/S Holston River	
Grant, Daniel	26		Sullivan	350	37	23 Oct 1782	365	28 Mar 1780	43	255	On the Big Creek	
Grant, Daniel	361		Hawkins	60	354	8 Mar 1793			78	486	N/S Holston River	
Grant, Elisha	837a	Sheppard, Nancy	Sumner	640	2328	20 May 1793	1522	24 Nov 1792	81	197	Salt Lick Fork	Yes
Grant, Elisha	908	Williams, Willoughby	Davidson	640	924	18 May 1789	1182		63	318	S/S Cumberland River	Yes
Grant, Ephraim	941	Ford, Elias	Davidson	640	957	18 May 1789			63	326	Beg at N/E cor of Suggs tract	Yes
Grant, Gilbert	1158	Harris, Edward	Sumner	640	2663	4 June 1796	2803	1 June 1795	88	355	Joining sd Harris Survey	Yes
Grant, James	153		Middle Dist	5000	156	17 June 1790	1497	1 Jan 1780	73	96	Waters of Tennessee River	
Grant, James	198		Middle Dist	5000	201	15 July 1793	1502	19 Feb 1784	76	494	Both Sides S/Fk Duck River	
Grant, James	200		Middle Dist	5000	203	15 July 1793	1499	19 Feb 1784	76	494	Both sides Mid/Fk Duck River	
Grant, Jas.	210		Middle Dist	5000	196	28 Dec 1792	1699	16 Apr 1784	78	460	N/S Duck River	
Grant, Jno.	1227		Davidson	640	191	10 July 1788	440	12 May 1784	66	410	N/S Cumberland River	
Grant, Joel	546	Robertson, James	Sumner	640	1750	29 Aug 1793	2569	4 Nov 1789	81	66	S/S Cumberland River	Yes
Grant, John	2085	Sheppard, Nancy	Davidson	640	2286	20 May 1793	1497		81	188	Small Creek of Duck River	Yes
Grant, John	409		Sumner	640	420	27 June 1793	442	12 May 1784	80	348	On Dry/Fk of Bledsoes Creek	
Grant, John	428		Sumner	640	439	27 June 1793	442	12 May 1784	80	354	Dry/Fk of Bledsoes Creek	
Grant, Lewis	277	Rice, Jno & Harriett	Tennessee	640	1857	20 May 1793	2052	26 Aug 1785	81	91	S/S of Cumberland River	Yes
Grant, Rubin	2069	Elliott, John	Davidson	640	2211	20 May 1793	1329		81	171	Lick Creek No waters of Duck River	Yes
Grasan, Jacob	544		Sullivan	300	527	17 Nov 1790	2379	27 Dec 1779	76	187	On path leads from Nancy Shotes	
Grate, David	522		Washington	100	785	16 Aug 1787	109	23 Aug 1786	64	147	E/S Sinking Creek	
Graves, Francis	1274		Sumner	2560	3016	10 Apr 1797	350	1 July 1796	90	300	Headwaters of Salt Lick Creek	Yes
Graves, Francis	2283	Webb, Charles	Davidson	640	2765	20 July 1796	3957		88	463	S/S Cumberland	Yes
Graves, Jonathan	1760		Green	3000	1437	25 Nov [illegible]	524	27 Oct 1783	96	15	N/S of Duck River	
Graves, Joseph	679	Wilkoff & Clark	Davidson	640	652	8 Dec 1787	2186		63	231	So. boundary Capt Towns survey	Yes
Graves, Absalom	1304		Washington	200	1190	4 Dec 1795	521	19 Oct 1778	89	431	Joining Peter Starnes	
Graves, Absalom	1375		Washington	200	1290	9 Dec 1797	1488	26 July 1779	96	13	On waters of Boons Creek	
Gray, Andrew	809	Baker, John	Sumner	640	2276	20 May 1793	3410	19 Nov 1792	81	186	Beg at a Sycamore	Yes
Gray, George	28		Washington	399	318	24 Oct 1782	1321	31 Mar 1779	43	305	Waters of Cedar Creek	
Gray, George	312		Washington	488	179	23 Oct 1782	866	30 Dec 1779	47	87	On Cedar Creek	
Gray, Henry	1356	Beard, Lewis	Sumner	1000	2779	16 Oct 1796	3738	10 Nov 1795	91	23	N/S of Cumberland River	Yes
Gray, Henry	2072	Hays, Robert	Davidson	1000	2214	30 May 1793	2607		81	172	N/S of Cumberland River	Yes
Gray, Jonathan	678	Hays, Narcissa	Sumner	274	202	20 May 1793	2312	24 Nov 1792	81	129	Salt Lik Fk of Big Barren River	Yes
Gray, Joseph & James	21		Tennessee	3840	1169	26 Nov 1789	3122	12 Dec 1785	74	163	N/S Cumberland River	
Gray, Peter	967	Donelson, Stockley	Davidson	640	984	18 May 1789		E#1679 &1780	63	333	Both sides of Smiths Fork	Yes
Gray, Robert	035		Sullivan	640	138	23 Oct 1782	315		43	324	On head of Kings Branch	
Gray, Robert	126		Sullivan	400	1251	6 June 1797	1731	25 Sep 1779	90	309	Beg at Geo. Gray's corner	
Gray, Robert	1327		Washington	200	194	10 Oct 1783	2774	20 Feb 1781	53	156	On Caney Creek	
Gray, Robert	187		Sullivan	640	62	23 Oct 1782	566		43	268	Waters of Muddy Creek	
Gray, Robert	51		Sullivan	560	691	9 Dec 1795	1815	E#1680 &1691	89	401	Beg at a white oak	
Gray, Robert Jr.	750		Sullivan	200	1931	20 May 1793	109	7 Oct 1775	81		Beg at a white oak	
Gray, Samuel	1995	Cobb, Jesse	Davidson	640		20 May 1793	1109		81	107	W/S Stones River	Yes
Gray, Sylvanus	050	McCall, Alex.	Middle Dist	640			387		81		S/S Watauga River	Yes
Gray, William	019		Washington	637			387	12 Sep 1778			S/S Watauga River	
Grayham, Richard	87		Middle Dist	2000	89	10 July 1788	683	28 Oct 1783	67	453	S/S Duck River	

Claimant:	File #:	Assignee:	County:	Acres:	Grant:	Grant Date:	Entry:	Entry Date:	Bk:	Pg:	Location by Stream Name:	Military:
Greate, David	523		Washington	100	785	10 Aug 1787	109	23 Aug 1786	64	147	E/S of Sinking Creek	
Green, Abraham	1924	Tatum, Howell	Davidson	640	1730	20 May 1793	2721		81	61	On waters of Whites Creek	Yes
Green, Alex	058		Green	5000	405(sic)		405	25 Oct 1783			On waters of Big Hatchey	
Green, Alexander	1677	Robertson, Jas of Valentine	Davidson	640	1602	23 Feb 1753	2697		76	313	W/S Harpeth Riv on mouth of Dry Cr.	Yes
Green, Andrew	047	Osborn, Jesse	Davidson	640			4771	12 Sep 1797			On head of Pond Creek	
Green, Burwell	2295	Allentharpe, John hrs	Davidson	640	2772	9 Sep 1796	1851		88	523	On Deer Creek	Yes
Green, Dempsey	654	Nelson, Robert	Tennessee	150	3231	17 Nov 1791	2488		94	168	N/Fk of W/Fk of Blooming Grove Cr.	Yes
Green, Demsey	415	Nelson, Robert	Davidson	640	387	15 Sep 1787	2488		63	144	Both sides of Red River	Yes
Green, Elizabeth	640		Green	400	681	11 July 1788	760	28 Feb 1783	66	454	Lying on Wt/S Clinch Mtn. on Flat Cr.	
Green, Elizabeth	641		Green	400	682	11 July 1788	1166	31 Oct 1783	66	454	On prong Bull R, cor of Jas Green	
Green, Francis	1093		Green	200	936	26 Dec 1791	84	20 Jan 1789	77	255	On waters of Bent Creek	
Green, James	613		Green	400	654	11 July 1788	879	29 Oct 1783	66	445	W/S of Clinch Mountain	
Green, James Jr.	663		Green	400	704	11 July 1788	702	29 Oct 1783	66	461	On head of Bull Run that runs into Clinch	
Green, James West	560		Davidson	4800	532	15 Sep 1787	430		63	191	First Big Creek below Harpeth	Yes
Green, Jesse	0122		Green	500			2660	28 Oct 1779			S/S French Broad River	
Green, Jesse	861		Green	300	811	27 Nov 1789	2660	28 Oct 1779	74	15	N/S of French Broad River	
Green, Jno	660		Green	400	701	11 July 1788	878	29 Oct 1783	66	461	W/S of Clinch Mountain	
Green, Jno. Jr.	654		Green	400	695	11 July 1788	666	28 Oct 1783	66	459	On waters of Bull Run that runs into Clinch	
Green, John & John Selvage	426		Eastern Dist	720	291	19 Feb 1797	759	28 Oct 1783	90	247	Little Et/Fk of Little Pigeon River	
Green, Jonathan	1267		Sumner	640	457	1 Mar 1787	544	23 July 1784	90	221	S/S Cumberland River	
Green, Joseph	612		Green	400	653	11 July 1788	1167	31 Oct 1783	66	444	Prong of Bull Run & In Wt/S Coper Ridge	
Green, Joseph	661		Green	500	702	11 July 1788	871	29 Oct 1783	66	461	Both sides N/Fk of Bull Run	
Green, Joseph	662		Green	1000	703	11 July 1788	401	25 Oct 1783	66	461	Lying chiefly on E/S of Flat Creek	
Green, Joseph Jr.	631		Green	400	672	11 July 1788	756	28 Oct 1783	66	451	Both sides N/Fk of Bull Run	
Green, Joseph Jr.	655		Green	400	696	11 July 1788	881	29 Oct 1783	66	459	On Flat Creek	
Green, Joseph Sr.	630		Green	400	671	11 July 1788	1050	29 Oct 1783	66	450	Prong of Bull Run that runs into Clinch River	
Green, Micajah	81	Lewis, Macajah Green	Western Dist	1000	81	10 July 1788	2636	25 May 1784	67	312	Waters of S/Fk of Forked Deer River	
Green, Nathaniel	2		Tennessee	25000				1784	69	210	Beg on S/branch of Duck River	
Green, Phillemer	671		Green	200	712	11 July 1788	2343	8 Dec 1779	66	464	N/S of Holston River	
Green, Randel	292	Fenner, Richard	Davidson	640	278	22 Mar 1787	2095		63	102	S/S of Cumberland River	Yes
Green, Richard	283		Sullivan	640	422	9 Aug 1787	1634	16 Sep 1779	61	441	On Clinch River	
Green, Robert	1004		Davidson	1006	1024	18 May 1789	1214		63	341	E. branches Halfpone Creek	Yes
Green, Samuel	1130	Harris, Edward	Sumner	640	2636	4 June 1796	2720	1 June 1795	88	346	Joining Harris Survey	Yes
Green, Samuel	258	Hadley, Joshua	Tennessee	228	1681	20 May 1793	3748	4 Mar 1792	81	49	W/Fk of Persons Creek	Yes
Green, Sarah	543		Hawkins	1000	416	29 July 1793	397	25 Oct 1783	80	281	N/S of Tennessee River	
Green, Thomas	627	Gubbins, William	Davidson	640	599	15 Sep 1787	1758		63	214	N/S Cumberland River	Yes
Green, Turnfold	670		Green	400	711	11 July 1788	882	29 Oct 1783	66	464	Wt/S of Clinch Mtn on Flat Cr.	
Green, William	16		Tennessee	640	1164	26 Nov 1789	431	31 Jan 1784	74	161	S/S of Sulphur Fork	
Green, William	665		Green	500	706	11 July 1788	755	29 Oct 1783	66	462	On Wt/S of Clinch Mountain on Flat Creek	
Green, William	672		Green	400	713	11 July 1788	880	29 Oct 1783	66	464	W/S of Clinch Mountain on Flat Creek	
Green, William	7		Robertson	228	2409	10 Feb 1804	3046	21 May 1800	118	299	On waters of Sulphur Fork	
Green, William	853		Green	100	834	13 Feb 1791	89	25 Apr 1789	73	379	Waters Long Cr., waters of Chuckey River	
Green, William (Heirs of)	079		Sumner	640			1809	21 Sep 1787			On waters of Big Barren	
Green, Zachariah	1269		Davidson	640	234	10 July 1788	752	16 July 1784	66	420	On Drakes Creek	Yes
Greenaway, Jnol	1201		Davidson	640	618	8 Oct 1784	66	10 Nov 1784	66	224	Lying on Wt Branches of Bartons Creek	

Earliest Tennessee Land Records

Claimant:	File #:	Assignee:	County:	Acres:	Grant:	Grant Date:	Entry:	Entry Date:	Bk:	Pg:	Location by Stream Name:	Military:
Greenaway, William	1094		Washington	252.5	1044	27 Nov 1792	344	2 Sep 1778	80	203	S/S of creek [unnamed]	
Greene, Jesse	1567		Green	500	1313	6 Jan 1795			83	158	S/S French Broad River	
Greenlee, James	1171		Washington	424	1129	7 July 1794	319	2 Sep 1778	81	620	N/S Noleychuckey	
Greer, Alex & Jas Robertson	1674	Capton, John	Davidson	640	1599	23 Feb 1793	2798		76	312	On headwaters of So. Harpeth River	Yes
Greer, Alexander	1904		Davidson	720	143	27 Apr 1793	835	30 Nov 1792	81	39	S. Harpeth Creek	
Greer, Alexander	401		Middle Dist	2500	340	17 Dec 1794	1437	27 Jan 1784	84	224	N/S Elk River	
Greer, Alexander & David	389		Western Dist	5000	390	27 Nov 1793			81	503	On waters of Big Hatchey	
Greer, Andrew	1062		Green	640	905	26 Dec 1790	122	26 Feb 1778	77	244	Beg W/S of Four Mile Creek	
Greer, Andrew	1192		Green	640	1035	26 Dec 1791	120	26 Feb 1778	77	294	Beg on Four Mile Creek	
Greer, Andrew	35	Bowner, Wm. Hrs.	Montgomery	1000	3244	20 Nov 1797	4769		81		W/S of Harpeth	Yes
Greer, Andrew	383		Middle Dist	2500	322	17 Dec 1794	1438	29 Jan 1784	84	215	On Cane Creek	
Greer, Andrew	403		Middle Dist	1000	342	17 Dec 1794	1448	29 Jan 1784	84	225	On Cane Creek	
Greer, Andrew	432		Middle Dist	1500	371	17 Dec 1794	1447	29 Jan 1784	84	239	N/S of Elk River	
Greer, Andrew	508		Washington	200	771	16 Aug 1787	1300	25 Mar 1786	64	143	On waters of Watagah	
Greer, Andrew	530		Washington	365	793	16 Aug 1787	978	2 Jan 1779	64	150	Bounded by Drury Goodwin	
Greer, Andrew	532		Washington	394	795	16 Aug 1787	2567	26 Sep 1780	64	151	Bounded by his survey	
Greer, Andrew	574		Washington	575	839	11 July 1788	960	2 Jan 1779	64	338	Bounded by John Shelby, Jr.	
Greer, Andrew	583		Sullivan	400	581	29 July 1793	1795	5 Oct 1779	76	474	Incl. Womack Old Fork	
Greer, Andrew & David	657		Hawkins	640	562	12 July 1794	332	22 Mar 1780	81	591	Waters of Blackwater	
Greer, Ann	147		Tennessee	1000	1398	26 Dec 1791	1140	9 Aug 1784	77	350	Both sides Duck River	
Greer, Ann	152		Tennessee	640	1405	20 Dec 1791	1142	9 Aug 1784	77	352	Both sides of Pine Creek	
Greer, Ann	433		Western Dist	1020	432	25 Oct 1802	1450	30 Jan 1784	115	421	Lying on the Fork Creek	
Greer, David	810		Hawkins	100	646	6 Jan 1795	3414	1 Feb 1780	83	168	S/S Clinch River	
Greer, John Gee	044	Dillenberry, Redmon	Sumner	640			4336	14 Oct 1797			On head branches	Yes
Greer, Jos & Jas Robertson	1673	McCay, John	Davidson	640	1592	23 Feb 1793	2016		76	310	S side of Harpeth River	yes
Greer, Joseph	273		Western Dist	1500	299	25 Apr 1789	2146	11 May 1784	70	259	On waters of Big Hatcha	
Greer, Joseph	275		Western Dist	1500	304(301?	25 Apr 1789	2148	11 May 1784	70	260	On the waters of Big Hatcha	
Greer, Joseph	277		Western Dist	1500	303	25 Apr 1789	2141	11 May 1784	70	262	On waters of Big Hatcha River	
Greer, Joseph	402		Middle Dist	2500	341	17 Dec 1794	1436	27 Jan 1784	84	224	On E Fk of Cane Creek	
Greer, Joseph	431		Middle Dist	2500	370	17 Dec 1794	1446	29 Jan 1784	84	239	On N/S of Elk River	
Greer, Joseph	544		Washington	415	809	11 July 1788	663, 2994	11 July 1788	64	333	On E/S of Doe River	
Greer, Ruth	430		Middle Dist	2625	369	17 Dec 1794	1445	29 Jan 1784	84	238	S/S of Elk River	
Greer, Ruth			Western Dist								See Middle Dist File 430	
Greers, Robert	328		Green	200	330	20 Sep 1787	73	20 Sep 1787	65	467	N/S of Nolechucky River	
Greers, Thomas & Alexander	38		Middle Dist	5000	40	10 July 1788	1433	27 Jan 1784	67	425	S/S of Duck River	
Gregg, Henry	968		Green	400	882	17 Nov 1790	928	29 Oct 1783	76	132	N/S French Broad River	
Gregg, Samuel	493		Green	200	295	20 Sep 1787	51	3 Apr 1780	65	517	On Meadow Creek	
Gregory, Isaac	263	Shackler, Phillip	Sumner	640	1220	10 Dec 1790	372	9 Dec 1785	74	338	On N/S Cumberland	
Gregory, William	618		Washington	96	712	26 Oct 1786	2424	11 Feb 1787	66	17	In Grasey Cove	Yes
Grice, Theophilus	2239	Stewart, Duncan	Davidson	640	2686	6 June 1796	3853		88	363	On S Harpeth River	Yes
Griffen, Jacob	290	Fenner, Richard	Davidson	640	276	22 Mar 1787	2096		63	101	S/S Cumberland River	Yes
Griffen, James	2388	Robertson, Jonathan	Davidson	274	3176	14 Sep 1797	1163		90	432	On S. Harpeth River	Yes
Griffen, William	463	Ford, John	Sumner	640	1610	27 Apr 1793	357		81	20	On a Fk of Roaring River	Yes
Griffen, William	940		Washington	200	917	17 Nov 1790	924	1 Jan 1779	76	150	On Roane Creek	Yes
Griffin, Edward	1499	Mountflorence, Jas C	Davidson	640	1056	26 Nov 1789	2183		74	102	N/S Cumberland River	Yes

Earliest Tennessee Land Records

Claimant:	File #:	Assignee:	County:	Acres:	Grant:	Grant Date:	Entry:	Entry Date:	Bk:	Pg:	Location by Stream Name:	Military:
Griffin, Edward	905	Simpson, Thomas	Sumner	452	2473	31 Dec 1793	3096	22 Dec 1792	81	434	On S/S of Cumberland River	Yes
Griffin, Isaac	816	Marr, John	Sumner	640	2287	20 May 1793	2417	19 Nov 1792	81	188	On S/S Big Barron River	Yes
Griffin, James	244		Tennessee	274	1621	27 Apr 1793	1163	13 Aug 1784	81	22	S/S of Cumberland River	
Griffin, James	745	Donelson, John	Sumner	640	2147	20 May 1793	3463	11 Apr 1788	81	160	Both sides of Cedar Lick Creek	Yes
Griffin, Joseph	183	Dickson, John	Tennessee	640	1463	4 Jan 1792	3661	10 Dec 1783	77	367	S/S of Cumberland River	Yes
Griffin, Joshua	195	Hart, Anthony	Tennessee	640	1481	4 Jan 1792	2719	30 Sep 1785	77	371	On S/S of Cumberland River	Yes
Griffin, Lemon	385	Sheppard, Benj.	Davidson	640	357	15 Sep 1787	2339	134	63	134	W. Fk of Drakes Creek	Yes
Griffin, Samuel	311	Rice, Jno. & others	Davidson	640	297	13 June 1787	2037		63	111	Beg at a large white oak	Yes
Griffin, William	152		Washington	104	20	23 Oct 1782	795	28 Dec 1778	47	9	S/S Roans Creek	
Griffis, Samuel	034	Barker, Lewis	Robertson	400				10 Jan 1794			W of Cumberland River	
Griffis, Samuel	864	Mountfforence, Jas C.	Davidson	1000	878	17 Jan 1789	2125		63	304	On Weakleys Creek	
Griffith, Henry	1118	Harris, Edward	Sumner	640	2624	4 June 1796	2455	1 June 1795	88	342	Joining said Harris survey	Yes
Grigg, James	804		Sullivan	500	747	17 Nov 1797			94	149	On the head of Lick Branch	
Griggs, Charles	541		Davidson	274	513	15 Sep 1787	993		63	185	On 1st Creek S/S Cumberland River	
Giles, Elitt	101		Hawkins	125	135	26 Dec 1791	992	4 Jan 1779	75	156	S/S Holston River	Yes
Grimes, Andrew	1599	Ford, John	Davidson	640	1292	10 Dec 1790	2454		74	363	On waters of Mill Creek	
Grimes, Benjamin	416		Tennessee	274	2455	31 Dec 1793	1942	27 July 1785	81	428	On Montgomery Fork	
Grimes, David	423		Sullivan	200	302	10 Nov 1784	1845	6 Oct 1779	69	177	On Fall Creek	
Grimes, James	1030		Washington	100	980	14 Jan 1793	2583	30 June 1780	79	278	On Little Limestone	
Grimes, James	187		Washington	200	55	23 Oct 1782	395	15 Sep 1778	47	26	On Sinking Creek	
Grimes, James	205		Washington	389	73	23 Oct 1782	329	29 Aug 1778	47	35	On a branch of Little Limestone Creek	
Grimes, James	68		Washington	355		23 Oct 1782	330	29 Aug 1770	44	263	On the Onion Branch	
Grimes, Simon	581	Sanford, Samuel	Sumner	640	1819	20 May 1793	2376	6 Aug 1792	81	83	On headwaters of E. Branches	Yes
Grinder, John	1754	Hays, Robert	Davidson	1000	1526	14 Jan 1793	1220		79	264	On waters of Harpeth River	Yes
Grinestaff, John	1307		Washington	100	1193	4 Dec 1795	1515	12 Aug 1779	89	432	On Little Doe	
Grise, Christopher	1541		Davidson	100	81	26 Nov 1789			74	167	On Heatons Lick Branch	
Grisham, Richard	352		Eastern Dist	100	291	6 June 1796		Martin Armstrong	88	383	Waters of Dumplin Creek	
Grissam, Thompson	1621		Green	370	1342	22 Feb 1792	1224	Dec 1789	84	296	On waters of Dumplin Creek	
Grissom, Robert	609	Stewart, Duncan	Tennessee	1000	3155	14 Sep 1797	4320	3 Jan 1779	90	424	N/S of Cumberland River	Yes
Grogan, Jacob	1963	Sanford, Samuel	Davidson	640	1825	20 May 1793	2375	26 Aug 1781	81	84	On waters of W. Harpeth	Yes
Grogan, James	384	Thomas, Richard	Sumner	274	1568	4 Feb 1793	2418	19 Nov 1792	79	293	E/S of Caney Fork	Yes
Grogan, John	697	Sheppard, Benj.	Davidson	1000	670	8 Dec 1787	2347		63	237	On Bizzells Salleen	Yes
Gross, Christopher	703		Hawkins	150	505	23 Apr 1794	984	3 Jan 1779	82	154	In Carters Valley	
Groves, James Sr.	510		Hawkins	100	383	29 July 1793	833	26 Aug 1781	80	272	On both sides of Big Creek	
Groves, John	80		Hawkins	400	53	27 Nov 1789			74	40	N/S of Holstein River	
Groves, John Sr.	477		Hawkins	100	349	29 July 1793	833	26 Aug 1781	80	263	Joining Carter's Valley	
Groves, John Sr.	51		Hawkins	400	36	18 May 1789	33	8 Feb 1780	72	250	On both sides of Big Creek	
Groves, Nicholas	1972	Donelson, John	Davidson	640	1859	20 May 1793			81	91	On a small S/Fk of Stones Creek	Yes
Groves, William	327	Allen, William	Tennessee	640	2076	20 May 1793	2126	9 Sep 1785	81	143	On 1st large Fork	Yes
Groves, William Berry	285		Western Dist	1500	274	25 Apr 1789	2149	11 May 1784	72	82	On waters of Big Hatcha River	
Grub, Jacob	299		Sullivan	200	438	9 Aug 1787	121	9 Feb 1780	61	457	On both sides of Little Sinking Creek	
Grubb, Abraham	86		Sullivan	510	97	23 Oct 1782	1657	17 Sep 1779	43	284	N/S of Holston River	
Gubbins, William	1554		Davidson	720	100	26 Nov 1789	762		74	173	Beg at an ash	
Gubbins, William	360	Dixon, Henry hrs.	Davidson	640	344	4 Sep 1787	1802		63	128	S/S Sulphur Fork	Yes
Gubbins, William	627	Green, Thomas hrs.	Davidson	640	599	15 Sep 1787	1758		63	214	N/S Cumberland River	Yes

Claimant:	File #:	Assignee:	County:	Acres:	Grant:	Grant Date:	Entry:	Entry Date:	Bk:	Pg:	Location by Stream Name:	Military:
Guchey, John	056		Tennessee	650	19			3 Aug 1819	52	299	Beg at a stake "Indian Lands"	
Gudger, William	480		Washington	99	472	13 Oct 1783	1988	16 Oct 1779	52	274	Indian Creek	
Guest, Joseph	426		Washington	185	418	13 Oct 1783	1087	6 Jan 1779			On Dunhams Creek	
Guffy, John	023	McLemore, Robert	Robertson	640	3387		5265	21 May 1800			Waters of Red River	Yes
Guice, Christopher	1425		Davidson	100	42	08 Oct 1787			68	158	On waters of Guice Creek	
Guice, Christopher	1626		Davidson	90	99	10 Nov 1790			74	388	On waters of Guice Creek	
Guille M. Devereaux	205(204)		Hawkins	640	192	26 Dec 1791	894	29 Oct 1783	77	311	S/S of Holston River	
Guille M. Devereax	114	Chemey, Robert	Davidson	640	100	14 Mar 1786	451		63	40	On Guices Creek	
Guin, Daniel	814	Davis, Joshua	Sumner	640	2282	20 May 1793	2358	19 Nov 1792	81	187	Beg at a sugar tree	Yes
Guin, Edward	289	Price, William	Tennessee	640	1916	20 May 1793	3297	3 Jan 1786	81	104	On the waters of Bartons Creek	Yes
Guin, Thomas	540	Williams, Willoughby	Davidson	365	512	15 Sep 1787	1111		63	185	S/S Cumberland River	Yes
Guinn, Edward	309	King, Anthony	Sumner	640	1517	10 Apr 1792	2519	6 Aug 1791	75	507	On waters of Spencers Creek	Yes
Guion, Samuel	1930	White, James	Davidson	640	1741	20 May 1793	3090		81	64	N/S of Cmberland River	Yes
Guion, William	344	Adair, James	Eastern Dist	274	2610	7 Mar 1796			88	331	On N/S Clinch River	Yes
Guist, Joshua	46		Hawkins	200	31	18 May 1789	4	22 Oct 1778	72	248	N/S Clinch River	Yes
Guist, Thomas	2066	Blount, Jno.G. & Thos.	Davidson	640	2204	20 May 1793	2515		81	169	S/S Harpeth River	Yes
Gumbell, Moses	976		Washington	400	953	17 Nov 1790	1801	14 Feb 1789	76	163	N/S Watauga River	Yes
Gun, Hardy	1147	Harris, Edward	Sumner	640	2653	4 June 1796	2718	1 June 1795	88	352	Joining Harris survey	Yes
Gunn, Abraham	995	Weakley, Robert	Davidson	640	1012	18 May 1789	2487		63	339	E/Fk Stones River	Yes
Gunn, Alexander	280	Rutherford, Griffith	Davidson	1000	266	14 Mar 1786	748		63	97	N/S Tennessee River	Yes
Gunn, John	366	Walker, George	Tennessee	1000	2239	20 May 1791	747	7 May 1784	81	178	S/S Cumberland River	Yes
Gunter, Joel	954	Dixon, Charles	Davidson	274	971	18 May 1789			63	329	On head branches of 1st Creek	Yes
Gunter, Samuel	1309	Donelson, Stockley	Sumner	205	3107	14 Sep 1797	4280	12 May 1797	90	405	Waters of Spencers Creek	Yes
Gurley, James	955	Logue, John	Davidson	1000	972	18 May 1789	1737		63	330	S/S Cumberland River	Yes
Gurley, Joseph	903	Smith, John	Sumner	640	2459	31 Dec 1793	488	12 Dec 1792	81	429	S/S Cumberland River	Yes
Gutherie, Adam	1379		Green	123	1234	27 Jan 1793	1829	6 Oct 1779	79	507	Beg at a post oak	
Gutherey, Francis	690		Hawkins	450	579	17 Jul 1794	2239, 1936		81	612	On N/S of Clinch River	
Guthrie, Robert	743		Washington	200	557	10 Nov 1784	2473	10 Mar 1780	69	126	S/S Gullens Branch	
Guthrop, John	038	Clark, Lardner	Not given	640			1384	7 Oct 1789			S/S Cumberland River	Yes
Guttery, Henry	1049	Douglas, John	Sumner	640	2512	20 Nov 1795	1425	23 Nov 1789	88	283	Beg at a Buckeye	Yes
Guttery, James	809	Simpson, Archibald	Hawkins	200	645	6 Jan 1795	379	3 Apr 1780	83	167	Joining where Mrs. Jane Evans now lives.	
Guyen, Williams	1060		Hawkins	200	769	21 Jan 1797	703	27 Sep 1780	91	115	Beg a black oak	
Gwaltney, Joshua	393	Sheppard, Benj.	Davidson	640	365	15 Sep 1787	2334		63	137	W/S Middle Fork of Drakes Creek	Yes
Gwin, Edward	181	Jenkins, Levi	Tennessee	640	1461	4 Jan 1792	2518	30 Sep 1785	77	366	S/S Cumberland River	
Gwin, James	863		Washington	522	847	18 May 1789	605	27 Mar 1779	72	219	Beg at a stake	
Gwin, John	1185		Green	100	1028	26 Dec 1791	2640		77	291	S/S of Dumplin Creek	
Gwin, John	1385	Hooker, John	Sumner	274	3310	6 Dec 1797	4088	27 Apr 1797	97	37	On waters of Big Barren	Yes
Gwin, John	1434	Jones, Elisha	Sumner	274	3309	6 Dec 1797	4034	8 May 1797	98	180	On Peytons Fork of Drakes Creek	Yes
Gwin, Wm.	1386	Strider, George	Sumner	411	3311	6 Dec 1797	1191	1797	97	37	On waters of Big Barren	Yes
Gwinn, Jacob	652	Dobbs & Bushnell	Davidson	640	625	15 Sep 1787	1686		63	222	On waters of Stewarts Creek	Yes
Gwins, Robert	1090		Davidson	640	64	17 Apr 1786	566	7 Aug 1784	66	56	Both sides Station Fork of Red River	Yes
Habbits, Andrew	1739		Green	59	1390	2 Dec 1796	441	22 Apr 1780	91	272	Beg at a white oak	
Hacker, Julious	1175		Washington	100	1133	7 July 1794	2485	10 Mar 1780	81	621	Beg on the side of a hill	
Hacker, John	387		Sullivan	640	266	10 Nov 1784	455	14 Apr 1780	69	167	On N/S of Holstein River	
Hackett, John	813		Green	250	814	11 Aug 1889			71	34	In fork of Tenn & Clinch Rivers	

Earliest Tennessee Land Records

Claimant:	File #:	Assignee:	County:	Acres:	Grant:	Grant Date:	Entry:	Entry Date:	Bk:	Pg:	Location by Stream Name:	Military:
Hackett, John	1052		Green	150	895	26 Dec 1791	81	16 Nov 1788	77	240	On N/S French Broad River	
Hackett, John	1075		Green	300	918	26 Dec 1791	569	22 May 1780	77	248	S/S of Clinch River	
Hackett, John	120		Eastern Dist	150	153	29 July 1793	93	25 Apr 1789	76	481	N/S of Holston River	
Hackett, John	137		Green	253	119	1 Nov 1786	619	21 Oct 1783	60	451	N/S Tennessee River	
Hackett, John	1413		Green	100	1225	27 Nov 1792	88	24 Apr 1789	80	162	On the head of Little Chuckey	
Hackett, John	142		Green	500	612	23 Aug 1788			64	345	N/S Holston River	
Hackett, John	148		Green	2000	618	23 Aug 1788	413	25 Oct 1783	64	347	N/S Tennessee River	
Hackett, John	174		Green	100	644	23 Aug 1788	2523	6 Apr 1780	64	356	N/S French Broad River	
Hackett, John	199		Green	800	156	20 Sep 1787	445	28 Oct 1783	65	415	N/S of Clinch River	
Hackett, John	200		Green	140	157	20 Sep 1787			65	416	In Cumberland Valley	
Hackett, John	209		Green	600	166	20 Sep 1787			65	419	N/S of Tennessee River	
Hackett, John	247		Green	214	204	20 Sep 1787	1880	24 Apr 1784	65	432	N/S of Holston River	
Hackett, John	376		Eastern Dist	200	227	28 Aug 1795	726	3 Sep 1778	89	81	On Lick Branch	
Hackett, John	455		Eastern Dist	1000	302	2 Dec 1800	670	28 Oct 1783	112	11	Waters of Turkey Creek	
Hackett, John	767		Green	225	572	23 Aug 1788	1021	15 Dec 1785	68	250	N/S of Tennessee River	
Hackett, John	773		Green	500	578	23 Aug 1788	1746	21 Apr 1784	68	253	N/S of Clinch River	
Hackett, John	782		Green	600	587	23 Aug 1788	282	27 Mar 1781	68	257	N/S Holston River on Little Meadow Creek	
Hackett, John	788		Green	640	593	23 Aug 1788	350	24 Mar 1780	68	259	N/S Holston River on Little Sinking Creek	
Hackett, John	790		Green	250	595	23 Aug 1788	614	27 Oct 1783	68	260	S/S of Clinch River	
Hackett, John	866	Hart, Wm.	Sumner	640	2379	20 May 1793	966	23 June 1792	81	298	On 1st large creek below Smith's Fork	Yes
Hackett, John & Donelson	215		Eastern Dist	5000	201	17 July 1794			81	613	At the mouth of Highawassa River	
Hackett, John Sr.	449		Eastern Dist	400	317	18 Dec 1802	2119		110	270	N/S Clinch River	
Hackett, John Sr.	450		Eastern Dist	600	318	15 Dec 1802	2119	30 Sep 1784	110	271	On the Grassy Valley	
Hackner, Daniel	789	King, Robt & Chas & Coop	Hawkins	640	629	12 July 1794	3355		82	223	In Stoney Fork Valley	Yes
Hacksaw, James	371	Hayes, Robert	Sumner	640	1537	14 Jan 1793	2382	30 Nov 1792	79	266	On waters of Madisons Creek	Yes
Haclatt, John	153		Eastern Dist	100	123	24 Dec 1792	74	5 Nov 1788	78	455	N/S Clinch River	
Hadden, Anna	744		Washington	100	558	10 Nov 1784	2107	31 Oct 1779	69	126	On Middle Fk of Big Limestone	
Hadden, Elisha	1077		Washington	100	1027	27 Nov 1792	2591	22 July 1780	80	184	On waters of Big Limestone	
Haddock, Admiral	944	McCutchin, John	Davidson	228	960	18 May 1789	1235		63	327	N/S E/Fk of Stones River	Yes
Haddock, Andrew	107	Nicholas, John	Davidson	1000	93	14 Mar 1786	1076		63	38	Both sides of Big Harpeth River	Yes
Haddock, Andrew	108	Brooks, Thomas	Davidson	429	94	14 Mar 1786	311		63	38	Joining Nathaniel Dickerson	Yes
Haddock, Peter	104	Pyette, Peter	Tennessee	640	1524	10 Apr 1792	449	19 Oct 1784	75	509	S/S Cumberland River	Yes
Haddock, William	565	King, Robert	Middle Dist	640	3086	30 Aug 1793	3172		90	393	On the Caney Fork	Yes
Hadley, John	535	Ralph, John heirs	Sumner	640	1729	20 May 1793			81	60	On waters of Collins River	Yes
Hadley, Josh	1412	Rogers, Austin	Sumner	228	3267	6 Dec 1797	4542	22 June 1797	98	152	On waters of Spring Creek	Yes
Hadley, Joshua	250	Thompson, Wm.	Sumner	640	1196	30 Nov 1790	3211	10 Nov 1787	74	320	On Big Barron River	Yes
Hadley, Joshua	251	Thompson, Ned	Sumner	640	1197	30 Nov 1790	3212	18 Nov 1787	74	321	N/F of Big Barron River	
Hadley, Joshua	258		Tennessee	228	1681	20 May 1793	3748	4 Mar 1792	81	49	On W/F of Persons Creek	
Hadley, Joshua	516	Dobbins, William	Sumner	640	1693	20 May 1793	1048	29 Aug 1792	81	52	On E/Fk of Bledsoe's Creek	Yes
Hadley, Joshua	1422		Sumner	228	3277	6 Dec 1797	4549	21 June 1797	98	158	On waters of Spring Creek	
Hadley, Joshua	020		Not Given									Yes
Hadley, Joshua	059		Green	2430			1637				On waters of Duck Creek	
Hadley, Joshua	077	Tilly, John	Middle Dist	400				12 Oct 1784				
Hadley, Joshua	080	Fenner, Robert	Sumner	640	2914	22 Dec 1792					On waters of Station Camp	Yes
Hadley, Joshua	081	McRace, Robert	Sumner	640		18 Oct 1787					On Punchin Camp Creek	

Claimant:	File #:	Assignee:	County:	Acres:	Grant:	Grant Date:	Entry:	Entry Date:	Bk:	Pg:	Location by Stream Name:	Military:
Hadley, Joshua	126	Joynes, Lewis	Tennessee	640	1632	23 Feb 1793	2666	30 Sep 1785	76	328	S/S Cumberland River	
Hadley, Joshua	1352	Lindsay, Isaac	Sumner	274	3171	4 Sep 1797	3936	8 Nov 1796	90	430	Headwaters of Dixons Creek	Yes
Hadley, Joshua	1358	Jones, Oliver	Sumner	640	2804	21 Dec 1796	3873	14 Oct 1796	91	475	E/S Caney Fork	Yes
Hadley, Joshua	1413	Ryan, Jeff	Sumner	228	3268	6 Dec 1797	4543	22 June 1791	98	152	Waters of Spring Creek	Yes
Hadley, Joshua	1414		Sumner	228	3269	6 Dec 1797	4545	22 June 1797	98	153	Waters of Spring Creek	Yes
Hadley, Joshua	1415		Sumner	220/228(	3270	6 Dec 1797	449	8 May 1797	98	154	Waters of Cedar Creek	Yes
Hadley, Joshua	1416		Sumner	228	3271	6 Dec 1797	4546	21 June 1797	98	154	Waters of Spring Creek	Yes
Hadley, Joshua	1417		Sumner	228	3272	6 Dec 1797	4547	21 June 1797	98	155	Beg at Samuel Jones S/E corner	Yes
Hadley, Joshua	1418		Sumner	228	3273	6 Dec 1797	4552	8 May 1797	98	155	Waters of Cedar Creek	Yes
Hadley, Joshua	1419		Sumner	228	3274	6 Dec 1797	4550	8 May 1797	98	156	Headwaters of Cedar Creek	Yes
Hadley, Joshua	1421		Sumner	640	3276	6 Dec 1797	4499	21 June 1797	98	157	Headwaters of Cedar Creek	Yes
Hadley, Joshua	165	McKinsey, Wm.	Tennessee	640	1427	20 Dec 1791	223	25 Oct 1783	77	358	Both sides Pine River	
Hadley, Joshua	2406	Stern, Andrew heirs	Davidson	640	2803	21 Dec 1796	3933		91	475	On West Harpeth River	Yes
Hadley, Joshua	45	Hunter, Elisha	Sumner	640	900	17 Jan 1789	3077	10 Nov 1787	63	311	On the ridge that divides &c	yes
Hadley, Joshua	46	Hill, Jas.	Sumner	640	901	17 Jan 1789	2733		63	311	E/Fk of Big Barren River	Yes
Hadley, Joshua	464	Gardner, Demsey	Davidson	274	436	15 Sep 1787	459		63	160	N/S of Cumberland River	Yes
Hadley, Joshua	495	Lewis, John	Sumner	640	1663	20 May 1793			81	44	Waters of E/Fk of Barren River	Yes
Hadley, Joshua	507		Sumner	640	1679	20 May 1793			81	48	Beg at an oak	Yes
Hadley, Joshua	512		Sumner	274	1689	20 May 1793	3207	12 Feb 1787	81	51	On the Fk Cumberland & Obids River	Yes
Hadley, Joshua	521		Sumner	640	1700	20 May 1793			81	53	W/S Caney Fork	Yes
Hadley, Joshua	524	McDonald, Wm. Hrs	Sumner	640	1708	20 May 1793	3143	10 Mar 1788	81	55	W/S Caney Fork	Yes
Hadley, Joshua	534	Albright, Jas heirs	Sumner	640	1728	20 May 1793	2828	10 Mar 1788	81	60	On waters of Collins River	Yes
Hadley, Joshua	548		Sumner	640	1753	29 Aug 1793			81	67	Waters of Station Camp Creek	Yes
Hadley, Joshua	576	Dobbins, William	Sumner	640	1693	20 May 1793	1048	29 Aug 1792	81	52	E/Fk of Bledsoes Creek	Yes
Hadley, Joshua	609		Middle Dist	1280	207	29 Apr 1801		Evans Cooper	112	389	W of Cumberland Mountain	
Hadley, Joshua	83		Davidson	3840	69	14 Mar 1786	59		63	28	N/S Duck River	
Hadley, Joshua, Assignee	1050		Sumner	400	177	2 Dec 1795			88	285	N/S Cumberland River	Yes
Hadley, Selby & Ant. Bledsoe	707		Sumner	640	2087	20 May 1793	3100	30 Nov 1792	81	146	Branches Middle Fk Goose Creek	Yes
Hadley, West	980	Ellis, James	Sumner	1000	2445	22 Feb 1795	3270	8 Aug 1792	84	319	A fork of Obeys River	Yes
Hadley, William	1019		Green	150	1246	29 July 1793	893	3 Dec 1778	76	487	N/S French Broad River	
Hadsock, Josiah	1936	Robertson, James	Davidson	640	1756	29 May 1793	2852		81	68	S/S Cumberland River	Yes
Hadson, Joel	1110	Harris, Edward	Sumner	640	2616	4 June 1796	2662	1 June 1795	88	338	Joining sd Harris survey	Yes
Hafter, Thomas	737	Colton, Thos.	Sumner	640	2130	20 May 1793	3257	9 Aug 1792	81	156	S/S Jinnings Creek	Yes
Haggard, Henry	331		Green	300	333	28 Sep 1787	663	28 Oct 1783	65	467	Lyles Creek	
Haggard, Henry & A. Hodges	798		Hawkins	300	215	30 Oct 1794			83	142	N/S Holston River	
Hagins, James	619	Ford, John	Davidson	640	591	15 Sep 1787	893		63	211	S/S Cumberland	
Hagley, David	1012		Green	600	1239	29 July 1793			76	486	N/S Holston	
Hague, John	304	Fuller, Wm.	Tennessee		1995	20 May 1793	3345	7 Jan 1786	81	123	Waters of Red River	
Hail, Abedmegp	934		Washington	200	911	17 Nov 1790	698	16 Dec 1778	76	148	Dry Fork of Sinking Creek	
Hail, Abednigo	1027		Washington	100	977	14 Jan 1793	296	4 Aug 1778	79	277	Branch of Big Limestone	
Hail, Alexander	1155		Washington	150	1113	7 July 1794	2911	28 Aug 1781	81	615	Beg at John Moseley's line	
Hail, Edward	822	McCullock, Benj.	Sumner	640	2300	20 May 1793	1785	20 Nov 1792	81	191	Abt 1 mile from the Old Station	Yes
Hail, Frederick	1365		Green	200	1220	27 Jan 1793	1400	12 Jan 1784	79	503	N/S Noleychuckey River	
Hail, Jno	156		Sullivan	640	166	18 Aug 1783	114	14 Mar 1778	45	273	On Bent Creek	
Hail, John	150		Sullivan	200	160	18 Aug 1783	165	14 Mar 1778	45	271	On Jno. Hunnycutts Creek	

Earliest Tennessee Land Records

Claimant:	File #:	Assignee:	County:	Acres:	Grant:	Grant Date:	Entry:	Entry Date:	Bk:	Pg:	Location by Stream Name:	Military:
Hall, Meshack	594		Washington	112	688	26 Oct 1786	1418	5 May 1779	66	6	Both sides Lick Creek	
Hall, Nicholas	507		Washington	200	770	16 Aug 1787	2682	12 Dec 1780	64	142	Waters of Sinking Creek	
Hall, Nicholas, Jr.	1000		Washington	400	972	26 Dec 1791	425	29 Apr 1780	77	300	Waters of Kendricks Creek	
Hall, Shadrach	793		Washington	200	2872	10 Nov 1784	2872	18 June 1781	69	140	Water of Lick Creek	
Hailie, Meshack	315		Washington	348	182	24 Oct 1782	767	24 Dec 1778	49	218	N/S Watauga River	
Hailie, Nicholas	116		Washington	640	284	24 Oct 1782	646	28 Nov 1778	40	290	On Sinking Creek	
Hailie, Nicholas	119		Washington	300/360(	287	24 Oct 1782	1569	2 Sep 1779	44	291	Sinking Creek	
Hailie, Philip	1490		Green	200	1253	12 July 1794	72	12 Mar 1784	81	579	N/S Noleychuckey River	
Hailey, David Jr.	326		Green	315	328	20 Sep 1787	866	29 Oct 1783	67	466	N/S Holston River, Richland Creek	
Hailey, David	219		Eastern District	320	162	30 Dec 1793			82	144	SE/S of Copper Creek	
Haily, Robert	793	McCulloch, Benj.	Sumner	274	2253	20 May 1793	3007	30 Nov 1792	81	181	On Defeated Creek	Yes
Hains, Abraham	1741		Green	100	1392	2 Dec 1796	507	28 Apr 1780	91	273	Beg at Drury Morris' corner	
Hains, Christopher	1540		Green	300	1300	17 July 1794	412	12 Apr 1780	81	609	Beg at a stake	
Hains, Christopher	1710		Green	300	1425	8 June 1797			90	321	Waters of Dumplin Creek	
Hains, Christopher	859		Hawkins	300	638	16 Jan 1795	368	14 Aug 1781	84	36	Beg at a white oak	
Hains, John & Lewis Harman	1018		Hawkins	400	784	8 Jan 1797	492	26 Apr 1780	90	209	On head of Lime Stone Fork	
Hains, Phillip	1909	Bostian, Jacob	Davidson	640	1671	20 May 1793	1714		81	46	1st large creek comes into Cumberland	
Hains, William	1973	Hord, John	Davidson	640	1867	20 May 1793	3604		63	93	S/S Cumberland on waters of Stones River	Yes
Hair, David	830	Armstrong, Andrew	Davidson	640	833	17 Jan 1789	3466		63	293	N/S Cumberland River	Yes
Hair, James	206	Dickson, John	Tennessee	640	1496	4 Jan 1792	1905		77	374	S/S Cumberland River	Yes
Hair, John	166	Smith, Oliver	Tennessee	640	1430	20 Dec 1791	1907		77	359	On Pine River	Yes
Hair, John	2438	Tatum & Wiggans	Davidson	640	3280	6 Dec 1797	4266		98	160	On waters of W/Fk of Stones River	Yes
Hair, William	149		Tennessee	640	1401	20 Dec 1791	1906		77	351	Both sides Pine River	Yes
Halcolm, William	875	Sugg, Acquilla	Davidson	1000	889	17 Jan 1789	1817		63	308	E/S Main E/FK Main E/Fk of Stones River	Yes
Halcom, Phillips	051	Lewis, Wm. T.	Not given	185	1640	23 Feb 1793		6 Dec 1792			Beg at 3 white oaks	Yes
Hale, Josiah	419	Cobb, Jesse	Tennessee	640	2465	31 Dec 1793	1208	26 Sep 1784	81	431	On Main head branches	Yes
Hale, Nathan	1233	Sanders, William	Sumner	1000	2506	12 Nov 1795	1623	21 Sep 1787	89	422	Beg at 2 beech trees	Yes
Hale, Nicholas	523		Washington	200	786	16 Aug 1787	2777	21 Feb 1781	64	148	In fork of Sinking Creek	
Hale, Phillip	952		Green	100	866	17 Nov 1790	720	21 May 1787	76	127	Incl. island on S/S Nolachucky River	
Hale, Shadrick	601		Washington	100	695	26 Oct 1786	720	21 Dec 1778	66	9	On waters of Lick Creek	
Hale, Shadrick	645		Washington	300	739	26 Oct 1786	510	17 Oct 1778	66	30	N/Fk (sic)	
Hale, Wm. Quate	1040		Green	200	1267	29 Jul 1793	1380	21 May 1777	76	491	Beg at a pine on Wm. Pursleys line	
Haley, David	170		Hawkins	150	103	16 Nov 1790	1492	19 Feb 1784	77	186	N/S Holston	
Haley, David	482		Green	250	484	20 Sep 1787	5	14 Oct 1785	65	513	N/S Holston	
Halfacre, Michael	1676		Green	290	1361	20 July 1796			88	492	N/S French Broad River	
Halfacre, Michael	329		Green	239	331	20 Sep 1787		21 Oct 1783	65	467	N/S French Broad River	
Halkins, Joseph	850		Green	200	831	13 Feb 1791	496	27 Sep 1789	73	378	Headwaters Horse Stamp–Fk of Lick Creek	
Hall, Clement	61		Davidson	3840	47	14 Mar 1786	555		63	20	Beg at 2 walnuts	Yes
Hall, David	082	Dowell, James	Sumner	274			598	20 Aug 1785			N/S Cumberland River	
Hall, David	1368	Stewart, Duncan	Sumner	274	3217	14 Sep 1797	591	20 Aug 1785	92(?)	12	N/S Cumberland River	
Hall, James	374	Hays, Robert	Sumner	640	1548	14 Jan 1793	285(?)	6 Feb 1792	79	269	E/Fk of Goose Creek	Yes
Hall, James	43		Western Dist	2000	43	10 July 1788	2616	24 May 1784	67	297	S/S Indian Creek	Yes
Hall, John	268		Sullivan	640	407	9 Aug 1787	1983	19 Oct 1779	61	426	Beg at Benjamin Mooneys corner	
Hall, John	744		Sullivan	135	675	13 Nov 1795	792	10 June 1780	89	277	S/S Holston River	
Hall, John	831		Sullivan	135	774	5 Dec 1798	792	10 June 1781	97	297	S/S Holston River	

Claimant:	File #:	Assignee:	Acres:	Grant:	Grant Date:	Entry:	Entry Date:	Bk:	Pg:	Location by Stream Name:	Military:
Hall, Philip	657		100	698	11 July 1788	266	22 Oct 1783	66	460	N of Nolichuckey River..Beg on his old line	
Hall, William	277		500	416	9 Aug 1787	2233	20 Nov 1779	61	435	In Powells Valley	
Hall, William	292		500	431	9 Aug 1787	2234	20 Nov 1779	61	450	S/S of Powells River	
Hall, William	293		500	432	9 Aug 1787	2232	20 Nov 1779	61	451	In Powells Valley on Gap Creek	
Hall, William	577		460	842	23 Aug 1788	43	26 Feb 1778	64	359	On Big Limestone	
Hall, William	600		200	694	26 Oct 1786	471	2 Oct 1780	66	8	Beg at a white oak	
Hallaway, William	1195		400	1148	6 Jan 1795	2926	10 Sep 1789	83	176	Joining a conditional line	
Hallaway, William	869		200	853	28 May 1789	462	1 Oct 1779	72	221	On Kendricks Creek	
Hallaway, William Jr.	879		200	863	18 May 1789	2767	8 Feb 1781	72	224	Beg at Wheellocks upper line	
Halley, Joshua	264		2560	1712	20 May 1793	3105	8 Dec 1785	81	56	S/S Cumberland River	
Haling, Silomon	882		2057	2401	7 Jan 1794	3730	19 Oct 1792	81	392	S/Fk of Abbetts River	
Halmark, George	311		350	313	20 Sep 1787	254	22 Oct 1783	65	462	Both sides Lick Creek	
Halsted, Jollef	2141	Averall, William	160	2418	7 Jan 1794	995		81	405	N/S Cumberland River	Yes
Ham, John	028	Dillenberry, Redmon	640	4408	14 Oct 1797					On Caney Fork	Yes
Hambleton, Alexander	629		250	577	27 June 1793	260	6 June 1789	80	373	Branch of Fall Creek	
Hambleton, James	303		170	442	9 Aug 1787	1022	1779	61	461	On Patesons Creek	
Hambleton, Jno	1268		640	233	10 July 1788	281	14 Feb 1784	66	419	Blooming Grove Cr N/S Cumberland River	
Hambleton, Joshua	622		400	570	27 June 1793	446	22 Apr 1780	80	370	N/S Holstein River	
Hambleton, Josiah	300		180	167	24 Oct 1782	253	3 Jul 1778	77	81	On both sides of Little Limestone	
Hambleton, Robert	245		125/135(	584	9 Aug 1787	773	15 Dec 1781	61	403	S/S Holstein River	
Hambleton, William	1147	Clendennin, John	229	990	26 Dec 1790	990(sic)	25 Oct 1783	77	278	N/S Holstein River	
Hamblin, Daniel	157		100	90	16 Nov 1790			77	181	N/S Holstein River	
Hamelton, Eliazer	2189		100	176	26 Mar 1791			86	378	Waters of Stones River	
Hamelton, Elijah	424	Rhone, John	640	2475	31 Dec 1793	2004	16 Aug 1785	81	435	Sturgeon Creek	
Hamelton, Hance	1958	Hamilton, Thomas	4800	1802	20 May 1793	676		81	80	S/S Cumberland River	Yes
Hamelton, James	424		75	313	5 June 1793	830	10 Aug 1781	80	157	N/S Holstein River	
Hamelton, Thomas	698		500	500	16 Dec 1793	1726, 1762	9 Oct 1779	82	101	N/S of Holston River	
Hamilton, George	083	Walker, John	640			1264	8 Dec 1792			On Lick Creek	
Hamilton, James	121	Kervin, Thomas	274	107	7 Mar 1786	363		63	43	On Stones River	Yes
Hamilton, James	372		618	311	17 Dec 1794	1551	26 May 1784	84	211	N/S Tennessee River	
Hamilton, James	416		640	355	17 Dec 1794	1552	26 Mar 1784	84	231	N/S Tennessee	
Hamilton, James	915		185(184)	724	7 Mar 1796	552	1 May 1780	88	202	N/S Holstein River	
Hamilton, Jno	1306		640	271	10 July 1788	567	9 Aug 1784	66	432	Wt/Fk of Station Camp Creek	
Hamilton, Jno.	1077		560	51	17 Apr 1786	86	13 Jan 1784	66	51	On Middle Fk & E/Fk of Station Camp Creek	
Hamilton, Jno.	2471	Morris, Wm. Heirs	1000	3405	3 Dec 1803	3277		118	139	N/S Cumberland River	Yes
Hamilton, John	397		500	389	13 Oct 1783	535	26 Oct 1778	52	260	On Mill Fork	
Hamilton, John	607	Crutcher, Anthony	640	579	15 Sep 1787	1845		63	207	N/S Cumberland River	Yes
Hamilton, John	897		640	2449	31 Dec 1793			81	426	Below Mouth of Obeys River	
Hamilton, John C.	1346		500	1263	19 July 1797	2047	27 Oct 1779	91	617	Waters of Lorrel Fork	
Hamilton, John C.	1371		300	1286	17 Nov 1797	2201	12 Nov 1779	94	144	Waters of Rones Creek	
Hamilton, Joseph & Elinor	365		835	1273	17 Dec 1794	1273	23 Dec 1783	84	209	Waters of Buffalo River Branch	
Hamilton, Robert	744		100	584	7 July 1794	227	26 May 1778	82	204	N/S Cumberland River	
Hamilton, Robert	925		25	707	2 Dec 1795	773	9 Apr 1781	88	263	S/S of Holston River	
Hamilton, Robert	926		400	708	2 Dec 1795	1184,804	1781, 1779	88	263	S/S Holston River	
Hamilton, Thomas	0134	Clifton, Daniel	640			1208	18 June 1792			On Waters of Red River	Yes

Claimant:	File #:	Assignee:	County:	Acres:	Grant:	Grant Date:	Entry:	Entry Date:	Bk:	Pg:	Location by Stream Name:	Military:
Hamilton, Thomas	1958	Hamilton, Hance	Davidson	4800	1802	20 May 1793	676		81	80	S/S Cumberland Riv S E/Fk of Stones Riv	Yes
Hamilton, Thomas	528	McClain, Jeremiah	Davidson	640	500	15 Sep 1787	1937		63	181	N/S Cumberland River	Yes
Hamilton, Thomas	53	Terrell, Clement	Tennessee	640	1258	10 Dec 1790	1054	26 May 1784	74	351	S/S Cumberland River	
Hamilton, Thomas	537	Cunningham, James	Davidson	640	509	15 Sep 1787	1938		63	184	Wt/S of Caney Fork	Yes
Hamilton, Thomas	981	Shaw, Robert	Sumner	243	2446	22 Feb 1795	1526	24 Nov 1786	84	319	On waters of Red River	Yes
Hamilton, Thomas	698		Hawkins	500	500	16 Feb 1793	1726, 72	9 Oct 1779	82	101	N/S Holston River	
Hamilton, Thos.	692	Fussell(?)	Sumner	640	2051	20 May 1793	853	28 Nov 1792	81	137	On the waters of Red River	
Hamilton, William	2236	Cross, Anthony hrs	Davidson	640	2607	7 Mar 1796	2119		88	330	E/S of Stones River	Yes
Hammel, Robert	1179		Green	200	1022	26 Dec 1791	2875	29 June 1781	77	289	On waters of Little Chuckey	
Hammer, Isaac	1525		Green	200	1286	12 July 1794	390	25 June 1792	81	590	N/S French Broad	
Hammer, Isaac	851		Hawkins	250	676	22 Feb 1795	2410	29 Jan 1780	83	434	S/S Holston River	
Hammer, John	923		Washington	200	900	17 Nov 1790	2602	5 Aug 1780	76	144	Beg in Chisolm's line	
Hammer, John	924		Washington	200	901	17 Nov 1790	2519	3 Apr 1780	76	144	Beg at a spanish oak	
Hammett, John	964	Donelson, Stockley	Davidson	640	981	18 May 1789	63	332	81		On Second Creek above Bradleys Lick	Yes
Hammock, Samuel	030		Middle Dist	640			2654				Assigned to Reading Blount	Yes
Hammon, James	200	Hart, Anthony	Sumner	640	1105	26 Nov 1789	2665	12 Mar 1788	74	131	W/S of Caney Fork River	Yes
Hammon, John B.	957		Davidson	357	974	18 May 1789	713		63	330	S/S Cumberland River	Yes
Hammond, Edmund	567	Blackface, William	Tennessee	640	3004	10 Apr 1797	1759		90	295	N/S Cumberland River	Yes
Hammond, Feston	902	Barrow, James	Sumner	640	2458	31 Dec 1793	2727	27 June 1788	81	429	A small fork of Smiths	Yes
Hammond, Joseph	101	Graham, Joseph	Tennessee	640	1519	10 Apr 1792	3082	30 Nov 1785	75	507	S/S Cumberland	Yes
Hammond, Matthew	278	Brown, John	Sumner	640	1270	10 Dec 1790	1713		74	355	S/S Cumberland River	Yes
Hammonds, John	209	Reed, Jesse	Sumner	640	1114	26 Nov 1789	2652	12 Mar 1788	74	136	W/S Caney Fork River	Yes
Hammonds, Ralph	1125	Harris, Edward	Sumner	640	2631	4 June 1796	3006	1 July 1795	88	344	Joins said Harris survey	Yes
Hammons, Willis	391	Sheppard, Benjamin	Davidson	640	363	15 Sep 1787	2336	8 Dec 1779	63	136	E/S East Fork of Drakes Creek	Yes
Hamner, Isaac	456		Green	200	458	20 Sep 1787	2337		65	504	On Limestone Fork of Tuckers Creek	
Hampton, Adam	1223		Davidson	640	187	10 July 1788	288	16 Feb 1784	66	409	S/S Richland Creek	
Hampton, Adam	1326		Davidson	320	12	18 Aug 1787	230	2 Feb 1784	64	125	On Sulphur Fork of Red River	
Hampton, Adam	1346		Davidson	320	32	8 Oct 1787	231	2 Feb 1784	68	134	Lying on Sulphur Fork of Red River	
Hampton, Andrew	767	Marshall, Charles	Davidson	640	740	11 July 1788	3005	30 Sep 1785	63	260	W/S of Elk Fork of Red River	Yes
Hampton, George	342	McColloch, Benj.	Tennessee	274	2141	20 May 1793	893	31 Dec 1778	81	159	Waters of Winters Creek	Yes
Hampton, Robert	598		Washington	200	692	26 Oct 1786	4291	14 Dec 1796	66	7	Beg at a white oak	
Hance, Job	1243	Blount, Jno. Gray	Sumner	640	2842	21 Jan 1797	1899		90	45	On Camp Creek	Yes
Hancock, Randolph	187	Oneill, Thomas	Middle Dist	640	1663	8 Mar 1793	540		76	342	On waters of Cumberland River	Yes
Handcock, Isham	945	Anderson, John	Davidson	1000	961	18 May 1789	328	24 Aug 1778	63	327	On waters of Caney Fork	Yes
Handerson, Daniel	179		Washington	250	47	23 Oct 1782	740		47	22	On a small creek called Bear Branch	
Handley, Samuel	1397	Armstrong, M.	Davidson	100	14	8 Oct 1787	813	28 Dec 1778	68	152	Situate on Cobbs Creek	
Handley, Samuel	381		Washington	200	373	13 Oct 1783	1593	3 Sep 1779	52	252	On a branch of Sinking Creek	
Handley, William	1436		Green	200	1247	27 Nov 1792	42	1 May 1792	80	170	N/S Nolichuckey a branch of Sinking Creek	
Hanes, Christopher	1717		Green	700	1396	21 Jan 1797		23 Mar 1780	91	123	Waters of Tuckers Creek	
Hanes, Jno & Lewis Harman	067		Green	300	329						On the headwaters of Lost Creek	
Hanes, Jno & Lewis Harmon	065		Green	300	318		3187				On the headwaters of Lost Creek	
Haney, Selley & A. Bledsoe	728		Sumner	640	2113	20 May 1793	81	152			On ridge bet waters of Goose Creek	Yes
Hankins, Edward	023		Hawkins	200			81	26 Feb 1778			Joining John Beard & Robert Randles	
Hankins, Edward	685	Sypert, Robert	Hawkins	228	2396	17 July 1794	3718		81	604	N/S Holston River	
Hankins, William	472		Hawkins	300	344(?)	29 July 1792	1111	14 July 1779	80	261	N/S Holston River	

Earliest Tennessee Land Records

Claimant:	File #:	Assignee:	County:	Acres:	Grant:	Grant Date:	Entry:	Entry Date:	Bk:	Pg:	Location by Stream Name:	Military:
Hankins, William	553		Hawkins	400	426	29 July 1793	508	16 Oct 1778	80	284	N/S of Holston River	
Hann, Adam	1120		Washington	200	1079	12 Jul 1794	2634	7 Sep 1780	81	562	On Buffaloe's Creek	
Hann...wes(?), Henry	466		Davidson	274	438	15 Sep 1787	996	15 Sep 1787	63	161	N/S of Cumberland River	Yes
Hanna, Samuel	475		Hawkins	200	347	29 July 1793	1428	28 Oct 1779	80	262	S/S Holston River on Sinking Creek	
Hannah, Jno.	277		Hawkins	500	288	14 Jan 1793	81	8 Feb 1780	78	341	N/S Holston River	
Hannah, John	061		Green	400			321	17 Mar 1780			In Carters Valley	
Hannah, John	1314		Washington	389	1234	26 Dec 1786	208	5 May 1778	90	204	On Clark's Branch	
Hannah, John	171	Wigbeys, John heirs	Tennessee	640	1441	20 Dec 1791	2350	29 Sep 1785	77	361	S/S Cumberland River	
Hannah, John	696		Washington	150	510	10 Nov 1784	2637	7 Sep 1780	69	108	Beg at a marked black oak	
Hannah, Jos.	456	Walton, William	Sumner	640	1593	27 Apr 1793	3255	19 Dec 1787	81	16	S/S Et/Fk of Roaring River	Yes
Hannah, Joseph	2213		Davidson	100	241	27 Feb 1796		16 Nov 1790	88	180	N/S Harpeth	
Hannah, Joseph	1481		Davidson	640	285	26 Nov 1789	404	10 Apr 1784	73	257	On Big Harpeth Creek	
Hannah, Rody	626	Humphries, Wm.	Sumner	640	1904	20 May 1793	2343	13 Dec 1792	81	101	On a small fork of Roaring River	Yes
Hannah, William	1480		Green	200	1243	12 July 1794	1059	8 Jan 1779	81	576	On waters of Roaring Fork	
Hannah, William	570		Hawkins	200	444	29 July 1793			80	288	S/S Holston River on Sinking Creek	
Hannah, William	956		Green	99	870	17 Nov 1790	2848	12 May 1781	76	128	On waters of McCarneys Creek	
Hannan, Andrew	042		Sullivan	100	2537	10 Apr 1780					Beg at a large white oak	
Hannan, John	1024		Washington	100	974	14 Jan 1793	1496	30 July 1779	79	277	Beg at a mulberry & forked walnut	
Hannan, John	1138		Green	640	981	26 Dec 1791	246	28 June 1780	77	275	On Nine Mile Creek	
Hannan, Joseph	2213		Davidson	100	241	27 Feb 1796		16 Nov 1790	88	180	N/S Harpeth	
Hanner, Rody	630		Sumner	640	1913	20 May 1793	2341	27 Nov 1792	81	103	On waters of W/Fk of Drakes Creek	Yes
Hansell, Charles	1637	Barrow, Sherrod	Davidson	640	1372	20 Apr 1791	2725		74	395	S/S Cumberland River	Yes
Haralson, Paul	1068		Hawkins	50	777	21 Jan 1797	47	8 Feb 1780	91	119	On headwaters of Fall Creek	
Haralson, Paul	1085		Hawkins	48	371	4 July 1797			91	393 (59	On Flat Creek	
Haralson, Paul	1086		Hawkins	25	378	4 July 1797			91	596	On Flat Creek	
Haralson, Paul	1749		Green	100	374	4 July 1797		12 Apl 1795	91	594	Waters of Dumplin Creek	
Haralson, Paul	1750		Green	100	375	4 July 1797			91	594	Beg at a pine	
Haralson, Paul	1751		Green	18	376	4 July 1797		25 May 1797	91	595	On Cumberland Mountain	
Haralson, Paul	1752		Green	30	377	4 July 1797			91	595	Waters of Dumplin Creek	
Haralson, Paul	1045		Hawkins	40	809	8 June 1797	137	12 Feb 1780	90	324	On Crooked Creek	
Harbenson, David	445		Green	400	447	20 Sep 1787	59	14 Mar 1784	65	501	On Bent Creek waters of Nolechuckey Riv	
Hardeman, Thomas	202		Washington	100	70	23 Ock 1782	544	29 Oct 1778	47	33	Beg at a Black oak &c	
Hardeman, Thomas	355		Washington	190	222	24 Oct 1782	654	26 Nov 1778	49	226	On Boons Creek	
Hardeman, Thomas	357		Washington	35	224	24 Oct 1782	1214	19 Feb 1779	49	227	On Boons Creek	
Harden, John	206		Green	400	163	20 Sep 1787	319	23 Oct 1783	65	418	Ridge dividing Holston & Fr Broad Waters	
Harden, John	207		Green	100	164	20 Sep 1787	64	12 May 1784	65	418	On Roseberrys Creek	
Harden, John	229		Green	200	186	20 Sep 1787	10	2 Oct 1783	65	426	S/S Holston River	
Harden, John	565		Davidson	228	537	15 Sep 1787	93		63	193	W Major Boctons Preemption &Blooming	Yes
Harden, Joseph	257		Washington	200	125	23 Oct 1782	2783	22 Feb 1781	47	61	Roaring Fork of Lick Creek	
Harden, Joseph	356		Washington	50	223	24 Oct 1782	2784	22 Feb 1781	49	227	Roaring Fork of Lick Creek	
Harden, Joseph	415		Green	200	417	20 Sep 1787	54	12 May 1781	65	493	S/S Holston River, branch called Loos Creek	
Harden, Joseph	55		Washington	300	345	24 Oct 1782	534	12 May 1781	43	316	On a Branch of Roaring Fork	
Harden, Joseph	864		Green	200	814	17 Nov 1789	2849	12 Apr 1781	75	17	Roaring Fork of Lick Creek	
Harden, Joseph	91		Green	400	49	1 Nov 1786	37	4 May 1784	59	410	Big Gap Creek	
Harden, Joseph & Joseph, Jr.	237		Green	300	194	20 Sept 1787	40	6 May 1784	65	429	N/S Holston River on Flat Creek	

Claimant:	File #:	Assignee:	County:	Acres:	Grant:	Grant Date:	Entry:	Entry Date:	Bk:	Pg:	Location by Stream Name:	Military:
Harden, Moses hr of Henry	1372		Sumner	640	3227	17 Nov 1797	3072	25 Oct 1796	94	166	Waters of Drakes Creed	Yes
Hardick, Richard	2321	Tatum, Howell	Davidson	640	2936	1 Mar 1797	905		90	211	On w Harpeth River	yes
Hardiman, Thomas	1307		Davidson	640	272	18 Jan 1784	163	10 July 1788	66	432	Beg at a Honey Locust marked DM	
Hardiman, Thomas	1703		Davidson	640	319	23 Feb 1793	52	5 Jan 1784	76	344	S/S Cumberland River	
Hardiman, Thomas	1753		Davidson	640	112	20 Dec 1791	367	23 Mar 1784	77	384	S/S Cumberland River on Little Harpeth	
Hardiman, Thomas	1826		Davidson	640	399	26 June 1793	162	19 Jan 1784	80	342	S/S Cumberland River	
Hardiman, Thomas	972		Hawkins	640	744	20 July 1796	905	29 Oct 1783	88	496	N/S Holston River	
Hardin, John	1371	McKee, Jno.	Sumner	640	3226	17 Nov 1797	2752	7 Nov 1791	94	165	Waters of Arringtons Fork	Yes
Hardin, John	2		Middle District	1000	4	10 Jul 1788	2127	10 May 1784	67	408	E/S Tennessee River	
Hardin, Joseph	115		Green	600	131	1 Nov 1786	318	23 Oct 1783	59	43	Both sides Big Gap Creek	
Hardin, Joseph	56		Middle District	3000	58	10 Jul 1788	1619	5 Apr 1784	67	439	N/S Tennessee River	
Hardin, Joseph	592		Green	200	273	20 Sep 1787	53	12 May 1784	66	164	S/S of Holston River	
Hardin, William	028		Middle Dist.	1700	30	10 July 1788	704	28 Oct 1783	67	421	N/S Duck River	
Hardison, Samuel	1028	Sheppard, John	Sumner	640	2565	8 Mar 1796	294	15 Aug 1792	88	188	Obeys River	Yes
Hardon, Benj., Sr.	1867	Kuykendall, Adam	Davidson	388	1604	27 Apr 1793	1230		81	18	Both sides Sulphur Fork of Red River	Yes
Hardon, Rovert	843	Phifer, Martin	Sumner	182	2346	20 May 1793	3695	27 Oct 1792	81	201	Kerkendoll's Branch	Yes
Hardy, John	028	Blount, Reading	Middle Dist.	640			2043					Yes
Hare, Lawrence	263	Murphree, Hardy	Davidson	914	249	14 Mar 1786	115		63	91	Both sides of Clear Creek	Yes
Haregrove, John	177		Tennessee	274	1454	20 Dec 1791	315	26 Nov 1783	77	364	N/S Red River	Yes
Hareygrove, Benjamin	1702		Green	240	1418	18 Feb 1797	146	7 Sep 1796	90	241	S/S Noleychucky River	
Hargatt, Frederick	92	Freeman, Richd.	Tennessee	640	1368	30 Nov 1790	1254	25 Oct 1784	74	393	N/S Cumberland River	
Harges, Abraham	239		Davidson	228	225	7 Mar 1786	439		63	83	Red River	
Hargess, Shadrack	120		Western Dist.	120	120	10 Jul 1788	636	28 Oct 1783	67	327	Both sides Looshatchee River	Yes
Harget, Fred	587	Supper, Nathan	Sumner	274	1828	20 May 1793	1252	22 Dec 1792	81	85	S/S Big Harpeth River	yes
Harget, Fred	588	Jones, James	Sumner	274	1829	20 May 1793	1435	27 Sep 1788	81	85	S/Fk of E/Fk of Stones River	yes
Harget, Fred	589	Tate, Wm.	Sumner	274	1830	20 May 1793	605	27 Sep 1788	81	85	S/Fk of E/Fk of Stones River	yes
Harget, Frederick	1948	Skipper, Jos. Heirs	Davidson	640	1782	20 May 1793	1253		81	74	E Fork of Jones Creek	Yes
Harget, Frederick	1954	Morris, Philemon	Davidson	274	1794	20 May 1793	577		81	78	S/S Cumberland River	Yes
Harget, Frederick	1955	Bradsher, John	Davidson	640	1796	20 May 1793	1126		81	78	S. Fork of Stones River	Yes
Harget, Frederick	1964	Simmons, Felix	Davidson	274	1827	20 May 1793	576		81	85	S/S Cumberland Riv- waters Little Harpeth	yes
Harget, Frederick	2229	Card, Joseph heirs	Davidson	640	2590	7 Mar 1796	1332		88	321	E/Fk of Turnbulls Creek	yes
Harget, Frederick	2237	Broadbent, Richard	Davidson	640	2608	7 Mar 1796	1337		88	330	On Murpheys Fork of Harpeth River	yes
Harget, Frederick	56		Davidson	1508	42	14 March 1786	226		63	18	Willow Creek & its waters	Yes
Harget, Fredrk & Jas Carney	640	Hall, John	Tennessee	2560	3084	12 Aug 1797	1078	2 June 1784	91	626	Both sides Millers Creek	
Hargett, Fred	274	Brown, James	Tennessee	274	1831	20 May 1793	1461	25 Nov 1784	81	86	S/S Cumberland River	
Hargrove, William	24		Davidson	2560	10	16 Feb 1786	314		63	5	N/S Cumberland River	Yes
Hargrove, William	742	Baker, John	Sumner	1000	2137	20 May 1793	3565	15 Aug 1792	81	158	W/S Caney Fork	Yes
Haris, Peter	145		Hawkins	300	179	26 Dec 1791	354	7 June 1784	75	175	N/S Holston River	
Harkin, John	952		Sumner	400	155	1 Dec 1794		11 Dec 1792	83	478	N/S Cumberland River	yes
Harle, William	478		Hawkins	200	350	29 July 1793	2040	27 Oct 1779	80	263	On Flat Creek	
Harlin, John	1004		Sumner	400	160	17 Dec 1794			84	335	S/S of Cumberland	
Harlin, Joshua	1002	Payton, John	Sumner	400	158	17 Dec 1794			84	334	N/S of Cumberland River	yes
Harlin, Joshua	1003	Payton, John	Sumner	400	159	17 Dec 1794			84	334	S/S Cumberland River	yes
Harlin, Reason	502		Hawkins	400	374	29 July 1793	130	26 Feb 1778	80	270	Poor Valley Creek	
Harman, Lewis	1063		Hawkins	400	772	21 Jan 1797	2066	27 Oct 1779	91	116	Valley that leads to Beaver Creek	

Claimant:	File #:	Assignee:	County:	Acres:	Grant:	Grant Date:	Entry:	Entry Date:	Bk:	Pg:	Location by Stream Name:	Military:
Harman, Lewis & Jno Hanes	1065		Hawkins	300	774	21 Jan 1797	432	19 Apr 1780	91	117	Beg. at 2 post oaks	
Harman, Lewis & Jno Hanes	1066		Hawkins	900	775	21 Jan 1797			91	118	Beg 2 small post oak grubs	
Harmand, Jno.	060		Green	200			516	15 Feb 1781			N/Fk Emerys River	
Harmon, John	1605		Green	150	1322	4 Feb 1795	2534	10 Apr 1780	84	107	On waters of Delaneys Creek	
Harmon, Lewis & John Hanes	01		Jefferson	900			57-793	1781 & 1787				
Harmon, Thomas	1668		Green	200	1373	27 Feb 1796	1060	8 Jan 1779	88	489	On waters of Lick Creek	
Harmons, Jacob	064		Green	600			371	3 June 1780			Beg at 2 Pines near a spring.	
Harnett, Ephraim	321	Williams, Willoughby	Middle District	640	2383	3 Feb 1795	2724	30 Nov 1792	83	383	W/S W/Fk Obeys River	yes
Harney, Selby & Ant. Bledsoe	702	Gilbreath, John	Sumner	640	2081	20 May 1793	3104	30 Nov 1792	81	144	N/S Cumberland	
Harney, Selby & Ant. Bledsoe	703	Burgess, George	Sumner	274	2082	20 May 1793	3208	18 Nov 1792	81	145	Bledsoes Creek	yes
Harney, Selby & Ant. Bledsoe	706	Mann, Thomas	Sumner	640	2086	20 May 1793	3019	18 Nov 1792	81	146	On head of small branch	yes
Harney, Selby & Ant. Bledsoe	710	Jackson, Robert	Sumner	274	2090	20 May 1793	3101	18 Nov 1792	81	147	Bledsoes Creek	yes
Harney, Selby & Ant. Bledsoe	833	Crisp, Wm.	Sumner	640	2319	20 May 1793	3012	30 Nov 1792	81	195	Middle Fk of Goose Creek	yes
Harney, Selby & Anthony	084	Jennings, Thomas	Sumner	640	3220	18 Nov 1792					On ridge bet Goose Creek & Trammels Cr	yes
Harney, Selley/Spelby	37		Davidson	7200	23	14 Mar 1786	98		63	10	N/S Cumberland River	yes
Harper, Fred	079	Lewis, James M.	Davidson	640			1509				On a small creek	yes
Harper, Frederick	2039	Blount, Jno.G & Thos	Davidson	640	2055	20 May 1793	2516		81	138	S/S of Big Harpeth	yes
Harper, Jesse	36		Eastern Dist	1250	36	11 July 1788	1384	25 June 1784	67	354	Heads of Bull Run and Beaverdam Creeks	yes
Harper, Johnston	1164	Harris, Edward	Sumner	640	2669	4 June 1796	2734	1 June 1795	88	357	Joining Mr Harris survey	
Harper, Robt. Glidlo	618		Green	5000	659(?)	11 July 1788	1383	23 June 1784	66	446	Adj. Henderson & Co.'s line	
Harper, William	674	Mann, John	Tennessee	640	3266	6 Dec 1797	4616		98	151	N/S of Cumberland River	yes
Harper/Hayer, Robert	637	Gilmore, Charles	Davidson	640	610	15 Sep 1787	2659		63	217	On waters of Stones Creek	yes
Harrell, Benjamin	662	John McNairy	Tennessee	640	3255	6 Dec 1797	4092		97	36	N/S of head of Piney Fork	yes
Harrell, Ephraim	320	Willoughby Williams	Middle Dist.	640	2382	3 Feb 1795			83	383	W/Fk of Obeys River	yes
Harrell, Holland	034	Donelson & Armstrong	Middle Dist.	640			1479					yes
Harrell, Holland	580	Eliza Williams	Middle Dist.	640	2787	20 Dec 1796	1479		91	322	On br. of Falling Water	yes
Harrell, Peter	418		Tennessee	535	2463	31 Dec 1793	1344	4 Nov 1784	81	431	W/Fk of Red River	yes
Harrewood, Thomas	811	Elijah Robertson	Davidson	640	814	20 Nov 1788	3314		63	286	Waters of Caney Fork	yes
Harrewood, Thomas	066	Sheppard, John	Middle Dist.	640			2805					yes
Harrington	838	Brock, Joseph	Davidson	640	841	17 Jan 1789	3351		63	295	On Sulphur Fork	yes
Harrington, Henry	781		Sumner	2560	2236	20 May 1793	1828	30 Nov 1792	81	177	On ridge bet. Bledsoes & Trammels Creek	yes
Harris, Abraham	1561	Buchanan, John	Davidson	640	1183	30 Nov 1790	2730		74	315	Headwaters of Mill Creek	yes
Harris, Christopher	1560		Green	900	208	30 Oct 1794	2258	22 Nov 1779	83	138	Dividing ridge bet Halston & Fr Broad Riv	
Harris, Claibourn	520	Douglass & Sharp	Sumner	640	1699	20 May 1793	884	25 Jan 1791	81	53	N/S Cumbrland River	yes
Harris, Edward	1163		Sumner	640	2668	4 June 1796	3881	1 June 1795	88	357	Joins sd Harris survey	Yes
Harris, Edward	1		Western Dist.	1000	1	10 July 1788	2370	25 May 1784	67	281	Both sides Clover Lick	
Harris, Edward	10		Western Dist	1000	10	10 July 1788	2330	25 May 1784	67	284	Clover Lick Creek	
Harris, Edward	11		Western Dist	1000	11	10 July 1788	2329	25 May 1784	67	284	Fk of Clover Lick Cr.	
Harris, Edward	1106		Sumner	640	2612	4 June 1796	856	1 June 1795	88	336	S/S Cumberland	yes
Harris, Edward	1107		Sumner	640	2613	4 June 1796	2760	1 June 1795	88	337	Joining Old Harris survey	
Harris, Edward	1108		Sumner	640	2614	4 June 1796	2747	1 June 1795	88	337	Joins sd Harris survey	yes
Harris, Edward	1109		Sumner	640	2615	4 June 1796	2662	1 June 1795	88	338	Joins sd Harris survey	yes
Harris, Edward	1110		Sumner	640	2616	4 June 1796	2478	1 June 1795	88	338	Joins sd Harris survey	yes
Harris, Edward	1111	Wood, Nath heirs	Sumner	640	2617	4 June 1796	2478	1 June 1795	88	339	Joins sd Harris survey	yes
Harris, Edward	1112	Powell, Peter heirs	Sumner	640	2618	4 June 1796	2470	1 June 1795	88	339	Joins sd Harris survey	yes

Claimant:	File #:	Assignee:	County:	Acres:	Grant:	Grant Date:	Entry:	Entry Date:	Bk:	Pg:	Location by Stream Name:	Military:
Harris, Edward	1113		Sumner	640	2619	4 June 1796	2780	1 July 1795	88	340	Joins sd Harris survey	yes
Harris, Edward	1114		Sumner	640	2620	4 June 1795	2698	1 June 1795	88	340	Joins sd Harris survey	yes
Harris, Edward	1115		Sumner	640	2621	4 June 1796	2659	1 July 1795	88	341	Joins sd Harris survey	yes
Harris, Edward	1116	Never, David	Sumner	640	2622	4June 1796	2677	4 June 1796	88	341	Joins sd Harris survey	yes
Harris, Edward	1117		Sumner	640	2623	4 June 1796	2757	1 June 1795	88	342	Joins sd Harris survey	yes
Harris, Edward	1118		Sumner	640	2624	4 June 1796	2455	1 June 1795	88	342	Joins sd Harris survey	yes
Harris, Edward	1119		Sumner	640	2625	4 June 1796	2462	1 June 1795	88	342	Joins sd Harris survey	yes
Harris, Edward	1120	Hubberts, Anthony	Sumner	640	2626	4 Jun 1796	2726	1 Jun 1795	88	343	Joining said Harris survey	Yes
Harris, Edward	1121	Duggin, John	Sumner	640	2627	4 June 1796	2799	1 June 1795	88	343	Joins sd Harris survey	yes
Harris, Edward	1122	Skippen, Hardy	Sumner	640	2628	4 June 1796	2775	1 June 1795	88	343	Joins sd Harris survey	yes
Harris, Edward	1123		Sumner	640	2629	4 June 1796	2951	1 June 1795	88	344	Joins sd Harris survey	yes
Harris, Edward	1124		Sumner	640	2630	4 June 1796	2770	1 June 1795	88	344	Joins sd Harris survey	yes
Harris, Edward	1125		Sumner	640	3631	4 June 1796	3006	1 July 1795	88	344	Joins sd Harris survey	Yes
Harris, Edward	1125		Sumner	640	3631	4 Jun 1796	3006	1 Jul 1795	88	344	Joins Harris Survey	Yes
Harris, Edward	1126		Sumner	640	2632	4 June 1796	2614	1 July 1795	88	345	Joins sd Harris survey	yes
Harris, Edward	1127	Peters, Titus	Sumner	640	2633	4 June 1796	2461	1 June 1795	88	345	Joins sd Harris survey	yes
Harris, Edward	1128		Sumner	640	2634	4 June 1796	3001	1 July 1795	88	345	Joins sd Harris survey	yes
Harris, Edward	1129	Chesnut, Jas.	Sumner	640	2635	4 June 1796	2996	1 June 1795	88	346	Joins sd Harris survey	yes
Harris, Edward	1130		Sumner	640	2636	4 June 1796	2720	1 June 1795	88	346	Joins sd Harris survey	yes
Harris, Edward	1131		Sumner	640	2637	4 June 1796	1808	1 June 1795	88	346	Joins sd Harris survey	yes
Harris, Edward	1132		Sumner	640	2638	4 June 1796	2649	1 June 1795	88	347	Joins sd Harris survey	yes
Harris, Edward	1133	Bagley, Isaac	Sumner	640	2639	4 June 1796	1807	1 June 1795	88	347	Joins sd Harris survey	Yes
Harris, Edward	1134		Sumner	640	2640	4 June 1796	2224	1 June 1795	88	347	Joins sd Harris survey	Yes
Harris, Edward	1135		Sumner	640	2641	4 June 1796	1992	1 June 1795	88	348	Joins sd Harris survey	Yes
Harris, Edward	1136	Sneed, Elbert	Sumner	640	2642	4 June 1796	2764	1 June 1795	88	348	Joins sd Harris survey	yes
Harris, Edward	1137		Sumner	640	2643	4 June 1796	2670	1 June 1795	88	348	Joins sd Harris survey	Yes
Harris, Edward	1138	Powers, Robt.	Sumner	640	2644	4 June 1796	2471	1 June 1795	88	349	Joins sd Harris survey	Yes
Harris, Edward	1139		Sumner	640	2645	4 June 1796	2452	1 June 1795	88	349	Joins sd Harris survey	Yes
Harris, Edward	1140		Sumner	640	2646	4 June 1796	2476	1 June 1795	88	349	Joins sd Harris survey	Yes
Harris, Edward	1141		Sumner	640	2647	4 June 1796	2672	1 June 1795	88	350	Joins sd Harris survey	Yes
Harris, Edward	1142		Sumner	640	2648	4 June 1786	2459	1 June 1785	88	350	Joins sd Harris survey	Yes
Harris, Edward	1143		Sumner	640	2649	4 June 1796	1400	1 June 1795	88	350	Joins sd Harris survey	Yes
Harris, Edward	1144		Sumner	640	2651	4 June 1796	1889	1 June 1795	88	351	Joins sd Harris survey	Yes
Harris, Edward	1145		Sumner	640	2650	4 June 1796	2458	1 June 1795	88	351	Joins sd Harris survey	Yes
Harris, Edward	1146		Sumner	640	2652	4 June 1796	1340	1 June 1795	88	351	Joins sd Harris survey	Yes
Harris, Edward	1147		Sumner	640	2653	4 June 1796	2718	1 June 1795	88	352	Joins sd Harris survey	Yes
Harris, Edward	1148	Praton, Josh	Sumner	640	2654	4 June 1796	2019	1 June 1795	88	352	Joins sd Harris survey	Yes
Harris, Edward	1149	Delaney, Michael	Sumner	640	2655	4 June 1796	3838		88	352	Joins sd Harris survey	Yes
Harris, Edward	1151	Kelly, Dugald	Sumner	640	2656	1 June 1795			88	353	Joins sd Harris survey	Yes
Harris, Edward	1152	Carter, Saml.	Sumner	640	2657	4 June 1796			88	353	Joins sd Harris survey	Yes
Harris, Edward	1153		Sumner	640	2658	4 June 1796	1414	1 June 1795	88	353	Joins sd Harris survey	Yes
Harris, Edward	1154	Collins, Dillard	Sumner	640	2659	4 June 1796	1135	1 June 1795	88	353	Joins sd Harris survey	Yes
Harris, Edward	1155	Collins, Burwell	Sumner	640	2660	4 June 1796	1134	1 June 1795	88	354	Joins sd Harris survey	Yes
Harris, Edward	1156		Sumner	640	2661	4 June 1796	1756	1 June 1795	88	354	none given	Yes
Harris, Edward	1157		Sumner	640	2662	4 June 1796	3857	1 June 1795	88	355	Joins sd Harris survey	Yes

Claimant:	File #:	Assignee:	County:	Acres:	Grant:	Grant Date:	Entry:	Entry Date:	Bk:	Pg:	Location by Stream Name:	Military:
Harris, Edward	1158		Sumner	640	2663	4 June 1796	2803	1 June 1795	88	355	Joins sd Harris survey	Yes
Harris, Edward	1159		Sumner	640	2664	4 June 1796	3840	1 June 1795	88	355	Joins sd Harris survey	Yes
Harris, Edward	1160	King, Andrew	Sumner	640	2665	4 June 1796	2463	1 June 1795	88	356	Joins sd Harris survey	Yes
Harris, Edward	1161		Sumner	640	2666	4 June 1796	3588	1 June 1795	88	356	Joins sd Harris survey	Yes
Harris, Edward	1162		Sumner	640	2667	4 June 1796	3830	1 June 1795	88	356	Joins sd Harris survey	Yes
Harris, Edward	1163		Sumner	640	2668	4 June 1796	3881	1 June 1795	88	357	Joins sd Harris survey	Yes
Harris, Edward	1164		Sumner	640	2669	4 June 1796	2734	1 June 1795	88	357	Joins sd Harris survey	Yes
Harris, Edward	1165		Sumner	640	2670	4 June 1796	2735	1 June 1795	88	357	Joins sd Harris survey	Yes
Harris, Edward	1166		Sumner	640	2671	4 June 1796	2434	1 June 1795	88	358	Joins sd Harris survey	Yes
Harris, Edward	1167		Sumner	640	2673	4 June 1796	1888	1 June 1795	88	358	Joins sd Harris survey	Yes
Harris, Edward	1168		Sumner	640	2873	4 June 1796	2425	1 June 1795	88	358	Joins sd Harris survey	Yes
Harris, Edward	1169	Smith, Charles	Sumner	640	2674	4 June 1796	2436	1 June 1795	88	359	Joins sd Harris survey	Yes
Harris, Edward	1170		Sumner	640	2675	4 June 1796	2772	1 June 1795	88	359	Joins sd Harris	Yes
Harris, Edward	1171		Sumner	640	2676	4 June 1796	3023	1 June 1795	88	359	Joins sd Harris	Yes
Harris, Edward	1172		Sumner	640	2677	4 June 1796	3032	1 June 1795	88	360	Joins sd Harris survey	Yes
Harris, Edward	1173		Sumner	640	2678	4 June 1796	2993	1 June 1795	88	360	Joins sd Harris	Yes
Harris, Edward	1174		Sumner	640	2679	4 June 1796	3028	1 June 1795	88	360	Joins sd Harris	Yes
Harris, Edward	1175		Sumner	640	2680	4 June 1796	952	1 June 1795	88	361	Joins sd Harris	Yes
Harris, Edward	1176		Sumner	640	2681	4 June 1796	2748	1 June 1795	88	361	Joins sd Harris	Yes
Harris, Edward	1177		Sumner	640	2682	4 June 1796	943	1 June 1795	88	361	Joins sd Harris survey	Yes
Harris, Edward	1178	Avery, Jas.	Sumner	2560	2684	4 June 1796	1312	1 June 1795	88	262	Joins sd Harris survey	Yes
Harris, Edward	1179	Shafferd, John	Sumner	640	3684	4 June 1796	2777	1 June 1795	88	362	Joins sd Harris survey	Yes
Harris, Edward	1180	Moye?, John	Sumner	640	2684	4 June 1796	1877	1 June 1795	88	363	Joins sd Harris survey	Yes
Harris, Edward	12		Western Dist	1000	12	10 July 1788	2340	25 May 1784	67	284	On Grove Creek	
Harris, Edward	13		Western Dist	1000	13	10 July 1788	2326	25 May 1784	67	285	Clover Lick Cr. of Obion River	
Harris, Edward	14		Western Dist	1000	14	10 July 1788	2368	25 May 1784	67	285	Both sides of Clover Lick Cr.	
Harris, Edward	1464		Sumner	154	3381	12 Dec 1801	500	11 Mar 1801	88	114	Head of a small branch	Yes
Harris, Edward	1464		Sumner	154	3381	12 Dec 1801	500	11 Jun 1801	114	88	On head of a small branch	Yes
Harris, Edward	1465	Killgoworth, John (?)	Sumner	560	3382	12 Dec 1801	500	21 Feb 1801	114	89	On Caney Form	Yes
Harris, Edward	1465		Sumner	560	3382	12 Dec 1801	500	21 Feb 1801	89	114	On Caney Fork	Yes
Harris, Edward	15		Western Dist	1000	15	10 July 1788	2373	25 May 1784	67	286	N/S Obion Riv. on a Creek	
Harris, Edward	16		Western Dist	1000	16	10 July 1788	2372	25 May 1784	67	286	On waters of Reelfoot River	
Harris, Edward	2		Western Dist	1000	2	10 July 1788	2369	25 May 1784	67	281	Both sides Richland Cr.	
Harris, Edward	2241		Sumner	640	2647	4 June 1796	2672	1 June 1795	88	350	Joins sd Harris survey	yes
Harris, Edward	282	Ray, William	Sumner	640	1278	10 Dec 1790	1206	22 Mar 1788	74	358	S/S Cumberland Riv.	yes
Harris, Edward	3		Western Dist	1000	3	10 July 1788	2367	25 May 1784	67	281	Both sides Richland Cr.	
Harris, Edward	332		Western Dist	640	332	18 May 1789	460	25 Oct 1783	72	274	N/S Obion Riv on a creek	
Harris, Edward	4		Western Dist	1000	4	10 July 1788	2371	25 May 1784	67	282	Clover Lick Cr.	
Harris, Edward	5	Godfrey, Clement	Montgomery	274	3410	19 Feb 1802	3589	19 Feb 1801	118	300	On the fork of McAdoo Creek	
Harris, Edward	5		Western Dist	1000	5	10 July 1788	2336	25 May 1784	67	282	Both sides Goose Creek	
Harris, Edward	5		Montgomery	274	3410	10 Feb 1802	3598	19 Feb 1801	118	300	On a fork of McAdo Creek	
Harris, Edward	6		Western Dist	1000	6	10 July 1788	2366	25 May 1784	67	282	Both sides Clover Lick	
Harris, Edward	7		Western Dist	1000	7	10 July 1788	2327	25 May 1784	67	283	A Fk of Clover Lick Creek	
Harris, Edward	8		Western Dist	1000	8	10 July 1788	2328	25 May 1784	67	283	On the waters of Long Fork Creek	
Harris, Edward	9		Western Dist	1000	9	10 July 1788	2327	25 May 1784	67	283	Clover Lick Creek	

Earliest Tennessee Land Records

Claimant:	File #:	Assignee:	County:	Acres:	Grant:	Grant Date:	Entry:	Entry Date:	Bk:	Pg:	Location by Stream Name:	Military:
Harris, Edward (ass. heirs)	1107		Sumner	640	2613	4 June 1796	856	1 June 1785	88	337	Joins sd Harris survey	yes
Harris, Elisha	046	Goodloe, Robert	Davidson	640			3052	9 Sep 1786			N/waters of Little Harpeth	Yes
Harris, George	530	Davis, Joshua	Davidson	640	502	15 Sep 1787	2355		63	181	Both sides of the Third Creek	Yes
Harris, Goldman	268	Briston, James	Sumner	228	1237	10 Dec 1790	1410	23 Mar 1787	74	344	Near head of E/Fk Goose Creek	Yes
Harris, Hardy	037	Hughlett, William	Middle Dist	640			2728					Yes
Harris, James	122		Sullivan	370	134	23 Oct 1782	273	9 Mar 1780	43	322	Sinking Creek	
Harris, James	1844		Davidson	640	344	27 Nov 1792	371	27 Mar 1784	81	7	Beg 40 poles below head of a spring	
Harris, James	2235		Davidson	228	2605	7 Mar 1796	1132		88	329	Poplar Creek	Yes
Harris, James	68		Sullivan	86	79	23 Oct 1782	684	3 Aug 1780	43	276	Sinking Creek	
Harris, James	77		Washington	200	245	23 Sep 1782	419	23 Sep 1778	44	269	Both sides N/Fk Beech Creek	
Harris, James	90		Washington	100	258	23 Oct 1782	420	23 Sep 1778	44	276	N/Fk of Beech Creek	
Harris, James W	253		Washington	199	121	23 Oct 1782	1429	8 June 1779	47	59	N/Fk of Beech Creek	
Harris, Joab	061	Sheppard, John	Middle Dist	640			2923					Yes
Harris, Job	2428	Dedrick, Geo. Michael	Davidson	640	3318	6 Dec 1797	2923		97	42	Waters of Overalls Creek	Yes
Harris, John	067	Sheppard, John	none given	640			2922	15 Aug 1792			Obeys River	Yes
Harris, John	1340		Davidson	320	26	18 Aug 1787	372	27 Mar 1784	68	131	Beg at ash & sugar tree at mo of West For	Yes
Harris, John	1514		Green	200	1275	12 July 1794	731	31 Jan 1781	81	586	S/S Nolichuckey River	
Harris, John	183	Murphree, Hardy	Davidson	640	169	7 Mar 1786	129		63	64	Joins his tract of 5760 acres	
Harris, John	224	Marshall, John	Sumner	228	1129	26 Nov 1789	1604	21 Sep 1787	74	143	Manskers Trace Creek	Ys
Harris, John	729		Hawkins	120	549	12 June 1794	1823		82	171	S/S Holston River	
Harris, Nathan	190	Dickson, John	Tennessee	640	1470	4 Jan 1792	1915	15 July 1785	77	369	S/S Cumberland River	Yes
Harris, Peter	145		Hawkins	300	179	25 Dec 1791	354	7June 1784	75	175	On N/S Holston River	
Harris, Peter	467	Armstrong, Martin	Davidson	1000	439	5 Sep 1787	1657		63	161	S/S Cumberland River	Yes
Harris, Peter	979		Hawkins	300	751	20 July 1796			88	500	N/S Holston River	
Harris, Richard	1866	Bond, John	Davidson	640	1601	27 Apr 1793	1588	23 Apr 1784	81	18	Head of S. Brs. of Stones Creek	Yes
Harris, Robert	307		Sullivan	1000	283	17 Dec 1794	1825		83	329	S/S Duck River	
Harris, Saml. & Thos. Fletche	600		Sullivan	600	555	25 Dec 1791	1431	8 June 1779	77	304	Poor Valley	
Harris, Samuel	020		Washington	400			51	26 Feb 1778			Beg at a sugar tree	
Harris, Samuel	10		Washington	240	10	15 Dec 1780	52	14 Sep 1778	36	10	N/Fk Doe River	
Harris, Samuel	17		Western Dist	5000	17	10 July 1788	1566	20 Mar 1784	67	286	N/Fk Looshatcher River	
Harris, Samuel	346		Washington	203	213	23 Oct 1782	399	17 Sep 1778	49	232	N/S Watauga River	
Harris, Samuel	480	Marshall, John	Davidson	228	452	15 Sep 1787	2274		63	165a	Moneyfork Creek	Yes
Harris, Samuel	5		Washington	400	5	15 Dec 1788	65	14 Sep 1778	36	5	Nobbs Lick Branch	
Harris, Samuel	582		Washington	480	807	11 July 1788	415	21 Sep 1778	65	629	Waters of Boons Creek	
Harris, Samuel	872		Washington	480	856	18 May 1789	415	12 Jan 1779	72	222	Waters of Boons Creek	
Harris, Samuel Jr.	444		Middle Dist	1000	383	17 Dec 1794	1804	23 Apr 1784	84	253	Wilson Valley	
Harris, Sherwood	721	Bledsoe, Isaac	Sumner	228	2105	20 May 1793	1712	31 July 1792	81	150	S/S Cumberland River	Yes
Harris, Thomas	1854		Davidson	2057	1579	27 Apr 1793	179		81	12	E. waters of W/Fk Stones River	Yes
Harris, Thomas	204	Willson, David	Tennessee	1000	1494	4 Jan 1792	1430	19 Nov 1784	77	374	S/S Cumberland River	Yes
Harris, Thomas	645		Sumner	1000	1938	20 May 1793	1432		81	109	Waters of Round Lick Creek	Yes
Harris, Thomas	844		Sumner	1000	2347	20 May 1793	1431		81	201	Waters of Round Lick Creek	Yes
Harris, Thomas	941	Conrad, Nichollas	Sumner	213	2465	22 Feb 1795	1540	14 Sep 1785	83	424	S/S Cumberland River	Yes
Harris, Thompson	218	Bledsoe, Isaac	Sumner	640	1123	26 Nov 1789	1203		74	140	E/S Bledsoes Creek	Yes
Harris, William	310	Rice, John & others	Davidson	640	296	13 June 1787	2129		63	111	Beg. at a large white oak	Yes
Harrison	389	Williams, Sampson	Sumner	640	366	26 June 1793	2380	17 Sep 1792	80	321	Obeds River	Yes

Claimant:	File #:	Assignee:	Acres:	Grant:	Grant Date:	Entry:	Entry Date:	Bk:	Pg:	Location by Stream Name:	Military:
Harrison, Augustine	791	Davis, Joshua	640	2250	20 May 1793	2422	19 Nov 1792	81	181	Caney Fork	Yes
Harrison, Daniel	021		300			15	25 Feb 1778			S/S Noleychuckey River	
Harrison, Daniel	1027		300	1254	29 July 1783	1275		76	489	S/S Noleychuckey River	
Harrison, Daniel	371		200	363	13 Oct 1783	1275	12 Mar 1779	52	248	On the Big Limestone	
Harrison, Daniel	403		81	395	13 Oct 1783	2442	20 Jan 1781	52	263	On waters of Big Limestone	
Harrison, Dempsey	740		387	2135	20 May 1793	592	31 July 1792	81	157	Beg at a poplar & white oak	Yes
Harrison, Francis	851	Phifer, Caleb	640	2355	20 May 1793	2069	27 Oct 1792	81	203	Bet Little Cedar Creek	Yes
Harrison, George	58	Tatum, Howell	640	1282	10 Dec 1790	1918	23 July 1785	74	359	Yellow Creek	Yes
Harrison, Gilbert	2032	Blair, James	640	2044	20 May 1793	3512		81	135	Headwaters of Mill Creek	Yes
Harrison, Henry	433	Blount, Reading	640	405	15 Sep 1787	109		63	150	So branches of Sycamore Creek	Yes
Harrison, Isaiah	1003		200	1230	29 July 1793	1230	12 Jan 1789	76	485	S/S Chuckey River	Yes
Harrison, James	716	Glasgow, James	640	689	8 Nov 1787	1568		63	243	Sinking Creek	Yes
Harrison, James	899		228	2453	31 Dec 1793	2292	21 Sep 1787	81	427	Rockey Creek	Yes
Harrison, Jesse	501		274	473	15 Sep 1787	841		63	172	S/S Cumberland River	Yes
Harrison, John	688	Davis, Joshua	640	661	8 Dec 1787	2421		63	234	Waters of Salleen Creek	Yes
Harrison, John Axley	1957	Todd, James	640	1801	20 May 1793	2009		81	79	Waters of Mill Creek	Yes
Harrison, Jonathan	335	Armstrong, Andrew	1000	321	28 May 1787	2127		63	119	One of the branches of Sulphur Fork	Yes
Harrison, Patrick	998	Dillard, William	400	154	17 Dec 1794			84	332	A Fork of Roaring River	Yes
Harrison, Robert	712	Balew, Thomas	640	2093	20 May 1793	2657	9 Sep 1792	81	147	Dishas Creek	Yes
Harrison, Thomas	698	Bonner, Jno & Jas	274	2070	20 May 1793	382	22 Aug 1785	81	142	S/S Cumberland River	Yes
Harrison, Thos.	127		1097	139	23 Oct 1782	386	11 Sep 1778	43	325	On Horse Creek	
Harrison, William	1345	Barbour, Richard	640	3147	14 Sep 1797	4096	3 Dec 1796	90	421	On Pipe Creek	Yes
Harrod, Barnet hr of Jas.	1835		640	329	27 Nov 1792	156	17 Jan 1784	81	4	N/S Cumberland River	
Harrod, Jas.	080	Robertson, Jas.	640			2188	5 June 1790			S/S Cumberland	Yes
Harrold, James	2291	Robeson, Jas.	640	2770	10 Sep 1796	2485	12 Mar 1788	88	491	S/S Cumberland River	Yes
Harrold, John	1376	Cook, Richard	1000	3238	24 Nov 1797	1501	13 Aug 1797	94	172	Bet. two creeks	Yes
Harrold, John	246		400	385	9 Aug 1787	610	10 June 1780	61	403	N/S of Holston River	Yes
Hars, Thomas	849		1000	2352	20 May 1793	1433	24 Oct 1788	81	202	Round Lick Creek	Yes
Hart, [no other name]	075	Tyrrell, William	640			3468	4 June 1796			N/S Cumberland River	Yes
Hart, Adam	1404	Hutson, Chamberlin	640	3334	6 Dec 1797	263	1 May 1797	97	53	Waters of Big Barron	Yes
Hart, Anthony	045	Cross, Randal	640			2485	12 Mar 1788			Headwaters of Hickmans Creek	
Hart, Anthony	1506	West, Cyprian	640	1063	26 Nov 1789	1501		74	110	N/S Cumberland River	Yes
Hart, Anthony	157	Nobles, Wm.	640	1414	20 Dec 1791	3516	8 Feb 1786	77	355	Beaver Creek	
Hart, Anthony	195	Griffin, Joshua heirs	640 acre	1481	4 Jan 1792	2719	30 Sep 1785	77	371	S/S Caney Fork River	Yes
Hart, Anthony	199		640	1104	26 Nov 1789	2483	12 Mar 1788	74	131	W/S Caney Fork River	
Hart, Anthony	200		640	1105	26 Nov 1789	2665	12 Mar 1788	74	131	W/S Caney Fork River	
Hart, Anthony	201		434	1106	26 Nov 1789	3118	12 Mar 1788	74	132	Waters of Collins River	Yes
Hart, Anthony	202		640	1107	26 Nov 1789	2809	12 Mar 1788	74	132	W/S Caney Fork River	Yes
Hart, Anthony	203		640	1108	26 Nov 1789	2492	12 Mar 1788	74	133	Headwaters of large creek	Yes
Hart, Anthony	204		640	1109	26 Nov 1789	2448	12 Mar 1788	74	132	W/S Caney Fork River	Yes
Hart, Anthony	468		2194	440	15 Sep 1787	869		63	162	First large creek - runs into Cumberland	Yes
Hart, Anthony	600	Lassiter, Saml heirs	640	572	15 Sep 1787			63	205	Trace near head of Gilkersons Creek	Yes
Hart, Anthony	601	Buck, Abraham heirs	640	573	15 Sep 1787	2707		63	205	S/S Big Barren River	Yes
Hart, Anthony	602	Riddick, Issac	640	574	15 Sep 1787	2957		63	205	N/S Cumberland River	Yes
Hart, Anthony	654		274	1964	20 May 1793	3510	19 Nov 1792	81	115	W/S Caney Fork	Yes

Earliest Tennessee Land Records

Page 221

Claimant:	File #:	Assignee:	County:	Acres:	Grant:	Grant Date:	Entry:	Entry Date:	Bk:	Pg:	Location by Stream Name:	Military:
Hart, Anthony	69	Daughtry, Lewis	Tennessee	640	1309	10 Dec 1790	1516	20 Jan 1785	74	368	N/S Cumberland River	Yes
Hart, Anthony	705(704)	Sellers, John	Davidson	640	678	8 Dec 1787	2763		63	239	S/S Cumberland River	Yes
Hart, Anthony	739	Colvin, Obed	Davidson	640	712	11 July 1788	3423		63	250	N/S Cumberland River	Yes
Hart, Anthony	743	Madry, Moses	Davidson	640	716	11 July 1788	3087		63	252	Head of Karrs & Nelson Creeks	Yes
Hart, Anthony	745	Baileon, Maon	Davidson	640	718	11 July 1788	3416		63	252	N/S Waters of Sycamore Creek	Yes
Hart, Anthony	775		Sumner	640	2228	20 May 1793	2249	19 Nov 1792	81	175	On Caney Fork	Yes
Hart, Anthony	840	Mills, John heirs	Davidson	640	845	17 Jan 1789	2812		63	296	Head of Browns Creek	Yes
Hart, Anthony	843	Colbert, Laurence	Davidson	640	848	17 Jan 1789	3422		63	297	Dividing Ridge bet. Sycamore & Halfpone	Yes
Hart, Anthony	863	Bailey, Morris	Davidson	640	877	17 Jan 1789	3420		63	304	W/FK Spring Creek	Yes
Hart, Anthony	495	Evans, Wm.	Tennessee	640	2495	26 Sep 1795	2801	30 Sep 1785	89	105	Willses Creek	
Hart, Antony	7021	Rivear, William	Davidson	640	675	8 Dec 1787	2815		63	238	W/S of Twinbulls Clay Lick	Yes
Hart, David	28		Sumner	274	785	11 July 1788	776	21 Sep 1787	63	275	Waters of Goose Creek	Yes
Hart, David	289		Western Dist	2250	278	18 Apr 1789	1254	24 Nov 1783	72	83	N/S Big Hatcher River	
Hart, Hardy	295	McCulloch, Benjamin	Tennessee	640	1968	20 May 1793	2655	30 Sep 1785	81	116	N/S Cumberland River	Yes
Hart, John	019	Buchanan, John	Sumner	640			1334	5 Nov 1790			Jenning Fk of Round Lick Creek	Yes
Hart, John Brynat	1023		Washington	100	973	14 Jan 1793	2394	10 Jan 1780	79	277	S/S Noleychucky River	
Hart, Joseph	017	Tyrrell, Wm. T.	Montgomery	640			3358				N/S Cumberland River	
Hart, Joseph	277		Middle Dist	1000	241	27 Nov 1793	69		81	507	N/S Duck River	
Hart, Joseph	36	Brock, Joseph	Sumner	640	861	17 Jan 1789	3358	17 May 1788	63	300	Waters of Red River	Yes
Hart, William	866	Hacket, John	Sumner	640	2379	20 May 1793	966	23 June 1792	81	208	On 1st large creek	Yes
Hartill, Hannah	1122		Washington	30	1081	12 July 1794	2281	27 Nov 1779	81	562	Beg at a black oak	
Hartley, John	2024	Donelson, John	Davidson	640	2026	20 May 1793	1647		81	131	On head of Stones Creek	Yes
Hartley, Joseph	351		Sumner	383	1438	20 Dec 1791	327	13 Nov 1788	77	360	S/S of Cumberland River	Yes
Hartsfield, John	1429	Leanon, Peter	Sumner	274	3303	6 Dec 1797	4089	27 Apr 1797	98	176	Waters of Big Barren	Yes
Harvewy, Augustus	53		Western Dist	2500	53	10 July 1788	1149	31 Oct 1783	67	300	On Cane Creek	
Harvey, Augustus	45		Western Dist	2500	45	10 July 1788	1148	31 Oct 1783	67	297	On Reelfoot River	
Harvey, Henderson	1111		Hawkins	165	831	15 Sep 1797	658	20 July 1780	94	137	N/S Holston River	
Harwood, Howell	1600	Lawrence, Adam	Davidson	1000	1302	10 Dec 1790	1711		74	366	On waters of Cumberland	Yes
Hasten, Oliver	2038	May, John	Davidson	640	2053	20 May 1793	3008		81	137	Bet head of Little Clear & Round Lick Cree	Yes
Hasten, Willis	367	Davis, Joshua	Tennessee	640	2245	20 May 1793	2423	30 Sep 1785	81	179	N/S Cumberland River	Yes
Haston, Daniel	201	Archer, Thomas	Tennessee	640	1490	4 Jan 1792	2344	24 July 1791	77	373	S/S Cumberland River	Yes
Hatches, David	582	Marshall, John	Davidson	640	554	15 Sep 1787	1613	16 Mar 1787	63	199	Many Fork Creek	Yes
Hatfield, Andrew	1334b	Hickman, Thomas	Sumner	640	3134	14 Sep 1797	4398	3 June 1797	90	417	Waters of Big Barren	Yes
Hatfield, Wm.	462		Green	400	683	11 Jul 1788	1164	25 Jan 1784	66	455	Both sides N/F Bull Run	
Hathcock, Amos	112	Tatum, Howell	Tennessee	640	1604	23 Feb 1793	2653	30 Sep 1785	76	314	Waters of Sulphur Fork	Yes
Hathcock, Fred	108	Foster, Anthony	Tennessee	228	1578	23 Feb 1793	3526	15 Feb 1786	76	302	S/S Cumberland	Yes
Hathcock, Holladay	718	Sheppard, Nancy	Davidson	640	691	11 Jul 1788	1763		83	243	Waters of Sycamore	Yes
Hathcock, John	106	Weakley, Polly	Tennessee	640	1571	23 Feb 1793	2489	20 Sep 1785	76	299	S/S Cumberland	Yes
Hatter, Michael	818		Green	200	819	18 Aug 1789	1089	16 Mar 1787	71	36	Waters of Nollachuckey River	
Hatter, Phillip	677		Green	100	718	11 July 1788	1510	27 Mar 1787	66	465	S/S Nolichuckey River	
Hatter/Hatlan, Sebastian	537		Washington	400	800	10 Aug 1787	2595	22 July 1780	64	152	Beg at a marked red oak	
Haughton, Levi	550	Molloy, Thomas	Tennessee	640	2975	5 Apr 1797	4127		90	276	S/S Cumberland River	Yes
Haun, Adam	1120		Washington	200	1079	12 July 1794	2634	7 Sep 1780	81	562	On Buffaloe Creek	
Haun, Sebastian	1121		Washington	400	1080	12 July 1794	1488	11 June 1779	81	562	On Fall Creek	
Hauston, James	7		Green	200	70	10 Nov 1786	127	21 Oct 1783	58	431	N/S Nolichuckie	

Claimant:	File #:	Assignee:	County:	Acres:	Grant:	Grant Date:	Entry:	Entry Date:	Bk:	Pg:	Location by Stream Name:	Military:
Hawkins, Elias	151		Washington	100	19	23 Oct 1782	1189	5 Feb 1779	47	9	S/S Roans Creek	
Hawkins, Elisha	198		Hawkins	400	186	26 Dec 1791	2062	27 Oct 1779	77	308	Clinch River	
Hawkins, John	581		Sullivan	283	579	29 July 1793	1101	9 Jan 1779	76	473	N/S Holston River	
Hawkins, John	821		Sullivan	5	764	17 Nov 1797	618	9 Feb 1796	94	159	Beg at a large spanish oak	
Hawkins, John	827		Sullivan	5	770	17 Nov 1797	618	2 June 1781	94	163	Beg at 3 white oaks	
Hawkins, John & Phillips	135	Simmons, Silas & Campbell	Tennessee	428	1647	23 Feb 1793	3125	13 Dec 1785	76	335	West side Red River	
Hawkins, Nicholas	246		Hawkins	240	234	26 Dec 1791			77	324	Both sides of Caney Creek	
Hawkins, Phileman	329		Western Dist	4000	329	18 May 1789	1732	17 Apr 1784	72	273	Indian Creek of Big Hatchee	
Hawkins, William	117		Western Dist	3510	117	10 July 1788	414	25 Oct 1783	67	226	S/Fk of Forked Deer River	
Hawley, Benjamin	96	Person, Thomas	Tennessee	640	1378	20 Dec 1791	1389	12 Nov 1784	75	504	Both/S of Taylors Creek	Yes
Hawley, Caleb	2030	McCulloh, Benj.	Davidson	640	2040	20 May 1793	3078		81	134	N/S Cumberland River	Yes
Hawley, Joseph	408	Person, Thomas	Tennessee	640	2434	18 Mar 1794	1291	1 Nov 1784	81	422	E. Br of Pine River	Yes
Hawley, William	1523	Ross, Joseph	Davidson	640	1080	26 Nov 1789	2265		74	120	N/S Cumberland River	Yes
Hawn, Adam	1294		Washington	100	1180	4 Dec 1795	819	29 Dec 1778	89	426	Beg at a small white oak	
Hawn, Sebastian	1296		Washington	200	1182	4 Dec 1795	2522	6 Apr 1780	89	427	N/S Noleychuckey River	
Hawthorn, William	1349	Stewart, Duncan	Sumner	640	3159	14 Sep 1797	4273	30 May 1797	90	425	Waters of Big Barren	Yes
Hay, Abraham	2262	Donelson, Stockley	Davidson	640	2726	20 Jul 1796	448		88	451	On the waters of Stones River	
Hay, Daniel	1017		Sumner	50	204	27 Feb 1795			88	163	N/S Cumberland River	
Hay, David	082		Not Given	50							N/S Cumberland River	
Hay, David	2304	Williams, Oliver	Davidson	640	455	5 Nov 1795			89	118	At a spring	Yes
Hay, David	2308	Armstrong, Martin	Davidson	50	197	27 Aug 1795			89	411	Waters of Dry Fork of Whites Creek	
Haybird, Samuel	1139		Davidson	640	116	17 Apr 1786	680	12 Feb 1785	66	178	Both/S Big Harpeth River	
Haycraft, Mark	2037	Buchanon, John	Davidson	640	2052	20 May 1793	1104		81	137	Both/S Cumberland River	Yes
Hayes, Charles	1572		Green	200	1318	6 Jan 1795	460	30 Sep 1778	83	162	Large Fk of Lick Creek	
Hayes, Charles	359		Washington	200	351	13 Oct 1783	2750	20 Jan 1781	52	244	Both/S Lick Creek	
Hayes, James	43		Green	30	106	1 Nov 1786	20	22 Nov 1783	58	467	Limestone Fk of Lick Cr.	
Hayes, James	676	Wheaton, Daniel	Tennessee	97	3293	6 Dec 1797	4324		98	169	E/FK of Barretts Creek	Yes
Hayes, Robert	2353	Sitgreaves, John	Davidson	640	3019	10 Apr 1797	1973		90	301	E/S Stones River	Yes
Hayes, Thomas	131	Henderson, Abra. Hrs	Tennessee	640	1639	23 Feb 1793	2571	30 Sep 1785	76	331	S/S Cumberland River	
Hayland, James	24		Hawkins	131	56	7 Apr 1790	690	8 Sep 1780	71	281	N/S Holston River joins Leepers Cr.	
Hayley, David	024		Hawkins	600	1239	29 July 1793	479	7 June 1784			N/S Holston	
Haynes, James	035	Story, Jonah	Robertson	274		2 Feb 1795	3544				N/Fk Red River	
Haynes, John	559	Williamson, John	Davidson	228	531	15 Sep 1787	1811		63	191	Waters of Mill Creek	Yes
Hays, Charles	155		Washington	400	23	23 Oct 1787	426	25 Sep 1778	47	10	Incl. Aaron Burfieson's Old Improvement	
Hays, Charles	425		Green	500	427	20 Sep 1787	34	1 May 1784	65	495	N/S of Tennessee River	
Hays, Charles	730		Washington	200	544	10 Nov 1784	1517	13 Aug 1779	69	120	Pinsons Creek	
Hays, Francis	1107		Hawkins	150	827	15 Sep 1797	311	21 Feb 1780	94	135	Lick Creek	
Hays, Hugh	1110		Davidson	640	87	17 Apr 1786	654	8 Jan 1785	66	171	At the entrance of Jones Bent	
Hays, Isaac	150	Ivey, Claborn	Tennessee	640	1403	20 Dec 1791	3148	16 Dec 1785	77	352	S/S Cumberland River	Yes
Hays, James	1486		Davidson	640	290	26 Nov 1789	204	29 Jan 1784	73	259	Head of 1st sm. cr. of Cumberland River	
Hays, James	1819		Davidson	640	392	26 June 1797	204	29 Jan 1784	80	339	S/S Cumberland River	
Hays, James	2468		Davidson	640	474	7 Oct 1802	38	31 Dec 1783	115	383	E/Fk of Station Camp Creek	
Hays, James	633		Sumner	640	1917	20 May 1793	2570	22 Dec 1792	81	104	Headwaters of S of Cedar Lick Cr.	Yes
Hays, John	069	Douglas, James	Sumner	274			1263	16 July 1786			E/waters E/Fk Station Camp Creek	Yes
Hays, John	360	Nolby, Anderson	Tennessee	640	2209	20 May 1793	2288	22 Oct 1785	81	171	Yellow Creek	Yes

Earliest Tennessee Land Records

Claimant:	File #:	Assignee:	County:	Acres:	Grant:	Grant Date:	Entry:	Entry Date:	Bk:	Pg:	Location by Stream Name:	Military:
Hays, John	427		Sumner	640	438	27 June 1793	848	18 Dec 1792	80	354	N/S Stones River	Yes
Hays, John	57	Mundine, Zebulon	Tennessee	640	1275	10 May 1793	2385	22 Oct 1785	74	357	S/S Cumberland River	
Hays, John	621		Sumner	274	1896	20 May 1793	2383	21 Dec 1792	81	99	A ridge abt 2 mi. above Little Cedar Lick	Yes
Hays, John	87	Burn, Andrew	Tennessee	640	1351	10 Dec 1790	2562	30 Sep 1785	74	382	S/S Cumberland River	
Hays, Narcissa	678		Sumner	274	2021	10 May 1793	2312	24 Nov 1792	81	129	Salt Lick Fork	Yes
Hays, Nathaniel	1050		Davidson	640	24	17 Apr 1786	655	8 Jan 1785	66	42	Spring Jones Bent S/S Cumberland	
Hays, Nicholas	1421		Green	300	1233	27 Nov 1792	2306	27 Nov 1779	80	165	Lick/Fk of Lick Creek	
Hays, Nicholas	517		Green	100	519	20 Sep 1787	2461	10 Mar 1780	65	528	Br. of Sinking Creek	
Hays, Patty	687	Thompson,?	Sumner	640	2041	20 May 1793	2337	29 Oct 1792	81	134	Thompsons Creek	Yes
Hays, Rachel	321	Abbott, Isaac	Tennessee	640	2038	20 May 1793	2340	29 Sep 1785	81	133	N/S Cumberland	
Hays, Robert	103		Middle Dist	5000	105	10 July 1788	2575	25 May 1782	67	461	Richland Creek	
Hays, Robert	1754	Grinder, John	Davidson	1000	1526	14 Jan 1793	1220		79	264	Waters of West Harpeth River	Yes
Hays, Robert	1755		Davidson	2560	1527	14 Jan 1793	368		79	264	W. Harpeth River	Yes
Hays, Robert	1756	Yancey, John	Davidson	640	1529	14 Jan 1793			79	264	Both/S of small fork of Stones River	Yes
Hays, Robert	1757	Ricks, Lewis	Davidson	640	1531	14 Jan 1793	2684		79	265	E/Branch of Stones River	Yes
Hays, Robert	1758	Williams, Wm.	Davidson	640	1534	14 Jan 1793	1970		79	266	On waters of Whites Creek	Yes
Hays, Robert	1759	Pollock, Benjamin	Davidson	640	1538	14 Jan 1793	1786	14 Jan 1793	79	267	Joins Hays which joins Bryans	Yes
Hays, Robert	1760	Rivell, John	Davidson	274	1539	14 Jan 1793	1864		79	267	Waters of Mancows Creek	Yes
Hays, Robert	1761	Balmore, John	Davidson	640	1540	14 Jan 1793	1749		79	267	Waters of West Harpeth	Yes
Hays, Robert	1762	Tanner, John	Davidson	640	1541	14 Jan 1793			79	267	Burch Creek	Yes
Hays, Robert	1763	Brownguary, Gasper	Davidson	640	1542	14 Jan 1793	2595		79	267	E Branches of Stones River	Yes
Hays, Robert	1764	Smalley, James Hrs.	Davidson	640	1544	14 Jan 1793	2239		79	268	To join Robert Barnet	Yes
Hays, Robert	1765	Thomas, John hrs	Davidson	640	1545	14 Jan 1793	3821		79	268	Waters of West Harpeth	Yes
Hays, Robert	1766	Wilkins, Benjamin	Davidson	640	1549	14 Jan 1793	1903		79	269	N/S Cumberland River	Yes
Hays, Robert	1773	Powell, Stephen	Davidson	640	1561	14 Jan 1793	1784		79	272	Waters of Manscows Creek	Yes
Hays, Robert	1774	Brittle, Benjamin	Davidson	640	1562	14 Jan 1793	1748		79	272	N/Branches of Stones River	Yes
Hays, Robert	1775	Armstrong, M.	Davidson	138	116	14 Jan 1793			79	273	N/S Cumberland River	
Hays, Robert	1776	Armstrong, M.	Davidson	120	118	14 Jan 1793			79	273	Dividing ridge bet Shains Fk.	
Hays, Robert	2072	Gray, Henry	Davidson	1000	2214	20 May 1793	2607		81	172	N/S Cumberland River	Yes
Hays, Robert	221	Galloway, John	Tennessee	1000	1547	14 Jan 1793	1757	23 Apr 1795	79	268	Waters of Red River	
Hays, Robert	222	Armstrong, M.	Tennessee	150	117	14 Jan 1793		23 Dec 1785	79	273	Dry Fk of W/Fk of Red River	
Hays, Robert	223	Armstrong, Martin	Tennessee	100	119	14 Jan 1793		5 May 1786	79	274	Waters of Spring Creek	
Hays, Robert	2398	Biggs, Nath	Davidson	640	2795	20 Dec 1796	2790		91	470	E/S Stones River	Yes
Hays, Robert	315	Reed, William	Eastern Dist.	640	2487	18 Aug 1795			87	509	Headwaters of Whites Creek	
Hays, Robert	365		Sumner	640	1528	14 Jan 1793	2782	6 Feb 1792	79	264	E/Fk of Goose Creek	Yes
Hays, Robert	366		Sumner	640	1530	14 Jan 1793	3496	9 Mar 1786	79	265	Waters of Manscows Creek	Yes
Hays, Robert	367		Sumner	640	1532	14 Jan 1793	2674	30 Nov 1792	79	265	Waters of Manscows Creek	Yes
Hays, Robert	368		Sumner	640	1533	14 Jan 1793	2737	5 Jan 1790	79	266	Waters of Maddisons Creek	Yes
Hays, Robert	369		Sumner	640	1535	14 Jan 1793	1774	3 Dec 1792	79	266	E/S Spencers Creek	Yes
Hays, Robert	370		Sumner	640	1536	14 Jan 1793	2959	25 Nov 1792	79	266	Waters of Rules Creek	Yes
Hays, Robert	371		Sumner	640	1537	14 Jan 1793	2382	30 Nov 1793	79	266	Waters of Madisons Creek	Yes
Hays, Robert	372		Sumner	640	1543	14 Jan 1793	2660	5 Jan 1790	79	268	Waters of Mansows Creek	Yes
Hays, Robert	373		Sumner	640	1546	14 Jan 1793		9 Mar 1786	79	268	Waters of Manscows Creek	Yes
Hays, Robert	374		Sumner	640	1548	14 Jan 1793	2851	6 Feb 1793	79	269	Waters of E/Fk Goose Creek	Yes
Hays, Robert	379		Sumner	640	1560	14 Jan 1793	2838	9 Apr 1788	79	271	Both Sides S/Fk of Smiths Fork	Yes

Earliest Tennessee Land Records

Claimant:	File #:	Assignee:	County:	Acres:	Grant:	Grant Date:	Entry:	Entry Date:	Bk:	Pg:	Location by Stream Name:	Military:
Hays, Robert	380		Sumner	640	1563	14 Jan 1793	2850	9 Apr 1788	79	272	S/S of Swifts Creek	Yes
Hays, Robert	381		Sumner	640	1564	14 Jan 1793	2970	9 Apr 1788	79	272	Both sides Smiths Fork	Yes
Hays, Robert	382		Sumner	640	1565	14 Jan 1793	2954	9 Apr 1788	79	272	Smiths Fork	Yes
Hays, Robert	383		Sumner	640	1560	14 Jan 1793	2949	9 Apr 1788	79	273	Both sides of Smiths Fork	Yes
Hays, Robert	422		Middle Dist	5000	361	17 Dec 1794	1760	27 Apr 1784	84	234	On Duck River	
Hays, Robert	450	Armstrong, Martin	Tennessee	150	238	27 Feb 1796		23 Dec 1785	88	179	Dry Fk of W/Fk of Red River	
Hays, Robert	457	Armstrong, M.	Tennessee	200	260	25 Feb 1796			88	195	Waters of Sulphur Fork	
Hays, Robert	46	Reed, Wm.	Not shown	640			3785	15 July 1795				
Hays, Robert	465	Parks, Saml.	Tennessee	640	2593	7 Mar 1796	2945	30 Sep 1785	88	323	Beg at a black oak	
Hays, Robert	466	Bennet, Henry	Tennessee	640	2594	7 Mar 1796	2837	30 Sep 1785	88	323	Beg at a Red Oak	
Hays, Robert	487	Armstrong, M.	Tennessee	200	318	10 Sep 1796			88	516	Waters of Sulphur Fork	
Hays, Robert	671	Butler, Edward	Davidson	1000	644	15 Nov 1787	1666		63	228	Bizzells Salteen (Sic)	Yes
Hays, Robert	672	James, William	Davidson	640	645	15 Nov 1787	376 (816)		63	229	N/S Cumberland River	Yes
Hays, Robert	782	Totewine, Winder Hrs.	Davidson	640	755	11 July 1788	1102		63	265	Head of Wartrace Creek	Yes
Hays, Robert	80		Middle Dist	1000	82	10 July 1788	2644	25 May 1782	67	450	N/S Duck River	
Hays, Robert	811		Sumner	640	2278	20 May 1793	2406	19 Nov 1792	81	186	On Caney Fork	Yes
Hays, Robert	821		Sumner	640	2298	20 May 1793	327(?)	3 Nov 1792	81	191	Waters of Dixon Creek	Yes
Hays, Robert & others	3		Davidson	640	1	20 Dec 1791			62	296	Molly's Lick & Spring	
Hays, Robt	028	Hays, John heirs	Tennessee	640			2820	30 Sep 1785			Brush Creek	
Hays, Robt	1758	Williams, Wm.	Davidson	640	1534	14 Jan 1793	1970	30 Sep 1785	79	266	Waters of Whites Creek	Yes
Hays, Samuel	1061		Davidson	640	35	17 Apr 1786	205	29 Jan 1784	66	46	N/S Stones Clover Creek br of Stones River	
Hays, Samuel	773	Alexander, George	Sumner	640	2225	20 May 1793	2266	1 Aug 1792	81	174	S/S Cumberland River	Yes
Hays, Sarah	141	Clifton, Richd.	Tennessee	640	1791	20 Dec 1791			77	349	N/S Tennessee River	
Hays, Stockley	658		Sumner	640	1975	20 May 1793	2443	19 Nov 1792	81	118	On Caney Fork	Yes
Hays, Stockley	812		Sumner	640	2279	20 May 1793	2360	18 Nov 1792	81	186	On Caney Fork	Yes
Hays, Theophilus	348		Sumner	411	1429	20 Dec 1791	304	13 Mar 1788	77	358	S/S Cumberland River	Yes
Hays, Thomas	1374	Cooke, Richard	Sumner	274	3236	24 Nov 1797	1197	20 Aug 1785	94	171	N/S Cumberland River	Yes
Hays, Thomas	81	Smith, Micajah	Tennessee	640	1337	10 Dec 1790	2342	29 Sep 1785	74	378	S/S Cumberland River	
Hays, Thos	115	Murray, Joshua hrs	Tennessee	640	1612	23 Feb 1793	2351	29 Sep 1735	76	318	S/S Cumberland River	
Hayse, William	660	Bushnell & Dobbs	Davidson	1000	633	15 Sep 1787			63	225	S/S Cumberland	
Haysworth, Absalom	792		Washington	150	606	10 Nov 1784	2863	29 May 1781	69	140	W/S Moore's land	Yes
Haywood, James	915	Sugg, Aquilla	Davidson	640	931	18 May 1789			63	320	Waters of 1st Creek	
Haywood, John	174		Middle Dist	5000	184	20 Dec 1791	388	25 Oct 1783	75	229	Waters of Richland Creek	Yes
Haywood, John	245		Sumner	1000	1150	26 Nov 1789	3112	10 Mar 1788	74	154	Both sides Caney Fork	
Haywood, John	2452	Woodley, Thos.	Davidson	640	2347	6 Dec 1797	3120		98	182	S/S Cumberland Rivewr	Yes
Haywood, John	409	Ellison, A.	Tennessee	640	2435	18 Mar 1794	1949	1 Aug 1785	81	422	S/S Cumberland River	Yes
Haywood, John	410	Medlin, Mills	Tennessee	640	2436	18 Mar 1794	3117	12 Dec 1785	81	422	S/S Cumberland River	
Haywood, John	411	Medlin, Zeland	Tennessee	640	2437	18 Mar 1794	1438	30 Nov 1785	81	422	S/S Cumberland River	
Haywood, Mordecai	416		Sullivan	300	295	10 Nov 1784	992	4 Jan 1779	69	174	N/Side of Holstein River	
Hayworth, Absalom	1146		Green	50	989	26 Dec 1790	2873	4 June 1781	77	278	Nolachuckey Riv below mouth of Sinking Cr	
Hayworth, George	315		Green	300	317	20 Sep 1787	1402	23 Oct 1783	65	463	On waters of Nolachuckey	
Head, Luke	813	McCulloch, Benjamin	Sumner	1000	2280	20 May 1793	3003	30 Nov 1792	81	187	Beg at a sugar tree	
Head, William	1198		Davidson	640	70	8 Oct 1787	534	19 July 1784	66	223	On the Middle Fk of Goose Creek	Yes
Headley, Wm.	1355		Green	100	1201	23 Feb 1793	401	17 Sep 1778	78	442	N/S Dumplin Creek	
Headrick, Jacob	826		Washington	200	640	10 Nov 1784	1144	28 Jan 1779	69	149	Beg at a hickory	

Claimant:	File #:	Assignee:	County:	Acres:	Grant:	Grant Date:	Entry:	Entry Date:	Bk:	Pg:	Location by Stream Name:	Military:
Heale, Nicholas	346		Hawkins	100	340	8 Mar 1793	827	28 July 1792	78	479	S/S Clinch River	
Hearn, George	543	Clark, Vachell	Sumner	640	1746	29 Aug 1793	3393		81	65	W/Fk Bartons Creek	Yes
Hearns, Joseph	1433		Green	400	1245	27 Nov 1792	1066	30 Dec 1783	80	169	Head of a creek that runs into Holston	
Heatherick, Jacob	962		Washington	107	939	17 Nov 1790	798	26 Dec 1778	76	157	On Roans Creek	
Heatherly, Evans	127		Washington	200	295	24 Oct 1782	1125	23 Jan 1779	44	296	Little Doe River	
Heatherly, Evans	34		Washington	200	324	24 Oct 1782	1126	14 Jan 1779	43	308	Little Doe River	
Heatherly, Evans	42		Washington	92	332	24 Oct 1782	1127	23 Jan 1779	43	311	Little Doe River	
Heaton, Amos	1028		Davidson	640	82	17 Apr 1786	338		65	411	N/S Cumberland River	
Heaton, Amos	1850		Davidson	640	351	27 Nov 1792	759	20 Aug 1785	81	9	N/S Cumberland River	
Heaton, Robert	1359		Davidson	320	42	8 Oct 1787	343	10 Mar 1784	68	138	On Red River	
Heaton, Robert	1841		Davidson	640	339	27 Nov 1792	547	23 July 1784	81	6	W/S of Harpeth River	
Heaton, Robt	218	Hogan, Jas.	Tennessee	320	105	20 Dec 1791	287	27 July 1790	77	382	S/S Cumberland River	
Hector, Lewis	1262	Motherall, Joseph	Sumner	640	2938	1 Mar 1797	2381	22 Oct 1791	90	212	On an Eastern Branch	Yes
Hedgepeth, Marmaduke	552	Wikoff & Clark	Davidson	274	524	15 Sep 1787	1953		63	189	S/S Cumberland River	Yes
Hedgpeth, John	538	Shelby, Evan	Davidson	640	510	15 Sep 1787	1662		63	184	N/S Cumberland River	Yes
Hedley, William	891		Green	100	842	24 Nov 1790	1201	21 Sep 1789	74	289	On waters of Dumplin Creek	
Hedrack, Jacob	20		Sullivan	300	31	23 Oct 1782	1301	19 Jan 1782	43	252	Beg at a white oak	
Hedrick, Jacob	568		Washington	220	833	11 July 1788	2138	6 Nov 1779	64	337	W/S of Doe River	
Hedspeth, Stephen	1379	Boyd, John Jr.	Sumner	640	3241	24 Nov 1797	4084	14 Apr 1797	94	173	On Waters of Smiths Fork	Yes
Heel, Joseh	073	Fenner, Richard	Sumner	640			2101	17 May 1788			N/S of Cumberland River	Yes
Henderson, Abrahm	131	Hayes, Thomas	Tennessee	640	1639	23 Feb 1793	2571	30 Sep 1785	76	331	S/S Cumberland River	Yes
Henderson, Andrew	1271		Green	400	1121	12 Jan 1793	541	27 Oct 1783	78	377	N/S French Broad River	
Henderson, Andrew	2372	Stewart, Duncan	Green	640	3093	14 Sep 1797	4167		90	398	S. Harpeth River	Yes
Henderson, Andrew	67		Green	236.5	63	28 Oct 1787	76	21 Oct 1783	59	386	N/S French Broad River	
Henderson, Archibald	109		Davidson	773	95	14 Mar 1786	168		63	39	On Beaver Creek	Yes
Henderson, Daniel	179		Washington	250	47	23 Oct 1782	328	24 Aug 1798	47	22	On a small creek	
Henderson, James	1521	Williams, Sampson	Davidson	640	1078	26 Nov 1789	3667		74	119	N/S Cumberland River	Yes
Henderson, James	375		Green	200	377	20 Sep 1787	65	21 Oct 1783	65	479	S/S Nolachuckey River	
Henderson, Jno	1104		Davidson	640	78	17 Apr 1786	346	10 Mar 1784	66	60	S/S Cumberland River	
Henderson, John	1380		Davidson	320	63	28 Oct 1787	345	10 Mar 1784	68	147	S/S Cumberland River	
Henderson, John	237		Sullivan	600	376	9 Aug 1787	277	15 July 1784	61	395	N/S Holston	
Henderson, Joseph	1214		Green	250	1214	May 1792	2181	17 Feb 1781	77	404	Ceader branch of Lick Creek	
Henderson, Joseph	1282		Davidson	640	247	10 July 1788	275	13 Feb 1784	66	424	S/S Cumberland River	
Henderson, Nathaniel	292	King, Thomas	Middle Dist	400	252	7 Jul 1794	1249	21 Nov 1783	82	200	On Clear Fork of Cumberland River	
Henderson, Nathaniel	489		Hawkins	300	361	29 July 1793	2253	22 Nov 1779	80	266	In Powells Valley on Rob Camp Creek	
Henderson, Nathaniel	514		Hawkins	200	387	29 July 1793	2242	22 Nov 1779	80	274	N/S Powells Mountain	
Henderson, Nathaniel	563		Hawkins	450	436	29 July 1793	2202	12 Sep 1779	80	286	On Black Water Creek	
Henderson, Nathaniel	588		Hawkins	640	462	29 July 1793	1619	2 Feb 1782	80	292	N/S Holston River	
Henderson, Nathaniel	609		Hawkins	400	483	29 July 1793	2061	10 Oct 1780	80	296	N/S Clinch River	
Henderson, Nathaniel	622		Hawkins	640	494	27 June 1793	1663	17 Sep 1779	80	359	Joining James Landmans	
Henderson, Nathaniel	663		Sullivan	640	611	12 July 1794	187	21 Mar 1778	81	598	N/S Holstein River	
Henderson, Nathaniel	1830		Middle Dist	400	252	7 July 179	1249	21 Nov 1783	82	200	Cleark Fk of Cumberland River	
Henderson, Pleasant	1830		Davidson	640	403	26 June 1793	106		80	342	Adj. Public Lands of Nashville	
Henderson, Pleasant	2182		Davidson	640	459	16 Dec 1793	106	15 Jan 1784	82	135	S/S Cumberland River	
Henderson, Richard	842		Hawkins	400	667	5 Dec 1794	2174	19 Nov 1779	83	413	Powell's Valley on Turkey Creek	

Claimant:	File #:	Assignee:	County:	Acres:	Grant:	Grant Date:	Entry:	Entry Date:	Bk:	Pg:	Location by Stream Name:	Military:
Henderson, Richard	843		Hawkins	400	668	5 Dec 1794	2204	12 Nov 1779	83	414	Beg at Geo Simpsons corner sugar tree	
Henderson, Richard	853		Hawkins	640	669	12 Dec 1794	1615	14 Sep 1779	83	441	In Powell's Valley near Cumberland Gap	
Henderson, Richard	854		Hawkins	250	670	12 Dec 1794	2251	22 Nov 1779	83	442	In Powell's Valley on Rob Camp Creek	
Henderson, Richard	855		Hawkins	300	671	12 Dec 1794	2257	22 Nov 1779	83	442	In Powell's Valley	
Henderson, Richard & others	858	Act of Assembly	Hawkins	200000	637	8 Jan 1795		1783	84	5	On Powells & Clinch River	
Henderson, Richard & others	995	Act of Assembly	Hawkins	200000	714	5 Dec 1795		1783	89	155	On Powell & Clinch Rivers	
Henderson, Robert	071	White, William	Middle Dist	307	2492		1131					Yes
Henderson, Robert	1458		Green	51	1218	27 Nov 1793	2088	15 Jan 1784	81	508	Beg at a red oak	
Henderson, Samuel	1235		Green	100	1085	12 Jan 1793			78	355	N/S French Broad River	
Henderson, Samuel	1288		Green	100	1138	12 Jan 1793	2359	16 Dec 1779	78	387	S/S Nolachuckey River	
Henderson, Samuel	321	Armstrong, Martin	Eastern Dist	127	258	7 Mar 1796			88	194	S/S Holston River	
Henderson, Samuel	486		Hawkins	640	358	29 July 1793	1588	12 Sep 1779	80	265	Powell's Valley below Cumberland Gap	
Henderson, Samuel	554		Hawkins	250	427	29 July 1793	2058	10 Oct 1783	80	284	On Bob Camp Creek	
Henderson, Samuel	585		Hawkins	640	459	29 July 1793	1639	17 Sep 1779	80	291	Near War Gap in Clinch Mountain	
Henderson, Samuel	602		Hawkins	250	476	29 July 1793	2249	22 Nov 1779	80	295	N/S Powell's Mountain	
Henderson, Simon	022	Slothart, Robert	Montgomery	640			4091	1797			On Head of a branch	Yes
Henderson, Simon	1313	Hickman, Thomas	Sumner	640	3113	14 Sep 1797	4091	6 May 1797	90	408	On Sinking Creek	Yes
Henderson, Thomas	423		Green	350	425	20 Sep 1787	355	23 Oct 1783	65	495	N/S Holston River at head of Garman Creek	
Henderson, Thomas	6		Eastern Dist	100	306	13 Mar 1801	1094	30 Oct 1783	112	361	N/S Clinch River	
Henderson, Thomas	665		Sullivan	300	613	9 July 1794	525 etc	1 Apr 1785	81	625	Both/S of Main Road	
Henderson, Thomas	7		Eastern Dist	200	307	13 Mar 1801	1094	30 Oct 1783	112	361	On Buffalow Creek	
Henderson, Thomas	8		Eastern Dist	1200	308	13 Mar 1801	1094	30 Oct 1783	112	362	NW/S of Clinch River	
Henderson, Thos.	600		Green	286	557	20 Sep 1787	352	21 Oct 1783	66	248	N/S Holstein River on German Creek	
Henderson, William	1766		Green	200	1442	31 Mar 1801	73	29 July 1790	112	369	On Hendersons Creek of Holleys Creek	
Henderson, William	1766		Green	200	1442	31 Mar 1801	73	29 July 1790	112	369	On Hendersons Creek of Holleys Cr	
Henderson, William	1767		Green	150	1443	31 Mar 1801	8713	29 July 1790	112	370	On Holleys Creek	
Henderson, William	883		Green	300	815	Sep 1790	1	29 July 1790	74	276	Beg at a black walnut	
Henderson, William	884		Green	300	816	Sep 1790	6	11 Sep 1783	74	276	Beg at a white oak	
Hendry, Wm.	622	Hickman, Ed	Tennessee	274	3185	14 Sept 1797	4071	3 Dec 1796	90	436	N/S Cumberland River	
Hendri ks, John	21	Anderson, Meede	Not given	400	199	8 June 1797						Yes
Hendrick, William	688		Sullivan	426	636	9 July 1794	309 - 1582	1779 & 1780	81	633	On Sinking Creek	
Hendricks, Jeremiah	1403		Sumner	640	3333	6 Dec 1797	3911	12 Oct 1796	97	52	S/S Cumberland River	Yes
Hendricks, John	021		Not given	400	199	8 June 1797					No Plat	
Hendricks, John	1311		Washington	15	329	29 Dec 1796			90	188	Waters of Watauga	
Hendricks, Joseph	449		Sumner	640	354	27 Nov 1792	554	27 July 1784	81	10	Both sides Cedar Lick Creek	Yes
Hendricks, Joseph	734	Robeson, Joel	Davidson	640	707	11 July 1788	1412		63	249	1st cr that empties in E. Fk of Stones River	Yes
Hendrix, John	022	McCormin, James	Not given	400								Yes
Hendrix, John	483	McCoy, Anon	Tennessee	400	192	20 July 1796		14 Apr 1792	88	473		Yes
Hendry, Wm.	621	Gore, Jonathan	Tennessee	274	3184	14 Sept 1797	4072	3 Dec 1796	90	435	Waters of Sairos Creek	
Hendry, Wm.	623		Tennessee	274	3168	14 Sep 1797	4070	3 Dec 1796	90	436	N/S Cumberland River	
Henley, John	212	Hill, Joseph heirs	Tennessee	640	1506	4 Jan 1792	3465	2 Feb 1786	77	377	S/S Red River	
Hennis, Benbury	37	Blount, John Gray	Tennessee	640	1219	10 Dec 1790	2517	30 Sep 1785	74	338	N/S Cumberland River	Yes
Henry, Isaac	1828		Davidson	640	401	26 June 1793	447		80	343	On Stewarts Creek	Yes
Henry, Isham	908	Smith, John	Sumner	640	2477	31 Dec 1793	2726	25 Nov 1789	81	435	S/S of Cumberland River	Yes
Henry, James	319		Sumner	640	312	17 Nov 1790	728	13 May 1785	76	185	Both sides Spencers Creek	Yes

Earliest Tennessee Land Records

Claimant:	File #:	Assignee:	County:	Acres:	Grant:	Grant Date:	Entry:	Entry Date:	Bk:	Pg:	Location by Stream Name:	Military:
Henry, James	772		Green	1000	577	23 Aug 1788	387	25 Oct 1783	68	252	E/S of Clinch River	
Henry, John	1261	Hill, Green	Green	100	1111	12 Jan 1793	2735	16 Jan 1781	78	370	Waters of Dumplin Creek	
Henry, John	166	Robertson, Elijah	Davidson	640	152	7 Mar 1786	1071		63	58	N/S TennesseeRiver	Yes
Henry, John	807		Davidson	640	810	20 Nov 1788	3262		63	285	E/Fk of Stones River	Yes
Henry, Jonathan	041	Donelson, Stockley	Robertson	640	413	27 June 1793	838	13 Aug 1796			Waters of Red River	Yes
Henry, Mary	402		Sumner	640	90	23 Oct 1782	823	17 April 1780	80	345	S/S Cumberland River	
Henry, Samuel	222		Washington	150	90	23 Oct 1782	823	17 April 1780	47	43	On Dry Creek	
Henry, Samuel	284		Eastern Dist	850	209	5 Dec 1794			84	89	S of the Ohio	
Henry, Samuel	78		Washington	578	246	23 Oct 1782	822	29 Dec 1778	44	269	W/S Buffalow Creek	
Henry, Samuel, Jr.	284		Washington	200	151	23 Oct 1782	523	17 April 1780	47	73	On Buffalow Creek	
Henry, Thomas	2223	Seagroves, John	Davidson	124	2528	8 Dec 1795	622		88	280	Waters of Dry Creek	Yes
Henry, William	013	Radley, Icabod	Knox	400	366	4 Juy 1797		14 Apr 1791			N/S of Holston River	
Henry, William	1080	Armstrong, Martin	Hawkins	200	366	4 Juy 1797			91	590	On Rasberrys Creek	
Henry, William	904		Hawkins	400	162	17 Dec 1794			84	336	N/S Holston River	
Henry, William	919		Hawkins	700	728	7 Mar 1796	1743	16 Sep 1779	88	204	S/S Clinch River	
Henry, Hugh	854		Green	100	835	13 Feb 1791	66	4 Jan 1785	73	379	N/S of place where Henry now lives	
Henver, James	845	Brock, Joseph	Davidson	640	850	17 Jan 1789	3352	16 Sep 1779	63	297	N/S Cumberland River	Yes
Heritage, Burwell	349	Barton, Samuel	Sumner	640	1433	20 Dec 1791	3660	21 May 1791			E/waters of Cedar Creek	Yes
Heritage, John	131		Green	640		15 July 1786	770	28 Oct 1783	60	350	N/S Nolachuckey River	
Herking, Burwell	349	Barton, Samuel	Sumner	640	1433	20 Dec 1791	3660	21 May 1793	77	359	On waters of Cedar Creek	
Herkleroad, Henry	315		Sullivan	640	461	20 Nov 1787	2046	24 May 1780	67	215	On Beaver Creek	
Herkleroad, Henry	537		Sullivan	640	514	27 Nov 1789	371	29 Mar 1780	74	27	Both sides of Beaver Creek	
Herklerod, Henry	541		Sullivan	625	518	27 Nov 1789	2005	22 Oct 1779	74	29	Both sides of Beaver Creek	
Herklerod, Henry	542		Sullivan	295	519	27 Nov 1789	480	17 June 1788	74	29	On both sides Beaver Creek	
Herklerode, Henry	619		Sullivan	150	567	27 June 1793	2378	27 Dec 1779	80	369	Geo. Emmets Junr. line	
Herklerode, Henry	624		Sullivan	278	572	27 June 1793	769	6 Apr 1781	80	371	Beg at a black oak & white oak	
Herly, John	332		Tennessee	640	2102	20 May 1793	243	25 Oct 1783	81	150	S/S of Cumberland River	Yes
Hern, Drury	472	Brown, John	Sumner	228	1636	27 Apr 1793	69	6 Dec 1789	81	26	Adjoining Browns tract	Yes
Herndon, Benjamin	1884	Ferrell, James	Davidson	274	1889	20 May 1793	42		81	98	On Harpeth River on the 1st bend	Yes
Herndon, Benjamin	76		Middle Dist	4000	78	10 July 1788	433	25 Oct 1783	67	448	N/S of Duck River	
Herndon, George	07	Medearis, John	Montgomery	640	3248	6 Dec 1797	4330	20 May 1797			Waters of the w/Fk of Red River	Yes
Herrell, James	91	Phillips & Campbell	Tennessee	640	1360	10 Dec 1793	2188	12 Sep 1785	74	385	S/S Cumberland River	Yes
Herrendon, James	565	Peyton, Ephraim	Sumner	640	1798	20 May 1793	3689	29 Nov 1792	81	79	On a small E/Fk of Bartons Creek	Yes
Herring, Henry	2427	White, James L.	Davidson	640	3247	30 Nov 1797	4087		94	177	E side of E/Fk of S. Harpeth River	Yes
Herring, Jacob	2084	Sheppard, Nancy	Davidson	640	2284	30 May 1793	1761	2 Jan 1778	81	187	On the 1st creek	Yes
Herrington, Charles	76		Washington	300	244	23 Oct 1782	973	5 Jan 1790	44	268	On Dunhams Creek	
Herrington, Drury	372	Hays, Robert	Sumner	640	1543	14 Jan 1793	2660	30 Sep 1785	79	268	Waters of Manscows Creek	Yes
Herrington, Richard	148	Robertson & Grier	Tennessee	640	1399	20 Dec 1791	2804	11 Apr 1797	77	351	Both sides of Pine River	Yes
Herrington, Samuel	0103	Nash, William	Sumner	640			4209				E/s E/Fk Stones River	Yes
Herrod, John	281		Eastern Dist	100	206	5 Jan 1795	1126	14 Jan 1779	84	54	N/S of Clinch River	
Hertherly, Evan	34		Washington	200	324	24 Oct 1782	629	17 July 1780	43	308	Little Doe River	
Hester, [not decipherable]	1351		Green	200	1197	23 Feb 1793			78	440	S/S Dumplin Creek	
Hester, John	2096	McCrory, James	Davidson	640	2315	20 May 1793	1965	17 July 1780	81	194	N/S Cumberland	Yes
Heston, Abram	652		Washington	50	746	26 Oct 1786	2102	30 Oct 1779	66	32	Beg 2 marked white oak saplings	
Hetherly, Hains	944		Washington	100	921	17 Nov 1790	1251	27 Feb 1779	76	151	On Little Doe	

Earliest Tennessee Land Records

Claimant:	File #:	Assignee:	County:	Acres:	Grant:	Grant Date:	Entry:	Entry Date:	Bk:	Pg:	Location by Stream Name:	Military:
Hewet, Ebenezer	049	McConnell, Robert	Davidson	640	416	15 Sep 1787	3770	11 Aug 1797	63	154	Waters of E. Fork of S. Harpeth	Yes
Hezard(Hubbard) Moses	444		Davidson	640	546	20 Sep 1787	626	21 Oct 1783	65	539	Meat Camp or Bartons Creek	Yes
Hibbard, Samuel	544		Green	246	546	20 Sep 1787	132		65	539	Alexanders Brank of Lick Creek	
Hibbard, Samuel	671		Hawkins	400	576	15 July 1794	141	10 Mar 1778	81	595	On Turkey Creek	
Hickison, Wm., Isaac, & John	425		Sumner	640	436	27 June 1793	594	30 Aug 1784	80	353	W. Branch of Goose Creek	Yes
Hickman, Charles	773	Fenner, Richard	Davidson	640	746	11 July 1788	2191		63	262	N/S Sycamore Creek	Yes
Hickman, Corbin	31a	Jones, Ambrose	Sumner	640	790	11 July 1788	3354	12 Sep 1787	63	277	N/S Cumberland River	Yes
Hickman, Ed	622	Hendry, William	Tennessee	274	3185	14 Sep 1797	4071	3 Dec 1796	90	436	N/S of Cumberland	Yes
Hickman, Edward	010		Davidson	640		18 Mar 1784	342	18 Mar 1784			Below the mouth of Red River	
Hickman, Edwin	2077	Stevens, John	Davidson	228	2234	20 May 1793	3588		81	177	On waters of Hickman Creek	Yes
Hickman, Edwin	2201		Davidson	100	217	27 Feb 1796		28 Nov 1792	88	169	On waters of Whites Creek	
Hickman, Edwin	2202		Davidson	25	219	27 Feb 1795		23 Feb 1786	88	170	An island in Cumberland River	
Hickman, Edwin	2210		Davidson	150	233	27 Feb 1796		27 June 1786	88	176	On a branch of Stumps Fk.	
Hickman, Edwin	369	Burrington, Demoey	Tennessee	274	2256	20 May 1793	2268	30 Sep 1785	81	182	Joins No. Boundary of John Hayes entry	
Hickman, Edwin	535	Campbell, Daniel	Davidson	640	507	15 Sep 1787	1700		63	183	N/S Cumberland River	Yes
Hickman, Edwin	578	Threabers, Hugh	Davidson	1000	550	15 Sep 1787	2603		63	197	S/S Cumberland	Yes
Hickman, Edwin	680		Sumner	640	2025	20 May 1793	2321	30 Nov 1792	81	130	Waters of Dixon Creek	Yes
Hickman, Edwin	784		Sumner	365	2241	20 May 1793	3121	22 Feb 1787	81	178	N/S Cumberland	Yes
Hickman, Edwin	795		Sumner	640	2255	20 May 1793	2329	30 Nov 1782	81	182	N/S Cumberland River	Yes
Hickman, Edwin	796		Sumner	640	2257	20 May 1793	2333	29 Oct 1792	81	182	On Lick Creek	Yes
Hickman, John	623	Hendry, William	Tennessee	274	3186	14 Sep 1797	4070	3 Dec 1796	90	436	N/S Cumberland River	Yes
Hickman, John	863		Sumner	640	2373	20 May 1793	2432	6 Jan 1786	81	207	S/S of Big Barren River	Yes
Hickman, Peter	781		Sullivan	60	713	18 Nov 1796	49	8 Feb 1780	91	89	Beg at a black oak	
Hickman, Thomas	012		Davidson	70				9 Aug 1786			N/S Cumberland	
Hickman, Thomas	085	Caney, Andrew	Sumner	640			4587	6 Apr 1797			Waters of Main E/Fk of B. Barren	Yes
Hickman, Thomas	086	Cowin, Absolim	Sumner	649			2447	4 June 1796			S/S Cumberland River	Yes
Hickman, Thomas	087	Morris, John & James	Sumner	640			1477	14 Sep 1796			N/S Cumberland River	Yes
Hickman, Thomas	1298		Sumner	640	3067	19 July 1797	4588	6 Apr 1796	90	377	S/S Cumberland River	Yes
Hickman, Thomas	1300		Sumner	640	3070	19 July 1797	4591	6 Apr 1797	90	378	S/S Cumberland	Yes
Hickman, Thomas	1304		Sumner	640	3075	19 July 1797	4647	6 Apr 1797	90	380	Waters of E/Fk of Big Barron	Yes
Hickman, Thomas	1306		Sumner	640	3079	19 July 1797	3902	6 Apr 1797	90	382	On waters of Big Barren	Yes
Hickman, Thomas	1313		Sumner	640	3113	14 Sep 1797	4091	6 May 1797	90	408	On Sinking Creek	Yes
Hickman, Thomas	1317		Sumner	640	3117	14 Sep 1797	4395	6 May 1797	90	410	On the waters of Big Barren	Yes
Hickman, Thomas	1329	Madison, Jno.	Sumner	640	3129	14 Sep 1797	4313	6 May 1797	90	415	Headwaters of Sinking Creek	Yes
Hickman, Thomas	1332		Sumner	640	3132	14 Sep 1797	4468	6 May 1797	90	416	On headwaters of Sinking Creek	Yes
Hickman, Thomas	1335		Sumner	640	3135	14 Sep 1797	4394	3 June 1797	90	417	On Salt Lick of Big Barren	Yes
Hickman, Thomas	1390		Sumner	365	3316	6 Dec 1797	3064	23 June 1797	97	41	On the Salt Lick Fork	Yes
Hickman, Thomas	1793	Armstrong, Martin	Davidson	100	135	29 Aug 1793		22 Nov 1792	80	326	S/S Cumberland River	
Hickman, Thomas	2199		Davidson	70	214	27 Feb 1796		1 Aug 1786	88	168	On Gaspers Creek	
Hickman, Thomas	2200		Davidson	320	215	27 Feb 1796		22 Dec 1792	88	168	On waters of Harpeth River	
Hickman, Thomas	2205		Davidson	100	225	27 Feb 1786			88	173	N/S Cumberland River	
Hickman, Thomas	2206		Davidson	38	226	27 Feb 1796		30 Nov 1792	88	173	N/S Cumberland River	
Hickman, Thomas	2208		Davidson	288	228	27 Feb 1796		17 Mar 17??	88	174	On waters of Brown Creek	
Hickman, Thomas	395		Davidson	70	142	29 Aug 1793			80	329	N/S Cumberland River	Yes
Hickman, Thomas	7		Sumner	274	704	11 July 1788	3456	30 Aug 1787	63	268	On waters of Caney Fork	Yes

Claimant:	File #:	Assignee:	County:	Acres:	Grant:	Grant Date:	Entry:	Entry Date:	Bk:	Pg:	Location by Stream Name:	Military:
Hickman, Thomas	766	Smith, Nathaniel hrs.	Davidson	640	739	11 July 1788	2776		63	260	Waters 1st Creek runs into E/Fk Stones Ri	Yes
Hickman, Thomas	769	Cross, Frederick	Davidson	640	742	11 July 1788	2712		63	261	Waters of 1st Creek on E/S of Stones Rive	Yes
Hickman, Thomas	771	Davis, James	Davidson	640	744	11 July 1788	1791		63	261	1st Creek on E/Fk of Stones River	Yes
Hickman, Thomas	785	Carron, James	Davidson	640	758	11 July 1788	2638		63	266	1st Creek in the E/Fk of Stones River	Yes
Hickman, Thos	1264		Sumner	640	2940	1 Mar 1797	1478	6 Apr 1797	90	213	N/S Cumberland River	Yes
Hickman, Thos	1301		Sumner	640	3069	19 July 1797	4648	6 Apr 1797	90	378	S/S Cumberland	Yes
Hickman, Thos	1303		Sumner	640	3074	19 July 1797	4664	6 Apr 1797	90	380	Waters of Big Barron River	Yes
Hickman, Thos	1328		Sumner	640	3128	14 Sep 1797	4314	3 June 1797	90	415	Waters of Big Barren	Yes
Hickman, Thos	259	Roberson, Cornelius	Tennessee	274	1684	20 May 1793	3557	10 Aug 1787	81	50	N/S Cumberland River	
Hickman, Thos	526		Sumner	640	1719	20 May 1793	2159	19 Nov 1792	81	58	W/S Caney Fork	Yes
Hickman, Thos.	1263		Sumner	640	2939	1 Mar 1797	3309	11 May 1795	90	212	N/S Cumberland River	Yes
Hickman, Thos	1265		Sumner	640	2941	1 Mar 1797	2586	14 Oct 1795	90	213	Waters of Hickmans Creek	Yes
Hickman, Thos.	1297		Sumner	640	3064	19 July 1797	4594	6 Apr 1797	90	376	S/S Cumberland	Yes
Hickman, Thos.	1299		Sumner	640	3068	19 July 1797	4590	6 Apr 1797	90	377	S/S Cumberland	Yes
Hickman, Thos.	1302	Fenwick, Nathaniel	Sumner	640	3071	19 July 1797	4700	6 Apr 1797	90	379	Headwaters of Round Lick Creek	Yes
Hickman, Thos.	1330		Sumner	640	3130	14 Sep 1796	4161	3 June 1797	90	415	On waters of Punchin Camp Creek	Yes
Hickman, Thos.	1333		Sumner	1000	3133	14 Sep 1797	4551	6 _ 1797	90	417	Waters of E Fork of Big Barren	Yes
Hickman, Thos.	1334		Sumner	640	3134	14 Sep 1797	4398	3 June 1797	90	417	Waters of Big Barren	Yes
Hickman, Thos.	1357		Sumner	640	2783	11 Dec 1796	1316	28 Oct 1796	91	296	N/S of Cumberland River	Yes
Hickman, Thos.	330		Sumner	640	1621	23 Feb 1793	3114	22 Dec 1792	76	322	Headwaters of Hickman's Creek	Yes
Hickman, Thos.	533		Sumner	1000	1727	20 May 1793	3661	15 Aug 1792	81	60	W/S of Caney Fork	Yes
Hicks, Daniel	198		Tennessee	428	1484	4 Jan 1792	239	25 Oct 1783	77	372	S/S of Cumberland River	
Hicks, David	895		Washington	300	959	15 Dec 1791	963	2 Jan 1779	75	148	Beg at 2 Sycamores	
Hicks, Hansel	034	Betts, William	Montgomery	274			1277				On Saline Creek	Yes
Hicks, Harris	1339	Hinds, John	Sumner	640	3139	14 Sep 1797	4445	6 May 1797	90	419	Waters of Big Barren	Yes
Hicks, Henry	219	Saunders, James	Davidson	640	205	7 Mar 1786	804		63	76	N/S Cumberland River	Yes
Hicks, Isaac	043		Sullivan	136			1058	13 Mar 1789			N/S Holston River	
Hicks, Isaac	1341	Hinds, John	Sumner	228	3141	14 Sep 1797	4311	6 May 1797	90	420	Waters of Big Barren	Yes
Hicks, Isaac	796		Sullivan	133	731	6 July 1797	305	10 Mar 1780	91	600	Beg at or near Walter Johnsons Corner	
Hicks, Jacob	09	Nelson, Robert	Montgomery	228	3082		1680	4 Nov 1785			Waters W/Fk of Red River	Yes
Hicks, James	1	Cherry, Willie	Wilson	228	3386	12 Dec 1801	5117	19 Aug 1800	114	91	On waters of Bartons Creek	Yes
Hicks, John	064	Sheppherd, John	Not given	640			2931	15 Aug 1792			On waters of Obeys Creek	Yes
Hicks, Jonathan	277		Green	300	279	20 Sep 1787	1345	12 Jan 1784	65	453	N/S Nolechuckey on Bats Branch	
Hicks, Reubin	1229	Donoho, Thomas	Sumner	1000	2500	12 Nov 1795	1651	1 Mar 1786	89	419	On Second Creek	Yes
Hicks, Robert	647	Bledsoe, Isaac	Sumner	228	1943	20 May 1793	346	31 July 1792	81	110	N/S of Cumberland River	Yes
Hicks, Shadrack	55		Sullivan	317	66	23 Oct 1782	509 & 510	19 Aug 1786	43	270	N/S Holston River	
Hicks, Stephen	044		Sullivan	50			705	13 Nov 1780			Beg at an old corner white oak	
Hicks, William	063	Shepperd, John	Not given	640			2932	15 Aug 1792			On Obeys River	Yes
Hickson, Joseph	1534		Green	60	1294	17 July 1794	2843	31 Mar 1784	81	607	On Middle Creek	
Highder, Michael	215		Washington	260	83	23 Oct 1782	796	28 Dec 1778	47	40	E. Branch of Buffalow Creek	
Hiland, Henry	1218		Davidson	640	182	10 July 1788	555	27 July 1784	66	407	Both sides of Harpeth River	
Hill, Bennett	1614	Carroll, Douglas	Davidson	428	1342	10 Dec 1790			74	379	On N. Cross Creek	Yes
Hill, Dan	1307		Sumner	640	3080	19 July 1797	4641	12 Apr 1797	90	383	Martins Creek	Yes
Hill, Green	166	Henry, John	Davidson	640	152	7 Mar 1786	1071		63	58	N/S of Tennessee River	Yes
Hill, Green	180	Humphries, Randolph	Davidson	640	166	7 Mar 1786	811		63	63	On waters of Little Harper & Mill Creek	Yes

Claimant:	File #:	Assignee:	County:	Acres:	Grant:	Grant Date:	Entry:	Entry Date:	Bk:	Pg:	Location by Stream Name:	Military:
Hill, Green	195	Randall, Andrew	Davidson	1000	181	7 Mar 1786	421		63	68	South of Duck River	Yes
Hill, Green	198	McCoy, John	Davidson	640	184	7 Mar 1786	1070		63	69	N/S of Tennessee River	Yes
Hill, Green	222	Driskiel, David	Davidson	274	208	7 Mar 1786	1057		63	77	N/S Cumberland River	Yes
Hill, Green	2293	Armstrong, Martin	Davidson	77	313	9 Sep 1796		11 July 1796	88	514	On waters of Mill Creek	
Hill, Green	243	Walker, Wm.	Davidson	640	229	7 Mar 1796	1067		63	84	On waters of Stones River	Yes
Hill, Hardy	671	Mann, John	Tennessee	1000	3258	6 Dec 1797	4613		98	146	On the waters of Saline Creek	Yes
Hill, Henry	030	Kuykendall, John hrs	Montgomery	640		5 May 1797	3875	5 May 1797			Waters of Little W/Fk of Red river	Yes
Hill, Henry	031	Laremore, Marmaduke	Montgomery	640			3872	5 May 1797			Waters of Little W/Fk of Red River	Yes
Hill, Henry	032	Parker, Thos.	Montgomery	640		5 May 1797	3806	5 May 1797			Waters of Little W/Fk of Red River	Yes
Hill, Henry	1070		Sumner	640	2518	10 Dec 1795	3872	8 Aug 1795	88	297	W/S of W/Fk of Obeys river	Yes
Hill, Henry	1071		Sumner	640	2519	10 Dec 1795	3875	8 Aug 1794	88	297	W/S of W/Fk of Obeys River	Yes
Hill, Henry	1072		Sumner	640	2520	10 Dec 1795	3806	8 Aug 1794	88	298	W/S of W/Fk of Obeys River	Yes
Hill, Isaac	658	Bushnell & Dobbs	Davidson	228	631	15 Sep 1787	1689		63	224	On waters of Stones River	Yes
Hill, James	135		Green	78	117	1 Nov 1786	113	21 Oct 1783	60	449	An island in Nollechucky River	
Hill, James	17		Green	400	80	1 Nov 1786	4	21 Oct 1783	58	441	N/S Nolichuckie River	
Hill, James	46	Hadley, Joshua	Sumner	640	901	17 Jan 1789	2733		63	311	E/Fk of Big Barren River	Yes
Hill, John	617	Melvin, George	Sumner	365	1882	20 May 1793	1458	19 Dec 1792	81	96	On a branch of Long Creek	Yes
Hill, John	876		Sumner	2560	2393	7 Jan 1793			81	389	S/S of W/Fk of Abbits Creek	Yes
Hill, Roberson	317	McCulloch, Benjamin	Tennessee	640	2018	20 May 1793	2658	30 Sep 1785	81	129	N/S of Cumberland River	Yes
Hill, Samuel	1200		Green	375	1044	_ Mar 1792	196	22 Oct 1784	77	338	Below Fk of French Broad & Nolachuckey	
Hill, William	0130		Green	182	182	17 Dec 1794	1559	26 Mar 1784			On Elk River	
Hill, William	1463		Green	2000	1223	27 Nov 1793	2649	25 May 1784	81	509	S/S Elk River	
Hill, William	1465		Green	2500	1225	27 Nov 1793	2181	14 May 1784	81	510	S/S Elk River	
Hill, William	343		Middle Dist	2500	182	7 Dec 1794			84	16	On Elk River	
Hill, William	594	Flowers, William	Middle Dist	274	3087	19 Aug 1797	1978	30 Apr 1780	92	2		Yes
Hill, William	597		Middle Dist	1500	362	9 Dec 1797	206	24 Oct 1783	96	9	W/S Richland Creek	Yes
Hill, Wm.	324	Ward, John	Tennessee	640	2068	20 May 1793	3465	2 Feb 1786	81	141	N/S Cumberland River	
Hills, Joseph	212	Henley, John	Tennessee	640	1506	4 Jan 1792			77	377	S/S of Red River	Yes
Hills, William	22		Washington	189	312	24 Oct 1782	16	21 Oct 1783	43	302	Beg at a poplar	
Hilton, Daniel	119	Hilton, Wm.	Tennessee	2560	1620	23 Feb 1793	1072	8 Jan 1779	76	322	Waters of Grices Creek	
Himes, Geo	644		Sullivan	275	592	27 June 1793	2458	1 June 1795	80	381	N/S Beaver Creek	
Hind, Anthony	1145	Harris, Edward	Sumner	640	2650	4 June 1796		3 Sep 1778	88	351	Join sd Harris survey	Yes
Hinds, Christopher	04		Jefferson	300			312					
Hinds, John	1311		Sumner	640	3111	14 Sep 1797	4331	6 May 1797	90	407	Waters of Big Barren River	Yes
Hinds, John	1316		Sumner	640	3116	14 Sep 1797	4393	10 May 1797	90	410	On Waters of Big Barren	Yes
Hinds, John	1318		Sumner	640	3118	14 Sep 1797	4315	6 May 1797	90	410	Waters of Big Barren	Yes
Hinds, John	1339		Sumner	640	3139	14 Sep 1797	4445	6 May 1797	90	419	Waters of Big Barren	Yes
Hinds, John	1340		Sumner	320	3140	14 Sep 1797	4465	6 May 1797	90	419	Waters of Big Barren	Yes
Hinds, John	1341		Sumner	228	3141	14 Sep 1797	4311	6 May 1797	90	420	Waters of Big Barren	Yes
Hinds, John	1342		Sumner	920	3142	14 Sep 1797		20 May 1797	90	420	On the Seventh Creek	Yes
Hinds, Joseph	324		Eastern Dist	400	264	7 Mar 1796	1344	12 Jan 1784	88	199	Both sides of Beaver Creek	
Hinds, Joseph	33		Eastern Dist	500	33	11 July 1788	1343	7 June 1784	67	353	On Bull Run	
Hinds, Joseph	34		Eastern Dist	400	34	11 July 1788			67	353	On Bull Run	
Hinds, Joseph	81		Middle Dist	5000	83	10 July 1788	550	27 Oct 1773	67	451	Both sides of Duck River	
Hinds, levi	437		Hawkins	980	315	24 June 1793	627	25 June 1784	80	191	Bet Blaine Sta. & Clinch Mtn.	

Claimant:	File #:	Assignee:	County:	Acres:	Grant:	Grant Date:	Entry:	Entry Date:	Bk:	Pg:	Location by Stream Name:	Military:
Hinds, Levi, Sylvanus & John	182	Hines, Simon & others	Eastern Dist	1000	137	24 June 1793	1531	13 Mar 1784	80	188	Cumberland Valley	
Hinds, Levy	35	Bynum, Eb.	Eastern Dist	200	35	11 July 1788			67	353	Waters of Beaverdam Creek	
Hinds, Samuel	443		Hawkins	493	321	24 June 1793	644	7 June 1784	80	193	A small Sinking Branch	
Hines, David	16		Washington	200	306	24 Oct 1782			43	299	On Coopers Creek	
Hines, Levi	126		Eastern Dist	200	158	29 July 1793		12 Jan 1779	76	482	Waters of Beaverdam Cr./Hines Valley	Yes
Hinton, Benj	1983		Davidson	640	1888	20 May 1793	915		81	98	Jones Cr. beg John Larkins corner	Yes
Hinton, John	031	Armstrong & Donelson	Middle Dist	640			2929					
Hippinstall, Jos	1248		Green	200	1098	12 Jan 1793	1418	5 June 1779	78	363	Waters of Tuckahoe River	
Hird, John	414		Sumner	640	425	27 June 1793	839	11 Dec 1792	80	349	S/S Cumberland River	
Hise, Jacob	1256		Green	50	1106	12 Jan 1793	2864	5 Jan 1792	78	367	S/S Nolichuckey River	
Hise, Jacob	1264		Green	100	1114	12 Jan 1793	362	30 Dec 1778	78	372	N/S Nolechuckey River	
Hise, Jacob	1409		Green	200	1221	27 Nov 1792	586	7 Nov 1780	80	161	N/S Nolechuckey River	
Hitchcock, John	416		Green	125	418	20 Sep 1787	163	22 Oct 1783	65	493	N/S Chuckey River on Little Chuckey	
Hitchcock, John	418		Green	82	420	20 Sep 1787	338	12 Jan 1784	65	494	Beg at a stake & beach	
Hitchcock, William	1493	Hunter, James	Davidson	640	1046	27 Nov 1789	3356		74	47	Waters of Spencers Creek	Yes
Hix, Isaac	799		Sullivan	13	742	17 Nov 1797	377	31 Mar 1780	94	146	Beg at a Walnut	
Hixon, Joseph	96		Green	100	54	1 Nov 1786	2731	16 Jan 1781	59	415	Beg post oak & pine trees	
Hobbs, Isaac	064	Sheppard, James	Middle Dist	640			2928					Yes
Hobbs, Isaac	2267	Tyrrell, Wm. T.	Davidson	640	2743	20 July 1796	2928		88	454	Waters of Mill Creek	Yes
Hobbs, Joel	036	Carmack, Joseph	Robertson	640			2925	13 Aug 1796			On Elk Fork of Red River	Yes
Hobbs, Moses	058	Shepphard, John	Middle Dist	640			2927					Yes
Hockett, John	813		Green	250	814	11 Aug 1789	425		11	34	In Fk of Tenn. & Clinch River	
Hoag, John	214		Middle Dist	1260	200				79	286	2nd lge creek runs in Elk River	
Hodge, Frances	1833		Davidson	640	323	27 Nov 1792	136	16 Jan 1784	81	2	Beg at 3 black oaks	
Hodge, Francis	1780		Davidson	640	360	26 June 1793	135	16 June 1784	80	319	N/S Cumberland River	
Hodge, John	068		Green	1260			2130	10 May 1784			E/S Tennessee River	
Hodges	852		Washington	500	843	17 Nov 1788	425	15 Sep 1788	70	11	Beg at a Sycamore	
Hodges, Benjamin	1622	Parsons, Harrison	Davidson	640	1358	10 Dec 1790	1080	22 Oct 1783	74	385	Beg 2 white oak trees	Yes
Hodges, Charles	54		Green	450	12	1 Nov 1786	330		59	373	Waters of Bent Creek	
Hodges, Drury	389		Green	300	391	20 Sep 1787	1421	21 Jan 1784	65	483	Lick Creek	
Hodges, Hardy	0104	Nash, William	Sumner	1000	2970	5 Apr 1797	1567	12 Apr 1797	90	274	S/S Fowling Creek	Yes
Hodges, Hardy	546	Malloy, Thomas	Tennessee	1000	2404	20 Dec 1793	1122	26 July 1784	81	419	S/S Cumberland River	Yes
Hodges, John	402	Glasgow, James	Tennessee	792	92	16 Nov 1790	1419	21 Jan 1784	77	182	S/S Cumberland River	Yes
Hodges, Welcom	159		Hawkins	500	540		1420	21 Jan 1784	65	536	S/S Holston	
Hodges, Welcom	538		Green	300	959	20 Sep 1787	1830		63	326	Both sides Lick Creek	
Hodgin, Holder	943	Donelson, Stockley	Davidson	640	86	18 May 1789		7 Feb 1784	66	171	S/S Cumberland River	Yes
Hogan, Daniel	1109		Davidson	640	361	17 Apr 1786	252		90	283	Sulphur Fork	
Hogan, Daniel	555		Tennessee	50	159	10 Apr 1797		13 Aug 1792	66	188	Both sides Drakes Creek	
Hogan, Edward	1182		Davidson	640	187	17 Apr 1786	278	13 Feb 1784	66	70	Both sides Sulphur Fork	Yes
Hogan, Humphrey	201	Christmas, John	Davidson	640	55	7 Mar 1786	50		63	23	S/S Cumberland River	Yes
Hogan, James	69	Hogan, Lemuel hr of Jas	Davidson	12000	3380	14 Mar 1786	324		63	87	On waters of Red River	Yes
Hogan, John	1463	Hogan, Wm.	Sumner	640	2693	10 Dec 1801	3831	10 Sep 1796	114	87	Adj. land of John Couch	
Hogan, John	469	McMullin, Michael	Tennessee	274	158	6 June 1796	3828	25 Jan 1795	88	88	Middle Fk of Station Camp Creek	
Hogan, Richard	1181		Davidson	640	3253	17 Apr 1796	276	13 Feb 1784	66	138	Flat Lick Fork	Yes
Hogan, Roger	660	McNary, John	Tennessee	274		6 Dec 1797	4741		97	34		Yes

Claimant:	File #:	Assignee:	County:	Acres:	Grant:	Grant Date:	Entry:	Entry Date:	Bk:	Pg:	Location by Stream Name:	Military:
Hogan, Rogers	023	Stothart, Robert	Montgomery	640			4741	1 Apr 1797	63	23	S/S Piney Fk of Elk River	Yes
Hogan, Samuel	69	Hogan, James heir	Davidson	12000	55	14 Mar 1786	324				S/S Cumberland River	Yes
Hogan, William	1181		Sumner	500	2694	6 June 1796	3827	29 Mar 1796	88	368	S/S Cumberland River	Yes
Hogan, William	1463		Sumner	640	3380	10 Dec 1801	3831	10 Sep 1796	114	87	Waters of Red River	Yes
Hogan, William (heirs of)	455		Sumner	1000	1592	27 Apr 1793			81	15	Both sides Caney Fork	Yes
Hogard, James	580		Sullivan	150	578	29 July 1793	185	21 Feb 1780	76	473	N/S Reedy Creek	
Hogg, James	286		Middle Dist	1000	240	30 Dec 1793	2290	12 Jan 1785	82	147	Waters of E/Fk Stone River	
Hogg, Thomas	1585	Lucas, Benjamin	Davidson	640	1246	10 Dec 1790			74	347	S/S Cumberland River	Yes
Hogg, Thomas	55	Mann, Robert	Tennessee	640	1271	10 Dec 1790	2428	30 Sep 1785	74	356	S/S Cumberland River	
Hogg, Thomas	740	Delaney, John	Davidson	640	713	11 July 1788	3080		63	251	Waters of Sycamore Creek	
Hogg, Thomas	78		Tennessee	640	1323	10 Dec 1780	2429	30 Sep 1785	74	373	S/S Cumberland River	
Hogg, Thos	026	Lucas, Benj.	Tennessee	640			2426	30 Sep 1785			S/S Cumberland River	
Hogg, William (Heirs of)	88		Sumner	1000			3613	4 Dec 1789			Both sides Caney Fork	Yes
Hoggard, William	1278	Dillonbarry, Redmon	Sumner	228	3037	8 June 1797	1924	7 Apr 1797	90	313	Waters of W/Fk of Paytons Creek	Yes
Hoggatt, James	1570	Armstrong, M.	Davidson	70	97	30 Nov 1790			74	323	N/S Cumberland River	
Hogges, Ambrose	186		Washington	200	54	23 Oct 1782	326	25 Aug 1778	47	25	Both sides Cherokee Creek	
Hogget, James	1743	Armstrong, M.	Davidson	160	136	4 Jan 1792	1741	4 May 1791	77	379	On Sulphur	
Hogget, Jess	517	Spencer, Jas.	Davidson	228	489	15 Sep 1787	1741		63	177	N/S Cumberland River	Yes
Hoggett, James	1408	Armstrong, M.	Davidson	60	25	8 Oct 1787	442	12 Nov 1785	68	154	N/S Cumberland River	
Hoggett, Solomon	1419		Green	150	1231	27 Nov 1792	405	19 Sep 1778	80	164	On Sinking Lick Br. of Lick Creek	
Hoggott, James	1412		Davidson	160	29	8 Oct 1787	446	21 Dec 1785	68	155	On Sulphur Creek	
Hoggott, James	1460		Davidson	60	62	18 May 1789	752	21 Dec 1786	71	222	Mouth of Sulphur Fork	
Hohamer, Philip	02	Welburn, Daniel	Robertson	640			1951	10 Feb 1796			On Clay Lick Branch	Yes
Holbrook, John	281	Graham, Joseph	Tennessee	640	1866	20 May 1793	1883	11 Jul 1785	81	93	On S side of Cumberland River	Yes
Holder, Isaac	654	Hart, Anthony	Sumner	274	1964	20 May 1793	3510	19 NOV 1792	81	115	On the W side of Caney Fork	Yes
Holderness, William	206	Bryant, Ambrose hrs	Davidson	640	192	7 Mar 1786	308		63	71	On waters of Goose Creek	Yes
Holderson, William	744	Emory, John	Davidson	640	717	11 Jul 1788	309		63	252	On head of Nelsons Creek Kerr Creek	Yes
Holdman, Mordeca	675	Clark, Lardner	Davidson	640	648	8 Dec 1787	1661		63	230	On waters of Hurricane Creek	Yes
Holebrook, John	214		Washington	300	82	23 Oct 1782	700	18 Dec 1778	47	40	Including a mill seat &c	
Holf---?, Mordice	675	Clark, Lardner	Davidson	640	648	8 Dec 1787	1661		63	230	On waters of Hurricane Creek	Yes
Hollan, Thomas	1625		Green	100	1345	22 Feb 1795	2273	15 Jun 1782	84	329	On N side of French Broad River	
Holland, Ben	063		Green	350			287	22 Oct 1783			S bank of French Broad River	
Holland, Benjamin	1007		Washington	300	979	26 Dec 1791	1048	7 Jan 1779	77	302	On Sinking Creek	
Holland, Benjamin	45		Sullivan	28			414	14 Apr 1780			Beg at a dogwood	
Holland, Benjamin	512		Washington	121	775	16 Aug 1787	2620	23 Aug 1780	64	144	Joining the land the said Holland lives on	
Holland, Benjamin	780		Washington	100	594	10 Nov 1784	1960	10 Oct 1779	69	136	On the Buffaloe Valley &c	
Holland, Charles	829	Brock, Joseph	Davidson	640	832	17 Jan 1789			63	293	On N side of Cumberland River	Yes
Holland, Chas.	050	Lewis, Wm. Terrell	Not given	640	4067		3476	26 May 1796			S side of Cumberland River	Yes
Holland, Daniel	010	Rowland, John	Robertson	640	3331	21 Apr 1797					On Spring Creek	
Holland, Den /sic/	665	Rowland, John	Tennessee	640	74	6 Dec 1797			97	50	On Spring Creek	
Holland, James	72		Middle District	5000	716	10 Jul 1788	421		67	446	On both sides of Duck River &c	
Holland, Joseph	47	Holland, Josiah	Not given	640				1 Jun 1785			On first creek N side Cumberland River	
Holland, Reason	278	Gillespie, George	Tennessee	274	1860	20 May 1793	252	25 Oct 1783	81	92	On N side of Cumberland River	Yes
Holland, Thomas	1625		Green	100	1345	22 Feb 1795	2273	15 Jun 1782	84	329	On N side of French Broad River	
Holland, William	526	Coonrod, Nicholas	Davidson	640	498	15 Sep 1787	715		63	180	N side of Cumberland River	Yes

Claimant:	File #:	Assignee:	County:	Acres:	Grant:	Grant Date:	Entry:	Entry Date:	Bk:	Pg:	Location by Stream Name:	Military:
Hollaway, John	300		Sullivan	50	439	9 Jul 1787	20	16 May 1783	61	458	On S side of N Fork of Holston River	
Hollaway, John	672		Sullivan	43	620	9 Jul 1794	620	23 Jun 1780	81	628	On N fork of Holston River	
Holley, Henry	2087	McAdams, John	Davidson	228	2290	20 May 1793	1691		81	189	On Bazzel Saleen /sic/	Yes
Holley, John	06	Coffery, John	Robertson	640	3000	10 Apr 1797	3844	13 Jan 1796			On head Spring of Clear Branch	Yes
Holley, John	109		Washington	250	277	24 Oct 1782	327	2 Sep 1778	44	286	W Fork of Holleys Branch	
Holley, John	325		Washington	300	192	24 Oct 1782	499	9 Oct 1778	49	223	On the N side of Noleychuckey River	
Holley, Jonathan	261		Washington	100	129	23 Oct 1782	497	9 Oct 1778	47	63	On Holleys Creek	
Holley, Nathaniel	1325	Shelby, David	Davidson	320	11	18 Aug 1787	506	2 Jul 1784	68	125	On waters of Sulfur Fork	
Holley, Nathaniel	345	Stone, Littleberry	Tennessee	640	2158	20 May 1793	3381	7 Jan 1786	81	162	On N side of Cumberland River	
Holley, Nathaniel	380	Hays, Robert	Sumner	640	1563	14 Jan 1793	2850	7 Apr 1788	79	272	On s/s of Swifts Creek	
Holliman, Kinchen	735	Gatlin, John	Sumner	228	2123	20 May 1793	3568	4 May 1791	81	155	on S side of Cumberland River	Yes
Hollingsworth, Thomas	805	Robertson, Elijah	Davidson	640	808	20 Nov 1788	3315		63	284	On waters of Collins River	Yes
Hollis, James	199	Few, David hr Arthur	Davidson	640	185	7 Mar 1786	728		63	69	On a branch of Halfpone Creek	
Hollis, James	39		Sullivan	200	50	23 Oct 1782	571	25 May 1780	43	261	On Fall Creek	
Hollis, James	427		Washington	450	419	13 Oct 1783	864	30 Dec 1778	52	275	On Holsteins River &c	
Hollis, James	453		Sullivan	420	332	10 Nov 1784	484	6 Oct 1778	69	188	On N fork of Horse Creek	
Hollis, James	59		Sullivan	200	70	23 Oct 1782	233	26 Feb 1780	43	273	On the waters of Fall Creek	
Hollis, James	95		Sullivan	500	106	23 Oct 1782	111	8 Feb 1780	43	288	On the waters of Fall Creek	
Hollway, William	1195		Washington	400	1148	6 Jan 1795	2926	10 Sep 1789	83	176	Conditional line Ezekial Smith &Jno Wheelock	
Hollomon, Aaron	062	Ross, William	Davidson	640			2663	23 Jun 1787			On Ridge bet. Red River & Station Camp	Yes
Holloway, John	1188	Donelson, Stockley	Sumner	640	2716	20 Jul 1796	2491	10 May 1796	88	445	On 1st creek E of Pond Lick Creek	Yes
Holloway, John Jr.	679		Sullivan	200	627	9 Jul 1794	647	12 Jul 1780	81	630	Land between 2 entries by Nathan Page	
Holly, Nathaniel	1325	Shelby, David	Davidson	320	11	18 Aug 1787	506	2 Jul 1784	68	125	On the waters of Sulphur Fork	Yes
Holmes, Andrew	2016	McCulloch, Benj.	Davidson	640	1978	20 May 1793	2456		81	119	On waters of Stones River	Yes
Holmes, Hardy	246		Davidson	2560	232	7 Mar 1786	212		63	85	On waters of Stones River	
Holmes, Richard	363		Western District	3000	369	20 Dec 1791	190	24 Sep 1785	75	219	On N Fork of Forked Deer River	
Holmes, Robert	365		Western District	1200	371	20 Dec 1791	31	13 Sep 1784	75	220	On Waters of S Fork of Rutherfords Fork	
Holmes, Robert	374		Western District	5000	380	20 Dec 1791	191	15 Sep 1784	75	226	On N Fork of Forked Deer River	
Holmes, Shadrack	159	Murphree, Hardy	Davidson	228	145	14 Mar 1786	739		63	55	On Eastens Creek	Yes
Holt, David	985		Hawkins	100	757	27 fEB 1796	216	21 Feb 1780	88	502	On N side of Holston	
Holt, Drury	984		Hawkins	50	756	27 Feb 1796	63	8 Feb 1780	88	502	N side of Clinch River	
Holt, Francis	1055		Washington	300	1005	27 Nov 1792	480	2 Oct 1778	80	178	On S side of Holston River	
Holt, Francis	211	Fenner, Richard	Sullivan	300	218	10 Oct 1783	480	5 Oct 1778	53	166	On S side of Holston River	
Holton, James	780		Davidson	640	753	11 Jul 1788	2190	19 Jul 1786	63	264	On N waters of Sycamore Creek	Yes
Homer, Chas	027	Tyner, Nich.	Tennessee	640			3401				On a branch	
Homer, William	841		Green	100	822	13 Feb 1790	85	3 Feb 1789	73	376	On waters of Bent Creek	
Honey, John	373		Green	200 (300	375	20 Sep 1787	182	10 Nov 1785	65	479	On waters of Nolechuckey	
Honeycut, Austin	431		Hawkins	300	320	5 Jun 1793			80	160	On S side of Holston River &c	
Honeycut, John	429		Hawkins	300	318	5 Jun 1793			80	159	On S side of Holston River &c	
Honeycut, John	430		Hawkins	250	319	5 Jun 1793			80	159	On S side of Holston River &c	
Honeycut, John	432		Hawkins	200	321	5 Jun 1793			80	160	On the S side of Holston River &c	
Honeycut, John	433		Hawkins	190	322	5 Jun 1793			80	160	On the S side of Holston &c	
Honeycut, John	238 /n	Dillonberry, Redmon	Washington	296	105	23 Oct 1782	1360	6 May 1779	47	51	S side of Holston River	
Hood, Archibald	30		Sumner	640			4462	19 Sep 1797			On waters of middle for &c	Yes
Hood, Charles	2150	Rice, John	Davidson	192	2451	31 Dec 1793	667		81	427	On N side of Cumberland River	Yes

Earliest Tennessee Land Records

Claimant:	File #:	Assignee:	County:	Acres:	Grant:	Grant Date:	Entry:	Entry Date:	Bk:	Pg:	Location by Stream Name:	Military:
Hood, Robert	243		Green	175	200	20 Sep 1787	131	31 Oct 1783	65	431	Beg at a white oak	
Hood, William	1804		Davidson	640	377	26 Jun 1793	289	16 Feb 1784	80	334	On Richland Creek	
Hood, William	2059	Love, Robert	Davidson	274	2163	20 May 1793	979		81	164	On N branches of Harpeth River	Yes
Hood, William	830		Hawkins	640	655	5 Dec 1794	2195	12 Nov 1779	83	407	S side of Powells River &c	
Hook, George	330		Tennessee	274	2085	20 May 1793	1879	11 Jul 1785	81	145	On E fork of Bartons Creek	
Hooker, John	1385	Gwin, John	Sumner	274	3310	6 Dec 1797	4088	27 Apr 1797	97	37	On waters of Big Barren	Yes
Hooks, Ephraim	291	Blount, William	Sumner	228	1299	10 Dec 1790	1307	30 Apr 1785	74	365	Beg at sugar tree	Yes
Hooks, John	1731	McCulloh, Benj.	Davidson	640	1446	20 Dec 1791	2000		77	362	On the dividing ridge &c	Yes
Hooks, William	1913	Barton, Saml.	Davidson	640	1686	20 Dec 1793	2731		81	50	On headwaters of Mill Creek	Yes
Hooper, Absolon; Ass.	1416		Davidson	230	33	8 Oct 1787		4 Nov 1784	68	156	On both sides of Whites Creek	
Hooper, Ennis	024	Stothart, Robert	Montgomery	274			4733	Apr 1797			On the Piney Fork	Yes
Hoover, Abraham	582	Saunders, Jacob	Tennessee	640	3029	10 Apr 1797	3937		90	305	S side of Cumberland River	
Hoover, Henry	684	Lenear, James	Davidson	640	657	8 Dec 1787	3460		63	233	On the S & E of Nicholas Coonrod's survey	Yes
Hoover, Henry heirs	684	Lenear, James	Davidson	640	657	8 Dec 1787	3460		63	233	On the S & E of Nicholas Coonrod's survey	Yes
Hoover, Matthias	626		Green	150	667	11 Jul 1788	12	29 Mar 1787	66	449	S/S Nolichuckey River joining Philip Sherreis	Yes
Hopewell, George	634	Wilson, David	Sumner	640	1923	20 May 1793	1032		81	105	On Station Camp	
Hopkin, George	1058		Green	200	901	26 Dec 1791		29 Oct 1783	77	242	N/S of French Broad River on the Sinking Cr	Yes
Hopkins, Agnes	1604		Green	300	1321	4 Feb 1795			84	106	On S side of Noley Chuckey River	
Hopkins, Isaac	055	McCall, Alex.	Middle District	274			1577					
Hopkins, John	753	Lenear, James	Davidson	640	726	11 Jul 1788	2806		63	255	On W of John Elliotts corner	Yes
Hopkins, John	753	Lenear, James	Davidson	640	726	11 Jul 1788	2806		63	255	On W of John Elliotts corner	Yes
Hopkins, Jonathan	422	Cobb, Jesse	Tennessee	1000	2468	31 Dec 1793	1564	21 Feb 1785	81	432	On both main forks of Guesses Creek	Yes
Hopkins, Jos.	86	McKinnie, Wm.	Tennessee	640	1348	10 Dec 1790	949	19 May 1784	74	381	On N side of Cumberland River	Yes
Hopkins, Joseph	458(6)	Wheaton, Charles	Tennessee	400	178	7 Mar 1796	178	10 Jan 1794	88	195	W of the Cumberland Mountain	Yes
Hopkins, Richard	639	Patton, Thomas	Sumner	218	1928	20 May 1793	1357	20 Nov 1786	81	107	On waters of Station Camp Creek	Yes
Hopper, William	774	Wycoff & Clark	Davidson	228	747	11 Jul 1788	1688		63	262	Lying on Gises Creek	Yes
Hopton, John	1226		Green	200	1076	12 Jan 1793	2714	4 Jan 1784	78	349	On S side of Noleychuckey River	
Horalson, Paul	1747		Green	54	372	4 Jul 1797			91	593	N side of Dumplin Creek	
Horalson, Paul	1748		Green	25	373	4 Jul 1797			91	593	N side of Dumplin Creek	
Hord, John	1973	Hains, William	Davidson	640	1867	20 May 1793	3604		81	93	S/S Cumberland Riv on waters of Stones	Yes
Hord, William	827		Hawkins	400	652	5 Dec 1794	1625	2 Feb 1780	83	406	On a fork of Black water	
Hord, William	1154		Hawkins	640	1872	21 Mar 1804	1627	16 Sep 1779	118	322	Beg on a South fork of Sycamore Creek	
Hord, William	133		Hawkins	200	167	26 Dec 1791	1990	19 Oct 1779	75	170	In Powells Valley	
Hord, William	211		Hawkins	600	198	26 Dec 1791	1705	22 Sep 1779	77	312	Powell Valley below Cumberland Gap	
Hord, William	216		Hawkins	300	203	26 Dec 1791	1628	16 Sep 1779	77	314	Lying on the head of War Creek	
Hord, William	636	King, Robert	Hawkins	600	504	27 Nov 1793	2235	22 May 1777	81	502	Near Powells River	
Hord, William	734 /sic/		Hawkins	200	659	5 Dec 1794	215	28 Feb 1785	83	409	In a valley s side of Wallins Ridge	
Hord, William	768		Hawkins	150	608	12 Jul 1794	863	8 Dec 1778	82	214	On the waters of Richland Creek	
Hord, William	824		Hawkins	350	649	5 Dec 1794	1802	8 Oct 1779	83	404	S side of Powells River	
Hord, William	825		Hawkins	300	650	5 Dec 1794	2197	12 Nov 1779	83	405	On the waters of Mulberry Creek &c	
Hord, William	826		Hawkins	640	651	5 Dec 1794	2194	29 Dec 1783	82	405	In Powells Valley on Gap Creek	
Hord, William	828		Hawkins	640	653	5 Dec 1794	1660	17 Sep 1779	83	406	On a creek formerly called Turkey Creek	
Hord, William	829		Hawkins	250	654	5 Dec 1794	2250	22 Nov 1779	83	407	S side of Powells Mountain &c	
Hord, William	831		Hawkins	400	656	5 Dec 1794	2055	10 Oct 1780	83	408	S side of Powells Mountain &c	
Hord, William	832		Hawkins	640	657	5 Dec 1794	1662	17 Sep 1779	83	408	S side of Clinch Mountain	

Claimant:	File #:	Assignee:	Acres:	County:	Grant:	Grant Date:	Entry:	Entry Date:	Bk:	Pg:	Location by Stream Name:	Military:
Hord, William	832		640	Hawkins	657	5 Dec 1794	1662	17 Sep 1779	83	408	Powells Valley above mouth of Old Town Cr	
Hord, William	833		640	Hawkins	658	5 Dec 1794	2191	12 Nov 1779	83	409	Beg at a white oak &c	
Hord, William	835		640	Hawkins	660	5 Dec 1794	2208	12 Nov 1779	83	410	On the waters of Turkey Creek	
Hord, William	836		400	Hawkins	661	5 Dec 1794	2057	10 Oct 1780	83	410	N side of Clinch River	
Hord, William	837		250	Hawkins	662	5 Dec 1794	2254	22 Nov 1779	83	411	On Powells River &c	
Hord, William	838		640	Hawkins	663	5 Dec 1794	1768	9 Oct 1780	83	411	On Mulberry Creek	
Hord, William	839		640	Hawkins	664	5 Dec 1794	1631	2 Feb 1780	83	412	On Clinch River	
Hord, William	840		640	Hawkins	665	5 Dec 1794	1770	1 Oct 1779	83	412	Beg at two white oaks &c	
Hord, William	841		640	Hawkins	666	5 Dec 1794	1667	17 Sep 1779	83	413(5)	S side of Powells River &c	
Hord, William	867		200	Hawkins	643	19 Jan 1795	2238	22 Nov 1779	84	48	On Indian Creek	
Hord, William	868		400	Hawkins	644	19 Jan 1795	1832	16 Aug 1791 (surv	84	48	On S side of Powells River	
Hord, William	874		300	Hawkins	644	5 Dec 1794	2203	2 Nov 1779	84	132	On both sides of Black Water Creek	
Hord, William	875		320	Hawkins	645	5 Dec 1795	2173	1 Nov 1780	84	133	On Powells River	
Hord, William	878		250	Hawkins	648	5 Dec 1794	1941	5 Feb 1780	84	137	In Powells Valley	
Hord, William & Robert King	636		600	Hawkins	504	27 Nov 1793	2235	22 Nov 1779	81	502	Near Powells River	
Horler, Thomas assignee	973		640	Sumner	2437	22 Feb 1795			84	315	On waters of Roaring River	Yes
Horn, Philip	048		150	Sullivan		12 Dec 1780	712				S side of Holstein River	
Hornback, Jno.	561		300	Green	241	20 Sep 1787	1377	1784	66	154	S/S Holstein Riv opposite the big bent /sic/	
Hornback, John	244		100	Green	201	20 Sep 1787	1007	9 Nov 1785	65	431	On the S side of Holston River	
Hornbeck, John	218		200	Hawkins	205	26 Dec 1791	1376	14 Jan 1784	77	315	Valley bet Hornbecks Creek and Lost Creek	
Horner, William	1399		200	Green	1211	27 Nov 1792	216	22 Oct 1783	80	155	On a small branch of Bent Creek	
Horner, William	699		200	Washington	513	10 Nov 1784	2611	13 Aug 1780	69	109	On waters of Sinking Creek	
Horner, William	742		100	Washington	556	10 Nov 1784	837	29 Dec 1778	69	126	On Sinking Creek	
Horner, Wm.	022		200	Washington							On waters of Sinking Creek &c	
Horseford, James	410	Mayberry, Francis	640	Eastern District	2497	10 Nov 1795	3803		89	424	Joining Hendersons N W line	Yes
Horton, James	624	Murphree, Hardy	640	Sumner	1901	20 May 1793	733	17 Dec 1792	81	100	On S side of Cumberland River	Yes
Hoskins, Jesse	64		146	Washington	232	23 Oct 1782	676	9 Dec 1778	44	261	E side of Rones Creek	
Hoskins, John	023		510	Washington			675	9 Dec 1778			On both sides of Rones Creek	
Hoskins, John	243		510	Washington	111	23 Oct 1782			47	54	On both sides of Rones Creek	
Hoss, Jacob	1325		400	Washington	1249	6 Jun 1797	2371	24 Dec 1779	90	308	Waters of Boone Creek	
Hough, Joseph	532		200	Green	534	20 Sep 1787	1458	2 Feb 1784	65	534	On the E side of French Broad River	
Houghton, Joshua	024		524	Washington	94	23 Oct 1782	742	23 Dec 1778			On S side of Wataughar /sic/ River	
Houghton, Joshua	226		352	Washington	175	24 Oct 1782	741	1 May 1779	47	45	N side of Watauga River	
Houghton, Joshua	308		640	Washington	397	24 Oct 1782	740	23 Dec 1778	47	84	S side of Watauga River	
Houghton, Joshua	405		324	Washington	281	13 Oct 1783	1388	22 May 1779	52	264	On the S side of Watauga River	
Houghton, Joshua, Jr.	113		200	Washington		24 Oct 1782			44	288	N side of Watauga River	
Houghton, Thomas	067		500	Sullivan		8 Feb 1780	30					
Houghton, Thomas	177		522	Washington	45	23 Oct 1782	301	10 Jul 1778	47	20	Beg at a white oak & hickory	
Houghton, Thomas	303		640	Middle Dist	209	30 Oct 1794			83	139	Upon a branch of Woolf /sic/ River &c	
House, Geo	062		50	Green		25 Feb 1796	2613				Joining Benjamin Odle &c	
House, George	1187		200	Washington	211	30 Oct 1794	1039		83	140	S of the river Ohio &c	
House, George	1251		100	Green	1101	12 Jan 1793	1039	8 Jan 1779	78	364	Beg. at a forked white oak	
House, George	1303		150	Green	1153	12 Jan 1793	2794	27 Feb 1781	78	396	On waters of Lick Creek	
House, George	1307		100	Green	1157	12 Jan 1793	1250	27 Feb 1779	78	398	On waters of Noleychuckey	
House, George	1603		400	Green	1320	4 Feb 1795	1067	8 Jan 1779	84	106	On waters of Lows Creek	

Earliest Tennessee Land Records

Claimant:	File #:	Assignee:	County:	Acres:	Grant:	Grant Date:	Entry:	Entry Date:	Bk:	Pg:	Location by Stream Name:	Military:
Houser, George	50		Western Dist	5000	50	10 Jul 1788	691	28 Oct 1784	67	299	On Housers Creek &c	
Houston, Daniel	950	Kerr, Joseph	Davidson	640	967	18 May 1789			63	328	On head branches of Gibsons Creek	Yes
Houston, James	464		Middle Dist	5000	403	17 Dec 1794	744	28 Oct 1783	84	263	On S side of Duck River	
Houston, Robert	018		Eastern Dist	300	2174			9 Nov 1779			On waters of Whites Mill Creek	
Houston, Robert	1032		Green	150	1259	29 Jul 1793	252	3 Mar 1780	76	490	N side of Holston River	
Houts, Christopher	1473		Green	275	1237	12 Jul 1794	1631	9 Apr 1784	81	574	On Little Gap Creek	
How, Daniel	1151		Davidson	640	128	17 Apr 1786	364	18 Mar 1786	66	181	On the N side of Big Harpeth	
Howard, Benjamin	1950	Blount, Thomas	Davidson	274	1789	20 May 1793	1553		81	76	On poplar creek a branch of S. Harpeth	Yes
Howard, Edmes /sic/	1142	Harris, Edward	Sumner	640	2648	4 Jun 1796	2459	1 Jun 1795	88	350	Joining said Harris survey	Yes
Howard, Edward	284	Dever, John	Sumner	228	1281	10 Dec 1790	203	28 Jun 1784	74	359	Waters of Middle fork of Station Camp Cre	Yes
Howard, Isaac	355	Donelly, James	Davidson	274	339	4 Sep 1787	550		63	126	On Clear Branch	Yes
Howard, John	045	Dillenberry, Redmon	Sumner	640			4206	3 Apr 1797			E side E Fork of Stones River	Yes
Howard, John	1400		Green	203	1212	27 Nov 1792	377	23 Oct 1783	80	155	Lying on both sides of Bent Creek	
Howard, John	174		Washington	99	42	23 Oct 1782	1754	29 Sep 1779	47	19	On Sinking Creek	
Howard, John, Senr	453		Green	200	455	20 Sep 1787	339	2 Sep 1778	65	503	On a branch of the Long fork	
Howard, Joseph	765		Davidson	274	738	11 Jul 1788	127		63	259	On Big Harpeth River	Yes
Howard, Joshua	129	Marchant, McCaleb	Davidson	274	115	7 Mar 1786	833		63	45	On both sides Whites & Heatons Creek	Yes
Howard, Joshua	1842		Davidson	320	342	27 Nov 1792	304	17 Feb 1784	81	7	On Willer Creek	
Howard, Richard	8	Mountflorence, J. C.	Tennessee	640	1156	26 Nov 1792	2131	9 Sep 1785	74	157	On N side of Sulphur Fork	Yes
Howard, Rich'd	288		Hawkins	150	299	14 Jan 1793	2289	27 Nov 1779	78	346	On N side of Holston River	
Howard, Solomon	511	Barker, Thomas	Davidson	220	483	15 Sep 1787	714		63	175	On S Fork of Red River	Yes
Howard, Thomas	687	Campbell, James	Sumner	320	131	27 Apr 1793	840	12 Dec 1792	81	36	On S side of Cumberland River	Yes
Howard, William	406	Lanier, James	Davidson	640	378	15 Sep 1787	3464		63	141	S side of Big Barren River	Yes
Howdyshall, Henry	1122		Davidson	640	99	17 Apr 1786	113	26 Jan 1784	66	174	Lying on Ashers Creek &c	
Howel, Ebenezer	2415	McConnell, Robert	Davidson	640	3208	14 Sep 1797			92	7	Waters of E Fork of S. Harpeth	Yes
Howel, John	03	Howel, John	Tennessee	640			1442	20 Nov 1784			Rite /sic/ hand fork of the 1st large creek	Yes
Howel, Taliaferro	033	McConnell, Robert	Tennessee	1000			4449	22 Dec 1796			S side of Cumberland River	Yes
Howel, Daniel	757	Wycoff & Clark	Davidson	640	730	11 Jul 1788	1980		63	257	On N side of Cumberland River	Yes
Howel, David W.	568		Hawkins	300	442	29 Jul 1793	813	7 Jul 1785	80	287	S side of Holston River on Lyons Creek	
Howel, David Wessel	551		Hawkins	200	424	29 Jul 1793	980	23 Jun 1784	80	283	On the S side of Holston River	
Howel, Frederick	2454	Good, William	Davidson	640	3350	12 Dec 1797	1441		98	184	On the waters of Harpeth River	Yes
Howel, Hall	1088		Hawkins	739	817	4 Jul 1797	2381	11 Apr 1790	91	598	S side of Holston River	
Howel, Henry	2349	Smith, John	Davidson	640	3011	10 Apr 1797	3642		90	298	Waters of Little Harpeth	Yes
Howel, Henry	999		Hawkins	300	701	27 Aug 1795	1374	20 May 1779	89	416	Beg at an ash	
Howel, Jesse	815	Looney, David	Sumner	640	2285	20 May 1793	278	21 Nov 1784	81	188	On N side of Cumberland River	Yes
Howel, John	134	Barton, Samuel	Tennessee	640	1644	23 Feb 1793	2651	30 Sep 1785	76	334	S side of Cumberland River &c	Yes
Howel, John	523	Douglass, Reuben	Davidson	640	495	15 Sep 1787	207		63	179	On waters of Station Camp Creek	Yes
Howel, John	523	Douglas, Reubin	Davidson	640	495	15 Sep 1787	207		63	179	On waters of Station Camp Creek	Yes
Howel, John, assignee	343		Sumner	640	1410	20 Dec 1791	2048	25 Nov 1789	77	354	On the S side of Cumberland River	Yes
Howel, John, assignee	353		Sumner	640	1440	20 Dec 1791	2365	25 Nov 1789	77	361	S side of Cumberland River	Yes
Howel, Peter	048	Fenner, Richard	Not given	640								Yes
Howel, Taliferro	2410	McConnell, Robert	Davidson	1000	3203	14 Sep 1797			92	5	S side of Cumberland river	Yes
Howel, Tatum & Wiggins	2438	Hair, John	Davidson	640	3280	6 Dec 1797	4266		98	160	On the waters of West fork of Stones River	Yes
Howel, Thomas	566		Hawkins	200	440	29 Jul 1793	659	20 Jul 1780	80	287	S side of Holston River &c	
Howser, John	331		Sullivan	97	471	10 Jul 1788	1800	5 Oct 1779	67	482	To include the double springs	

Claimant:	File #:	Assignee:	County:	Acres:	Grant:	Grant Date:	Entry:	Entry Date:	Bk:	Pg:	Location by Stream Name:	Military:
Howser, John	702		Washington	200	516	10 Nov 1784	2310	27 Nov 1779	69	110	On branches of Lick Creek	
Howser, Nicholas /sic/	328		Sullivan	50	468	10 Jul 1788	1799	5 Oct 1779	67	480	On both sides of Cherokee Creek	
Howson, Nicholas /sic/	794		Sullivan	52	726	2 Dec 1796	441,-825	1780,-1781	91	278	Begin at said Howser's /sic/ corner	
Hubbard, James	64		Green	1000	22	1 Nov 1786	492	25 Oct 1784	59	386	N side of Tennessee River	
Hubbard, James	809		Washington	150	623	10 Nov 1784	2809	5 Mar 1781	69	145	Beg at a red oak	
Hubbard, James & Wm. Tho	877		Green	600	837	27 Nov 1789	802	29 Oct 1783	74	34	On N side of Tennessee River	
Hubbart, Jas. & W. T. Lewis	89		Green	600	47	1 Nov 1786	747	28 Oct 1783	59	408	N side of French Broad	
Hubbart, James	0126		Green	400	111	1 Nov 1780	40	21 Oct 1783			N side of French Broad River	
Hubbart, James	1598		Green	200	1340	22 Feb 1795			83	439	N side of French Broad River	
Hubbart, James	248		Green	250	205	20 Sep 1787	42	21 Oct 1783	65	432	On the N side of French Broad River	
Hubbart, James	34		Green	600	97	1 Nov 1786	39	21 Oct 1783	58	458	On an island in French Broad River	
Hubbart, James	37		Green	400	100	1 Nov 1786	1062	3 Jan 1779	58	461	On the N side of French Broad River	
Hubbart, James	48		Green	400	111	1 Nov 1786	392	21 Oct 1783	58	472	Upon the N side of French Broad River	
Hubbart, James	585		Green	100	266	20 Sep 1787	350	22 Oct 1783	66	162	On Dumplin Creek &c	
Hubbart, Jas. & W.T. Lewis	89		Green	600	47	1 Nov 1786	747	28 Oct 1783	39	408	N side of French Broad	
Hubbart, Zebulon	573	Keay, Jonathan	Davidson	228	545	15 Sep 1787	1805		63	196	On Red River	Yes
Hubbert, James	1080		Green	200	923	26 Dec 1791	270	9 Mar 1780	77	250	On Dumplin Creek	
Hubbert, James	1086		Green	300	929	26 Dec 1791	2503	27 Mar 1780	77	252	On the N side of French Broad River	
Hubbert, James	182		Green	200	652	11 Jul 1788	1524	24 Feb 1784	64	359	On the N side of Dumplin Creek	
Huberts, Anthony	1120	Harris, Edward	Sumner	640	2626	4 Jun 1796	2726	1 Jun 1795	88	343	Joining said Harris survey	Yes
Hubert, James	789		Green	400	594	23 Aug 1788	41	1 Nov 1786	68	260	Lying on the N side of the French Broad Riv	
Huck, John	285		Middle Dist	1000	239	30 Dec 1793	2291	12 Jan 1785	82	146	On the waters of the E fork of Stones River	
Huck, Thomas	1722	McCullough, Benj.	Davidson	640	1418	20 Dec 1791	1999		77	356	On the dividing ridge	Yes
Hudder, John	647	Caswell, Wm hr Wm.	Davidson	640	620	15 Sep 1787	483		63	220	N side of Joseph Brock's entry	Yes
Huddleston, Robert	1445	Overton, John	Sumner	640	3357	25 May 1800	1144	17 Feb 1797	108	40	On a W Fork of Dixons Creek	Yes
Huddleston, Robert	1683	Overton, John	Davidson	640	1616	23 Feb 1793	1144		76	320	On an Eastern branch of the W Fork of Har	Yes
Huddleston, William	1680	Clark, Lardner	Davidson	640	1608	23 Feb 1793	1143		76	316	On the waters of Richland Creek	Yes
Hudgen, Holder	1061	King, William	Sumner	640	2538	10 Dec 1795	1830	8 Aug 1795	88	292	On a creek called Lick Creek	Yes
Hudgins, James	1238	Donelson, Stockley	Sumner	640	2814	12 Jan 1797	3801	7 Aug 1796	90	28	On Martin's Creek	Yes
Hudler, Joseph	210	Caswell, William	Tennessee	640	1500	4 Jan 1792	480	9 Mar 1784	77	375	S side of Cumberland River &c	Yes
Hudler, Lemuel	669	Caswell, William	Tennessee	274	3343	6 Dec 1797	481		97	59	On Red River	Yes
Hudlow, Joseph	2432	Mann, John	Davidson	640	3260	6 Dec 1797	4611 /sic/		98	147	On the waters of first Creek	Yes
Hudson, Chamberlain	1960	Smith, Robert	Davidson	640	1805	20 May 1793	1464		81	80	On Hays Creek	Yes
Hudson, George	247	Dix, William	Sumner	640	1152	26 Nov 1789	1428	21 Sep 1787	74	155	On waters of Bradleys Lick Creek	Yes
Hudson, Miles	1669	Robertson, James	Davidson	274	1593	23 Feb 1793	3611		76	309	On the waters of Richland Creek	Yes
Hues, David	25		Washington	200			1145	30 Jan 1779			On Coopers Creek	
Hues, Francis	387		Washington	300	379	13 Oct 1783	23	25 Feb 1778	52	255	On Camp Creek	
Hues, Henry	19		Sullivan	200	30	23 Oct 1782	519	28 Apr 1780	43	251	Beg at a hickory & beech	
Hues, Henry	38		Sullivan	200	49	23 Oct 1782	631	5 Jul 1780	43	261	On a branch of Reedy Creek	
Hues, John	278		Washington	200	146	23 Oct 1782	853	30 Dec 1778	47	71	On a branch of Buffalow Creek	
Hues, William	026		Washington	189			2642	9 Sep 1780			Beg at a poplar cor to Jno. Stuart	
Hues, William	258		Washington	200	126	23 Oct 1782	821	29 Dec 1778	47	62	On Aulston Choles Branch	
Hues, William	683		Washington	50	497	10 Nov 1784	2868	4 Jun 1781	69	104	Joining E & W line of tract &c	
Huff, John	176		Green	400	646	11 Jul 1788	176	7 Oct 1783	64	357	On the N side of French Broad River	
Huff, Peter	955		Green	300	869	17 Nov 1790	19	21 Oct 1783	76	128	N side of French Broad River	

Claimant:	File #:	Assignee:	County:	Acres:	Grant:	Grant Date:	Entry:	Entry Date:	Bk:	Pg:	Location by Stream Name:	Military:
Huffman, David	707		Washington	146	521	10 Nov 1784	1297	23 Mar 1779	69	112	On Cherokee Creek	
Huffman, Peter	545		Sullivan	312	528	17 Nov 1790	243	27 Jun 1778	76	187	Both sides of Horse Creek &c	
Huffman, Daniel	692		Sullivan	150	640	9 Jul 1794			81	635	On S side of Holston River	
Huggins, James	139		Middle District	1000	141	10 Jul 1788	418	25 Oct 1783	67	477	On the S side of Duck River, &c	
Hughes, Bartley	029	Dillonberry, Redmon	Sumner	640			4389	14 Oct 1797			On dividing ridge &c	Yes
Hughes, Burwell	2258		Davidson	640	2722	20 Jul 1796	2930		88	450	On waters of Hurricane & Harts Spring Cre	Yes
Hughes, David	234		Sullivan	150	373	9 Aug 1787	790,-2130	1779 & 1781	61	392	On White Top Creek	
Hughes, David	321		Washington	600	188	24 Oct 1782	269	24 Jul 1778	49	221	On both sides of Little Limestone Creek	
Hughes, Frances	1265		Green	640	1115	12 Jan 1793	2338	5 Sep 1792	78	373	On S side Nolichuckey River	
Hughes, Henry	492		Davidson	640	467	15 Sep 1787	963		63	169	On Middle Fork of Station Camp Creek	Yes
Hughes, James	235		Sullivan	220	374	9 Aug 1787	223	22 Feb 1780	61	393	On White Top Creek	
Hughes, James	818		Sullivan	200	761	17 Nov 1797	1105	18 May 1773			On White Top Creek	
Hughlet, William	051	Lynch, George hrs.	Middle District	640			2526					
Hughlet, James hrs.	052	Lanbrick, James hrs.	Middle District	640			2524					
Hughlet, William	443	Freeman, Nathan	Davidson	640	415	15 Sep 1787	64		63	154	On S side of Cumberland River	Yes
Hughlett, William	037	Harris, Hardy heirs	Middle District	640			2728					
Hughlett, William	042	Mott, Abraham heirs	Middle District	640			2138					
Hughlett, William	043	Long, James heirs	Middle District	640			2668					
Hughlett, William	044	Ash, Stephan heirs	Middle District	640			2830					
Hughlett, William	046	Bunnett, John heirs	Middle District	640			2794					
Hughlett, William	047	Merrell, Henry heirs	Middle District	640	2		2750					
Hughlett, William	113		Western District	500	113	10 Jul 1788	463	25 Oct 1783	67	324	On the N Fork of Forked Deer River &c	
Hughlett, William	1201		Green	600	1045	Mar 1792			77	338	On the Whitehorn Fork of Bent Creek	
Hughlett, William	26		Western District	500	26	10 Jul 1788	998	29 Oct 1783	67	290	On the S Fork of Forked Deer River	
Hughlett, William	391		Green	600	393	20 Sep 1787	1291	7 Jun 1784	65	483	On the Whitehorn Fork of Bent Creek	
Hughlett, William	579	Vaughan, Abraham	Davidson	640	551	15 Sep 1787	930		63	198	On both sides of second large branch	Yes
Hughlett, William	925	Boone, Jacob heirs	Davidson	640	941	18 May 1789	2831		63	322	On the waters of Sulphur Fork	Yes
Hughlett, William	983		Sumner	640	2448	22 Feb 1795			84	320	On E side of W Fork of Obeys River	Yes
Hughlett, William, Assignee	960		Sumner	640	2423	22 Feb 1795			84	308	On E side of W Fork of Obeys River	Yes
Hughlett, William, Assignee	962		Sumner	640	2425	22 Feb 1795			84	309	On E side of W Fork of Obeys River	Yes
Hughlett, William, Assignee	964		Sumner	640	2427	22 Feb 1795			84	310	On E side of W Branch of Obeys River	Yes
Hughlett, William, Assignee	965		Sumner	640	2428	22 Feb 1795			84	310	On E side of W Fork of Obeys River	Yes
Hughlett, William, Assignee	969		Sumner	640	2432	22 Feb 1795			84	312	On E side of W Fork of Obeys River	Yes
Hughlett, Wm.	045	Berry, John heirs	Middle District	640	2793							
Hughlett, Wm., Assignee	985		Sumner	640	2450	22 Feb 1795			84	321	On E side of W Fork of Obeys River	Yes
Hughlett, Wm., Assignee	990		Sumner	640	2472	22 Feb 1795			84	324	On E side of W Fork of Obeys River	Yes
Hughitt, William	331		Western District	3000	331	18 May 1793	1082	30 Oct 1783	72	273	On the Obrian /sic/ River	
Hughs, Aaron	1238		Green	500	1088	12 Jan 1793	502	24 Mar 1786	78	357	On N side of Holston	
Hughs, Abner	047		Sullivan	150	1088		544	9 Apr 1780			Beg at a white oak & Sugar tree	
Hughs, Aron	0136		Green	500	1088	12 Jan 1793	502				N side Holston	
Hughs, Burwell	2258	Doneison, Stockley	Davidson	640	2722	20 Jul 1796	2930		88	450	On waters of Hurricane & Harts Spring Cre	Yes
Hughs, David	767		Sullivan	150	698	20 Jul 1796	2130,-790	1779 & 1781	91	82	Beg, at a pine & white oak	
Hughs, David, Assignee	354		Sumner	274	1450	20 Dec 1791	3483	11 Oct 1786	77	363	On the N side of Red River	Yes
Hughs, Frances /sic/	066		Green	50	262	23 Oct 1782	967	9 Oct 1797			On the head of Mill Fork of Big Limestone	
Hughs, Francis /sic/	94		Washington	99	262	23 Oct 1782	967	2 Jan 1779	44	279	On waters of Sinking Creek	

Claimant:	File #:	Assignee:	County:	Acres:	Grant:	Grant Date:	Entry:	Entry Date:	Bk:	Pg:	Location by Stream Name:	Military:
Hughs, George	065	Sheppard, John	Not given	640	297	10 Nov 1784	2849	15 Aug 1792	69	175	On Obeys River	Yes
Hughs, Henry	418		Sullivan	200	582	27 Jun 1793	814	28 Jun 1781	80	376	On S side of Holstin River	
Hughs, Henry	634		Sullivan	150	582	27 Jun 1793	544	29 Apr 1780	80	376	On the waters of Reedy Creek	
Hughs, Henry	636		Sullivan	100	584	27 Jun 1793	250	3 Mar 1780	80	377	On a fork of Reedy Creek	
Hughs, James	818		Sullivan	200	761	17 Nov 1797	1105	18 May 1773	94	157	N side of Holstin River	
Hughs, Robert	1284		Green	100	1134	12 Jan 1793			78	385	On waters of Long Creek	
Hughs, Thomas	534		Sullivan	424	529	13 Feb 1791	410	11 Apr 1780	73	384	On White Top &c	
Hughs, Thomas	888		Washington	99	865	27 Nov 1789	404	19 Sep 1778	74	35	Bet. Watauga & Holstien /sic/ Rivers	
Hughs, William	1240		Washington	85	1212	20 Jul 1796	2422	1 Feb 1780	88	505	Line bet. Sullivan and Washington Counties	
Hughs, William	847		Green	400	828	13 Feb 1791	1004	1 May 1790	73	377	On the waters of Dumpling Creek	
Huglett, William, Assignee	983		Sumner	640	2448	22 Feb 1795			84	320	On E side of W Fork of Obeys River	Yes
Hugs, Nathaniel	116		Davidson	316	102	7 Mar 1786	27		63	41	On Sinking Creek	Yes
Hules /?/, William	785		Sullivan	68	717	2 Dec 1796	825	26 Jul 1781	91	274	Beg at Archibald McGahagans corner	
Humphrees, William	1136		Washington	50	1094	12 Jul 1794	2983	24 Sep 1783	81	567	Upon the Ceader /sic/ Branch	
Humphrey, Joseph	2118	Weakley, Robert	Davidson	640	2382	14 Dec 1793 /?/	1328		81	385	On S side of Big Harpeth River	yes
Humphrey, Richard	100		Washington	150	268	24 Oct 1782	342	2 Sep 1778	44	282	N side of Noleychuckey River	
Humphries, David	633	Hays, James	Sumner	640	1917	20 May 1793	2570	22 Dec 1792	81	104	On head waters of S of Cedar Lick Creek	Yes
Humphries, David, Assignee	872		Sumner	274	2388	7 Jan 1794	1093	19 Dec 1792	81	388	On E side of Cedar Lick Creek	Yes
Humphries, Elijah	633	Reaves, David heirs	Hawkins	640	2391	8 Jan 1794			81	389	In Powells Valley	
Humphries, Elijah	871		Sumner	640	1287 (a)	7 Jan 1794	2858	12 Oct 1792	81	387	On a small creek &c	Yes
Humphries, Henry	886	Sugg, Geo. Augustus	Davidson	640	902	17 Jan 1789	2457		63	312	On E side of main E Fork of Stones River	Yes
Humphries, James	651	Wilson, David	Sumner	166	1958	20 May 1793	3697	20 Sep 1791	81	114	On waters of Station Camp Creek	Yes
Humphries, Randolph	180	Hill, Green	Davidson	640	166	7 Mar 1786	811		63	63	On waters of Little Harper /sic/ & Mill Creek	Yes
Humphries, William	626	R /?/ Hannah	Sumner	640	1904	20 May 1793	2343	13 Dec 1792	81	101	On a small fork of Roaring River	yes
Humphry, Jno	627		Washington	100	721	26 Oct 1786	2495	11 Mar 1780	66	21	On Watauga River &c	
Hunbar /?/, Samuel	1067		Green	50	910	26 Dec 1791	184	12 Nov 1779	77	245	On the waters of Lick Creek	
Huneycut, Alston	136		Washington	175	351	24 Oct 1782	1551	25 Aug 1779	45	274	On the S side of Holston River &c	
Huneycutt, Jno	132		Washington	300	347	23 Oct 1782	630	24 Nov 1778	45	267	On Dry Creek	
Huneycutt, Jno.	133		Washington	163	348	23 Oct 1782	628	24 Nov 1778	45	267	On the S side of Holston River	
Hunnecut, Alston	134		Washington	100	349	23 Oct 1782	1357	6 May 1779	45	267	On the S side of Holston River &c	
Hunneycut, John	0103		Washington	300			630	25 Nov 1778				
Hunneycutt, Jno.	135		Washington	250	360	23 Oct 1782	629	24 Nov 1778	45	268	On the S side of Holston River	
Hunneycutt, John	248		Washington	98	116	23 Oct 1782	631	24 Nov 1778	47	57	S side of Holston River	
Hunt, Anderson	445		Middle District	5000	364	17 Dec 1794	539	27 Oct 1783	84	253	On S side of Duck River	
Hunt, David	208	Marshall, John	Sumner	640	1133	26 Nov 1789	1619	21 Jan 1786	74	135	On both sides of a Creek	yes
Hunt, Elisha	155		Davidson	640	141	4 Mar 1786	117		63	54	On head of Long Fork of Sycamore Creek	yes
Hunt, James	591	Ballentine, Maltise	Robertson	640	3060		3753	24 Dec 1796			W waters of Spring Creek	
Hunt, James	038	Maltrie	Tennessee	640	3060	19 Jul 1797			90	374	W waters of Spring Creek	
Hunt, Jesse	1003		Washington	136	975	26 Dec 1791	2028	26 Oct 1779	77	301	On the waters of Sinking Creek	
Hunt, Jesse	1009		Washington	80	981	26 Dec 1791	2621	1 Aug 1780	77	303	Joining an entry &c	
Hunt, John	100		Hawkins	500	134	26 Dec 1791			75	155	On N side of Holston River	
Hunt, John	205		Eastern District	200	177	8 Apr 1794			81	560	Bet. First and Second Creek	
Hunt, John	73		Hawkins	100	73	26 Nov 1789	639	10 Jul 1780	73	3	On the N side of Holston River &c	
Hunt, John	976		Hawkins	40	748	20 Jul 1796	161	4 Sep 1780	88	499	On Second Creek	
Hunt, John, Jr.	096		Sullivan	100			1278	12 Mar 1779			On a branch of Holson River	

Claimant:	File #:	Assignee:	County:	Acres:	Grant:	Grant Date:	Entry:	Entry Date:	Bk:	Pg:	Location by Stream Name:	Military:
Hunt, John, Jr.	605		Sullivan	100	560	26 Dec 1791	1356	13 Jul 1786	77	306	Joining Wm. Mitchells line	
Hunt, Memucan /?/	145	Glaze, Samuel	Davidson	1000	131	14 Mar 1786	860		63	51	West Fork of Harpeth River	yes
Hunt, Mimican	341		Western District	5000	348	10 Aug 1791	1841	24 Apr 1784	75	88	2nd large creek that emptied into Tenn. River	
Hunt, Mimucam	357		Western District	5000	364	10 Aug 1791	1857	24 Apr 1784	75	93	On waters of S Fork of Obion River	
Hunt, Mimucan	342		Western District	5000	349	10 Aug 1791	1842	24 Apr 1784	75	88	2nd large creek that empties into Tenn. River	
Hunt, Mimucan	343		Western District	5000	350	10 Aug 1791		24 Apr 1784	75	89	30 mi nearly due W course fr mouth Duck Riv	
Hunt, Mimucan	344		Western District	5000	351	10 Aug 1791	1844	24 Apr 1784	75	89	On Beaver Creek	
Hunt, Mimucan	345		Western District	5000	352	10 Aug 1791	1845	24 Apr 1784	75	89	On Beaver Creek	
Hunt, Mimucan	346		Western District	5000	353	10 Aug 1791	1846	24 Apr 1784	75	90	On Beaver Creek	
Hunt, Mimucan	347		Western District	5000	354	10 Aug 1791	1847	24 Apr 1784	75	90	On right hand fork of Beaver Creek	
Hunt, Mimucan	348		Western District	5000	355	10 Aug 1791	1848	24 Apr 1784	75	90	On waters of Beaver Creek	
Hunt, Mimucan	349		Western District	5000	356	10 Aug 1791	1849	24 Apr 1784	75	91	On waters of Beaver Creek	
Hunt, Mimucan	350		Western District	5000	357	10 Aug 1791	1850	24 Apr 1784	75	91	On waters of Beaver Creek	
Hunt, Mimucan	351		Western District	5000	358	10 Aug 1791	1851	24 Apr 1784	75	91	On waters of Beaver Creek	
Hunt, Mimucan	352		Western District	5000	359	10 Aug 1791	1852	24 Apr 1784	75	92	On waters of Beaver Creek	
Hunt, Mimucan *	353		Western District	5000	360	10 Aug 1791	1853	24 Apr 1784	75	92	On crooked Creek	
Hunt, Mimucan	354		Western District	5000	361	10 Aug 1791	1855	24 Apr 1784	75	92	On Crooked Creek	
Hunt, Mimucan	355		Western District	5000	362	10 Aug 1791	1855	24 Apr 1784	75	93	On Crooked Creek	
Hunt, Mimucan	356		Western District	5000	363	10 Aug 1791	1856	24 Apr 1784	75	93	On waters of S Fork of Obion River	
Hunt, Mimucan /?/	340		Western District	5000	347	10 Aug 1791	1757	22 Apr 1784	75	91	On waters of S Fork of Obion River &c	
Hunt, Minecan /?/	338		Western District	5000	345	10 Aug 1791	1755	22 Apr 1784	75	88	2nd large creek that empties in Tenn. River	
Hunt, Minucan	339		Western District	5000	346	10 Aug 1791	1756	27 Apr 1784	75	87	2nd large creek that empties into Tenn. River	
Hunt, Uriah	1006		Washington	250	978	26 Dec 1791	1778	25 Dec 1778	77	302	On the waters of Sinking Creek	
Hunt, Uriah	159		Washington	300	27	23 Oct 1782	671	9 Dec 1778	47	12	On both sides of Boons Creek	
Hunt, Uriah	24		Washington	119	79	23 oct 1782	1494	29 Jul 1779	47	38	On waters of Boons Creek	
Hunter, Caleb	318		Washington	93	185	24 Oct 1782	297	4 Aug 1778	49	219	On the waters of Mill Creek	
Hunter, Caleb	422		Washington	166	414	13 oct 1783	1484	26 Jul 1779	52	272	On the waters of Big Limestone	
Hunter, Elisha	45	Hadley, Joshua	Sumner	640	900	17 Jan 1789	3077	10 Nov 1787	63	311	On the ridge that divides &c	yes
Hunter, James	1490		Davidson	640		27 Nov 1789			74	37	On waters of Spencers Creek	yes
Hunter, James	1493	Hitchcock, Wm heirs	Davidson	640	1046	27 Nov 1794	3356		74	47	On waters of Spencers Creek	yes
Hunter, James	392		Middle District	1000	331	17 Dec 1794	1944	29 Apr 1784	84	220	On E Fork of Stones River	
Hunter, James	394		Middle District	1000	333	17 Dec 1794	1946	29 Apr 1784	84	221	On Stones River	
Hunter, James	842		Washington	300	656	10 Nov 1784	1972	19 Oct 1779	69	153	Joining Hosea Rose &c	
Hunter, Jas or Alex Nelson	360		Middle District	1500	299	17 Dec 1794	1949	29 Apr 1784	84	207	On N side of Duck River	
Hunter, John	546		Washington	57	811	11 Jul 1788	2753	26 Jan 1781	64	333	On ---- /sic/ or near Cherokee Cr	
Hunter, John, Sr.	1052		Washington	200	1002	27 Nov 1792	1732	25 Sep 1779	80	177	On the waters of Branch Creek	
Hunter, John, Sr.*	518		Washington	170	781	16 Aug 1787	2450	23 Feb 1780	64	146	Beg on Taylor's line &c	
Hunter, Robert	396		Green	200	398	20 Sep 1787	103	26 Feb 1778	65	485	On the N side of Holston River	
Hunter, Robt.	0121		Green	200	398	20 Sep 1787	811	29 Oct 1783			Bet. Richland & Gearman Creek	
Hunter, Solomon	66	Jones, Seburn	Tennessee	1000	1304	10 Dec 1790	3353	15 Jun 1790	74	367	On N side of Duck River	
Hunter, Theophilus	60		Middle District	3316 (23	62	10 Jul 1788	763	28 Oct 1783	67	441	On N side of Cumberland River	yes
Hunter, Timothy	067	Sheppard, John	Middle District	640			2926				On S side of Duck River &c	
Huse, David	025		Washington	200			1145	30 Jan 1779				yes
Huse, Samuel	023	Cates, Joshua	not given	640			4307					yes

Claimant:	File #:	Assignee:	County:	Acres:	Grant:	Grant Date:	Entry:	Entry Date:	Bk:	Pg:	Location by Stream Name:	Military:
Huss, Francis	387		Washington	300	379	13 Oct 1782	23	25 Feb 1778	52	255	On Camp Creek	
Huston, Archibald	317		Middle District	800	293	17 Dec 1794	1815	23 Apr 1784	83	334	On the headwaters of Caney Spring Creek	
Huston, James	806		Green	640	800	19 Nov 1788	5	24 Feb 1778	70	6	On the N side of French Broad River	
Hutcheson, James	949		Green	100	863	17 Nov 1790	1034	29 Oct 1783	76	126	S side of Nolechuckey River	
Hutcheson, William	1106		Green	150	949	26 Dec 1791	82	16 Mar 1788	77	262	On the waters of Cove Creek	
Hutchings, Edward	983	Bright, Simon	Davidson	1000	1000	18 May 1789	2786		63	336	On N side of Cumberland River	yes
Hutchings, Thomas	069		Green	600			1062	30 Oct 1783			On the waters of Bull Run	
Hutchings, Thomas	16		Eastern District	640	16	11 Jul 1788	478	25 Apr 1780	67	346	On McCrarys Creek of Holston River	
Hutchings, Thomas	17		Eastern District	400	17	11 Jul 1788	938	25 Jun 1784	67	347	On Beaverdam Creek	
Hutchings, Thomas	18		Eastern District	640	18	11 Jul 1788	1015	29 Oct 1783	67	347	On McCrarys Creek of Holston River &c	
Hutchings, Thomas	19		Eastern District	640	19	11 Jul 1788			67	347	On Beaverdam Creek	
Hutchings, Thomas	20		Eastern District	640	20	11 Jul 1788	659	-- Nov ---	67	348	Adj James Whites survey on Sinking Creek	
Hutchings, Thomas	21		Eastern District	500	21	11 Jul 1788	917	29 Oct 1783	67	348	On Beaverdam Creek	
Hutchings, Thomas	22		Eastern District	640	22	11 Jul 1788	352	24 Mar 1780	67	349	On waters of Sinking Creek of Holston River	
Hutchings, Thomas	23		Eastern District	300	23	11 Jul 1788	432	19 Apr 1780	67	349	On Beaverdam Creek	
Hutchings, Thomas	459	Sutherland, George	Tennessee	274	2529	8 Dec 1795	1520	20 Jan 1785	88	280	On both sides of Sulphur Fork	
Hutchins, James	1563	Buchanan, John	Davidson	640	1185	30 Nov 1790	1095		74	316	On waters of Millcreek	yes
Hutchins, Robert	301	Mountflorence, Jas C.	Davidson	640	287	22 Mar 1787	2033		63	107	S side of Cumberland River	yes
Hutchins, Smith (?)	325		Green	200	327	20 Sep 1787	94	17 Jan 1784	65	466	On the waters of Lick Creek	
Hutsen, Chamberlain	355	McFarland, Walter	Tennessee	640	2185	20 May 1793	2139	9 Sep 1785	81	167	On the waters of Bartons Creek	yes
Hutson, Chamberlain, Ass	1404		Sumner	640	3334	6 Dec 1797	263	1 May 1797	97	53	On waters of Big Barren	yes
Hutson, Isaac	1001	Nichols, John	Davidson	640	1018	18 May 1789	1764		63	341	On Weakley Creek	yes
Hutson, John	481	Marshall, John	Davidson	640	453	15 Sep 1787	1610		63	165a	On Money Fork Creek	
Hutton, William	1136		Green	1200	979	26 Dec 1791	745	13 Feb 1781	77	274	On Bakers Creek	
Hutton, William	428		Washington	200	420	13 Oct 1783	873	31 Dec 1778	52	275	On the Little Limestone Creek	Yes
Hy, Abraham	2262	Donelson, Stockley	Davidson	640	2726	20 July 1796	448		88	451	Waters of Stones River	yes
Hyde, Andrew	420	Dyer, Joel	Eastern District	110	2946	1 Mar 1797	4490		90	216	Joining lines with James Armstrong	
Hyland, James	258		Sullivan	300	397	9 Aug 1787	1930	15 Oct 1779	61	416	On Calvats (?) Creek	
Hyland, James	35		Hawkins	344	67	7 Apr 1790			71	287	On the S side of Holston River	
Hynds, Jno.	219	Mayberry, Frances	Middle District	4400	199	24 Jun 1793	531	27 Oct 1783	80	189	On Wolf River	yes
Hynes, Hardy	724	Sheppard, Nancy	Davidson	640	697	11 Jul 1788	1760		63	245	On waters of Sulphur Fork	
Hynight, Thos.	046		Sullivan	200			667	12 Aug 1780			On Beaverdam Creek	
Iddens, Benjamin	1417		Green	20	1229	27 Nov 1792	3	20 Dec 178(?)	80	163	On the head of Sinking Creek	yes
Igley, Samuel	128	Armstrong, Richard	Tennessee	640	1634	23 Feb 1793	2808	30 Sep 1785	76	329	On the waters of Wells Creek	
Illegible	0104 (?)		Sullivan									
Ingles, John	442		Davidson	3840	414	15 Sep 1787	294		63	153	On waters of Bledsoes Creek	yes
Ingles, Thomas	19		Hawkins	400	15	23 Aug 1788	99	21 Oct 1783	67	434	On the S side of Holston River &c	
Ingles, Thomas	803		Green	100	608	23 Aug 1788	2679	11 Dec 1780	65	265	Beg on the E side of McCartneys branch	
Inglish, William	541		Green	640	543	20 Sep 1787		29 Dec 1778	65	538	Situate on House Creek	
Ingram, Andrew	117		Hawkins	300	151	26 Dec 1791			75	164	On both sides of the Nose Branch	
Ingram, Edwin	745		Washington	300	559	10 Nov 1784	185	19 Mar 1778	69	127	On head spring of Buffaloe Creek	
Ingram, John	358		Hawkins	100	351	8 Mar 1793	2664	14 Nov 1780	78	485	On S side of Holston River	
Ingram, Mary	711		Sullivan	388	656	5 Dec 1794	41	8 Feb 1780	84	163	On Caney Creek	
Ingram, William	713		Sullivan	222	658	4 Dec 1794	1723	20 Sep 1779	84	164	In Carters Valley	
Ingram, William	701		Sullivan	200	646	5 Dec 1794	45	8 Feb 1780	84	159	On Caney Creek	

Earliest Tennessee Land Records

Claimant:	File #:	Assignee:	County:	Acres:	Grant:	Grant Date:	Entry:	Entry Date:	Bk:	Pg:	Location by Stream Name:	Military:
Ingram, William	709		Sullivan	276	654	5 Dec 1794	40	8 Feb 1780	84	162	On Caney Creek	
Ingram, William	717		Sullivan	457	662	4 Dec 1794	625	24 Jun 1780	84	167	On Caney Creek	
Ingrim, George	963	Donelson, Stokley	Davidson	640	980	18 May 1789			63	332	On both sides of a fork of Smiths Fork	yes
Inman, Abednego	216		Green	100	173	20 Sep 1787	308	23 Oct 1783	65	421	On the S side of Holston River	
Inman, Abednego	6		Green	150	69	10 Nov 1786	564	11 Aug 1785	58	430	On the S side of Holstein River	
Inman, Abednego	68		Green	200	26	1 Nov 1786	501	24 Oct 1778	59	387	S side of Holston River	
Inman, Shadrach	221		Green	200	178	20 Sep 1787	114	21 Oct 1783	65	423	Lying on the N side of Nolechuckey River	
Inman, William	2390	Deaderick, J. & Geo.	Davidson	320	3178	14 Sep 1797	4263		90	433	Waters of W. Harpeth River	yes
Ireland, John	88		Eastern District	50	77	17 Nov 1790	1982	15 Oct 1779	76	168	N side of Holstein River	
Ireson, James	1627		Davidson	100	100	10 Nvo 1790	1066	30 Jun 1785	74	388	On N boundary of Logans	
Ireson, James	1628	Armstrong, Martin	Davidson	100	101	10 Nov 1790	938	31 Apr 1785	74	389	On N boundary of Mitchell's pre-emption	
Irvin, Robert	13		Washington	100	302	24 Oct 1782	2702	22 Dec 1780	43	298	On the waters of Great Limestone	
Irvin, Robert	223		Washington	50	91	23 Oct 1782	2701	22 Dec 1780	47	44	On waters of Great Limestone	
Irvine, Robert	347		Washington	55	214	24 Oct 1782	2229	28 Nov 1779	49	232	On the waters of Great Limestone	
Irwin, Andrew	179	Settleworth, Andrew	Tennessee	640	1458	20 Dec 1791	2521	15 Sep 1789	77	366	On the waters of Sulphur Fork of Red River	
Irwin, Henry, Jr. ass	632		Sumner	5760	1915	20 May 1793	2290	29 Nov 1792	81	103	On S side of Cumberland River &c	yes
Irwin, James, ass	14		Maury	4000	30	14 Jul 1812	2056	30 Nov 1784	126	438	On N Fork of Big Tom Bigby	
Irwin, John	2175		Davidson	640	452	27 Nov 1793	763	27 Aug 1785	81	498	On S side of Cumberland River	yes
Irwin, John, ass	342		Sumner	640	1406	20 Dec 1791	489	18 May 1791	77	353	On the S side of Cumberland River	yes
Irwin, Joseph	2420	Brinkley, Jeremiah hrs	Davidson	640	3224	19 Oct 1797			92	91	West side of South Harpeth	yes
Irwin, Joseph	2421	Benton, Sol	Davidson	640	3225 (22	19 Oct 1797	2561		92	92	Waters of S Harpeth	
Irwin, Robert	148		Middle District	2600	144	20 Nov 1788	1936	29 Apr 1784	72	126	On the Main West fork of Stones River	
Irwin, Robert	157		Middle District	3200	158	6 Dec 1790	682	28 Oct 1783	74	245	On Richland Creek	
Irwin, Robert	1633	Orr, Nathan	Davidson	640	1366	30 Nov 1790			74	392	On waters of Little Harpeth	yes
Irwin, Robert	1634	Jordan, Fountain	Davidson	640	1367	30 Nov 1790	754		74	1367	On S side of Cumberland River	yes
Isabell, Thomas	20		Green	200	83	1 Nov 1786	1676	18 Sep 1779	58	444	On both sides of Lick Creek	
Isbell, Jason	691		Green	100	732	11 Jul 1788	367	25 Oct 1783	66	470	S/S Fr Broad River above mouth Big Pigeon	
Isbell, Thomas	512	Atway, Hardy	Davidson	640	484	15 Sep 1787	2781		63	175	On South side of Big Barren	yes
Isbell, Thomas	758	Smith, Arthur	Davidson	640	731	11 Jul 1788	1988		63	257	Side side of Big Barren River	yes
Isbell, Thomas	762	Dooston, Abraham	Davidson	640	735	11 Jul 1788	2505		63	258	S side of Big Barren River	yes
Ish, John	1130		Green	640	973	26 Dec 1791	2876	29 Dec 1781	77	272	On the S side of Holstein River	
Ish, John	1131		Green	200	974	26 Dec 1791	2407	24 Jan 1780	77	273	On the S side of Holstein River	
Isley, Phillip	815		Eastern District	400	217	30 Oct 1794			83	143	S side of Holston River	
Issabell /sic/, Thomas	83		Sullivan	276	758	17 Nov 1797	417,-14	15 Apr 1780	94	155	Waters of Reedy Creek	
Ives, James	1982		Green	100	41	1 Nov 1786	1677	18 Sep 1779	59	402	On waters of Lick Creek	
Ivey, Clabein /sic/	150	Hays, Isaac	Davidson	640	1887	20 May 1793	543		81	97	S W side Harpeth on head of Trace Creek	yes
Ivey, Curtis	59		Tennessee	640	1403	20 Dec 1791	3148	16 Dec 1785	77	352	On the South side of Cumberland River	
Ivey, David	448	Barbey, John	Davidson	2560	45	14 Mar 1786	177		63	19	On both sides Harpeth River	yes
Ivey, Elisha	1119	Harris, Edward	Sumner	274	420	15 Sep 1787	821	1 Jun 1795	63	155	S side of Cumberland River	yes
Jack, (no other name)	058		Tennessee	640	2625	4 Jun 1796	2462		88	342	Joining said Harris survey	yes
Jack, Jeremiah	1074		Washington	53	1024	27 Nov 1792	2169	3 Aug 1819	80	183	Beg at a stake &c	
Jack, Jeremiah	109		Green	300	125	1 Nov 1786	27	9 Nov 1779	59	428	On the S side of Nolichucky River	
Jack, Jeremiah	276		Washington	320	144	23 Oct 1782	639	21 Oct 1783	47	70	S side Nolachuckie River	
Jack, Jeremiah	761		Washington	50	575	10 Nov 1784	2169	25 Nov 1778	69	131	On S side of Nolachucka River	

Claimant:	File #:	Assignee:	Acres:	County:	Grant:	Grant Date:	Entry:	Entry Date:	Bk:	Pg:	Location by Stream Name:	Military:
Jack, Joseph	272		207	Sullivan	411	9 Aug 1787	33	8 Feb 1780	61	430	Om Carters Valley on Big Creek	
Jack, Samuel	1523		400	Green	1284	12 Jul 1794	1237	23 Jun 1784	81	589	Beg at a pine	
Jack, Samuel	1543		200	Green	1303	17 Jul 1794			81	610	On N/S French Broad River	
Jack, Samuel	1721		130	Green	1400	21 Jan 1797			91	125	N side French Broad River	
Jack, Samuel	973		530	Hawkins	745	20 Jul 1796	594	7 Jun 1780	88	497	On S side of Holston River	
Jackson, Andrew, ass	1099		640	Sumner	2599	7 Mar 1796	1793	12 Nov 1795	88	326	Beg at a small white oak	yes
Jackson, Andrew, ass	1100		428	Sumner	2600	7 Mar 1796	1676	12 Nov 1795	88	326	On a sinking fork	
Jackson, Andrew, ass	333		640	Sumner	1635	23 Feb 1793	1348	19 Mar 1790	76	329	S side of Cumberland River &c	yes
Jackson, Fred.	1661	Robertson, James	640	Davidson	1584	23 Feb 1793	1916		76	305	S side of Warpath /sic/ River	
Jackson, Jacob	533		200	Green	535	20 Sep 1787	152	22 Oct 1783	65	534	N/S of Long Creek on the Sinking Creek	
Jackson, James	1604	Bell, Robert	228	Davidson	1327	10 Dec 1790	1928		74	374	On waters of Mill Creek	yes
Jackson, Jeremiak /sic/	778	Sheppard, Martin Gard.	640	Davidson	751	11 Jul 1788	1498		63	264	On waters of Sulphur Fork of Red River	yes
Jackson, Job	2305	Clark, Lardner	640	Davidson	2499	18 Nov 1795	2572		89	136	On a branch of the last big creek	yes
Jackson, John	1397		300	Green	1209	27 Nov 1792	1460	2 Feb 1784	80	153	On Limestone Fork	
Jackson, John	267	Weakley, Robert	274	Tennessee	1734	20 May 1793	375	4 Nov 1783	81	62	N side of Cumberland River &c	yes
Jackson, John	424		180	Sullivan	303	10 Nov 1784	316	10 Mar 1780	69	177	In Carters Valley	
Jackson, Josiah	676	Twinbull, William	640	Davidson	649	8 Dec 1787	1810		63	230	On headwaters of Spring Creek	yes
Jackson, Peter	645		75	Sullivan	593	27 Jun 1793	2321	27 Nov 1779	80	381	On the drains of Hendricks Creek	
Jackson, Phillip	1689	Robertson, Elijah	640	Davidson	1648	23 Feb 1793	2196		76	336	On Flat Creek of Harpeth River	yes
Jackson, Robert	623		50	Sullivan	571	27 Jun 1793	235	26 Feb 1780	80	371	Beg a a Cranberry and White oak	
Jackson, Robert	710	Harney & Bledsoe	274	Sumner	2090	20 May 1793	3101	18 Nov 1792	81	147	On Bledsoes Creek	yes
Jackson, Robertson	400	Sheppard, Benj.	640	Davidson	372	15 Sep 1787			63	139	On both sides of E Fork of Drakes Creek	yes
Jackson, Thomas	0105		5000	Washington			1521	20 Feb 1784				
Jackson, Thomas	108		400	Eastern District	97	17 Nov 1790	93	8 Feb 1780	76	175	S side of Clinch River	
Jackson, Thomas	445		200	Hawkins	327	14 Jun 1793	197	21 Feb 1780	80	195	On Roseberry Creek	
Jackson, Thomas	447		640	Hawkins	325	24 Jun 1793	1655	17 Sep 1779	80	194	On the N side of Holston River &c	
Jackson, Thomas	448		640	Hawkins	326	24 Jun 1793	2172	8 Nov 1779	80	194	On the N side of Holston River &c	
Jackson, Thomas	449		200	Hawkins	327	24 Jun 1793	197	21 Feb 1780	80	195	On Roseberry Creek	
Jackson, Thomas	478	Dixon, Tilmon	640	Sumner	1649	27 Apr 1793	2201	25 Feb 1788	81	29	Adjoining a pre-emption &c	yes
Jackson, Thomas	5		5000	Smith & Middle	376	15 Nov 1800	1521	20 Feb 1784	108	203	On the waters of Obeys River	
Jackson, Thomas	56		200	Hawkins	41	18 May 1789	91	21 Oct 1783	72	252	On the S side of Holeson River &c	
Jackson, Thomas	707	Harney & Bledsoe	640	Sumner	2087	20 May 1793	3100	30 Nov 1792	81	146	On branches of Middle Fork of Goose Cree	yes
Jackson, Thomas	856		300	Hawkins	672	18 Apr 1795	118	8 Nov 1786	83	462	S side of Holston River	
Jackson, Thos. & C. Riggs	631		300	Hawkins	493	27 Jun 1793	2206	12 Nov 1779	80	359	On the S side of Spring Creek	
Jackson, Thos. & E. Friel	910		640	Green	110	26 Dec 1791	2193	12 Nov 1779	75	182	On N side of Holston River	
Jackson, Thos. & E. Triel	118		200	Hawkins	172	6 Dec 1791	817	13 Ju; 1781	75	164	E side of Flat Creek &c	
Jackson, William	1141		100	Washington	1099	12 Jul 1794	2136	25 Dec 1792	81	569	Beg on the fork of Doe River	
Jackson, William	1165		200	Washington	1123	7 Jul 1794	2919	29 Aug 1781	81	618	Beg at a stake	
Jackson, William	680		274	Davidson	653	8 Dec 1787	184		63	231	On E side of Big Harpeth	yes
Jackson, Thos & Edw Freel	510		640	Green	110	26 Dec 1791	2193	12 Nov 1779	75	182	On N side of Holston River	
Jacob,	059		640	Tennessee	3			3 Aug 1819			Beg at a black oak & hickory	
Jacobs, Abraham	701	Bledsoe, Anthony	640	Sumner	2073	20 May 1793	2133	20 May 1786	81	142	On the Round Lick Creek	yes
Jacobs, Benjamin	18	McCawley, Matthew	640	Davidson	4	16 Feb 1786	290		63	3	On both sides of a small creek	yes
Jacobs, Daniel	651	Bushnell & Dobbs	1000	Davidson	624	15 Sep 1787	1674		63	222	On waters of Stones River	yes
Jacobs, Peter	2051	Dixon, Tilmon	640	Davidson	2126	20 May 1793	1405		81	155	On S side of Cumberland River	yes

Claimant:	File #:	Assignee:	County:	Acres:	Grant:	Grant Date:	Entry:	Entry Date:	Bk:	Pg:	Location by Stream Name:	Military:
Jacobs, William	2369	Stewart, Duncan	Davidson	640	3090	14 Sep 1797	4012		90	397	On a Western branch of S. Harpeth River	yes
Jacobs, Ambrose	644	Baker, John	Sumner	640	1935	20 May 1793	3406	19 Nov 1792	81	108	On W side of Caney Fork	yes
James, Charles	08	Donelson, Stokley	Robertson	640			3469	13 Aug 1796			On Spring Creek	yes
James, Charles	824	Brock, Joseph	Davidson	640	827	17 Jan 1789	3469		63	291	On N side of Cumberland River	yes
James, Daniel	089	Cason, William	Sumner	640			522	3 Jan 1787			N side of Cumberland River	yes
James, Daniel	1020		Sumner	70	222	27 Feb 1796			88	172	On waters of Drakes Creek	
James, Daniel	2188		Davidson	50	174	26 Mar 1795			86	377	On N side of Cumberland	
James, Daniel	892	Cason, William	Davidson	640	908	17 Jan 1789			63	313	On N side of Cumberland River	
James, Daniel & Jas. Russell	1895	Rule, Henry	Davidson	320	119	27 Apr 1793	844	15 Dec 1792	81	33	Joining entry of 62 acres of James Russell	
James, George	241		Eastern District	60000 /s	203	30 Oct 1794	11 warrants		83	136	On a great bend of the Tennessee River &c	
James, George	712		Hawkins	10,000 /	532	12 Jun 1794	457,-1498	1783, 1784	82	164	W of Hawkins Courthouse in Poor Valley	
James, John	1742		Green	3791	1393	18 Dec 1796	2579	25 May 1784	91	312	Waters of Duck River	
James, John	200	Rice, John	Tennessee	640	1488	4 Jan 1792	79	27 Oct 1783	77	373	S side of Cumberland River	yes
James, Johnson	803		Sullivan	81	746	17 Nov 1797	14	1 Apr 1780	95	148	Beg at two white oaks	
James, Joseph T.	1617		Green	200	1329	18 Jan 1795	1833	6 Oct 1779	84	156	On waters of Long Creek	
James, Miles	2347	Gillingham, James	Davidson	640	2995	10 Apr 1797	3934		90	291	On Harpeth River	
James, Thomas	2395		Davidson	50	321	11 Dec 1796			91	297	N side of Cumberland River	yes
James, William	672	Hays, Robert	Davidson	640	645	15 Nov 1787	876		63	229	On the N side of Cumberland River	yes
Jamieson, William	709		Sumner	1000	2089	20 May 1793	1169	20 Aug 1783	81	147	On waters of W fork of Goose Creek	yes
Jamison, Benjamin	553		Green	100	233	20 Sep 1787	2300	27 Mar 1786	66	152	On the waters of Stories or Hollies Creek	
Jamison, George	1511		Green	200	1272	12 Jul 1794	861	29 Oct 1783	81	585	On Burneys Branch	
Jamison, Roger	1312	McConnell, Robert	Sumner	357	3112	14 Sep 1797	4302	6 May 1797	90	408	Waters of Big Barren	yes
Jarmany, Peter	1999	Brown, John & Hagg	Davidson	640	1939	20 May 1793	2345		81	109	On the waters of Mill Creek	yes
Jarmigan, Thomas	1541		Green	100	1301	17 Jul 1794			81	609	On N side of Nolichuckey River	
Jarratt, Jacob	2371	Stewart, Duncan	Davidson	640	3092	14 Sep 1797	4013		90	398	On a E fork of S Harpeth River	yes
Jarvis, Joel	2297	McNary, John	Davidson	640	2775	9 Sep 1796	3009		88	524	On E side of Stones River	yes
Jarvis, Lewis	1415	Hadley, Joshua	Sumner	220 (228	3270	6 Dec 1797	4491	8 May 1797	98	154	On the waters of Cedar Creek	yes
Jay, Simon	633	Robertson, James	Tennessee	640	3197	14 Sep 1797	3921		90	442	On the ridge	yes
Jefferson, Joel	016	Armstrong & Donelson	Middle District	640			2933					yes
Jeffrees, Thomas	5		Grainger, Easter	650	304	13 Mar 1801	605	27 Oct 1783	112	360	On Tyes Branch	
Jeffres, John	703	Wells, Haydon	Davidson	274	676	8 Dec 1787	321		63	239	N side of Cumberland River	yes
Jeffreys, John	623	Marshall, John	Davidson	640	595	15 Sep 1787	2275		63	212	On N Fork of Money Fork Creek	yes
Jeffreys, Thomas	1621	Tiffin, Thomas	Davidson	520	1357	10 Dec 1790	214		74	384	On waters of Station Camp Creek	yes
Jeffries, Thomas	17		Knox, Eastern D	350	305	13 Mar 1801	605	27 Oct 1783	112	360	On the S side of Beaverdam Creek	yes
Jenkins, Burwell	336	Barton, Samuel	Sumner	274	1645	23 Feb 1793	1939	18 Nov 1792	76	334	On Bartons Creek near the head	Y
Jenkins, Demsey	232		Davidson	320	218	7 Mar 1786	145		63	80	On waters of Stones River	
Jenkins, John	590	Weakley, Robert	Tennessee	640	3059	19 Jul 1797	4332		90	373	N side of Cumberland River	yes
Jenkins, Josiah	42	Bracken, J. G.	Tennessee	640	1233	10 Dec 1790	2853	30 Sep 1785	74	342	On S side of Cumberland River	yes
Jenkins, Levi	181	Gwin, Edward	Tennessee	640	1461	4 Jan 1792	2518	30 Sep 1785	77	366	S side of Cumberland River	yes
Jenkins, Roland	909		Washington	248	886	17 Nov 1790	118	2 Feb 1779	76	139	On Roans Creek	yes
Jenkins, William	628		Davidson	274	600	15 Sep 1787	1943		63	214	On the Wartrace Creek	
Jennett, Lewis	699	Sheppard, Benjamin	Davidson	1000	672	8 Dec 1787	2302		63	237	On a small Creek &c	yes
Jennings, Edmund	410		Sumner	640	421	27 Jun 1793		19 Aug 1791	80	348	On the N Fork of Smiths Fork	yes
Jennings, Edward	014		Davidson	200	341						On Dixons Creek	yes
Jennings, Thomas	084	Harney, Selby	Sumner	640			3220	18 Nov 1792			On ridge bet. Goose & Trammel Creeks	yes

Claimant:	File #:	Assignee:	County:	Acres:	Grant:	Grant Date:	Entry:	Entry Date:	Bk:	Pg:	Location by Stream Name:	Military:
Jennings, William	166		Sullivan	120	173	10 Oct 1783	2030	20 Oct 1780	53	147	Joining Moses Looney & Evans Orphans	
Jennings, William	1788		Davidson	640	370	26 Jul 1793	459	24 May 1784	80	322	On Stones River	
Jennins, Edmond	542		Tennessee (?) /s	200	341	19 Feb 1797			90	253	On Dixons Creek	
Jennison /?/, James	112		Davidson	640	98	14 Mar 1786	644		63	40	On Camp Creek	yes
Jermany, Thomas	1168	Harris, Edward	Sumner	640	2873	4 Jun 1796	2425	1 Jun 1795	88	358	Joining said Harris survey	yes
Jermagan, Thomas	24		Green	1000	87	1 Nov 1786	487	23 Oct 1783	58	448	On the S side of Holston River	
Jermagan, Thomas	93		Green	200	51	1 Nov 1786	1247	7 Jun 1784	59	412	N side of Nolichuckie River	
Jermagin, Gardner	71	Phillips, Mann	Tennessee	274	1313	10 Dec 1790	1866	25 Jun 1785	74	370	On N side of Red River	yes
Jerves, Willoughby	2112		Davidson	274	2369	20 May 1793	991		81	206	On W side of Harpeth River	yes
Jessop, Andrew	239	Armstrong, Andrew	Sumner	640	1144	26 Nov 1789	2807	7 Oct 1789	74	151	On head of Drakes Creek	yes
Jessop, Isaac	2227	Donelson, Stockley	Davidson	640	2557	7 Mar 1796			88	309	On waters of Stones River	yes
Jeth, Tanner	878	Sugg, Geo Augustus	Davidson	640	892	17 Jan 1789	2197		63	309	On a small fork &c	
Jett, Peter	031	McCulloch, Benj.	Tennessee	640			2012	16 Aug 1785			On the waters of Red River on the S side	yes
Jetts, Jeremiah	1718	Benjamin McCulloh	Davidson	640	1386	20 Dec 1791	2015		77	347	On Knob Creek of Duck River	yes
Jewell, Samuel	1156	Edward Harris	Sumner	640	2661	4 Jun 1796	3756	1 Jun 1795	88	354	Joining a survey of Harris	yes
Jiles, John	1107		Washington	100	1057	27 Nov 1792	2844	30 Apr 1781	80	207	Beg at a white oak saplin	
Jimmerson, Thomas	238	Reed, Alexander	Sumner	228	1143	26 Nov 1789	875	9 Aug 1785	74	150	On N side of Cumberland River	yes
Jimmerson, William	622	Montgomery, William	Davidson	640	594	15 Sep 1787	1168		63	212	On S side of Cumberland River	yes
Jinings, Edward, Ass.	919		Sumner	640	165	9 Jan 1794	320	13 Sep 1792	81	443	On waters of Smith Fork	
Jinkins, Abraham	639	Samuel Martin	Davidson	357	612	15 Sep 1787	414		63	218	On S side of Cumberland River	yes
Jinkins, William	1023	Griffith Rutherford	Davidson	640	1041	18 May 1789	2065		63	346	On E Fork of Stones River	yes
Job, William	669		Green	500	710	11 Jul 1788	50	21 Oct 1783	66	463	Locust tree standing bank French Broad Riv	
Jobe, David	1085		Robertson	200	1035	27 Nov 1792			80	200	On Burch Creek	
Jobe, David	1090		Washington	300	1040	27 Nov 1792	2553	2 May 1780	80	201	On the W side of Burch Creek	
Jobe, David	1091		Washington	80	1041	27 Nov 1792	2507	22 Mar 1783	80	202	Beg at 3 sycamores &c	
Jobe, David	1092		Washington	200	1042	27 Nov 1792	595	22 Mar 1783	80	202	Beg at a white & Red oak	
Jobe, Samuel	105		Washington	200	273	24 Oct 1782	622	24 Nov 1778	44	284	On Kindrick /sic/ Creek	
Jobe, Samuel	322		Washington	512	189	24 Oct 1782	621	24 Nov 1778	49	221	On Hendricks Creek	
Joens, Matthew	360		Western District	3498	366	20 Dec 1791	2158	12 May 1784	75	218	On Forked Deer River	
John, (no other name)	057		Tennessee	640	14			9 Aug 1819			Beg at a red oak & 2 chestnuts	
John, Ebenezer	254		Hawkins	300	242	26 Dec 1791	695	16 Oct 1780	77	327	On Lost Creek	
Johnson, Arthur	1378	Boyd, John Jr..	Sumner	640	3240	24 Nov 1797	4093	14 Apr 1797	94	173	Waters of Smiths Fork	yes
Johnson, Henry	07	Dobson, Elias	Robertson	640							On waters of Red River	
Johnson, Henry, Jr.	536	Eth(?) Wm. Heirs	Tennessee	640	2928	19 Feb 1797	2646	30 Sep 1785	90	250	Waters of Sulphur Fork	
Johnson, Henry, Jr.	537		Tennessee	640	2929	19 Feb 1797			90	250	Waters of Spring Creek	
Johnson, Henry, Jr., Ass	020	Flesher, Robert	Robertson	640	2929		1834	13 Aug 1796			On waters of Spring Creek	
Johnson, Holland	049		Not given	428			613	6 Jul 1784			S side of Cumberland River	
Johnson, Isaac	1383		Davidson	190	66	8 Oct 1787	4	26 Dec 1783	68	148	Beg at a red oak I.J., 1784, &c	
Johnson, Jacob	546		Green	200	548	20 Sep 1787	280	22 Oct 1783	65	540	On the N side of Nolachuckey	
Johnson, James	049		Sullivan	92			89	8 Feb 1780			On Kindricks /sic/ Creek	
Johnson, Jas.	1283		Green	300	1133	12 Jan 1793	37	21 Oct 1783	78	384	On S side of Nolachuckay River	
Johnson, John & J. M. Lewis	06		Western District	5000			1133,-1176	31 Oct 1783			On waters of Cumberland River	
Johnson, Richard	115	Edwards, David	Davidson	640	101	14 Mar 1786	699	Surv'd 17 Oct 1797	63	41	On Sycamore Creek	yes
Johnson, Samuel	073		Washington	80							On waters of Big /sic/ Limestone	yes
Johnson, Thomas	1575	Cox, Charles	Davidson	228	1224	10 Dec 1790	3452		74	339	On waters of Cripple Creek	yes

Earliest Tennessee Land Records

Claimant:	File #:	Assignee:	County:	Acres:	Grant:	Grant Date:	Entry:	Entry Date:	Bk:	Pg:	Location by Stream Name:	Military:
Johnson, Thomas	1686	McGloskins, Alex	Davidson	640	1628	23 Feb 1793	1728		76	326	On the waters of Stones River	yes
Johnson, Thomas	687		Washington	200	501	10 Nov 1784	2218	14 Nov 1779	69	105	On Lick Creek waters	
Johnson, Thos.	072		Tennessee	50			24	25 Jul 1789			Beg at a poplar Saplin &c	
Johnson, Walter	654		Sullivan	40	602	5 Jun 1793	239	29 Feb 1780 /sic/	81	337	On a branch above Benj. Looneys old place	
Johnson, Walter	655		Sullivan	100	603	5 Jun 1793	409	10 Apr 1780	81	338	Beg at a dogwood	
Johnson, William	538	Bailey, Robert heirs	Tennessee	640	2932	19 Feb 1797			90	251	Waters of Red River	
Johnson, William	539	Reid, Fran heirs	Tennessee	640	2933	19 Feb 1797			90	251	Beg at a hickory	
Johnson, William	551		Green	150	231	20 Sep 1787	203	22 Oct 1783	66	151	On Mosse /sic/ Creek &c	
Johnson, Wm.	018	Bailey, Robert	Robertson	640	2932	640	1584	25 Jul 1796			On waters of Red River	
Johnson, Wm.	04	Boyd, Francis	Robertson	640	2933	19 Feb 1797	3072	25 Jul 1796			Beg a hickory	
Johnston, (no other name)	060		Tennessee	640	5			8 Sep 1819			Beg at a post oak	
Johnston, Amelia	284		Western District	1000	273	25 Apr 1789	2522	25 May 1784	72	82	On the waters of Big Hatcha River &c	
Johnston, Ann	126 (127)		Eastern District	100	159	29 Jul 1793	775	28 Oct 1783	76	482	In Powells Valley	
Johnston, Aquilla, Ass	318		Eastern District	50	242	27 Feb 1796		Martin Armstrong	88	181	An island in Clinch River	
Johnston, Archibald	51	Anderson, Daniel	Tennessee	640	1256	10 Dec 1790	2854	30 Sep 1785	74	351	On N side of Cumberland River	yes
Johnston, Benjamin	2108	Lytle, Archibald	Davidson	390	2354	20 May 1793	118		81	203	On E side of Harpeth River	yes
Johnston, Benjamin	650	Atkinson, Charlton	Sumner	228	1954	20 May 1793	1199	6 Apr 1785	81	113	On Bledsoes Creek	yes
Johnston, Benjamin	666		Tennessee	640	3335	6 Dec 1797	3859		97	53	Adjoining Hugh Williamsons S boundary	yes
Johnston, Briton	322	Burton, Robert	Davidson	640	308	13 Jun 1787	1145		63	114	On a branch of Smith's Creek	
Johnston, Crafford	1602		Davidson	640	1308	10 Dec 1790			74	368	On N side of Cumberland River	
Johnston, Daniel	172	Cloud, Peter	Davidson	274	158	7 Mar 1786	735		63	60	On Hospens Creek	yes
Johnston, David	1009		Green	300	1236	29 Jul 1793	726	28 Oct 1783	76	485	N side of French Broad River	
Johnston, David	1108		Green	200	951	26 Dec 1791	815	29 Oct 1783	77	263	On the N side of French Broad River	
Johnston, David	1165		Green	100	1008	26 Dec 1791	101	25 June 1789	77	284	S/S Chuckey River on Matthews Branch	
Johnston, David	971		Green	44	885	17 Nov 1790	33	11 Mar 1784	76	133	In the forks of Long Creek &c	
Johnston, David, Sr.	1156		Green	200	999	26 Dec 1791	121	21 Oct 1783	77	281	N/S French Broad River on Long Creek	
Johnston, E /?/	963		Hawkins	200	877	17 Nov 1790	801	13 May 1780	76	130	N side of Holston River	
Johnston, Equela /sic/	366	Sheppard, Nancy	Davidson	640	359	8 Mar 1793	2297	27 Nov 1779	78	488	On S side of Beaverdam Creek	
Johnston, Hardy	720	Harris, Edward	Davidson	640	693	11 Jul 1788	1769		63	244	On waters of Sulphur Fork	yes
Johnston, Harmon	1108		Sumner	640	2614	4 Jun 1796	2740	1 Jun 1795	88	337	Joining sd Harris' survey	yes
Johnston, Henry	231		Davidson	640	217	7 Mar 1786	612		63	80	N side of Tennessee River	yes
Johnston, Henry	287		Tennessee	640	1903	20 May 1793	8	15 Oct 1783	81	101	On S side of Cumberland River &c	
Johnston, Holland	774		Sumner	428	2226	20 My 1793			81	175	On S side of Cumberland River	
Johnston, Howell	19	Sanders, James	Sumner	640	776	11 Jul 1788	3519	21 Sep 1787	63	272	On third large creek &c	yes
Johnston, Hudson	359		Hawkins	300	352	8 Mar 1793	1836	7 Oct 1779	78	486	Joining /?/ above and Ingram below	yes
Johnston, Isaac	1039		Davidson	640	13	17 Apr 1786	86	5 Feb 1789	66	38	Beg. at a small red oak marked I. J.	
Johnston, Isaac	1063		Davidson	640	37	17 Apr 1786	2150	10 Jan 1784	66	47	S boundary of Isaac Johnstons tract #3	
Johnston, Isaac	362		Washington	100	354	13 Oct 1783	394	15 Sep 1776	52	245	On S branch of the Horse Stamp Branch &c	
Johnston, Isaac	404		Washington	100	396	13 Oct 1783	545	29 Oct 1778	52	263	Joining his other tract	
Johnston, James	012	Tyrrell, William	Montgomery	1000			1063	4 Jun 1796			On Flat Lick of Little W Fork of Red River	yes
Johnston, James	1085		Green	150	928	26 Dec 1791	86	5 Feb 1789	77	251	On the S side of Nolachuckey River	
Johnston, James	446		Middle District	2200	385	17 Dec 1794	2150	11 May 1764	84	254	On N Fork of Duck River	
Johnston, James	595		Green	600	552	20 Sep 1787	123	21 Oct 1783	66	247	On the S side of Nolichuckey River &c	
Johnston, Jno.	1125		Davidson	640	102	17 Apr 1786	314	27 Feb 1786	66	175	Lying on the waters of Dry Creek	
Johnston, Jno. & J. M. Lewis	397		Western District	5000	398	27 Nov 1793			81	506	About 14 miles from the Masippia /sic/ River	

Claimant:	Assignee:	County:	Acres:	Grant:	Grant Date:	Entry:	Entry Date:	Bk:	Pg:	Location by Stream Name:	Military:
Johnston, Jno. & J. M. Lewis		Western District	5000	399	27 Nov 1793	1713	16 Apr 1784	81	506	About 15 miles from the Masippia /sic/	
Johnston, John		Green	120	991	26 Dec 1791	103	24 Jul 1789	77	278	On the N side of Chuckey River	
Johnston, John		Washington	640	1162	22 Feb 1795	2718	16 Jan 1781	84	292	Joining his former survey	
Johnston, John		Washington	640	1163	22 Feb 1794	267	23 Jul 1778	84	292	Adjoining his former survey &c	
Johnston, John		Washington	640	1164	22 Feb 1795	1962	19 Oct 1779	84	293	Joining his former survey &c	
Johnston, John		Washington	600	1165	22 Feb 1795	1064	8 Jan 1779	84	293	Joining his former survey &c	
Johnston, John		Washington	640	1166	22 Feb 1795	263	23 Jul 1778	84	294	Joining his former survey &c	
Johnston, John		Washington	640	1167	22 Feb 1795	266	23 Jul 1778	84	294	Joining his former survey &c	
Johnston, John		Washington	640	1168	22 Feb 1795	1961	19 Oct 1779	84	295	Joining his former survey &c	
Johnston, John		Washington	640	1169	22 Feb 1795	261	22 Jul 1778	84	295	On waters of Puncheon Camp Creek	
Johnston, John		Green	200	1203	23 Feb 1793	771	9 Apr 1781	78	443	On N side of Bays Mountain	
Johnston, John	Cantrell, Stephen	Sumner	228	3332	6 Feb 1797	4141	6 Feb 1797	97	51	On waters of Manshoes /sic/ & Madisons	yes
Johnston, John		Green	100	1240	27 Nov 1792	808	28 Dec 1778	80	167	Joining 640 acres of David Campbell	
Johnston, John	Cole, William Pample	Tennessee	1500	1396	20 Dec 1791	246	25 Oct 1783	77	350	On the E Fork of Pine River	
Johnston, John	Rowel, Andrew	Tenn	640	1397	20 Dec 1791	1789	23 Apr 1785	77	350	On the fork of Pine River	
Johnston, John	Whitfield, Bryant	Tennessee	640	1765	20 May 1793	1529	2 Feb 1785	81	70	On N side of Cumberland River &c	yes
Johnston, John		Sullivan	211	436	9 Aug 1787	1728	25 Sep 1779	61	455	On the waters of Beaver Creek	
Johnston, John		Green	100	314	20 Sep 1787	1416	17 Jan 1784	65	462	Clay Lick Creek waters of French Broad	
Johnston, Joseph	Williams, Etheldred	Summer	2560	350	1 Mar 1797	3994	21 Nov 1796	90	215	On Caney Fork	yes
Johnston, Joseph		Sullivan	200	188	10 Nov 1784	535	29 Apr 1780	69	195	Beg at John Gillihans corner	
Johnston, Kines /?/		Green	200	188	20 Sep 1787	1245	11Nov 1763	65	427	On the N/S Holstein River on Flatt Creek	
Johnston, Lancelet	Paden, Thomas	Tennessee	640	2167	20 Nov 1793	1853	15 Jun 1785	8153	165	On the W side of Red River	
Johnston, Peter	Phillips, Phillip	Davidson	640	1076	26 Nov 1789	2192		74	118	On waters of Stones River	yes
Johnston, Rice	Jones, Ambrose	Tennessee	274	2263	20 May 1793	3720	2 Jan 1790	81	184	On the waters of Sulphur Fork	yes
Johnston, Robert	Rose, Abraham	Davidson	640	674	8 Dec 1787	1179		63	238	N side of Cumberland River	yes
Johnston, Samuel		Washington	200	1214	4 Dec 1795	1276	12 Mar 1779	89	332	On a branch of Sinking Creek	
Johnston, Samuel	Williams, Sampson	Sumner	185	1629	23 Feb 1793	1141	22 Oct 1791	76	326	N side of Cumberland River	yes
Johnston, Seth		Eastern District	100	26	11 Jul 1788	582	5 May 1780	67	350	On Beaverdam Creek &c	
Johnston, Thomas	McGloskey, Alexander	Davidson	640	2296	20 May 1793		81		81	190	On waters of Stones River	yes
Johnston, Thomas		Washington	150	193	24 Oct 1782	504	12 Oct 1778	49	223	On the waters of Lick Creek	
Johnston, Thomas	Willard, James	Tennessee	640	2314	20 May 1793	3031	30 Sep 1785	81	194	Beg. at a red oak	
Johnston, Thomas		Tennessee	206	134	16 Dec 1793	45	14 Sep 1789 (date)	81	395	On waters of Sulphur Fork	
Johnston, Thomas		Tennessee	61	239	27 Feb 1796		14 Sep 1792	88	179	On waters of Sulphur Fork	
Johnston, Thomas		Tennessee	74	184	26 Mar 1795		21 Aug 1792	89	95	On Sulphur Fork	
Johnston, Thomas		Sullivan	50	655	5 Dec 1794	817	12 Jul 1781	84	163	On Walkers fork of Horse Creek	
Johnston, Thomas		Washington	347	609	10 Nov 1784	2826	27 Mar 1781	69	141	Beg at a black oak	
Johnston, Thomas		Green	640	887	17 Nov 1790	70	26 Feb 1778	76	133	Bent creek incl Crab Orchard and Big Lick	
Johnston, Thomas, Ass.		Davidson	65	162	9 Jan 1794		22 Dec 1792	81	442	On N side of Cumberland River	
Johnston, Thos	Smith, Owen	Tennessee	640	2186	20 May 1793	1847	15 June 1785	81	167	On the waters of Sulphur Fork of Red River	
Johnston, Thos & Armstrong		Tennessee	100	208	27 Feb 1796	43		88	165	On Spring Creek	
Johnston, Thos.		Tennessee	124	128	16 Dec 1793		17 Aug 1792	81	393	On Sulphur Fork	
Johnston, Thos.		Tennessee	278	129	16 Dec 1793	44	13 Jul 1790 (date	81	393	On the waters of Sulphur Fork	
Johnston, Thos.		Tennessee	200	130	16 Dec 1793		14 Nov 1792 (sur.)	81	393	On Millers Creek	
Johnston, Thos.		Tennessee	160	131	16 Dec 1793		12 Nov 1792	81	394	On Calclas /sic/ Creek	
Johnston, Thos.		Tennessee	54	132	16 Dec 1793		9 Feb 1792	81	394	On Sulphur Fork of Red River	

Claimant:	File #:	Assignee:	County:	Acres:	Grant:	Grant Date:	Entry:	Entry Date:	Bk:	Pg:	Location by Stream Name:	Military:
Johnston, Thos.	394		Tennessee	130	135	16 Dec 1793			81	395	On Sulpur Fork of Red River	
Johnston, Thos.	395		Tennessee	228	136	16 Dec 1793		2 May 1789	81	395	On Woods Branch	
Johnston, Thos.	428		Tennessee	130	158	9 Jan 1794		21 Jul 1791	81	441	On S Fork of Red River	
Johnston, Thos.	429		Tennessee	137	159	9 Jan 1794		1 Nov 1792 (dated	81	441	On Sulphur Fork of Red River	
Johnston, Thos.	432		Tennessee	50	163	9 Jan 1794		7 Sep 1791	81	443	Beg. at a poplar Saplin	
Johnston, Thos.	435		Tennessee	50	181	9 Jan 1794		21 Aug 1792 (date	81	449	On waters of Sulphur Fork	
Johnston, Thos.	445		Tennessee	206	216	27 Feb 1796		7 Jan 1794	88	169	On waters of Sulphur Fork	
Johnston, Thos.	447		Tennessee	54	221	27 Feb 1796		9 Jan 1792	88	171	On Sulphur Fork of Red River	
Johnston, Thos.	449		Tennessee	50	236	27 Feb 1796	18	20 Nov 1790 (date	88	178	On waters of Sulphur Fork	
Johnston, Walter	361		Sullivan	260	240	10 Nov 1784	2010	24 Oct 1779	69	159	In Stanleys Valley	
Johnston, William	200	Chunney, John	Davidson	428	186	7 Mar 1786	983		63	69	On Red River	yes
Johnston, William	934	Brehon, James G.	Davidson	640	950	18 May 1789	3388		63	324	On the Caney Fork	yes
Johnston, Zophar	936		Green	100	850	17 Nov 1790	2537	10 Apr 1780	76	121	Corner of a survey of Wm. Hannah's land	
Johnston, Zophar, Sr.	1633		Green	100	1336	18 Aug 1795	2360	18 Dec 1779	87	502	On waters of Little Chuckie & Pigeon Creek	
Jolley, Henry	1166		Washington	100	1124	7 Jul 1794			81	618	On the War Road	
Jolley, William	648		Sullivan	100	596	27 Jun 1793	739	2 Jun 1789	80	382	Beg. near Charles Dencans /sic/ line	
Jonakin /sic/, Thomas	311		Washington	300	178	24 Oct 1782	1579	7 Sep 1779	47	86	Bet. a survey said Jonakin now lives on &c	
Jonakin, Thomas	1016		Green	2960 /?/	1243	29 Jul 1793	389	25 Oct 1783	76	487	N side of Holston and Richland Creek	
Jonakin, Thomas	121		Washington	640	289	24 Oct 1782	673	9 Dec 1778	44	292	On Cedar Creek	
Jonekin, Thomas	0144		Green	3960			389	12 Nov 1791			N side Holston	
Jonekin, Thomas	100		Green	640	58	1 Nov 1786	23	21 Oct 1783	59	419	Upon Nolichuckie River	
Jones, Abraham	048	Jones, Brinson	Davidson	640			845	17 Oct 1785			On waters of Harpeth	
Jones, Absolom	050	Enjamin /sic/ McCulloch	Davidson	640			2461	9 Mar 1786			N side of Cumberland River	
Jones, Allen	820		Sumner	1000	2295	20 May 1793	1014	2 Jun 1785	81	190	On both sides of a trace &c	yes
Jones, Ambrose	1436		Sumner	640	3349	9 Dec 1797	1507	12 Apr 1788	98	183	On E side of Cedar Lick Creek	yes
Jones, Ambrose	31		Sumner	640	790	11 Jul 1788	3354	12 Sep 1787	63	277	On N side of Cumberland River	yes
Jones, Ambrose	370	Johnston, Rice	Tennessee	274	2263	20 May 1793	3720	2 Jan 1790	81	184	On the waters of Sulphur Fork	yes
Jones, Ambrose	788	Ray, Daniel	Davidson	640	791	11 Jul 1788	2741		63	277	On E side of Stones River	
Jones, Ambrose	868	Bennett, William's hrs.	Davidson	640	883	17 Jan 1789	1507	12 Apr 1788	63	305	On E side of Cedar Creek	yes
Jones, Benjamin	635	Linton, Hezekiah	Davidson	640	608	15 Sep 1787	192		63	216	On North side of Cumberland River	yes
Jones, Benjamin	709	Taylor, Thomas	Davidson	320	682	8 Dec 1787	3389		63	240	On E waters of Whites Creek	yes
Jones, Binford	2351	Smith, John	Davidson	640	3013	10 Apr 1797	3940		90	299	S side of Cumberland River	yes
Jones, Brittain	2444	Tatum & Wiggins	Davidson	640	3286	6 Dec 1797	4267		98	164	On the waters of Overalls /sic/ Creek &c	yes
Jones, Daniel	27		Sumner	1234	784	11 Jul 1788	1288	21 Jan 1786	63	275	On head of a creek &c	yes
Jones, Darlin /sic/	1186		Washington	259 & 24	1073	11 Jul 1794	1439	11 Jun 1779	82	245	Beg. on a chestnut	
Jones, David	1567		Davidson	1096	1200	13 Aug 1796	1297		74	322	On S side of Red River	yes
Jones, David	3	Onagood, Thomas	Robertson	640	2927	19 Feb 1797			90	249	On waters of Red River	
Jones, David	535		Tennessee	640	1297	30 Nov 1790					On waters of Red River	
Jones, David	564		Hawkins	144	437	29 Jul 1793	64	8 Feb 1780	90	286	S Side of Holston on Buck Creek	yes
Jones, David	776		Davidson	1000	749	11 Jul 1788	385		80	263	On West Fork of Red River	
Jones, David & D. Stewart	1367		Sumner	1000	3216	14 Sep 1797	3283	1 Jun 1797	63	12	On Indian Creek	yes
Jones, Elisha	1434	Gwin, John	Sumner	274	3309	6 Dec 1797	4034	8 May 1797	92	180	On Peytons Fork of Drakes Creek	yes
Jones, Evan	1456		Sumner	640	3373	20 Sep 1801	583	2 Aug 1789	98	59	On N side of Cumberland River	yes
Jones, Hardy	247		Davidson	360	233	7 Mar 1786	178		111	86	South side of Cumberland River	yes
Jones, Harwood	1281		Green	200	1131	12 Jan 1793			78	383	On a drain /sic/ of Loss /sic/ Creek	yes

Earliest Tennessee Land Records

Claimant:	File #:	Assignee:	County:	Acres:	Grant:	Grant Date:	Entry:	Entry Date:	Bk:	Pg:	Location by Stream Name:	Military:
Jones, Harwood	188		Green	2500	145	23 Apr 1787	2620	25 May 1784	65	161	Lying on Mosey /sic/ Cr Branch of Holston	
Jones, Henry	167	Pratt, Peter	Tennessee	640	1431	20 Dec 1791	2050	26 Aug 1785	77	359	On both sides of Garners Creek	
Jones, Hezekiah	691	Davis, Joshua	Sumner	228	2048	20 May 1793	2356	29 Nov 1792	81	136	On the waters of Dixons Creek	yes
Jones, Jacob	1777		Davidson	640	355	26 Jun 1793	552	27 Jul 1784	80	318	On both sides of a small creek &c	
Jones, Jacob	225		Tennessee	640	362	26 Jun 1793			80	320	On a creek that empties into Red River	
Jones, Jacob	280	Gambrill, Bradley	Sumner	640	1273	10 Dec 1790	2460	14 Nov 1789	74	356	On waters of Bartons Creek	yes
Jones, James	1453		Green	100	1263	27 Nov 1792	2420	2 Feb 1780	80	175	On the Cedar Branch of Lick Creek	
Jones, James	27	Spear Fort	Montgomery	640			3733	4 Jun 1796			In the Fork of Brush Creek	yes
Jones, James	588	Harget, Frederick	Sumner	274	1829	20 May 1793	1435	27 Sep 1788	81	85	On S Fork of E Fork of Stones River	yes
Jones, John	0141	Cobb, Jesse	Sumner	640			1486	12 Jan 1785 (dated)			On both sides of the road	yes
Jones, John	1172		Green	200	1015	26 Dec 1791	1516	15 Aug 1779	77	287	On the E side of Lick Creek	
Jones, John	1478		Green	300	1241	12 Jul 1794	2737	16 Jan 1781	81	575	On S side of Nolichuckey River	yes
Jones, John	536	Allen, Samuel	Davidson	640	508	15 Sep 1787	2162		63	183	On head of Gilbesons /sic/ Creek	yes
Jones, John	849	Thompson, Samuel	Davidson	640	854	17 Jan 1789	2021		63	298	On waters of Caney Fork	yes
Jones, John	946		Green	966	860	17 Nov 1790	1265	6 Dec 1783	76	125	W fork of Stones River	
Jones, Joshua	348	Tuton, Oliver	Davidson	640	333	29 Aug 1787	1771		63	124	N side of Cumberland River	yes
Jones, Josiah	1721	Brickell, James	Davidson	1000	1393	20 Dec 1791	720		77	349	S boundary of Gen. Summers /?/ survey	yes
Jones, Josiah	800	Davis, Joshua	Sumner	228	2261	20 May 1793	2359	29 Nov 1792	81	183	On the waters of Dixons Creek	yes
Jones, Kedar /sic/	886a	Motheral, John	Sumner	640	2413	7 Jan 1794	2198	19 Dec 1792	81	403	On ridge &c	yes
Jones, Lazerus	714		Sumner	337	2096	20 May 1793	584	31 Jul 1792	81	148	Beg on S bank of Cumberland River	yes
Jones, Martin	685	McCulloh, Benjamin	Sumner	1000	2034	20 May 1793	2193	30 Nov 1792	81	133	On W Fork of Peytons Creek	yes
Jones, Matthew	360		Western Dist	3498	366	20 Dec 1791	2158	12 May 1784	75	218	On Forked Deer River	
Jones, Nathaniel	72	Jones, Samuel	Davidson	2560	58	14 Mar 1786	160		63	24	South side of Cumberland River	yes
Jones, Nathaniel	98		Middle District	1350	100	10 Jul 1788	708	28 Oct 1783	67	458	On the S side of Duck River &c	
Jones, Norwood	1087		Hawkins	500	816	4 Jul 1797	597	7 Jun 1784	91	597	N side of Holston River	
Jones, Oliver	1358	Hadley, Joshua	Sumner	640	2804	21 Dec 1796	3873	14 Oct 1796	91	475	N side of Caney Fork	yes
Jones, Peter	491	Donelson, Stockley	Sumner	640	1653	20 May 1793	1834		81	42	On E side of Stones River	yes
Jones, Philip	1006		Davidson	2560	1023	18 May 1789	260		63	342	On head waters of Cedar Lick Creek	yes
Jones, Philip	583	Williams, Eliza	Middle District	640	2790	20 Dec 1796	1278		91	324	Waters of Caney Fork	yes
Jones, Richard	0125	Wilburn, Daniel	Sumner	640			1998	20 Jul 1796			Beg at Stockey Donelson corner	yes
Jones, Richard	1184		Washington	35	1069	30 Dec 1793	3002	26 Mar 1784	82	142	On the waters of Redins Branch	
Jones, Richard	1431	Wilburn, Daniel	Sumner	640	3306	6 Dec 1797	1998	20 Jul 1796	98	178	About 3 miles N of Pond Lick	yes
Jones, Richard	2160		Davidson	40 (50) / 173		9 Jan 1794	1770	6 Sep 1786	81	446	On waters of Jaspers Creek	
Jones, Samuel	351	Tuton, William	Davidson	640	336	29 Aug 1787			63	125	S side of Cumberland River	yes
Jones, Samuel	72	Jones, Nathaniel (heir)	Davidson	2560	58	14 Mar 1786	160		63	24	S side of Cumberland River	yes
Jones, Seburn	36	Leary, Luke	Tennessee	640	1218	10 Mar 1790	856	14 May 1784	74	337	On N side of Cumberland River	
Jones, Seburn	66	Hunter, Sol.	Tennessee	1000	1304	10 Dec 1790	3353	15 Jan 1790	74	367	On N side of Cumberland River	
Jones, Shadrack	073		Tennessee	640			552	16 Apr 1792			On a creek that empties into Red River	
Jones, Shadrack	1782		Davidson	640	363	26 Jun 1793	553	27 Jul 1784	80	320	On the fork of Stones River &c	
Jones, Solomon	768		Sullivan	240	699	20 Jul 1796	372,-711	1780,-1781	91	83	Waters of Muddy Creek	
Jones, Stephen	032	Barton, Samuel	Davidson	640			3654	14 Dec 1795			E side of Stones River	
Jones, Stephen	352	Baron, Samuel	Sumner	640	1439	20 Nov 1791	2195	19 Nov 1790	77	361	On the waters of Cedar Creek	yes
Jones, Taylor	1562	Nelson, Robert	Davidson	640	1184	30 Nov 1790	3654		74	316	On E side of Big Harpeth River	yes
Jones, Theophilus	368	Hayes, Robert	Sumner	640	1533	14 Jan 1793	2737	5 Jan 1790	79	266	On waters of Madisons Creek	yes
Jones, Thomas	106	Clark, Lardner	Davidson	228	92	14 Mar 1786	1232		63	37	On both sides of a branch	yes

Claimant:	File #:	Assignee:	County:	Acres:	Grant:	Grant Date:	Entry:	Entry Date:	Bk:	Pg:	Location by Stream Name:	Military:
Jones, Thomas	1308		Washington	100	1194	4 Oct 1795	2575	30 May 1780	89	433	On Cobs Creek	
Jones, Thomas	192		Sumner	50	68	18 May 1789			71	225	On the waters of Drakes Creek	yes
Jones, Tignall	129		Middle District	2100	131	10 Jul 1788	701	28 Oct 1783	67	472	Lying on the S side of Duck River	
Jones, Underhill	549	Malloy, Thomas	Tennessee	640	2974	5 Apr 1797	3920	8 Dec 1795	90	275	S side of Cumberland River	yes
Jones, William	1994	Jesse Cobb	Davidson	389	1920	20 May 1793			81	105	On Brown Creek	yes
Jones, William	947		Green	1000	861	17 Nov 1790	1465	6 Feb 1784	76	125	W Fork of Stones River	
Jones, Wm.	085	Cobb, Jessie	Davidson	389			1487	8 Jan 1785			On Browns Creek	yes
Jonston /sic/, Hugh	86		Hawkins	200	78	13 Feb 1791	1727	25 Sep 1779	74	285	On waters of Holstein /sic/	
Joperton, Taylor	1715	McCulloch, Benjamin	Davidson	640	1383	21 Dec 1791	2194		77	346	On the dividing ridge bet. &c	yes
Jordan, Fountain	1634	Erwin, Robert	Davidson	640	1367	30 Nov 1790	754		74	392	On S side of Cumberland River	
Jordan, James	367		Eastern District	300	282	20 Jul 1796	1863	7 Oct 1779	88	494	On a branch of Tuckahoe Creek	
Jordan, John	452	Williams, Willoughby	Davidson	640	424	15 Sep 1787	1167		63	157	S side of Richland Creek	yes
Jordan, Jones	1097	Easton, James	Sumner	640	2588	7 Mar 1796	3932	5 Jun 1795	88	320	On S side of Cumberland River	yes
Jordan, Joseph	1165	Harris, Edward	Sumner	640	2670	4 Jun 1796	2735	1 Jun 1795	88	357	Joining said Harris survey	yes
Jordan, Lewis	980		Washington	400	957	17 Nov 1790	2821	19 Mar 1781	76	164	On the waters of Little Limestone	
Jordan, Pilate /sic/	29	William Cookran	Tennessee	640	1193	30 Nov 1790	2736	30 Sep 1785	74	319	S of Cumberland River	
Jordan, Ptolomy	022	Dillenberry, Redmond	Sumner	640			4416	14 Oct 1797			E waters Middle Fork Drakes Creek	yes
Jordan, River	1208	Barton, Samuel	Sumner	400	164	26 Mar 1795		20 Nov 1792	89	92	On Bartons Creek	yes
Jordan, River	1210	Barton, Samuel	Sumner	400	167	26 Mar 1795		5 Dec 1792	89	93	On S side of Cumberland River	yes
Jordan, Robert	258		Davidson	640	244	7 Mar 1786	842		63	89	Large creek running into Tenesse /sic/ Riv	yes
Jordan, Thomas	298	McCulloch, Benjamin	Tennessee	640	1972	20 May 1793	2081	1 Sep 1785	81	117	On S side of Cumberland	yes
Joslin, Benjamin	437	Robertson, James R.	Tennessee	480	183	26 Mar 1795		19 Apr 1792	86	412	On the SW side of Big Harpeth River	yes
Joyner /Joiner/, Freeman	891	Barrow, Sherrod	Sumner	640	2407	20 Jan 1794	2739	2 Mar 1786	81	420	On E side of Caney Fork	yes
Joyner /Joiner/, Stephen	1531	Thompson, Robert	Davidson	640	1088	26 Nov 1789	1917		74	125	On waters of Hurricane Creek	yes
Joyner, Joel	1864	Nichols, John	Davidson	640	1598	27 Apr 1793	1075		81	17	On W bank of Big Harpeth River	yes
Joyner, Lewis	126	Hadley, Joshua	Tennessee	640	1632	23 Feb 1793	2666	30 Sep 1785	76	328	S side of Cumberland River &c	yes
Joyner, Thomas	919	Brahen, James Gliester	Davidson	2560	935	18 May 1789	3551		63	321	On S side of Cumberland River	yes
Judge, Thomas	384	McClurd, Thomas	Tennessee	228	2378	20 May 1793	1227	2 Oct 1784	81	208	On S side of Cumberland	
Jules, John	1107		Washington	100	1057	27 Nov 1792	2844	30 Apr 1781	80	207	Beg at a white oak saplin	
Justice, David	612		Middle District	2000	391	25 Oct 1802	528	27 Oct 1783	115	421	On both sides of Duck River	
Justice, Moses	97		Eastern District	250	86	17 Nov 1790			76	171	On the waters of Big Creek	
Kanady, Daniel	38		Washington	394	328	24 Oct 1782	259	22 Jul 1778	43	309	On the head of the Mill Fork of Lick Creek	
Kanady, Daniel	396		Washington	120	388	13 Oct 1783	1505	10 Aug 1779	52	359	Beg at 2 white oaks and sourwood	
Kanady, David	398		Washington	300	390	13 Oct 1783	2811	12 Mar 1781	52	260	On the 1st branch &c	
Kanady, David	496		Davidson	640	468	15 Sep 1787	961		63	170	On waters of Station Camp Creek	
Kanday, Abraham	947	Laurey, Daniel	Davidson	640	963	18 May 1789	2523		63	327	Headwaters of Barlows & Cedar Lick Creek	yes
Kannady /sic/, Daniel	467		Washington	43.5	459	13 Oct 1783	2801	28 Feb 1781	52	293	On big Limestone waters	yes
Kannady, Abraham	1799		Davidson	640	372	26 June 1793	842	14 Dec 1792	80	331	On the S waters of Big Harpeth River	
Karr, George	783		Washington	100	597	10 Nov 1784	855	30 Dec 1778	69	137	On waters of Little Limestone	
Karr, Jean /?/	023		Sullivan	400			1897	6 Oct 1779				
Karr, Joseph	23		Middle District	1854	25	10 Jul 1788	1648	16 Apr 1784	67	418	On the N side of Duck River	
Karr, Robert	540	Malloy, Thomas	Tennessee	12	339	19 Feb 1797			90	252	Joining said Karrs S boundary	yes
Karr, Samuel	75		Middle District	1000	77	10 Jul 1788	1651	16 Apr 1784	67	448	On both sides of the N fork of Duck River	
Karr, Walter	782		Washington	100	596	10 Nov 1784			69	137	On waters of Cherokee	
Keagey, John	571	Childers, John hrs.	Tennessee	640	3009	10 Apr 1797	3931		90	297	N side of Cumberland River	

Claimant:	File #:	Assignee:	County:	Acres:	Grant:	Grant Date:	Entry:	Entry Date:	Bk:	Pg:	Location by Stream Name:	Military:
Kear /sic/, Robert	70		Green	300	28	1 Nov 1786	1407	17 May 1779	59	389	Beg in a spring	
Kearr /sic/, Robert	727	Crocker, Abraham	Davidson	274	700	11 Jul 1788	3426		63	246	On Sulphur Fork of Red River	yes
Keay, Jonathan	573	Hubbart, Zebulon	Davidson	228	545	15 Sep 1787	1805		63	196	On Red River	Yes
Keay, Jonathan	573	Hubbart, Zebulon	Davidson	228	545	15 Sep 1787	1805		63	196	On Red River	yes
Keentz /Kuntz?/, Phillip	070		Green	200		23 Sep 1789		24 Jun 1780			On Swan Pon /sic/ Creek	
Keeny, Jno.	683		Green	67	724	11 Jul 1788	1399	17 Jan 1784	66	467	Fr Broad incl Ige island opp Robert Lamb	
Keiller, Frederick	319		Sullivan	640	455	28 Nov 1787	928	1 Jan 1779	67	218	On the S side of Holston River	
Keith, Daniel	279		Washington	200	147	23 Oct 1782	299	4 Aug 1778	47	71	On the waters of Big Limestone Creek	
Keith, Daniel	73		Washington	99	241	23 Oct 1782	1317	30 Mar 1779	44	266	S side of Nobs Creek	
Keith, Jno	12		Giles	450	15	14 Jul 1812	2728	9 Jan 1781	126	432	Lying and being on Big Creek	
Keith, Jno.	10		Giles	640	13	14 Jul 1812	1595	24 Sep 1779	126	431	Being and lying on Robertsons Fork	
Keith, Jno.	11		Giles	500	14	14 Jul 1812	2722	5 Jan 1781	126	431	Being and lying on Dry Fork	
Keith, Jno.	17		Maury	600	34	14 Jul 1812	61	26 Feb 1778	126	440	On waters of Catheys Creek	
Keith, Jno.	21		Giles	440	52	15 Jul 1812	27	26 Feb 1778	126	447	Lying on Big Creek	
Keith, Jno.	4		Maury	640	16	14 Jul 1812	2726	8 Jan 1781	126	432	E side of Catheys Creek	
Keith, John to James Taylor	01		Carter								Deed - no other info	
Keithly, John	650		Tennessee	100	408	14 Sep 1797			92	20	On Spring Creek	
Keller, Frederick	747		Sullivan	150	686	9 Dec 1795	165	15 Jun 1792	89	395	On a small branch &c	
Kelley, Alex & A. Lackey	1120		Green	1000	963	26 Oct 1791			77	268	On the Tennessee River &c	
Kelley, Alex & Jno. Kelley	1123		Green	640	966	26 Dec 1791			77	269	Beg at a black oak &c	
Kelley, Alexander	112		Eastern District	500	128	1 Nov 1786	284	1 Nov 1786	59	431	On waters of S side of Nolichuckie River	
Kelley, Alexander	169		Eastern District	600	133	14 Jan 1793	1443		79	290	On S side of Holston River	
Kelley, Alexander & /blank/	1119		Green	640	962	26 Oct 1791	60	7 Oct 1779	77	268	On the N side of Tennessee River	
Kelley, Charles	1496	Pasmore, David	Davidson	580	1053	26 Nov 1789	418		74	103	On N side of Cumberland River	yes
Kelley, John	207		Middle District	5000	193	5 Dec 1792			78	458	On the Harding Creek	
Kelley, John	364	Long, Nicholas	Tennessee	640	2223	20 May 1793	468	24 Feb 1784	81	174	On S side of Cumberland River	yes
Kelley, John	682	King, Robert	Hawkins	640	2393	17 Jul 1794	3139		81	603	On the Sycamore Creek	yes
Kelley, Joshua	732		Washington	138	546	10 Nov 1784	2929	3 Sep 1781	69	121	Incl where John Bearden formerly lived	
Kelley, William	2441	Tatum & Wiggins	Davidson	640	3283	6 Dec 1797	4166		98	162	On the waters of W Fork of Stones River	yes
Kellum, John	158		Green	500	628	23 Aug 1788	2528	25 May 1784	64	350	On the N side of Tennessee River	
Kelly, Alex	139		Hawkins	40	173	26 Dec 1791	2115	26 Mar 1785	75	173	An island in Holson /sic/ River	
Kelly, Alexander	158		Eastern District	200	128	14 Jan 1793	363	5 Sep 1778	79	288	On S side of Holston River	
Kelly, Dugald	1151	Harris, Edward	Sumner	640	2656	4 Jun 1796	3832	1 Jun 1795	81	353	Joining the said Harris survey	yes
Kelly, John	178		Green	100	648	11 Jul 1788	1405	17 Jan 1784	64	357	S/S Nollechuckey River in bent /sic/ of river	
Kelly, Thomas	2152	Brown, William	Davidson	274	2471	31 Dec 1793	984		81	433	On Whites Creek	yes
Kelsey, Hugh	1077		Green	100	920	26 Dec 1791	241	22 Oct 1783	77	249	N/S French Broad River on Kelsey Mill Creek	
Kelsey, Hugh	765		Green	225	570	23 Aug 1788	98	29 Oct 1783	68	249	Lying on the N side of French Broad River	
Kelsey, Samuel	1056		Washington	190	1006	27 Nov 1792	760	23 Dec 1778	80	178	Joining lands of Beadsley /sic/ Gambles &c	
Kelsey, Samuel	788		Washington	93	602 (3)	10 Nov 1784	2645	24 Sep 1780	69	139	On Boons Creek	
Kelso, Hugh	0118		Green	200			98	16 May 1790			N side of French Broad River	
Kelso, Hugh	979		Green	640	1206	29 Jul 1793	901	29 Oct 1783	76	467	Beg at an oak N bank of French Broad River	
Kelver, John	152		Eastern District	400	122	24 Dec 1792	1927	15 Oct 1779	78	454	On N side of Clinch River	
Kemp, David	078	King, Robert	Middle District	640			2520				N side of Clinch River	yes
Kemp, Joseph	613	Faison, Jas.	Tennessee	274	3172	14 Sep 1797	4033	25 Nov 1796	90	430	S side of Cumberland River	
Kenady, Robert	408		Middle District	880	347	17 Dec 1794	2038	3 May 1784	84	227	On N side of Elk River	

Claimant:	File #:	Assignee:	County:	Acres:	Grant:	Grant Date:	Entry:	Entry Date:	Bk:	Pg:	Location by Stream Name:	Military:
Kenady, Robert	458		Middle District	400	397	17 Dec 1794	2026	3 May 1784	84	260	On S side of Elk River	
Kenbro, Duke	06		Jefferson	100				15 Dec 1796 (surveyed)			S side of Holston River	
Kendey, James	431		Sumner	640	442	27 Jun 1793	815	19 Jun 1785	80	355	On Jennings Fork &c	
Keneday /sic/, Jacob	165		Hawkins	400	98	16 Nov 1790	2175	9 Nov 1779	77	184	On the S side of Holston River &c	
Kenedy, Anthony	100	Bude, Samuel	Tennessee	640	1516	10 Apr 1792	3408	29 Jan 1786	75	506	On S side of Cumberland River	yes
Kenedy, John	1183		Washington	200	1068	30 Dec 1793			82	142	On the waters of Nolachuckey &c	
Kenedy, John	2		Jefferson	150	1445	10 Aug 1803		26 Oct 1779	110	345	Joining of John Canada /sic/	
Kenedy, Moses	591		Washington	100	685	26 Oct 1786	2699	19 Dec 1780	66	4	On the waters of Lick Creek &c	
Kenedy, Moses	615		Washington	100	709	26 Oct 1786	2775	20 Feb 1780	66	5	Beg in the middle of a large spring	
Kener, Frances	412		Sullivan	500	291	10 Nov 1784	1036	6 Jan 1779	69	173	On N side of Holston River	
Keneday, Thomas	1206		Washington	50	1160	5 Dec 1794	1776	1 Oct 1779	83	417	On the drains of Big Limestone	
Kennedy, Andrew	16		Maury	640	32	14 Jul 1812	2136	30 Nov 1784	126	439	On both sides of Middle Fork	
Kennedy, David	1365		Washington	200	1015	27 Nov 1792	1968	19 Oct 1779	80	180	On waters of Knaves Branch	
Kennedy, Jacob	796		Hawkins	200	636	12 Jul 1794	1746	24 Sep 1779	82	225	On the N side of Holston River &c	
Kennedy, James	2462		Davidson	640	469	23 Apr 1800	429	7 May 1784	107	361	On Cedar Creek	
Kennedy, Jno, Wm, Thos.	443		Washington	399	435	13 Oct 1783	367	8 Sep 1778	52	282	Joining Daniel Kennedys survey	
Kennedy, Jno.	2		Maury	1435	3	14 Jul 1812	660	28 Oct 1783	126	427	Lying and being on a main fork	
Kennedy, John	1765		Green	150	1445	10 Aug 1803	2019	26 Aug 1779	110	345	Joining of John Canada /sic/	
Kennedy, Thomas	1266		Davidson	640	231	10 Jul 1788	636	18 Mar 1784	66	419	On the S side of Cumberland River	
Kenner, Hawson	253		Hawkins	640	241	26 Dec 1791	1036	6 Jan 1779	77	327	On Stock Creek	
Kenner, Hawson	41	Kenner, Thomas, decd	Hawkins	254	26	18 May 1789	561	30 Oct 1778	72	247	On the S side of Holston River &c	
Kenney, Thomas	1000	Payton, Ephraim	Sumner	480	156	17 Dec 1794		11 Dec 1792	84	333	On S side of Cumberland	yes
Kenney, Thomas	999	Payton, Ephraim	Sumner	480	155	17 Dec 1794		11 Dec 1792	84	332	On S side of Cumberland	yes
Kenor, Redham /sic/	467		Hawkins	100	339	29 Jul 1793			80	260	On the N side of Holston River	
Kenor, Rodham	050		Sullivan	100			688	8 Sep 1780			N side of Holston River	
Kent, Thomas	593	Sanders, William	Davidson	640	565	15 Sep 1787	1617		63	202	On N branch of Maney Fork Creek	yes
Ker, John	2343	Malloy, Thomas	Davidson	640	2987	10 Apr 1797	3630		90	288	On Harpeth River	yes
Ker, Joseph	950	Houston, Daniel	Davidson	640	967	18 May 1789			63	328	On head branches of Gibsons Creek	yes
Kerchin /Kirchin/, Godfrey	789		Washington	640	603	10 Nov 1784	1794	5 Oct 1779	69	139	Including the blew /sic/ spring	
Kerchin, Godfrey	777		Washington	250	591	10 Nov 1784	2656	26 Sep 1780	69	135	Below the blew /sic/ spring	
Kerdendall, Mathew	346		Sumner	428	1426	20 Dec 1791	3455	25 Oct 1786	77	358	On the Middle Fork of Red River	yes
Kerdendall, Matthew	610		Sumner	640	1867	20 May 1793	1964	6 Feb 1792	81	93	On Station Camp Creek	yes
Kerkendall, Jane	377		Sumner	274	1557	14 Jan 1793	1863	15 Feb 1787	79	271	Beg at a sugar tree	yes
Kerkendoll, Jane	612		Sumner	79-1/4	1871	20 May 1793	1693	22 Aug 1792	81	94	Beg at a double elm	yes
Kerney, Arthur	1492	Donelson, John	Davidson	420	1045	27 Nov 1789	1196		74	47	On S side of Cumberland River	yes
Kerr, Andrew	45		Green	5000	108	1 Nov 1786	2222	21 May 1784	58	469	Upon the N side of Tennessee River	
Kerr, David	134		Green	150	116	1 Nov 1786	923	1 Nov 1786	60	448	On the N side of Nolichuckie River	
Kerr, George	489		Washington	100	674	8 Dec 1787	2294	27 Nov 1779	60	447	Lying on the S side of Little Limestone	
Kerr, Joseph	713	Fox, Francis	Davidson	274	686	8 Dec 1787	498	16 apr 1784	63	242	On a branch of Big Harpeth River	yes
Kerr, Joseph	83		Middle District	2000	85	10 Jul 1788	1647	16 apr 1784	67	452	On the N side of Duck River &c	
Kerr, Patrick	612		Sullivan	200	565	Mar 1792	1653	19 Oct 1788	77	332	On a branch of the waters of Holston River	
Kerr, Robert	1175		Green	200	1018	26 Dec 1791	233	1 Nov 1786	77	288	Joining his old survey	
Kerr, Robert	12		Davidson	228	6	16 Feb 1786	567	16 Jan 1785	63	3	On Sulphur Lick Creek	
Kerr, Robert	371		Davidson	228	6	16 Feb 1786			63	3	(inter leaf) /sic/	
Kerr, Samuel	659		Sullivan	200	607	5 Jun 1793	458 -1862	1779 -1780	81	339	On waters of Fall Creek	

Claimant:	File #:	Assignee:	County:	Acres:	Grant:	Grant Date:	Entry:	Entry Date:	Bk:	Pg:	Location by Stream Name:	Military:
Kerr, Samuel	90		Middle District	1000	92	10 Jul 1788	1650	16 apr 1784	67	455	On the N side of Duck River &c	
Kerr, William	1509		Green	89	1270	12 Jul 1794			81	585	On S side of Holston River	
Kervin, Thomas	121	Hamilton, James	Davidson	274	107	7 Mar 1786	363		63	43	On Stones River	yes
Kethley, John	649		Tennessee	46	407	14 Sep 1797			92	19	On Spring Creek	
Key, Job	620		Sullivan	100	568	27 Jun 1793	158	14 Mar 1781	80	369	Beg at a white oak &c	
Key, Jonathan	1458		Not given	579	818	25 Sep 1800			109	257	On the N E side	
Keykendall, Peter	797		Washington	150	611	10 Nov 1784	2327	8 Apr 1780	69	141	On Sinking Creek	
Kidwell, Elijah	241	Beard, John Lewis	Davidson	640	227	7 Mar 1786	601		63	83	On Harpeth River	yes
Kien, John	1066		Green	200	909	26 Dec 1791			77	245	On the N side of French Broad River &c	
Kilgore, Thomas	1064		Davidson	640	38	17 Apr 1786	187	26 Jan 1784	66	47	Lying on a branch of Dry Creek	
Kilgore, Thomas	1365		Davidson	800	48	8 Oct 1787	186	26 Jan 1784	68	140	On the S side of Cumberland River	
Kilgore, Thomas	2310	Carter, Humphrey	Davidson	640	2511	27 Aug 1795	778		89	414	Between Red River & Sulphur Fork	yes
Kilgore, Thos.	1100		Davidson	640	74	17 Apr 1786	185	26 Jan 1784	66	59	On the S Fork of Red River	
Killingsworth, John	1465	Harris, Edward	Sumner	560	3382	12 Dec 1801	500	21 Feb 1801	114	89	On Caney Fork	yes
Kilpatrick /sic/, Michael	0127		Green	1000	379	17 Dec 1794	737	28 Oct 1783			N side of Elk River	
Kilpatrick, John	20	Sanders, James	Sumner	228	777	11 Jul 1788	1646	12 Feb 1787	63	272	On waters of Cumberland River	yes
Kilpatrick, Joseph	71		Middle District	800	73	10 Jul 1788	518	27 Oct 1783	67	446	On both side of Duck River &c	
Kilpatrick, Michael	440		Middle District	1000	379	17 Dec 1794			84	251	On N side of Elk River	
Kimberland, Jacob	1186		Davidson	640	163	17 Apr 1786	622	15 Nov 1784	66	189	On the waters of Bledsoes Creek &c	
Kimbro, Duke	1716		Green	100	383	19 Jul 1797		15 Dec 1796	90	369	S side of Holstein River	
Kimbro, Duke	1743		Green	100	362	4 Jul 1797			91	588	S side of Holston River	
Kimbrough, Jesse	855		Green	250	836	13 Feb 1791	91	25 Apr 1789	73	379	Kelseys Creek the waters of French Broad	
Kincade, Andrew	505		Green	200	501	20 Sep 1787	276	22 Oct 1783	65	524	N/S Holston River back from said river	
Kincade, Joseph	409		Sullivan	970	288	10 Nov 1784	970	8 Jun 1780	69	172	In Carters Valley	
Kincaid, David	51		Eastern District	200	48	18 May 1789	732	11 Feb 1781	72	259	On the S/S Clinch River in Homes's Valley	
Kincaid, Jos. & Jas. Brigham	03		Middle District	400			1104	11 Jan 1779				
Kincannon, Andrew	180		Sullivan	483	187	10 Oct 1783	53	8 Feb 1780	53	152	On big creek for heirs of Castleton Brooks	
Kincannon, Andrew	184 (195)		Sullivan	226	202	10 Oct 1783	54	8 Feb 1780	53	159	Nettle place for heirs of Castleton Brooks	
Kincannon, Matthew	463	McCoy, Eli	Davidson	640	435	15 Sep 1787			63	160	On waters of Second Creek	yes
Kincannon, Matthew	731	Darby, Patrick	Davidson	640	704	11 Jul 1788	2415		63	248	Lying on Second Creek	yes
Kindle, Geo & Martin Snyder	1287		Washington	150	1202	9 Dec 1795			89	402	Joining a 100 acre tract &c	
King Robert	699	Forgey, Jas.	Hawkins	500	501	16 Dec 1793	67		82	101	On the N side of Clinch River	
King, Andrew	1160	Harris, Edward	Sumner	640	2665	4 Jun 1796	2463	1 Jun 1795	88	356	Joining said Harris survey	yes
King, Anthony	309	Gwinn, Edward	Sumner	640	1517	10 Apr 1792	2519	6 Aug 1791	75	507	On waters of Spencers Creek	yes
King, Edmund	1989	Ford, John	Davidson	640	1905	20 May 1793	953		81	101	On N side of Cumberland River	yes
King, Edward	2260	Donelson, Stockley	Davidson	640	2724	20 Jul 1796	953		88	451	On waters of Harts Spring Branch	yes
King, Edward	287		Washington	640	154	24 Oct 1782	444	28 Sep 1778	47	74	N side of Watauga River	
King, Enoch	320	McCulloh, Benjamin	Tennessee	640	2033	20 May 1793	1639	22 Mar 1785	81	132	On S side of Cumberland River	yes
King, Enock /sic/	2073	Wilson, John	Davidson	640	2215	20 May 1793	3088		81	172	On Yellow Creek	yes
King, George	123	King, Robert (heir)	Davidson	640	109	7 Mar 1786	784		63	43	On Calebs Creek	yes
King, Henry	424		Washington	200	1083	12 Jul 1794	1490	27 Jul 1779	81	563	Beg at a white oak	yes
King, Jacob	2374	Stewart, Duncan	Davidson	640	3095	14 Sep 1797	4011		90	399	E Fork of S Harpeth River	yes
King, James	059	Dixon, Tilmon	Sumner	3840							On a creek of Stones River	
King, James	1069	King, William	Sumner	640	2546	10 Dec 1795	809	8 Aug 1795	88	296	Joining an entry of Robert King	yes
King, James	129		Hawkins	300	163	26 Dec 1791	2395	25 May 1784	75	169	On head of Richland Creek	yes

Claimant:	File #:	Assignee:	County:	Acres:	Grant:	Grant Date:	Entry:	Entry Date:	Bk:	Pg:	Location by Stream Name:	Military:
King, James	296		Eastern District	5000	209	7 Feb 1795			84	153	Bet the River Holston & Clinch	
King, James	370		Hawkins	300	304	14 Jan 1793			79	292	On N Fork of Bent Creek	
King, James	382		Hawkins	100	503	27 Jan 1793	458	24 Apr 1780	79	492	On waters of Richland Creek	
King, James	399		Hawkins	100	520	27 Jan 1793	458	24 Apr 1780	79	497	On the Richland Creek	
King, James	785		Hawkins	100	625	12 Jul 1794	458		82	221	On Richland Creek	
King, James	821		Hawkins	5000	645	31 Jan 1795			83	371	Bet the River Holston and French Broad	
King, James	822		Hawkins	5000	646	31 Jan 1795	1657	20 Dec 1794	83	372	Both sides of Clinch River	
King, James	826		Green	50	807	18 May 1789	765	28 Oct 1785	72	244	On the N side of Holston &c	
King, James	869		Hawkins	5000	643	3 Jan 1795	1656	15 Apr 1784	84	65	Joining his former survey	
King, James	870		Hawkins	5000	644	31 Jan 1795	1658	16 Apr 1784	84	65	On both sides of Clinch River	
King, James	936		Hawkins	5000	718(710)	8 Dec 1795			88	275	Between Holston & French Broad	
King, James	937		Hawkins	5000	719	8 Dec 1795	782		88	275	Between Tiver Holston and French Broad	
King, James & Co	733		Sullivan	3000		7 Mar 1796	843	14 Mar 1795	88	234	Beg at three white oaks on the Virginia line	
King, James & Co	741		Sullivan	640	2689	6 Jun 1796			88	365	Both sides of Beaver Creek	
King, John	061	Robertson, James	Davidson	274			960	23 Apr 1785			On waters of Big Harpeth	
King, John	123		Hawkins	400	157	26 Dec 1791	702	27 Oct 1780	75	167	On S side of Holston River	
King, John	2063		Davidson	457	2188	20 May 1793	2286		81	168	On the E Fork of Duck River	yes
King, John	214		Sullivan	400	221	10 Oct 1783	78	8 Feb 1780	53	167	On the N side of Holston River	
King, John	294		Washington	200	161	24 Oct 1782	461	30 Sep 1778	47	78	On both sides of Stoney Creek	
King, John	667		Sullivan	200	615	9 Jul 1794	1829	7 Oct 1779	81	626	On a branch known as Grant's Branch	
King, John	89		Sullivan	400	100	23 Oct 1782	1847	6 Oct 1779	43	286	On the N side of Holston River	
King, John	974		Hawkins	500	746	20 Jul 1796			88	498	On the Lick Branch	
King, John, Sr.	644		Hawkins	150	514	23 Apr 1794	494	7 Apr 1780	81	553	On N side of Holston River	
King, Joseph	447	Ward, Ennis	Davidson	274	419	15 Sep 1787	683		63	155	On meat camp of Bartons Creek	yes
King, Rbert /sic/	1559-a		Green	1000	205	30 Oct 1794			83	137	N side of Tenn. River &c	yes
King, Richard	202	Hart, Anthony	Sumner	640	1107	26 Nov 1789	2809	12 Mar 1788	74	132	On W side of Caney Fork River	yes
King, Robert	052		Sullivan	50			655	17 Jul 1780			In an island in Holston River	
King, Robert	068		Sullivan	150			487				On a fork of Sycamore Creek	
King, Robert	1031		Hawkins	200	794	22 Feb 1797	671	19 Aug 1780	90	227	On a branch of Holston River	
King, Robert	1039	Parry, Francis heirs	Hawkins	640	2957	22 Feb 1797	8748 /?/		90	233	On a branch of Clinch River	
King, Robert	1040	Prescott, Isaac heirs	Hawkins	640	2958	22 Feb 1797			90	233	N side of Clinch River	
King, Robert	122		Hawkins	300	156	12 Jan 1793	400	25 Apr 1783	75	166	On N side of Holston River	
King, Robert	1301		Green	500	1151	12 Jul 1794	1477	19 Feb 1784	78	395	On N side of Holston	
King, Robert	1494		Green	500	1257	12 Jul 1794	979	20 Sep 1787	81	580	On N side of Holston	
King, Robert	1500		Green	200	1262	12 Nov 1794			81	582	On S side of Clinch River	
King, Robert	1558		Green	150	1230	12 Jun 1794			82	183	On a fork of Sycamore Creek &c	
King, Robert	167		Green	200	637	23 Aug 1788	1280	24 Dec 1783	64	354	N/S Holston opposite Little Horseshoe bottom	
King, Robert	225		Hawkins	500	212	26 Dec 1791	732	28 Oct 1783	77	317	On the N side of Holston River	
King, Robert	252		Hawkins	600	240	26 Dec 1791	473	19 Apr 1780	77	326	Beg on two white oaks	
King, Robert	271		Eastern District	300	206	4 Jan 1795	1352	12 Jan 1784	84	40	On N side of Holston River	
King, Robert	309		Eastern District	400	128	30 Oct 1794			85	324	On N side of Tennessee	
King, Robert	346		Eastern District	287	256	7 Mar 1796	357	23 Oct 1783	88	332	On S side of Clinch River	
King, Robert	347	McAllister, John	Eastern District	274	2690	6 Jun 1796	3955		88	366	On Wallings Ridge	
King, Robert	363		Eastern District	500	279	20 Feb 1796			88	465	On N side of Holston	
King, Robert	378		Hawkins	300	499	27 Jan 1793	369	28 Mar 1780	79	490	On N fork of Bent Creek	

Claimant:	File #:	Assignee:	County:	Acres:	Grant:	Grant Date:	Entry:	Entry Date:	Bk:	Pg:	Location by Stream Name:	Military:
King, Robert	379		Hawkins	40	500	27 Jan 1793		10 Oct 1791	79	491	In an island in Holston River	
King, Robert	384		Hawkins	400	505	27 Jan 1793			79	492	On N side of Holston River	
King, Robert	390		Green	200	392	20 Sep 1787	848	11 Jul 1780	65	483	On Siam /sic/ Creek on the S/S Holston River	
King, Robert	396		Hawkins	50	517	27 Jan 1793			79	496	Lying in an island in Holston River	
King, Robert	419	Dodd, Jesse	Eastern District	274	2942	1 Mar 1797	4487		90	214	N side of Holston River	
King, Robert	424		Eastern District	400	292	1 Mar 1797	27	26 Aug 1781	90	229	Both sides of Sinking Creek &c	
King, Robert	425		Eastern District	150	293	1 Mar 1797	673	19 Aug 1780	90	230	N side of Cumberland River	
King, Robert	448		Green	300	450	20 Sep 1787	104	21 Oct 1783	65	501	On the S side of Nolachuckey River	
King, Robert	488		Hawkins .	270	360	29 Jul 1793	1005	7 Jun 1784	80	266	S side of Clinch River	
King, Robert	511	Bean, William	Middle District	640	2691	6 Jun 1796	3447		88	366	On N side of Spring Creek	yes
King, Robert	525	Garner, Thomas heirs	Middle District	640	2943	1 Mar 1797	4605		90	214	Waters of Caney Fork	yes
King, Robert	526	Gibson, Charles	Middle District	640	2951	1 Mar 1797			90	2951	N of Cumberland Mountain	yes
King, Robert	529		Middle District	2500	338	1 Mar 1797	2253	24 May 1784	90	235	On Camp Creek	
King, Robert	530		Middle District	2500	339	1 Mar 1797	2252	24 May 1784	90	236	On the mouth of a branch of Cane Creek	
King, Robert	531		Middle District	2500	340	1 Mar 1787	2258	24 May 1784	90	236	On a branch of Caney Fork	
King, Robert	532		Middle District	2500	341	1 Mar 1787	2254	24 May 1784	90	236	On Cain Creek	
King, Robert	533		Middle District	2500	342	1 Mar 1797	2259	30 Nov 1784	90	237	Including a spring	
King, Robert	536	McCoy, Patrick N.	Middle District	640	2960	2 Mar 1797	3939		90	255	On Camp Creek	yes
King, Robert	563	Swann, Thomas heirs	Middle District	640	3084	12 Aug 1797	3187		90	392	On a branch of Cumberland River	yes
King, Robert	564	Miles, Jacob heirs	Middle District	640	3085	12 Aug 1797	3176		90	392	On a branch of Caney Fork	yes
King, Robert	565	Haddock, Wm. Heirs	Middle District	640	3086	30 Aug 1797			90	393	On the Caney Fork	yes
King, Robert	596		Middle District	640	362	29 Jan 1798	96	8 /blank/			On a branch of Caney Fork	
King, Robert	636		Hawkins	600	504	27 Nov 1793	2235	22 Nov 1779	81	502	Near Powells River	
King, Robert	675	Bean, Henry	Hawkins	640	2385	12 Jul 1794			81	601	In a valley known as Calf Killers Valley	
King, Robert	682	Kelly, John heirs	Hawkins	640	2393	17 Jul 1794	3139		81	603	On the Sycamore Creek	
King, Robert	683	Dickner, David	Hawkins	640	2394	17 Jul 1794			81	603	N side of Wallens Ridge	
King, Robert	699	Forgey, Jas	Hawkins	500	501	16 Dec 1793	67		82	101	On N side of Clinch River	
King, Robert	705		Hawkins	40	525	12 Jun 1794	325	17 Mar 1780	82	161	On the N side of Clinch River &c	
King, Robert	710		Hawkins	200	530	12 Jun 1794	644	11 Jul 1780	82	163	On the S side of Holston River &c	
King, Robert	711		Hawkins	640	531	12 Jun 1794	167	16 Oct 1784	82	163	On the N side of Walling Ridge	
King, Robert	716		Hawkins	140 (150	536	12 Jun 1794	486	26 Apr 1780	82	166	On Kentuckey River	
King, Robert	721		Hawkins	250	541	12 Jun 1794	504	28 Apr 1780	82	168	On the N side of Wallings Ridge &c	
King, Robert	739		Hawkins	400	559	12 Jun 1794	325	17 Mar 1780	82	174	On the N side of Holston &c	
King, Robert	746		Hawkins	640	586	7 Jul 1794	1664	18 Sep 1779	82	205	On Renfrows Creek	
King, Robert	757		Hawkins	300	597	12 Jul 1794	400	25 Oct 1783	82	210	On the N side of Holston River	
King, Robert	778		Hawkins	300	618	12 Jul 1794	1395	16 Jan 1784	82	219	On German Creek &c	
King, Robert	812		Hawkins	200	648	6 Jan 1795	644	11 Jul 1780	83	169	N side of Clinch River	
King, Robert	860		Hawkins	640	639	16 Jan 1795	400	8 Apr 1780	84	37	On N side of Clinch River	
King, Robert	864		Hawkins	640	640 /sic/	4 Jan 1795		8 Jan 1780	84	46	On N side of Clinch River	
King, Robert	959		Hawkins	100	280	6 Jun 1796			88	378	On Powells River	
King, Robert & Isham Shilby /	1130		Hawkins	400	850	29 Jan 1798	634	14 Jun 1780	96	7	N side of Clinch Mountain	
King, Robert & Jas. Glasgow	943		Hawkins	258	263	6 Jun 1796		M. Armstrong	88	371	On Powells River	
King, Robert & Jas. Glasgow	946		Hawkins	250	266	6 Jun 1796		M. Armstrong	88	373	On both sides of Powells River	
King, Robert & Jas. Glasgow	947		Hawkins	300	267	6 Jun 1796		M. Armstrong	88	373	On both sides of Powells River	
King, Robert & Jas. Glasgow	949		Hawkins	200	269	6 Jun 1796		M. Armstrong	88	374	On Powells River	

Earliest Tennessee Land Records

Claimant:	File #:	Assignee:	County:	Acres:	Grant:	Grant Date:	Entry:	Entry Date:	Bk:	Pg:	Location by Stream Name:	Military:
King, Robert & Jas. Glasgow	952		Hawkins	375	272	6 Jun 1796		M. Armstrong	88	375	On Powells River	
King, Robert & Jas. Glasgow	953		Hawkins	200	273	6 Jun 1796		M. Armstrong	88	375	On S side of Powells River	
King, Robert & Jas. Glasgow	955		Hawkins	450	275	6 Jun 1796		M. Armstrong	88	376	On both sides of Powells River	
King, Robert & Jas. Glasgow	956		Hawkins	100	276	6 Jun 1796		M. Armstrong	88	377	On Stanleys Valley	
King, Robert & John Blair	783		Hawkins	200	623	12 Jul 1794	2669	19 Nov 1780	82	221	On German Creek	
King, Robert & John Latham	422	Phillips, Richard	Eastern District	274	2952	1 Mar 1797			90	219	S side of the Great Road	
King, Robert & Wm. Terrell	801		Hawkins	200	637	6 Jan 1795			83	163	On Clinch River &c	
King, Robert etal	1019		Hawkins	428	2944	1 Mar 1797	4440		90	215	In Powells Valley	
King, Robert, etal	025		Hawkins	640			2245	22 Nov 1779			In Stoney Fork Valley	
King, Robert, heir of George	123		Davidson	640	109	7 Mar 1786	784		63	43	On Calebs Creek	yes
King, Robert; Parks & Campb	658		Hawkins	200	563	12 Jul 1794	2392	3 Jan 1780	81	591	On N side of Sycamore Creek	
King, Robt & Geo.Christian	1035		Hawkins	240	798	1 Mar 1797	191	21 Feb 1780	90	229	On the head of Bull Creek	
King, Robt & Jas Cobb	031	Stephenson, Jonathan	Eastern District	640			4753					
King, Robt & Jas. Cooper	717		Hawkins	400	537	12 Jun 1794	1029	6 Jan 1779	82	166	On the waters of Powells River	
King, Robt & Jas. Cooper	942	Brickel, Nathaniel R. heirs	Hawkins	640	2692	6 Jun 1796	3924		88	367	On Stoney Fork Valley	
King, Robt & Jas. Galsgow /sl	954		Hawkins	200	274	6 Jun 1796		Martin Armstrong	88	376	On a branch of Stock Creek	
King, Robt & Jas. Glasgow	349		Eastern District	200	279	6 Jun 1796			88	378	On N side of Holston River	
King, Robt & Jas. Glasgow	944		Hawkins	500	264	6 Jun 1796		Martin Armstrong	88	372	On N side of Wallens Ridge	
King, Robt & Jas. Glasgow	950		Hawkins	262	270	6 Jun 1796		Martin Armstrong	88	374	On N side of Powells River	
King, Robt & Jas. Glasgow	951		Hawkins	200	271	6 Jun 1796		Martin Armstrong	88	374	On a creek known as Longs Creek	
King, Robt & Jas. Glasgow	958		Hawkins	100	278	6 Jun 1796		Martin Armstrong	88	377	On N side of Clinch River	
King, Robt & John Thompson	1023	Bellews, Charles	Hawkins	274	2953	1 Mar 1797	4482		90	219	On Caney Valley Creek	
King, Robt & N. Henderson	793		Hawkins	640	633	12 Jul 1794	1600	12 Sep 1779	82	224	At the end of Powells Mountain	
King, Robt & Nathaniel Hend	998		Hawkins	640	700	27 Aug 1795	911	29 Oct 1783	89	415	On N side of Clinch River	
King, Robt & Walter	784	Henderson, Nathaniel	Hawkins	250	624	12 Jul 1794			82	221	Lying near the fork of Powell Mountain	
King, Robt & Wm. Patterson	966		Hawkins	250	310	20 Jul 1794			88	443	On Richland Creek	
King, Robt.	078	Kemp, David heirs	Middle District	640			2520					
King, Robt. & Jas. Glasgow	945		Hawkins	150	265	6 Jun 1796		Martin Armstrong	88	372	On Powells River	
King, Robt. & Jas. Glasgow	948		Hawkins	200	268	6 Jun 1796		Martin Armstrong	88	373	On Powells River	
King, Robt. & Jas. Glasgow	957		Hawkins	100	277	6 Jun 1796		Martin Armstrong	88	377	On Powells River	
King, Robt. & John Rhea	709		Hawkins	640	529	12 Jun 1794			82	163	On the N side of Clinch River &c	
King, Robt. & Thos.	6		Hawkins	600	19	23 Aug 1788		17 Apr 1780	64	360	Joining above a survey of 600 acres &c	
King, Robt. & Thos.	7		Hawkins	1280	25	23 Aug 1788		2 Jan 1779	64	360	On Wolf River (Middle District)	
King, Thomas	010		Middle District	600			422	17 Apr 1780			On Brimstone Creek	
King, Thomas	026		Hawkins	200			1002	2 Jan 1779			N side of Holston River	
King, Thomas	1012		Washington	640	961	May 1792	1664	17 Sep 1779	77	400	On W Fork of Turkey Creek	
King, Thomas	1029		Hawkins	100	792	22 Feb 1797	324	17 Mar 1780	90	226	N side of Clinch Mountain	
King, Thomas	1030		Hawkins	100	793	22 Feb 1797	324	17 Mar 1780	90	227	N side of Clinch Mountain	
King, Thomas	1089		Hawkins	640	818	19 Jul 1797	381	3 Apr 1780	91	613	On Puncheon Camp Creek	
King, Thomas	1090		Hawkins	640	819	19 Jul 1797	380	10 Apr 1780	91	613	Waters of Clinch River	
King, Thomas	1091		Hawkins	640	820	19 Jul 1797	406	10 Apr 1780	91	614	In the Grassy Valley	
King, Thomas	1092		Hawkins	640	821	19 Jul 1797	325	17 Mar 1780	91	614	Waters of Sycamore Creek	
King, Thomas	1253		Washington	300	1225	20 Jul 1796	1355	6 May 1779	88	510	On waters of Nobb Creek	
King, Thomas	1378		Green	300	1233	27 Jan 1793	1939	15 Oct 1779	79	507	On N side of Holston River	
King, Thomas	1407		Green	300	1219	27 Nov 1792	824	26 Jul 1781	80	157	On Third Creek	

Claimant:	File #:	Assignee:	County:	Acres:	Grant:	Grant Date:	Entry:	Entry Date:	Bk:	Pg:	Location by Stream Name:	Military:
King, Thomas	1412		Green	640	1224	27 Nov 1792	15	21 Feb 1780	80	162	N/S Holston River on a br Beaverdam Creek	
King, Thomas	1422		Green	640	1234	27 Nov 1792	457	24 Apr 1780	80	165	Waters of the N Fork of Turkey Creek	
King, Thomas	1485		Green	640	1248	12 Jul 1794	1219	16 Dec 1779	81	577	On head of W Fork of Turkey Creek	
King, Thomas	1498		Green	34	1261	12 Jul 1794	558	24 Apr 1780	81	581	On an island in Clinch River	
King, Thomas	1554		Green	640	1219	8 Apr 1794	458	24 Apr 1780	82	156	On a creek known as Fourth Creek	
King, Thomas	1699		Green	300	1422	22 Feb 1797	1734	27 Jan 1794	90	230	N side of Clinch River	
King, Thomas	183		Green	400	792	20 Nov 1788	1363	11 May 1779	64	471	On the N side of Holston River &c	
King, Thomas	184		Green	600	793	20 Nov 1788	1008	29 Oct 1783	64	471	Head of creek known as McCrays Creek	
King, Thomas	185		Green	1200	794	20 Nov 1788	1725	16 Apr 1784	64	471	On the N side of Holston River, etc	
King, Thomas	232		Hawkins	640	219	26 Dec 1791	1665	17 Sep 1779	77	320	On No side of Holston River	
King, Thomas	329		Sullivan	2000 (20	469	10 Jul 1788			67	481	On the N side of Holston River	
King, Thomas	381		Hawkins	100	502	27 Jan 1793	131	19 Feb 1780	79	491	On Patersons Mill Creek	
King, Thomas	428		Sullivan	640	307	10 Nov 1784	1684	20 Sep 1779	69	179	On N side of Holstin River	
King, Thomas	558		Hawkins	100	431	29 Jul 1793	482		80	285	N side of Clinch Mountain	
King, Thomas	598		Sullivan	100	553	26 Dec 1791			77	304	In two Islands in Holstein River	
King, Thomas	677	Nobles, John heirs	Hawkins	640	2387	12 Jul 1794	3675		81	601	On Indian Creek	
King, Thomas	678	Maples, Marmaduke	Hawkins	518	2388	12 Jul 1794	3579		81	601	On E side of Holston River	
King, Thomas	751		Hawkins	150	591	7 Jul 1794	2172	9 — 1779	82	207	On the N side of Holston River	
King, Thomas	752		Hawkins	200	592	7 Jul 1794	2222	26 Nov 1779	82	208	On Puncheons Camp Creek	
King, Thomas	754		Hawkins	150	594	7 Jul 1794	1022	5 Jan 1778	82	208	S side of Clinch River &c	
King, Thomas	760		Hawkins	300	600	12 Jul 1794	2116	4 Nov 1779	82	211	On a creek known as Buckeye Creek	
King, Thomas	761		Green	640	580	11 Jul 1788	1248	12 Nov 1779	68	219	On a creek known as Sinking Creek	
King, Thomas	766		Hawkins	600	606	12 Jul 1794	930	29 Oct 1783	82	213	N side of Clinch Mountain &c	
King, Thomas	777		Green	400	582	23 Aug 1788	811	7 Feb 1785	68	254	On the N/S Holston River on the Third Creek	
King, Thomas	779		Green	100	585	23 Aug 1788	2223	16 Nov 1779	68	256	Lying on the N side of Holston River	
King, Thomas	779		Hawkins	600	619	12 Jul 1794	935	27 Oct 1783	82	219	On the N side of Clinch River &c	
King, Thomas	811		Hawkins	640	647 (674	6 Jan 1795			83	168	On E Fork of Emerys River &c	
King, Thomas	903	Owens, William	Hawkins	640	2030	2 Feb 1795	216	21 Feb 1780	84	327	On N Fork of Emerys River	
King, Thomas	924		Hawkins	64	706	2 Dec 1795	216	21 Feb 1780	88	263	On W Fork of Wilson Creek	
King, Thomas	969		Hawkins	100	741	20 Jul 1796	1028	21 Feb 1780	88	495	On Russels Creek	
King, Thomas & Jas. Cooper	691		Hawkins	400	580	17 Jul 1794	1028	6 Jan 1779	81	612	On N side of Clinch River	
King, Thomas & others	789	Hackner, Daniel	Hawkins	640	629	12 Jul 1794	3355		82	223	In Stoney Fork Valley	
King, Thomas & others	1489		Green	300	1252	12 Jul 1794	322	25 Jan 1786	81	579	On S side of Clinch River	
King, Thomas & Robert	204		Hawkins	300	191	26 Dec 1791	1682	23 Oct 1783	77	310	On the N side of Holston River	
King, Thomas & Robert	51		Middle District	5000	53	10 Jul 1788	1682	16 Apr 1784	67	436	Lying about four miles fr the great salt lick	
King, Thomas & Robert	69		Middle District	2500	71	10 Jul 1788	1689	16 Apr 1784	67	445	At a place known by the name of the banks	
King, Thomas & Robert	759		Green	400	578	11 Jul 1788	702	27 Oct 1780	68	218	On Brimstone Creek	
King, Thomas & Robert	760		Green	1000	579	11 Jul 1788	741	28 Oct 1783	68	218	On the S side of Clinch River &c	
King, Thomas & S.Donelson	076		Middle District	5000	576	11 Jul 1788	1723	16 Apr 1784			Green County on the waters of Wolf River	
King, Thomas (?) /sic/	027		Hawkins	300			365	28 Mar 1780			On N Fork of Bent Creek	
King, Thomas (?) /sic/	27		Hawkins	300			365	28 Mar 1780			On N Fork of Bent Creek	
King, Thomas (?) /sic/	071		Green	200			2222	16 Nov 1779			On the N side of Holston River	
King, Thos.	072		Green	50				9 Feb 1785				
King, Thos. & John Callun	725		Hawkins	400	543	12 Jun 1794	822	6 Jul 1781	82	169	On the N Fork of Sycamore Creek	
King, Thos. & Robt	16		Hawkins	1000	12	23 Aug 1788	1079	30 Oct 1783	67	433	Creek known as Brimstone Creek	

Claimant:	File #:	Assignee:	County:	Acres:	Grant:	Grant Date:	Entry:	Entry Date:	Bk:	Pg:	Location by Stream Name:	Military:
King, Thos. & Robt	17		Hawkins	1280	13	23 Aug 1788	2671,2275	19 Dec 1780	67	433	On Wolf River, Etc	
King, Thos. & Robt.	758		Green	1000	577	11 Jul 1788			68	218	On the N side of Tenn River &c	
King, Thos. & S.Donelson	575		Green	5000	576	11 Jul 1788			68	217	On the waters of Wolf River &c	
King, Thos. & S.Donelson	756		Green	5000	575	11 Jul 1788			68	217	On Spring Creek the waters of Wolf River	
King, Thos.& John Rhea	043		Hawkins	640			452	24 Apr 1780			S side of Clinch River	
King, Walter	1025		Washington	640	975	14 Dec 1791	478	25 Apr 1780	79	277	On S side of Nolachuckey River	
King, Walter	1026		Washington	300	976	14 Jan 1793	119	9 Feb 1780	79	277	On draughts of E Fork &c	
King, Walter	1028		Washington	640	978	14 jan 1793	1618	14 Se 1779	79	278	In Bumpass Cove	
King, Walter & James Brook	281		Hawkins	640	292	14 Jan 1793	2192	Oct 1779	78	343	On the Swan Pond Creek	
King, Walter & L.Newhouse	1016		Washington	640	965	14 Jan 1793	2160	6 Nov 1779	79	275	On E Fork of Cherokee Creek	
King, Walter & L.Newhouse	1019		Washington	640	968	14 Ja 1793	205	14 Apr 172	79	275	On S side of Nolachuckey River	
King, Walter & Robert	028		Hawkins	250			1947	12 Oct 1779			Near the foot of Powells Mountain	
King, Walter & Robert	747		Hawkins	190	587	12 May 1794	1027	6 Jan 1779	82	206	On the N side of Clarks River &c	
King, Walter;, John Sevier, Sr.	727		Sullivan	1000	672	27 Aug 1795	182,-193	1778 & 1780	87	522	On N side of Holston River	
King, William	1069		Sumner	640	2546	10 Dec 1795	809	8 Aug 1795	88	296	Joining an entry of Robert King	yes
King, William	485		Sullivan	400	496	18 May 1789	440	22 Apr 1780	71	9	On Holstons River beg at a beach /sic/	
King, William	090	Modlin, Ezekiel	Sumner	640			3781	8 Aug 1795			On Little Lick Creek	yes
King, William	1053		Sumner	640	2530	10 Dec 1795	3034	8 Aug 1795	88	289	On a creek called Lick Creek	yes
King, William	1054	Boyce, Seth	Sumner	640	2531	10 Dec 1795	1333	8 Aug 1795	88	289	On a creek called Lick Creek	yes
King, William	1055		Sumner	640	2532	10 Dec 1795			88	290	On Little Lick Creek	yes
King, William	1056		Sumner	640	2533	10 Dec 1795	1584	8 Aug 1795	88	290	Joining an entry of Robert King	yes
King, William	1057		Sumner	640	2534	10 Dec 1795			88	291	On Little Lick Creek &c	yes
King, William	1058		sumner	640	2535	10 Dec 1795	504	8 Aug 1795	88	291	On Salt River	yes
King, William	1059		Sumner	640	2536	10 Dec 1795			88	291	Joining an entry of Robt. King	yes
King, William	1061		Sumner	640	2538	10 Dec 1795	1830	8 Aug 1795	88	292	On a creek called Lick Creek	yes
King, William	1062		Sumner	640	2539	10 Dec 1795	505		88	293	On a creek called Lick Creek	yes
King, William	1063		Sumner	640	2540	10 Dec 1795	503		88	293	On a creek called Lick Creek	yes
King, William	1064		Sumner	640	2541	10 Dec 1795	441		88	294	On a creek called Lick Creek	yes
King, William	1065		Sumner	640 /?/	2542 /?/	10 Dec 1795 /?	798 /?/	8 Aug 1793 /?/	88 /?/	294 /?/	On Little Lick Creek /?/	yes
King, William	1066		Sumner	640	2643	10 Dec 1795			88	295	Joining an entry of Robt. King	yes
King, William	1068		Sumner	640	2545	10 Dec 1795			88	296	On Little Lick Creek	yes
King, William	253		Eastern District	200	206	6 Jan 1795	1494	25 Nov 1784	83	174	S side of Clinch River	
King, William	261		Sullivan	270	400	9 Aug 1787	116	8 Feb 1780	61	419	On the waters of Reedy Creek	
King, William	685		Sullivan	463	633	9 Jul 1794	117,-440	Feb & Apr 1780	81	632	Beg at a forked sycamore	
King, William	872		Green	340	822	27 Nov 1789	15	30 Jun 1787	74	22	Beg at a marked hickory	
King, William	876		Green	300	826	27 Nov 1789	15	30 Jan 1787	74	24	Beg at a stake	
King, John	061	Robertson, James	Davidson	274			960	23 Apr 1785			On waters of Big Harpeth River	yes
King, Thomas	185		Green	1200	794	20 Nov 1788	1725	16 Apr 1784	64	471	N/S Holston River nr a mile from said river	
Kings, Thomas & Robert	5		Middle District	1000	7	10 Jul 1788			67	409	On a branch of Wolf River	
Kings, Thos. & Robt	17		Hawkins	1280	13	23 Aug 1788	2691,-2275	19 Dec 1780	67	433	On Woolf /sic/ River &c	
Kingsberry, John	70		Davidson	4800	56	14 Mar 1786	383		63	23	On Beaver Creek	yes
Kinkaid, Joseph	119		Sullivan	600			1734	27 Sep 1779			S side of Holston River	
Kinkaid, Joseph	56		Sullivan	250	67	23 Oct 1782	190	25 Apr 1778	43	271	On the S side of Holston River &c	
Kinkead, Joseph	749		Sullivan	700	688	9 Dec 1795	644,-1734	1779,-1780	89	396	S of the river Ohio	
Kinney, Robert	054	Molloy, Thomas	Davidson	640			4629	27 Mar 1797			On Swan Creek	yes

Earliest Tennessee Land Records

Claimant:	File #:	Assignee:	County:	Acres:	Grant:	Grant Date:	Entry:	Entry Date:	Bk:	Pg:	Location by Stream Name:	Military:
Kirby, Edmund;	2119	Decem, Francis	Davidson	640	2395	7 jan 1794	1299		81	390	On both sides of Half Pone Creek	yes
Kirk, John	133		Davidson	1000	119	7 Mar 1786	793		63	47	South side of Red River	yes
Kirkendale, Joseph	455		Washington	100	447	13 Oct 1783	2846	12 Apr 1781	52	288	On the Roaring Fork of Lick Creek	
Kirkendall, John	030	Hill, Henry	Montgomery	640			3875	5 May 1797			On waters of Little West Fork of Red River	yes
Kirkendall, John	1071	Hill, Henry	Sumner	640	2519	10 Dec 1795	3875	8 Aug 1794	88	297	On W side of W Fork of Obeys River	yes
Kirkendall, Peter	1763		Green	900	1440	13 Dec 1798	2327	8 Apr 1780	97	298	On Sinking Creek	
Kirkland, William	2099	Sheppard, Nancy	Davidson	640	2324	20 May 1793	2073		81	196	On 1st creek which Continental Line cross	yes
Kirkpatrick, Alexander	195		Sumner	640	1051	27 Nov 1789	3374	25 Apr 1788	71	289	On the N side of Cumberland River	yes
Kirkpatrick, Hugh	961		Green	100	875	17 Nov 1790	1733	17 Apr 1784	76	130	On Bowman's branch a fork of Bent Creek	
Kirkpatrick, Jacob	1649		Green	200	1348	28 Aug 1795	55	8 Feb 1780	87	523	On waters of Bent Creek	
Kirkpatrick, John	0128		Green	1000	332	17 Dec 1794	1934	28 Apr 1784			On Buffalow River	
Kirkpatrick, John	393		Middle District	1000	332	17 Dec 1794			84	220	On Buffalo River	
Kirkpatrick, John;	1855	Boyd, John	Davidson	476	1580	27 Apr 1793	1382		81	12	On waters of Harpeth	yes
Kirkpatrick, John;	2196		Davidson	30	201	27 Feb 1796		26 Feb 1792	88	162	On waters of Richland Creek	
Kirkpatrick, Michael;	1858	McDonald, Arthur	Davidson	640	1585	27 Apr 1793	897		81	14	On waters of Big Harpeth	yes
Kirkpatrick, Michael;	1859	Burnsides, David	Davidson	360	1586	27 Apr 1793	222		81	14	On waters of Big Harpeth	yes
Kirkpatrick, Michael;	1882	Gillespie, David	Davidson	274	1625	27 Apr 1793	161		81	25	On waters of Big Harpeth	yes
Kirkpatrick, Robert	401		Hawkins	100 (100	522	27 Jan 1793	1037	29 Oct 1783	79	498	On N side of Holston River	
Kirkpatrick, Robert	977		Green	300	891	17 Nov 1790	1039	29 Oct 1783	76	135	On Plum Creek including the war path	
Kissinger, John	1832		Davidson	640	319	27 Nov 1792	469	5 Jun 1784	81	1	On waters of Harpeth River	
Kite, Demsey	1393	Davis, James	Sumner	640	3320	6 Dec 1797	3989	17 Jun 1797	97	43	On waters of Cedar Creek	yes
Kite, Richard	1302		Washington	150	1188	4 Dec 1795	1434	19 May 1785	89	430	On Watery Fork of Gap Creek	
Kite, Robert	069		Sullivan	200			1015	20 Oct 1779				
Kite, William	059	Sheppard, John	Not given	640			2856	15 Aug 1792			On Obeys River	yes
Kites, Charles	596	Donelson, Stockley	Tennessee	274	3076	19 Jul 1797	4143		90	381	N side of Cumberland River	
Kitrine, Laurence /sic/	502		Sullivan	1276	513	18 May 1789	47 -48	13 Nov 1783	71	17	Including two warrants	
Kitt, Solomon	291		Western District	5000	280	25 Apr 1789	2078	5 May 1784	72	84	On both sides of Big Hatcha /sic/ river	
Kitt, Solomon	292		Western District	5000	281	25 Apr 1789	2076	5 May 1784	72	84	On both sides of Big Hatcha /sic/ river	
Kitt, Solomon	314	Stokes, John hrs	Davidson	640	300	13 Jun 1787	1687		63	112	South side of Cumberland	yes
Knight, James	2363	Swaggerty, Abraham	Davidson	640	3061	19 Jul 1797	140		90	374	On first fork of West Fork	yes
Knight, Miles	618	McAustin, John	Tennessee	1000	3180	14 Sep 1797	238		90	434	S side of Cumberland River	yes
Knight, Morgan	18	Taylor, James P.	Giles	640	38	14 Jul 1812	198	14 Jul 1812	126	442	On Pigeon Root /sic/	yes
Knight, Samuel	462	Matthews, Musserdan	Davidson	274	434	15 Sep 1787	217	23 Dec 1809	63	160	On waters of Station Camp Creek	yes
Knox, John	311		Sumner	3840	1521	10 Apr 1792	1255	21 Sep 1787	75	508	On both sides of N fork of Smiths Fork	
Kolb, Robert /sic/	492		Sullivan	400	503	18 May 1789	1931	15 Oct 1779	71	13	On Stock Creek	
Koil, Solomon	180		Hawkins	100	113	16 Nov 1790	308	16 Mar 1780	77	188	On the N side of Holston River	
Koil, Robert /sic/	051		Sullivan	100								
Koin, John	449		Davidson	571	421	15 Sep 1787	839	31 Dec 1778	63	156	South side of Cumberland River	yes
Koons, Phillip	960		Washington	233	937	17 Nov 1790	914	15 Oct 1779	76	156	On a fork of Roans Creek	
Koyl, Robert	606		Sullivan	300	561	26 Dec 1791	1928		77	306	On the N side of Holston River &c	
Krauss, Gottlob;	1555	Ready, John	Davidson	640	1171	26 Nov 1789	2155	14 Feb 1784	74	173	On E fork of Stones River	yes
Kuckindale, Simon	1036		Davidson	640	10	17 Apr 1786	232		66	37	Lying on Karpers /sic-Kaspers?/ Creek &c	
Kuntz, Phillip	105		Hawkins	200	139	26 Dec 1791			75	158	On Swan Pond Creek	
Kuykendal, Abram	274		Washington	200	142	23 oct 1782	716	19 Dec 1778	47	69	On waters of great Limestone	
Kuykendal, Abram	281		Washington	200	148	23 Oct 1782	228	26 May 1778	47	72	On waters of Great Limestone	

Claimant:	File #:	Assignee:	Acres:	Grant:	County:	Entry:	Entry Date:	Bk:	Pg:	Location by Stream Name:	Military:
Kuykendal, Abram	342		100	209	Washington	2528	8 Apr 1780	49	230	On the waters of Great Limestone	
Kuykendal, John	341		150	208	Washington	2529	8 Apr 1780	49	230	On the waters of Great Limestone	
Kuykendall, Adam	1867	Harden, Benj.	388	1604	Davidson	1230		81	18	On both sides of Sulphur Fork of Red River	yes
Kuykendall, Joseph	1256	Malden, James	1640	221	Davidson	354	12 Mar 1784	66	416	On the Middle Fork of Red River	
Kuykendall, Samuel	907	Crafford, Hugh	274	2476	Sumner	3470	2 Jun 1785	81	435	Both sides W Fork of Station Camp Creek	yes
Kuykindall, Benjamin	1175		640	152	Davidson	153	17 Jan 1784	66	186	On the Middle Fork of Station Camp Creek	
Kyler, Joseph	709		200	750	Green	51	21 Oct 1783	66	477	On the S side of Nolichuckey River &c	
Kyles, Robert	169		200	102	Hawkins	1015	16 Nov 1790	77	186	On Caney Creek	
Lacey, John	1711		200	1426	Green	193	8 Jul 1797	90	321	S/S Holston River & French Broad River	
Lackay, Archibald	1127		200	970	Green	1919	11 Oct 1779	77	271	On the waters of Tennessee River &c	
Lackay, James Woods	157		400	127	Eastern District		14 Jan 1793	79	288	On N side of Holston River	
Lackay, Samuel	211		640	197	Middle District		14 Jan 1793	79	285	On Mill Creek	
Lackey, James	1124		100	967	Green		26 Dec 1791	77	270	On the S side of Holsten River &c	
Lackey, James	246		276	203	Green	175	20 Sep 1787	65	432	On French Broad River &c	
Lackey, James & Andrew	1712		150	1427	Green	7	23 Dec 1779	90	322	Waters of Lick Creek	
Lackey, James Wood /sic/	313		5000	218	Eastern District		18 Aug 1795	87	505	At the head of Lackey Creek	
Lackey, James Woods	1049		345	813	Hawkins	2187	12 Nov 1779	90	326	S side of Holston River	
Lackey, James Woods	1121		500	964	Green	794	10 Jun 1781	77	269	S side of French Broad River &c	
Lackey, James Woods	1122		300	965	Green	431	19 Apr 1780	77	269	On the N side of Tennessee River &c	
Lackey, James Woods	256		1500	203	Eastern District			83	245	On Little River on waters of Holston	
Lackey, James Woods	271		640	282	Hawkins			78 /?/	338	On S side of Holston River	
Lackey, James Woods	688		1000	577	Hawkins			81	611	On N side of Clinch River	
Lackey, James Woods etal	1	S. Donelson	1000	815	Grainger			91	597	In Powells Valley	
Lackey, James Woods etal	244		1000	207	Eastern District			83	130 (13	N side of Tennessee River	
Lackey, James Woods etal	984		53	1211	Green			76	468	Beg. at a pine tree &c	
Lackey, Jas W & Wm Terrell	272		1200	207	Eastern District	1723	16 Apr 1784	84	41	On Six Mile Creek	
Lackey, Jas. & McClung	1126		1000	969	Green			77	271	On Little River	
Lackey, Jas. W.	1455	Woods, Jno.	200	1651	Green			81	41	Beg. at a white oak	
Lackey, Jas. W. & others	1642		1000	1345	Green	368	8 Feb 1780	87	512	On N side of Lick Creek	
Lackey, Jas. W. & others	269		200	280	Hawkins	723	7 Jun 1784	78	337	On N side of Holston River	
Lackey, Jas. W. & Terrell	303		-000 /si	212	Eastern District			84	288	On S side of Tennessee River	
Lackey, Jas. W. & W. Tyrrell	1047		240	811	Hawkins	2193	26 Feb 1778	90	325	S side of Holston River	
Lackey, Jas. W. & W. Tyrrell	1050		500	814	Hawkins	697	3 Nov 1783	90	327	On waters of Buck Creek	
Lackey, Jas. W. & W. Tyrrell	1704		1000	1420	Green	2329	25 May 1789 (178	90	242	Beg at a marked black oak	
Lackey, John	344	Ross, William	640	329	Davidson	2745	28 Jul 1787	63	122	On ridge bet. Red River & Station Camp Cr	
Lackey, William	493		200	365	Hawkins	1406	24 May 1779	80	268	S side of Holston River &c	
Lackey,Jas & Wm Terrell	293		10000	210	Eastern District		1 Feb 1795	84	150	Lying on Eanstenaughty /?/ Creek	
Lackey,V W & Robt Young	019		5354		East District	2130-517-472					
Lacy, Hopkins & Math Lively	301		640	1991	Tennessee	2133	9 Sep 1785	81	122	On S side of Cumberland River	
Lacy, Hopkins & Thos Malloy	266	Scarborough, Nathan	640	1717	Tennessee	3683	10 Dec 1788	81	57	On the first creek N of Cumberland	
Lain, Aquilla	266		100	405	Sullivan	1244	24 Feb 1779	61	424	On the S side of Holston River	
Lain, Corban	466		150	468	Green		20 Sep 1787	65	507	Beg. at a Spanish oak	
Lain, Duttain /sic/	198		100	66	Washington	573	23 Oct 1782	47	32	On the waters of Lick	
Lain, Dutton	165		150 (100	33	Washington	371	9 Sep 1778	47	15	On waters of Lick Creek	
Lain, Joel	1301		640	266	Davidson	48	1 Jan 1784	66	430	Harpeth River below mouth of Jones Creek	

Claimant:	File #:	Assignee:	County:	Acres:	Grant:	Grant Date:	Entry:	Entry Date:	Bk:	Pg:	Location by Stream Name:	Military:
Lain, Joel	132		Middle District	2000	134	10 Jul 1788	751	28 Oct 1783	67	473	On the S side of Duck River	
Lain, John	504	Lytle, Archibald	Sumner	640	1675	20 May 1793	2742	30 Nov 1792	81	47	On Lick Creek	yes
Lain, John Fuller	014		Washington	103			600	23 Mar 1779			On S side of Boons Creek	
Lain, Lamberth	256		Sullivan	316	395	9 Aug 1787	207	20 Apr 1778	61	414	On the South side of Holston River	
Lain, Richard	269		Sullivan	100	408	9 Aug 1787	1541	24 Aug 1779	61	427	In a bend on the South side of Holston	
Lain, Thomas	190		Hawkins	100	123	16 Nov 1790	615	18 Jun 1780	77	191	Lying on Graveley Valley	
Laine, Thomas	061	Donelson, Stockley	Sumner	640			3095	10 May 1796			On First Creek E of Pond Lick Creek	yes
Lains, John	314		Washington	399	181	24 Oct 1782	1174	1 Feb 1779	49	217	On Cedar Creek	
Lamb, Abner	177		Davidson	2560	163	14 mar 1786	864		63	62	North side of Cumberland River	yes
Lamb, Gibbs	188	Dickson, James	Tennessee	640	1468	4 Jan 1792	251	25 oct 1783	77	368	On both sides of Jones Creek	yes
Lamb, Gideon	282		Davidson	6171	268	14 Mar 1786	969		63	98	South side of Cumberland River	yes
Lamb, Hugh	651		Hawkins	200	521	May 1794	2256	22 Nov 1779	81	554	Beg. at a poplar	
Lamb, John	469	Messingale, Solomon	Sumner	640	1628	27 Apr 1793	1715	30 Nov 1792	81	24	On a small fork of Smiths Fork	yes
Lamb, Nathan	1969	Donelson, John	Davidson	640	1847	20 May 1793	2522		81	89	On E of Wm. Stewarts preemption	yes
Lamb, Robert	948		Green	640	862	17 Nov 1790	117	21 Oct 1783	76	125	N side of French Broad &c	
Lambert, Aaron	205	Queen, Michael	Tennessee	2102	1495	4 Jan 1792	1356	23 May 1791	77	374	On both sides of Pine River	
Lambert, Aaron	468	Davis, Arch	Tennessee	274	2601	7 Mar 1796	1399	16 Nov 1784	88	327	On both sides of Pine River	
Lambert, Aron	385	Dixon, Thomas	Tennessee	640	2381	14 Dec 1793	1341	4 Nov 1784	81	385	On N side of Cumberland River	
Lambert, Henry	723	Sheppard, Nancy	Davidson	640	696	11 Jul 1788	2082		63	245	On waters of Kaspers Creek	yes
Lamberth, Daniel	621		Sullivan	140	569	27 Jun 1793	1778	21 Feb 1780	80	370	On Sinking Creek	
Lambrick, James	052	Hughlett, William	Middle District	640			2524				On the N side of Duck River	yes
Lanair /sic/, William	124		Middle District	1500	126	10 Jul 1788	771	28 oct 1783	67	470	On the N side of Duck River	
Lanbrick, James hrs.	52	Hughlett, William	Middle District	640			2524					
Lancaster, John	274		Sumner	2560	1265	10 Dec 1790	101	23 Sep 1785	74	354	On W side of Caney Fork	yes
Lancaster, John	374	Boone, Aaron	Tennessee	640	2289	20 May 1793	1994	16 Aug 1785 /178	81	189	On N side of Cumberland River	
Lancaster, John	375	Surles, Joseph	Tennessee	640	2307	20 May 1793	2238	12 Sep 1785	81	192	On N side of Cumberland River	
Lancaster, John	562		Sumner	640	1785	20 May 1793	2220	2 Jun 1792	81	75	On head waters of a creek &c	yes
Lancaster, John	778		Sumner	640	2232	20 May 1793	2225	2 Sep 1792	81	176	On head waters of Bartons Creek	yes
Lancaster, John	802		Sumner	640	2267	20 May 1793	2226	2 Jun 1792	81	184	On S side of Cumberland River	yes
Land, Joseph	15		Maury	640	31	14 Jul 1812	2241	30 Nov 1784	126	439	On S side of Duck River	
Landers, Abram	344		Middle District	879	296	17 Dec 1794	700	28 Oct 1783	84	74	On Duck River	
Landers, Abram	345		Middle District	2000	297	17 Dec 1794	1793	23 Apr 1784	84	74	In Wilsons Valley	
Lane, Aquilla	073		Green	240	74	1 Nov 1786	1312	1 Nov 1786			N side French Broad River	
Lane, Aquilla	11		Green	240	74	1 Nov 1786	2288	27 Nov 1779	58	435	On the N side of French Broad River	
Lane, Corbin	027		Washington	46			2102	31 Oct 1779			Joining his other lands	
Lane, Corbin	1360		Green	46	1215	27 Jan 1793	2362	18 Dec 1775	79	502	Joining his other lands	
Lane, Duton /sic/	1496		Green	100	1259	12 Jul 1794	407	21 Sep 1778	81	581	On first branch of Cedar Creek	
Lane, Isaac	581		Washington	76	752	26 Oct 1786	2822	23 Mar 1781	65	164	Joining William Beans land	
Lane, James	211	Jesse Reed	Sumner	640	1116	26 Nov 1789	2744	12 Mar 1788	74	137	On W side of Caney Fork River	
Lane, Jesse	306	John Rice	Davidson	640	292	13 Jun 1787	865		63	109	On Millers Creek	yes
Lane, Jesse	869	John Rice	Davidson	640	884	25 Apr 1789			63	306	Lying adjoining Rices claim	yes
Lane, Richard	053		Sullivan	66			541	29 Apr 1780			Beg at Alex Moores corner	
Lane, Thomas	691	Cobb, Jesse	Davidson	274	664	8 Dec 1787	1261		63	235	On Brush Creek	yes
Lane, Tidiance /sic/	1249		Green	100	1099	12 Jan 1793			78	363	Beg. in the hollow of Bent Creek	yes
Lane, William	402		Sullivan	100	281	10 Nov 1784	1177	1 Feb 1779	69	171	On South side of Holstin River	

Earliest Tennessee Land Records

Page 262

Claimant:	File #:	Assignee:	County:	Acres:	Grant:	Grant Date:	Entry:	Entry Date:	Bk:	Pg:	Location by Stream Name:	Military:
Laney, Jeremiah	1370		Green	50	1225	27 Jan 1793	2284	8 Apr 1791	79	505	Beg. at a sugar tree	
Langdon, Jonathan	076		Green	100			1535	23 Aug 1779			On the waters of French Broad River	
Langdon, Jonathan	1393		Green	640	1205	27 Nov 1792	946	2 Jan 1779	80	151	Lying in Grassey Creek	
Langdon, Jonathan	820		Green	200	821	11 Aug 1789	1415	17 Jan 1784	71	37	N fr French Broad Riv & on waters thereof	
Langford, Peter	850	Armstrong, Andrew	Davidson	640	855	17 Jan 1789	2206		63	298	N boundary of Robert Nelson's Sugar Cam	yes
Langhan, Elias	173		Middle District	1000	183	20 Dec 1791	689	28 Apr 1783	75	229	On Clear Fork of Cumberland River	
Langston, David	470		Sumner	640	1630	27 Apr 1793	2676	1 Dec 1792	81	24	On the Dividing Ridge &c	yes
Langston, Josiah	32	Fenner, Richard	Sumner	640	843	11 Jun 1789	2103	17 Mar 1788	63	295	On N side of Cumberland	yes
Langston, Samuel	1307	Hill, Daniel	Sumner	640	3080	19 Jul 1797	4641	12 Apr 1797	90	383	Martins Creek	yes
Lanham, Abel	443		Green	200 ?/l	445	20 Sep 1787	1474	19 Feb 1784	65	500	Lying on Bent Creek &c	
Laniar /sic/, James	1012	Oats, Daniel	Davidson	640	1029	18 May 1789	2538		63	343	On Middle Fork of Red River	yes
Lanier, Alexander	607		Sumner	640	1861	20 May 1793	1390	8 Aug 1795	81	92	On S side of Main Smiths Fork	yes
Lanier, Edward	2086	McCullough, Benjamin	Davidson	640	2288	20 May 1793	2288		81	188	On the waters of Stones River	yes
Lanier, James	32	Blount, Jno.G & Thos.	Davidson	2560	18	14 Mar 1786	475		63	8	On waters of Harpeth River	
Lanier, James	406	Howard, William	Davidson	640	378	15 Sep 1787	3464		63	141	S side of Big Barren River	Yes
Lanier, James	572	Lee, Henry	Davidson	640	544	15 Sep 1787	3359		63	195	South side of Big Barren River	yes
Lanier, James	576	Starn, Peter	Davidson	640	548	15 Sep 1787	3479		63	197	South side of Barren River	yes
Lanier, James	763	Bear, Jesse	Davidson	640	736	11 Jul 1788	3449	not given	63	259	On main Salt Lick Fork	yes
Lanier, James	764	Everitt, Thomas hrs	Davidson	640	737	11 Jul 1788	3461		63	259	Main Salt Lick Fork of Big Barrow /sic/ Rive	yes
Lanier, James	779	Mann, Francis	Davidson	640	752	11 Jul 1788	3362		63	264	On S/S main East fork of Big Barron River	yes
Lanier, James;	742	Smart, John hrs	Davidson	640	715	11 Jul 1788	3481		63	251	South side of Reves Creek	yes
Lanier, James;	324	Wiggle, Dempsey	Davidson	640	310	28 Jun 1787	2346		63	115	South side of Big Barron River	yes
Lanier, James;	406	Howard, William	Davidson	640	378	15 Sep 1787	3463		63	141	S side of Big Barren River	yes
Lanier, James;	417	Sally, Thomas	Davidson	640	389	15 Sep 1787	3377		63	145	South side of Big Barren River	yes
Lanier, James;	603		Sumner	640	1853	20 May 1793			81	90	On waters of Smiths Fork	yes
Lanier, James;	730	Rhodes, Jacob	Davidson	640	703	11 Jul 1788	3476		63	247	On South side of Kerrs Creek	yes
Lanier, Lewis	557		Middle District	2000	356	8 Jun 1797	2289	25 May 1784	90	345	On Cane Creek	
Lanier, Peter	877	Sugg, Aquilla	Davidson	640	891	17 Jan 1789	2464		63	309	On W side of Main E Fork of Stones River	yes
Lanier, Robert	1533	Anderson, Daniel	Davidson	640	1090	26 Nov 1797	2205		74	126	On S side of Cumberland River	yes
Lanier, Robert	555		Middle District	640	354	8 Jun 1797	1997	30 Apr 1784	90	344	On Tennessee River	
Lanier, Robert	556		Middle District	640	355	8 Jun 1797	1998	30 Apr 1784	90	345	At the south of Russells Creek	
Lanier, Robert	559		Middle District	640	358	8 Jun 1797	1999	30 Apr 1784	90	346	On Matthews Creek	
Lanier, Robert	560		Middle District	5000	359	8 Jun 1797	2288	25 May 1784	90	346	On Elk River	
Lanier, Robert	561		Middle District	640	360	8 Jun 1797	1996	30 Apr 1784	90	347	E side of Russells Creek	
Lanier, Robert	562		Middle District	500	361	8 Jun 1797	1995	30 Apr 1784	90	347	W side of Elk River	
Lard, James	459		Hawkins	640	331	29 Jul 1793	501	28 Apr 1780	80	258	In Powells Valley	
Lard, James	471		Hawkins	640	343	29 Jul 1793	287	10 Mar 1780	80	261	On Powells Valley	
Lard, James	491		Hawkins	640	363	29 Jul 1793	126	9 Feb 1780	80	267	In Powells Valley on the Boundary line	
Laremore, Marmaduke	031	Hill, Henry	Montgomery	640			3872	5 May 1797			On waters of Little W Fork of Red River	yes
Largan, Wm.	916		Green	150	830	17 Nov 1790	819	29 Oct 1763	76	115	S side of Nolechuckey River &c	
Lark, James	6		Maury	150	21	14 Jul 1812	2315	27 Nov 1779	126	434	On waters of Catheys Creek	
Larkin, John	567	McDaniel, Hugh	Davidson	1000	539	15 Sep 1787	768		63	194	On Jones Creek	
Larkins, David	371		Hawkins	300	325	27 Jul 1793	1920	11 Oct 1779	79	488	On S side of Holston River	yes
Larkins, Stephen	1430	Leamon, Peter	Sumner	274	3304	6 Dec 1797	4037	27 Apr 1797	98	177	On the waters of Big Barren &c	yes
Larrimore, Marmaduke	1070	Hill, Henry	Sumner	640	2518	10 Dec 1795	3872	8 Aug 1795	88	297	On W side of W Fork of Obeys River	yes

Claimant:	File #:	Assignee:	County:	Acres:	Grant:	Grant Date:	Entry:	Entry Date:	Bk:	Pg:	Location by Stream Name:	Military:
Larrimore, T.	797	Saunders, John	Hawkins	400	2	19 Jul 1794	4323		82	227	S/S Holstein River on Honeycutts Creek	yes
Larrimore, William	677	Wheaton, Daniel	Tennessee	640	3296	6 Dec 1797	537	19 Jul 1784	98	172	On W Fork of Barretts Creek	
Larymore, Edward	1812		Davidson	640	385	26 Jun 1793		19 Jul 1784	80	337	Two sugar trees on bank of Cumberland Riv	yes
Lash, Christian	1505	Bryan, John hrs.	Davidson	640	1062	26 Nov 1789	2788		74	109	On N side of Cumberland River	yes
Lassiter, Jacob	1559	Nelson, Robert	Davidson	640	1181	640	712		74	315	On N side of Cumberland River	yes
Lassiter, James	610	Stewart, Duncan	Tennessee	1000	3156	14 Sep 1797	4047		90	424	N side of Cumberland River	yes
Lassiter, Samuel	600	Hart, Anthony	Davidson	640	572	15 Sep 1797	2671		63	205	On the trace near head of Gilkersons Creek	
Laster, James	871	Humphries, Elijah	Sumner	640	2387a	7 Jan 1794	2858	12 Oct 1792	81	387	On a small creek &c	yes
Laster, Josiah	068	Sheppard, John	Not given	640			2857	15 Aug 1792			On Obeys River	yes
Lath, Abner	832	Baker, John	Sumner	640	2318	20 May 1793	3413	19 Nov 1792	81	195	Beg. at a white oak &c	yes
Latham, Jno.	1059		Davidson	640	33	17 Apr 1786	111	15 Jan 1784	66	45	On the Wt Fork of Station Camp Creek	
Latham, Phineas	288		Tennessee	1000	1910	20 may 1793	623	22 Apr 1784	81	102	On S/S of Cumberland River on Dyers Creek	
Lathem, John;	1022	Reaves, Samuel	Hawkins	200	2949	1 Mar 1787	4505		90	217	Both sides of Caney Fork	
Lathim, James	152		Hawkins	178	328	29 Jul 1793	1741	27 Sep 1779	76	466	N side of Holston &c	
Lathim, Jno. & Donelson	1033		Hawkins	640	796	22 Feb 1797	155	12 Mar 1778	90	228	Both sides of Poore Valley Creek	
Latimer, Jonathan,	364		Sumner	50	107	4 Jan 1792		14 May 1791	77	379	On a Wt branch of Station Camp Creek	
Laton, William	224	Drake, Jonathan	Davidson	640	210	7 Mar 1786	608		63	78	North side of Cumberland River	
Lauchlin /sic/, John	761		Sullivan	80	740	28 Jul 1797	295	10 Mar 1780	90	388	Beg at the white oak	
Lauderdail /sic/, Wm.	1092		Davidson	640	66	17 Apr 1786	250	6 Feb 1784	66	56	On the Wt Fork of Goose Creek	yes
Laughlin, John	201		Sullivan	400	208	10 Oct 1783	92	10 Mar 1780	53	162	N/S Holston River, beginning at 2 white oaks	
Laughlin, Alexander	121		Sullivan	720	133	23 Oct 1782	296-197	Mar & May, 1780	43	321	Both sides of Sinking Creek	
Laughlin, Alexander	156		Hawkins	300	89	16 Nov 1790	1132	30 oct 1783	77	181	On the N side of Holston River	
Laughlin, Cornelius	1389	Donelson, John	Sumner	640	3314	6 Dec 1797	4635	10 Apr 1797	97	39	On a S branch of Falling Creek	yes
Laughlin, James	123		Sullivan	456	135	23 Oct 1782	444	22 Apr 1780	43	322	On the North side of Holston River	
Laughlin, John	202		Sullivan	320	209	10 Oct 1783			53	162	Beg at Alex. Grabs corner white oak	
Laurence, Adam	2057	Estridge, Thomas	Davidson	640	2154	20 May 1793	1466		81	161	On S side of Cumberland River	yes
Laurence, Adam;	267		Sumner	640	1230	10 Dec 1790	606	31 Dec 1784	74	341	On N side of Cumberland River	yes
Laurey, Daniel	947	Kanady, Abraham	Davidson	640	963	18 May 1789	2523		63	327	Bet. head waters of Barlows Creek &c	yes
Law, Abraham*	053	Mabene, James, Admr.	Davidson	640			1957	15 Jun 1786	63		On waters of Battleground Creek	yes
Lawless, Matthew	513	Allen, Peggy	Davidson	640	485	15 Sep 1787	2059		63	176	On N side of Sulphur Fork	yes
Lawrence, Adam	1600		Davidson	1000	1302	10 Dec 1790	1711		74	366	On waters of Cumberland	yes
Lawrence, John	743	William Lytle	Sumner	640	2140	20 May 1793	2034	20 Mar 1786	81	158	On S side of Cumberland River	yes
Lawrence, Josiah	069	John Sheppard	Middle District	640			2859				South side of Cumberland River	yes
Lawrence, Nathaniel	99		Davidson	2560	85	14 Mar 1786	352		63	35	South side of Cumberland River	yes
Lawrimore, Thos.	077	Wood, Robt.	not given	400							In the little valley	yes
Laws, Wm & hrs. of John	460		Tennessee	1000	2513	4 Dec 1795	3833	3 Feb 1795	88	286	Beg. at two black oaks	
Lawson, John	377	Kerkandoll, Jane	Sumner	274	1557	14 Jan 1793	1863	15 Feb 1787	79	271	Beg at a sugar tree	yes
Lawson, Randolph /sic/	454		Eastern District	500	322	18 Dec 1802	2527	25 May 1784	110	273	On Poor Valley Creek	
Lawson, William	299	Montflorence, J. C.	Davidson	640	285	22 mar 1787	2054		63	105	N side of Cumberland River	yes
Laxkey /sic/, James Woods	256		Eastern District	1500	203	1 Jan 1795	976		83	245	On Little River on the waters of Holston River	
Laydon, Thomas	494		Davidson	274	466	15 Sep 1787			63	169	On third creek the S/S Cumberland River	
Layman John	948		Washington	200	925	17 Nov 1790	2121	4 Nov 1779	76	152	On the waters of Nolachuckey	yes
Laymen (Leamons), John /sic/	029		Washington	200			271	27 Jul 1778			Beg. white oak on Mr. Rogers 1-1/2 /?/ line	
Laymen, John	028		Washington	100			2122	4 Nov 1779			On Bumperses /sic/ Creek	
Laymen, Jno.	642		Washington	150	736	26 Oct 1786	884	27 Sep 1783	66	29	Beg at marked poplar &c	

Claimant:	File #:	Assignee:	County:	Acres:	Grant:	Grant Date:	Entry:	Entry Date:	Bk:	Pg:	Location by Stream Name:	Military:
Laymoord, John	633		Washington	20	727	26 Oct 1786	2434	23 Feb 1780	66	24	Beg. at a marked white oak &c	
Laymoord, Jno.	639		Washington	50	733	26 Oct 1786	2433	23 Feb 1780	66	27	Beg at a marked white oak &c	
Lea, James	020		Eastern District	500							Beg. on a poplar	
Lea, James	1119		Hawkins	300	849	11 Dec 1797			95	354	S side of Holston River	
Lea, James	1132		Hawkins	300	849	11 Dec 1797			96	8	S side of Holston River	
Lea, James	145		Eastern District	200	115	20 Dec 1791			78	329	On N side of Holston River	
Lea, James	153		Hawkins	400	329	29 Jul 1793	5	24 Feb 1778	76	466	On N side of Holston River	
Lea, James	1722		Green	70	1401	21 Jan 1797		15 Nov 1796	91	125	Beg at a pine	
Lea, James	1723		Green	125	1402	21 Jan 1797		15 Nov 1796	91	126	Waters of Bent Creek	
Lea, James	29		Sumner	228	786	11 Jul 1788	545	21 Oct 1783	63	275	On W fork of Goose Creel	yes
Lea, James	410		Hawkins	300	531	27 Jan 1793	2207	19 May 1784	79	501	On head of Mossy Creek	
Lea, Luke	108		Hawkins	150	142	26 Dec 1791	156	16 Feb 1780	75	160	On n side of Holson River	
Lea, Micajah	282		Hawkins	400	293	14 Jan 1793	156	16 Feb 1780	78	343	On waters of Robinsons Creek	
Lea, William	143		Eastern District	280	112	-- Mar 1792 /sic/	20	8 Feb 1780	77	332	On the waters of Beaver Creek	
Lea, William	82		Hawkins	300	55	27 Nov 1789	936	13 Sep 1783	74	41	On N side of Holston	
Leader, John	1991	Mufree, Hardy	Davidson	640	1907	20 May 1793	738		81	102	On S W side of Big harpeth River	yes
Leamon, Peter	1429		Sumner	274	3303	6 Dec 1797	4089	27 Apr 1797	98	176	On the waters of Big Barren	yes
Leamon, Peter	1430		Sumner	274	3304	6 Dec 1797	4037	27 Apr 1797	98	177	On the waters of Big Barren	yes
Lean, John Fuller	849		Washington	150	663	10 Nov 1784			69	155	On S side of Boons Creek	
Learey, Robt.	470		Tennessee	50	297	20 Jul 1796			88	438	To include an island in Cumberland River	
Leary, Bennett;	2419		Davidson	104	404	14 Sep 1797	3728	7 Jun 1788	92	18 /sic/	Waters of Mill Creek	
Leary, Luke	36	Jones, Seburn	Tennessee	640	1218	10 Mar 1790	856	14 May 1784	74	337	On N side of Cumberland River	yes
Leath, Josiah	128		Green	640	5	15 Jul 1786	179	22 Oct 1782	60	347	Upon French Broad River	
Leath, Josiah	816		Green	225	817	11 Aug 1789	143	2 Oct 1782	71	36	Joining sd. Leath's former survey	
Leath, Josiah	816		Green	225	817	11 Aug 1789	143	2 Oct 1782	71	36	Joining sd. Leath's former survey	
Leatherdale, John	408		Green	200	410	20 Sep 1787	162	2 Oct 1783	65	487	On the N side of Nolechuckey River	
Leavoin, John	019	Allen, Sarah	Montgomery	640	246	-- Mar 1792 /sic/	2157	11 Mar 1797	77	334	Piney Fork of Little West Fork of Red River	yes
Lee, Ellenor	258		Hawkins	200	1222	10 Dec 1790	2342	8 Jun 1778	74	339	On the S side of Holstein River	
Lee, Hardy	38	Anderson, Daniel	Tennessee	640	11	1 Nov 1786	2935	30 Sep 1785	59	372	On N side of Cumberland River	yes
Lee, James	53		Green	218	113	-- Jul 1792 /sic/	1261	6 May 1785	74	448	Beg. on Brittain Smiths line	
Lee, James	75		Eastern District	500	1068	-- Jul 1792 /sic/	101	21 Oct 1783	65	447	On N side of Holston River	
Lee, James	905		Green	290	253	-- Jul 1792	1068	4 Jan 1779	74	445	Joining plantation he now lives on	
Lee, James	95		Hawkins	200	254	-- Jul 1792	102	26 Feb 1778	74	446	On both side of Powie's /sic/ River	
Lee, James	96		Hawkins	500		-- Jul 1792	70	21 Oct 1783	74		In Powells Valley	
Lee, James,	2224	Cothram, John	Davidson	228	2514	8 Dec 1795	1417	5 Nov 1790	88	287	On waters of Sycamore	yes
Lee, James;	1052		Sumner	640	2516	8 Dec 1795	192	4 May 1784	88	288	On Jinnings Fork	yes
Lee, Jas.	029	Crockran, John	Tennessee	228							N side of Cumberland River	yes
Lee, Jno.	607		Green	220	564	20 Sep 1787	1849	5 Nov 1790	66	250	On the S side of Nolichuckey River &c	
Lee, John	1051		Sumner	640	2515	8 Dec 1795	374	23 oct 1783	88	287	On Jinnings Fork &c	
Lee, Nicholas	401		Green	120	403	20 Sep 1787	2214	23 Oct 1783	65	486	On Robinson Creek &c	
Lee, Peter	384	Shepherd, Benjamin	Davidson	640	356	15 Sep 1787	2136	5 Nov 1779	63	134	On both sides of E Fork of Drakes Creek	yes
Lee, Thomas	1406		Green	100	1218	27 Nov 1792	269	22 Oct 1783	80	157	On the S side of Holston River &c	
Lee, Thomas	462		Green	520	464	20 Sep 1787	217	22 Oct 1783	65	505	On the S/S Holston River in Carters Valley	
Lee, Thomas	605		Green	540	562	20 Sep 1787	217	22 Oct 1783	66	250	S/S Holston River in Carters Valley	
Lee, Thomas	684		Green	120	725	11 Jul 1788	1309	4 Jul 1784	66	468	Head of Flat Creek incl a Limestone Spring	

Claimant:	File #:	Assignee:	County:	Acres:	Grant:	Grant Date:	Entry:	Entry Date:	Bk:	Pg:	Location by Stream Name:	Military:
Lee, Timothy	88	Brekon, James	Tennessee	640	1352	10 Dec 1790	2934	30 Sep 1785	74	383	On S side of Cumberland River	yes
Leebo, Isaac	822		Sullivan	100	765	17 Nov 1794	85	8 Feb 1780	94	160	South bank of Holston River	
Leech, Joseph	387		Western District	5000	387	27 Nov 1794	2275-76-77	24 May 1784	81	503	On waters of Missippia /sic/	yes
Leek, Henry	572	Lanier, James	Davidson	640	544	15 Sep 1787	3359	19 Mar 1780	63	195	S side of Big Barren River	
Leeper, Andrew	102		Sullivan	540	113	23 Oct 1782	386	19 Mar 1780	43	292	On the North side of Holston River	
Leeper, G.	074		Green	640			386	7 Apr 1780			On the N side of Holston River	
Leeper, George	1242		Davidson	640	207	10 Jul 1788	143	16 Jan 1784	66	413	On the N side of the Cumberland River &c	
Leeper, George	1650		Green	168	1349	28 Aug 1795	2043	27 Oct 1779	87	523	On N side of Nolychuckey River	
Leeper, Guion	1491		Green	400	1254	12 Jul 1794	1816	6 oct 1779	81	579	On N side of Tennessee	
Leeper, Guyon	308		Sullivan	640	447	9 Aug 1787	386	7 Apr 1780	61	466	On the North side of Holston River	
Leeper, John	403		Sullivan	450	282	10 Nov 1784	51	8 Feb 1780	69	171	On North side of Holstin River	
Leeper, Mary	21		Sullivan	250	32	23 Oct 1782	1690	21 Sep 1779	43	252	Beg. at three white oaks	
Leeper, Matthew	1700		Green	640	1416	19 Feb 1797	160	22 Oct 1783	90	240	On Richland Creek	
Leepers, James; heirs of	1815		Davidson	640	388	26 Jul 1793	142	16 Jan 1784	80	337	Beg. at a honey locust	
Legars, James	704	Bledsoe, Anthony	Sumner	365	2083	20 May 1793	1052	8 Jul 1785	81	145	On Tramill's Creek	yes
Legatts /h/, John	1703		Green	100	1419	19 Feb 1797	22	13 Dec 1779	90	242	Waters of Elk Creek	
Legget, Elias	1928	Weakley, Robert	Davidson	640	1739	20 May 1793	2465		81	63	On S side of Cumberland River &c	yes
Legget, John Joseph Dobson	1212	Brotherton, Thomas	Green	300	1056	May 1792	2200	12 Nov 1779	77	402	On Big Gap Creek	
Legget, John Joseph Dobson	1211		Green	153	1055	– May 1792			77	402	Beg at a white oak &c	
Lemare, Lewis	835	Bledsoe, Anthony	Sumner	274	2321	20 May 1793	3012	18 Nov 1792	81	195	On Bledsoes Creek	yes
Lemertin, John	1103		Washington	300	1053	27 Nov 1792			80	206	On Little Doe River	
Lemmons, William	369		Washington	200	361	13 Oct 1783	324	29 Aug 1778	52	247	On the head spring of Mitchells Branch	
Lenear, James	684	Hoover, Henry heirs	Davidson	640	657	8 Dec 1787	3338		63	233	S & E of Nicholas Cooneods /sic/ survey	yes
Lenear, James	704	Childers, Robert hrs	Davidson	640	677	8 Dec 1787	2806		63	239	On Brush Creek	yes
Lenear, James	753	Hopkins, John	Davidson	640	726	11 Jul 1788	3823		63	255	On West of John Elliotts corner	yes
Lennon, Ephraim	1407	Smith, Robert	Sumner	640	3339	6 Dec 1797	536	22 Dec 1795	97	56	Both sides of Falling Creek	yes
Lennon, Ephraim	636	Stewart, Duncan	Tennessee	1000	2791	20 Dec 1796	4640	10 Apr 1797	91	467	S side of Cumberland River	yes
Lenoir, Charles	1387	Donelson, John	Sumner	640	3312	6 Dec 1797	406	25 Oct 1783	97	38	On a S branch of Falling Creek	yes
Lenoir, Wm. & Wm. T. Lewis	150		Green	3500	620	23 Aug 1788	294	23 Oct 1783	64	348	N/S Tennessee River & Holeston River	
Leper /sic/, Andrew	552		Green	250	232	20 Sep 1787	453	18 May 1784	66	151	On the N side of Nolichuckey River &c	
Lesever, Mary & Margaret	1480		Davidson	640	284	26 Nov 1789	733	5 Feb 1781	73	256	On the S side of Cumberland River &c	
Lester, William	464		Sullivan	187	343	10 Nov 1784	2276		69	192	On Fall Branch of Horse Creek	
Letches, William	484	Marsgall, John	Davidson	640	456	15 Sep 1787	4414	14 Oct 1797	63	166	On Moneyfork Creek	yes
Letchmore, Watson	040	Dillenberry, Redmon	Sumner	640			2276	1 Mar 1786			On dividing ridge &c	yes
Lethis, William	0135	Young, Samuel	Sumner	640			92				On the Many Fork	yes
Lett, James	141	McDowd, Josiah	Davidson	274	127	14 Mar 1786	405		63	49	N side of Cumberland River	yes
Lewellen, Thomas	1726	Cartwright, Robert	Davidson	224	1437	20 Dec 1791	45	21 Oct 1783	77	360	On the waters of Dry Creek	yes
Lewis, Andrew	815		Green	640	816	11 Aug 1789	707	19 Dec 1778	71	35	Including a large island in French Broad Rlv	
Lewis, Aaron	031		Washington	100			434				On both sides Lick Creek	
Lewis, Aaron	033		Washington				1506				Beg at a large B. oak &c	
Lewis, Aaron	30		Washington	150			710	10 Aug 1779	69	95	N side of Limestone Fork of Lick Creek	
Lewis, Aaron	659		Washington	200	473	10 Nov 1784	710	19 Dec 1778	69	95	Including a cedar spring	
Lewis, Aaron	662		Washington	100	476	10 Nov 1784	705	19 Dec 1778	69	96	On both sides of Limestone Fork	
Lewis, Aaron	663		Washington	146	477	10 Nov 1784	1507	10 Aug 1779	69	96	On E end of Cedar Spring survey	
Lewis, Aaron	665		Washington	150	479	10 Nov 1784	706	19 Dec 1778	69	97	On N side of Limestone Fork	

Claimant:	File #:	Assignee:	County:	Acres:	Grant:	Grant Date:	Entry:	Entry Date:	Bk:	Pg:	Location by Stream Name:	Military:
Lewis, Aaron	694		Washington	100	508	10 Nov 1784	709	19 Dec 1772	69	107	On both sides of Lick Creek	
Lewis, Aaron	694		Washington	100	508	10 Nov 1784	709	19 Dec 1772	69	107	On both sides of Lick Creek	
Lewis, Aaron	93		Washington	140	261	23 Oct 1782	537	26 Oct 1778	44	278	S Fork of Cherokee Creek	
Lewis, Aaron, Jr.	032		Washington	109-1/2			711	19 Dec 1772			On Sinking Branch &c	
Lewis, Amos	074	Tyrrel, William	Davidson	228			1485				On Leepers Fk of Harpeth	
Lewis, Amos	2281	Punch, John	Davidson	274	2762	20 Jul 1796	1485		88	462	On Leepers Fork of Harpeth River	yes
Lewis, Andrew	030		Washington	150			1506	10 Aug 1779			N side of Limestone Fork of Lick Creek	
Lewis, Andrew, Jr.	1631		Green	300	1334	21 Jul 1795	944	29 Oct 1793	87	357	In French Broad River	
Lewis, Charles	669	Clark, Lardner	Davidson	640	642	15 Nov 1787	1835		63	228	On waters of Salleen /sic/	yes
Lewis, David	1141	Harris, Edward	Sumner	640	2647	4 Jun 1796	2672	1 Jun 1795	88	350	Joining said Harris survey	yes
Lewis, Elizabeth W.	358		Middle District	2500	297	17 Dec 1794	1766	23 Apr 1784	84	206	1 mi below 1st lge cr emptying into Elk River	
Lewis, Elizabeth W.	368		Middle District	2500	307	17 Dec 1794	1767	23 Apr 1784	84	210	Joining Elizabeth Lewis survey #1766	
Lewis, George	04		Western District	4000			2661	1 Jan 1787			On Chittahomome /sic/ River	
Lewis, Hugh:	1547		Davidson	100	87	26 Nov 1789			74	170	On Brush Creek	
Lewis, J. M. & John Johnson	397		Western District	5000	398	27 Nov 1793			81	506	About 14 miles from the Masippia /sic/	
Lewis, J. M. & John Johnson	6		Western District	5000			1133,-1176	31 Oct 1783			Bounded by John Johnstons line &c	
Lewis, J. M. &Jno Johnston	398		Western District	5000	399	27 Nov 1793	1713	16 Apr 1784	81	506	About 15 miles from the Masippia /sic/	
Lewis, James M.	079	Harper, Fred	Davidson				1509				On a small creek	
Lewis, James M.	2215		Davidson	274	246	27 Feb 1796			88	182	Beg at two ashes	
Lewis, James Martin	194		Eastern District	2500	166	27 Nov 1793	402	25 Oct 1783	81	506	On the Tenessee /sic/ River	
Lewis, James Martin	589		Middle District	2000	331	20 Dec 1796	424	25 Oct 1783	91	326	Waters of Richland Creek	
Lewis, James Martin	590		Middle District	2000	332	20 Dec 1796	603	27 Oct 1783	91	327	Waters of Richland Creek &c	
Lewis, James, Sr.	087		Not given	500			1209	4 Nov 1783				
Lewis, Jas. M.	398		Western District	5000	399	27 Nov 1793	1713	16 Apr 1784	81	506	About 15 miles from the Masippia /sic/	
Lewis, Jobe	1591		Green	100	1333	22 Feb 1795			83	436	Bounded by John Johnstons line &c	
Lewis, Joel	129	Rainey, James	Tennessee	1463	1637	23 Feb 1793	56	21 oct 1783	76	330	Joining N boundary of Thompsons preemp	
Lewis, Joel	257		Davidson	640	243	7 Mar 1786	273		63	89	On both sides E Fork of Yellow Creek	yes
Lewis, Joel & Benj. Gooden	628		Green	300	669	11 Jul 1788	344	23 Oct 1783	66	450	On Big Goss /sic/ Creek &c	
Lewis, John	419	Nichols, John	Davidson	640	391	15 Sep 1787	1772		63	146	W side of Sycamore Creek	yes
Lewis, Jonathan	861	Ford, John	Davidson	274	874	17 Jan 1789	1642		63	303	On N side of Cumberland	yes
Lewis, Joshua	1397	Barnes, Henry	Sumner	640	3324	6 Dec 1797	4247	17 Jun 1797	97	46	Waters of Round Lick Creek	yes
Lewis, Joshua	405	Buchanan, John	Davidson	640	377	15 Sep 1787	1773		63	141	On Stones River	yes
Lewis, Matthew	249	Drew, John	Sumner	640	1174	29 Nov 1790	2135	23 Mar 1789	74	234	On N side of Cumberland River	yes
Lewis, Micajah Green	645	Lewis, Wm. T. heir Macajah	Davidson	3840	618	15 Sep 1787	54	27 Oct 1783	63	220	On S side of Cumberland River	yes
Lewis, Nathan	118		Middle District	5000	120	10 Jul 1788	569	12 Aug 1779	67	467	On Richland Creek	yes
Lewis, Nathan	054		Sullivan	120			666				Beg. at Geo. Hines corner	
Lewis, Nathan	091		Washington	20		-- Jun 1784 /sic/	827				Upon a spur of Iron Mtn.	
Lewis, Nathan	1265		Washington	100	1203	4 Dec 1795	2709	1 Jan 1781	89	326	On Gap Creek	
Lewis, Nathan	1266		Washington	200	1204	4 Dec 1795	1733	27 Sep 1779	89	327	On Dry Creek	
Lewis, Nathan	1274		Washington	100	1212	4 Dec 1795	666	17 Apr 1794	89	330	On a large branch of N Fork &c	
Lewis, Nathan	1284		Washington	22	1222	4 Dec 1795	138	16 Sep 1794	89	337	On a branch of Indian Creek	
Lewis, Nathan	304		Sullivan	200	443	9 Aug 1787			61	462	Beg. at George Hines' corner	
Lewis, Nathan	509		Washington	200	772	16 Aug 1787	2891	9 Aug 1781	64	143	On the waters of Gap Creek	
Lewis, Nathan	639		Sullivan	78	587	27 Jun 1793	138	12 Feb 1780	80	378	On the North side of Holston River	
Lewis, Nathan	729		Sullivan	400	689	9 Dec 1795	136-1623	7 Apr 1794	88	159	South of the River Ohio	

Claimant:	File #:	Assignee:	County:	Acres:	Grant:	Grant Date:	Entry:	Entry Date:	Bk:	Pg:	Location by Stream Name:	Military:
Lewis, Nathan	730		Sullivan	80	690	9 Dec 1795	137	12 Feb 1780	88	160	South of the River Ohio	
Lewis, Nathan	731		Sullivan	20	200	27 Feb 1796			88	161	On a spur of the Iron Mountain	
Lewis, Nathan	732		Sullivan	200	692	17 Feb 1796	726	12 Jan 1781	88	161	Beg at Job Keds corner	
Lewis, Nathan	811		Sullivan	100	754	17 Nov 1797	137	12 Feb 1780	94	153	On Holston River	
Lewis, Nathaniel	260		Sullivan	450	399	9 Aug 1787	136-1623	2 Feb 1780	61	418	On Beaver Creek	
Lewis, Richard	2403	Stewart, Charles	Davidson	640	2800	6 Jun 1796	1367 or 3867 /sic/		91	473	S W side of Big Harpeth River	yes
Lewis, Sampson W.	2117	Murphree, Hardy	Davidson	640	2380 (a)	20 May 1793	150		81	208	On S W side of Big Harpeth River	yes
Lewis, Samuel	1082		Green	100	925	26 Dec 1791	50	10 May 1784	77	250	Joining entry on head of McCartneys Br	
Lewis, Samuel	1465		Davidson	100	70	18 May 1789		29 Apr 1786	71	225	Sugar tree on the W side of Sulphur Creek	
Lewis, Samuel	1466		Davidson	100	73	18 May 1789		1 Apr 1786	71	226	On Sulphur Creek	
Lewis, Samuel	992		Green		1219	29 Jul 1793	2001	22 Oct 1779	76	483	Head Jas McCarrens Br including the spring	
Lewis, Seth & Geo Walker	271	Duffnel, David	Tennessee	497	1784	20 May 1793	1184	15 Sep 1784	81	75	On Beaverdam Creek	
Lewis, Thomas	1282	Dillonberry, Remon	Sumner	640	3141	8 Jun 1797	4055	29 Mar 1797	90	314	On waters of 32 Mile Creek	yes
Lewis, Tollfarrow	392		Western District	2500	393	27 Nov 1793	631,-920	27 & 29 Oct 1783	81	504	On waters of Tennessee River	
Lewis, William	365		Tennessee	274	2227	20 May 1793	144	22 Oct 1783	81	175	Waters 1st branch below Pleasant Cr	
Lewis, William	378	John Gray & Thomas Bloun	Tennessee	640	2330	20 May 1793	3186 /r/	14 Dec 1785	81	197	On S side of Cumberland River	yes
Lewis, William F.	1688	Williams, Jesse	Davidson	640	1646	23 Feb 1793	3134		76	335	S side of Cumberland River	yes
Lewis, William T	66		Hawkins	500	51	18 May 1789	1175	31 Oct 1783	72	256	On the S side of Clinch River &c	
Lewis, William T	119		Middle District	5000	121	10 Jul 1788	1135	30 Oct 1783	67	468	On Big Creek	
Lewis, William T.	136		Middle District	5000	138	10 Jul 1788	1136	30 Oct 1783	67	475	Lying on the S side of Duck River &c	
Lewis, William T.	156		Western District	1490	156	10 Jul 1788	2635	25 May 1784	67	357	On S Fork of Forked Deer River	
Lewis, William T.	163		Western District	1500	163	10 Jul 1788	2637	25 May 1784	67	360	On each side of S Fork of Forked Deer River	
Lewis, William T.	166		Western District	1000	166	19 Jul 1788	2639	25 May 1784	67	361	On the waters of Reelfoot River &c	
Lewis, William T.	386		Middle District	200	325	17 Dec 1794	1764	23 Apr 1784	84	217	1st large creek that empties into Elk River	
Lewis, William T.	54		Hawkins	500	39	18 May 1789	749	28 Oct 1783	72	251	On a creek that runs into Clinch River &c	
Lewis, William T.	60		Western District	1000	60	10 Jul 1788	2638	25 May 1784	67	303	On waters of N Fork of Forked Deer River	
Lewis, William T.	60		Hawkins	400	45	18 May 1789	1180	31 Oct 1783	72	254	On a creek that empties into Clinch River &c	
Lewis, William T.	63		Middle District	5000	65	10 Jul 1788	1138	30 Oct 1783	67	442	Lying on Big Creek &c	
Lewis, William T.	64		Hawkins	500	49	18 May 1789	748	28 Oct 1784	72	255	On the S side of Clinch River &c	
Lewis, William T.	65		Middle District	5000	67	10 Jul 1788	1140	30 Oct 1783	67	443	On the west side of Richland Creek	
Lewis, William Terrel	155		Western District	1000	155	10 Jul 1788	2633	25 May 1784	67	357	On the waters of N Fork of Forked Deer River	
Lewis, William Terrel	2054	Morrison, Joel	Davidson	640	2143	20 May 1793	3132		81	159	On the waters of Stones River	yes
Lewis, William Terrel	2056	Pitts, Matthew	Davidson	640	2146	20 May 1793	3092		81	160	On the waters of Stones River	yes
Lewis, William Terrel	208		Eastern District	1463	1498	4 Jan 1792	55	21 Oct 1783	77	375	On both sides of Yellow Creek	
Lewis, William Terrel	214		Eastern District	1000	200	12 Jul 1794	757	28 Oct 1783	84	597	On N side of Tennessee River	
Lewis, William Terrel	385		Middle District	2500	324	17 Dec 1794	2183	14 May 1784	84	216	On Main Elk River	
Lewis, William Terrel	389		Middle District	1500	328	17 Dec 1794	1765	23 Apr 1783	84	218	Head of 1st large creek emptying into Elk Riv	
Lewis, William Terrel	413		Middle District	2500	352	17 Dec 1794	2186	14 May 1784	84	230	Joining the above entry #2185	
Lewis, William Terrel	418		Middle District	2500	357	17 Dec 1794	2184	14 May 1784	84	232	Joining the above entry #2183	
Lewis, William Terrel	85		Middle District	5000	87	10 Jul 1788	1137	30 Oct 1783	67	452	On Globe Creek	
Lewis, William Terrel	113		Middle District	5000	115	10 Jul 1788	1139	3 Nov 1783	67	465	On both side of Richland Creek	
Lewis, William Terrell	1483		Davidson	320	287	26 Nov 1789	735	10 May 1785	73	257	On the s side of Cumberland River &c	
Lewis, William Terrell	330		Western District	1500	330	18 May 1793	2188	14 May 1784	72	273	On the head of the Long Fork of the Miss.	
Lewis, William Terrell	50		Hawkins	400	35	18 May 1789			72	250	On the N side of Clinch River	
Lewis, William Terrell, heir of	645		Davidson	3840	618	15 Sep 1787	54		63	220	On South side of Cumberland River	yes

Earliest Tennessee Land Records

Claimant:	File #:	Assignee:	County:	Acres:	Grant:	Grant Date:	Entry:	Entry Date:	Bk:	Pg:	Location by Stream Name:	Military:
Lewis, William Tyrrel /sic/	2364	Wetherington, Joseph	Davidson	264	3065	19 Jul 1797	3891	19 Jul 1797	90	376	Waters of Leepers Fork	yes
Lewis, William Tyrrell	561	Eason, Mason heirs	Tennessee	640	2996	10 Apr 1797	3615	29 Nov 1788	90	291	On Dry Fork of Spring Creek	
Lewis, Wm T & PeterMcNairy	583		Green	300	264	20 Sep 1787	919	20 May 1782	66	162	On the head of the Wt Fork of Flatt Creek	
Lewis, Wm. & Wm. Lytle, Jr.	531		Tennessee	274	2849	21 Jan 1797			90	49	On Spring Creek	
Lewis, Wm. L. & Wm. Tyrrell	052	Tarrent, Manlore	Not given					6 Dec 1792			Beg at three white oaks	
Lewis, Wm. T.	051	Halcom, Phillip	Not given	185	1640	23 Feb 1793	147	22 Oct 1783			N side of French Broad River	
Lewis, Wm. T.	075		Green	640						341		
Lewis, Wm. T.	139	Waters, Wm. Heirs	Tennessee	640		26 Dec 1792	3603	14 Aug 1788	76		On the waters of Red River	
Lewis, Wm. T.	650		Green	2500	691	11 Jul 1788	1388	15 Jan 1783	66	457	Adjoining Hardeson & Comps. line	
Lewis, Wm. T.	817		Sumner	640	2292	20 May 1793	3091	27 Nov 1792	81	189	On Magness Fork of Bledsoes Creek	yes
Lewis, Wm. T. & Phil. Holwell	132		Tennessee	185	1640	23 Feb 1793			76	332	Beg at white oak Fred. Stumps W boundary	
Lewis, Wm. T. & W Tyrrell	528		Tennessee	274	2844	21 Jan 1797	3137	16 Dec 1785	90	46	On the Barren Fork	
Lewis, Wm. T. & Wm. Terrell	029	Parr, Josiah	Montgomery	274	410	27 May 1796	425	27 Sep 1796			On Spring Creek	yes
Lewis, Wm. T. & Wm. Tyrrell	028	Sugg, John	Montgomery	274							On the Barren Fork of the Little West Fork	yes
Lewis, Wm. T. & Wm. Tyrrell	53 /?/	Locklove, Jonathan	Not given	640	3521	26 May 1796					On S side of Cumberland	
Lewis, Wm. T. & Wm. Tyrrell	532		Tennessee	640	2851	21 Jan 1797			90	50	S side of Cumberland River	
Lewis, Wm. T. & Wn., Tyrrell	050	Holland, Charles	Not given	640			3476	26 May 1796			S side Cumberland River	
Lewis, Wm. Terrell	089		Not given	1000		Note about grants /sic/	1018	25 Jun 1784				
Lewis, Wm. Terrel	2041	Williams, Nathan	Davidson	228	2058	20 May 1793	3089	29 oct 1783	81	139	On the N side of Cumberland	yes
Lewis, Wm. Terrel	363		Middle District	2500	302	17 Dec 1794	4057	29 Mar 1797	84	208	Joining the above entry 2184	
Lewis, Wm. Terrel	376		Western District	4000	340	17 Nov 1790	2667	5 Mar 1791	76	166	on a branch of Big Ha cher /sic/ River	
Lewis, Wm. Terrell	694		Sumner	640	2061	20 May 1793	2664	14 Nov 1780	81	139	On Bledsoes Creek	yes
Lewis, Wm. Terrell	082		Middle District	75			2743	7 May 1784				
Lewis, Wm. Terrell	645		Green	500	686	11 Jul 1788	1387	3 Jan 1784	66	456	Alexanders Cr the waters of Nolichuckey	
Lewton, Leonard	1279	Dillon Barry, Remond	Sumner	640	3038	8 Jun 1797	922	21 May 1779	90	313	On Spring Creek	yes
Libbincutt /sic/, John	068	Sugg, Geo. A.	Davidson	640				16 Feb 1784			Bet. waters Whites Creek & Marrowbone	yes
Light, Jacob	494		Washington	100	757	16 Aug 1787		20 Jul 1786	83	478	Including Leaches improvement &c	
Lilly, John	347	Buxton, William	Davidson	640	332	28 Jul 1787	1357	23 Oct 1783	63	123	N side of Cumberland River	yes
Lincoln, Isaac	536		Washington	265	799	16 Aug 1787			64	152	Beg. at a marked Ash &c	
Lindsay, Caleb;	037		Montgomery								On Spring Creek	
Lindsay, David	432		Green	400	434	20 Sep 1787	3936	10 Nov 1784	65	497	Waters Lick Creek & Plum Creek	
Lindsay, Isaac	1352	Hadley, Joshua	Sumner	274	3171	14 Sep 1797		8 Nov 1796	90	430	Head waters of Dixons Creek	yes
Lindsay, Isaac;	951		Sumner	400	154	1 Dec 1787	192	14 Apr 1792	83	216	Beg at Wm. Dillards lower corner	yes
Lindsay, James	428		Middle District	1000	367	17 Dec 1794	2103	7 May 1784	84	237	On both sides of Duck River	
Lindsay, David	481		Green	640	483	20 Sep 1787	1356	3 Jan 1784	65	513	On Plum Creek & Chum Camp Creek	
Lindsay, Isaac	1089		Davidson	640	63	17 Apr 1786	298	16 Feb 1784	66	55	On the N side of Cumberland River &c	
Linear, James	1459		Davidson	180	61	18 May 1789	285	20 Jul 1786	71	222	Joining E boundary of Capt. Vance's claim	
Linsey, Isaac	1364		Davidson	320	47	8 Oct 1787		23 Oct 1783	68	140	At the mouth of Mills Creek	
Linton, Hezekiah	581	Linton, Jesse heirs	Davidson	1000	553	15 Sep 1787	587	15 Sep 1787	63	198	North side of Cumberland River	yes
Linton, Hezekiah	635	Jones, Benjamin	Davidson	640	608	15 Sep 1787	192		63	216	On N side of Cumberland River	yes
Linton, Hezekiah	724	Linton, Jesse heirs	Sumner	640	2108	20 May 1793	586	21 Nov 1792	81	151	On Trammels Creek	yes
Linton, James	581	Linton, Hezekiah , hr. Jess	Davidson	1000	553	15 Sept 1787	587		63	198	N side of Cumberland River	yes
Linton, Silas	210		Davidson	640	196	7 Mar 1786	829		63	73	South side of Cumberland River	yes
Linton, William	36		Davidson	1417	22	14 Mar 1786	625		63	9	On Parsons Creek	yes
Linton, Wm.	0102		Sullivan	640			1665	17 Sep 1779				yes

Earliest Tennessee Land Records

Claimant:	File #:	Assignee:	County:	Acres:	Grant:	Grant Date:	Entry:	Entry Date:	Bk:	Pg:	Location by Stream Name:	Military:
Lipe, Daniel	029		Hawkins	170							In Carters Valley	
Lippencut, William	430	Barbour, Richard	Eastern District	640	3145	14 Sep 1797	4185		90	421	Beg. & cornering on 2 hickorys	
Lipton, Joseph	429		Washington	572	421	13 Oct 1783			52	276	On Limestone Creek	
Lisbee, Aaron	463		Sullivan	125	348	10 Nov 1784	789	27 May 1781	69	192	On Waters of Horse Creek	
Lisk, James	071		not given	640			894	9 Apr 1788			Waters of 1st creek S/S Cumberland River	
Liskow, Thomas	182	Clark, Lardner	Davidson	640	168	7 Mar 1786	816		63	63	In the fork of Mill Creek	yes
List of Returns	080		Washington									
List of Warrants	O16		Sullivan					6 Sep 1797				
Lister, John	463		Green	280	465	20 Sep 1787	1392	16 Aug 1784	65	506	On the S side of Nolachuckey	
Little, Jonas	0122	Watson, John	Sumner	640			4637	10 Apr 1797			N Fork of Bradleys Creek	yes
Little, Andrew	75		Sullivan	300	86	23 oct 1782	1037	7 Jan 1779	43	279	On the S side of Holston River	
Little, George	0123	Watson, John	Sumner	640			4637	10 Apr 1797			On N Fork of Bradleys Creek	yes
Little, George	7		Sullivan	247	18	23 Oct 1782	1040	7 Jan 1779	43	246	On the North side of Holston River	
Little, Jonas	197		Washington	320	65	23 Oct 1782	825	29 Dec 1778	47	31	On Bush Creek	
Little, Mathias	63		Sullivan	120	74	23 Oct 1782	669-1038	17 Aug 1780	43	274	On the S/S of Holston River on Indian Creek	
Little, Matthias	334		Sullivan	100	474	10 Jul 1788	1546	13 Feb 1787	67	483	Beg. at an ash tree	
Little, Matthias	511		Washington	100	774	16 Aug 1787	1141	27 Jan 1779	64	144	On the waters of Dry Creek	
Little, Matthias	534		Washington	200	797	16 Aug 1787	663	14 Aug 1781	64	151	Beg. at a gum &c	
Little, Matthias	650		Sullivan	90	598	27 Jun 1793	2739	16 Jan 1781	80	383	Beg at Jacob Nedver's cor hickory saplin	
Little, Valentine	76		Sullivan	100	87	23 Oct 1782	665	11 Aug 1780	43	280	On the South side of Holston River	
Littrell, Hugh	1967		Davidson	2260	1845	20 May 1793	850		81	88	On W branches of Big Harpeth	yes
Lively, Matthew	301	Lacey, Hopkins	Tennessee	640	1991	20 May 1793	2133	9 Sep 1785	81	122	On S side of Cumberland River	yes
Livingston, William	1103		Hawkins	220	399	19 Jul 1797		Martin Armstrong /	91	623	N side of Clinch River	
Lock, James	750	Zealott, Jonathan	Davidson	274	723	11 Jul 1788	3234		63	254	On the Main Tennessee River	yes
Lock, James	948	Zealott, William	Davidson	274	964	18 May 1789	3233		63	328	On waters of E Fork of Stones River	yes
Lock, John	011		Middle District	2000			1789	23 Apr 1784			N side of the N bank of Duck River	
Lock, John	252	Wilson, David	Sumner	357	1198	30 Nov 1790	596	5 Jan 1785	74	321	On N side of Cumberland River	yes
Lock, Matthew	1877	Davenport, Jos.	Davidson	640	1618	27 Apr 1793	2067		81	22	On both sides of South Harpeth	yes
Lock, Matthew	32		Middle District	5000	34	10 Jul 1788	420	25 Oct 1783	67	423	On both sides the N fork of Duck River	
Lock, Matthew	989	Wise, John	Davidson	428	1006	18 May 1789	1229		63	338	On N side of E Fork of Stones River	yes
Lock, Matthew	990	Rayford, Morrice	Davidson	236	1007	18 May 1789	1301		63	338	On S branch of E Fork of Stones River	yes
Lock, Richard	34		Middle District	2000	36	10 Jul 1788	1790	23 Apr 1784	67	423	Headwaters of West Fork of Stones River	
Lock, William	2061	Tatum, Brainam	Davidson	640	2166	20 May 1793	885	1 May 1780	81	164	On waters of W Harpeth	yes
Lock, Wm.	0121		Sullivan	200			553				Beg. at a white oak	
Lockart, John	1888		Davidson	321	1648	27 Apr 1793	571		81	29	On S side of Cumberland River	
Lockart, John	641		Sumner	640	1930	20 May 1793	1996	19 Nov 1792	81	107	On W side of Caney Fork	yes
Lockett, Pleasant	1582		Davidson	40	1243	10 Dec 1790		2 Sep 1785	74	346	On N side of Cumberland River	yes
Lockhart, Samuel	525		Davidson	5760	497	15 Sep 1787	563		63	180	At mouth of Indian Creek	yes
Lockhart, Samuel	57		Middle District	3000	59	10 Jul 1788	1922	24 Apr 1784	67	439	Lying on the S side of Elk River	
Lockhart, Samuel	64		Middle District	2000	66	10 Jul 1788	1921	24 Apr 1784	67	443	On the N side of Elk River &c	
Locklove, Jonathan	053	Lewis, Wm. T. & Wm.	Not given	640			3521	26 May 1796			On S side of Cumberland	yes
Locust, Arthur	607	Gorham, James C.	Tennessee	640	3150	14 Sep 1797	4064		90	423	Waters of W Fork of Red River	yes
Locust, Francis	606	Gorham, John	Tennessee	640	3151	19 Sep 1797	4065		90	422	Waters of W Fork of Red River	yes
Locust, Thomas	1137	Harris, Edward	Sumner	640	2643	4 Jun 1796	2670	1 Jun 1795	88	348	Joining said Harris survey	yes
Logan, Benjamin	1185		Davidson	640	162	17 Apr 1786	88	14 Jan 1784	66	189	On the S side of Cumberland River &c	yes

Earliest Tennessee Land Records

Claimant:	File #:	Assignee:	County:	Acres:	Grant:	Grant Date:	Entry:	Entry Date:	Bk:	Pg:	Location by Stream Name:	Military:
Logan, Hugh	1825		Davidson	640	398	26 Jun 1793	785	4 Feb 1786	80	341	On both sides of the S Fork of Stones Creek	
Logan, William	1655		Green	200	1354	27 Aug 1795	1059	28 Jun 1794	87	526	N side of Nolychuckey River	
Loggins, William	1167		Davidson	640	144	17 Apr 1786	616	16 Nov 1784	66	185	On the E t Fork of Whites Creek	
Loggins, William	558		Middle District	640	357	8 Jun 1797	2117	8 May 1784	90	345	On Flat Creek	
Logue, John	955	Gurley, James	Davidson	1000	972	18 May 1789	1737		63	330	On S side of Cumberland River	yes
Lomack, William	2296	Casbol, Robert	Davidson	274	2774	10 Sep 1796	3205		88	524	On W side of Stones River	yes
Lomas, William	158		Davidson	274	144	14 Mar 1786	693		63	55	North side of Cumberland River	yes
Long, Benjamin	37		Sullivan	200	48	23 Oct 1782	1729	25 Sep 1779	43	260	On the waters of Sinking Creek	
Long, Haywood	2105	Smith, Oliver	Davidson	640	2335	20 May 1793	2669		81	199	On both sides of S Harpeth	yes
Long, James	043	Hughlett, William	Middle District	640			2668					yes
Long, John	132		Hawkins	225	166	26 Dec 1791	1397		75	170	On N side of Holston River	
Long, John	138		Sullivan	640	151	23 Oct 1782	319-318	15 Jan 1782	43	331	Carters Valley joining Ellisons, Taylors,&Hunt	
Long, John	484		Hawkins	600	356	29 Jul 1793	1644	16 Sep 1779	80	265	N side of Clinch River &c	
Long, John	824		Green	640	812	26 Nov 1789	1644	16 Sep 1779	71	383	On the N side of Holston River &c	
Long, Joseph	236		Green	300	193	20 Sep 1787	1673	18 Sep 1779	65	429	On the S side of Clinch River in Hinds Valley	
Long, Lunsford	367		Western District	2500	373	20 Dec 1791	2197	25 May 1784	75	221	2nd large or emptying into Tennessee River	
Long, Lunsford	369		Western District	2500	375	20 Dec 1791	2196	15 May 1784	75	222	2nd large or emptying into Tennessee River	
Long, Nehemiah	66		Davidson	1785	52	14 Mar 1786	109		63	22	On waters of Halfpone Creek	yes
Long, Nicholas	0129		Green	2000	329	19 Dec 1794	2198	15 May 1784			On Duck River	
Long, Nicholas	149		Middle District	5000	145	18 May 1789	415	23 Oct 1783	72	257	On the S side of Duck River	
Long, Nicholas	1520		Green	200	1281	12 Jul 1794	816	2 May 1779	81	588	Beg. at a white oak	
Long, Nicholas	2048	Barber, Joshua	Davidson	274	2080	20 May 1793	2287		81	144	On Marrowbone Creek	yes
Long, Nicholas	230		Middle District	500 (500	210	1 Jan 1793	549	27 Oct 1783	80	211	On the S side of Duck River	
Long, Nicholas	236		Middle District	5000	216	1 Jan 1793	533	27 Oct 1783	80	213	On the S side of Duck River	
Long, Nicholas	285	Richardson, William	Tennessee	640	1895	20 May 1793	466	24 Feb 1784	81	99	On S side of Cumberland River &c	
Long, Nicholas	286	Thomas, Lemuel	Tennessee	640	1897	20 May 1793	465	24 Feb 1784	81	99	On S side of Cumberland River &c	
Long, Nicholas	290		Tennessee	640	1918	20 May 1793	6	15 Oct 1783	81	104	On S side of Cumberland Creek /sic/ &c	
Long, Nicholas	329	Swanson, John	Tennessee	640	2079	20 May 1793	3060	30 Nov 1785	81	144	On N side of Cumberland River	
Long, Nicholas	351	Lucy, Burrell	Tennessee	640	2179	20 May 1793	467	24 Feb 1784	81	166	On S side of Cumberland River	
Long, Nicholas	352	Symonny, James	Tennessee	640	2180	20 May 1793	12	15 Oct 1783	81	166	On S side of Cumberland River	
Long, Nicholas	354	Underdue, Dempsey	Tennessee	640	2183	20 May 1793	5		81	167	On S side of Cumberland River	
Long, Nicholas	358	Copeland, Kedar	Tennessee	640	2203	20 May 193	9		81	169	Beg on an Elm	
Long, Nicholas	363	Glandon, Major	Tennessee	1000	2220	20 May 1793	10	15 Oct 1783	81	173	On N side of Tennessee River	
Long, Nicholas	364	Kelly, John	Tennessee	640	2223	20 May 1793	468	24 Feb 1784	81	174	On S side of Cumberland River	
Long, Nicholas	366		Western District	3000	372	20 Dec 1791	2225	21 May 1778	75	221	2nd lge or emptying into Tennessee River	
Long, Nicholas	372		Western District	5000	378	20 Dec 1791	2226	21 May 1784	75	223	2nd large or emptying in Tennessee River	
Long, Nicholas	390		Middle District	2000	329	17 Nov 1794			84	219	On Duck River	
Long, William	1589	Shelton, David	Davidson	640	1260	10 Dec 1790	1002		74	352	On waters of Round Lick Creek	yes
Loomis, Jonathan	73		Davidson	3940	59	14 Mar 1786	666		63	24	On Cedar Creek	yes
Loomis, Nathaniel	1134		Hawkins	640	852	17 Dec 1798	2189	12 Nov 1779	97	301	S E side of Clinch River	
Loomis, Nathaniel	1135		Hawkins	400	853	17 Dec 1798	171	18 Mar 1778	97	302	Both sides of Holston River	
Loomis, Nathaniel	1764		Green	640	1441	17 Dec 1798	174	18 Mar 1778	97	299	On Tellico River	
Loomiss, Nathaniel	1		Sevier	640	1298	10 Jun 1799			101	347	On South side French Broad River	
Looney, Absolom	423		Hawkins	640	311	27 Nov 1792	2189	12 Nov 1779	80	151	On the S E side of Clinch River	
Looney, Benjamin	173		Sullivan	260	180	10 Oct 1783	94	8 Feb 1780	53	149	On the head of Possum Creek	

Claimant:	File #:	Assignee:	County:	Acres:	Grant:	Grant Date:	Entry:	Entry Date:	Bk:	Pg:	Location by Stream Name:	Military:
Looney, David	0103		Sullivan	279			1895	15 Feb 1780			Beg. at a white oak &c	
Looney, David	1053		Davidson	640	21	17 Apr 1786	295	16 Feb 1784	66	43	Lying on the Wt Fork of Station Camp Creek	
Looney, David	1097		Davidson	640	71	17 Apr 1786	297	16 Feb 1784	66	58	Lying on the Wt Fork of Station Camp Creek	
Looney, David	164		Sullivan	179 (320	171	10 Oct 1783			53	146	Beg. at a white oak	
Looney, David	23	Howell, Jesse	Sumner	350 (357	780	11 Jul 1788	455	21 Sep 1787	63	273	On waters of Caney Fork	yes
Looney, David	390		Sullivan	560 (600	269	10 Nov 1784			69	167	In Stanleys Valley	
Looney, David	411		Sullivan	200	290	10 Nov 1784	635	6 Jun 1780	69	173	On the Widow Kirk's Mill Creek	
Looney, David	457		Sumner	411	1594	27 Apr 1793	497	26 Jan 1785	81	16	On Upper Fork of Goose Creek	yes
Looney, David	483		Sullivan	320	493	17 Nov 1788	1895	7 Oct 1779	70	12	Beg at 2 white oaks and a sowerwood /sic/	
Looney, David	549		Sullivan	150	532	17 Nov 1790	828	31 Jul 1781	76	189	Joining his first survey where he lives	
Looney, David	550		Sullivan	235	533	17 Nov 1790	663	8 Aug 1780	76	189	On Muddy Creek	
Looney, David	815	Howell, Jesse	Sumner	640	2285	20 May 1793	278	21 Nov 1784	81	188	On N side of Cumberland River	Yes
Looney, David	815		Sumner	640	2285	20 May 1793	278	21 Nov 1784	8	188	On N side of Cumberland River	yes
Looney, John	167		Hawkins	200	100	16 Nov 1790	682	Sep 1780	77	185	On the No side of Holston River &c	
Looney, John	91		Sullivan	160	102	23 Oct 1782	95	8 Feb 1780	43	287	On Possum Creek in Stanley Valley	
Looney, John, Jr.	844		Hawkins	100	669	5 Dec 1794	1495	1785	83	414	S side of Clinch River &c	
Looney, Moses	0120		Sullivan	200			605	7 Jun 1780			On Holston River	
Looney, Moses	171	Potts, Nathan orphans	Sullivan	300	178	10 Oct 1783	344	24 Mar 1780	53	149	On the head spring of Diver's Run	
Looney, Moses	194		Sullivan	383 (393	201	10 Oct 1783	2077	26 Oct 1779	53	159	Beg at three Chestnut Oak Saplings	
Looney, Moses	2		Knox	19	142	7 Jan 1794		20 Jul 1792	81	398	In the river of Holston	
Looney, Moses	303		Hawkins	200	266	24 Dec 1792			78	450	On Holston River	
Looney, Moses	343		Sullivan	394	483	10 Jul 1788	1846	6 Oct 1779	67	487	Incl Improvement & Island in Holston River	
Looney, Moses	358		Eastern District	200	275	20 Jul 1796	2041	27 Oct 1779	88	435	On N side of Holston River	
Looney, Moses	628	Robertson, James	Tennessee	640	3192	14 Sep 1797	3874		90	439	W side of Bartons Creek	yes
Looney, Peter	1105		Davidson	640	79	17 Apr 1786	96	14 Jan 1784	66	61	On Sinking Creek &c	
Looney, Peter	1232		Davidson	640	196	10 Jul 1788	293	16 Feb 1784	66	411	On the S side of Cumberland River	
Looney, Peter	1313		Davidson	640	279	10 Jul 1788	476	7 Jun 1785	66	434	On an Eastern branch of Drakes Creek	
Looney, Peter;	1016		Sumner	40	203	27 Feb 1795	1962	6 Jan 1790	88	163	Beg at a hornbeam	
Looney, Robert	1451		Davidson	640	97	10 Jul 1788	719	2 May 1785	68	235	Lying on Station Camp Creek	
Losson, John	035	McCulloch, Benjamin	Tennessee	640			2992	30 Sep 1785			S side of Cumberland River	
Love, David	2142	Young, Daniel	Davidson	2057	2419	7 Jan 1794	339		81	406	On N side of Cumberland River	yes
Love, James	870		Green	100	820	27 Nov 1789	110	12 Feb 1789	74	21	On N side of Chuckey River	yes
Love, Josiah, Ass	207		Sumner	640	1112	26 Nov 1789	3472	10 Oct 1789	74	135	On N side of Cumberland River	yes
Love, Josiah, Ass	248		Sumner	640	1153	26 Nov 1789	1490	12 Jun 1787	74	155	On N fork of Red River	yes
Love, Phillip	1637		Green	400	1340	27 Aug 1795	1962	10 Oct 1779	87	510	On Caney Fork of Spring Creek	
Love, Robert	1201		Washington	100	1154	1 Jan 1795	1398	24 May 1779	83	234	Joining lands of John & Martin Webbs	
Love, Robert	2059	Hood, William	Davidson	274	2163	20 May 1793	979	27 Nov 1792	81	164	On N branches of Harpeth River	
Love, Robert	416		Hawkins	300	304	27 Nov 1792	1036	29 Oct 1783	80	149	S side of Holston River	
Love, Robert	638		Washington	300	732	26 Oct 1786	531	23 Oct 1778	66	732	On both sides of Indian Creek &c	
Love, Robert, Jr.	24		Giles	500	55	23 Apr 1813	1956	30 Nov 1784	127	330	On Richland creek of Elk River	
Love, Thomas	1068		Green	80	911	26 Dec 1790	106	16 Jul 1789	77	246	On the S side of Noleychuckey River &c	
Love, Thomas	1585		Green	80	132	4 Feb 1795	38		83	403	S side of Noleychuckey River	
Love, Thomas	1873	Brooks, Giles	Davidson	640	1613	27 Apr 1793	3415		81	21	On waters of W Fork of Stones River	yes
Love, Thomas	239		Green	300	196	20 Sep 1787			65	429	On the S side of Nolichuckey River	
Love, Thomas	725	Pettes, Stephen	Davidson	640	698	11 Jul 1788	1508	26 Feb 1778	63	246	On both sides of Sycamore Creek	yes

Claimant:	File #:	Assignee:	County:	Acres:	Grant:	Grant Date:	Entry:	Entry Date:	Bk:	Pg:	Location by Stream Name:	Military:
Lovelady, Joseph	1282		Green	100	1132	12 Jan 1793	1480	24 Jun 1779	78	384	On S side of Noluchuckey River	
Lovelady, Marshall	407		Green	100	409	20 Sep 1787	29	20 Sep 1787	65	487	On the Cedar branch	
Loveletty, Joseph	1162		Green	100	1035	26 Dec 1791	29	26 Jul 1787	77	283	On the S side of Nolachuckey River	
Lovell, John	661	McNairy, John	Tennessee	640	3254	6 Dec 1797	4634		97	35	On the ridge	yes
Lovell, Thomas	1608		Davidson	100	1331	10 Dec 1790		1 Jun 178- /sic/	74	376	On N side of Cumberland River	
Loving, Henry	1113		Davidson	640	90	17 Apr 1786	133	16 Jan 1784	66	172	On the waters of Bledsoes Creek &c	
Low, Aquilla	227		Green	400	184	20 Sep 1787	361	23 Oct 1783	65	425	On Bent Creek	
Low, Aquilla	228		Green	270	185	20 Sep 1787	192	22 Oct 1783	65	426	On the N side of Nolechuckey &c	
Low, John	353		Hawkins	640	361	8 Mar 1793	942	29 Oct 1783	78	483	On waters of Big Sinking Creek	
Low, Jonathan	1051	John Lee	Sumner	640	2515	8 Dec 1795	1849	5 Nov 1790	88	287	On Jinning Fork &c	yes
Low, Joshua	1432		Green	100	1244	27 Nov 1792	2417	2 Feb 1780	80	168	On the N side Nolichuckey River	
Lowary, William	1442		Green	250	1252	27 Nov 1792	35	24 Jan 1787	80	172	On French Broad River Beg at a stake	
Lowe, Marvel	1336	Stansil, Peter heirs	Sumner	640	3136	14 Sep 1797	4444	15 May 1796	90	418	On Salt Lick Fork of Big Barren	yes
Lowe, Robert	33		Maury	620	62	21 Dec 1815	318	10 Dec 1778	130	99	On a head branch of Fountain Creek	
Lowell, James	43	Brecken, J.G.	Tennessee	640	1234	10 Dec 1790	2877	30 Sep 1785	74	343	On N side of Cumberland River	yes
Lowell, Zadock	472	Glasgow, James	Davidson	228	444	15 Sep 1787	1150		63	163	On N Boundary of Maj. Bartons preemptio	yes
Lowman, Mark	9	Thomas, Philemon	Sumner	640	766	11 Jul 1788	3011	20 Sep 1787	63	269	On some of the branch &c	yes
Lowry, Elizabeth	1508		Green	150	1269	12 Jul 1794	505	15 Oct 1778	81	584	Beg. at a conditional line Edwards old place	
Lowry, Jane	451		Hawkins	100	329	24 Jun 1793	827	28 Jul 1781	80	195	On Chamberlains Branch	
Lowry, Mary	455		Hawkins	100	333	24 Jun 1793	827	28 Jul 1781	80	196	On the Long Branch waters of Long Creek	
Lowry, Robert	450		Hawkins	100	328	24 Jun 1793	827	28 Jul 1781	80	195	Beg at a black gum marked M	
Loyd, John	1098		Green	150	941	26 Dec 1791	2793	27 Feb 1781	77	258	Waters of Nolachuckey on Meadow Creek	
Loyd, John	204		Green	200	161	20 Sep 1787	15	17 Oct 1783	65	417	On a branch of Nolechuckey River	
Loyd, Lenord, heirs of	1862		Davidson	640	1591	27 Apr 1793	282	28 Jul 1783	81	15	On a small creek of Richland	yes
Lubo, Henry	700		Green	200	741	11 Jul 1788	688	25 Jun 1797	66	474	On the N side of Holeston River &c	
Lucas, Ball	076	Fowler, David	Sumner	640			4528				On waters of White oak Creek	yes
Lucas, Benjamin	1191	Hogg, Thomas	Tennessee	640			2426	30 Sep 1785			S side of Cumberland	yes
Lucas, Benjamin	1484		Green	640	1034	26 Dec 1791	18	24 Feb 1778	77	294	Beg, at an Elm & Maple tree	
Lucas, Benjamin	1585	Hogg, Thomas	Davidson	640	288	26 Nov 1789	450	18 Jun 1784	73	258	On Big Harpeth River	
Lucas, Matthew	1261	Dillon Barry, Redmond	Davidson	640	1246	10 Dec 1790	1056		74	347	On S side of Cumberland River	yes
Lucas, Valentine	754		Davidson	228	3040	8 Jun 1797	782	29 mar 1797	90	314	On Turkey Creek	yes
Lucas, William	1222		Davidson	640	727	11 Jul 1788	491		63	255	On Spring Creek of Red River	yes
Lucas, William	513		Washington	440	186	10 Jul 1788	1173	18 Jun 1784	66	408	Beg, at two small sugar trees & a dogwood	
Luchars, Richard	1435	Gideon Pillow	Sumner	440	776	16 Aug 1787	2450	1 Feb 1779	64	144	On Cedar Creek &c	
Luck, Thomas	540		Green	640	3346	6 Dec 1797	1296		98	181	On the waters of Round Lick Creek	yes
Ludspeak Ptl, Christopher	680		Green	400	512 (542)	20 Sep 1787	1245	26 Dec 1783	65	537	On the N side of French Broad River &c	
Ludwell, Richard	353	Tuton, William	Davidson	122	338	11 Jul 1788	3659	10 Dec 1788	63	125	S side of Cumberland River	yes
Luellin, Daniel	189	Totevine, William	Tennessee	224	1469	29 Aug 1792	467	24 Feb 1784	77	368	S side of Chuckey River &c	
Luey, Burrel	351	Long, Nicholas	Tennessee	640	2179	20 May 1793	4314		81	166	On N side of Cumberland River	yes
Lumblyer, Simon	1328	Hickman, Thomas	Sumner	640	3128	14 Sep 1797	4315	3 Jun 1797	90	415	Waters of Big Barren	yes
Lumbyes, David	1318	Hinds, John	Sumner	640	1267 (7)	14 Sep 1797	817	6 May 1797	90	410	On the waters of Big Barren	yes
Lusk, Joseph	1037		Green	640		29 Jul 1793	1371		76	491	On the waters of Little Chucka	yes
Lusk, Joseph	21		Green	200	84	1 Nov 1786	854	22 Dec 1784	58	445	Beg upon a hickory	
Lusk, Robert	800		Washington	260	614	10 Nov 1784		30 Dec 1778	69	142	On a branch of Buffalow Creek	

Claimant:	File #:	Assignee:	County:	Acres:	Grant:	Grant Date:	Entry:	Entry Date:	Bk:	Pg:	Location by Stream Name:	Military:
Lussey, Josiah	597		Washington	640	691	26 Oct 1786	382	12 Jan 1779	66	7	Beg. at 3 marked ash trees &c	
Lust, Robert	290		Washington	50	157	24 Oct 1782	1253	1 Mar 1779	47	76	On draft of Buffalow Creek	
Luter, Andrew	22	Eaton, John	Tennessee	640	1170	26 Nov 1789	3520	8 Feb 1786	74	164	On N side of Cumberland River	yes
Lyle, David	1107		Green	320	950	26 Dec 1791	142	21 Oct 1783	77	262	On the N side of French Broad River	
Lyle, Henry	101		Washington	123	269	24 Oct 1782	919	1 Jan 1779	44	282	E side of Doe River	
Lyle, John	1044		Washington	200	994	14 Jan 1793	702	19 Dec 1778	79	284	Beg. at the beg. cor. of his former survey	
Lyle, John	107		Washington	640	275	24 Oct 1782	701	19 Dec 1778	44	285	On Little Limestone	
Lyle, Samuel	50		Washington	50	340	24 Oct 1782	1240	25 Feb 1779	43	315	On the waters of Lick Creek	
Lyles, Benjamin	655	Bushnell & Dobbins	Davidson	640	628	15 Sep 1787	1672		63	223	On S side of Cumberland	yes
Lynch, George hrs.	051	Hughlet, William	Middle District	640			2526					
Lynch, John	1256		Washington	200	1228	27 Feb 1796	2549	25 Apr 1780	88	511	On both sides of Wataugah	yes
Lynch, John	356	Phifer, Caleb	Sumner	640	1477 (?)	4 Jan 1792	3239	27 Oct 1791	77	370	On the dividing line &c	
Lynch, John	901		Washington	100	878	17 Nov 1790	2376	27 Nov 1779	76	137	On the draughts of Wattauga River	
Lyndsay, James	161		Middle District	250	171	20 Dec 1791	22	12 Jan 1786	75	224	On Catheys Creek	
Lyne, Edward	285		Sullivan	640	424	9 Aug 1787	289	10 Mar 1780	61	443	In Powells Valley on the N/S Powells River	
Lynn, Adam	1351		Davidson	50	1	8 Oct 1787		30 May 1785	68	135	On Shanes Fork of Gaspers Creek	
Lynn, Adam	1352		Davidson	50	2	8 Oct 1787		16 Mar 1786	68	136	On Shanes Fork of Gaspers Creek	
Lynn, Jonathan	05	Wells, Haydon & John Give	Montgomery	640			4636	28 Aug 1797			S side of Cumberland River	yes
Lynn, Stephen	164		Davidson	1000	150	7 Mar 1786	635		63	57	On Thompsons Creek	yes
Lynnes, John	111	Robertson & Shepherd	Tennessee	640	1598	23 Feb 1793	2525	30 Sep 1785	76	311	S side of Cumberland River &c	
Lynsey, Isaac	1013		Sumner	280	181	26 Mar 1795			86	381	On S side of Cumberland River	
Lynsey, Isaac	1026		Sumner	640	253	640			88	185	On S side of Cumberland River	
Lyon, Ezekiel	034		Washington	100			463	24 Apr 1775			On head of Boons Creek	
Lyon, John	590		Sullivan	100	588	29 Jul 1793	831	26 Aug 1781	76	475	Incl plantation where Jonathan Hickman lives	
Lyon, John	936		Washington	100	913	17 Nov 1790	1540	24 Aug 1779	76	148	On the waters of Boons Creek	
Lyon, Nathaniel	1014		Green	200	1241	29 Jul 1793	1278	16 Mar 1779	76	486	N side of Holstons River	
Lyon, Nathaniel	74		Eastern District	100	69	27 Nov 1789	362	24 Mar 1780	74	34	On side of Holstien	
Lyon, Nathaniel	9		Sullivan	300	20	23 Oct 1782	1180	2 Feb 1779	43	247	Beg. at Walnut & Beach on bank of the river	
Lyons, John	290		Green	250	292	20 Sep 1787	948	29 Oct 1783	65	456	On S side of Holsten River on Caney Creek	
Lyons, Nathaniel	90		Hawkins	600	68	-- Sep 1790			74	294	On S of Holston River	
Lytle, Archibald	091	Stephenson, Peter	Sumner	274			3545	19 Dec 1792			S Fork Cedar Lick Creek	yes
Lytle, Archibald	092	Flood, Frederick	Sumner	640			1052	24 Mar 1787			S side of Cumberland River	yes
Lytle, Archibald	093	Dennet, William	Sumner	640			170 (??)	24 Mar 1787			S side of Cumberland River	yes
Lytle, Archibald	094	Brannon, James	Sumner	1000			1467	23 Jun 1788			S side Cumberland River	yes
Lytle, Archibald	15		Davidson	7200	1		1		63	1	West Fork of Stones River	yes
Lytle, Archibald	420	Robeson, John	Davidson	640	392	15 Sep 1787	1171		63	146	On Second Creek	yes
Lytle, Archibald	504		Sumner	640	1675	20 May 1793	2742	30 Nov 1792	81	47	On Lick Creek	yes
Lytle, Archibald	602		Middle District	3000	367	23 Jan 1800	11	4 Jan 1786	106	369	On Cedar River	
Lytle, Archibald	613		Sumner	1000	1872	20 May 1793	1202	31 Jul 1792	81	94	On the waters of Bartons Creek	yes
Lytle, Archibald	650		Sumner	228	1954	20 May 1793	1199	6 Apr 1785	81	113	On Bledsoes Creek	yes
Lytle, Archibald	713		Sumner	640	2095	20 May 1793	1050	6 Apr 1788	81	148	On Bledsoes Creek	yes
Lytle, Archibald	722		Sumner	640	2106	20 May 1793	1198	6 Apr 1785	81	151	On the Brushey Fork of Bledsoes Creek	yes
Lytle, Archibald	783	Blackmore, Geo. D.	Sumner	640	2240	20 May 1793	1718		81	178	On S side of Cumberland River	yes
Lytle, William	1069 ?		Hawkins	100	778	21 Jan 1797	391	7 Apr 1780	91	119	On a branch of Lyons Creek	yes
Lytle, William	1070		Hawkins	600	779	21 Jan 1797	774	-- Jun 1784 /sic/	91	120	S side of Clinch River	

Claimant:	File #:	Assignee:	County:	Acres:	Grant:	Grant Date:	Entry:	Entry Date:	Bk:	Pg:	Location by Stream Name:	Military:
Lytle, William	1295		Sumner	3000	201	19 Jul 1797	5	4 Jan 1786	90	371	On Obids /sic/ River	
Lytle, William	1423		Sumner	640	3297	6 Dec 1797	1968	13 Jun 1796	98	172	Adjoining his survey &c	yes
Lytle, William	1425		Sumner	640	3299	6 Dec 1797	1028	9 Mar 1797	98	174	On the E side of Bartons Creek	yes
Lytle, William	1426		Sumner	640	3300	6 Dec 1797	1020	13 Jun 1796	98	174	On the waters of Big Cedar Lick Creek	yes
Lytle, William	306	Welch, William	Tennessee	1000	2002	20 May 1793	224	25 Oct 1783	81	125	On the N side of Duck River	
Lytle, William	403		Davidson	3840	375	15 Sep 1787	4		63	140	South side of Cumberland River	yes
Lytle, William	433		Eastern District	300	284	21 Jan 1797	356	24 Mar 1780	91	120	S side of Holston River	
Lytle, William	743		Sumner	640	2140	20 May 1793	2034	26 Mar 1786	81	158	On S side of Cumberland River	yes
Lytle, William	758		Sumner	640	2169	20 May 1793	2034	20 Mar 1786	81	165	On Plesan /sic/ Run	yes
Lytle, William	930		Sumner	640	2381	9 Jan 1795	1060	8 Jul 1785	83	236	N side of Cumberland River	yes
Lytle, William,	1424		Sumner	640	3298	6 Dec 1797	1043	13 Jun 1796	98	173	On the waters of Big Cedar Lick Creek	yes
Lytle, William,	655		Sumner	853	1966	20 May 1793	274	21 Mar 1792	81	116	On s side of Cumberland River	yes
Lytle, William, Jr.	1003		Hawkins	255	389	17 Oct 1796			90	14	On N side of Holston River	
Lytle, Wm.	032		Robertson	640							On Red River	
Lytle, Wm.	033		Robertson	640							On Red River	
Lytle, Andrew	2022	Lytle, William	Davidson	640	2000	20 May 1793	261		81	124	On big Harpeth River	yes
Lytle, William	2022	Lytle, Andrew	Davidson	640	2000	20 May 1793	261		81	124	On Big Harpeth River	yes
Lytle, Wm, Jr.	012	Armstrong, Martin	Knox	255							On waters of Holston River	
m	42		Green	200	105	1 Nov 1786	2849	12 May 1781	58	466	Beg upon a white oak	
Mabbey, William	2079	Buchanon, John	Davidson	640	2244	20 May 1793	2064	15 Jun 1786	81	179	On Mill Creek	yes
Mabene, James; Admr.	53	Law, Abraham	Davidson	640			1997 /?/		84		On waters of Battleground Creek	
Maberry, Fr. & T. Jackson	222		Eastern District	640	165	23 Apr 1794	693	14 Dec 1784	82	154	On the S E side of Clinch River &c	
Maberry, Francis	1151		Hawkins	640	868	27 Jun 1801	303	30 Mar 1780	111	16	In Powell's Valley	
Maberry, Francis	409		Eastern District	1000	229	9 Nov 1795	2507	25 May 1784	89	424	The N side of the Tennessee	
Maberry, James	256		Hawkins	640	244	Mar 1792	17	4 Feb 1780	77	333	On the S side of Holston River &c	
Mabins, Charles,	988 (788)		Sumner	640	2452	22 Feb 1792			84	323	On Main Fork of Obeys River	yes
Mabury, F. & Thos. Jackson	113		Hawkins	320	147	26 Dec 1791			75	162	On E side of Dodsons Creek	
Mabury, F. & Thos. Jackson	131		Hawkins	607	165	26 Dec 1791	355	24 Mar 1780	75	169	On N side of Holstons River	
Macan, John	75		Davidson	1097	61	14 Mar 1786	186		63	25	E side of Buffaloe Creek	yes
Macay, John	1234		Washington	50	1206	27 Feb 1796	2895	11 Aug 1795	88	298	Upon Wattagah River	
MacCollum, Isaac	290	Curtis, Thomas	Eastern District	224	2397	8 Feb 1795	1703		84	137	On W side of Cumberland Mountain	yes
Machie, Wm.	122	Stewart, George heirs	Tennessee	1000	1625	23 Feb 1793	3563	20 Oct 1787	76	324	N side of Cumberland River &c	
MacKary, John	2297	Jarvis, Joel	Montgomery	640	2775	9 Sep 1796	3009		88	524	On E side of Stones River	yes
Mackey, Jno.	1274		Davidson	640	239	10 Jul 1788	642	28 Dec 1784	66	421	At fork of Blooming Grove the first creek	
Macklemore, John	2399	Stewart, Duncan	Davidson	640	2796	6 Jun 1796	3848		91	470	S W side of Big Harpeth River	yes
Mackleway, John	942	Cantwell, Stephen	Davidson	1000	958	18 May 1789	450		63	326	On N side of Cumberland River	yes
Maclin, William	1712		Davidson	180	125	23 Feb 1793			76	347	On the waters of Stones River	
Macomes, Aquilla	2064	Moore, William	Davidson	640	2189	20 May 1793	1248		81	168	On Duck River	yes
Macon, John	95	Person, Thomas	Tennessee	640	1377	20 Dec 1791	1388	12 Nov 1784	75	504	On W side of Bushes Meat House	yes
Madearis, John	06	Mullis, James hrs.	Montgomery	640	3249	6 Dec 1797	4329	20 May 1797			On Fletchers Fork of Red River	
Madearis, John	07		Montgomery	640	3248	6 Dec 1797	4330	20 May 1797			Waters of the West Fork of Red River	yes
Madison, Gabriel	1783		Davidson	640	364	26 Jun 1793	568	11 Aug 1784	80	320	On a Big Fork of Harpeth River	
Madison, John	1329	Hickman, Thomas	Sumner	640	3129	14 Sep 1797	4313	6 May 1797	90	415	On head waters of Sinking Creek	yes
Madry, Darling	452	Martin, George	Sumner	228	1575	27 Apr 1793	1241	11 Jul 1791	81	11	Headwaters of Middle Fork of Sulphur Fork	yes
Madry, John	055	Mulherin, James	Davidson	333			698	19 Sep 1785			S side of Cumberland River	yes

Earliest Tennessee Land Records

Claimant:	File #:	Assignee:	County:	Acres:	Grant:	Grant Date:	Entry:	Entry Date:	Bk:	Pg:	Location by Stream Name:	Military:
Madry, Moses	743	Hart, Anthony	Davidson	640	716	11 Jul 1788	3087		63	252	On head of Kerrs & Nelsons Creek	yes
Madry, William	265		Davidson	357	251	7 Mar 1786	981		63	92	On waters of Hays Creek	yes
Magary, Hugh	016		Davidson	640		31 Dec 1783	37				Beg, one mile South of the Spring	
Magbee, William	1096		Hawkins	100	389	19 Jul 1797		Martin Armstrong / 91		618	S side of Holston River	
Magbee, Wm	137		Washington	398			503	14 Oct 1778			On Lick Creek	
Magbee, Wm.	036		Washington	394			515	19 Oct 1778			On the Fall Branch	
Magby, Robert	594	Donelson, Stockley	Tennessee	640	3066	19 Jul 1797	2811		90	376	N side of Cumberland River	yes
Mahan, David	35		Sullivan	236	46	23 Oct 1782	1863	6 Oct 1779	43	259	On a branch of Bever /sic/ Creek &c	
Mahan, James	357		Green	300	359	20 Sep 1787	262	22 Oct 1783	65	475	On Lick Creek	
Mahan, Jno.	562		Green	300	242	20 Sep 1787	263	22 Oct 1783	66	154	On both sides of Lick Creek &c	
Maiden, Benjamin	764		Green	500	583	11 Jul 1788	959	29 Oct 1783	68	220	On the S side of Holston River	
Mailin, William	138		Tennessee	2560		26 Dec 1792	3713	20 Dec 1789	76	341	On the waters of Red River	
Mains, William	761	Burgess, William	Sumner	274	2174	20 May 1793	3209	19 Dec 1792	81	166	On E branch of Middle Fork of Goose Cree	yes
Mallabey, James	357	Weakley, Robert	Davidson	640	341	4 Sep 1787	3282		63	127	N side of Cumberland River	yes
Mallet, Daniel	287		Western District	5000	276	25 Apr 1789	1761		72	83	On both sides of Big Hatcha River	
Mallock (Metlock), David	695		Washington	540	509	10 Nov 1784	606	12 Sep 1782	69	108	Beg at a red /sic/ on W bank of Doe River	
Malloy, Thomas	1211		Davidson	2500	176	10 Jul 1788	24	29 Dec 1783	66	367	Beg. at the mouth of the 1st creek	
Malloy, Thomas	1270		Sumner	1000	2976	5 Apr 1797	2629	7 Oct 1796	90	276	N side of Cumberland River	yes
Malloy, Thomas	1322		Davidson	320	8	18 Aug 1787	696	26 Mar 1785	68	123	Beg at an ash and elm &c	
Malloy, Thomas	1342	Kilgore, Thomas	Davidson	320	28	18 Aug 1787	695	26 Mar 1785	68	131	Beg at a box elder &c	
Malloy, Thomas	1653		Davidson	640	304	17 Nov 1790	537	19 Jul 1784	76	182	Beg. 2 sugar trees on the Cumberland	
Malloy, Thomas	2190		Davidson	50	179	26 Mar 1795			86	379	On Heatons Lick Branch	
Malloy, Thomas	2326	Davidson, James heirs	Davidson	640	2971	5 Apr 1797	3627		90	274	N side of Cumberland River	yes
Malloy, Thomas	2327		Davidson	72	351	10 Apr 1797	51		90	279	On Overalls Creek	
Malloy, Thomas	2328		Davidson	150	352	10 Apr 1797	50		90	280	Waters of Overall Creek	
Malloy, Thomas	2335	Brocken, Joseph heirs	Davidson	640	2979	10 Apr 1797	3164		90	285	S side of Cumberland River	yes
Malloy, Thomas	2336	Pendergrass, Wm. Heirs	Davidson	640	2980	10 Apr 1797	3186 (3180) /sic/		90	285	Waters of Harpeth	yes
Malloy, Thomas	2337	Bosten, Andrew	Davidson	228	2981	10 Apr 1797	1859		90	286	On Overalls Creek	yes
Malloy, Thomas	2338	Copeland, Joab	Davidson	640	2982	10 Apr 1797	1040		90	286	On Harpeth River	yes
Malloy, Thomas	2339	Alexander, Cameron	Davidson	491	2983	10 Apr 1797			90	286	S side of Cumberland River	yes
Malloy, Thomas	2340	Sion, Bradley	Davidson	220	2984	10 Apr 1797			90	287	On Pigeon Creek	yes
Malloy, Thomas	2341	Perkins, Jesse heirs	Davidson	640	2985	10 Apr 1797	3963		90	287	On Hapeth River /sic/	yes
Malloy, Thomas	2342	Ruth, Edward	Davidson	640	2986	10 Apr 1797	3629		90	287	Waters of Harpeth River	yes
Malloy, Thomas	2343	Kerr, John	Davidson	640	2987	10 Apr 1797	3630		90	288	On Harpeth River	yes
Malloy, Thomas	2344	Baird, Joseph heirs	Davidson	640	2989	10 Apr 1797	3943		90	289	On Harpeth River	yes
Malloy, Thomas	2345	Morris, Phillip heirs	Davidson	640	2990	10 Apr 1797	3638		90	289	On Harpeth River	
Malloy, Thomas	2346	Melchior, Fain	Davidson	640	2991	10 Apr 1797	3634		90	289	On waters of Little Harpeth River	yes
Malloy, Thomas	54	Roberts, Kinney	Davidson	640			4629	27 Mar 1797			On Swan Creek	
Malloy, Thomas	546	Hodges, Hardy heirs	Tennessee	1000	2970	5 Apr 1797	1567		90	274	S side of Cumberland River	
Malloy, Thomas	548	Cullifee, James	Tennessee	640	2973	5 Apr 1797	4251		90	275	S side of Cumberland River	
Malloy, Thomas	556	Curry, Thomas heirs	Tennessee	350	2978	10 Apr 1797	3577	13 Dec 1787	90	284	S side of Cumberland River	
Malloy, Thomas	558	Cobb, Zebb heirs	Tennessee	640	2992	10 Apr 1797	2841		90	290	S side of Cumberland River	
Malloy, Thos.	2334	Williams, Thomas	Davidson	640	2977	10 Apr 1797	473		90	284	Waters of Harpeth River	yes
Malloy, Thos.	544	Meere, Abraham heirs	Tennessee	1000	2968	5 Apr 1797	2207		90	273	On Barnetts Creek	
Malloy, Thos.	545	Richey, Thos. Heirs	Tenessee	1000	2969	5 Apr 1797	3961		90	273	S side of Cumberland River	

Earliest Tennessee Land Records

Claimant:	File #:	Assignee:	County:	Acres:	Grant:	Grant Date:	Entry:	Entry Date:	Bk:	Pg:	Location by Stream Name:	Military:
Malloy, Thos.	547	Nelson, Giles	Tennessee	274	2972	5 Apr 1797	1454		90	274	On Lick Creek	
Malloy, Thos.	549	Jones, Underhill heirs	Tennessee	640	2974	5 Apr 1797	3920	8 Dec 1795	90	275	S side of Cumberland River	
Malloy, Thos.	550	Haughton, Levi heirs	Tennessee	640	2975	5 Apr 1797	4127		90	276	S side of Cumberland River	
Malloy, Thos.	557	Glover, Samuel heirs	Tennessee	1000	2988	10 Apr 1797	3724		90	288	On Yellow Creek	
Malone, Jacob	039	Dilenberry, Redmon	Sumner	640			4390	14 Oct 1797			On waters of Middle Fork	yes
Man, John	424	Nelson, Robert	Davidson	640	396	15 Sep 1787	730		63	147	On N side of Cumberland River	yes
Manafee, Jarrott	1143		Davidson	640	120	17 Apr 1786	482	9 Jun 1784	66	179	On both sides of Big Harpeth	
Manasco, James	604		Hawkins	60	478	29 Jul 1793	312	16 Mar 1780	80	295	On the N side of Holston River	
Manasco, James	90		Eastern District	300	79	17 Nov 1790	1844	7 Oct 1779	76	169	S/S Holstein River on waters of Dry Creek	
Manasco, James	91		Eastern District	300	80	17 Nov 1790	1486	19 Feb 1784	76	169	S side of Holston River	
Mancher /sic/, Kasper	1347		Davidson	640	33	8 Oct 1787	89	14 Jan 1784	68	134	Lying on left hand fork of Kaspers Creek	
Mancher /sic/, Kasper	1349		Davidson	320	35	8 Oct 1787	393	5 Apr 1784	68	134	Lying on the headwaters of Red River	
Maneese, James	396		Middle District	1000	335	17 Dec 1794				221	On first creek that empties into Elk River	
Manefee, Jonas	1224		Davidson	584	188	10 Jul 1788	529	17 Jul 1784	84	409	S/S Cumberland River & on Browns Creek	
Mangold, Thomas	1364	Tatum, Ho & Henry Wiggin	Sumner	640	3212	14 Sep 1797	4171	29 Jun 1797	66	10	Waters of Stones River	yes
Manifee, John	302		Sullivan	250	441	9 Aug 1787	1986	16 Oct 1779	92	460	On the waters of Reedy Creek	
Manifee, Jonas	013		Davidson	590			529	17 Jul 1784	61		On the S side of Cumberland	
Manley, William	1665	Robertson, James	Davidson	274	1588	23 Feb 1793	148		76	306	On Otter Creek &c	yes
Manly, Adam	557	Murfree, Hardy	Sumner	640	1776	20 May 1793	718	17 Dec 1792	81	73	On S side of Cumberland River	yes
Manly, Mark	254	Archer, Laticia heiress	Davidson	640	240	7 Mar 1786	215		63	88	S side of Cumberland River	yes
Manly, Solomon	113	Murfree, Hardy	Davidson	640	99	14 Mar 1786	141		63	40	On both sides of Spring Creek	
Mann, Arnold	1685	White, James	Davidson	228	1624	23 Feb 1793	3689		76	324	Cumberland River in said Whites Bent /sic/	yes
Mann, Francis	779	Lenier, James	Davidson	640	752	11 Jul 1788	3362		63	264	On S side of Main E Fork of Big Barren Riv	yes
Mann, James	1203		Green	500	1047	Mar 1792	296	23 Oct 1783	77	339	On Magarts /sic/ Creek	
Mann, John	021	Brayboy, John	Montgomery	600			4572	27 Mar 1797			On Williams Creek	yes
Mann, John	2331		Davidson	40	356	10 Apr 1797			90	281	S side of Cumberland River	
Mann, John	2431	McFurson, Roger	Davidson	640	3259	6 Dec 1797	4360		98	147	On the waters of Marrowbone Creek	yes
Mann, John	2432	Hadlow, Joseph heirs	Davidson	640	3260	6 Dec 1797	4611		98	147	On the waters of First Creek	yes
Mann, John	2433	Pickle, Jonas	Davidson	640	3261	6 Dec 1797	4361		98	148	On Cumberland & Harpeth Rivers	yes
Mann, John	2434	Dunlap, Thomas heirs	Davidson	640	3263	6 Dec 1797	4139		98	149	On head waters of Trace Creek of Harpeth	yes
Mann, John	2435	Mullen, Michael	Davidson	640	3264	6 Dec 1797	1018		98	150	On a large branch on Harpeth River	yes
Mann, John	670	Finley, Abraham heirs	Tennessee	640	3257	6 Dec 1797	2913		98	146	On Barretts Creek &c	
Mann, John	671	Hill, Hardy	Tennessee	1000	3258	6 Dec 1797	4613		98	146	On the waters of Saline Creek	
Mann, John	672	Worwick, Walter	Tennessee	640	3262	6 Dec 1797	1471		98	149	On Barretts Creek	
Mann, John	673	Fowler, Abraham	Tennessee	640	3265	6 Dec 1797	4770		98	151	On the head of Barretts Creek	
Mann, John	674	Harper, Wm. Heirs	Tennessee	640	3266	6 Dec 1797	4616		98	151	On the N side of Cumberland River &c	
Mann, Robert	55	Hogg, Thomas	Tennessee	640	1271	10 Dec 1790	2428	30 Sep 1785	74	356	On S side of Cumberland River	yes
Mann, Thomas	706	Harney, S. & A. Bledsoe	Sumner	640	2086	20 May 1793	3019	18 Nov 1792	81	146	On head of a small branch &c	yes
Mannin, Timothy	862	Fort, Elias	Sumner	228	2370	20 May 1793	3589	9 Sep 1788	81	206	Joining his other entry	yes
Manning, John	541	Ewing, Alexander	Sumner	640	1743	20 May 1793	1513	6 May 1780	81	64	On both sides of Cedar Lick Creek	yes
Manns, Jacob	643		Hawkins	250	512	23 Apr 1794	1765	6 May 1780	81	552	On S side of Holston River	
Mansoor /sic/, Casper	1128		Davidson	640	105	17 Apr 1786	90	14 Jan 1784	66	175	Lying on both sides of Kaspers Creek	
Manshaw, George	1535	Gilmour, Charles	Davidson	640	1092	26 Nov 1789	3514		74	127	On N side of Cumberland River	
Mansher /sic/, Gasper	1350		Davidson	640	36	8 Oct 1787	54	5 Jan 1784	68	135	Lying on West waters of Kaspers Creek	yes
Mansker, George	1120		Davidson	640	97	17 Apr 1786	100	14 Jan 1784	66	174	Lying on Station Camp Creek &c	

Claimant:	File #:	Assignee:	County:	Acres:	Grant:	Grant Date:	Entry:	Entry Date:	Bk:	Pg:	Location by Stream Name:	Military:
Manson, John	2279	Buckanan, John	Davidson	640	2759	20 Jul 1796	2529		88	461	On waters of Harricane /sic/ Creek &c	yes
Manson, John	712a	Payne, Josiah	Sumner	640	2481	31 Dec 1793	2529	22 Dec 1792	81	437	On W side of Caney Fork	yes
Maples, Marmaduke	349		Middle District	640	2398	1 Feb 1795			84	149	On N side of Cumberland Mountain /sic/	yes
Maples, Marmaduke	678	King, Thomas	Hawkins	518	2388	12 Jul 1794	3579		81	601	On N side of Holston River	yes
March, Febreas /sic/	1109	Harris, Edward	Sumner	640	2615	4 Jun 1796	2747	1 Jun 1795	88	338	Joining said Harris survey	yes
Marchant, Caleb	129	Howard, Joshua	Davidson	274	115	7 Mar 1786	833		63	45	On both sides Whites & Heatons Creek	yes
Mardera, James	464	Donelson, S.	Tennessee	640	2576	7 Mar 1796	2939	30 Sep 1785	88	314	On W branch of Sulphur Fork	yes
Mares, James	1379		Davidson	320	62	8 Oct 1787	317	28 Feb 1784	68	146	Beg. on line of David Shannons preemption	
Marley, Robert	340	Murray, James heirs	Davidson	640	325	1 Aug 1787	1775		63	121	Beg. at a Lynn & Sugar tree	yes
Marley, Robert	341	Anderson, Chas heirs	Davidson	640	326	1 Aug 1787	3106 (2106) /sic/		63	121	Beg at a white oak & Ashe	yes
Marley, George heirs	343	Barlow, George heirs	Davidson	640	328	1 Aug 1787	2109		63	122	On waters of Spring Creek	yes
Marr, John	39		Middle District	1000	41	10 Jul 1788	490	25 Oct 1783	67	426	On the waters of Elk River	
Marr, John, Jr.	242	Beard, John Lewis	Davidson	640	228	7 Mar 1786	748		63	84	On Harpeth River	yes
Marr, John, Sr.	608	Roberson /sic/, James	Davidson	335	580	15 Sep 1787	750		63	207	On S side of Cumberland River	
Marr, John;	816		Sumner	640	2287	20 May 1793	2417	19 Nov 1792	81	188	On S side of Big Barren River	yes
Mars, Timothy	296	Mountflorence, James Cole	Davidson	640	282	22 Mar 1787	2094		63	104	S side of Cumberland River	yes
Marsh, Eli	563	Brown, Morgan	Tennessee	640	2998	10 Apr 1797	3943		90	292	S side of Cumberland River	yes
Marshall, Bartlett	748		Hawkins	200	588	7 Jul 1794	991	29 Oct 1783	82	206	On the S side of Holston &c	
Marshall, Charles	767	Hampton, Andrew	Davidson	640	740	11 Jul 1788	3474		63	260	On W side of Elk Rork of Red River	yes
Marshall, Dixon	77		Davidson	2560	63	14 Mar 1786	1401		63	26	North side of Cumberland River	yes
Marshall, Emanuel	3	Barton, Joseph	Wilson	640	3389	12 Dec 1801	3612		114	92	On waters of Round Lick Creek	yes
Marshall, George	1502	McCarty, Jacob	Davidson	228	1059	26 Nov 1789	870		74	107	On Sulfer /sic/ Fork	yes
Marshall, Henry	186		Hawkins	450	119	16 Nov 1790	2205	12 Nov 1779	77	190	On the N side of Holston River &c	
Marshall, Henry	99		Hawkins	300	133	26 Dec 1791	2199	12 Nov 1779	75	155	On N side of Holston River	
Marshall, John	1511		Davidson	(?)	1068	26 Nov 1789	2269		74	113	Beg. on the Virginia line	
Marshall, John	206		Sumner	640	1111	26 Nov 1789	2269		74	134	Beg at an ash	yes
Marshall, John	208		Sumner	640	1113	26 Nov 1789	1619	21 Jan 1786	74	135	On both sides of a creek	yes
Marshall, John	222		Sumner	640	1127	26 Nov 1789	1620	21 Jan 1786	74	142	Both sides Head Creek of big Barren River	yes
Marshall, John	223		Sumner	640	1128	26 Nov 1789	2270	9 Feb 1787	74	143	On waters of Caney Fork	yes
Marshall, John	224		Sumner	228	1129	26 Nov 1789	1604	21 Sep 1787	74	143	On Manskers Trace Creek	yes
Marshall, John	225		Sumner	640	1130	26 Nov 1789	1612	9 Feb 1787	74	144	First creek emptying into E Fk of Stones Ri	yes
Marshall, John	226		Sumner	640	1131	26 Nov 1789	1624	21 Jan 1786	74	144	On a creek of S. Fork &c	yes
Marshall, John	227		Sumner	640	1132	26 Nov 1789			74	145	On Collins River	yes
Marshall, John	228		Sumner	640	1133	26 Nov 1789	1608	21 Jan 1786	74	145	On Main S Fork of Big Barren River	yes
Marshall, John	229		Sumner	228	1134	26 Nov 1789	1601	21 Sep 1787	74	146	On Manskers Trace Creek	yes
Marshall, John	230		Sumner	640	1135	26 Nov 1789	1607		74	146	On the creek &c	yes
Marshall, John	473	Young, William heirs	Davidson	640	445	15 Sep 1787	2285		63	163	On Money Fork Creek	yes
Marshall, John	474	West, Francis heirs	Davidson	640	446	15 Sep 1787	1611		63	164	On Money Fork Creek	yes
Marshall, John	475	Glover, Jones heirs	Davidson	228	447	15 Sep 1787	2273		63	164	On Station Camp Creek	yes
Marshall, John	476	Valentine, P.	Davidson	640	448	15 Sep 1787	2279		63	164	On the Money Fork Creek	yes
Marshall, John	477	Woodrough, John heirs	Davidson	640	449	15 Sep 1787	2284		63	165	On Money Fork Creek	yes
Marshall, John	478	Savage, Ransom	Davidson	357	450	15 Sep 1787	2293		63	165	On waters of Stones River	yes
Marshall, John	479	Rigens, Joel	Davidson	640	451	15 Sep 1787	2282		63	165	On Hurricane Creek	yes
Marshall, John	48	Hutson, John	Davidson	640	453	15 Sep 1787	1610		63	165a	On Money Fork Creek	yes
Marshall, John	480	Harris, Samuel	Davidson	228	452	15 Sep 1787	2274		63	165a	On Money Fork Creek	yes

Earliest Tennessee Land Records

Claimant:	File #:	Assignee:	County:	Acres:	Grant:	Grant Date:	Entry:	Entry Date:	Bk:	Pg:	Location by Stream Name:	Military:
Marshall, John	481	Hutson, John heirs	Davidson	640	453	15 Sep 1787	1610		63	165a	On Money Fork Creek	yes
Marshall, John	482	Ward, Benjamin	Davidson	640	454	15 Sep 1787	2281		63	165	On Money Fork Creek	yes
Marshall, John	483	Clark, William	Davidson	640	455	15 Sep 1787	2271		63	166	On Money Fork Creek	yes
Marshall, John	484	Letches, William	Davidson	640	456	15 Sep 1787	2276		63	166	On Money Fork Creek	yes
Marshall, John	485	White, George heirs	Davidson	640	457	15 Sep 1787	1618		63	166	On Money Fork Creek	yes
Marshall, John	486	Duncan, William	Davidson	228	458	15 Sep 1787	1602		63	167	On Money Fork Creek	yes
Marshall, John	487	Matthews, Richard	Davidson	640	459	15 Sep 1787	1615		63	167	On waters of S Fork of Maney Fork Creek	yes
Marshall, John	488	Carroll, Harwell	Davidson	640	460	15 Sep 1787	1605		63	167	On Money Fork Creek	yes
Marshall, John	582	Hatches, David heirs	Davidson	640	554	15 Sep 1787	1613		63	199	On Money Fork Creek	yes
Marshall, John	623	Jeffries, John heirs	Davidson	640	595	15 Sep 1787	2275		63	212	On N Fork of Money Fork Creek	yes
Marshall, John	97	Morris, Wm.	Sumner	640			2277	21 Jan 1787			Beg. in the VA line at a white oak	yes
Marshall, John	98	Beavears, John	Sumner	640			1609	9 Feb 1787			On a fork of Caney Fork	yes
Marshall, William	1362		Davidson	320	45	8 Oct 1787	192	27 Jan 1784	68	139	On the waters of Big Harpeth	
Marshall, William	273		Middle District	400	142	27 Apr 1793	3	4 Jan 1786	81	39	On N side of Duck River	
Marshall, William	364		Hawkins	335	357	8 Mar 1793	1205	1779	78	488	On N side of Clinch River	
Marsom, Samuel	887	Crockley, Allen	Davidson	640	903	17 Jan 1789	3425		63	312	On the Spring Creek	yes
Martain, George	038		Washington	294			721	25 Dec 1779			On a branch of Lick Creek	
Martin, Alex.	209		Middle District	2000	195	5 Dec 1792	2		78	459	On S side of Duck River	
Martin, Alexander	16		Davidson	2314	2	14 Mar 1786			63	2	On Big Harpeth River	yes
Martin, Andrew	1180		Green	200	1023	26 Dec 1791	507	15 Oct 1778	77	289	On the head of Second Creek	yes
Martin, Archibald	490		Davidson	297	462	15 Sep 1787	848		63	168	On both sides of Stones Creek	yes
Martin, Bastian	480		Sumner	150	122	27 Apr 1793	1786	12 Sep 1786	81	30	On a branch of Red River	
Martin, Geo.	09		Sullivan	100	732		732 /sic/	21 Dec 1778			On waters of Lick Creek	
Martin, George	1200		Sumner	320	317	10 Sep 1796	1241	11 Jul 1791	88	516	On N side of Cumberland River	
Martin, George	452		Sumner	228	1575	27 Apr 1793	732	21 Dec 1778	81	11	Headwaters of Middle Fork of Sulphur Fork	yes
Martin, George	861		Washington	100	868	26 Nov 1789	1786	23 Apr 1784	71	385	On the Lick Creek	
Martin, George & others	14		Middle District	3243	16	10 Jul 1788	394		67	414	On the S side of Duck River &c	
Martin, Henry	284	Williams, Willoughby	Davidson	640	270	24 Jan 1787	3366	19 Aug 1788	63	99	On both sides Buzzard Creek	yes
Martin, Isaac	060	Robertson, James	Davidson	320			1908	31 Dec 1779			S side Harpeth River	yes
Martin, James	1069		Washington	100	1019	27 Nov 1792	458	25 Oct 1783	80	181	Beg. at a black oak &c	
Martin, James	108		Western District	5000	108	10 Jul 1788	1019	8 Oct 1779	67	323	On both sides of Obion River	
Martin, James	168		Washington	186	36	23 Oct 1782	114		47	16	Beg at a stake &c	
Martin, James	275		Davidson	1114	261	14 Mar 1786	563	27 Oct 1783	63	95	On West Harpeth River	yes
Martin, James	39		Western District	5000	39	10 Jul 1788	269	10 Dec 1790	67	295	On the Obion River &c	
Martin, James	493		Washington	100	756	16 Aug 1787	240	17 Jan 1780	64	137	Beg. at a white oak &c	
Martin, James	497		Washington	68	360	16 Aug 1787	2401	17 Jan 1780	64	139	Beg. at a cor. red oak &c	
Martin, James	938		Washington	100	915	17 Nov 1790	2140		76	149	Joining his 1st entry &c	
Martin, John	315	Rice, John & others	Davidson	640	301	13 Jun 1787	2922		63	112	On N side of Tenesee /sic/ River	yes
Martin, Jos. & Jno. Hackett	151		Green	500	621	23 Aug 1788	387	5 Sep 1781	64	348	On the S side of Clinch River &c	
Martin, Joseph	1220		Davidson	640	184	10 Jul 1788	600	31 Mar 1784	66	408	On the So side of Cumberland River &c	
Martin, Joseph	1296		Davidson	640	261	10 Jul 1788	610	9 Oct 1784	66	426	On the waters of Stones River	
Martin, Joseph	1323		Green	300	1173	12 Jan 1793	269	23 Nov 1778	78	409	On Sinking Creek	
Martin, Joseph	1597	McVey, Eli	Davidson	640	1288	10 Dec 1790		1779,-1781	74	361	On W side of Stones River	yes
Martin, Joseph	189		Sullivan	400	196	10 Oct 1783	766,-1789		53	157	On the N side of Holston River	
Martin, Joseph	212		Sullivan	400	219	10 Oct 1783	98-99	1778	53	166	On the S side of Holston River	

Claimant:	File #:	Assignee:	County:	Acres:	Grant:	Grant Date:	Entry:	Entry Date:	Bk:	Pg:	Location by Stream Name:	Military:
Martin, Joseph	62		Washington	299	230	23 Oct 1782	610	23 Nov 1778	44	260	On Sinking Creek	
Martin, Joshua	227	Porter, John	Davidson	274	213	7 Mar 1786	35		63	79	On waters of Harpeth River	yes
Martin, Josiah	766		Washington	100	580	10 Nov 1784	1449	1 Nov 1779	69	132	Beg at a marked white oak	
Martin, Josiah	798		Washington	200	612	10 Nov 1784	254	17 Oct 1778	69	141	Beg. at a marked white oak	
Martin, Nicholas	207	Love, Josiah	Sumner	640	1112	26 Nov 1789	3472	10 Oct 1789	74	135	On N side of Cumberland River	yes
Martin, Patrick	876		Davidson	1000	890	17 Jan 1789	1824		63	309	On both sides Main E Fork of Stones River	yes
Martin, Richard	29	Lee, James	Sumner	228	786	11 Jul 1788	565	21 Oct 1786	63	275	On West Fork of Goose Creek	yes
Martin, Richard	376		Green	300	378	20 Sep 1787	2823	27 Mar 1785	65	480	Upon the waters of Clinch River	
Martin, Robert	262	Clark, Lardner	Davidson	428	248	7 Mar 1786	1209	25 Oct 1783	63	91	On waters of Stones River	yes
Martin, Robert	75		Western District	5000	75	10 Jul 1788	480		67	309	On the Obion River &c	
Martin, Samuel	639	Jinkins, Abraham	Davidson	357	612	15 Sep 1787	414		63	218	On South side of Cumberland River	yes
Martin, Thomas	287	Glasgow, James	Davidson	228	273	24 Jan 1787	1152		63	100	On N side of Cumberland River	yes
Martin, Thos. & Samuel	1309		Davidson	640	274	10 Jul 1788	374	29 Mar 1784	66	433	Beg at the Et side of large pond at an elm.	
Martin, William	283	Williams, Willoughby	Davidson	640	269	24 Jan 1786	1212		63	98	E side of Blooming Grove	yes
Martin, William Capt.	1457		Sumner	1280	410	30 Oct 1801			111	109	On head of Little Cedar Creek	yes
Martin, William, Capt.	1458		Sumner	1280	411	30 Oct 1801			111	109	Bet. the head of Cedar Creek & Round Lic	yes
Masey, Zebulon	025	Sloan, John	Not given	640							On the waters of Watauga	yes
Massingale, Henry	966		Washington	150	943	17 Nov 1790	2661	10 Nov 1780	76	158	On the waters of Watauga	
Maslin, William	1907 /r/		Davidson	11.25	120	23 Feb 1793			76	345	N side of Cumberland River	
Mason, Joan	61	O'Bryan, Laurence	Tennessee	640	1295	10 Dec 1796	1797	4 May 1785	74	364	N side of Cumberland River	yes
Mason, Phillip	414	Donelson, S. & Robt. Youg	Eastern District	1000	2806	28 Dec 1796	2066		90	206	In the Grassy Valley	yes
Mason, Robert	964		Washington	100	941	17 Nov 1790	2904	23 Aug 1781	76	158	On the Island Fork	
Mason, Samuel	1257		Davidson	640	222	10 Jul 1788	312	16 Feb 1784	66	417	On the N side of Cumberland River	
Massengill, Henry	417		Washington	100	409	13 Oct 1783	843	30 Dec 1778	52	270	On Watauga River	
Massey, James	1879	Massey, Reubin heir	Davidson	640	1623	27 Apr 1793			81	23	On E branches of the fork of Stones River	yes
Massey, James	1884	Massey, Thomas heir	Davidson	640	1642	27 Apr 1793			81	27	On a small fork of Stewarts Creek	yes
Massey, Thomas	1623		Davidson	640	1363	10 Dec 1790			74	386	On a small fork of Stewarts Creek	
Massey, Zebulon	538	Williams, Etheldred	Middle District	640	2962	2 Mar 1797	3995		90	256	Both sides of Caney Fork	yes
Massingale, Michael	154		Washington	150	22	23 Oct 1782	1053	8 Jan 1779	47	10	On head of Hicory /sic/ Creek	
Massingale, Solomon	469	Donelson, Stockley	Sumner	640	1628	27 Apr 1793	1715	30 Nov 1792	81	24	On a small creek of Smiths Fork	yes
Massingell, Henry	1320	Knight, Samuel	Washington	300	1241	5 Apr 1797	972	2 Jan 1779	90	278	On Watauga River	
Massingell, Henry	1341	Banks, Robert	Washington	100	1262	30 Dec 1796	1537	24 Aug 1779	91	541	On Coopers Creek	
Massingill, Henry	1319	Stewart, Duncan	Washington	200	1240	5 Apr 1797	2651	19 Sep 1780	90	278	On Watauga River	
Massingill, Henry	367	Hart, Anthony	Washington	220	359	13 Oct 1783	844	30 Dec 1778	52	246	On Watauga River	
Masterson, Charles	436		Sumner	640	321	27 Nov 1792	457	22 May 1784	81	2	On some of W branches of Drakes Creek	yes
Matchett, Edward	1248	Donelson, Stockley	Sumner	640	2855	21 Jan 1797	1455	7 Aug 1796	90	52	Waters of Martins Creek	yes
Mathews, Mussenden /sic/	462	Knight, Samuel	Davidson	274	434	15 Sep 1787	217		63	160	On waters of Station Camp Creek	yes
Matthew, Gilbert	1273	Banks, Robert	Sumner	182	3015	10 Apr 1797	3904	22 Nov 1796	90	299	On the Cainey /sic/ Fork	yes
Matthews, Charles	2375	Stewart, Duncan	Davidson	640	3096	14 Sep 1797	4001		90	399	E Fork of S Harpeth	yes
Matthews, Gilbert	201	Hart, Anthony	Sumner	434	1106	26 Nov 1789	3118	12 Mar 1788	74	132	On waters of Collins River	yes
Matthews, Jacob	146		Davidson	640	132	14 Mar 1786	300		63	51	On Williams Creek	yes
Matthews, Jeremiah & C. Hill	1291		Green	640	1141	12 Jan 1793	6	24 Feb 1778	78	388	Beg at a white oak	
Mathews, Joel	499		Green	200	501	20 Sep 1787	63	21 Oct 1783	65	522	S/S Nolachucky River & on the Flag Branch	yes
Matthews, John	2046	Baker, Charles	Davidson	274	2069	20 May 1793	3036		81	141	On a small branch of Gaspers Creek	yes
Matthews, Joseph	272	Gerard, Charles	Tennessee	640	1788	20 May 1793	1595	24 Apr 1785	81	76	On S side of Cumberland River	yes

Claimant:	File #:	Assignee:	County:	Acres:	Grant:	Grant Date:	Entry:	Entry Date:	Bk:	Pg:	Location by Stream Name:	Military:
Matthews, Richard	487	Marshall, John	Davidson	640	459	15 Sep 1787	1615		63	167	On waters of S Fork of Maney Fork or Cr	yes
Matthews, William	1865	Alexander, Ebenezer	Davidson	640	1599	27 Apr 1793	2437		81	17	On S side of Cumberland River	yes
Matticks, Valentine	289		Hawkins	300	300	14 Jan 1793	2126	4 Nov 1779	78	347	On Wm. Doaks Creek	
Mattimore, William	1366	Tatum, Ho. & Henry Wiggin	Sumner	640	3214	14 Sep 1797	4260	16 Feb 1797	92	11	Waters of Stones River	yes
Mattock, Moore	039		Washington	200			749	23 Dec 1778			On Clear Fork of Horse Creek	yes
Mattock, Moore	520		Washington	200	783	16 Aug 1787	1316	30 Mar 1779	64	147	On the waters of Boons Creek &c	
Mattock, Moore	547		Sullivan	200	530	17 Nov 1790			76	188	On the Clear Fork of Horse Creek	
Mattock, Nicholas	1213		Sumner	427	2492	26 Sep 1795	1426	19 Sep 1785	89	103	Lying near 2 miles W of a large spring	yes
Mattock, William	484	Lytle, Archibald	Sumner	320	25	27 Apr 1793	819	1 Sep 1792	81	35	On Bartons Creek	yes
Matton, William	722		Sumner	640	2106	20 May 1793	1198	6 Apr 1785	81	151	On the Brushey Fork &c	yes
Maulden, Ambrose	695		Sumner	274	2062	20 May 1793	3459	9 Aug 1786	81	140	On Red River	yes
Maulden, Molton	1308		Davidson	650	273	10 Jul 1788	311	20 Feb 1784	66	432	On the Sulphur Fork a branch of Red River	
Mauris, John	1768		Green	100	1444	17 Apr 1801	2361	10 Dec 1783	112	385	N side of Nollychuckey River	
Maxey, Jesse	1327		Davidson	640	13	18 Aug 1787	659	10 Jan 1785	68	125	Elm & black gum Thos. Sharpes N W corner	
Maxwell, Geo. & F. Mayberry	174		Eastern District	500	129	24 Jun 1793	1738	2 Feb 1780	80	186	Joining the N W line of Henderson survey	
Maxwell, George	1316		Davidson	320	2	18 Aug 1787	194	27 Jan 1784	68	121	On Kaspers Creek	
Maxwell, George	1787	McNeal, Archibald heirs	Davidson	640	369	26 Jun 1793	709	16 Apr 1785	80	322	On the S side of Harpeth	
Maxwell, George	368		Sullivan	160	247	10 Nov 1784	779	22 Apr 1781	69	161	On N side of Holston River	
Maxwell, George	48		Sullivan	200	59	23 Oct 1782	1692	21 Sep 1779	43	266	On Sinking Creek	
Maxwell, George	619		Hawkins	300	315	15 Jul 1793			80	300	On the S Fork of Big Buffalow Creek	
Maxwell, Jesse	1187		Davidson	562	164	17 Apr 1786	257	9 Feb 1784	66	189	On the S side of Cumberland River &c	
Maxwell, Jesse	1442	Franklin, James	Davidson	320	88	10 Jul 1788	681	19 Feb 1785	68	231	On the N side of Cumberland River	
Maxwell, Jesse	150		Middle District	400	147	18 May 1789	58		73	257	On the S side of Richland Creek &c	
Maxwell, Nathaniel	45		Sullivan	300	56	23 Oct 1782	1695	21 Sep 1779	43	265	On the S Fork of Muddy Creek	
Maxwell, Samuel	273		Middle District	150	412	9 Aug 1787	554	1 May 1780	61	431	On the West side of Spring Creek	
Maxwell, Thomas	224		Middle District	720	204	27 Nov 1792	2012	1 May 1784	80	209	On the S side of Duck River	
Maxwell, William & Moses	448		Sullivan	612	327	10 Nov 1784	780	22 Apr 1781	69	186	Beg at 3 black oaks	
Maxwell, John	1785		Davidson	640	367	26 Jun 1793	112	15 Jan 1784	80	321	On the waters of the W Fork of Mill Creek	
May, Abraham	1762	Welborn, Daniel	Green	100	1439	2 Dec 1797	175	19 Feb 1780	96	no #	N side of Long Creek	
May, John;	569	Hasten, Oliver heir	Tennessee	1000	3006	10 Apr 1797	2210		90	295	N of Red River	yes
May, Major /sic/	2038		Davidson	640	2053	20 May 1793			81	137	Bet head of Little Cedar Cr and Round Lick	yes
May, Saml, Jr. & Thos. King	575	Wells, Hayden	Tennessee	640	3022	10 Apr 1797	758		90	302	S side of Cumberland River	yes
May, Thomas	657		Sullivan	300	605	5 Jun 1793			81 ?	338	On the Long Creek	
	137	Nelson, John	Davidson	274	123	14 Mar 1786	759		63	48	N side of Cumberland River	yes
Mayberry F & Thos. Jackson	149		Hawkins	250	183	26 Dec 1791	1778	2 Oct 1779	75	176	On E Fork of Dodsons Creek	
Mayberry F & Thos. Jackson	351		Hawkins	640	345	8 Mar 1793	1616	14 Sep 1779	78	482	On waters of Sinking Creek	
Mayberry, Fr. & Geo. Hynds	219		Middle District	4400	199	24 Jun 1793	531	27 Oct 1783	80	189	On Wolf River	
Mayberry, Fr. & T. Jackson	105		Eastern District	150	94	17 Nov 1790	705	13 Nov 1780	76	174	N side of Holston River	
Mayberry, Frances	175		Eastern District	640	130	24 Jun 1793	1954	12 Feb 1780	80	186	N side of Clinch River &c	
Mayberry, Frances	218		Middle District	200	198	24 Jun 1793	459	24 Apr 1780	80	189	About 1 mile from Obeys River	
Mayberry, Francis	176		Eastern District	640	131	24 Jun 1792	1666	7 Sep 1779	80	186	Joining Henderson & Co. N W line	
Mayberry, Francis	177		Eastern District	640	132	24 Jun 1793	1766	1 Oct 1779	80	187	Joining Henderson and Companys sur	
Mayberry, Francis	178		Eastern District	550	133	24 Jun 1793	2172	13 May 1784	80	187	In Powells Valley	
Mayberry, Francis	179		Eastern District	300	134	24 Jun 1793	558	6 May 1780	80	187	On the S side of Clinch River	
Mayberry, Francis	180		Eastern District	1000	135	24 Jun 1793	2169	13 May 1784	80	188	In Powells Valley	

Earliest Tennessee Land Records

Claimant:	File #:	Assignee:	County:	Acres:	Grant:	Grant Date:	Entry:	Entry Date:	Bk:	Pg:	Location by Stream Name:	Mill
Mayberry, Francis	197		Eastern District	50 (60) /	169	23 Apr 1793	556	6 May 1780	81	557	On waters of Long Creek	
Mayberry, Francis	30		Eastern District	640	30	11 Jul 1788	693	13 Sep 1780	67	352	On the S E side of Clinch River &c	
Mayberry, Francis	410	Horseford, James heirs	Eastern Dist	640	2497	10 Nov 1795	3803		89	424	Joining Hendersons NW line	
Mayberry, Francis	438		Hawkins	800	316	24 Jun 1793	120,-459	1780	80	191	On the E Fork of Flatt Creek	
Mayberry, Francis	439		Hawkins	100	317	24 Jun 1793	459	24 Apr 1780	80	191	On the S side of Holston River	
Mayberry, Francis	440		Hawkins	1280	318	24 Jun 1793	2382,-2170	30 May 1784	80	192	On the E Fork of Flat Creek	
Mayberry, Francis	637		Hawkins	5000	506	23 Apr 1794	2566	4 Mar 1793	81	551	On S side of Holston River	
Mayberry, J. & Jno Smith	452		Hawkins	640	330	24 Jun 1793			80	195	On the S side of Holston River	
Mayberry, James	031		Hawkins	400	332			10 Sep 1778		185	On the N side of Holston River	
Mayberry, James	171		Eastern Dist	150	126	24 Jun 1793	381	27 Nov 1780	80	196	On the E Fork of Flatt Creek	
Mayberry, James	454		Hawkins	400	332	24 Jun 1793	708	1779,-1780	80	197	In Powells Valley on Little Cove Creek	
Mayberry, James	457		Hawkins	300	335	24 Jun 1793	1926,-2494	7 Jun 1780	80	180	In Powell's Valley	
Mayberry, James	81		Eastern Dist	300	106	26 Dec 1791	586,-2196	12 Nov 1779	75	180	On N side of Clinch River	
Mayberry, James	82		Eastern District	500	107	26 Dec 1791	2196	28 Apr 1780	75	463	On the waters of Tuckaho Creek	
Maybury, Francis	1599		Green	200	1331	18 Apr 1795	505	8 Feb 1780	83	321	On the S side of Holston River & c	
Maybury, James	237		Hawkins	640	224	26 Dec 1791	184	16 May 1780	77	174	Lying on head of the W Fork of Mill Creek	
Mayfield, James	1124		Davidson	640	101	17 Apr 1786	565	6 Jan 1784	66	29	On S side of Cumberland River	yes
Mayfield, Spencer	477	Williams, Sampson	Sumner	228	1647	27 Apr 1793	245	23 Jun 1792	81	41	On Mill Creek	yes
Mayfield, Sutterline	117	Copeland, Stephen heir	Davidson	640	783	7 Mar 1786	1539		63	89	E Fork of Mill Creek	yes
Mayfield, Sutterline	256	Morrison, Robert	Davidson	640	242	7 Mar 1786	783		63	320	On S side of Cumberland River	yes
Mays, John	30	Cockran, William	Tennessee	640	1194	30 Nov 1790	641	30 Sep 1785	74	294	On head of Clear Branch of Long Creek	
Mays, Maj /sic/	1065	King, William	Sumner	640	2542	10 Dec 1795	2749	8 Aug 1795	88	588	On Little Lick Creek	
Mays, William	1519		Green	400	1280	12 Jul 1794	758	26 Jan 1781	81	167	S side of Holston River &c	
Maze, Henry	808		Hawkins	200	644	6 Jan 1795	2755	4 Feb 1787	83	312	On Cherokee Creek	
McAdams, James	43		Washington	400	333	24 Oct 1782	2671	29 Dec 1779	43	189	On Bazzel Saleen	yes
McAdams, John	2087	Holley, Henry	Davidson	228	2290	20 May 1793	829		81	256	On waters of Caney Fork	yes
McAdoe, James	1039	Easton, James	Sumner	640	2701	27 Mar 1796	3968	11 May 1795	88	49	Beg at two white oaks &c	
McAdone, Arthur	1071		Davidson	640	45	17 Apr 1786	244	6 Feb 1784	66	420	On the S side of Holston on Morse Creek	
McAdow, John	211		Green	300	168	20 Sep 1787	102	2 May 1785 surv.	65	65	On Bullard Creek	
McAdow, John	265		Washington	200	133	23 Oct 1782	861	30 Dec 1778	47	480	Known by the name of Chestnut Ridge	
McAdow, John	377		Green	50	379	20 Sep 1787	238		65	290	On the Dry Valley	
McAleb, Archibald M.	461		Washington	95	453	13 Oct 1783	1255	1 Mar 1779	52	212	On the N side of Holston River &c	
McAlister, Jno. & J Shields	762		Hawkins	300	602	12 Jul 1794	1939	15 Oct 1779	82	501	Beg at a black oak	
McAllister, Thos. & others	1115		Washington	640	1073	27 Nov 1793	2358	22 Nov 1788	81	489	Waters of Cumberland on Spring Creek	
McAmish, James	1030		Green	1000	1257	29 Jul 1793	2422	25 May 1784	76	499	On the head of Fall Creek &c	
McAndrews, Andrew	440		Sumner	800	442	20 Sep 1787	501	22 oct 1783	65	142	On N side of Cumberland River	yes
McAustine, John	221	Baker, John	Tennessee	640	1126	26 Nov 1789	3402	2 Jun 1788	74	434	S side of Cumberland	
McBee, James, Jr.	618	Knight, Miles	Washington	1000	3180	14 Sep 1797	238		90	95	On or near the head of Flat Branch	
McBee, John Griffith	661		Washington	400	475	10 Nov 1784	811 /9117/	31 Dec 1778	69	269	On waters of Stewarts Creek	yes
McBee, William	1767		Davidson	4800	1550	14 Jan 1793	554		79	158	On N side of Holston River	
McBee, William; Ass	317		Eastern District	40	199	24 Feb 1795			88	1344	On Nobb Creek	
McBride, James	772		Washington	358	586	10 Nov 1784	758	27 Jul 1783	69	158	S side of Holston River	yes
McBride, James	909	Robertson, Elijah	Hawkins	6 & 15 p	198	24 Feb 1796		Martin Armstrong	88		On the waters of Caney Fork	yes
McBride, James	029	Robertson, Elijah	Davidson	640	812	20 Nov 1788	3281	22 Mar 1788	63	285	On waters of Caney Fork	yes
	809		Davidson	640			3281					

Earliest Tennessee Land Records

Claimant:	File #:	Assignee:	County:	Acres:	Grant:	Grant Date:	Entry:	Entry Date:	BK:	Pg:	Location by Stream Name:	Military:
McBride, William	313		Washington	500	180	24 Oct 1782	376	9 Sep 1778	49	217	On Mill Creek	
McBroom, John	391		Sullivan	282	270	10 Nov 1784	1881	6 Oct 1779	69	168	On N side of Holstein River	
McBroom, John	67		Hawkins	100	52	18 May 1789	662	26 Jul 1780	72	256	In Carter's Valley	
McBroom, Thomas	1013		Hawkins	150	335	29 Dec 1796		Martin Armstrong	90	194	Waters of Richland Creek	
McBroom, Thomas	428		Hawkins	350	317	5 Jun 1793	391	3 Jun 1781	80	159	N side of Holston River	
McBroom, Thomas	787		Hawkins	500	627	12 Jul 1794	485	15 Feb 1781	82	222	On both sides of Big War Creek	
McBroom, Thomas, Jr.	496		Sullivan	233	507	18 May 1789	1757	30 Sep 1779	71	14	In Carter's Valley	
McBroom, William	124		Hawkins	500	158	26 Dec 1791	336	23 Oct 1783	75	167	On S side of Holston River	
McBroom, William	334		Green	400	336	20 Sep 1787	951	29 Oct 1783	65	468	On the N side of Holston River &c	
McBroom, William	380		Green	100	382	20 Sep 1787	68	22 Oct 1783	65	481	On the Burnt Cabbin Spring	
McBroom, William	414		Green	100	416	20 Sep 1787	1222	5 Nov 1783	65	493	Near the Blue Spring	
McBroom, William	857		Hawkins	200	673	18 Apr 1795			83	463	On the waters of Roseberry Creek &c	
McBrooms, W.	081		Green	200			1430	28 Apr 1792			On the waters of Rosemery Creek	
McCabe, Peter	1642	Donelson, John	Davidson	640	1520	10 Apr 1792	2574		75	508	On S side of Cumberland River	yes
McCafferty, James, Ass	679	Conway, Joseph	Tennessee	640	3402	17 May 1803	1450	22 Jul 1785	110	319	On Sinking or Little W Fork of Red River	
McCain, James	095	Shute, William	Sumner	640			510	22 Oct 1785			On E branch of Drakes Creek	yes
McCain, Joseph	216		Middle District	600	202	14 Jan 1793	1651	7 Sep 1779	79	287	On a creek known as Cold Water	
McCaleb, Archibald	249		Eastern District	300	202	6 Jan 1795	397	8 Apr 1780	83	172	N/S Holston River on E fork of Turkey Creek	
McCall, Alex	053	Perkins, Isaac	Middle District	274			3203	19 Dec 1785				
McCall, Alex, Ass	935		Sumner	274	2459	22 Feb 1795			83	421	On the main fork of Obeys River &c	yes
McCall, Alex, Ass	946		Sumner	640	2470	22 Feb 1795			83	427	On the main fork of Obeys River &c	yes
McCall, Alex.	048	Gray, George	Middle District	228			1571 (1574)					
McCall, Alex.	050	Gray, Silvanus	Middle District	640			1109					
McCall, Alex.	054	Ready, Hezekiah heirs	Middle District	640			2950	30 Sep 1785				
McCall, Alex.	055	Hopkins, Isaac	Middle District	274			1577					
McCall, Alex.	056	Charlescraft, Jas.	Middle District	228			1576					
McCall, Alex. Ass.	954	Moore, James Lt. Assn.	Sumner	2560	2417	22 Feb 1795			84	305	On Main Fork of Obeys River	yes
McCall, Alex. Ass;	049		Middle District	2560			545					
McCall, Alexander	717		Sumner	640	2099	20 May 1793	1009	21 Nov 1792	81	149	On waters of Rocky Creek	yes
McCall, Alexander, Ass	932		Sumner	228	2456	22 Feb 1795			83	420	On the Main Fork of Obeys River &c	yes
McCall, Alexander, Ass	933		Sumner	228	2457	22 Feb 1795			83	420	On the Main Fork of Obeys River	yes
McCall, Alexander, Ass	970		Sumner	228	2434	22 Feb 1795			84	313	On Main Fork of Obeys River	yes
McCall, Alexander, Ass	978		Sumner	274	2442	22 Feb 1795			84	317	On Main Fork of Obeys River	yes
McCall, Peter	0118		Sullivan	300			1743	28 Sep 1779			Beg at a poplar on side of a large ridge	
McCall, Peter	379		Sullivan	300	258	10 Nov 1784	547,-1822	6 Oct 1779	69	164	Beg at a white oak & ash	
McCall, Robert	1665		Green	124	287	6 Jun 1796			88	381	Joining lands entered by Jos. Lusk	
McCalleb, Archibald	458		Green	150	460	20 Sep 1787	2860	23 May 1781	65	504	On the N side of French Broad River &c	
McCallister, John	1019a		Washington	400	969	14 Jan 1793	640	25 Nov 1778	79	276	On Big Limestone	
McCallister, John	347	King, Robert	Eastern District	274	2690	6 Jun 1796	3955		88	366	On Walling Ridge	yes
McCallu, Isaac	04		Middle District	400							Waters of Main West Fork of Stones River	
McCallum, Isaac, Ass	950		Sumner	400	154	26 Mar 1795			83	451	W of the Cumberland Mountain	yes
McCallum, Isaac, Ass.	949		Sumner	400	153	26 Mar 1795			83	450	W of the Cumberland Mountain	yes
McCamel, Andrew	473		Hawkins	350	345	29 Jul 1793	490	26 Apr 1780	80	262	On the waters of Whites Creek	yes
McCamon, Isaac, Ass.	1437		Sumner	357	3352	12 Dec 1797	5009	27 Nov 1797	98	185	On both sides of Sinking Creek	yes
McCane, James	1135		Davidson	640	112	17 Apr 1786	99	10 Jan 1784	66	177	On Station Camp Creek &c	

Claimant:	File #:	Assignee:	County:	Acres:	Grant:	Grant Date:	Entry:	Entry Date:	Bk:	Pg:	Location by Stream Name:	Military:
McCaney, Samuel	942		Green	375	856	17 Nov 1790	642	28 Oct 1783	76	123	On the watery fork of Caney Branch	
McCann, Hugh	1771	Newman, Anthony	Davidson	640	1555	14 Jan 1793	920		79	270	On waters of W Harpeth	yes
McCann, James	2459		Davidson	400	205	15 Mar 1800			105	444	West of the Cumberland Mountains	
McCann, Michael	614	Bledsoe, Isaac	Sumner	640	1873	20 May 1793	1719	27 Jul 1786	81	94	On N side of Cumberland River &c	yes
McCann, Nathaniel	555		Davidson	2560	527	15 Sep 1787	191		63	190	South side of Cumberland	yes
McCarmack, Martin,	1022		Sumner	320	229	27 Feb 1796	1982	25 Feb 1796	88	175	On N side of Cumberland River	
McCarmey, Samuel	1531		Green	150	1291	17 Jul 1794	1487	7 May 1793	81	606	Beg at a pine	
McCarmick, Robert	19		Middle District	2000	21	10 Jul 1788	2267	24 May 1784	67	416	On the S side of Duck River	
McCarming, James	137		Sullivan	300	150	23 Oct 1782	166	19 Feb 1780	43	331	On Muddy Creek &c	
McCarrel, John	256		Washington	400	124	23 Oct 1782			47	61	On Sinking Creek	
McCarty, Benjamin	492		Hawkins	100	364	29 Jul 1793	411	28 Jul 1780	80	267	On the N side of Holston River &c	
McCarty, Flourane	175	Gamble, Edmund	Tennessee	822	1452	20 Dec 1791	1172	26 Aug 1784	77	364	On the S side of Red River	yes
McCarty, Jacob	1502	Marshall, Geo.	Davidson	228	1059	26 Nov 1789	870		74	107	On Sulphur Fork	yes
McCarty, Jacob	489	Elliott, John	Tennessee	480	158	26 Mar 1795			89	89	W of Cumberland Mountain	
McCarty, James	2		Hawkins	300	1	10 Jul 1788	359	7 Jun 1784	64	328	On the S side of Holston	
McCarty, James	577		Hawkins	250	451	29 Jul 1793	516	23 Oct 1783	80	290	On the N side of Holston River	
McCarty, James	786		Hawkins	100	626	12 Jul 1794	994	Jun 1784	82	222	On the N side of Holston River &c	
McCarty, William	548		Hawkins	400	421	29 Jul 1793	370	1 Jan 1784	80	283	Valley on the N side of the Clinch Mountain	
McCarty, Wm.	150		Eastern District	400	120	24 Dec 1792	57	8 Feb 1780	78	453	In the Valley N side of Clinch River	
McCarver, Archibald	520		Hawkins	50 (55)	393	29 Jul 1793	242	28 Jun 1780	80	275	S side of Holston River	
McCaulley, John	1301	Hickman, Thomas	Sumner	640	3069	19 Jul 1797	4648	6 Apr 1797	90	378	S side of Cumberland River	
McCaulley, John	923		Sumner	320	180	9 Jun 1794			81	448	On S side of Jinnings Rreek	
McCawley, Matthew	19		Davidson	1761 (76	5	16 Feb 1786	104		63	3	Both sides small or two miles above Brush	yes
McCawley, Matthew	18	Jacobs, Benjamin	Davidson	640	4	16 Feb 1786	290		63	3	On both sides of a small creek	yes
McCay, John	1673	Greer, Jos & Jas Robertson	Davidson	640	1592	23 Feb 1793	2016		76	310	S side of Harpeth River	yes
Mocay, Spruce	88		Western District	1000	88	10 Jul 1788	2645	25 May 1785	67	315	Waters of the N Fork of Forked Deer River	
McClain, Jeremiah	528	Hamilton, Thomas	Davidson	640	500	15 Sep 1787	1937	15 May 1780	63	181	N side of Cumberland River	yes
McClaland, Andrew	686		Sullivan	400	634	9 Jul 1794	562	10 Mar 1788	81	632	On S side of the N Fork	
McClammey, Joseph	37		Sumner	2560	865	17 Jan 1789	1969	22 Oct 1783	63	301	On Caney Fork River	yes
McClanahan, Alexander	909		Green	475	896	31 Oct 1791	158	4 Dec 1779	75	123	On N side of French Broad River	
McCleary, Abraham	1178		Green	200	1021	26 Dec 1791	2331	5 Jul 1799	77	289	On the N side of French Broad River	
McCleary, Abraham	932		Green	100	846	17 Nov 1790	1461	3 May 1779	76	120	N side of French Broad River	
McCleary, Patrick	349		Green	100	351	27 Sep 1787	840		65	473	On Sinking Creek &c	
McCleary, Samuel	222		Middle District	500	202	27 Nov 1792			80	208	On the S side of Duck River	
McCleland, James	266	Nelson, Robert	Davidson	429	252	7 Mar 1786	258		63	92	E side of the Big Harpeth River	yes
McClellen, William	1		Knox	15	141	7 Jan 1794		7 Jan 1779	81	397	It being the first Island in Holston	
McClenan, Abraham	52		Sullivan	505 (504	63	23 Oct 1782	1046		43	268	On Beaver and White Top Creeks	
McCloud, Chas	276		Hawkins	200	287	14 Jan 1793			78	340	On S side of Holston River	
McCloud, Daniel	898	Ray, William	Sumner	640	2452	31 Dec 1793	2143	28 Nov 1792	81	427	On W side of Caney	yes
McClung, Charles	1149		Hawkins	200	871	3 May 1803	643	15 Apr 1780	110	324	On E Fork of Poplar Creek	
McClung, Charles	137		Eastern District	1000	103	6 Sep 1791	1911	24 Apr 1784	77	222 (7)	In the fork bet. Holston & Clinch River	
McClung, Charles	16		Knox, fr Hawkins	200	871	3 May 1803		15 Apr 1780	110	324	On E Fork of Poplar Creek	
McClung, Charles	184		Eastern District	200	161	27 Jun 1793	2596	25 May 1784	80	368	S side of Clinch River on Conners Creek	
McClung, Charles	582		Hawkins	150	456	29 Jul 1793	943	29 Oct 1783	80	291	On the N side of Holston River &c	
McClung, Chas.	154		Eastern District	400	124	24 Dec 1792	1290	24 Dec 1783	78	455	On N side of Holston River	

Claimant:	File #:	Assignee:	County:	Acres:	Grant:	Grant Date:	Entry:	Entry Date:	Bk:	Pg:	Location by Stream Name:	Military:
McClung, Hugh	120		Green	800	136	1 Nov 1786	816	29 Oct 1783	59	439	N side of Tennessee River	
McClung, Hugh	967		Hawkins	250	739	20 Jul 1796	53		88	495	On the Valley Fork	
McClung, Chas & Jas Lackey	1126		Green	1000	969	26 Dec 1791			77	271	On Little River	
McClurd, Thomas	384	Judge, Thomas	Tennessee	228	2378	20 May 1793	1227	2 Oct 1784	81	208	On S side of Cumberland	
McClure, Hardyman	659	McNary, John	Tennessee	640	3252	6 Dec 1797	4695		97	33	On the head of Piney Fork &c	yes
McClure, Matthew	471		Middle District	1000	263	6 Dec 1794	2067	4 May 1784	85	334	On N side of Elk River	
McClure, Matthew	472		Middle District	2000	264	6 Dec 1794	2066	4 May 1784	85	334	On N side of Elk River	
McClure, Michael	797	Robertson, Elijah	Davidson	640	800	20 Nov 1788	3316		63	281	On S side of Cumberland River	yes
McClure, Nathan	1324		Davidson	320	10	18 Aug 1787	376	30 Mar 1784	68	124	On Whites Creek	
McClure, Nathan	1896		Davidson	320	121	27 Apr 1793	377	30 Mar 1784	81	34	On Big Harpeth River	
McClure, Thomas	986		Washington	65	1063	29 Jul 1793	2748	24 Jan 1781	76	477	Joining William Rickey's &c	
McClure, William	457		Davidson	4840	429	15 Sep 1787	743		63	158	North side of Cumberland River	yes
McCobb, Bryan	248		Eastern District	100	1330	10 Dec 1794			83	154	E/Fk Obeys a S branch of Cumberland River	
McCofferty, James	2472	Prescott, Austin	Davidson	640	3406	22 Dec 1803	3123		118	139	Beginning at James Gatlins west boundary	yes
McColl, Archibald	760	Bledsoe, Isaac	Sumner	640	2173	20 May 1793	1010	31 Jul 1792	81	166	On N side of Cumberland River	yes
McCollister, James	05	Barton, Samuel	Sumner	640			1158				On E side of Bartons Creek	yes
McComb, Jesse	213		Middle District	1794	199	14 Jan 1793			79	286	On 2nd large creek that runs into Elk River	
McConial, Patrick	642	Perry, Sion	Sumner	497	1932	20 May 1793	3363	17 Nov 1792	81	108	On waters of Middle Fork &c	yes
McConnel, Jacob	610		Green	200	567	20 Sep 1787	231	22 Oct 1783	66	251	On Clear Creek &c	
McConnel, Robert	2413	Burden, Thomas	Davidson	640	3206	14 Sep 1797	4577		92	6	W/S South Harpeth Beg at a White oak	yes
McConnel, Robert,	2414	Collet, John heirs	Davidson	640	3207	14 Sep 1797	4691		91	7	On South Harpeth River	yes
McConnel, Robert, Ass	1312		Sumner	357	3112	14 Sep 1797	4302	6 May 1797	90	408	Waters of Big Barron	yes
McConnel, Robert, Ass	1314		Sumner	1000	3114	14 Sep 1797	4688	15 May 1797	90	409	Including forks of Puncheon Camp Creek	yes
McConnel, Robert, Ass	1315		Sumner	640	4115	14 Sep 1797	4589	6 May 1797	90	409	Including forks of Puncheaon Camp Creek	yes
McConnel, Robert, Ass	1319		Sumner	640	3119	14 Sep 1797	4592	6 May 1797	90	411	On Puncheaon Camp Creek	yes
McConnel, Robert, Ass	1320		Sumner	1000	3120	14 Sep 1797	4476	15 May 1797	90	411	Joining an entry of his own &c	yes
McConnel, Robert, Ass	1321		Sumner	228	3121	14 Sep 1797	4726	3 Jun 1797	90	412	On the waters of Big Barren	yes
McConnel, Robert, Ass	1322		Sumner	1000	3122	10 Sep 1797	4705	15 May 1797	90	412	On waters of Big Barren	yes
McConnel, Robert, Ass	1323	Sherkley, Thomas	Sumner	1000	3123	14 Sep 1797	4702	15 May 1797	90	413	Waters of Big Barron	yes
McConnel, Robert, Ass	1324		Sumner	640	3124	14 Sep 1797	4595	6 May 1797	90	413	Joining his entry	yes
McConnel, Robert, Ass	1325		Sumner	640	3125	14 Sep 1797	3951	6 May 1797	90	413	Waters of Big Barren	yes
McConnel, Robert, Ass	1326		Sumner	1000	3126	14 Sep 1797	4450	15 May 1797	90	414	On the waters of Big Barren	yes
McConnel, Robert, Ass	1327		Sumner	274	3127	14 Sep 1797	4658	6 May 1797	90	414	Waters of Big Barren	yes
McConnell, Robert;	2411	Potter, Francis	Davidson	228	3204	14 Sep 1797	4104		92	6	Waters of E Fork of S Harpeth	yes
McConnell, Peter;	2408	Broomfield, Peter	Davidson	228	3201	14 Sep 1797	4080		92	4	East of South Harpeth	yes
McConnell, Robert	?	Bagley, John heirs	Davidson	640	3202	14 Sep 1797	4689		92	5	West side of South Harpeth	yes
McConnell, Robert	033	Howell, Tallefarro	Tennessee	1000			4449	22 Dec 1796		6	S side of Cumberland River	Yes
McConnell, Robert	2410	Howell, Talliferro heirs	Davidson (Tenn)	1000	3203	14 Sep 1797	4689	none	92	5	S side of Cumberland River	yes
McConnell, Robert	2412	Crossey, Anthony	Davidson	640	3205	14 Sep 1797	4586		92	6	W/S South Fork above the Hurricane	yes
McConnell, Robert	2415	Howel, Ebenezer	Davidson	640	3208	14 Sep 1797			92	7	Waters of E Fork of South Harpeth	yes
McConnell, Robt.	049	Hewet, Ebenezer	Davidson	640			3770	11 Aug 1797			Waters E Fork of S Harpeth	
McConnell, Robert	2409	Bagley, John heirs	Davidson	640	3202	14 Sep 1797	4689	none	92	5	West side of South Harpeth	yes
McConnough, Samuel	636	Willoughby, Matthew	Sumner	640	1925	20 May 1793	2141	11 Feb 1786	81	106	On E/S Main Middle Fork of Bledsoe Creek	yes
McConough, Dougald	308	Riston, Abr. & Elisha Rice	Davidson	640	294	13 Jun 1787	2142		63	110	Beg at an ash & elm	yes
McCool, Gabriel	1368		Green	200	1223	27 Jan 1793	305	8 Aug 1778	79	504	On head of McCartneys Creek	

Claimant:	File #:	Assignee:	County:	Acres:	Grant:	Grant Date:	Entry:	Entry Date:	Bk:	Pg:	Location by Stream Name:	Military:
McCord, David	112		Washington	200	280	24 Oct 1782	235	17 Oct 1778	44	288	On E side of Big Limestone Creek	
McCord, David	252		Washington	250	120	23 Oct 1782	235	19 Jun 1778	47	59	On Big Limestone Creek	
McCord, David	411		Washington	100	403	13 Oct 1783	2088	11 Oct 1780	52	267	On a branch of Big Limestone	
McCord, James	17		Washington	200	307	24 Oct 1782	1475	16 Jul 1779	43	300	On the waters of Great Limestone &c	
McCord, James	372		Washington	100	364	13 Oct 1783	2091	11 Oct 1780	52	248	On the N side of his former survey	
McCord, James	388		Washington	150	380	10 Oct 1783	1247	15 Jun 1780	52	255	On the N side of the S fork &c	
McCord, James	395		Washington	500	387	13 Oct 1783	1248	27 Feb 1779	56	259	On the fork of Big Limestone Creek	
McCord, James	469		Washington	100	461	13 Oct 1783	2092	30 Oct 1779	52	294	On the E side of his former survey	
McCorkell, Samuel & Joseph	1106		Washington	420	1056	27 Dec 1792	1293	21 Mar 1779	80	207	On the S side of Holston River	
McCorkle, Samuel	638		Sullivan	400	586	27 Jun 1793	1023	5 Jun 1779	80	377	On the S side of Holston River	
McCormack, William	362		Sullivan	100	241	10 Nov 1784	931	1 Jan 1779	69	159	On S side of Holstein River	
McCormack, William	526		Sullivan	100	542	26 Nov 1789	1329	7 Apr 1779	73	51	On the S side of Holeson /sic/ River	
McCormack,Wm &H Rowan	1123	Parker, Charles	Hawkins	365	842	2 Nov 1797	4754		96	3	Both sides of Lawhaus Creek	yes
McCormack,Wm &H Rowan	1141		Hawkins	400	859	24 Dec 1798			97	306	On waters of Sycamore Creek	
McCormickis, John	2265	Tyrrell, Wm.	Davidson	640	2471	20 Jul 1796	3967		88	453	On N side of Cumberland River	yes
McCoskey, John	689		Greene	100	730	11 Jul 1788	25	30 Dec 1783	66	469	On the N side of Nolichuckey &c	
McCowen, James	079		Middle District	400	205	15 Mar 1800					West of the Cumberland Mountains	
McCoy, Alexander	1304	Hickman, Thomas	Sumner	640	3075	19 Jul 1797	4647	6 Apr 1797	90	380	Waters of Main E Fork of Big Barron	yes
McCoy, Anan,Wm Murphy	360		Eastern District	640	277	20 Jul 1796	14	8 Feb 1780	88	436	In Hindes's valley	
McCoy, Ananias	139		Eastern District	262	105	6 Sep 1791	1308	4 Jan 1784	77	223	On the W Fork of Third Creek	
McCoy, Ananias	481	Robinson, Henry	Tennessee	400	189	20 Jul 1796			88	471	W side of Cumberland Mountain	
McCoy, Ananias	482	Darrow, Benjamin	Tennessee	480	190	20 Jul 1796	11	14 Apr 1792	88	472	W of Cumberland Mountain	
McCoy, Ananias	483	Hendrix, John	Tennessee	400	192	20 Jul 1796		14 Apr 1792	88	473	W of Cumberland Mountain	
McCoy, Ananias	484	Bolic, John	Tennessee	480	193	20 Jul 1796	12	14 Apr 1792	88	473	W of Cumberland Mountain	
McCoy, Ananias	485	Robinson, Henry	Tennessee	400	194	20 Jul 1796	15	14 Apr 1792	88	474	W of the Cumberland Mountain	
McCoy, Ananias	486	Darrow, Benjamin	Tennessee	480	195	20 Jul 1796	10	14 Apr 1792	88	474	W of Cumberland Mountain	
McCoy, Annanias	778		Green	200	583	23 Aug 1788	1217	5 Nov 1783	68	255	On the N side of Clinch River	
McCoy, Annanias	097		Washington	300			901	31 Dec 1778				
McCoy, Annanias	102		Green	500	60	1 Nov 1786	519	27 Oct 1783	59	421	N side of Tennessee River	
McCoy, Annanias	122		Eastern District	640	155	29 Jul 1793			76	481	NW/S Clinch on the Valley Fork of Big Creek	
McCoy, Annanias	176		Eastern District	200	149	29 Jul 1793			76	480	N side of Tennessee River &c	
McCoy, Annanias	213		Eastern District	1000	199	12 Jul 1794			81	597	On N side of Tennessee River	
McCoy, Annanias	469		Hawkins	1200	341	29 Jul 1793	1725		80	260	N side of Tennessee &c	
McCoy, Annanias	521		Middle District	480	188	20 Jul 1796			88	471	W of Cumberland Mountain	
McCoy, Annanias	522		Middle District	400	191	20 Jul 1796			88	472	On waters of Main W Fork of Stones River	
McCoy, Annanias	529		Hawkins	640	402	29 Jul 1793			80	277	N side of Clinch River &c	
McCoy, Annanias	598		Hawkins	600	472	29 Jul 1793	192	21 Feb 1783	80	294	On the N side of Tennessee River	
McCoy, Annanias	766		Green	400	571	23 Aug 1788	130	16 May 1785	68	249	Lying on the S side of Clinch River	
McCoy, Annanias	781		Green	640	586	23 Aug 1788			68	256	On the N side of Tenn. River &c	
McCoy, Annanias	795		Green	640	600	23 Aug 1788	83	26 Feb 1778	68	262	On the N side of ClinchRiver &c	
McCoy, Annanias	821		Green	300	822	11 Aug 1789			71	37	On the N side of Clinch River	
McCoy, Armanidas	23		Green	500	86	1 Nov 1786	1455	2 Feb 1784	58	447	On the N side of Tennessee	
McCoy, Daniel	077		Green	93							On the waters of Middle Creek	
McCoy, Daniel	2109	Wilson, David	Davidson	549	2357	20 May 1793	26		81	203	On E fork of Harpeth River	yes
McCoy, Daniel	860	Winchester, David	Sumner	640	2367	20 May 1793	3652	23 May 1792	81	205	Beg at 3 Sycamores	yes

Earliest Tennessee Land Records

Claimant:	File #:	Assignee:	County:	Acres:	Grant:	Grant Date:	Entry:	Entry Date:	Bk:	Pg:	Location by Stream Name:	Military:
McCoy, Dugald	1044	Easton, James	Sumner	640	2706	27 Mar 1796	1716	11 May 1795	88	258	Joining said Eastons survey	yes
McCoy, Dugald, heirs of	194		Tennessee	640	1478	4 Jan 1792	1367	9 Nov 1784	77	371	S side of Cumberland River	
McCoy, Eli	463	Kincannon, Mathew	Davidson	640	435	15 Sep 1787			63	160	On waters of Second Creek	yes
McCoy, James	2226	Donelson, S. & Wm. Terrel	Davidson	640	2550	7 Mar 1796			88	305	On the waters of Stones River	yes
McCoy, James	629	Robertson, James	Tennessee	640	3193	14 Sep 1797	3957		90	440	On Bartons Creek	yes
McCoy, John	198	Hill, Green	Davidson	640	184 7/l	7 Mar 1786	1070		63	69	N side of Tenessee River	yes
McCoy, John	2169	Williams, Willoughby	Davidson	640	2490	1 Apr 1794	1777		81	451	On waters of Stones River	yes
McCoy, Morris	373	Hays, Robert	Sumner	640	1546	14 Jan 1793		9 Mar 1780	79	268	On waters of Mauscaws Creek /sic/	yes
McCoy, Patrick	536	King, Robert M.	Middle District	640	2960	2 Mar 1797	3939		90	255	On Camp Creek	yes
McCoy, Roger	048	Cobb, Jos, Duke, & McDani	Hawkins	640			3841					yes
McCoy, Spruce	32		Eastern District	5000	32	11 Jul 1788	1426	19 Feb 1784	67	352	On Beaverdam Creek &c	
McCoy, Spruce, Ass	834		Sumner	640	2320	20 May 1793	3133	27 Nov 1792	81	195	On N side of Cumberland River	yes
McCra, Robert	216		Tennessee	25	111	20 Dec 1791		15 Nov 1790	77	380	On the Sulphur Fork of Red River	
McCraw, Samuel	687	Bryner, William heir of	Davidson	640	660	8 Dec 1787	2789		63	233	On head drafts of Sycamore	yes
McCraw, William	794		Hawkins	640	634	12 Jul 1794	1618	14 Sep 1779	82	225	On the S side of Clinch River &c	
McCray, Daniel	557		Washington	200	822	11 Jul 1788	290	3 Aug 1778	64	335	Beg. below Aaron Pensons Creek	
McCray, Wm. & David White	294		Middle District	800	254	7 Jul 1794	1215	5 Nov 1783	82	201	SW side of Clear Fork of Cumberland River	
McCrory, James	2019	Davidson, Thomas	Davidson	640	1990	20 May 1793	3570		81	122	On Harpeth waters	yes
McCrory, James	2096	Hester, John	Davidson	640	2315	20 May 1793	1965		81	194	On N side of Cumberland	yes
McCrory, Thomas	2005	Moore, James	Davidson	230	1949	20 May 1793			81	112	Beg at a dogwood	yes
McCrory, Thomas	418	Bardiner, James heirs of	Davidson	640	390	15 Sep 1787	1982		63	145	Where Big S road leaves Big Harper water	yes
McCrory, Thomas	733	Bennet, William	Davidson	640	706	11 Jul 1788	2111		63	248	On South waters of Big Harpeth	yes
McCrory, Thomas	760	Beabey, Abraham heirs	Davidson	640	733	11 Jul 1783	1984		63	258	On West side of Stones River	yes
McCroskey, Jno	693		Greene	200	734	11 Jul 1788	2340	16 Dec 1779	66	471	E/S Browns line on W/S side of Holleys Cr	
McCroskey, John	1010		Greene	100	1237	29 Jul 1793	43	7 May 1784	76	486	On Hollies Creek	
McQuestion, James	1503		Davidson	640	1060	26 Nov 1789	948		74	108	On South side of Cumberland River	yes
McCuisten, James	267	Pyatt, Peter	Davidson	428	253	7 Mar 1786	318		63	92	E Fork of Mill Creek	yes
McCullah, Joseph	254		Green	500	211	20 Sep 1787			65	434	On S/S of Holston River	
McCullah, Joseph	446		Green	148	448	20 Sep 1787	1238	7 Jul 1783	65	501	On the S side of Holston River	
McCullers, Joseph	030		Hawkins	92			787	Jun 1785			S side of the Holston River	
McCulloch, Alexander	41		Western District	3000	41	10 Jul 1788	2568	25 May 1784	67	296	On Looshatcher River &c	
McCulloch, Alexander	42		Western District	2000	42	10 Jul 1788	2569	25 May 1784	67	296	On both sides of Looshatcher River &c	
McCulloch, Benj.	034	Dunn, Thomas heirs	Tennessee	640			2008	16 Aug 1785			On Red River	
McCulloch, Benj.	035	Losson, John	Tennessee	640			2992	30 Sep 1785			S side Cumberland River	
McCulloh, Benj.	050	Jones, Absalom	Davidson	640			2461	9 Mar 1786			N side of Cumberland River	
McCulloch, Benjamin, Ass	829		Sumner	640	2309	20 May 1793	2011	26 Nov 1792	81	193	On ridge bet Bartons Creek & Stones River	yes
McCulloch, Joseph	1497	McCulloch, Robert hr Jos	Davidson	640	1054	26 Nov 1789	1722		74	104	On S Fork of McAdows Creek	yes
McCullock, Alex	2271	Casey, John	Davidson	640	2749	20 Jul 1796	556		88	457	On a large creek of the Tenn River	yes
McCullock, Benjamin	31	Jitts, Peter heirs	Tennessee	640			2012	16 Aug 1785			On the waters of Red River on the S side	
McCulloh, Benj.	1729	Wright, Peter	Davidson	640	1444	26 Dec 1791	2257		77	362	Knob Creek the waters of Duck River	yes
McCulloh, Benj.	299	Russell, Peter	Tennessee	640	1973	20 May 1793			81	117	On the waters of Red River	
McCulloh, Benj.	314	Baker, Peter	Tennessee	640	2015	20 May 1793			81	128	On S side of Cumberland River	
McCulloh, Benj.	317	Hill, Roberson	Tennessee	640	2018	20 May 1793	2658	30 Sep 1785	81	129	On N side of Cumberland River	
McCulloh, Benj.	323	Steell, Hardy	Tennessee	640	2060	20 May 1793	2074	1 Sep 1785	81	139	N side of Cumberland River	
McCulloh, Benj.	368	Tucker, Wiley	Tennessee	640	225	20 May 1793	2244	12 Sep 1785	81	181	On N side of Cumberland River	

Claimant:	File #:	Assignee:	County:	Acres:	Grant:	Grant Date:	Entry:	Entry Date:	Bk:	Pg:	Location by Stream Name:	Military:
McCulloh, Benj. Ass	2092	Yarbrough, David heirs	Davidson	640	2302	20 May 1793	2263		81	191	On S side of Cumberland River	yes
McCulloh, Benjamin	051	Seymore, Edward	Davidson	640			2014	26 Nov 1793			On waters of Stones River	
McCulloh, Benjamin	1715	Taylor, Jopaton	Davidson	640	1383	21 Dec 1791	2194		77	346	Dividing ridge bet. Duck & Harpeth Rivers	yes
McCulloh, Benjamin	1716	Curlee, Thomas	Davidson	640	1384	20 Dec 1791	1975		77	347	On Knob Creek of Duck River	yes
McCulloh, Benjamin	1717	Barker, Nicholas	Davidson	640	1385	20 Dec 1791	2498		77	347	On Knob Creek of Duck River	yes
McCulloh, Benjamin	1718	Jitts, Jeremiah	Davidson	640	1386	20 Dec 1791	2015		77	347	On Knob Creek of Duck River	yes
McCulloh, Benjamin	1719	Baker, Peter	Davidson	640	1387	20 Dec 1791	2499		77	348	On Knob Creek of Duck River	yes
McCulloh, Benjamin	1720	Welborn, John	Davidson	640	1388	20 Dec 1791	2077		77	348	Dividing ridge bet. Duck River & Harpeth	yes
McCulloh, Benjamin	1722	Huck, Thomas	Davidson	640	1418	20 Dec 1791	1999		77	356	On the dividing ridge	yes
McCulloh, Benjamin	1727	Bracken, Matthias	Davidson	640	1442	20 Dec 1791	2500		77	361	On Knob Creek of Duck River	yes
McCulloh, Benjamin	1730	Davis, James	Davidson	640	1445	20 Dec 1791	2080		77	362	Dividing ridge bet Duck River & Harpeth	yes
McCulloh, Benjamin	1731	Hocks, John	Davidson	640	1446	20 Dec 1791	2000		77	362	Dividing ridge bet Duck River and Harpeth	yes
McCulloh, Benjamin	2015	Ducanna, James	Davidson	640	1970	20 May 1793	2510		81	117	On Snow Creek the waters of Duck River	yes
McCulloh, Benjamin	2016	Holmes, Andrew	Davidson	640	1978	20 May 1793	2456		81	119	On waters of Stones River	yes
McCulloh, Benjamin	2023	Parker, Arthur	Davidson	1000	2024	20 May 1793	2261		81	130	On Lepers Lick Creek waters of Duck River	yes
McCulloh, Benjamin	2024(a)	Thomas, Jeremiah	Davidson	640	2030	20 May 1793	2693		81	132	On N side of Cumberland River	yes
McCulloh, Benjamin	2025	Barber, James	Davidson	640	2031	20 May 1793	3322		81	132	On the waters of Duck River	yes
McCulloh, Benjamin	2026	Echols, Abner	Davidson	640	2032	20 May 1793	3222		81	132	On N side of Cumberland River	yes
McCulloh, Benjamin	2027	Richardson, James	Davidson	640	2035	20 May 1793	2816		81	133	On Snow Creek	yes
McCulloh, Benjamin	2028	Nobles, Robert	Davidson	274	2036	20 May 1793	3014		81	133	On N side of Cumberland River	yes
McCulloh, Benjamin	2029	Brass(Bass), Moses	Davidson	640	2039	20 May 1793	3221		81	134	On N side of Cumberland River	yes
McCulloh, Benjamin	2030	Hawley, Caleb	Davidson	640	2040	20 May 1793	3078		81	134	On N side of Cumberland River	yes
McCulloh, Benjamin	2081	Flood, Elisha	Davidson	640	2266	20 May 1793	2013		81	184	On waters of Stones River	yes
McCulloh, Benjamin	2083	Bowman, Jesse	Davidson	640	2281	20 May 1793	2834		81	187	On waters of Leepers Lick Creek	yes
McCulloh, Benjamin	2086	Lanier, Edward	Davidson	640	2288	20 May 1793			81	188	On the waters of Stones River	yes
McCulloh, Benjamin	2091	Thomas, Thomas	Davidson	640	2299	20 May 1793	2819		81	191	On Leepers Creek	yes
McCulloh, Benjamin	2116	Pool, John	Davidson	640	2376	20 May 1793	2006		81	207	On waters of Stones River	yes
McCulloh, Benjamin	2195(a)	Tucker, Willey	Davidson	640	2483	18 Aug 1795			87	507	On N side of Cumberland River	yes
McCulloh, Benjamin	295	Hart, Hardy	Tennessee	640	1968	20 May 1793	2655	30 Sep 1785	81	116	N side of Cumberland River &c	
McCulloh, Benjamin	296	Parker, Elias	Tennessee	640	1969	20 May 1793	2079	1 Sep 1785	81	116	On S side of Cumberland River	
McCulloh, Benjamin	298	Jordan, Thos.	Tennessee	640	1972	20 May 1793	2081	1 Sep 1785	81	117	On S side of Cumberland River	
McCulloh, Benjamin	300	Taylor, Benjamin	Tennessee	640	1976	20 May 1793	2243	12 Sep 1785	81	118	On waters of Blooming Grove Creek	
McCulloh, Benjamin	307	Toomer, Joseph	Tennessee	640	2008	20 May 1793	2244	12 Sep 1785	81	126	S side of Cumberland River	
McCulloh, Benjamin	308	Bently, Isaac	Tennessee	640	2009	20 May 1793	2078	1 Sep 1785	81	126	On N side of Cumberland River	
McCulloh, Benjamin	309	Thompson, Joshua	Tennessee	640	2010	20 May 1793	2240	12 Sep 1785	81	127	Head of sm drane emptying into Winters Cr	
McCulloh, Benjamin	310		Tennessee	640	2011	20 May 1793	2983	30 Sep 1785	81	127	On S side of Red River	
McCulloh, Benjamin	311	Flory, Frances	Tennessee	640	2012	20 May 1793	2010	16 Aug 1785	81	127	On S side of Cumberland River	
McCulloh, Benjamin	312	Grandall, John	Tennessee	640	2013	20 May 1793	2007	16 Aug 1785	81	127	On S side of Cumberland River	
McCulloh, Benjamin	313	McFascon, Henry	Tennessee	640	2014	20 May 1793	2466	30 Sep 1785	81	128	On S side of Cumberland River	
McCulloh, Benjamin	315	Shorte, Abraham	Tennessee	640	2016	20 May 1793	2493	20 Sep 1785	81	128	On S side of Cumberland River	
McCulloh, Benjamin	316	Fisher, Joel	Tennessee	640	2017	20 May 1793	2989	30 Sep 1786	81	128	On S side of Cumberland River	
McCulloh, Benjamin	318	Thornhill, John	Tennessee	640	2019	20 May 1793	2242	12 Sep 1785	81	129	On S side of Cumberland River	
McCulloh, Benjamin	319	Medlin, Elijah	Tennessee	274	2023	20 May 1793	1631	22 Mar 1785	81	130	On the Deafster /sic/ Creek &c	
McCulloh, Benjamin	320	King, Enoch	Tennessee	640	2033	20 May 1793	1639	22 Mar 1785	81	132	On S side of Cumberland River	
McCulloh, Benjamin	342	Hampton, George	Tennessee	274	2141	20 May 1793	3005	30 Sep 1785	81	159	On waters of Winters Creek	

Claimant:	File #:	Assignee:	County:	Acres:	Grant:	Entry:	Grant Date:	Entry Date:	Bk:	Pg:	Location by Stream Name:	Military:
McCulloh, Benjamin	343	Edens, John	Tennessee	640	2144	2647	20 May 1793	30 Sep 1785	81	159	On S Side of Cumberland River	
McCulloh, Benjamin	78		Western District	5000	78	2570	10 Jul 1788	25 May 1784	67	310	On the N side of Forked Deer River &c	
McCulloh, Benjamin, Ass	297	Shanks, James		640	1971	2237	20 May 1793	12 Sep 1785	81	147	On S side of Cumberland River	
McCulloh, Benjamin, Ass	373		Tennessee	640	2280		20 May 1793		81	187	On Red River	
McCulloh, Benjamin, Ass	656		Sumner	640	1967	2991	20 May 1793	16 Nov 1792	81	116	On the waters of Bledoes Creek	yes
McCulloh, Benjamin, Ass	659		Sumner	640	1977	3022	20 May 1793	16 Nov 1792	81	118	On the waters of Bledsoe's Creek	yes
McCulloh, Benjamin, Ass	660		Sumner	640	1979	2999	20 May 1793	16 Nov 1792	81	119	On the waters of Bledsoes Creek	yes
McCulloh, Benjamin, Ass	685		Sumner	1000	2034	2193	20 May 1793	30 Nov 1792	81	133	On W Fork of Peytons Creek	yes
McCulloh, Benjamin, Ass	789		Sumner	274	2248	3002	20 May 1793	30 Nov 1792	81	180	On the Defeated Creek	yes
McCulloh, Benjamin, Ass	790		Sumner	274	2249	1632	20 May 1793	30 Nov 1792	81	180	On the Defeated Creek	yes
McCulloh, Benjamin, Ass	793		Sumner	274	2253	3007	20 May 1793	30 Nov 1792	81	181	On the Defeated Creek	yes
McCulloh, Benjamin, Ass	813		Sumner	1000	2280	3003	20 May 1793	30 Nov 1792	81	187	Beg at a sugar tree	yes
McCulloh, Benjamin, Ass	822		Sumner	640	2300	1985	20 May 1793	26 Nov 1792	81	191	About 1 mile from the Old Station	yes
McCulloh, Joseph	110		Eastern District	492	99	751	17 Nov 1790	30 Feb 1781	76	176	N/S Clinch River both sides of Loss Creek	
McCulloh, Joseph	164		Hawkins	399	97	44	16 Nov 1790	8 Feb 1780	77	184	On the S side of Clinch River &c	
McCulloh, Joseph	494		Hawkins	200	366	169	29 Jul 1793	27 Jun 1780	80	268	S side of Clinch River &c	
McCulloh, Joseph	500		Hawkins	300	372	989	29 Jul 1793	2 Jan 1779	80	270	In Henders Valley	
McCulloh, Joseph	505		Hawkins	250	377	1949	29 Jul 1793	12 Oct 1779	80	271	On the S side of Clinch River &c	
McCulloh, Joseph	599		Hawkins	150	473	1564	29 Jul 1793	31 Aug 1779	80	294	S side of Clinch River &c	
McCulloh, Joseph	615		Hawkins	200	490	609	29 Jul 1793	9 Jun 1780	80	297	S side of Clinch River &c	
McCulloh, Joseph	87		Eastern District	150	76	689	17 Nov 1790	8 Sep 1780	76	168	S side of Clinch River	
McCulloh, Robert, Ass	864		Sumner	640	2375	1997	20 May 1793	26 Nov 1792	81	207	On headwaters of Bartons Creek	yes
McCulloh, Thomas	245		Eastern District	300	210		30 Oct 1794		83	139	S of the Ohio on S side of Holston River	
McCullough, Benjamin	2055	Blough, Benjamin	Davidson	640	2145	1991	20 May 1793		81	159	On the waters of Stones River	yes
McCullum, Isaac	2294	Upchurch, Charles	Davidson	228	2771	3894	9 Sep 1796		88	523	On waters of Harpeth	yes
McCumber, Humphrey	2380	Donelson, Stockley	Davidson	1000	3106	4254	14 Sep 1797		90	405	On the Falling Creek	yes
McCusster, James, Jr.	138		Middle District	2626 26	140	1276	10 Jul 1788	23 Dec 1783	67	476	Lying on Duck River &c	
McCustin, Beginning	808		Green	200	806	69	20 Nov 1788	12 May 1784	70	30	On the waters of Loud Creek	
McCutchan, Patrick	1153		Davidson	640	130	260	17 Apr 1786	19 Feb 1784	66	182	On the N side of Harpeth River	
McCutchen, Samuel	1281		Davidson	640	246	259	10 Jul 1788	9 Feb 1784	66	423	On Little Harpeth Rivers	
McCutchen, James	1902		Davidson	320	139	715	27 Apr 1793	26 Apr 1785	81	38	On Big Harpeth River	
McCutchen, James	1907		Davidson	320	146	782	27 Apr 1793	18 Dec 1785	81	40	On waters of Harpeth River	
McCutchin, Samuel	1321		Davidson	320	7	261	18 Aug 1787	9 Feb 1781	68	123	On Little Harpeth River	
McCutchin, John	944	Haddock, Admiral	Davidson	228	960	1235	18 May 1789		63	327	On E side of E fork of Stones River	yes
McDaak /sic/, John	1959	Thompson, Jason	Davidson	284	1804	3541	20 May 1793		81	80	On S side of Cumberland River &c	yes
McDalton, Joseph	2012	Bond, John Senr	Davidson	20	1959	3542	20 May 1793		81	114	Being part of a 274 &c	yes
McDaniel, Alexander	1186	Donelson, Stockley	Sumner	640	2708	3912	20 Jul 1796	9 May 1796	88	444	On branches of Spencers Creek	yes
McDaniel, Alexander	251	Dickey, Thomas	Davidson	1000	237	1222	7 Mar 1786		63	87	On waters of W Harpeth River	yes
McDaniel, Hugh	567	Larkin, John (their)	Davidson	1000	539	768	15 Sep 1787		63	194	On Jones Creek	yes
McDaniel, Hugh	874	McIver, Alexander	Sumner	640	2390	2925	7 Jan 1794	8 Aug 1795	81	388	On a creek &c	yes
McDaniel, I.	48	McDaniel, I., Cobb, & P. Du	Hawkins	640		3841						
McDaniel, James	295		Sullivan	140	434	641	9 Aug 1787	10 Jul 1780	61	453	On the waters of Hannahs Creek	
McDaniel, John	44	Blount, John Gray	Tennessee	640	1235	2532	10 Dec 1790	30 Sep 1785	74	343	On N side of Cumberland River	yes
McDaniel, Larkin	037	Rice, John	tennessee	640		1792		25 Apr 1785			On both side of the N Fork &c	yes
McDaniel, Thomas	290	Ross, Henry	Sumner	274	1298	3294	10 Dec 1790	14 Mar 1789	74	365	On S side of Cumberland River	yes

Claimant:	File #:	Assignee:	County:	Acres:	Grant:	Grant Date:	Entry:	Entry Date:	Bk:	Pg:	Location by Stream Name:	Military:
McDaniel,/or McDonald, Thos	1571		Davidson	640	1204	10 Nov 1790	458		74	331	On Harpeth River	yes
McDaniels, Allen	08	Blount, John Gray	Tennessee	640			2533	30 Oct 1785			S side of Spring Creek	yes
McDonald, Arthur	1858	Kirkpatrick, Michael	Davidson	640	1585	27 Apr 1793	897		81	14	On waters of Big Harpeth	yes
McDonald, Colin	036	Dowd, Cornelius	Middle District	640			3811					yes
McDonald, James	0117		Sullivan	200			640	10 Jul 1780			N side Holston River W fork Richland Creek	
McDonald, James	356		Green	100	358	20 Sep 1787	8	22 Oct 1783	65	474	Near the S end of Clinch Mountain &c	
McDonald, james	924		Green	100	838	17 Nov 1790	642	14 Oct 1785	76	117	N side of Holston River &c	
McDonald, John	016	Lewis, W. T. & Wm. Tyrrell	Montgomery	640			458				On Williams Creek	yes
McDonald, John	267		Green	400	234	20 Sept 1787	2066	12 Apr 1786	65	439	On the N side of Holston River &c	
McDonald, Magnus	1076		Davidson	640		17 Apr 1786	776	7 Jun 1785	66	51	On the S side of Cumberland River	
McDonald, William	524	Hadley, Joshua	Sumner	640	1708	20 May 1793	3143	10 Mar 1788	81	55	On W side of Caney Fork	yes
McDowd, Josiah	141	Lett, James	Davidson	274	127	14 Mar 1786	92		63	49	North side of Cumberland River	yes
McDowell, James	1611		Green	1000	1323	1 Feb 1795			84	151	On S side of French Broad River	
McDowell, Joseph	1517	Bartie, John heirs	Davidson	640	1074	26 Oct 1789	2045		74	117	On E side of Mill Creek	yes
McDowell, Joseph	1529	Faigan, George heirs	Davidson	640	1086	26 Nov 1789	2031		74	124	On Mill Creek	yes
McDowell, Joseph	47	Brown, John	Davidson	1737	33	14 Mar 1786	800		63	13	On Pleasant Creek	yes
McDown, Joseph	024	Brewer, Joseph	Not given	640			4333					yes
McDuel, Willis	2034	Buckanon, John	Davidson	640	2047	20 May 1793	2573		81	136	On the waters of Mill Creek	yes
McDugald, Archibald	24	Bowman, William	Sumner	320	781	11 Jul 1788	2530	1 Mar 1787	63	274	On both sides of Long Branch	yes
McDunniald, James	150		Hawkins	200	184	26 Dec 1791			75	177	On N side of Holson River	
McElwis, James	355		Hawkins	400	348	8 Mar 1793			78	484	On E side of Holston River	
McEnis, James	812		Green	200	813	11 Aug 1789	2828	28 Mar 1781	71	34	On the W side of Sinking Creek	
McEntire, John	200		Hawkins	640	188	26 Dec 1791	693	13 Sep 1780	77	309	In the Grassey Valley	
McEueen, David	052	Wood, Isham	Davidson	274		26 Mar 1791	1868	26 Mar 1791			On waters of Big Harpeth River	
McEwen, Alexander	892		Washington	105	867	13 Feb 1791	2871	16 Jun 1781	74	287	On S side of Great Limestone	
McFadden, James	1386		Davidson	320	69	8 Oct 1787	403	10 Apr 1784	68	149	On Red River, &c	
McFarland, Benjamin	1020		Green	200	1247	29 Jul 1793	566	27 Oct 1783	76	488	N side of French Broad River	
McFarland, Benjamin	1718		Green	127	1397	21 Jan 1797	54	20 Jan 1780	91	124	N side of French Broad River	
McFarland, Benjamin	395		Middle District	1000	334	17 Dec 1794	1945	29 Apr 1784	84	221	On E side of Stones River	
McFarland, John	1824		Davidson	640	397	26 Jun 1793	826	20 Nov 1792	80	341	On the head of Stones Creek	
McFarland, Robert	171		Green	400	641	23 Aug 1788	314	23 Aug 1783	64	355	On the branch of Sinking Creek	
McFarland, Robert	817		Green	200	818	11 Aug 1789	525	27 Oct 1783	71	36	On the S side of Nollichuckey River &c	
McFarland, Walter	355	Hutsen, Chamberlain	Tennessee	640	2185	20 May 1793	2139	9 Sep 1785	81	167	On the waters of Bartons Creek	yes
McFarlin, Alex.	1290		Green	200	1140	12 Jan 1793	1397	29 Apr 1786	78	388	Beg at a hickory tree	
McFarlin, Alexander	1532	McFarlin, John heir	Davidson	640	1089	26 Nov 1789	3364	17 Sep 1778	74	125	Bet. Cedar Lick Creek & Spences Creek	yes
McFarlin, Alexander	67		Washington	300	235	23 Oct 1782	397		44	262	Beg above head of Big Spring	
McFarlin, Alexander	88		Green	200	46	1 Nov 1786	1332	24 Oct 1779	59	407	Known by the name of the Meadows	
McFarlin, Jas.	473		Tennessee	100	307	20 Jul 1796			88	442	On N side of Sulphur Fork	
McFarlin, John	1420	Hadley, Joshua	Sumner	228	157	6 Dec 1797	4551	8 May 1797	98	157	On the waters of Cedar Creek	
McFarlin, John	371		Sullivan	100	250	10 Nov 1784	1258	2 Mar 1779	69	162	On head of Clear Fork of Horse Creek	yes
McFarlin, John, heir of Alex	1532		Davidson	640	1089	26 Nov 1789	3364		74	125	Between Cedar Lick & Spencers Creek	yes
McFarlin, Joseph	350		Green	228	352	20 Sep 1787	1390	16 Jan 1786	65	473	On the S side of Nolachuckey	
McFarlin, Morgan, heir	032		Tennessee	640			1363	9 Nov 1784			S side of Red River	
McFarlin, Thomas	1331		Davidson	320	17	18 Aug 1787	504	1 Jul 1784	68	127	On the N side of Cumberland River	
McFarlin, William	1044		Green	100	1271	29 Jul 1793	77	16 Nov 1788	76	492	N/S Nolychuckey on waters of Bent Creek	

Earliest Tennessee Land Records

Claimant:	File #:	Assignee:	County:	Acres:	Grant:	Entry:	Grant Date:	Entry Date:	Bk:	Pg:	Location by Stream Name:	Military:
McFarson, Richard	1104		Washington	200	1054	2744	27 Nov 1792	27 Jan 1781	80	206	On the draft of Lick Creek &c	
McFarson, Roger	2431	Mann, John	Davidson	640	3259	4360	6 Dec 1797		98	147	On the waters of Marrowbone Creek	yes
McFascon, Henry	313	McCulloh, Benjamin	Tennessee	640	2014	2466	20 May 1793	30 Sep 1785	81	128	On S side of Cumberland River	yes
McFashion, Caleb	470	Langston, David	Sumner	640	1630	2676	27 Apr 1793	1 Dec 1792	81	24	On the dividing ridge &c	yes
McFatter, Daniel	143		Tennessee	640	1394		20 Dec 1791		77	349	On the S side of Red River	
McFeeters, Samuel	396		Sullivan	300	275	125	10 Nov 1784	26 Feb 1778	69	169	On S side of Holstein River	
McFeeters, Samuel	430		Sullivan	640	309	1272	10 Nov 1784	8 Mar 1779	69	179	On Duncans Branch	
McFeeters, Samuel	52		Washington	99	342	220	24 Oct 1782	26 May 1778	43	315	On Boldings Creek	
McFerron, Andrew	495		Green	250	497	1464	20 Sep 1787	2 Feb 1784	65	517	On the W side of Richland Creek	
McFerson, Duncan	558	McPherson, John	Davidson	640	530	2612	15 Sep 1787		63	191	N side of Cumberland	yes
McFoy, Morrie	1123	Harris, Edward	Sumner	640	2629	2751	4 Jun 1796	1 Jun 1795	88	344	Joining said Harris survey	yes
McGauhey, Saml & others	1109		Green	3000	952	822	26 Dec 1791		77	263	Beg at a Beech tree &c	
McGauhey, Saml & others	1110		Green	300	953	2849	26 Dec 1791	29 Oct 1783	77	264	On the S side of French Broad River	
McGauhey, William	42		Green	200	105	373	1 Nov 1786	12 May 1781	58	466	Beg upon a white oak	
McGavock, David	1066		Davidson	640	40		17 Apr 1786	29 Mar 1784	66	48	Beg at a large black oak	
McGavock, David, Ass of	1737		Davidson	228	1485		4 Jan 1792		77	372	On S side of Little Harpeth	
McGeary, Samuel	998		Green	200	1225	1408	29 Jul 1793	17 Jan 1784	76	484	On the Cedar Branch of Long Creek	
McGee, John, hr/Jesse Steed	282		Western District	1035	308	1751	25 Apr 1789	21 Apr 1784	70	265	On the waters of Big Hatcher River &c	
McGee, Peter, heirs	196		Tennessee	1000	1482	1362	4 Jan 1792	9 Nov 1784	77	371	On the S side of Cumberland River &c	
McGert, John	080		Green	50		326		11 Jun 1793			Joining survey where McGert now lives	
McGibbony, Patrick, Lieut.	1450		Sumner	1920	3359	317	29 Sep 1800	22 Sep 1787	108	129	On the waters of Big Barren River	yes
McGill, James	245	.	Green	260	202	15	20 Sep 1787	21 Oct 1783	65	431	On Sinking Creek	
McGill, William	508		Green	200	510	16	20 Sep 1787	21 Oct 1783	65	525	N side of Nolachuckey on Sinking Creek	
McGinnis, John	1236		Washington	200	1208	1179	20 Jul 1796	2 Feb 1779	88	503	On a small branch of Little Limeston creek	
McGirt, John	161		Green	165	631	762	23 Aug 1788	28 oct 1783	64	352	On the waters of French Broad River	
McGist, John	372		Hawkins	50	326		27 Jul 1793		79	488	Joining survey where sd McGist now lives	
McGlavock, James, Ass of	1334		Davidson	640	20	67	18 Aug 1787	8 Jan 1784	68	128	Beg at a hickory & mulberry &c	
McGloskins, Alexander	1686	Johnson, Thomas	Davidson	640	1628	1728	23 Feb 1793		76	326	On the waters of Stones River	yes
McGlouren, Alexander	2089	Johnston, Thomas	Davidson	640	2296		20 May 1793		81	190	On waters of Stones River	yes
McGound, Thomas	1244	Blount, John Grey	Sumner	640	2843	4249	21 Jan 1797	13 Dec 1796	90	46	On Camp Creek	yes
McGown, Andrew	1629		Green	466	1349	1852	22 Feb 1795	Dec 1780	84	331	On N side of French Broad River	
McGown, Samuel	1467		Davidson	60	74	2867	18 May 1789	29 Jul 1787	71	227	On Whites Creek	
McGrayhen, Archibald	680		Sullivan	93	628	737	9 Jul 1794	6 Feb 1781	81	630	On a branch of Kendricks Creek	
McGuacock, William	1141		Davidson	640	118	191	17 Apr 1786	26 Jan 1784	66	179	On both sides of Arrington Creek &c	
McGuaivock /sic/, Wm.	1205		Davidson	320	77	189	8 Oct 1787	26 Jan 1784	66	225	Lying on both sides of Arringtons Creek	
McGuesten, John	1383	Davidson, John	Sumner	640	3250	4644	24 Nov 1797	13 May 1797	97	32	On waters of Cedar Creek	yes
McGuire, Michael	1395	Morrow, John & James	Sumner	640	3322	1391	6 Dec 1797	13 Mar 1797	97	45	On the head of N Fork of Red River	yes
McIlhattan, Abram	12		Maury	1000	28	1470	14 Jul 1812	24 /sic/	126	437	On a small branch	
McIlhekee, Jno. Russell	331	Heir of Miles	Tennessee	2560	3094	1087	20 May 1793	2 Jun 1784	81	148	On the waters of Sulphur Fork	
McIlyhia, John	1588	Braiden, Charles	Davidson	1000	1259	1235	10 Dec 1790		74	352	On waters of Spring Creek	yes
McIntire, John	828		Green	640	809	435	18 May 1789	26 Jan 1781	72	244	On the head waters of Second Creek	
McIntosh, Benj.,	215		Tennessee	50	108	66	20 Dec 1791	19 Sep 1789	72	379	In the Barrons &c	
McIntosh, Tos.	217		Tennessee	100	115		20 Dec 1791	18 Sep 1789 (surv)	77	381	On the W side of the Upper Trace Creek	
McIntrof, Christopher	1087		Washington	550	1037	431	27 Nov 1792	25 Sep 1778	80	200	Beg at a Buck &c	
McIver, Alexander, Ass	874		Sumner	640	2390	2925	7 Jan 1794	8 Aug 1795	81	388	On a creek &c	yes

Claimant:	File #:	Assignee:	County:	Acres:	Grant:	Grant Date:	Entry:	Entry Date:	Bk:	Pg:	Location by Stream Name:	Military:
McKadon, William	728	Adcock, Joshua	Davidson	274	701	11 Jul 1788	438	5 oct 1786	63	247	South side of Red River	yes
McKain, James	1464		Davidson	50	69	18 May 1789	2999		71	225	On the waters of Drakes Creek	
McKain, James, Ass	894		Sumner	640	2444	18 Mar 1794			81	424	On E side of Bledsoes Creek	yes
McKanish, William	1678		Green	200	1383	18 Jul 1796	4	30 Aug 1784	88	493	The head of Roaring Fork	
McKay, Alexander, Ass	856		Sumner	640	2361	20 May 1793			81	204	On waters of Drakes Creek	yes
McKee, Alexander	283		Western District	1000	338	11 Aug 1789	575	27 Oct 1783	71	245	On the E side of Grove Creek	
McKee, Alexander	67		Western District	1500	67	10 Jul 1788	2631	25 May 1784	67	306	On the E side of Grove Creek &c	
McKee, Alexander	799		Washington	300	613	10 Nov 1784	1041	7 Jan 1779	69	142	Beg at 2 marked white oaks	
McKee, John	1241		Washington	200	1213	20 Jul 1796	1913	2 Jan 1792	88	505	Upon Knaves Branch	
McKee, Matthew	130		Hawkins	400	164	26 Dec 1791	1706	22 Sep 1779	75	169	On S Side of Holston River	
McKeel, Joshua	286	Casselman, Jacob	Sumner	640	1287	10 Dec 1790	3471	26 Jun 1788	74	361	On waters of Bartons Creek	yes
McKenie, John	341	Rice, John & Harriet	Tennessee	640	2138	20 May 1793	2144	9 Sep 1785	81	158	On N side of Cumberland River	yes
McKenney, Daniel	1380	Boyd, John Jr	Sumner	640	3242	24 Nov 1797	4102	14 Apr 1797	94	174	Waters of Smiths Fork	yes
McKenny, Alexander	330	Hickman, Thomas	Sumner	640	1621	23 Feb 1793	3114	22 Dec 1792	76	322	Headwaters of Hickmans Cr a br Caney Fk	yes
McKenny, Charles	192	Russel, Samuel	Tennessee	640	1472	4 Jan 1792	847	12 May 1784	77	369	Wt side of the Wt Fork of Jones Creek	yes
McKey, Alex	096	Dundelow, Benj.	Sumner	640			2568	29 Aug 1792			Beg at a white oak &c	yes
McKinley, Daniel	706	Carnahan, Andrew	Davidson	640	679	8 Dec 1787	1265		63	239	On waters of Big Harpeth	yes
McKinney, Robert	1271	Adams, Jacob	Sumner	640	2999	10 Apr 1797	936	12 Jan 1797	90	293	S Side of Cumberland River	yes
McKinnie, William	86	Hopkins, Joseph	Tennessee	640	1348	10 Dec 1790	949	19 May 1784	74	381	On N side of Cumberland River	yes
McKinns, Timothy	1697	Campbell, M. & Phillip Philli	Davidson	640	1658	23 Feb 1793	3390	19 Nov 1792	76	339	On the waters of Stones River	yes
McKinsey, Hugh	501	Barton, Samuel	Sumner	640	1670	20 May 1793	1717	19 Nov 1792	81	46	On Bartons Creek	yes
McKinsey, William	165	Hadley, Joshua	Tennessee	640	1427	20 Dec 1791	223	25 Oct 1783	77	358	On both side of Pine River	yes
McKissack, Daniel, Ass	785		Sumner	640	2242	20 May 1793	3252	18 Nov 1792	81	179	On S side of Cumberland River	yes
McKissick, James	112		Middle District	1000	114	10 jul 1788	2587	24 May 1784	67	465	Removed from joining David Smith's entry	
McKnight, Patrick	663	McNairy, John	Tennessee	640	3256	6 Dec 1797	4101		97	36	On the ridge	yes
McKnight, William,	2288	White, Robert	Davidson	400	196	20 Jul 1796			88	475	On Whites Creek	
McKnight, Wm.	054	White, Robert	Not given	400				10 Jan 1794			On Whites Creek	
McKonley, Samuel	168		Sullivan	150	175	10 Oct 1783	623	24 Jun 1780	53	148	Joining Cresley Weavers former survey	
McLauddin - see McLaughlin												
McLaughlan, Samuel	2110	Smith, David		274	2363	20 May 1793	849		81	204	On E side of Harpeth	yes
McLaughland, Henry	476		Davidson	100	468	13 Oct 1783	1485	26 Jul 1779	52	297	On the Mill Fork &c	
McLaughlin, John	431		Washington	200	423	13 Oct 1783	1060	8 Jan 1779	52	277	On the N side of Big Limestone Creek	
McLaughlin, John	893		Washington	200	868	13 Feb 1791	1039	17 May 1779	74	288	On W side of Big Limestone	
McLaughlin, Neil	1227	Montgomery, William	Sumner	400	175	27 Aug 1795		1 Nov 1792	89	413	On Drakes Creek	yes
McLaughlin, Neill	1207	Carter, Charles	Sumner	400	163	26 Mar 1795			89	91	On Bledsoes Lick Creek	yes
McLaughlin, Thomas	62		Hawkins	400	47	18 May 1789	1945	12 Oct 1779	72	255	On the N side of Holston River &c	
McLean, Ephraim	123		Western District	1000	123	10 Jul 1788	2213	20 May 1784	67	328	On the S side of Duck River	
Mclean, Ephraim	1330		Davidson	320	16	18 Aug 1787	5	26 Dec 1783	68	127	On the N side of Cumberland	
McLean, Ephraim	159		Western District	2500	159	10 Jul 1788	2219	21 May 1784	67	358	On the waters of Obion River	
McLean, Ephraim	398		Middle District	1100	337	17 Dec 1794	773	28 Oct 1773	84	222	On N side of Duck River	
McLean, Ephraim, Sr.	155		Middle District	5000	151	27 Nov 1789	1567	1 Apr 1784	74	44	On N side of Duck River	
McLean, Ephraim;	1332	Dunham, Daniel	Davidson	320	18	18 Aug 1787	6	26 Dec 1783	68	127	On the N side of Cumberland River	
McLean, George	40		Western District	1000	40	10 Jul 1788	2214	20 May 1784	67	295	On Flatt Creek &c	
McLear, Robert	1116		Green	800	959	26 Dec 1791	135	29 Feb 1778	77	267	On Ellejoy Creek	
Mclemore, Amos	26		Giles	200	57	23 Apr 1813	1083	8 Jan 1779	127	330	On Big Creek	

Earliest Tennessee Land Records

Claimant:	File #:	Assignee:	County:	Acres:	Grant:	Grant Date:	Entry:	Entry Date:	Bk:	Pg:	Location by Stream Name:	Military:
McLemore, Robt	023		Robertson	640	3387		5365	21 May 1800			On waters of Red River	
McLin, John	421		Middle District	5000	360	17 Dec 1794	1778	23 Apr 1784	84	234	On Middle Fork of Elk River	
McLin, William	367		Middle District	5000	306	17 Dec 1794	1770	23 Apr 1784	84	210	On Elk River	
McMacken, John	667		Washington	200	481	10 Nov 1784	476	2 Oct 1778	69	97	Beg at 3 white oaks	
McMacken, Thos.	1252		Green	100	1102	12 Jan 1793	2443	28 Feb 1785	78	365	On Mill Creek	
McMahan, Daniel	216	Aldridge, William	Davidson	228	202	7 Mar 1786	685		63	75	On waters of Big Harpeth River	yes
McMahan, John	176		Washington	540	44	23 Oct 1782	478	2 Oct 1778	47	20	On Knob Creek	
McMahan, John	386		Washington	300	378	13 Oct 1783	477	2 Oct 1778	52	254	Beg at a chestnut on Cobbs line	
McMahan, John	442		Washington	150	434	13 Oct 1783	1167	1 Feb 1779	52	282	Beg at a black oak	
McMahan, John Blair	188		Washington	100	56	23 Oct 1782	1168	1 Feb 1779	47	26	Joining S E line of plantation, etc.	
McMahan, John Blair	244		Washington	300	112	23 Oct 1782	473	2 oct 1778	47	55	On head spring of Knobb Creek	
McMahan, John Blair	288		Washington	300	155	2 Oct 1782	474	2 Oct 1778	47	75	On head spring &c	
McMains, Thos.	1306		Green	200	1156	12 Jan 1793	271	7 Jul 1788	78	398	On Limestone Fork	
McMin, John	63		Hawkins	250	48	18 May 1789	753	10 Mar 1781	72	255	On the N side of Holston River &c	
McMin, Joseph	288		Middle District	400	244	12 Jun 1794	2176	9 Nov 1774	82	181	On the Clear Fork of Cumberland Mountain	
McMordie, Francis	2		Transylvania			26 Jan 1786			69	314		
McMordie, Francis	4 (3)		Tennessee								Letter from Adam Boyd making him attorney	
Mcmoren, Domnick	2011	Standley, James	Davidson	274	1957	20 May 1793	1105	26 Jan 1786	69	314	On waters of W Fork of Mill Creek	yes
McMullin, Joseph	1686		Green	200	1367	7 Dec 1785	1488	2 May 1794	81	113	On waters of Lick Creek	
McMullen, Alexander	402		Hawkins	100	523	27 Jan 1793	2667	19 Nov 1780	89	224	On S side of Holston River	
McMullen, Alexander	405		Hawkins	100	526	27 Jan 1793	2182	11 Nov 1779	79	498	On S side of Holston River	
McMullen, Isaac	1086	Tyrrell, W. & S. Donelson	Sumner	640	2577	7 Mar 1796	2863	2 Nov 1795	79	499	On S side of Holston River	yes
McMullin, Alexander	1065		Green	200	908	26 Dec 1791	2125	12 May 1784	88	315	On head of the Pond Lick Creek	
McMullin, Alexander	541		Hawkins	120	414	29 Jul 1793	926	29 Oct 1782	77	245	On the E Fork of Swan Pond Creek	
McMullin, Alexander	565		Green	200	245	20 Sep 1787	312	1 Dec 1797	80	281	On S side of Holsten River &c	
McMullin, Alexander	708		Hawkins	300	528	12 June 1794	1653	31 Oct 1778	66	155	On the S side of Holsten River	
McMullin, Alexander	72		Green	500	30	1 Nov 1786	279	22 Oct 1783	82	162	On the S side of Holston &c	
McMullin, Alexander, Ass	0138		Green	300	245	20 Sep 1787	318	Mar 1785	59	391	S side of Holston River	
McMullin, Joshua	806	Woodard, Noah	Sumner	369	2273	20 May 1793	1233	25 Oct 1786	81	185	On Arringtons Fork of Red River	yes
McMullin, Michael	469	Hogan, John	Tennessee	274	2693	6 Jun 1796	3828	25 Jan 1795	88	367	Adjoining land of John Couch &c	yes
McMullin, William	543		Sullivan	252	520	27 Nov 1789	1739	27 Sep 1779	74	30	On waters of Fall Creek	
McMullins, Alexander	224		Hawkins	250	211	26 Dec 1791	1483	19 Feb 1784	77	317	Lying on Turkey Creek	
McMurray, John	115		Sullivan	280	127	24 Oct 1782	1215	22 Feb 1779	43	318	On the S Fork of Big Creek &c	
McMurray, Samuel (Wm.)	34		Sullivan	239	45	23 Oct 1782	1257	2 Mar 1779	43	259	On the S Fork of Big Creek &c	
McMurray, Samuel, Ass	030	Porter, Samuel	Tennessee	320			3372	7 Jan 1786			N side of Cumberland River	
McMurray, Wm. & Saml	1270		Green	640	1120	12 Jan 1793	205	3 Jan 1784	78	377	On Crooked Creek	
McMurry, Jno.	1166		Davidson	640	143	17 Apr 1786	612	30 Oct 1784	66	185	On the waters of Big Harpeth &c	
McMurry, John	1367		Davidson	320	50	8 Oct 1787	690	25 Feb 1785	68	141	On the N side of Big Harpeth	
McMurry, Samuel	1273		Davidson	640	238	10 Jul 1788	613	30 Oct 1784	66	421	Beg at a hickory S W corner to James Todd	
McMurry, Samuel	1337		Davidson	320	233	18 Aug 1787	713	25 Apr 1785	68	129	Beg at a black walnut marked S. M.	
McMurry, Thomas	1323		Davidson	320	9	18 Aug 1787	328	3 Mar 1784	68	124	On the S side of Cumberland River	
McMurtey, Joseph	938		Green	100	852	17 Nov 1790			76	122	Beg at a big chestnut tree &c	
McMurtree, John	795	Robertson, Elijah	Davidson	640	798	20 Nov 1788	2615		63	280	On waters of the first creek	
McMurtry, John	1813		Davidson	640	386	26 Jun 1793	574	12 Apr 1784	80	336	On the middle fork of Jaspers Creek	yes
McMurtry, Joseph	0124		Green	100			2915	22 Oct 1788			Beg at a big chestnut	

Claimant:	File #:	Assignee:	County:	Acres:	Grant:	Entry:	Grant Date:	Entry Date:	Bk:	Pg:	Location by Stream Name:	Military:
McMurtry, Joseph	338		Green	300	340	30	20 Sep 1787	21 Oct 1783	65	469	On both sides of Camp Creek	
McMurty, William	2	Donelson, Stockley	Montgomery	640		2615		13 Feb 1797			On 1st branch N side of Cumberland River	yes
McNabb, Baptist	204		Washington	600	72	686	23 Oct 1782	10 Dec 1778	47	34	On W side of Buflow (sic) Creek	
McNabb, Baptist	51		Washington	112	341	2367	24 Oct 1782	23 Dec 1779	43	315	Joining his other survey &c	
McNabb, Jno.	611		Green	432	568	17	20 Sep 1787	21 Oct 1783	66	251	On Big Pigeon River &c	
McNabb, John	466		Washington	300	458	13	13 Oct 1783	24 Feb 1778	52	293	On Nollechuckie River &c	
McNabb, William	240		Washington	507	108	793	23 Oct 1782	26 Dec 1778	47	52	On a branch of Sinking Creek	
McNair, James	509		Hawkins	400	382	1004	29 Jul 1793	29 Oct 1783	80	272	N side of Holston River &c	
McNair, James & Robt. King	1030		Hawkins	200	795	989	22 Feb 1797	29 Oct 1783	90	228	On a branch of Indian Creek	
McNairy, John	494	Pendegrass, Jno.	Tennessee	640	2493	1876	26 Sep 1795	4 Jul 1785	89	104	On W Fork of Gillon Creek	
McNairy, John	5		Davidson	200	3		20 Dec 1791		62	298	On the South bank of Cumberland River	
McNairy, John	601		Middle District	1003 (13	366	101	6 Jun 1797		101	346	On the head waters of Big Harpeth River	
McNairy, John	661	Lovell, John heirs	Tennessee	640	3254	4634	6 Dec 1797		97	35	On the Ridge	
McNairy, John	662	Harrell, Benj.	Tennessee	640	3255	4092	6 Dec 1797		97	36	N side of the head of Piney Fork	
McNairy, John	663	McKnight, Pat	Tennessee	640	3256	4101	6 Dec 1797		97	36	On the ridge	
McNamee, Joseph & Peter	035	Wilson, Adam	Washington	300		233		18 Jun 1778			Including a big spring on the wagon road	
McNamee, Peter	030		Eastern District	100		1466		14 Jan 1780			Hawkins Co.	
McNamee, Peter	220		Hawkins	250	207	1466	26 Dec 1791	14 Jan 1780	77	316	On the N side of Holston River &c	
McNamee/McNemee, Peter	238		Washington	570	106	876	23 Oct 1782	31 Dec 1778	47	51	On Shipmans Fork	
McNamee/McNemee, Peters	027		Eastern District	100		1466		14 Jan 1780			Knox County on Second Creek	
McNare, James	1061		Green	200	904	986	26 Dec 1791	29 Oct 1783	77	243	On the S side of Holstein River	
McNare, James	516		Hawkins	100	389	1000	29 Jul 1793	29 Oct 1783	80	274	An island in Holston River	
McNare, James	581		Hawkins	390	455	380	29 Jul 1793	1779	80	290	S side of Holston River &c	
McNary, Jno. & Robt Nelson	3050	Oneel, Isham	Tennessee	640	1996	2680	20 May 1793	24 Nov 1792	81	123	On S side of Cumberland River	
McNary, John	659	McClure, Hardyman	Washington	640	3252	4695	6 Dec 1797		97	33	On the head of Piney Fork &c	
McNary, John	660	Hogan, Roger	Tennessee	274	3253	4741	6 Dec 1797		97	34	On the Flat Lick Fork	
McNear, James, Ass	322		Sumner	640	315	737	17 Nov 1790	30 May 1785	70	186	On Bledsoes Creek &c	
McNeel, Absalom	115	Shackle, Phillip	Sumner	640		3540		25 May 1791			S side of Cumberland River	
McNeeley, William, Ass	1015		Sumner	400	2484				87	508	On S side of Cumberland River	yes
McNeeley, Wm.,	521	White, Walter	Davidson	640	493	2036	15 Sep 1787		63	178	South side of Cumberland River	yes
McNees, James	434		Sumner	640	318	512	27 Nov 1792	6 Jul 1784	81	1	On N side of Cumberland River	yes
McNees, John	1591	Reaves, Benja.	Davidson	640	1264	1108	10 Dec 1790		74	353	On N side of Cumberland River	yes
McNees, John	1593	Howell, James	Davidson	640	1276	2866	10 Dec 1790		74	357	On waters of Bear Branch	yes
McNees, John	1593	Price, Micajah	Davidson	640	1263	2947	10 Dec 1790		74	353	On a branch of the Duck Spring Creek	yes
McNees, John	793	Mott, Edge	Davidson	640	796	2938	23 Aug 1788		63	279	On N side of Cumberland River	yes
McNees, John	794	Stewart, Andrew	Davidson	640	797	3546	23 Aug 1788		63	279	On N side of Cumberland River	yes
McNeese, Jas	396	Overton, John	Tennessee	274	2410		7 Jan 1794		81	402	On N side of Sycamore Creek	
McNeese, John	1034	Blount, John Gray	Sumner	3840	2571		7 Mar 1796		88	191	On waters of Caney Fork	yes
McNeese, John	135	Mears, Timothy	Sumner	640	121	442	14 Mar 1786		63	47	West side of Harpeth River	yes
McNeese, John	792	McWilliams, Jesse	Davidson	1000	795	2864	23 Aug 1788		63	278	On North side of Cumberland River	yes
McNeill, John	1126	Harris, Edward	Sumner	640	2632	2614	4 Jun 1796	1 Jul 1795	88	345	Joining said Harris survey	yes
McNess, John	013	Blount, John Gray	Sumner	3840				10 Jun 1795			S side of Cumberland Road	yes
McNess, John	790		Davidson	1000	793	2896	23 Aug 1788		63	277	On N side of Cumberland River	yes
McNess, John	791	Appleton, John	Davidson	1000	794	3530	23 Aug 1788		63	278	On waters of Duck Spring Creek	yes
McNett, Robert	451		Washington	50	443	2090	13 Oct 1783	30 Oct 1779	52	286	On the waters of Big Limestone	

Claimant:	File #:	Assignee:	County:	Acres:	Grant:	Grant Date:	Entry:	Entry Date:	Bk:	Pg:	Location by Stream Name:	Military:
McNiell, Zebulon	2309	Tyrrel, Wm. & Robt. King	Davidson	1000	2510	27 Aug 1795	3542		89	414	On both side of Salt River	yes
McNitt, Anthony	1001		Washington	35	973	26 Dec 1791	2458	8 Mar 1780	77	300	On Limestone	
McNulty, John	1189	Donelson, Stockley	Sumner	640	2711	20 Jul 1796	3846	19 Mar 1796	88	445	On Spencers Creek	yes
McNutt, George	954		Green	50	868	17 Nov 1790	2897	1 May 1787	76	127	N side of Holston River	
McNutt, Robert	233		Green	200	190	20 Sep 1787	640	10 Jul 1780	65	427	On the N side of Holston River	
McNutty, John	1759		Green	182	1430 [?]	17 Nov 1797	2249	22 Nov 1779	94	146	Waters of Pigeon Creek	
McPharen, Jas	1258		Green	350	1108	12 Jan 1793	7	6 Dec 1783	78	368	On S side of Lick Creek	
McPheran, James	1395		Green	300	1207	27 Nov 1792	150	22 Oct 1783	80	152	On the waters of Roaring Fork of Lick Creek	
McPhern, Andrew	342		Green	400	344	20 Sep 1787	151	22 Oct 1783	65	470	On Long Creek	
McPherson, Abel	559	Wheaton, Daniel	Tennessee	1000	2993	10 Apr 1797	1575		90	290	E Fork of Yellow Creek	yes
McPherson, John	558	McPherson, Duncan heirs	Davidson	640	530	15 Sep 1787	2612		63	191	North side of Cumberland	yes
McPherson, William	460		Green	250	462	20 Sep 1787	8	6 Sep 1783	65	505	On the N side of Nolachuckey River &c	
McQuillin, William	614	Pipkin, Lewis	Tennessee	640	3173	14 Sep 1797	4016	26 Nov 1796	90	431	On N side of Cumberland River	uillin
McQuinn, Alexander	701		Washington	50	515	10 Nov 1784	2271	16 Jun 1781	69	110	On W side of Alexander Campbell's land	
McRace, Roger	081	Hadley, Joshua	Sumner	640				18 Oct 1787			On Puntchin [sic] Camp Creek	
McRae, David	1594		Davidson	1000	1279	10 Dec 1790	1621		74	358	On N side of Cumberland River	yes
McRae, Reuben	1305	Brewer, Sterling	Sumner	1000	3077	19 Jul 1797	4294	27 Apr 1797	90	381	Waters of Big Barren	yes
McRandels, Joseph	234		Green	130	191	20 Sep 1787	35	11 Mar 1784	65	428	On N side of Nolechuckey River	yes
McRea, Saml	620	Foster, Thomas	Tenn	640	3182	14 Sep 1797			90	435	S side of Cumberland River	
McRea, William	399		Middle District	308	338	17 Dec 1794	2588	10 Apr 1782	84	223	On Main Elk River	
McRee, John	1371a	Hardin, John	Sumner	640	3226	17 Nov 1797	2752	7 Nov 1791	94	165	Waters of Arrington's Fork of Red River	yes
McRees, John	2289	Tyrrel, William	Davidson	3840	2769	12 Aug 1796			88	480	Including the mouth of Bull Run	yes
McRory, James, heir of Thos	48		Davidson	3840	34	14 Mar 1786	30		63	14	North Fork of McAdoes	yes
McRory, John	682	Brown, David heirs	Davidson	640	655	8 Dec 1787	1267		63	232	On S waters of Big Harpeth	yes
McRory, Thomas	48	McRory, James (heir)	Davidson	3840	34	14 Mar 1786	30		63	14	North Fork of McAdoes	yes
McRoy, James, Ass	560		Sumner	640	1781	20 May 1793	2293	12 Jul 1788	81	74	On Cripple Creek &c	yes
McShadden, Archibald	1029		Green	400	1256	29 Jul 1793			76	489	On Doaks & Dry Creek &c	
McSpedden, John	159		Green	300	629	23 Aug 1788	134	22 (?) 1783	64	351	On the N side of French Broad River	
McSpidden, Archibald	156		Green	100	926	23 Aug 1788	1286	16 Mar 1780	64	350	On the N side of French Broad	
McTuney, Alexander	653	Overton, John	Sumner	640	1963	20 May 1793	2919	14 Nov 1792	81	115	On small creek which runs into Smith's For	yes
McVey, Eli	1597	Martin, Joseph	Davidson	640	1288	10 Dec 1790	269		74	361	On W side of Stones River	yes
McVey, Eli	713	Lyttle, Archibald	Sumner	640	2095	20 May 1793	1050	6 Apr 1788	81	148	On Bledsoe's Creek	yes
McVey, Eli	82	Phillips, P & Campbell	Tennessee	640	1338	10 Dec 1790	1738	24 Apr 1785	74	378	On S side of Cumberland River	yes
McVey, John	1598	Elliott, John	Davidson	640	1289	10 Dec 1790	270	27 Apr 1780	74	362	On W Fork of Stones River	yes
McWherter, James	296		Sullivan	320	435	9 Aug 1787	496	27 Apr 1780	61	454	In Carters Valley	yes
McWhirter, George	1655		Davidson	640	306	17 Nov 1790	455	20 May 1784	76	183	Beg at an ash on Cumberland River	
McWhirter, William, Ass	412		Sumner	640	423	27 Jun 1793	673	29 Jan 1785	80	349	On the main middle fork of Gooses Creek	
McWhiter [?], James	364		Sullivan	142	243	10 Nov 1784	500	27 Apr 1780	69	159	On Carters Valley	
McWilliams, Jesse	792	McNeese, John	Davidson	1000	795	23 Aug 1788	2864		63	278	On N side of Cumberland River	
Meadaris, John	1943		Davidson	3840	1771	20 May 1793	19		81	72	On W Fork of Stones River	yes
Meadow, John	079		Green	50			2263	22 Mar 1779			Beg at a white oak	
Meadows, Abraham	417	Shacker, Phillip	Tennessee	274	2462	31 Dec 1793	1536	5 Feb 1785	81	430	On waters of Sulphur Fork of Red River	yes
Meafee, Azariah	667	Berry, Thomas	Davidson	640	640	15 Nov 1787	1112		63	227	On small creek that empties into Tennesse	yes
Meaglin, Robert	599		Washington	200	693	26 Oct 1786	736	22 Dec 1778	66	8	On a large spring &c	yes
Meares, Abraham	544	Malley, Thomas	Tennessee	1000	2968	5 Apr 1797	2207		90	273	On Barretts Creek	yes

Claimant:	File #:	Assignee:	County:	Acres:	Grant:	Grant Date:	Entry:	Entry Date:	Bk:	Pg:	Location by Stream Name:	Military:
Mears, Alexander, Ass.	754		Sumner	428	2159	20 May 1793	89	23 Aug 1792	81	163	On waters of W Fork of Drakes Creek	yes
Mears, Timothy	135	McNeese, John	Davidson	640	121	14 Mar 1786	442		63	47	W side of Harpeth River	yes
Mears, Willis	821	Hays, Robert	Sumner	640	2298	20 May 1793	2327	3 Nov 1792	81	191	On waters of Dixons Creek	yes
Meban, Alexander	901		Green	2000	822	10 Nov 1790	1622	5 Apr 1784	74	332	On Tennessee River	
Mebane, Alexander	882		Green	1000	817	6 Dec 1790	2123	20 Nov 1784	74	244	On First Sinking Branch	
Mebane, Alexander	902		Green	500	823	10 [blank] 1790			74	332	On a fork of Nine mile Creek	
Mebane, Alexander	903		Green	250	824	10 Nov 1790	1064	28 Feb 1784	74	332	Cornering on two small black oaks	
Mebane, Alexander, Ass	253		Sumner	640	1205	10 Nov 1790			74	333	On waters of SW Fork of Caney Fork	yes
Mebane, Alexander, Ass	254		Sumner	640	1206	10 Nov 1790			74	333	On E boundary of Phillips & Campbells	yes
Mebane, Alexander, Ass	255		Sumner	640	1207	10 Nov 1790			74	333	On Cainey Fork River	yes
Mebane, Alexander, Ass	256		Sumner	640	1208	10 Dec 1790			74	334	On W Fork of Caney Fork	yes
Mebane, Alexander, Ass	257		Sumner	640	1209	10 Dec 1790			74	334	On SW Fork of Caney Fork	yes
Mebane, Alexander, Ass	258		Sumner	640	1210	10 Dec 1790			74	334	On S side of Cumberland River	yes
Mebane, Alexander, Ass	259		Sumner	640	1211	10 Dec 1790			74	335	On waters of SW Fork of Caney Fork	yes
Mebane, Alexander, Ass	260		Sumner	640	1212	10 Dec 1791			74	335	On waters of SW Fork of Caney Fork	yes
Mebane, Alexander, Ass	261		Sumner	640	1213	10 Dec 1790			74	335	On waters of SW Fork of Caney Fork	yes
Mebane, Alexander, Ass	262		Sumner	640	1214	10 Dec 1790			74	330	On waters of SW Fork of Caney Fork	yes
Mebane, Chas.	060	Bailey, Wm. Henry heirs	Middle District	640			3757		74	383	On Meat Camp	yes
Mebane, James	1620	Wright, Adam	Davidson	1000	1354	10 Dec 1790	863	21 May 1784	112	295	Waters of Eagle Creek	
Mebane, James, Jr	16		Smith	5000	379	27 Dec 1800	2220	21 May 1784	112	294	Waters of Woolf [sic] River	
Mebane, James, Sr	15		Smith	5000	378	27 Dec 1800	2221		63	6	On both sides W Fork of Big Harpeth River	yes
Mebane, Robert	27	Mebane, Wm heir of Robt	Davidson	7200	13	14 Mar 1786	162	19 Nov 1784	77	355	On both sides of Pine River	yes
Medlin, Elisha	158	Bailey, Thomas	Tennessee	640	1415	20 Dec 1791	1437	22 Mar 1785	81	130	On the Deafster (?) Creek	yes
Medlin, Elisha	319	McCulloh, Benjamin	Tennessee	274	2023	20 May 1793	1631	12 Dec 1785	81	422	On S side of Cumberland River	yes
Medlin, Mills	410	Haywood, John	Tennessee	640	2436	18 Mar 1794	3117	30 Nov 1785	81	422	On S side of Cumberland River	yes
Medlin, Zeland	411	Haywood, John	Tennessee	640	2437	18 Mar 1794	1438				On Holston River	
Medlock, Chas	032		Hawkins	16							S side of Holston	
Medlock, John	033		Hawkins	100			467	2 Oct 1778	76	477	S side of Holston River	
Medlock, John	985		Washington	100	1062	29 Jul 1793	769	30 Dec 1783	77	383	On the waters of Stones Creek	
Medlock, William	1751		Davidson	320	109	20 Dec 1791	2183	12 Nov 1779				
Meek, Adam	0102		Washington	300			51	10 May 1784				
Meek, Adam	0149		Green	25			813	29 Oct 1783			S side of Holston River	
Meek, Adam	051		Hawkins	300			48	8 Feb 1780				
Meek, Adam	070		Sullivan	250								
Meek, Adam	1046		Hawkins	100	810	8 Jun 1797			90	325	Including his improvements	
Meek, Adam	1223		Green	100	1073	12 Jan 1793	2065	29 Mar 1787	78	348	Upon Holleys Creek	
Meek, Adam	1227		Green	200	1077	12 Jan 1793	375	12 Jan 1779	78	350	On N side of Holston	
Meek, Adam	1242		Green	200	1092	12 Jan 1793	1528	17 Aug 1779	78	360	On N side of Holston River	
Meek, Adam	1269		Green	100	1119	12 Jan 1793	1374	14 Jan 1784	78	376	On Mossey Creek	
Meek, Adam	1286		Green	200	1136	12 Jan 1793	61	12 May 1784	78	386	On a draft of Beaver Dam Creek	
Meek, Adam	167		Eastern District	400	131	14 Jan 1793			79	289	On N side of Tennessee River	
Meek, Adam	186		Green	600	143	23 Apr 1787	337	23 Oct 1783	65	161	On the S side of Holston River &c	
Meek, Adam	187		Green	100	144	23 Apr 1787			65	161	On the S side of Holston River &c	
Meek, Adam	191		Green	600	829	Sep 1790	588	23 Apr 1787	74	293	Dividing ridge bet Holston & French Broad	
Meek, Adam	192		Green	100	149	23 Apr 1787	83	12 May 1784	65	162	On the S side of Holston River &c	

Claimant:	File #:	Assignee:	County:	Acres:	Grant:	Grant Date:	Entry:	Entry Date:	Bk:	Pg:	Location by Stream Name:	Military:
Meek, Adam	193		Green	600	150	23 Apr 1787	351	23 Oct 1783	65	163	On the N side of Holston River &c	
Meek, Adam	194		Green	488	151	23 Apr 1787	828	29 Oct 1783	65	163	Valley bet. Sinking Creek and Beaver Creek	
Meek, Adam	195		Green	200	152	23 Apr 1787			65	163	On the S side of Holston River &c	
Meek, Adam	287		Hawkins	200	298	14 Jan 1793			78	346	On N side of Holston River	
Meek, Adam	311		Middle District	1000	287	17 Dec 1794			83	331	S side of Duck River	
Meek, Adam	463		Hawkins	200	335	29 Jul 1793	56	6 Jul 1779	80	259	S side of Holston River &c	
Meek, Adam	481		Hawkins	500	353	29 Jul 1793	1981	18 Mar 178_	80	264	On Flatt Creek	
Meek, Adam	503		Hawkins	350	375	29 Jul 1793	2183	12 Nov 1779	80	270	On Boyle Spring Branch	
Meek, Adam	507		Hawkins	300	380	29 Jul 1793	1389	12 Nov 1789	80	271	Joining James Creswell &c	
Meek, Adam	51		Hawkins	300	380	29 Jul 1793	1389	23 May 1779	80	271	Joining James Creswell &c	
Meek, Adam	561		Hawkins	200	434	29 Jul 1793	1281	16 Mar 1779	80	285	S side of Holston River on Lyons Creek	
Meek, Adam	70		Hawkins	200	434	29 Jul 1793	1281	16 Mar 1779	80	285	S Side of Holston River on Lyons Creek	
Meek, Adam	898		Sullivan	250			48	8 Feb 1780				
Meek, Adam & David Stuart	898		Green	600	829	Sep 1790	588	23 Apr 1787	74	293	Dividing ridge bet Holston & French Broad	
Meek, Adam, Jr	191		Green	300 (200	148	23 Apr 1787	13	17 Oct 1783	65	162	On the S side of Holston River &c	
Meek, Jeremiah	190		Green	200	147	23 Apr 1787	1030	29 Oct 1783	65	162	On the S side of Holston River	
Meek, Moses	483		Green	400	485	20 Sep 1787	259	28 Oct 1783	65	513	On Lick Creek	
Meek, Moses	040		Washington	100			464	1 Oct 1778			Beg at a black oak & hickory	
Meek, Moses	1013		Washington	108	962	14 Jan 1793			79	274	Bet. Chas Young's & Wm. Hesel's line	
Meek, Moses	1032		Washington	100	982	14 Jan 1793	464	1 Oct 1778	79	279	Beg at a spanish & white oak	
Meeks, Moses	776		Washington	100	590	10 Nov 1784			69	135	On Brush Creek	
Meeks, Robt	1976	Blount, John G. & Thos.	Davidson	274	1878	20 May 1793	524		81	96	On Harpeth River	
Meenece, James [not clear]	387		Middle District	1000	326	17 Dec 1794	1881	24 Apr 1784	84	217	On S side of Cumberland River	yes
Meezlies, Micajah	411	Nichols, John	Davidson	640	383	15 Sep 1787	2575		63	143	E side of Cumberland River	
Meginson, Thomas	1840		Davidson	640	338	27 Nov 1792	638	18 Dec 1784	81	6	Three small sugar trees & a white oak	yes
Mehon, James	1287	Barry, Redmond Dillion	Sumner	640	3046	8 Jun 1797	4062	29 Mar 1797	90	316	On 32 mile creek	
Meidkiff, Isiah	1102(?)		Hawkins	250	397	19 Jul 1797		Martin Armstrong	91	622	S side of Holston River	yes
Melbourne, Solomon	1698	Phillips, P. & Michael Cam	Davidson	1000	1659	23 Feb 1793	517	7 Aug 1796	76	340	On the waters of Stones River &c	
Mellekin, James	360		Green	150	362	20 Sep 1787	2609	13 Aug 1780	65	475	On the S Fork of Cedar Branch of Lick Creek	yes
Mellone, Micheal	782		Sullivan	200	714	18 Nov 1796	293	10 Nov 1780	71	90	Nside of Holston River	
Melone, Jno & Zach Casteel	1697		Green	200	1361	12 Nov 1795	2425	15 Feb 1780	89	418	On waters of Lick Creek	
Melone, John	79		Sullivan	200	90	23 Oct 1782	1758	30 Sep 1779	43	281	On the waters of Beaver Creek	
Melone, William	114		Sullivan	100	125	23 Oct 1782	229	25 Feb 1780	43	318	On the waters of Beaver Creek	
Melory, Thomas	064	Donelson, Stockley	Davidson	640	1577	27 Apr 1793	569	3 Apr 1784	74	390	On the waters of Watauga River	
Melton, Daniel	730		Sumner	1000	336	27 Nov 1792	2616	7 Aug 1796	81	12	On W side of Mill Creek	
Melton, John	2233	Robeson [sic], James	Davidson	640	335	20 May 1793	1170	6 Apr 1785	81	5	On N side of Cumberland River	yes
Melvin, George, Ass	617		Davidson	640	2596	7 Mar 1796	133	24 Apr 1789	88	324	On E Fork of Turnbulls Creek	yes
Melvin, Thomas	1099		Sumner	365	1882	20 May 1793	1458	19 Dec 1792	81	96	On a branch of Long Creek	yes
Mences, James	1631		Washington	140 (144	1049	27 Nov 1792	1334	8 Apr 1779	80	204	On the waters of Watauga River	yes
Mences, James	1853	Speirpoint, Joseph	Davidson	320	101	10 Nov 1792	418	3 Apr 1784	74	390	On W side of Mill Creek	
Mences, James	445		Sumner	640	336	27 Nov 1792	511	6 Jul 1784	81	12	On N side of Cumberland River	
Mences, Jam's	0134		Green	1000	335	17 Dec 1794	1882	24 Apr 1789	81	5	On E Fork of Barton's Creek	yes
Mendinghall, Martin, Ass	961		Hawkins	200	289	6 Jun 1796		Martin Armstrong	88	382	First large creek that empties into Elk River	
Meness, James	1647		Davidson	640	298	17 Nov 1790	78	12 Jan 1784	76	180	On S side of Holston River	
Meness, James	396		Middle District	1000	335	17 Dec 1794			84	221	First large creek that empties into Elk River	

Claimant:	File #:	Assignee:	County:	Acres:	Grant:	Grant Date:	Entry:	Entry Date:	Bk:	Pg:	Location by Stream Name:	Military:
Mennett, Benjamin	571	Merritt, Stephen heir	Davidson	640	543	15 Sep 1787	958		63	195	South side of Cumberland River	yes
Meredith, Benjamin	1285	Barry, Redmond Dillion	Sumner	640	3044	8 Jun 1797	4036	29 Mar 1797	90	316	On Doe Creek	yes
Merer, Abraham	354	Williams, Willoughby	Middle District	1000	2403	5 Feb 1795			84	184	On E side of W Fork of Obeys River	yes
Merrell, Henry heirs	47	Hughlett, William	Middle District	640	2		2750					
Merrell, Benjamin	1004		Green	300	1231	29 Jul 1793	2116	4 Nov 1779	76	485	N side of Clinch River &c	
Merriott, John	1744		Green	150	363	4 Jul 1797		19 Dec 1795	91	588	Waters of Little Chucka	
Merritt, Benjamin	43		Sullivan	200	54	23 Oct 1782	383	10 Sep 1778	43	264	On a branch of Horse Creek &c	
Merritt, William	191	Dickson, John	Tennessee	640	1471	4 Jan 1792	1910	15 Jul 1785	77	369	S side of Cumberland River	yes
Mertain, Andrew	310		Washington	200	177	24 Oct 1782	871	31 Dec 1778	47	85	On both forks of Cedar Creek	
Merton, Joseph	21		Washington	150	311	24 Oct 1782	874	31 Dec 1778	43	302	On Cedar Fork Branch &c	
Messar, Benjamin	1472	Armstrong, Martin	Davidson	274	1048	17 Nov 1789	575		71	282	On the E waters of Cedar Lick	yes
Messar, Richard	074		Sullivan	200	542	17 Nov 1790			76	192	On Beech Creek &c	
Messar, Richard	559		Washington	200			1277	12 Mar 1779			On Beech Creek	
Messick, Jacob	543		Davidson	2560	515	15 Sep 1787	553		63	186	South side of Cumberland River	yes
Messingale, Henry	681		Washington	400	495	10 Nov 1784	935	1 Jan 1779	69	103	On Wataugha /sic/ River	
Messingale, Henry	686		Washington	200	500	10 Nov 1784	2393	3 Jan 1780	69	105	On waters of Wataugha /sic/	
Metts, Willis	722	Sheppard, Nancy	Davidson	640	695	11 Jul 1788	2093		63	245	On waters of Sulphur Fork	yes
Mewhisaw, John	2045	Sheppard, Nancy	Davidson	640	2065	20 May 1793	1494		81	140	On N side of Cumberland on N Cross Cree	yes
Michal, Kimberland	1117		Davidson	640	94	17 Apr 1786	688	21 Feb 1785	66	173	On the Dry Fork of Bledsoes Creek	
Middleton, James	325		Tennessee	1000	2074	20 May 1793	1459	23 Nov 1784	81	143	On both sides of Yellow Creek	
Middleton, Solomon	883	Ford, John	Davidson	640	897	17 Jan 1789	921		63	311	On N side of Cumberland River	yes
Midgett, Jacob	388	Sheppard, Benjamin	Davidson	640	360	15 Sep 1787	2301		63	135	On Main Fork of Big Barren	yes
Midkiff, Isaac	442		Eastern District	100	396	19 Jul 1797			91	622	N side of Holston River	
Midkiff, John	441		Eastern District	50	395	19 Jul 1797			91	621	N side of the Big Ridge	
Migley, Demsey	1962	Sanford, Samuel	Davidson	640	1820	20 May 1793	2398		81	83	On waters of West Harpeth	yes
Milburn, William	1390		Green	100	1245	27 Jan 1792	506	15 Oct 1778	79	511	On N side of Nolechuckey	
Miles, Henry	1301		Washington	100	1187	4 Dec 1795	2664	26 Sep 1780	89	429	On the E side of the river	
Miles, Jacob	364	King, Robert	Middle District	640	3085	12 Aug 1797	3176		90	393 (39	On a branch of the Caney Fork	yes
Milhorn, George	854		Washington	200		17 Nov 1788		10 Mar 1788	65	13	Beg at a white oak &c	
Millekin, John, Sr	846		Green	100	827	13 Feb 1791	2765	17 Sep 1779	73	377	On the S fork of Horse Camp &c	
Miller, Abraham	1419		Davidson	46	34	8 Oct 1787		1779 & 1780	68	156	Wartrace Creek of Sulphur Fork of Red River	
Miller, Adam	099	Roberts, Richard	Sumner	640			942	25 Nov 1789			S side of Cumberland River	yes
Miller, Alexander	1134		Green	200	977	26 Dec 1791	194	6 Apr 1778	77	274	Beg at two white oaks &c	
Miller, Andrew	1135		Green	300	167	20 Sep 1787	380	23 Oct 1783	65	419	On the S side of Nolechuckey River &c	
Miller, Andrew	1279		Green	100	1129	12 Jan 1793	1401	17 Jan 1784	78	382	On S side of Nolechuckey River	
Miller, Andrew	210		Green	300	978	26 Dec 1791	137	10 Mar 1788	77	274	On Nine Mile Creek	
Miller, Daniel	318		Sullivan	248	454	28 Nov 1787	1654	17 Sep 1779	67	217	On the waters of Beaver Creek	
Miller, Daniel	32		Sullivan	600	43	23 Oct 1782	264,-1654	1779 & 1780	43	358	On the branches of Beaver Creek	
Miller, Frederick	158		Western District	4000	158	10 Jul 1788	633	28 Oct 1783	67	358	On Reelfoot River &c	
Miller, Gasper	1169		Green	200	1012	26 Dec 1791	548	29 Oct 1778	77	286	Joining Sandy Armstrong's land	
Miller, Henry	1130		Washington	100	1088	12 Jul 1794	483	6 Oct 1778	81	565	Beg at a big white oak tree	
Miller, Jacob	1048		Washington	50	998	27 Nov 1792	1171	1 Feb 1779	80	176	Beg at a white oak &c	
Miller, James	459		Eastern District	640	315	25 Oct 1802	1938	5 Jan 1785	115	420	On Fourth Creek	
Miller, James	545	Douglass, Edward	Davidson	640	517	15 Sep 1787	1216		63	186	On waters of Station Camp Creek	yes
Miller, James	707	Blount, Reading	Davidson	640	2146	8 Dec 1787	2146		63	240	Headwaters Long Fork of Sycamore Creek	yes

Earliest Tennessee Land Records

Claimant:	File #:	Assignee:	County:	Acres:	Grant:	Grant Date:	Entry:	Entry Date:	Bk:	Pg:	Location by Stream Name:	Military:
Miller, John	382		Sullivan	150	261	10 nov 1784	1751	28 Sep 1779	69	165	On waters of Possom Creek	
Miller, John	524		Sullivan	270	540	26 Nov 1789	469	25 Apr 1780	73	49	On the N side of Holston River	
Miller, John	572		Sullivan	248	570	29 July 1793	264	7 Mar 1780	76	471	On the waters of Beaver Creek &c	
Miller, John	651		Sullivan	353	599	27 June 1793	469	29 Apr 1780	80	383	On the N side of Holston	
Miller, John	840	Hart, Anthony	Davidson	640	845	17 Jan 1789	2812		63	296	On head of Browns Creek	
Miller, John &Jos Brown	1363		Washington	100	1280	30 Jun 1797	2635	7 Sep 1780	92	57	Waters of Big Limestone	
Miller, John Lough	928		Hawkins	50	710	2 Dec 1795	700	28 Oct 1780	88	264	On N side of Holston River	
Miller, John West	628		Sullivan	150	576	27 Jun 1793	2455	7 Mar 1780	80	373	Including a small spring by a large rock	
Miller, Jordan	735		Sullivan	72	678	2 Dec 1795	1239	24 Feb 1779	88	268	On S side of Holston River	
Miller, Matthias	569		Hawkins	100	443	29 Jul 1793	761	20 Mar 1781	80	288	On the N side of the N Fork	
Miller, Peter	905		Hawkins	184	693	16 Jul 1795	1373	20 May 1779	87	422	On S side of Holston River	
Miller, Richard	669	Ramsey, Allen	Sumner	365	2071	20 May 1793	1084	4 Jun 1791	81	142	On S side of Cumberland River	yes
Miller, Solomon	263	Robertson, James	Tennessee	640	1711	20 May 1793	2865	30 Sep 1785	81	56	On S side of Cumberland River	yes
Miller, Thomas	640		Sullivan	291	588	27 Jun 1793	517	29 Apr 1780	80	378	Beg at a locust Sourwood	
Miller, Thomas	918		Washington	200	895	17 Nov 1790	540	26 Sep 1778	76	142	On Stoney Creek	
Milligan, John	274		Middle District	250	147	27 Apr 1793	71		81	40	On S side of Duck River	
Milliken, Jas.	1244		Green	200	1124	12 Jan 1793	209	7 May 1778	78	380	On N side of Noleychuckey	
Millner, John	1644		Davidson	640	295	17 Nov 1790	561	2 Aug 1784	76	180	On the head of Milners Creek	
Mills, Ann	1475		Green	100	1239	12 Jul 1794	391	4 Aug 1781	81	575	Beg at a hickory	
Mills, Benj. & Isaac Bledsoe	601		Sumner	1142	1851	20 May 1793	1443	5 Oct 1792	81	90	On S side of Cumberland River & c	yes
Mills, Daniel	367	Hays, Robert	Sumner	640	1532	14 Jan 1793	2674	30 Nov 1792	79	285	On waters of Manscows Creek	yes
Mills, Elijah	2256	Donelson, Stockley	Davidson	640	2716	20 Jul 1796	1323		88	447	On waters of Stones River &c	yes
Mills, Jacob	997	Douglass, Edward	Sumner	400	153	17 Dec 1795		20 Nov 1792	84	331	W of Cumberland Mountain	yes
Mills, James	68		Davidson	3840	54	14 Mar 1786	546		63	22	Large creek running Into Tennessee River	yes
Mills, Jesse	780	Taylor, Wm. & John	Sumner	640	2235	20 May 1793	2808	30 Nov 1792	81	177	On the waters of Dixons Creek	yes
Mills, Randel, Ass	1398	Donelson, Stockley	Sumner	640	3326(?)	6 Dec 1797	3065	23 Jun 1797	97	47	On Salt Lick Fork of Big Barren	yes
Mills, William	026		Not given	285			1322					yes
Mills, William	026		Not given	285								
Mills, William	1041	Armstrong, James	Hawkins	280	2959	22 Feb 1797			90	234	Waters of Caney Creek	yes
Milner, John	228		Tennessee	640	405	27 Jun 1793	561	1 Jun 1789	80	342a	On the head of Milners Creek	
Mims, Jacob	759		Sullivan	140	758	28 Jul 1797	248	2 Mar 1780	90	387	Beg at a Beech tree	
Minahaw, Micajah	2466	Robertson, David	Davidson	640	3401	14 pr 1803	1846	12 Mar 1803	110	319	Lying in the ridge above Leepers Fork	yes
Miner, John	78		Sullivan	250	89	23 Oct 1782	68	8 Feb 1780	43	281	On the N side of Holston River	
Miness, Benjamin	1246		Davidson	640	211	10 Jul 1788	5405	12 Apr 1784	66	414	Head of Leages Creek br of Big Barren River	
Minory, George	1557	Drew, John	Davidson	640	1173	29 Nov 1790	2145		74	234	On S side of Cumberland River	yes
Minshaw, David	056	Robertson, David	Davidson	640			1846	29 Oct 1786			On Big Ridge above fork of Harpeth	yes
Minshaw, Micajah	566	Blackface, William	Tennessee	640	3002	10 Apr 1797	3641		90	294	S side of Cumberland River	yes
Mintore, John	041	Dillenberry, Redmon [sic]	Sumner	640			4334	14 Oct 1797			On headwaters of W Fork &c	yes
Mires, Jacob	182		Washington	300	50	23 Oct 1782	792	26 Oct 17__	47	23	On Big Limestone Creek	yes
Mires, John	398	Brown, James, heirs of	Tennessee	274	2424	31 Dec 1793	823	11 May 1784	81	407	On Pine River	
Misse, Thos.	071		Sullivan	300			2198				On both sides of Stock Creek	
Mitchel, Jacob	408	Nelson, Robert	Davidson	640	380	15 Sep 1787	2576		63	142	On Pasture Creek	yes
Mitchel, Jacob	041		Washington	200			618	24 Nov 1778			On Lick Creek waters	
Mitchel, James	479		Washington	300	471	13 Oct 1783	352	4 Sep 1778	52	299	On the W Fork of Big Limestone	
Mitchel, Robert	406		Sumner	640	417	27 Jun 1793	734	30 May 1785	80	347	On both sides of Cedar Lick Creek	

Claimant:	File #:	Assignee:	County:	Acres:	Grant:	Grant Date:	Entry:	Entry Date:	Bk:	Pg:	Location by Stream Name:	Military:
Mitchel, Samuel	0100	Moore, Daniel	Sumner	228			4100	21 Jun 1797	47	58	On Johnstons Creek	yes
Mitchel, Thomas	251		Washington	200	119	23 Oct 1782	3	4 Sep 1778	81	170	On an E branch &c	
Mitchell, Abraham	2067	Person, Thomas	Davidson	228	2206	20 May 1793	1723		81	170	On E side of Harpeth River	yes
Mitchell, Andrew	363		Green	200	365	20 Sep 1787	167	22 Oct 1783	65	476	On Lick Creek	
Mitchell, James	1392		Green	200	1247	27 Jan 1793			79	511	On Lick Creek	
Mitchell, James	689		Washington	200	503	10 Nov 1784	1384	30 Mar 1779	69	106	On S side of N Fork of Big Limestone	
Mitchell, Joab	153		Sullivan	540	163	18 Aug 1783	164,-159	14 Mar 1778	45	272	On the So side of Holston River &c	
Mitchell, Joab	154		Sullivan	640	164	18 Aug 1783	20	21 Feb 1778	45	272	On the S side of Holston River	
Mitchell, Joab	155		Sullivan	300	165	18 Aug 1783	57	26 Feb 1778	45	273	On the So side of Holston River	
Mitchell, John	02	Alford, William	Tennessee	640			775	1 May 1784			On the 4th large creek &c	yes
Mitchell, John	197	Flatt, John	Tennessee	640	1483	4 Jan 1792	937	18 Nov 1791	77	372	S side of Cumberland River &c	
Mitchell, John	681	Donelson, John	Sumner	640	2027	20 May 1793	3473	10 Feb 1787	81	131	On the N Fork of Stones	yes
Mitchell, John	934		Hawkins	300	716	8 Dec 1796	1186	1 Nov 1783	88	274	The N side of Holston River	
Mitchell, John	211		Davidson	274	197	7 Mar 1786	146		63	73	On waters of Stones River	yes
Mitchell, Joseph	042		Washington	100			2932	7 Aug 1783			On Boones Creek	
Mitchell, Mark	043		Washington	300			2514	30 Mar 1780			On waters of Boons Creek	
Mitchell, Mark	144		Sullivan	200	154	18 Aug 1783	20	25 Feb 1778	45	268	On Honeycutts Creek &c	
Mitchell, Mark	145		Sullivan	300	155	18 Aug 1783	20	25 Feb 1778	45	269	On Dodsons Creek	
Mitchell, Mark	146		Sullivan	300	156	18 Aug 1783	20	25 Feb 1778	45	269	On Dodsons corner &c	
Mitchell, Mark	147		Sullivan	300	157	18 Aug 1783	20	25 Feb 1778	45	270	On Dodsons Creek	
Mitchell, Mark	148		Sullivan	300	158	18 Aug 1783	20	25 Feb 1778	45	270	On Dodsons Corner	
Mitchell, Mark	149		Sullivan	600	159	18 Aug 1783	164	14 Mar 1778	45	271	At the head of Bent Creek	
Mitchell, Mark	151		Sullivan	340	161	18 Aug 1783	19	25 Feb 1778	45	271	On S side of Holston River &c	
Mitchell, Mark	152		Sullivan	400	162	18 Aug 1783	20	25 Feb 1778	45	272	On Jno Honeycutts Creek &c	
Mitchell, Mark	232		Middle District	500	212	1 Jan 1793	419	25 Apr 1783	80	212	Lying S side of Duck River	
Mitchell, Mark	666		Green	300	707	11 Jul 1788	440	25 Oct 1783	66	462	On the S side of Holston River &c	
Mitchell, Mark	693		Hawkins	400	495	16 Dec 1793	58	26 Feb 1778	82	99	On the S side of Holston River &c	
Mitchell, Mark, Ass	911a		Hawkins	283	256	7 Mar 1796		Martin Armstrong	88	193	On S side of Holston River	
Mitchell, Richard	151		Hawkins	640	185	26 Dec 1791	68	26 Feb 1778	75	177	On German Creek	
Mitchell, Thomas	685		Washington	60	499	10 Nov 1784	2800	28 Feb 1781	69	104	On waters of Big Limestone	yes
Mitchell, Thomas	549		Davidson	1000	521	15 Sep 1787	121	29 Mar 1797	63	188	On waters of Stones River	
Mitchell, William	685		Washington	60	499	10 Nov 1784	2800	28 Feb 1781	69	104	On waters of Big Limestone	
Mitchell, Wm.	1042		Davidson	640	16	17 Apr 1786	246	6 Feb 1784	66	39	Branches on the E Fork of White Creek	
Mock, Henry	473		Sullivan	200	362	10 Nov 1784	1821	6 Oct 1779	69	196	On N side of Holstein River	
Mock, Henry	690		Sullivan	450	638	9 Jul 1794	256-1818	2 Oct 1789	81	634	On Rock Bottom Branch	
Modlin, Ezekial	090	King, William	Sumner	640			3781	8 Aug 1795			On Little Lick Creek	yes
Modlin, Ezekial	656	Beaird, Joseph	Hawkins	640	2482	23 May 1794	3781		81	556	N side of Clinch River	yes
Mohon, James	1287	Barry, Redmond Dillion	Sumner	640	3046	8 Jun 1797	4062	29 Mar 1797	90	316	On 32 Mile Creek	yes
Moburn, David	127	Boyd, John	Tennessee	274	1633	23 Feb 1793	518	20 Apr 1784	76	328	On Wells Creek	yes
Molay, Thomas;	22	White, Henry	Davidson	228	8	16 Feb 1786	516		63	4	S side of Cumberland River	yes
Molley, Thomas;	2230	Moore, Marmaduke	Davidson	640	2591	7 Mar 1796	975		88	322	On Harpeth River	yes
Molley, Thomas;	08	Cameron, Alexander, hrs of	Montgomery	491	2983		3636	30 Dec 1796			S side of Cumberland River	yes
Molloy, Thomas	1025	Spencer, Whilliam heirs	Davidson	640	1043	11 May 1789	2587		63	346	S side of Cumberland River	yes
Molloy, Thomas	1411		Davidson	160	28	18 Oct 1787			68	155	Southern boundary Malloys Guardright #695	yes
Molloy, Thomas	2333	Sharkin, James heirs	Davidson	640	460	10 Apr 1797	538	19 Jul 1784	90	284	S side of Cumberland	

Claimant:	File #:	Assignee:	County:	Acres:	Grant:	Grant Date:	Entry:	Entry Date:	Bk:	Pg:	Location by Stream Name:	Military:
Molloy, Thomas	2333		Davidson	160	28	18 Oct 1787	510	7 Sep 1796	68	155	Southern boundary Malloys Guardright #695	
Molloy, Thos. & Wm. Shute	015		Davidson	640			937						
Moncrieff, Thomas	5033		Davidson	274	475	15 Sep 1787	228			172	South side of Cumberland River	yes
Money, Benjamin	539		Sullivan	401	516	27 Nov 1789	228	22 Feb 1789	74	28	On S side of Holston River	
Monhouse, Daniel	293	Mountflorence, James C.	Davidson	640	279	22 Mar 1787	2044		63	102	N side of Cumberland River	yes
Monk, Israel	1283	Barry, Redmond Dillion	Sumner	640	3042	8 Jun 1797	4061	29 Mar 1797	90	315	On 32 Mile Creek	yes
Monk, Notingham	2070	Ryan, Thomas	Davidson	274	2212	20 May 1793	1272		81	171	On W Fork of Lick Creek	yes
Montflorence	92	Cooley, Samuel	Davidson	1428	78	14 Mar 1786	397		63	32	On both sides of Red River	yes
Montflorence, James Cole	852	Batchelor, George	Davidson	640	858	17 Jan 1789	1870		63	299	On S side of Cumberland River	yes
Montflorence, James Cole	852	Batchelor, George heirs	Davidson	640	858	17 Jan 1789	1879		63	299	On South side of Cumberland River	yes
Montflorence, James Cole	92	Cooley, Samuel	Davidson	1428	78	14 Mar 1786	397		63	32	On both sides of Red River	yes
Montford, Henry	77		Middle District	5000	79	10 Jul 1788	1143	21 Oct 1783	67	449	On the S side of Duck River &c	
Montfort, Joseph	88		Davidson	3840	74	14 Mar 1786	340		63	30	On Main E Fork of Stones River	yes
Montgomery & Armstrong	017		Davidson	640	175	8 Dec 1787	147	16 Jan 1784			N side of Cumberland River	
Montgomery, Alexander	184		Hawkins	300	117	16 Nov 1790	1747	26 Mar 1785	77	189	On the S side of Holston River &c	
Montgomery, Alexander	673		Sumner	228	2004	20 May 1793	3632	29 Aug 1792	81	125	On the waters of Drakes Creek	yes
Montgomery, Alexander	845		Green	450	826	13 Feb 1791	2017	10 Oct 1780	73	377	On the waters of Long Creek	
Montgomery, Jas.	1219	Armstrong, Martin	Sumner	300	191	27 Aug 1795			89	408	On S side of Cumberland River	
Montgomery, Michael	1036		Hawkins	640	785	22 Feb 1797	776	1 May 1781	90	7857	S bank of Holston River	
Montgomery, Michael	12		Sumner	640	769	11 Jul 1788	1625		63	270	On waters of Collins River	
Montgomery, Michael	4		Sumner	228	761	11 Jul 1788	1653	9 Feb 1787	63	267	On waters of Collins River	yes
Montgomery, Michael	1136	Bowen, Henry	Hawkins	640	854	24 Dec 1798	147	18 Feb 1780	97	302	On the head of Barren Creek	yes
Montgomery, Robert	1193		Davidson	640	170	17 Apr 1786	93	14 Jan 1784	66	190	On the Wt Fork of Bledsoes Creek &c	
Montgomery, Samuel	907		Green	220	894	31 Oct 1791	1142	27 Jan 1779	75	121	On N side of French Broad River	
Montgomery, William	1277		Davidson	640	242	10 Jul 1788	483	9 Jun 1784	66	422	On the S side of Cumberland River	
Montgomery, William	622	Gimmerson, William	Davidson	640	594	15 Sep 1787	1168		63	212	On S side of Cumberland River	yes
Montgomery, William	881		Washington	33		13 Feb 1791	2632	5 Sep 1780	73	382	On the waters of Big Limestone	
Montgomery, William, Ass	1227		Sumner	400	175	27 Aur 1795	95		89	413	On Drakes Creek	yes
Montgomery, Wm.	1085		Davidson	640	59	17 Apr 1786	95	14 Jan 1784	66	54	Lying on both sides of Drakes Creek &c	
Moodey, Andrew	110		Hawkins	100	144	26 Dec 1791			75	161	In Carters Valley	
Mooney, George	102		Eastern District	199	91	17 Nov 1790	1856	6 Oct 1779	76	173	On S side of Holston River	
Moor, Jas.	558		Green	130	238	20 Sep 1787	856	29 Oct 1783	66	153	On the N side of Holston River &c	
Moor, William	0101	Owens, David & Francis	Sumner	640			3712				Head forks of Woolf River	yes
Moore, Alexander	480		Green	400	482	20 Sep 1787	177	22 Oct 1783	65	512	On Meadow Creek	
Moore, Alexander	719		Sullivan	81	664	4 Dec 1794	190	21 Feb 1780	84	168	Beg at Aquilla Lanes corner	
Moore, Ann	931		Green	200	845	17 Nov 1790	648	28 Oct 1783	76	120	On Cedar Creek	
Moore, Ann	887		Washington	240	864	27 Nov 1789	949	2 Jan 1779	74	35	Beg at a white oak	
Moore, Anne	644		Washington	191	738	26 Oct 1786	949	2 Jan 1779	66	29	Beg at a white oak &c	
Moore, Anthony	044		Washington	100			1446	21 Jun 1779			On head of Francis Holleys Creek	
Moore, Anthony	077		Washington	200			2875	29 Jun 1781				
Moore, Anthony	1034		Green	200	1261	29 Jul 1793	2875	29 Jun 1781	76	490	On the headwaters of Stones Creek	
Moore, Anthony	1220		Green	150	1220	May 1792	2597	25 May 1784	77	407	N side of Chuckey River	
Moore, Anthony	82		Green	100	40	1 Nov 1786	1445	21 Jun 1779	59	401	On head of Storeys Creek	
Moore, Anthony	82		Green	100	40	1 Nov 1786	1445	21 Jun 1779	59	401	On head of Storeys Creek	
Moore, Arthur	1208		Green	640	1052	Mar 1792	883	29 Oct 1783	77	241	On Tuckahoe Creek	

Earliest Tennessee Land Records

Claimant:	File #:	Assignee:	County:	Acres:	Grant:	Grant Date:	Entry:	Entry Date:	Bk:	Pg:	Location by Stream Name:	Military:
Moore, Benjamin	392		Hawkins	100	513	27 Jan 1793	2092	13 Jun 1784	79	495	Beg at a white oak	
Moore, Daniel	0100	Mitchell, Samuel	Sumner	228			4100	21 Jun 1797			On Johnstons Creek	yes
Moore, Davis John	1041	Easton, James	Sumner	640	2703	27 Mar 1796	3969	11 Mar 1795	88	257	On waters of the Caney Fork	yes
Moore, Demsey	1381		Sumner	780	3243	24 Nov 1797	233	13 Jul 1797	94	177	Between two creeks	yes
Moore, Elijah	159	Moore, William	Tennessee	3840	1416	20 Dec 1791	32		77	355	On both sides of Duck River	yes
Moore, Elijah	44		Davidson	3840	30	14 Mar 1786	234		63	12	On both sides of Duck River	yes
Moore, Elizabeth	034		Hawkins	640	1116	7 Jul 1794	15	24 Feb 1778			Beg at lower end and Island in Tennessee River	
Moore, Elizabeth	1158		Washington	640	1116	7 Jul 1794			81	616	Beg at lower end of an island	
Moore, Freeman	634	Robertson, James	Tennessee	640	3198	14 Sep 1797	4375	22 Dec 1796	90	442	On the Ironwork's fork	yes
Moore, Isaac	597		Davidson	3840	569	15 Sep 1787	1086		63	204	On the first large creek	yes
Moore, James	0137		Green	200	1169	12 Jan 1793	360	7 Jun 1784			Beg at 2 black oaks	
Moore, James	049	McCall, Alex	Middle District	2560			545					yes
Moore, James	1168		Washington	200	1126	7 Jul 1794	1408	24 May 1779	81	619	On Bushey Creek	
Moore, James	1198		Green	640	1042	Mar 1792	1048	1 Oct 1779	77	337	Head of Limestone Fork of Tuckahoe Creek	
Moore, James	1199		Green	250	1043	Mar 1792	1322	10 Jan 1784	77	337	Near the lead mines	
Moore, James	1258		Davidson	640	223	10 Jul 1788	533	19 Jul 1784	66	417	On the Et side of Mill Creek	
Moore, James	1319		Green	200	1169	12 Jan 1793	2021	26 Oct 1779	78	405	On head of Emmanuels (?) branch	
Moore, James	2005	McCrory, Thomas	Davidson	230	1949	20 May 1793	1445		81	112	Beg at a dogwood	yes
Moore, James	2114		Davidson	12000	2372	20 May 1793	23		81	206	On Harpeth River beg at a post oak	yes
Moore, James	212		Green	200	169	20 Sep 1789	857	29 Oct 1783	65	420	Below the mouth of Mossey Creek &c	
Moore, James	232		Washington	300	100	23 Oct 1782	979	2 Jan 1779	47	49	On Little Sinking Creek	
Moore, James	314	Thompson, Robt & Jac Jon	Eastern District	228	2486	18 Aug 1795	3764		87	509	On S side of Holston River	yes
Moore, James	340		Washington	300	207	24 Oct 1782	511	17 Oct 1778	49	229	On Little Limestone	
Moore, James	389		Hawkins	382	510	27 Jan 1793	1332	22 Nov 1783	79	494	On Long Fork of Buffalow	
Moore, James	89		Hawkins	100	81	13 Feb 1791	348	12 Jul 1780	74	287	On Upper Fork of Possums Creek	
Moore, Jas & Ephraim Murry	1263		Washington	150	1201	4 Dec 1795	2534	25 Dec 1794	89	325	On waters of Cherokee	
Moore, John	425	Templeton, Thomas	Tennessee	428	2485	31 Dec 1793	1644	14 Apr 1785	81	438	On Sulphur Fork of Red River	
Moore, John	461		Green	100	463	20 Sep 1787	36	22 Oct 1783	65	505	On the S side of Nolachucky River	
Moore, John	564		Washington	50	829	11 Jul 1788	2880	2 Jul 1781	64	336	On the N side of Watauga River	
Moore, Joseph	432		Sullivan	150	311	10 Nov 1784	536	29 Apr 1780	69	180	On S bank of Holstein River	
Moore, Joseph	529		Sullivan	260	532	13 Feb 1791	190	21 Feb 1780	73	380	On the big Bend of Holstein River &c	
Moore, Marmaduke	2230	Molley, Thomas	Davidson	640	2591	7 Mar 1793	975		88	322	On Harpeth River	yes
Moore, Morris	1856	Weakley, Robert	Davidson	640	1581	27 Apr 1793	1092(?)	22 Apr 1794	81	13	On S side of Cumberland River	yes
Moore, Moses	078		Green	200			1479	22 Apr 1794			N side of Noleychuckey River	
Moore, Moses	1053		Washington	200	1003	27 Nov 1792	355	5 Sep 1778	80	177	On the waters of Big Limestone &c	
Moore, Moses	353	Gerard, Charles	Tennessee	640	2181	20 May 1793	3050	26 Nov 1785	81	166	On S side of Cumberland River	yes
Moore, Moses	475		Washington	431	467	13 Oct 1783	354	5 Sep 1778	52	297	On the waters of Big Limestone &c	
Moore, Nicholas	649	Allen, Alexander	Davidson	640	622	15 Sep 1787	2136		63	221	E side of Sulphur Fork	yes
Moore, Peter	1110		Washington	100	1065	27 Jun 1793	1250	27 Feb 1779	80	391	On the N Fork of Kendricks Creek	
Moore, Robert	1094		Davidson	640	68	17 Apr 1786	379	30 Mar 1784	66	57	Beg at 3 Black oaks	
Moore, Samuel	1129		Davidson	640	106	17 Apr 1786	631	8 Dec 1784	66	176	On the W Fork of Harpeth River	
Moore, Samuel	1191		Davidson	640	168	17 Apr 1786	381		66	190	Forked cottonwood & sycamore on river	
Moore, Samuel	1325		Green	200	1175	12 Jan 1793	1778		78	410	On Little Sinking Creek	
Moore, Samuel	1966	Rice, John & Harriett	Davidson	640	1843	20 May 1793	1469	15 Jul 1779	81	88	On S side of Cumberland River	yes
Moore, Samuel	729		Washington	150	543	10 Nov 1784			69	119	Near the head of Little Sinking Creek	

Claimant:	File #:	Assignee:	County:	Acres:	Grant:	Grant Date:	Entry:	Entry Date:	Bk:	Pg:	Location by Stream Name:	Military:
Moore, Samuel	796		Washington	100	610	10 Nov 1784	1470	1 Jul 1779	69	141	On Little Sinking Creek	
Moore, Thomas	6	Rawls, Gabriel	Robertson	228	3408	10 Feb 1804	185	9 Dec 1800	118	298	On N side of Cumberland	
Moore, William	1181		Washington	100	1139	7 Jul 1794	2137	5 Nov 1779	81	622	On Roans Creek	
Moore, William	1235		Davidson	640	200	10 Jul 1788	45	1 Jan 1784	66	412	On the waters of Stones River	
Moore, William	1389		Davidson	100	6	8 Oct 1787			68	150	On the N side of Cumberland River	
Moore, William	2064	Mason, Aquilla	Davidson	640	2189	20 May 1793	1248		81	168	On Duck River	yes
Moore, William	2394		Davidson	274	320	29 Dec 1796		30 Aug 1785	91	297	N side of Cumberland River	
Moore, William	286		Western District	1320	275	25 Apr 1789	589	27 oct 1783	72	82	On the waters of Big Hatcher River &c	
Moore, William	441		Green	100	443	20 Sep 1787	1450	2 Jun 1779	65	500	On Holleys Creek of Nolachucky	
Moore, William	542		Green	300	544	20 Sep 1787	202	22 Oct 1783	65	538	On Meadow Creek	
Moore, William	6		Smith	1280	3364	14 Nov 1800	7	11 Aug 1800	108	205	On the waters of Jennings Creek	
Moore, William	679	Owens, Francis	Hawkins	640	2389	12 Jul 1794			81	602	On Head Fork of Woolf River	
Moore, William	884		Washington	358	869	16 Nov 1790	611	23 Nov 1779	73	398	On the N side of Noleychuckay River	
Moore, William , Ass	766		Sumner	1000	2200	20 May 1793	3	19 Dec 1792	81	168	On S branches of E Fork of Stones River	yes
Moore, Wm.	159	Moore, Elijah	Tennessee	3840	1416	25 Dec 1791	32		77	355	On both sides of Duck River	
Moore, Wm. & Thos. Hutchin	754		Green	2000	573	11 Jul 1788	1443	21 Jan 1784	68	216	On the NW side of Clinch River	
Moran, John	2062	Standen, John	Davidson	503	2176	20 May 1793	3688		81	167	On SW side of Big Harpeth River	yes
Moran, John	810	Buel, Ambrose (heir)	Sumner	1000	2277	20 May 1793	2070	24 Nov 1792	81	186	On S side of Cumberland River	yes
More, Benjamin	043	Foster, Anthony	Not Given	640			3051	19 Dec 1792			On waters of Stones River	yes
Morefield, John	119		Sullivan	177	131	23 Oct 1782	788	26 Dec 1778	43	320	On the mouth of Horse Creek	
Morehead, James	639		Tennessee	944	2794	20 Dec 1796	1187		91	469	N side of Cumberland River	
Moreland, William	1300		Washington	100	1186	4 Dec 1795	2120	4 Nov 1779	89	429	On Rones Creek	
Morgan, Adonijah	1232		Green	200	1082	12 Jan 1793	515	2 Apr 1792	78	353	Beg at a double white oak	
Morgan, Adonijah	1427		Green	200	1239	27 Nov 1792	514	19 Oct 1778	80	167	Beg at four white oaks	
Morgan, Bennet	1733		Davidson	850-1/2	1455	20 Dec 1791	360		77	365	On the waters of Hay's Creek	yes
Morgan, Charles	289		Sullivan	640	428	9 Aug 1787	2231	20 Nov 1779	61	447	In Powells Valley &c	
Morgan, Griffin	1525	Frazer, George	Davidson	640	1082	26 Nov 1789	2492		74	121	On N side of Cumberland River	yes
Morgan, Hardy	188	Beaird, Joseph	Eastern District	640	1659	15 Jul 1793	2467		81	43	Beg at a walnut	yes
Morgan, Humphrey	2145	Robertson, James	Davidson	640	2429	31 Dec 1793	2468	27 Apr 1784	81	409	On both sides of Big Harpeth River	yes
Morgan, Isaac, Ass	839		Sumner	640	2341	20 May 1793	3043	5 Jun 1788	81	200	On S side of Cumberland River	yes
Morgan, Jacob	516	Robertson, Elijah	Davidson	640	488	15 Sep 1787	2209		63	177	N side of Cumberland River	yes
Morgan, James	070	Sheppard, John	Not given	640			2862	15 Aug 1792			On Obeys River	yes
Morgan, Jno	1164		Davidson	640	141	17 Apr 1786	423	29 Apr 1784	66	184	On the Dry Fork of Bledsoes Creek	
Morgan, Lewis	203	Hart, Anthony	Sumner	640	1108	26 Nov 1789	2860	12 Mar 1788	74	133	On headwaters of a large creek	yes
Morgan, Peter	1917	Phillips, Jonathan	Davidson	352	1706	20 May 1793	3656		81	55	On N side of Mill Creek	yes
Morgan, Richard	1033		Green	300	1260	29 Jul 1793	1744	27 Apr 1784	76	490	N side of French Broad River &c	
Morgan, Richard	1055		Green	100	241	26 Dec 1790	87	15 Feb 1789	77	241	On the waters of Dumplin Creek	
Morgan, Richard	1143	Harris, Edward	Sumner	640	2649	4 Jun 1796	1400	1 Jun 1795	88	350	Joining Harris survey	yes
Morgan, Thomas	1050		Green	50	893	26 Dec 1791	2283	27 Nov 1779	77	239	S side of Nolachuckey River on Camp Creek	
Morgan, William	1355	Barry, Redmond D.	Sumner	640	2778	10 Oct 1796	2860	12 Aug 1796	91	23	On Martins Creek	
Morgan, William	582		Sullivan	100	580	29 Jul 1793	1181	3 Feb 1779	76	473	N side of Holston River &c	
Morgan, William	635	Sellers, Matthew	Tennessee	640	2780	17 Oct 1796	3769		91	23	On the main W Fork of Red River	yes
Morgan, William	666	Berry, Thomas	Davidson	274	639	15 Nov 1787	1398	16 Oct 1779	63	227	On small creek emptying into Tennessee	yes
Morison, Peter	198		Sullivan	630	205	10 Oct 1783	1984	24 Nov 1778	53	160	On the N side of Holston River	yes
Morral, John	045		Washington	400			624				On Sinking Creek	

Claimant:	File #:	Assignee:	County:	Acres:	Grant:	Grant Date:	Entry:	Entry Date:	Bk:	Pg:	Location by Stream Name:	Military:
Morrason, Peter	508		Sullivan	510	526	7 Apr 1790	1984	19 Oct 1779	71	288	On the Plumb Branch	
Morrel, John	045		Washington	400			624	24 Nov 1778			On Sinking Creek	
Morrel, John	242		Sullivan	87	381	9 Aug 1787	885	31 Dec 1778	61	400	On the S side of Holston Roiver	
Morris, Benjamin	041		Middle District	640			1476				Assn. To Armstrong & Donelson	yes
Morris, Drewy	784		Washington	100	598	10 Nov 1784	1775	1 Oct 1779	69	137	On Middle Fork of Cedar Creek	
Morris, Drury	147		Washington	199	15	23 Oct 1782	360	5 Sep 1778	47	7	Including a big spring &c	
Morris, Drury	233		Washington	97	101	23 Oct 1782	361	5 Sep 1778	47	49	On Cedar Creek	
Morris, Drury	910		Washington	100 (50)	887	17 Nov 1790	2225	16 Nov 1779	76	140	On Cedar Creek	
Morris, Gideon	095		Washington	200			1727	25 Sep 1779				
Morris, Gideon	259		Washington	198	127	23 Oct 1782	641	25 Nov 1778	47	62	On a branch of Lick Creek	
Morris, Gideon	474		Green	400	476	20 Sep 1787	198	22 Oct 1783	65	510	On a branch of Holsten River &c	
Morris, Gideon	83		Hawkins	200	75	13 Feb 1791	1425	1779	74	284	On N side of Holstein River	
Morris, James	1263	Hickman, Thomas	Sumner	640	2939	1 Mar 1797	3309	11 May 1795	90	212	N side of Cumberland River	yes
Morris, James	189	Beaird, Joseph	Eastern Dist	640	1660	15 Jul 1793	3777		81	44	Beg at two Buckeyes	yes
Morris, John	1566		Green	100	1312	6 Jan 1795	2687	11 Dec 1780	83	158	N side of Nolachuckey River	
Morris, John	283		Green	100	285	20 Sep 1787	50	10 May 1784	65	454	Beg at white oak corner to James Hawkins	
Morris, John	326	Foster, Anthony	Sumner	640	2579	23 Feb 1793	1745	4 Oct 1785	76	303	S side of Cumberland River	yes
Morris, John & James	087	Hickman, Thomas	Sumner	640			1477	14 Sep 1796			N side of Cumberland River	yes
Morris, Philamon	1954	Harget, Frederick	Davidson	274	1794	20 May 1793	577		81	78	On S side of Cumberland River	yes
Morris, Phillip	2345	Malloy, Thomas	Davidson	640	2990	10 Apr 1797	3638		90	289	On Harpeth River	yes
Morris, Richard	674	Donelson, Stockley	Hawkins	250	2384	12 Jul 1794			81	600	In Hinds Valley	yes
Morris, Shadrack	322		Washington	200	322	24 Oct 1782	1162	1 Feb 1779	43	307	On the head of said Morris Spring Branch	
Morris, Shadrack	337		Washington	598 (298	204	24 Oct 1782	1161	1 Feb 1779	49	228	On the waters of Lick Creek	
Morris, Shadrack	350		Washington	299	217	24 Oct 1782	1128	25 Jan 1779	49	233	On a branch of Lick Creek	
Morris, William	097	Marshall, John	Sumner	640			2277	21 Jan 1787			Beg in the VA line &c	yes
Morris, William	138	Brown, James	Davidson	640	124	14 Mar 1786	1065		63	48	On a creek S side of Sulphur Fork	yes
Morris, William	2471	Hamilton, Jno	Davidson	1000	3405	3 Dec 1803	3277		118	139	On N side of Sulphur Fork	yes
Morrison, Alexander	766	Moore, William	Sumner	1000	2200	20 May 1793	3	19 Dec 1792	81	168	On S branches of E Fork of Stones River	yes
Morrison, James	555		Sullivan	100	538	17 Nov 1790	581	3 May 1780	76	191	On the waters of Beech Creek	
Morrison, Joel	2054	Lewis, William Terrel	Davidson	640	2143	20 May 1793	3132		81	159	On the waters of Stones River	yes
Morrison, Michael	162		Hawkins	200	95	16 Nov 1790	270	22 Oct 1783	77	183	On the N side of Holston River &c	
Morrison, Michael	351		Sullivan	300	230	10 Nov 1784	133	12 Feb 1780	69	156	On N side of Holston River	
Morrison, Michael	547		Hawkins	250	420	29 Jul 1793	1003	29 Oct 1783	80	282	On the N side of Holston River &c	
Morrison, Patrick	474		Sullivan	300	353	10 Nov 1784	661	26 Jul 1780	69	197	On N side of Garrotts Branch	
Morrison, Patrick	904		Washington	200	881	17 Nov 1790	2226	16 Nov 1779	76	138	On Lick Creek &c	
Morrison, Peter	196		Sullivan	300	203	10 Oct 1783	299,-1985	1779,-1780	53	150	On the N side of Holston River	
Morrison, Peter	198		Sullivan	630	205	10 Oct 1783	1984	16 Oct 1779	53	160	On the N side of Holston River	
Morrison, Peter	218		Sullivan	80	225	10 Oct 1783	529	29 Apr 1780	53	168	On the E side of the North Fork of Holston	
Morrison, Peter	508		Sullivan	510	526	7 Apr 1790	1984	19 Oct 1779	71	288	On the Plumb Branch	
Morrison, Robert	1635	Morrison, Thos.	Davidson	640	1369	30 Nov 1792			74	393	Headwaters of W Fork of Cedar Lick Creek	yes
Morrison, Robert	256	Mayfield, Sutterline	Davidson	640	242	7 Mar 1786	641		63	89	E Fork of Mill Creek	yes
Morrison, Thomas	1376		Green	600	1231	27 Jan 1793	990	29 Oct 1783	79	507	On a creek on N side of Clinch Mountain	
Morrison, Thomas	601		Sullivan	53.5	556	26 Dec 1791	564	31 Oct 1778	77	305	In an Island of Holston River	
Morrison, Thos.	1635	Morrison, Robt.	Davidson	640	1369	30 Nov 1792			74	393	Headwaters of W Fork of Cedar Lick Creek	yes
Morrison, William	1142		Davidson	640	119	17 Apr 1786	564		66	???	On the waters of Rockey Creek	yes

Claimant:	File #:	Assignee:	County:	Acres:	Grant:	Grant Date:	Entry:	Entry Date:	Bk:	Pg:	Location by Stream Name:	Military:
Morriss, John	326	Foster, Anthony	Sumner	640	1579	23 Feb 1793	1745	4 Oct 1785	76	303	S side of Cumberland River	yes
Morrow, Alexander	115		Washington	300	283	24 Oct 1782	809	28 Dec 1778	44	289	On head of Big Limestone Creek	
Morrow, Andrew & John	362		Hawkins	640	355	8 Mar 1793	449	10 Sep 1785	78	487	On S side of Clinch River	
Morrow, John & James	1395		Sumner	640	3322	6 Dec 1797	1391	13 Mar 1797	97	45	On the head of N Fork of Red River	yes
Morrow, Samuel	761	Bowman, William	Davidson	640	734	11 Jul 1788	2531		63	258	W & N side of land Wm Harrison lives on	yes
Morrow, Thomas	207	Dickson, James	Tennessee	640	1497	4 Jan 1792	3657	10 Dec 1788	77	375	S side of Cumberland River	yes
Morrow, William	1746		Green	200	365	4 Jul 1797			91	599	Joining a survey of 327 acres	
Morrow, William	452		Green	170	454	20 Sep 1787	858	30 Dec 1778	65	502	On the S side of Nolachuckey River	
Morrow, William	526		Green	327	528	20 Sep 1787	139	21 Oct 1783	65	531	Beg at a post oak on Richland Creek	
Morrow, Wm.	900		Green	400	831	Sep 1790	1556	29 Aug 1779	74	293	Incl. Cross roads on the waters of 9 Mile	
Morrow, John	1035		Green	100	1262	29 Jul 1793	2671	28 Nov 1780	76	490	N side of French Broad River	
Morrows, John	1391		Sumner	640	3317	6 Dec 1797	1045	25 Oct 1796	97	41	On the head of the first big branch	yes
Morthrell, John	2324	Armstrong, M.	Davidson	49.5	348	1 Mar 1787			90	224	N side of Cumberland River	
Morton, Jones	1656	White, James	Davidson	274	1572	23 Feb 1793	1940		76	299	N side of Cumberland River &c	yes
Morton, William	909	Williams, Willoughby	Davidson	1000	925	18 May 1789			63	318	On waters of Caney Fork	
Moseley, John	293		Washington	49.5	160	24 Oct 1782	1342	16 Apr 1779	47	77	On a branch of Cedar Creek	
Moseley, Samuel	1107		Davidson	640	81	17 Apr 1786	443	12 May 1784	66	61	On both sides of Cedar Lick Creek &c	
Moses, Mayer	083		Middle District	2000	1777	23 Apr 1784					On both sides of the Middle Fork of Elk River	
Moses, Mayer	086		Middle District	3000			1774	23 Apr 1784			On Middle Fork of Elk River	
Mosier, Fran & B Robinson	1537	Saunders, James	Davidson	914	1094	26 Nov 1789	2299,-1249		74	128	On N side of Cumberland River	yes
Mosier, Samuel	586	Smith, Daniel	Davidson	640	558	15 Sep 1787	2300		63	200	S side of Cumberland River	yes
Mosland, John	889	Brooks, Stephen	Davidson	640	905	17 Jan 1789	3515		63	313	On waters of Stones River	yes
Moslander, Abel	026	Armstrong, John	Middle District	2560			851					yes
Mosley, Demsey	646	Sugg, Noah	Sumner	640	1940	20 May 1793	1887	29 Nov 1792	81	109	On the N boundary of Alex. McClure	yes
Mosley, Joseph	1426	Lyttle, William	Sumner	640	3300	6 Dec 1797	1020	13 Jun 1796	98	174	On the waters of Big Cedar Lick Creek	yes
Mosley, Joseph	2456		Davidson	640	464	9 Dec 1799	255	9 Feb 1784	103	446	S side of Cumberland River	
Mosley, Samuel	1285		Davidson	640	250	10 Jul 1788	445	12 May 1784	66	425	On branch of the Sulphur Fork of Red River	
Mosley, Samuel	1288		Davidson	640	253	10 Jul 1788	446	12 May 1784	66	426	On the Sulphur Fork of Red River &c	
Mosley, Samuel	1749		Davidson	320	106	20 Dec 1791	444	12 May 1784	77	382	On the headwaters of Hays Creek	
Moss, William	429		Middle District	5000	368	17 Dec 1794	1435	27 Jan 1784	84	238	On W Fork of Cane Creek	
Mosuire, Francis	817	Lewis, William T.	Sumner	640	2292	20 May 1793	3091	27 Nov 1792	81	189	On Magness Fork of Bledsoes Creek	yes
Motheral, John, Ass	887		Davidson	640	2417	7 Jan 1794	2378	19 Dec 1792	81	405	On waters of E Fork of Gooses Creek	yes
Motheral, Samuel	1723	Williams, Peter heirs	Davidson	640	1420	20 Dec 1791			77	356	S/S Cumberland waters of Spencers Creek	yes
Motheral, Joseph, Ass	1262		Sumner	640	2938	1 Mar 1797	2381	22 Oct 1791	90	212	On an Eastern branch of Spencers Creek	yes
Motherell, John, Ass	886		Sumner	640	2413	7 Jan 1791	2198	19 Dec 1792	81	403	On ridge of head of Seeder(sic) Lick Creek	yes
Motherill, John	1747		Davidson	40	113	20 Dec 1791			77	381	On a branch of Whites Creek	
Motherill, John, Ass.	265		Sumner	228	1225	10 Mar 1790	1826	9 Mar 1790	74	340	On N side of Cumberland River	yes
Motherill, Samuel	0102	Tusson, Charles	Sumner	640			2245	13 Mar 1787			S side of Cumberland River	yes
Mott, Abraham heirs	042	Hughlett, William	Middle District	640			2138					yes
Mott, Benjamin	615	Toomer, Henry	Tennessee	1000	3174	14 Sep 1797	889		90	431	S side of Cumberland River	yes
Mott, Daniel	209	Dickson, Edward	Tennessee	640	1499	4 Jan 1790	3723	23 Nov 1790	77	375	S side of Cumberland River	yes
Mott, Daniel	363	Vann, William	Sumner	640	1508	4 Jan 1792	3730	18 Nov 1791	77	378	S side of Cumberland River &c	yes
Mott, Edge	793	McNees, John	Davidson	640	796	23 Aug 1788	2938		63	279	On N side of Cumberland River	yes
Mountflorence & Fenner	241		Sumner	228	1146	26 Nov 1789	1599	11 Jun 1789	74	152	Bet. Middle Fork & N Fork of Red River	yes
Mountflorence, James	293	Monhouse, Daniel heirs	Davidson	640	279	22 Mar 1787	2044		63	102	North side of Cumberland River	yes

Claimant:	File #:	Assignee:	County:	Acres:	Grant:	Grant Date:	Entry:	Entry Date:	Bk:	Pg:	Location by Stream Name:	Military:
Mountflorence, James C	864	Griffis, Samuel	Davidson	1000	878	17 Jan 1789	2125		63	304	On Weakleys Creek	yes
Mountflorence, James Cole	1498	Boone, James heirs	Davidson	640	1055	26 Nov 1789	1493		74	104	On N side of Cumberland River	yes
Mountflorence, James Cole	1499	Griffin, Edward heirs	Davidson	640	1056	26 Nov 1789	2183		74	105	On N side of Cumberland River	yes
Mountflorence, James Cole	1500	Bowman, Robert heirs	Davidson	640	1057	26 Nov 1789	3035		74	100(?)	On N side of Cumberland River	yes
Mountflorence, James Cole	1580	Powell, John	Davidson	228	1241	10 Dec 1790	1289		74	245	On south west side of Harpeth	yes
Mountflorence, James Cole	242		Sumner	274	1147	26 Nov 1790	1285	23 Mar 1789	74	152	On N side of Cumberland River	yes
Mountflorence, James Cole	287		Sumner	1000	1290	10 Dec 1790	3391	12 Jun 1787	74	362	On N side of Cumberland River	yes
Mountflorence, James Cole	294	Sims, Thomas, heirs of	Davidson	640	280	22 Mar 1787	2057		63	103	Beg at a red oak & two sugar trees	yes
Mountflorence, James Cole	295	Hawkins, Joseph heirs	Davidson	640	281	22 Mar 1787	2098		63	103	South side of Cumberland River	yes
Mountflorence, James Cole	296	Mars, Timothy heirs	Davidson	640	282	22 Mar 1787	2094		63	104	South side of Cumberland River	yes
Mountflorence, James Cole	297	Polk, John	Davidson	1000	283	22 Mar 1787	2149		63	104	Beg at a small sugar tree and elm	yes
Mountflorence, James Cole	298	Nelson, John heirs	Davidson	640	284	22 Mar 1787	2062		63	105	South side of Cumberland River	yes
Mountflorence, James Cole	299	Lawson, William heirs	Davidson	640	285	22 Mar 1787	2054		63	105	North side of Cumberland River	yes
Mountflorence, James Cole	300	Norvell, William	Davidson	640	286	22 Mar 1787	2097		63	106	South side of Cumberland River	yes
Mountflorence, James Cole	301	Hutchins, Robert	Davidson	640	287	22 Mar 1787	2033		63	107	South side of Cumberland River	yes
Mountflorence, James Cole	326	Collins, Samuel heirs	Davidson	640	312	28 Jun 1787	2176		63	116	North side of Cumberland River	yes
Mountflorence, James Cole	327	Cobb, Peter heirs	Davidson	640	313	28 Jun 1787	2175		63	116	South side of Cumberland River	yes
Mountflorence, James Cole	332 (333)	Britt, Sherrard heirs	Davidson	640	319	28 Jun 1787	2169		63	119	South side of Sulphur Fork	yes
Mountflorence, James Cole	34		Sumner	640	857	17 Jan 1789	2184	19 Mar 1788	63	299	On S side of Cumberland River	yes
Mountflorence, James Cole	34		Sumner	640	857	17 Jan 1789	2184	10 Mar 1788	63	299	On S side of Cumberland River	yes
Mountflorence, James Cole	40		Sumner	640	872	17 Jan 1789	1480	17 May 1788	63	303	On N side of Cumberland River	yes
Mountflorence, James Cole	41		Sumner	640	873	17 Jan 1789	1481	17 May 1788	63	303	On waters of Red River	yes
Mountflorence, James Cole	6		Tennessee	1000	1154	26 Nov 1789	3556	1 Aug 1787	74	150	On N side of Cumberland River	
Mountflorence, James Cole	7		Tennessee	640	1155	26 Nov 1789	2120	9 Sep 1785	63	156	On N side of Sulphur Fork of Red River	
Mountflorence, James Cole	777	Brown, Jesse heirs	Davidson	1000	750	11 Jul 1788	2112		63	263	On E side of W Fork of Station Camp Cree	yes
Mountflorence, James Cole	8		Tennessee	640	1156	26 Nov 1789	2131	9 Sep 1785	74	157	On N side of Sulphur Fork	Yes
Mountflorence, James Cole	859	Reaves, Benjamin heirs	Davidson	1000	869	17 Jan 1787	2153		63	302	On Weakley Creek	yes
Mountflorence, James Cole	859		Tennessee	640	1156	26 Nov 1789	2131	9 Sep 1785	74	157	On N side of Sulphur Fork	
Moveal, Henry	1176	Harris, Edward	Sumner	640	2661	4 Jun 1796	2748	1 Jun 1795	88	361	Joining said Harris	yes
Moys, Gardner	303	Breakey, Andrew	Davidson	428	289	3 May 1787	1324		63	108	On Gilkersons Creek	yes
Moys, George	606	Bonner, John & James	Davidson	228	578	15 Sep 1787	380		63	207	On S side of Cumberland River	yes
Moys, John	1180	Harris, Edward	Sumner	2560	2684	4 Jun 1796	1877	1 Jun 1795	88	363	Joining said Harris	yes
Muckleroy, John	616	Benton, Jesse	Sumner	274	1881	20 May 1793	3129	19 Dec 1792	81	96	On the Otter Fork of Bledsoes Creek	yes
Mulaby, John	229		Hawkins	300	216	2 Dec 1791	171	19 Feb 1780	77	319	On the S side of Holston River	
Mulanin, Richard	1737		Green	100	1388	2 Dec 1796	6	3 Jun 1780	91	271	On a branch of Lick Creek	
Mulford, Portis	413	Nelson, Robert	Davidson	640	385	15 Sep 1787	2491		63	144	On Goose Creek	yes
Mulharren, James	1009	Bailey, Ethelred heirs	Davidson	640	1026	18 May 1789			63	343	On Hickmans Creek	yes
Mulheren, James	2130		Davidson	40	149	7 Jan 1794		20 Mar 1792	81	400	S side of Cumberland River	
Mulherin, John	055	Madry, John	Davidson	333			698	19 Sep 1785			S side of Cumberland River	
Mulherin, James	913	Cobb, Anthony heirs	Davidson	640	929	18 May 1789			63	319	On waters of Caney Fork	yes
Mulherin, James	926	Avery, Estridge heirs	Davidson	640	942	18 May 1789			63	323	On Hickmans Creek	yes
Mulherin, James	929	Roberts, Elijah heirs	Davidson	640	945	18 May 1789			63	323	On Hickmans Creek	yes
Mulherin, James	933	Doly, James heirs	Davidson	640	949	18 May 1789			63	324	On waters of Caney Fork	yes
Mulherin, Jno	1031		Davidson	640	5	17 Apr 1786	11	26 Dec 1783	66	35	On Overalls Creek beg at a black walnut	
Mulherran, James	2128		Davidson	100	147	7 Jan 1794		Dec 1792	81	399	On S side of Cumberland River	

Earliest Tennessee Land Records

Claimant:	File #:	Assignee:	County:	Acres:	Grant:	Grant Date:	Entry:	Entry Date:	Bk:	Pg:	Location by Stream Name:	Military:
Mulherren, James	2129		Davidson	60	148	7 Jan 1794		Dec 1792	81	400	On S/S Cumberland River on Otter Creek	
Mulherren, James	2132		Davidson	60	151	7 Jan 1794		20 Mar 1792	81	401	On S side of Cumberland River	
Mulherren, James, Ass	2131		Davidson	200	150	7 Jan 1794		22 Dec 1792	81	400	On the W side of Stones River	
Mulherrin, James	1176		Davidson	640	153	17 Apr 1786	87	14 Jan 1787	66	187	Black oak & honey locust on Cumberland	
Mulherrin, James	2132		Davidson	100	152	7 Jan 1794		20 Mar 1792	81	401	On S side of Cumberland River	
Mulherrin, James	2135	Roberts, Elijah heirs	Davidson	640	2409	7 Jan 1794	3319		81	402	On S side of Cumberland River	yes
Mulherrin, James	2136	Rountree, Arthur	Davidson	640	2411	7 Jan 1794	3323		81	403	On S side of Cumberland River	yes
Mulherrin, James	2137	Doty, James	Davidson	640	2412	7 Jan 1794	3306		81	403	On Stones River	yes
Mulherrin, James	2138	Cobbs, Anthony	Davidson	640	2414	7 Jan 1794	3305		81	404	On S side of Cumberland River	yes
Mulherrin, James	2139	Avery, Estridge	Davidson	640	2415	7 Jan 1794	3299		81	404	S/S Cumberland on waters of Mill Creek	yes
Mulherrin, James	2140	Bailey, Ethelred heirs	Davidson	640	2416	7 Jan 1794	3329		81	405	On Stones River	yes
Mulherrin, James	912	Rountree, Arthur	Davidson	640	928	18 May 1789			63	319	On Caney Fork	yes
Mulherrin, James, Ass	2134		Davidson	40	153	7 Jan 1794		Dec 1792	81	401	On S side of Cumberland River	yes
Mulherrin, John,	1420		Davidson	396	37	8 Oct 1787		27 Jun 1785	68	157	On both sides of Mill Creek	
Mulhollan, Thomas	431		Western Dist	500	430	7 Dec 1797	454	25 Oct 1783	96	18	S side of Tennessee River	
Mulinix, Richard	1736		Green	50	1387	2 Dec 1796	580	3 Jun 1780	91	271	On Lick Creek	
Mulinix, Richard	1738		Green	35	1389	2 Dec 1796	580	1 Jun 1780	91	272	On Lick Creek	
Mulkey, William (or John)	153	Robertson, J. & Alex Greer	Tennessee	640	1407	20 Dec 1791	2810	30 Sep 1785	77	353	On both sides of Pine River	yes
Mullans, William	1146	Mann, John	Hawkins	200	864	9 Mar 1797 (99	671	19 Aug 1780	100	344	On Little Mulberry Creek	
Mullen, Michael	2435	Gatling, John	Davidson	640			1018		98	150	On a large branch on Harpeth River	yes
Mullen, William	044	Fletcher, Joseph heirs	Not given	365	1168	26 Nov 1789	3342	2 Jan 1786	74	163	On N side of Cumberland River	yes
Mullet, Theodore	20		Tennessee	640	418	15 Sep 1787	13	13 Nov 1780	63	155	South side of Big Harpeth	yes
Mullin, Malone	446		Davidson	228			705	24 Apr 1780			Including plantation where said Mullins	
Mullings, Flour	062		Sullivan	50			459				On a branch of Lick Creek	
Mullinix, Leny [?]	082		Green	50	344	10 Nov 1784	38	26 Feb 1778	69	193	Beg at an old corner Beech tree	
Mullins, John	465		Montgomery	200	3249	6 Dec 1797	4329	20 May 1797	74	363	On Fletchers Fork of Red River	yes
Mullis, James	06	Medearin, John	Sullivan	640	1293	10 Dec 1790	2427		81	191	On N side of Cumberland River	
Mulloys, Thomas, Ass	288		Sumner	228	2301	20 May 1793	2385	19 Nov 1792	74	357	On E side of Caney Fork	
Mundine, Joshua	823	Davis, Joshua	Sumner	640	1275	10 Dec 1790	2383	22 Oct 1785	81	99	On S side of Cumberland River	yes
Mundine, Zebulon	57	Hays, John	Tennessee	640	1896	20 May 1793	1256	21 Dec 1792	70	259	On the ridge & c	yes
Munding, Richard	621	Hays, John	Sumner	274	200	25 Apr 1789	1257		70	261	On the ridge & c	yes
Munford, Robinson	274		Western Dist	5000	302	25 Apr 1789	38	24 Nov 1783	81	507	On the S side of Big Hatcha River	yes
Munford, Robinson	276		Western Dist	5000	242	27 Nov 1793	2098	24 Nov 1783	70	264	On the E side of the Miss River	
Munoe [?], James	278		Middle District	250	306	25 Apr 1789	4257				On the S of Cumberland River	
Munsford, Robinson	280		Western Dist	5000	3284	6 Dec 1797	2528				On the waters of Big Hatcha River &c	
Murbee, Patrick	2442	Tatum, H. & H. Wiggins	Davidson	640	1192	30 Nov 1790	2534	6 May 1784	98	163	On the waters of Overalls Creek	
Murdock, Allen	28	Cockran, William	Tennessee	640	914	18 May 1789	893	30 Sep 1785	74	319	On S side of Cumberland River	yes
Murdock, McCloud	898	Blount, Reading	Davidson	640	229	26 Dec 1791	2294	29 Oct 1783	63	316	On N branch of E Fork of Stones River	yes
Murfey, William	242		Hawkins	200				24 May 1784	77	323	Above road between Brown Cr & Spring Cr	yes
Murfree, Hardy	082		Tennessee	5000			2294				Resolution of Assembly	
Murfree, Hardy	113	Manly, Solomon	Davidson	640	99	14 Mar 1786	141		63	40	On both sides of Spring Creek	
Murfree, Hardy	1991	Leader, John	Davidson	640	1907	20 May 1793	738		81	102	On SW side of Big Harpeth River	yes
Murfree, Hardy	2117	Lewis, Simpson W. heirs	Davidson	640	2380(a)	20 May 1793	150		81	208	On SW side of Big Harpeth River	yes
Murfree, Hardy	248	Perkins, Adam	Davidson	640	234	7 Mar 1786	732		63	86	On a branch of the Fork of Big Creek	yes
Murfree, Hardy	426		Western District	5000	425	6 Dec 1796	2292	25 May 1784	91	281	On N Fork of Obion River	yes

Claimant:	File #:	Assignee:	County:	Acres:	Grant:	Grant Date:	Entry:	Entry Date:	Bk:	Pg:	Location by Stream Name:	Military:
Muffree, Hardy	427		Western District	500	426	6 Dec 1796	2652	25 May 1784	91	286	S side of Obion River	
Muffree, Hardy	428		Western District	5000	427	6 Dec 1796	2293	25 May 1784	91	282	S side of Obions River	
Muffree, Hardy	583	Nichols, Wm. Sr.	Tennessee	640	3030	10 Apr 1797	3567		90	305	Waters of W Fork of Red River	
Muffree, Hardy	82	Winborn, John heirs	Davidson	2560	68	14 Mar 1786	113		63	28	On both sides of Cedar Creek	yes
Muffree, Hardy, Ass	557		Sumner	640	1776	20 May 1793	718	17 Dec 1792	81	93	On S side of Cumberland River	yes
Muffree, Hardy, Ass	886		Sumner	280	2421	7 Jan 1794	1563	23 Aug 1792	81	406	On waters of Drakes Creek	yes
Muffree, Hardy, Ass.	624		Sumner	640	1901	20 May 1793	733	17 Dec 1792	81	100	On S side of Cumberland River &c	yes
Muffree, William Harden	128		Middle District	5000	130	10 Jul 1788	1187	1 Nov 1783	67	472	Lying on the SE side of Richland Creek	
Muffrey, Hardy, Ass	1182		Sumner	320	2696	6 Jun 1796	142	17 Dec 1792	88	369	On S side of Cumberland River	yes
Murphey, Henry	12		Middle District	5000	144	10 Jul 1788	1156	30 Oct 1783	67	413	On the head waters of Harpeth River	
Murphey, Henry	295		Washington	400	162	24 Oct 1782	1114	14 Jul 1779	47	78	On Lick Creek	
Murphey, John	116		Green	640	132	1 Nov 1786	221	22 Oct 1783	59	435	On both sides Lick Creek	
Murphey, John	1506		Green	100	1267	12 Jul 1794			81	584	On Woolf Creek	
Murphey, John	281		Sullivan	100	420	9 Aug 1787	763	24 Mar 1781	61	439	Joining Nathaniel Bormans line &c	yes
Murphey, John	353		Sullivan	100	232	10 Nov 1784	1169	1 Feb 1779	69	157	On a branch of Holston River	
Murphey, Levy	422		Sullivan	100 (150)	301	10 Nov 1784	180	21 Feb 1780	69	177	Near Holstein River	
Murphey, Patrick	916	Whittaker, John	Sumner	640	2487	31 Dec 1793	3076	19 Jul 1788	81	438	On waters of E Fork of Stones River	yes
Murphey, William	1054		Green	150	897	16 Dec 1790	1476	19 Feb 1784	77	241	Beg at a stake on John Evans line	
Murphey, William	126		Washington	130	294	24 Oct 1782	1115	14 Jan 1779	44	295	On both sides Cherokee Creek	
Murphey, William	163		Washington	150	31	23 Oct 1782			47	14	On both sides of Cherokee Creek	
Murphey, William	264		Washington	94	132	23 Oct 1782	625	24 Nov 1778	47	64	N side of Nolachuckey River	
Murphey, William	270		Washington	100	138	23 Oct 1782	632	25 Nov 1778	47	67	N side of Nolachuckey River	
Murphey, William	306		Washington	300	173	24 Oct 1782	1113	14 Jan 1779	47	84	On both sides of Lick Creek	
Murphree, Archibald	648	Dowell, James	Davidson	274	621	15 Sep 1787	197		63	221	On the waters of Drakes Creek	yes
Murphree, Hardy	113	Mahley, Solomon	Davidson	640	99	14 Mar 1786	141		63	40	On both sides of Spring Creek	yes
Murphree, Hardy	148	Archer, Baker	Davidson	640	134	14 Mar 1786			63	52	On waters of Wolf Creek	yes
Murphree, Hardy	159	Holmes, Shadrack	Davidson	228	145	14 Mar 1786	739		63	55	On Eatons Creek	yes
Murphree, Hardy	161	Powell, William	Davidson	440	147	14 Mar 1786	134		63	56	On waters of Wolf Creek	yes
Murphree, Hardy	168	Williams, Theophelus heirs	Davidson	640	154	7 Mar 1786	719		63	58	On both sides of Spring Creek	yes
Murphree, Hardy	183	Harris, John	Davidson	640	169	7 Mar 1786	129		63	64	Joining his tract of 5760 acres	yes
Murphree, Hardy	184	Horton, James	Sumner	640	1901	20 May 1793	733	17 Dec 1792	81	100	On S side of Cumberland River	Yes
Murphree, Hardy	184	Williams, John	Davidson	274	170	7 Mar 1786	721		63	64	On both sides of E Fork Whites Creek	Yes
Murphree, Hardy	244		Davidson	274	230	7 Mar 1786	734		63	84	Headwaters Long Fork of Sycamore Creek	yes
Murphree, Hardy	263		Davidson	914	249	14 Mar 1786	115		63	91	On both sides of Cedar Creek	yes
Murphree, Hardy	519	Wiggins, Matthew	Davidson	274	491	15 Sep 1787	731		63	178	Bet the old & new trace	yes
Murphree, Hardy	53		Davidson	5760	39	14 Mar 1786	107		63	16	On Murphreys Fork	yes
Murphree, Hardy	57	Burton, John	Davidson	1168	43	14 Mar 1786	172		63	18	South side of Cumberland River	yes
Murphrey, Hardy	229	Carter, Robert	Davidson	228	215	7 Mar 1786	736		63	79	Both sides of E Fork of Station Camp Cree	yes
Murphrey, Solomon	836		Washington	150	650	10 Nov 1784	2610	18 Aug 1780	69	152	On E side of a line &c	
Murphy, Archibald	125		Western Dist	3210	125	10 Jul 1788	435	25 Oct 1783	67	329	On Obion River &c	
Murphy, Archibald	375		Western Dist	4350	339	17 Nov 1790	1950	29 Apr 1784	76	166	On S Fork of Forked Deer River	
Murphy, Hugh	616	Murphy, Archibald heir	Tennessee	640	3175	14 Sep 1797			90	431	S side of Cumberland River	
Murphy, William	415		Eastern District	80	338	8 Jan 1797			90	208	On Blases Creek	
Murphy, William	416		Eastern District	50	339	8 Jan 1797			90	208	In the Fish Trap Island	
Murphy, William & others	360		Eastern District	640	277	20 Jul 1796	14	8 Feb 1780	88	436	In Hindes's Valley	

Earliest Tennessee Land Records

Claimant:	File #:	Assignee:	County:	Acres:	Grant:	Grant Date:	Entry:	Entry Date:	Bk:	Pg:	Location by Stream Name:	Military:
Murphy, Wm.	335		Hawkins	400	329	8 Mar 1793	2085	29 Oct 1779	78	474	In Hinches Valley	
Murral, Matthew	369	Hays, Robert	Sumner	640	1535	14 Jan 1793	1774	3 Dec 1792	79	266	On E side of Spencers Creek	yes
Murral, Thomas	250		Sullivan	150	309	9 Aug 1787	1375	20 May 1779	61	408	On the N side of Holston River	
Murray, Joshua	115	Hays, Thomas	Tennessee	640	1612	23 Feb 1793	2351	29 Sep 1785	76	318	S side of Cumberland River	yes
Murray, Samuel	1800		Davidson	640	373	26 Jun 1793	125	15 Jan 1784	80	331	On Spring Branch of Rockey Creek	
Murray, Shadrach	565		Washington	150	830	11 Jul 1788	2884	1 Aug 1785	64	336	On a branch of Sinking Creek &c	
Murray, Thomas	1702	Murray, Samuel heirs	Davidson	640	318	23 Feb 1793	125		76	343	In ceded territory on N/S Cumberland River	
Murray, Thomas	2360		Davidson	75	382	19 Jul 1797	697		90	368	N side of Cumberland River	
Murray, Titus	233		Tennessee	640	447	27 Jun 1793	47	22 Nov 1792	80	357	On the first creek below Indian Town Creek	
Murray, William	1399		Davidson	100	16	8 Oct 1787		4 Jul 1785	68	153	Waters Hurricane Cr running in Stones River	
Murray, William	1418		Davidson	163	35	8 Oct 1787		4 Jul 1784	68	156	Beg at a hackberry on John Thomas's line	
Murrel, Jacob	2010	Smith, Oliver	Davidson	640	1656	20 May 1793	1900		81	113	On SW side of Big Harpeth	yes
Murrel, John	242		Sullivan	87	381	9 Aug 1787	885	31 Dec 1778	61	400	On the S side of Holston River	
Murrel, Thomas	593		Hawkins	127	467	29 Jul 1793	1376	20 May 1779	80	293	On the S side of Holston	
Murrell, Benjamin	1057		Hawkins	100	766	11 Jan 1797	1240	8 Feb 1780	91	113	S side of Holston River	
Murrell, Henry	047	Hughlett, William	Middle District	640			2750					yes
Murrell, Thomas	779		Sullivan	50	711	18 Nov 1796	664	26 Jul 1780	91	88	S side of Holston River	
Murrey, Morgan	935		Washington	50	912	17 Nov 1790	1331	7 Apr 1779	76	148	S side of Sinking Creek ridge	
Murrey, Thomas	906		Washington	300	883	17 Nov 1790	849	30 Dec 1778	76	138	On the S Fork of Sinking Creek &c	
Murrey, Thomas	955		Washington	90	932	17 Nov 1790	1330	7 Apr 1779	76	155	Including a big spring	
Murry, Ephraim & J. Moore	1263		Washington	150	1201	4 Dec 1790	2534	25 Dec 1794	89	325	On waters of Cherokee	
Murry, James	340	Marley, Robert	Davidson	640	325	1 Aug 1787	1775		63	121	Beg at a Lynn & Sugar tree	yes
Munson, Samuel	890	Underwood, Howell	Davidson	640	906	17 Jan 1789	2696		63	313	On head of W Fork of Spring Creek	yes
Murtes, Zedikiah	350	Williams, Willoughby	Middle District	640	2399	30 Jan 1795	2861		84	182	On W side of W Fork of Obeys River	yes
Muzie, Thomas	120		Hawkins	300	154	26 Dec 1791			75	165	On both sides of Stock Creek	
Myer, Jacob	1481		Green	100	1244	12 Jul 1794	2735	16 Jan 1781	81	576	On S side of Nolechuckey River	
Myer, Martin	512		Sullivan	386	528	26 Nov 1789	2211	12 Nov 1779	73	43	On the waters of Beaver Creek	
Myers, Christopher	937		Green	100	851	17 Nov 1790	70	10 May 1784	76	122	Both sides of Long Creek	
Myers, Jacob	1421		Davidson	400	38	8 Oct 1787	240	1 Mar 1780	68	157	Lying on the E side of Stones River	
Myers, John	1094		Green	200	937	26 Dec 1791	138	10 Mar 1778	77	256	On the waters of Nolachuckey &c	
Myers, William	1392	Robb, William	Sumner	640	3319	6 Dec 1797	1721	29 Aug 1796	97	43	On E waters of Spring Creek	yes
Myham, William	64	Anderson, Daniel	Tennessee	640	1301	10 Dec 1790	3486	26 Feb 1786	74	366	On N side of Cumberland River	yes
Mynet, George	592		Hawkins	200	466	29 Jul 1793	1701	21 Sep 1779	80	293	N side of Holston River	
Myres, Jacob	2259	Donelson, Stockley	Davidson	640	2723	20 Jul 1796	1960		88	450	On waters of Stones River	yes
Nailen, Bryant Ward	209		Sullivan	200	216	10 Oct 1783	240		53	165	On a branch of Horse Creek	
Nare, Henry	1193		Green	200	1036	26 Dec 1791	138	10 Mar 1778	77	327	S/S Nolaychuckey River on Little Lick Creek	
Narress, David	580	Smith, Jacob	Tennessee	640	3027	10 Apr 1797	2678		90	304	S side of Cumberland River	yes
Nash, Abner	130		Western District	1000	130	10 Jul 1788	2344	25 May 1784	67	330	On both sides of N Fork of Obion River	
Nash, Abner	131		Western District	1000	131	10 Jul 1788	2343	25 May 1784	67	331	On E side of N Fork of Obion River	
Nash, Abner	132		Western District	1000	132	10 Jul 1788	2361	25 May 1784	67	331	On waters of N Fork of Obion River	
Nash, Abner	133		Western District	1000	133	10 Jul 1788	2363	25 May 1784	67	331	On S side of N Fork of Obion River	
Nash, Abner	134		Western District	1000	134	10 Jul 1788	2355	25 May 1784	67	332	On the waters of S Fork of Obion River &c	
Nash, Abner	135		Western District	1000	135	10 Jul 1788	2351	25 May 1784	67	332	On the N of Obion River &c	
Nash, Abner	136		Western District	1000	136	10 Jul 1788	2347	25 May 1784	67	333	On both sides of N Fork of Obion River &c	
Nash, Abner	137		Western District	1000	137	10 Jul 1788	2359	25 May 1784	67	333	On waters of the N Fork of Obion River &c	

Earliest Tennessee Land Records

Claimant:	File #:	Assignee:	County:	Acres:	Grant:	Grant Date:	Entry:	Entry Date:	Bk:	Pg:	Location by Stream Name:	Military:
Nash, Abner	138		Western District	1000	138	10 Jul 1788	2358	25 May 1784	67	333	On the N Fork of Obion River	
Nash, Abner	139		Western District	1000	139	10 Jul 1788	2349	25 May 1784	67	334	On both sides of Grove Creek &c	
Nash, Abner	140		Western District	1000	140	10 Jul 1788	2348	25 May 1784	67	334	On the N Fork of Obion River &c	
Nash, Abner	141		Western District	1000	141	10 Jul 1788	2362	25 May 1784	67	334	On the N Fork &c	
Nash, Abner	142		Western District	1000	142	10 Jul 1788	2346	25 May 1784	67	335	On the N Fork of Obion River &c	
Nash, Abner	143		Western District	1000	143	10 Jul 1788	2365	25 May 1784	67	335	On the N side of N Fork of Obion River	
Nash, Abner	144		Western District	1000	144	10 Jul 1788	2341	25 May 1784	67	335	On both sides of N Fork of Obion River	
Nash, Abner	145		Western District	1000	145	10 Jul 1788	2357	25 May 1784	67	336	On the waters of N Fork of Obion River	
Nash, Abner	146		Western District	1000	146	10 Jul 1788	2360	25 May 1784	67	336	N Fork of Obion River	
Nash, Abner	147		Western District	1000	147	10 Jul 1788	2356	25 May 1781	67	336	On the waters of the N Fork of Obion River	
Nash, Abner	148		Western District	1000	148	10 Jul 1788	2352	25 May 1784	67	337	On both sides Grove Creek &c	
Nash, Abner	149		Western District	1000	149	10 Jul 1788	2353	25 May 1784	67	337	On the waters of the S Fork of Obion River	
Nash, Abner	150		Western District	1000	150	10 Jul 1788	2364	25 May 1784	67	337	On both sides of N Fork of Obion River &c	
Nash, Abner	151		Western District	1000	151	10 Jul 1788	2350	25 May 1784	67	338	On both sides of N Fork of Obion River	
Nash, Abner	152		Western District	1000	152	10 Jul 1788	2354	25 May 1784	67	338	On the waters of S & N Fork of Obion River	
Nash, Abner	153		Western District	1000	153	10 Jul 1788	2342	25 May 1784	67	338	on the E side of the N Fork of Obion River	
Nash, Abner	154		Western District	1000	154	10 Jul 1788	2345	25 May 1784	67	339	On the N fork of Obion River &c	
Nash, Francis	524	Sanders, James	Davidson	640	496	15 Sep 1787	443		63	179	S side of Cumberland River	yes
Nash, Francis	717	Nash, Sarah heiress	Davidson	12000	690	5 Nov 1787	755		63	243	On the first big creek below Harpeth	yes
Nash, John	754	Mears, Alexander	Sumner	428	2159	20 May 1793	89	23 Aug 1792	81	163	On waters of W Fork of Drakes Creek	yes
Nash, Joseph	665	Alexander, Robert	Sumner	640	1985	20 May 1793	3206	18 Nov 1792	81	120	On the ridge &c	yes
Nash, Sarah hr of Francis	717	Harrington, Samuel	Sumner	12000	690	5 Nov 1787	755		63	243	On the first big creek below Harpeth	yes
Nash, William	0103		Sumner	640			4209	11 Apr 1797			E side E Fork of Stones River	yes
Nash, William	0104	Hodges, Hardy	Sumner	1000	1567	12 Apr 1797					S side Fowling Creek	yes
Nash, William	1860	Brumley, Wm.	Davidson	640	1588	27 Apr 1793			81	14	On S side of Cumberland River	yes
Nash, William	2198	Armstrong, M.	Davidson	300 (640	213	27 Feb 1795			88	167	On S side of Cumberland River	
Nash, William	2216	Anderson, John's heirs	Davidson	200	247	27 Feb 1796		21 Dec 1792	88	183	On E side of Stones River	
Nash, William	2298	Anderson, John's heirs	Davidson	640	2776	9 Sep 1796	3736		88	525	On E side of Stones River	yes
Nash, William	759	Rigbey, Ezekial	Davidson	640	732	11 Jul 1788	2577		63	257	On E side of Stones River	yes
Nash, William	808		Sullivan	200	751	17 Nov 1797	268	6 Mar 1780	94	151	Waters of Reedy Creek	yes
Nash, William	920	Cabbert, Richard	Davidson	640	936	18 May 1789			63	321	E Fork First Creek above Stones Lick Cree	yes
Nash, William	921		Davidson	640	937	18 May 1789	2783		63	321	1st Cr abv Stones Lick on Stones River	yes
Nash, William	922	Simmons, Isaac heirs	Davidson	640	938	26 Dec 1791	1752		63	322	Waters 1st Cr above Stones Lick Cr	yes
Nash, William	923	Reaves, Foster	Davidson	640	939	18 May 1789	2235		63	322	On waters of W Fork of First Creek	yes
Nash, William	923	Reaves, Foster	Davidson	640	939	18 May 1789			63	322	On waters of W Fork of First Creek	yes
Nash, William, Ass	1353		Sumner	1000	3183	14 Sep 1797	4203	20 Feb 1797	90	435	E side of Stones River	yes
Nash, Wm.	1021		Sumner	100	224	27 Feb 1795			88	172	On n side of Cumberland River	
Nash, Wm.	924	Whitten, Isom heirs	Davidson	640	940	18 May 1789			63	322	On N side of Cumberland River	
Nation, Joseph	1059		Green	113	902	26 Dec 1791	1752	21 Apr 1784	77	243	On the waters of Little Chuckey Creek	yes
Nations, John	677	Tatum, James	Davidson	640	650	8 Dec 1787	2533		63	230	Lying bet. Clay Lick & Battleground	yes
Nave, John	094		Washington	200			3132	26 Feb 1778				
Neal, Andrew	452		Middle District	2000	391	17 Dec 1794	570	27 Oct 1783	84	257	On N side of Duck River	
Neal, Matthew	360		Hawkins	200	353	8 Mar 1793	750	30 Feb 1781	78	486	On the N side of Holston River	
Neal, Nicholas	73		Green	200	31	10 Nov 1786	58	21 Oct 1783	59	392	On Clear Creek	
Neal, Petter (sic)	93		Hawkins	400	251	Jul 1792	79	26 Feb 1778	74	444	On S side of Holston River	

Earliest Tennessee Land Records

Claimant:	File #:	Assignee:	County:	Acres:	Grant:	Grant Date:	Entry:	Entry Date:	Bk:	Pg:	Location by Stream Name:	Military:
Neal, Whitaker	859	Pipkin, Phillip	Sumner	640	2365	20 May 1793	3412	19 Nov 1792	81	205	On w side of Caney Fork	yes
Neave, Titer	332		Washington	300	199	23 Oct 1782	369	8 Sep 1778	49	199	On the S side of Watauga	
Nedeaver, George	641		Sullivan	50	589	27 Jun 1793	898	31 Dec 1778	80	379	On the waters of Indian Creek	
Nedeaver, Jacob	075		Washington	15			1165	1 Feb 1779			On both sides Indian Creek	
Nedeaver, Jacob	324		Sullivan	400	464	10 Jul 1788	1835	5 Mar 1787	67	478	Includes an Island on Holston River	
Nedeaver, Jacob	325		Sullivan	1050	465	10 Jul 1788			67	478	On both sides of Indian Creek	
Nedeaver, Jacob	332		Sullivan	200	472	10 Jul 1788	1414	26 May 1779	67	482	On both sides of Colboths Creek	
Neeley, Alexander	422		Sumner	640	433	27 Jun 1793	422	28 Apr 1784	80	352	On the E Fork of Gooses Creek	
Neeley, Andrew	397		Eastern District	300	239	27 Nov 1795	168	17 Mar 1778	89	293	On S side of French Broad River	
Neeley, Isaac	1230		Davidson	640	194	10 Jul 1788	66	6 Jan 1784	66	410	On the N side of Cumberland River	
Neeley, John	398		Eastern District	640	240	27 Nov 1795	31	26 Feb 1778	89	293	On S bank of French Broad River	
Neeley, William	280		Middle District	250	247	12 Jul 1794			81	599	On S side of Buffalo River	
Neeley, William, Ass	339		Middle District	2004	166	12 Dec 1794			83	440	S side of Buffalo River near the fork	
Neeley, Wm. & Samuel	1248		Davidson	640	213	10 Jul 1788	65	6 Jan 1784	66	414	On the N side of Cumberland River &c	
Neill, Benjamin	213		Hawkins	640	200	26 Dec 1791	898	7 Jun 1784	77	313	Beg at a black oak and pine	
Neilly, Andrew	890		Washington	300	867	2 Dec 1790	168	17 Mar 1778	74	230	On S bank of French Broad River	
Neilly, John	891		Washington	640	868	2 Dec 1790	307	26 Feb 1778	74	230	On S bank of French Broad River	
Neilson, Hugh	1654		Green	550	1353	28 Aug 1795	307	23 Oct 1783	87	526	Beg on the N side of Nolychuckey River	
Neilson, Hugh	958		Green	66	872	17 Nov 1790	1337	12 Jan 1784	76	129	N side of Nolachuckey River	
Neilson, William	1530		Green	100	1290	17 Jul 1794			81	606	S side of Nolichuckey	
Neilson, William, Ass	0148		Green	228			3438	15 May 1795			S side French Broad	
Nelms, Charles	242	Mountflorence, JC & R.Fen	Sumner	274	1147	26 Nov 1789	2285	23 May 1789	74	152	On N side of Cumberland River	yes
Nelms, Jesse	339	Rice, John & Harriet	Tennessee	640	2129	20 May 1793	2147	9 Sep 1785	81	156	On S side of Cumberland River	yes
Nelson, Alex	248	Curry, John	Tennessee	640	1624	27 Apr 1793	1885	15 Aug 1785	81	25	On S boundary of Mills Ramseys survey	
Nelson, Alex or Jas Hunter	360		Middle District	1500	299	17 Dec 1794	1949	29 Apr 1784	84	207	On N side of Duck River	
Nelson, Alexander	1116		Hawkins	300	836	16 Sep 1797	276	9 Mar 1780	94	139	N side of Holston River	
Nelson, Alexander	173	Ward, Drury	Tennessee	274	1449	20 Dec 1791	182	24 Oct 1783	77	363	S side of Red River	
Nelson, Alexander	1810	Gower, Russell	Davidson	640	383	26 Jun 1792	322	1 Mar 1784	80	336	Beg at two oaks on a ridge	
Nelson, Alexander	362		Middle District	2000	301	17 Dec 1794	1948	29 Apr 1784	84	207	Beg at Robt Espays SE corner	
Nelson, Alexander	391		Middle District	1000	330	17 Dec 1794	1943	29 Apr 1784	84	219	On Stones River	
Nelson, Alexander	65		Davidson	763	51	14 Mar 1786	180		63	21	E side of Big Harpeth River	
Nelson, Collins	240	Baker, John	Sumner	640	1145	26 Nov 1789	3404	14 Jun 1788	74	151	On N side of Cumberland River	yes
Nelson, Daniel	1371		Green	200	1226	27 Jan 1793	143	10 Mar 1778	79	505	On waters of Noleychuckey	yes
Nelson, Estride	804	Robertson, Elijah	Davidson	640	807	20 Nov 1788	3317		63	283	On waters of Caney Fork	yes
Nelson, Giles	547	Malley, Thomas	Tennessee	274	2972	5 Apr 1797	1454		90	274	On Lick Creek	yes
Nelson, Hugh, Ass	1645		Green	640	2485	27 Aug 1795	1258	8 Jan 1795	87	512	On waters of Spring Creek	
Nelson, James	656	Nelson, Robert	Tennessee	1280	3233	17 Nov 1797			94	169	S side of the Piney Fork	
Nelson, Jesse	040	Donelson, Stockley	Not given	640			1314	9 Jun 1796			On waters of Mill Creek	yes
Nelson, John	036	Freeman, David heirs	Tennessee	640			1880	11 Jul 1785			S Fork of the Silcan [sic]	yes
Nelson, John	114		Middle District	5000	116	10 Jul 1788	1108		67	466	On the West waters of Richland Creek	
Nelson, John	117	May, Thomas	Middle District	5000	119	10 Jul 1788	1109	30 Oct 1783	67	467	On Robertsons Creek	
Nelson, John	137		Davidson	274	123	14 Mar 1786	759		63	48	On N side of Cumberland River	
Nelson, John	272		Davidson	4800	258	14 Mar 1786	37		63	94	On Nelsons Creek	
Nelson, John	298	Mountflorence, James Cole	Davidson	640	284	22 Mar 1787	2062		63	105	On S side of Cumberland River	yes
Nelson, John	49		Middle District	5000	51	10 Aug 1788	1110	30 Oct 1783	67	436	Headwaters Robertsons & Richlands Creek	

Claimant:	File #:	Assignee:	County:	Acres:	Grant:	Grant Date:	Entry:	Entry Date:	Bk:	Pg:	Location by Stream Name:	Military:
Nelson, John	492	Patterson, Hugh	Tennessee	640	2489	17 Apr 1793	1884	11 Jul 1785	89	101	On S fork of the Tokers (?)	
Nelson, John & Alex	246	Bentley, John	Tennessee	640	1630	17 Jul 1794	6	16 Jan 1781	81	24	On N side of Cumberland River	
Nelson, Johnston	1535		Green	200	1295				81	607	On Little Lick Creek	
Nelson, Nathaniel	318	Rice, John & others	Davidson	640	304	13 Jun 1787	2038		63	113	N side of Tennessee River	yes
Nelson, Robert	010	Browners, John	Montgomery	60	3232	17 Nov 1797	2531	20 Jul 1797			N side of Cumberland River	yes
Nelson, Robert	026	Winningham, Thomas	Robertson	200	340	19 Feb 1797		7 Jul 1788			On Red River	yes
Nelson, Robert	074	Heaton, Amos	Tennessee	640			828	21 Nov 1792			W of the W fork of Red River	yes
Nelson, Robert	09		Montgomery	228	3082		1680	4 Nov 1785	75	509	On E side of Sycamore Cr	
Nelson, Robert	102	Atkinson, John	Davidson	358	1522	10 Apr 1792	198	8 May 1784	68	132	On N side of Cumberland River	
Nelson, Robert	1343	Armstrong, M.	Davidson	320	29	16 Aug 1787	757	15 Aug 1785	68	151	On S side of Cumberland River	
Nelson, Robert	1391	Armstrong, M.	Davidson	250	10	8 Oct 1787	849	14 Apr 1785	68	151	Abt 3 mil below mouth of Red River	
Nelson, Robert	1391	Armstrong, M.	Davidson	250	8	8 Oct 1787	850	14 Apr 1785	68	151	On N side of Cumberland River	
Nelson, Robert	1392	Armstrong, M.	Davidson	150	9	8 Oct 1787	1153	22 Jul 1785	68	151	Abt 3 mil below mouth of Red R	
Nelson, Robert	1393	Armstrong, M.	Davidson	250	10	8 Oct 1787	850	14 Apr 1785	68	151	On N side of Cumberland River	
Nelson, Robert	1394	Armstrong, M.	Davidson	60	11	8 Oct 1787	1154	20 Jul 1785	68	151	On N side of Cumberland River	
Nelson, Robert	1395	Armstrong, M.	Davidson	200	12	8 Oct 1787	554	3 Jan 1785	68	152	On N side of Cumberland River	
Nelson, Robert	1396	Armstrong, M.	Davidson	100	13	8 Oct 1787	1068	30 Jun 1785	68	152	On Caledbs Creel	
Nelson, Robert	1559	Lassiter, Jacob	Davidson	640	1181	30 Nov 1790			74	315	On N side of Cumberland River	yes
Nelson, Robert	1562	Jones, Taylor	Davidson	640	1184	30 Nov 1790			74	316	On E side of Big Harpeth River	yes
Nelson, Robert	1568	Armstrong, M.	Davidson	3	94	30 Nov 1790	2195	30 Jul 1786	74	323	On first island above mouth of Red River	
Nelson, Robert	1643		Davidson	640	294	17 Nov 1790	332	3 Mar 1784	76	179	On N side of Red River	
Nelson, Robert	169	Sugg, Michael	Tennessee	640	1434	20 Dec 1791	3547	15 Feb 1786	77	360	On the N side of Cumberland River	
Nelson, Robert	17		Tennessee	274	1165	26 Mar 1789			74	161	On Red River	
Nelson, Robert	172	Shoecraft, Abraham	Tennessee	640	1447	20 Dec 1791	2092	1 Sep 1785	77	362	Joining W boundary Saml. Henleys cor	yes
Nelson, Robert	1732	Dowden, Samuel	Davidson	640	1448	20 Dec 1791	1286		77	363	N side Harpeth on mouth br of Nelson Cr	yes
Nelson, Robert	1739	Wadsworth, William	Davidson	640	1504	4 Jan 1792	1554		77	377	On E side of Big Harpeth River	yes
Nelson, Robert	2036	Rose, Samuel	Davidson	640	2050	20 May 1793	3074		81	137	On E side of Big Harpeth River	yes
Nelson, Robert	2301	Nelson, James	Davidson	280	165	26 Mar 1795			89	92	On Nelsons Creek	
Nelson, Robert	2423	Burden, James' heirs	Davidson	510	3230	17 Nov 1787			94	167	On S side of Big Harpeth	yes
Nelson, Robert	256	Thomas, Zock	Tennessee	320	149	27 Apr 1793	827	25 Nov 1792	81	41	On flat branch of Keers (sic) Cr	
Nelson, Robert	26	Gamble, Edmond	Tennessee	274	1189	16 Nov 1790	1867	26 Jun 1785	74	318	On a creek called Blooming Grove	yes
Nelson, Robert	261		Tennessee	357	247	7 Mar 1786	262		63	90	Joining James Shaws (?) pre-emption	yes
Nelson, Robert	266	McCleland, James	Davidson	429	252	7 Mar 1786	258		63	92	On E side of Big Harpeth River	yes
Nelson, Robert	401	Stedman, Isaiah	Davidson	640	373	15 Sep 1787	2543		63	140	On Sulphur Fork of Red River	yes
Nelson, Robert	404	Tow, Christoher	Davidson	640	376	15 Sep 1787	3119		83	141	North boundary of Tops' claim	yes
Nelson, Robert	407	Orange, Wm. Heirs	Davidson	640	378	25 Sep 1787	2056		63	142	North side of Cumberland River	yes
Nelson, Robert	408	Mitchell, Jacob	Davidson	640	380	15 Sep 1787	2576		63	142	On Pasture Creek	yes
Nelson, Robert	412	Ginn, Henry heirs	Tennessee	640	2443	18 May 1789	2453	30 Sep 1785	81	424	On both sides of Red River	
Nelson, Robert	413	Mulford, Pertie heirs	Davidson	640	385	15 Sep 1787	2491		63	144	On Goose Creek	yes
Nelson, Robert	414	Strader, George	Davidson	1000	386	15 Sep 1787	1886		63	144	On Big Harpeth	yes
Nelson, Robert	415	Green, Dempsey	Davidson	640	387	15 Sep 1787	2488		63	144	Both sides Red River abt 3 mi fr Clarks Mill	
Nelson, Robert	421	Fulcher, James	Davidson	640	393	15 Sep 1787	2121		63	146	On Groves Creek	yes
Nelson, Robert	424	Man, John heirs	Davidson	640	396	15 Sep 1787	730		63	147	On N side of Cumberland River	yes
Nelson, Robert	436		Tennessee	640	350	5 Dec 1794			83	415	N side of Cumberland River	
Nelson, Robert	438	White, Robert	Tennessee	400	171	26 Sep 1794		20 Dec 1794	86	529	Joining Saml. Henleys survey	

Claimant:	File #:	Assignee:	County:	Acres:	Grant:	Grant Date:	Entry:	Entry Date:	Bk:	Pg:	Location by Stream Name:	Military:
Nelson, Robert	446	Armstrong, M.	Tennessee	28	218	27 Feb 1796			88	170	On waters of Sulphur Fork	
Nelson, Robert	456	Armstrong, M.	Tennessee	40	254	27 Feb 1796		30 May 1792	88	187	Name of Wm Johnston was erased	
Nelson, Robert	471		Tennessee	60	304	20 Jul 1796			88	441	On N side of Red River	
Nelson, Robert	491	Tyhen, Thos	Tennessee	640	2488	26 Sep 1795	1995	16 Aug 1785	89	101	On N side of Red River	
Nelson, Robert	493	Pendergrass, John	Tennessee	640	2490	26 Sep 1795	1881	11 Jul 1785	89	102	On N side of Red River	
Nelson, Robert	562	Sharpe, John	Tennessee	428	2997	10 Apr 1797	671		90	292	On N side of Cumberland River	
Nelson, Robert	589	Carrick, Zach heirs	Tennessee	1000	3057	19 Jul 1797	4402		90	372	Main head of a South fork	
Nelson, Robert	598		Tennessee	28	3082	19 July 1797		28 Dec 1792	90	363	W of the W fork	
Nelson, Robert	653	Stewart, Duncan	Tennessee	320	3229	17 Nov 1797	2453		94	167	On Little W Fork of Red River	yes
Nelson, Robert	654	Green, Dempsey	Tennessee	150	3231	17 Nov 1791	2488		94	168	N fork of W fork of Blooming Grove	
Nelson, Robert	655	Browners, John	Tennessee	60	3232	17 Nov 1797	2531	15 Feb 1786	94	169	N side of Cumberland River	
Nelson, Robert	656	Nelson, James	Tennessee	1280	3233	17 Nov 1797			94	169	S side of the Piney Fork	
Nelson, Robert	673	Beard, John's hr James	Davidson	640	3230	8 Dec 1787			63	229	On N side of Big Harpeth	yes
Nelson, Robt & Jno McNary	880	Pulleu, Sam (hr of George)	Davidson	640	894	17 Jan 1789	2472		63	310	On N side of Cumberland River	yes
Nelson, William	3050	Oneel, Isham	Tennessee	640	1996	20 May 1793	2680	24 Nov 1792	81	123	On S side of Cumberland River	
Nelson, William	046		Washington	460			43	21 Sep 1779			Beg at a stake	
Nelson, William	047		Washington	460			43	26 Feb 1778			Beg at a stake	
Nelson, William	1082		Washington	187	1032	27 Nov 1792	2516	3 Apr 1780	80	199	On the dreans of Knobs Creek	
Nelson, William	1183		Green	200	1026	26 Dec 1791	2346	11 Dec 1779	77	291	On W side of Chuckey Riv on Sinking Fk	
Nelson, William	131		Washington	220	299	24 Oct 1782	754	23 Dec 1778	44	298	Beg at a black & white oak	
Nelson, William	1646		Green	365	2486	28 Aug 1795	1439	15 May 1795	87	513	On N side of French Broad River	
Nelson, William	1647		Green	228	2487	28 Aug 1795	1439	20 Sep 1792	87	513	On S side of French Broad River	
Nelson, William	286	Glasgow, James	Davidson	640	272	24 Jan 1787	1313		63	99	On the War Trace Cr	yes
Nelson, William	63		Green	300	21	1 Nov 1786	180	22 Oct 1782	59	382	S side of Nolechuckie	yes
Nelson, William	98		Green	640	56	1 Nov 1786	56	21 Oct 1783	59	417	S side of Nolechuckie	yes
Nelvin, Robert	49	Williams, Willoughby	Tennessee	1000	2622	10 Nov 1790	2625	30 Jul 1790	74	347	On S side of Cumberland River	yes
Nervear, David	1116	Harris, Edward	Sumner	640	2622	4 Jun 1796	2677	1 Jun 1795	88	341	Joining said Harris survey	yes
Netherlon, Henry	1361		Green	100	1216	27 Jan 1793	836	17 Aug 1781	79	502	On the fork of French Broad etc	
Nevil, George	1329	Day, Ransom	Davidson	320	15	18 Aug 1787	117	15 Jan 1784	68	126	On the S side of Cumberland River	
Neville, George	1297		Davidson	640	262	10 Jul 1788	438	12 May 1784	66	429	Beg mouth of 1st cr below Little Harpeth	
Neville, George	187	Gambling, James	Davidson	350	173	7 Mar 1786	832		63	65	On Red River	yes
Neville, George	4	Adams, Howell	Montgomery	323	3379	1 Dec 1801	173				On middle fork of Bartons Creek	yes
Newberry, William	463	Donelson & Tyrrell	Tennessee	640	2573	7 Mar 1796	2940	30 Sep 1785	88	313	On head branches of Carrs Creek	yes
Newbery, Henry	1363		Green	150	1218	27 Jan 1793	1796	1 Oct 1779	79	503	On waters of Lick Creek	
Newby, Matthew	342	Ervin, John	Sumner	640	1406(?)	20 Dec 1791	489	18 May 1791	77	353	On S side of Cumberland River	yes
Newby, Robert	927	Read, John	Davidson	640	943	18 May 1789	1547		63	323	On S side of Cumberland River	yes
Newby, Worley (?)	1669		Green	150	1374	27 Feb 1796	537	26 May 1778	88	489	On waters of Lick Creek	
Newell, John	2043	Sheppard, Nancy	Davidson	640	2063	20 May 1793	1504		81	140	On N side of Cumberland River	yes
Newell, William	1161		Davidson	640	138	17 Apr 1796	481	9 Jun 1784	66	183	On head of Little Haprer	
Newhouse, Joseph	295	Mountflorence, James Cole	Davidson	640	281	22 Mar 1787	2098		63	103	On S side of Cumberland River	yes
Newhouse, Lewis	1016	King, Watter	Washington	640	965	14 Jan 1793	2160	6 Nov 1779	79	275	On E fork of Cherokee Creek	
Newhouse, Lewis	1019	King, Watter	Washington	640	968	14 Jan 1793	205	14 Apr 1772	79	275	On S side of Nolechuckey River	
Newhouse, Lewis	989		Washington	640	961	26 Dec 1791	268	22 Jul 1778	77	295	In Bumpass cove	
Newhouse, Lewis	990		Washington	300	962	26 Dec 1791	2140	6 Nov 1779	77	296	In Bumpass cove	
Newhouse, Lewis	991		Washington	640	963	26 Dec 1791	48	26 Feb 1778	77	296	On S side of Nolachucky River	

Earliest Tennessee Land Records

Claimant:	File #:	Assignee:	County:	Acres:	Grant:	Grant Date:	Entry:	Entry Date:	Bk:	Pg:	Location by Stream Name:	Military:
Newland, Eli	342	Rainey, James	Davidson	320	327	1 Aug 1787	1730	23 Oct 1778	63	122	On W Fork of Spring Creek	yes
Newland, George	1005		Washington	50	301	26 Dec 1791	528		77	301	Lying on Sinking Creek	
Newland, George	1008		Tennessee	320	980	26 Dec 1791			77	303	Beg at a locust	
Newman, Anthony	125		Middle District	5000	127	10 Jul 1788	2160	13 May 1784	67	470	On N side of Duck River	
Newman, Anthony	1771	McCam, Hugh	Davidson	640	1555	14 Jan 1793	920		79	270	On waters of West Harpeth	yes
Newman, Anthony	2120	Cox, Thomas	Davidson	640	2396	7 Jan 1794	1549		81	390	On waters of Roaring Waters	yes
Newman, Isaac	07		Jefferson	228							On waters of Dumplin Creek	
Newman, Isaac	1008		Green	200	1235	29 Jul 1793			76	485	On a draft of Dumplin Creek	
Newman, Isaac	1608	Cates, Wm.	Green	46	1354	4 Feb 1795		1 Nov 1794	84	139	On waters of Dumplin Creek	
Newman, Isaac	1682		Green	228	315	10 Sep 1796	3967	8 Mar 1796	88	515	On waters of Dumplin Creek	
Newman, Isaac	1753		Green	228	3055	4 Jul 1797			91	599	On waters of Dumplin Creek	
Newman, Isaac	275		Hawkins	100	286	14 Jan 1793	1967	14 Oct 1779	78	340	On S side of Holston River	
Newman, Isaac	635		Hawkins	100	503	27 Nov 1793	897	29 Oct 1783	81	502	On N side of Holston River	
Newman, Isaac	986		Hawkins	200	316	10 Sep 1796			88	515	Beg at a post oak	
Newman, Jno.	573		Green	100	253	20 Sep 1787	11	11 Mar 1779	66	158	Adj his former survey on Lick Cr	
Newman, John	272		Green	600	229	20 Sep 1787	833	29 Sep 1783	65	441	On Lick Creek	
Newman, John	310		Middle District	1000	286	17 Dec 1794	1805	23 Apl 1784	83	331	On headwaters of Harpeth	
Newman, John	554		Green	50	234	20 Sep 1787	2472	10 Mar 1780	66	152	Adj his former survey on Lick Cr	
Newsham, Aaron	2065	Whitfield, Bryant	Davidson	640	2201	20 May 1793	1502		81	169	On E side of Stones River	yes
Newsom, Aaron	1436	Jones, Ambrose	Sumner	640	3349	9 Dec 1797	1507	12 Apr 1788	98	183	On E side of Cedar Lick Cr	yes
Newsom, Crafford	731	Payton, Ephraim	Sumner	640	2117	20 May 1793	3650	29 May 1792	81	153	On N side of Cumberland River	yes
Newtom. Estridge	1691	Phillips, Phillip & Campbell	Davidson	1000	1652	23 Feb 1793	3155		76	337	On waters of Stones River	yes
Newton, Francis	1725	Tatum, Howell	Davidson	640	1422	20 Dec 1791	3681		77	357	On N side of Cumberland River	yes
Newton, Henry	2040	Turnbull, William	Davidson	640	2057	20 May 1793	3662		81	138	On waters of Big Harpeth	yes
Newton, Joseph	2368	Stewart, Duncan	Davidson	640	3089	14 May 1797	4007		90	396	On W side of S Harpeth River	yes
Niceley, Michael	813		Sullivan	250	756	17 Nov 1797	2212-331	12 Jun 1796	94	154	North side of Holston River	
Nichelson, Richard	1539		Green	200	1299	17 Jul 1794	95	26 Feb 1778	81	608	On waters of Swan Pond Creek	
Nichelson, Samuel	1869		Davidson	1000	1607	27 Apr 1793	779		81	19	Sm Cr on N/S Cumberland River	yes
Nicholas, James	322		Green	400	324	20 Sep 1787	274	29 Oct 1783	65	465	On N bank of Holston River	
Nichold, John	932	Freelers, John	Davidson	640	948	18 May 1789	2617		63	324	Sm Cr on E fork of Stones River	yes
Nicholet, John	715	Bud, Samuel	Davidson	640	688	8 Sep 1793	1788		63	242	W side of Milners Creek	yes
Nicholls, John	1579	Smith, Stephens heirs	Davidson	640	1240	10 Dec 1790	646		74	345	In the fork of Red River	yes
Nicholls, Hancock	139		Davidson	640	125	14 Mar 1786	1764		63	49	On E fork of Camp Creek	yes
Nicholls, John	1001	Hutson, Isaac heirs	Davidson	640	1018	18 May 1789	2589		63	341	On Weakley Creek	yes
Nicholls, John	1002	Winkle, Josiah heirs	Davidson	640	1019	18 May 1789	2590		63	341	On Barretts Creek	yes
Nicholls, John	1021	Venters, William heirs	Davidson	640	1039	18 May 1789	2588		63	345	On 1st creek of Duck River	yes
Nicholls, John	1474	Spruel, Richard	Davidson	640	1050	27 Nov 1789	2581		71	283	On N/S of Cumberland River	yes
Nicholls, John	153	Therogool, Francis	Davidson	773	139	14 Mar 1786	824		63	53	South side of Cumberland River	yes
Nicholls, John	1864	Joyner, Joel	Davidson	640	1598	27 Apr 1793	1075		81	17	On W bank of Big Harpeth River	yes
Nicholls, John	1919	White, Benjamin	Davidson	640	1713	20 May 1793	924		81	56	On W side of Harpeth River	yes
Nicholls, John	2467	Warren, H. heirs	Davidson	640	3403	30 May 1803	2589	8 May 1786	110	320	On waters of Harpeth River	yes
Nicholls, John	265		Tennessee	640	1714	20 May 1793	3084	5 Dec 1785	81	57	On S side of Cumberland River	yes
Nicholls, John	409	Cole, Martin	Davidson	1000	381	15 Sep 1787	90		63	142	On waters of Station Camp Cr.	yes
Nicholls, John	411	Measles, Micajah	Davidson	640	383	15 Sep 1787	2575		63	143	North side of Cumberland River	yes
Nicholls, John	419	Lewis, John	Davidson	640	391	15 Sep 1787	1772		63	146	W side of Sycamore Creek	yes

Claimant:	File #:	Assignee:	County:	Acres:	Grant:	Grant Date:	Entry:	Entry Date:	Bk:	Pg:	Location by Stream Name:	Military:
Nichols, John	422	Cooker, John heirs	Davidson	640	394	15 Sep 1787	2565		63	147	On waters of Sulpher Fork	yes
Nichols, John	425	Cole, Jas or Edward heirs	Davidson	640	397	15 Sep 1787	1848		63	148	N side of Cumberland River	yes
Nichols, John	426	Salter, John	Davidson	457	398	15 Sep 1787	1848		63	148	On the N/S of Cumberland River	yes
Nichols, John	427	Wiggins, Jacob	Davidson	1000	399	15 Sep 1787	1934		63	148	On W/S of Caney Fork	yes
Nichols, John	428	Crook, William heirs	Davidson	1000	400	15 Sep 1787	2601		63	149	Lying on Spring Creek	yes
Nichols, John	429	Sparkman, Edward	Davidson	640	401	15 Sep 1787	2579		63	149	On N/S of Cumberland River	yes
Nichols, John	430	Fist, Samuel heirs	Davidson	640	402	15 Sep 1787	1189		63	149	On E side of Caney Fork	yes
Nichols, John	453	Williams, Willoughby	Davidson	640	425	15 Sep 1787	1183		63	157	N of survey at Turnbulls Clay Lick	yes
Nichols, John	459	Ridley, Berriman	Davidson	640	431	15 Sep 1787			63	159	N side of Cumberland River	yes
Nichols, John	500		Sumner	640	1669	20 May 1793			81	46	On the Caney Fork	yes
Nichols, John	505		Sumner	640	1677	20 May 1793			81	48	On the Caney Fork	yes
Nichols, John	506		Sumner	640	1678	20 May 1793			81	48	On the Caney Fork	yes
Nichols, John	509		Sumner	640	1685	20 May 1793			81	50	On the Caney Fork	yes
Nichols, John	510		Sumner	640	1687	20 May 1793			81	50	On the Caney Fork	yes
Nichols, John	511		Sumner	640	1688	20 May 1793			81	51	On the Caney Fork	yes
Nichols, John	514		Sumner	1000	1691	20 May 1793			81	51	On waters of Caney Fork	yes
Nichols, John	515		Sumner	640	1692	20 May 1793			81	51	On the Caney Fork	yes
Nichols, John	518		Sumner	640	1697	20 May 1793			81	53	On Caney Fork	yes
Nichols, John	519		Sumner	640	1698	20 May 1793			81	53	On S side of Cumberland River	yes
Nichols, John	523		Sumner	640	1705	20 May 1793			81	54	On the Caney Fork	yes
Nichols, John	525		Sumner	640	1710	20 May 1793			81	56	On W Fork of Caney Fork	yes
Nichols, John	527		Sumner	640	1720	20 May 1793			81	58	On W side of Caney Fork	yes
Nichols, John	529		Sumner	640	1722	20 May 1793			81	59	On headwaters of Hickmans Cr.	yes
Nichols, John	539		Sumner	640	1736	20 May 1793			81	62	On W side of Caney Fork	yes
Nichols, John	735	Collier, Josiah	Davidson	640	708	11 Jul 1788	3566		63	249	Headbranch nr Wm. Borms survey	yes
Nichols, John	752	Daniel, Benjamin	Davidson	640	725	11 Jul 1788	2567		63	255	N side of Fenners Survey	yes
Nichols, John	74	Webb, John	Middle District	1900	76	10 July 1788	548	27 Oct 1783	67	447	On S side of Duck River	yes
Nichols, William Jr.	583	Murfree, Hardy	Tennessee	640	3030	10 Apr 1797	3567	19 Sep 1797	90	305	Waters of W Fk of Red River	yes
Nicholson, Isaac	043	Dillenberry, Redmond	Sumner	640			4464	19 Sep 1797			Head of Maxels Fork of Red River	yes
Nicholson, Isaac	1421	Hadley, Joshua	Sumner	640	3276	6 Dec 1797	4499	21 June 1797	98	157	On Headwaters of Cedar Creek	
Nickelson, James	31	Cockran, William	Tennessee	640	1195	30 Nov 1790	2753	30 Sep 1785	74	320	On S side of Cumberland River	
Nicklas, Isaac	027	Barber, Joseph	not given	274			4212					yes
Nicklas, Isaac	027		not given	274			4212					yes
Nichols, John	107	Haddock, Andrew	Davidson	1000	93	14 Mar 1786	1076		63	38	On both sides of Big Harpeth Riv	yes
Nicolas, Richard	1352	Barry, Redmond D.	Sumner	640	3167	14 Sep 1797	4245	20 Feb 1797	90	429	On the Falling Creek	yes
Nixon, Robert	815	Robertson, Elijah	Davidson	640	818	20 Nov 1788	3318		63	288	On waters of Caney Fork	yes
Noble, Mark	024	Barco, John	Robertson	274	3385		4188	17 Jul 1800			On Brush Creek	
Noble, Mark	1423	Armstrong, M.	Davidson	100	40	8 Oct 1787		21 Jan 1786	68	157	On Sycamore Creek	
Noble, Mark	1611		Davidson	320	103	10 Oct 1790	755	6 Aug 1786	74	377	On head of Josiah Ramseys Mill Cr	
Noble, Mark	364	Armstrong, M.	Davidson	200	6	4 Sep 1787		6 Aug 1785	63	130	N side of Sycamore Creek	
Noble, Mark	4		Robertson	274	3385	12 Dec 1801	4212		114	90	On Brush Creek	
Nobles, Robert	2028	McCulloh, Benjamin	Davidson	274	2036	20 May 1793	3014	8 Feb 1786	81	133	On N/S of Cumberland River	yes
Nobles, William	157	Hart, Anthony	Tennessee	640	1414	20 Dec 1791	3516		77	355	On Beaver Creek	yes
Nobles, John	677	King, Thomas	Hawkins	640	2387	12 July 1794	3675		81	601	On Indian Creek	yes
Nodding, William	1357		Washington	300	1274	19 Oct 1797	1495	29 Jul 1779	92	50	On Little Limestone	yes

Earliest Tennessee Land Records

Page 315

Claimant:	File #:	Assignee:	County:	Acres:	Grant:	Grant Date:	Entry:	Entry Date:	Bk:	Pg:	Location by Stream Name:	Military:
Nodding, William	709		Washington	300	523	10 Nov 1784	1495	29 Jul 1779	69	113	E of entry made by Aaron Burleson	
Noddy, William	844		Washington	500	658	10 Nov 1784	289	3 Aug 1778	69	154	On Little Limestone	
Nolby, Anderson	360	Hays, John	Tennessee	640	2209	20 May 1793	2288	22 Oct 1785	81	171	On Yellow Creek	yes
Nolley, Dixon	2234	Robeson, James	Davidson	640	2598	2 Mar 1796	1330		88	325	On S Harpeth	yes
Nording, William	083		Green	200			681	10 July 1783			On Camp Creek	
Norman, Thomas	784	Hickman, Edwin	Sumner	365	2241	20 May 1793	3121	22 Feb 1787	81	178	N side of Cumberland River	yes
Norris, George	06	Service Rights	Knox	100							On Flat Creek	
Norris, George	461		Middle District	1280	400	17 Dec 1794	2024	3 May 1784	84	261	On N side of Elk River	
Norris, George	78	Hogg, Thomas	Tennessee	640	1323	10 Dec 1790	2429	30 Sep 1785	74	373	S side of Cumberland River	yes
Norris, Robert	833	Valentine, Daniel	Davidson	640	836	17 Jan 1789	3606		63	294	On waters of Caney Fork	yes
Norris, Thomas	626	Davis, Samuel	Davidson	357	598	15 Sep 1787	1463	15 Sep 1787	63	213	On N boundary of James Brown	yes
Norris, Ezekiel	471		Sumner	640	1632	27 Apr 1793	3692	15 Feb 1791	81	25	S side of Cumberland River	yes
North, John	977		Washington	100	954	17 Nov 1790	2128	4 Nov 1779	76	163	Beg at a red oak, etc.	
North, Samuel	084		Middle District	3000			1776	23 Apl 1784			Middle fork of Elk River	
Norton, Jeremiah	2386	Donelson, John	Davidson	1000	3169	14 Sep 1797	4246		90	429	S side of Falling Creek	yes
Norton, William	1876		Davidson	640	1617	27 Apr 1793	3062		81	22	On headbranches of Stones Cr	yes
Norwester, John	1340	Hinds, John	Sumner	320	3140	14 Sep 1797	4465	6 May 1797	90	419	Waters of Big Barron	yes
Norwood, John	1331		Washington	200	1255	6 Jun 1797	197	6 Apr 1778	90	311	S side of Watauga River	
Norwood, Theophillus	1311	Hinds, John	Sumner	640	3111	14 Sep 1797	4331	6 May 1797	90	407	Waters of Big Barron	yes
Norwood, William	831	Anderson, Daniel	Davidson	640	834	17 Jan 1789	3369		63	293	On waters of Caney Fork	yes
Nowell, James	1593	McNess, John	Davidson	640	1276	10 Dec 1790	2866		74	357	On waters of Bear Branch	yes
Nowell, William	300	Mountflorence, James Cole	Davidson	640	286	22 Mar 1787	2097		63	106	S side of Cumberland River	
Nowells, John	145		Washington	400	13	25 Oct 1782	333	29 Aug 1778	47	6	N side of Watauga River	yes
Nowland, Jesse	042	Dillenberry, Redmond	Sumner	640			4466	19 Sep 1797			On head branches, etc	
Nowland, John	268		Middle District	250	116	27 Apr 1793	32	27 Feb 1782	81	33	On waters of W Fork of Tenn Riv	
Nowlin, Bryant Ward	06		Sullivan	200			680				On a branch of Horse Creek	
Nowlin, John	145		Washington	400	13	22 Oct 1782	333	29 Aug 1778	47	6	N side of Watauga River	
Nucus, Aaron	120	Bond, John	Tennessee	640	1622	23 Feb 1793	1835	14 June 1785	76	323	Abt 5 miles fr mouth of Red River	yes
Nunnery, Androwson	864	McCulloh, Benjamin	Sumner	640	2375	20 May 1793	1997	26 Nov 1792	81	207	On headwaters of Bartons Creek	yes
Oats, Daniel	1012	Lanier, James	Davidson	640	1029	18 May 1789	2538		63	343	On middle fork of Red River	yes
Obarr, Daniel	011	Bledsoe, Isaac	Sumner	457			1408	2 Aug 1785			At mouth of Bledsoes Creek	yes
Obarr, Michael	457	Dixon, Tilghman	Sumner	457	1839	20 May 1793	1407	20 Aug 1785	81	87	N side of Cumberland River	yes
O'Barr, Michael	73	Anderson, Daniel	Tennessee	640	1317	10 Dec 1790	1658	19 June 1790	74	371	On S side of Cumberland River	yes
Obarr, Robert	596	Dixon, Tilghman	Sumner	596	1839	20 May 1793	1407	20 Aug 1785	81	87	On N side of Cumberland River	yes
O'Bryan, Robert	60	Robertson, Henry	Tennessee	640	1291	10 Dec 1790	1796	4 May 1785	74	362	On N side of Cumberland River	
O'Bryan, Laurence	61	Mason, John	Tennessee	640	1295	10 Dec 1790	1797	4 May 1785	74	364	On N side of Cumberland River	
O'Bryan, Laurence	75	Buckingham, Wm.	Tennessee	640	1320	10 Dec 1790	1798	4 May 1785	74	372	On Brush Creek	
O'Carrill, Henry	1322	McConnel, Robert	Sumner	1000	3122	10 Sep 1797	4705	15 May 1797	90	412	On waters of Big Barren	yes
O'Conner, Sullivan	037	Dillenberry, Redmond	Sumner	274			518	19 Sep 1797			On Dividing Ridge	yes
Odel, William	048		Washington	239				24 Nov 1778			Including a spring, etc.	
Odell, Benjamin	1047		Washington	120	997	27 Nov 1792	2508	31 Mar 1780	80	176	On Brush Creek	
Odell, Benjamin	1047		Washington	120	997	27 Nov 1792	2508	31 Mar 1780	80	176	On Brush Creek	
Odell, William	162		Washington	440	30	23 Oct 1782	318	31 Mar 1779	47	13	On waters of Big Limestone	
Odell, William	162		Washington	440	30	23 Oct 1782	318	31 Mar 1779	47	13	On waters of Big Limestone	
Odemeal, Bartholomew	838		Washington	200	652	10 Nov 1784	2759	6 Feb 1781	69	152	Near head of Bear Tree Hollow	

Earliest Tennessee Land Records

Claimant:	File #:	Assignee:	County:	Acres:	Grant:	Grant Date:	Entry:	Entry Date:	Bk:	Pg:	Location by Stream Name:	Military:
Oden, James	366		Sullivan	200	245	10 Nov 1784	145	15 Feb 1780	69	160	On a br of Cavatts Mill Creek	
Odeneal, Bartholomew	1034		Washington	100	984	14 Jan 1793	2527	8 Apr 1780	79	280	On both sides of Big Limestone	
Odle, Caleb	831		Washington	80	645	10 Nov 1784	2506	29 Mar 1780	69	150	Beg at a chesnut corner	
Odle, Isaac	393		Washington	300	385	13 Oct 1783	1252	30 Feb 1779	52	258	On a branch of Lick Creek	
Odum, Dickerson	2383	Barry, Redmond D.	Davidson	640	3165	14 Sep 1797	4244		90	428	On E branch of Stones River	yes
Offield, James	116		Sullivan	200	128	23 Oct 1782	647	28 Nov 1778	43	318	On the S side of Holston River	
Ofiel, James	769		Sullivan	50	700	28 Jul 1796	87	8 Feb 1780	91	83	Beg at an ash	
Ogdon, Dempsey	031	Dillenberry, Redmond	Sumner	640			4410	14 Oct 1797			Headwaters of Middle Fork (?)	yes
Oglesby, Nehemiah	032	Dillenberry, Redmond	Sumner	640			4417	14 Oct 1797			Headwaters of Middle Fork (?)	yes
Oglesby, Richard	432	Blount, Reading	Davidson	640	404	15 Sep 1787			63	150	N side of Cumberland River	yes
Old, Henry	062		Tennessee	640	10			9 Aug 1819			Both sides of Tuckasedge River	
Oliver, Elijah	058		not given	640			1418	1 Mar 1786			On waters of Second Creek	yes
Oliver, Andrw	801	Saunders, James	Sumner	274	2262	20 May 1793	5	7 Sep 1783	81	183	On N side of Cumberland River	yes
Olliphant, John	379		Green	50	381	20 Sep 1787	603	21 Apl 1784	65	480	On the Carneys Creek	
Olliver, Andrew	282	Williams, Willoughby	Tennessee	640	1868	20 May 1793	2537		81	93	Both sides of Sulphur Lick Creek	
Oneal, Archer	692	Willson, John	Davidson	640	665	8 Dec 1787	680	26 Apl 1784	63	235	On mouth of War Trace Creek	yes
Oneal, Charles	257	Gist, Joshua	Tennessee	853	1655	20 May 1793	272	27 Jul 1778	81	42	On N side of Cumberland River	yes
Oneal, Cornelius	653		Washington	200	747	26 Oct 1786	273	27 Jul 1778	66	33	Beg at a marked poplar	yes
Oneal, Cornelius	654		Washington	200	748	26 Oct 1786	2536		66	33	Be at 3 marked buckeyes	
Oneal, Matthias	2049	Carson, James	Davidson	640	2115	20 May 1793	922	1 Jan 1779	81	153	On both sides of Stones Creek	yes
Oneal, Robert	616		Washington	200	710	26 Oct 1786	934	1 Jan 1779	66	16	S side of Nolechuckey River	
Oneal, Robert	886		Green	400	818	Sep 1790	2680	24 Nov 1792	74	277	On Horse Creek	
Oneal,(?) Isham	305	McNary & Nelson	Tennessee	640	1996	20 May 1793	4170	6 May 1797	81	123	On S side of Cumberland River	yes
Onealey, Thomas	1338	Brooks, Matthew	Sumner	640	3138	14 Sep 1797	2681		90	418	N fork of Big Barren	yes
Oneall, Thomas	189	Oneall, Isham heirs	Middle District	640	1665	8 Mar 1793	2681		76	34	On waters of Cumberland River	yes
O'Neil, Isham	189	Oneall, Isham	Middle District	640	1665	8 Mar 1793	965	18 May 1784	76	343	On the waters of Cumberland Riv	yes
O'Neil, James	039	Robertson, Elijah	Tennessee	640			2536	29 Oct 1787			N side of Cumberland River	yes
O'Neil, Matthew	035	Carson, James	Davidson	640			2635	4 Oct 1792			On both sides of Stones Creek	yes
Oneil, Thomas	055	Chappel, Edward	not given	640							On N side of Tennesy River	
Oneill, Thomas	140	Chappelle, Wm. Heirs	Tennessee	640	1662	18 Mar 1793	1899		76	342	N side of Tenn River, etc.	yes
Oneill, Thomas	187	Hancock, Ann	Middle District	640	1663	8 Mar 1793	3019		76	342	On waters of Cumberland River	yes
Oneill, Thomas	188	Parrish, Mark	Middle District	1000	1664	8 Mar 1793	2986		76	343	On waters of Cumberland River	yes
Oneill, Thomas	1889	Belwood, Sam'l.	Davidson	640	1571	25 May 1793			81	30	On N side of Holston	yes
Onsley, John	1327	McConnell, Robert	Sumner	274	3127	14 Sep 1797	4659 (?)	6 May 1797	90	414	On waters of Big Barren	yes
Oo-lak-not-too	061		Tennessee	640	4			3 Aug 1819			Beg post oak Johnstone SW corner	
Ore, James	1152		Hawkins	1000	866	2 May 1801	1641	30 Nov 1784	112	389	N side of Holston River	
Ore, James	2251	Adams, Arthur	Davidson	274	2592	7 Mar 1798			88	322	N side of Holston River	yes
Ore, James	305		Hawkins	25	270	24 Feb 1792	1744	28 Sep 1779	78	451	On Carman Creek	
Ore, James	373		Hawkins	500	327	27 Jul 1793	85	17 Nov 1791	79	489	On both sides of Carman Creek	
Ore, James	408		Eastern District	500	232	12 Nov 1795	1178	30 Oct 1783	89	418	The N side of Holston River	
Ore, James	451		Eastern District	617	319	15 Dec 1802	2224	12 Jan 1785	110	271	On E side of Holstons River	
Ore, James	452		Eastern District	177	320	15 Dec 1802	2224	12 Jan 1785	110	272	On N side of Holstons River	
Ore, James	453		Eastern District	440	321	15 Dec 1802	2224	12 Jan 1785	110	272	On E side of Emeries River	
Ore, James	866	Rhodes, Christian	Hawkins	400	642	4 Jan 1795			84	47	Beg at a beach and popular	
Ore, James	929		Hawkins	640	711	2 Dec 1795	2582	10 Sep 1783	88	265	On N side of Holston River	

Claimant:	File #:	Assignee:	County:	Acres:	Grant:	Grant Date:	Entry:	Entry Date:	Bk:	Pg:	Location by Stream Name:	Military:
Ore, James	930		Hawkins	500	713	2 Dec 1795	918	29 Oct 1783	88	266	On N side of Holston River	
Orell, James	072	Ellison, Joseph	Sumner	274			3015	2 Apr 1787			N branch of Bradleys Lick Creek	
Orme, James (sic)	1092	Easton, James	Sumner	640	2583	7 Mar 1796	3858	22 Jul 1795	88	318	N/S of a large fork of Caney Fork	yes
Orr, James	542	Richman, Mark	Davidson	640	514	15 Sep 1787	2539		63	185	S side of Cumberland River	yes
Orr, Nathan	1633	Erwin, Robert	Davidson	640	1366	30 Nov 1790			74	392	On waters of Little Harpeth	yes
Orr, Robert	316		Green	223	318	20 Sep 1787	218	27 Oct 1783	65	464	On S side of Noleychuckey River	
Orr, Robert	371		Green	100	373	20 Sep 1787	1231	7 Nov 1783	65	478	On S side of Noleychuckey River	
Orr, Samuel	2100	Sheppard, Nancy	Davidson	640	2325	20 May 1793	1765		81	196	2nd Cr Continental Line crosses	yes
Orrange, William	407	Nelson, Robert	Davidson	640	378	15 Sep 1787	2056		63	142	N side of Cumberland River	yes
Orrell, Thomas	1695	Phillips and Campbell	Davidson	1144	1656	23 Feb 1793	1283		76	339	On the Chickmauga Trace	yes
Orth, Adam	184 (37)		Sullivan	640	191	10 Oct 1783	991	4 Jan 1779	53	154	N side of Holston River	
Orth, Adam	200		Sullivan	600	207	10 Oct 1783	2266-73	22 Nov 1779	53	151	N side of Holston River	
Orth, Adam	210		Sullivan	352	217	10 Oct 1783	2265	22 Nov 1779	53	165	N side of Holston River	
Orth, Adam	213		Sullivan	640	220	10 Oct 1783	990	4 Jan 1779	53	166	N side of Holston River	
Orth, Adam	215		Sullivan	320	222	10 Oct 1783	2268	22 Nov 1779	53	167	N side of Holston River	
Orth, Adam	216		Sullivan	640	223	10 Oct 1783	2267	22 Nov 1779	53	167	N side of Holston River	
Osborn, Jessee	047	Green, Andrew	Davidson	640			4771	15 Sep 1797			On head of Pond Creek	yes
Osburn, Edward	908		Green	200	895	31 Oct 1791	1548	24 Aug 1779	75	122	N side of French Broad River	
Ostin, William	298	Phillips and Campbell	Sumner	640	1345	10 Dec 1790	3684	13 Mar 1790	74	330	N side of Cumberland River	yes
Ouran, Timothy	1363	Tatum and Wiggin	Sumner	640	3211	14 Sep 1797	4169	16 Feb 1797	92	9	Waters of Stones River	yes
Ouss, Jonathan	2385	Dillenberry, Redmond	Davidson	640	3168	14 Sep 1797	4243		90	429	Branches of Suggs Cr & Stones R	yes
Ouster, Ferryman	1332	Hickman, Thomas	Sumner	640	3132	14 Sep 1797	4468	6 May 1797	90	416	On headwaters of Sinking Cr	yes
Outlaw, Alexander	129		Green	640	6	15 Jul 1786			60	348	S side of Nolachucki River	
Outlaw, Alexander	130		Green	640	7	15 Jul 1786	366	23 Oct 1783	60	349	N side of Nolauchuchey River	
Outlaw, Alexander	132		Green	640	9	15 Jul 1786	107	21 Oct 1783	60	351	N side of Nolauchuchey River	
Outlaw, Alexander	133		Green	5000	10	15 Jul 1786	398	21 Oct 1783	60	352	N side of Tennessee River	
Outlaw, Alexander	1563		Green	1300	1310	Aug 1794	171	28 May 1784	83	146	N side of French Broad River	
Outlaw, Alexander	1564		Green	1640	1311	Aug 1794	915	29 Oct 1783	83	147	N side of French Broad River	
Outlaw, Alexander	1565		Green	2000	1312	Aug 1794	2338	25 May 1784	83	147	N side of French Broad River	
Outlaw, Alexander	362	Lewis, Wm. Tyrell	Green	5000	364	20 Sep 1787	381	25 Oct 1783	65	476	N side of Tennessee River	
Outlaw, Alexander	57		Green	400	15	1 Nov 1786	216	24 Oct 1786	59	376	On both sides Bent Creek	
Outlaw, Alexander	574(3)		Sullivan	244	572	29 Jul 1793	829	2 Aug 1781	76	471	N side of Holston River	
Outlaw, Alexander	86		Green	640	44	1 Nov 1786	109	22 Oct 1783	59	405	On Holston River	
Outler, Aaron	279	Phillips, Philip	Sumner	640	1272	10 Dec 1790	2867	25 Feb 1786	74	356	Adj. S boundary line of a tract	yes
Overall, William	1169		Davidson	640	146	17 Apr 1786	130	15 Jan 1784	66	185	A hickory on bank of Overall	
Overall, William	1189		Davidson	640	166	17 Apr 1786	131	20 Jan 1784	66	190	On Overalls Creel	
Overall, William	1247	King, Martin	Davidson	640	212	10 Jul 1788	301	16 Feb 1784	66	414	S side of Cumberland River	
Overall, William	1843		Davidson	640	343	27 Nov 1792	598	13 Sep 1784	81	7	On Turners Creek	
Overstreet, John	113	Tatum, Howell	Tennessee	640	1605	23 Feb 1793	2679	3 Sep 1785	76	315	On waters of Sulphur Fork	yes
Overton, Edward	372	Fort, Elias	Tennessee	640	2271	20 May 1793	1528	2 Feb 1785	81	185	On Buds Creek	yes
Overton, John	081		Middle District	400	204	15 Mar 1800					W of Cumberland Mountain	
Overton, John	1445		Sumner	640	3357	25 May 1800	1144	17 Feb 1797	108	40	On a West fork of Dixons Creek	yes
Overton, John	1457		not given	400	204	17 Feb 1800			106	369	Between North Continental Line	yes
Overton, John	1457		not given	400	204	17 Feb 1800			106	369	Between North Continental Line	
Overton, John	1683	Huddleston, Robert	Davidson	640	1616	23 Feb 1793	1144		76	320	E branch of West Fork of Harpeth	yes

Claimant:	File #:	Assignee:	County:	Acres:	Grant:	Grant Date:	Entry:	Entry Date:	Bk:	Pg:	Location by Stream Name:	Military:
Overton, John	2003	Phillips, Zebulon	Davidson	640	1947	20 May 1793	3645		81	111	On W branch of Stones Creek	yes
Overton, John	2004	Buck, William	Davidson	640	1948	20 May 1793	2102		81	111	W/S West fork of Big Harpeth Riv	yes
Overton, John	294		Tennessee	274	1965	20 May 1793	3156	16 Dec 1785	81	115	North side of Cumberland River	
Overton, John	514	Fry, Buell	Middle District	400	181	20 Jul 1796			88	467	W side Main W Fork of Stones Riv	
Overton, John	515	Marion, Frederick	Middle District	480	182	20 Jul 1796			88	468	W of Cumberland Mountain	
Overton, John	516		Middle District	640	183	20 Jul 1796			88	468	W of Cumberland Mountain	
Overton, John	517		Middle District	640	184	20 Jul 1796			88	469	W side Main W Fork of Stones Riv	
Overton, John	518	Marion, F.	Middle District	480	185	20 Jul 1796			88	469	W of Cumberland Mountain	
Overton, John	519	McConn, James	Middle District	400	186	20 Jul 1796			88	470	W of Cumberland Mountain	
Overton, John	520	Tilley, John	Middle District	400	187	20 Jul 1796			88	470	W of Cumberland Mountain	
Overton, John	635		Sumner	640	1924	20 May 1793	3485	13 Nov 1792	81	106	Both sides of Red or Lick Creek	yes
Overton, John	649		Sumner	1000	1951	20 May 1793	3341	19 Nov 1792	81	112	On the Cedar Lick Creek	yes
Overton, John	653		Sumner	640	1963	20 May 1793	2919	14 Nov 1792	81	115	On a small creek etc.	yes
Owen, John	033	Dillenberry, Redmond	Sumner	640			4469	1 Sep 1797			On Dividing Ridge	yes
Owen, Thomas	7		Maury	5000	22	14 Jul 1812	1507	19 Feb 1784	126	434	On both sides of Big Tombigby Cr.	
Owens, Christopher	111	Bowers, Giles	Davidson	640	97	14 Mar 1786	477		63	39	S side Big Harpeth River	yes
Owens, Don & Fran	0101	Moor, William	Sumner	640			3712				Head fork of Wolf River	yes
Owens, Elijah	703		Washington	200	517	10 Nov 1784	2689	19 Dec 1780	69	111	On Sinking Creek	
Owens, Elijah	841		Washington	100	655	10 Nov 1784	2619	23 Aug 1780	69	153	Bet Thomas Berry & Moses Cavates	
Owens, Elijah	841		Washington	100	655	10 Nov 1784	2619	23 Aug 1780	69	153	Lying between Thos Murry, &c (?)	
Owens, Francis	679	Moore, William	Hawkins	640	2389	12 Jul 1794		1 Sep 1797	81	602	On head fork of Woolf River	yes
Owens, James	572		Washington	87	837	11 Jul 1788	2774	17 Feb 1781	64	338	On Cedar Creek	
Owens, John	12		Sullivan	200	23	23 Oct 1782	366	28 Mar 1780	43	248	On W side of Coles Ridge	
Owens, John	426		Sumner	640	437	27 Jun 1793	217	30 Jan 1784	80	353	S side of Cumberland River	
Owens, Jonathan	816		Sullivan	40	759	17 Nov 1797	377	21 May 1780	94	156	N side of Holston River	
Owens, Owen	725		Washington	150	539	10 Nov 1784	366	8 Sep 1778	69	118	Upon Little Sinking Creek	
Owens, William	1137		Hawkins	200	855	24 Feb 1798	85	8 Feb 1780	97	303	On waters of Poor Valley	
Owens, William	365		Green	200	367	20 Sep 1787	2889	29 Oct 1779	65	477	N side of Holston River	
Owens, William	903	King, Thomas	Hawkins	640	2478	22 Feb 1795	2030		84	327	On E Fork of Emerys River	yes
Owens, Elijah	703		Washington	200	517	10 Nov 1784	2689	19 Dec 1780	69	111	On Sinking Creek	
Owins, Joseph	760		Sullivan	100	739	28 Jul 1797	178	21 Sep 1780	90	387	Beg at said Owens old corner	
Owins, William	1113		Hawkins	100	833	15 Sep 1797	631	8 Feb 1780	94	138	N side of Holston River	
Pable, John	723		Washington	200	537	10 Nov 1784	2134	5 Nov 1779	69	117	On waters of Nolechuckee	
Pace, Demcey	1985	Smith, Oliver	Davidson	640	1890	20 May 1793	1894		81	98	On Duck River	yes
Padgett, Thomas	377	Armstrong, Martin	Davidson	640	349	15 Sep 1787	1298		63	132	On Sturgeons Creek	yes
Padon, Thomas	346	Johnston, Lancelot	Tennessee	640	2167	20 May 1793	1853	15 Jun 1785	81	165	On W side of Red River	yes
Page, Abraham	747	Sheppard, Nancy	Sumner	640	2149	20 May 1793	1500	24 Nov 1792	81	160	On Salt Lick Fork, etc	yes
Page, William	11		Maury	400	27	14 Jul 1812		14 Apr 1793	126	437	On S side of Duck Creek (River ?)	
Page, William	9		Maury	400	25	14 Jul 1812		14 Apr 1812	126	436	On both sides of Duck River	
Paget, Sarah, heiress	334	Stevens, Joseph	Tennessee	640	2111	20 May 1793	3149	16 Dec 1785	81	152	On S side of Cumberland River	
Pain, Arne	06	Barton, Samuel	Sumner	640			3666	5 Dec 1789			Bet head of Round Lick & Cedar Crs	yes
Pain, John	07	Barton, Samuel	Sumner	640			3665	19 Dec 1789			On Jennings For of Round Lick Cr.	yes
Pain, John	525		Hawkins	400	398	29 Jul 1793	819	14 Jul 1788	80	276	On Dodsons Creek	
Pain, Josiah	544		Sumner	1000	1747	20 May 1793	237	30 Dec 1785	81	65	On E side of Cumberland River	yes
Pain, William Jr.	580		Hawkins	400	454	29 Jul 1793	467	24 Apr 1780	80	290	On waters pf Beaver Creek	

Claimant	File #	Assignee	County	Acres	Grant	Grant Date	Entry	Entry Date	Bk	Pg	Location by Stream Name	Military
Paker, William	042	Fisher, Frederick	Davidson	640			3140	12 Sep 1790	61	456	On Dividing Ridge	yes
Palate, Ann	298		Sullivan	147	437	9 Aug 1787	643	10 Jul 1780			Beg at a small white oak, etc.	yes
Pall, Jacob	077	Tyrell & Jas Easton	Davidson	640			4213	12 Jun 1797			On Harpeth River	yes
Palmer, Benjamin	579	Sanford, Samuel	Sumner	640	1817	20 May 1793	2390	6 Aug 1792	81	83	Nead head of N branch of Roaring Riv	yes
Palmer, Elisha	80	Tatum, Howell	Tennessee	640	1326	10 Dec 1790	3679	10 Dec 1788	74	374	On S side of Cumberland River	yes
Palmer, Joseph	533	Davis, Joshua	Davidson	640	505	15 Sep 1787	2430	15 Sep 1787	63	182	On 3rd creek VA line crosses	yes
Pamberly, John	983		Hawkins	90	755	27 Feb 1796	63	8 Feb 1780	88	502	On head of Caney Creek	
Panel, Daniel	1289	Williams, Sampson	Sumner	640	3048	8 Jun 1797	4707	5 Apr 1797	90	317	On head branches of Turkeys Cr	yes
Paramore, Matthew	444		Washington	200	436	13 Oct 1783	1477	21 Jul 1779	52	283	On Lick fork of Lick Creek	
Parberry, James	283		Hawkins	300	294	14 Jan 1793	416	23 Oct 1783	78	344	On N side of Holston River	
Parees, Robert	374		Green	100	376	20 Sep 1787	1219	22 Feb 1779	65	479	On Sinking Creek	
Parish, Henry	1998	Blount, John G. & Thos.	Davidson	274	1937	20 May 1793	1552		81	109	On W side of Big Harpeth	yes
Parish, Nicholas	618	Blount, John G. & Thos.	Sumner	274	1883	20 May 1793	1550		81	97	On Jones Cr, waters of Harpeth	yes
Parker, Arthur	1863	Williams, Sampson	Davidson	228	1595	27 Apr 1793	364	4 Jun 1792	81	16	On S side of Cumberland River	yes
Parker, Arthur	2023	McCulloh, Benjamim	Davidson	1000	2024	20 May 1793	2261		92	130	On Lepers Lick	yes
Parker, Benj (heir of Wm)	1360		Sumner	640	462	2 Aug 1797	699	5 Apr 1785	96	1	On Station Camp Creek	
Parker, Charles	1123	McCormack & Rowan	Davidson	365	842	2 Nov 1797	4754		80	3	Both sides of Lawhaus Creek	yes
Parker, Charles	1792	Armstrong, Martin	Davidson	100	134	29 Aug 1793			80	325	On N side of Cumberland River	
Parker, Charles	649		Sullivan	50	597	27 June 1783	283		88	382	On S side of Holston River	
Parker, Hillary	2255	Donelson, Stockley	Davidson	640	2715	20 Jul 1796	3807		74	447	On waters of Stones River	yes
Parker, Isom	306	Barrow, Betsy	Sumner	640	1375	20 Apr 1791	2756	20 Nov 1790	90	396	On E side of Jennings Fork	yes
Parker, James	1321	McConnel, Robert	Sumner	228	3121	14 Sep 1797	4726	3 Jun 1797	74	412	On waters of Big Barren	yes
Parker, Jeptha	1601	Clark, Lardner	Davidson	1000	1306	10 Dec 1790	87		90	367	On waters of Harrian (?) Creek	yes
Parker, John	1337	Brooke, Matthew	Sumner	640	3137	14 Sep 1797	4158	5 May 1797	91	418	Waters of N fork of Big Barren Cr	yes
Parker, John	780		Sullivan	140	712	18 Mar 1796	227	21 Feb 1780	81	88	Beg at a white oak, etc	
Parker, Joseph	848	Fishburn, Phillip	Sumner	1000	2351	20 May 1793	1492	27 Oct 1792	81	202	At the head of Flinns Creek	yes
Parker, Samuel	679		Sumner	3840	2022	20 May 1793	170	17 Jun 1785	81	130	Both sides of Cumberland River	yes
Parker, Simon	748	Steed, Jesse	Sumner	640	2151	20 May 1793	548	3 Feb 1790	88	161	On waters of Pound Lick Creek	yes
Parker, Thomas	032	Hill, Henry	Montgomery	640	3806		3806	5 May 1797			Waters of Little West Fork of Red Riv.	yes
Parker, Thomas	1072	Hill, Henry	Sumner	640	2520	10 Dec 1795	190	8 Aug 1794	72	298	W side of W fork of Obeys River	yes
Parker, William	05		Sullivan	55	22	18 May 1789	2353	21 Feb 1780			Beg at Alex Fords corner	
Parker, William	37		Hawkins	580	451	13 Oct 1783	881	16 Dec 1779	52	245	N side of Clinch River, etc.	
Parker, William	459		Washington	450	667	8 Dec 1787	2090	12 Jan 1781	63	289	On Stoney Creek	
Parker, William	694	Sheppard, Nancy	Davidson	640					63	236	On Hays's Creek	yes
Parker, William & Jno Carter	096		Washington								Cavit	
Parkerson, James	38	Parkerson, Rebecca (heir)	Davidson	2560	24	14 Mar 1786	2560		63	10	On head of 1st big creek (??)	yes
Parkerson, Rebecca	38	Parkerson, James	Davidson	2560	24	14 Mar 1786	2560		63	10	On head of 1st big creek (??)	yes
Parkes, George	499		Middle District	5000	299	26 Sep 1795	447	25 Oct 1783	86	529	On S side of Cumberland River	
Parkison, Peter	1076		Washington	200	1026	27 May 1792	1809		80	183	In the fork of Doe River	
Parks, David	420		Middle District	1000	359	17 Dec 1794	1978	23 Apr 1784	84	233	On N fork of Duck River	
Parks, George	744		Sumner	640	2142	20 May 1793	1781	24 Nov 1793	81	159	On Jinnings Fork, etc.	yes
Parks, Hugh	167		Middle District	640	177	20 Dec 1791	2945	28 Feb 1779	75	226	On headwaters of Big Harper Riv	
Parks, Samuel	465	Hays, Robert	Tennessee	640	2593	7 Mar 1796	3292	30 Sep 1785	88	323	Beg at a black oak	yes
Parks, Solomon	1990		Davidson	733	1906	20 May 1793	3094		81	101	On E fork of Lick Creek	yes
Parmely, Ephraim	694	Lewis, Wm. Tyrell	Sumner	640	2061	20 May 1793		27 Mar 1792	81	139	On Bledsoes Creek	yes

Claimant:	File #:	Assignee:	County:	Acres:	Grant:	Entry:	Grant Date:	Entry Date:	Bk:	Pg:	Location by Stream Name:	Military:
Parmore, Ezekiel	786		Washington	100	600	1566	10 Nov 1784	10 Jul 1780	69	138	On W side of Big Limestone	
Parmore, Matthew	416		Washington	200	408	2320	13 Oct 1783	27 Nov 1779	52	269	On N fork of Lick Creek	
Parnel, Joshua	1094	Easton, James	Sumner	640	2585	2219	7 Mar 1796	22 Jul 1795	88	319	N side of large fork of Caney Fork	yes
Parr, George	1201	Scott, Joshua	Sumner	182	2773	3696	10 Sep 1796	3 Aug 1796	88	524	On waters of Station Camp Creek	yes
Parr, Joseph	1734		Davidson	274	1456		20 Dec 1791		77	365	On the head of Holstons Creek	
Parr, Josiah	029	Lewis & Tyrrell	Montgomery	274		410		27 May 1796			On Spring Creek	
Parr, William	131		Davidson	274	117	992	7 Mar 1786		63	46	North side of Cumberland River	yes
Parrees, Robert	525		Green	100	527	806	20 Sep 1787	28 Dec 1778	65	531	On Sinking Creek	yes
Parres, Joseph	562		Washington	200	827		11 Jul 1788		64	336	On waters of Sinking Creek	
Parrett, John	298		Green	640	300	244	20 Sep 1787	22 Oct 1785	65	458	On Clear Creek	
Parrish, Mark	188	O'Neale, Thomas	Middle District	1000	1664	3019	8 Mar 1783(93)		76	343	On waters of Cumberland River	yes
Parrot, Benjamin	040	Stewart & Robertson	Tennessee	640	3215	4434		22 Dec 1796			On headwaters of Johnsons Cr.	yes
Parrott, William	400		Green	100	482(?)	2162	20 Sep 1787	6 Nov 1779	65	486	On Lick Creel	
Parry, Francis	1039	King, Robert	Hawkins	640	2957	4748	22 Feb 1797		90	233	On a branch of Clinch River	yes
Parsons, Harrison	1622	Hodges, Benja.	Davidson	640	1358	1080	10 Dec 1790		74	385	Beg at two white oak trees	yes
Partin, John	98		Eastern District	200	87	389	17 Nov 1790	7 April 1780	76	172	On S side of Holston River	
Pasmore, David	1496	Kelly, Charles	Davidson	580	1053	418	26 Nov 1789		74	103	On N side of Cumberland River	yes
Pasmore, David	952	Berry, John	Davidson	1000	969	361	18 May 1789		63	329	On the bank of a small creek	yes
Pasmore, David	992	Right, Isaac	Davidson	365	1009	417	18 May 1789		63	338	On waters of Stones River	yes
Pasmore, Enoch	1974	Rice, John & Harriett	Davidson	640	1869	1724	20 May 1793		81	94	On S side of Cumberland River	yes
Passmore, Joseph	819	Sheppard, Nancy	Sumner	640	2294	2091	20 May 1793	29 Oct 1792	81	190	Bet middle & east forks of Goose Cr	yes
Passmore, Joshua	044	Tatum, Howell	Tennessee	640		3513		8 Feb 1786			E side of Cumberland River	yes
Pasture, Thomas	529		Davidson	2560	501	299	15 Sep 1787		63	181	E side of Big Harpeth River	yes
Pate, Matthew	381		Green	100	383	16	20 Sep 1787	17 Oct 1783	65	401	On N side of Nolechuckey River	
Pate, William	2448	Wheaton, Daniel	Davidson	640	3291	4289	6 Dec 1797		98	168	Dividing waters Cumberland & Harpeth	yes
Pater, Reese	414		Middle District	2000	353	1272	17 Dec 1794	23 Dec 1783	84	230	Both sides of Weakleys Creek	
Patterson, Mark	873		Sumner	640	2389		7 Jan 1794		81	388	On Sinking Creek	yes
Patterson, Hardy	1574	Clark, Lardner	Davidson	640	1217	1659(?)	10 Dec 1790		74	337	On Big Harpeth River	yes
Patterson, James	01		Western District	2500		2561	31 Jul 1787	25 May 1784			E side of Mississippi River	
Patterson, James	171		Hawkins	100	104	717	16 Nov 1790	25 Jun 1784	77	186	On N side of Holston River	
Patterson, James	223		Sullivan	226	362	76	9 Aug 1787	8 Feb 1780	61	381	On both sides of the big road	
Patterson, James	224		Sullivan	200	363	232	9 Aug 1787	24 Feb 1780	61	382	In the fork of Fall Creek	
Patterson, James	23		Western District	1000	23	2334	10 Jul 1788	25 May 1784	67	289	Waters of Long Fork, &c	
Patterson, James	234		Hawkins	100	221	988	26 Dec 1791	29 Oct 1783	77	320	Near Roseberry Creek	
Patterson, James	24		Western District	1000	24	2333	18 Jul 1788	25 May 1784	67	289	Waters of Long Fork, &c	
Patterson, James	36		Sullivan	265	47	231	23 Oct 1782	25 Feb 1780	43	260	Waters of Fall Creek	
Patterson, James	379		Western District	2500	343	2364	17 Nov 1790	25 May 1784	76	167	On the Mississippi	
Patterson, James	385		Western District	5000	385	2622	27 Nov 1793	25 May 1784	81	502	On waters of Mississippi (?)	
Patterson, James	394		Western District	5000	395	2557	27 Nov 1793	25 May 1784	81	505	On waters of Mississippi (?)	
Patterson, James	395		Western District	5000	396	2560	27 Nov 1793	12 Jan 1785	81	505	On waters of Mississippi (?)	
Patterson, James	570		Sullivan	44	568	2217	29 Jul 1793	13 Nov 1779	76	470	N side of Holstein River	
Patterson, Jesse	58		Washington	298	226	188	23 Oct 1782	19 Mar 1778	44	258	S side of Holston River	
Patterson, Jesse	1659	Robertson, James	Davidson	320	1582	1337	23 Feb 1793		76	304	Both sides of Big Harpeth River	yes
Patterson, Jno	577		Green	200	258	49	20 Sep 1787	10 May 1784	66	160	On a branch of Long Creek &C	
Patterson, John	084		Green	100		32		1 Nov 1779			Head of Francis Holleys Creek	

Earliest Tennessee Land Records

Claimant:	File #:	Assignee:	County:	Acres:	Grant:	Grant Date:	Entry:	Entry Date:	Bk:	Pg:	Location by Stream Name:	Military:
Patterson, John	1031		Green	200	1258	29 Jul 1793	46	10 May 1784	76	490	On a small branch of Long Creek	
Patterson, John	1053		Green	300	896	26 Dec 1791	1736	17 Apr 1784	77	240	On S side of Holston River	
Patterson, John	27		Washington	200	317	24 Oct 1782	872	31 Dec 1778	43	305	On head of Caney Fork Branch	
Patterson, John	314		Green	100	316	20 Sep 1787	38	5 May 1784	65	463	Joining the North &c (?)	
Patterson, John	392		Green	300	394	20 Sep 1787	48	10 May 1784	65	484	On N side of Holston River	
Patterson, John	447		Green	200	449	20 Sep 1787	1411	17 Jan 1784	65	501	On a small branch of Long Creek	
Patterson, John	790		Hawkins	150	630	12 Jul 1794	1878	7 Oct 1779	82	223	On the N side of Holston River	
Patterson, John	921		Hawkins	250	730	7 Mar 1796	1360	9 Mar 1779	88	205	On N side of Holston River	
Patterson, Robert	101		Sullivan	250	112	23 Oct 1782	1854	6 Oct 1779	43	291	N side of Holston River	
Patterson, Robert	1401		Green	287	1213	27 Nov 1792	357	23 Oct 1785	80	155	N side of Holston River	
Patterson, Samuel	411		Middle District	2500	350	17 Dec 1794	1818	23 April 1784	84	229	N side of Duck River	
Patterson, William	072		Sullivan	100			645	11 July 1780			In Carters Valley	
Patterson, William	153		Washington	400	21	23 Oct 1782	359	5 Sep 1778	47	9	On a branch of Watauga River	
Patterson, William	523		Green	500	525	20 Sep 1787	353	23 Oct 1783	65	530	On N side of Holston River	
Patterson, William	88		Sullivan	187	99	23 Oct 1782	37	6 Feb 1780	43	285	In Carters Valley	
Pattes, Stephen	725		Davidson	640	698	11 Jul 1788	1508		63	246	On both sides of Sycamore Creek	yes
Patton, Anthony	868		Green	8	818	27 Nov 1789	112	10 Jul 1789	74	19	On French Broad River	
Patton, Elijah	166		Middle District	100	176	20 Dec 1791	2069	5 May 1784	75	226	On Knob Creek	
Patton, Elijah	28		Western District	1000	28	10 Jul 1788	2068	5 May 1784	67(?)	290	Waters of S & Rutherford Forks	
Patton, Henry	1622		Green	200	1343	22 Feb 1793	415	14 Apr 1780	84	297	On N side of French Broad River	
Patton, John	1179		Washington	430	1137	7 Jul 1794	4 Warrants	4 diff dates	81	622	Beg at a black oak	
Patton, John	440	Blount, John G. & Thos.	Davidson	7200	412	15 Sep 1787	354	6 Apr 1780	63	153	On E fork of 3rd Big Creek	yes
Patton, Joseph	049		Washington	200			252	1 Apl 1784			On N side of Holston River	
Patton, Robert	63		Western District	1000	63	10 Jul 1788	1569	1 Apl 1784	67	304	On Rutherford Fork of Obion Riv	
Patton, Saml, Jr	37	Nichols, Thomas	Middle District	1000	39	10 Jul 1788	2284	24 May 1784	67	425	On the S side of Duck River	
Patton, Samuel, Jr.	54		Middle District	1500	56	10 Jul 1788	1801	3 Apl 1784	67	438	On the S side of Duck River	
Patton, Samuel, Sr.	8		Middle District	520	10	10 Jul 1788	1800	23 Apr 1784	67	410	Lying on Duck River	
Patton, Thomas	639		Sumner	218	1928	20 May 1793	1357	20 May 1786	81	107	On waters of Station Camp Creek	yes
Paul, James	085		Green	640			292	23 Oct 1783			S W side of French Broad River	
Paul, James	2350	Smith, John	Tennessee	640	3012	10 Apl 1797	3182		90	298	On Lick Crek	
Paul, James	830		Green	250	803 (?)	5 Jul 1790	51	20 Jun 1787	73	98	Be at a white walnut &c	
Paul, James	960		Green	640	874	17 Nov 1790	305	23 Oct 1783	76	129	W side of Holston River	
Paul, Norris	1348	Stewart, Duncan	Sumner	640	3158	14 Sep 1797	4154	30 May 1797	90	425	On waters of Big Barren	yes
Payne, Charles	104		Eastern District	200	93	17 Nov 1790	1378	21 May 1779	76	174	On Iry Cr, S side of Holston River	
Payne, Charles	493		Sullivan	100	504	18 May 1780	1397	21 May 1777	71	13	N side of Holston River	
Payne, Charles	573		Hawkins	200	447	29 Jul 1793	562	31 Aug 1778	80	289	S side of Holston River	
Payne, George	1314		Davidson	640	280	10 Jul 1788	744	14 June 1785	66	435	On W fork of Station Camp Creek	
Payne, Henry	0125		Green	150			1422	21 Jan 1784			On the N side of French Broad Riv	
Payne, Henry	1095		Green	150	938	26 Dec 1791	1422	21 Jan 1784	77	256	On head of McCloardye Cr	
Payne, Henry	896		Green	350	827	Sep 1790	950	29 Oct 1783	74	292	On N side of French Broad River	
Payne, John	028	Terrell, Wm.	Eastern District	200				29 Mar 1780			Knox County	
Payne, John	098	Terrell, Wm.	not given	1000			369	2 Apl 1782				
Payne, John	257		Hawkins	200	245	Mar 1792	22	26 Feb 1778	77	334	On N side of Holston River	
Payne, John	264		Eastern District	500	663	7 Feb 1795	1211	4 Nov 1783	83	390	On Fourth Creek	
Payne, John	287		Eastern District	640	210	5 Feb 1795	1962	5 Feb 1780	84	130	On N side of Clinch River	

Claimant:	File #:	Assignee:	County:	Acres:	Grant:	Grant Date:	Entry:	Entry Date:	Bk:	Pg:	Location by Stream Name:	Military:
Payne, John	823		Hawkins	500	663	7 Feb 1795			83	390	On Fourth Creek	
Payne, Josiah	1607	Armstrong, M.	Davidson	78	1330	10 Dec 1790			74	375	On E side of Cumberland River	
Payne, Josiah	2194		Davidson	121	186	26 Sep 1795		8 Aug 1795	86	530	On Wm. Stewarts corner	
Payne, Josiah	912		Sumner	640	2481	31 Dec 1793	2529	22 Dec 1792	81	437	On W side of Caney Fork	yes
Payne, Matthew	1160		Davidson	640	137	17 Apr 1786	526	15 Jul 1784	66	183	Lying on mouth of Pasgers Creek	
Payne, Peter	562	Lancaster, John	Sumner	640	1785	20 May 1793	2220	2 Jun 1792	81	75	On headwaters of a creek	yes
Payne, Thomas	807		Washington	500	621	10 Nov 1784	1271	8 Mar 1779	69	144	On Flanarys Fork	
Payne, Thomas	811		Washington	450	625	10 Nov 1784	1270	8 Mar 1779	69	145	On Rones Creek	
Payne, Thomas Jr.	961		Washington	132 (?)	938	17 Nov 1790			76	157	On Roans Creek	
Payne, Thos. Jr.	050		Washington	140			1102	9 Jan 1779			On Flanarys Fork	
Payne, William	1093	Smith, John & Jos Cobb	Hawkins	640	822	19 Jul 1797	111	26 Feb 1778	91	615	On Blairs Creek	
Payne, William	212		Hawkins	300	199	26 Dec 1791	56	26 Feb 1778	77	313	N S of Holston Riv	
Payne, William	33		Sullivan	420	44	23 Oct 1782	467	24 Apr 1780	43	258	On right hand fork of Dodsons Cr.	
Payne, William	490		Sullivan	300	501	18 May 1789	650	13 Jul 1780	71	12	On left hand fork of Dodson Cr	
Payne, William	495		Sullivan	300	506	18 May 1789	1385	21 May 1779	71	14	S side of Holston River	
Payne, William	516		Sullivan	200	532	26 Nov 1789	579	3 May 1780	73	46	On S side of Holston River	
Payne, William	607		Washington	200	701	26 Oct 1786	562	26 Oct 1778	66	122	Joining Mark Mochells claim	
Payne, William Jr.	223		Eastern District	400	166	23 Apr 1794	819	14 Jul 1781	82	155	N S Clinch Riv on Sp Fk of Sycamore	
Payner, Peter	175		Davidson	274	161	7 Mar 1796	997		63	61	South S of Cumberland River	yes
Peale, Daniel	130	Peale, James	Davidson	640	116	7 Mar 1786	1346		63	46	On lge or running into TN River	yes
Pearce, Daniel	1526		Green	600	1287	12 Jul 1794	725	1 Jan 1781	81	590	On N/S of Nolichuckey River	
Pearce, James	1074		Green	640	917	26 Dec 1791	6	15 Aug 1785	77	248	Beg at two persimmons	
Pearce, James	1150		Green	150	993	26 Dec 1791	68 (?)	20 Nov 1788	77	279	Beg post oak on Moses Moore	
Pearce, James	1161		Green	300	1004	26 Dec 1791	78	22 Oct 1783	77	283	On N side of Nolechuckey River	
Pearce, James	12		Washington	100	301	24 Oct 1782	302	5 Aug 1778	43	298	On Little Limestone	
Pearce, James	202	Pearce, John (heir)	Davidson	640	188	7 Mar 1786	725		63	70	S/S of Cumberland River	yes
Pearce, John	1675		Green	200	1380	20 July 1796	6	24 Feb 1778	88	492	Beg at a white oak	
Pearce, John	202	Pearce, John (heir of Jas)	Davidson	640	188	7 Mar 1786	725		63	70	S side of Cumberland River	yes
Pearce, Robert	1059		Hawkins	140	768	21 Jan 1797	47	8 Feb 1778	91	114	On head waters of Whites Creek	
Pearce, Theophilus	930	Lytle, William	Sumner	640	2381	8 Jan 1795	1060	8 Jul 1785	83	236	On N side of Cumberland River	yes
Pearce, Thomas	127	Edwards, David	Davidson	640	113	7 Mar 1786	700		63	45	On Station Camp Creek	yes
Pearer, Nehemiah	736		Davidson	640	709	11 Jul 1788	934		63	249	Bet head of Calebs & Millers Cr.	yes
Pearl, James	2468a	Weakley, R. & Thos Bedfor	Davidson	3840	3390	12 Dec 1801	3042	30 Aug 1780	114	93	Lying on Stones River	yes
Pearpoint, Larkin	546		Sullivan	83	529	17 Nov 1790	679		76	188	Joining a former entry of Thomas Braggs	
Pearsall, Jos.	234		Middle District	1000	214	1 Jan 1793	2111	4 May 1784	80	212	On the S side of Duck River	
Pearson, Christian	300		Eastern District	200	209	22 Feb 1795	1851	7 Oct 1779	84	286	Upon Stock Creek	
Pearson, James	2047	Prescote, Thomas	Davidson	1000	2078	20 May 1793	3055		81	144	On Cripple Creek	yes
Pearson, James	2080	Cormack, John	Davidson	640	2265	20 May 1793	3038		81	184	On Cripple Creek	yes
Peat, Matthew	280		Green	72	382(282)	20 May 1787		23 Oct 1783	65	453	On N/S of Nolichuckey River	
Peat, Matthew	388		Green	200	390	20 Sep 1787	298	23 Oct 1783	65	483	On N/S of Nolichuckey River	
Peaton, Nancy	1181		Green	300	1024	26 Dec 1791	471	25 Oct 1783	77	290	Beg at a sugar tree	
Peble, John	1613		Green	300	1325	5 Dec 1784	880	31 Dec 1778	84	154	Joining Gillespie	
Peck, Joseph	304		Eastern District	400	213	22 Feb 1795	1282	7 Jun 1784	84	288	On S side of Little River	
Pecking, James	704		Sullivan	100	649	5 Dec 1794			84	160	Beg at a white oak	
Pemberton, John	302		Washington	300	169	24 Oct 1782	1265	8 Mar 1779	47	82	N side of Holston River	

Claimant:	File #:	Assignee:	County:	Acres:	Grant:	Grant Date:	Entry:	Entry Date:	Bk:	Pg:	Location by Stream Name:	Military:
Pemberton, John	427		Sullivan	306	306	10 Nov 1784	129	9 Feb 1780	69	178	Beg at red oak & dogwood saplin	
Pemberton, William	53		Sullivan	200	64	23 Oct 1782	165	18 Feb 1780	43	269	On both sides of Sinking Creek	
Pender, Thomas	1275	Fell, Watson	Tennessee	640	3017	10 Apl 1797	3181		90	300	Abt 1 1/2 miles below Dyers Creek	yes
Pendergrass, John	205	Robertson, James	Davidson	274	191	7 Mar 1786	274		63	71	On waters of Big Harpeth River	yes
Pendergrass, John	493	Nelson, Robert	Tennessee	640	2490	26 Sep 1795	1881	11 Jul 1785	89	102	N side of Red River	yes
Pendergrass, John	494	McNairy, John	Tennessee	640	2493	26 Sep 1795	1876	4 Jul 1785	89	104	On W fork of Gillon Creek	yes
Pendergrass, John	599	Robertson, James	Davidson	274	571	15 Sep 1787	271		63	204	S side of Cumberland River	yes
Pendergrass, William	2336	Malloy, Thos.	Davidson	640	2980	10 Apr 1797	3180		90	285	Waters of Harpeth	yes
Peners, Thomas	582	Sanford, Samuel	Sumner	640	1821	20 May 1793	2391	6 Aug 1792	81	84	Near headwaters of a small creek	yes
Peney, Francis	2268	Coghill, James	Davidson	1000	2746	20 Jul 1796	2620	2 Apr 1780	88	455	On lge fork of Tennessee River	
Penkerton, John	04		Sullivan	10			507				Beg at Jno Karwoods old point	
Penney, James	1316		Washington	220	1236	19 Feb 1797	1134	25 Jan 1779	90	246	Waters of Watauga River	yes
Pennington, Isaac	250	Tyner, Nicholas	Davidson	266	236	7 Mar 1786	707		63	87	On Red River	
Pennington, Jacob	1344	Ballard, Frances	Davidson	320	30	18 Aug 1787	224	4 Feb 1784	68	132	On Spring Creek of Red River	
Peoples, John	1135		Washington	100	1093	12 Jul 1794	2373	25 Feb 1779	81	567	A branch of Buffalo	
Peoples, John	914		Washington	100	891	17 Nov 1790			76	141	On branch of Buffalow River	
Peoples, William	1178		Washington	100	1136	7 Jul 1794	1109	13 Jan 1779	81	621	Beg at 2 mulberry trees	
Perkins, Adam	1735	Cummins, George	Davidson	274	1475	4 Jan 1792	1726		77	370	S side of Cumberland River	yes
Perkins, Adam	248	Murphree, Hardy	Davidson	640	234	7 Mar 1786	732		63	86	On branch of fork of Big Creek	yes
Perkins, Constant	208		Hawkins	400	195	26 Dec 1791	910	7 Jan 1784	77	312	On N side of Holston River	
Perkins, Constantine	168	Poor, John	Tennessee	640	1432	20 Dec 1791	3071	30 Nov 1785	77	359	On waters of Sulphur Fork of Red R	
Perkins, Constantine	629		Green	640	670	11 Jul 1788	909	29 Oct 1783	66	450	On N side of Holston River	
Perkins, Daniel	915		Green	100	829	17 Nov 1790	58	12 May 1784	76	114	Joins Johnstons on Mossy Creek	
Perkins, George	953		Washington	100	930	17 Nov 1790	1713	24 Sep 1779	76	155	On 1st fork of Little Doe River	yes
Perkins, Isaac	053	McCall, Alex	Middle District	274			3203	19 Dec 1785		135	On Cambells Creek	
Perkins, Isaac	897		Washington	100	874	17 Nov 1790	2920	29 Aug 1781	76	505	On N side of Cumberland River	yes
Perkins, James	1640	Whitsell, William	Davidson	640	1513	10 Apr 1792	611		75	287	On Harpeth River	yes
Perkins, James	2342	Malloy, Thos.	Davidson	640	2986	10 Apl 1797	3179		90	431	N side of Cumberland River	yes
Perkins, Lewis	614	McQuillin, Wm. (heirs)	Tennessee	640	3173	14 Sep 1797	4016	26 Nov 1786	75	168	Bet Wm Johnson & Jones Survey	
Perkins, Nicholas	127		Hawkins	200	161	26 Dec 1791	142	10 Mar 1778	75	171	On S side of Holston River	
Perkins, Nicholas	134		Hawkins	640	168	26 Dec 1791			75	174	On S side of Holston River	
Perkins, Nicholas	144		Hawkins	400	178	26 Dec 1791	884	7 June 1784	81	556	On N side of French Broad River	
Perkins, Nicholas	1467		Green	100	1217	23 May 1794	2566	30 May 1780	82	155	On waters of Dumplin Creek	
Perkins, Nicholas	1553		Green	300	1218	27 Nov 1793	907	29 Oct 1783	88	382	On Dumplin Creel	
Perkins, Nicholas	1666		Green	100	288	6 Jun 1796		12 Dec 1795	77	311	On N side of Holston River	
Perkins, Nicholas	206		Hawkins	200	193	26 Dec 1791	659	1 Sep 1789	80	150	On waters of Money Creek	
Perkins, Nicholas	419		Hawkins	640	307	27 Nov 1792	889	29 Oct 1783	80	151(8)	Beg at Lees corner at a post oak	
Perkins, Nicholas	420		Hawkins	640	308	27 Nov 1792	887	27 Oct 1783	81	554	On S side of Holston River	
Perkins, Nicholas	648		Hawkins	300	518	May 1794			82	175	On S side of Holston River	
Perkins, Nicholas	740		Hawkins	150	560	12 Jun 1794	1385	15 Jan 1784	88	499	On N side of Holston River	
Perkins, Nicholas	977		Hawkins	387	749	20 Jul 1796	889	29 Oct 1783	82	166	On N side of Holston River	
Perkins, Nicholas Tate	718		Hawkins	400	538	12 Jun 1794	2183	11 Nov 1779			In forks of Doe River	
Perkinson, Peter	082		Washington	200	338	24 Oct 1782	666		43	314	On the Cow Pasture Branch	
Perrimore, Matthew	48		Washington	500	810	18 May 1789			72	245	On N side of Holston River	
Perrin, Joseph	829		Green	200								

Claimant:	File #:	Assignee:	County:	Acres:	Grant:	Grant Date:	Entry:	Entry Date:	Bk:	Pg:	Location by Stream Name:	Military:
Perry, David	102		Washington	222	270	24 Oct 1782	459	30 Sep 1778	44	283	On N side of Big Limestone	
Perry, David	610		Sullivan	450	565	26 Dec 1791	414	22 Sep 1778	77	308	On Kendricks Creek	
Perry, David	769		Washington	200	583	10 Nov 1784	2615	14 Aug 1780	69	133	On waters of Kendricks Creek	
Perry, George	293		Middle District	300	253	7 Jul 1794	1528	24 Feb 1784	82	200	On Clear Fork of Cumberland River	
Perry, John	1736	Ford, Thomas	Davidson	228	1476	4 Jan 1792	1573		77	370	On S side of Cumberland River	yes
Perry, Robert	340	Porterfield, John	Tennessee	640	2133	20 May 1793	3061	30 Nov 1785	81	157	Joining James Sanders Survey	yes
Perry, Sion	642		Sumner	497	1932	20 May 1793	3363	17 Nov 1792	81	108	On Middle Fork Station Camp Cr	yes
Perry, Sion	662		Sumner	640	1982	20 May 1793	3664	5 May 1790	81	120	On head of Red River	yes
Perry, William	1084	Donelson, S & W. Tyrrel	Sumner	640	2574	7 Mar 1796	2946	2 Nov 1795	88	313	On br of Pond Lick Creek	yes
Perry, William	1087	Donelson, S & W. Tyrrel	Sumner	640	2578	7 Mar 1796	2941		88	315	On a branch of Pond Lick Creek	yes
Perryman, Benoni	917		Green	200	831	17 Nov 1790	1537	17 Mar 1784	76	115	N side of Holston River	
Perryman, James	581	Williams, Eliza	Middle District	640	2788	20 Dec 1796	1523		91	322	Both sides of the Caney Fork	
Person, Nathan	579	Williams, Eliza	Middle District	640	2786	20 Dec 1796	1339		91	321	Waters of the Caney Fork	
Person, Thomas	2067	Mitchel, Abraham	Davidson	228	2206	20 May 1793	1723		81	170	On N side of Harpeth River	
Person, Thomas	405	Thomas, Ann	Tennessee	228	2431	18 Mar 1794	1292	1 Nov 1784	81	421	On Bushes Meat House fk of Pine R	
Person, Thomas	406	Gist, Robert	Tennessee	640	2432	1 Nov 1784	1294	1 Nov 1784	81	421	W Branch of Pine River	
Person, Thomas	407	Inman(?), George	Tennessee	228	2433	18 Mar 1794	1542	12 Feb 1785	81	421	On Waters of Beaver Creek	
Person, Thomas	408	Hawley, Joseph	Tennessee	640	2434	18 Mar 1794	1291	1 Nov 1784	81	422	E branch of Pine River	
Person, Thomas	94	Williams, George	Tennessee	228	1361	20 Dec 1791	1543	12 Feb 1785	75	503	Both sides of Beaver Creek	
Person, Thomas	95	Macon, John	Tennessee	640	1377	20 Dec 1791	1388	12 Nov 1784	75	504	W side of Bushes Meat House	
Person, Thomas	96	Bosley, Jacob	Tennessee	640	1378	20 Dec 1791	1389	12 Nov 1784	75	504	On Both sides of Taylors Creek	
Person, Thomas	97	Ballard, Peter	Tennessee	640	1379	20 Dec 1791	2166	12 Sep 1785	75	504	Both sides of Bushes Meat House	
Person, Thomas	98	Tucker, Saml	Tennessee	640	1380	20 Dec 1791	3253	24 Dec 1785	75	505	Both sides of Bushes Meat House	
Person, Thos	95		Tennessee	640	1377	20 Dec 1791	1388	12 Nov 1784	75	504	W side of Bushes Meat House	
Persythe, Joseph	033	Blount, Reading	Middle District	640			2150					yes
Perth, George	317		Sumner	640	310	17 Nov 1790	683	15 Feb 1785	76	184	On waters of Sycamore Creek	
Perth, George	318		Sumner	640	311	17 Nov 1790	798	12 Feb 1788	76	185	On waters of Sycamore Creek	
Pervice, James	1942	Brown, John & John & John Davie	Davidson	640	1793	20 May 1793	2813		81	70	On SW side of Harpeth River	yes
Pervice, James	244	Brown, John	Sumner	640	1149	26 Nov 1789	2813	19 Apr 1788	74	153	On S side of Cumberland River	yes
Perviehouse, John	1049		Washington	50	999	27 Nov 1792	1096	9 Feb 1779	80	176	On dreams of Watauga River	
Pervin, John	467	Barnet, Robert	Sumner	287	1624	27 Apr 1793	3677	17 Feb 1790	81	23	On S side of Cumberland River	yes
Peters, Coonrod	109		Sullivan	287	120	23 Oct 1782	162, 1658	1779 & 1780	43	295	On waters of White Top Creek	
Peters, Daniel	502	Bledsoe, Anthony	Sumner	274	1673	20 May 1793	3018	30 May 1780	81	47	On waters of Middle Fork	yes
Peters, Elizabeth T.	392		Eastern District	640	234	17 Nov 1795	1756	16 Sep 1779	89	290	On N side of Clinch River	
Peters, George	1127		Washington	100	1086	12 Jul 1794			81	564	On Doe River	
Peters, James Jr.	399		Eastern District	640	241	27 Nov 1795	1718	16 Sep 1779	89	294	N side of Clinch River	
Peters, Thomas	336	Canady, James	Eastern District	640	2511	20 Nov 1795	2114		88	282	On N side of Clinch River	
Peters, Titus	1127	Harris, Edward	Sumner	640	2633	4 Jun 1796	2461	1 Jun 1795	88	345	Joining sd Harris survey	yes
Petiet, Benjamin	1203		Davidson	640	75	8 Oct 1792	75	10 Jan 1784	66	224	Lying on Whites Creek	
Petree, Adam	1177		Washington	300	1135	7 Jul 1794	2712	4 Jan 1781	81	621	Beg at a chestnut	
Petterson, John	408		Hawkins	200	529	27 Jan 1793	450	6 Oct 1783	79	500	On N side of Holston River	
Pettigrew, Hara(?)	416	Blair, John	Davidson	1000	388	15 Sep 1787	2022		63	145	On water of Spring Creek	yes
Pettit, Benjamin	1316		Green	200	1166	12 Jan 1793	2038	27 Oct 1779	78	403	On Alexanders Creek	
Pettit, Nehamiah	1070		Green	35	913	26 Dec 1791	3002	26 Mar 1784	77	246	Waters of Lick Creek on Alexander	yes
Pettit, Nehamiah	1586		Green	40	133	4 Feb 1795	2712	28 Jul 1794	83	404	E side of French Broad River	

Claimant:	File #:	Assignee:	County:	Acres:	Grant:	Grant Date:	Entry:	Entry Date:	Bk:	Pg:	Location by Stream Name:	Military:
Petty, John	1015	Bailes, Barnabas	Davidson	228	1032	18 May 1789	1821		63	344	On E fork of Whites Creek	yes
Pevehouse, Abraham	439		Eastern District	320	296	19 Jul 1797	2187	12 Mar 1779	91	616	Place Pevehouse now lives on	
Pevehouse, Abraham	664		Hawkins	300(350)	569	12 Jul 1794	1339	6 Oct 1779	81	593	On S side of Powells River	
Peveshouse, John	900		Washington	100	877	17 Nov 1790	2029	26 Oct 1779	76	136	On branch of S fork of Cobbs Cr	
Peveshouse, John	902		Washington	100	879	17 Nov 1790	1674	18 Sep 1779	76	137	On S fork of Cobbs Creek	
Pevy, Nehniah	2240	Randolph, Benjamin	Davidson	1000	2687	6 Jun 1796	3869		88	364	On headwaters of Sulphur Fork	yes
Pew, Arthur	199	Hollis, James	Davidson	640	185	7 Mar 1786	728		63	69	On a branch of Halfpone Cr	yes
Pew, Lewis	804	Williams, Willoughby	Sumner	640	2269	20 May 1793	2053	4 Feb 1786	81	185	On W fork of Goose Creek	yes
Peyton, Ephraim	1000		Sumner	480	156	17 Dec 1794		11 Feb 1792	84	333	On S side of Cumberland River	yes
Peyton, Ephraim	1018	Armstrong, M.	Sumner	200	205	27 Feb 1796			88	163	On N side of Cumberland River	
Peyton, Ephraim	1260		Davidson	640	225	10 Jul 1788	664	19 Jan 1785	66	417	On Bledsoes Cr beg at a pine & red oak	
Peyton, Ephraim	1837		Davidson	640	332	27 Nov 1792	154	17 Jan 1784	81	4	On Station Camp Creek	
Peyton, Ephraim	345		Sumner	289	1412	20 Dec 1791	1537	9 Dec 1785	77	354	On Peytons Creel	yes
Peyton, Ephraim	416		Sumner	640	427	27 Jun 1793	829	26 Nov 1792	80	350	On S side of Cumberland River	yes
Peyton, Ephraim	565		Sumner	640	1798	20 May 1793	3689	29 Nov 1792	81	79	On small E Fork of Peytons Cr	yes
Peyton, Ephraim	831		Sumner	640	2117	20 May 1793	3650	29 Nov 1792	81	153	On N side of Cumberland River	yes
Peyton, Ephraim	929		Sumner	640			1534	9 Dec 1785	81	637	On Dixie Creek	yes
Peyton, Ephraim	999		Sumner	480	155	17 Dec 1794		11 Dec 1792	84	332	On S side of Cumberland River	yes
Peyton, Jno.	1188		Davidson	640	165	17 Apr 1786	170	24 Jan 1784	66	190	On W fork of Station Camp Cr.	
Peyton, John	0105	Armstrong, M.	Sumner	86				2 Dec 1795			On fork of Drakes Creek	yes
Peyton, John	1002		Sumner	400	158	17 Dec 1794			84	334	On N side of Cumberland River	yes
Peyton, John	1003		Sumner	400	159	17 Dec 1794			84	334	On S side of Cumberland River	yes
Peyton, John	331		Sumner	365	1627	23 Feb 1793			76	325	Both sides of Jennings Creek	yes
Peyton, John	419		Sumner	640	430	27 Jun 1793	741	2 Jun 1785	80	351	On the main first fork	
Peyton, John	567		Sumner	228	1800	20 May 1793	3731	7 Jul 1792	81	79	Both sides tract leads	yes
Peyton, John	676		Sumner	640	2007	20 May 1793	3673	25 Nov 1789	81	126	On S side of Cumberland River	yes
Peyton, John	922		Sumner	240	179	9 Jan 1794			81	448	On the dividing ridge	
Peyton, John & Ephraim	1223	Armstrong, M.	Sumner	10	196	27 Aug 1795			89	410	On S side of Cumberland River	
Peyton, Thomas	0106	Church, Christopher	Sumner	640			3256	19 Dec 1787			On both sides of Jennings Creek	yes
Phelps, Elisha	1651		Davidson	640	392	17 Nov 1790	736	30 May 1785	76	181	On the waters of Bartons Creek	
Phelps, James	034	Dillenberry, Redmod	Sumner	1000			4470	14 Oct 1797			On W branches of Trammels Cr	yes
Phelps, William	334	Williams, Willoughby	Middle District	640	2393	31 Jan 1795	3287	24 Oct 1787	83	391	W/S of W Fork of Obeys River	yes
Phelps, Garrett	371	Conrod, Nicholas	Tennessee	640	2264	20 May 1793	3564	24 Oct 1787	81	184	On head branch of Buds Cr	yes
Phew, Richard	47	Ford, John	Sumner	640	965	18 May 1789	2217	20 Sep 1788	63	328	E Fork of Puncheon Camp Cr.	yes
Phifer, Caleb	100		Middle District	5000	102	10 Jul 1788	623	27 Oct 1783	67	459	On Failing Creek	
Phifer, Caleb	356		Sumner	640	1477	4 Jan 1792	3239	21 Oct 1791	77	370	On the dividing ridge	yes
Phifer, Caleb	851		Sumner	640	2355	20 May 1793	2069	27 Oct 1792	81	203	Bet Little Cedar Creek	yes
Phifer, Martin	36		Middle District	8373	38	10 Jul 1788	677	27 Oct 1783	67	424	On N side of Duck River	
Phifer, Martin Jr.	102		Middle District	5000	104	10 Jul 1788	632	28 Oct 1783	67	460	On Falling Creek	
Phifer, Martin Jr.	843		Sumner	182	2346	20 May 1793	3695	27 Oct 1795	81	201	On Kuykendolls Branch	yes
Phifer, Martin Jr.	853		Sumner	182	2358	20 May 1793	3704	27 Oct 1792	81	203	On Kuykendolls Branch	yes
Phifer, Martin Jr.	94		Davidson	1143	80	14 Mar 1786	25		63	33	North side of Cumberland River	yes
Philips, Isaac	426	Cornelius, Elijah heirs	Tennessee	640	2486	31 Dec 1793	2713	30 Sep 1785	81	438	Red [Riv] beginning at cedar bluff	
Phillips James	929		Washington	200	906	17 Nov 1790	509	17 Oct 1778	76	146	On SE fork of Stoney Creek	
Phillips P & M. Campbell	296		Sumner	640	1316	10 Dec 1790	2366	23 Jun 1788	74	371	On Round Lick Creek	yes

Claimant:	File #:	Assignee:	County:	Acres:	Grant:	Grant Date:	Entry:	Entry Date:	Bk:	Pg:	Location by Stream Name:	Military:
Phillips P & M. Campbell	298		Sumner	640	1345	10 Dec 1790	3684	23 Mar 1790	74	380	On N side of Cumberland River	yes
Phillips P & M. Campbell	72	Grace, James	Tennessee	640	1315	10 Dec 1790	2124	9 Sep 1785	74	370	On S side of Cumberland River	
Phillips P & M. Campbell	82	Movey, Eli	Tennessee	640	1338	10 Dec 1790	1738	24 Apr 1785	74	378	On S side of Cumberland River	
Phillips, Abraham	281		Western Dist	1500	307	25 Apr 1789	2175	13 May 1784	70	264	On waters of Big Hatcha	
Phillips, David	2332		Davidson	15	358	10 Apr 1797		2 Jan 1797	90	282	N side o Cumberland River	
Phillips, David	616		Davidson	228	588	15 Sep 1787	15		63	210	S/S of Big Harpeth River	yes
Phillips, George	340	Cassleman, Benjamin	Sumner	640	1400	20 Dec 1791	181	26 June 1788	77(?)	351	S side of Cumberland River	yes
Phillips, James	1377		Sumner	224	3239	24 Nov 1797	1927	13 Jul 1747	94	172	Between two creeks	yes
Phillips, John	231		Tennessee	640	445	27 Jan 1793	161	13 Sep 1784	80	356	On Richland Creek	
Phillips, Jonathan	1917	Morgan, Peter heirs	Davidson	352	1706	20 May 1793	3656		81	55	On E side of Mill Creek	yes
Phillips, Mann	1215		Sumner	640	2496	26 Sep 1795	1243	8 Aug 1795	89	105	Both sides of Pond Lick	yes
Phillips, Mann	50	Sweet, William	Tennessee	228	1250	10 Dec 1790	322	27 Mar 1783	74	348	On fork of Bud River	
Phillips, Mann	636	Andrews, Thomas	Davidson	640	609	15 Sep 1787	2258		63	217	On S side Big Barren River	yes
Phillips, Mann	661		Sumner	640	1980	20 May 1793	2255	30 Nov 1792	81	119	On waters of Dixons Creek	yes
Phillips, Mann	678	Clark, William	Davidson	640	651	8 Dec 1787	1785		63	231	Middle fork of Red River	yes
Phillips, Mann	71	Jernigan, Gardner	Tennessee	274	1313	10 Dec 1790	1866	25 Jun 1785	74	370	On N side of Red River	
Phillips, Mann	710	Wilkins, Jordan heirs	Davidson	640	683	8 Dec 1787	2256		63	241	On waters of the Salleen	yes
Phillips, Mann	711	Willson, John	Davidson	640	684	8 Dec 1787	2075		63	241	Beg at a poplar & white oak	yes
Phillips, Mann	787		Sumner	640	2246	20 May 1793	2259	30 Nov 1792	81	180	On waters of Dixons Creek	yes
Phillips, Michael	825		Sumner	640	2304	20 May 1793	2253	30 Dec 1792	81	192	On waters of Dixons Creek	yes
Phillips, Oswald	863	Hickman, John Marr	Sumner	640	2373	20 May 1793	2432	6 Jan 1786	81	207	S side of Big Barren River	yes
Phillips, P & M. Campbell	1371	Stephenson, Hugh	Sumner	400	202	14 Sep 1797			92	20	Waters of Goose Creek	yes
Phillips, P & M. Campbell	0107	Bradley, John	Sumner	640			2172	3 Mar 1787			W Fork of Drakes Creek	yes
Phillips, P & M. Campbell	1618	Barnett, Henry	Davidson	640	1349	10 Dec 1790			74	382	On E side of Stones River	
Phillips, P & M. Campbell	1690	Saunders, Isaac Heirs	Davidson	640	1651	23 Feb 1793	2960		76	337	1 1/2 miles from Black Fox Creek	yes
Phillips, P & M. Campbell	1691	Newton, Estridge	Davidson	1000	1652	23 Feb 1793	3155		76	337	On waters of Stones River	yes
Phillips, P & M. Campbell	1692	Tate, William	Davidson	274	1653	23 Feb 1793	43		76	338	Adj their Survey No. 1066	yes
Phillips, P & M. Campbell	1693	Turner, Wm.	Davidson	640	1654	23 Feb 1793	3382		76	338	On waters of Stones River	yes
Phillips, P & M. Campbell	1694	Saunders, Richard	Davidson	640	1655	23 Feb 1793	3151		76	338	On waters of Stones River	yes
Phillips, P & M. Campbell	1695	Orrell, Thomas	Davidson	1144	1656	23 Feb 1793	1283		76	339	On Chicamauga tr abt 2 mi fr Black Pea	yes
Phillips, P & M. Campbell	1696	Watson, Everett	Davidson	640	1657	23 Feb 1793	2700		76	339	On waters of Stones River	yes
Phillips, P & M. Campbell	1697	McKims, Timothy	Davidson	640	1658	23 Feb 1793	3390		76	339	On waters of Stones River	yes
Phillips, P & M. Campbell	1698	Melbourne, Solomon	Davidson	1000	1659	23 Feb 1793	517		76	340	On waters of Stones River	yes
Phillips, P & M. Campbell	1699	Conners, James	Davidson	428	1660	23 Feb 1793	106		76	340	Abt 3 mi from Black Foxes Camp	yes
Phillips, P & M. Campbell	1700	Buell, Samuel	Davidson	640	1661	23 Feb 1793	3152		76	341	W side of Chicamauga	yes
Phillips, P & M. Campbell	266		Sumner	640	1229	10 Dec 1790			74	341	On E Fork of Drakes Creek	yes
Phillips, P & M. Campbell	281		Sumner	640	1277	10 Dec 1790	3451	4 Mar 1790	74	358	On waters of Bartons Creek	yes
Phillips, P & M. Campbell	301		Sumner	1000	1361	10 Dec 1790			74	386	On McNeeleys Creek	yes
Phillips, P & M. Campbell	438		Sumner	640	325	27 Nov 1792	804	11 Mar 1790	81	3	On waters of Caney Fork	
Phillips, P & M. Campbell	439		Sumner	640	326	27 Nov 1792	806	11 Mar 1790	81	3	On waters of Caney Fork	
Phillips, P & M. Campbell	440		Sumner	640	327	27 Nov 1792	802	11 Mar 1790	81	3	On waters of Caney Fork	
Phillips, P & M. Campbell	441		Sumner	640	328	27 Nov 1792	799	11 Mar 1790	88	3	On waters of Caney Fork	
Phillips, P & M. Campbell	442		Sumner	640	331	27 Nov 1792	803	11 Mar 1790	81	?	On waters of Caney Fork	
Phillips, P & M. Campbell	443		Sumner	640	333	27 Nov 1792	800	11 Mar 1790	81	5	On waters of Caney Fork	
Phillips, P & M. Campbell	446		Sumner	640	341	27 Nov 1792	801	11 Mar 1790	81	6	On waters of Caney Fork	

Earliest Tennessee Land Records

Claimant:	File #:	Assignee:	County:	Acres:	Grant:	Grant Date:	Entry:	Entry Date:	Bk:	Pg:	Location by Stream Name:	Military:
Phillips, P. & M. Campbell	91	Harrell, James	Tennessee	640	1360	10 Dec 1790	2188	12 Sep 1785	74	385	On S side of Cumberland River	
Phillips, P. & M.Campbell	433		Sumner	640	317	27 Nov 1792	805	11 Mar 1790	81	1	On waters of Caney Fork	
Phillips, Phillip	1519	Johnston, Peter	Davidson	640	1076	26 Nov 1789	2192		74	118	On waters of Stones River	yes
Phillips, Phillip	275	Campbell, Michael	Sumner	640	1267	10 Dec 1790	2541	23 Sep 1785	74	354	On E side of Caney Fork	
Phillips, Phillip	279		Sumner	640	1272	10 Dec 1790	2867	25 Feb 1786	74	356	Adjoining Tract No. 2250	
Phillips, Phillip	292		Sumner	640	1300	10 Dec 1790	3373	23 Jun 1788	74	365	On Small W Fk of Round Lick Cr	yes
Phillips, Phillip	295		Sumner	1000	1314	10 Dec 1790	1675	23 Sep 1785	74	370	On McNeeleys Creek	yes
Phillips, Phillip	85	Trotter, Thomas	Tennessee	640	1346	10 Dec 1790	3505	8 Feb 1786	74	381	On S side of Cumberland River	yes
Phillips, Richard	235		Davidson	274	221	7 Mar 1786	220		63	81	South side of Richland Creek	yes
Phillips, Richard	422	King, Robt & John Latham	Eastern District	274	2952	1 Mar 1797	4500	15 Feb 1780	90	219	S side of Great Road	yes
Phillips, Thomas	573	Phillips, Thos (heir of Bush)	Tennessee	640	3020	10 Apr 1797	1954		90	301	1st br falls in Cumb. below Harpeth	
Phillips, William	349	Tuton, Oliver	Davidson	640	334	29 Aug 1797	1780		63	124	S side of Cumberland River	yes
Phillips, William	478	Tyrell & Lyttle	Tennessee	640	2740	20 Jul 1796	1030	26 May 1784	88	453	On waters of Spring Creek	yes
Phillips, Zebulon	2003	Overton, John	Davidson	640	1947	20 May 1793	3645		81	111	W branch of Stones Creek	yes
Pickens, James	03		Sullivan	100			2426	15 Feb 1780			Beg at a black oak	
Pickens, James	1659		Green	200	1363	2 Dec 1795	2144	6 Nov 1789	88	271	On waters of Lick Creek	
Pickens, James	1695		Green	200	1370	9 Dec 1795	1583	12 Sep 1779	89	404	On waters of Lick Creek	
Pickens, James	260		Washington	250	128	23 Oct 1782	234	18 Jun 1778	47	63	On Big Limestone Creek	
Pickens, James	421		Washington	42	413	13 Oct 1783	2697	19 Dec 1780	52	272	Adj. Chadd Morris's upper survey	
Pickens, James	433		Washington	275	425	13 Oct 1783	2695	19 Dec 1780	52	278	On waters of Lick Creek	
Pickens, James	447		Washington	100	439	13 Oct 1783	2687	18 Dec 1780	52	284	On waters of Lick Creek	
Pickens, John	402		Washington	200	394	13 Oct 1783	248	1 Jul 1778	52	262	On waters of Lick Creek	
Pickens, John	477		Washington	100	469	13 Oct 1783	2747	20 Jan 1781	52	298	On waters of Lick Creek	
Pickle, John	928		Sumner	640	2382	27 Sep 1794	1740	9 Aug 1794	81	637	On ridge that divides waters, etc.	yes
Pickle, Jonas	2433	Mann, John	Davidson	640	3261	6 Dec 1797	4361		98	148	On Cumberland & Harpeth Rivers	yes
Pickle, Richard	390	Sheppard, Benjamin	Davidson	274	362	15 Sep 1787	2311		63	136	N side of Cumberland River	yes
Pierce, James	364		Green	129	366	20 Sep 1787	1293	24 Dec 1783	65	477	On S side of Nolachuckey River	
Pierce, Jeremiah	1612	Pierce, Wm.	Davidson	328	104	10 Dec 1790	712	22 Apr 1785	74	377	On waters of W. Harper River	
Pierce, John	2143	Pierce, Hardy's heir	Davidson	640	2422	31 Dec 1793	726		81	407	At 1 1/2 mi south of Harpeth River	yes
Pierce, Joseph	664	Weakley, Robert	Tennessee	640	3315	6 Dec 1797	4382		97	40	N side of Cumberland River	yes
Piercifield, Samuel	631		Washington	100	725	26 Oct 1786	714	19 Dec 1778	66	23	Incl. Jacob Hambleton's improv.	
Piercifield, Samuel	650		Washington	100	744	28 Oct 1786	2127	4 Nov 1779	66	32	Joining end of Jacob Hambleton	
Pierson, Samuel	140	Beck, Williams	Davidson	640	126	14 Mar 1786	513		63	49	S side of Cumberland River	yes
Pike, Samuel	062	Donelson & Terrell	Sumner	3840			1566	2 Nov 1795	126	436	On a fork of Pond Lick Creek	yes
Pillow, Abner	10		Maury	400	26	14 Jul 1812	3450		98	181	On a small creek	
Pillow, Gidion	1435		Sumner	640	3346	6 Dec 1797	832	29 Dec 1779	43	301	On waters of Pound Lick Creek	yes
Pinson, Joseph	20		Washington	120	310	24 Oct 1782	2872	17 Jan 1789	63	298	On Cherokee Creek.	
Pipkin, Willis	848	Anderson, Daniel	Sumner	640	853	17 Jan 1789	3412	19 Nov 1792	81	205	On N side of Cumberland River	yes
Pipkins, Philip, Ass.	859		Sumner	320	2365	20 May 1793	126	1 Sep 1792	81	35	On W side of Caney Fork	yes
Pirtle, George, Ass.	485		Sumner	640	1952	27 Apr 1793	2682		81	112	Both sides of Middle Fork of Goose Creek	yes
Pitman, Isom	2007	Smith, Oliver	Davidson	640	3094	20 May 1793	4157		81	399	On both sides of S. Harpeth	yes
Pitman, John	2373	Stewart, Duncan	Davidson	401	530	14 Sep 1797			90	384	On S Harpeth River	yes
Pitner, John	535		Sullivan	640	1509	13 Feb 1791	1913(?)		73	378	On the S side of Holston River	
Pitnor, John	214	Dickson, James	Tennessee	640	2146	4 Jan 1792	3092	15 Jul 1785	77	160	S side of Cumberland River	yes
Pitts, Matthew	2056	Lewis, William Terrel	Davidson	640		20 May 1793			81		On waters of Stones River	yes

Earliest Tennessee Land Records

Claimant:	File #:	Assignee:	County:	Acres:	Grant:	Grant Date:	Entry:	Entry Date:	Bk:	Pg:	Location by Stream Name:	Military:
Platt, John	197	Mitchell, John	Tennessee	640	1483	4 Jan 1792	937	18 Nov 1791	77	372	S side of Cumberland River	yes
Plemon, Peter	250		Washington	200	118	23 Oct 1782	1290	19 Mar 1779	47	58	S branch of Lick Creek	
Pleney, Francis	355	Williams, Willoughby	Middle District	1000	2404	5 Feb 1795			84	185	On both sides of W fork of Obeys	yes
Plumley, George	1660	Robertson, James	Davidson	640	1583	23 Feb 1793	1276		76	304	On Warpath River	yes
Poe, John	035	Donelson & Armstrong	Middle District	640			3776					yes
Pogue, Robert	65		Sullivan	150	76	23 Oct 1782	560	15 May 1780	43	275	On Youngs River (run)	
Poland, John	1079		Washington	230	1029	27 Nov 1792	834	29 Dec 1778	80	198	On S side of a hill	
Polk, Charles, Jr.	62		Middle District	5000	64	10 Jul 1788	536	27 Oct 1783	67	442	On W side of Richland Creek	
Polk, Ezekial	220	Stephens, Thomas	Davidson	640	206	7 Mar 1786	814		63	76	On Richland Creek	yes
Polk, Ezekial	3		Middle District	2000	5	10 Jul 1788	1	4 Jan 1786	67	408	On N branch of Elk River	
Polk, Ezekial, Jr.	73		Middle District	5000	75	10 Jul 1788	635	28 Oct 1783	67	447	On N side of Duck River &c	
Polk, James	24		Middle District	5000	26	10 Jul 1788	606	27 Oct 1783	67	419	On N side of Duck River	
Polk, John	297	Mountflorence, James Cole	Davidson	1000	283	22 Mar 1787	2149		63	104	Beg at a small sugar tree & elm	yes
Polk, Thomas	109		Middle District	2000	111	10 Jul 1788	1103	30 Oct 1783	67	463	On S side of Duck River &c	
Polk, Thomas	110		Middle District	5000	112	10 Jul 1788	667	28 Oct 1783	67	464	On N side of Duck River	
Polk, Thomas	116		Middle District	5000	118	10 Jul 1788	1112	30 oct 1783	67	466	On Richland Creek	
Polk, Thomas	133		Middle District	5000	135	10 Jul 1788	1111	30 oct 1783	67	474	On head waters of Richland Creek	
Polk, Thomas	25		Middle District	5000	27	10 Jul 1788	1113	30 Oct 1783	67	419	On S side of Duck River	
Polk, Thomas	386		Tennessee	2191	2383	14 Dec 1793	157	22 Oct 1783	81	385	On Defeated Camp Creek	
Polk, Thomas	4		Middle District	5000	6	10 Jul 1788	1099	30 Oct 1783	67	409	On the head waters of Harpeth River	
Polk, Thomas	40		Middle District	5000	42	10 Jul 1788	1223	6 Nov 1783	67	426	On waters of Elk River &c	
Polk, Thomas	43		Middle District	5000	45	10 Jul 1788	1102	30 Oct 1783	67	427	On E waters of Richland Creek	
Polk, Thomas	46		Middle District	5000	48	10 Jul 1788	1101	30 Oct 1783	67	428	Lying on Richland Creek	
Polk, Thomas	47		Middle District	3000	49	10 Jul 1788	1104	30 Oct 1783	67	429	Lying on N branches of Richland Creek	
Polk, Thomas	47		Western District	5000	47	10 Jul 1788	1055	29 Oct 1783	67	298	On waters of Looshatcher River	
Polk, Thomas & Ezekial	91		Middle District	5000	93	10 Jul 1788	817	29 Oct 1783	67	455	Beg on a Sugar tree & two poplars	
Polk, William	1		Sumner	200	370	17 Apr 1800	1942	29 Apr 1784	106	454	In Middle District &c	
Polk, William	1217		Davidson	640	181	10 Jul 1788	2	14 Dec 1783	66	368	S/S Cumberland River & on Browns Creek	
Polk, William	144		Middle District	5000	148	11 Aug 1789	453	25 Oct 1783	71	245	On S side of Duck River	
Polk, William	1443		Sumner/Smith	2000	370	17 Apr 1800			106	454	In the Middle District &c	yes
Polk, William	1446		Sumner/Smith	640	373	26 May 1800		30 Apr 1784	108	40	Principally on S side of Obeds River	yes
Polk, William	1447		Sumner	5000	274	26 May 1800		25 May 1784	108	41	On both sides of Obeds River	yes
Polk, William	156		Middle District	5000	157	6 Dec 1790	622	27 Oct 1783	74	244	On both sides of Beaver Creek	
Polk, William	2		Smith	330	371	17 Apr 1800	1994	30 Apr 1784	106	455	In the Middle District &c	
Polk, William	3		Smith-Sumner	640	373	26 May 1800	1663	30 Apr 1784	108	39	Prin. on S side of Obeds River	
Polk, William	4		Smith-Sumner	5000	374	26 May 1800	2295	25 May 1784	108	41	On both sides of Obeds River	
Polk, William	48		Western District	5000	48	10 Jul 1788	2524	25 May 1784	67	299	On Indian Creek &c	
Polk, William	480		Middle District	640	272	6 Dec 1794	1940	29 Apr 1784	85	337	On N side of Duck River	
Polk, William	487		Middle District	1000	279	6 Dec 1794	1992	23 Apr 1784	85	339	On S side of Duck River	
Polk, William	488		Middle District	5000	280	6 Dec 1794	1988	30 Apr 1784	85	340	On S side of Duck River	
Polk, William	489		Middle District	700 (750	281	6 Dec 1794	1991	30 Apr 1784	85	340	On N side of Duck River	
Polk, William	49		Western District	2000	49	10 Jul 1788	2525	25 May 1784	67	299	On waters of S Fork of Forked Deer River	
Polk, William	490		Middle District	640	282	6 Dec 1794	1968	30 Apr 1784	85	341	On N side of Duck River	
Polk, William	491		Middle District	5000	283	6 Dec 1794	1982	30 Apr 1784	85	341	On N side of Duck River &c	
Polk, William	492		Middle District	5000	284	6 Dec 1794	1987	30 Apr 1784	85	341	On N side of Duck River	

Claimant:	File #:	Assignee:	County:	Acres:	Grant:	Grant Date:	Entry:	Entry Date:	Bk:	Pg:	Location by Stream Name:	Military:
Polk, William	493		Middle District	1000	285	6 Dec 1794	1980	30 Apr 1784	85	342	On W side of Richland Creek	
Polk, William	56		Western District	3000	56	10 Jul 1788	2526	25 May 1784	67	302	On the Miss. River &c	
Polk, William	604		Middle District	500	372	17 Apr 1800	1984		106	456	On S side of Lick Creek	
Polk, William	98		Davidson	1888	84	14 Mar 1786	163		63	34	Both sides West Fk of Big Harpeth River	yes
Pollock, Benjamin	1759	Hays, Robert	Davidson	640	1538	14 Jan 1793	1786		79	267	To join Hays which joins Bryans	yes
Polson, John	824	Davis, Joshua	Sumner	228	2303	20 May 1793	2357	30 Nov 1792	81	192	On waters of Dixons Creek	yes
Pond, John	415	Prince, Robert	Tennessee	274	2454	31 Dec 1793	1239	4 Oct 1785	81	428	On E side of Brush Creek	yes
Ponder, William	217		Davidson	318	203	7 Mar 1786	124		63	75	On waters of Stones River	yes
Pooe, David	931		Davidson	640	947	18 May 1789	1064		63	324	On N side of Cumberland River	yes
Pool, John	2116	McCulloh, Benjamin	Davidson	640	2376	20 May 1793	2006		81	207	On waters of Stones River	yes
Poor, John	168	Perkins, Constant	Tennessee	640	1432	20 Dec 1791	3071	30 Nov 1785	77	359	On the waters of Sulphur Fork of Red River	yes
Poor, Moses	25		Eastern District	300	25	11 Jul 1788	1329	12 Jan 1784	67	350	Beaverdam Cr including the Cedar Spring	
Pooram, John	1206	Barton, Samuel	Sumner	400	162	26 Mar 1795			89	91	On Bartons Creek	yes
Pooram, John	1212	Barton, Samuel	Sumner	400	169	26 Mar 1795		10 Nov 1792	89	94	On Bartons Creek &c	yes
Pope, Samuel	1151	Donelson, Stockley	Sumenr	640	2714	20 Jul 1796	3879	8 Jun 1796	88	446	On 1st creek E of Pond Lick Creek	yes
Pope, Samuel	1951	Thompson, Jason	Davidson	274	1790	20 May 1793	1120		81	76	On waters of White Creek	yes
Pope, Valentine	536		Sullivan	300	531	13 Feb 1791	986	15 Oct 1785	73	385	On waters of Fall Creek &c	
Pope, William	1390	Hickman, Thomas	Sumner	365	3316	6 Dec 1797	3064	23 Jun 1797	97	41	On the Salt Lick Fork	yes
Porter, Benjamin	1178		Davidson	640	155	17 Apr 1786	94	14 Jan 1784	66	187	Station Camp Creek at Jno Wethers line	
Porter, David	316		Eastern District	5000	219	28 Aug 1795	1720		87	524	On S side of Holston River	
Porter, David	375		Davidson	1000	226	28 Aug 1795	495	27 Oct 1783	89	80	On the Crab Orchard Valley	
Porter, John	227	Martin, Joshua	Davidson	274	213	7 Mar 1786	35		63	79	On waters of W Harpeth River	yes
Porter, Joshua	015	Bonner, John & James	Sumner	640			1825	13 Sep 1785			N side of Cumberland River	yes
Porter, Rees	370		Middle District	640	309	17 Dec 1794	1628	9 Apr 1784	84	211	On S side of Duck River	
Porter, Rees	454		Middle District	540	393	17 Dec 1794	2245	30 Nov 1784	84	258	On S side of Duck River	yes
Porter, Rees, Ass	726	Perry, Robert	Sumner	640	2110	20 May 1793	1735	Nov 1792	81	152	On Jinning Fork &c	
Porter, Reese	366		Middle District	640	305	17 Dec 1794	1627	10 Apr 1784	84	209	On S side of Duck River	yes
Porter, Rese [sic]	204		Middle District	1000	197	27 Nov 1797	1271	23 Dec 1783	78	426	On N side of Duck River	
Porter, Samuel	030	McMurray, Samuel	Tennessee	320		7 Jan 1786	3372	7 Jan 1786			N side of Cumberland River	yes
Porter, Wiliam [sic]	413	Bonner, John & James	Tennessee	640	2445	31 Dec 1793	1823	11 Jun 1785	81	425	On S side of Sycamore	yes
Porterfield, James	288		Western Dist	5000	277	25 Apr 1789	491	25 Oct 1783	72	83	On E side of Miss. River &c	
Porterfield, John	181		Middle District	5000	163	17 Dec 1790	578	22 Oct 1783	76	177	On Globe Creek &c	
Porterfield, John	340	Perry, Robert	Tennessee	640	2433	20 May 1793	3061	30 Nov 1785	81	157	N boundary of James Saunders survey	
Porterfield, John	927	Thompson, William	Sumner	228	2381	27 Sep 1794	3127	16 Jul 1786	81	637	Waters of E Fork of Middle Fork &c	yes
Porterfield, Seth	801		Sullivan	48	743	17 Nov 1797	377	31 Mar 1780	94	147	N side of Holston River	
Portlock, Caleb	2042		Davidson	274	2059	20 May 1793	3574		81	139	On waters of West Harpeth	yes
Posey, Joseph	1311		Green	150	1161	12 Jan 1793	10	9 Oct 1778	78	400	On S side of Richland Creek	
Poterfield, James [sic]	288		Western District	5000	277	25 Apr 1789	491	25 Oct 1783	72	83	On E side of Miss. River &c	
Potter, Daniel	7	Green, William	Robertson	228	3409	10 Feb 1804	3046	21 May 1800	118	299	On waters of Sulphur Fork	yes
Potter, Francis	2411	McConnel, Robert	Davidson	228	3204	14 Sep 1797	4104		92	6	Waters of E Fork of S. Harpeth	yes
Potter, John	30		Washington	320	320	24 Oct 1782	926	1 Jan 1779	43	306	On both sides of Rones Creek	
Potter, John	615		Davidson	228	587	15 Sep 1787	14		63	210	South side of Big Harpeth River	yes
Pounds, Zachariah	592	Sanford, Samuel	Sumner	640	1834	20 May 1793	2392	6 Aug 1792	81	86	On head waters of Roaring River	yes
Powell, Benjamin	0127	Williams, Sampson	Sumner	640			506	22 Nov 1796			On 32 Mile Creek	yes
Powell, Demsey	10		Middle District	1977	12	10 Jul 1788	740	28 Oct 1783	67	411	On Duck River &c	

Claimant:	File #:	Assignee:	County:	Acres:	Grant:	Grant Date:	Entry:	Entry Date:	Bk:	Pg:	Location by Stream Name:	Military:
Powell, Francis	0120	Tuton, William	Sumner	640	1782	8 Sep 1797			74	345	E side W Fork of Stones River	yes
Powell, John	1580	Mountflorence, James C.	Davidson	228	1241	10 Dec 1790	1289				On S W side of Harpeth	yes
Powell, Matthew	1361	Tatum, Howell	Sumner	640	3209	14 Sep 1797	3897	16 Mar 1797	91	8(?)	On E Fork of Bledsoes Creek	yes
Powell, Nicholas	072	Tuton, William	Davidson	640			1781	13 Apr 1797			W Fork of Stones River	yes
Powell, Peter	1112	Harris, Edward	Sumner	640	2618	4 Jun 1796	2470	1 Jun 1795	88	339	Joining sd Harris survey	yes
Powell, Stephen	1773	Hays, Robert	Davidson	640	1561	14 Jan 1793	1784		79	272	On waters of Mauscaws [sic] Creek	yes
Powell, Thomas	1182	Muffrey, Hardy	Sumner	320	2696	6 Jun 1796	142	17 Dec 1792	88	369	On S side of Cumberland River	yes
Powell, Thomas	215		Davidson	320	201	7 Mar 1786	142		63	74	On waters of Stones River	yes
Powell, William	161	Murphree, Hardy	Davidson	440	147	14 Mar 1786	134		63	56	On waters of Wolf Creek	yes
Powers, James	732		Sumner	1200	2118	20 May 1793	1228	17 Mar 1786	81	154	On head waters of Drakes Creek	yes
Powers, Jessey	02		Sullivan	50			705	13 Nov 1780			Beg at a white oak	
Powers, Robert	1138	Harris, Edward	Sumner	640	2644	4 Jun 1796	2471	1 Jun 1795	88	349	Joining sd Harris survey	yes
Poynter, John	763		Sumner	508	2178	20 May 1793		22 Mar 1788	81	167	On the waters of Caney Fork	yes
Prather, John	738		Washington	200	552	10 Nov 1784	2752	26 Jun 1781	69	124	Upon Kendricks Creek	
Praton, Joshua	1148	Harris, Edward	Sumner	640	2654	4 Jun 1796	2019	1 Jun 1795	88	352	Joining sd Harris survey	yes
Pratt, James	2379	Donelson, Stockley	Davidson	274	3105	14 Sep 1797	4278		90	404	On the Falling Creek	yes
Pratt, Peter	167	Jones, Henry	Tennessee	640	1431	20 Dec 1791	2050	26 Aug 1785	77	359	On both sides of Garners Creek	yes
Pratt, Zebulon	790	McColloch, Benjamin	Sumner	274	2249	20 May 1793	1632	30 Nov 1792	81	180	On the Defeated Creek	yes
Prescot, Aaron	1	Stewart, Duncan	Sumner	640	3099	14 Sep 1797	4232	30 May 1797	90	401	Waters of Big Barren	yes
Prescot, Charles	2370	Stewart, Duncan	Davidson	640	3091	14 Sep 1797	4010		90	397	On S Harpeth River	yes
Prescote, Isaac	1040	King, Robert	Hawkins	640	2958	22 Feb 1797	4749		90	233	N side of Clinch River	yes
Prescote, Thomas	2047	Pearson, James	Davidson	1000	2078	20 May 1793	3055		81	144	On Cripple Creek	yes
Prescote, Willoughby	606	Young, John	Sumner	365	1858	20 May 1793	1535	3 Feb 1786	81	91	On a branch of Drakes Creek	yes
Prescott, Austin	2472	McCofferty, James	Davidson	640	3406	22 Dec 1803	3123		118	139	Beg at Jas. Gatlins W boundary	yes
Prescott, Jonathan	042	Weakley, Robert	Robertson	640			3982	15 Feb 1797			N side of Cumberland River	yes
Preston, George	350		Hawkins	200	344	8 Mar 1793		21 Mar 1780	78	481	On 3rd Creek below a survey of McCoys	
Pretherow, Alex	1231		Green	400	1081	12 Jan 1793	1556	12 Aug 1792	78	352	End of tenth line of Adonijah Morgan's tract	
Pretor, George	322	Williams, Willoughby	Middle District	640	2383	3 Feb 1795	2619		83	384	W side of W Fork of Obeys River &c	yes
Prewet, Joshua	070	Thomas, Isaac	Davidson	274			541	7 Feb 1786			On Main E Fork of Mill Creek	yes
Prewitt, William	840		Washington	150	654	10 Nov 1784	1117	15 Jan 1779	69	153	On Lick Creek	
Prewit, David	378		Green	115	380	20 Sep 1787	119	21 Oct 1783	65	400	On Little Chuckey	
Price, James	1162		Washington	100	1120	7 Jul 1794	1164	1 Feb 1779	81	617	On Indian Creek	
Price, James	272	Wikoff, Wm. & Lardner Clar	Sumner	274	1254	10 Dec 1790	2268	9 Apr 1788	74	349	On S side of Cumberland River	yes
Price, Jonathan	012	Batts, Simon	Robertson	228			1694	1 Nov 1794			On Beaverdam Creek	
Price, Jonathan	028	Ewing, Robert	Robertson	110	306	20 Jul 1796		2 Feb 1787			On Beaverdam Creek	
Price, Jonathan	472	Armstrong, M. heirs	Tennessee	110	306	20 Jul 1796			88	442	On Beaverdam Creek	
Price, Jonathan	480	Batts, Simon	Tennessee	228	2763	20 Jul 1796	1644	[torn]	88	462	On Beaverdam Creek	
Price, Micajah	1590	McNees, John	Davidson	640	1263	10 Dec 1790	2947		74	353	On a branch of the Duck Spring Creek	yes
Price, Mordecai	878		Washington	400	862	18 May 1789	644	28 Nov ―――	72	224	On Sinking Creek	
Price, Rice	874	Sugg, Aquilla	Davidson	640	887	17 Jan 1789	2218		63	308	On the 1st creek above Stones Lick Creek	yes
Price, Robert	146		Hawkins	400	180	26 Dec 1791			75	175	On both sides of the road	
Price, Samuel	224	Thomas, Richard	Tennessee	385	1567	4 Feb 1793	2433	30 Sep 1785	79	293	Joining E boundary of a tract of 400 acres	yes
Price, Thomas	024	Foster, Anthony	Tennessee	640			1556	14 Feb 1785			N side of Cumberland River	yes
Price, William	03		Western Dist	4000	2(?)		2662	1 Jan 1787			On the Chittahoma River	
Price, William	289	Gwin, Edward	Tennessee	640	1916	20 May 1793	3297	2 Jan 1786	81	104	On the waters of Bartons Creek	yes

Claimant:	File #:	Assignee:	County:	Acres:	Grant:	Grant Date:	Entry:	Entry Date:	Bk:	Pg:	Location by Stream Name:	Military:
Price, William	604	Castleman, Jacob	Davidson	640	576	15 Sep 1787	951		63	207	S side of Cumberland River	yes
Pridgen, Ezekiah	680	Hickman, Edwin	Sumner	640	2025	20 May 1793	2321	30 Nov 1792	81	130	On waters of Dixons Creek	yes
Pridgeon, Marmaduke	599	Stewart, Duncan	Tennessee	640	3101	14 Sep 1797	4554	9 Feb 1797	90	402	S side of Cumberland River	yes
Pridgeon, William	609	Williams, Willoughby	Davidson	274	581	15 Sep 1787	1121		63	208	S side of Cumberland River	yes
Priest, Martin	535		Hawkins	100	408	29 Jul 1793	717	21 Dec 1780	80	279	On Fourth Creek	
Prigmore, Joseph	1719		Green	200	1398	21 Jan 1797	104	8 Feb 1780	91	124	Waters of Long Creek	
Prim, Abraham	1594	McRae, David	Davidson	1000	1279	10 Dec 1790	1621		74	358	On N side of Cumberland River	yes
Prince, John	1142		Washington	100	1100	12 Jul 1794	495	8 Oct 1778	81	569	On Cobbs Branch	
Prince, Robert	415	Pond, John	Tennessee	274	2454	31 Dec 1793	1239	4 Oct 1785	81	428	On E side of Brush Creek	
Pritchard, James	361		Tennessee	640	2210	20 May 1793	2029	26 Aug 1785	81	171	On both sides of Blounts Creek	
Pritchet, Edward	073	Sypress, Thomas	not given	640			3759	3 Aug 1792			N E side Little Tenn. River	yes
Pritchett, Thomas	1758		Green	271	1435	17 Nov 1796	2197	12 Nov 1779	95	146	Beg at a white oak	
Privet, Rosana	450	Flemings, William	Sumner	274	1572	27 Apr 1793	542	12 Oct 1792	81	10	On N side of Cedar Lick of Creek	yes
Privett, Sinclair, Ass.	489		Sumner	320	138	27 Apr 1793	519	10 Jul 1784	81	38	On N side of Cumberland	yes
Procheth (?), James	1131		Davidson	640	108	17 Apr 1786			66	176	On a So Fork of Little Harpeth	
Proctor, William	1181	Hogan, William	Sumner	500	2694	6 Jun 1796	3827	29 Mar 1796	88	368	On S side of Cumberland River	yes
Proctor, William	479	Tyrrell, William	Tennessee	228	2744	21 Jan 1797	1532	3 Feb 1785	88	455	On or near head of Kilgores Station Branch	yes
Proudford, James	1024	Donelson, S. & John Latha	Hawkins	275	2954	1 Mar 1797	4501		90	220	Beg at a white oak & sugar tree	yes(?)
Provence, John	103		Sullivan	300	114	23 Oct 1782	1730	21 Sep 1779	43	292	On the branches of Sinking Creek	
Province, John	1250	Blount, John Gray	Sumner	640	2854	21 Jan 1797	4293	14 Dec 1796	90	51	On Camp Creek	yes
Province, John	1803	Killoer, Andrew	Davidson	640	376	26 Jun 1793	595	7 Sep 1784	80	334	On both sides of Big Harpeth River	
Prowford, John	152	Greer, Ann	Tennessee	640	1405	29 Jul 1793	1142	9 Aug 1784	77	352	On both sides of Pine River	yes
Pruett, Martin	1042		Green	100	1269	22 Feb 1795	416	21 May 1781	76	492	On Lick Creek	
Pruitt, Isaac	852		Hawkins	300	677	26 Dec 1791	1090	14 Apr 1780	83	434	On the waters of Whites Creek	
Pryor, Joseph	1105		Green	200	948	20 May 1793	3724	9 Jan 1779	77	261	On Cove Creek	
Pryor, William, Ass.	752		Sumner	640	2156	4 Dec 1795	2574	8 Feb 1792	81	162	On waters of Middle Fk of Drakes Creek	yes
Pue, David	1295		Washington	50	1181	20 May 1793	2089	30 May 1780	89	426	Beg at 2 white oaks	
Pugh, David	830	Sheppard, Nancy	Sumner	640	2310	15 Sep 1787	2330	29 Oct 1792	81	193	On E waters of Roaring River	yes
Pugh, Frederick	394	Sheppard, Benjamin	Davidson	640	366	7 Jan 1789	2472		63	137	On both sides E Fork of Drakes Creek	yes
Pulley, George	880	Nelson, Robert	Davidson	640	894	7 Mar 1786	705		63	310	On N side of Cumberland River	yes
Pulley, James	191	Brickell, James	Davidson	278	177	20 May 1793	2329	30 Nov 1792	63	66	On waters of Richland Creek	yes
Pulley, Jessey	795	Hickman, Edwin	Sumner	640	2255	20 Jul 1796	1485		81	182	On N side of Cumberland River	yes
Punch, John	2281	Lewis, Amos	Davidson	274	2762	20 Apr 1791	2754	17 Dec 1783	88	462	On Leepers Fk of Harpeth River	yes
Purceil, Barnet	304	Barrow, Sherrod	Sumner	640	1371	7 Mar 1786	132	20 Nov 1790	74	394	On waters of Collins River	yes
Purdie, James	181		Davidson	281	167	26 Jun 1793	487		63	63	South side of Cumberland River	yes
Purnal, Thaney, heir of Mary	1807		Davidson	640	380	17 Apr 1786	323	14 Jun 1784	80	335	Beg at a small sugar tree	
Purnell, William	1146		Davidson	640	123	20 May 1793	2755	1 Mar 1784	66	180	On the waters of Big Harpeth River	yes
Pursley, John	1638	Barrow, Henry	Davidson	640	1373	4 Jun 1796	2757		74	395	On S side of Cumberland River	yes
Purton, Elexana	1117	Harris, Edward	Sumner	640	2623	10 Jul 1788	2335	1 Jun 1795	88	342	Joining sd Harris survey	
Purviance, James	22		Western Dist	1000	22	17 Dec 1799	778	25 May 1784	67	288	On the waters of the Long Fork &c	
Purviance, John	465		Middle District	3000	404	6 Jan 1795	1273	29 Oct 1783	84	263	On Indian Creek	
Pyatt, John	1198		Washington	100	1151	7 Mar 1786	318	11 Mar 1779	83	178	Beg at a large white oak (chestnut)	
Pyatt, Peter	267	McCuistian, James	Davidson	428	253	10 Apr 1792	449		63	92	E Fork of Mill Creek	yes
Pyette, Peter	104	Haddock, Peter	Tennessee	640	1524	4 Jan 1792	1356	19 Oct 1784	75	509	On S side of Cumberland	
Quinn, Michael	205	Lambert, Aaron	Tennessee	2102	1495			23 May 1791	77	374	On both sides of Pine River	yes

Earliest Tennessee Land Records

Claimant:	File #:	Assignee:	County:	Acres:	Grant:	Grant Date:	Entry:	Entry Date:	Bk:	Pg:	Location by Stream Name:	Military:
Quinton, William	1628		Green	150	1348	22 Feb 1796	2786	30 Apr 1780	84	330	On N side of French Broad River	
Rabb, Wm.	1392	Myers, Wm. Heirs	Sumner	640	3319	6 Dec 1797	1721	29 Aug 1796	97	43	On E waters of Spring Creek	yes
Radley, Ichabod	013	Henry, William	Knox	400				14 Apr 1791			N side Holston River	yes
Radley, Jonas	2391	Stewart, Charles	Davidson	640	3188	14 Sep 1797	4014		90	437	On South Harpeth River	yes
Raines, Simon (Ephraim)	260	Robertson, Eliz.	Tennessee	640	1703	20 May 1793	1838	14 Jun 1785	81	54	On E waters of Pine River	yes
Rainey, James	257	Lewis, Joel	Davidson	640	243	7 Mar 1786	273		63	89	On both sides of East Fork of Yellow Creek	yes
Rainey, James	342	Newland, Eli	Davidson	320	327	1 Aug 1787	1730		63	122	On waters of W Fork of Spring Creek	yes
Rainey, Joseph	1100		Green	100	943	26 Dec 1791			77	259	On Dumplin Creek	
Rainey, William	20		Middle District	4000	22	10 Jul 1788	425	25 Oct 1783	67	417	On Smiths Creek	
Rainey, William	3		Green	300	66	1 Nov 1786	83	26 Sep 1786	58	427	On N side of French Broad River	
Rainey, William	442		Green	200	444	20 Sep 1787	84	21 Oct 1783	65	500	On the S side of Holsten River	
Rainney, Jos.	051		Washington	100			596	20 Nov 1778			Lying on Dumpling	
Rains, Charles	057	Robertson, Elijah	Davidson	640			1839	16 Mar 1786			N side of Cumberland River	yes
Rains, Jno.	1119		Davidson	640	96	17 Apr 1786	201	29 Jan 1784	66	173	S/S Cumberland River on Browns Cr	
Rains, John	666	Webb, Lewis heirs	Sumner	640	1986	20 May 1793	3386	28 Jun 1788	81	121	On waters of Cedar Lick Creek	yes
Ralford, John	310	McCulloh, Benjamin	Tennessee	640	2011	20 May 1793	2983	30 Sep 1785	81	127	On S side of Red River	yes
Ramage, Alexander	226	Thompson, Jasson	Davidson	640	212	7 Mar 1786	815		63	78	On waters of Mill Creek	yes
Ramsey, Allen	1941		Davidson	1097	1762	20 May 1793	137		81	69	On S side of Harpeth River	yes
Ramsey, Allen	465	Story, Caleb	Sumner	640	6157	27 Apr 1793	903	11 Jun 1791	81	21	On S side of Cumberland River	yes
Ramsey, Allen	697	Branch, Job	Sumner	350	2067	20 May 1793	1436	11 Jun 1791	81	141	On S side of Cumberland River	yes
Ramsey, Allen	699	Miller, Rich'd	Sumner	365	2071	20 May 1793	1084	4 Jun 1791	81	142	On S side Cumberland River	yes
Ramsey, Andrew	275	Phillips & Campbell	Sumner	640	1267	10 Dec 1790	2541	23 Sep 1785	74	354	On E side of Caney Fork	yes
Ramsey, Danl	67	Ramsey, Solomon	Tennessee	1000	1305	10 Dec 1790	2875	30 Sep 1785	74	367	On N side of Cumberland River	
Ramsey, Danl	090		Green	50				26 Sep 1797			Adjoining his other survey on Blum Creek	
Ramsey, Francis A.	10		Green	90	73	1 Nov 1786	33	11 Mar 1784	58	434	Joining Washington County line	
Ramsey, Francis A.	1221		Green	150	1065	May 1792	1696	23 Mar 1780	77	407	N side of Chuckey River	
Ramsey, Francis Alex	1673		Green	150	1378	20 Jul 1796	1378	11 Dec 1783	88	491	Joins survey includes the Swan Pond	
Ramsey, Francis Alex.	2		Green	100	65	1 Nov 1786	2852	12 May 1784	58	426	Joining lands of R. Kerr & J. Lusk	
Ramsey, Francis Alex.	273		Hawkins	640	284	14 Jan 1793	136	15 May 1789	78	339	On N side of Holston River	
Ramsey, Francis Alexander	052		Washington	400			594	27 Oct 1783			Joining land of Brittain Hutton	
Ramsey, Francis Alexander	1123		Washington	70	1082	12 Jul 1794	11	4 Oct 1783	81	563	Upon that Fork of Big Limestone &c	
Ramsey, Francis Alexander	46		Green	200	109	1 Nov 1786	1529	24 Feb 1784	58	470	Upon a water of Holstein River	
Ramsey, Francis Alexander	47		Green	300	110	1 Nov 1786	304	13 Sep 1786	58	471	Joining his other survey	
Ramsey, Francis Alexander	61		Green	400	19	1 Nov 1786	1368	11 May 1779	59	380	Upon Conners Mill Creek	
Ramsey, Francis Alexander	78		Green	200	36	1 Nov 1786	1231	23 Feb 1779	59	397	In Conners Mill Creek	
Ramsey, Francis Alexander	8		Green	300	71	1 Nov 1786	346	23 Oct 1783	58	432	On Dumplin Creek	
Ramsey, Henry	08	Barton, Samuel	Sumner	640			3668	28 Nov 1789			Bet head Round Lick & Cedar Cr	yes
Ramsey, Henry	1208		Davidson	960	80	8 Oct 1787	661	11 Jan 1785	66	226	N/S Cumberland & E/S Bledsoes Cr	
Ramsey, Joel	1408	Smith, John	Sumner	274	3340	6 Dec 1797	3735	26 Jan 1796	97	57	Waters of Station Camp	yes
Ramsey, John	1285		Green	200	1135	12 Jan 1793	228	22 Oct 1783	78	385	Beg at a poplar	
Ramsey, John	39	Mills (no other name given)	Tennessee	640	1223	10 Dec 1790			74	339	On S side of Cumberland River	
Ramsey, John	933		Green	100	847	17 Nov 1790	2333	15 Sep 1786	76	120	N side of Nolechuckey River	
Ramsey, Joseph	1497		Green	100	1260	12 Jul 1794	256	3 Mar 1780	81	581	On waters of Nolichuckey	
Ramsey, Josiah	1048		Davidson	640	22	17 Apr 1786			66	41	Beg at black oak & white oak &c	
Ramsey, Josiah	1207		Davidson	640	79	8 Oct 1787	226	31 Jan 1784	66	226	Lying on waters of Halfpone Cr	

Claimant:	File #:	Assignee:	County:	Acres:	Grant:	Grant Date:	Entry:	Entry Date:	Bk:	Pg:	Location by Stream Name:	Military:
Ramsey, Josiah	361	Armstrong, M.	Davidson	200	3	4 Sep 1787			63	129	On Sycamore Creek	
Ramsey, Josiah	363	Armstrong, M.	Davidson	200	5	4 Sep 1787			63	130	On Ramsey's Fork	
Ramsey, Josiah	87		Sullivan	200	98	23 Oct 1782	282	9 Mar 1780	43	285	On S Fork of Renfrows Creek	yes
Ramsey, Matthew	1871		Davidson	2697	1609	27 Apr 1793	154		81	20	On W Fork of Stones River	
Ramsey, Matthew	422		Western Dist	3300	423	20 Jul 1796	2436,35,32	25 May 1784	88	431	On waters of N Fork of Obion R	
Ramsey, Mills	1681	Clark, Lardner	Davidson	640	1610	23 Feb 1793	2956		76	317	N side of W Harpeth River	yes
Ramsey, Robert	54		Sullivan	500	65	23 Oct 1782	818-677	1780-1781	43	270	Fall Riv inc plant., Ramsey lives on	
Ramsey, Solomon	67	Anderson, Daniel	Tennessee	1000	1305	10 Dec 1790	2875	30 Sep 1783	74	367	On N side of Cumberland River	yes
Ramsey, William	12		Tennessee	640	1160	26 Nov 1789	711	29 Apr 1784	74	159	On N side of Cumberland River	
Ramsey, William	872	Rice, John	Davidson	640	55	25 Apr 1789			63	307	On head of John Milners Creek	yes
Ramsey, Wm.	038	Whitley, Sol.	Tennessee	640			3280	28 Dec 1785			N side of Cumberland River	
Randall, Andrew	195	Hill, Green	Davidson	1000	181	7 Mar 1786	421		63	68	On S side of Duck River	yes
Randall, John	553	Williby, Andrew	Sumner	640	1769	20 May 1793	2058	21 Nov 1792	81	75	On Drakes Cr waters of Big Barron	yes
Randals, William	273		Washington	200	141	23 Oct 1782	144	10 Mar 1778	47	68	N side of Nolachuckey River	
Randolph, Benjamin Fitz	2240	Pevy, Nehemiah	Davidson	1000	2687	6 Jun 1796	3869		88	364	On head waters of Sulphur Fork	yes
Randolph, James	332		Green	600	334	20 Sep 1787	75	18 Apr 1785	65	468	On N side of French Broad River	
Randolph, James	471		Washington	302	463	13 Oct 1787	542	28 Oct 1779	52	295	On a branch of Big Limestone Cr	
Randolph, Thomas	366		Washington	200	358	13 Oct 1783	1347	24 Apr 1779	52	246	On a branch of Big Limestone	
Randols, James	65		Hawkins	200	50	18 May 1789	2244	22 Nov 1779	72	256	On the N side of Holston River &c	
Range, James	1086		Washington	100	1036	27 Nov 1792			80	200	Beg at a marked dogwood	
Range, James	1088		Washington	100	1038	27 Nov 1792	2858	9 Dec 1783	80	201	Beg at a marked poplar &c	
Rankin, David	1010		Washington	100	959	- May 1792	2676	19 Nov 1780	77	399	On the head of Stones Creek	
Rankin, David	1011		Washington	100	960	- May 1792	1410	25 May 1779	77	400	On the head branch of Stones Creek	
Rankin, David	1011		Green	100	1238	29 Jul 1793	1760	30 Sep 1779	76	486	N side of Nolachuckey River &c	
Rankin, David	1518		Green	200	1279	12 Jul 1794	2675	19 Nov 1780	81	587	On Stones Creek	
Rankin, David	240		Green	200	197	20 Sep 1787	2675	28 Nov 1780	65	430	On the head of Stones Creek	
Rankin, David	927		Green	100	841	17 Nov 1790	2676	28 Nov 1780	76	118	Beg at a white oak	
Rankin, James	1537		Green	100	1297	17 Jul 1794	1936	11 Oct 1779	81	608	On waters of Swan Pond Creek	
Rankin, James	263		Hawkins	200	274	14 Jan 1793	2075	28 Oct 1779	78	333	N side of Holston River &c	
Rankin, Richard	1615		Green	110	1327	4 Feb 1795	622	24 Jun 1780	84	155	On Dumplin Creek	
Rankin, Thomas	086		Green	400		13 Aug 1779	1520				N side of Dumpling Creek	
Rankin, Thomas	1204		Green	400	1048	- Mar 1792	2165	8 Nov 1779	77	340	On side of Dumplin Creek	
Rankin, Wm.	1278		Green	100	1128	12 Jan 1793	2483	- Jun 1780	78	382	On Little Chuckey Creek	
Rankins, Richard	1101		Green	300	944	26 Dec 1791	1094	24 May 1779	77	259	On the waters of Dumplin Creek	
Rankins, Thomas	1083		Green	150	926	26 Dec 1791	62	12 May 1784	77	251	On Dumplin Creek	
Rape, Francis	836	Sheppard, Nancy	Sumenr	640	2322	20 May 1793	2083		81	195	On E waters of Roaring River	yes
Raper, John, pt. Cont Line	1-a (?)		Wilson	274	3360	18 Oct 1800	3741	- Jul 1800	108	132	On waters of Jennings Fork	
Raper, Robert	1410		Sumner	503	3344	6 Dec 1797	3742	20 Jun 1797	97	59	On waters of Spring Creek	yes
Rawlings, Aaron	375		Hawkins	200	496	27 Jan 1793	1968	14 Oct 1779	79	489	On the head draughts of the third	
Rawlings, Aaron	377		Hawkins	100	498	27 Jan 1793	1296	8 Jul 1779	79	490	On a branch of Big Sinking Creek	
Rawlings, Aaron	420		Washington	200	412	13 Oct 1783	2817	14 Mar 1781	52	271	On S side of Carrick Branch	
Rawlings, Asabel	1235		Washington	200	1207	20 Jul 1796	1486	20 Jul 1779	88	503	Beg on a chestnut	
Rawlings, Asahael	882		Washington	400	867	16 Nov 1790	624	24 Nov 1778	73	397	On head of Sinking Creek	
Rawlings, Asahall	883		Washington	200	868	16 Nov 1790	2684	13 Dec 1780	73	397	On Lick Creek &c	
Rawlings, Asahall	885		Washington	200	870	16 Nov 1790	2683	12 Dec 1780	73	398	On Lick Creek &c	

Earliest Tennessee Land Records

Claimant:	File #:	Assignee:	County:	Acres:	Grant:	Grant Date:	Entry:	Entry Date:	Bk:	Pg:	Location by Stream Name:	Military:
Rawlings, Asahel	385		Washington	200	377	13 Oct 1783	2812	14 Mar 1781	52	254	On Cane Creek &c	
Rawlings, Asahel	397		Hawkins	640	518	27 Jan 1793	1442	12 Jan 1779	79	497	Head draughts W fk Big Sinking Cr	
Rawlings, Asahel	398		Hawkins	200	519	27 Jan 1793			79	497	On draughts of Third Creek	
Rawlings, Asahel	446		Washington	640	438	13 Oct 1783	2906	28 Aug 1781	52	284	On both sides of Lick Creek	
Rawlings, Asahel	449		Washington	268	441	13 Oct 1783			52	285	On N side of Nolechucke River	
Rawlings, Asahil	751		Washington	30	565	10 Nov 1784	2694	19 Dec 1780	69	128	Adjoining S side of Sloans land	
Rawlings, Ashael	864	Rawlings, Ezekiel	Washington	200	848	18 May 1789	2751	20 Jan 1781	72	219	On the Limestone Fork & c	
Rawlings, Ashel	053		Washington	200			391	12 Apr 1778			On drafts of Little Fork of Third Creek	
Rawlings, Daniel	1022		Washington	150	972	14 Jan 1793	2799	28 Mar 1781	79	277	On waters of Little Limestone	
Rawlings, Daniel	1033		Washington	440	983	14 Jan 1793	108	30 Mar 1779	79	279	Joining the Lick Creek Knobbs	
Rawlings, Daniel	363		Washington	200	355	13 Oct 1783	2818	14 Mar 1781	52	245	On W side of Lick Creek &c	
Rawlings, Daniel	930		Washington	300	146	17 Nov 1790	728	21 Dec 1780	76	146	On Lick Creek &c	
Rawlings, Ezekial (Ashael?)	865		Washington	200	849	18 May 1789	2685	28 Mar 1783	72	220	On waters of Lick Creek	
Rawlings, Ezekial (Ashael?)	866		Washington	150	850	18 May 1789	2695	28 Mar 1783	72	220	Bet Richeys & Stevensons	
Rawlings, John	376		Hawkins	250	497	27 Jan 1793	2181	11 Nov 1779	79	490	On head draughts of 2nd Cr	
Rawlings, John	438		Washington	200	430	13 Oct 1783	2816	14 Mar 1781	52	280	On waters of Lick Creek	
Rawlings, Michael	054		Washington	180			2698	19 Dec 1780			On W/S Shade Morris upper survey	
Rawlings, Michael	055		Washington	150			2798	28 FEb 1781			On Little Limestone	
Rawlings, Michael	1369		Green	150	1224	27 Jan 1793			79	505	On Little Limestone	
Rawlings, Michael	395		Hawkins	100	516	27 Jan 1793	1539	24 Aug 1779	79	496	On head spring of Little Fork 3rd Cr	
Rawlings, Michael	406		Hawkins	200	527	27 Jan 1793	2282	27 Nov 1779	79	500	Joining S/S a tract of John Hacketts	
Rawlings, Michael	407		Hawkins	640	528	27 Jan 1793	2907	27 Apr 1792	79	500	On the Planet Br [sic] of Turkey Cr	
Rawlings, Michael	435		Washington	200	427	13 Oct 1783	2813	14 Mar 1781	52	279	On Cane Creek	
Rawlings, Michael	877		Washington	50	861	18 May 1789	2749	29 Dec 1778	72	224	On the waters of Big Limestone	
Rawlings, Nathan	374		Hawkins	100	495	27 Jan 1793	831	20 Jan 1781	79	489	On E side of Second Creek	
Rawlings, Nathan	409		Hawkins	400	530	27 Jan 1793	1327	4 Apr 1779	79	501	On draughts W Fork Big Sinking Cr	
Rawlings, Nathaniel	432		Washington	300	424	13 Oct 1783	2815	14 Mar 1781	52	277	On waters of Lick Creek	
Rawlings, Nathaniel	450		Washington	200	442	13 Oct 1783	2814	14 Mar 1781	52	286	On S Fork of Cane Creek &c	
Rawls, Gabriel	6	Moore, Thomas	Robertson	228	3408	10 Feb 1804	185	9 Dec 1800	118	298	On N side of Cumberland River	
Ray, Archibald	1014	Anderson, James	Davidson	640	1031	18 May 1789			63	344	On Smiths Fork	yes
Ray, Archibald	1373	Andrews, James	Sumner	640	3228	17 Nov 1797	1705	24 Feb 1787	94	166	On N branches of Smiths Fork	yes
Ray, Archibald	839	Morgan, Isaac	Sumner	640	2341	20 May 1793	3043	5 Jun 1788	81	200	On S side of Cumberland River	yes
Ray, Benjamin	528		Green	320	530	20 Sep 1787	188	22 Oct 1783	65	532	On Richland Creek	
Ray, Daniel	788	Jones, Ambrose	Davidson	640	791	11 Jul 1788	2741		63	277	On E side of Stones River	
Ray, David	135		Hawkins	300	169	26 Dec 1791	941	29 Oct 1783	75	171	On Buffaloe Creek	yes
Ray, James	2		Davidson	640	3	10 Apr 1784	39	8 Apr 1784	56	314	On branch of Wt Fork of Mill Creek	
Ray, James	74		Washington	199	242	23 Oct 1782	270	25 Jul 1778	44	267	On a branch of Cherokee Creek	
Ray, John	552		Hawkins	200	425	29 Jul 1793			80	284	On the waters of Fourth Creek	
Ray, John	613		Sullivan	250 (200	566	24 Dec 1793			78	489	On waters of South Creek	
Ray, Joseph	394		Green	150	396	20 Sep 1787	1552	26 Aug 1779	65	484	On head of McCartneys Branch	
Ray, Stephen	213	Edwards, David	Davidson	640	199	7 Mar 1786	701		63	74	On a branch of Sycamore Creek	yes
Ray, Thomas	579		Green	150	260	20 Sep 1787	189	22 Oct 1783	66	160	On Little Chuckey Beg a post oak	
Ray, William	0109	German, Benj.	Sumner	365			1166				W side Caney Fork	
Ray, William	1509	Walker, Richard Shewell	Davidson	1000	1066	26 Nov 1789	2363	22 Dec 1792	74	112	On S side of Cumberland River	yes
Ray, William	1861	Reaves, Nehemiah	Davidson	228	1589	27 Apr 1793			81	15	On N side of Cumberland River	yes

Earliest Tennessee Land Records

Claimant:	File #:	Assignee:	County:	Acres:	Grant:	Grant Date:	Entry:	Entry Date:	Bk:	Pg:	Location by Stream Name:	Military:
Ray, Wm.	282	Harris, Edward	Sumner	640	1278	10 Dec 1790	1206	22 Mar 1788	74	358	On S side of Cumberland River	yes
Ray, Wm.	638	Cloud, Daniel	Sumner	640	1927	20 May –			81	106	On W side of Caney Fork	yes
Ray, Wm.	895	Underhill, Jas.	Sumner	640	2446	31 Dec 1793	3039	18 Dec 1792	81	425	On W side of Caney Fork	yes
Ray, Wm.	898	McCloud, Danl.	Sumner	640	2452	31 Dec 1793	2143	28 Nov 1792	81	427	On W side of Caney	yes
Rayford, John	414	Cobb, Jesse	Tennessee	640	2448	31 Dec 1793	1236	16 Oct 1784	81	426	On S side of Cumberland River	yes
Rayford, Maurice	990	Lock, Matthew	Davidson	236	1007	18 May 1789	1301		63	338	On S branch of E Fork of Stones River	yes
Rayior, Archibald	418		Sumner	640	429	27 Jun 1793			80	351	On waters of Bledsoes Creek	yes
Rayly, John	577 (6)		Sullivan	200	575	29 Jul 1793	192	30 Mar 1778	76	472	Both sides of Indian Creek	
Raymore, Daniel	431	Blount, Reading	Davidson	640	403	15 Sep 1787			63	150	On S branches of Sycamore Creek	yes
Raynor, Amos	358	Weakley, Robert	Davidson	640	342	4 Sep 1787	2578		63	128	N side of Cumberland River	yes
Rea, John	1550		Green	940	1215	30 Dec 1793	1215	24 Aug 1780	82	143	Both sides Little R on cone of mtn	
Reaby, Abraham	760	McCrory, Thomas	Davidson	640	733	11 Jul 1788	1984		63	258	On W side of Stones River	yes
Read, Alexander	1542	Armstrong, M.	Davidson	100	82	26 Nov 1789			74	168	On waters of Manskers Creek	
Read, Alexander	1543	Armstrong, M.	Davidson	50	83	26 Nov 1789			74	168	On a branch of Whites Creek	
Read, Alexander	1544	Armstrong, M.	Davidson	50	84	26 Nov 1789			74	169	On N side of Cumberland River	
Read, Alexander	1545	Armstrong, M.	Davidson	228	85	26 Nov 1789			74	169	On the side of Cumberland River	
Read, Alexander	20 (29?307?)		Western District	600	30	10 Jul 1788	2163	13 May 1784	67	291	On waters of S Fork of Obion Riv	
Read, Henry	361		Western District	5000	367	20 Dec 1791	198	26 Sep 1785	75	219	On N Fork of Forked Deer River	
Read, James	880		Sumner (?)	3840	2399	7 Jan 1794			81	391	Joining John Gees tract	yes
Read, William	323		Green	400	325	20 Sep 1787	1323	12 Jan 1784	65	465	On Beaverdam Creek	
Read, William	347		Green	400	349	20 Sep 1787	1335	12 Jan 1784	65	472	On Beaverdam Creek	
Ready, William	54	Hickman, Thomas	Sumner	640	3074	19 Jul 1797	4664	6 Apr 1797	90	380	Waters of Big Barren River	yes
Ready, Hezekiah	054	McCall, Alex	Middle District	640	202	10 Jul 1788	2950	30 Sep 1785				yes
Realing, Lewis	1237		Davidson	640	885	25 Apr 1789	727	13 May 1785	66	412	Waters of Mill Creek beg white oak	yes
Realy, Ezekial	870	Rice, John	Davidson	428	611	15 Sep 1787			63	306	Lying adjoining his entry	yes
Rearden, Dennis heir	638	Rearden, William's heir	Davidson	1000	159	7 Mar 1786	662		63	217	S side of Cumberland River	yes
Rearden, Dudley	173	Rearden, Nancy & Eliz., heir	Davidson	640	143	14 Mar 1786	703		63	60	S side of Cumberland River	yes
Rearden, Jeremiah	157	Anderson, William	Davidson	174	601	27 Aug 1788	746		63	55	E side of Big Harpeth	yes
Rearden, Thomas	796		Green	400	2950	1 Mar 1797			68	262	On waters of Long Creek	
Reardon, Jeremiah	421	Brown, Claiborne	Eastern District	200	3157	14 Sep 1797	4509		90	218	In a row of knobs	
Reason, John	1347	Stewart, Duncan	Sumner	640	702	11 Jul 1788	4259	30 May 1797	90	425	Waters of Big Barren	yes
Reason, William	729		Davidson	412			256		63	247	On Millars Creek	yes
Reasons, Thomas	01	Alford, William	Tennessee	640	1264	10 Dec 1790	1069	31 May 1784	74	353	On the R hand fk of 1st large creek &c	yes
Reaves, Benjamin	1591	McNees, John	Davidson	640	869	17 Jan 1787	1108		63	302	On N side of Cumberland River	yes
Reaves, Benjamin	859	Mountflorence, James Cole	Davidson	1000	2391	7 Jan 1794	2153		81	389	On Weakley Creek	yes
Reaves, David	633	Humphries, Elijah	Hawkins	640	939	18 May 1794	2683		63	322	In Powell's Valley	yes
Reaves, Foster	923	Nash, William	Davidson	640	551	10 Nov 1784	797	28 Dec 1778	69	123	On waters of W Fork of 1st Creek	yes
Reaves, George	737		Washington	640	1319	4 Feb 1795	2537	10 Apr 1780	84	105	On waters of Watauga River	yes
Reaves, John	1602		Green	100	3328	6 Dec 1797			97	48	On head branch of Little Chucka	
Reaves, Jordan	2430	Saunders, Wm.	Davidson	274	1589	27 Apr 1793	1268		81	15	N side of Big Harpeth River	yes
Reaves, Nehemiah	1861	Ray, William	Davidson	228	2949	1 Mar 1797	1932		90	217	On N side of Cumberland River	yes
Reaves, Samuel	1022	Latham, John	Hawkins	200	731	26 Oct 1786	4505		66	26	Both sides of the Caney Fork	yes
Reaves, William	637		Washington	200	347	1 Mar 1797	886	31 Dec 1778	90	223	Beg at an oak	yes
Reavis, Dabiel [sic]	2323	Armstrong, M.	Davidson	50							S side of Cumberland River	yes
Rector, Benjamin	1145		Green	200	988	26 Dec 1791	988	21 Jan 1785	77	277	On W side of Lick Creek	

Claimant:	File #:	Assignee:	County:	Acres:	Grant:	Grant Date:	Entry:	Entry Date:	Bk:	Pg:	Location by Stream Name:	Military:
Rector, Maxililian [sic]	056			180			2465	10 Mar 1780			On waters of Big Limestone	
Redden, John	794		Washington	250	608	10 Nov 1784	3373	1 Sep 1778	69	140	On Charles Creek	
Redden, John	815		Washington	100	629	10 Nov 1784	1224	22 Feb 1779	69	146	Beg at 2 white oaks	
Reddick, Isaac	602	Hart, Anthony	Davidson	640	574	15 Sep 1787	2957		63	205	N side Cumberland River	yes
Reddick, Peter	10	Sanders, James	Sumner	640	767	11 Jul 1788	2227	25 Nov 1786	63	269	On head of S Fork of Bradleys Lick Creek	yes
Redding, Robert	130	Turner, Benj. Heirs	Tennessee	640	1638	23 Feb 1793	1413	16 Nov 1784	76	331	Bet. Grices & Yellow Creek	
Reditt, Samuel	733		Sumner	366	2119	20 May 1793	3566	15 Feb 1791	81	154	On both sides E Fork Dicksons Cr	yes
Redley, George	369		Sullivan	129 (179)	248	10 Nov 1784	1969	14 Oct 1779	69	161	On waters of Horse Creek	
Redley, George	425		Sullivan	200	304	10 Nov 1784	1977	14 Oct 1779	69	177	Inc the Pond Spring	
Redy, Jacob	1555	Krauss, Gotlob	Davidson	640	1171	26 Nov 1789	2155		74	173	On E Fork of Stones River	
Reed, Alexander	1551	Armstrong, M.	Davidson	200	91	26 Nov 1789			74	171	On ridge bet. Whites & Masters Cr	yes
Reed, Alexander	2243	Armstrong, M.	Davidson	228	85	26 Nov 1789			74	169	On [sic] side of Cumberland River	
Reed, Alexander	2243	Armstrong, M.	Davidson	30	290	6 Jun 1796			88	383	Joining W side of sd Reeds 300 acres	
Reed, Alexander	238	Jimmerson, Thomas	Sumner	228	1143	26 Nov 1789	875	9 Aug 1785	74	150	On N side of Cumberland River	yes
Reed, Alexander	364	Armstrong, M.	Davidson	50	83	26 Nov 1789			74	168	On a branch of Whites Creek	
Reed, Alexander	479	Armstrong, M.	Sumner	300	120	27 Apr 1793			81	30	On S side of Cumberland River	
Reed, Andrew	364		Washington	100	356	13 Oct 1783	558	30 Oct 1778	52	245	On the Cedar Fork of Lick Creek	
Reed, Andrew	389		Washington	300	381	13 Oct 1783	556	30 Oct 1778	52	256	Near Godfrey Isbells entry	
Reed, Andrew	59		Washington	150	227	23 Oct 1782	555	30 Oct 1778	44	258	On Cove Creek	
Reed, Andrew Cortier	328		Hawkins	200	322	8 Mar 1793	1648	19 Sep 1779	78	470	In Hinds Valley	
Reed, Benjamin	134		Davidson	640	120	7 Mar 1786	130		63	47	On waters of Little Harpeth	yes
Reed, Daniel	1071		Green	260	914	26 Dec 1791	107	2 Dec 1789	77	247	N/S Nolachuckey River on Pidgeon Creek	
Reed, Daniel	377		Washington	100	369	13 Oct 1783	2802	28 Feb 1781	52	250	On waters of Big Limestone	
Reed, David	366		Green	200	368	20 Sep 1787	1340	12 Jan 1784	65	477	On waters of Little Chuckey	
Reed, Guilford	1401	Roberts, Delilah	Sumner	640	3330	6 Dec 1797	4670	17 Jun 1797	97	50	On waters of Cedar Creek	yes
Reed, Guilford Dudley, heir	2149	Reid, James' heir	Davidson	3840	2450	31 Dec 1793	296		81	426	On W Fork of Harpeth River	yes
Reed, Henry	358		Western District	5000	365	15 Dec 1793			75	148	Waters of N Fork of Forked Deer R	
Reed, Jacob	1075		Washington	200	1025	27 Nov 1792	1913	9 Oct 1779	80	183	On Neaves Branch	
Reed, Jesse	209	Hammonds, Ralph	Sumner	640	1114	26 Nov 1789	2652	12 Mar 1788	74	136	On W side of Caney Fork River	yes
Reed, Jesse	209		Washington	100			1211	15 Feb 1779			On Neaves Branch	
Reed, Jesse	211	Lane, James	Sumner	640	1116	26 Nov 1789	2744	12 Mar 1788	74	137	On W side of Caney Fork River	yes
Reed, Jesse	212	Billego, John	Sumner	640	1117	26 Nov 1789	3417	12 Mar 1788	74	137	On W side of Caney Fork	yes
Reed, Jesse	213	Richards, Jesse	Sumner	640	1118	26 Nov 1789	1977	12 Mar 1788	74	138	On S W side of Caney Fork River	yes
Reed, Jesse	214	Bass, Jonathan	Sumner	640	1119	26 Nov 1789	3419	12 Mar 1788	74	138	On head waters of Collins river	yes
Reed, Jesse	231	Backhonham, John	Sumner	640	1136	26 Nov 1789	2633	12 Mar 1788	74	147	On waters of Hickmans Creek	yes
Reed, Jesse	232	Browning, Baker	Sumner	640	1137	26 Nov 1789	3421	12 Mar 1788	74	147		yes
Reed, Jesse	233	Dorman, West	Sumner	640	1138	26 Nov 1789	3427	12 Mar 1788	74	148	On W side of Caney Fork River	yes
Reed, Jesse	234	Yancey, George	Sumner	640	1139	26 Nov 1789	3509	12 Mar 1788	74	148	On W side of Caney Fork	yes
Reed, Jesse	235	Forrest, Matthew	Sumner	640	1140	26 Nov 1789	2715	12 Mar 1788	74	149	On W side of Caney Fork River	yes
Reed, Jesse	236	Walker, Walter	Sumner	640	1141	26 Nov 1789	3507	12 Mar 1788	74	149	On waters of Collins River	yes
Reed, Jesse	237	Williams, Phillips	Sumner	640	1142	26 Nov 1789	3506	12 Mar 1788	74	150	On W side of Caney Fork River	yes
Reed, Jesse	270	Asobrow, Wm. Jno.	Sumner	640	1115	26 Nov 1789	3501	12 Mar 1788	74	136	On W side of Caney Fork River	yes
Reed, Jesse	460	Delvay, George	Davidson	274	432	15 Sep 1787	3429		63	159		yes
Reed, Jesse	591	Besall, Elisha	Davidson	640	563	15 Sep 1787	2003		63	202	S side of Big Barren River	yes
Reed, Jesse	598	Thompson, Ahab	Davidson	640	570	15 Sep 1787			63	204	S side of Big Barren River	yes

Claimant:	File #:	Assignee:	County:	Acres:	Grant:	Grant Date:	Entry:	Entry Date:	Bk:	Pg:	Location by Stream Name:	Military?
Reed, John	057		Washington	100			1211	15 Feb 1779			On Neaves Branch	
Reed, John	1006		Green	150	1233	29 Jul 1793	166	27 Nov 1792	76	485	Beg at a black walnut &c	
Reed, John	1448		Green	150	1258	27 Nov 1792	1487	26 Jul 1779	80	173	N side incl.mouth of Meadow Cr	
Reed, John	927	Newby, Robert	Davidson	640	943	18 May 1789	1547		63	323	On S side of Cumberland River	yes
Reed, Joseph	1085	Donelson, Stockley	Sumner	640	2575	7 Mar 1796	2948	2 Nov 1795	88	314	On head of Pond Lick Creek	yes
Reed, Michael	303		Green	132	305	20 Sep 1787	1339	12 Jan 1784	65	460	On Buffaloe branch of Pigeon Cr	
Reed, Phelps	1440		Sumner	3000	369	17 Feb 1800	1052	6 Apr 1798	106	370	On waters of Wolf River	yes
Reed, Robert	058		Washington	500			1032	6 Jan 1779			On S side of Clinch River	
Reed, Robert	542		Hawkins	500	415	29 Jul 1793	1918	11 Oct 1779	80	281	S side of Clinch River &c	
Reed, Robert	735		Hawkins	640	555	12 Jun 1794	30	24 Jun 1780	82	173	On S E side of Clinch River	
Reed, Robert	738		Hawkins	500	558	12 Jun 1793	1068	30 Oct 1783	82	174	On S side of Clinch River	
Reed, Robt	323		Hawkins	675	317	8 Mar 1793	1522	23 Feb 1784	78	468	On N side Tennessee River	
Reed, Samuel	675		Green	400	716	11 Jul 1788	404 [?]	2 Apr 1789	66	465	S side Nolechuckey R on Big Cr	
Reed, Solomon	093		Green	100							On waters of Wolf Creek	
Reed, Solomon	216	Anderson, Daniel	Sumner	640	1341	27 Aug 1795	2230	23 Mar 1789	87	510	On N side of Cumberland River	yes
Reed, Stephen	216		Green	640	1121	26 Nov 1789	1286	16 Mar 1779	74	139	On E side of Clinch River	
Reed, W.	310		Hawkins	400	304	8 Mar 1793	3966	11 Mar 1795	78	461	On waters of Caney Fork	yes
Reed, Walson	1040	Easton, James	Sumner	640	2702	27 Mar 1796		6 Apr 1794	88	256	On waters of Bever Creek	
Reed, Walson	299		Eastern District	400	152	22 Feb 1795	3785	15 Jul 1795	84	285	On head waters of Whites Creek	yes
Reed, William	046	Hays, Robert	not given	640				9 Aug 1819			On both sides of Tuckaseige R	
Reed, William	063		Tennessee	640	28		1374	23 Jul 1784	59	423	On waters of Little Chuckey	
Reed, William	104		Green	100	62	1 Nov 1786	4664	6 Apr 1797	90	380	Waters of Big Barren River	yes
Reed, William	1303	Hickman, Thomas	Sumner	640	3074	19 Jul 1797	2080	29 Oct 1779	78	461	ON N W side of Emerys River	yes
Reed, William	309		Hawkins	400	303	8 Mar 1793	675	28 Oct 1783	87	509	On head waters of Whites Creek	yes
Reed, William	315	Hays, Robert	Eastern District	640	2487	18 Aug 1795					On S side of Clinch River	
Reed, Wm.	087		Green	800			1093	9 Jan 1779			In Hinds Valley	
Reed, Wm.	308		Hawkins	400	302	5 Mar 1793			78	460	On N side of Clinch River	
Reed, Wm.	311		Hawkins	400	305	8 Mar 1793			78	462	Both S of Willow fk of Beaverdam Cr	
Reed, Wm.	312		Hawkins	400	306	8 Mar 1793			78	462	On N side of Clinch River	
Reed, Wm.	313		Hawkins	640	307	8 Mar 1793			78	463	On N W side of Emerys River	
Reed, Wm.	314		Hawkins	640	308	8 Mar 1793	468	24 Apr 1780	78	464	On N side Clinch River	
Reed, Wm.	315		Hawkins	640	309	8 Mar 1793			78	464	On N side of Clinch River	
Reed, Wm.	316		Hawkins	640	310	8 Mar 1793			78	465	On S E side of Clinch River	
Reed, Wm.	317		Hawkins	640	311	8 Mar 1793			78	465	On S side of Clinch River	
Reed, Wm.	318		Hawkins	800	312	8 Mar 1793			78	466	On the forks of Grassey Creek	
Reed, Wm.	319		Hawkins	600	313	8 Mar 1793	1671	18 Sep 1779	78	466	In Beaver Creek Valley	
Reed, Wm.	320		Hawkins	250	314	8 Mar 1793	1094	9 Jan 1779	78	467	On S side of Clinch River	
Reed, Wm.	321		Hawkins	250	315	8 Mar 1793	545	29 Apr 1780	78	467	On S side of Clinch River	
Reed, Wm.	322		Hawkins	300	316	8 Mar 1793	590	7 Jun 1780	78	467	On S side of Clinch River	
Reed, Wm.	390	Armstrong, M.	Sumner	200	128	29 Aug 1793			80	323	On both sides of the Caney Fork	
Reed, Wm. & Abrm Swagerty	326		Hawkins	640	320	8 Mar 1793	243	27 Jun 1778	78	469	On N side of Clinch River	
Reed, Wm. & Abrm Swagerty	324		Hawkins	640	318	8 Mar 1793	1720	24 Sep 1779	78	468	On N side of Clinch River	
Reed, Wm. & Abrm Swagerty	325		Hawkins	640	319	8 Mar 1793	1961	10 Oct 1779	78	469	On N side of Clinch River	
Reed, Wm. & Abrm Swagerty	327		Hawkins	640	321	8 Mar 1793	194	21 Sep 1780	78	470	On N side of Clinch River	
Reedpeth, John	274	Lancaster, John	Sumner	2560	1265	10 Dec 1790	101	23 Sep 1785	74	354	On W side of Caney Fork	yes

Earliest Tennessee Land Records

Claimant:	File #:	Assignee:	County:	Acres:	Grant:	Grant Date:	Entry:	Entry Date:	Bk:	Pg:	Location by Stream Name:	Military:
Rees, George, Jr.	306		Middle District	640	282	17 Dec 1794	836	29 Oct 1783	83	329	S side of Duck River	
Reese, John	1142		Green	200	985	20 Dec 1791	105	6 Jul 1789	77	276	On Pidgeon Creek	
Reese, David	2		Washington	90	2	15 Dec 1778	59	14 Sep 1778	36	2	On both sides of Doe River	
Reese, David	4		Washington	320	4	15 Dec 1778	63	14 Sep 1778	36	4	On waters of Lick Creek	
Reese, David	6		Washington	400	6	15 Sep 1778	64	14 Sep 1778	36	6	On heads of a branch &c	
Reese, James	229		Middle District	500	209	1 Jan 1793	674	28 Oct 1783	80	210	On S side of Duck River	
Reese, John	597	Tatum, Barnard	Sumner	228	1840	20 May 1799	1732	31 Jul 1792	81	87	On S side of Cumberland River	yes
Reese, Roger	768	Shelton, David	Sumner	274	2208	20 May 1793	235	Nov 1783	81	170	On N side of Cumberland River	yes
Reese, William	350	Shelton, David	Sumner	274	1436	20 Dec 1791	236	18 May 1791	77	360	On Round Lick Branch	yes
Reeves, Frederick	1398		Green	500	1210	27 Nov 1792		23 Dec 1791	80	154	On Little Sinking Creek	
Regans, John	720	White, William	Sumner	228	2104	20 May 1793	602	31 Jul 1792	81	150	On waters of Spring Creek	yes
Reid, John	421	Cobb, Jesse	Tennessee	640	2467	31 Dec 1793	1279	28 Oct 1784	81	432	On head branches &c	yes
Reiley, Edmond	0113	Sanders, James	Sumner	640			1874	10 Apr 1797			On waters of Bradleys Lick Creek	yes
Reiley, Edmond	604	Gorham, J. C.	Tennessee	640	3148	14 Sep 1797	4348		90	422	N side of Cumberland River	yes
Reiley, Ezekial	1100	A. Jackson & S. Donelson	Sumner	428	2600	7 Mar 1796	1676	12 Nov 1795	88	326	On a Sinking Fork	yes
Reiley, Thomas	806	Robertson, Elijah	Davidson	640	809	20 Nov 1788	3322		63	284	On waters of Caney Fork	yes
Reily, John	541		Washington	100	804	16 Aug 1787	2841		64	153	Northeasterly side of 1st big ridge &c	yes
Relph, Lewis	4	Montgomery, Michael	Sumner	228	761	11 Jul 1788	1653	9 Feb 1787	63	267	On waters of Collins River	yes
Renfro, Stephen	10		Sullivan	200	21	23 Oct 1782	1605	13 Sep 1779	43	247	N/S Holston R at mouth of Beva Cr	
Renfro, Stephen	15		Sullivan	70	26	23 Oct 1782	1759	30 Sep 1779	43	249	S side of Holston River	
Renfroe, James	232		Tennessee	640	446	27 Jun 1793	503	1 Nov 1792	80	356	On N side of Red River	
Renfroe, Jesse	230		Tennessee	640	444	27 Jun 1793	623	22 Nov 1792	80	256	On S side of Cumberland	
Renn, Aaron	802	Lancaster, John	Sumner	640	2267(7)	20 May 1793	2226	2 Jun 1792	81	184	On S side Cumberland River	yes
Rentfro, Joseph	1820		Davidson	640	393	26 Jun 1793	542	21 Jul 1784	80	339	Beg at a poplar	
Rentfro, Peter	1272		Davidson	640	237	10 Jul 1788	581	17 Aug 1784	66	421	Beg ash & elm Wm Hays N E cor	
Rentfroe, William	1291		Davidson	640	256	10 Jul 1788	623	15 Nov 1784	66	427	Beg at a black oak on Cantrils line	
Resner [?], Michael	607		Hawkins	250	481	29 Jul 1793	307	7 Dec 1792	80	296	Lying above 2nd fork of Opossum	
Reutledge, Thomas, Jr.	227		Middle District	640	207	1 Jan 1793	2654	25 May 1784	80	210	On the S side of Duck River	
Revert, James	434	Blount, Reading	Davidson	640	406	15 Sep 1787	2152		63	151	N branches of Marrowbone Creek	yes
Reyley, John	518	Fenner, Richard	Davidson	640	490	15 Sep 1787	2540		63	177	N of survey for Philip Alston	yes
Reynolds, Henry	411		Green	300	413	20 Sep 1787	34	21 Oct 1783	65	492	On both sides Camp Creek	
Reynolds, Henry	679		Washington	300	493	10 Nov 1784			69	102	Beg at a stake	
Reynolds, Robert	1048		Green	300	892	6 Sep 1791	2131	5 Nov 1779	77	223	On a branch of W Fork of Flatt Cr	
Reynolds, Silvester	035	Dillenberry, Redmon	Sumner	640							On dividing ridge	
Reynolds, William	581	Barton, Samuel	Tennessee	640	3028	10 Apr 1797	4391	22 Sep 1797	90	304	N side of Cumberland River	yes
Rhaiford, Philip	2252		Davidson	274	305	20 Jul 1796	1033		88	442	On waters of Harpeth	yes
Rhea, Archibald	1132		Green	300	975	26 Dec 1791			77	273	On S/S French Broad & Holstein River	
Rhea, Jno & Chas McClung	115		Eastern District	500	148	29 Jul 1793	1378	14 Jan 1784			S side of Clinch River	
Rhea, Jno, Annanias McCoy	286	Lackey, James W.	Eastern District	3000	211	4 Feb 1795	15	24 Feb 1778	76	480	In the Bend of Tennessee River	
Rhea, John	01		Sullivan	353		5 Jan 1779	1021		84	104	On W side of Holston River on Beaver Cr	
Rhea, John	0124		Sullivan	640			18,-19	24 Apr 1780			On W side of Indian Creek	
Rhea, John	0126		Sullivan	200			338	10 Mar 1780			In the Little Valley	
Rhea, John	078		Sullivan	640				24 Apr 1780			Joining above the former entry	
Rhea, John	079		Sullivan	640				24 Apr 1780			On the N side of Tenn. River	
Rhea, John	091		not given	1000			1279					

Earliest Tennessee Land Records

Claimant:	File #:	Assignee:	County:	Acres:	Grant:	Grant Date:	Entry:	Entry Date:	Bk:	Pg:	Location by Stream Name:	Military:
Rhea, John	1054		Hawkins	100	764	21 Jan 1797	1145	9 Feb 1779	91	113	N side of Holston River	
Rhea, John	130		Sullivan	400	142	23 Oct 1782	34	8 Feb 1780	43	326	On both sides of Caney Creek	
Rhea, John	1616		Green	100	1328	5 Jan 1795	1328	1 Oct 1779	84	156	On N side of Nolechuckey River	
Rhea, John	264		Hawkins	300	275	14 Jan 1793			78	334	In the Little Valley	
Rhea, John	268		Hawkins	250	279	14 Jan 1793	160		78	336	On waters of Fourth Creek	
Rhea, John	282		Eastern District	640	207	5 Jan 1795			84	55	On E side of Clinch River	
Rhea, John	288		Eastern District	640	211	5 Feb 1795			84	131	On N side of Tennessee River	
Rhea, John	289		Eastern District	640	212	5 Feb 1795	448	24 Apr 1778	84	132	On N side of Tennessee River	
Rhea, John	322		Sullivan	209	458	28 Nov 1787	2112	2 Nov 1779	67	220	On S side of Holston River	
Rhea, John	37		Eastern District	1000	37	11 Jul 1788			67	354	On a large creek of Clinch River	
Rhea, John	5		Hawkins	193	4	10 Jul 1788	803	13 Jun 1781	64	329	On the N side of Holston River &c	
Rhea, John	736		Sullivan	500	679	8 Dec 1795	2264	22 Nov 1779	88	268	On S side of Holston River	
Rhea, John	738		Sullivan	400	681	8 Dec 1795	400	24 Apr 1780	88	269	On N side of Beaver Creek	
Rhea, John	739		Sullivan	2320	682	8 Dec 1795	3 warrants	3 entry dates	88	269	On Beaver Dam Creek	
Rhea, John	742		Sullivan	640	674	11 May 1795	85	8 Feb 1780	89	83	On N side of Holston River	
Rhea, John	991		Hawkins	600	694	28 Aug 1795	376	31 Mar 1780	89	81	On waters of Beaver Creek	
Rhea, John & Geo. Gordon	1640		Green	1920	1343	27 Aug 1795			87	511	On waters of Spring & Wolf Creek	
Rhea, John & James Adair	170		Eastern District	640	134	14 Jan 1793	727	26 Jan 1781	79	290	On Caney Creek	
Rhea, John & James Sterling	704		Hawkins	640	515	8 Apr 1794	450	24 Apr 1780	82	156	On W side of Holston River	
Rhea, John & Robert King	645		Hawkins	640	516	22 Apr 1794	455	24 Apr 1780	81	553	On Big War Creek	
Rhea, John & Robert King	815		Hawkins	640	651	6 Jan 1795	448	24 Apr 1780	83	170	N side of Clinch River	
Rhea, John & Robert King	861		Hawkins	640	640	16 Jan 1795	448	24 Apr 1780	84	37	On N side of Clinch River	
Rhea, John & Robert King	863		Hawkins	640	642	16 Jan 1795	451	24 Apr 1780	84	39	On N side of Clinch River	
Rhea, John & Thomas King	191		Eastern District	640	163	5 Jun 1793	453	24 Apr 1780	81	339	On both sides of E Fork Emerys R	
Rhea, John & Wm. Terrell	353		Eastern District	1000	270	4 Mar 1796			88	408	On S side of Holston River	
Rhea, John & Wm. Terrell	502		Middle District	200	309	7 Mar 1796			88	197	On Little Lick Creek	
Rhea, John & Wm. Terrell	503		Middle District	500	310	7 Mar 1796	459	24 Apr 1780	88	197	On a fork of the Caney Fork	
Rhea, John & Wm. Terrell	504		Middle District	640	311	7 Mar 1796	776	1 May 1787	88	198	On waters of Colley Fork	
Rhea, John & Wm. Tyrrell	080		Middle District	3234			1786				N/S new road leading to Nashville	
Rhea, John, Ass.	080		Sullivan	200	844	2 Nov 1797	364	20 Mar 1780	96	4	Both sides of Lawhons Creek	
Rhea, Joseph & Robert King	1125		Hawkins	640	709	17 Nov 1796	653	15 Jul 1780	91	87	N side of Holston River	
Rhea, Matthew	777		Sullivan	20- [sic]	680	8 Dec 1795	127	11 Feb 1780	88	268	On N side of Holston River	
Rhea, Wm & Joseph Rhea	737		Sullivan	200	1052	26 Nov 1789	803	13 Jun 1781	74	102	On S side of Cumberland River	yes
Rhen [?], Peter	1495		Davidson	428	296		528	23 Jun 1783			N side of Tinisee (sic) River	
Rhodes, Christian	089		Green	5000	296		1351	22 Feb 1795			N side of Holston River	
Rhodes, Christian	1048		Hawkins	200	812	8 Jun 1797	1725	15 Sep 1779	90	326	On S side of Holston River	
Rhodes, Christian	270		Hawkins	200	281	14 Jan 1793			78	337	On S side of Holston River	
Rhodes, Christian	469		Middle District	5000	296	22 Feb 1795			84	291	Waters Clear Fk of Cumberland R	
Rhodes, Christian	663		Hawkins	400	568	12 Jul 1794	123	9 Feb 1780	81	592	On Big War Creek	
Rhodes, Christian	920		Hawkins	600	729	7 Mar 1796	1772	16 Sep 1779	88	205	On S side of Holston River	
Rhodes, Christian & [blank]	378		Sullivan	640	257	10 Nov 1784	619	23 Jun 1783	69	164	W side of N Fork of Holsten River	
Rhodes, Christian etal	885	McCurty, James	Hawkins	750	145	4 Feb 1795		Martin Armstrong	84	144	Opposite the horse shoe bent	
Rhodes, Christian etal	890		Hawkins	500	151	1 Feb 1795		Martin Armstrong	84	148	Including the Well Spring	
Rhodes, Christian, Ass.	348	Armstrong, M.	Middle District	1000	150	1 Feb 1795			84	147	S W Clear Fork of Cumberland R	
Rhodes, Christian, Ass.	884		Hawkins	250	144	24 Feb 1795			84	143	On S side of Richland Ridge	

Earliest Tennessee Land Records

Claimant:	File #:	Assignee:	County:	Acres:	Grant:	Grant Date:	Entry:	Entry Date:	Bk:	Pg:	Location by Stream Name:	Military:
Rhodes, Christian, Ass.	888	Armstrong, M.	Hawkins	300	148	1 Feb 1795			84	146	On head of fork of German Creek	
Rhodes, Christian, Ass.	889	Armstrong, M.	Hawkins	550	149	1 Feb 1795			84	147	On S side of the valley knobs	
Rhodes, Jacob	730	Lanier, James	Davidson	640	703	11 Jul 1788	3476		63	247	On S side of Kerrs Creek	yes
Rhodes, Joseph	1953		Davidson	3840	1792	20 May 1793	607		81	77	On main W Fork of Stones River	yes
Rhone, John	424	Hamelton, Elijah	Tennessee	640	2475	31 Dec 1793	2004	16 Aug 1785	81	435	On Sturgeon Creek	yes
Rhymes, Jesse	14	Williams, James heirs	Tennessee	1000	1163	26 Nov 1789	2024	24 Aug 1785	74	160	On N side of Cumberland River	
Rhymes, Jesse	15	Williams, Jos.	Tennessee	640	1164	26 Nov 1789	2025	24 Aug 1785	74	160	On N side of Cumberland River	
Rice, Abraham	1080		Washington	100	1030	27 Nov 1792			80	198	Joining Moses Emroys &c	
Rice, Daniel	1952	Smith, Robert	Davidson	640	1791	20 May 1793	277		81	77	On waters of Big Harpeth River	yes
Rice, Daniel	920		Green	200	834	17 Nov 1790	1236	13 Sep 1786	76	116	S side of Nolachuckey River &c	
Rice, Henry	021		Eastern District	640			779	25 Feb 1778			N side of Clinch River	
Rice, Henry	081		Sullivan	200			680	24 Aug 1780				
Rice, Henry	468		Sullivan	643	347	10 Nov 1784	1755	30 Sep 1779	69	194	On N side of Holston River	
Rice, Henry	488		Green	640	490	20 Sep 1787	324	17 Mar 1780	65	515	N side Clinch River in Bald Valley	
Rice, Henry	759		Hawkins	200	599	12 Jul 1794			82	211	N/S Holston R on Sinking Spring	
Rice, Henry	814		Hawkins	640	650	6 Jan 1795	126		83	170	S side of Holston River	
Rice, Jno,Elisha &Abra Risto	313	Dominas, Domina heirs	Davidson	1000	299	13 Jun 1787	2602		63	112	On Middle Fork of Drakes Creek	yes
Rice, Jno.	21		Smith (Middle)	1666	387	6 Feb 1802	2073	5 May 1784	114	392	On waters of Roaring River	
Rice, Jno.	308		Smith (Middle Di	933-1/3	389	6 Feb 1802	520	27 Oct 1783	114	393	On waters of Roaring River	
Rice, Jno.	667		Green	300	708	11 Jul 1788	802	13 Jun 1788	66	463	On the N W side of Clinch River &c	
Rice, Jno. Etal	308	McConough, Dougald heirs	Davidson	640	294	13 Jun 1787	2142		63	110	Beg at an ash & elm	yes
Rice, Jno. Etal	309	Lowel, Obediah	Davidson	640	295	13 Jun 1787	2584		63	110	On a branch of Smiths Creek	yes
Rice, Jno. Etal	310	Harris, William heirs	Davidson	640	296	13 Jun 1787	2129		63	111	Beg at a large white oak	yes
Rice, Jno. Etal	311	Griffin, Samuel heirs	Davidson	640	297	13 Jun 1787	3037		63	111	Beg at a large white oak	yes
Rice, Jno. Etal	315	Martin, John heirs	Davidson	640	301	13 Jun 1787	2140		63	112	ON N side of Tennessee River	yes
Rice, Jno. Etal	318	Nelson, Nathaniel heirs	Davidson	640	304	13 Jun 1787	2038		63	113	N side of Tennessee River	yes
Rice, Jno. Etal	319	Ferrell, Jacob heirs	Davidson	640	305	13 Jun 1787	767		63	114	N side of Roaring River	yes
Rice, Jno. Etal	320	Simpson, Moses heirs	Davidson	640	306	13 Jun 1787	2055		63	114	Beg at a sycamore	yes
Rice, Jno. Etal	321	Vintress, John heirs	Davidson	640	307	13 Jun 1787	2160		63	114	Small creek coming into main TN	yes
Rice, Jno. Etal	323	Stevens, Henry heirs	Davidson	640	309	13 Jun 1787	2582		63	115	On Smith's Creek	yes
Rice, John	037	McDaniel, Larkin heirs	Tennessee	640			1792	25 Apr 1785			On both sides of the North Fork &c	
Rice, John	083		Sullivan	640			1633	16 Sep 1779				
Rice, John	112		Hawkins	140	146	26 Dec 1791			75	162	In Sizemores Valley	
Rice, John	1319	Porter, John	Davidson	320	5	18 Aug 1787	181		68	122	Abt 3 miles below mouth of Red R. &c	
Rice, John	1339	Porter, Wm.	Davidson	320	25	18 Aug 1787	182	22 Feb 1780	68	130	In fork of Red River & Cumberland	
Rice, John	1443	Ballard, Francis	Davidson	320	89	10 Jul 1788			68	232	Lying on Smith Fork of the Caney Fork	
Rice, John	1586	Realey, Ezekial	Davidson	228	1249	10 Dec 1790			74	348	Adjoining his entry as Assn. of Wm. Ramsey	
Rice, John	1592	Lane, Jesse	Davidson	640	1266	10 Dec 1790			74	354	Joining sd Rice's claim	
Rice, John	1610	Ramsey, Wm.	Davidson	640	1333	10 Dec 1790	180	26 Jan 1784	74	376	On head of John Milners Creek	
Rice, John	1629	Armstrong, M.	Davidson	168	102	10 Nov 1790			74	389	Beg at a red oak	
Rice, John	166		Hawkins	100	99	16 Nov 1790	167	19 Feb 1780	77	185	N/S of Holston River	
Rice, John	176		Hawkins	640	109	16 Nov 1790	430	19 Apr 1780	77	187	On S side of Clinch River	
Rice, John	187		Hawkins	300	120	16 Nov 1790	465	24 Apr 1780	77	190	Lying in Standleys Valley	
Rice, John	191		Hawkins	640	124	16 Nov 1790	1633	23 Jul 1783	77	191	On So side of Clinch River	
Rice, John	20		Smith	1666	385	6 Feb 1802	2073	5 May 1784	114	391	On West of Cumberland Mountain	

Earliest Tennessee Land Records

Claimant:	File #:	Assignee:	County:	Acres:	Grant:	Grant Date:	Entry:	Entry Date:	Bk:	Pg:	Location by Stream Name:	Military:
Rice, John	200	Joines, John	Tennessee	640	1488	4 Jan 1792	79	27 Oct 1783	77	373	S side of Cumberland River	
Rice, John	21		Smith (Middle)	1666	387	6 Feb 1802	2073	5 May 1784	114	392	On Roaring River	
Rice, John	2150	Hood, Charles	Davidson	192	2451	31 Dec 1793	667		81	427	On N side of Cumberland River	yes
Rice, John	22	Blanset, Frederick	Sumner	228	779	11 Jul 1788	1930	21 Sep 1787	63	273	On waters of Caney Fork	yes
Rice, John	221		Washington	177	89	23 Oct 1782	651	25 Dec 1778	47	43	S side of Holston River	
Rice, John	23		Smith (Middle Di	388	388	6 Feb 1802	520	27 Oct 1783	114	393	On waters of Roaring River	
Rice, John	24		Smith (Middle Di	933	389	6 Feb 1802	520	27 Oct 1783	114	393	On waters of Roaring River	
Rice, John	25		Smith(Middle)	933	390	6 Feb 1802	520	27 Oct 1783	114	393	On waters of Roaring River	
Rice, John	293		Western District	5000	282	25 Apr 1789	2075	5 May 1784	72	85	On waters of Big Hatcher River	
Rice, John	294		Western District	5000	283	5 Apr 1789	382	25 Oct 1783	72	85	On the Chickasaw Bluff	
Rice, John	295		Western District	5000	284	25 Apr 1789	2097	6 May 1784	72	86	On big Hatcha River	
Rice, John	296		Western District	5000	285	25 Apr 1789	2203	15 May 1784	72	86	On Big Hatcha River	
Rice, John	297		Western District	5000	341	17 Nov 1790	2142	11 May 1784	76	166	On Big Hatcha River	
Rice, John	297		Western District	5000	286	25 Apr 1789	2200 [?]	15 May 1784	72	86	On both sides of Big Hatcha River	
Rice, John	298		Western District	5000	287	25 Apr 1789	2074		72	87	On waters of Big Hatcha River &c	
Rice, John	299		Western District	5000	288	25 Apr 1789	2095	6 May 1784	72	87	On S side of Hatcha River	
Rice, John	300		Western District	5000	289	25 Apr 1789	2096	6 May 1784	72	87	On S side of Big Hatcha River	
Rice, John	301		Western Dist	5000	290	25 Apr 1789	1255	24 May 1783	72	88	Waters of Big Hatcha River	
Rice, John	302		Western District	5007	291	25 Apr 1789	2201	15 May 1784	72	88	On waters of Big Hatcha River	
Rice, John	303		Western District	5000	292	25 Apr 1789	2094	6 May 1784	72	88	On S side of Big Hatcha River &c	
Rice, John	304		Western District	5000	293	25 Apr 1789	2205	15 May 1784	72	89	On waters of Big Hatcha River	
Rice, John	305		Western District	5000	294	25 Apr 1789	2204	15 May 1784	72	89	On both sides Big Hatcha River	
Rice, John	306	Lane, Jesse	Davidson	640	292	13 Jun 1787	865		63	109	On Millers Creek	yes
Rice, John	306		Western District	5000	295	25 Apr 1789	2077	5 May 1784	72	90	On waters of Big Hatcha River	
Rice, John	307	Barker, Levy	Davidson	640	293	13 Jun 1787	1088		63	109	Fork of Cumberland & Red Rivers	yes
Rice, John	307		Western District	5000	296	25 Apr 1789	2199	15 May 1784	72	90	On both sides of Big Hatcha River	
Rice, John	308		Western District	5000	297	25 Apr 1789	2202	15 May 1784	72	91	On Big Hatcha River &c	
Rice, John	323		Hawkins	100	99	16 Nov 1790	167	19 Feb 1780	77	185	Lying on N side of Holston River	
Rice, John	344	McDonald, William	Sumner	640	1411	20 Dec 1791			77	354	On both sides of the N Fork &c	yes
Rice, John	37		Washington	74	327	24 Oct 1782	651	27 Nov 1778	43	309	On the side of Holston River	
Rice, John	501		Hawkins	250	373	29 Jul 1793	1948	2 Oct 1779	80	270	On N side of Copper Ridge	
Rice, John	611		Middle District	1000	384	15 Jan 1802	1258	24 Nov 1783	114	391	On middle fork of Roaring River	
Rice, John	611		Western District	2500	290	25 Apr 1789	1255	24 Nov 1783	72	88	On waters of Big Hatcha River	
Rice, John	622	Fleming, William	Sumner	640	1898	20 May 1793	1188	12 Oct 1792	81	100	On S side of Cumberland River	yes
Rice, John	668		Sullivan	400	616	9 Jul 1794	2236	22 Nov 1779	81	626	On Black Water Creek	
Rice, John	685	Tracey, James	Davidson	274	658	8 Dec 1787	1201		63	233	On waters of E Fork of Mill Creek	yes
Rice, John	74	Stoveall, John	Tennessee	640	1318	10 Dec 1790	1136	9 Aug 1784	74	371	On N side of Cumberland River	
Rice, John	79	Ferrell, Wm.	Tennessee	640	1324	10 Dec 1790	1077	1 Jun 1784	74	373	On N side of Cumberland River	
Rice, John	80		Western District	5000	80	10 Jul 1788	2072	5 May 1784	67	311	On S side of Big Hatcha &c	
Rice, John	800		Hawkins	68	636	6 Jan 1795	63	8 Feb 1780	83	162	On both sides of Mill Creek &c	
Rice, John	869	Lane, Jesse	Davidson	640	884	25 Apr 1789			63	306	Lying adjoining Rices claim	yes
Rice, John	870	Realy, Ezekial	Davidson	428	885	25 Apr 1789			63	306	Lying adjoining his entry	
Rice, John	871	Armstrong, M.	Davidson	168	54	25 Apr 1789			63	306	Beg at a red oak	
Rice, John	872	Ramsey, Wm.	Davidson	640	55	25 Apr 1789			63	307	On head of John Milners Creek	
Rice, John & Co.	056	Borough, Joel (?)	not given	1000			1668	20 Sep 1788			N side of Cumberland River	

Claimant:	File #:	Assignee:	County:	Acres:	Grant:	Grant Date:	Entry:	Entry Date:	Bk:	Pg:	Location by Stream Name:	Military:
Rice, John & Harriet S.	1966	Moore, Samuel	Davidson	640	1843	20 May 1793	1778		81	88	On S/S Cumberland River Sams Cr	yes
Rice, John & Harriet S.	1974	Pasmore, Enock	Davidson	640	1869	20 May 1793	1724		81	94	S/S Cumberland River	yes
Rice, John & Harriot	339	Nelms, Jesse	Tennessee	640	2129	20 May 1793	2147	9 Sep 1785	81	156	On S side of Cumberland River	
Rice, John & Harriot	341	McKinis, John	Tennessee	640	2138	20 May 1793	2144	9 Sep 1785	81	158	On N side of Cumberland River	
Rice, John & Harriot S.	277	Grant, Lewis	Tennessee	640	1857	20 May 1793	2052	26 Aug 1785	81	91	On S side of Cumberland River	
Rice, John & John Sapington	312	Wright, John	Davidson	640	298	13 Jun 1787	2060		63	111	On Therrs Creek of Sulphur Fork	yes
Rice, John, Sapington & Co.	316	Wooten, Thomas heirs	Davidson	640	302	13 Jun 1787	2254		63	113	West Fork of Jones's Creek	yes
Rice, Spencer	622		Green	347	663	11 Jul 1788	103	20 Oct 1783	66	448	On S side of Nolichuckey River	
Rice, William	115		Hawkins	250	149	26 Dec 1791	2260	22 Nov 1779	75	163	On S side of Holston River	
Rich, James	1423	Lytle, William	Sumner	640	3297	6 Dec 1797	1968	13 Jun 1796	98	172	Adjoining his survey &c	yes
Richards, Clement	936	Blount, Reading	Davidson	640	952	18 May 1789	2154		63	325	On waters of Caney Fork	yes
Richards, Henry	508	Tatum, Howell	Sumner	640	1682	20 May 1793	2475	10 Apr 1792	81	49	On waters of Bledsoes Creek	yes
Richards, Jacob	2052		Davidson	342	2132	20 May 1793	228		81	157	On N side of Cumberland River	yes
Richards, James	1979		Davidson	357	1884	20 May 1793	1829		81	97	On Lick Creek N waters of Duck River	yes
Richards, Jesse	213	Reed, Jesse	Sumner	640	1118	26 Nov 1789	1977	12 Mar 1788	74	138	On S W side of Caney Fork River	yes
Richards, John	1013	Buckanan, John	Davidson	640	1030	18 May 1789	1981		63	343	On Stones River	yes
Richards, John	195		Hawkins	100	128	16 Nov 1790	676	10 Jun 1785	77	193	On N side of Holston River	
Richards, John	482		Hawkins	100 (150	354	29 Jul 1793	100	8 Feb 1780	80	264	Joins plantat. where he now lives	
Richards, Joseph	1359	Wynne, Robert	Sumner	640	3054	4 Jul 1797	4029	25 Nov 1796	91	599	Waters of Caney Fork	yes
Richards, Stephen	183		Hawkins	400	116	16 Nov 1790	3207	18 Oct 1779	77	189	On the N side of Clinch Mountain &c	
Richards, Stephen	251		Hawkins	640	239	26 Dec 1791	1921	11 Oct 1779	77	326	On the N side of Clinch Mountain	
Richards, Stephen	3		Hawkins	158	2	10 Jul 1788	2095	26 Oct 1779	64	328	On N side of Holston River &c	
Richards, Stephen	4		Hawkins	315	3	10 Jul 1788	295	10 Mar 1780	64	329	On N side of Clinch Mountain	
Richardson, Amos	1289		Washington	100	1204	9 Dec 1795	2349	11 Dec 1779	89	403	On a dry branch of Little Doe	
Richardson, James	156		Washington	99	24	23 Oct 1782	1440	11 Jun 1779	47	11	On Little Sinking Creek	
Richardson, James	2027	McCulloh, Benjamin	Davidson	640	2035	20 May 1793	2816		81	133	On Snow Creek	yes
Richardson, James	289	Fenner, Richard	Davidson	640	275	22 Mar 1787	2542		63	100	On Sulphur Fork of Red River	yes
Richardson, James	906		Green	300	1069	Jul 1792	916	29 Oct 1783	74	447	Joining McHoods line	
Richardson, John	1139		Washington	50	1097	12 Jul 1794	2363	20 Dec 1770	81	568	Beg at a chesnut	yes
Richardson, John	186		Davidson	274	172	7 Mar 1786	391		63	65	On waters of Browns Creek	yes
Richardson, John	382		Green	240	384	20 Sep 1787	173	22 Nov 1784	65	481	On a branch of Lick Creek &c	
Richardson, William	285	Long, Nicholas	Tennessee	640	1895	20 May 1793	466	24 Feb 1784	81	99	On S side of Cumberland River	yes
Richeson, James	177		Green	640	647	11 Jul 1788	166	10 Oct 1784	64	357	On S side Nolichuckey River	
Richeson, Jesse	014	Gilliam, Charles	Knox	328			1945	20 Apr 1793			S side Holston River	yes
Richeson, Jesse	348	Gillam, Charles	Eastern Dist	328	2695	6 Jun 1796			88	368	On S side of Holston River	yes
Richeson, Joseph	1389		Green	40	1244	27 Jan 1793	2882	22 Jul 1781	79	511	On waters of Nolechuckey	
Richey, Gideon	15		Green	250	78	1 Nov 1786	179	21 Oct 1783	58	439	On N or N W/S of Nolichuckie Riv	
Richey, Thomas	523		Hawkins	300	396	29 Jul 1793			80	276	On Third Creek	
Richey, William	407		Washington	55	399	13 Oct 1783	2742	20 Jan 1781	52	265	On big Limestone Creek	
Richey, William	437		Washington	200	429	13 Oct 1783	2924	10 Sep 1781	52	280	On W side of Lick Creek	
Richman, Mark	542	Orr, James heirs	Davidson	640	514	15 Sep 1787	2539		63	185	S side of Cumberland	yes
Richy, Thomas	545	Malloy, Thomas	Tennessee	1000	2969	5 Apr 1797	3961		90	273	S side of Cumberland River	yes
Rickey, John	254		Washington	491	122	23 Oct 1782	1091	8 Jan 1779	47	60	On Horse Pasture Branch	
Rickey, John	339		Washington	318	206	24 Oct 1782	292	4 Aug 1778	49	229	On both sides of Big Limestone Cr	yes
Rickey, John	54		Washington	198	344	24 Oct 1782	612	22 Nov 1778	43	316	On the Lick Fork of Lick Creek	yes

Claimant:	File #:	Assignee:	County:	Acres:	Grant:	Grant Date:	Entry:	Entry Date:	Bk:	Pg:	Location by Stream Name:	Military:
Rickey, Thomas	908		Hawkins	100	696	18 Aug 1795	869	31 Dec 1778	87	507	On Third Creek	
Rickey, William	169		Washington	200	37	23 Oct 1782	295	4 Aug 1778	47	17	On waters of Lick Creek	
Rickey, William	170		Washington	300	38	23 Oct 1782	338	1 Sep 1778	47	17	On a branch of Limestone	
Rickey, William	24		Washington	600	314	24 Oct 1782	870	31 Dec 1778	43	303	On waters of Big Limestone Creek	
Rickey, William	763		Washington	200	577	10 Nov 1784	1179	2 Feb 1779	69	131	On a small branch &c	
Ricks, Lewis	1757	Hays, Robert	Davidson	640	1531	14 Jan 1793	2684		79	265	On E branches of Stones River	yes
Ridden, John	1615	Blair, John	Davidson	640	1343	10 Dec 1790	696		74	380	On waters of Stones River	yes
Riddick, John	33		Hawkins	150	65	7 Apr 1790	1129	19 May 1779	71	286	On the S side of Holston River &c	
Riddick, Joseph	576	Rose, Thomas	Tennessee	640	3023	10 Apr 1797	1386		90	302	On Collin[-?-]'s Creek	yes
Riddle, James	0177		Green	300			278	22 Oct 1783			On Little Chuckey	
Rider, Jno.	651		Washington	100	745	26 Oct 1786	2444	28 Feb 1780	66	32	On Sinking Creek &c	
Riding, Robert	124		Tennessee	274	1630	23 Feb 1793	3273	26 Dec 1785	76	327	Bet. Grices & Yellow Creek	
Ridley, Berriman	459	Nichols, John	Davidson	640	431	15 Sep 1787	1933		63	159	N side of Cumberland River	yes
Ridley, George	133		Sullivan	400	146	23 Oct 1782	638	16 May 1780	43	328	On S side of Holston River &c	
Ridley, George	1652		Davidson	640	303	17 Nov 1790	46	1 Jan 1788	76	182	S/S Cumber. waters of Browns Cr	
Ridley, George	49		Hawkins	200	34	18 May 1789	1978	19 Oct 1779	72	250	On head of Russells Creek	
Ridley, George	57		Sullivan	200	68	23 Oct 1782	222	24 May 1778	43	271	On S side of Holston River &c	
Ridley, George	917		Hawkins	500	726	7 Mar 1796			88	203	On S side of Holston River	
Ridley, George, Sr.	763		Green	500	582	11 Jul 1788	582 [sic]	25 Oct 1783	68	219	On N side of Holsten River	
Rieley, Thomas	689		Sullivan	100	637	9 Jul 1794	718	21 Dec 1780	81	634	Joins tract formerly John Stewarts	
Reeves, John	1153		Green	80	996	26 Dec 1791	104	4 Jul 1789	77	280	On the head of a branch of Little Chuckey	
Rife, Abraham	059		Washington	100			2536	10 Apr 1780			Joining Moses Emory's	
Rife, Abraham	715		Washington	100	529	10 Nov 1784	856	30 Dec 1778	69	115	Upon a branch of Little Limestone	
Rigby, Ezekial	759	Nash, William	Davidson	640	732	11 Jul 1788	2577		63	257	On E side of Stones River	yes
Rigens, Joel	479	Marshall, John	Davidson	640	451	15 Sep 1787	2282		63	165	On Hurricane Creek	yes
Riggis, Edward	426		Green	1000	428	20 Sep 1787	428 [sic]	25 Oct 1783	65	496	On S side of Holston &c	
Riggs, Clisby & Tho Jackson	500		Hawkins	300	493	27 Jun 1793	2206	12 Nov 1779	80	359	On the S side of Spring Creek	
Riggs, Clisby & Tho Jackson	631		Hawkins	300	493	27 Jun 1793	2206	12 Nov 1779	80	359	On the S side of Spring Creek	
Riggs, Edward	500		Green	445	502	20 Sep 1787	650	28 Oct 1783	65	522	On N side of the Knobbs &c	
Riggs, Edward	619		Green	200	660	11 Jul 1788	608	28 Oct 1785	66	447	On S side of Holston River	
Riggs, Jesse	292		Green	70	294	20 Sep 1787	672	28 Oct 1783	65	457	S side of Holston River on Fall Cr	
Riggs, Saml.	0125		Sullivan	200			472	25 Apr 1780			On Fall Creek	
Riggs, Samuel	1377		Green	40	1232	27 Jan 1793	1232 [sic]	25 Apr 1792	79	507	Joining a survey of 1000 acres &c	
Riggs, Samuel	404		Hawkins	200	525	27 Jan 1793			79	499	On Fall Creek	
Right, Isaac	992	Pasmore, David	Davidson	365	1009	18 May 1789	417		63	338	On waters of Stones River	yes
Rights, Francis	223		Middle District	1230	203	27 Nov 1792	1548	22 Mar 1784	80	209	On N side of Duck River	
Rights, John	55		Western Dist	5000	55	10 Jul 1788	690	28 Oct 1783	67	301	On Housers Creeks &c	
Rigsby, Frederick	20	Bosley, James	Davidson	274	6	16 Feb 1786	751		63	3	S side of Cumberland River	yes
Riley, John	1672	Robertson, Jas & Ben. Josli	Davidson	640	1596	23 Feb 1793	1729		76	310	S side of Big Harpeth River	yes
Riley, John	445 or(6)		Sullivan	200	324		900	31 Dec 1778	69	185	On Indian Creek	
Riley, Samuel	817	Robertson, Elijah	Davidson	640	820	20 Nov 1788	3321		63	289	On waters of Caney Fork	yes
Rillom, John	1424	Lytle, William	Sumner	640	3298	6 Dec 1797	1043	13 Jun 1796	98	173	On waters of Big Cedar Lick Cr	yes
Ring, John	940		Green	1011	854	17 Nov 1790	1263	6 Dec 1783	76	123	On the waters of Duck River	
Ring, William	778	Lancaster, John	Sumner	640	2232	20 May 1793	2225	2 Sep 1792	81	176	On head waters of Bartons Creek	yes
Rinkle, George	022		Eastern Dist	300			488	25 Sep 1783			S side French Broad River	

Claimant:	File #:	Assignee:	County:	Acres:	Grant:	Grant Date:	Entry:	Entry Date:	Bk:	Pg:	Location by Stream Name:	Military:
Riston, Abraham	1024	Straughan, Larker	Davidson	640	1042	18 May 1789	472	25 Apr 1780	63	346	On Spencers Creek	
Ritchey, William	190		Eastern Dist	200	162	5 Jun 1793	2751	20 Jan 1781	81	339	On Second Cr waters of Holston	yes
Ritchey, William	375		Washington	150	367	13 Oct 1783	2751	20 Jan 1781	52	249	On W side of Lick Creek &c	
Ritchey, William	458		Washington	299	450	13 Oct 1783	436	25 Sep 1778	52	289	On the Sinking Fork of Lick Creek	
Ritchie, William	851		Washington	300	842	10 Nov 1788	233	18 Jun 1778	70	1	On waters of Little Limestone	
Ritledge, John	484		Middle District	3000	276	6 Dec 1794	1775	23 Apr 1784	85	338	On Middle Fork of Elk River	
Ritter, Jacob	085		Middle District	3000	1775	23 Apr 1784					On the middle fork of Elk River	
Rivell, John	1760	Hays, Robert	Davidson	274	1539	14 Jan 1793	1864		79	267	On waters of Mauscows Creek	
Rivers, William	702	Hart, Anthony	Davidson	640	675	8 Dec 1787	2815		63	238	On W of Twinbulls Clay Lick	yes
Roach, Jordan	712	Hays, Robert	Washington	400	526	8 Nov 1784	1034	6 Jan 1779	69	114	Beg at a white oak	yes
Roach, Moses	382	Hays, Robert	Sumner	640	1565	14 Jan 1793	2954	9 Apr 1788	79	272	On Smiths Fork	
Roads, Christian	045		Hawkins	200								yes
Roads, Christian	076		Washington	300			794	4 Jan 1779			N side of Holston River	
Roads, Christian	082		Sullivan	100			175	19 Feb 1780				
Roads, Christian etal	267	Menifee, John	Sullivan	1280	406	9 Aug 1787	302-303	10 Mar 1780	61	425	On the N side of Holston River &c	
Roan, David	1937	Robertson, James	Davidson	640	1757	29 May 1793			81	68	Hollis Fk, Heatons Fk of Whites Cr	yes
Robards, James	288		Sullivan	100	427	9 Aug 1787	2119	4 Nov 1779	61	446	On waters of Reedy Creek	
Robards, Lewis	1241		Davidson	640	206	10 Jul 1788	399	6 Apr 1784	66	413	On S/S Cumberland River	
Robb, William	544	Stolcop, William	Davidson	357	516	15 Sep 1787	173		63	186	On waters of Goose Creek	yes
Robbins, James	812	Hays, Stockley	Sumner	640	2279	20 May 1793	2360	18 Nov 1792	81	186	On Caney Fork &c	yes
Robbins, Samuel	1423		Green	100	1235	27 Nov 1792			80	165	On N side of Nolichucky River	
Robenson, Charles	238	Hargett & Randel	Middle District	1000	211	12 Jan 1793	2612	25 May 1784	80	298	On a creek called Cold Water	
Robenson, Charles	239		Middle District	100(?)	212	12 Jan 1793	2608	25 May 1784	80	298	On a river called Buffellow River &c	
Robenson, Charles	329		Washington	500	643	10 Nov 1784	857	30 Dec 1778	69	150	On N side Nolachuckey River	
Roberson, Cornelius	259	Hickman, Thomas	Tennessee	274	1684	20 May 1793	3557	11 Aug 1787	81	50	On N side of Cumberland River	
Roberson, Daniel	0143		Green	100			494	27 Oct 1783			N side Holston River	yes
Roberson, James	608	Marr, John Sr.	Davidson	335	580	15 Sep 1787	750	1 Oct 1779	63	207	On S side of Cumberland River	yes
Roberson, John	239		Sullivan	640	378	9 Aug 1787	1763		61	397	On the N side of Holston River	
Roberson, John	31		Washington	200	301	24 Oct 1782	833	29 Dec 1778	43	307	On a branch of Big Limestone Cr	
Roberson, John	420	Lytle, Archibald	Davidson	640	392	15 Sep 1787	1171		63	146	On Second Creek	yes
Roberson, Jonathan Fryers	2192		Davidson	480	182	26 Mar 1795			86	412	On S of Harpeth River	
Roberson, Moses	553		Sullivan	620	536	17 Nov 1790	186	20 Mar 1778	76	536	On Horse Creek	
Roberson, Samuel	1454		Green	100	1264	27 Nov 1792	2851	12 Apr 1781	80	175	N/S Nolechuckey R on Franks Cr	
Roberson, Willoughby	383	Sheppard, Benjamin	Davidson	640	355	15 Sep 1787	2319	15 Sep 1787	63	134	Both sides 3rd lge or of Big Barren	yes
Robert, Edmund	26		Washington	300	316	24 Oct 1782	842	30 Dec 1778	43	304	On the Cedar Branch &c	
Roberts, David	669		Sullivan	250	617	9 Jul 1794	2120	4 Nov 1779	81	627	On waters of Reed Creek	
Roberts, David (heirs)	055		Sullivan	250	2118	4 Nov 1779					In the rich valley	
Roberts, Deliiah	1401	Reed, Guilford	Sumner	640	3330	6 Dec 1797	4670	17 Jun 1797	97	50	On waters of Cedar Creek	yes
Roberts, Edmund	503		Green	300	505	20 Sep 1787	2139	4 Nov 1779	65	523	On Ceader (sic) Branch	
Roberts, Elijah	1536		Davidson	640	1093	26 Nov 1789			74	127	On S side of Cumberland river	
Roberts, Elijah	2135	Mulherin, James	Davidson	640	2409	7 Jan 1794	3319		81	402	On S side of Cumberland river	yes
Roberts, Elijah	262	Hay, Archibald	Tennessee	640	1707	20 May 1793			81	55	On Main E Fork of Bends Creek	
Roberts, Elijah	929	Mulherin, James	Davidson	640	945	18 May 1789			63	323	On Hickmans creek	yes
Roberts, Elisha	023		Eastern Dist	200				14 Jul 1797			Waters of Flat Creek	
Roberts, Elisha	024		Eastern Dist	200							On Mountain Fork of Flat Creek	

Claimant:	File #:	Assignee:	County:	Acres:	Grant:	Grant Date:	Entry:	Entry Date:	Bk:	Pg:	Location by Stream Name:	Military:
Roberts, George	441		Sullivan	505	320	10 Nov 1784	976	22 Jan 1779	69	183	On both sides of Robinsons Creek	
Roberts, George	597		Sullivan	150	552	26 Dec 1791	1774	1 Oct 1779	77	303	Joins plantation he now lives on	
Roberts, Hardy	1538	Craddock, John	Davidson	640	1095	26 Nov 1789	2474		74	129	Waters W Fork of Station Camp Cr	yes
Roberts, Henry	596		Sullivan	35	594	29 Jul 1793	231	24 Feb 1780	76	477	N/S Holston waters of Reedy Cr	
Roberts, Henry	599		Sullivan	300	554	26 Dec 1791	543	29 Apr 1780	77	304	On both sides of Reedy Creek	
Roberts, Henry	734		Sullivan	150	677	2 Dec 1796	1741	27 Sep 1779	88	267	On waters of Reedy Creek	
Roberts, Henry	795		Hawkins	200	635	12 Jul 1794	1814 [?]	7 Oct 1779	82	225	On a small creek N/S Clinch Mtn	
Roberts, Isaac	1786		Davidson	640	368	26 Jun 1793	470	7 Jun 1784	80	322	N/S Cumberland on Halfpone Cr	
Roberts, Isaac	599		Western Dist	5000	382	29 Jul 1793	1705	8 May 1787	76	479	On the waters of Obion River	
Roberts, J.	01	Williamson, George	Montgomery	640			1554	15 Oct 1790			On McFaddins Fork	yes
Roberts, James	152		Green	50	622	23 Aug 1788	2524	[?] Apr 1780	64	348	On Big Limestone	
Roberts, James	299		Hawkins	150	262	24 Dec 1792	827	28 Jul 1781	78	448	On S side of Holston River	
Roberts, Jesse	664	Yancey, John	Davidson	640	637	15 Nov 1787	1841		63	226	Beg at N side of Cumberland River	yes
Roberts, John	141		Eastern Dist	250	110	-- Mar 1792	1935	11 Oct 1779	77	331	On a branch of Beaver Creek	
Roberts, John	476	Donelson, Stockley	Tennessee	640	2721	20 Jul 1796	2814	30 Sep 1785	88	449	On waters of Sulphur Fork	yes
Roberts, Joshua	1020	Wallace, William	Davidson	640	1038	18 May 1789	2760		63	345	1st creek above Stones Lick Cr	yes
Roberts, Obed	1388	Armstrong, M.	Davidson	640	5	8 Oct 1787			68	150	On Camp Cr the N waters Duck R	
Roberts, Reuben	1060		Washington	50	1010	27 Nov 1792	2024	26 Oct 1779	80	179	On both sides of Dry Run	
Roberts, Reuben, heirs of	1399		Sumner	228	3327	6 Dec 1797			97	48	On the Round Lick Creek	
Roberts, Richard	099	Miller, Adam	Sumner	640			942	25 Nov 1789			S side of Cumberland River	yes
Roberts, Sampson	1140	Harris, Edward	Sumner	640	2646	4 Jun 1796	2476	1 Jun 1795	88	349	Joining sd Harris survey	yes
Roberts, Shadrack	265	Motherall, John	Sumner	228	1225	10 Mar 1790	1826	9 Mar 1790	74	340	On N side of Cumberland River	yes
Roberts, Thomas W.	1428	Barton, Samuel	Sumner	640	3302	6 Dec 1797	4663	20 Jun 1797	98	176	On waters of Round Lick Creek	yes
Roberts, Venson	956	Dixon, Tilman	Davidson	308	973	18 May 1789			63	330	On small fork of Big Harpeth River	yes
Roberts, William	335		Sullivan	3000 (?)	475	10 Jul 1788	2123	4 Nov 1779	67	484	Lying in Rich Valey &c	
Roberts, William	970		Hawkins	40	742	20 Jul 1796	49	8 Feb 1780	88	496	On waters of Roseberrys Creek	
Roberts, William & Co.	816		Hawkins	132	652	6 Jan 1795	63	8 Feb 1780	83	171	On the waters of Clinch River &c	
Roberts, Wm.	142		Eastern Dist	200	111	-- Mar 1792	22	26 Feb 1778	77	332	Hinds Valley on waters of Beaver Cr	
Robertson, Alexander	16		Middle Dist	2000	18	10 Jul 1788	639	28 Oct 1783	67	415	On Duck River &c	
Robertson, Charles	1049		Green	600	893	6 Sep 1791	77 [sic]	21 Oct 1783	77	224	N side of French Broad River	yes
Robertson, Charles	1728	Duncan, Jesse	Davidson	274	1443	20 Dec 1791	539		77	361	N/S Cumber& waters of Whites Cr	
Robertson, Charles	181		Green	300	651	11 Jan 1788	48	20 Oct 1783	644	358	S/S Nolichuckey River on Cove Cr	
Robertson, Charles	323		Washington	257	190	24 Oct 1782	685	9 Dec 1778	49	190	On the E branch of Sinking Creek	
Robertson, Chas.	109	Baker, Jos.	Tennessee	640	1581	23 Feb 1793	1035	26 May 1784	76	303	Cr Chickasaw Tr Cr aft Warpath	
Robertson, David	056		Davidson	640			1840	29 Oct 1786			Big Ridge, Lepers Fork of Harpeth	
Robertson, David	2466	Minshew, Wm. Heirs	Davidson	640	3401	14 Apr 1803	1846	29 Oct 1796	110	319	Ridge above Leepers Fk of Harpeth	yes
Robertson, Elijah	029	McBride, James	Davidson	640			3281	22 Mar 1788			On the waters of Caney Fork	
Robertson, Elijah	039	Oneil, James	Tennessee	640			965	18 May 1784			N side Cumberland River	
Robertson, Elijah	057	Rains, Charles	Davidson	640			1839	16 Mar 1786			N side of Cumberland River	
Robertson, Elijah	058	White, Charles	Davidson	640			515	14 Feb 1784			Abt 2 miles S of Nashville	
Robertson, Elijah	1005	Shaw, John	Sumner	640	169	26 Mar 1795	3376	28 Jun 1788	86	375	On the Cold Creek	yes
Robertson, Elijah	104		Middle District	5000	106	10 Jul 1788	1043	29 Oct 1783	67	461	On the S side of Duck River &c	
Robertson, Elijah	1254		Davidson	640	219	10 Jul 1788	19	29 Dec 1783	63	416	W oak&dogw line of Public survey	
Robertson, Elijah	136	Jackson, Philip heirs	Tennessee	640	1649	23 Feb 1793			76	336	N side of Cumberland River &c	
Robertson, Elijah	137	Suerlock, Eph.	Tennessee	640	1650	23 FEb 1793	1837	14 Jun 1785	76	336	N side of Cumberland River &c	

Earliest Tennessee Land Records

Claimant:	File #:	Assignee:	County:	Acres:	Grant:	Grant Date:	Entry:	Entry Date:	Bk:	Pg:	Location by Stream Name:	Military:
Robertson, Elijah	144	Wood, Titus heirs	Tennessee	640	1395	20 Dec 1791	79	8 Feb 1780	77	350	On both sides of Pine River &c	
Robertson, Elijah	157		Sullivan	447	167	18 Oct 1783		8 Feb 1780	45	214	Beg two basket [sic] white oaks	
Robertson, Elijah	158		Sullivan	329(?)	168	11 Oct 1783	80	8 Feb 1780	45	275	Beg at the mouth of Clouds Creek	
Robertson, Elijah	159		Sullivan	490	169	11 Oct 1783	1996	22 Oct 1779	45	275	Beg at an ash &c	
Robertson, Elijah	1658		Davidson	960	1580	23 Feb 1793	852		76	303	Big Harpeth R at mouth of Buffaloe	yes
Robertson, Elijah	1689	Jackson, Philip heirs	Davidson	640	1648	23 Feb 1793	2196		76	336	On Flat Creek of Harpeth River	yes
Robertson, Elijah	1706		Davidson	640	322	23 Feb 1793	20	29 Dec 1783	76	345	S/S Harpeth on or big South leads up	
Robertson, Elijah	18		Middle District	5000	20	10 Jul 1788	651	28 Oct 1783	67	416	On Richland Creek &c	
Robertson, Elijah	2184		Davidson	300	158	22 Feb 1795			84	283	On waters of Stones River	
Robertson, Elijah	2185	White, Wm.	Davidson	20	159	22 Feb 1795			84	284	Being an island below Nashville	
Robertson, Elijah	2318		Davidson	640	2781	29 Nov 1796			90	15	About 2 miles S of Nashville	yes
Robertson, Elijah	336		Western Dist	100	336	18 May 1789			72	276	On N side of Woolf River &c	
Robertson, Elijah	337		Western District	500	337	18 May 1789	1996	22 Oct 1779	72	276	On the E side of Harris's Fork &c	
Robertson, Elijah	516	Morgan, Thos. Heir of Jaco	Davidson	640	488	15 Sep 1787	2209		63	177	N side of Cumberland River	yes
Robertson, Elijah	625	Thomas, Amos heir of Britt.	Davidson	640	597	15 Sep 1787			63	213	On N side of Cumberland River	yes
Robertson, Elijah	795	McMurtree, John	Davidson	640	798	20 Nov 1788	2615		63	280	On waters of the first creek	yes
Robertson, Elijah	796	Caldwell, Wm.	Davidson	640	799	20 Nov 1788	3303		63	280	On waters of Caney Fork	yes
Robertson, Elijah	797	McClane, Michael	Davidson	640	800	20 Nov 1788	3316		63	281	On S side of Cumberland River	yes
Robertson, Elijah	798	Dudley, Matthias	Davidson	640	801	20 Nov 1788			63	281	On waters of Hickmans Creek	yes
Robertson, Elijah	799	Willard, Stephen	Davidson	640	802	20 Nov 1788	3326		63	282	On waters of Caney Fork	yes
Robertson, Elijah	800	Stockley, Alexander Sgt.	Davidson	1000	803	20 Nov 1788	3324		63	282	On S side of Cumberland River	yes
Robertson, Elijah	802	Garrison, William	Davidson	640	805	20 Nov 1788	3312		63	283	On S side of Cumberland River	yes
Robertson, Elijah	803	Gordin, Hastin	Davidson	640	806	20 Nov 1788	3313		63	283	On waters of Caney Fork	yes
Robertson, Elijah	804	Nelson, Estridge	Davidson	640	807	20 Nov 1788	3317		63	283	On waters of Caney Fork	yes
Robertson, Elijah	805	Holingsworth, Thomas	Davidson	640	808	20 Nov 1788	3315		63	284	On waters of Caney Fork	yes
Robertson, Elijah	806	Reily, Thomas	Davidson	640	809	20 Nov 1788	3322		63	284	On waters of Collins River	yes
Robertson, Elijah	807	Henry, John	Davidson	640	810	20 Nov 1788	3262		63	284	On waters of Caney Fork	yes
Robertson, Elijah	808	Watkins, Evan	Davidson	640	811	20 Nov 1788	3327		63	285	On E Fork of Stones River	yes
Robertson, Elijah	809	McBride, James heirs	Davidson	640	812	20 Nov 1788	3281		63	285	On S side of Cumberland	yes
Robertson, Elijah	810	Caldwell, Lemuel heirs	Davidson	640	813	20 Nov 1788			63	285	On waters of Caney Fork	yes
Robertson, Elijah	811	Harrell, Thomas	Davidson	640	814	20 Nov 1788	3314		63	286	On waters of Caney Fork	yes
Robertson, Elijah	812	Diggs, William heirs	Davidson	640	815	20 Nov 1788	3310		63	286	On waters of Caney Fork	yes
Robertson, Elijah	813	Dunbar, Isaac heirs	Davidson	640	816	20 Nov 1788	3307		63	287	On waters of Caney Fork	yes
Robertson, Elijah	814	Black, Peter heirs	Davidson	640	817	20 Nov 1788	3300		63	287	On waters of Caney Fork	yes
Robertson, Elijah	815	Nixon, Robert	Davidson	640	818	20 Nov 1788	3318		63	287	On waters of Caney Fork	yes
Robertson, Elijah	817	Riley, Samuel heirs	Davidson	640	820	20 Nov 1788	3321		63	288	On waters of Caney Fork	yes
Robertson, Elijah	876(816)	Gale, Stephen heirs	Davidson	640	819	20 Nov 1788	3311		63	288	On waters of Caney Fork	yes
Robertson, Elijah	94		Middle District	5000	96	10 Jul 1788	1045	29 Oct 1783	67	457	On the head of Fountain Creek	yes
Robertson, Elijah, Ass.	2212		Davidson	65	237	27 Feb 1796	4373	29 Jul 1790	88	178	Abt 4 mi southwardly fr Nashville	
Robertson, Elijah, Ass.	325	Pea, Nicholas	Sumner	640	1576	23 Feb 1793	3335	28 Jun 1788	76	301	On Cold Creek a fork of Smith Fork	
Robertson, Elisha	1444		Davidson	320	90	10 Jul 1788	18	29 Dec 1783	68	232	Beg at N/W cor of public survey	
Robertson, Elizabeth	260	Raines, Simon	Tennessee	640	1703	20 May 1793	1838	14 Jun 1785	81	54	On E waters of Pine River	
Robertson, F. & Jno. Jackson	120		Middle District	4000	122	10 Jul 1788	2159	13 May 1784	67	468	On the N side of Duck River	
Robertson, Hardy	2090	Sheppard, Nancy	Davidson	640	2297	20 May 1793	2085		81	190	On E Fork of Stones River	yes
Robertson, Henry	60	O'Bryan, Laurence	Tennessee	640	1291	10 Dec 1790	1796	4 May 1785	74	362	On N side of Cumberland River	yes

Earliest Tennessee Land Records

Claimant:	File #:	Assignee:	County:	Acres:	Grant:	Grant Date:	Entry:	Entry Date:	Bk:	Pg:	Location by Stream Name:	Military:
Robertson, Hooker	676	Donelson, Stockley	Hawkins	300	2366	12 Jul 1794	3548		81	601	On S side of Clinch River	yes
Robertson, Isaac	1115	Harris, Edward	Sumner	640	2621	4 Jun 1796	2759	1 Jul 1795	88	341	Joining sd Harris survey	yes
Robertson, J. & Hugh Leeper	79		Middle District	2034	81	10 Jul 1788	730	28 Oct 1783	67	450	On the N side of Duck River &c	
Robertson, James	020	Armstrong, M.	Davidson	150			986	May 1785			S side Cumberland River	
Robertson, James	029	Elliott, Samuel	not given					20 Sep 1795				yes
Robertson, James	029		not given					20 Sep 1795				
Robertson, James	057	Dunning, James	not given	357			4200	17 Mar 1797			W Fork Jones Creek	
Robertson, James	059	Boon, David	Davidson	640			2632	3 Dec 1792			Hollises Fork of Natond [?] Fork of Whites Cr	
Robertson, James	060	Martin, Isaac	Davidson	320			3366	19 Aug 1788			S side of Harpeth River	
Robertson, James	061	King, John	Davidson	274			960	23 Apr 1785			On waters of Big Harpeth River	
Robertson, James	08	Armstrong, M.	Davidson	100	2	16 Feb 1786			63	1	In the bent of Cumberland River	
Robertson, James	080	Harrold, Jas.	Davidson	640			2188	5 Jun 1790			S side of Cumberland River	
Robertson, James	1022	Cates, Benj.	Davidson	365	1582	20 May 1793	3058		81	58	On E side of Harpeth River	yes
Robertson, James	1099		Davidson	640	73	17 Apr 1786	10	26 Dec 1783	66	59	Beg at a sugar tree & white oak	
Robertson, James	1306	Hickman, Thomas	Sumner	640	3079	19 Jul 1797	3902	6 Apr 1797	90	382	On waters of Big Barron	yes
Robertson, James	1355		Davidson	2000	38	8 Oct 1787	9	26 Dec 1783	68	137	Beg at the mouth of small Glade Br	
Robertson, James	1377		Davidson	320	60	8 Oct 1787	12	26 Dec 1783	68	146	In the bent of Cumberland River &c	
Robertson, James	1438		Green	50	1248	27 Nov 1792	96	16 May 1789	80	170	Joins Anthony Kelly & his own land	
Robertson, James	1613		Davidson	620	1341	10 Dec 1790	682		74	379	On S side of Cumberland River	yes
Robertson, James	1659	Patterson, Jesse	Davidson	320	1582	23 Feb 1793	1337		76	304	Big Harpeth @ mo Mountain cedars	yes
Robertson, James	1660	Plumley, Geo.	Davidson	640	1583	23 Feb 1793	1276		76	304	On Harpeth inc the Big Clay Lick	yes
Robertson, James	1661	Jackson, Fra. Heirs	Davidson	640	1584	23 Feb 1793	1916		76	305	S/S Harpeth inc mo of Turnbulls Cr	yes
Robertson, James	1662	Rogers, Michael	Davidson	274	1585	23 Feb 1793	1551		76	305	Sm cr emptying S of Little Harpeth	yes
Robertson, James	1663	Tippe, Jno.	Davidson	228	1586	23 Feb 1793	209		76	305	On both sides Big Harpeth River	yes
Robertson, James	1664	Edmonds, Abel	Davidson	275	1587	23 Feb 1793	1415		76	306	On waters of West Harpeth River	yes
Robertson, James	1665	Manly, William	Davidson	274	1588	23 Feb 1793	148		76	306	On Otter branch of Little Harpeth	yes
Robertson, James	1666	Allgood, H. heirs	Davidson	640	4589	23 Feb 1793	1350		76	307	On the waters of Little Harpeth	yes
Robertson, James	1667	Rogers, Patrick	Davidson	2560	1591	23 Feb 1793	3135		76	307	On Harpeth River	yes
Robertson, James	1669	Hudson, Miles	Davidson	274	1593	23 Feb 1793	3611		76	309	On the waters of Richland Creek	yes
Robertson, James	1701		Davidson	640	317	23 Feb 1793	665	19 Jan 1785	76	343	On the N waters of Little Harpeth	
Robertson, James	1708	Armstrong, M.	Davidson	1000	121	23 Feb 1793			76	346	Robertson's pre nr Fletchers Lick	
Robertson, James	1710	Armstrong, M.	Davidson	34.5	123	23 Feb 1793			76	346	S side Cumberland River	
Robertson, James	175		Green	200	645	11 Jul 1788	461	23 Mar 1786	64	356	On Ceadar (sic) Branch	
Robertson, James	1908	Barnes, Burwell heir of Tho	Davidson	640	1667	20 May 1793	752		81	45	On S branches of Big Harpeth R	yes
Robertson, James	1911	Dillard, John	Davidson	357	1676	20 May 1793	808		81	48	On Harpeth River	yes
Robertson, James	1926	Faithfull, William	Davidson	640	1737	20 May 1793	910		81	63	On Harpeth River	yes
Robertson, James	1933	Willis, Wilton	Davidson	640	1752	29 Aug 1793	3279		81	67	Joins Barnabas Boyles	yes
Robertson, James	1934	Shockley, Isaac heirs	Davidson	640	1754	29 Aug 1793	1818		81	67	Joins Barnabas Boyle	yes
Robertson, James	1935	Dix, (Dees?) Abraham	Davidson	640	1755	29 Aug 1793	1891		81	68	On N side of Cumberland River	yes
Robertson, James	1937	Roan, David	Davidson	640	1757	29 May 1793			81	68	Hollis Fk Heatons Fx of Whites Cr	yes
Robertson, James	1938	Ward, Jas.	Davidson	640	1758	29 May 1793	1896		81	68	N/S Cumberland on Bull Run	yes
Robertson, James	196	Davie, Richard	Davidson	274	182	7 Mar 1786	29		63	68	S side of Cumberland River	yes
Robertson, James	205	Pendergrass, Job	Davidson	274	191	7 Mar 1786	274		63	71	On waters of Big Harpeth River	yes
Robertson, James	2145	Morgan, Humphrey heirs	Davidson	640	2429	31 Dec 1793			81	409	Both sides of Big Harpeth River	yes
Robertson, James	223	Deal, James	Davidson	274	209	7 Mar 1786	756		63	77	On bent of Cumberland River	yes

Earliest Tennessee Land Records

Page 348

Claimant:	File #:	Assignee:	County:	Acres:	Grant:	Grant Date:	Entry:	Entry Date:	Bk:	Pg:	Location by Stream Name:	Military:
Robertson, James	228	White, Jacob	Davidson	274	214	7 Mar 1786	275		63	79	On the bent of Cumberland River	yes
Robertson, James	2286	Daniel, Ephraim heirs	Davidson	640	2760	20 Jul 1796			88	464	On both sides of Big Harpeth River	yes
Robertson, James	367	Armstrong, M.	Davidson	100	2	16 Feb 1786			63	1 (interl	In the bent of Cumberland River	
Robertson, James	42		Middle District	3000	44	10 Jul 1788	8	4 Jan 1786	67	427	On Weakleys Creek &c	
Robertson, James	546	Grant, Joel heirs	Sumner	640	1750	29 Aug 1793	2569	4 Nov 1789	81	66	On S side of Cumberland River	yes
Robertson, James	549	Davis, Moses	Sumner	640	1759	29 May 1793	3457	4 Jul 1789	81	69	S side Cumberland River &c	yes
Robertson, James	550		Washington	200	815	11 Jul 1788	2297	27 Nov 1779	64	334	On Amton's [sic] Fork of Lick Cr	
Robertson, James	599	Pendergrass, John	Davidson	274	571	15 Sep 1787	271		63	204	S side of Cumberland River	yes
Robertson, James	628	Looney, Moses heirs	Tennessee	640	3192	14 Sep 1797	3874		90	439	W side of Bartons Creek	
Robertson, James	629	McCoy, James heirs	Tennessee	640	3193	14 Sep 1797	3957		90	440	On Bartons Creek	
Robertson, James	630	Rollins, Patrick heirs	Tennessee	640	3194	14 Sep 1797	4192		90	440	On Middle Fork of Bartons Creek	
Robertson, James	631	Rose, Terry heirs	Tennessee	640	3195	14 Sep 1797	4191	11 Sep 1797	90	441	On the ridge	
Robertson, James	632	Edge, Jos. Heirs	Tennessee	640	3196	14 Sep 1797	3064	14 Aug 1795	90	441	Near the head of Bartons Creek	
Robertson, James	633	Jay, Simon heirs	Tennessee	640	3197	14 Sep 1797	3921		90	442	On the ridge	
Robertson, James	634	Moore, Freeman, heirs	Tennessee	640	3198	14 Sep 1797	4376	22 Dec 1796	90	442	On the Iron Works Forks	
Robertson, James	641	Trimnal, Dennis heirs	Tennessee	640	3199	14 Sep 1797	3919	25 Jan 1797	92	11	Waters of Bartons Creek	
Robertson, James	643	[blank] heirs of	Tennessee	640	3215	14 Sep 1797			92	11	On head waters of Johnstons Cr	
Robertson, James	676	Peyton, John	Sumner	640	2007	20 May 1793	3673	25 Nov 1789	81	126	On S side of Cumberland River	yes
Robertson, James	71		Western District	2000	71	10 Jul 1788	465	25 Oct 1783	67	307	On both sides Looshatcher River	
Robertson, James	76		Western District	1000	76	10 Jul 1788	1646	16 Apr 1784	67	310	On the Obion River &c	
Robertson, James etal	111	Symms, John heirs	Tennessee	640	1598	23 Feb 1793	2525	30 Sep 1785	76	311	S side of Cumberland River &c	
Robertson, James etal	148	Harrington, Richard	Tennessee	640	1399	20 Dec 1791	2804	30 Sep 1785	77	351	On both sides of Pine River	
Robertson, James etal	153	Mulkey, Wm.	Tennessee	640	1407	20 Dec 1791	2810	30 Sep 1785	77	353	On both sides of Pine River	
Robertson, James etal	1671	Staniand, James	Davidson	640	310	23 Feb 1793	1251		76	310	Big Harpeth mi below mo of Brush	yes
Robertson, James etal	1672	Riley, John	Davidson	640	1596	23 Feb 1793	1729		76	310	S side of Big Harpeth River	yes
Robertson, James etal	1673	McCay, John	Davidson	640	1597	23 Feb 1793	2016		76	310	Harpeth below mouth of S Harpeth	yes
Robertson, James R.	437	Joslin, Benj.	Tennessee	480	183	26 Mar 1765		19 Apr 1792	86	412	On S W side of Big Harpeth River	
Robertson, James Randolph	1684	Ashe, Charles	Davidson	640	1618	23 Feb 1793	1355		76	321	On Big Harpeth River	yes
Robertson, Jas.	110	Campbell, Jas.	Tennessee	640	1590	23 Feb 1793	1274	28 Oct 1784	76	307	S side of Cumberland River	
Robertson, Jas.	1668	Conner, Davey	Davidson	640	1592	23 Feb 1753	1016		76	308	On Harpeth River Big Clay Lick	yes
Robertson, Jas.	1670	Bennett, Peter heirs	Davidson	640	1594	23 Feb 1793	2706		76	309	Harpeth above the Big Clay Lick	yes
Robertson, Jas.	190	Smith, Samuel	Davidson	428	176	7 Mar 1786	169		63	66	E side of W Fk of Harpeth River	yes
Robertson, Jas.	263	Miller, Sol.	Tennessee	640	1711	20 May 1793	2865	30 Sep 1785	81	56	On S side of Cumberland River	
Robertson, Jas.	642	Denning, Jas.	Tennessee	357	3200	14 Sep 1797		2 Sep 1786	92	4	W Fork of Jones Creek	
Robertson, Jas., Ass.	1709		Davidson	14	122	23 Feb 1793			76	346	Isle in Cumb abt 1 mi abv Richland	
Robertson, Jesse	458	Cooper, Robert	Sumner	274	1597	27 Apr 1793	1731	27 Nov 1792	81	17	On S bank of Cedar Lick Creek	yes
Robertson, Jesse	820	Clark, Lardner	Davidson	1000	823	17 Jan 1789	844		63	290	On waters of W Harpeth River	yes
Robertson, John	311		Sullivan	100	462	18 Jul 1788	312	14 Mar 1780	64	339	On N side of Holston River	
Robertson, Jonathan F.	2388	Griffen, James	Davidson	274	3176	14 Sep 1797	1163		90	432	On S Harpeth River	yes
Robertson, Jonathan Fier	2404	Sessums, Abel, heirs	Davidson	640	2801	6 Jun 1796	3852		91	473	S W side of Big Harpeth River	yes
Robertson, Jonathan Tier	2405	Tew, Alexander	Davidson	640	2802	6 Jun 1796	3862		91	474	S W side of Big Harpeth	yes
Robertson, Joseph	292	Phillips, P. & M. Campbell	Sumner	640	1300	10 Dec 1790	3373	23 Jun 1788	74	365	On small W Fork of Round Lick Creek	yes
Robertson, Lewis	487		Green	200	489	20 Sep 1787	1993	22 Jan 1787	65	515	On the N side of Holston River	
Robertson, Mark	019		Davidson	640							no plat	
Robertson, Mark	1338		Davidson	640	24	18 Aug 1787	15	29 Dec 1783	68	130	Waters of Spencers Cr	

Earliest Tennessee Land Records

Claimant:	File #:	Assignee:	County:	Acres:	Grant:	Entry:	Entry Date:	Bk:	Pg:	Location by Stream Name:	Military:
Robertson, Mark	68		Middle District	5000	70	571	27 Oct 1783	67	444	Lying on N side of Duck River &c	
Robertson, Michael	0110	Clower, Wm.	Sumner	640		1857	1 Apr 1788			S side of Cumberland River	yes
Robertson, Michael	35		Middle District	1500	37	640 [?]	27 Oct 1783	67	424	On N side of Duck River &c	
Robertson, Patsey	801	Dudley, Bennet	Davidson	640	804	3308		63	282	On waters of Caney Creek	yes
Robertson, Patsey	819	Steps, Abraham heirs	Davidson	1000	822	3392		63	290	On Caney Fork	yes
Robertson, Patsy	818	Roper, Stephen heirs	Davidson	1000	821	3320		63	289	On waters of Caney Fork	yes
Robertson, Thomas	091		Green	20			25 Oct 1797			On the waters of Lick Creek	
Robertson, Thomas	092		Green	130			25 Oct 1797			On the waters of Lick Creek	
Robertson, William	196		Green	478	153	1251	22 Nov 1783	65	414	On the N Holston River on Big Cr	
Robertson, Charles	1017		Washington	50	966	1473	10 Jul 1779	79	275	On Cherokee Creek	
Robeson, Charles	190	Harget & Randal	Middle District	1000	204	2610	25 May 1784	76	478	Beg at Red oak & Black oak	
Robeson, Charles	1914	Harget & Randal	Middle District	1000	204	2610	25 May 1784	76	478	Beg at Red oak & Black oak	
Robeson, Charles	192	Harget & Randal	Middle District	1000	206	2607	25 May 1785	76	478	On waters of Sycamore River	
Robeson, Charles	192		Middle District	1000	206	2607	25 May 1785	76	478	On waters of Sycamore	
Robeson, Charles	193	Harget & Randal	Middle District	1000	207	2609	25 May 1784	76	478	Beg at a white oak &c	
Robeson, Charles	737	George, John	Davidson	640	710	573	11 Jul 1788	63	250	On head of Calebs Creek	yes
Robeson, Charles	350	Clark, Jas. & Wm.	Tennessee	640	2177	3687	20 May 1793	81	167	On the Elk Fork of Red River	yes
Robeson, Edward	456		Middle District	2200	395	1640	14 Apr 1784	84	259	On S side of Elk River	
Robeson, Elizabeth	1914	Robeson, James	Davidson	320	1694			81	52	On S side of Harpeth River	yes
Robeson, Isaac	1025		Green	200	1252			76	488	On Antons Fork of Lick Creek	
Robeson, James	1778	Robeson, Isaac	Davidson	320	1694			81	52	On S side of Harpeth River	yes
Robeson, James	1778		Davidson	640	356	169	24 Jan 1784	80	318	Beg at small hickory & horn beam	
Robeson, James	1918	Esteridge, Thomas heirs	Davidson	640	1709	670	20 May 1793	81	55	On both sides Big Harpeth River	yes
Robeson, James	2232	Bonds, William	Davidson	640	2595	1336	7 Mar 1793	88	324	On S Harpeth	yes
Robeson, James	2233	Melton, John heirs	Davidson	640	2596	1331	7 Mar 1796	88	324	On E Fork of Turnbulls Creek	yes
Robeson, James	2234	Nolley, Dixon heirs	Davidson	640	2598	1330	7 Mar 1796	88	325	On S Harpeth	yes
Robeson, James	2291	Harrold, James	Davidson	640	2770		10 Sep 1790	88	491	On S side of Cumberland River	yes
Robeson, James	369		Middle District	1000	308	1645	16 Apr 1784	84	210	On E Fork of Stones River	
Robeson, James	447	Folk, Chris heirs	Middle District	675	386	1643	15 Apr 1784	84	254	On N side of Duck River	
Robeson, James	467		Tennessee	640	2597	1335	3 Nov 1784	88	325	On the Upper West Fork	
Robeson, James etal	379		Middle District	1280	318	2004	1 May 1784	84	214	On W Fork of Stones River	
Robeson, Joel	734	Hendricks, Joseph	Davidson	640	707	1412	11 Jul 1788	63	249	On the first creek &c	yes
Robeson, John	755		Hawkins	200	595	653	19 Jul 1780	82	209	On the S side of Clinch River &c	
Robeson, Mark	1808		Davidson	640	381	16	29 Dec 1783	80	335	Beg @ hackberry E/S Richland Cr	
Robeson, Mark	1827		Davidson	640	400	16	29 Dec 1783	80	342	Beg @ a hackberry marked M.R.	
Robeson, Patrick	756	Bonner, John & James	Sumner	640	2162	1453	14 Apr 1792	81	163	On dividing ridge	yes
Robeson, William	732		Hawkins	300 (340)	552	107	12 Jun 1794	82	172	On the S side of Beaver Creek	
Robeson, William, Ass	319		Eastern District	103	251	987	27 Feb 1796	88	185	On N side of Holston River	
Robins, John	383	Hays, Robert	Sumner	640	1566	2949	14 Jan 1793	79	273	On both sides Smiths Fork	yes
Robins, John	383	Hays, Robert	Sumner	640	1566	2949	9 Apr 1788	79	273	On both sides of Smiths Fork	yes
Robinson, Charles	7		Washington	640	7	275	14 Sep 1778	36	7	On S side of Holston River &c	
Robinson, Charles	949		Washington	38	926	1511	17 Nov 1790	76	153	On the waters of Nolachuckey	
Robinson, Charles	950		Washington	190	927	1423	17 Nov 1790	76	153	N side of Nolechuckey River	
Robinson, Col. Chas.	060		Washington	50			5 May 1779			On Nolachuckey	
Robinson, Daniel	931		Hawkins	200	714	1285	2 Dec 1795	88	266	On head of Richland Creek	

Claimant:	File #:	Assignee:	County:	Acres:	Grant:	Grant Date:	Entry:	Entry Date:	Bk:	Pg:	Location by Stream Name:	Military:
Robinson, Hargett & Randal	237		Middle District	1000	210	12 Jan 1793	2613	25 May 1784	80	298	On a river called Buffalow River	
Robinson, Hargett & Randal	240		Middle District	1000	213	12 Jan 1793	2601	25 May 1784	80	299	On a river called Sycamore River	
Robinson, Hargett & Randal	241		Middle District	1000	214	12 Jan 1793	2602	25 May 1784	80	299	On a creek called Cold Water	
Robinson, Hargett & Randal	242		Middle District	1000	215	12 Jan 1793	2603	25 May 1784	80	299	On a river called Sycamore River	
Robinson, Henry	028	McCoy, Ananias	not given	400								yes
Robinson, Henry	28		not given	400								
Robinson, Henry	485	McCoy, Anan:	Tennessee	400	194	20 Jul 1796	15	14 Apr 1792	88	474	W of the Cumberland Mountain	yes
Robinson, Jacob	77		Tennessee	428	1322	10 Dec 1790	525	20 Apr 1784	74	373	On S side of Cumberland River	
Robinson, James	1936	Haddock, Josiah	Davidson	640	1756	29 May 1793	2852	4 Nov 1779	81	68	On S side of Cumberland River	yes
Robinson, James	767		Washington	300	581	10 Nov 1784	2126	4 Nov 1779	69	133	On Amton's Fork of Lick Creek	
Robinson, James	800		Green	100	605	23 Aug 1788	2174	13 May 1784	68	264	On the S side of Clinch River	
Robinson, James	925		Green	200	839	17 Nov 1790	547	27 Oct 1783	76	118	S/S Holston River on Robisons Cr	
Robinson, Jesse	1613	Robertson, James	Davidson	620	1341	10 Dec 1790	682	27 Oct 1783	74	379	On S side of Cumberland River	yes
Robinson, John	735		Washington	100	549	10 Nov 1784	2530	6 Apr 1780	69	122	Inc the Chickinquimin Thicket	
Robinson, Jos.	0146		Green	200			2498	20 Nov 1780			On Hintons Fork of Lick Creek	
Robinson, Lewis	088		Green	150	826		1476	12 Aug 1797			N side of Holston River	
Robinson, Lewis	1106		Hawkins	150	826	12 Aug 1797			91	625	N side of Holston River	
Robinson, Rossdon [?]	486		Washington	100	671	1 Nov 1786	2991	4 Oct 1783	60	444	Beg at a marked white oak &c	
Robinson, Samuel	0145		Green	100			2277	27 Nov 1779			N side Noley Chuckey	
Robinson, Thos.	641		Washington	200	735	26 Oct 1786	513	19 Oct 1778	66	28	Beg at a marked white oak &c	
Robison, Daniel	1084		Green	100	927	26 Dec 1791			77	251	On N side of Holstein River &c	
Robison, Daniel	1495		Green	200	1258	12 Jul 1794	9	21 Oct 1783	81	581	At a place called Mulberry Bottom	
Robison, David	380		Washington	100	372	13 Oct 1783	2624	28 Aug 1780	52	251	On waters of Big Limestone	
Robison, David	473		Washington	400	465	13 Oct 1783	232	18 Jun 1778	52	296	On waters of Big Limestone &c	
Robison, David	986		Green	300	1213	29 Jul 1793	243	22 Oct 1783	76	469	Both sides of Little Chuckie	
Rochester, Nicholas	247		Tennessee	1000	1623	27 Apr 1793	1452	22 Nov 1784	81	25	On Duck River	
Rock, Jordan	676		Green	640	717	11 Jul 1788	583	18 Jan 1787	66	465	On Holston River &c	
Roddy, James	1064		Hawkins	232	773	21 Jan 1799	143	5 Feb 1780	91	117	S side of Holston River	
Roddy, James	118		Green	220	134	1 Nov 1786	169	22 Oct 1783	59	437	Upon Bent Creek	
Roddy, James	121		Green	267	137	1 Nov 1786	1289	24 Dec 1783	59	440	On waters of Burnt Cabbin Branch	
Roddy, James	275		Washington	275	143	23 Oct 1782	785	26 Dec 1778	47	69	S side of Watauga River	
Roddye, James	110		Green	640	126	1 Nov 1786	168	22 Oct 1783	59	429	On waters of Bent Creek	
Rodes, C. & J. Manfield	135		Sullivan	200 (120	148	23 Oct 1782			43	330	On the North Fork &c	
Rodes, Christian	102		Hawkins	300	136	26 Dec 1791	142		75	156	On N side of Holson River	
Rodes, Christian	104		Hawkins	300	138	26 Dec 1791			75	157	On N side of Holson River	
Rodes, Christian	109		Hawkins	300	143	26 Dec 1791	834	27 Aug 1781	75	160	On N side Holson River	
Rodes, Christian	141		Hawkins	640	175	26 Dec 1791			75	173	On N side of Holson River	
Rodes, Christian	562		Hawkins	5000	435	29 Jul 1793	1873		80	286	N side of Holston River &c	
Rodes, Lewis	376	Barton, Samuel	Sumner	640	1556	14 Jan 1793	2952	19 Dec 1789	79	270	Near headwaters of Jining Fork &c	yes
Rodgers, James	1039		Washington	600	989	14 Jan 1793	899	31 Dec 1778	70	282	On waters of Little Sinking Creek	
Rodgers, Joseph	0114		Sullivan	640			1621	15 Sep 1779			On N side of Holson River	
Rodgers, Joseph	338		Sullivan	500	478	10 Jul 1788	243	21 Mar 1760	67	485	On S of Holston River &c	
Rodgers, Robert	35		Washington	280	325	24 Oct 1782	917	1 Jan 1779	43	308	On waters of Cherokey Creek	
Roe, Dempsey	1166	Harris, Edward	Sunner	640	2671	4 Jun 1796	2434	1 Jun 1795	88	358	Joining sd Harris survey	yes
Roe, Samuel	1		Williamson	228	3369	5 Mar 1801	3	24 Nov 1800	112	354	Waters of W Harpeth	

Claimant:	File #:	Assignee:	County:	Acres:	Grant:	Grant Date:	Entry:	Entry Date:	Bk:	Pg:	Location by Stream Name:	Military:
Roe, Terry	030	Robinson, James	not given	640			4191				ON Bledsoes Creek	yes
Rogan, Hugh	488		Sumner	320	1-37 [sic]	27 Apr 1793	499	28 Jun 1784	81	38	ON Bledsoes Creek	yes
Rogers, Abraham	302	Dew, John	Sumner	640	1362	10 Dec 1790	3571	4 Dec 1789	74	386	On both sides of Caney Cork	yes
Rogers, Absolom	1134	Harris, Edward	Sumner	640	2640	4 Jun 1796	2224	1 Jun 1795	88	347	Joining sd Harris survey	yes
Rogers, Arthur	225	Marshall, John	Sumner	640	1130	26 Nov 1789	1612	9 Feb 1787	74	144	On first creek &c	yes
Rogers, Austin	1412	Hadley, Joshua	Sumner	228	3267	6 Dec 1797	4542	22 Jun 1797	98	152	On the waters of Spring Creek	yes
Rogers, Benjamin	1017	West, Joseph heirs	Davidson	357	1034	18 May 1789	1950	18 May 1789	63	344	On N side of Red River	yes
Rogers, Daniel	818	Sheppard, Nancy	Sumner	640	2293	20 May 1793	2084	29 Oct 1792	81	190	On E branch of Roaring River	yes
Rogers, Elisha	037	Blount, John G. & Thomas	not given	640			1548	14 Jun 1792			On Harpeth River	yes
Rogers, Elisha	2104	Blount, John Gray & Thos.	Davidson	640	2333	20 May 1793			81	198	On Harpeth River	yes
Rogers, James	1076	Donelson, Stockley	Sumner	640	2553	7 Mar 1796	2951	2 Nov 1795	88	307	On head of Pond Lick Creek	yes
Rogers, James	1222		Green	200	1066	May 1792	143	10 Mar 1778	77	408	N side of Noleychuckey River &c	
Rogers, Jesse	365		Sullivan	640	244	10 Nov 1784			69	160	N side of Holston River	
Rogers, Joseph	293	Cobb, Jesse	Tennessee	640	1946	20 May 1793	1175	28 Aug 1784	81	111	On both sides of the 2nd large cr	yes
Rogers, Joseph	719		Hawkins	300	539	12 Jun 1794	1653,-560	1780	82	167	N side of Holston River &c	
Rogers, Joseph	733		Hawkins	250	553	12 Jun 1794	503	28 Apr 1780	82	172	On N side of Holston River	
Rogers, Joseph	85		Eastern Dist	200	74	17 Nov 1790	1379	21 May 1779	76	167	S side of Holstein River on Dry Cr	
Rogers, Mark	195	Kirkpatrick, Alexander	Sumner	640	1051	27 Nov 1789	3374	25 Apr 1788	71	289	On N side of Cumberland River	yes
Rogers, Mary	187	Rogers, William	Tennessee	640	1467	4 Jan 1792	3289	28 Dec 1785	77	368	S side of Cumberland River &c	
Rogers, Michel	1662	Robertson, James	Davidson	274	1585	23 Feb 1793	1551		76	305	On a small creek &c	yes
Rogers, Nicholas	571		Sullivan	50	569	29 Jul 1793	2217	13 Nov 1779	76	470	N side of Holston River	
Rogers, Parker	2376	Stewart, Duncan	Davidson	640	3097	14 Sep 1797	4032		90	400	On S Harpeth a br of Big Harpeth	yes
Rogers, Patrick	1667	Robertson, James	Davidson	2560	1591	23 Feb 1793	3135		76	307	On Harpeth River	yes
Rogers, Thomas	813		Washington	100	627	10 Nov 1784	1966	14 Oct 1779	69	146	Beg at a red oak	
Rogers, Thos. & David	035		Hawkins	250			2612	13 Aug 1783			N side of Clinch Mtn.	
Rogers, William	509		Sullivan	325	495	6 May 1789	1622,-1719	21 Sep 1779	72	124	Including the spring &c	
Roles, Horatio	1084		Davidson	640	58	17 Apr 1786	213	30 Jan 1784	66	54	On Deshas Fork of Bledsoes Cr	
Roller, Battice	037	Bushnell, E. & Wm. Dobbin	Davidson	1000			1673	12 Aug 1785			S side of Cumberland	yes
Roller, Henry	814		Sullivan	100	757	17 Nov 1797	14	1 Feb 1780	94	155	N side of Holstein River	
Rollins, James	1956	Buchanon, John	Davidson	640	1797	20 May 1793	1654		81	78	On S road bet. Big & Little Harpeth	yes
Rollins, Patrick	630	Robertson, James	Tennessee	640	3194	14 Sep 1797	4192		90	440	On Middle Fork of Bartons Creek	yes
Rolston, David	1609	Armstrong, M.	Davidson	200	1332	10 Dec 1790	1332		74	376	On N side of Cumberland River	
Rolston, Isaac	29 [?]	Blount, Wm.	Davidson	1240	15	14 Mar 1786	977		63	7	N side of Tennessee River	yes
Rolston, Robert	31	Blount, Wm.	Davidson	1097	17	14 Mar 1786	1004		63	8	On waters of Harpeth River	yes
Rook, Thomas	630		Sullivan	115	578	27 Jun 1793	581	3 Jun 1786	80	374	On the Clear Fork of Horse Creek	
Roper, James	551	Wikoff, Wm. & Lardner Clar	Davidson	274	523	15 Sep 1787	2267		63	188	On waters of North Cross Creek	yes
Roper, Richard	190	Armstrong, Crutcher, & Sm	Sumner	228	65	18 May 1789	1921	12 Aug 1785	71	223	On waters of Station Camp Creek	yes
Roper, Stephen	818	Robertson, Patsey	Davidson	1000	821	20 Nov 1788	3320		63	289	On waters of Caney Fork	yes
Rose, Andrew	2426	White, James L.	Davidson	640	3246	30 Nov 1797	4105		94	176	W side of Harpeth	yes
Rose, Hosea	249		Washington	299	117	23 Oct 1782	224	26 May 1778	47	57	S Fork of Cherokee Creek	
Rose, Hosea	596		Washington	100	690	26 Oct 1786	1965	13 Oct 1779	66	6	On the N Fork of the Cherokee Cr	
Rose, Hosea	933		Washington	320	147	17 Nov 1790	1045	19 Feb 1787	76	147	Beg at a white oak &c	
Rose, Terry	631	Robertson, James	Tennessee	640	3195	14 Sep 1797	4191	11 Sep 1797 (surv)	90	441	On the ridge	yes
Rose, Thos.	576	Riddick, Joseph heirs	Tennessee	640	3023	10 Apr 1797	1386		90	302	On Callinders Creek	yes
Rose, William	2033	Walker, George	Davidson	428	2046	20 May 1793	3200		81	136	On N side of Cumberland River	yes

Claimant:	File #:	Assignee:	County:	Acres:	Grant:	Grant Date:	Entry:	Entry Date:	Bk:	Pg:	Location by Stream Name:	Military:
Roseberry, William	238		Green	200	195	20 Sep 1787	2341	8 Dec 1779	65	429	On the N side of Holston River	
Roseberry, William	31		Hawkins	300	63	7 Apr 1790	1737	17 Apr 1787	71	285	On the N side of Holston River &c	
Roseberry, William	353		Green	250	355	20 Sep 1787	984	29 Oct 1783	65	474	On grassy plains Roseberrys Creek	
Roseberry, William	36		Hawkins	400	68	7 Apr 1790	843	6 Oct 1779	71	287	On N side of Holston River &c	
Roseberry, William	99		Eastern District	200	88	17 Nov 1780			76	172	On S side of Holstein River	
Ross, Abram	701	Johnston, Robert	Davidson	640	674	8 Dec 1787	1179		63	238	N side of Cumberland River	yes
Ross, David	0105		Sullivan	100			766	8 Mar 1781			N side of Holston River	
Ross, David	0106		Sullivan	100			770	6 Apr 1781			N side of Holston River	
Ross, David	1		Hawkins	3000	1	12 Jun 1794	842	13 Feb 1792	62	311	Joining sd Rosses Iron works	
Ross, David	282		Sullivan	200	421	9 Aug 1786	380	10 Sep 1778	61	440	On the S side of Holston River	
Ross, David	43		Hawkins	100	28	18 May 1789	812	28 Dec 1778	72	247	S/S Holston George Ridleys oor	
Ross, David	436		Hawkins	100	314	24 Jun 1793	182	21 Feb 1780	80	190	On S E side of N Fork of Holston	
Ross, David	586		Sullivan	400	584	29 Jul 1793	1970	14 Oct 1779	76	474	On Holston River	
Ross, David	591		Sullivan	2288	589	29 Jul 1793	23		76	476	On the waters of Reedy Creek &c	
Ross, David	617		Sullivan	640	566	24 Jun 1793	286	8 Feb 1780	80	189	Beg at a white oak & hickory	
Ross, David	670		Sullivan	55	618	9 Jul 1794	205	10 Mar 1780	81	627	On Holston River	
Ross, David	694		Sullivan	100	610	12 Jun 1794	841	20 Mar 1789	82	183	S side of Holston &c	
Ross, David	695		Sullivan	2888	611	12 Jun 1794	30	29 Feb 1792	82	184	On the waters of Reedy Creek &c	
Ross, David	713		Hawkins	410	533	12 Jun 1794	1630	5 May 1789	82	164	On the S side of Holston River &c	
Ross, David	715		Hawkins	400	535	12 Jul 1794	646	16 Sep 1779	82	165	On S side of Holston River &c	
Ross, David, Ass.	975		Hawkins	30	747	20 Jul 1796		14 Mar 1789	88	498	On island in Holston River	
Ross, Henry	290	McDaniel, Thos.	Sumner	274	1298	10 Dec 1790	3294		74	365	On S side of Cumberland River	yes
Ross, Henry	623	McDaniel, Thos.	Sumner	274	1899	20 May 1793			81	100	On S side of Cumberland River	yes
Ross, James	154	Bond, Elisha	Davidson	224	140	14 Mar 1786	28		63	54	On Sinking Creek	yes
Ross, John	067	Douglass, Edward	Sumner	182		23 Mar 1790	3708		88	460	N side of Harricane Creek &c	yes
Ross, John	2278	Buckanan, John	Western District	1000	1712	8 May 1797	2051	23 Mar 1790	88	460	On a fork of the Obion River	yes
Ross, Joseph	02		Davidson	640	2758	20 July 1796	2663		81	137	On S side of Cumberland River	yes
Ross, Joseph	1510	Yarlet, James	Davidson	640	1067	26 Nov 1789	3400		74	112	On S side of Cumberland River	yes
Ross, Joseph	1523	Hawley, Wm.	Davidson	640	1080	26 Nov 1789	2265		74	120	On N side of Cumberland River	yes
Ross, Nicholas	03	Barton, Samuel	Sumner	640			4574	20 Mar 1797	81	28	S side of Cumberland River	yes
Ross, Samuel	2036	Nelson, Robert	Davidson	640	2050	20 May 1793	3074		81	137	On E side of Big Harpeth	yes
Ross, Samuel, heirs of	476		Sumner	640	1645	27 Apr 1793		23 Jun 1787	81	28	On S side of Cumberland River	yes
Ross, William	062	Hollomon, Aaron	Davidson	640	265	23 Jun 1787	67		63	96	Ridge bet Red & Station Camp Cr	yes
Ross, William	279	Sharpe, Benj.	Davidson	1000		14 Mar 1786	2694		63	120	On Sinking Creek	yes
Ross, William	336	Rucker, Gray	Davidson	640	322	28 Jul 1787	2694		63	120	On waters of Red River	yes
Ross, William	337	Boon, Elisha heirs	Davidson	640	322	28 Jul 1787			63	120	On the waters of Red River	yes
Ross, William	344	Lackey, John heirs	Davidson	640	329	28 Jul 1787	2745		63	122	Ridge bet. Red R & Station Camp Cr	yes
Ross, William	345	[blank] heirs	Davidson	640	330	28 Jul 1787			63	123	Ridge bet Red R & Station Camp Cr	yes
Ross, William	345	Ross, William	Davidson	640		23 Jun 1787			74		On Ridge bet. Red River & Station Camp	Yes
Ross, ??????	303		Sumner	640	2365	15 Dec 1790	2663	23 Jun 1787	74	387	On waters of Sycamore Creek	Yes
Rotchel, Job, heir of Isaiah	240		Davidson	640	226	7 Mar 1786	727		63	83	Bet Red River & Sulphur Fork	yes
Rothwell, David	514	Armstrong, Martin	Davidson	640	48(6)7	15 Sep 1787	279		63	176	On headwaters Marrowbone Cr	yes
Rothwell, William	2348	Blackface, William	Davidson	640	3003	10 Apr 1797	288		90	294	On Harpeth River	yes
Round (Rounaval), David	1037		Davidson	640	11	17 Apr 1786	348	11 Mar 1784	66	37	Lying on Whites Creek &c	yes
Roundtree, Archer	912	Mulherin, James	Davidson	640	928	18 May 1789			63	319	On Caney Fork	yes

Claimant:	File #:	Assignee:	County:	Acres:	Grant:	Grant Date:	Entry:	Entry Date:	Bk:	Pg:	Location by Stream Name:	Military:
Rountree, Archer	2136	Mulherrin, James	Davidson	640	2411	7 Jan 1794	3323	25 May 1784	81	403	On S side of Cumberland River	yes
Routledge, Thomas Jr.	227		Middle District	640	207	1 Jan 1793	2654		80	210	On S side of Dicl Rover	
Row, George	255	Beck, William	Davidson	640	241	7 Mar 1786	514		63	88	At a poplar & dogwood	yes
Row, Jesse	359	Wilson, David & John Dicks	Sumner	428	1487	4 Jan 1792	2393	1 Apr 1788	77	372	N side of Cumberland River &c	yes
Row, Jesse	580	Sanford, Samuel	Sumner	640	1818	20 May 1793	512	18 Aug 1790	81	83	On S side of Cumberland River	yes
Rowan, Abraham, Jr.	1296	Brewer, Sterlin	Sumner	1000	3058	19 Jul 1797	4477	27 Apr 1797	90	373	Waters of Big Barren	yes
Rowan, Francis	1060		Green	100	903	26 Dec 1790	1463	22 Jun 1779	77	243	On Clay Creek	
Rowan, Francis	1103		Green	200	946	26 Dec 1791	1234	7 Nov 1783	77	260	N/S French Broad R on Clay Lick	
Rowan, Francis	1384		Green	200	1239	27 Jan 1793	1406	17 Dec 1788	79	509	On waters of Clay Creek	
Rowan, H. & W. McCormack	1121		Hawkins	400	840	2 Nov 1797	39	8 Feb 1780	96	1	Waters Clear Fork of Cumberland	
Rowan, H. & W. McCormack	1122		Hawkins	400	859	24 Dec 1798		10 Mar 1780	97	306	On waters of Sycamore Creek	
Rowan, H. & W. McCormack	1122		Hawkins	640	841	2 Nov 1797	303		96	2	Waters of Powells River	
Rowan, H. & W. McCormack	1140		Hawkins	400	859	24 Dec 1798			97	306	On waters of Sycamore Creek	
Rowan, H. & W. McCormack	1140		Hawkins	640	858	24 Dec 1798	27	8 Feb 1780	97	305	On the head of Puncheon Camp	
Rowan, H. & W. McCormack	1384	Parker, Charles	Hawkins	365	842	2 Nov 1797	4754		96	3	Both sides of Lawhaus Creek	yes
Rowan, Henry	1028		Hawkins	100	791	1 Mar 1797	107	8 Feb 1780	90	226	Including a cabin & spring	
Rowan, Henry	1043		Green	1000	1270	29 Jul 1793			76	492	On head waters of Nine Mile Creek &c	
Rowan, Henry	1142		Hawkins	320	860	24 Dec 1798	363	10 Mar 1780	97	306	Joining the walnut grove	
Rowan, Henry	1143		Hawkins	640	861	24 Dec 1798	47	8 Feb 1780	97	307	On S Fk of Cumberland River	
Rowan, Henry	1144		Hawkins	320	862	24 Dec 1798	363	10 Mar 1780	97	308	On Spring Cr called Walnut Grove	
Rowan, Henry	814		Green	550	815	11 Aug 1789	44	26 May 1783	71	335	On Tuckeho Creek &c	
Rowan, Henry & Jas Boovey,	074		Sullivan	640			126	9 Feb 1780				
Rowan, John Latham	1139		Hawkins	640	857	24 Dec 1798	48	8 Feb 1780	97	304	Waters of Powells River	
Rowan, Simon	648	Sugg, Noah	Sumner	640	1944	20 May 1793	3523	29 Nov 1792	81	110	Joining assignee of Benj Woolard	yes
Rowan, Susannah	1138		Hawkins	200	856	24 Dec 1798	744	12 Feb 1781	97	304	Waters of Russells Creek	
Rowan, William	063	Goodrum, Thomas	Davidson	640			3663	17 Mar 1790			On waters of Little Harpeth	
Rowan, William	064	Goodrum, Thomas	Davidson	640			63663(?)	17 Apr 1790			On waters of Little Harpeth River	
Rowell, Andrew	146	Johnston, John	Tennessee	640	1397	20 Dec 1791	1789	23 Apr 1785	77	350	On the fork of Pine River	yes
Rowlan, Samuel	268	Burnes, James	Tennessee	640	1742	20 May 1793	3250	24 Dec 1785	81	64	On the waters of Red River	yes
Rowland, James	0111		Sumner	640			1204	21 Sep 1787			On waters of Goose Creek	yes
Rowland, James	2186	Connod, Nicholas	Davidson	274	2433	22 Feb 1795	3251		84	313	Waters of Sulphur Fork of Red R	yes
Rowland, James	962		Davidson	640	979	18 May 1789			63	331	On waters of Goose Creek	
Rowland, John	010	Holland, Daniel	Robertson	640			4067	21 Apr 1797			On Spring Creek	yes
Rowler, Martain	57		Washington	312	143	23 Oct 1782			43	327	On Fall Creek &c	
Rowler, Martin	0113		Sullivan	312			1850	6 Oct 1779			On Fall Creek	
Rowles, Martin	137		Hawkins	300	171	26 Dec 1791	1750	28 Sep 1779	75	172	In Powells Valley	
Rowlins, Ashil	677		Washington	121.25	491	10 Nov 1784	2693	7 Dec 1780	69	101	On waters of Lick Creek	
Royal, James	1970		Davidson	640	1849	20 May 1793	460		81	89	On S side of Big Harpeth River	yes
Rozier, Jordon Heir	1369		Sumner	640	3223	14 Sep 1797	4008	14 Aug 1797	92	16	On head of Indian Creek	yes
Ruble, Peter	1245		Washington	50	1217	20 Jul 1796	2442	8 Feb 1780	88	506	On waters of Cherokee Creek	
Rubles, John	1355		Washington	100	1272	19 Oct 1797	1238	24 Feb 1779	92	49	On head draughts of Brush Creek	
Ruddell, Cornelius	1263		Davidson	640	228	10 Jul 1788	738	30 May 1784	66	418	On Stones River beg atwhite oak	
Rule, Henry	1264		Davidson	640	229	10 Jul 1788	772	9 Nov 1785	66	418	On Et side of Harpers Creek	
Rumbolt, Joseph	061		Washington	200			2902	23 Aug 1781			Beg on a white oak	
Runnels, Moses	1306		Washington	100	1192	4 Dec 1795	1514	12 Aug 1779	89	432	On Cobs Creek	

Earliest Tennessee Land Records

Claimant:	File #:	Assignee:	County:	Acres:	Grant:	Grant Date:	Entry:	Entry Date:	Bk:	Pg:	Location by Stream Name:	Military:
Runnels, William	149		Washington	104	17	23 Oct 1782	764	24 Dec 1778	47	8	On Roans Creek	
Rush, William	185	Beard, Joseph	Eastern District	640	1656	15 Jul 1793	2761		81	43	Beg at two beech trees	yes
Russal, George	559		Green	300	239	20 Sep 1787	349	23 Oct 1783	66	153	On the head of Fall Creek &c	
Russel, Brice	149		Eastern District	300	119	24 Dec 1792			78	453	In the Grassey Valley	
Russel, Buckner	26		Smith	126	3392	25 Oct 1802	3580	21 Aug 1800	115	436	On Jennings Creek	
Russel, David	1440		Green	200	1250	27 Nov 1792	71	21 Oct 1783	80	171	N/S of Nolichuckey on Richland Cr	
Russel, George	1259		Washington	300	1198	18 Nov 1795	525	23 Oct 1778	89	141	On S E Fork of Big Limestone Cr	
Russel, George	303		Washington	99	170	24 Oct 1782	1683	20 Sep 1779	47	82	On waters of Boons Creek	
Russel, George	336		Washington	591	203	24 Oct 1782	1047	7 Jan 1778	49	227	Inc his manner plantation	
Russel, George	559		Green	300	239	20 Sep 1787	349	23 Oct 1783	66	153	On head of Fall Creek	
Russel, George	595		Washington	100	689	26 Oct 1786	1683	20 Sep 1779	66	6	Beg at sd Russell's No corner &c	
Russel, James	1415	Armstrong, M.	Davidson	100	32	8 Oct 1787			68	156	On S side of Cumberland River	
Russel, James	2470		Davidson	274	3395	25 Dec 1802	274	14 Apr 1801	115	438	On N side of Cumberland River	yes
Russel, James	692	Hamilton, Thomas	Sumner	640	2051	20 May 1793	853	28 Nov 1792	81	137	On the waters of Red River	yes
Russel, Jas.	075	Armstrong, M.	Tennessee	100		2 Jul 1785 (located)		2 Jul 1785 (located)			Beg at a red oak & sugar tree	
Russel, John	530	White, Thomas	Sumner	640	1723	20 May 1793	1790	21 Apr 1787	81	59	On a branch that empties &c	
Russel, John	534		Green	300	536	20 Sep 1787	187	29 Nov 1784	65	534	On N side of Nolachuckey	
Russel, Robt. S.	021		Davidson	640			400	6 Apr 1784			W Fork of Stewarts Creek	
Russel, Samuel	192	McKenney, Charles	Tennessee	640	1472	4 Jan 1792	847	12 May 1784	77	369	Wt side of Wt Fork of Jones Creek	
Russel, William	60		Washington	50	228	23 Oct 1782	1682	20 Sep 1779	44	259	On Boons Creek	
Russell, Andrew	723		Sullivan	145	668	5 Dec 1794	327	19 Mar 1780	84	170	On N side of Holston	
Russell, Brian	121		Eastern District	400	154	29 Jul 1793	1803	7 Oct 1779	76	481	On the head of the first branch &c	
Russell, Brice	565		Sullivan	150	548	17 Nov 1790	416	14----1780(?)	76	194	N side of Holstein River &c	
Russell, Brice	671		Sullivan	320	619	9 Jul 1794	748	14 Feb1781	81	627	Beg on an ash	
Russell, Bryce	99		Sullivan	640	110	23 Oct 1782	1852	6 Oct 1779	43	290	On the N side of Holston River	
Russell, Daniel	418		Eastern District	100	290	8 Jan 1797	1928	17 Oct 1779	90	209	S side of French Broad River	
Russell, David	0116		Green	100			1033	29 Oct 1783			S side of Knowlachucky River	
Russell, David	1100		Washington	100	1050	27 Nov 1792	1742	27 Sep 1779	80	205	On waters of Big Limestone	
Russell, George	390		Washington	100	382	13 Oct 1783	626	24 Nov 1778	52	256	On Cedar Branch	
Russell, George	470		Sullivan	74	349	10 Nov 1784	1393	24 May 1779	69	195	On said Russells Valley	
Russell, George	593		Green	600	274	20 Sep 1787	115	21 Oct 1783	66	165	On Fall Creek &c	
Russell, Jas & D. James	011	Giwins, George	Montgomery	640			1019	14 Aug 1797			On Small East Fork of Yellow Creek	yes
Russell, Jas.	1895	Rule, Henry	Davidson	320	119	27 Apr 1793	844	15 Dec 1792	81	33	Joining entry of 62 acres of James Russell	
Russell, John	554	Armstrong, M.	Tennessee (?)	20	360	10 Apr 1797	1393	21 Sep 1785	90	283	On the first island in Cumberland River &c	
Russell, John	680		Washington	48	494	10 Nov 1784			69	102	Beg at a black oak	
Russell, John	825		Washington	400	639	10 Nov 1784	715	19 Dec 1778	69	149	On Boons Creek	
Russell, John	981		Hawkins	100	753	20 Jul 1796	1244	6 Jul 1779	88	501	S of Holston River	
Russell, Robert	273	Wiggins, Levi	Sumner	640	1261	10 Dec 1790			74	352	On waters of Round Lick Creek	yes
Russell, Uriah	495	Sanders, William	Davidson	640	467	15 Sep 1787	2280		63	170	On Money Fork Creek	yes
Russell, William	301		Eastern District	200	210	3 Jan 1795	1020	29 Oct 1783	84	286	On S side of Clinch River	
Russie, David	1210		Green	300	1054	May 1792	855	29 Oct 1783	77	401	On N side of River on Richland Cr	
Russie, Thomas	1741	Armstrong, M.	Davidson	100	104	4 Jan 1792			77	378	S/S Cumberland & both sides of Pond Creek	
Rusters, David	328	Williams, Willoughby	Middle District	640	2390	3 Feb 1795	2621	12 Nov 1791	83	387	W side of W Fork of Obeys River	yes
Ruswell, Mattheas	761		Hawkins	300	601	12 Jul 1794	1875	7 Oct 1779	82	211	On N side of Holston River &c	
Ruth, Edward	2341	Malloy, Thomas	Davidson	640	2985	10 Apr 1797	3629		90	287	Waters of Harpeth River	yes

Claimant:	File #:	Assignee:	County:	Acres:	Grant:	Grant Date:	Entry:	Entry Date:	Bk:	Pg:	Location by Stream Name:	Military:
Ruth, John	1388	Donelson, John	Sumner	640	3313	6 Dec 1797	4667	10 Apr 1797	97	39	On a S branch of Falling Creek	yes
Rutherford, Elizabeth	427		Middle District	640	366	17 Dec 1794	2104	7 May 1784	84	237	On both sides of Camp Creek	
Rutherford, Griffith	1		Middle District	5000	3	10 Jul 1788	2086	6 May 1784	67	289	Lying on S side of Duck River &c	
Rutherford, Griffith	1023	Jinkins, William heirs	Davidson	640	1041	18 May 1789	2065		63	346	On E Fork of Stones River	yes
Rutherford, Griffith	280	Gunn, Alexander	Davidson	1000	266	14 Mar 1786	748		63	97	N side of Tennessee River	yes
Rutherford, Griffith	37		Western District	3000	37	10 Jul 1788	2249	24 May 1784	67	294	On S side of Forked Deer River &c	
Rutherford, Griffith	74		Western District	3000	74	10 Jul 1788	18	12 Jan 1786	67	309	On S side of Forked Deer River &c	
Rutherford, Griffith	991	Cruder, Jacob	Davidson	428	1008	18 May 1789	3225		63	338	On E Fork of Stones River	yes
Rutherford, Henry	075		Sullivan [?]	3000	368	20 Dec 1791	370	28 Sep 1785			Waters of Rutherfords fk of Obion River	
Rutherford, Henry	076		Sullivan [sic]	3000			192	15 Sep 1784			On Rutherford Fork of Obion River	
Rutherford, Henry	111		Western District	250	111	10 Jul 1788	21	12 Jan 1786	67	324	S/S Fked Deer Riv E of Boyds Lake	
Rutherford, Henry	114		Western District	250	114	10 Jul 1788	23	13 Jan 1786	67	325	On S side of Forked Deer River &c	
Rutherford, Henry	135		Middle District	5000	137	10 Jul 1788	733	28 Oct 1783	67	475	Lying on Fork of Forked Deer River	
Rutherford, Henry	1390		Davidson	378	7	8 Oct 1787		2 Nov 1785	68	150	Lying on Sycamore Creek &c	
Rutherford, Henry	160		Middle District	250	170	20 Dec 1791	20		75	224	On Catheys Creek	
Rutherford, Henry	34		Western District	2000	34	10 Jul 1788	19	12 Jan 1786	67	293	On S side of Forked Deer River	
Rutherford, Henry	362		Western District	3000	368	20 Dec 1791			75	219	On Rutherfords Fork of Obion R	
Rutherford, Henry	364		Western District	3000	370	20 Dec 1791			75	220	Waters Rutherfords Fork of Obion	
Rutherford, Henry	76	Armstrong, M.	Davidson	378	7	8 Oct 1787		2 Nov 1785	68	150	On Sycamore Cr where lower path crosses	
Rutherford, John	107		Middle District	5000	109	10 Jul 1788	2085	6 May 1784	67	462	On S Fork of Forked Deer River	
Rutherford, Margret Chamber	468		Middle District	1000	407	17 Dec 1794	2109	30 Nov 1784	84	265	On both sides of Camp Creek	
Rutledge, John	476		Middle District	3000	268	6 Dec 1794	1771	23 Apr 1784	85	336	On Middle Fork of Elk River	
Rutledge, John	477		Middle District	5000	269	6 Dec 1794	1780	23 Apr 1780	85	336	On S Fork of Elk River	
Rutledge, John	478		Middle District	5000	270	6 Dec 1794	1779	23 Apr 1784	85	336	On Elk River	
Rutledge, John	479		Middle District	5000	271	6 Dec 1794	1783	23 Apr 1784	85	337	On S Fork of Elk River	
Rutledge, John	481		Middle District	5000	273	6 Dec 1794	1784	23 Apr 1784	85	337	On S Fork of Elk River	
Rutledge, John	483		Middle District	2000	275	6 Dec 1794	1777	23 Apr 1784	85	338	Joining survey of Rutledge	
Rutledge, John	483		Middle District	5000	287	6 Dec 1794	1781	23 Apr 1784	85	342	On S Fork of Elk River	
Rutledge, John	485		Middle District	3000	277	6 Dec 1794	1776	23 Apr 1784	85	339	Both sides Middle Fork of Elk River	
Rutledge, John	486		Middle District	3000	278	6 Dec 1794	1773	23 Apr 1784	85	339	On Middle Fork of Elk River	
Rutledge, John	495		Middle District	3000	288	6 Dec 1794	1774	23 Apr 1784	85	343	Joining Wm. Frazier's entry	
Rutledge, John	566		Middle District	5000	315	6 Dec 1796	1830	17 Apr 1784	91	282	On a large creek	
Rutledge, John	567		Middle District	5000	316	6 Dec 1796	1835,-1837	23 Apr 1784	91	283	On Main Fork of Elk River	
Rutledge, John	568		Middle District	5000	317	6 Dec 1796	1833	23 Apr 1784	91	283	On Main Fork of Elk River &c	
Rutledge, John	569		Middle District	5000	318	6 Dec 1796	1834,-1836	23 Apr 1784	91	284	On a branch &c	
Rutledge, John	570		Middle District	500	319	6 Dec 1796	1832	23 Apr 1784	91	284	On the Main Fork of Elk River &c	
Rutledge, Sarah	641		Davidson	2560	614	15 Sep 1787	190		63	218	On waters of Stones River	yes
Rutledge, Thomas	170		Middle District	1103	180	20 Dec 1791	2653	25 May 1784	75	228	On S side of Duck River	
Rutledge, William	203		Sullivan (?)	450	210	10 Oct 1783			53	163	On a branch of White Top Creek	
Rutledge, William	641	Rutledge, Sara heiress	Davidson	2560	614	15 Sep 1787	190		63	218	On waters of Stones River	yes
Rutledge, William	482		Middle District	3000	274	6 Dec 1794	1772	23 Apr 1784	85	338	Joining survey of sd Rutledge	
Rutledge, John	494		Middle District	5000	286	6 Dec 1794	1782	23 Apr 1784	85	342	On S Fork of Elk River	
Ryal, Joseph	151	Donaldson, John	Davidson	640	137	14 Mar 1786	1074		63	53	On waters of Big Harpeth River	yes
Ryal, William	2402	Davis, John	Davidson	640	2799	6 Jun 1796	3868		91	472	S W side of Big Harpeth River	yes
Ryan, Cornelius	454	Armstrong, Martin	Davidson	640	426	15 Sep 1787	389		63	157	S side of Richland	yes

Claimant:	File #:	Assignee:	County:	Acres:	Grant:	Grant Date:	Entry:	Entry Date:	Bk:	Pg:	Location by Stream Name:	Military:
Ryan, Cornelius	863	Gillespie, James	Sumner	640	2368	20 May 1793	955	21 Oct 1791	81	205	N side of Cumberland River	yes
Ryan, Jeffrey	1411	Hadley, Joshua	Sumner	228	3268	6 Dec 1797	4543	22 Jun 1797	98	152	On waters of Spring Creek	yes
Ryan, John	859		Washington	100 (150	866	26 Nov 1789	2423	11 Feb 1780	71	384	On Clear Fork of Lick Creek	
Ryan, Thomas	2070	Monk, Notingham	Davidson	274	2212	20 May 1793	1272		81	171	On W Fork of Lick Creek	yes
Rymond, Daniel	803	Sloss, John	Sumner	640	2268	20 May 1793	917	28 Nov 1792	81	184	On S side of Cumberland River	yes
Sage, Edward	677	David, Joshua	Sumner	640	2020	20 May 1793	2437	29 Oct 1792	81	129	On Crabapple Creek	yes
Sale of Salt Licks	038		Montg/Sumn									
Sallers, Sebert	972		Green	200	886	17 Nov 1790	71	12 May 1784	76	133	On head waters of Meadow Creek &c	
Sally, Thomas	417	Lanier, James	Davidson	640	389	15 Sep 1787	3377		63	145	S side of Big Barren River	
Salmon, Vincent	638	Searcey, Richard	Tennessee	1000	2793	20 Dec 1796	240	25 Oct 1783	91	468	N side of Cumberland River	yes
Salter, John	426	Nichols, John	Davidson	457	398	15 Sep 1787	1848		63	148	On N side of Cumberland	yes
Sample, George	475		Green	160	477	20 Sep 1787	185	22 Oct 1783	65	510	On waters of Little Chuckey	
Sample, Samuel	497		Hawkins	150	369	29 Jul 1793	49	10 May 1785	80	269	S side of Holston River &c	
Sample, Samuel	550		Green	150	230	20 Sep 1787	49	10 May 1784	66	151	On S side of Holston River &c	
Sample, Samuel	591		Green	200	272	20 Sep 1787	47	10 May 1784	66	164	On S side of Holston River	
Samples, Saml	095		Green	300			14	29 Aug 1783			N side of Chuckey River	
Samples, Thomas	46		Washington	100	336	24 Oct 1782	336	1 Sep 1778	43	313	On E side of Big Limestone Creek	yes
Sampson, David	1971	Sugg, George A.	Davidson	640	1850	20 May 1793	3480		81	90	On S/S Cumberland River black oak	
Sampson, George	887	Motheral, John	Sumner	640	2417	7 Jan 1794	2378	19 Dec 1792	81	405	On waters of E Fork of Goose Creek	yes
Sampson, Joab	366	Hays, Robert	Sumner	640	1530	14 Jan 1793	3496	9 Mar 1786	79	265	On waters of Munscows Creek	yes
Sams, Rue (Price)	823		Washington	100	637	10 Nov 1784	1491	27 Jul 1779	69	148	Beg at a small white oak	
Samuel, Jones	26		Davidson	3840	112 [?]	14 Mar 1786	176		63	6	On Spring & Cedar Creek	
Sanderlin, Isaac	794	Davis, Joshua	Sumner	640	2254	20 May 1793	2435	29 Oct 1792	81	182	On the dividing ridge	yes
Sanderlin, Leevi	552	Burgess, William	Sumner	228	1768	20 May 1793	3020	20 Dec 1792	81	75	On W Fork of Goose Creek	yes
Sanders, James	0112	Reed, William	Sumner	640			1874	10 Apr 1797			On waters of Bradly Lick Creek	yes
Sanders, James	0113	Reid, John	Sumner	640			1874	10 Apr 1797			on waters of Bradleys Lick Creek	yes
Sanders, James	058	Oliver, Elijah	not given	640			1418	1 Mar 1786			On waters of Second Creek	
Sanders, James	1034		Davidson	640	8	17 Apr 1786	171	24 Jan 1784	66	36	Lying Middle Fk of Station Camp Cr	
Sanders, James	1414	Armstrong, M.	Davidson	200	31	8 Oct 1787			68	156	On Rockey Cr on N/S Cumberland	
Sanders, James	1537	Armstrong, M.	Sumner	50	72	18 May 1789			71	226	On N side of Cumberland River	
Sanders, James	1537	Mosier, Francis heirs	Davidson	914	1094	26 Nov 1789	2299		74	128	On N side of Cumberland River	yes
Sanders, James	1537	Robinson, Benj.	Davidson	914	1094	26 Nov 1789	1249		74	128	On N side of Cumberland River	yes
Sanders, James	2314	Adkison, Michael heirs	Davidson	640	2503	12 Nov 1795			89	420	On Second Creek	yes
Sanders, James	245	Simpson, John	Davidson	640	231	7 Mar 1786	49		63	85	N side of Cumberland River	yes
Sanders, James	317	Slawson, Ezekial heirs	Davidson	632	303	13 Jun 1787	2583		63	113	Heads W branches of Drakes Cr	yes
Sanders, James	524	Nash, Francis heirs	Davidson	640	496	15 Sep 1787	443		63	179	S side of Cumberland River	yes
Sanders, James	770	Donohoe, William	Davidson	640	743	11 Jul 1788	1419		63	261	On Second Creek	yes
Sanders, James	980	Breadlowes, Spencer heirs	Davidson	640	997	18 May 1789			63	336	On E branch of E Fork of Stones R	yes
Sanders, James, Ass.	10		Sumner	640	767	11 Jul 1788	2227	25 Nov 1786	63	269	Head S Fork of Bradleys Lick Cr	yes
Sanders, James, Ass.	11		Sumner	640	768	11 Jul 1788	3524	21 Sep 1787	63	269	On Bradleys Lick Creek	yes
Sanders, James, Ass.	1232		Sumner	640	2504	12 Nov 1795	2650	21 Sep 1787	89	421	On Many Fork Creek	yes
Sanders, James, Ass.	1235		Sumner	640	2508	12 Nov 1795	2980	22 Sep 1787	89	422	On the Many Fork Creek	yes
Sanders, James, Ass.	1236		Sumner	200	2509	12 Nov 1795	1603	30 Mar 1786	89	423	On N side of Cumberland River	yes
Sanders, James, Ass.	15		Sumner	640	772	11 Jul 1788	3027	20 Sep 1787	63	271	On Cumberland River	yes
Sanders, James, Ass.	16		Sumner	228	773	11 Jul 1788	1655	21 Oct 1786	63	271	On waters of Goose Creek	yes

Claimant:	File #:	Assignee:	County:	Acres:	Grant:	Grant Date:	Entry:	Entry Date:	Bk:	Pg:	Location by Stream Name:	Military:
Sanders, James, Ass.	18		Sumner	464	775	11 Jul 1788			63	272	On W Fork of Station Camp Creek	yes
Sanders, James, Ass.	19		Sumner	640	776	11 Jul 1788	3519	21 Sep 1787	63	272	On third large creek &c	yes
Sanders, James, Ass.	20		Sumner	228	777	11 Jul 1788	1646	12 Feb 1788	63	272	On waters of Cumberland River	yes
Sanders, James, Ass.	21		Sumner	640	778	11 Jul 1788	3497	21 Sep 1787	63	273	At the forks of Bradleys Lick Cr	yes
Sanders, James, Ass.	2315		Davidson	640	2505	12 Nov 1795			89	421	On waters of Second Creek	
Sanders, James, Ass.	30		Sumner	640	787	11 Jul 1788	523	8 Jul 1784	63	276	Beg at the N bank of Cumberland River	yes
Sanders, James, Ass.	48		Sumner	640	1035	18 May 1789	2781	25 Nov 1786	63	344	On S Fork of Bradleys Creek	yes
Sanders, James, Ass.	716		Sumner	228	2098	20 May 1793	3487	21 Sep 1787	81	149	Beg at 2 sugar trees & an elm	yes
Sanders, Jas.	193	Armstrong, M.	Sumner	228	71	18 May 1789			71	226	On N side of Cumberland River	
Sanders, John	1528		Green	200	1288	17 Jul 1794	1804	7 Oct 1779	81	605	Beg at a walnut	
Sanders, Peter	979	Drake, Jonathan	Davidson	640	996	18 May 1789	3158		63	335	On Racoon Creek	yes
Sanders, William	365	Floyd, Charles heirs	Davidson	640	345	15 Sep 1787	1614		63	130	On Money Fork Creek	yes
Sanders, William	489	Duke, Sherod	Davidson	640	461	15 Sep 1787	2272		63	168	S fork of Money Fork Creek	yes
Sanders, William	495	Russell, Uriah	Davidson	640	467	5 Sep 1787	2280		63	170	On Maney Fork Creek	yes
Sanders, William	499	Tatton, James	Davidson	640	471	15 Sep 1787	2278		63	171	On Maney Fork Creek	yes
Sanders, William	584	Vinson, Moses heirs	Davidson	640	556	15 Sep 1787	1606		63	199	On Maney Fork Creek	yes
Sanders, William	585	Vinson, William	Davidson	640	557	15 Sep 1787	2298		63	200	On N Fork of Maney Fork	yes
Sanders, William	593	Kent, Thomas	Davidson	640	565	15 Sep 1787	1617		63	202	On N branch of Money Fork Creek	yes
Sanders, William, Ass.	1230		Sumner	640	2501	12 Nov 1795	1813	21 Jan 1786	89	419	On waters of Big Barren River	yes
Sanders, William, Ass.	1231		Sumner	1000	2502	12 Nov 1795	1622	21 Jan 1786	89	420	Lying on Big Barren	
Sanders, William, Ass.	1233		Sumner	640	2506	12 Nov 1795	1623	21 Sep 1787	89	422	Beg at 2 beech trees	yes
Sanders, William, Ass.	1234		Sumner	640	2507	12 Nov 1795			89	422	On waters of Goose Creek	yes
Sanders, William, Ass.	217		Sumner	640	1122	26 Nov 1789	1616	9 Feb 1787	74	140	On waters of Caney Fork	yes
Sanders, William, Ass.	2225	Watkins, Jno. Heir of Bur.	Davidson	640	2517	8 Dec 1795	2283		88	288	A Fork of S Fork of Many Fork Cr	yes
Sanders, William, Ass.	31	Gillingham, James	Sumner	640	788	11 Jul 1788	805	9 Feb 1787	63	276	On waters of Collins River	
Sanderson, William	560		Tennessee	640	2994	10 Apr 1797	3983		90	291	N side of Cumberland River	yes
Sanford, Samuel	1961	Cook, Jonah	Davidson	640	1816	20 May 1793	2371		81	83	On waters of W Harpeth	yes
Sanford, Samuel	1962	Wigley, Demsey	Davidson	640	1820	20 May 1793	2398		81	83	On waters of West Harpeth	
Sanford, Samuel	1963	Grogan, Jacob	Davidson	640	1825	20 May 1793	2375		81	84	On waters of W Harpeth	yes
Sanford, Samuel, Ass.	512		Sumner	640	1809	20 May 1793	2402	6 Aug 1792	81	81	Headwaters E branches Roaring R	
Sanford, Samuel, Ass.	571		Sumner	640	1808	20 May 1793	2367	6 Aug 1792	81	81	On head of a branch &c	yes
Sanford, Samuel, Ass.	573		Sumner	640	1810	20 May 1793	2400	6 Aug 1792	81	81	On head waters of First Creek &c	
Sanford, Samuel, Ass.	574		Sumner	640	1811	20 May 1793	2373	6 Aug 1792	81	82	Lying on called Crabapple Creek	yes
Sanford, Samuel, Ass.	575		Sumner	640	1812	20 May 1793	2374	11 Oct 1792	81	82	On waters of E Fork of Goose Creek	
Sanford, Samuel, Ass.	576		Sumner	640	1813	20 May 1793	2397	6 Aug 1792	81	82	On head of 1st large creek &c	yes
Sanford, Samuel, Ass.	577		Sumner	640	1814	20 May 1793	2403	6 Aug 1792	81	82	On N side of Cumberland River	
Sanford, Samuel, Ass.	578		Sumner	640	1815	20 May 1793	2399	30 Nov 1792	81	82	On Jining Fork &c	
Sanford, Samuel, Ass.	579		Sumner	640	1817	20 May 1793	2393	6 Aug 1792	81	83	Near head E branch of Roaring R	yes
Sanford, Samuel, Ass.	580		Sumner	640	1818	20 May 1793	512	18 Aug 1790	81	83	On S side of Cumberland River &c	yes
Sanford, Samuel, Ass.	581		Sumner	640	1819	20 May 1793	2376	6 Aug 1792	81	83	Headwaters E branches Roaring R	yes
Sanford, Samuel, Ass.	582		Sumner	640	1821	20 May 1793	2391	6 Aug 1792	81	84	Near headwaters of small creek &c	yes
Sanford, Samuel, Ass.	583		Sumner	640	1822	20 Dec 1792	2394	20 Dec 1792	81	84	On side at head of Cedar Lick Cr	yes
Sanford, Samuel, Ass.	584		Sumner	640	1823	20 May 1793	2377	6 Aug 1792	81	84	On head of E branch of Roaring River	yes
Sanford, Samuel, Ass.	585		Sumner	640	1824	20 May 1793	2369	6 Aug 1792	81	84	On W Fork of Roaring River	yes
Sanford, Samuel, Ass.	586		Sumner	640	1826	20 May 1793	2395	6 Aug 1792	81	85	On W Fork of Roaring River	yes

Earliest Tennessee Land Records

Claimant:	File #:	Assignee:	County:	Acres:	Grant:	Grant Date:	Entry:	Entry Date:	Bk:	Pg:	Location by Stream Name:	Military:
Sanford, Samuel, Ass.	590		Sumner	640	1832	20 May 1793	2396	17 Aug 1792	81	86	On waters of Caney Fork	yes
Sanford, Samuel, Ass.	591		Sumner	640	1833	20 May 1793	2370	6 Aug 1792	81	86	On the dividing ridge &c	yes
Sanford, Samuel, Ass.	592		Sumner	640	1834	20 May 1793	2392	6 Aug 1792	81	86	On head waters of Roaring River	yes
Sanford, Samuel, Ass.	593		Sumner	640	1835	20 May 1793	2372	10 Dec 1792	81	86	On S Fork of Cedar Creek	
Sanford, Samuel, Ass.	826		Sumner	640	2305	20 May 1793	2401	6 Aug 1792	81	192	On headwaters of the first &c	yes
Sans, Joseph	1375		Washington	300	1297	6 Jun 1799	968	2 Jan 1779	101	346	On the N Fork of Rones Creek	
Saunderlin, Thomas	381	Sheppard, Benjamin	Davidson	640	353	15 Sep 1787	2338		63	133	E Fork of Drakes Creek	
Saunders, Andrew	0121	Tyrrell, William	Sumner	428			1278				Adj. Wm. Hays surveys	
Saunders, Daniel	1353	Nash, William	Sumner	1000	3183	14 Sep 1797	4203	20 Feb 1797	90	435	E side of Stones River	yes
Saunders, Edward	019	Bradshaw, John	Robertson	640	3014	11 Nov 1796	1506				Waters of Sulphur Fork Red River	
Saunders, Edward	2352	Bradshaw, John heirs	Tennessee	640	3014	10 Apr 1797			90	299	Waters of Sulphur Fork	
Saunders, Isaac	1690	Phillips, P. & Michael Cam	Davidson	640	1651	23 Feb 1793	2960		76	337	1-1/2 mile from Black Fox Creek	yes
Saunders, Jacob	582	Hoover, Abraham	Tennessee	640	3029	10 Apr 1797	3937		90	305	S side of Cumberland River	yes
Saunders, James	076	Armstrong, M.	Tennessee	200			762	4 Apr 1785			On Rockey Creek	
Saunders, Jas. & I.Bledsoe	219	Hicks, Wm heir of Henry	Davidson	640	205	7 Mar 1786	804		63	76	N side of Cumberland River	yes
Saunders, John	1011	Armstrong, M.	Sumner	100	177	26 Mar 1795			86	378	Waters of Trammels Creek	
Saunders, John	875	Larrimore, T.	Hawkins	400	2	19 Jul 1794			82	227	S side of Holston River on Honeycuts Creek	
Saunders, Peter	043	Donelson, Stockley	Robertson	640	2392	7 Jan 1793	1739	19 Sep 1792	81	389	On waters of Red River	yes
Saunders, Richard	1694	Phillips, P. & Michael Cam	Davidson	640	1655	23 Feb 1793	3158	13 Aug 1796			On waters of Red River	yes
Saunders, Thomas	1284	Barry, Redmon Dillon	Sumner	640	3043	8 Jun 1797	3151		76	338	On waters of Stones River	yes
Saunders, William	2430	Reaves, Jordan	Davidson	274	3328	6 Dec 1797	4063	29 Mar 1797	90	315	Inc forks of Turkey & Spring Creeks	yes
Saunders, William	90		Davidson	2560	76	14 Mar 1786	1268		97	48	N side of Big Harpeth River	yes
Savage, James	583	Sanford, Samuel	Sumner	640	1822	27 Nov 1792	2394	20 Dec 1792	63	31	On ridge at the head of Cedar Lick	yes
Savage, John	1414		Green	200	1226	20 May 1793	301	3 Oct 1783	81	84	On waters of Nolechuckey River	yes
Savage, Joseph	586	Sanford, Samuel	Sumner	640	1826	20 May 1793	2395	6 Aug 1792	80	163	On W Fork of Roaring River	yes
Savage, Micajah	493	Bradley, James	Davidson	220	465	15 Sep 1787	2291		81	85	On head of Cranes Creek	yes
Savage, Ransom	167		Davidson	560	153	7 Mar 1786	135		63	169	Beg at Peter Cloud N W corner	yes
Savage, Ransom	478	Marshall, John	Davidson	357	450	15 Sep 1787	2293		63	58	On waters of Stones River	yes
Saws, David	156		Tennessee	640	1413	20 Dec 1791	639	23 Apr 1784	77	354	On Spring Creek	yes
Sawyer, Jno.	1106		Davidson	640	80	17 Apr 1786	479	7 Jun 1784	66	61	Lying Middle Fork of Bledsoes Cr	
Sawyer, Miller	441		Davidson	1000	413	15 Sep 1787			63	153	E side of Caney Fork	yes
Sawyer, Miller	551		Sumner	274	1766	19 Dec 1792	3215		81	70	On Otter Fork of Bledsoes Creek	yes
Sawyer, Thomas	269		Davidson	274	255	7 Mar 1786	827		63	93	S side of Cumberland River	yes
Sawyer, Willis	911	King, William	Sumner	640	2480	31 Dec 1793	3799		81	436	On Harts Creek	
Sawyers, Sampson	1713		Davidson	640	355	29 Jul 1793			76	479	S/S Cumberland N E Big Harpeth R	
Sayers, John	1356		Davidson	320	39	8 Oct 1787	679	12 Feb 1785	68	137	On a branch of Arringtons Creek	
Sayman (Layman), John	759		Washington	150	573	10 Nov 1784	828	29 Dec 1778	69	130	On N Fork of Cherokee Creek	
Scales, Joseph	236		Hawkins	640	223	26 Dec 1791	902	7 Jan 1784	77	321	On S side of Holston River &c	
Scalf, John	362		Tennessee	297	2217	20 May 1793	585	21 Apr 1784	81	172	On N side of Cumberland River	yes
Scalp, James	8		Davidson	640	765	29 Jul 1793	3025	20 Sep 1787	63	268	On head of some branches &c	
Scarbrough, Nathan	266	Thomas, Philemon	Sumner	640	1717	11 Jul 1788	3683	10 Dec 1788	68	57	On 1st creek N of Cumberland	yes
Scavrons, John	242	Lacy, Hopkins & T. Malloy	Tennessee	640	1596	20 May 1793	2157	9 Sep 1785	81	16	On both sides of Cumberland River	yes
Schakley, Philip, Ass.	264	Allen, Sarah	Sumner	640	1221	27 Apr 1793	373	9 Dec 1795	74	338	On N side of Cumberland River	yes
Schenocker, Elias	819		Sullivan	188	762	17 Nov 1797	377, -49	8 Feb 1780	96	158	N side of Holstein River	yes

Earliest Tennessee Land Records

Claimant:	File #:	Assignee:	County:	Acres:	Grant:	Grant Date:	Entry:	Entry Date:	Bk:	Pg:	Location by Stream Name:	Military:
Scogin, Humphrey	693		Washington	200	507	10 Nov 1784	1371	18 May 1779	69	107	Beg on the S side of Rock Creek	
Scot, Burrel	126		Hawkins	150	160	26 Dec 1791	481	26 Apr 1780	75	168	Beg at a white oak	
Scott, D.	1074		Davidson	640	48	17 Apr 1786	51	2 Jan 1784	66	50	Bet at an Elm tree	
Scott, David	1125		Green	400	968	26 Dec 1791	293	23 Oct 1783	77	270	On a branch of Crooked Creek	
Scott, Geo & Ralph Fleming	1287		Davidson	640	252	10 Jul 1788	516	10 Jul 1784	66	425	On Millers Cr of Richland of Red R	
Scott, George	1255		Davidson	640	220	10 Jul 1788	514	7 Jul 1784	66	416	Waters of Big Harpeth	
Scott, George	188		Sumner	640	277	10 Jul 1788	794	22 Sep 1787	66	434	On Puncheon Camp Creek	yes
Scott, James	673		Sullivan	200	621	9 Jul 1794	189	25 Mar 1780	81	628	On E side of Holston River	
Scott, James, Ass.	770		Sumner	182	2218	20 May 1793	3698	19 Dec 1792	81	173	On S side of Cumberland River	yes
Scott, John	129		Sullivan	220	141	23 Oct 1782	1685	20 Sep 1779	43	326	On the N side of Holston River	
Scott, John	140		Sullivan	110	153	23 Oct 1782	294	10 Mar 1780	43	332	On N side of Holston River &c	
Scott, John	170		Sullivan	100	177	10 Oct 1783	2605	13 Aug 1780	53	148	On S side of Holston River	
Scott, John	174		Sullivan	100	181	10 Oct 1783	2869	4 Jun 1781	53	150	On S side of Holston River	
Scott, John	379		Washington	135	371	10 Oct 1783	1163	1 Feb 1779	52	251	On N/S Watauga River	
Scott, John	928	Pickle, John	Sumner	640	2382	27 Sep 1794	1740	9 Aug 1794	81	637	On ridge that divides waters &c	yes
Scott, Joshua & John Payton	1007	Armstrong, Martin	Sumner	100	171	26 Mar 1795			86	376	On the Wolf Branch	yes
Scott, Joshua etal	0114	Crow, Wm.	Sumner	228			4714	12 May 1797			E side of W Fork Station Camp Cr	yes
Scott, Joshua, Ass.	1201		Sumner	182	2773	10 Sep 1796	3696	3 Aug 1796	88	524	On waters of Station Camp Creek	yes
Scott, Marmaduke	144	Thomas, William	Davidson	640	130	14 Mar 1786	416		63	50	On both sides of E Fork Yellow Cr	yes
Scott, Marmaduke	590	Sears, Robert	Davidson	640	562	15 Sep 1787	912	5 Mar 1791	63	201	N side of Cumberland River	yes
Scott, Overstreet	066	Sugg, Geo. A.	Davidson	640			1893				Bet. Whites Creek & Marrowbone	
Scott, Samuel	1074	Scott, Jas. Heir	Davidson	640	48	17 Apr 1786	51	2 Jan 1784	66	50	Beg at an elm tree	
Scott, Samuel	17		Smith Middle Di	5000	380	27 Dec 1800	2580	25 May 1784	112	295	Waters of Woolf River	
Scott, William	188		Sullivan	300	195	10 Oct 1783	2664	13 Aug 1780	53	156	On N side of Holston River	
Scott, William	197		Sullivan	200	204	10 Oct 1783	810	15 Jun 1781	53	150	On S side of Holston River	
Scrogs, Ebenezer	771		Washington	300	585	10 Nov 1784	662	8 Dec 1778	69	134	Beg at a white oak	
Scull, John Gamber	1639		Davidson	1127	1376	15 Dec 1791	1300		75	125	On a creek of Duck River	yes
Scull, John Gembier	236		Davidson	1127	222	7 Mar 1786			63	82	On a creek of Duck River	yes
Scutchings, Meredy	1124	Harris, Edward	Sumner	640	2630	4 Jun 1796	2770	1 Jun 1795	88	344	Joining sd Harris survey	yes
Scutchins, Samuel	976	Tuton, William	Davidson	640	993	18 May 1789	1898	18 Dec 1789	63	335	On Mulherrins Creek	yes
Seaborn, Edward	1207		Green	200	1051	Mar 1792	2890		77	341	On N side of Dumplin Creek	
Seabourn, Edward	852		Green	200	833	13 Feb 1791	831	29 Oct 1783	73	378	On the waters of Dumpling Creek	
Seaburn, Edward	1244		Green	200	1094	12 Jan 1793	2111	8 Nov 1779	78	361	On waters of Dumplin Creek	
Seaburn, Edward	1245		Green	100	1095	12 Jan 1793	1404	1 Mar 1790	78	361	On waters of Dumplin Creek	
Seagroves, John	2223	Henry, Thomas	Davidson	124	2528	8 Dec 1795	622		88	280	On waters of Dry Creek	yes
Seal, Frances	2075	Anderson, Matthew	Davidson	182	2222	20 May 1793			81	174	On waters of Drakes Creek	yes
Seales, Joseph	1187		Green	640	1030	26 Dec 1791	904	29 Oct 1783	77	292	On Bent Creek	
Seals, Francis	02	Anderson, Matthew	Sumner	182			3707	29 Aug 1792			On waters of Drakes Creek	yes
Seamon, John	1035		Washington	100	985	14 Jan 1793	2572	30 May 1780	79	280	On Cherokee Creek	
Seamons, John	1043		Washington	200	993	14 Jan 1793	1472	5 Jul 1779	79	283	On Cherokee	
Seamons, John	1108		Washington	200	1058	27 Nov 1792			80	207	S side of river Ohio	
Searcey (Learcey), Luke	36	Jones, Seburn	Tennessee	640	1218	10 Mar 1790	856	14 May 1784	74	337	On N side of Cumberland River	yes
Searcey, Reuben	133	Spanns, Mills	Tennessee	228	1641	23 Feb 1793	883	19 May 1784	76	332	N side of Cumberland River	
Searcey, Robert	023		Davidson	21				22 Dec 1792			S side of Cumberland River	
Searcey, Robert	2387	Bandy, James heirs	Davidson	640	3170	14 Sep 1797	4003		90	430	E side of S Harpeth	yes

Claimant:	File #:	Assignee:	County:	Acres:	Grant:	Grant Date:	Entry:	Entry Date:	Bk:	Pg:	Location by Stream Name:	Military:
Searchwell, Joshua	356	Taitt, William	Davidson	640	340	4 Sep 1787	2234		63	127	W branches of Half Pone Creek	yes
Searcy, Bennet, Ass.	1916	Stillwell, Simon heirs	Davidson	640	1702	20 May 1793	2585		81	54	On S side of Cumberland River	yes
Searcy, Bennet, Ass.	888		Sumner	640	2428	31 Dec 1793	2994	30 Nov 1792	81	409	Bet. Bartons Creek & Stones River	yes
Searcy, Richard etal	417		Sumner	640	428	27 Jun 1793	796	6 May 1788	80	350	On waters of Cedar Lick Creek	yes
Searcy, Robert	638	Salmon, Vincent	Tennessee	1000	2793	20 Dec 1796	240	25 Dec 1783	91	469	N side Cumberland River	
Sears, Arthur	21	Sanders, James	Sumner	640	778	11 Jul 1788	3497	21 Sep 1787	63	273	At forks of Bradleys Lick Creek	yes
Seasever, John	050	Dillenberry, Redmond	Sumner	640			4215	28 Oct 1797			E side of E Fork of Stones River	yes
Seebery, Alston	2455	Good, William	Davidson	640	3351	12 Dec 1797	1273		98	185	On Swan Creek &c	yes
Seener, Peter	853	Phifer, Martin	Sumner	182	2358	20 May 1793	3704	27 Oct 1792	81	203	On Keykendolls Branch	yes
Seers (?), Robert	590	Scott, Marmaduke	Davidson	640	562	15 Sep 1787	912		63	201	N side of Cumberland River	yes
Seers, John	0120	Armstrong, Martin	Green	120							N side Noley Chuckey	yes
Self, Joseph	1372		Green	100	1227	27 Jan 1793	398	19 Sep 1778	79	505	On big Gap Creek	
Sellars, Nathan	1706		Green	160	343	19 Feb 1797	343	4 Aug 1794	90	254	On Bays Mountain	
Sellars, Robert	389		Sullivan	300	268	10 Nov 1784	1288	16 Mar 1779	69	167	On S side of Holstein River	
Sellers, Daniel, heirs of	1875		Davidson	640	1616	27 Apr 1793	1366		81	21	On E side of Persons Survey	yes
Sellers, John	705	Hart, Anthony	Davidson	640	678	8 Dec 1787	2763		63	239	S side of Cumberland River	yes
Sellers, Matthew	635	Morgan, Wm.	Tennessee	640	2780	17 Oct 1796	3769		91	23	On Main West Fork of Red River	
Semple, Robert	1276	Warner, Hardin	Tennessee	320	3018	10 Apr 1797	3885		90	300	On E Fork of Barretts Creek	
Sers, James	293	Barton, Samuel	Sumner	640	1311	10 Dec 1790	3653	28 Nov 1789	74	369	Beg at a white oak	
Sessums, Abel	2404	Robertson, Jonathan F.	Davidson	640	2801	6 Jun 1796	3852		91	473	S W side of Big Harpeth River	yes
Setgreaves, John	2353	Hayes, Robert	Davidson	640	3019	10 Apr 1797	1973		90	301	E side of Stones River	yes
Settleworth, Andrew	179	Erwin, Andrew	Tennessee	640	1458	20 Dec 1791	2521	15 Sep 1789	77	366	On the waters of Sulphur Fork	yes
Severes, Geo.	0122		Sullivan	200			765	28 Mar 1781			Beg. at M. Adams corner Elm	yes
Severs, George	631		Sullivan	200	580	27 Jun 1793	765	30 May 1780	80	375	On N side of Holston River	
Severs, Robert	1054		Washington	100	1004	27 Nov 1792	2564	30 May 1780	80	178	On N Fork of Cherokee Creek	
Sevier, Charles	196	Harget & Randall	Middle District	1000	209	29 Jul 1793	2611	25 May 1784	76	482	On waters of Tennessee	
Sevier, James	1317		Washington	250	1237	19 Feb 1797	2098	30 Oct 1779	90	247	S side of Nolachucky River	
Sevier, Jno.	549	Caswell, Richard	Green	200	569	15 Nov 1787	1286	7 Jun 1784	65	564	On N side of Tennessee River	
Sevier, John	1134		Washington	300	1092	12 Jul 1794			81	566	On S side of Nolichuckey River	
Sevier, John	15		Middle District	2115	17	10 Jul 1788	1047	29 Oct 1783	67	414	On S side of Duck River &c	
Sevier, John	1641		Green	640	1344	27 Aug 1795	1703	6 May 1780	87	511	On S side of French Broad River	
Sevier, John	1690		Green	640	1366	27 Nov 1795	1763	20 Apr 1780	89	288	On S side of Noleychuckey River	
Sevier, John	374		Eastern District	10500	225	28 Aug 1795	12 Warrants		89	80	On Crow Creek	
Sevier, John	505		Middle District	32000	300	27 Nov 1795	36 warrants		88	262	On waters of Cumberland River	
Sevier, John	6		Middle District	1000	55	10 Jul 1788	2592	25 May 1784	67	437	On N side of Tennessee River	
Sevier, John	675		Middle District	1000	8	10 Jul 1788	2593	25 May 1784	67	410	Lying on both sides of Buffaloe R	
Sevier, John etal	189		Washington	640	489	10 Nov 1784			69	100	Incl plantation where John Wood lived	
Sevier, John etal	593		Green	500	146	23 Apr 1787	1288	24 Dec 1783	65	161	On N side of Tennessee River	
Sevier, John etal	76		Sullivan	200	591	29 Jul 1793	1340	15 Apr 1779	76	476	N side of Holston River	
Sevier, John, Jr.	1188		Green	357-1/2	34	1 Nov 1786	396	25 Oct 1783	59	395	Including the Island in French Broad River	
Sevier, John, Jr.	1189		Washington	5660	1141	10 Sep 1794			83	143	Beg at 2 small hickorys	
Sevier, John, Jr.	1190		Washington	8590	1142	10 Sep 1794			83	144	On waters of Stoney Creek	
Sevier, John, Jr.	1191		Washington	5660	1143	10 Sep 1794			83	144	Beg at 2 small hicorys &c	
Sevier, John, Jr.	1192		Washington	6090	1144	Sep 1794			83	145	On waters of Stoney Creek	
Sevier, John, Jr.			Washington	7750	1145	10 Sep 1794			83	145	On waters of Stoney Creek &c	

Claimant:	File #:	Assignee:	County:	Acres:	Grant:	Grant Date:	Entry:	Entry Date:	Bk:	Pg:	Location by Stream Name:	Military:
Sevier, John, Jr.	1193		Washington	7880	1146	10 Sep 1794			83	146	On the waters of Stoney Creek	
Sevier, John, Sr.	1190		Sumner	25060	228	28 Aug 1795			89	81	On waters of Cumberland River	yes
Sevier, John, Sr.	1203		Sumner	6040	229	27 Aug 1795			89	82	On S side of Cumberland River	yes
Sevier, John, Sr.	1689		Green	3000	1365	27 Nov 1795	2362	7 May 1780	89	287	On S side of Nolechuckey River &c	
Sevier, Robert	343		Washington	200	210	24 Oct 1782	1191	4 Feb 1779	49	230	On the N Fork of Cherokey Creek	
Sevier, Valentine, Sen.	733		Washington	360	547	10 Nov 1784	799	28 Dec 1778	69	121	On Wataugha River	
Sevirs, Valentine	626		Washington	500	720	26 Oct 1786	800	28 Dec 1778	66	21	Beg at a marked white oak &c	
Sevil, Daniel	471	Norris, Ezekial	Sumner	640	1632	27 Apr 1793	3692	15 Feb 1791	81	25	On S side of Cumberland River	yes
Sexton, Jeremiah	1968		Davidson	640	1846	20 May 1793	834		81	89	Below first bluff S/S Cumberland	yes
Sexton, William	185		Davidson	640	171	7 Mar 1786	826		63	64	S side of Cumberland River	yes
Seymore, Edward	051	McCulloch, Benjamin	Davidson	640			2014	26 Mar 1792			On waters of Stones River	yes
Seymore, Solomon	554	Standley, John	Davidson	228	526	15 Sep 1787	96		63	198	On Beaverdam Creek	yes
Seymore, William	851	Douglas, Edward	Davidson	274	856	17 Jan 1789	97		63	299	Waters W Fork of Station Camp Cr	yes
Seypear, Robert	337		Green	600	339	20 Sep 1787	1193	5 Nov 1783	65	469	On Slate Stone Creek &c	
Shackler, Philip	0132	Young, John	Sumner	1000	375		375	27 Mar 1786			Middle Fork of Drakes Creek	yes
Shackler, Philip, Ass.	263		Sumner	640	1220	10 Dec 1790	372	9 Dec 1785	74	338	On N side of Cumberland	yes
Shackler, Philip, Ass.	297		Sumner	640	1326	10 Dec 1790	1533	9 Dec 1785	74	374	On N side of Cumberland River	yes
Shackler, Philip, Ass.	914		Sumner	640	2483	31 Dec 1793			81	437	On Little W Fork of Red River	yes
Shackler, Philip, Ass.	915		Sumner	640	2484	31 Dec 1793			81	437	On Round Lick Creek	yes
Shackler, Philip	042	Dickson, Joel	Tennessee	640			1801	11 May 1785			On Little West Fork of Red River	
Shackler, Philip	417	Meadows, Abraham	Tennessee	274	2462	31 Dec 1793	1536	5 Feb 1785	81	430	On waters of Sulphur Fork	
Shackley, Philip	0115	McNeel, Absalom	Sumner	640			3540	25 May 1791			S side of Cumberland River	yes
Shackley, Philip	0116	Weeks, Benj.	Sumner	640			1804	9 Dec 1785			N side Cumberland River	yes
Shaden, Alexander	848		Green	200	829	13 Feb 1791	1607	3 Jan 1780	73	377	On waters of French Broad	
Shaffer, Henry	437	Blount, Reading	Davidson	640	409	15 Sep 1787			63	152	N side of Cumberland River	yes
Shaffer, Richard, Ass.	205		Sumner	640	1110	26 Nov 1789	3446	12 Mar 1788	74	134	On W side of Caney Fork River	yes
Shafferd, John	1179	Harris, Edward	Sumner	640	2684	4 Jun 1796	2777	1 Jun 1795	88	362	Joining sd Harris survey	yes
Shakler, Philip	755	Young, John	Sumner	1000	2161	20 May 1793	374	8 Oct 1788	81	163	On Middle Fork of Drakes Creek	yes
Shane, Morris	1083		Davidson	640	57	17 Apr 1786	291	16 Feb 1784	66	53	Lying on the Fork of Gaspers Cr	
Shaner, Martin	293		Hawkins	400	256	24 Dec 1792	86	8 Feb 1780	78	445	In Stanley Valley	
Shanks, Holden	983		Washington	50	1060	29 Jul 1793	2701	20 Dec 1780	76	469	Joining the land he now lives on	
Shanks, James	297	McCulloh, Benjamin	Tennessee	640	1971	20 May 1793	2237	12 Sep 1785	81	117	On S side of Cumberland River	yes
Shanks, Moses	459		Green	500	461	20 Sep 1787	1354	13 Jan 1784	65	504	On the waters of Lick Creek &c	
Shannon, David	1056		Davidson	640	30	17 Apr 1786	320	28 Feb 1784	66	44	Lying on a N branch of Whites Cr	
Shannon, Robert	2361	Armstrong, M.	Davidson	21.75	384	19 Jul 1797		2 Sep 1796	90	369	Waters of Richland Creek	
Shannon, Samuel	1461		Davidson	82	63	18 May 1789	3141	17 Jan 1787	71	222	On the waters of Whites Creek	
Shannon, Samuel	1577	Askin, William	Davidson	640	1231	10 Dec 1790	2630	26 Jan 1785	74	342	On waters of Stones River	yes
Shannon, Samuel	867	Acock, Robert	Davidson	228	881	17 Jan 1789	1482	22 Dec 1785	63	305	On waters of Whites Creek	yes
Sharp Fellow	064		Tennessee	640	2		67	6 Sep 1819			Beg at a stake in the mountain	
Sharp, Abner	19		Western District	2000	19	10 Jul 1788	2658	25 May 1784	67	287	On N side of Loosahatcher River	
Sharp, Anthony	1385		Davidson	320	68	7 Oct 1787	671		68	149	On Middle Fork of Goose Creek	yes
Sharp, Anthony	50		Davidson	3840	36	14 Mar 1786	52		63	14	On Big Harpeth River	yes
Sharp, Benjamin	279	Ross, Wm.	Davidson	1000	265	14 Mar 1786	67		63	96	On Sinking Creek	
Sharp, Edward	59		Western District	5000	59	10 Jul 1788	384	25 Oct 1783	67	303	On N side of N Fork Forked Deer R	yes
Sharp, John	142		Sullivan	700	155	23 Oct 1782	442	21 Feb 1780	43	333	On N side of Holston River	yes

Claimant:	File #:	Assignee:	County:	Acres:	Grant:	Grant Date:	Entry:	Entry Date:	Bk:	Pg:	Location by Stream Name:	Military:
Sharp, John	449		Sullivan	116	328	10 Jul 1784	442	22 Apr 1780	69	186	On both sides of Hoistin River	
Sharp, John	514		Sullivan	146	530	26 Nov 1789	1269	8 Mar 1779	73	45	On waters of Holston River	
Sharp, John	754		Sullivan	29	733	28 Jul 1797	177	21 Sep 1780	90	385	N bank of Holston River	
Sharp, John	756		Sullivan	717	735	28 Jul 1797	176,-1063	1779 & 1780	90	385	Beg at 2 red oaks & cherry	
Sharp, John etal	757		Sullivan	100	736	28 Jul 1797	1786	24 Jul 1796	90	386	Beg at Jno. Sharpes old corner	
Sharp, Jonas	354	Weakley, Robt.	Green	1000	1257	29 Jul 1793	2422	25 May 1784	76	489	Waters Cumberland River on Spring Creek	
Sharp, Thomas	455		Davidson	640	338	4 Sep 1787	2580		63	126	N side of Cumberland River &c	yes
Sharp, Thomas Rine	20		Sullivan	593	334	10 Nov 1784	491	26 Apr 1780	69	189	On N side of Holstein River	
Sharp, William	18		Western District	1000	20	10 Jul 1788	2657	25 May 1784	67	287	On waters of the Long Fork	
Sharp, William	3		Western District	5000	18	10 Jul 1788	1565	28 Mar 1784	67	287	On S side of Obrian River &c	
Sharpe, Anthony	551		Washington	400	3	15 Dec 1778	53	14 Sep 1778	36	3	Lower W Fork of Indian Creek	
Sharpe, Anthony	83		Sullivan	100	534	17 Nov 1790	66	1 Aug 1778	76	189	N side of Holstein	
Sharpe, Anthony etal	61		Western District	3500	83	10 Jul 1788	409	25 Oct 1783	67	313	On N Fork of Forked Deer River	
Sharpe, Anthony etal	67		Middle District	1000	63	10 Jul 1788	2284	10 May 1784	67	441	Removed frm N/S E Fork of Duck R	
Sharpe, Anthony etal	7		Middle District	1000	69	10 Jul 1788	2283	24 May 1784	67	444	On S side of Duck River &c	
Sharpe, Anthony, Ass.	492		Middle District	1000	9	10 Jul 1788	2282	24 May 1784	67	410	On S side of Duck River &c	yes
Sharpe, John	49		Sumner	1000	1654	20 May 1793	2107	10 Oct 1785	81	42	On N side of Cumberland River	
Sharpe, John	725		Sullivan	620	60	23 Oct 1782	176,179	20 & 21 Feb 1780	84	267	Beg 2 red oaks hicory & white oak	
Sharpe, John	755		Sullivan	397	670	5 Dec 1794	1594	12 Sep 1779	84	171	On Sinking Creek	
Sharpe, Joseph	562	Nelson, Robert	Tennessee	47	734	28 Jul 1797	491	26 Apr 1780	90	385	On Sharps Creek	yes
Sharpe, Thomas	127		Middle District	428	2997	10 Apr 1797	671		90	292	N side of Cumberland River	
Sharpe, Thomas	48		Middle District	400	129	10 Jul 1788	47		67	471	Lying on Weakleys Creek	
Sharpe, Thomas Reid	46		Western District	250	50	10 Jul 1788	46		67	429	On Weakleys Creek	
Sharpe, Thos.	1280		Davidson	1000	245	10 Jul 1788	2656	25 May 1784	66	298	On waters of the Long Fork &c	
Sharpe, William	1364		Washington	640	1293	18 Dec 1797	660	10 Jan 1785	66	423	Beg at a hickory & sweet gum	
Sharpe, William	1365		Washington	200	1294	18 Dec 1797	418	23 Sep 1778	92	196	Upon Doe River	
Sharpe, William	218		Washington	200	86	23 Oct 1782	419	23 Sep 1778	92	197	Both sides of Little Branch	
Sharpe, William	625		Washington	140	791	26 Oct 1786	457	28 Sep 1778	47	41	Both sides of Gap Creek	
Sharpe, William	773		Washington	400	587	10 Nov 1784	156	12 Mar 1778	66	20	Upon Cape Creek &c	
Sharpe, William	8		Washington	600	8	15 Dec 1788	54	26 Feb 1778	69	134	On Little Doe of Rones Creek	
Shatswood, Robt	1051		Davidson	400	25	17 Apr 1786	55	14 Sep 1778	36	8	On Doe River &c	
Shavor, Michael	1111		Davidson	640	88	17 Apr 1786	101	14 Jan 1784	66	42	On Wt Fork of Stewarts Creek	
Shaw, Benjamin	649		Washington	189	743	17 Apr 1786	2554	2 May 1780	66	171	Lying on Station Camp Creek	
Shaw, Daniel	161		Tennessee	2560	1419	26 Oct 1786	1794	27 Apr 1785	66	31	On the head of Wolf Branch &c	
Shaw, Francis	1272		Western District	200	1210	20 Dec 1791	1234	27 Feb 1779	77	356	On both sides of Duck River	yes
Shaw, Harmon	024	Dillenberry, Redmon	Sumner	640	240	4 Dec 1795	4335	19 Sep 1797	89	330	On a branch of Big Limestone	
Shaw, James	1275		Davidson	640	83	10 Jul 1788	146	16 Jan 1784	66	421	On waters of Mackersfield Creek	yes
Shaw, James	1437	Purnell (?), Wm.	Davidson	320	87	10 Jul 1788	651	6 Jan 1785	68	230	Adjoining river on S by Nelsons on the N	
Shaw, James	1441	Redwell, Robt.	Davidson	320	169	10 Jul 1788	652	6 Jan 1785	68	231	A beech on W/S South Cross Cr	
Shaw, John	1005	Roberson, Elijah	Sumner	640	126	26 Mar 1795	3376	28 Jun 1788	86	375	Beg hickory on S Cross Creek	
Shaw, John	156		Eastern District	250	188	14 Jan 1793	95	26 Feb 1778	79	288	On the Cold Creek	yes
Shaw, Robert	1216	Armstrong, M.	Sumner	50		27 Aug 1795	8 [?]		89	407	On Lick Branch of Sinking Creek	
Shaw, Robert	1905	Elliot, John	Davidson	274	1773	20 May 1793	3295		81	72	On S side of Cumberland River	yes
Shaw, Robert, Ass.	981		Sumner	243	2446	22 Feb 1795	1526	24 Nov 1786	84	319	On waters of Red River	yes

Claimant:	File #:	Assignee:	County:	Acres:	Grant:	Grant Date:	Entry:	Entry Date:	Bk:	Pg:	Location by Stream Name:	Military:
Shaw, Williams	1010	Best, John	Davidson	640	1027	18 May 1789	3442		63	343	On N side of Cumberland River	yes
Shaw, Zacharias	230	Marshall, John	Sumner	640	1135	26 Nov 1789	1607		74	146	E side of E Fork of Stones River	yes
Shedden, Alexanders	1552		Green	200	1217	8 Apr 1794	1479	21 Jul 1779	82	152	On N side of French Broad River	
Shelbey, David	459		Sullivan	200	338	10 Nov 1784	638	10 Jul 1780	69	190	Stephen Rentfroes & John Crotchets line	
Shelbey, Evan	1245		Davidson	640	210	10 Jul 1788	369	23 Mar 1786	66	414	On Askers Creek beg an elm tree	
Shelby, Avan	129		Washington	640	297	24 Oct 1782	84	26 Feb 1778	44	297	On both sides of Buffalow Creek	
Shelby, David	1901	Hay, David	Davidson	2200 (?)	136	27 Apr 1793	669	24 Jan 1785	81	37	On Arringtons Creek	
Shelby, David	2185	Armstrong, M.	Sumner	48.5	303	20 Jul 1796			88	441	E/S Middle Fork of Station Camp Cr	
Shelby, David	2185	Shelby, David	Davidson	320	11	18 Aug 1787	506	2 Jul 1784	68	125	On the waters of Sulphur Fork	
Shelby, David	435		Sullivan	100	314	10 Nov 1784	152	16 Feb 1780	69	181	On N side of Holstin River	
Shelby, David, Ass.	1198		Sumner	640	2761	20 Jul 1796			88	461	On W side of Drakes Creek	yes
Shelby, David, Ass.	1205		Sumner	400	160	26 Mar 1795		29 Nov 1792	89	90	On Middle Fork of Goose's Creek	yes
Shelby, David, Ass.	276		Sumner	640	1268	10 Dec 1790	1919	6 Sep 1785	74	355	Branch that runs into Drakes Cr	yes
Shelby, David, Ass.	536		Sumner	1000	1730	20 May 1793	1138	22 Aug 1785	81	61	N side of Cumberland River &c	yes
Shelby, David, Ass.	537		Sumner	640	173	20 May 1793	2122	22 Oct 1785	81	61	On W Fork of Station Camp Creek	yes
Shelby, E. & J. Montgomery	1292		Davidson	640	257	10 Jul 1788	433	10 May 1784	66	427	On N side of Cumberland River &c	
Shelby, Evan	056		Sullivan	640			1196.,1197	8 Feb 1779			On Cainey Creek	
Shelby, Evan	059		Sullivan	425			1198	8 Feb 1779			S side Holston River	
Shelby, Evan	129		Washington	640	297	24 Oct 1782	84	26 Feb 1778	44	297	On both sides Buffalow Creek	
Shelby, Evan	1361	Standley, Robert	Davidson	1200	44	8 Oct 1787	241	6 Feb 1784	68	139	On Stewarts Creek	
Shelby, Evan	1617		Davidson	428	1347	10 Dec 1790	1106		74	381	N side of Cumberland	yes
Shelby, Evan	538	Hedgpeth, John	Davidson	640	510	15 Sep 1787	1662		63	184	N side of Cumberland River	yes
Shelby, Evan, Sr.	057		Sullivan	408			2052	23 Oct 1779			On Caney Creek	
Shelby, Evan, Sr.	058		Sullivan	203			2071	25 Oct 1779			On both sides of Beaver Creek	
Shelby, Evan, Sr.	060		Sullivan	400			1195	8 Feb 1779			On Caney Creek	
Shelby, Evan, Sr.	061		Sullivan	396			1199	10 Feb 1779			On Big Creek beg at a red oak	
Shelby, Isaac	1033		Davidson	640	7	17 Apr 1786	501	25 Jun 1784	66	36	Matersons Cr at two sugar trees	
Shelby, Isaac	1078		Hawkins	400	805	10 Apr 1797	1285	16 Mar 1779	91	570	N side of Holston River	
Shelby, Isaac	1371		Davidson	500 (500	54	8 Oct 1787	240	6 Feb 1784	68	143	A large hickory red oak & dogwood	
Shelby, John	0112		Sullivan	400			1524	13 Aug 1779			On N side of Holson River	
Shelby, John	1353		Davidson	2500	3	8 Oct 1787	166	24 Jan 1784	68	136	Bet at a sugar tree	
Shelby, John	24		Sullivan	100	35	23 Oct 1782	1611	13 Sep 1779	43	254	On Sinking Creek	
Shelby, John	489		Sullivan	300	500	18 May 1789	1432	9 Jun 1779	71	11	On N side of Holesons River &c	
Shelby, John	500		Sullivan	200	511	18 May 1789	1433	9 Jan 1779	71	16	In Carters Valley	
Shelby, John	505		Sullivan	509	523	7 Apr 1790	150	16 Feb 1780	71	280	Beg at a white oak	
Shelby, John	69		Washington	640	237	23 Oct 1782	301	6 Aug 1778	44	263	Beg at a large poplar &c	
Shelby, John, Sr.	584		Sullivan	346 (376	582	29 Jul 1793	753	10 Mar 1781	76	474	Inc plantation sd Shelby now lives	
Shelby, Moses	1384		Davidson	1200	67	8 Oct 1787	242	6 Feb 1784	68	148	Beg at four Mulberry trees &c	
Shelby, Moses	2191		Davidson	50	180	26 Mar 1795		7 Oct 1786	86	380	On E side of Stones River	
Shelby, Philip	269		Washington	100	137	23 Oct 1782	490	9 Oct 1778	47	67	N side of Watauga River	
Sheldon, David	1011	Armstrong, Martin	Hawkins	200	331	29 Dec 1796			90	192	N side Hoston River	
Shell, Arnold	2		Sullivan	200	123	23 Oct 1782	1798	12 Jun 1781	43	297	S side Holston River	
Shell, Arnold	58		Sullivan	450	69	23 Oct 1782	718	19 Dec 1778	43	272	On S side of Holston River	
Shelley, David	1770	Goodson, James	Davidson	640	1553	14 Jan 1793	1756		79	270	On N side of Cumberland River	yes
Shelley, David	447		Sumner	640	350	27 Nov 1792	761	22 Aug 1785	81	9	On Bledsoes Creek	

Claimant:	File #:	Assignee:	County:	Acres:	Grant:	Grant Date:	Entry:	Entry Date:	Bk:	Pg:	Location by Stream Name:	Military:
Shelton, David	125		Western District	3000	128	10 Jul 1788	678	28 Oct 1783	67	330	On Beaverdam Creek	
Shelton, David	1311		Davidson	640	276	10 Jul 1788	536	19 Jul 1784	66	433	A maple on bank of Cumberland	
Shelton, David	1589	Long, William	Davidson	640	1260	10 Dec 1790	1002		74	352	On waters of Round Lick Creek	yes
Shelton, David	471	Thompson, Nathan	Davidson	640	443	15 Sep 1787	764		63	163	S side of Cumberland River	yes
Shelton, David, Ass	768		Sumner	274	2208	20 May 1793	235	Nov 1783	81	170	On N side of Cumberland River	yes
Shelton, David, Ass.	350		Sumner	274	1436	20 Dec 1791	236	18 May 1791	77	360	On the Round Lick Branch	yes
Shelton, Lewis	70		Sullivan	285	81	23 Oct 1782	717	19 Dec 1778	43	277	On Horse Creek	
Shelton, Stephen	833		Washington	250	647	10 Nov 1784	1468	12 Jul 1779	69	151	On N Fork of Kendricks Creek	
Shepard, John	058	Hobbs, Moses heirs	Middle District	640			2927					
Shepard, John	059	Sorrel, Thomas heirs	Middle District	640			2961					
Sheppard, Benjamin	378	Curganus, Jeremiah	Davidson	640	356	15 Sep 1787	2304		63	132	Both sides Middle Fork Drakes Cr	yes
Sheppard, Benjamin	379	Betts, Jonathan	Davidson	640	351	15 Sep 1787	2309		63	132	W side of E Fork of Drakes Creek	yes
Sheppard, Benjamin	380	Colby, Absalmon	Davidson	640	352	15 Sep 1787	2306		63	133	On both sides of Large Creek	yes
Sheppard, Benjamin	381	Saunderlin, Thomas	Davidson	640	353	15 Sep 1787	2338		63	133	East Fork of Drakes Creek	yes
Sheppard, Benjamin	382	Cator, John	Davidson	640	354	15 Sep 1787	2323		63	133	East Fork of Drakes Creek	yes
Sheppard, Benjamin	383	Robertson, Willoughby	Davidson	640	355	15 Sep 1787	2319		63	134	3rd large creek of Big Barren	yes
Sheppard, Benjamin	384	Lee, Peter	Davidson	640	356	15 Sep 1787	2214		63	134	E Fork of Drakes Creek	yes
Sheppard, Benjamin	385	Griffin, Lamon	Davidson	640	357	15 Sep 1787	2339		63	134	West Fork of Drakes Creek	yes
Sheppard, Benjamin	386	Goodin, Enos	Davidson	640	358	15 Sep 1787	2328		63	135	S side of Big Barren River	yes
Sheppard, Benjamin	387	Covenan, Benjamin	Davidson	640	359	15 Sep 1787	2335		63	135	W Fork of Drakes Creek	yes
Sheppard, Benjamin	388	Midget, Jacob	Davidson	640	360	15 Sep 1787	2301		63	135	On Main Fork of Big Barren	yes
Sheppard, Benjamin	389	Galloway, Richard	Davidson	640	361	15 Sep 1787	2322		63	136	W side of E Fork of Drakes Creek	yes
Sheppard, Benjamin	390	Pickles, Richard	Davidson	274	362	15 Sep 1787	2311		63	136	N side of Cumberland River	yes
Sheppard, Benjamin	391	Hammons, Abraham	Davidson	640	363	15 Sep 1787	2336		63	136	E side of E Fork of Drakes Creek	yes
Sheppard, Benjamin	392	Batts, Sampson heirs	Davidson	640	364	15 Sep 1787	2320		63	137	E Fork of Drakes Creek	yes
Sheppard, Benjamin	393	Guatney, Joshua	Davidson	640	365	15 Sep 1787	2334		63	137	W/S Middle Fork of Drakes Creek	yes
Sheppard, Benjamin	394	Pugh, Richard heirs	Davidson	640	366	15 Sep 1787	2330		63	137	On both sides E Fork of Drakes Creek	yes
Sheppard, Benjamin	398	Basded, Jacob	Davidson	640	370	15 Sep 1787	2332		63	139	N side of Cumberland River	yes
Sheppard, Benjamin	399	Fairfax, William heirs	Davidson	640	371	15 Sep 1787	2310		63	139	W Fork of Drakes Creek	yes
Sheppard, Benjamin	400	Jackson, Roberson heirs	Davidson	640	372	15 Sep 1787	2303		63	139	E Fork of Drakes Creek	yes
Sheppard, Benjamin	561	Gaylord, Aaron	Davidson	640	533	15 Sep 1787	2317		63	192	Middle Fork of Drakes Creek	yes
Sheppard, Benjamin	562	Flood, Zachariah	Davidson	640	534	15 Sep 1787	2318		63	192	S side of Big Barren River	yes
Sheppard, Benjamin	696	Dukes, Elisha	Davidson	1000	669	8 Dec 1787	2347		63	237	Small or empties N/S Tennessee	yes
Sheppard, Benjamin	697	Grogan, John	Davidson	1000	670	8 Dec 1787	2315		63	237	On Bizzells Salleen	yes
Sheppard, Benjamin	698	Gitt, Wm heir of Jesse	Davidson	1000	671	8 Dec 1787	2302		63	237	To join an entry of John Holleys	yes
Sheppard, Benjamin	699	Jennett, Lewis	Davidson	1000	672	8 Dec 1787	2307		63	237	Small Creek named Hays Creek	yes
Sheppard, Benjamin	700	Fairfax, Frederick	Davidson	640	673	8 Dec 1787	2326		63	238	On N side of Cumberland River	yes
Sheppard, Benjamin, Ass.	569		Sumner	640	1806	20 May 1793	2305	30 Nov 1792	81	81	On waters of Dixons Creek	yes
Sheppard, Benjamin, Ass.	570		Sumner	640	1807	20 May 1793		30 Nov 1792	81	81	On waters of Dixons Creek	yes
Shepard, Jno.	061	Harris, Joab heirs	Middle District	640	2923		2912					
Sheppard, Jno.	1033		Sumner	640	2570	8 Mar 1796	294	15 Aug 1792	88	190	On Obeys River	yes
Sheppard, Jno., Ass.	1028		Sumner	640	2565	8 Mar 1796	2971	15 Aug 1792	88	188	On Obeys River	yes
Sheppard, Jno., Ass.	1029		Sumner	640	2566	8 Mar 1796	2644	15 Aug 1792	88	188	On waters of Obeys River	yes
Sheppard, Jno., Ass.	1030		Sumner	640	2567	8 Mar 1796	2910	15 Aug 1791	88	189	On waters of Obeys River	yes
Sheppard, Jno., Ass.	1031		Sumner	640	2568	8 Mar 1796			88	189	On Obeys River	yes

Claimant:	File #:	Assignee:	County:	Acres:	Grant:	Grant Date:	Entry:	Entry Date:	Bk:	Pg:	Location by Stream Name:	Military:
Sheppard, Jno., Ass.	1032		Sumner	640	2569	8 Mar 1796	2643		88	190	On waters of Obeys River	yes
Sheppard, John	01	Allison, David	Sumner	1714	3750	8 Jan 1795					On headwaters of Flinns Creek	yes
Sheppard, John	05		Knox	640	2407	12 Dec 1794			84	298	On Obeys River	
Sheppard, John	057	Finley, Abraham heirs	Middle District	640			2913					
Sheppard, John	059	Kite, William	not given	640			2856	15 Aug 1792			On Obeys River	
Sheppard, John	060	Washington, Dred	not given	640			2969	15 Aug 1792			On waters of Obeys River	
Sheppard, John	061	Winborn, John	not given	640							On Obeys River	
Sheppard, John	062	Filigena, Wm heirs	Middle District	640			2848					
Sheppard, John	062	Wingfield, Jacob	not given	640			2966	15 Aug 1792			On Obeys River	
Sheppard, John	063	Hicks, Wm.	not given	640			2932	15 Aug 1792			On Obeys River	
Sheppard, John	063		Middle District	640								
Sheppard, John	064	Hicks, John	not given	640			2931	15 Aug 1792			On waters of Obeys River	
Sheppard, John	064	Hobbs, Isaac heirs	Middle District	640			2928					
Sheppard, John	064	Hughes, George	Not given	640			2849	15 Aug 1792			On Obeys River	Yes
Sheppard, John	065	Hughs, George	not given	640			2849	15 Aug 1792			On Obeys River	
Sheppard, John	066	Harrewood, Thomas heirs	Middle District	640			2805					
Sheppard, John	066	Tilton, Richard	not given	640			2962	15 Aug 1792			Waters of Obeys River	
Sheppard, John	067	Harris, John	not given	640			2922	15 Aug 1792			On Obeds River	
Sheppard, John	067	Hunter, Timothy	Middle District	640			2926					yes
Sheppard, John	068	Garrett, Jesse heirs	Middle District	640			2916					
Sheppard, John	068	Laster, Josiah	not given	640			2857	15 Aug 1792			On Obeds River	
Sheppard, John	069	Gooding, Wm.	not given	640			2921	15 Aug 1792			On Obeys River	
Sheppard, John	069	Lawrence, Josiah	Middle District	640			2859					
Sheppard, John	070	Dundels, Hugh heirs	Middle District	640			2911					
Sheppard, John	070	Morgan, James	not given	640			2862	15 Aug 1792			On Obeys River	
Sheppard, John	14		Knox	640	2416	12 Dec 1794			84	304	On Obeys River	
Sheppard, John	2220	Allison, David	Davidson	1714	2522	8 Dec 1795			88	277	On headwaters of Flinns Creek	yes
Sheppard, John	4		Hawkins (Knox)	640	2416	12 Dec 1794			84	304	On Obeys River	
Sheppard, John	6		Knox	640	2408	12 Dec 1794			84	298	On Obeys River	
Sheppard, John	620	Gatlin, John	Sumner	640	1892	20 May 1793	906	4 Jun 1795	81	98	On S side Cumberland River	yes
Sheppard, John	620	Gatlin, John	Sumner	640	1819	20 May 1793	906	4 Jun 1795	81	98	S/S of Cumberland River	yes
Sheppard, John	7		Knox fr. Hawkins	640	2409	12 Dec 1794			84	299	On Obeys River	
Sheppard, John	7		Knox	640	2409	12 Dec 1794			84	299	On Obeys River	
Sheppard, John	872		Hawkins	640	2399	1 Jan 1795			84	99	On waters of Obeys River	
Sheppard, John	896		Hawkins	640	2410	12 Dec 1794			84	300	On Obeys River	
Sheppard, John	9		Knox	640	2411	12 Dec 1794			84	300	On Obeys River	
Sheppard, John, Ass.	08		Knox	640	2410	12 Dec 1794			84	300	On Obeys River	
Sheppard, John, Ass.	10		Knox	640	2412	12 Dec 1794			84	301	On waters of Obeys River	
Sheppard, John, Ass.	11		Knox	640	2413	12 Dec 1794			84	302	On Obeys River	
Sheppard, John, Ass.	12		Knox	640	2414	12 Dec 1794			84	302	On Obeys River	
Sheppard, John, Ass.	13		Knox	640	2415	12 Dec 1794			84	303	On Obeys River	
Sheppard, John, Ass.	5		Hawkins	640	2407	12 Dec 1794			84	298	On Obeys River	
Sheppard, John, Ass.	871		Hawkins	640	2398	1 Dec 1794			84	99	On waters of Obeys River	
Sheppard, John, Ass.	872		Hawkins now Kn	640	2399	1 Jan 1795			84	99	On waters of Obeys River	
Sheppard, John, Ass.	894		Hawkins	640	2408	12 Dec 1794			84	298	On Obeys River	

Claimant:	File #:	Assignee:	County:	Acres:	Grant:	Entry:	Grant Date:	Entry Date:	Bk:	Pg:	Location by Stream Name:	Military:
Sheppard, John, Ass.	895		Hawkins	640	2409		12 Dec 1794		84	299	On Obeys River	
Sheppard, John, Ass.	897		Hawkins	640	2411		12 Dec 1794		84	300	On Obeys River	
Sheppard, John, Ass.	898		Hawkins	640	2412		2 Dec 1794		84	301	On waters of Obeys River	
Sheppard, John, Ass.	899		Hawkins	640	2413		12 Dec 1794		84	302	On Obeys River	
Sheppard, John, Ass.	900		Hawkins	640	2414		12 Dec 1794		84	302	On Obeys River	
Sheppard, John, Ass.	901		Hawkins	640	2415		12 Dec 1794		84	303	On Obeys River	
Sheppard, John, Ass.	902		Hawkins	640	2416		12 Dec 1794		84	304	On Obeys River	
Sheppard, Martha	168		Middle District	2000	178	1042	20 Dec 1791	29 Oct 1783	75	227	On Richland Creek	
Sheppard, Martin Gardner	778	Jackson, Jeremiah heirs	Davidson	640	751		11 Jul 1788		63	264	Waters of Sulphur Fork of Red R	yes
Sheppard, Nancy	2043	Newell, John	Davidson	640	2063	1504	20 May 1793		81	140	On N side of Cumberland River	yes
Sheppard, Nancy	2044	Carrol, William	Davidson	640	2064	1754	20 May 1793		81	140	2nd creek that the boundary line crosses	yes
Sheppard, Nancy	2045	Mewshaw, John	Davidson	640	2065	1494	20 May 1793		81	140	On N side Cumberland on N Cross Creek	yes
Sheppard, Nancy	2084	Herring, Jacob heirs	Davidson	640	2284		20 May 1793		81	187	On the first creek	yes
Sheppard, Nancy	2085		Davidson	640	2286	1497	20 May 1793		81	188	On a small creek of Duck River	yes
Sheppard, Nancy	2090	Robertson, Hardy	Davidson	640	2297	2085	20 May 1793		81	190	On E Fork of Stones River	yes
Sheppard, Nancy	2093	Cotton, Ephraim	Davidson	640	2311	1752	20 May 1793		81	193	On head of Jinings Creek	yes
Sheppard, Nancy	2095	Clark, Jno heir of Josiah	Davidson	640	2313	2088	20 May 1793		81	194	On W Fork of Bledsoes Creek	yes
Sheppard, Nancy	2098	Crab, Richard	Davidson	640	2323	1751	20 May 1793		81	196	On E Fork of E Fork of Stones R	yes
Sheppard, Nancy	2099	Kirkland, John heir of Wm	Davidson	640	2324		20 May 1793		81	196	1st creek continental line crosses	yes
Sheppard, nancy	2100	Orr, Samuel heirs	Davidson	640	2325		20 May 1793		81	196	2nd creek continental line crosses	yes
Sheppard, Nancy	2101	Floyd, Joseph	Davidson	640	2326	1766	20 May 1793		81	196	2nd or cont line crosses aft Stones	yes
Sheppard, Nancy	2102	Chester, Robert	Davidson	640	2327	1495	20 May 1793		81	197	On waters of Duck River	yes
Sheppard, Nancy	693	Bennett, Joseph	Davidson	640	666	2090	8 Dec 1787		63	236	Small cr or on N/S Tennessee River	yes
Sheppard, Nancy	694	Parker, John heir of Wm.	Davidson	640	667	2086	8 Dec 1787		63	236	On Hayses Creek	yes
Sheppard, Nancy	695	Cooper, Jacob heir of Nat.	Davidson	640	668	2086	8 Dec 1787		63	236	On N side of Tennessee River	yes
Sheppard, Nancy	695	Hynes, Hardy heirs	Davidson	640	697	1760	11 Jul 1788		63	245	On waters of Sulphur Fork	yes
Sheppard, Nancy	718	Holladay, Hathoock	Davidson	640	691	1763	11 Jul 1788		63	243	On waters of Sycamore	yes
Sheppard, Nancy	719	Carraway, Thomas	Davidson	640	692	1865	11 Jul 1788		63	244	On waters of Caspers Creek	yes
Sheppard, Nancy	720	Johnston, Hardy	Davidson	640	693	1769	11 Jul 1788		63	244	On waters of Sulphur Fork	yes
Sheppard, Nancy	721	Ballard, James heirs	Davidson	640	694	1350	11 Jul 1788		63	244	On waters of Sycamore	yes
Sheppard, Nancy	72?	Metts, Willis heirs	Davidson	640	695		11 Jul 1788		63	245	On waters of Sulphur Fork	yes
Sheppard, Nancy		Lambert, Henry	Davidson	640	696	2082	11 Jul 1788		63	245	On waters of Kaspers Creek	yes
Sheppard, Nancy		Hynes, Hardy	Davidson	640	697	1760	11 Jul 1788		63	245	On waters of Sulphur Fork	yes
Sheppard, Nancy, Ass.			Sumner	640	2066	2087	20 May 1793	29 Oct 1792	81	141	On W Fork of Roaring River	yes
Sheppard, Nancy, Ass.	747		Sumner	640	2149	1500	20 May 1793	24 Nov 1792	81	160	On Salt Lick Fork &c	yes
Sheppard, Nancy, Ass.	818		Sumner	640	2293	2084	20 May 1793	19 Oct 1792	81	190	Situated on E branch of Roaring R	yes
Sheppard, Nancy, Ass.	819		Sumner	640	2294	2091	20 May 1793	29 Oct 1792	8	190	Bet Middle & E Fork of Goose Cr	yes
Sheppard, Nancy, Ass.	830		Sumner	640	2310	2089	20 May 1793	29 Oct 1792	81	193	On E waters of Roaring River	yes
Sheppard, Nancy, Ass.	836		Sumner	640	2322	2083	20 May 1793		81	195	On E waters of Roaring River	yes
Sheppard, Nancy, Ass.	837		Sumner	640	2328	1522	20 May 1793	24 Nov 1792	81	197	On Salt Lick Fork of Big Barren R	yes
Sheppard, Valentine	019	Armstrong & Donelson	Middle District	640		2690						yes
Sheppard, William	506	Davis, Samuel	Davidson	357	478	1205	15 Sep 1787		63	173	N side of Cumberland River	yes
Sheppard, William	507	Castle, Thomas	Davidson	274	479	1855	15 Sep 1787		63	174	N side Cumberland River	yes
Sheppard, William	988	Baxter, Samuel	Davidson	1000	1005	267	18 May 1789		63	337	On N side of Cumberland River	yes
Sheppard, William, Ass.	663		Sumner	640	1983	2826	20 May 1793	24 Nov 1792	81	120	On both sides of Hickmans Creek	yes

Claimant:	File #:	Assignee:	Acres:	Grant:	County:	Location by Stream Name:	Bk:	Pg:	Entry Date:	Entry:	Grant Date:	Military:
Sheppard, William, Ass.	779		640	2233	Sumner	On waters of Hickmans Creek	81	176	24 Nov 1792	2791	20 May 1793	yes
Sheppard, William, Ass.	797		640	2258	Sumner	On waters of Hickmans Creek	81	183	24 Nov 1792	2827	20 May 1793	yes
Sheppard, Wm.	116	Simmons, Wm.	640	1613	Tennessee	N side of Cumberland River	76	318	24 Dec 1785	3261	23 Feb 1793	
Sheppard, Wm.	284		1000	238	Middle District	On S side of Elk River	82	146	27 Apr 1784	1928	30 Dec 1793	
Sheppard, Wm. Etal	1675	Bushop, Wm.	640	1600	Davidson	Both sides of South Harpeth River	76	312		2795	23 Feb 1793	yes
Sheppard, Wm. Etal	1676	Carson, John	640	1601	Davidson	S/S Harpeth below Fletcher's Lick	76	313		2797	23 Feb 1793	yes
Sheppard, Wm. Etal	175		5000	185	Middle District	On Richland Creek	75	231	27 Oct 1783	581	20 Dec 1791	
Sheppeard, John, Ass.	175		640	2414	Hawkins (Knox)	On Obeys River	84	302			12 Dec 1794	
Sherkey, Patrick	269		6.25	164	Eastern District	In an island in Holston River	83	430			22 Feb 1795	
Sherkey's Patrick	077	Armstrong, M.	6.25		Tennessee	In an island in Holston River			16 May 1794	16		
Sherkley, Robert	1323	McConnel, Robert	1000	3123	Sumner	Waters of Big Barren	90	413	15 May 1797	4702	14 Sep 1797	yes
Sherlock, Demsey	025	Dillenberry, Redman	640		Sumner	On E Fork &c			14 Oct 1797	4474		yes
Shermentine, Hezekiah	567	Peyton, John	228	1800	Sumner	On both sides of the road &c	81	79	7 Jul 1792	3731	20 May 1793	yes
Sherrel, Adam	213		400	81	Washington	On both sides of Onion Branch	47	39	31 Jul 1778	279	23 Oct 1782	
Sherrell, Adam	536		300	538	Green	On N side of Nolachuckey River	65	535	22 Oct 1783	178	20 Sep 1787	
Sherrell, John	801		250	606	Green	On Dry Fork of Caney Branch	68	264	27 Oct 1783	554	23 Aug 1788	
Sherrell, Martha	286		100	153	Washington	S side of Nolachuckey River	47	74	23 Dec 1778	761	24 Oct 1782	
Sherri, Aquilla	535		300	537	Green	Lying on Cove Creek	65	535	23 Oct 1783	369	20 Sep 1787	
Sherrin, William	45		750	47	Middle District	On both sides of Duck River	67	428	11 May 1784	2151	10 Jul 1788	
Sherrod, Robert	563	Gilmore, Charles	640	535	Davidson	N side of Cumberland River	63	192		1979	15 Sep 1787	yes
Sherrol, Samuel	272		312	140	Washington	S side of Nolachuckey River	47	68	7 Dec 1778	660	23 Oct 1782	
Sherwood, Edward	1870	Bond, John	640	1608	Davidson	On head branches of Stones Cr	81	19		1592	27 Apr 1793	yes
Shield, John	935		200	849	Green	Red oak on S/S Nolachuckey River	76	121	31 Mar 1783	963	17 Nov 1793	
Shields, Henry	1036		300	986	Washington	Beg at a white oak & hicory	79	280	14 Mar 1781	2819	14 Jan 1793	
Shields, Henry	1113		100	1071	Washington	On N side of Rich Mountain	81	500	9 Nov 1779	1512	27 Nov 1793	
Shields, John	1046		200	1273	Green	Beg post oak on line of Vent Fines	76	493	7 Jun 1784	1355	29 Jul 1793	
Shields, John	1326		400	1176	Green	Beg at a white oak &c	78	411	22 Apr 1779	728	12 Jan 1793	
Shields, John	1457		500	1217	Green	Beg at a post oak & pine	81	507	28 Oct 1783	761	27 Nov 1793	
Shields, John	1460		640	1220	Green	Beg at a white oak	81	508	29 Oct 1783	888	27 Nov 1793	
Shields, John	1461		400	1221	Green	Beg at a poplar tree	81	509	25 Jun 1784	1236	27 Nov 1793	
Shields, John	1471		1000	1235	Green	Beg at a white oak	81	573	17 Jan 1784	1404	18 Jul 1794	
Shields, John	403		400	524	Hawkins	On S side of Holston River	79	499	9 Mar 1780	2460	27 Jan 1793	
Shields, John	481		100	666	Washington	Beg at a white oak tree	59	354	3 Apr 1784	3003	15 Jul 1786	
Shields, John	880		50	866	Washington	Beg at a large white oak &c	73	97	7 Aug 1783	2931	5 Jul 1790	
Shields, John etal	106		640	1073	Washington	Beg on a black oak	81	501	22 Nov 1788	2358	27 Nov 1793	
Shields, John etal	1115	McAllister, John	640	1073	Washington	Beg a black oak	81	501	22 Nov 1788	2358	27 Nov 1793	
Shields, John etal	980		640	467	Green	Beg at an oak &c	76	467			29 Jul 1793	
Shields, Patrick	106		50	117	Sullivan	On Clear Fork of House Creek	43	294	13 Sep 1779	1392	23 Oct 1782	
Shilks, Lewis	423	Cobb, Jesse	640	2469	Tennessee	On Main E Fork of Guesses Creek	81	433	28 Aug 1784	1174	31 Dec 1793	yes
Shipley, Ely	0111		300		Sullivan	On N side of Holson River			24 Aug 1780	677,-189		
Shipley, Richard	344		400	484	Sullivan	On the waters of Fall Creek	67	488	22 Apr 1780	445	10 Jul 1788	
Shober, Gottlieb	528		1000	337	Middle District	S side of Elk River	90	235	10 Oct 1793	1019	1 Mar 1797	
Shockley, Isaac	1934	Robertson, James	640	1754	Davidson	Joins Barnabas Boyles on East	81	67	29 Aug 1793	1818	29 Aug 1793	yes
Shoecraft, Abraham	172	Nelson, Robert	640	1447	Tennessee	Joining the W boundary &c	77	362	1 Sep 1785	2092	20 Dec 1791	yes
Shoemakey, John	633		200	581	Sullivan	Inc a spring at Eatons Ridge	80	375	1 Jul 1780	629	27 Jun 1793	

Earliest Tennessee Land Records

Page 368

Claimant:	File #:	Assignee:	County:	Acres:	Grant:	Grant Date:	Entry:	Entry Date:	Bk:	Pg:	Location by Stream Name:	Military:
Shore, William	651		Green	200	692	11 Jul 1788	251	31 Dec 1786	66	458	On Grassey Creek	
Shores, Jacob, Ass.	693		Sumner	640	2056	30 May 1793	3602	4 Jun 1791	81	138	On S side of Cumberland River	yes
Shores, John	287		Green	170	289	20 Sep 1787	252	22 Oct 1783	65	455	On Lick Creek	
Short, James	413		Green	150	415	20 Sep 1787	323	31 Aug 1785	65	492	Below Poor Valley Creek &c	
Short, James	427		Hawkins	150	316	5 Jun 1793	1398	23 Jun 1784	80	158	Lying on the Barrons	
Short, Peter	130		Middle District	1075	132	10 Jul 1788	553	27 Oct 1783	67	473	On the waters of Duck River	
Short, William	162	Tatom, Howell	Tennessee	640	1423	20 Dec 1791	2627	30 Sep 1785	77	357	S side of Cumberland River	yes
Shorte, Abraham	315	McCulloh, Benjamin	Tennessee	640	2016	20 May 1793	2493	20 Sep 1785	81	128	On S side Cumberland River	yes
Shoults, Christian	1089		Washington	229	1039	27 Nov 1792	826	29 Dec 1778	80	201	Including of an old improvement	
Shoun, Sarah	697		Sullivan	150	642	6 Jan 1795	883	1 Dec 1778	83	180	S side of Holstein River	
Shrite, John	0108		Sullivan	400			2080	28 Oct 1779			Joining Anthony Bledsoe	
Shrites, John	0107		Sullivan	400			2080	29 Oct 1779			On waters of Steele Creek	
Shutes, David	86		Eastern District	50	75	17 Nov 1790	742	12 Feb 1789	76	168	S/S Holstein waters Honeycutts Cr	
Shults, Martin	301		Sullivan	160	440	9 Aug 1787	1531	19 Aug 1779	61	459	On S side of Holstein River	
Shurley, John	889		Washington	639	982	22 Nov 1790	237	2 Jun 1778	74	196	On Cherokee Creek	
Shute, Jesse	470		Davidson	640	442	15 Sep 1787	624		63	162	S side of Cumberland River	yes
Shute, John	264		Sullivan	400	403	9 Aug 1787			61	422	Joins Anthony Bledsoes entry#207	
Shute, Thomas, Ass.	1047		Sumner	1000	2526	8 Dec 1795	1100		88	279	Near head of Flinns Creek	yes
Shute, William	095	McCain, James	Sumner	640			510	22 Oct 1785		629	On E branch of Drakes Creek	yes
Shutes, John	676		Sullivan	400	624	19 Jul 1794			81	629	Joins where Anthony Bledsoe lived	
Sides, Peter	434	Armstrong, M.	Tennessee	150	172	9 Jan 1794	576	20 Aug 1785	81	446	ON Red River	
Sidewell, Richard	533		Hawkins	400	406	29 Jul 1793	403	8 Apr 1780	80	278	On head springs of Knob Creek	
Siduskey, Emanuel	801		Washington	640	615	10 Nov 1784	932	1 Jan 1779	69	142	Beg at a marked black oak	
Siduskey, Emanuel	802		Washington	100	616	10 Nov 1784	2706	28 Dec 1780	69	143	On N E cor his former survey	
Sikes, James	065	Sugg, Geo. A.	Davidson	640			2686	5 Mar 1791			Bet. Whites Creek & Marrowbone	yes
Simerlin, John	062		Washington	300			734	22 Dec 1778			On Little & Main Doe Rivers	
Simmon, Felix	1964	Harget, Frederick	Davidson	274	1827	20 May 1793	576		81	85	On S side of Cumberland River	yes
Simmon, Leonard & Phillip	1385	Bushnell, E. & Wm. Dobbin	Green	100	1240	27 Jan 1793	1411	12 May 1785	79	509	On Little Chuckey	yes
Simmons, Aliason	659		Davidson	1000	632	15 Sep 1787	1660		63	224	On waters of Stones River	yes
Simmons, Benjamin	630	Wills, George	Davidson	428	602	15 Sep 1787	672		63	215	On a branch of the Sulphur Fork	yes
Simmons, David	20		Giles	200	51	15 Jul 1812	2720	4 Jan 1781	126	447	On Big Creek	
Simmons, Holden	1403	Hendricks, Jeremiah	Sumner	640	3333	6 Dec 1797	3911	12 Oct 1796	97	52	S side of Cumberland River &c	yes
Simmons, Isaac	922	Nash, William	Davidson	640	938	18 May 1789	2235		63	322	1st creek above Stones Lick Cr	yes
Simmons, Islar	135	Hawkins, Phillips & Campbe	Tennessee	428	1647	23 Feb 1793	3125	13 Dec 1785	76	335	W side of Red River &c	yes
Simmons, James	15	Sanders, James	Davidson	640	772	11 Jul 1788	3027	20 Sep 1787	63	271	On Cumberland River	yes
Simmons, John	746	Bryan, Morgan	Davidson	274	719	11 Jul 1788	1557		63	253	On Beaverdam Creek	yes
Simmons, Joshua	90	Brekon, J. C.	Tennessee	640	1355	10 Dec 1790	2879	10 Dec 1790	74	384	On S side of Cumberland River	yes
Simmons, Leonard	1578		Green	150	1329	4 Feb 1795	314	10 Mar 1780	83	397	On waters of Little Chuckey River	
Simmons, Malia	060	Donelson, John	Sumner	640			1946	8 Jun 1796			N branches of Cedar Lick Creek	yes
Simmons, Richard	842	Wilson, James	Sumner	282	2345	20 May 1793	3700		81	201	On waters of Sinking Creek	yes
Simmons, William	116	Sheppard, William	Tennessee	640	1613	23 Feb 1793	3261	24 Dec 1785	76	318	N side of Cumberland River &c	yes
Simms, Drury	25	Bowman, William	Sumner	640	782	11 Jul 1788	2818	23 Mar 1787	63	274	On N side of N Fork of Red River	yes
Simms, Job	1677		Green	574	1382	20 Jul 1796	1375	17 Nov 1789	88	492	On both sides of Lick Creek	
Simms, Job	707		Green	574	748	11 Jul 1788			66	477	On Lick Creek &c	
Simons, Peter	827	Blount, Reading	Sumner	640	2306	20 May 1793	1637	22 Aug 1785	81	192	On both sides of War Trace Creek	yes

Claimant:	File #:	Assignee:	County:	Acres:	Grant:	Grant Date:	Entry:	Entry Date:	Bk:	Pg:	Location by Stream Name:	Military:
Simpkins, Abel	1051		Washington	300	1001	27 Nov 1792	1989	19 Oct 1779	80	177	On Doe River	
Simpkins, Joseph	2446	Goodrich & Wheaton	Davidson	640	3288	6 Dec 1797	4427		98	166	On Dog Creek of Harpeth River	yes
Simpson, Andrew	1404		Green	200	1216	27 Nov 1792	153	20 Sep 1787	80	156	On the Dry Fork of Lick Creek	
Simpson, Andrew	489		Green	250	491	20 Sep 1787	2559	18 May 1780	65	515	On S side of Lick Creek &c	
Simpson, Dred	823	Brock, Joseph	Davidson	640	826	17 Jan 1789	3482		63	291	On N side of Cumberland River	yes
Simpson, Henry	0110		Sullivan	200			1987	19 Oct 1779			On waters of Reedy Creek	
Simpson, Henry	408		Sullivan	100	287	10 Nov 1784	1790	2 Oct 1779	69	172	On N side of Holston River &c	
Simpson, Henry	413		Sullivan	200	292	10 Nov 1784	1075	8 Jan 1779	69	174	On waters of Reedy Creek	
Simpson, Henry	506		Sullivan	200	524	7 Apr 1790	1815	6 Oct 1779	71	287	On the waters of Reedy Creek	
Simpson, Henry	609		Sullivan	200	564	26 Dec 1791	187,-1789	2 Oct 1779	77	307	On waters of Reedy Creek	
Simpson, Henry	696		Sullivan	300	612	12 Jun 1794	1790,-1987	2 Oct 1779	82	184	On waters of Reedy Creek	
Simpson, Jack	1326	McConnel, Robert	Sumner	1000	3126	14 Sep 1797	4450	15 May 1797	90	414	On waters of Big Barren	yes
Simpson, John	036		Hawkins				1627				Affidavit of Entry	
Simpson, John	245	Saunders, James	Davidson	640	231	7 Mar 1786	49		63	85	N side of Cumberland River	yes
Simpson, Moses	320	Rice, John & others	Davidson	640	306	13 Jun 1787	2055		63	114	Beg at a sycamore	yes
Simpson, Samuel	618	Woodard, Noah	Davidson	640	590	15 Sep 1787	901		63	211	On N fork of Red river	yes
Simpson, Smith	668	Funk, Henry	Tennessee	274	3342	6 Dec 1797	3268		97	58	S side of McAdows Creek	yes
Simpson, Thomas	2		Sumner	640	6	27 Sep 1794	1987		62	319	On waters of Mattersons Creek	
Simpson, Thomas, Ass.	905		Sumner	452	2473	31 Dec 1793	3096	22 Dec 1792	81	434	On S side of Cumberland River	yes
Simpson, William	1095		Davidson	640	69	17 Apr 1786	30	30 Dec 1783	66	57	On the head of Little Harpeth &c	
Simpson, William	1197		Davidson	640	174	17 Apr 1786	31	30 Nov 1783	66	191	S/S Cumberland R & waters Mill Cr	
Simpson, William	573		Sullivan	400	571	29 Jul 1793	2037	27 Oct 1779	76	471	On the waters of Reedy Creek	
Sims, Bartlet	094		Green	640			990	19 May 1779			N side of Holston River	
Sims, Bartlet	669		Hawkins	300	574	12 Jul 1794	1880	7 Oct 1779	81	594	On N side of Holston River	
Sims, Bartlett	447		Sullivan	90	326	10 Nov 1784			69	185	On N side of Holston River	
Sims, Jobe	0100		Green	100			415	14 Apr 1780			Beg on a conditional line	
Sims, Thomas	294	Montflorence, James Cole	Davidson	640	280	22 Mar 1787	2057		63	103	Beg at a red oak & 2 sugar trees	yes
Simson, Henry	666		Sullivan	200	614	9 Jul 1794	1957	3 Feb 1780	81	626	On waters of Reedy Creek	
Simson, Leonard & Philip	1385		Green	100	1240	27 Jan 1793	1411	12 May 1785	79	509	On Little Chuckey	
Singleton, Henry	103	Welch, John	Tennessee	640	1523	10 Apr 1792	861	14 May 1784	75	509	On S side of Cumberland River	yes
Singleton, John	928		Green	300	842	17 Nov 1790	246	22 Oct 1783	76	119	S side of Clinch River	
Sitgreaves, John	25		Western District	5000	25	10 Jul 1788	2299	25 May 1784	67	290	On N Fork of Loosahatcher River	
Sitgreaves, John	789	Williams, Samuel	Davidson	640	792	Jul 1788	1456		63	277	On E Fork of Buffalow Creek	yes
Sitgreaves, Joseph	041	Combs, William	Tennessee	640		30 Sep 1765	2642				On the waters of Bartons Creek	
Sitgreaves, Joseph	160		Western District	5000	160	10 Jul 1788	2300	25 May 1784	67	359	On N Fork of Loosahatcher River	yes
Siven, Joseph	987	Blount, Reading	Sumner	640	2452	22 Feb 1795	2546	30 Sep 1792	84	322	On Main Fork of Obeys River	
Skaggs, James	753		Hawkins	150	593	7 Jul 1794	1469	10 Jun 1779	82	208	On the N side of Holston River	yes
Skelton, Ralph	160		Hawkins	200	93	16 Nov 1790	151	15 Feb 1780	77	183	On S side of Holston River	
Skerret, Isidore	854	Zarlett, Zachariah	Davidson	640	862	17 Jan 1789			63	300	On E Fork of Stones River	
Skerrett, Isidore	866	Zarlett, Timothy	Davidson	640	880	17 Jan 1789	3398		63	305	On E Fork of Stones River	yes
Skidmore, John	194		Hawkins	178	127	16 Nov 1790	519	29 Apr 1780	77	192	On N side of Holston River &c	
Skinner, Samuel	528	Barton, Samuel	Sumner	640	1721	20 May 1793	2231	18 Nov 1792	81	58	On waters of Bartons Creek	yes
Skipper, Hardy	1122	Harris, Edward	Sumner	640	2628	4 Jun 1796	2775	1 Jun 1793	88	343	Joining sd Harris survey	yes
Skipper, Joseph	1948	Harget, Frederick	Davidson	640	1782	20 May 1793	1253		81	74	On E Fork of Jones Creek	yes
Skipper, Nathan	587	Harget, Frederick	Sumner	274	1828	20 May 1793	1252	22 Dec 1792	81	85	On S side of Big Harpeth River	yes

Claimant:	File #:	Assignee:	County:	Acres:	Grant:	Grant Date:	Entry:	Entry Date:	Bk:	Pg:	Location by Stream Name:	Military:
Skipton, Andrew	982	Brehon, James G.	Davidson	640	999	18 May 1789	2882		63	336	Beg at the S E corner &c	yes
Slade, Nathaniel	14	Booman, William	Sumner	640	771	11 Jul 1788	2544	22 Jan 1787	63	270	On N side of N Fork of Red River	yes
Slade, William	1005		Davidson	1607	1022	18 May 1789	511		63	342	On Cedar Lick Creek	yes
Slaughter, Constantine	1265	Hickman, Thomas	Sumner	640	2941	1 Mar 1797	2586	14 Oct 1795	90	213	Waters of Hickmans Creek	yes
Slawson, Ezekiah	317	Sanders, James	Davison	632	303	13 Jun 1787	2583		63	113	On heads W branches Drakes Cr	yes
Sloan, Archibald	1114		Washington	200	1072	27 Nov 1793	99	26 Feb 1778	81	501	On N Fork of Nine Mile Creek	
Sloan, Archibald	827		Washington	200	641	10 Nov 1784	2707	20 Dec 1780	69	149	On E side of his former entry	
Sloan, Archibald	988		Washington	640	960	26 Dec 1791	721	21 Dec 1778	77	295	Beg at a white oak &c	
Sloan, David	326	Graham, Joseph	Tennessee	640	2075	20 May 1793	1882	11 Jul 1785	81	143	On 2nd large creek &c	yes
Sloan, John	185	Paul, Steph	Tennessee	640	1465	4 Jan 1792			77	367	S side of Cumberland River	
Sloan, John	467		Middle District	1000	406	17 Dec 1794	2176	13 May 1784	84	264	On S side of Duck River	
Sloss, John	217		Middle District	5000	203	14 Jan 1793	2		79	287	On Elk River	
Sloss, John, Ass.	466		Sumner	640	1620	27 Apr 1793	211	10 Sep 1788	81	22	On Smiths Fork of Caney Fork	yes
Sloss, John, Ass.	803		Sumner	640	2268	20 May 1793	917	28 Nov 1792	81	184	On S side of Cumberland River	yes
Slothart, Robert	022		Montgomery	640			4091	1797			On the head of a branch	yes
Slothart, Robt, Ass.	024		Montgomery	274			4733	-- Apr 1797			On the Piney Fork	yes
Slothart, Robt.	023		Montgomery	640			4741	1 Apr 1797			S side of Piney River of Elks River	yes
Slothart, Robt. Ass.	025		Montgomery	640			4106				On the head of a draft &c	yes
Slump, Frederick & Molloy	551		Tennessee	640	353	10 Apr 1797	57		90	280	S side of Cumberland River	
Smalley, James	1764	Hays, Robert	Davidson	640	1544	14 Jan 1793	2239		79	268	To join Robert Barnett	yes
Smalling, Solomon	790		Sullivan	100	722	2 Dec 1796	580	3 Jun 1781	91	277	Beg at 3 white oaks	
Smart, John	742	Lanier, James	Davidson	640	715	11 Jul 1788	3481		63	251	S side of Rives Creek	
Smart, Thomas	540	Donelson, William	Sumner	640	1740	20 May 1793	3577	8 Aug 1795	81	64	On both sides of Cedar Lick Creek	yes
Smeeler, Jacob	1557		Green	400	1229	12 Jun 1794	1557	13 Aug 1779	82	183	On the head of Holleys Creek	
Smiley, Jonathan	70	Anderson, Daniel	Tennessee	640	1310	10 Dec 1790	2884	30 Sep 1785	74	369	On N side of Cumberland River	yes
Smiley, Andrew	1507		Green	100	1268	12 Jul 1794	100	21 Oct 1783	81	584	On head of Blue Spring Branch	
Smiley, Andrew	1529		Green	100	1289	17 Jul 1794			81	605	On waters of Lick Creek	
Smith, Aaron	666		Hawkins	100	571	12 Jul 1794	622	24 Jun 1780	81	593	On S side of Holston River	
Smith, Abraham	574	Benton, Juliah heirs	Tennessee	640	3021	10 Apr 1797	3629		90	302(7)	N side of Cumberland River	
Smith, Alexander	188		Hawkins	100	121	16 Nov 1790	132	12 Feb 1780	77	190	On S side of Holston River	
Smith, Alexander	887a	Thompson, Jason	Sumner	640	2425	31 Dec 1793	1352	13 Nov 1790	81	408	On E waters of Spring Creek	yes
Smith, Arthur	47		Sullivan	250	58	23 Oct 1782	2054	27 Oct 1779	43	266	On Kindricks Creek	
Smith, Arthur	758	Isbell, Thomas	Davidson	640	731	11 Jul 1788	1988		63	257	S side of Big Barren River	yes
Smith, Bartholomew	441		Eastern District	320	298	19 Jul 1798	2188	12 Nov 1779	91	617	S side of Richland Creek	
Smith, Bartholomew&Pleasan	1000		Hawkins	200	699	12 Nov 1795	1587	12 Sep 1779	89	416	On N side of Tennessee River	
Smith, Benjamin	122		Western District	3000	122	10 Jul 1788	2403	25 May 1784	67	327	On N Fork of Forked Deer River	
Smith, Benjamin	157		Western District	1500	157	10 Jul 1788	1626	26 May 1784	67	357	On Spring Cr branch of Long Fork	
Smith, Benjamin	157		Western District	3000	31	10 Jul 1788	2404	25 May 1784	67	292	On the waters of Forked Deer River	
Smith, Benjamin	165		Western District	165	165	10 Jul 1788	2401	25 May 1784	67	361	On the Forked Deer River &c	
Smith, Benjamin	2273	Donelson, John	Davidson	274	2751	20 Jul 1796	1116		88	457	On Stones Creek	yes
Smith, Benjamin	233		Davidson	420 (428	219	7 Mar 1786	663		63	81	On waters of Stones River	yes
Smith, Benjamin	352	Tuton, William	Davidson	224 (274	337	29 Aug 1787	1633		63	125	N side of Cumberland River	yes
Smith, Benjamin	401		Western District	5000	400	9 Jan 1795	2413	25 May 1784	83	188	S waters S Fork of Forked Deer R	
Smith, Benjamin	402		Western District	5000	401	9 Jan 1795	2415	25 May 1784	83	188	On S Fork of Forked Deer River	
Smith, Benjamin	403		Western District	5000	402	9 Jan 1795	2406	25 May 1784	83	189	N waters of S Fork of Forked Deer River	

Earliest Tennessee Land Records

Claimant:	File #:	Assignee:	County:	Acres:	Grant:	Grant Date:	Entry:	Entry Date:	Bk:	Pg:	Location by Stream Name:	Military:
Smith, Benjamin	404		Western District	5000	403	9 Jan 1795	2627	25 May 1784	83	189	On the S Fork of Forked Deer Riv	
Smith, Benjamin	405		Western District	3000	404	9 Jan 1795	2408	25 May 1784	83	190	On waters S Fork of Forked Deer	
Smith, Benjamin	406		Western District	2000	405	9 Jan 1795	2420	25 May 1784	83	190	N waters S Fork of Forked Deer R	
Smith, Benjamin	407		Western District	3000	406	9 Jan 1795	2407	25 May 1784	83	191	S Fork of S Fork of Forked Deer R	
Smith, Benjamin	408		Western District	5000	407	9 Jan 1795	2421	25 May 1784	83	191	On S Fork of Forked Deer River	
Smith, Benjamin	409		Western District	5000	408	9 Jan 1794	2628	25 May 1784	83	192	On the Forked Deer River	
Smith, Benjamin	410		Western District	5000	409	9 Jan 1795	2409	25 May 1784	83	192	On S Fork of Forked Deer River	
Smith, Benjamin	411		Western District	3000	410	9 Jan 1795	2419	25 May 1784	83	193	S waters of S Fork of Forked Deer	
Smith, Benjamin	412		Western District	5000	411	9 Jan 1795	2416	25 May 1784	83	193	On N side of S Forked Deer River	
Smith, Benjamin	413		Western District	5000	412	9 Jan 1795	2414	25 May 1784	83	194	On S Fork of Forked Deer River	
Smith, Benjamin	414		Western District	5000	413	9 Jan 1795	2410	25 May 1784	83	194	S waters S Fork of Forked Deer R.	
Smith, Benjamin	415		Western District	5000	414	9 Jan 1795	2418	25 May 1784	83	195	On S waters of S Fork of Forked Deer River	
Smith, Benjamin	416		Western District	5000	415	9 Jan 1795	2417	25 May 1784	83	195	On waters S Fork of Forked Deer R	
Smith, Benjamin	417		Western District	5000	416	9 Jan 1795	2411	25 May 1784	83	196	N side of S Fork of Forked Deer R.	
Smith, Benjamin	418		Western District	5000	417	9 Jan 1795	2412	25 May 1784	83	196	On N waters of S Fork of Deer R	
Smith, Benjamin	84		Western District	4000	84	10 Jul 1788	2405	5 May 1784	67	313	On waters of Forked Deer River	
Smith, Benjamin	89		Western District	5000	89	10 Jul 1788	2402	25 May 1784	67	315	On Forked Deer River &c	
Smith, Britian	1449		Green	200	1259	27 Nov 1792	473	25 Oct 1783	80	174	On the head of Bent Creek	
Smith, Britian, Jr.	352		Green	500	354	20 Sep 1787	475	7 Oct 1785	65	473	On the S side of Holstein River	
Smith, Brtin	220		Sullivan	100	207	10 Nov 1784	785	27 May 1781	55	217	On S side of Holstein River &c	
Smith, Britton	1440	Reed, Phelps	Sumner	3000	369	17 Feb 1800	1052	6 Apr 1798	106	370	On waters of Wolf River	yes
Smith, Britton	317		Green	200	319	20 Sep 1787	859	29 Oct 1783	65	464	On S Fork of Holsten River &c	
Smith, Bryan	237		Davidson	342	223	7 Mar 1794	147		63	82	On waters of Stones River	yes
Smith, Charles	1169	Harris, Edward	Sumner	640	2674	4 Jun 1796	2436	1 Jun 1795	88	359	Joining sd Harris	yes
Smith, Chas.	44	Williamson, George	Robertson	640			1787	17 Oct 1796			On waters of Brush Creek	yes
Smith, Clement	245	Smith, Thomas	Tennessee	640	1629	27 Apr 1793	589	21 Apr 1784	81	24	On W Fork of Red River	
Smith, Daniel	1373		Davidson	3140	56	8 Oct 1787	40 & 41	31 Dec 1783	68	144	N/S Cumberland at mouth of Drakes Creek	
Smith, Daniel	1491	Allen, Jesse	Davidson	220	1044	27 Nov 1789	3227		74	46	On S side of Cumberland River	yes
Smith, Daniel	189	Armstrong, M.	Sumner	50	60	18 May 1789	1684		71	221	On the E branch of Drakes Creek	
Smith, Daniel	274	McLaughlen, Samuel	Davidson	274	2363	20 May 1793	849		81	204	On E side of Harpeth	yes
Smith, Daniel	409		Middle District	1000	348	17 Dec 1794	1572	1 Apr 1784	84	228	On N side of Duck River	
Smith, Daniel	586	Mosier, Samuel heirs	Davidson	640	558	15 Sep 1787	2300		63	200	S side of Cumberland River	yes
Smith, Daniel, Ass.	13		Sumner	640	770	11 Jul 1788	195	9 Mar 1784	63	270	Head E branches of Drakes Creek	yes
Smith, Daniel, Ass.	2127		Davidson	26	146	7 Jan 1794			81	399	On S side of Cumberland River	
Smith, Daniel, Ass.	3		Sumner	274	760	11 Jul 1788	2998	3 Oct 1787	63	267	Head E branches of Drakes Creek	yes
Smith, Drury, heirs	072		not given	640							no plat	
Smith, Edward	1164		Washington	200	1122	7 Jul 1794	918	1 Jan 1779	81	617	On Doe River	
Smith, Edward	491		Washington	100	754	16 Aug 1787	735	26 Apr 1779	64	136	Beg at a marked black walnut &c	
Smith, Edward	739		Washington	600	553	10 Nov 1784	325	1 Apr 1784	69	124	Beg at a marked beech tree	
Smith, Ephraim	247		Hawkins	640	235	26 Dec 1791	18 & 19	8 Feb 1780	77	325	On N side of Clinch River	
Smith, George	03		Jefferson	250			104	26 Feb 1778				
Smith, George	092		Sullivan	100			1814	6 Oct 1779			Beg a white oak on Jno. Bayleys line	
Smith, George	1007		Green	250	1234	29 Jul 1793			76	485	On the Panther Creek	
Smith, George	637		Sullivan	100	585	27 Jun 1793			80	377	Beg at a white oak	
Smith, Henry	1657	Foster, Anto. & W. T. Lewis	Davidson	640	1574	23 Feb 1793	11		76	300	On waters of Whites Creek	yes

Claimant:	File #:	Assignee:	County:	Acres:	Grant:	Entry:	Entry Date:	Bk:	Pg:	Location by Stream Name:	Military:
Smith, Hezekiah	561	Walker, G. & J. Deaderick	Sumner	228	1783	1941	10 Jun 1792	81	75	On N side of Cumberland River	yes
Smith, Jacob	580	Narress, David heirs	Tennessee	640	3027	2678	10 Apr 1797	90	304	S side of Cumberland River	
Smith, James	2366	Beard, Lewis	Davidson	640	3081	3737	19 Jul 1797	90	383	On Leepers Fork of Harpeth	yes
Smith, James	244		Hawkins	400	232		26 Dec 1791	77	324	On N side of Clinch Mountain &c	
Smith, James	260	Cotten, Thomas	Davidson	640	246	723	7 Mar 1786	63	90	S side of Cumberland River	yes
Smith, James	415		Sullivan	200	294	1806	10 Nov 1784			Place where James Blythe lived	
Smith, James, heir of Joseph	086	Cotton, Thomas	Davidson	640	2512	874	6 Oct 1779	69	174	On waters of Stones River	
Smith, Jeremiah	1508		Davidson	274	1065	526	7 Apr 1784	74	111	On Overalls Creek	
Smith, Jno. & Jas.Mayberry	452		Hawkins	640	330		26 Nov 1789 24 Jun 1793	80	195	On the S side of Holston River	
Smith, Joab	067	Sugg, Geo. A.	Davidson	640		2477	29 Jun 1791			On dividing ridge &c	yes
Smith, Joel	435	Blount, Reading	Davidson	640	407	2545	15 Sep 1787	63	151	S branches of Sycamore Creek	yes
Smith, John	030	Glasgow, James	Davidson	640		1115	25 Aug 1785			On waters of Sulphur Fork	yes
Smith, John	043		Tennessee	640		1376	11 Nov 1784			S side of Cumberland River	
Smith, John	1239		Green	500	1089	268	1 Nov 1786	78	357	Beg at a white oak	
Smith, John	1291		Washington	100	1196	839	12 Jan 1793	89	417	On S side of Noleychuckey River	yes
Smith, John	1993	Buchanan, John	Davidson	640	1919	1099	12 Nov 1795	81	104	On waters of Mill Creek	
Smith, John	22		Green	300	85	1053	20 May 1793	58	446	On the N of Nolihuckie [sic] River	yes
Smith, John	2349	Howell, Henry	Davidson	640	3011	3642	1 Nov 1786	90	298	Waters of Little Harpeth	yes
Smith, John	2350	Paul, James heirs	Tennessee	640	3012	3182	10 Apr 1797	90	298	On Lick Creek	
Smith, John	2351	Jones, Binford	Davidson	640	3013	3940	30 Oct 1783	90	299	S side of Cumberland River	yes
Smith, John	260		Hawkins	250	247	2252	10 Apr 1797	77	398	N side of Holstein River &c	
Smith, John	261		Hawkins	400	248	1246	22 Nov 1779	77	399	N/S Holstein R Dry Fork of Turkey	yes
Smith, John	302	Breakey, Andrew	Davidson	640	288		12 Jun 1784	63	107	On waters of Sulphur Fork	
Smith, John	31		Green	500	94	1	3 May 1787	58	455	On Robertsons Creek	yes
Smith, John	400		Sumner	640	411	2797	1 Nov 1786	80	345	On Main E Fork of Roaring River	
Smith, John	406		Washington	100	398	571	21 Oct 1783	52	264	On Little Limestone &c	
Smith, John	508	Armstrong, Martin	Davidson	640	480	3170	- Nov 1792	63	174	S side Cumberland	yes
Smith, John	572	Graham, Peter heirs	Tennessee	640	3010	774	27 Feb 1781	90	297	S side of Cumberland River	
Smith, John	691		Sullivan	100	639	487	19 Dec 1785	81	634	Bet. Jno. Rheas & McCaland	yes
Smith, John	767	Whitfield, Bryant	Sumner	640	2202	937	21 Apr 1781	81	169	On the waters of Stones River	
Smith, John	818	Payne,Wm & Jos. Cobb	Washington	100	632	111	21 Dec 1792	69	147	On waters of Little Limestone	yes
Smith, John & others	1093		Hawkins	640	822	488	1 Jan 1779	91	615	On Blairs Creek	
Smith, John, Ass	903		Sumner	640	2459	3735	26 Feb 1778	81	429	On S side of Cumberland River	yes
Smith, John, Ass.	1408		Sumner	274	3340	2726	12 Dec 1792	97	57	Waters of Station Camp	
Smith, John, Ass.	908		Sumner	640	2477	672	26 Jan 1796	81	435	On S side of Cumberland River	yes
Smith, John, Ass.	913		Sumner	274	2482	267	25 Nov 1789	81	437	On Round Lick Creek	yes
Smith, John, Sr.	539		Green	500	541	751	19 Jul 1797	65	537	S/S Holsten R on branch of Fall Cr	yes
Smith, Joseph	125		Sullivan	150	37	441	31 Dec 1793	43	323	On Clear Fork of Horse Creek &c	
Smith, Joseph	190		Sullivan	44	197		6 Dec 1797	53	157	On S side of Holston River	
Smith, Joseph	2313	Cotton, Thomas	Davidson	640	2512	384	31 Dec 1793	89	415	On waters of Stones River	yes
Smith, Joseph	31		Sullivan	50	42	383	22 Oct 1783	43	257	White oak John Crawfords E cor	
Smith, Micajah	61		Sullivan	30	72	2342	23 Sep 1787	43	273	On the Big Ridge &c	
Smith, Michael	81	Hays, Thomas	Tennessee	640	1337	651	10 Dec 1790	74	378	On S side of Cumberland River	yes
Smith, Michael	165		Davidson	640	151	882	7 Mar 1786	63	57	A small branch of Cumberland	yes
Smith, Michael	225		Washington	374	93		21 Dec 1778	47	45	On both sides of Stoney Creek	yes

Earliest Tennessee Land Records

Claimant:	File #:	Assignee:	County:	Acres:	Grant:	Grant Date:	Entry:	Entry Date:	Bk:	Pg:	Location by Stream Name:	Military:
Smith, Nehemiah	766	Hickman, Thomas	Davidson	640	739	11 Jul 1788	2776		63	260	On waters of 1st Creek &c	yes
Smith, Nicholas	395		Green	335	397	20 Sep 1787	174	8 Jan 1785	65	484	On White Horn a cr of Bent Creek	
Smith, Oliver	149	Hair, William	Tennessee	640	1401	20 Dec 1791	1906	15 Jul 1785	77	351	On both sides of Pine River	
Smith, Oliver	155	Callson, William	Tennessee	640	1409	20 Dec 1791	2640	30 Sep 1785	77	353	On both sides of Pine River	
Smith, Oliver	166	Hair, John	Tennessee	640	1430	20 Dec 1791	1907	18 May 1788	77	359	On Pine River	
Smith, Oliver	1986	Brown, William	Davidson	274	1893	20 May 1793	3717		81	99	On S side of S Harpeth	yes
Smith, Oliver	1985	Pace, Demsey	Davidson	640	1890	20 May 1793	1894		81	98	On Duck River beg at an ash	yes
Smith, Oliver	2007	Pitman, Ison heirs	Davidson	640	1952	20 May 1793	2682		81	112	On both sides of S Harpeth	yes
Smith, Oliver	2010	Murrell, Jacob	Davidson	640	1656	20 May 1793	1900		81	113	On S W side of Big Harpeth	yes
Smith, Oliver	2018	Ward, David	Davidson	640	1989	20 May 1793	1890		81	121	S W side Big Harpeth on Jones Cr	yes
Smith, Oliver	2105	Long, Heywood heirs	Davidson	640	2335	20 May 1793			81	199	On both sides of South Harpeth	yes
Smith, Owen	356	Johnston, Thomas	Tennessee	640	2186	20 May 1793	1847	15 Jan 1785	81	167	On waters of Sulphur Fork &c	yes
Smith, Peter	356	Williams, Willoughby	Middle District	1000	2405	5 Feb 1795	2622		84	185	On E side of W Fork of Obeys R	yes
Smith, Peter	73		Sullivan	300	84	23 Oct 1782			43	279	A poplar on the side of large ridge &c	
Smith, Redick	589	Woodard, Thomas	Davidson	640	561	15 Sep 1787	1231		63	201	N side of Red River	yes
Smith, Reuben	142	Daugherty, George	Davidson	640	128	14 Mar 1786	424		63	50	E Fork of Buffaloe Creek	yes
Smith, Robert	1184		Green	200	1027	26 Dec 1791	636	10 Jul 1780	77	291	On waters of Tuckahoe Creek	
Smith, Robert	13		Middle District	5000	15	10 Jul 1788	1883	24 May 1784	67	413	Lying on Duck River &c	
Smith, Robert	1952	Rice, Daniel	Davidson	640	1791	20 May 1793	277		81	77	On waters of Big Harpeth River	yes
Smith, Robert	1960	Hudson, Chamberlain	Davidson	640	1805	20 May 1793	1464		81	80	On Hays Creek	yes
Smith, Robert	1975		Davidson	1828	1876	20 May 1793	188		81	95	On S side of Stones River	yes
Smith, Robert	474		Middle District	2640	266	6 Dec 1794	1794	23 Apr 1784	85	335	On N side of N Fork of Duck River	
Smith, Robert	475		Middle District	2000	267	6 Dec 1794	1797	23 Apr 1784	85	335	On N side of N Fork of Duck River	
Smith, Robert	608		Hawkins	200	482	29 Jul 1793	823	26 Jul 1781	80	296	On Buck Creek	
Smith, Robert	94		Hawkins	300	252	20 Dec 1791	16	24 Feb 1778	74	445	Joining John Smiths land	
Smith, Robert Washington	319		Middle District	2500	295	17 Dec 1794	1796	23 Apr 1784	83	335	S side of Duck River &c	
Smith, Robert Washington	459		Middle District	2000	398	17 Dec 1794	1795	23 Apr 1784	84	260	On N side of N Fork of Duck River	
Smith, Robert, Ass.	459		Sumner	640	3339	6 Dec 1797	3823	22 Dec 1795	97	56	Both sides of Falling Creek	yes
Smith, Robt.	302		Hawkins	300	265	24 Dec 1792	506	29 Apr 1780	78	449	On S side of Holston River	
Smith, Saml.	110		Sullivan	250	121	23 Oct 1782	1200	31 Dec 1778	43	296	On S side of Holston River &c	
Smith, Saml.	190	Robertson, James	Davidson	428	176	7 Mar 1786	169	10 Feb 1779	63	66	E side of W Fork of Harpeth River	
Smith, Saml.	646		Sullivan	100	594	27 Jun 1793	2180	11 Nov 1779	80	381	On waters of Indian Creek	
Smith, Saml., Sr.	30		Hawkins	400	62	7 Apr 1790	1235	7 Nov 1783	71	285	On S side of Holston River	
Smith, Samuel	138		Hawkins	50	172	26 Dec 1791	596	3 Jul 1779	75	172	In an island in Holson River	
Smith, Samuel	1510		Green	400	1271	12 Jul 1794	413	12 Apr 1780	81	585	On N side of Tennessee	
Smith, Samuel	346		Sullivan	57	486	10 Jul 1788	890	31 Dec 1778	67	489	Joins Solomon Smith & John Reley	
Smith, Samuel	81		Sullivan	630	92	23 Oct 1782	891	31 Dec 1778	43	282	On S side of Holston River	
Smith, Seth	1219		Green	200	1063	– May 1792	416	22 Sep 1778	77	407	On Stories Creek	
Smith, Solomon	380		Sullivan	400	259	10 Nov 1784	892	31 Dec 1778	69	165	On S side of Holstein River	
Smith, Stephen	1579	Nichols, John	Davidson	640	1240	10 Dec 1790	1788		74	345	In the fork of Red River	yes
Smith, Thomas	1382	Barton, Samuel	Sumner	1000	203	6 Dec 1797			97	32	S side of Cumberland River	yes
Smith, Thomas	2264	Donelson, Stockley	Davidson	465	2728	20 Jul 1796	1379		88	452	On waters of Leepers Fork	yes
Smith, Thomas	33	Crutcher, Anthony	Sumner	640	844	17 Jan 1789	303	28 Jul 1784	63	296	On N side of Cumberland River	yes
Smith, Thomas	482		Sullivan	200	492	17 Nov 1788	630	5 Jun 1780	70	10	Beg at a dogwood & white oak	
Smith, Thomas	568		Davidson	640	540	15 Sep 1787	1361		63	194	N side of Cumberland River	yes

Earliest Tennessee Land Records

Claimant:	File #:	Assignee:	County:	Acres:	Grant:	Grant Date:	Entry:	Entry Date:	Bk:	Pg:	Location by Stream Name:	Military:
Smith, Thomas	627		Sumner	100	1908	20 May 1793	2596	23 Sep 1785	81	102	On the Caney Fork River	yes
Smith, Thomas	643	Cummins, George	Sumner	640	1934		3325		81	108	S/S Cumberland River	yes
Smith, Thomas	739		Sumner	274	2134	20 May 1793	588	20 Aug 1785	81	157	On Bledsoes Creek	yes
Smith, Thomas	747		Washington	50.50	561	10 Nov 1784	2219	14 Nov 1779	69	127	Joining Gideon Moris &c	
Smith, Thomas	920	Hinds, John	Sumner	920	3142	14 Sep 1797		20 May 1797	90	420	On the Seventh Creek	yes
Smith, Thomas	947		Washington	100	924	17 Nov 1790	2903	23 Aug 1781	76	152	On the Island Fork	
Smith, Thomas	963		Washington	100	940	17 Nov 1790	2898	23 Aug 1781	76	157	Incl head spring David Powey's Br	
Smith, Thos. Hr of Clement	245		Tennessee	640	1629	27 Apr 1793	589	21 Apr 1784	81	24	On W Fork of Red River	
Smith, Tilghman	969		Green	164	883	17 Nov 1793	1372	17 Nov 1790	76	132	Beg at a black oak &c	
Smith, Tilman	1439		Green	50	1249	27 Nov 1792	39	6 May 1784	80	171	On a branch of Lick Creek	
Smith, William	080		not given	640			964				no plat	
Smith, William	1055		Hawkins	100	765	21 Jan 1797	217	21 Feb 1780	91	113	Waters of Swan Pond Creek	
Smith, William	1131		Hawkins	200	851	29 Jan 1798	377		96	7	S side of Clinch River	
Smith, William	118	Allen, John	Davidson	640	104	7 Mar 1786	599		63	42	E Fork of Buffaloe Creek	yes
Smith, William	1236		Davidson	640	201	10 Jul 1788		9 Oct 1784	66	412	E Fk of Mill Cr Beg at a white oak	
Smith, William	1375	Cook, Richard	Sumner	1000	3237	24 Nov 1797	1375	13 Jul 1797	94	171	On W Fork of Drakes Creek	yes
Smith, William	179		Hawkins	200	112	16 Nov 1790	217	21 Feb 1780	77	188	In the Piney Valley	
Smith, William	287		Sullivan	100	426	9 Aug 1787	2011	24 Oct 1779	61	445	On S side of Holston River	
Smith, William	373		Middle District	640	312	17 Dec 1794	1439	27 Jan 1784	84	212	On Cane Creek	
Smith, William	439		Green	150	441	20 Sep 1787	954	20 Jun 1785	65	499	On N side of Holston River	
Smith, William	444		Sullivan	41	323	10 Nov 1784	730	27 Jun 1781	69	184	On S side of Holston River	
Smith, William Bailey	480	Thompson, Robert	Sumner	480	1252	10 Dec 1790	1246	29 Sep 1787	74	349	On S side of Cumberland River	yes
Smith, Wm.	787		Washington	450	601	10 Nov 1784	1344	9 Apr 1779	69	138	Beg on W side of Rones Creek	
Smith, Wm. & John Davis	011		Knox	100							On waters of Swan Pond Creek	
Smithly, Thomas	255	Glass, George	Tennessee	320	127	27 Apr 1793	841	14 Dec 1792	81	35	On S side of Cumberland River	
Smithwick, Edmond	643	Cummins, George	Sumner	640	1934	20 May 1793	3325		81	108	On S side of Cumberland River &c	yes
Smithwick, James	1912	Tatum, Howell	Davidson	640	1680	20 May 1793	1157		81	49	On N side of Cumberland River	yes
Smyth, John	114	Clark, Lardner	Tennessee	640	1609	23 Feb 1793	2063	26 Aug 1785	76	317	On Wells Creek	yes
Sneed, Elbet	373		Washington	100	365	13 Oct 1783	1955	13 Oct 1779	52	249	On Little Limestone &c	
Snell, James	1136	Harris, Edward	Sumner	640	2642	4 Jun 1796	2764	1 Jun 1795	88	348	Joining sd Harris survey	yes
Snider, Frederick	527	Cypell, Robt.	not given	274	4999	15 Sep 1787	1641		63	180	West side of Wattrace Creek	yes
Snider, Michael	081		Sullivan	358			45	13 mar 1784			On waters of Whites Creek	
Snoddy, Thomas	810		Green	80	753	17 Nov 1797	2030	15 Mar 1788	94	152	Waters of Beaver Creek	
Snoddy, Thomas etal	1298		Green	100	1148	12 Jan 1793	791	18 Feb 1782	78	393	Waters of Sinking Fork of Long Cr	
Snoddy, William	1515		Davidson	200	1276	12 Jul 1794	804	28 Dec 1778	81	586	Waters of Sinking Fork of Long Cr	
Snodgrass, John	1183		Sullivan	640	160	17 Apr 1786	219	30 Jan 1784	66	188	On Middle Fork of Station Camp Cr	
Snodgrass, Robt., heirs of	410		Sullivan	174	289	10 Nov 1784	293	10 Mar 1780	69	173	Beg at a forked chestnut	
Snodgrass, William	0109		Sullivan	300			439	21 Apr 1780			On head waters of S Reedy Creek	
Snodgrass, William	567		Sullivan	100	550	17 Nov 1790	139	17 Mar 1789	76	195	Beg at a white oak &c	
Snodgrass, William	748		Sullivan	100	687	9 Dec 1795	1823	7 Oct 1779	89	396	S of the Ohio	
Snodgrass, William	825		Sullivan	640 (600)	768	17 Nov 1797	2211	12 Nov 1779	94	161	Beg 2 swamp white oaks & an ash	
Snodgrass, William	829		Sullivan	400	772	17 Nov 1797	236,439	28 Feb 1780	94	163	Beg at a white oak	
Snodgrass, William, Sr.	823		Sullivan	150	766	17 Nov 1797	618,-347	24 Mar 1780	94	160	Beg at a dogwood & hickory	
Snyder, Frederick	0117		Sumner	640				17 Mar 1784			On Drakes Creek	yes
Snyder, George etal	1264	Kindle, George	Washington	100	1202	4 Dec 1795	2985	8 Sep 1783	89	326	On S side of Little Limestone	

Claimant:	File #:	Assignee:	County:	Acres:	Grant:	Grant Date:	Entry:	Entry Date:	Bk:	Pg:	Location by Stream Name:	Military:
Scott, James	673		Sullivan	200	621	9 Jul 1794	189	25 Mar 1780	81	628	On N side of Holston River	
Scott, John	379		Washington	135	371	13 Oct 1783	1163	1 Feb 1779	52	251	On N side of Watavgo River	
Scott, John	419		Washington	150	411	13 Oct 1783	2378	27 Nov 1779	52	271	On N side of Wataughgar River	
Scott, John	724		Washington	150	538	10 Nov 1784	2761	6 Feb 1781	69	118	Beg at a small white oak	
Scott, John, Ass.	396		Sumner	640	407	27 Jun 1793	739	30 May 1785	80	343A	On S side of Cumberland River	yes
Solomon, Stephen	1400	Walker, Henry	Sumner	640	3329	6 Dec 1797	4380	29 Aug 1797	97	49	On 1st large fk of Round Lick Cr	yes
Somberland, James	270	Gerard, Charles	Tennessee	274	1767	20 May 1793	1284	20 Oct 1784	81	71	On S side of Cumberland River	yes
Sorrell, Thomas	059	Shepard, John	Middle District	640			2961					yes
Sotherland, David	235		Hawkins	150	222	26 Dec 1791	819	14 Jul 1781	77	320	On S side of Holston River &c	
Southerland, George	11	Saunders, James	Sumner	640	768	11 Jul 1788	3524	21 Sep 1787	63	269	On Bradleys Lick Creek	yes
Southerland, John	517	Boyd, Robert	Sumner	274	1695	20 May 1793	210	11 Sep 1792	81	52	On waters of Drakes Creek	yes
Southerland, William	2050	Dixon, Tilighman	Davidson	640	2125	20 May 1793	1519		81	155	On a branch of Stones Creek	yes
Southerlin, David	111		Hawkins	300	145	26 Dec 1791			75	161	On S side of Holston River	
Southrun, James	731		Washington	300	545	10 Nov 1784	1415	29 May 1779	69	120	Beg at a red oak	
Sowell, Lewis	2277	Buckanan, John	Davidson	640	2757	20 Jul 1796	1031		88	460	On waters of Harricane Creek	yes
Spaight, Jesse etal	1639	Gordon, Wm. & George	Green	1040	1342	27 Aug 1795	1764	7 Jun 1782	87	511	On waters of Spring Creek	
Spain, Austin	777		Sumner	428	2231	20 May 1793	3559	24 Nov 1792	81	176	On head waters of Hickmans Cr	yes
Spain, Eps.	749	Gerard, Charles	Sumner	1000	2152	20 May 1793	3560	10 Nov 1789	81	161	On S side of Cumberland River	yes
Spain, Thomas	533	Hickman, Thomas	Sumner	1000	1727	20 May 1793	3561	15 Aug 1792	81	60	On W side of Caney Fork	yes
Spain, William	757	Gerard, Charles	Sumner	1000	2165	20 May 1793	3562	10 Nov 1789	81	164	On S side of Cumberland River	yes
Spann, James	781	Winchester, James & Geor	Davidson	228	754	11 Jul 1788	3116		63	265	On E side of Bledsoes Creek	yes
Spann, Willis	133	Searcy, Reuben	Tennessee	228	1641	23 Feb 1793	883	19 May 1784	76	332	N side of Cumberland River	yes
Spar, Henry	263		Sullivan	200	402	9 Aug 1787	707	23 Nov 1780	61	421	Bet Robert Snodgrass & Simon Ellit	
Sparckman, Edward	429	Nickols, John	Davidson	640	401	15 Sep 1787	2579		63	149	N side of Cumberland River	yes
Sparkman, William	18	Brehon, James Gloster	Tennessee	640	1160	26 Nov 1789	2880	30 Sep 1785	74	162	On waters of Sulphur Fork	yes
Sparks, Samuel	608		Washington	50	702	26 Oct 1786	2901	1 Nov 1779	66	12	On Sinking Creek &c	
Spauldin, Edward	659	McCulloh, Benjamin	Sumner	640	1977	20 May 1793	3022	16 Nov 1792	81	118	On waters of Bledsoes Creek	yes
Spear, Seth	1513	Eaton, John	Davidson	640	1070	26 Nov 1789	3499		74	114	On N side of Cumberland River	yes
Spears, Thomas	025	Stothart, Robert	Montgomery	640			4106				On the head of a draft &c	
Spedman, Simon	1365	Tatum, Ho & Henry Wiggon	Sumner	640	3213	14 Sep 1797	4264	29 Jul 1797	92	10	Waters of Stones River &c	
Speer, Henry	656		Green	200	697	11 Jul 1788	148	10 May 1785	66	459	Bent Cr waters of Nolichucky	
Speight, Frances	686	Davis, Joshua	Sumner	640	2037	20 May 1793	2361	18 Nov 1792	81	133	On the Caney Fork	yes
Speight, Joseph	494	Coit, Farwell	Sumner	640	1662	23 Aug 1793	3769	27 Oct 1793	81	44	On waters of Cumberland	yes
Spence, Jacob	797		Green	100	602	23 Aug 1788	1218	22 Feb 1779	68	263	On Holleys Creek &c	
Spence, James	517	Hoggett, James	Davidson	228	489	15 Sep 1787	1741		63	177	N side of Cumberland River	yes
Spence, Job	512	Hadley, Joshua	Sumner	274	1689	20 May 1793	3207	12 Feb 1787	81	51	On forks of Cumberland & Oblds R	yes
Spencer, Thomas	188	Chester, David	Davidson	1000	174	7 Mar 1786	70		63	65	N side of Cumberland River	yes
Spencer, Thomas Sharpe	1448	Fletcher, Benjamin	Davidson	320	94	10 Jul 1788	273	13 Feb 1784	68	234	On the waters of Big Harper River	
Spencer, Thomas Sharpe	1449		Davidson	320	95	10 Jul 1788	272	13 Feb 1784	68	234	On the waters of Big Harper River	
Spencer, Thos.	1043		Davidson	640	17	17 Apr 1786	274	13 Feb 1784	66	39	On the Et of Station Camp Creek	
Spencer, Thomas	1116		Davidson	640	93	17 Apr 1786	277	13 Feb 1784	66	173	Lying both sides of Drakes Creek	
Spencer, William	1025	Molloy, Thomas	Davidson	640	1043	11 May 1789	2587		63	346	On N side of Cumberland River	
Spencer, Wm, heir of Hon'l	04		Grainger								Sam'l Spencer, Letters concerning	
Spierpoint, Joseph	1853	Mences, James	Davidson	640	1577	27 Apr 1793	569		81	12	N side of Cumberland River	yes
Spinns, James	462		Hawkins	200	334	29 Jul 1793	513	14 Feb 1781	80	259	N side of Holston River &c	

Claimant:	File #:	Assignee:	Acres:	Grant:	Grant Date:	Entry:	Entry Date:	Bk:	Pg:	Location by Stream Name:	Military:
Spinns, James	743		200	583	7 Jul 1794	144	15 Feb 1780	82	204	On N side of Holston River &c	
Spoolman, William	295	Phillips, P. & M. Campbell	1000	1314	10 Dec 1790	1675	23 Sep 1785	74	370	On McNeeleys Creek	yes
Sprite, Henry	635		466	583	27 Jun 1793	1693	21 Sep 1779	80	376	Where Jesse Maxwell lived	
Spruel, Richard	1474	Nichols, John	640	1050	27 Nov 1789	2581		71	283	On N side of Cumberland River	yes
Spurgeon, John	367		100	369	20 Sep 1787	1191	1 Nov 1783	65	477	On S side of Nolachuckey River	
Spurgin, John	812		194	755	17 Nov 1797	335	22 Mar 1780	94	153	N side of Holstein River	
Spurgin, William	494		400	505	18 May 1789	2352	16 Dec 1779	71	13	On S side of Holston River	
Spurgin, William	501		300	512	18 May 1789	1875	12 Feb 1780	71	17	On the S side of Holston River &c	
Spurr, Spencer	338	Taylor, Thomas	640	1389	20 Dec 1791	918	25 Nov 1789	77	348	S side of Cumberland River &c	yes
Spyers, Absolam	218		360	204	7 Mar 1786	128		63	75	N side of Cumberland River	yes
Squires, John	625	Stewart, Charles	320	3189	14 Sep 1797	358	4 Dec 1783	90	438	S side of Cumberland	
Stacey, Simon	422		100	310		2183	12 Nov 1779	80	151	S side of Holston River &c	
Stafford, Josiah	291	Cobb, Jesse	274	1921	27 Mar 1792	1483		81	105	On both sides of Red River	yes
Stallions, James	1920	Foster, Anthony	640	1715	20 May 1793	1743		81	57	On waters of W Harpeth	yes
Stamland, Robert, heir of Ben	1988		1000	1900	20 May 1793	1250		81	100	N/S Harpeth above mo Hunting Camp Cr	yes
Stanaland, James	1671	Robertson, Jas. & Jno. Dav	640	310	23 Feb 1793	1251		76	310	On Big Harpeth &c	yes
Stanbrough, Solomon	098		150			528	29 Apr 1780			On waters of Little Sinking Creek	
Stancel, Peter	1336	Lowe, Marvel	640	3136	14 Sep 1797	4444	15 May 1796	90	418	On Salt Lick Fork of Big Barron	
Standen, John	2062	Moran, John	503	2176	20 May 1793	3688		81	167	On S W side of Big Harpeth River	yes
Standfield, Thomas	821		606	635	10 Nov 1784	475 (9)	26 Feb 1778	69	148	Including the Old Indian Camp	yes
Standifer, William	892		300	155	22 Feb 1795			84	280	On N of Clinch River	
Standiford, Wm.	032	Armstrong, M.	300							N side Clinch River	
Standley, James	2011	McMoran, Domin[-?-]	274	1957	20 May 1793	1105		81	113	On waters of W Fork of Mill Creek	yes
Standley, John	554	Seymore, Solomon	228	526	15 Sep 1787	96		63	198	On Beaver Dam Creek	yes
Standley, Jonathan	046	Williams, Willoughby	274							S side of Cumberland River	yes
Standley, Robert	1617	Shelby, Evan	428	1347	10 Dec 1790	1282	29 Oct 1784	74	381	N side of Cumberland River	yes
Stanfield, (John) Thomas	501		300	503	20 Sep 1787	1106	7 May 1784	65	523	On a branch of Lick Creek	
Stanfield, William	1754		150	1431	30 Jun 1797	44	2 Sep 1778	92	58	Beg at an ash	
Stanley, Hancock	1170	Harris, Edward	640	2675	4 Jun 1796	45	1 Jun 1795	88	359	Joining said Harris	yes
Stanly, Robert	2450	Wheaton, Daniel	640	3294	6 Dec 1797	2772		98	170	On the E Fork of Swan Creek	yes
Starkey, William	31	Sanders, William	640	788	11 Jul 1788	4290	9 Feb 1787	63	276	On waters of Colins River	yes
Starn, Peter	576	Lanier, James	640	548	15 Sep 1787	805		63	197	S side of Barren River	yes
Starnes, Adam	997		150	1224	29 Jul 1793	3479	19 Sep 1778	76	484	On Lick Creek	
Starr, Adam	871		300	821	27 Nov 1789	405	28 Oct 1783	74	21	Beg at a white oak	
Starr, Hance	1857		640	1582	27 Apr 1793	664		81	13	On N side of Kerrs Creek	
Starr, Henry	038	Dillenberry, Redmon	640			3069	14 Oct 1797			On waters of Middle Fork &c	yes
State of Tennessee	0-					4472	20 May 1790			List of Returns	
Steadham, Tobias	07	Blount, John Gray	640			2817	30 Sep 1785			S side of Red River	yes
Stearn, William	1035		640	9	17 Apr 1786	118	15 Jan 1785	66	37	Red River Thos. Kilgores S E corner	
Stedham, Isaiah	401	Nelson, Robert	640	373	15 Sep 1787	2543		63	140	On Sulphur Fork of Red River	yes
Stedmore, George	329	Bledsoe, Anthony	640	1617	23 Feb 1793	3024	18 Nov 1792	76	320	W br of Middle Fork of Goose Cr	yes
Steed, Jesse	167		1500	167	10 Jul 1788	407	25 Oct 1783	67	362	On S side of Looshatcher River	
Steed, Jesse	555	Allison, David	357	1774	20 May 1793	549	7 Oct 1791	81	72	On 1st creek below Obids River	
Steed, Jesse	96		2560	82	14 Mar 1786	53		63	34	Waters Main W Fork of Harpeths River	yes
Steed, Jesse, Ass.	748		640	2151	20 May 1793	548	3 Feb 1790	81	161	On waters of Paun Lick Creek	yes

Claimant:	File #:	Assignee:	County:	Acres:	Grant:	Grant Date:	Entry:	Entry Date:	Bk:	Pg:	Location by Stream Name:	Military:
Steedman, John	1171	Harris, Edward	Sumner	640	2674 (76)	4 Jun 1796	3023	1 Jul 1795	88	359	Joining sd Harris	yes
Steedmore, Peter	670	Bledsoe, Anthony	Sumner	640	1997	20 May 1793	3026	18 Nov 1492	81	123	On the E Fork of Joes (?) Creek	yes
Steel, David (Jno.)	683		Sullivan	600	631	9 Jul 1794			81	631	Inc where sd Steel now lives	
Steel, John, Trustee	312		Middle District	080 128	288	7 Dec 1794	2039	3 May 1784	83	331	N side of Elk River	
Steel, Joseph	42	Fenner, Richard	Sumner	640	875	17 Jan 1789	3478	19 Feb 1788	63	303	On N side of Cumberland River	yes
Steel, Ninian	097		Green	300			664				On waters of Holston River	
Steel, Robert	1080		Davidson	640	54	17 Apr 1786	280	14 Feb 1784	66	52	In the fork of Bledsoes Creek	
Steel, Robert	604		Washington	200	698	26 Oct 1786	1995	21 Oct 1779	66	10	Below Joseph Martins entry	
Steel, Robert	635		Washington	150	729	26 Oct 1786	455	28 Sep 1788	66	25	Adjoining John Gelielomds entry	
Steel, Robert	93		Sullivan	400	104	23 Oct 1782	772,-1820	1779,-1781	43	287	On N side of Holston River &c	
Steel, William	585		Washington	150	679	26 Oct 1786	2370	23 Dec 1779	66	2	On the head of Sinking Creek	
Steel, Zachariah	1073		Davidson	640	47	17 Apr 1786	197	28 Jan 1784	66	50	Trace below his spring	
Steel, John	473		Middle District	1280	265	6 Dec 1794	2022	3 May 1784	85	335	On S side of Elk River	
Steele, Nancy Nesfield	2124	Armstrong, M.	Davidson	500	139	7 Jan 1794		30 Nov 1792	81	397	On waters of Stones River	
Steeley, Jeremiah	078	Boyd, John	not given	274			3453				no plat	yes
Steell, Hardy	323	McCulloch, Benj.	Tennessee	640	2060	20 May 1793	2074	1 Sep 1785	81	139	N side of Cumberland River	yes
Steell, John, heirs of	42		Sumner	640	875	17 Jan 1789	3478	19 Feb 1788	63	303	On N side of Cumberland River	yes
Steelley, Jeremiah	078		not given	274			3453				no plat	
Stephens, John	1162	Harris, Edward	Sumner	640	2667	4 Jun 1796	3830	1 Jun 1795	88	356	Joining sd Harris survey	yes
Stephens, Thomas	220	Polk, Ezekial	Davidson	640	206	7 Mar 1786	814		63	76	On Richland Creek	yes
Stephenson, Hughey	1946	Whitfield, Bryant	Davidson	365	1778	20 May 1793	1530		81	73	On E side of Stones River	yes
Stephenson, John etal	1371	Perkins, John	Sumner	400	202	14 Sep 1797			92	20	Waters of Goose Creek	yes
Stephenson, Peter	091	Lytle, Archibald	Sumner	274	323	24 Oct 1782	3545	19 Dec 1792	43	307	S Fork Cedar Lick Creek	yes
Stephenson, Robert	33		Washington	45	1142	12 Jan 1793	1454	22 Jun 1779	78	389	On Lick Fork of Lick Creek	
Stephenson, Robt.	1292		Green	300	729	1 Jul 1788	861	23 May 1781	63	250(6)	On Lick Creek	yes
Stepp, John	756	Thompson, Thomas	Davidson	640	822	20 Nov 1788	1451	6 Oct 1778	63	290	1st creek below Stones Lick Creek	yes
Steps, Abraham	819	Robertson, Patsey	Davidson	1000	1264	12 Jul 1794	3392	22 Oct 1779	81	583	On Caney Fork	yes
Sterling, John	1503		Green	80	931	17 Nov 1790	485	21 May 1781	76	154	On a branch of Dumpling Creek	
Stevens, Edmond	954		Washington	50	1086	12 Jan 1793	2002	6 Nov 1779	78	356	On the Limestone Fork &c	
Stevens, Edmund	1236		Green	100	1155	12 Jan 1793	2858		78	397	On Lick Creek	
Stevens, Edmund	1305		Green	100	309	13 Jan 1787	2162		63	115	On Lick Creek	
Stevens, Henry	323	Rice, John & others	Davidson	640	1222	27 Nov 1793	2582	19 Oct 1779	81	509	On Smiths Creek	yes
Stevens, James	1462		Green	150	2392	31 Jan 1795	5172		83	390	On N of French Broad River	
Stevens, James	333	Williams, Willoughby	Middle District	640	2234	20 May 1793	2691		81	177	W side of W Fork of Obeys River	yes
Stevens, John	2077	Hickman, Edwin	Davidson	228	2111	20 May 1793	3588		81	152	On waters of Hickman's Creek	yes
Stevens, Jos. (Sarah Pagets)	334	Padget, Sarah (hr of Jos.)	Tennessee	640	699	11 Jul 1788	3149	16 Dec 1785	66	460	On S side of Cumberland River	yes
Stevens, Wm.	658		Green	220	533	10 Nov 1784	1051	29 Oct 1783	69	116	On a creek that makes into Clinch River &c	
Stevenson, Hugh	719		Washington	150	666	11 Jul 1788	2476	10 Mar 1780	66	449	Beg at a white oak	
Stevenson, J. & H. Jones	625		Green	500	1037	18 May 1789	62	21 Oct 1783	63	345	On E side of Big Pigeon River &c	
Stevenson, James	1019	Thompson, Robert	Davidson	640	2395	17 Jul 1794	3477		81	603	Bet. Cedar Lick Creek & Spencers Creek	yes
Stevenson, Jonathan	031	King, Robert & Joseph Cob	Eastern District	640	4753	20 May 1793	4753		83	165	On S side of Wallings Ridge	yes
Stevenson, Peter	684	Donelson, S. & Joseph Bea	Hawkins	1000	2169	23 Aug 1788	3545	20 Mar 1786	81	279	On Pleasan Run	yes
Stevenson, William	758	Lytle, William	Sumner	640	2034	20 May 1793	2034		81	416	On N side of Cumberland River	yes
Stewart, Andrew	794	McNees, John	Davidson	640	797	20 Mar 1786	3546		63	279	On N side of Cumberland River	yes
Stewart, Charles	1204		Washington	70	1158	5 Dec 1794	2616	19 Aug 1786	83	416	On head of Limestone	yes

Claimant:	File #:	Assignee:	County:	Acres:	Grant:	Grant Date:	Entry:	Entry Date:	Bk:	Pg:	Location by Stream Name:	Military:
Stewart, Charles	2391	Radley, Jonas heirs	Davidson	640	3188	14 Sep 1797			90	437	On South Harpeth	yes
Stewart, Charles	2403	Lewis, Richard heirs	Davidson	640	2800	6 Jun 1796	1367or3867		91	473	S W side of Big Harpeth River	yes
Stewart, Charles	624	Stone, Arthur heirs	Tennessee	640	3187	14 Sep 1797	3996		90	437	N side of Cumberland	
Stewart, Charles	625	Squires, John	Tennessee	320	3189	14 Sep 1797	358	4 Dec 1783	90	438	S side of Cumberland	
Stewart, Charles	626	Bird, John heirs	Tennessee	640	3190	14 Sep 1797	438		90	438	S side of Cumberland River	
Stewart, Charles	627	Bradshaw, Ephraim heirs	Tennessee	640	3191	14 Sep 1797	3860		90	439	Head waters of Johnstons Creek	
Stewart, Charles	627		Washington	70	1158	5 Dec 1794	2616	19 Aug 1786	83	416	On the head of Limestone	
Stewart, David	1194		Green	500	1037	26 Dec 1791			77	328	On the N side of French Broad River	
Stewart, David	1315		Washington	50	1235	26 Dec 1796	2475	22 Mar 1796	90	205	Beg on/near David Stewarts line	
Stewart, David	181		Washington	292	49	23 Oct 1782	737	22 Dec 1778	47	23	On a branch of Big Limestone Cr	
Stewart, David etal	506		Washington	200	769	16 Aug 1787			64	142	On the N side of Holston River &c	
Stewart, Duncan	1368		Sumner	274	3217	14 Sep 1797	591	20 Aug 1785	91	12	N side of Cumberland River	yes
Stewart, Duncan	2239	Green, Theophilus heirs	Davidson	640	2686	6 Jun 1796	3853		88	363	On S Harpeth River	yes
Stewart, Duncan	2241	Cannon, Edward heirs	Davidson	640	2688	6 Jun 1796	3863		88	364	On S side of Harpeth River	yes
Stewart, Duncan	2367	Garvey, Matthew heirs	Davidson	640	3088	14 Sep 1797	4000		90	396	E side of Harpeth River	yes
Stewart, Duncan	2368	Newton, Joseph	Davidson	640	3089	14 Sep 1797	4007		90	396	W side of S Harpeth River	yes
Stewart, Duncan	2369	Jacobs, William heirs	Davidson	640	3090	14 Sep 1797	4012		90	397	On Western br of S Harpeth River	yes
Stewart, Duncan	2370	Pascot, Charles heirs	Davidson	640	3091	14 Sep 1797	4010		90	397	On S Harpeth River	yes
Stewart, Duncan	2371	Jarrett, Jacob heirs	Davidson	640	3092	14 Sep 1797	4013		90	398	On an E Fork of S Harpeth River	yes
Stewart, Duncan	2372	Henderson, Andrew	Davidson	640	3093	14 Sep 1797	4167		90	398	On S Harpeth River	yes
Stewart, Duncan	2373	Pitman, John	Davidson	640	3094	14 Sep 1797	4157		90	399	On S Harpeth River	yes
Stewart, Duncan	2374	King, Jacob	Davidson	640	3095	14 Sep 1797	4011		90	399	E Fork of S Harpeth	yes
Stewart, Duncan	2375	Matthews, Charles heirs	Davidson	640	3096	14 Sep 1797	4001		90	399	E Fork of S Harpeth	yes
Stewart, Duncan	2376	Rogers, Parker	Davidson	640	3097	14 Sep 1797	4032		90	400	On S Harpeth a br of Big Harpeth	yes
Stewart, Duncan	2377	Colbey, John	Davidson	640	3098	14 Sep 1797	4151		90	400	On S Harpeth River	yes
Stewart, Duncan	2378	Davis, Benj	Davidson	640	3100	14 Sep 1797	4233		90	402	On an E Fork of S Harpeth	yes
Stewart, Duncan	2399	Maclemore, John	Davidson	640	2796	6 Jun 1796	3848		91	470	S W side of Big Harpeth River	yes
Stewart, Duncan	2400	Wright, Abraham heirs	Davidson	1000	2797	6 Jun 1796	3854		91	471	S W side of Big Harpeth River	yes
Stewart, Duncan	2416	Williams, James heirs	Davidson	3840	3219	14 Sep 1797			92	13(?)	On S Harpeth River	yes
Stewart, Duncan	598	Pridgion, Marmaduke heirs	Tennessee	640	3101	14 Sep 1797	4554	9 Feb 1797	90	402	S side of Cumberland River	
Stewart, Duncan	599	Campbell, Patrick	Tennessee	428	3218	14 Sep 1797	91		92	13	S side of Cumberland River	
Stewart, Duncan	600	Edge, Thos heirs	Tennessee	640	3102	14 Sep 1797	4433	22 Dec 1796	90	403	S side of Cumberland River &c	
Stewart, Duncan	601	Clark, Benj. Heirs	Tennessee	640	3103	14 Sep 1797	4435		90	403	S side of Cumberland River &c	
Stewart, Duncan	602	Clark, Nell heirs	Tennessee	640	3161	14 Sep 1797	1365	9 Nov 1784	90	426	N side of Cumberland River	
Stewart, Duncan	603	White, Stephen	Tennessee	1000	3110	14 Sep 1797			90	406	S side of Cumberland River	
Stewart, Duncan	609	Gressum, Robert heirs	Tennessee	1000	3155	14 Sep 1797	4320		90	424	N side of Cumberland River	
Stewart, Duncan	610	Lassiter, Jas.	Tennessee	1000	3156	14 Sep 1797	4047		90	424	N side of Cumberland River	
Stewart, Duncan	611	White, John heirs	Tennessee	1000	3160	14 Sep 1797	534		90	426	S side of Cumberland River	
Stewart, Duncan	612	Lennon, Eph heirs	Tennessee	1000	2791	20 Dec 1796	536		91	467	S side of Cumberland River	
Stewart, Duncan	627	Young, John	Tennessee	228	2792	20 Dec 1796	557		91	468	S side of Cumberland River	
Stewart, Duncan	645	Bateman, Wm. Heirs	Tennessee	6000 (?)	3104	14 Sep 1797	4441	22 Dec 1796	90	404	S side of Cumberland River &c	
Stewart, Duncan	645	Williams, Arthur	Tennessee	640	3220	14 Sep 1797	4006		92	14	S side of Cumberland River	
Stewart, Duncan	646	Gray, James heirs	Tennessee	1000	3221	14 Sep 1797	4442		92	14	N side of Cumberland River	
Stewart, Duncan	648		Tennessee	63	406	14 Sep 1797		14 Aug 1795	91	19	E side of W Fork of Red River	
Stewart, Duncan	651	Armstrong, M.	Tennessee	67	405	14 Sep 1797		14 Aug 1797	92	18	On Wells Creek	

Claimant:	File #:	Assignee:	County:	Acres:	Grant:	Grant Date:	Entry:	Entry Date:	Bk:	Pg:	Location by Stream Name:	Military:
Stewart, Duncan	653	Ginn, Thos.	Tennessee	320	3229	17 Nov 1797	2453		94	167	On Little West Fork of Red River	
Stewart, Duncan	657	Young, John	Tennessee	228	3234	20 Nov 1797	557	11 Aug 1797	94	170	On the Piney Fork	
Stewart, Duncan etal	040	Parrot, Benjamin heirs	Tennessee	640	3215		4434	22 Dec 1796			On headwaters of Johnsons Creek	
Stewart, Duncan etal	653		Sumner	1000	3216	14 Sep 1797	3283	1 Jun 1797	92	12	On Indian Creek	yes
Stewart, Duncan, Ass.	1308		Sumner	640	3099	14 Sep 1797	4232	30 May 1797	90	401	Waters of Big Barren	yes
Stewart, Duncan, Ass.	1331		Sumner	640	3131	14 Sep 1797	941	27 May 1785	90	416	N side of Cumberland River &c	yes
Stewart, Duncan, Ass.	1346		Sumner	640	3154	14 Sep 1797	4258	30 May 1797	90	424	On the ridge	yes
Stewart, Duncan, Ass.	1347		Sumner	640	3157	14 Sep 1797	4259	30 May 1797	90	425	Waters of Big Barren	yes
Stewart, Duncan, Ass.	1348		Sumner	640	3158	14 Sep 1797	4154	30 May 1797	90	425	Waters of Big Barren	yes
Stewart, Duncan, Ass.	1349		Sumner	640	3159	14 Sep 1797	4273	30 May 1797	90	425	Waters of Big Barren	yes
Stewart, George	122	Maclin, William	Tennessee	1000	1625	23 Feb 1793	3563	20 Oct 1787	76	324	N side of Cumberland River	yes
Stewart, James	722		Washington	350	536	10 Nov 1784	231	27 Aug 1778	69	117	Beg at a white oak	
Stewart, James	810		Washington	200	624	10 Nov 1784	2314	27 Nov 1779	69	145	On S Fork of Lick Creek	
Stewart, James & Robert	741		Washington	150	555	10 Nov 1784	708	19 Dec 1778	69	125	On N Fork of Cherokee Creek	
Stewart, John	1446	Fitzworth, Isaac	Davidson	320	92	10 Jul 1788	365	22 Mar 1784	68	233	On Red River	
Stewart, John	1553		Davidson	320	99	26 Nov 1789	509	5 Jul 1784	74	172	Both sides Sulphur Fork of Richland Creek	
Stewart, John	238	Thompson, James	Davidson	274	224	7 Mar 1786	454		63	82	On waters of Richland Creek	yes
Stewart, John	585	Armstrong, M.	Tennessee	186	385	19 Jul 1797			90	369	N side of Cumberland River	
Stewart, John, Ass.	1366		Davidson	640	49	8 Oct 1787	137	16 Jan 1784	68	141	S/S side of Sulphur Fork of Red R	
Stewart, Robert, Ass.	896		Sumner	640	2447	31 Dec 1793	3674	5 Dec 1789	81	425	On headwaters of Spring Creek	yes
Stewart, Thomas	199		Washington	148.5	67	23 Oct 1782	1400	24 May 1779	47	32	Including a spring &c	
Stewart, William	1831		Davidson	640	404	26 Jun 1793	520	12 Jul 1784	80	342(a)	S/S of Big Harpeth River	
Stewart, William	784		Davidson	640	757	11 Jul 1788	659		63	266	On n side of Cumberland River	yes
Stewart, Wm.	1624	Weymouth, Corbyn	Davidson	365	1364	10 Dec 1790	485		74	387	On N side of Cumberland River	yes
Stilwell, Jeremiah	1260	Donelson, Stockley	Sumner	640	2738	21 Jul 1798	213	4 Apr 1785	90	187	W/s of W Fork of Obeys River &c	yes
Stilwell, Simon	1916	Searcey, Ben & Geo Walke	Davidson	640	1702	20 May 1793	2585		81	54	On S side of Cumberland River	yes
Stillwill, David	460	White, Thomas	Sumner	403	1602	27 Apr 1793	1224	8 Mar 1788	81	18	On both sides of Jinnings Creek	yes
Stinson, James	334		Washington	180	201	24 Oct 1782	1349	30 Apr 1779	49	227	On E branch of Little Limestone Cr	
Stinson, James	384		Washington	147	376	13 Oct 1783	1042	7 Jan 1779	52	253	On branch of Little Limestone Cr	
Stinson, James	836		Green	150	822	19 Nov 1790	1445	25 Jun 1779	73	277	On Joseph Gists Fork of Lick Cr	
Stinson, John	879	Sugg, George A.	Davidson	640	893	1789	2236		63	309	On 1st Creek &c	
Stobbotie, James	334	Casselman, Andrew	Sumner	640	1636	23 Feb 1793	3525	3 Dec 1792	76	330	On the N boundary	yes
Stockkey, Alexander	800	Robertson, Elijah	Davidson	1000	803	20 Nov 1788	3324		63	282	On S side of Cumberland River	yes
Stockton, Thomas	107		Green	400	123	1 Nov 1786	3	29 Oct 1783	59	426	N side of French Broad River	
Stockton, Thomas	1253		Green	160	1103	12 Jan 1793			78	365	On N side of French Broad River	
Stockton, Thomas	485		Green	100	487	20 Sep 1787	341	23 Oct 1783	65	514	On N side of French Broad River &c	
Stockton, Thos.	1330		Green	30	1072	24 Dec 1792	897	16 May 1789	78	429	Joining his former survey	
Stockton, William	324		Washington	300	191	24 Oct 1782	1050	29 Dec 1778	49	222	On a branch of Lick Creek	
Stockton, Wm.	155		Eastern District	300	125	24 Dec 1792	1050	20 Oct 1779	78	450	Confluence of Holston & Little Riv	
Stoke, Adam	579		Sullivan	200	577	29 Jul 1793	473	Aug & Nov 1780	76	473	On a branch of Reedy Creek	
Stokely, John	276	Shelby, David	Sumner	640	1268	10 Dec 1790	1919	6 Sep 1785	74	3556	Branch that runs into Drakes Cr	yes
Stokes, John	314	Kitt, Solomon	Davidson	640	300	13 Jun 1787	1687		63	112	S side of Cumberland	yes
Stokes, John	36		Western District	2500	36	10 Jul 1788	2651	5 May 1784	67	294	S/S of N fork of Forked Deer River	
Stokes, John	58		Western District	2500	58	10 Jul 1788	2650	5 May 1784	67	302	N/S of N Fork of Forked Deer River	
Stokes, Peter	59	Brekon, Jas. G.	Tennessee	640	1286	10 Dec 1790	3379	7 Jan 1786	74	361	On S side of Cumberland River	yes

Claimant:	File #:	Assignee:	County:	Acres:	Grant:	Grant Date:	Entry:	Entry Date:	Bk:	Pg:	Location by Stream Name:	Military:
Stolcop, William	544	Robb, William	Davidson	357	516	15 Sep 1787	173		63	186	On waters of Goose Creek	yes
Stone, Arthur	624	Stewart, Charles	Tennessee	640	3187	14 Sep 1797	3996		90	437	N side of Cumberland	yes
Stone, John	0135		Green	200	176	8 Apr 1794	1348	12 Jan 1784			On the N side of Holston River	
Stone, John	1014		Green	200	1242	29 Jul 1793		20 Oct 1783	76	486	N side of Nolychuckie River	
Stone, John	204		Eastern District	200	176	8 Apr 1794			81	559	On N side of Holston River	
Stone, John	305	Barrow, James	Sumner	640	1374	20 Apr 1791	2771	20 Nov 1790	74	396	On E side of Jennings Fork	yes
Stone, John	429		Eastern District	50	380	19 Jul 1797			90	368	E side of Second Creek	
Stone, John	986	Brehon, James Gloster	Davidson	640	1003	18 May 1789	2881		63	337	On N side of Cumberland River	yes
Stone, Littleberry	345	Holley, Nathaniel	Tennessee	640	2158	20 May 1793	3381	7 Jan 1786	81	162	On N side of Cumberland River	yes
Stone, Littleberry	429	Stone, Littleberry	Tennessee	640	2158	20 May 1793	3381	7 Jan 1786	81	162	On N side of Cumberland River	
Stone, Sylvanus	578	Brenaman, Melchior	Tennessee	640	3025	10 Apr 1797	3938		90	303	N side of Cumberland River	yes
Stone, William	790		Washington	486	604	10 Nov 1784	801	28 Dec 1778	69	139	On Boon Creek	
Stoner, John	770		Sullivan	100	701	20 Jul 1796	49	8 Feb 1780	91	84	Beg at 2 chestnuts & 2 white oaks	
Storm, Andrew	2406	Hadley, Joshua	Davidson	640	2803	21 Dec 1796	3933		91	475	On W Harpeth River	yes
Stormer, Henry	353	Williams, Willoughby	Middle District	1000	2402	5 Feb 1795	2623		84	184	On E side of W Fork of Obeys R	yes
Story, Caleb	465	Ramsey, Allen	Sumner	640	1615	27 Apr 1793	903	11 Jun 1791	81	21	On S side of Cumberland River	yes
Story, Jonah	035	Haynes, James	Robertson	274			3544	2 Feb 1795			N Fork of Red River	yes
Story, William, heirs of	1885		Davidson	640	1643	27 Apr 1793	855		81	27	On first large branch above Cobbs	yes
Stothart, Robert	1630	Stothart, Robert	Montgomery	274			4733	Apr 1797			On the Piney Fork	yes
Stoub, Peter	1630		Green	200	1312	9 Jul 1792			85	324	On N side of Holston River	Yes
Stout, Hosea	422		Green	100	424	20 Sep 1787	3933		91	495	S/S of Nolachucky River on Lick Cr	
Stout, Hosea	596		Green	200	553	20 Sep 1787	1742	21 Apr 1784	65	247	On S side of Nolechuckey River &c	
Stout, Samuel	68		Hawkins	640	54	18 May 1789	892	7 Jun 1784	66	301	On N side of Holson River &c	
Stoveall, John	74	Rice, John	Tennessee	640	1318	10 Dec 1790	1136	9 Aug 1784	72	371	On N side of Cumberland River	yes
Stowbridge, John	027	Dillenberry, Redmon	Sumner	640			4387	22 Sep 1797	74		On dividing ridges &c	yes
Strader, George	414	Nelson, Robert	Davidson	1000	386	15 Sep 1787	1886		63	144	On Big Harpeth	yes
Stradley, Edward	1398	Miller, Randal	Sumner	640	3326	6 Dec 1797	3065	23 Jun 1797	97	47	On Salt Lick Fork of Big Barren	yes
Stradley, James	2009	Cobb, Jesse	Davidson	640	1955	20 May 1793	1128		81	113	On waters of Stones River	yes
Strand, John	708	Blount, Reading	Davidson	640	681	8 Dec 1787	2548		63	240	On Sycamore Creek	yes
Strather, John & Jno. Gooch	23		Giles	5000	54	30 Sep 1812	436	24 Jun 1784	123	26	Lying on Richland Creek	yes
Stratin, Joab	935	Brehon, James G.	Davidson	640	951	18 May 1789	3498		63	324	On waters of Mulherins Creek	yes
Straughan, Richard	1024	Riston, Abraham	Davidson	640	1042	18 May 1789	944		63	346	On Spencers Creek	yes
Strider, George	1386	Gwin, William	Sumner	411	3311	6 Dec 1797	1191	~ 1797	97	37	On waters of Big Barron	yes
Stringer, John	1331	Stuart, Duncan	Sumner	640	3131	14 Sep 1797	941	27 May 1785	90	416	N side of Cumberland River	yes
Stringer, Josiah	2071		Davidson	264	2113	20 May 1793	1162		81	171	On S W side of Big Harpeth	yes
Stringer, Lineage	2263	Donelson, Stockley	Davidson	640	2727	20 Jul 1796	3185		88	452	On waters of Stones River	yes
Stringer, James	401	Glasgow, James	Tennessee	521	2403	20 Dec 1793	1107	14 Jun 1784	81	419	On N side of Cumberland River	yes
Stringer, Simon	063	Donelson, Stockley	Sumner	640			3185	13 Apr 1795			W side of W Fork of Obeys River	yes
Striplin, Newton	217	Sanders, William	Sumner	640	1122	26 Nov 1789	1616	9 Feb 1787	74	140	On waters of Caney Fork	yes
Strong, George	026	Dillenberry, Redmon	Sumner	640			4337	16 Sep 1797			On head of Shanes Branch	yes
Strowd, William	1104		Hawkins	200	824	10 Aug 1797	1728		91	624	N W side of Powells River	yes
Stuart, David	096		Green	400			1921	15 Oct 1779			On Sinking Fork of Russels Creek	
Stuart, David	101		Knox, Eastern D	1000	301	15 Nov 1800		25 Oct 1780	108	204	On N side of Tennessee River	yes
Stuart, David	101		Green	59	59	1 Nov 1786	17	27 Oct 1783	59	420	N side of Tennessee River	
Stuart, David	15		Eastern District	1000	301	15 Nov 1800	427	25 Oct 1783	108	204	On N side of Tennessee River	

Claimant:	File #:	Assignee:	County:	Acres:	Grant:	Grant Date:	Entry:	Entry Date:	Bk:	Pg:	Location by Stream Name:	Military:
Stuart, David	180		Green	250	650	11 Jul 1788	758	28 Oct 1783	64	358	N side of French Broad River	
Stuart, David	215		Green	200	172	20 Sep 1787	2493	11 Mar 1780	65	421	On N side of Tennessee River	
Stuart, David	235		Green	300	192	20 Sep 1787	1920	15 Oct 1779	65	428	On N side of Holsten River &c	
Stuart, David	271		Green	200	228	20 Sep 1787	2287	27 Nov 1779	65	441	On waters of Russels Creek &c	
Stuart, David	271		Green	300	256	20 Sep 1787	1923	6 Feb 1786	66	159	On So side of Powell River &c	
Stuart, David	576		Green	400	257	20 Sep 1787	29	17 Jan 1784	66	160	On the Sinking Fork of Russels Cr	
Stuart, David	578		Green	470	259	20 Sep 1787	162	14 Mar 1778	66	160	On Russels Creek &c	
Stuart, David	581		Green	500	262	20 Sep 1787	2288	27 Nov 1779	66	161	N/S Tennessee River joining Thos. Kings	
Stuart, David	94		Green	40	52	1 Nov 1786			59	413	N side of Tennessee River	
Stuart, David & Adam Willson	55		Green	420	13	1 Nov 1786	512	27 Oct 1783	59	374	N side of Holston River	
Stuart, David & John Hill	219		Green	368	176	20 Sep 1787	2529	25 May 1784	65	422	S/S of French Broad River &c	
Stuart, David & Thos. Keef	566		Green	160	246	20 Sep 1787	1138	1 Feb 1779	66	156	On N side of Holsten River &c	
Stuart, David & Wm. Cocke	560		Green	400	254	20 Sep 1787	381	30 Mar 1786	66	158	On waters of Clinch River & War	
Stuart, David etal	099		Green	200			1183	4 Feb 1779			N side of Holsten River	
Stuart, David etal	560	Douglas, Jonathan	Green	640	240	20 Sep 1787	1914	11 Oct 1779	66	154	On S side of Holston River &c	
Stuart, David etal	688		Green	640	729	11 Jul 1788	1225	28 Dec 1781	66	469	On S side of Holsten River	
Stuart, David, Jno. McNabb &c	99	Denton & Baldridge	Green	155	722	11 Jul 1788	1741	26 Feb 1787	66	467	In fork of Big Pigeon & French Broad River	
Stuart, James	122		Washington	397.5	290	24 Oct 1782	365	5 Sep 1778	44	293	On waters of Boons Creek	
Stuart, James	1381		Washington	150	1302	17 Apr 1801	520	19 Oct 1778	112	386	On head waters of Cherokee Cr	
Stuart, James	1383		Washington	300	1309	31 Oct 1803	1124	22 Jan 1779	117	50	Joining 2 nobs	
Stuart, James	2		Carter(?)	300	1301	17 Apr 1801	1356	6 May 1779	112	386	Upon Buffalo Creek	
Stuart, James	231		Washington	285	99	23 Oct 1782	300	5 Aug 1778	47	48	S side of Nolachuckey	
Stuart, James	517		Hawkins	200	390	29 Jul 1793	1060	17 May 1779	80	274	N side Holston River &c	
Stuart, James	632		Washington	300	726	26 Oct 1786	322	25 Aug 1778	66	24	Beg at 2 dogwood saplings &c	
Stuart, James & Robert	063		Washington				982	2 Jan 1779			On waters of Lick Creek	
Stuart, James & Robert	578		Washington	200	843	20 Nov 1788	320	25 Aug 1778	64	468	In the Limestone Cove &c	
Stuart, James & Robert	579		Washington	100	844	20 Nov 1788	1450	19 Jun 1779	64	469	In the Limestone Cove &c	
Stuart, James & Robert	580		Washington	200	845	20 Nov 1788	321	25 Aug 1778	64	469	On the Limestone Cove	
Stuart, Jas. & Robt.	095		Sullivan	100								
Stuart, Joseph	490		Green	400	492	20 Sep 1787	1417	19 Jan 1784	65	516	On white horn a branch of Bent Cr	
Stuart, Thomas	227		Washington	148.5	95	23 Oct 1782	1399	24 May 1779	47	45	Including the head spring &c	
Stuart, William	1192		Davidson	640	169	17 Apr 1786	247	6 Feb 1784	66	190	E/S Stones R & S/S of public road	
Stubblefield, Robert	701		Hawkins	300	503	23 Apr 1794			82	153	N/S Holston R joining Wm. Cock	
Stubblefield, Robert L.	499		Washington	100	762	16 Aug 1787	620	24 Nov 1778	64	139	On head of Gammons Branch	
Stubblefield, Robert Lockaley	517		Sullivan	100	533	20 Nov 1789	714	15 Dec 1780	73	46	On waters of Sinking Creek	
Stubblefield, Robt. Luxley	280		Hawkins	300	291	14 Jan 1793	277	22 Oct 1783	78	342	N side of Holston River	
Stubblefield, Thomas	0118		Sumner	640			1990	9 Feb 1796			On waters of Second Creek	yes
Stubblefield, Weight [sic]	357		Sullivan	95	236	10 Nov 1784	534	29 Apr 1780	69	158	Beg at Garret Fitgeralds corner	
Stubblefield, Wiet	506		Hawkins	400	379	29 Jul 1793	1925	15 Oct 1779	80	271	On N side of Holston River	
Stubblefield, William	520		Sullivan	160	536	26 Nov 1789	1014	5 Jan 1773	73	47	On S side of Holston River &c	
Stuchen, Jacob	476		Hawkins	100	348	29 Jul 1793	2068	28 Oct 1779	80	262	On N side Opossum Creek	
Stump, Christopher	2144	Dodson, John	Davidson	274	2423	31 Dec 1793	1679		81	407	On waters of Whites Creek	yes
Stump, Fred	2330	Armstrong, M.	Davidson	50	355	10 Apr 1797			90	281	Waters of Second Creek	
Stump, Frederick	022	Nelson, Robert	Davidson								N side Cumberland River	
Stump, Frederick	1102		Davidson	640	76	17 Apr 1786	139	16 Jan 1784	66	60	Lying on White Creek &c	

Claimant:	File #:	Assignee:	County:	Acres:	Grant:	Grant Date:	Entry:	Entry Date:	Bk:	Pg:	Location by Stream Name:	Military:
Stump, Frederick	1315		Davidson	320	1	20 Jul 1787	1578	21 Nov 1785	67	60	On N side of Cumberland River	
Stump, Frederick	1400	Armstrong, M.	Davidson	150	17	8 Oct 1787			68	153	On W of Jacob Stumps survey	
Stump, Frederick	1402	Armstrong, M.	Davidson	150	19	8 Oct 1787	608	7 Feb 1785	68	153	On Dry Fork of Whites Creek	
Stump, Frederick	1403	Armstrong, M.	DAvidson	100	20	8 Oct 1787	109	9 Jul 1785	68	153	Boundary William Mitchells preemp	
Stump, Frederick	1900		Davidson	320	135	27 Apr 1793			81	37	On N side of Cumberland River	
Stump, Frederick	2193	Armstrong, M.	Davidson	274	185	26 Sep 1795			86	530	On waters of Whites Creek	
Stump, Frederick	2329	Armstrong, M.	Davidson	100	354	10 Apr 1797			90	281	Waters of Whites Creek	
Stump, Frederick etal	2329	Armstrong, M.	Tennessee	640	353	10 Apr 1797	57		90	280	S side of Cumberland River	
Stump, Frederick, Ass.	1650		Davidson	640	301	17 Nov 1790	138	16 Jan 1784	76	181	On Whites Creek	
Stumps, John	437		Eastern District	1000	288	21 Jan 1797	356-2317	1780 1779 [sic]	91	123	On Lick Creek	
Stute, John	401		Sullivan	600	280	10 Nov 1784			69	170	On Frk of Buck Creek	
Styron, Samuel	670	Clark, Lardner	Davidson	640	643	15 Nov 1787	1578		63	228	On the Salleen	yes
Suarlock, James	896	Price, Rice	Davidson	2560	912	18 May 1789			63	315	On both sides Harpeth River	
Sugg, Aquilla	874	Halcolm, William heirs	Davidson	640	887	17 Jan 1789	2218		63	308	1st creek above Stones Lick Cr	yes
Sugg, Aquilla	875	Martin, Patrick	Davidson	1000	889	17 Jan 1789	1817		63	308	E/S Main E Fork of Stones River	yes
Sugg, Aquilla	876	Lanier, Peter	Davidson	1000	890	17 Jan 1789	1824		63	309	Both sides Main E Fork of Stones Riv	yes
Sugg, Aquilla	877	Cherry, Jonathan	Davidson	640	891	17 Jan 1789	2464		63	309	W side of Main E Fork of Stones R	yes
Sugg, Aquilla	891	Blacknell, John heirs	Davidson	640	907	17 Jan 1789	2446		63	313	On 2nd creek above Stewarts Cr	yes
Sugg, Aquilla	902	Fowler, Joshua heirs	Davidson	640	918	18 May 1789			63	317	On E side of Stones River	
Sugg, Aquilla	904	Berk, Meradeth heirs	Davidson	640	919	18 May 1789			63	317	On S side of Cumberland River	
Sugg, Aquilla	910	Davis, Jesse heirs	Davidson	640	926	18 May 1789			63	319	E Fork First Creek above Stones R	
Sugg, Aquilla	911	Haywood, James	Davidson	640	927	18 May 1789			63	319	E side of Main E Fork of Stones R	
Sugg, Aquilla	915	Pollard, Matthew heirs	Davidson	640	931	18 May 1789			63	320	1st creek above Stones Lick Cr	yes
Sugg, Aquilla	917	Parker, Solomon	Davidson	640	933	18 May 1789			63	320	On head waters of First Creek &c	
Sugg, Aquilla	918	Sanders, Job	Davidson	640	934	18 May 1789			63	321	On second creek above Stewarts	
Sugg, Aquilla	971		Davidson	640	988	18 May 1789			63	334	On headwaters of First Creek	
Sugg, Aquilla, Ass.	904	Sikes, James	Davidson	640	920	18 May 1789			63	317	On S side of Cumberland River	
Sugg, Geo. A.	065	Sikes, James	Davidson	640			2686	5 Mar 1791			Bet. Whites Creek & Marrow Bone	yes
Sugg, Geo. A.	066	Scott, Overstreet	Davidson	640			1893	5 Mar 1791			Bet. Whites Creek & Marrow Bone	
Sugg, Geo. A.	067	Smith, Joab	Davidson	640			2477	29 Jun 1791			Bet. Whites Cr & Marrowbone	
Sugg, Geo. A.	068	Libbincutt, John	Davidson	640			2667	5 Mar 1791			Bet. Whites Cr & Marrow Bone	
Sugg, Geo. A.	069	Flimin, Samuel	Davidson	640			2802	29 Jun 1791			On head waters of Marrow Bone	
Sugg, Geo. A.	905	Peters, John	Davidson	640	921	18 May 1789			63	317	On S side of Cumberland River	
Sugg, Geo. A., Ass.	973		Davidson	640	990	18 May 1789			63	334	On main E Fork of Stones River	
Sugg, Geo. A., heirs	974		Davidson	640	991	18 May 1789			63	334	Waters 1st cr above Stones Lick Cr	
Sugg, Geo. A., heirs											Head waters W Fork of the First Cr	
Sugg, George A.	1971	Sampson, David	Davidson	640	1850	20 May 1793	3480		81	90	S/S Cumberland River	yes
Sugg, George A.	2111	Weatherby, Isaac heirs	Davidson	640	2366	20 May 1793	2626		81	205	On S side of Cumberland River	yes
Sugg, George A.	879	Stinson, John heirs	Davidson	640	893	1789	2236		63	309	On 1st creek above Stones Lick Cr	yes
Sugg, George A.	970	Benford, Isaac heirs	Davidson	640	987	18 May 1789			63	333	On S side of Cumberland River	
Sugg, George A.	972	Sanders, Applewhite heirs	Davidson	640	989	18 May 1789			63	334	Head waters 1st creek above Stones Lick	
Sugg, George Agustus	886	Humphries, Henry heirs	Davidson	640	902	17 Jan 1789	2457		63	312	E side of Main E Fork of Stones R	yes
Sugg, George Agustus	969	Sanders, John heirs	Davidson	640	986	18 May 1789			63	333	On 2nd creek above Stewarts Cr	
Sugg, George Augustus	878	Jeth, Fenner heirs	Davidson	640	892	17 Jan 1789	2197		63	309	On small fk 1st cr above Stewarts Cr	yes
Sugg, John	028	Lewis, W. T. & Wm. Tyrrell	Montgomery	274			425	27 Sep 1796	77		On Barren Fork of Little West Fork	yes
Sugg, Michael	169	Nelson, Robert	Tennessee	274	1434	20 Dec 1791	3547	15 Feb 1786	77	360	On the N side of Cumberland River	yes

Earliest Tennessee Land Records

Claimant:	File #:	Assignee:	County:	Acres:	Grant:	Grant Date:	Entry:	Entry Date:	Bk:	Pg:	Location by Stream Name:	Military:
Sugg, Noah	671		Sumner	640	2001	20 May 1793	2076	29 Nov 1792	81	124	Joining assignee Benjamin Woolard	yes
Sugg, Noah, Ass.	648		Sumner	640	1944	20 May 1793	3523	29 Nov 1792	81	110	Joining Benjamin Woolard	yes
Sugg, Noah, Ass.	652		Sumner	640	1962	20 May 1793	2331	29 Nov 1792	81	115	On the Pond Lick Creek	yes
Suggs, Noah, Ass.	646		Sumner	640	1940	20 May 1793	1887	29 Nov 1792	81	109	E boundary of Alexander McClure	yes
Sullivan, James	1626		Green	100	1346	22 Feb 1795	102	26 Feb 1778	84	329	On S side of Dumplin Creek	
Sullivan, James	5	Tatum, Howell	Tennessee	640	1103	26 Nov 1789	3680	10 Dec 1788	74	130	On N side of Cumberland River	yes
Sullivan, John	1652		Green	200	1351	28 Aug 1795	575	20 Feb 1781	87	525	On N side of Nolychuckey River	
Sullivan, Michael	193	Campbell, Wm.	Tennessee	640	1473	4 Jan 1792	795	4 May 1784	77	369	S side of Cumberland River	
Sullivan, Port	2424	White, James L.	Davidson	640	3244	30 Nov 1797	4443		94	175	J. Robertson Sheppards S E cor	
Sullivant, Lucas	673	Carter, John	Hawkins	228	2382	12 Jul 1794	3727		81	600	On N side of Clinch River	
Summers, George	598		Sumner	288	1841	20 May 1793	2294	28 Jun 1788	81	88	On N side of Smiths Fork	yes
Summers, James	207		Davidson	857	193	7 Mar 1786	310		63	72	On Red River	yes
Summers, John	1083		Sumner	3840	2564	7 Mar 1796	230	15 Oct 1795	88	312	Both sides of a fork of Pond Lick	yes
Sumner, Francis	370	Hays, R. & Edmond Jinings	Sumner	640	1536	14 Jan 1793	2959 [?]	26 [?] Nov 1792	79	266	The waters of Rules Creek	yes
Sumner, Jacob	681	Bud, Samuel	Davidson	640	654	8 Dec 1787	2958		63	232	On ridge bet. Milners & Brush Cr	yes
Sumner, Jethro	1852		Davidson	12000	1574	27 Apr 1793	166		81	11	On waters of Big Harpeth River	yes
Sumner, Jethro	9		Middle District	1470	11	10 Jul 1788	1633	10 Apr 1784	67	411	On E waters of Richland Creek &c	
Sumner, William	037		Hawkins	150			2623	28 Aug 1780			S side of Holston River	
Surcy, Robert	1711	Armstrong, M.	Davidson	21	124	23 Feb 1793			76	347	S side of Cumberland River	yes
Surles, Joseph	375	Lancaster, John	Tennessee	640	2307	20 May 1793	2238	12 Sep 1785	81	192	On N side of Cumberland River	yes
Surlock, Ephraim	137	Robertson, Elijah	Tennessee	640	1650	23 Feb 1793	1837	14 Jun 1785	76	336	N side of Cumberland River	yes
Sutherland, George	459	Hutchings, Thomas	Tennessee	274	2529	8 Dec 1795	1520	20 Jan 1785	88	280	On both sides of Sulphur Fork	
Sutton, Bailey	619	Edge, Jno.	Tennessee	640	3181	14 Sep 1797	3865	12 Oct 1795	90	434	Waters of Bartons Creek	
Sutton, James	1072		Green	200	915	26 Dec 1791	2910	17 Aug 1787	77	247	N side of French Broad River &c	
Swagerty, Abraham	1017		Hawkins	640	761	28 Dec 1796	349	24 Mar 1780	90	204	N side of Clinch River	
Swagerty, Abraham	1347		Green	300	1193	23 Feb 1793	1844	3 Oct 1787	78	438	S side of Beays Mountain	
Swagerty, Abraham	1348		Green	400	1194	23 Feb 1793	86	7 Oct 1784	78	438	On N side of French Broad River	
Swagerty, Abraham	1349		Green	200	1195	23 Feb 1793	1195	23 Sep 1788	78	439	On N side of French Broad River	
Swagerty, Abraham	1350		Green	200	1196	23 Feb 1793	1196	7 Mar 1780	78	439	On N side of French Broad River	
Swagerty, Abraham	1696		Green	500	1394	28 Dec 1796	967	27 Oct 1783	90	205	N side of French Broad River	
Swagerty, Abraham	339		Sullivan	640			1767	1 Oct 1793			On S side Clinch River	
Swagerty, Abraham	339		Hawkins	640	333	8 Mar 1793	2758	5 Feb 1781	78	476	On S side Clinch River	
Swagerty, Abraham	340		Hawkins	640	334	8 Mar 1793			78	476	On waters of Beaverdam Creek	
Swagerty, Abraham	341		Hawkins	200	335	8 Mar 1793			78	477	On S side of Clinch River	
Swagerty, Abraham	342		Hawkins	640	336	8 Mar 1793	654	16 Jul 1780	78	477	1st creek below mouth of Clinch R	
Swagerty, Abraham	343		Hawkins	640	337	8 Mar 1793			78	478	In Beavercreek Valley	
Swagerty, Abram	0123		Sullivan	640			214	21 Feb 1780			In Beavercreek Valley	
Swagerty, Abram	163		Green	1000	633	23 Aug 1788	67	26 Feb 1778	64	352	On S side of Clinch River &c	
Swagerty, Abram	164		Green	640	634	23 Aug 1788	1229	7 Nov 1783	64	353	On S side of Clinch River &c	
Swagerty, Frederick	1356		Green	200	1202	23 Feb 1793	2422	5 Feb 1780	78	442	Beg at sd Swagertys line	
Swagerty, Frederick	1358		Green	100	1204	23 Feb 1793	230	22 Oct 1783	78	443	Beg at a white oak	
Swagerty, Abraham	106		Green	200	64	1 Nov 1786	225	22 Oct 1783	59	425	On Clear Creek	
Swagerty, Abraham	113		Green	300	129	1 Nov 1786	140		59	432	On Clear Creek	
Swagerty, Abraham	2363	Knight, Jesse	Davidson	640	3061	19 Jul 1797			90	374	On 1st fork of West Fork	yes
Swaggerty, Abraham	784		Green	500	589	23 Aug 178-[si]	2120	4 Nov 1779	64	258	On N side of Clinch River &c	

Claimant:	File #:	Assignee:	Acres:	County:	Grant:	Grant Date:	Entry:	Entry Date:	Bk:	Pg:	Location by Stream Name:	Military:
Swaggerty, Frederick	123		200	Green	139	1 Nov 1786	226	22 Oct 1783	59	442	On a branch of French Broad R	
Swaggothy, Frederick	111		400	Green	127	1 Nov 1786	227	22 Oct 1783	59	430	On Clear Creek	
Swan, James	1425		100	Green	1237	27 Nov 1792	100	16 May 1789	80	166	On waters of Little Chuckey	
Swann, Thomas	563	King, Robert	640	Middle District	3084	12 Aug 1797	3187		90	392	On a branch of Cumberland River	yes
Swanson, Edward	1811		640	Davidson	384	26 Jun 1797	428	5 May 1784	80	336	E side of W Fork of Harpeth	
Swanson, John	329	Long, Nicholas	640	Tennessee	2079	20 May 1793	3060	30 Nov 1785	81	144	On S side of Cumberland River	yes
Swearance, John etal	713		200	Washington	527	10 Nov 1784	1043	7 Jan 1779	69	114	On both sides of Little Limestone	
Swearance, John etal	791		91	Washington	605	10 Nov 1784	2986	27 Sep 1783	69	140	On a branch of Little Limestone	
Swearingham, Zan or Van	1290	Coman, James	640	Sumner	3049	8 Jun 1797	4181	5 Apr 1797	90	318	On a branch or small creek	yes
Sweat, David	1996	Blount, John Gray & Thom	640	Davidson	1933	20 May 1793	946	27 Nov 1783	81	108	On the waters of Leapers Creek	yes
Sweat, William	50	Phillips, Mann	228	Tennessee	1250	10 Dec 1790	322	27 Nov 1783	74	348	In fork of Red River	yes
Sweetain, Edward	280		100	Washington	148	23 Oct 1782	909	31 Dec 1778	47	72	S side of Rones Creek	
Sweeton, Edward	1697		200	Green	1395	28 Dec 1796	2894	20 Aug 1781	90	205	On Tuckahoe Creek	
Sweeton, Edward, Ass.	910		50	Hawkins	235	27 Feb 1796			88	177	On S side of Holston River	
Swegerthy, Abraham	113		300	Green	129	1 Nov 1786	225	22 Oct 1783	59	432	On Clear Creek	
Swingle, George	1653		300	Green	1352	28 Aug 1795			87	525	On N side of French Broad River	
Swingle, John	1202		200	Green	1046	-- Mar 1792	321	23 Oct 1783	77	339	On N side of French Broad River	
Swingle, John	1374		200	Washington	1289	9 Dec 1797	2457	8 Mar 1780	96	12	On Indian Creek	
Swingle, Michael & John	1197		400	Green	1041	-- Mar 1792			77	337	On N/S French Broad River &c	
Syfret, Thomas	265	Worley, James	1000	Eastern District	2396	4 Feb 1795	3798		83	399	Northeastwardly side Little TN R	
Sykes, Simpson	750	Bond, John	640	Sumner	2153	20 May 1793	945	3 Mar 1790	81	161	On waters of Round Lick Creek	yes
Sylvester, Luke	461	Walton, William	640	Sumner	1603(?)	27 Apr 1793	3147	19 Dec 1787	81	18	On waters of Roaring River	yes
Symmony, James	352	Long, Nicholas	640	Tennessee	2180	20 May 1793	12	15 Oct 1783	81	166	On S side of Cumberland River	yes
Sypert, Robert	685	Hankins, Edward	228	Hawkins	2396	17 Jul 1794	3718		81	604	On N side of Holston River	yes
Sypret, Thomas	073	Pritchett, Edward	640	not given			3759	3 Aug 1792			N E side of Tennessee River	
Sypret, Thomas, Ass.	266		640	Eastern District	2397	4 Feb 1795			83	400	Northeasterly of Little Tennessee	
Tackell, Phillip	802		94	Hawkins	638	6 Jan 1795	379	3 Apr 1780	83	163	S side of Clinch River &c	
Tackett, George	1205		200	Green	1049	-- Mar 1792	2247	22 Jul 1784	77	340	Waters of Limestone Fork	
Taddis, Andrew	613	Clark, Lardner	640	Davidson	585	15 Sep 1787	1190		63	209	1st small or N/S Cumberland River	yes
Tadlock, Joshua	393		100	Green	395	20 Sep 1787	1904	8 Oct 1779	65	484	On waters of Lick Creek	
Tadlock, Thomas	968		100	Washington	945	17 Nov 1790	2423	11 Feb 1780	76	159	Branch of Clear Fork of Lick Creek	
Tagard, John	085		400	Sullivan			123	9 Feb 1780				
Taitt, Wm.	087	Nelson, Robt.	640	Davidson			2537	9 Jun 1796			On mouth of Western Creek	
Taitte, William	356	Searchnuit, Joshua	640	Davidson	340	4 Sep 1787	2234		63	127	W branches of Half Pone Creek	yes
Talbot, Matthew	292		526	Washington	159	24 Oct 1782	643	28 Nov 1778	47	77	On head of Bush Creek	
Talbot, Matthew	382		640	Middle District	321	17 Dec 1794	1432	27 Jan 1784	84	215	On both sides of Stones River	
Talbot, Matthew	828		400	Washington	642	10 Nov 1784	725	21 Dec 1778	69	149	On both sides of Gap Creek	
Talbot, Matthew, Sr.	349		500	Washington	216	23 Oct 1782	2570	30 May 1780	49	233	On N side of Wattaga River	
Talbot, Thomas	148		200	Washington	16	23 Oct 1782	1441	27 Jan 1784	47	7	On both sides of Gap Creek	
Talbot, Thomas	386		1000	Western District	386	27 Nov 1793	1927	27 Apr 1784	81	503	On first fork of Leeskacker [?]	
Talbot, Thomas	388		2000	Middle District	327	17 Dec 1794			84	218	On waters of Duck River	
Taliafarrow, James	436	Blount, Reading	640	Davidson	408	15 Sep 1787			63	151	Ridge bet. Sycamore & Marrowbone	yes
Talley, John	398		140	Sullivan	277	10 Nov 1784	420	2 Apr 1784	69	170	Beg at a poplar & white oak	
Talley, John	472		350	Sullivan	351	10 Nov 1784	419	15 Apr 1780	69	196	On N side of Holstein River	
Tally, John	0115			Sullivan								

Claimant:	File #:	Assignee:	County:	Acres:	Grant:	Grant Date:	Entry:	Entry Date:	Bk:	Pg:	Location by Stream Name:	Military:
Talton, James	499	Sanders, Williams	Davidson	640	471	15 Sep 1787	2278		63	171	On Maney Fork Creek	yes
Talton, Thomas	1106	Harris, Edward	Sumner	640 [?]	2612	4 Jun 1796	2965	1 Jun 1795	88	336	On S side of Cumberland River	yes
Tann, Ephraim	741	Thomas, Micajah	Davidson	640	714	11 Jul 1788	1585		63	251	On S waters of Sycamore Creek	yes
Tann, Joseph	071	Thomas, Micajah	Davidson	640			1586	20 Dec 1792			On waters of Stones River	yes
Tanner, John	028	Hays, Robert	Tennessee	640			2820	30 Sep 1785			On Brush Creek	yes
Tarbet, John	1073		Washington	149	1023	27 Nov 1792	1309	29 Mar 1779	80	182	On dreans of Watauga River	
Tarpin, Solomon, heirs of	2322		Davidson	640	458	1 Mar 1797	588	21 Aug 1784	90	222	Both sides Red River	
Tarrant, Manlove	052	Lews, Wm. T. & Wm. Tyrre	not given									yes
Tate, Adam, heir of Joseph	348		Tennessee	3840	2170	20 May 1793	684	26 Apr 1784	81	165	On S side of Cumberland River	
Tate, Caleb	183		Middle District	500	165	17 Nov 1790	1683	16 Apr 1784	76	178	On a branch the waters of Elk River	
Tate, Caleb	184		Middle District	5000	166	17 Dec 1790	1715	16 Apr 1784	76	178	W side of Richland Creek	
Tate, James, Rev.	74		Davidson	1553	60	14 Sep 1786	58		63	25	S side of Tennessee River	yes
Tate, John	939		Washington	50	916	17 Nov 1790	489	7 Oct 1778	76	149	On Elk River &c	
Tate, Samuel	210		Washington	455	78	23 Oct 1782	255	11 Jul 1778	47	37	On both sides Watauga River	
Tate, Samuel	602		Washington	150	696	26 Oct 1786	909	31 Dec 1778	66	9	Beg at a marked white oak &c	
Tate, Samuel	756		Washington	50	570	10 Nov 1784	2896	20 Aug 1781	69	129	Upon Roans Creek	
Tate, Samuel	779		Washington	100	593	10 Nov 1784	909	15 Mar 1784	69	136	On Rones Creek	
Tate, Samuel	925		Washington	78	902	17 Nov 1790	1571	2 Sep 1779	76	145	On Little Doe (?) &c	
Tate, Samuel	945		Washington	50	922	17 Nov 1790	487	7 Oct 1778	76	151	Elk [sic] C branch of Watauga R	
Tate, Samuel	971		Washington	500	948	17 Nov 1790	255	11 Jun 1778	76	160	On Watauga &c	
Tate, Thomas	825	Armstrong, Andrew	Davidson	640	828	23 Feb 1793	3384	17 Jan 1789	63	292	On N side of Red River	yes
Tate, William	1692	Phillips, Phillip & Mi. Camp	Davidson	270or27	1653	23 Feb 1793	43		76	338	Adjoining a suvey of their No. 106	yes
Tate, William	539	Gifford, James	Davidson	428	511	15 Sep 1787	3081		63	184	On Red River	yes
Tatem, Samuel	976		Green	100	890	17 Nov 1790	138	21 Oct 1783	76	134	N side of French Broad River &c	
Tatem, William	926		Washington	100	903	17 Nov 1790	488	7 Oct 1778	76	145	On Elk Creek &c	
Tatham, William	097		Sullivan	300			597	30 Nov 1792			On N side of Holston River	
Tatham, William	098		Sullivan	300			596	25 Sep 1784			In the Grassey Valley	
Tatham, William	099		Sullivan	300			585	7 Jun 1780			N side of Holston River	
Tatham, William	1001		Hawkins	500	694	9 Nov 1795	1827	6 Oct 1779	89	423	On Roseberry Creek	
Tatham, William	226	Richardson & McCoy	Sullivan	500	365	9 Aug 1787	410	8 Apr 1780	61	384	On the Reedy Creek	
Tatham, William	227	Richardson & McCoy	Sullivan	640	366	9 Aug 1787	399	8 Apr 1780	61	385	On Reedy Fork	
Tatham, William	228	Richardson & McCoy	Sullivan	300	367	9 Aug 1787	404	8 apr 1780	61	386	On Reedy Creek	
Tatham, William	229	Richardson & McCoy	Sullivan	500	368	9 Aug 1787	397		61	387	On Reedy Creek	
Tatham, William	230	Richardson & McCoy	Sullivan	300	369	9 Aug 1787	398	8 Apr 1780	61	388	On Reedy Creek	
Tatham, William	231	Richardson & McCoy	Sullivan	300	370	9 Aug 1787	405	8 Apr 1780	61	389	On Reedy Creek	
Tatham, William	265	Richardson & McCoy	Sullivan	640	404	9 Aug 1787	400	8 Apr 1780	61	423	On Reedy Creek	
Tatham, William	290		Middle District	640	250	7 Jul 1794	100	6 Oct 1779	82	199	Clear Fork of Cumberland River	
Tatham, William	466		Hawkins	300	338	29 Jul 1793			80	260	In a valley bet. 3rd and 4th Creeks	
Tatham, William	483		Hawkins	300	355	29 Jul 1793			80	264	On N side of Holston River &c	
Tatham, William	555		Hawkins	300	428	29 Jul 1793			80	284	Beg at a post oak	
Tatham, Wm. Etal	456		Hawkins	640	334	24 Jun 1793	1831	3 Feb 1780	80	197	On S side of Holston River	
Tatom, Absalom	024		Davidson	5000							Both sides W Fork Big Harpeth	
Tatom, Absalom	208		Middle District	4534	194	24 Dec 1792	613	10 Jul 1784	78	459	Main W Fork of Stones River	
Tatom, Barnard	1310	Kittrell, Isaac	Davidson	640	275	18 Jul 1788	50	1 Jan 1784	66	433	On N side of Cumberland River	
Tatom, Bernard	569	Currin, Elisha heirs	Davidson	640	541	15 Sep 1787	665		63	194	S side of Cumberland River	yes

Claimant:	File #:	Assignee:	County:	Acres:	Grant:	Grant Date:	Entry:	Entry Date:	Bk:	Pg:	Location by Stream Name:	Military:
Tatom, Howell	044	Parmore, Joshua	Tennessee	640	1605	23 Feb 1793	3513	8 Feb 1786	76	315	N side Cumberland River	
Tatom, Howell	113	Short, Wm.	Tennessee	640	1423	20 Dec 1791	2679	3 Sep 1785	77	357	Waters of Sulphur Fork of Red R	
Tatom, Howell	162	Chason, Joshua	Tennessee	640	1606	23 Feb 1793	2627	30 Sep 1785	77	357	S side of Cumberland River &c	yes
Tatom, Howell	1679	Newbran, Francis	Davidson	224	1422	20 Dec 1791	1640		76	315	N/S Cumberland on Willis Mill Cr	yes
Tatom, Howell	1725	Saunders, Julius	Davidson	640	111	20 Dec 1791	3681		77	357	N/S Cumberland on Marrow Bone Cr	
Tatom, Howell	220	Jackson, Andrew	Tennessee	960	1635	23 Feb 1793	808	7 May 1790	77	384	On Yellow Creek	yes
Tatom, Howell	333	Sullivan, James heirs	Sumner	640	1103	26 Nov 1789	1348	19 Mar 1790	76	329	S side of Cumberland River &c	
Tatom, Howell	5		Tennessee	640			3680	10 Dec 1788	74	130	On N side of Cumberland River	yes
Tatom, James	101		Davidson	2560	87	14 Mar 1786	335		63	36	Beg at a large Ash & Sugar tree	yes
Tatom, William	589	Harget, Frederick	Sumner	274	1830	20 May 1793	605	27 Sep 1788	81	75	On S Fork of E Fork of Stones R	yes
Tatum, Absolom	275		Middle District	3000	148	27 Apr 1793	10	4 Jan 1786	81	40	Waters of W Fork of Stones River	yes
Tatum, Bainard	2061	Lock, William	Davidson	640	2166	20 May 1793	885		81	164	On waters of W Harpeth	yes
Tatum, Bernard	725		Sumner	228	2109	20 May 1793	1733	5 Oct 1792	81	151	On S side of Cumberland River	yes
Tatum, Bernard, Ass.	597		Sumner	228	1840	20 May 1793	1732	31 Jul 1792	81	87	On S side of Cumberland River &c	yes
Tatum, Bernard, Ass.	727		Davidson	640	2112	20 May 1793	664	31 Jul 1792	81	152	On S side of Cumberland River	yes
Tatum, Harrall etal	2440	Austin, Thomas	Sumner	640	3282	6 Dec 1797	4156		98	162	On waters of Overalls Creek	yes
Tatum, Ho & Henry Wiggins	1370	Armstrong, Martin	Davidson	80	401	14 Sep 1797			92	16	Waters of Goose Creek	
Tatum, Ho & Henry Wiggins	2284	Martial, Solomon heirs	Davidson	640	2766	20 Jul 1796	4265		88	463	On waters of Murphys Fork	yes
Tatum, Ho & Henry Wiggins	2439	Branton, Levi	Davidson	640	3281	6 Dec 1797	4166		98	161	Overalls Creek of Stones River	yes
Tatum, Ho & Henry Wiggins	2441	Kelley, William heirs	Davidson	640	3283	6 Dec 1797	4257		98	162	Waters of W Fork of Stones River	yes
Tatum, Ho & Henry Wiggins	2442	Murbee, Patrick	Davidson	640	3284	6 Dec 1797	4160		98	163	On waters of Overalls Creek	yes
Tatum, Ho & Henry Wiggins	2443	Bolton, Thomas	Davidson	640	3285	6 Dec 1797	4267		98	164	Waters of Overalls Creek	yes
Tatum, Ho & Henry Wiggins	2444	Jones, Brittain	Davidson	640	3286	6 Dec 1797	4270		98	164	Waters of Overalls Creek	yes
Tatum, Ho & Henry Wiggins	2445	Trayham, John heirs	Davidson	640	3287	6 Dec 1797			98	165	Waters of Overalls Creek	yes
Tatum, Howell	112	Hatchcock, Amos heirs	Tennessee	640	1604	23 Feb 1793	2653	30 Sep 1785	76	314	On waters of Sulphur Fork	yes
Tatum, Howell	1912	Smithwick, Edmund heirs	Davidson	640	1680	23 Feb 1793	1157		81	49	On N side of Cumberland River	yes
Tatum, Howell	1923	Williamson, George	Davidson	640	1720	20 May 1793			81	59	On waters of W Harpeth River	yes
Tatum, Howell	1924	Green, Abraham	Davidson	640	1730	20 May 1793	2721		81	61	On waters of Whites Creek	yes
Tatum, Howell	1925	Williams, Jacob heirs	Davidson	274	1733	20 May 1793	3484		81	61	On waters of Whites Creek	yes
Tatum, Howell	2321	Hardick, Richard	Davidson	640	2936	1 Mar 1797	905		90	211	On West Harpeth River	yes
Tatum, Howell	2417	Armstrong, M.	Davidson	15	402	14 Oct 1797		26 Jun 1797	92	17	Beg at a hickory & elm	
Tatum, Howell	2436	Blamer, John heirs	Davidson	540	3278	6 Dec 1797	3041		98	158	On waters of Arrington Creek	yes
Tatum, Howell	2437	Cowan, Joseph	Davidson	220	3279	6 Dec 1797	3637		98	160	On waters of Overalls Creek	yes
Tatum, Howell	2453	Williamson, Geo.	Davidson	640	3348	6 Dec 1797	1724		98	183	Waters of Overalls Creek	yes
Tatum, Howell	47	Cox, Thos.	Tennessee	274	1239	10 Dec 1790	1244	20 Feb 1790	74	344	On S Cumberland River	yes
Tatum, Howell	58	Harrison, Geo.	Tennessee	640	1282	10 Dec 1790	1918	23 Jul 1785	74	359	On Yellow Creek	yes
Tatum, Howell	80	Palmer, Elisha	Tennessee	640	1326	10 Dec 1790	3679	10 Dec 1788	74	374	On S side of Cumberland River	yes
Tatum, Howell	821		Sumner	3565	824	17 Jan 1789	341	10 Mar 1788	63	291	On S side of Cumberland River	
Tatum, Howell	83	Easins, Thos.	Tennessee	640	1339	10 Dec 1790	1368	9 Nov 1784	74	378	On S side of Cumberland River	
Tatum, Howell	84	Thompson, Thos.	Tennessee	640	1340	10 Dec 1790	3648	10 Dec 1788	74	379	On S side of Cumberland River	
Tatum, Howell, Ass.	1361		Sumner	640	3209	14 Sep 1797	3897	16 Mar 1797	91	8	On E Fork of Bledsoes Creek	
Tatum, Howell, Ass.	1362		Sumner	320	3210	4 Oct 1797	4262	26 Jun 1797	92	8	Waters West Fork of Gooses Cr	yes
Tatum, Howell, Ass.	1362		Sumner	640	3211	14 Sep 1797	4169	16 Feb 1797	92	9	On waters of Stones River	
Tatum, Howell, Ass.	1364		Sumner	640	3212	14 Sep 1797	4171	29 Jun 1797	92	10	Waters of Stones River	yes
Tatum, Howell, Ass.	1365		Sumner	640	3213	14 Sep 1797	4264	29 Jul 1797	92	10	Waters of Stone River	yes

Claimant:	File #:	Assignee:	County:	Acres:	Grant:	Grant Date:	Entry:	Entry Date:	Bk:	Pg:	Location by Stream Name:	Military:
Tatum, Howell, Ass.	1366		Sumner	640	3214	14 Sep 1797	4260	16 Feb 1797	92	11	Waters of Stones River &c	yes
Tatum, Howell, Ass.	508		Sumner	640	1682	20 May 1793	2475	10 Apr 1792	81	49	On waters of Bledsoes Creek	yes
Tatum, Howell, Ass.	532		Sumner	304	1726	20 May 1793	1744	7 Jun 1792	81	60	On N side of Cumberland River	yes
Tatum, Howell, Ass.	532		Sumner	640	1735	20 May 1793	2564	5 Oct 1786	81	62	On N side of Cumberland River	
Tatum, James	677	Nations, John	Davidson	640	650	8 Dec 1787	2533		63	230	Bet the Clay Lick & Battleground	yes
Tatum, John	239	Whitard, William	Tennessee	274	1578	27 Apr 1793	595	25 Apr 1784	81	12	On W Fork of Red River	yes
Tatum, Howell	2418	Armstrong, Martin	Davidson	84	403	14 Sep 1797		26 June 1787	92	17	Near Nashville	
Taunt, Jesse	951		Davidson	1000	968	18 May 1789	615		63	329	E waters of Ceader(sic) Lick Cr	yes
Taunt, Thomas	132		Davidson	640	118	7 Mar 1786	616		63	46	On Blounts Creek	yes
Taunt, William	2074		Davidson	640	2221	20 May 1793	614		81	173	On N side of Harpeth River	yes
Taylor, Andred	297		Washington	450	164	24 Oct 1782	44	4 Apr 1779	47	79	On both sides of Buffalow Creek	
Taylor, Andrew	1163		Washington	640	1121	7 Jul 1794	1328	4 Apr 1779	81	617	On waters of Buffaloe Creek	
Taylor, Andrew	266		Washington	31	134	23 Oct 1782	1499	5 Aug 1779	47	65	Beg at 2 white oaks	
Taylor, Archibald	0144		Sumner	640			266	10 Feb 1792			On waters of Bledsoes Creek	
Taylor, Archibald	397		Sumner	640	408	27 Jun 1793	267	10 Feb 1784	80	343a	On S side of Cumberland River &c	
Taylor, Archibald	826		Sullivan	50	769	17 Nov 1793	47	8 Feb 1780	94	162	Beg at a black oak & ash	
Taylor, Benjamin	300	McCulloh, Benjamin	Tennessee	640	1976	20 May 1793	2243	12 Sep 1785	81	118	On waters of Blooming Grove Cr	yes
Taylor, Christopher	331		Washington	205	198	24 Oct 1782	214	20 May 1778	49	225	E side of Little Limestone	
Taylor, Christopher	928		Washington	100	905	17 Nov 1790	2989	29 Sep 1783	76	146	Beg at 2 white oaks &c	
Taylor, Christopher, Ass.	873		Hawkins	360	643	4 Feb 1795			84	104	On N side of Holston River	
Taylor, David	1411		Green	100	1223	27 Nov 1792	1405	24 May 1779	80	162	Three white oaks on Moores line	
Taylor, David	28		Green	200	91	1 Nov 1786	775	24 Dec 1763	58	452	Upon the N side of Nolilhuckie R	
Taylor, Elijah	1017	Etherington, Margaret	Rutherford	274			3549		82	423	Branch of Sandy Run of Broad R	
Taylor, George	1559		Green	200	1231	11 Jul 1794	2539	10 Apr 1780	82	245	Beg on a beech	
Taylor, George	345		Washington	200	212	24 Oct 1782	916	8 Oct 1779	49	231	On Frank Holley's branch	
Taylor, Henry	1350		Washington	165	1267	19 Oct 1797	26434(7)	9 Sep 1780	92	45	Waters of Little Limestone	
Taylor, Isaac	1097		Green	200	940	26 Dec 1791	1526	13 Jul 1779	77	257	On French Broad River	
Taylor, Isaac	1154		Washington	50	1112	7 Jul 1794	2395	12 May 1784	81	614	Beg at a bush &c	
Taylor, Isaac	12		Green	200	75	1 Nov 1786	56	1 Nov 1786	58	436	On N side of Tennessee River	
Taylor, Isaac	1293		Green	200	636	23 Aug 1788	45	8 May 1784	64	353	On N side of Holsten River &c	
Taylor, Isaac	1293		Washington	250	1179	4 Dec 1795	817	29 Dec 1779	89	426	Beg at a chesnut	
Taylor, Isaac	143		Green	640	613	23 Aug 1788	128	16 May 1785	64	345	On S side of Clinch River &c	
Taylor, Isaac	22		Hawkins	200	18	23 Aug 1788	1782	4 Feb 1779	67	435	On S side of Holston River &c	
Taylor, Isaac	260		Green	200	217	20 Sep 1787	303	23 Oct 1783	65	436	On waters of Sinking Creek	
Taylor, Isaac	50		Green	4000	113	1 Nov 1786	2223	21 Nov 1784	68	474	Upon N side of Tennessee River	
Taylor, Isaac	566	Bledsoe, Isaac	Sumner	640	1799	20 May 1793	3631	10 Apr 1789	81	79	On waters of Bledsoes Creek	yes
Taylor, Isaac	571		Green	400	251	20 Sep 1787	829	29 Oct 1783	66	157	On N side of Tennessee River &c	
Taylor, Isaac	69		Green	600	27	1 Nov 1786	712	28 Oct 1783	59	388	S side Holston River	
Taylor, Isaac	798		Green	250	603	23 Aug 1788	814	29 Oct 1783	68	263	On Dumplin Creek &c	
Taylor, Isaac	867		Washington	300	791	16 Aug 1787	2065	26 May 1786	64	149	On W side of Gap Creek	
Taylor, Isaac	867		Green	500	817	27 Nov 1789	14	17 Oct 1763	74	19	On side of Chuckey River	
Taylor, Isaac	885		Green	300	817	-- Sep 1790	1262	4 Dec 1783	74	277	On Dumplin Creek	
Taylor, Isaac	889		Green	300	821	-- Sep 1790	302	27 Oct 1783	74	281	On mouth of Dumpling Creek	
Taylor, Isaac	890		Green	300	822	-- Sep 1790	1298	27 Oct 1783	74	281	On Belfey Creek	
Taylor, Isaac	893		Green	300	824	-- Sep 1790	291	23 Oct 1783	74	290	On N side of French Broad River	

Claimant:	File #:	Assignee:	County:	Acres:	Grant:	Grant Date:	Entry:	Entry Date:	Bk:	Pg:	Location by Stream Name:	Military:
Taylor, Isaac	897		Green	200	828	-- Sep 1790	28	17 Jan 1783	74	292	Ridge known by Bradshers Gap	
Taylor, Isaac	95		Green	100	53	1 Nov 1786	30	29 Jan 1784	59	414	S side of Clear Creek	
Taylor, Isaac	97		Green	200	55	1 Nov 1786	1041	29 Oct 1783	59	416	On a branch of French Broad R	
Taylor, Isaac	99		Green	500	57	1 Nov 1786	522	27 Oct 1783	59	418	On both sides Holston River	
Taylor, Isaac	995		Green	100	1222	29 Jul 1793	2325	3 Dec 1779	76	484	On the waters of --- [sic]	
Taylor, Isaac & Robt. Young.	177		Hawkins	640	110	16 Nov 1790	502	11 Oct 1778	77	188	On N side of Tennessee River &c	
Taylor, James	671		Washington	640	845	10 Nov 1784	903	31 Dec 1778	69	99	On S side Wataugha River	
Taylor, James	775		Davidson	535	748	11 Jul 1788	559		63	263	On waters of Mill Creek	yes
Taylor, James P.	18		Giles	640	38	14 Jul 1812	198	23 Dec 1809	126	442	On Pigeon Root [sic]	
Taylor, James, Ass.	475		Sumner	640	1641	27 Apr 1793	810	5 Jun 1784	81	27	On both sides of Sulphur Fork &c	yes
Taylor, Jefrey	667	Cobb, Jesse	Sumner	640	1987	20 May 1793	1119	30 Nov 1792	81	121	On Cedar Creek	yes
Taylor, John	0116		Sullivan	30			521	29 Apr 1780			Beg at his old corner white oak	
Taylor, John	337		Hawkins	1500	331	8 Mar 1793	2273		78	475	On N side of Tennessee River	
Taylor, John	520	Bryan, John	Davidson	430	492	15 Sep 1787	225		63	178	N side of Cumberland River	yes
Taylor, John	662	Perry, Sion	Sumner	640	1982	20 May 1793	3664	5 May 1790	81	120	On head branches of Red River	yes
Taylor, Joseph	0103		Green	250			4	24 Feb 1778			Beg at a marked hickory	
Taylor, Joseph	113		Eastern District	100	146	29 Jul 1793	791	7 Jun 1787	76	480	N/S of Holston River inc an Island	
Taylor, Joseph	194		Middle District	300	208	29 Jul 1793	521	11 Aug 1789	76	478	S side of Cumberland River	
Taylor, Joseph	659		Hawkins	200	564	12 Jul 1794	1853	5 Feb 1780	81	591	On N side of Holston River	
Taylor, Matthew	1239		Washington	100	1211	20 Jul 1796	1436	11 Jun 1779	88	504	On Dry Creek	
Taylor, Nathaniel	1020		Washington	100	970	14 Jan 1793	2786	24 Feb 1781	79	276	Beg at a hickory	
Taylor, Nathaniel	1129		Hawkins	400	848	12 Dec 1797	1008	4 Jan 1779	96	6	Waters of Russells Creek	
Taylor, Nathaniel	1149		Washington	100	1107	17 Jul 1794	1436	11 Jul 1779	81	613	Beg at James Moores corner	
Taylor, Nathaniel	1152		Washington	100	1110	7 Jul 1794	2654	26 Sep 1780	81	614	Beg at a black oak	
Taylor, Nathaniel	1242		Washington	640	1214	20 Jul 1796	74	26 Feb 1778	88	505	On waters of Lorrells Fork	
Taylor, Nathaniel	1243		Washington	50	1215	20 Jul 1796	682	9 Dec 1778	88	506	On waters of Little Doe	
Taylor, Nathaniel	1244		Washington	320	1216	20 Jul 1796	557	30 Oct 1778	88	506	On branch of Little Doe	
Taylor, Nathaniel	1255		Washington	200	1227	27 Feb 1796	687	10 Dec 1778	88	511	Joining Edward Shipleys land	
Taylor, Nathaniel	1310		Washington	200	1231	17 Oct 1796	738	22 Dec 1778	90	14	Beg at a post oak &c	
Taylor, Nathaniel	18		Maury	500	35	14 Jul 1812	2721	5 Jan 1781	126	440	Being & lying on a small fork	
Taylor, Nathaniel, Ass.	3		Giles	450	5	14 Jul 1812	2723	7 Jan 1781	126	428	On Big Creek of Richland Creek	
Taylor, Nathaniel, Ass.	6		Giles	200	8	14 Jul 1812	432	25 Sep 1778	126	429	Lying on fork of Big Creek	
Taylor, Nathaniel, Ass.	7		Giles	260	9	14 Jul 1812	2736	14 Jan 1781	126	429	On Big Creek	
Taylor, Nathaniel, Ass.	9		Giles	200	11	14 Jul 1812	2734	12 Jan 1781	126	430	On fork of Big Creek	
Taylor, Nathaniel	968		Hawkins	500	740	27 Feb 1796	2047	27 Oct 1779	88	495	Beg at a dogwood	
Taylor, Nathaniel, Ass.	19		Maury	300	36	14 Jul 1812	127	4 Mar 1778	126	441	Being & lying on a small fork	
Taylor, Nathaniel, Ass.	2		Giles	1000	4	14 Jul 1812	2121	12 Jan 1785	126	427	On Big Creek of Richland Creek	
Taylor, Nathaniel, Ass.	20		Maury	1000	37	14 Jul 1812	1164	24 Dec 1811	126	441	On a fork of Catheys Creek	
Taylor, Nathaniel, Ass.	3		Maury	640	12	14 Jul 1812	2724	7 Jan 1781	126	430	On a branch of Catheys Creek	
Taylor, Nathaniel, Ass.	4		Giles	100	6	14 Jul 1812	712	- Dec 1779	126	428	On Big Creek	
Taylor, Nathaniel, Ass.	5		Giles	540	7	14 Jul 1812	1159	1 Feb 1779	126	429	Lying on a branch of Big Creek	
Taylor, Nathaniel, Ass.	8		Giles	540	10	14 Jul 1812	2738	19 Jan 1781	126	430	On Richland Creek	
Taylor, Parmanus	1102		Green	65	945	26 Dec 1791	92	29 Apr 1789	77	260	On N side of French Broad River	
Taylor, Permanus	369		Green	200	371	20 Sep 1787	368	8 Sep 1778	65	478	On waters of Lick Creek	
Taylor, Phillip	164		Tennessee	1757	1425	20 Dec 1791	193	24 Oct 1783	77	357	On both sides of Duck River	

Claimant:	File #:	Assignee:	County:	Acres:	Grant:	Grant Date:	Entry:	Entry Date:	Bk:	Pg:	Location by Stream Name:	Military:
Taylor, Thomas	0104		Green	150			317	17 Mar 1780			In Carters Valley	
Taylor, Thomas	0119	Waggoner, James	Sumner	640			1850	5 Dec 1785		158	On Dixons Creek	yes
Taylor, Thomas	106		Hawkins	236	140		317, -1783	1780 & 1779	75		In Carters Valley	
Taylor, Thomas	1267		Washington	100	1205	26 Dec 1791	2597	28 Jul 1780	89	327	Beg at a white oak	
Taylor, Thomas	1273		Washington	100	1211	4 Dec 1795	2597	28 Jul 1780	89	330	On Indian Creek	
Taylor, Thomas	150	Cole, Jesse	Davidson	640	136	14 Mar 1786	1210		63	52	E side of W Fork of Harpeth River	yes
Taylor, Thomas	2287	Frazier, John	Davidson	251	180	20 Jul 1796		12 May 1796	88	465	On E Fork of Whites Creek	
Taylor, Thomas	708	Jones, Benjamin	Davidson	320	682	8 Dec 1787	3389		63	240	On E waters of Whites Creek	yes
Taylor, Thomas, Ass.	219		Sumner	429	1124	26 Nov 1789	1656	9 Apr 1788	74	141	On S side of Cumberland River	yes
Taylor, Thomas, Ass.	338		Sumner	640	1389	20 Dec 1791	918	25 Nov 1789	77	348	S side of Cumberland River &c	yes
Taylor, Wm & John, Ass.	780		Sumner	640	2235	20 May 1793	2808	30 Nov 1792	81	177	On the waters of Dixons Creek	yes
Teenan, James	1160		Green	620	1003	26 Dec 1791	1523	24 Oct 1784	77	282	On S side of Clinch River	
Teer, William	125	Buxton, Wm.	Davidson	640	111	7 Mar 1786	652		63	44	S side of Cumberland River	yes
Telifair, Elizabeth	1687		Green	100	1363	27 Nov 1795	1817	6 Oct 1779	89	287	On N side of Noleychuckey River	
Teman, Robert	926		Green	370	840	17 Nov 1790			76	118	N side of Clinch River	
Temple, Major	5		Green	240	68	1 Nov 1786	66	21 Oct 1783	58	429	On a branch of Richland Creek	
Templeton, James	124		Western District	920	124	10 Jul 1788	1575	1 Apr 1784	67	328	Waters Rutherfords Fork of Obion	
Templeton, Thomas	2325	Donelson, John	Davidson	1000	2919	19 Feb 1797	2624		90	248	Both sides of Stones Creek	yes
Templeton, Thomas	425	Moore, John	Tennessee	428	2485	31 Dec 1793	1644	14 Apr 1785	81	438	On Sulphur Fork of Red River	yes
Tennessee papers,	00--	Fragments of papers	Sumner									
Tennessee papers,	130	Fragments of papers	Green	100			85					yes
Terrell, William	0106		Davidson	640	190	10 Jul 1788	199	25 Jan 1784	66	409	N side Noley Chuckey River	
Terrell, William	1226		Green	360	1233	12 Jun 1794			81	572	Overalls Cr branch of Stones River	
Terrell, William	1469	Hadley, Joshua	Tennessee	2560	1712	30 Oct 1793	3105	8 Dec 1785	81	56	On S side of Cumberland River	yes
Terrell, William	264		Eastern District	300	208	4 Jan 1795	193	21 Feb 1780	84	41	On N side of Tennessee River	
Terrell, William & Jas. Beaird	273	Boxley, Joseph	Eastern District	640	2399	1 Feb 1795			84	150	On S side of Clinch River	
Terrell, William, Ass.	294		Green	100	1365	4 Feb 1795			84	139	On head waters of Potters Creek	
Terrell, Wm & S Donelson	1609	McCoy, James	Davison	640	2550	7 Mar 1796			88	305	On the waters of Stones River	yes
Terrell, Wm. & John Cowan	1570		Green	376	1316	6 Jan 1795			83	160	In Sinking Cane Valley	
Terrell, Wm. & S. Donelson	1570		Green	640	1283	12 Jul 1794			81	589	On a branch of Sycamore Creek	
Terrell, Nimrod	1522	Barbour, Richard	Sumner	1000	3144	14 Sep 1797	4758	27 Feb 1797	90	420	On Flat Creek	yes
Terrell, William	1561		Green	640	212	30 Oct 1794			83	140	S side of Clinch River &c	yes
Terrell, William	235		Eastern District	100	190	12 Jun 1794			82	180	Head of Lower Fork of Third Creek	
Terrell, William	243		Eastern District	300	206	30 Oct 1794			83	137	In valley leading into Powells River	
Terrell, William	311		Eastern District	600	216	18 Aug 1795			87	504	On waters of Gost(sic) Creek	
Terrell, William	312		Eastern District	640	217	18 Aug 1795			87	504	On S side of Holston River	
Terrell, William	665		Hawkins	200	570	12 Jul 1794			81	593	On S side of Powells River	
Terrell, William	667		Hawkins	400	572	12 Jul 1794			81	594	On both sides of Powells River	
Terrell, William	707		Hawkins	60	529	12 Jun 1794			82	162	Elm stump on bank of Holston &c	
Terrell, William	737		Hawkins	300	557	12 Jun 1794			82	174	On N side of Holston River &c	
Terrell, William	737		Eastern District	600	216	18 Aug 1795			87	504	On waters of Gost [sic] Creek	
Terrell, William	805		Hawkins	100	641	6 Jan 1795	1263	-- Mar 1779	83	168	On waters of Caney Creek	
Terrell, William	818		Hawkins	1000	640	28 Jan 1794			83	362	N side of Clinch River	
Terrell, William & John Payne	347		Middle District	1000	138	4 Feb 1795			84	140	On Woolf River	

Claimant:	File #:	Assignee:	Acres:	Grant:	County:	Grant Date:	Entry:	Entry Date:	Bk:	Pg:	Location by Stream Name:	Military:
Terrell, William, Ass.	065		640		Middle District				84	149	On N side of Holston River	
Terrell, Wm & Jos. Beard	292		2000	209	Eastern District	1 Feb 1795					N side Noley Chuckey	
Terrell, Wm. & Geo. Gordon	0119		250		Green						N side of Noleychuckey River	
Terrell, Wm. & Geo. Gordon	1587		250	160	Green	22 Feb 1795	1630	9 Apr 1784	83	428	N side of Noleychuckey River	
Terrell, Wm. & Geo. Gordon	1589		480	1331	Green	21 Feb 1795	2166	8 Nov 1779	83	435	N side of French Broad River &c	
Terrell, Wm. & John Payne	263		200	211	Eastern District	3 Feb 1795			83	382	N side of Holston River	
Terrell, Wm. & Jos. Beaird	276		640	211	Eastern District	4 Jan 1795			84	44	On S side of Clinch River	
Terrell, Wm. & Joseph Beaird	259		2000	206	Eastern District	28 Jan 1794			83	365	N/S Clinch R on head of Big Barren	
Terrell, Wm. & Joseph Beard	270		640	205	Eastern District	4 Jan 1795			84	39	On N side of Clinch River	
Terrell, Wm. & Robt. King	806		640	642	Hawkins	6 Jan 1795			83	165	On Sycamore Creek &c	
Terrell, Wm. & S. Donelson	803		476	639	Hawkins	6 Jan 1795			83	164	On Panther Creek	
Terrell, Wm. & Wm T. Lewis	90		1000	90	Western District	10 Jul 1788	2030 (2632	25 May 1784	67	316	Both sides S Fork Forked Deer R	
Terrentine, Alexander	456	Wilson, John	640	428	Davidson	15 Sep 1787			63	158	N side of Sulphur Fork	yes
Terrill, William	351	Lewis, Amos	228		Davidson		1485				On Leepers Fork of Harpeth	yes
Terry (Tirey), John	351		100	218	Washington	24 Oct 1782	1444	21 Jun 1779	49	224	On waters of Cherokey Creek	
Terry, John	1287		100	1137	Green	12 Jan 1793	1302	1 Jan 1784	78	386	On S side of Holston River	
Tetner, Henry	668	Clark, Lardner	1000	641	Davidson	15 Nov 1787	2605		63	227	On Bizzells Salleen &c	yes
Teuton, Caleb	1103	Farmer, Thomas	640	2604	Sumner	7 Mar 1796	760		88	328	On N side of Obeys River	yes
Tew, Alexander	2405	Robertson, Jonathan	640	2802	Davidson	6 Jun 1796	3862(?)		91	474	S W side of Big Harpeth	yes
Thaxton, James	54		4352	40	Davidson	14 Mar 1786	208		63	17	Head branches W Fork of Harpeths R	yes
The Bear going in the hole	066		640	16	Tennessee			9 Aug 1819			2 wild cherry trees & small red oak	
The Fence	067		640	20	Tennessee			8 Sep 1819			Beg plumb bush on bank Tennessee River	
The Wolf	068		640	27	Tennessee			9 Aug 1819			Maples on N Fk of Tennessee	
Theregood, Francis	153	Nichols, John	773	139	Davidson	14 Mar 1786	824		63	53	S side of Cumberland River	yes
Thomas, Asa	405	Persons, Thomas	228	2431	Tennessee	18 Mar 1794	1292	1 Nov 1784	81	421	Branch Bushes Meat House Fork	yes
Thomas, Benjamin	633		640	605	Davidson	15 Sep 1787	777		63	216	On Lick Fork of Jones's Creek	yes
Thomas, Brittain	625	Robertson, Elijah	640	597	Davidson	15 Sep 1787	1832		63	213	On N side of Cumberland River	yes
Thomas, Caleb	1177	Harris, Edward	640	2682	Sumner	4 Jun 1796	943	1 Jun 1795	88	361	Joining sd Harris	yes
Thomas, Isaac	070	Prewet, Joshua	274		Davidson		541	7 Feb 1786			On main E Fork of Mill Creek	
Thomas, Isaac	1036		100	1263	Green	29 Jul 1793	31	29 Jan 1784	76	491	On a fork of Stockleys Mill Creek	
Thomas, Isaac	1527		274	1084	Davidson	26 Nov 1789			74	122	On Main E Fork of Mill Creek	
Thomas, Isaac	799		100	604	Green	23 Aug 1788	31	29 Jan 1784	68	263	Beg at a white oak	
Thomas, Jeremiah	017	Donelson, Stockley	640	2030	Robertson	20 May 1793	1589	30 Jul 1796			On Sulphur Fork of Red River	yes
Thomas, Jeremiah	2024a	McCulloh, Benjamin	640	76	Davidson	8 Oct 1787	2693		81	132	On N side of Cumberland River	yes
Thomas, Jessee	1204		320	1036	Davidson	18 May 1789	271	12 Feb 1784	66	225	Small or of N side of Big Harpeth R	
Thomas, Jethro	1018	Thomas, Micajah	640	103	Davidson	17 Apr 1786	1589		63	345	On E fork of Stones River	
Thomas, Jno.	1126		640	17	Davidson	14 Jul 1812	292	16 Feb 1784	66	175	N/S Cumberland cor James Espys	
Thomas, Jno., Ass.	13		640	18	Giles	14 Jul 1812 /	169	13 Mar 1778	126	432	Lying & being on Big Creek	
Thomas, Jno., Ass.	14		500	19	Giles	14 Jul 1812	1017	4 Jan 1779	126	433	On Lynn Creek	
Thomas, Jno., Ass.	15		300	33	Giles	14 Jul 1812	1035	4 Jan 1779	126	433	Lying on Big Creek	
Thomas, Jno., Ass.	17		640	20	Giles	14 Jul 1812	1024	4 Jan 1779	126	439	On water of Big Creek	
Thomas, Jno., Ass.	5		500	3375	Maury	14 Jul 1812	1018	4 Jan 1779	126	434	On the W side of Catheys Creek	
Thomas, John	13	Good, William	640	1545	Smith	26 Oct 1801	1271	23 Sep 1785	111	97	On E side of Caney Fork River	
Thomas, John	1765	Hays, Robert	640	817	Davidson	14 Jan 1793	3821		79	268	On waters of W Harpeth	yes
Thomas, John	552		200		Washington	11 Jul 1788	2855	9 Apr 1781	64	334	Beg in John Callahans line	yes

Claimant:	File #:	Assignee:	County:	Acres:	Grant:	Grant Date:	Entry:	Entry Date:	Bk:	Pg:	Location by Stream Name:	Military:
Thomas, John	909	Good, William	Sumner	297	2478	31 Dec 1793	1271	29 Jul 1792	81	436	On Whites Fork of New River	yes
Thomas, Joseph	1016		Hawkins	400	760	26 Dec 1796	5	24 Jan 1778	90	203	N side of Linch Mountain	
Thomas, Lemuel	286	Long, Nichols	Tennessee	640	1897	20 May 1793	465	24 Feb 1784	81	99	S side of Cumberland River &c	yes
Thomas, Martin	354	Hughs, David	Sumner	274	1450	20 Dec 1791	3483	11 Oct 1786	77	363	On N side of Red River	yes
Thomas, Micajah	071	Tann, Joseph	Davidson	640			1586	20 Dec 1792			On waters of Stones River	
Thomas, Micajah	1018	Thomas, Jethro	Davidson	640	1036	18 May 1789	1589		63	345	On N fork of Stones River	yes
Thomas, Micajah	117	Parr, Joseph heirs	Tennessee (?)	640	1615	23 Feb 1793			76	319	On waters of Stones River	
Thomas, Micajah	607		Middle District	1000	382	15 Sep 1801	2498	30 Nov 1784	111	50	On waters of Woolf River	
Thomas, Micajah	741	Tann, Ephraim	Davidson	640	714	11 Jul 1788	1585		63	251	On S waters of Sycamore Creek	yes
Thomas, Philemon, Ass.	8		Sumner	640	765	11 Jul 1788	3025	20 Sep 1787	63	268	Head branches of Bradley Lick Creek	yes
Thomas, Philemon, Ass.	9		Sumner	640	766	11 Jul 1788	3011	20 Sep 1787	63	269	N branches of Bradleys Lick Cr	yes
Thomas, Richard	147		Davidson	228	133	14 Mar 1786	798		63	51	On Parsons Creek	yes
Thomas, Richard	224	Price, Saml.	Tennessee	365	1567	4 Feb 1793	2433	30 Sep 1785	79	293	E boundary 400 acres Jas McCown	
Thomas, Richard, Ass.	313		Sumner	640	1526	20 Nov 1792	2005	26 Nov 1785	75	510	On both sides of Flinns Lick Creek	yes
Thomas, Richard, Ass.	384		Sumner	274	1568	4 Feb 1793	2418	19 Nov 1792	79	293	On E side of Caney Fork	yes
Thomas, Richard, Ass.	385		Sumner	640	1569	4 Feb 1793	2321	30 Nov 1792	79	293	On waters of Dixons Creek	yes
Thomas, Richard, Ass.	386		Sumner	640	1570	4 Feb 1793	2313	30 Nov 1785	79	294	On E Fork of Stones River	yes
Thomas, Ross	528	Lewis, W. T. & W. Tyrrell	Tennessee	274	2844	21 Jan 1797	3137	16 Dec 1785	90	46	On the Barren Fork	yes
Thomas, Thomas	2091	McCulloh, Benjamin	Davidson	640	2299	20 May 1793	2819		81	191	On Leepers Lick Creek	yes
Thomas, William	144	Scott, Marmaduke	Davidson	640	130	14 Mar 1786	416		63	50	Both sides of E Fork of Yellow Cr	yes
Thomas, William	370		Sullivan	440	249	10 Nov 1784	39,-285	Feb & Mar 1780	69	161	Beg at a large white oak	
Thomas, William	714	Thompson, Thomas	Davidson	640	687	8 Dec 1787	818		63	242	On W Fork of Jones's Creek	yes
Thomas, William, Ass.	1681		Green	400	1386	10 Sep 1796		13 Sep 1787	88	494	On N side French Broad River	
Thomas, Wm & Jas.Hubbard	637		Green	600	837	27 Nov 1789	802	29 Oct 1783	74	34	On N side of Tennessee River	
Thomas, Wm & Jas.Hubbard	877	Hubbard, James	Green	600	837	27 Nov 1789	802	29 Oct 1783	74	34	On N side of Tennessee River	
Thomas, Wm.	877		Green	600	837	27 Nov 1789	802	29 Oct 1783	74	34	On N side of Tennessee River	
Thomas, Zebulon	637	Baker, John	Sumner	640	1926	20 May 1793	3405	19 Nov 1792	81	106	On W side of Caney Rork	yes
Thomason, John	374		Davidson	640	346	15 Sep 1787	640		63	131	W Fork of Red River	yes
Thomason, John	848		Hawkins	200	673	22 Feb 1795	134	30 Apr 1779	83	432	N side of Holston River	
Thombell, John	318	McCulloh, Benjamin	Tennessee	640	2019	20 May 1793	2242	12 Sep 1785	81	129	On S side of Cumberland River	yes
Thompson, Ahab	598	Reed, Jesse	Davidson	640	570	15 Sep 1787			63	204	S side of Big Barren River	yes
Thompson, Andrew	1096		Davidson	640	70	17 Apr 1786	351	11 Mar 1784	66	58	Lying on Sulphur Fork of Red River	
Thompson, Andrew	391		Washington	100	383	13 Oct 1783	2296	27 Nov 1779	52	257	On waters of Big Limestone	
Thompson, Asabel	015	Tyrrell, Wm. & Wm. T. Lewi	Montgomery	640			3504	30 Dec 1796			On W Fork of 1st Creek	yes
Thompson, Chas.	1082		Davidson	640	56	17 Apr 1786	350	11 Mar 1784	66	53	N Fork Cumberland & Richland Cr	
Thompson, Daniel	620		Davidson	274	592	15 Sep 1787	78		63	211	S side of Cumberland River	yes
Thompson, David	899	Blount, Reading	Davidson	640	915	18 May 1789	2551		63	316	On N side of Cumberland River	yes
Thompson, James	1155		Davidson	640	132	17 Apr 1786	104	15 Jan 1784	66	182	Ridge Fletchers Lick & Richland	
Thompson, James	238	Stewart, John	Davidson	274	224	7 Mar 1786	454		63	82	On waters of Richland Creek	yes
Thompson, James	480		Sullivan	150	359	10 Nov 1784	611	17 Oct 1788	69	199	In Carters Valley	
Thompson, Jason	1487	Armstrong, M.	Davidson	104	97	20 Nov 1790		21 Jan 1789	73	278	On Mill Creek	
Thompson, Jason	1488	Brown, Isaac	Davidson	640	1201	16 Mar 1791	3678		73	278	On Mill Creek & Stones River	yes
Thompson, Jason	1512	Davis, Jonathan	Davidson	640	1069	26 Nov 1789	3458		74	114	Lying on Mill Creek	yes
Thompson, Jason	1528	Alexander, Joseph heirs	Davidson	640	1085	26 Nov 1789	3441		74	123	On E waters of Spring Creek	yes
Thompson, Jason	1540	Colanch, Peter heirs	Davidson	640	1097	26 Nov 1789	3454		74	130	On E waters of Mill Creek	yes

Claimant:	File #:	Assignee:	County:	Acres:	Grant:	Grant Date:	Entry:	Entry Date:	Bk:	Pg:	Location by Stream Name:	Military:
Thompson, Jason	184	Branner, Joseph	Tennessee	640	1464	4 Jan 1792	2348	20 Jul 1791	77	367	S side of Cumberland River	
Thompson, Jason	1951	Pope, Samuel	Davidson	274	1790	20 May 1793	1120		81	76	On waters of White Creek	yes
Thompson, Jason	1959	McDash, John	Davidson	284	1804	20 May 1793	3541		81	80	S/S Cumber R waters of Brown Cr	yes
Thompson, Jason	828	Conester, John heirs	Davidson	640	831	17 Jan 1789			63	292	On waters of Mill Creek	
Thompson, Jason, Ass.	887		Sumner	640	2425	31 Dec 1793	1352	13 Nov 1790	81	408	On E waters of Spring Creek	yes
Thompson, Jasson	226	Ramage, Alexander	Davidson	640	212	7 Mar 1786	815	7 Mar 1786	63	78	On waters of Mill Creek	yes
Thompson, John	093		Sullivan	150			560	15 May 1780			Beg gum & white ash N/S Reedy Creek	
Thompson, John	1241		Green	150	1091	12 Jan 1793	364	5 Sep 1778	78	359	Adjoining the seven islands tract	
Thompson, John	1517		Green	300	1278	12 Jan 1794	721	1 Jan 1781	81	587	On N side Nolichuckey River	
Thompson, John	1522	Bunnington, Wm.	Davidson	640	1079	26 Nov 1789	2407		74	119	On East waters of Mill Creek	yes
Thompson, John	1635		Green	168.5	1338	18 Aug 1795	1525	24 Feb 1784	87	503	On N side of Nolychucka River	
Thompson, John	336		Sullivan	200	476	10 Jul 1788			67	484	Lying on Cates Branch &c	
Thompson, John	538		Hawkins	200	411	29 Jul 1793	2248	22 Nov 1779	80	280	On Mulberry Creek	
Thompson, John	614		Hawkins	240	489	29 Jul 1793	1447	21 Jun 1779	80	297	N side of Clinch River &c	
Thompson, John	787	Wycoff & Clark	Davidson	640	789	11 Jul 1788	2165		63	276	On S side of Cumberland River	yes
Thompson, John	992		Hawkins	640	702	12 Nov 1795	1626	16 Sep 1779	89	144	On N side of Clinch River	
Thompson, John	994	Roberts, Wm.	Hawkins	250	704	12 Nov 1795	696	16 Oct 1780	89	145	On N side of Clinch Mountain	
Thompson, Joshua	1326		Washington	50	1250	6 Jun 1797	2496	11 May 1780	90	309	On Lick Creek	
Thompson, Joshua	309	McCulloh, Benjamin	Tennessee	640	2010	20 May 1793	2248	12 Sep 1785	81	127	On head of a small drain &c	yes
Thompson, Laurence	2088	Coffey, John	Davidson	1806	2291	20 May 1793	2240		81	189	On E Fork of Stones River	yes
Thompson, Lawrance	2303	Coffey, John	Davidson	1806	2491	26 Sep 1795	790		89	103	On E Fork of Stones River	
Thompson, Nathan	471	Shelton, David	Davidson	640	443	15 Sep 1787	764		63	163	S side of Cumberland River	yes
Thompson, Ned	251	Hadley, Joshua	Sumner	640	1197	30 Nov 1790	3212	18 Nov 1787	74	321	On waters of E Fork &c	yes
Thompson, Rich'd	364		Hawkins	200	356	8 Mar 1793	1865	6 Oct 1779	78	487	In Hinds Valley	
Thompson, Robert	025		Davidson	100			675	5 Mar 1785			On waters John Fletchers Lick Cr	
Thompson, Robert	1019	Stevenson, James	Davidson	640	1037	18 May 1789	3477		63	345	Bet. Cedar Lick Cr & Spencers Cr	yes
Thompson, Robert	1299		Davidson	640	264	10 Jul 1788	103	15 Jan 1784	66	429	Joining Wm. Collingsworth pre-emption	
Thompson, Robert	1429	Armstrong, R.	Davidson	100	46	8 Oct 1787	676	5 Mar 1785	68	159	On waters of Richland Creek	
Thompson, Robert	1531	Joiner, Stephen heirs	Davidson	640	1088	26 Nov 1789	1917		74	125	On waters of Hurricane Creek	yes
Thompson, Robert	189	Cates, Mathew	Middle District	274	175	7 Mar 1786	1011		63	66	W side of Big Harpeth River	yes
Thompson, Robert	225		Davidson	500	205	27 Nov 1792	1549	23 Mar 1784	80	209	On N side of Duck River	
Thompson, Robert, Ass.	9	Armstrong, M.	Davidson	100	3	16 Feb 1786			63	2	Waters of John Fletchers Lick Cr	
Thompson, Robert, Ass.	189		Davidson	100	3	16 Feb 1786			63	2	On waters of John Fletchers Lick Creek	
Thompson, Robt. Etal	270	Moore, James	Sumner	480	1252	10 Dec 1790	1246	29 Sep 1787	74	349	On S side of Cumberland River	yes
Thompson, Rosiah; Susanah	314		Eastern District	228	2486	18 Aug 1795	3764		87	509	On S side of Holston River	
Thompson, Samuel	2461	Thompson, John & others	Davidson	640	468	23 Jan 1800	500	28 Jun 1784	106	368	On a branch of Stewarts Creek	
Thompson, Samuel	1019	King, Robt,R. Muir, J. Berry	Hawkins	428	2944	1 Mar 1797	4440		90	215	In Powells Valley	yes
Thompson, Samuel	208		Green	200	165	20 Sep 1787	144	21 Oct 1783	65	419	On the N side of French Broad R	
Thompson, Samuel	849	Jones, John	Davidson	640	854	17 Jan 1789	2021		63	298	On waters of Caney Fork	yes
Thompson, Thomas	1290		Davidson	640	255	10 Jul 1788	132	15 Jan 1784	66	426	S/S Cumb R & waters Browns Cr	yes
Thompson, Thomas	149	Buckhannon, John	Davidson	640	135	14 Mar 1786	817		63	52	On waters of Mill Creek	
Thompson, Thomas	714	Thomas, William	Davidson	640	687	8 Dec 1787	818		63	242	On W Fork of Jones's Creek	yes
Thompson, Thomas	756	Stepp, John	Davidson	640	729	11 Jul 1788	1451		63	256	On 1st creek below Stones Lick Creek	yes
Thompson, Thomas	84	Tatum, Howell	Tennessee	640	1340	10 Dec 1790	3648	10 Dec 1788	74	379	On S side of Cumberland River	yes
Thompson, Thos & Saml.	31	Cotton, John	Middle District	4260	33	10 Jul 1788	1252	24 Nov 1783	67	422	On N side of Duck River &c	yes

Earliest Tennessee Land Records

Claimant:	File #:	Assignee:	County:	Acres:	Grant:	Entry:	Grant Date:	Entry Date:	Bk:	Pg:	Location by Stream Name:	Military:
Thompson, Thos.	038		Hawkins	200		990	15 Sep 1787		63	156	N side of Holston &c	
Thompson, William	451		Davidson	428	423						On N Cross Creek	yes
Thompson, William	927	Porterfield, John	Sumner	228	2381	3127	27 Sep 1794	16 Jul 1780	81	637	On waters of E Fork &c	yes
Thomson, Henry	710		Green	2000	751	602	11 Jul 1788	28 Oct 1783	66	478	S/S of French Broad River &c	
Thomson, Henry	094		Sullivan	200		339		21 Mar 1785			On Coles Branch	
Thomson, John	848		Hawkins	200	673	134	20 Feb 1795	30 Apr 1779	83	432	N side of Holston River &c	
Thomson, John etal	994		Hawkins	250	704	696	12 Nov 1795	16 Oct 1780	89	145	On N side of Clinch Mountain	
Thornbury, Henry	1724		Green	170	1403	1943	21 Jan 1797	5 Feb 1780	91	126	Joining Thornbury's he now lives on	
Thornbury, Joseph	597		Hawkins	150	471	1441	29 Jul 1793	31 Jun 1779	80	294	On waters of Beaver Creek	
Thornton, William	700		Washington	300	514	693	10 Nov 1784	16 Dec 1778	69	110	On Cherokee Creek	
Thornton, Yancey, Ass.	1442		Sumner	228	3354		7 Apr 1800		106	439	On both sides of Middle Fork	yes
Thornton, Yancey, Ass.	1441		Sumner	228	3353	3975	9 Apr 1800	23 Mar 1797	106	438	On waters of Paytons Creek	yes
Thow, Thomas	339	Barton, Samuel	Sumner	640	1390	1952	20 Dec 1791	21 May 1791	77	348	On E waters of Cedar Creek	yes
Thrift, Abraham	1377	Philips, Isaac	Sumner	224	3239	1927	24 Nov 1797	13 Jul 1797	94	172	Bet. two creeks	yes
Thurrill, Abraham	1159	Harris, Edward	Sumner	640	2664	3840	4 Jun 1796	1 Jun 1795	88	355	Joining Harris survey	yes
Thrust, Edward	940	Blount, Reading	Davidson	640	956	2552	18 May 1789		63	326	On E Fork of Stones River	
Tiers, Jas.	1546	King, Robt.	Green	250	1306	995	17 Jul 1794	29 Oct 1783	81	611	On S side of Holston River	
Tiffin, Thomas	1621	Jeffreys, Thomas	Davidson	520	1357	214	10 Dec 1790		74	384	On waters of Station Camp Creek	yes
Tigh, John	64		Washington	200		500		10 Oct 1778			On head of Muddy Fork of Cedar Cr	
Tight, John	390		Hawkins	200	511		27 Jan 1793		79	494	On head of Muddy Fork of Cedar Cr	
Tilghman, Bililtha	1047	Shute, Thomas	Sumner	1000	2526	1100	8 Dec 1795		88	279	Near head of Flinns Creek	yes
Tillet, Andrew	011	Weakley, Samuel	Robertson	640		4396		9 Mar 1794			On N waters of Sycamore Creek	yes
Tilley, Lewis	1020	Donelson, S. & Jas. Latha	Hawkins	274	2947	4517	1 Mar 1797		90	216	N side of the great road	yes
Tilman, John	872	Humphries, David	Sumner	274	2388	1093	7 Jan 1794	19 Dec 1792	81	388	On E side of Cedar Lick Creek	yes
Tilton, Richard	066	Sheppard, John	not given	640		2962		15 Aug 1792			Waters of Obeys River	yes
Tipper, John	1663	Robertson, James	Davidson	228	1586	209	23 Feb 1793		76	305	On Big Harpeth River	
Tippel, George	031	Paisley, Robt.	not given	640		4221 [?]						yes
Tippet, George	031		not given	640		4221 [?]						yes
Tipton, Jacob	428		Green	200	430	1427	20 Sep 1787	10 May 1785	65	496	Beg at a white oak	
Tipton, Jacob	548		Washington	100	813	1469	11 Jul 1788	5 Jul 1779	64	334	On W side of Doe River	
Tipton, John	0101		Green	1000	18	1816		16 Dec 1779			Being the E Fork &c	
Tipton, John	218		Eastern District	1000	202		12 Jul 1794		81	625	On E Fork of Emerys River	
Tipton, John	517		Washington	600	780	236	16 Aug 1787	13 Jun 1778	64	146	Beg at 3 white oak saplins &c	
Tipton, John	726		Washington	150	540	601	10 [?] Nov 178	21 Oct 1778	69	118	Beg at a chesnut	
Tipton, Jonathan	1299		Washington	50	1185	2363	4 Dec 1795	20 Dec 1779	89	428	Beg at a sugar tree	
Tipton, Jonathan	158		Washington	150	26	517	23 Oct 1782	19 Oct 1778	47	12	N fork of Cherokee Creek	
Tipton, Jonathan	329		Washington	566	196	1092	24 Oct 1782	9 Jan 1779	49	224	On both sides of Cherokee Creek	
Tipton, Joseph	0105		Green	285		1492		26 Jan 1786			On Lick Creek	
Tipton, Joseph	065		Washington	572		2546		10 Apr 1780			On Sinking Creek	
Tipton, Joseph	1081		Washington	400	1031	656	27 Nov 1792	28 Nov 1778	80	198	On Bush Creek	
Tipton, Joseph	1332		Washington	200	1256	2870	6 Jun 1797	16 Jun 1781	90	312	S side of Watauga River	
Tipton, Joseph	386		Green	400	388	1428	20 Sep 1787	27 Jun 1784	65	482	On Lick Creek	
Tipton, Wm.	0102		Green	200		750		17 Dec 1779			On the waters of Lick Creek	
Tipton, Wm.	1556		Green	200	1228		12 Jun 1794		82	182	On the waters of Lick Creek	
Titsworth, Isaac	132		Sullivan	286	145	691	24 Oct 1782	16 Dec 1778	43	328	On Horse Creek &c	

Claimant:	File #:	Assignee:	Acres:	Grant:	Grant Date:	Entry:	Entry Date:	Bk:	Pg:	Location by Stream Name:	Military:
Titsworth, Isaac, Jr.	352		400	231	10 Nov 1784	692	16 Dec 1778	69	156	Fall Branch waters of Horse Cr	
Titsworth, Thomas	180 (181)		400	188	10 Oct 1783	224	17 Oct 1778	53	153	On Horse Creek	
Tittle, John	1145		100	1103	12 Jul 1794	906	31 Dec 1778	81	570	On both sides of Indian Creek	
Titus, Ebenezer	1133		640	110	17 Apr 1786	725	7 May 1785	66	177	Lying on the Et branches of Mill Cr	
Titus, Ebenezer	1234		640	198	10 Jul 1788	127	15 Jan 1784	66	411	On waters of Big & Little Harper &c	
Titus, Ebenezer	1335		320	21	18 Aug 1787	689	22 Feb 1785	68	129	On the N waters of Little Harpeth	
Titus, Ebenezer	1378		320	61	8 Oct 1787	30	30 Dec 1783	68	146	Dry Creek N side of Cumberland R	
Titus, Martin	590	Sanford, Samuel	640	1832	20 May 1793	2396	17 Aug 1792	81	86	On the waters of Caney Fork	yes
Todd, James	1284		640	249	10 Jul 1788	72	10 Jan 1784	66	424	On S side of Cumberland River &c	
Todd, James	1957	Harrison, John Axley	640	1801	20 May 1793	2009		81	79	On the waters of Mill Creek	yes
Todd, James, Ass.	2209		54.5	231	27 Feb 1796			88	175	On S side of Cumberland River	
Todd, James, Ass.	901	Woods, Thomas heirs	640	917	18 May 1789	2480		63	316	On waters of Caney Fork	yes
Todd, John	261	Weakley, Robert	640	1704	20 May 1798	2778	30 Sep 1785	81	54	On N side of Cumberland River	yes
Todd, Josiah	015	Donelson, Stockley	640			1590	13 Aug 1796			On waters of Red River	yes
Todd, Low, Sr.	704		300	745	11 Jul 1788	735	28 Oct 1783	66	475	On S side of Nolichuckey River &c	
Tolar, Danl	836	Anderson, Daniel	640	839	17 Jan 1789	1383		63	294	On N side of Cumberland River	yes
Tolbert, Thomas	353		116	220	24 Oct 1782	1344	11 May 1779	49	225	On the N side of Wattauga River	
Tolbot, Thomas	106		1000	106	10 Jul 1788	1440	27 Jan 1784	67	322	Both sides of Loosahatcher River	
Tolbott, Matthew	354		640	221	24 Oct 1782	645	28 Nov 1778	49	225	On S side of Watauga River	
Tolbott, Thomas	11		2000	13	10 Jul 1788	1434	27 Jan 1784	67	412	Lying on Duck River &c	
Tolbott, Thomas	770		60	584	10 Nov 1784	824	29 Dec 1778	69	133	On S side of Roans Creek	
Tolock, Arthur	755	Gilmore, Charles	640	728	11 Jul 1788	3503		63	256	On N side of Cumberland River	yes
Tommas, Isaac	263		291	131	23 Oct 1782	1451	21 Jun 1779	47	64	S side of Watauga River	
Tomson, James	488		200	499	18 May 1789	338	19 Jan 1781	71	11	On N side of Holeson River &c	
Toney, Anthony	602	Coleman, Spilley	640	1852	20 May 1793	57	8 Jul 1785	81	90	On Second Creek &c	yes
Tood, James	982		600	1209	29 Jul 1793	20	21 Oct 1783	76	468	S side of Nolechuckey River	
Tool, John	330		29.5	332	20 Sep 1787	2622	10 May 1783	65	467	On Browns Creek	
Tool, John	769		640	574	23 Aug 1788	591	27 Oct 1783	68	251	On N side of Holston River	
Tool, John	771		400	576	23 Aug 1788	57	12 May 1784	68	251	On N side of Holston River	
Toole, John	41		100	104	1 Nov 1786	1470	29 Jun 1779	58	465	Abt 3/4 mi from Joseph Fowlers	
Toole, John	662		200	567	12 Jul 1794	34	26 Feb 1780	81	592	On N side of Holston River	
Tooley, Henry & James	14	Tuton, Oliver	636	3376	26 Oct 1801	1780	21 Jul 1801	111	98	Beg at a sweet gum & beach	
Toomer, Henry	307		2020	24	14 Jul 1812	2120	30 Nov 1784	126	435	On both sides of Robertsons Fork	
Toomer, Henry	615	Mott, Benj.	1000	3174	14 Sep 1797	889		90	431	S side Cumberland River	
Toomer, Joseph	307	McCulloh, Benjamin	640	2008	20 May 1793	2244	12 Sep 1785	81	126	S side Cumberland River	yes
Toomer, Henry	331		5000	296	4 Feb 1795	2002	1 May 1784	83	388	On E Fork of Elk Creek	
Top, Roger	290		170	429	9 Aug 1787	518	19 Apr 1780	61	448	A white oak under the knobs	
Topp, John	026	Topp, Roger	960			329	3 Mar 1784			S side of Cumberland River	
Topp, John	1452	Topp, Roger	640	281	25 Nov 1786	330	3 Mar 1784	65	17	On the waters of Bledsoes Creek	
Topp, John	1453		640	281	25 Nov 1788			70	21	On waters of Bledsoes Creek	
Topp, John, Ass.	401		640	412	27 Jun 1793	333	3 Mar 1784	80	345	On S side of Cumberland River	
Topp, Rodger	74		170	85	23 Oct 1782	28	26 Feb 1778	43	279	On S side of Holston River	
Topp, Roger	1300		640	265	10 Jul 1788	332	3 Mar 1784	66	430	On N side of Red River &c	
Topp, Roger	247		200	386	9 Aug 1787	513	28 Apr 1780	61	405	On both sides of Rice's Mill Creek	
Topp, Roger	530		700	533	13 Feb 1791	1703	21 Sep 1779	73	380	On the N side of Holston River	

Earliest Tennessee Land Records

Claimant:	File #:	Assignee:	County:	Acres:	Grant:	Grant Date:	Entry:	Entry Date:	Bk:	Pg:	Location by Stream Name:	Military:
Topp, Roger	769		Hawkins	90	609	12 Jul 1794	28	26 Feb 1778	82	214	On S side of Holston	
Torbett, Samuel	758		Washington	100	572	10 Nov 1784			69	130	On N side of Watauga River	
Torbitt, John	352		Washington	150	219	24 Oct 1782	1312	29 Mar 1779	49	225	Beg at a white oak	
Torbitt, John	553		Washington	200	818	11 Jul 1788	981	2 Jan 1779	64	335	On N side of Watauga River	
Torrentine, Alexander, heirs	456	Wilson, Jno by J. Torrentin	Davidson	640	428	15 Sep 1787			63	158	N side of Sulphur Fork	yes
Torry, Thomas	771		Sullivan	117	702	20 Jul 1796	227	21 Feb 1780	91	84	Beg at a large poplar	
Totevine, Colburn	628	Whitfield, Bryant	Sumner	1000	1909	20 May 1793	1096	21 Dec 1792	81	102	On waters of Stones River	yes
Totevine, Winder	081	Coast, John	Davidson	640			1102	7 Sep 1796			On Harpeth River	yes
Totevine, Winder	782	Hays, Robert	Davidson	640	755	11 Jul 1788	1102		63	265	On head of War Trace Creek	yes
Totevine, Wm.	182	Dickerson, Henry	Tennessee	640	1462	4 Jan 1792	3676	10 Dec 1788	77	367	S side of Cumberland River	
Totevine, Wm.	189	Luellen, Daniel	Tennessee	640	1469	20 Jan 1792	3659	10 Dec 1788	77	368	S side of Cumberland River	
Toulter, Wm.	1354		Green	100	1200	23 Feb 1793			78	441	On S side of Clear Creek	
Tow, Christopher	404	Nelson, Robert	Davidson	640	376	15 Sep 1787	3119		63	141	N boundary of Tops claim	yes
Towel, Obediah	309	Rice, J, A Rista, & Elisha Ri	Davidson	640	295	13 Jun 1787	2584		63	110	On a branch of Smiths Creek	yes
Towel, Stephen	1425	Lytle, William	Sumner	640	3299	6 Dec 1797	1028	9 Mar 1797	98	174	On N side of Burtons Creek	yes
Towler, Absolam	178	Armstrong, Thomas	Davidson	640	164	7 Mar 1786	86		63	62	Joining James Armstrong's 7200 acres	yes
Towning, James	226	Marshall, John	Sumner	640	1131	26 Nov 1789	1624	21 Jan 1786	74	144	On a creek of S Fork &c	yes
Towns, Ozwald [?]	2176		Davidson	640	453	27 Nov 1793	617	10 Nov 1784	81	499	On E side of Stones River	
Tracey, James	685	Rice, John	Davidson	274	658	8 Dec 1787	1201		63	233	On waters of E Fork of Mill Creek	yes
Tracey, Nathaniel	365		Washington	150	357	13 Oct 1783	1957	10 Oct 1779	52	246	On a branch of Lick Creek	
Tracey, Nathaniel	430		Washington	200	422	13 Oct 1783	1956	10 Oct 1779	52	276	On a branch of Lick Creek	
Trammell, Phillip	1221	Armstrong, Martin	Sumner	30	194	27 Aug 1795			89	410	Beg at a black oak	
Trammill, Phillip	1049		Davidson	640	23	17 Apr 1786	313	20 Feb 1784	66	41	Lying on N side of Cumberland R	yes
Trapp, Martin	607	Lanier, Alexander	Sumner	640	1861	20 May 1793	1390	8 Aug 1795	81	92	On S side of Main Smiths Fork	yes
Traxal, Adam	772		Sullivan	32	703	20 Jul 1796	49	8 Feb 1780	91	85	Beg at a hickory	
Trayham, John	2445		Davidson	640	3287	6 Dec 1797	4270		98	165	On waters of Overalls Creek &c	yes
Trayner, James, heirs of	1880		Davidson	640	1626	27 Apr 1793	287		81	23	Below fork of Nelsons Creek	yes
Treadway, William	307	Tatum, H. & H. Wiggins	Sullivan	150	446	9 Aug 1787	652	15 Jul 1780	61	465	On S side of N Fk of Holston River	
Trebell, Speiller	2151	Bushop, Colden	Davidson	640	2464	31 Dec 1793	2796		81	431	On waters of Whites Creek	yes
Tredway, William	360		Sullivan	300	239	10 Nov 1784	493	17 Apr 1784	69	158	On N side of N Fk of Holstein River	
Tribute, Jonathan	1026		Green	100	1253	29 Jul 1793		13 Jul 1789	76	489	N/S Nolychuckey waters Meadow Cr	
Triel, Edward & T. Jackson	118		Hawkins	200	172	6 Dec 1791	817	13 Jul 1781	75	164	E side of Flat Creek &c	
Trimble, John	4		Green	500	67	1 Nov 1786	57	15 Jul 1784	58	428	On S side of Nollichuckie River	
Trimble, William	120		Washington	474	288	24 Oct 1782	665	8 Dec 1778	44	292	On both sides of Little Limestone	
Trimnal, Dennis	641	Robertson, James	Tennessee	640	3199	14 Sep 1797	3919	25 Jan 1797	92	3	Waters of Bartons Creek	yes
Tripp, John	979	Blount, Reading	Sumner	640	2444	22 Feb 1795	2550	30 Sep 1785	84	318	On Main Fork of Obeys River	yes
Trotter, John	1098		Washington	300	1048	27 Nov 1792	215	24 May 1778	80	204	Beg at a black oak &c	
Trotter, John	1102		Washington	50	1052	27 Nov 1792	1482	26 Jul 1789	80	205	On Big Limestone Creek	
Trotter, John	505		Washington	63	768	16 Aug 1787	2487	10 Mar 1780	64	142	Beg at a hickory	
Trotter, Richard	101		Middle District	4100	103	10 Jul 1788	630	27 Oct 1783	67	460	On Falling Creek	
Trotter, Richard	309		Middle District	2000	285	17 Dec 1794	1838	23 Apr 1784	83	330	On Duck river	
Trotter, Samuel	408		Washington	100	400	13 Oct 1783	2477	10 Mar 1780	52	265	On E side of Big Limestone	
Trotter, Samuel	462		Washington	100	454	13 Oct 1783	2478	10 Mar 1780	52	291	On branch of Mill Creek	
Troublefield, Benjamin	46	Anderson, Daniel	Tennessee	640	1238	10 Dec 1790	2888	30 Sep 1785	74	344	On N side of Cumberland River	yes
Trousdale, John	54	Gibson, John	Tennessee	640	1262	10 Dec 1790	2104	2 Sep 1784	74	353	On N side of Cumberland River	

Claimant:	File #:	Assignee:	County:	Acres:	Grant:	Grant Date:	Entry:	Entry Date:	Bk:	Pg:	Location by Stream Name:	Military:
Trousdel, James	1		Davidson	640	1	4 Dec 1784	3505	8 Feb 1786	42	342	Beg 1/4 mile S of the Spring	yes
Trouter, Thomas	85	Phillips, P.	Tennessee	640	1346	10 Dec 1790			74	381	On S side of Cumberland River	yes
Truebuck, George	024	Armstrong & Donelson	Middle District	640	2462		2974					yes
Truelock, Sutton	074	White, William	Middle District	274	1446		1446					yes
Truet, Stephen	865	Baker, Obediah	Sumner	640	2377	20 May 1793	509	10 Sep 1788	81	207	On Smiths Fork	yes
Truett, Franklin	1101	Farmer, Thomas	Sumner	640	2602	7 Mar 1796	673		88	327	On S side of Obeys River	yes
Truett, Peter	0130	Winchester, James & Geor	Sumner	640			3670	8 Dec 1789	84	315	N side of Cumberland River	yes
Truett, Solomon	973	Horter, Thomas	Sumner	640	2437	22 Feb 1795					On waters of Roaring River	yes
Tryall, Christopher	343	Howell, John	Sumner	640	1410	20 Dec 1791	2048	25 Nov 1789	77	354	On S side of Cumberland River	yes
Tucker, Gray	336	Ross, William	Davidson	640	322	28 Jul 1787	2694		63	120	On waters of Red River	yes
Tucker, James	1981		Davidson	640	1886	20 May 1793	929		81	97	On S W side of Big Harpeth	yes
Tucker, Jno.	1060		Davidson	640	34	17 Apr 1786	155	17 Jan 1784	66	46	Bet the forks of Mill Creek	
Tucker, Joseph	1116		Washington	37	1075	12 Jul 1794	2916	28 Aug 1781	81	560	Head of a branch of Big Limestone	yes
Tucker, Samuel	98	Person, Thomas	Tennessee	640	1380	20 Dec 1791	3253	24 Dec 1785	75	505	Both sides of Bushes Meat House	yes
Tucker, Wiley	368	McCulloh, Benjamin	Tennessee	640	2251	20 May 1793	2244	12 Sep 1785	81	181	On N side Cumberland River	yes
Tucker, Willey	2195a	McCulloh, Benjamin	Davidson	640	2483	18 Aug 1795			87	507	On N side of Cumberland River	yes
Tucker, William	960	Donelson, Stokley	Davidson	640	977	18 May 1789			63	331	Both sides of a N Fork of Smiths Cr	yes
Tucker, Wm. & Joshua Wrigh	1391		Green	150	1246	27 Jan 1793	1294	30 May 1792	79	511	Inc place where they now live on	
Tulley, Samuel	066		Washington	320			2913	28 Aug 1781			On right hand fk of Cobbs Creek	
Tully, Charles	981		Green	570	1208	29 Jul 1793	1638	16 Sep 1791	76	468	Beg at Lewis upper corner	
Tully, Michael	946		Washington	300	923	17 Nov 1790	628	16 Sep 1779	76	152	On Doe River &c	
Turman, Ignatius	1		Jefferson	600	1	3 Dec 1792	336	22 Oct 1783	78	456	On N E side of Big Pigeon River	
Turnbull, William	2040	Newton, Henry	Davidson	640	2057	20 May 1793	3662		81	138	On waters of Big Harpeth	yes
Turnbull, William	690	Warren, Thomas	Davidson	640	663	8 Dec 1787	2061		63	235	On head waters of Spring Creek	yes
Turnbull, William, Ass.	2162		Davidson	150	175	9 Jan 1794		18 Apr 1785	81	447	On waters of Mill Creek	yes
Turnbull, William, Ass.	2164		Davidson	40	177	9 Jan 1794		12 Apr 1791	81	447	Beg at a hickory	
Turner, Abraham	987	Brehon, James G.	Davidson	640	1004	18 May 1789	2887		63	337	S of James Cole Mountflorence	yes
Turner, Andrew	568	Blackface William	Tennessee	640	3005	10 apr 1797	4397		90	295	S side of Cumberland River	yes
Turner, Benjamin	130	Redding, Robert	Tennessee	640	1638	23 Feb 1793	1413	16 Nov 1784	76	331	Bet. Grices & Yellow Creek	yes
Turner, Daniel	1816		Davidson	640	389	26 Jun 1793	776	3 Nov 1785	80	338	On N side of Cumberland River	
Turner, Daniel	2365	Weakley, Robt & Saml	Davidson	640	3072	19 Jul 1797	3984		90	379	S side Cumberland River	
Turner, Jacob, heir of	277		Davidson	3840	263	14 Mar 1786			63	96	N side of Cumberland River	yes
Turner, James	878		Green	500	828	27 Nov 1789	1218	5 Nov 1783	74	35	2nd or below mouth French Broad R	yes
Turner, Simon	1317		Sumner	640	3117	14 Sep 1797	4395	6 May 1797	90	410	On waters of Big Barren	
Turner, Thomas (heir of Ben)	341	Hickman, Thomas	Middle District	2560	2481	18 Apr 1795	3690		83	464	At the Painter Spring &c	yes
Turner, Walter	02		Hawkins	300	431	31 Apr 1780	431 [sic]	31 Apr 1780 [sic]			S side of Holston River	
Turner, Walter	1061		Hawkins	300	770	21 Jan 1797			91	115	S side of Holston River	
Turner, William	1693	Phillips, Phillip & M. Camp	Davidson	640	1654	23 Feb 1793	3382	9 Mar 1780	76	338	On waters of Stones River	yes
Turney, H. & J. Thompson	997		Hawkins	100	696		276	8 Feb 1780	89	276	In the Cainey Valley	
Turney, Henry	1108		Hawkins	300	829	16 Sep 1797	57		94	136	S side of Big Creek	
Turney, Henry	1121		Davidson	640	98	17 Apr 1786	179	26 Jan 1784	66	174	Lying on both sides Turneys Branch &c	yes
Turney, Henry	1221		Davidson	640	185	10 Jul 1788	571	12 Aug 1784	66	408	On Goose Creek	
Turney, Henry	169		Sullivan	300	176	10 Oct 1783	276	9 Mar 1780	53	178	On Big Creek	
Turney, Peter	1091		Davidson	640	65	17 Apr 1786	178	26 Jan 1784	66	56	Hackberry & red o Isaac Johnstons	
Turney, Peter	1450		Davidson	640	96	10 Jul 1788	723	4 May 1785	68	234	N W cor Capt James Bradley	

Claimant:	File #:	Assignee:	County:	Acres:	Grant:	Grant Date:	Entry:	Entry Date:	Bk:	Pg:	Location by Stream Name:	Military:
Turney, Peter	209		Hawkins	200	196	26 Dec 1791	1490	27 Dec 1780	77	312	On N side of Holstein River	
Turney, Peter	369		Hawkins	500	303	14 Jan 1793			79	291	On the N side of Holston River	
Turpin, Jesse & James	12		Smith&Sumner	640	476	24 Aug 1803		16 Jun 1800	110	433	Waters of Middle Fk of Goose Cr	
Turpin, Jesse & James	1455		Sumner	640	476	24 Aug 1803	862	16 Jun 1800	110	433	Waters of Middle Fk of Goose Cr	
Turpin, Solomon	229		Tennessee	640	406	27 Jun 1793	588	26 Nov 1792	80	342a	On Red River	
Tuton, Oliver	14	Tooley, Henry & James	Smith	636	3376	26 Oct 1801	1780	21 Jul 1801	111	98	Beg at a sweet gum & beech	yes
Tuton, Oliver	348	Jones, Joshua	Davidson	640	333	29 Aug 1787	1771		63	124	N side of Cumberland River	yes
Tuton, Oliver	349	Phillips, Wm.	Davidson	640	334	29 Aug 1787	1780		63	124	N side of Cumberland River	yes
Tuton, William	0120	Powell, Francis	Sumner	640			1782	8 Sep 1797			E side W Fk Stones River	yes
Tuton, William	072	Powell, Nicholas	Davidson	640			1781	13 Apr 1797			W Fk of Stones River	
Tuton, William	350	Brannor, Michael	Davidson	274	335	29 Aug 1787	1636		63	124	On Caney Fork River	yes
Tuton, William	351	Jones, Samuel	Davidson	640	336	29 Aug 1787	1770		63	125	S side of Cumberland River	yes
Tuton, William	352	Smith, Benjamin	Davidson	224 (274	337	29 Aug 1787	1633		63	125	N side of Cumberland	yes
Tuton, William	353	Ludwell, Richard	Davidson	224	338	29 Aug 1787	1245		63	125	S side of Cumberland River	yes
Tuton, William	827	Burden, Archibald	Davidson	640	830	17 Jan 1789	3494		63	297	On N side of Cumberland River	yes
Tuton, William	844	Underwood, Shadrack	Davidson	640	849	17 Jan 1789	1593		63	297	On N side Cumberland River	yes
Tuton, William	865	Boyer, Thomas	Davidson	640	879	17 Jan 1789	3491		63	304	On N side Cumberland River	yes
Tuton, William	976	Scutchins, Samuel	Davidson	640	993	18 May 1789	1898		63	335	On Mulherin Creek	yes
Tuton, William	977	Exum, Etheldred	Davidson	640	994	18 May 1789	1899		63	335	On Caney Fork	yes
Tutson, William, Ass.	43		Sumner	640	882	17 Jan 1789	3493	5 Jun 1788	63	305	On N side Red River	yes
Tutson, Charles	0102	Motherell, Samuel	Sumner	640			2245	13 Mar 1787			S side Cumberland River	yes
Twigg, Daniel	611		Davidson	240	583	15 Sep 1787	1215		63	208	On waters of Station Camp Creek	yes
Twinbull, William	676	Jackson, Josiah	Davidson	640	649	8 Dec 1787	1810		63	230	On head waters of Spring Creek	yes
Tyler, Owen	045		Tennessee	640	1191	30 Nov 1790	242	25 Oct 1783			Both sides Middle Fk of Bartons Cr	
Tyler, Owen	1565		Davidson	640	2637	4 Jun 1796			74	319	Both sides Middle Fk of Bartons Creek	
Tyner, Arthur	1131	Harris, Edward	Sumner	640	2637	4 Jun 1796	1808	1 Jun 1795	88	346	Joining a survey of sd Harris	yes
Tyner, Arthur	547	Anglin, Cornelius	Davidson	274	519	15 Sep 1787	708		63	187	On Second Creek	yes
Tyner, Lewis	2285	Homer, Charles	Davidson	640	2767	20 Jul 1796	440		88	464	On a large creek of Tenn River	yes
Tyner, Nicholas	027	Pennington, Isaac	Tennessee	640			3401	19 Jan 1786			On a branch	
Tyner, Nicholas	250	Tyner, Nich	Davidson	266	236	7 Mar 1786	707	19 Jul 1786	63	87	On Red River	yes
Tyner, Nicholas	250	McDonald, John	Tennessee	640			3401				On a branch	
Tyrell, Wm & W. T. Lewis	1547		Montgomery	640			458				On Williams Creek	yes
Tyrrel, William	1547		Green	200	1307	7 Jul 1794	14	8 Feb 1780	81	623	On N side of Holston River	
Tyrell, Wm & others	360		Eastern District	640	277	20 Jul 1796		22 Aug 1797	88	436	In Hindes's Valley	
Tyrrell, William	01		Knox	100				4 Jun 1796			Flat Lick of Little West Fk of Red R	yes
Tyrrell, William	012		Montgomery	1000			1063				Adj Wm. Hays surveys	yes
Tyrrell, William	0121	Saunders, Andrew	Sumner	428			1278				N side Cumberland River	yes
Tyrrell, William	013		Montgomery	1142			80	21 Dec 1796			On the Ridge Fk of Flatt Creek	
Tyrrell, William	02		Knox	200							On Stones River	
Tyrrell, William	028	Henry, William	Davidson	640			650	6 Jan 1785				
Tyrrell, William	07		Knox	150								
Tyrrell, William	073		Davidson	228			3953	27 May 1796			Dividing ridge bet. Duck & Harpeth	yes
Tyrrell, William	074	Lewis, Amos	Davidson	228			1485				On Leepers Fork of Harpeth	
Tyrrell, William	074	West, Levi	not given	428			1165	26 May 1796			Creek emptying in Cumberland Riv	
Tyrrell, William	075	Bullock, John	Davidson	228			461	27 May 1796			On waters of Duck	

Claimant:	File #:	Assignee:	County:	Acres:	Grant:	Grant Date:	Entry:	Entry Date:	Bk:	Pg:	Location by Stream Name:	Military:
Tyrrell, William	075	Hart	not given	640			3468	4 Jun 1796	90	56	N side of Cumberland River	
Tyrrell, William	1006		Eastern District	200	782	21 Jan 1797	149	15 Feb 1780			N side of Holston River	
Tyrrell, William	2265	McCormick, John heirs	Davidson	640	2741	20 Jul 1796	3067		88	453	On N side of Cumberland River	yes
Tyrrell, William	2266	Cook, Frederick heirs	Davidson	640	2742	20 Jul 1796	3066		88	454	On N side of Cumberland River	yes
Tyrrell, William	2267	Hobbs, Isaac heirs	Davidson	640	2743	20 Jul 1796	2928		88	454	On waters of Mill Creek	yes
Tyrrell, William	2289	Blount, John Gray	Davidson	3840	2769	12 Aug 1796			88	480	Inc the mouth of Bull Run	yes
Tyrrell, William	2354	Gee, Capt. James heirs	Davidson	3840	3031	10 Apr 1797	38		90	306	Waters of Mill Creek & Stewarts Cr	yes
Tyrrell, William	2358	Cyprett, Robert	Davidson	358	3952	8 Jun 1797	45		90	319	Waters of White Creek	yes
Tyrrell, William	355		Eastern District	500	272	20 Jul 1796	964	29 Oct 1783	88	434	On S side of Holston River	
Tyrrell, William	423		Western District	1000	424	20 Jul 1796	2532	25 May 1784	88	431	On N Fork of Forked Deer River	
Tyrrell, William	529		Tennessee	1000	2845	21 Jan 1797			90	47	On Flat Lick Fork	
Tyrrell, William & Jas. Woods	1701		Green	428	2846	21 Jan 1797	970	29 Oct 1783	90	47	Creek emptying in Cumberland Riv	
Tyrrell, William & Wm. Lytle	013		Middle District	1165	1417	19 Feb 1797		1784	90	241	Waters of Bent Creek	
Tyrrell, William & Wm. Lytle	2320	Burnham, Isaac	Davidson	640	2853	21 Jan 1797	1194		90	51	On waters of West Harpeth	yes
Tyrrell, William & Wm. Lytle	325		Eastern District	200	265	7 Mar 1796	392	29 Mar 1780	88	199	A branch that empties into Clinch	
Tyrrell, William & Wm. Lytle	329		Eastern District	200	269	7 Mar 1796			88	201	On Beaverdam Creek	
Tyrrell, William, Ass.	1195		Sumner	1000	2745	20 Jul 1796	2628	1796	88	455	On N side of Cumberland River	yes
Tyrrell, William, Ass.	1293		Sumner	640	3053	8 Jun 1797	57	17 Mar 1784	90	319	Both sides of Drakes Creek	yes
Tyrrell, William, Ass.	354		Eastern District	1000	271	20 Jul 1796			88	433	On N side of Holston River	
Tyrrell, William, Ass.	362		Eastern District	25	298	20 Jul 1796			88	439	Being in an Island	
Tyrrell, William, Ass.	964		Hawkins	298	734	20 Jul 1796	1221	23 Jun 1784	88	432	On both sides of Caney Creek	
Tyrrell, Wm & Wm. Lytle	2319	Wainwright, Obediah	Davidson	600	2847	21 Jan 1797	1032		90	48	Lge or emptying into West Harpeth	yes
Tyrrell, Wm.	477	Coffield, Benj.	Tennessee	1607	2739	20 Jul 1796	398		88	452	Headwaters of Half Pone Creek	
Tyrrell, Wm.	479	Proctor, Wm.	Tennessee	228	2744	20 Jul 1796	1532	3 Feb 1785	88	455	Near head of Kilgores Station Br	
Tyrrell, Wm.	584	Dunnick, Peter	Tennessee	360	3032	10 Apr 1787	3711		90	306	On W fork of Williams Creek	
Tyrrell, Wm. & James	076	Easton, Samuel Wistner	Davidson	640			4073	12 Jun 1797			E side of Harpeth River	
Tyrrell, Wm. & Jas. Easton	077	Pall, Jacob	Davidson	640			4213	12 Jun 1797			On Harpeth River	
Tyrrell, Wm. & Jno. Buckanna	2253		Davidson	180	311	20 Jul 1796			88	444	On waters of Mill Creek	
Tyrrell, Wm. & John Rhea	012		Middle District	3234			458	9 Jul 1796				
Tyrrell, Wm. & Paul Harrelson	912		Hawkins	290			3358	13 Jul 1795				
Tyrrell, Wm. & Robt King	2309	McNeill, Zebulon heirs	Davidson	200	259	7 Mar 1796	3217		88	194	On Roseberrys Creek	yes
Tyrrell, Wm. & Wm. Lytle	1241		Sumner	1000	2510	27 Aug 1795	3543		89	414	On both sides of Salt River	yes
Tyrrell, Wm. & Wm. Lytle	478	Phillips, Wm.	Tennessee	1000	2840	21 Jan 1797	893	11 Apr 1796	90	44	S side of Cumberland River	yes
Tyrrell, Wm. & Wm. Lytle	014	Vickers, Marmaduke	Montgomery	640	2740	20 Jul 1796	1030	26 May 1784	88	453	On waters of Spring Creek	yes
Tyrrell, Wm. & Wm. Lytle	050		Hawkins	640			1038	13 Feb 1797			On Elk Creek	
Tyrrell, Wm. & Wm. T. Lewis	015	Thompson, Asabel	Montgomery	200	3504	30 Dec 1796	1563	11 Mar 1794			On the Beaver Dam River	yes
Tyrrell, Wm. & Wm. T. Lewis	016	McDonald, John	Montgomery	640							On W Fk of First Creek	
Tyrrell, Wm. & Wm. T. Lewis	017	Harts, Joseph	Montgomery	640							On Williams Creek	
Tyrrell, Wm. & Wm. T. Lewis	018		Montgomery	640							N side of Cumberland River	yes
Tyrrell, Wm. & Thos. Chapman	913		Hawkins	290								yes
Tyson, Aaron	896	Stewart, Robert	Sumner	1000	722	7 Mar 1796	3674		88	201	In the Grassey Valley	yes
Tyson, Grisham	1037	Easton, James	Sumner	640	2447	31 Dec 1793		5 Dec 1789	81	425	On headwaters of Spring Creek	yes
Underdu, Demsey	034		not given	640	2699	27 Mar 1796			88	255	On waters of Caney Fork	yes
Underdue, Demsey	034		[torn off]	640								yes

Claimant:	File #:	Assignee:	County:	Acres:	Grant:	Grant Date:	Entry:	Entry Date:	Bk:	Pg:	Location by Stream Name:	Military:
Underdue, Demsey	354	Long, Nicholas	Tennessee	640	2183	20 May 1793	5		81	167	On S side of Cumberland River	yes
Underhill, James	895	Ray, William	Sumner	640	2446	31 Dec 1793	3039	18 Dec 1792	81	425	On W side of Caney Fork	yes
Underwood, Howell	890	Munson, Samuel	Davidson	640	906	17 Jan 1789	2696		63	313	On head of W Fork of Spring Cr	yes
Underwood, James	307	Barrow, Matthew	Sumner	640	1376	20 Apr 1791	2779	20 Nov 1790	74	396	On W side of Jening Fk	yes
Underwood, Shadrack	844	Tuton, William	Davidson	640	849	17 Jan 1789	1593		63	297	On N side of Cumberland	yes
Upchurch, Charles	2294	McCallum, Isaac	Davidson	228	2771	9 Sep 1796	3894		88	523	On waters of W Harpeth	yes
Upton, Joseph	576	Sanford, Samuel	Sumner	640	1813	20 May 1793	2397	6 Aug 1792	81	82	On head of 1st large creek	yes
Upton, Willis	657	Davis, Joshua	Sumner	640	1974	20 May 1793	2440	19 Nov 1792	81	118	On the Caney Fork &c	yes
Utter, Abraham	256		Green	300	213	20 Sep 1787	1876	6 Oct 1779	65	435	On N side of Clinch River &c	
Vaick, Adrian	279		Western District	5000	305	25 Apr 1789	2079	5 May 1784	70	263	Lying both sides of Big Hatcha R	
Valentine, Danl	833	Norris, Robert	Davidson	640	836	17 Jan 1789	3606		63	294	On waters of Caney Fork	yes
Valentine, Peter	476	Marshall, John	Davidson	640	448	15 Sep 1787	2279		63	164	On Money Fork Creek	yes
Valentine, Silas	63	Brekon, James G.	Tennessee	640	1297	10 Dec 1790	2889	30 Jul 1790	74	364	On S side of Cumberland River	yes
Valentine, Thomas	1677	Greer, A. & J. Robertson	Davidson	640	1602	23 Feb 1793	2697		76	313	W side of Harpeth River &c	yes
Vance, David	072	White, William	Middle District	1097	2460		1925					yes
Vance, David	33		Middle District	1000	35	10 Jul 1788	804	29 Oct 1783	67	423	Head Eastern br W/F of Stones R	
Vance, David	86		Middle District	1000	88	10 Jul 1788	803	29 Oct 1783	67	453	On S side of Duck River &c	
Vance, David & others	606		Middle District	5000	377	19 Nov 1800	1576	1 Apr 1784	109	418	On both sides of Elk River	
Vance, Davis	19		Washington	400	309	24 Oct 1782	1915	11 Oct 1779	43	201	On Cane Brake Branch	
Vance, Elijah	338		Tennessee	228	2127	20 May 1793	1305	2 Nov 1784	81	156	On Spring Creek	
Vance, John	018	Donelson, S. & Wm. Tyrrell	Tennessee	2560			330	27 Nov 1783			On W branches of Sulphur Fk	yes
Vance, John	614		Davidson	3840	586	15 Sep 1787	329		63	209	On N side of Cumberland River	yes
Vance, Joseph	1111		Green	1000	954	26 Dec 1791			77	264	On head of Sinking Branch &c	
Vance, Samuel	108		Green	250	124	1 Nov 1786	1463	7 May 1785	59	427	On Little Chuckey	
Vanderfield, William	5	Bowman, William	Sumner	640	762	11 Jul 1788	2822	29 Dec 1786	63	267	On both sides of N Fk of Red River	yes
Vandyke, Charles	073	Williams, Etheldred	Middle District				4767					yes
Vanhouser, Valentine	1305		Washington	100	1191	4 Dec 1795	565	3 Oct 1795	89	431	On a branch of Cobbs Creek	
Vankoozer, Jacob	839		Green	70	820	13 Feb 1791	718	21 Oct 1783	73	375	On the waters of Bent Creek	
Vann, William, Ass.	363		Sumner	640	1508	4 Jan 1792	3730	18 Nov 1791	77	378	S side of Cumberland River	yes
Vansendt, Isaiah	951		Green	356	865	17 Nov 1790	1617	2 Apr 1784	76	126	3 large oaks on the top of a ridge	
Vanters, Jesse	143		Sullivan	550	156	23 Oct 1782	1602	12 Sep 1779	43	334	Beg at William Delaneys white oak corner	
Vanunts, George	610		Washington	150	704	26 Oct 1786			66	13	Inc a large spring &c	
Vanzant, Isaac	1090		Green	285	933	26 Dec 1791	1616	1 Apr 1784	77	254	S/S of Nolachuckey River on Cove Creek	
Vanzant, Isaac & Jas. Pearce	1089		Green	210	932	26 Dec 1791	79	16 Nov 1788	77	253	S side of Nolachuckey River	
Varner, Samuel	1345	Hollis, Jas.	Davidson	640	31	18 Aug 1787	432	10 May 1784	68	132	On the waters of Whites Creek	
Vaughan, Abraham	579	Hughlett, William	Davidson	640	551	15 Sep 1787	930		63	198	Both sides of second large branch	Yes
Vaughan, James	1641	Dixon, Tilmon	Davidson	640	1515	10 Apr 1792	1518		75	506	On head of branch of Stones Cr	yes
Vaughn, Abraham	579	Hughlett, William	Davidson	640	551	15 Sep 1787	930		63	198	On both sides of 2nd large branch	yes
Vawter, Philemon	13		Sullivan	100	24	23 Oct 1782	734	6 Feb 1781	43	248	Beg @ foot of a knob	
Vawter, Philemon	25		Sullivan	54	36	23 Oct 1782	735	6 Feb 1781	43	255	On Holston River	
Veach, Nathaniel	1692		Green	100	1368	27 Nov 1795	494	27 Oct 1783	89	289	S side Noleychuckey on Owen Cr	
Venters, Arthur	987	Brehon, James G.	Davidson	640	998	18 May 1789			63	336	On N side Cumberland River	yes
Venters, William	1021	Nichols, John	Davidson	640	1039	18 May 1789	2588		63	345	On 1st creek of Duck River	yes
Venus & Thomas	486		Sumner	480	130	27 Apr 1793	824	19 Nov 1792	81	36	Beg at a black walnut	yes
Venus, Margaret	548		Sullivan	400	531	17 Nov 1790	2034	27 Oct 1779	76	188	Waters of N Fk of Holstein River	yes

Claimant:	File #:	Assignee:	County:	Acres:	Grant:	Grant Date:	Entry:	Entry Date:	Bk:	Pg:	Location by Stream Name:	Military:
Venus, Patrick	1113	Harris, Edward	Sumner	640	2619	4 Jun 1796	2780	1 Jul 1795	88	340	Joining sd Harris survey	yes
Verell, Wm.	025	Curry, Thompson	Robertson	357	3374	29 Sep 1801	4530	21 May 1800			On waters of Sycamore Creek	
Vickers, Marmaduke	014	Tyrrell, Wm. & Wm. Lyttle	Montgomery	640			1038	13 Feb 1797			On Elk Creek	yes
Vickery, Henry	554	Deaderick, John	Sumner	640	1770	20 May 1793	1963	10 Mar 1792	81	75	On N side of Cumberland River &c	yes
Vickory, John	016	Donelson, Stockley	Robertson	640			521	13 Aug 1796			On waters of Elk Fk of Red River	yes
Vicroy, John	856	Brock, Joseph	Davidson	640	864	17 Jan 1789	521		63	301	On N side of Cumberland River	yes
Vincent, Geo.	0114		Green	130			414	14 apr 1780			Beg at a Spanish oak &c	
Vincent, George	091		Sullivan	97			1800	6 Oct 1779			Inc the Double Spring	
Vincent, George	1111		Washington	150 (150	1066	27 Jun 1793	2501	22 Mar 1780	80	391	On upper end Capt. Geo. Ruse [?] survey	
Vincent, George	643		Sullivan	150	591	27 Jun 1793	1170	1 Feb 1779	80	380	On a branch of Cedar Clear Creek	
Vincent, George	690		Green	100	731	11 Jan 1788	1798	6 Oct 1779	66	470	On both sides of Cherokee River	
Vincent, Thomas	254		Sullivan	150	393	9 Aug 1787	1273	11 Mar 1779	61	412	On the N fk of Horse Creek	yes
Vincent, Thomas	712		Sullivan	150	657	5 Dec 1794	817	12 Jul 1781	84	164	lPlantation Thos Buckner now lives	
Vincet, George	116		Hawkins	400	150	26 Dec 1791	226	22 Feb 1780	75	164	On S side of Holson River	
Viney, Thomas	1433	Wilburn, Daniel	Sumner	640	3308	6 Dec 1797	2001	14 Jul 1797	98	180	On the S side of Cumberland River	yes
Vinson, Chatline	365	Hays, Robert	Sumner	640	1528	14 Jan 1793	2782	6 Feb 1792	79	264	On E fk of Gooses Creek	yes
Vinson, George	48	Sanders, James	Sumner	640	1035	18 May 1789	2781	25 Nov 1786	63	344	On S Fork of Bradleys Creek	yes
Vinson, Moses	584	Sanders, William	Davidson	640	556	15 Sep 1787	1606		63	199	On Money Fork Creek	yes
Vinson, Thomas	313	Thomas, Richard	Sumner	640	1526	20 Nov 1792	2005	26 Nov 1785	75	510	On both sides Flinns Lick Creek	yes
Vinson, William	585	Sanders, William	Davidson	640	557	15 Sep 1787	2298		63	200	On N Fork of Maney Fork	yes
Vintress, John	321	Rice, John & others	Davidson	640	307	13 Jun 1787	2160		63	114	Small creek emptying in Main Tenn	yes
Vinzant, Garrat	289		Washington	200	156	24 Oct 1782	242	27 Jun 1778	47	76	Sinking Fork of Lick Creek	
W. Territory Returns	112		Green					30 Sep 1783				
Waddel, John	255		Washington	270	123	23 Oct 1782	546	29 Oct 1779	47	60	S side of Nolachuckey River	
Waddle, David	219		Davidson	140	206	10 Nov 1784	1820(?)	6 Oct 1779	55	216	On the N side of HolsteinRiver &c	
Waddle, John	1312		Green	200	1162	12 Jan 1793	1428	17 Nov 1792	78	401	Beg 2nd line of his former survey	
Waddle, John	224		Green	600	181	20 Sep 1787	82	21 Oct 1783	65	424	2 sweet gums S bank of Broad R	
Waddle, John	358		Washington	179	225	24 Oct 1782	347	29 Oct 1778	49	228	On S side of Nolachuckey River	
Waddle, Seth	978		Hawkins	300	750	20 Jul 1796	35	8 Feb 1780	88	500	Joining survey purc of Jno Looney	
Wade, Andrew	1128		Washington	200	1087	12 Jul 1794	1448	15 Mar 1793	81	564	Beg at a white oak	
Wade, David	599		Sumner	228	1842	20 May 1793	347	3 Dec 1783	81	88	On N Fork of Red River	yes
Wade, David	50		Sullivan	100	61	23 Oct 1782	1593	12 Sep 1779	43	267	On Holston River &c	
Wade, Edward, Sr.	66		Sullivan	30	77	23 Oct 1782	1699	22 Sep 1770	43	275	Beg at a corner red oak &c	
Wade, Edward, Sr.	010		Sullivan	30 (100)	246	10 Nov 1784	1708	24 Sep 1779			On Garretts Branch	
Wade, James	367	Robertson, James	Davidson	640	1758	29 May 1793	1222	1 Apr 1780	69	160	On Jarratts Branch	
Wade, Thomas	1938		Middle District	5000	320	12 Dec 1796	1896		81	68	On N side of Cumberland River	yes
Wade, Thomas	571		Middle District	5000	321	12 Dec 1796	1721	16 Apr 1784	91	304	Waters of the Caney Fork	
Wade, Thomas	572		Middle District	5000	322	12 Dec 1796	1684	16 Apr 1784	91	304	On Caney Fork &c	
Wade, Thomas	573		Middle District	5000	323	12 Dec 1796	1693	12 Mar 1784	91	304	On Caney Fork &c	
Wade, Thomas	574		Middle District	5000	324	12 Dec 1796	1718	12 Mar 1784	91	305	On Caney Fork	
Wade, Thomas	575		Middle District	5000	325	12 Dec 1796	1720	16 Apr 1784	91	305	Caney Fork	
Wadsworth, William	576	Nelson, Robert	Davidson	640	1504	4 Jan 1792	1714	16 Apr 1784	91	306	On Camp Creek	
Waggoner, Daniel	1739		Washington	200	1134	7 Jul 1794	1554	4 Mar 1780	77	377	On E side of Big Harpeth	yes
Waggoner, David	1176		Davidson	100	1203	9 Dec 1795	2491		81	621	Beg at a red oak	
	1288		Davidson	100			1188	16 Apr 1794	89	402	On N Fk of Rones Creek	

Claimant:	File #:	Assignee:	County:	Acres:	Grant:	Grant Date:	Entry:	Entry Date:	Bk:	Pg:	Location by Stream Name:	Military:
Waggoner, David	908		Washington	112	885	17 Nov 1790	2413	1 Jan 1780	76	139	On waters of Roans Creek	
Waggoner, David	978		Washington	460	955	17 Nov 1790	915	31 Nov 1790	76	164	On Roans Creek	yes
Waggoner, James	0119	Taylor, Thomas	Sumner	640			1850	5 Dec 1785			On Dixons Creek	
Waggoner, Philip	1670		Green	150	1375	20 Jul 1796	2534	19 Dec 1794	88	490	Joining Matthias Hoovers	
Waggoner, Daniel	1173		Washington	100	1131	7 Jul 1794	2099	30 Oct 1779	81	620	Beg at a large white oak	
Waggoner, George	348		Green	400	350	20 Sep 1787	1023	29 Oct 1783	65	472	On both sides of Lick Creek	
Waggoner, Henry	377		Sullivan	500	256	10 Nov 1784	1143	28 Jan 1779	69	164	On S side of Holstin River	
Waggoner, John	285		Green	200	287	20 Sep 1787			65	455	On a Fk of Camp Creek &c	
Wainright, Obediah	2319	Tyrrell, Wm. & Wm. Lytle	Davidson	640	2847	21 Jan 1797	1032		90	48	Lrge or that runs into West Harpeth	yes
Walderson, James	609		Washington	217	703	26 Oct 1786	2905	28 Aug 1781	66	12	Joining Joseph Duncan &c	
Walderson, James	71		Sullivan	50	82	23 Oct 1782	284	9 May 1780	43	278	On Jarrats Branch &c	
Waldrupe, James	130		Washington	247	298	24 Oct 1782	784	26 Dec 1778	44	297	On Jarrets Branch	
Waling, Elisha	660		Hawkins	200	565	12 Jul 1794	2551	2 May 1780	81	591	Adjoining former surv of Walling	
Walker [Wallen], Joseph	262		Sullivan	640	401	9 Aug 1787			61	420	On N side of Clinch River	
Walker, Aaron	858	Alexander, Robert	Sumner	274	2364	20 May 1793	3030	18 Nov 1792	81	205	On Deans Lick Creek	yes
Walker, Allen	174	Walker(?), Wm.	Tennessee	1000	1451	20 Dec 1791	2364	30 Sep 1785	77	363	On both sides of Duck River	
Walker, David	1167		Green	200	1010	26 Dec 1790	1075	8 Jan 1779	77	285	On Clear Creek	
Walker, David	144		Eastern District	200	114	20 Dec 1791	1488	26 Jul 1779	78	328	On N side of Holston	
Walker, David	146		Eastern District	250	116	20 Dec 1791			78	329	On N side of Holston River	
Walker, David	173		Green	100	643	23 Aug 1788	612	12 Jun 1780	64	356	On N side of Holston River	
Walker, Felix	510		Sullivan	640	526	26 Nov 1789	132	26 Feb 1778	73	43	On Buck Creek	
Walker, Felix	619		Washington	500	713	26 Oct 1786	1339	15 Apr 1779	66	17	Upon Sinking Creek &c	
Walker, Geo & Seth Lewis	2078	Barnes, William heirs	Davidson	640	2238	20 May 1793	1256		81	178	On S side of Cumberland River	yes
Walker, Geo.	1025	Armstrong, M.	Sumner	40	252	27 Feb 1796		15 Dec 1792	88	185	Beg at a Spanish oak	yes [?]
Walker, Geo.	550		Sumner	640	1764	20 May 1793	2164	16 Jul 1792	81	70	On Drakes Creek	yes
Walker, Geo. Ass.	1893	Armstrong, M.	Davidson	22	127	27 Apr 1793			81	32	On N side of Cumberland River	yes
Walker, George	2033	Rose, William	Davidson	428	2046	20 May 1793	3200		81	136	On N side of Cumberland River	yes
Walker, George	2053	Duggin, William	Davidson	640	2139	20 May 1793	1159		81	158	On S side of Cumberland River	yes
Walker, George	2153	Gibson, William	Davidson	640	2472	31 Dec 1793	686		81	434	On S side of Cumberland River	
Walker, George	2197	Armstrong, M.	Davidson	50	202	27 Feb 1795			88	162	On waters of Whites Creek	
Walker, George	251	Armstrong, M.	Tennessee	100	123	27 Apr 1793		11 Nov 1792	81	31	On Clay Lick Branch	
Walker, George	366	Gunn, John	Tennessee	1000	2239	20 May 1793	747	7 May 1784	81	178	On S side of Cumberland River	
Walker, George	453	Armstrong, M.	Tennessee	137	248	27 Feb 1796	39	18 Dec 1792	88	183	On Sulphur Fk of Red River	
Walker, George, Ass.	2207		Davidson	65	227	27 Feb 1796			88	174	Abt 4 mi Southerly from Nashville	
Walker, George, Ass.	2250		Davidson	247	301	20 Jul 1796			88	440	On waters of W Harpeth River	
Walker, George, Ass.	561		Sumner	228	1783	20 May 1793	1841	10 Jun 1792	81	75	On N side of Cumberland River	yes
Walker, Green	1114	Harris, Edward	Sumner	640	2620	4 Jun 1796	2698	1 Jun 1795	88	340	Joining sd Harris survey	yes
Walker, Henry, Ass.	1400		Sumner	640	3329	6 Dec 1797	4380	29 Aug 1797	97	49	On 1st large fork of Round Lick Cr	yes
Walker, James	71		Green	200	29	1 Nov 1786	153	15 Feb 1786	59	390	N side of French Broad River	
Walker, Jno.	1252		Davidson	640	217	10 Jul 1788	686	19 Feb 1785	66	415	On N side of Cumberland River	
Walker, John	083	Hamilton, George	Sumner	640			1264	8 Dec 1792			On Lick Creek	yes
Walker, John	1038		Davidson	640	12	17 Apr 1786	265	10 Feb 1784	66	38	Head of Gibsons Cr at a white oak	
Walker, John	1625	Armstrong, M.	Davidson	21 (22)	98	10 Nov 1790			74	388	On N side of Cumberland River	
Walker, John	215		Middle District	1300	201	14 Jan 1793	1620	5 Apr 1784	79	287	On a branch of Duck River	yes
Walker, John	273		Davidson	1709	259	14 Mar 1786	249		63	94	On a creek of Duck Creek	

Claimant:	File #:	Assignee:	County:	Acres:	Grant:	Grant Date:	Entry:	Entry Date:	Bk:	Pg:	Location by Stream Name:	Military:
Walker, John	32		Green	250	95	1 Nov 1786	137	16 Feb 1785	58	456	Beg upon a white oak	
Walker, John	457		Green	175	459	20 Sep 1787	820	29 Oct 1783	65	504	On Meadow Creek	
Walker, John	892		Sumner	357	2438	31 Dec 1793	423	18 Dec 1792	81	423	On W bank of Caney Fork River	yes
Walker, John, Ass.	429		Sumner	640	440	27 Jun 1793	710	17 Mar 1785	80	354	On Spencers Creek	
Walker, John, Ass.	881		Sumner	640	2400	7 Jan 1794	781	26 Jul 1784	81	392	On S side of Cumberland River	yes
Walker, Joseph	262		Sullivan	640	401	9 Aug 1787			61	420	On N/S of Clinch River	
Walker, Moses	541	Daves, John	Sumner	228	1402	20 Dec 1791	326	22 Oct 1785	77	352	Adjoining the W boundary of Richard Hage	yes
Walker, Phelix	552		Sullivan	640	535	17 Nov 1790	132	9 Mar 1778	76	189	On Buck Creek	
Walker, Philip	279		Middle District	250	246	12 Jul 1794	28	24 Jan 1787	81	599	On N side of Elk River	
Walker, Phillip	1159		Davidson	640	136	17 Apr 1786	579	14 Aug 1784	66	183	Corner of Jas. Scotts pre-emption	
Walker, Phillip, Ass.	282		Middle District	300	249	12 Jul 1794	36	24 Jan 1787	81	599	Joining his other survey	
Walker, Phillip, Ass.	340		Middle District	300	167	12 Dec 1794			83	441	Joining his other survey on N/S	
Walker, Phillip, Ass.	342		Middle District	250	168	1 Dec 1794			83	479	N [? W]/S Elk River on Steels Cr	
Walker, Pritheas [?]	342		Green	317	566	20 Sep 1789	47	21 Oct 1783	66	251	On Cone Creek &c	
Walker, Richard Shewell	1509	Ray, William	Davidson	1000	1066	26 Nov 1789	2363		74	112	On S side of Cumberland River	yes
Walker, Robert & Samuel	1464		Green	1000	1224	27 ------	1629	27 Nov 1783	81	510	On s side of Elk River	
Walker, Robert, Sr.	122		Middle District	700	124	10 Jul 1788	2227	21 May 1784	67	469	Lying on Fork of Weakleys Creek	
Walker, Robert, Sr.	1466		Green	1200	1226	27 Nov 1793	1266	13 Dec 1783	81	510	On S side of Elk River	
Walker, Samuel	1070		Davidson	640	44	17 Apr 1786	239	5 Feb 1784	66	49	Lying on W Fork of Mill Creek	
Walker, Walter	236	Reed, Jesse	Sumner	640	1141	26 Nov 1789	3507	12 Mar 1788	74	149	On waters of Collins River	yes
Walker, William	1001		Green	235	1228	29 Jul 1793			76	484	N side of French Broad River	
Walker, William	1091		Green	100	934	26 Dec 1791	83	16 Nov 1788	77	254	On the waters of Lyons Creek	
Walker, William	174	Walker, Allen	Tennessee	1000	1451	20 Dec 1791	2364	30 Sep 1785	77	363	On both sides of Duck Creek	yes
Walker, William	243	Hill, Green	Davidson	640	229	7 Mar 1786	1067		63	84	On waters of Stones River	yes
Walker, William	321		Green	272	323	20 Sep 1787	1307	4 Jan 1784	65	465	On N side of French Broad River	yes
Walker, Wm.	642		Davidson	1000	615	15 Sep 1787	1878		63	219	On S side of Sulphur Fork	
Wall, Frithman(?)	286		Hawkins	25	297	14 Jan 1793	59	10 May 1784	78	345	On S side of Holston River	yes
Wall, Joel	609		Green	317	566	20 Sep 1789	47	21 Oct 1783	66	251	On Cove Creek	
Wall, John	2076		Davidson	1000	2230	20 May 1793	2027		81	176	On waters of W Fk of Stones R	yes
Wall, John	026		Eastern District	234	military			1795			"No Good"	
Wall, John	09		Knox	4 plats								
Wall, John, Ass.	330		Eastern District	640	712	2 Dec 1795	1759	6 Sep 1779	88	265	On N side of Holston River	
Wallace, Brown	032	Blount, Reading	Middle District	640			2553					
Wallace, James	313		Middle District	800	289	17 Dec 1794	1824	23 Apr 1784	83	332	N side of Duck River	yes
Wallace, John	1		Washington	240	1	15 Dec 1778	49	14 Sep 1778	36	1	On N Fk of Doe River	
Wallace, John	9		Washington	400	9	15 Dec 1778	66	14 Sep 1778	33	9	On a branch &c	
Wallace, Joseph	41		Sullivan	280	52	23 Oct 1782	127	11 Feb 1780	43	262	On N side of Holston	
Wallace, Matthew	1315		Green	200	1165	12 Jan 1793	54	12 May 1784	78	403	On Long Creek	
Wallace, Matthew	320		Green	200	322	20 Sep 1787			65	465	On Little Gap Creek	
Wallace, Thomas	479		Sullivan	250 (258	358	10 Nov 1784	540	29 Apr 1780	69	199	On Beaver Creek	
Wallace, William	671	Sugg, Noah	Sumner	640	2001	20 May 1793	2076	29 Nov 1792	81	124	Joining assignee of Benj Woolard	
Wallace, William	0115		Green	200			144				N/S French Broad River	
Wallace, William	1020	Roberts, Joshua heirs	Davidson	640	1038	18 May 1789	2760	21 Oct 1783	63	345	First creek above Stones Lick Cr	yes
Wallace, William	298		Green	200		27 Jun 1793	144				N side of French Broad River	yes
Wallace, William	625		Sullivan	200	573	27 Jun 1793	270	9 Mar 1780	80	372	N side of Holstein River	

Claimant:	File #:	Assignee:	County:	Acres:	Grant:	Grant Date:	Entry:	Entry Date:	Bk:	Pg:	Location by Stream Name:	Military:
Wallace, William	96		Sullivan	300	107	23 Oct 1782	1647	17 Sep 1779	43	289	Beg at a spruce pine &c	
Wallace, William	999		Green	200	1226	29 Jul 1793	52	10 May 1784	76	484	N side of French Broad River	
Wallace, William, Ass.	298		Eastern District	475	157	22 Feb 1795			84	282	On E Fk of Pistol Creek	
Wallace, Wm.	089		Sullivan	500			1646	16 Sep 1779			2 Bl Oak walnuts on the road	
Wallen, Elisha	239		Hawkins	640	226	26 Dec 1791	1589	12 Sep 1779	77	322	In Powells Valley	
Wallen, Elisha	240		Hawkins	400	227	26 Dec 1791	2059	27 Oct 1779	77	322	On N side of Clinch River	
Wallen, Elisha	907		Hawkins	100	695	18 Aug 1795	2456 (2436	27 Feb 1780	87	506	On N side of Holsten	
Waller, John	1359		Green	640	266	23 Feb 1793	266	27 Oct 1779	78	444	On S side of Clinch River	
Waller, John	301		Hawkins	640	264	24 Dec 1792	2245	22 Nov 1779	78	449	Caney Valley	
Wallice, Wm.	89		Sullivan	500			1646	16 Sep 1779			Beg at 2 black walnuts on the road	
Wallin, Elisha	233		Sullivan	461	372	9 Aug 1787	28	8 Feb 1780	61	391	Beg on bank of river	
Wallin, Elisha	620		Hawkins	250	316	15 Jul 1793	1944	19 Oct 1779	80	301	On the waters of Mulberry Creek	
Wallin, John	03		Grainger	200				no date				
Wallin, John	229		Eastern District	100	184	12 Jun 1794	495	27 Apr 1780	82	178	On road of German Cr to KY	
Wallin, Stephen	800		Sullivan	16	743	17 Nov 1797	14	1 Feb 1780	94	147	S side of Holston River	
Walling, Berriman	546		Hawkins	600	419	29 Jul 1793	2241	22 Nov 1779	80	282	S side of Cumberland Mountain	
Walling, Elisha	1128		Hawkins	640	847	9 Dec 1797	2351	12 Sep 1779	96	6	In Powells Valley	
Walling, Elisha	181		Hawkins	200	114	16 Nov 1790	1786	2 Oct 1779	77	189	On N side of Bays Mountain	
Walling, Elisha	248		Hawkins	300	236	26 Dec 1791	477	25 Apr 1780	77	325	On N side Holston River &c	
Walling, Elisha	512		Hawkins	400	385	29 Jul 1793	985	2 Jan 1779	80	273	N side of Wallings Ridge	
Walling, Elisha	528		Hawkins	200	452	29 Jul 1793	382	3 Apr 1780	80	290	On top of Valley Knob	
Walling, Elisha	530		Hawkins	300	403	29 Jul 1793	15	24 Feb 1778	80	278	N side of Clinch River &c	
Walling, Elisha	532		Hawkins	100	405	29 Jul 1793	101	8 Feb 1780	80	278	On S side of Copper Ridge	
Walling, Elisha	536		Hawkins	640	409	29 Jul 1793	3	8 Feb 1780	80	279	On N side of Powells Mountain	
Walling, Elisha	557		Hawkins	400	430	29 Jul 1793	473	25 Apr 1780	80	285	On N side of Holston River &c	
Walling, George	612		Hawkins	400	486	29 Jul 1793	70	8 Feb 1780	80	297	On N side of Holston River &c	
Wallis, George	221	Williams, John	Davidson	857	207	7 Mar 1786	306		63	76	On Middle Fork of Goose Creek	yes
Walter, Peter	1353		Washington	100	1270	19 Oct 1797	1535	10 Apr 1780	92	47	On a small branch	
Walton, Jesse	242		Washington	452	110	23 Oct 1782	249	2 Jul 1778	47	54	S side of Nolachuckey River	
Walton, William	1748	Blanchard, John	Davidson	640	1501	4 Jan 1792	3693		77	376	West side of Kaspers Creek	yes
Walton, William	276		Davidson	3840	262	14 Mar 1786	110		63	95	N side Cumberland River	yes
Walton, William, Ass.	451		Sumner	640	1573	27 Apr 1793	3259	19 Dec 1787	81	11	Both sides of a fk of Roaring River	yes
Walton, William, Ass.	456		Sumner	640	1593	27 Apr 1793	3255	19 Dec 1787	81	16	On S side of E Fk of Roaring River	yes
Walton, William, Ass.	461		Sumner	640	1603	27 Apr 1793	3147	19 Dec 1787	81	18	On waters of Roaring River	yes
Ward, Benjamin	482	Marshall, John	Davidson	640	454	15 Sep 1787	2281		63	165	On Money Fork Creek	yes
Ward, Benjamin	540		Washington	300	803	16 Aug 1787	966	2 Jan 1779	64	153	Beg at a marked chestnut tree	
Ward, Benjamin	873		Washington	300	857	18 May 1789	966	8 Apr 1784	72	222	Beg at a larage chesnut tree &c	
Ward, Charles	635	Overton, John	Sumner	640	1924	20 May 1793	3485	13 Nov 1792	81	106	On both sides of Red or Lick Creek	yes
Ward, David	2018	Smith, Oliver	Davidson	640	1989	20 May 1793	1890		81	121	On S W side of Big Harpeth &c	yes
Ward, Drury	173	Nelson, Alexander	Tennessee	274	1449	20 Dec 1791	182	24 Oct 1783	77	363	S side of Red River	yes
Ward, Edward	436		Sullivan	100	315	10 Nov 1784			69	181	On Jarrotts Branch	
Ward, Ennis	447	King, Joseph	Davidson	274	419	15 Sep 1787	683		63	155	On Meat Camp or Bartons Creek	yes
Ward, Isaac	658	Hays, Stokeley	Davidson	640	1975	20 May 1793	2443		63	118	On Caney Fork &c	yes
Ward, Jesse	825	Phillips, Mann	Sumner	640	2304	20 May 1793	2253	30 Nov 1792	81	192	On waters of Dixons Creek	yes
Ward, John	324	Hill, William	Tennessee	640	2068	20 May 1793	206	24 Oct 1783	81	141	On N side of Cumberland River	yes

Claimant:	File #:	Assignee:	County:	Acres:	Grant:	Grant Date:	Entry:	Entry Date:	Bk:	Pg:	Location by Stream Name:	Military:
Ward, John	654	Bushnell, E. & Wm. Dobbin	Davidson	1000	627	15 Sep 1787			63	223	Both sides Main W Fk of Stones R	yes
Ward, John	967		Green	400	881	17 Nov 1790	209	22 Oct 1789	77	131	S side of French Broad River	
Ward, John, Ass.	887	Armstrong, Martin	Hawkins	200	147	4 Feb 1795			84	145	On N side of Holston River	
Ward, Solomon	641	Lockart, John	Sumner	640	1930	20 May 1793	1996	19 Nov 1792	81	107	On W side of Caney Fork	yes
Ward, William	622		Washington	250	716	26 Oct 1786	1085	6 Jan 1779	66	19	On both sides of Brush Creek	
Ward, William	624		Washington	200	718	26 Oct 1786	2628	28 Aug 1780	66	20	Beg at a white oak sapling &c	
Ward, William	746		Washington	640	560	10 Nov 1784	11	24 Feb 1779	69	127	Beg at an ash	
Ware, George	570	Welborn, Daniel	Tennessee	274	3008	10 Apr 1797	3430	2 Feb 1786	90	297	S side of Red River	
Warmack, Jacob	63		Washington	262	231	23 Oct 1782	433	23 Sep 1778	44	260	W/S of Fains Branch	yes
Warner, Harden	1276	Semple, Robert	Tennessee	320	3018	10 Apr 1797	3885		90	300	On E Fork of Barritts Creek	
Warner, Hezekiah	2467	Nichols, John	Davidson	640	3403	30 May 1803	2589	8 Mar 1786	110	320	On waters of Harpeth River	yes
Warren, Edward	090		Sullivan	370			1103	9 Jan 1779			Beg at a spanish oak	
Warren, Edward	2148	Glasgow, James	Davidson	228	2442	18 Mar 1794	1155		81	424	On waters of Stones River	yes
Warren, Richard	1161	Harris, Edward	Sumner	640	2666	4 Jun 1794	3888	1 Jun 1795	88	356	Joining sd Harris survey	yes
Warren, Robert, Ass.	1581		Green	40	128	4 Feb 1795		10 May 1794	83	401	On Little Chuckey Creek	
Warren, Robert, Ass.	1582		Green	80	129	8 Feb 1795		25 Aug 1794	83	402	On Little Chuckey Creek	
Warren, Samuel	461	Bradley, James	Davidson	640	433	15 Sep 1787	2103		63	159	2nd creek a branch of Stones R	yes
Warren, Thomas	690	Turnbull, William	Davidson	640	663	8 Dec 1787	2061		63	235	On head waters of Spring Creek	yes
Warren, William	0108		Green	100			637	19 Jul 1780	63		On S side of Holstein River	
Warren, William	303	Cobb, Jesse	Tennessee	228	1994	20 May 1793	1161	28 Aug 1784	81	123	On both sides of Red River	yes
Warren, William	519		Sullivan	100	535	20 Nov 1789			73	47	On S side of Holstein River	
Warrick, William	792		Sullivan	50	724	2 Dec 1796			91	278	Inc where he now lives	
Warton, Edward	534	Davis, Joshua	Davidson	640	506	15 Sep 1787	2441		63	183	E side of Caney Fork &c	yes
Warwick, Robert	16	Sanders, James	Sumner	228	773	11 Jul 1788	1655	21 Oct 1786	63	271	On waters of Goose Creek	yes
Warwick, Shadrack	05	Blount, Thomas	Tennessee	640	1474	26 Nov 1784					On Rite hand fork of 1st large cr	yes
Washington, Dred	060	Sheppard, John	not given	640			2969	15 Aug 1792			On waters of Obeys River	yes
Washington, Etheldred (Wm)	212		Davidson	1000	198	7 Mar 1786	562		63	73	On Parsons Creek	yes
Washington, William	544	Pain, Josiah	Sumner	1000	1747	20 May 1793	237	20 Dec 1785	81	65	S side of Cumberland River	yes
Washington, William, heir	212		Davidson	1000	198	7 Mar 1786	562		63	73	On Parsons Creek	yes
Waters, John	033	Creesey, Thos & Wm Murr	Montgomery	1000	3394		5033	13 Oct 1800			On waters of Pleasant Creek	yes
Waters, William	139	Lewis, Wm. T.	Tennessee	640		26 Dec 1792	3603	14 Aug 1788	76	341	On waters of Red River	yes
Waters, William	556		Davidson	2011	528	15 Sep 1787	1444		63	190	S side of Cumberland	yes
Watkins, Burwell	2225	Sanders, William	Davidson	640	2517	8 Dec 1795	2283		88	288	On Fk of S Fk of Many Fk Creek	yes
Watkins, Evan	808	Robertson, Elijah	Davidson	640	811	20 Nov 1788	3327		63	285	On S side of Cumberland	yes
Watkins, Walter	1965	Blair, James	Davidson	274	1838	20 May 1793	3508		81	87	On waters of Mill Creek	yes
Watson, David	923		Hawkins	60	705	2 Dec 1795	63		88	262	In Carters Valley Knobbs	yes
Watson, Everat	1696	Phillips, Phillip & M. Camp	Davidson	640	1657	23 Feb 1793	2700	8 Feb 1780	88	339	On waters of Stones River	yes
Watson, Jacob	1518	Gilmore, Charles	Davidson	640	1075	26 Nov 1789	3281		76	117	On N side of Cumberland River	yes
Watson, John	0107		Green	200	2		2908	28 Aug 1781	74		Beg at a white oak	
Watson, John	0122	Little, Jonas	Sumner	640			4637	10 Apr 1797			N fork Bradleys Creek	yes
Watson, John	0123	Little, George	Sumner	640			4637	10 Apr 1797			On N Fork of Bradley Creek	yes
Watson, Lett	451		Green	100	453	20 Sep 1787			81	502	Joining Edwards claim	
Watson, Micajah	1983	Herndon, Benjamin	Davidson	640	1888	20 May 1793	915		65	98	On Jones Creek	yes
Watson, William	599		Tennessee	365	3026	10 Apr 1797	3786		90	304	N side Cumberland River	yes
	018	Armstrong & Donelson	Middle District	640			2893					yes

Claimant:	File #:	Assignee:	County:	Acres:	Grant:	Grant Date:	Entry:	Entry Date:	Bk:	Pg:	Location by Stream Name:	Military:
Watson, William	285		Washington	300	152	24 Oct 1782	719	19 Dec 1779	47	74	On Sinking Creek	
Watson, William	498		Washington	100	761	16 Aug 1787	597	21 Nov 1778	64	139	Bet Brush & Sinking Creeks	
Watson, William	526.....		Washington	200	789	16 Aug 1787	2505	29 Mar 1780	64	149	Upon Sinking Creek	
Watt, James	29		Middle District	1200	31	10 Jul 1788	432	25 Oct 1783	67	421	On S side of Duck River &c	
Waughmocks, Jesse	572	Sanford, Samuel	Sumner	640	1809	20 May 1793	2402	6 Aug 1792	81	81	On head waters &c	yes
Weaken, Stephen	1466	Cook, Richard	Sumner	540	3384	12 Dec 1801	654	7 Mar 1801	114	90	Beg at an oak	yes
Weakley, Polly	106	Hathcock, John heirs	Tennessee	640	1571	23 Feb 1793	2489	20 Sep 1785	76	299	S side Cumberland River	
Weakley, Robert	042	Prescott, Jonathan	Robertson	640			3982	15 Feb 1797			N side of Cumberland River	
Weakley, Robert	106		Middle District	2000	108	10 Jul 1788	1788	23 Apr 1784	67	462	On N side of Duck River &c	yes
Weakley, Robert	1560	Winstell, Thomas heirs	Davidson	640	1182	30 Nov 1790	2252		74	315	On S side of Cumberland River	yes
Weakley, Robert	1748	Armstrong, M.	Davidson	38	114	20 Dec 1791			77	381	On N waters of Little Harpeth	
Weakley, Robert	1789		Davidson	125	131	29 Aug 1793			80	324	On waters of Whites Creek	
Weakley, Robert	1790		Davidson	15	132	29 Aug 1793			80	324	On waters of Whites Creek	
Weakley, Robert	1794		Davidson	90	136	29 Aug 1793			80	326	On Little Harpeth	
Weakley, Robert	1795		Davidson	30	137	29 Aug 1793			88	327	On Little Harpeth	
Weakley, Robert	1856	Moore, Morris	Davidson	640	1581	27 Apr 1793	1892		81	13	On S side of Cumberland River	yes
Weakley, Robert	1887	Crabb, Benjamin	Davidson	428	1640 (6)	27 Apr 1793	3126		81	28	On S side of Cumberland River	yes
Weakley, Robert	1927	Demcey, David	Davidson	274	1738	20 May 1793	1347		81	63	On S side of Cumberland River	yes
Weakley, Robert	1928	Legget, Elias heirs	Davidson	640	1739	20 May 1793	2465		81	63	On the waters of Stewarts Cr	yes
Weakley, Robert	1931	Ferebe, David heirs	Davidson	200	1745	20 May 1793	2648		80	65	Waters of Stones River	yes
Weakley, Robert	196		Davidson	640	138	29 Aug 1793			81	327	On N side of Big Harpeth	
Weakley, Robert	2118	Humphrey, Joseph heirs	Davidson	640	2382	4 Dec 1793	1328		81	385	On S side of Big Harpeth River	yes
Weakley, Robert	226	_arkins, Benajah heirs	Davidson	640	1015	18 May 1789	3397	15 Dec 1792	63	340	On E Fk of Stones River	yes
Weakley, Robert	226		Tennessee	200	141	29 Aug 1793			80	328	On N waters of Sycamore Creek	
Weakley, Robert	2392	Armstrong, M.	Davidson	200	337	21 Jan 1797		4 Nov 1783	91	127	On N waters of Big Harpeth	
Weakley, Robert	267	Jackson, John	Tennessee	274	1734	20 May 1793	375	10 Jan 1786	81	62	N side of Cumberland River &C	
Weakley, Robert	272	Hughs, Jesse	Middle District	250	141	27 Apr 1793	1787	23 Apr 1784	81	39	On S side of Cumberland River	
Weakley, Robert	33		Western District	2000	33	11 Jul 1788	3282		67	292	On waters of Obion River &c	
Weakley, Robert	357	Mallebey, James	Davidson	640	341	4 Sep 1787	2578		63	127	N side Cumberland River	
Weakley, Robert	358	Raynor, Amos	Davidson	640	342	4 Sep 1787	1753		63	128	N side of Cumberland River	
Weakley, Robert	359	Crawford, John heirs	Davidson	640	343	4 Sep 1787			63	128	W side of Sycamore Creek	
Weakley, Robert	362	Armstrong, M.	Davidson	200	4	4 Sep 1787			63	129	On both sides of Red River	
Weakley, Robert	393		Sumner	70	139	29 Aug 1793			80	328	On N side of Cumberland	
Weakley, Robert	55		Middle District	2000	57	10 Jul 1788	1799	23 Apr 1784	67	438	On Weakleys Creek &c	
Weakley, Robert	664	Pierce, Joseph heirs	Tennessee	640	3315	6 Dec 1797	4382		97	40	N side of Cumberland River	yes
Weakley, Robert	993	Dedrick, Jacob	Davidson	640	1010	18 May 1789	2264		63	339	On E Fk of Stones River	yes
Weakley, Robert	995	Gunn, Abraham heirs	Davidson	640	1012	18 May 1789	2487		63	339	On E Fk of Stones River	yes
Weakley, Robert	996	Zealot, Nelson heirs	Davidson	640	1013	18 May 1789	3396		63	339	On waters of Halfpone Creek	yes
Weakley, Robert etal	2468	Pearl, James	Davidson	3840	3390	12 Dec 1801	3042	5 Nov 1792	114	93	Lying on Stone River	yes
Weakley, Robert, Ass.	323		Sumner	320	1573	23 Feb 1793	3527	30 Nov 1792	76	300	On W Branch of Drakes Creek	
Weakley, Robt	078	Armstrong, M.	Tennessee	100	1704	20 May 1798	2778	30 Sep 1785			On N waters of Sycamore Creek	
Weakley, Robt	261	Todd, John heirs	Tennessee	640	338	4 Sep 1787	2580		81	54	On N side of Cumberland River	
Weakley, Robt	354	Sharpe, Jonas heirs	Davidson	640	3059	19 Jul 1797			63	126	On N side of Cumberland River	yes
Weakley, Robt	590		Tennessee	640			4332		90	373	N/S Cumberland waters of Sycamore Cree	
Weakley, Robt	597	Prescott, Jonathan heirs	Tennessee	640	3078	19 Jul 1797			90	381	N side of Cumberland River	yes

Claimant:	File #:	Assignee:	County:	Acres:	Grant:	Grant Date:	Entry:	Entry Date:	Bk:	Pg:	Location by Stream Name:	Military:
Weakley, Robt & Samuel	2363	Turner, Daniel heirs	Davidson	640	3072	19 Jul 1797	3984		90	379	S side of Cumberland River	yes
Weakley, Robt, Ass.	196		Sumner	640	1052	27 Nov 1789	3428	3 Jun 1786	71	289	On Maddesons Creek	yes
Weakley, Saml	595	Tillet, Andrew heirs	Tennessee	640	3073	19 Jul 1797			90	379	N waters of Sycamore Creek	
Weakley, Samuel	011	Tillet, Andrew	Robertson	640			4396	9 Mar 1794			On N waters of Sycamore Creek	
Wear, Hugh	1113		Green	640	956	26 Dec 1791			77	266	On head of Pistol Creek	
Wear, Jno.	584		Washington	100	677	26 Oct 1786	3000	16 Feb 1784	66	1	Beg at a stake	
Wear, John	1420		Green	200	1232	27 Nov 1792	41	26 Feb 1778	80	164	On the N side Nolichuckey River &c	
Wear, Samuel	1114		Green	700	957	26 Dec 1791			77	266	On Crooked Creek	
Wear, Samuel	1477		Green	100	1240	12 Jul 1793	2161	6 Nov 1779	81	575	On a branch of Lick Creek	
Wear, Samuel	307		Eastern District	627	215	22 Feb 1795			84	290	On W Fk of Little Pigeon River	
Wearren, Edward	588		Sullivan	400	586	29 Jul 1793	1103,-1760	11 Mar 1789	76	475	On a branch of White Top	
Weatherby, Isaac	2111	Sugg, Geo. A.	Davidson	640	2366	20 May 1793	2626		81	205	On S side of Cumberland River	yes
Weatherington, Jacob	985	Brehon, James Gloster	Davidson	640	1002	18 May 1789	2892		63	337	On waters of Red River	yes
Weatherington, Jesse	835	Anderson, Daniel	Davidson	640	838	17 Jan 1789	2891		63	294	N side of Cumberland River	yes
Weathers, Benjamin	1270	Malloy, Thomas	Sumner	1000	2976	5 Apr 1797	2629	7 Oct 1796	90	276	N side of Cumberland River	yes
Weatherspoon, William	610	Kerkendoll, Matthew	Sumner	640	1867	20 May 1793	1964	6 Feb 1792	81	93	On Station Camp Creek	yes
Weaver, Christian	384		Sullivan	540	263	10 Nov 1784	896	31 Dec 1778	69	166	On S side of Holstein River	
Weaver, Christian	491		Sullivan	300	502	18 May 1789	895	31 Dec 1778	71	12	On Underwoods Branch	
Weaver, John	1045	Easton, James	Sumner	640	2707	27 Mar 1796	1130	30 Nov 1792	88	258	On waters of Caney Fork	yes
Weaver, Michael	225		Sullivan	500	364	9 Aug 1787	412	12 Apr 1780	61	383	On N side of Holstein River	
Weaver, Moses	1003	Cantrell, Stephen	Davidson	274	1020	18 May 1789			63	341	On head branches of 2nd Creek	yes
Weaver, Samuel	663	Sheppard, William	Sumner	640	1983	20 May 1793	2826	24 Nov 1792	81	120	On both sides of Hickmans Creek	yes
Weaver, Samuel	808		Washington	600	622	10 Nov 1784	533	26 Oct 1778	69	144	A small branch of Little Limestone	
Weaver, William	1000	Cathey, Richard	Davidson	640	1017	18 May 1789	1734		63	340	On E Fork of Stones River	yes
Webb, Benjamin	1286		Washington	50	1201	9 Dec 1795	136	16 Sep 1794	89	401	Upon a branch of Dry Creek	
Webb, Benjamin	92		Sullivan	240	103	23 Oct 1782	1039	7 Jan 1779	43	287	S side of Holstein	
Webb, Charles	2283	Graves, Francis	Davidson	640	2765	20 Jul 1796	3057		88	463	On S side of Cumberland	yes
Webb, David	94		Sullivan	575	105	23 Oct 1782	1070	8 Jan 1779	43	288	On S side of Holstein River	
Webb, George	067		Washington	613			1071	8 Jan 1779			On Beaver Creek	
Webb, George	199		Sullivan	613	206	10 Oct 1783			53	151	On Bever Creek	
Webb, Giles	588	Glasgow, James	Davidson	640	560	15 Sep 1787	149		63	201	S side of CumberlandRiver	yes
Webb, John	128		Sullivan	620 (622	140	23 Oct 1782	140	12 Feb 1780	43	325	On S side of Holstein	
Webb, John	1444	Good, William	Sumner	640	3356	6 May 1800	1462	23 Sep 1785	107	367	On S side of Cumberland River	yes
Webb, John	247		Washington	550.5	115	23 Oct 1782	668	8 Dec 1778	47	56	S side of Indian Creek	
Webb, John	74		Green	100	32	1 Nov 1786 .	61	21 Oct 1783	59	393	S side of Nolachuckie River	
Webb, John	910	Good, William	Sumner	640	2479	31 Dec 1793	1462	29 Jul 1792	81	436	On Whites Fork of New River	yes
Webb, Joshua	1197	Donelson, John	Sumner	640	2755	20 Jul 1796	3056	3 Jan 1796	88	459	On both sides of Cedar Lick Creek	yes
Webb, Lewis	666	Rains, John	Sumner	640	1986	20 May 1793	3386	28 Jun 1788	81	121	On waters of Cedar Lick Creek	yes
Webb, Martin	217		Washington	100	85	23 Oct 1782	1123	22 Jan 1779	47	41	Joining sd Webbs former entry	
Webb, Martin	25		Washington	400	315	24 Oct 1782	516	19 Oct 1778	43	304	In the Grassey Cove &c	
Webb, Richard	434		Green	150	436	20 Sep 1787	64	21 Oct 1783	65	498	On N side of Chuckey River &c	
Webb, William	1595		Green	190	1337	22 Dec 1795	479	27 Nov 1788	83	438	N side of Noleychuckey River	
Webster, Reubin	513		Green	200	515	20 Sep 1787	315	23 Oct 1783	65	527	On S side of Holston	
Webster, Richard	123		Tennessee	640	1626	23 Feb 1793	3576	12 Dec 1787	76	325	S side of Cumberland River	yes
Weddell, John	702		Hawkins	300	504	23 Apr 1794	382	10 Sep 1778	82	153	On N side of Holston	

Claimant:	File #:	Assignee:	County:	Acres:	Grant:	Grant Date:	Entry:	Entry Date:	Bk:	Pg:	Location by Stream Name:	Military:
Wedener, Lewis	039		Hawkins	480	788	19 Feb 1797	1748	28 Sep 1779			On Possum Creek	
Weeks, Benjamin	0116	Shackley, Philip	Sumner	640			1804	9 Dec 1785			N side of Cumberland River	yes
Weeks, Benjamin	357	West, Eli	Tennessee	640	2187	20 May 1793	1396	13 Nov 1784	81	168	On S side of Cumberland River	yes
Weeks, Cornelius	870	Evans, Thomas	Sumner	428	2387	31 Dec 1793	1569	12 Dec 1785	81	387	On waters of Station Camp	
Weeks, John	774		Sullivan	46	705	20 Jul 1796	49	8 Feb 1780	91	86	Beg at a spanish oak	
Weeks, Levi	359	West, Eli	Tennessee	500	2205	20 May 1793	1381	11 Jan 1794	81	170	On S side of Cumberland River	yes
Weeks, Silas	297	Shackler, Philip	Sumner	640	1325	10 Dec 1790	1533	9 Dec 1785	74	374	On N side of Cumberland River	yes
Weeks, Theophilus	1576	Edmunson, Thomas	Davidson	258	1226	20 Sep 1787	1806		74	340	On W Fork of Mill Creek	
Weer, John	299		Green	200	301		2530	25 May 1784	65	459	On N side of Noleychuckey River	
Weir, Samuel	892		Green	200	823	– Sep 1790	823 [sic]	12 May 1784	74	290	On N Fork of Crooked Creek	yes
Welbern, Daniel	0124	Amus, James	Sumner	640			1948	20 Jul 1796			On both sides Pond Lick Creek	
Welborn, Daniel	02	Hohamer, Phillip	Robertson	640			1951	10 Feb 1796			On Clay Lick Branch	
Welbum, Daniel	569	May, Abraham heirs	Tennessee	1000	3006	10 Apr 1797	2210		90	295	N of Red River	yes
Welbum, Daniel	570	Ware, Geo.	Tennessee	274	3008	10 Apr 1797	3430	2 Feb 1786	90	297	S side of RedRriver	yes
Welbum, Daniel, Ass.	0143		Sumner	640	3007	10 Apr 1797	1974	16 Sep 1796			S of Cumberland River	yes
Welbum, Daniel, Ass.	1272		Sumner	640	1523	10 Apr 1797	861		90	296	S of Cumberland River	
Welch, John	103	Singleton, Henry	Tennessee	640	975	10 Apr 1792	1213	14 May 1784	75	509	On S side of Cumberland River	yes
Welch, John	143		Davidson	1580	2002	18 May 1789	224		63	330	On E Fork of Stones River	yes
Welch, William	306	Lyttle, William	Tennessee	1000	410	20 May 1793	2555	25 Oct 1783	81	125	On N side of Duck River	yes
Welch, William	438	Blount, Reading	Davidson	640	172	15 Sep 1787	306		63	152	S branches of Sycamore Creek	yes
Welloughbey, Andrew	165		Sullivan	342	564	15 Sep 1787	2591	14 Mar 1780	53	147	On both sides Sinking Creek	
Wells, Daniel	592	Colson, Isaac	Davidson	640			4717	21 Sep 1797	63	202	On N side of Cumberland River	yes
Wells, Hayden	03	Good, John	Montgomery	228			4681	14 Jun 1797			Beg on E bundary of Wm. Shaw	yes
Wells, Hayden	04	White, Elijah	Montgomery	640			42				S side of Cumberland River	
Wells, Hayden	586	Armstrong, M.	Tennessee	44	386	19 Jul 1797	758		90	370	N side of Red River	
Wells, Hayden	575		Tennessee	640	3022	10 Apr 1797	43		90	302	S side of Cumberland River	
Wells, Haydon	587	Armstrong, M.	Tennessee	40	387	19 Jul 1787	172		90	370	S side of Red River	yes
Wells, Haydon & John Owens	05	Lynn, Jonathan heirs	Montgomery	640	463- [?]	28 Aug 1797	119	24 Jan 1784	66	180	S side of Cumberland	
Wells, Headon	1147		Davidson	640	124	17 Apr 1786	1582		63	72	Beg at a hickory &c	yes
Wells, John	209	Branton, Brittain heirs	Davidson	640	195	7 Mar 1786			97	47	On waters of Stones River	yes
Wells, Lewis	2429		Davidson	640	3325	6 Dec 1797					On a branch of Stones River	yes
Wells, Samuel	032	McNeeley, William	not given	400								yes
Wells, Samuel	032		not given				2881	22 Jul 1781	66	19	On N side of Wataugah River	
Wells, William	623		Washington	100	717	26 Oct 1786	3032	1 Jun 1795	88	360	Joining sd Harris survey	yes
Wells, Zebulon	1172	Harris, Edward	Sumner	640	2677	4 Jun 1796	2158	29 Nov 1790	74	233	On N side Cumberland River	yes
Welsh, Thomas	1556	Drew, John	Davidson	640	1172	29 Nov 1790	3237	1 Aug 1792	81	174	On S side of Cumberland River	yes
Wesley, John	772	Alexander, George	Sumner	274	2224	20 May 1793	1501		74	110	On N side of Cumberland River	yes
West, Cyprian	1506	Hart, Anthony	Davidson	640	1063	26 Nov 1789	1396	13 Nov 1784	81	168	On S side of Cumberland River	
West, Eli	357	Weaks, Benj.	Tennessee	640	2187	20 May 1793	2205	20 May 1793 [s	81	170	On S side of Cumberland River	yes
West, Eli	359	Weaks, Levi	Tennessee	500	2205	20 May 1793	1381	10 Jan 1794 [sic]	81	170	On S side of Cumberland River	yes
West, Eli	914	Collins, John	Davidson	428	930	18 May 1789	679		63	320	On S side of Cumberland River	
West, Francis	474	Marshall, John	Davidson	640	446	15 Sep 1787	1611		63	164	On Money Fork Creek	yes
West, Joseph	1017	Rogers, Benjamin	Davidson	357	1034	18 May 1789	1950		63	344	On N side of Red River	yes
West, Levi	074	Tyrrell, William	not given	428			1165	26 May 1796			A cr empties into Cumberland R	yes
West, Levi	283	Bonner, James	Sumner	428	1280	10 Dec 1790			74	359	On head waters of Goose Creek	yes

Earliest Tennessee Land Records

Claimant:	File #:	Assignee:	County:	Acres:	Grant:	Grant Date:	Entry:	Entry Date:	Bk:	Pg:	Location by Stream Name:	Military:
West, Thomas	1614		Green	117	1326	5 Dec 1794	2799	28 Feb 1781	84	154	Part of plantation West once lived	
West, Thomas	265		Hawkins	300	276	14 Jan 1793	1747	28 Sep 1779	78	334	In the knobs of Richland Creek	
West, Thomas	278		Hawkins	640	289	14 Jan 1793	129	26 Feb 1778	78	341	S side of Holston	
West, Thomas	569		Green	300	249	20 Sep 1787	260	6 Mar 1786	66	157	On S side of Holston River &c	
West, Thomas	830		Washington	85	644	10 Nov 1784	2862	29 May 1781	69	150	Joining James Rogers	
Wester, Fulgom	079		Washington	60				19 Oct 1797			On waters of Big Limestone	
Weston, Aquilla	1409	Bradon, Alexander	Sumner	1000	3341	6 Dec 1797	4683	8 May 1797	97	57	On waters of Big Barron	yes
Westwardhall, Francis	264	Shackler, Philip	Sumner	640	1221	10 Dec 1790	373	9 Dec 1795	74	338	On N side of Cumberland River	yes
Weymouth, Corbyn	1624	Stewart, William	Davidson	365	1364	10 Dec 1790	485		74	387	On N side of Cumberland River	yes
Wha-a-kah or Grass Grows	069		Tennessee	640	9			9 Aug 1819			A stake on top of a high mountain	
Wharton, James	1280	Barry, Redmond Dillin	Sumner	640	3039	8 Jun 1797	4044	20 Mar 1797	90	314	Both sides of the road	yes
Wheeler, James	161		Washington	97	29	23 Oct 1782	422	23 Sep 1778	47	13	Joining John Stewarts land	
Wheeler, James	245		Washington	200	113	23 Oct 1782	747	23 Dec 1778	47	56	On Clear Fork of Horse Creek	
Wheeler, James	280		Sullivan	100	419	9 Aug 1786	559	11 May 1780	61	438	Bet. Horse Creek & Lick Creek	
Wheeler, John	282		Washington	99	149	23 Oct 1782	748	23 Dec 1778	47	72	On Clear Fork of Horse Creek	
Wheeler, Stephen	1322		Washington	100	1243	5 Apr 1797	403	19 Sep 1778	90	279	Waters of Beaver Dam Creek	
Wheeler, Stephen	1323		Washington	200	1244	5 Apr 1797	2050	27 Oct 1779	90	279	Waters of Beaver Dam	
Wheeler, Stephen	1324		Washington	100	1245	5 Apr 1797	4723	22 Oct 1778	90	279	On the Beaverdam Creek	
Whealey, Isum	790	McNees, John	Davidson	1000	793	23 Aug 1788	2896		63	277	On N side of Cumberland River	yes
Wheallock, John	1196		Washington	400	1149	6 Jan 1795	916	31 Dec 1778	83	177	On or near head of Kendricks Cr	
Wheallock, John	1199		Washington	200	1152	6 Jan 1795	1448	19 Jun 1779	83	179	On waters of Horse Creek	
Wheallock, John	1200		Washington	100	1153	6 Jan 1795	616	23 Nov 1778	83	180	On Kendricks Creek	
Wheallock, John	868		Washington	100	852	18 May 1789	2773	17 Feb 1781	72	221	On drafts of Kendricks Creek	
Wheaock, John	916		Washington	100	893	17 Nov 1793	2172	16 Feb 1781	76	142	On draught of Kendricks Creek	
Wheaton & Lisdale	2451	Briggs, Wm. Heirs	Davidson	640	3295	6 Dec 1797	2317		98	171	Bet. Marrowbone & Sycamore Cr	yes
Wheaton, Charles	458	Hopkins, Joseph	Tennessee	400	178	7 Mar 1796		10 Jan 1794	88	195	W of the Cumberland Mountain	Yes
Wheaton, Charles	677	Larremore, William heirs	Tennessee	640	3296	6 Dec 1797	4323		98	172	On W Fork of Barretts Creek	
Wheaton, Daniel	2448	Pate, William heirs	Davidson	640	3291	6 Dec 1797(99)	4289		98	168	Waters Cumberland & Harpeth	yes
Wheaton, Daniel	2449	Carter, Isaac heirs	Davidson	640	3292	6 Dec 1797	4325		98	169	On W Fork of Sams Creek	yes
Wheaton, Daniel	2450	Stanley, Robert heirs	Davidson	640	3294	6 Dec 1797	4290		98	170	On E Fork of Swan Creek	yes
Wheaton, Daniel	559	McPherson, Abel	Tennessee	1000	2993	10 Apr 1797	1575		90	290	E Fork of Yellow Creek	
Wheaton, Daniel	676	Hayes, James	Tennessee	97	3293	6 Dec 1797	4324		98	169	On E Fork of Barretts Creek	
Wheeler, Benjamin	06	Blount, John Gray	Tennessee	640			2824	30 Sep 1785			S side Spring Creek	yes
Wheeler, Empery	124	Underwood, Elizabeth etal	Davidson	640	110	7 Mar 1786	710		63	44	S side of Cumberland River	yes
Wheeler, Empery heirs	124	Wheeler, Mourning (heir)	Davidson	640	110	7 Mar 1786	710		63	44	S side of Cumberland	yes
Wheeler, Isaac	744	Parks, George	Sumner	640	2142	20 May 1793	1978	24 Nov 1792	81	159	On Jining Fork &c	yes
Wheeler, Mourning & Elizab	124	Wheeler, Empery	Davidson	640	110	7 Mar 1786	710		63	44	S side of Cumberland	yes
Wheeler, Samuel	345	Adair, James	Eastern District	274	2611	7 Mar 1796			88	332	On N side of Clinch	
Wheeler, Stephen	1247		Washington	400	1219	27 Feb 1796	15	25 Feb 1778	88	507	On Beaverdam Creek	
Wheeler, Stephen	787		Sullivan	100	719	2 Dec 1796	580	3 Jun 1781	91	276	On Beaver Dam Creek	
Wheeler, David (heir)	787	Jones, Allen (hr of David)	Sumner	1000	2295	20 May 1793	1014	2 Jun 1785	81	190	On both sides of a trace &c	yes
Whillock, John	1031		Washington	200	981	14 Jan 1793	2760	6 Sep 1790	79	279	On headwaters of Kindreds Creek	
Whitaker, John, Ass.	629		Sumner	640	1912	20 May 1793	3248	19 Jul 1788	81	103	On waters E Fork of Stones River	yes
Whitaker, John, Ass.	631		Sumner	640	1914	20 May 1793	3249	19 Jul 1788	81	103	On the dividing ridge	yes
Whitaker, Josiah	015	Armstrong & Donelson	Middle District	640			2963					yes

Claimant:	File #:	Assignee:	County:	Acres:	Grant:	Grant Date:	Entry:	Entry Date:	Bk:	Pg:	Location by Stream Name:	Military:
Whitaker, Thos.	1313		Green	200	1163	12 Jan 1793	1391	16 Jan 1784	78	401	On Blacks Creek	
Whitakers, Joseph	826	Anderson, Daniel	Davidson	640	829	17 Jan 1789	2894		63	292	On waters of Caney Fork	yes
Whitard, Wm.	239	Tatum, John	Tennessee	274	1578	27 Apr 1793	595	25 Apr 1784	81	12	On W Fork of Red River	
Whitard, Wm.	241	Coyard, David	Tennessee	274	1590	27 Apr 1793	597	21 Apr 1784	81	15	Both sides of W Fork of Red River	
White, Archibald	1277		Washington	200	1215	4 Dec 1795	2555	2 May 1788	89	332	On waters of Watauga River	
White, Benjamin	1919	Nichols, John	Davidson	640	1713	20 May 1793	924		81	56	On W side of Harpeth River	yes
White, Daniel	8	Coon, Conrod	Robertson(David	228	3411	10 Feb 1804	1123		118	300	On both sides of Sycamore Creek	yes
White, David	294		Middle District	800	254	7 Jul 1794	1215	5 Nov 1783	82	201	SW side of Clear Fork of Cumberland River	
White, David & Wm. McCray	294		Middle District	800	254	7 Jul 1794	1215	5 Nov 1783	82	201	S/W of the Clear Fork of Cumberland River	
White, Doctor James	1791		Davidson	20	133	29 Aug 1793			80	325	On S side of Cumberland River	
White, Elijah	04	Wells, Hayden	Montgomery	640			4681	14 Jun 1797			S side of Cumberland River	yes
White, Ezekial	214		Davidson	274	200	7 Mar 1786	122		63	74	On waters of Stones River	yes
White, George	485	Marshall, John	Davidson	640	457	15 Sep 1787	1618		63	166	On Money Fork Creek	yes
White, George heirs	1038	White, George heirs	Davidson	640	457	15 Sep 1787	1618		63	166	On Money Fork Creek	yes
White, Henry	079	Armstrong, M.	Tennessee	150	367			6 May 1797			Beg at a Post oak & hickory	
White, Henry	1038		Green	100	1265	29 Jul 1793	75	4 Nov 1788	76	491	Around 2 squares of his 200 acres	
White, Henry	1081		Hawkins	150	367	4 Jul 1797			91	591	In the Little Valley	
White, Henry	1364		Green	240	1219	27 Jan 1793	75	4 Jan 1779	79	503	On N side of Holston River	
White, Henry	22	Molloy, Thomas	Davidson	228	8	16 Feb 1786	516	20 Apr 1784	63	4	S side of Cumberland River	yes
White, Henry	267		Hawkins	200	278	14 Jan 1793	1108	13 Jan 1779	78	336	On S side of Holston River	
White, Isaac	1207		Washington	400	1161	5 Dec 1794	515	19 Oct 1778	83	418	On the Fall Branch of Horse Creek	
White, Isaac	125		Green	200	141	1 Nov 1786	81	21 Oct 1783	59	444	Lying on Long Creek	
White, Jacob	228	Robertson, James	Davidson	274	214	7 Mar 1786	275		63	79	On the bent of Cumberland River	yes
White, Jacob	534	Coman, James	Middle District	1000	2934	22 Feb 1797	4686		90	238	On a fork of Caney Fork	yes
White, Jacob, Jr.	010	Bledsoe, Anthony	Sumner	274			276	19 Dec 1792			On Otter Fork of Bledsoes Creek	yes
White, James	144		Green	100	614	23 Aug 1788	668	28 Oct 1783	64	346	Adjoining his 400 acre survey	
White, James	160		Green	1000	630	23 Aug 1788	1739	17 Apr 1784	64	351	On N side of Holston River &c	
White, James	1656	Morton, Jonas	Davidson	274	1572	23 Feb 1793	1940		76	299	N/S Cumberland in mouth of White Bend	yes
White, James	1661		Green	350	1366	2 Dec 1795	245	22 Oct 1783	88	271	Upper end of 1st island in Holston	
White, James	1685	Mann, Arnold	Davidson	228	1624	23 Feb 1793	3689		76	324	Cumberland River in White Bent	yes
White, James	1930	Guion, Samuel	Davidson	640	1741	20 May 1793	3090		81	64	On N side of Cumberland	yes
White, James	2122	Armstrong, M.	Davidson	20	133	16 Dec 1793			81	394	On S side of Cumberland River	
White, James	2178	Armstrong, M.	Davidson	25	128	8 Apr 1794		4 Apr 1791	81	557	On N side of Cumberland River	
White, James	218		Green	800	175	20 Sep 1787	1527	20 Sep (no yeae)	65	422	On N side of Clinch	
White, James	2306	Armstrong, M.	Davidson	36.75	187	18 Nov 1795		31 Mar 1785	89	136	On S side of Cumberland River	
White, James	359		Green	112	361	20 Sep 1787			65	475	In the 1st island in Holston River	
White, James	445		Eastern District	555	299	20 Oct 1797	1479	19 Feb 1784	92	92	N side Holston River	
White, James	776		Green	320	581	23 Aug 1788	1489	19 Feb 1784	68	254	On N side of Holston River &c	
White, James	862		Green	400	812	27 Nov 1789	54	21 Oct 1783	74	16	On N side of French Broad River	
White, James L.	2424	Sullivan, Port heirs	Davidson	640	3244	30 Nov 1797	4443		94	175	Robertsons & Sheppards S E cor	yes
White, James L.	2425	Goodson, Wm.	Davidson	640	3245	30 Nov 1797	4083		94	176	E side of E Fork of S Harpeth	yes
White, James S.	2427	Herring, Henry	Davidson	640	3247	30 Nov 1797	4087		94	177	E side of E Fk of S Harpeth	yes
White, James, Ass.	2244		Davidson	35	292	20 Jul 1796		31 Mar 1784	88	437	On S side of Cumberland	
White, James, Ass.	2245		Davidson	35	293	20 Jul 1796		4 Apr 1791	88	437	On N side of Cumberland River	
White, James, Ass.	2247		Davidson	179	296	20 Jul 1796		28 Nov 1792	88	438	Beg at a beach	

Earliest Tennessee Land Records

Claimant:	File #:	Assignee:	County:	Acres:	Grant:	Grant Date:	Entry:	Entry Date:	Bk:	Pg:	Location by Stream Name:	Military:
White, James, Ass.	533	Armstrong, M.	Tennessee	40	349	1 Mar 1797			90	224	Inc. the Island	
White, James, Ass.	906		Hawkins	600	694	18 Aug 1795	939	29 Oct 1783	87	505	Beg at a pine & black oak	yes
White, James, Sr.	2426	Rose, Andrew	Davidson	640	3246	30 Nov 1797	4105		94	176	W side of Harpeth	yes
White, Jas & Jas Cozbee	548		Green	2100	550	20 Sep 1787	457	25 Oct 1784	65	541	On N side of Holston River &c	
White, Jas, Heir of Thomas	994		Davidson	3840	1011	18 May 1789	102		63	339	In large bent of Cumberland River	yes
White, John	078	Brown, Frederick	Davidson	640			2042	24 Jan 1791			On waters of Little Harpeth	
White, John	1280		Washington	640	1218	4 Dec 1795	568	2 Nov 1778	89	334	Beg at the mouth of Nobb Creek	
White, John	1451		Green	100	1261	27 Nov 1792	1783	2 Oct 1779	80	174	Ridge bet Sinking Creek & Lick Cr	
White, John	179		Davidson	228	165	7 Mar 1786	133		63	62	W Fk of Big Harpeth River	yes
White, John	611	Stewart, Duncan	Tennessee	1000	3160	14 Sep 1797	534		90	426	S side of Cumberland River	yes
White, Joseph	1092		Green	953	935	26 Dec 1791	1393	16 Jan 1784	77	255	At an elm at the Buffelow Ford	
White, Martha	846		Hawkins	200	671	22 Feb 1795	102	6 Feb 1778	83	431	N/S Holston on Douglads Branch	
White, Richard	81		Washington	465	249	23 Oct 1782	653	22 Apr 1779	44	371	On both sides of Rones Creek	
White, Richard	959		Washington	270	936	17 Nov 1790	2492	10 Mar 1780	76	156	On waters of Roans Creek	
White, Robert	033	Winton, John	not given	400								yes
White, Robert	033		not given	400								
White, Robert	054	McKnight, Wm.	not given	400				10 Jan 1794				
White, Robert	1157	Harris, Edward	Sumner	640	2662	4 Jun 1796	3857	1 Jun 1795	88	355	On Whites Creek	yes
White, Robert	438	Nelson, Robert	Tennessee	400	171	26 Sep 1795		20 Dec 1794	86	529	Joining Harris survey	yes
White, Solomon	1157		Davidson	640	134	17 Apr 1786	69	8 Jan 1784	66	183	Joined Samuel Henleys survey	yes
White, Solomon	1426	Armstrong, M.	Davidson	150	43	8 Oct 1787	1285	20 Aug 1785	68	158	On Red River	
White, Stephen	603	Stewart, Duncan	Tennessee	1000	3110	14 Sep 1797	535	21 Oct 1783	90	406	On Red River	yes
White, Thomas	617		Green	350	658	11 Jul 1788	49	2 Jun 1784	66	446	S side of Cumberland River	yes
White, Thomas	640	Harget, F. & J. Carney	Tennessee	2560	3084	12 Aug 1797	1078	2 Jun 1784	91	626	E side of Big Pigeon River	yes
White, Thomas (heir)	994		Davidson	3840	1011	18 May 1789	102		63	339	Both sides of Millers Creek	yes
White, Thomas, Ass.	460		Sumner	403	1602	27 Apr 1793	1224	8 Mar 1788	81	18	Large bent of Cumberland River	yes
White, Thomas, Ass.	530		Sumner	640	1723	20 May 1793	1790	21 Apr 1787	81	59	On both sides of Jinnings Creek	yes
White, Thomas, Ass.	542		Sumner	640	1744	20 May 1793	2639	25 apr 1787	81	65	A branch that empties in E Fk &c	yes
White, Thomas, Ass.	611		Sumner	228	1870	20 May 1793	73	21 Oct 1783	81	94	On waters of E Fk of Goose Creek	yes
White, Walter	521	McNeeley, William	Davidson	640	493	15 Sep 1787	2036	14 Feb 1784	63	178	On N side of Red River	yes
White, William	058	Robertson, Elijah	Davidson	640	2492		515				S side of Cumberland River	
White, William	071	Henderson, Robert	Middle District	307	2460		1131				Abt 2 miles S of Nashville	
White, William	072	Vance, David	Middle District	1097	2462		1925					
White, William	074	Trulock, Sutton	Middle District	274			1446					
White, William	19		Smythe	357	3383	12 Dec 1801	3725	2 Jun 1800	114	89	On waters of Jenning Creek	
White, William	203		Davidson	274	189	7 Mar 1786	702		63	70	On waters of Whites Creek	yes
White, William	2318	Robertson, Elijah	Davidson	640	2781	29 Nov 1796	515		90	15	Abt 2 miles S of Nashville	yes
White, William	271		Washington	136	139	23 Oct 1782	752	23 Dec 1778	47	67	On Fall Branch of Horse Creek	
White, William, Ass.	720		Sumner	228	2104	20 May 1793	602	31 Jul 1792	81	150	On waters of Spring Creek	yes
White, William, Ass.	936		Sumner	1097	2460	22 Feb 1795			83	422	On Brimstone Creek	yes
White, William, Ass.	938		Sumner	274	2462	22 Feb 1795			83	423	On Brimstone Creek	yes
White, William, Ass.	956		Sumner	307	2419	22 Feb 1795			84	306	On Brimstone Creek	yes
Whitehead, William, Ass.	708		Sumner	243	2088	20 May 1793	820	21 Nov 1792	81	146	On Spring Creek	yes
Whitehouse, Joel	355		Sumner	274	1474	4 Jan 1792	1118	18 Nov 1791	77	370	N side of Cumberland River	
Whiteman, William	526	Hickman, Thomas	Sumner	640	1719	20 May 1793	2159	19 Nov 1792	81	58	On W side of Caney Fork	yes

Claimant:	File #:	Assignee:	County:	Acres:	Grant:	Grant Date:	Entry:	Entry Date:	Bk:	Pg:	Location by Stream Name:	Military:
Whitenbeigen, Jos.	1331		Green	300	1073	26 Dec 1792	1072	5 Dec 1779	78	429	Joining James Moores land	
Whitenberger, Fredrick	1405		Green	300	1217	27 Nov 1792	36	21 Jul 1779	80	156	On a draft of Richland Creek	
Whitenberger, Frederick	1601		Green	200	1333	27 Apr 1795	1989	16 Oct 1779	83	491	N side of Nolechuckey River	
Whitenberger, Fredk	695		Green	300	736	11 Jul 1788	164	22 Oct 1783	66	472	N side of Nolichuckey River &c	
Whitesides, Jenkins etal	3		Grainger	1000	312	30 Oct 1801	3594	25 May 1784	111	108	On S side of Powells River	
Whitesides, William	394		Washington	148	386	13 Oct 1783	1958	10 Oct 1779	52	258	On a branch of Lick Creek	
Whitfield, Bryant	1946	Stephenson, Hughey	Davidson	365	1778	20 May 1793	1530		81	73	On E side of Stones River	yes
Whitfield, Bryant	1977	Frost, William	Davidson	640	1879	20 May 1793	3247		81	96	On head waters of Piney River	yes
Whitfield, Bryant	1992	Boss, Esau	Davidson	274	1911	20 May 1793	1531		81	103	On E side of Stones River	yes
Whitfield, Bryant	2065	Newnham, Aaron	Davidson	640	2201	20 May 1793			81	169	On E side of Stone River	yes
Whitfield, Bryant	269	Johnston, John	Tennessee	640	1765	20 May 1793	1529	2 Feb 1785	81	70	On N side of Cumberland River	yes
Whitfield, Bryant, Ass.	628		Sumner	1000	1909	20 May 1793	1096	21 Dec 1792	81	102	On waters of Stones River	yes
Whitfield, Bryant, Ass.	767		Sumner	640	2202	20 May 1793	487	21 Dec 1792	81	169	On waters of Stones River	yes
Whitfield, Jesse	071	Easton, James	Sumner	640				11 Mar 1795			On waters of Caney Fork	yes
Whitfield, Jesse	1264	Hickman, Thomas	Sumner	640	2940	1 Mar 1797	1478		90	213	N side of Cumberland River	yes
Whitfield, Jesse	186	Donelson, Stockley	Eastern District	640	1657	15 Jul 1793			81	43	Beg at a stake	yes
Whitfield, Lewis	114		Eastern District	1000	147	29 Jul 1793	600	27 Oct 1783	76	480	N side of Tennessee River &c	
Whitfield, Needham	634		Green	500	675	11 Jul 1788	557	27 Oct 1783	66	452	Bet. Clinch Mountain & Clinch River	
Whitfield, Needham	635		Green	400	676	11 Jul 1788	714	28 Oct 1783	66	452	On a prong of Bull Run &c	
Whitfield, Needham	636		Green	400	677	11 Jul 1788	868	29 Oct 1783	66	452	On both sides of Fk of Bull Run	
Whitfield, Needham	647		Green	400	688	11 Jul 1788	869	29 Oct 1784	66	456	On Bull Run &c	
Whitfield, William	642		Green	400	683	11 Jul 1788	1164	25 Jan 1784	66	455	Both sides E Fork of Bull Run	
Whitfield, William	648		Green	400	689	11 Jul 1788	870	29 Oct 1783	66	457	W/S ridge on prong of Bull Run	
Whitfield, William	659		Green	400	700	11 Jul 1788	872	29 Oct 1782	66	460	On both sides the N fk of Bull Run	
Whitfield, Wilson	023	Dillenberry, Redmon	Sumner	100			4112	6 Sep 1797			On Fk of Red River	yes
Whitfield, Wm, Jos. Green etal	308		Green	2500	310	20 Sep 1787	513	27 Oct 1783	65	461	On the N bank of Tennessee River	
Whitley, Hance	716	Saunders, James	Sumner	228	2098	20 May 1793	3487	21 Sep 1787	81	149	Beg at 2 sugar trees &c	yes
Whitley, Solomon	038	Ramsey, William	Tennessee	640			3280	28 Dec 1785			N side of Cumberland River	yes
Whitman, John	886		Washington	150	871	16 Nov 1790	1951	19 Oct 1779	73	399	On head of Clarks Branch	
Whitnall, Blount	643		Davidson	824	616	15 Sep 1787	2026	23 Nov 1793	63	219	On mouth of Big Harpeth River	yes
Whitner, Lewis	1043		Hawkins	480	807	8 Jun 1797	1713	23 Nov 1792	90	323	On Possum Creek	
Whitner, Lewis	339		Sullivan	300	479	10 Jul 1788	1749	28 Sep 1779	67	486	In Stanley Valley Manly Town	
Whitner, Lewis	576		Hawkins	70	450	29 Jul 1793	1752	29 Sep 1779	80	289	On Oposum Creek	
Whitney, James	2228	Donelson, Stockley & Willia	Davidson	640	2561	7 Mar 1796	46		88	311	On waters of Stones River	yes
Whitsell, Philip	387		Tennessee	1000	2386	31 Dec 1793	744	29 Apr 1784	81	387	On S side of Cumberland River	
Whitsell, William	1640	Perkins, James	Davidson	640	1513	10 Apr 1792	611		75	505	On N side of Cumberland River	yes
Whitsett, John	949	Cane, William heirs	Davidson	640	966	18 May 1789			63	328	On both sides of Smiths Fork	
Whitson, Thomas	1160		Washington	100	1118	7 Jul 1794	1714	23 Nov 1792	81	616	Beg at a white oak	
Whitson, Thomas	1161		Washington	50	1119	7 Jul 1794	2026	23 Nov 1793	81	617	Beg at a white oak	
Whitson, Thomas	1170		Washington	100	1128	7 Jul 1794	1713	23 Nov 1792	81	619	On side of Black Mountain	
Whitson, Thomas	1278		Washington	50	1216	4 Dec 1795	2032	26 Oct 1779	89	333	Beg at a black walnut	
Whitson, Thomas	1279		Washington	100	1217	4 Dec 1795	2033	26 Oct 1779	89	333	On waters of Little Doe	
Whitson, William	692		Green	282	733	11 Jul 1788	46	21 Oct 1783	66	474	On N E side of Big Pigeon River	
Whittaker, John, Ass.	916		Sumner	640	2487	31 Dec 1793	3076	19 Jul 1788	81	438	Waters of E Fork of Stones River	yes
Whittenborough, Frederick	1273		Green	200	1123	12 Jan 1793	19	7 Mar 1780	78	379	Beg at a Spanish oak	

Earliest Tennessee Land Records

Claimant:	File #:	Assignee:	County:	Acres:	Grant:	Grant Date:	Entry:	Entry Date:	Bk:	Pg:	Location by Stream Name:	Military:
Whitton, Isum	924	Nash, William	Davidson	640	940	18 May 1789	2783		63	322	On N side of Cumberland River	yes
Whood, William	1286	Barry, Redmon Dillon	Sumner	640	3045	8 Jun 1797	4045	29 Mar 1797	90	316	Cumberland road takes the mountain	yes
Wicker, James	1512		Green	100	1273	12 Jul 1794	1033	20 Feb 1793	81	585	Beg at a poplar	
Wicks, Zachariah	773		Sullivan	143	704	20 Jul 1796	227	21 Feb 1780	91	85	Waters of Reedy Fork	
Widener, Lewis	476		Sullivan	280	355	10 Nov 1784			69	198	On Possum Creek	
Wier, Hugh	679		Green	200	720	11 Jul 1788	33	21 Oct 1783	66	466	On N side of Nolichuckey	
Wier, Samuel	711		Washington	200	525	10 Nov 1784	2480	10 Mar 1780	69	113	On head waters of W Fk &c	
Wiet, Elijah	781		Washington	100	595	10 Nov 1784	2690	19 Dec 1780	69	137	On waters of Sinking Creek	
Wigbey, Samuel	171	Hannah, John	Tennessee	640	1441	20 Dec 1791	2350	29 Sep 1785	77	361	S side Cumberland River	yes
Wiggins, Charter	901	Barrow, Henry	Sumner	640	2457	31 Dec 1793	2785	4 Mar 1786	81	429	On Buffaloe Creek	yes
Wiggins, Henry & Ho Tatum	2438	Hair, John	Davidson	640	3280	6 Dec 1797	4266		98	160	On the waters of West Fork of Stones Rive	Yes
Wiggins, Jacob	427	Nichols, John	Davidson	1000	399	15 Sep 1787	1934		63	148	W side of Caney Fork	yes
Wiggins, Matthew	519	Murfree, Hardy	Davidson	274	491	15 Sep 1787	731		63	178	Bet the old & new trace	yes
Wiggins, Noah	673	Montgomery, Alexander	Sumner	228	2004	20 May 1793	3632	29 Aug 1792	81	125	On waters of Drakes Creek	yes
Wiggins, Thomas	1534	Craddock, John	Davidson	640	1091	26 Nov 1789	1448		74	126	On N side of Red River	yes
Wiggle, Demsey	324	Lanier, James	Davidson	640	310	28 Jun 1787	2346		63	115	S side of Big Barren River	yes
Wigley, Thomas	689	Davis, Joshua	Davidson	640	662	8 Dec 1787	2442		63	234	Beg at S E corner of 1000 acres	yes
Wikoff, Wm & Lardn. Clark	757	Clark, Daniel Howell heirs	Davidson	640	730	11 Jul 1788	1980		63	257	On N side of Cumberland River	yes
Wikoff & Clark	44		Middle District	250	46	10 Jul 1788	41	1 May 1786	67	428	On Weakleys Creek	
Wikoff & Clark	54		Western District	1000	54	10 Jul 1788	25	12 Jan 1786	67	301	On Reelfoot River &c	
Wikoff & Clark	57		Western District	400	57	10 Jul 1788	26	12 Jan 1786	67	302	On Reelfoot River &c	
Wikoff & Clark	621	Burke, Charles	Davidson	640	593	15 Sep 1787	1947		63	212	N side of Cumberland River	yes
Wikoff & Clark	679	Graves, Joseph	Davidson	640	652	8 Dec 1787	2186		63	231	S boundary of Captain Fawn	yes
Wikoff & Clark	82		Western District	390	82	10 Jul 1788	24	12 Jan 1786	67	312	On the Reelfoot	
Wikoff, William	094	Downing, George	not given	274			1460	8 Dec 1785			E Fk of N Cross Creek	
Wikoff, William	1745	Armstrong, M.	Davidson	228	110	20 Dec 1791			77	380	N/S Cumberland bel Marrowbone	
Wikoff, William, Ass. [?]	080	Bushnell, Eusebius	Tennessee	228				15 Jul 1788			N side Cumberland River	
Wikoff, Wm & Lardner Clark	081		Tennessee	357			19	9 Dec 1785			W Fk of N Cross Creek	
Wikoff, Wm.	347	Easter, Moses	Tennessee	640	2168	20 May 1793	2046	26 Aug 1785	81	165	On N side of Red River	
Wikoff, Wm. & Lardner Clark	082		Tennessee	228	86	26 Nov 1789	1612	29 Nov 1785	74	170	On waters of Puzzle Creek	
Wikoff, Wm. & Lardner Clark	1546	Armstrong, M.	Davidson	228	86	26 Nov 1789	1612	29 Nov 1785	74	170	On waters of Puzzle Creek	
Wikoff, Wm. & Lardner Clark	1606	Armstrong, Martin	Davidson	357	1329	10 Dec 1790	1254		74	375	On W Fork of N Cross Creek	
Wikoff, Wm. & Lardner Clark	272	Roger, James	Sumner	274	523	10 Dec 1790	2268	9 Apr 1788	74	349	On S side Cumberland River	yes
Wikoff, Wm. & Lardner Clark	551	Hedgepeth, Marmaduke	Davidson	274	523	15 Sep 1787	2267		63	188	On waters of N Cross Creek	yes
Wikoff, Wm. & Lardner Clark	552	McCulloh, Benjamin	Davidson	274	524	15 Sep 1787	1953		63	189	S side of Cumberland River	yes
Wilborn, John	1720		Davidson	640	1388	20 Dec 1791	2077		77	348	On the dividing ridge &c	yes
Wilborn, Daniel	0125	Jones, Richard	Sumner	640			1998	20 Jul 1796			Beg at Stockley Donelsons corner	yes
Wilburn, Daniel	678	Hockamer, Philip	Tennessee	640	3305	6 Dec 1797	1998	20 Jul 1796	98	178	Dry Lick Branch of SulphurFfork	
Wilburn, Daniel, Ass.	1431		Sumner	640	3306	6 Dec 1797	1998	20 Jul 1796	98	178	About 3 mi E of Pond Lick	yes
Wilburn, Daniel, Ass.	1432		Sumner	640	3307	6 Dec 1797	1948	20 Jul 1796	98	179	Abt 3 mi E of Pond Lick	yes
Wilburn, Daniel, Ass.	1433		Sumner	640	3308	6 Dec 1797	2001	14 Jul 1797	98	180	On the E side of Cumberland River	yes
Wilburn, Robert	323	Weakley, Robert	Sumner	320	1573	23 Feb 1793	3527	5 Nov 1792	76	300	On W branch of Drakes Creek	yes
Wilcock, David	646	Caswell, Richard, heir of W	Davidson	640	619	15 Sep 1787	479		63	220	On N boundary of his other survey	yes
Wilcockson, George	01		Sevier-Green	150							N side French Broad River	
Wilcockson, George	1499		Green	150	1262	12 Jul 1794	416	14 Apr 1780	81	582	On Dumplin Creek	

Earliest Tennessee Land Records

Claimant:	File #:	Assignee:	County:	Acres:	Grant:	Grant Date:	Entry:	Entry Date:	Bk:	Pg:	Location by Stream Name:	Military:
Wilcockson, George	1634		Green	400	1337	18 Aug 1795	591	10 Nov 1788	87	503	On N side of French Broad River	
Wilcockson, George	1745		Green	150	364	4 Jul 1797			91	589	N side French Broad River	
Wilcockson, William	92		Green	150	50	1 Nov 1786	1745	21 Apr 1784	59	411	On waters of Dumplin Creek	
Wilcoxon, George	1715		Green	640	1430	8 Jun 1797	925	29 Oct 1783	90	326	N side of French Broad	
Wilcoxson, George	1499		Green	150	1262	12 Jul 1794	416	14 Apr 1780	81	582	On Dumplin Creek	
Wilder, Joab	613		Washington	50	707	26 Oct 1786	2023	26 Oct 1779	66	14	Beg at a marked pine &c	
Wilder, Randal	41	Breckon, J. G.	Tennessee	1000	1228	10 Dec 1790	2895	30 Sep 1785	74	341	On S side of Cumberland River	yes
Wilder, Robert	570	Sheppard, Benjamin	Sumner	640	1807	20 May 1793	2305	30 Nov 1792	81	81	On waters of Dixons Creek	yes
Wiley, William	724		Sullivan	150	669	5 Dec 1794	622	24 Jun 1780	84	171	On waters of Hoes Creek	
Wilheight, Adam	875		Washington	200	859	18 May 1789	2887	1 Aug 1781	72	223	Beg at 2 white oaks &c	
Wilkerson, Moses	1348		Davidson	320	34	8 Oct 1787	208	29 Jan 1784	68	134	The creek joining his other survey	yes
Wilkerson, Moses	1369		Davidson	320	52	8 Oct 1787	209	29 Jan 1784	68	142	Beg on creek at a red oak	yes
Wilkerson, Thomas	1155		Green	100	998	26 Dec 1791	1545	25 Aug 1779	77	281	On waters of Nolychucky	yes
Wilkes, Francis	412	Allison, John	Davidson	228	384	15 Sep 1787	1091		63	143	On N boundary of his other claim	yes
Wilkeson, John	290	Long, Nicholas	Tennessee	640	1918	20 May 1793	6	15 Oct 1783	81	104	On S side of Cumberland River	yes
Wilkins, Benjamin	1766	Hays, Robert	Davidson	640	1549	14 Jan 1793	1903		79	269	On N side of Cumberland	yes
Wilkins, Elisha	163	Dickson, John	Tennessee	640	1424	20 Dec 1791	1909	15 Jul 1785	77	357	On both sides of Pine River	yes
Wilkins, Jordan	710	Phillips, Mann	Davidson	640	683	8 Dec 1787	2256		63	241	On waters of the Salleen	yes
Wilkins, Joseph	361	Williamson, Thomas	Sumner	640	1492	4 Jan 1792	2324	11 Nov 1787	77	373	On S side of Cumberland River	yes
Wilkins, Joseph	402	Nelson, Robert	Davidson	640	374	15 Sep 1787	2701		63	140	N side of Cumberland River	yes
Wilkins, William	1051	Gaylord, Thomas	Hawkins	156	3153		1736		90	423	N side Holston River	yes
Wilkins, William	661	Phillips, Mann	Sumner	640	1980	20 May 1793	2255	30 Nov 1792	81	119	On waters of Dixons Creek	yes
Willaba, Matthew	85		Hawkins	640	77	13 Feb 1791	169	7 Sep 1779	74	285	On S side Holston River	
Willaba, Matthew	88		Hawkins	640	80	13 Feb 1791			74	286	Beg on a bank of a Creek	
Willard, James	376	Johnston, Thomas	Tennessee	640	2314	20 May 1793	3031	30 Sep 1785	81	194	Beg at a red oak	yes
Willard, Stephen	799	Robertson, Elijah	Davidson	640	802	20 Nov 1788	3326		63	282	On waters of Caney Fork	yes
Willcocks, Isaac	1645		Davidson	320	296	17 Nov 1790	437	12 May 1784	76	180	On waters of Mill Creek	
Wilhelm, Andrew	1620		Green	200	1341	22 Feb 1795	250	30 May 1780	84	296	On N side of French Broad River	
Wilhite, Adam	365		Hawkins	200	358	8 Mar 1793	268	9 Mar 1780	78	488	On Beaverdam Creek	
Wilhite, Matthias	646		Green	200	687	11 Jul 1788	2509	30 Mar 1780	66	456	On Dumpling Creek	
Williams, Alexander	409		Green	411	411	20 Sep 1787	1564	29 Oct 1783	65	491	On Lick Creek & Camp Creek	
Williams, Allen	571		Hawkins	100	445	29 Jul 1793	649	28 Nov 1778	80	288	On S side of Holston River	
Williams, Amos	1067		Hawkins	50	776	21 Jan 1797	47	8 Feb 1780	91	776	S side of Holston River	
Williams, Arthur	645	Stewart, Duncan	Tennessee	640	3220	14 Sep 1797	4006		92	14	S side Cumberland River	yes
Williams, Curtice	1427	Armstrong, M.	Davidson	100	44	8 Oct 1787		6 Dec 1785	68	158	1st sm or above Blooming Grove	
Williams, Curtice	1605	Armstrong, M.	Davidson	100	1328	10 Dec 1790	1653	6 Dec 1785	74	375	On N side of Cumberland River	
Williams, Curtis	425		Washington	98	417	13 Oct 1783	1518	13 Aug 1779	52	274	On waters of Lick Creek	
Williams, Daniel	1027	Armstrong, M.	Sumner	300	255	27 Feb 1796			88	187	Waters of Middle Fk of Cedar Lick	
Williams, Daniel	1148		Davidson	640	125	17 Apr 1786	82	12 Jan 1784	66	180	On N side Cumberland	
Williams, Daniel	1752		Davidson	320	110	20 Dec 1791	164	19 Jan 1784	77	383	On Hays Creek	
Williams, Daniel	1997	Dowde, John	Davidson	640	1936	20 May 1793	932		81	109	On S W side of Big Harpeth	yes
Williams, Daniel	2389	Dillebo, Andrew heirs	Davidson	640	3177	14 Sep 1797	4005		90	432	On S Harpeth	yes
Williams, Daniel, Capt.	93		Tennessee	2285	1382	20 Jan 1792	3083	3 Dec 1785	75	185	S side Cumberland River	yes
Williams, Daniel, Sr.	889		Sumner	250		7 Jan 1794	68	3 Oct 1788	81	409	On Obeds River	yes
Williams, David	2401	Crumpler, Ratford	Davidson	640	2798	6 Jun 1796	3861		91	471	S W side of Big Harpeth River	yes

Claimant:	File #:	Assignee:	County:	Acres:	Grant:	Grant Date:	Entry:	Entry Date:	Bk:	Pg:	Location by Stream Name:	Military:
Williams, Edmond	1234		Green	200	1084	12 Jan 1793	727	21 Dec 1778	78	354	On Clear Creek	
Williams, Edmond	207		Washington	640	75	23 Oct 1782	726	21 Dec 1778	47	36	S side of Bufflow Creek	
Williams, Edmond	66		Washington	500	234	23 Oct 1782			44	262	S side of Buffalow Creek	
Williams, Edmund	068		Washington	200			197	6 Apr 1778			On Clear Creek	
Williams, Edmond	069		Washington	200			196	6 Apr 1778			Clear Creek formerly Camp Creek	
Williams, Edmond	070		Washington	200			198	6 Apr 1778			On Clear Creek	
Williams, Edmond	1228		Green	200	1078	12 Jan 1793			78	350	On Clear Creek	
Williams, Edmund	285		Hawkins	200	296	14 Jan 1793			78	345	On Clear Creek	
Williams, Edmond	348		Washington	400	215	24 Oct 1782	728	21 Dec 1778	49	232	On S E side of Bufflow Creek	
Williams, Edmund	549		Washington	100	814	11 Jul 1788	1514	12 Aug 1779	64	334	Beg at a pine	
Williams, Edmond	570		Washington	100	835	11 Jul 1788	2049	27 Oct 1779	64	337	On E Fork of Dry Creek	
Williams, Edmund	605		Washington	100	699	26 Oct 1786	1515	12 Aug 1779	66	11	On Indian Creek &c	
Williams, Edward	1112		Hawkins	100	832	15 Sep 1797	833	15 Aug 1781	94	137	Branch that empties into Holston	
Williams, Edward	1114		Hawkins	50	834	15 Sep 1797	175	19 Feb 1780	94	138	N side of Great Road	
Williams, Edward	498	Wright, John	Sumner	640	1660	20 May 1793	1051	20 Nov 1792	81	45	On S side Cumberland River	
Williams, Eliza	577	Corbin, James heirs	Middle District	640	2784	20 Dec 1796	1315		91	321	In Calf Killers Valley	yes
Williams, Eliza	578	Clark, Abraham heirs	Middle District	640	2785	20 Dec 1796	1597		91	321	On Cain Creek	
Williams, Eliza	579	Person, Nathan heirs	Middle District	640	2786	20 Dec 1796	1339		91	321	Waters of the Caney Fork	yes
Williams, Eliza	580	Harrell, Holland heirs	Middle District	640	2787	20 Dec 1796	1479		91	322	On branch of Falling Water	yes
Williams, Eliza	581	Perrymore, James heirs	Middle District	640	2788	20 Dec 1796	1523		91	322	Both sides of Caney Fork	yes
Williams, Eliza	582	Duggan, Jesse heirs	Middle District	640	2789	20 Dec 1796	1160		91	323	Both sides of Caney fFrk	yes
Williams, Eliza	583	Jones, Phillip	Middle District	640	2790	20 Dec 1796	1278		91	324	Waters of Caney Fork	yes
Williams, Eliza	584		Middle District	5000	326	20 Dec 1796	2200	24 May 1784	91	324	On N Cumberland Mountain	
Williams, Eliza	585		Middle District	2500	327	20 Dec 1796	2257	24 May 1784	91	325	N side Cumberland Mountain	
Williams, Eliza	586		Middle District	2500	328	20 Dec 1796	2255	24 May 1784	91	325	N side of Cumberland Mountain	
Williams, Eliza	587		Middle District	2500	329	20 Dec 1796	2256	24 May 1784	91	326	In Walnut Valley	
Williams, Eliza	588		Middle District	1000	330	20 Dec 1796	1292	24 Dec 1784	91	326	On Flat Creek	
Williams, Etheldred	073	Vandyke, Charles heirs	Middle District	640			4767					
Williams, Etheldred	537	Faircloth, Wm.	Middle District	730	2961	2 Mar 1797	4077		90	256	Creek known as Mill Creek	yes
Williams, Etheldred	538	Massey, Zebulon heirs	Middle District	640	2962	2 Mar 1797	3995		90	256	Both sides of Caney Fork	yes
Williams, Etheldred	539	Biggs, Robt.	Middle District	640	2963	2 Mar 1797	3941		90	257	On the Northward Path	yes
Williams, Etheldred etal	1266		Sumner	2560	2945	1 Mar 1797	3994	21 Nov 1796	91	215	On Caney Fork	yes
Williams, George	1260		Washington	155	1200	4 Dec 1795	1530	17 Aug 1779	89	316	Beg at a white ash	
Williams, George	94	Person, Thomas	Tennessee	228	1381	20 Dec 1791	1543	12 Feb 1785	75	503	On both sides of Beaver Creek	yes
Williams, Harbert	1026	Armstrong, Thomas & Jam	Davidson	1000		15 Sep 1797	862	30 Nov 1784	63	347	On S side of Cumberland	yes
Williams, Henry	8		Maury	1000	23	14 Jul 1812	1759	30 Nov 1784	126	435	On both sides of Big Tom Bigby Cr	
Williams, Isaac	040		Hawkins	200			2336	8 Dec 1779			S/S Holston River in Valley &c	
Williams, Jacob	1925	Tatum, Howell	Davidson	274	1733	20 May 1793	3484		81	61	On waters of Whites Creek	yes
Williams, James	14	Rhymes, Jesse	Tennessee	1000	1163	26 Nov 1789	2024	24 Aug 1785	74	160	On N side of Cumberland River	yes
Williams, James	2221	Blount, Redding	Davidson	274	2523	8 Dec 1795	1629		88	278	On S W side of Big Harpeth River	yes
Williams, James	2416	Stewart, Duncan	Davidson	3840	3219	14 Sep 1797			92	13-(?)	On S Harpeth River	
Williams, James	700		Hawkins	100	502	16 Dec 1793	982	29 Oct 1783	82	102	On N/S Holston River on Flat Creek	yes
Williams, Jesse	1688	Lewis, William T.	Davidson	640	1646	23 Feb 1793	3134		76	335	S side of Cumberland	yes
Williams, John	184	Murphree, Hardy	Davidson	274	170	7 Mar 1786	721		63	64	Both sides of E Fk of Whites Creek	yes
Williams, John	221	Wallis, George	Davidson	857	207	7 Mar 1786	306		63	76	On Middle Fk of Goose Creek	yes

Earliest Tennessee Land Records

Claimant:	File #:	Assignee:	County:	Acres:	Grant:	Grant Date:	Entry:	Entry Date:	Bk:	Pg:	Location by Stream Name:	Military:
Williams, John	480		Hawkins	440	352	29 Jul 1793	2255	22 Nov 1779	80	263	N side of Powells River	
Williams, John	523		Middle District	1000	312	6 Jun 1796	2506	25 May 1784	89	509	On waters of Caney Fork	
Williams, John	53		Washington	200	343	24 Oct 1782			43	316	On head spring of a branch &c	
Williams, John	560	McRory, James	Sumner	640	1781	20 May 1793	3293	12 Jul 1788	81	74	Cripple Creek waters of Stones R	yes
Williams, John	589		Hawkins	640	463	29 Jul 1793	2209	12 Nov 1779	80	292	On Turkey Creek	
Williams, John	595		Hawkins	640	469	29 Jul 1793	1590	12 Sep 1779	80	294	Near Cumberland Gap	
Williams, John	711	Blount, Reading	Sumner	274	2092	20 May 1793	1634	22 Aug 1785	81	147	On N side of Cumberland River	yes
Williams, John Pugh	868		Sumner	1371	2384	14 Dec 1793	3223	18 Sep 1785	81	386	On Cumberland River	yes
Williams, John, Lt.	102		Davidson	1144	88	14 Mar 1786	529		63	36	N side of Cumberland River	yes
Williams, John, Sr.	1109		Hawkins	89	828	14 Sep 1797	459	24 Apr 1780	94	136	N side of Holston River	
Williams, Jonathan	1314		Green	100	1164	12 Jan 1793	2763	8 Feb 1787	78	402	N side of Nolachuckey	
Williams, Jos.	1229		Green	50	1079	12 Jan 1793	2182	4 Nov 1779	78	351	S side of Nolechuckey River	
Williams, Joseph	1410		Green	200	1222	27 Nov 1792	514	19 Oct 1778	80	161	On a Fk of Clear Creek	
Williams, Joseph	15	Rhymes, Jesse	Tennessee	640	1164	26 Nov 1789	2025	24 Aug 1785	74	160	On N side of Cumberland River	yes
Williams, Joseph	498		Hawkins	640	370	29 Jul 1793	2207	12 Mar 1779	80	269	Near the head of Turkey Creek	
Williams, Joseph	559		Hawkins	400	432	29 Jul 1793	2063	27 Oct 1779	80	285	On Clinch River &c	
Williams, Joseph	611		Hawkins	640	485	29 Jul 1793	1769	1 Oct 1779	80	297	In Powells Valley	
Williams, Joseph	770		Hawkins	400	610	12 Jul 1794	483	25 Oct 1783	82	215	On N Fk of Clear Creek	
Williams, Mosson	143		Davidson	228	129	14 Mar 1786	151		63	50	On waters of Stones Creek	yes
Williams, Nathan	2041	Lewis, Wm. Terrel	Davidson	228	2058	20 May 1793	3089		81	139	On N side of Cumberland	yes
Williams, Nathaniel	58		Davidson	2560	44	14 Mar 1786	33		63	18	N side of Cumberland River	yes
Williams, Oliver	027	Hay, Joseph	Davidson	640			678	12 Feb 1785			At a spring	
Williams, Oliver	1891	Armstrong, Martin	Davidson	100	124	27 Apr 1793			81	31	On waters of Brown Creek	yes
Williams, Oliver	2304	Hay, David	Davidson	640	455	5 Nov 1795			89	118	At a spring	yes
Williams, Oliver	352	Williams, Willoughby	Middle District	1000	2401	5 Feb 1795	2627		84	183	On E side of W Fk of Obeys River	yes
Williams, Peter	1723	Motheral, Samuel	Davidson	640	1420	20 Dec 1791	2247		77	356	S side Cumberland River	yes
Williams, Peter	536	Shelby, David	Sumner	1000	1730	20 May 1793	1138	22 Aug 1785	81	61	N side of Cumberland	yes
Williams, Phillip	237	Reed, Jesse	Sumner	640	1142	26 Nov 1789	3506	12 Mar 1788	74	150	On W side of Caney Fork River	yes
Williams, Ralph	013	Tyrrell, William	Montgomery	1142			80	21 Dec 1796			N side of Cumberland River	yes
Williams, Robert	1037		Hawkins	400	786	22 Feb 1797	396	22 Oct 1779	90	231	In Carters Valley	yes
Williams, Robert	1330	Hickman, Thomas	Sumner	640	3130	14 Sep 1796	4161	3 Jun 1797	90	415	Waters of Punchin Camp Creek	yes
Williams, Robert	347		Sumner	274	1428	20 Dec 1791	291	13 Mar 1788	77	358	S side Cumberland River	yes
Williams, Robt	257		Sullivan	400	396	9 Aug 1787	2053	27 Oct 1779	61	415	In Carters Valley &c	yes
Williams, Sampson	0127	Powell, Benjamin	Sumner	640			506	22 Nov 1796			On 32 Mile Creek	yes
Williams, Sampson	0128		Sumner	640			764	1 Sep 1780			On Obeds River	yes
Williams, Sampson	1504	Colden, Phillip	Davidson	428	1061	26 Nov 1789	3424		74	108	On N side of Cumberland River	yes
Williams, Sampson	1521	Henderson, James	Davidson	640	1078	26 Nov 1789	3667		74	119	On N side of Cumberland River	yes
Williams, Sampson	1863	Parker, Arthur	Davidson	228	1595	27 Apr 1793	364		81	16	On S side of Cumberland River	yes
Williams, Sampson	2097	Baxter, Thomas	Davidson	640	2317	20 May 1793	2410		81	194	On Mill Creek & Stewarts Creek	yes
Williams, Sampson	2242	Dawson, Isaac	Davidson	274	2697	6 Jan 1796	1983		88	371	On the dividing ridge	yes
Williams, Sampson	389		Sumner	640	366	26 Jun 1793	2380	17 Sep 1792	80	321	On Obeds River	yes
Williams, Sampson	883	Armstrong, Martin	Sumner	100	136	7 Jan 1794			81	396	On waters of Rockey Creek	yes
Williams, Sampson	884	Armstrong, Martin	Sumner	274	138	7 Jan 1794			81	396	On S side Cumberland	
Williams, Sampson etal	0126	Elliott, John	Sumner	642		7 Jan 1791	1875		90		N side Cumberland River	yes
Williams, Sampson, Ass.	1289		Sumner	640	3048	8 Jun 1797	4707	5 Apr 1797	90	317	One of head branches Turkey Cr	yes

Claimant:	File #:	Assignee:	County:	Acres:	Grant:	Entry:	Grant Date:	Entry Date:	Bk:	Pg:	Location by Stream Name:	Military:
Williams, Sampson, Ass.	2123		Davidson	640	137		7 Jan 1794	10 Jul 1789	81	396	On a Fork of Harpeth	
Williams, Sampson, Ass.	312		Sumner	185	1629	1141	23 Feb 1793	22 Oct 1791	76	326	N side of Cumberland River	yes
Williams, Sampson, Ass.	44		Sumner	640	888	1708	17 Jan 1789	24 Mar 1787	63	308	On Little Fork of Spencers Creek	yes
Williams, Sampson, Ass.	477		Sumner	228	1647	1539	27 Apr 1793	23 Jun 1792	81	29	On S side of Cumberland River	yes
Williams, Sampson, Ass.	640		Sumner	640	2275		20 May 1793		81	186	Abt 3 miles from Bledsoes Lick	yes
Williams, Samuel	1327		Washington	200	1292	197	9 Dec 1797	6 Apr 1778	96	14	On the Long Branch	
Williams, Samuel	267	Stigreaves, John	Washington	384	135	310	23 Oct 1782	25 Aug 1778	47	66	S side of Nolachuckey River	
Williams, Samuel	789	Armstrong & Donelson	Davidson	640	792	1456	11 Jul 1788		63	277	On E Fork of Buffalow Creek	yes
Williams, Solomon	040		Middle District	640		1395						yes
Williams, Theophilus	168	Murphree, Hardy	Davidson	640	154	719	7 Mar 1786		63	58	On both sides of Spring Creek	yes
Williams, Theophilus	381	Hays, Robert	Sumner	640	1564	2970	14 Jan 1793	9 Apr 1788	79	272	On both sides of Smiths Fork	yes
Williams, Thomas	2334	Malloy, Thos.	Davidson	640	2977	473	10 Apr 1797		90	284	Waters of Harpeth River	yes
Williams, Thomas	360		Washington	10	352	1441	13 Oct 1783	12 Jun 1779	52	344	On the Gap of a mountain	yes
Williams, Thomas	441		Washington	200	433	2304	13 Oct 1783	27 Nov 1779	52	281	On the 1st fork &c	
Williams, Thomas	45	Blount, John Gray	Tennessee	640	1236	2825	10 Dec 1790	30 Sep 1785	74	343	On N side of Cumberland River	yes
Williams, Turner	1318		Davidson	320	4	22	18 Aug 1787	29 Dec 1783	68	122	On the N side of Cumberland	
Williams, Turner	978	Elliot, Wm heir of Joseph	Green	100	995	2537	18 May 1789		63	335	On Smiths Fork of Caney Fork	yes
Williams, Weston	1696		Davidson	640	1371	1970	9 Dec 1795	10 Apr 1780	89	404	On waters of Nolachuckey	yes
Williams, William	1758	Hayes, Robert	Sumner	640	1534	1327	14 Jan 1793		79	266	On waters of Whites Creek	
Williams, William, Ass.	1104		Sumner	640	2606	2710	7 Mar 1796	22 May 1795	88	329	On S side of Woolf River	yes
Williams, Willoughby	336	Cross, Silas heirs	Middle District	640	2395	2627	31 Jan 1795		83	392	On E side of W Fork of Obeys River	
Williams, Willoughby	352	Williams, Oliver heirs	Middle District	640	2401	1282	5 Feb 1795		84	183	On E side of W Fk of Obeys River	yes
Williams, Willoughby	046	Standley, Jonathan	Tennessee	1000		2705		29 Oct 1784			S side of Cumberland River	yes
Williams, Willoughby	075	Butworth, James heirs	Middle District	274		1180						
Williams, Willoughby	076	Fryer, Wm.	not given	228				3 Aug 1789			On Sulphur Fork	
Williams, Willoughby	2167	Davis, William	Davidson	640	2488	2842	1 Apr 1794		81	451	On waters of Stones River	yes
Williams, Willoughby	2168	Davidson, Amos	Davidson	640	2489	2844	1 Apr 1794		81	451	On waters of Stones River	yes
Williams, Willoughby	2169	McCoy, John	Davidson	640	2490	1777	1 Apr 1794		81	451	On waters of Stones River	yes
Williams, Willoughby	2170	Danley, Solomon heir	Davidson	640	2491	2845	1 Apr 1794		81	451	On waters of Stones River	yes
Williams, Willoughby	2171	Capehart, John	Davidson	640	2492	2840	1 Apr 1794		81	452	On waters of Stones River	yes
Williams, Willoughby	2172	Beates, John	Davidson	640	2493	1746	1 Apr 1794		81	452	On waters of Stones River	yes
Williams, Willoughby	2173	Cowan, James	Davidson	640	2494	2839	1 Apr 1794		81	452	On waters of Stones River	yes
Williams, Willoughby	282	Oliver, Andrew	Tennessee	640	1868	603	20 May 1793	24 Apr 1784	63	93	On both sides of a creek	yes
Williams, Willoughby	283	Martin, William	Davidson	640	269	1212	24 Jan 1786		63	98	E side of Blooming Grove	yes
Williams, Willoughby	284	Martin, Henry	Davidson	640	270	394	24 Jan 1787		63	99	On both sides Buzzard Creek	yes
Williams, Willoughby	320	Harrell, Ephraim heirs	Middle District	640	2382	2724	3 Feb 1795		83	383	W side of W Fork of Obeys River	yes
Williams, Willoughby	321	Harnett, Ephraim heirs	Middle District	640	2383	2619	3 Feb 1795		83	383	W side of W Fork of Obeys River	yes
Williams, Willoughby	322	Pretor, George heirs	Middle District	640	2384	1181	3 Feb 1795		83	384	W side of W Fork of Obeys River &c	yes
Williams, Willoughby	323	Fryer, Josiah	Middle District	640	2385	2709	3 Feb 1795		83	384	W side of W Fk of Obeys River &c	yes
Williams, Willoughby	324	Bullard, Waker(?)	Middle District	640	2386	2708	3 Feb 1795		83	385	W side of W Fk of Obeys River &c	yes
Williams, Willoughby	325	Bunton, James	Middle District	640	2387	2711	3 Feb 1795		83	385	W side of W Fk of Obeys River &c	yes
Williams, Willoughby	326	Chamberlain, Henry heirs	Middle District	640	2388	2717	3 Feb 1795		83	386	W side of W side of Obeys River	yes
Williams, Willoughby	327	Gerris, Joshua heirs	Middle District	640	2389		3 Feb 1795		83	386	W side of W side of Obeys River	yes
Williams, Willoughby	328	Rusters (?), David heirs	Middle District	640	2390		3 Feb 1795		83	387	W side of W Fk of Obeys River &c	yes
Williams, Willoughby	329	Bentford, James heirs	Middle District	640	2391		3 Feb 1795		83	387	W side of W Fork of Obeys River	yes

Claimant:	File #:	Assignee:	County:	Acres:	Grant:	Grant Date:	Entry:	Entry Date:	Bk:	Pg:	Location by Stream Name:	Military:
Williams, Willoughby	33	Hopewell, George heirs	Tennessee	640	1201	10 Nov 1790	2691		74	330	On N side of Cumberland River	yes
Williams, Willoughby	333	Stevens, James	Middle District	640	2392	31 Jan 1795			83	390	W side of W Fk of Obeys River	yes
Williams, Willoughby	334	Phelps, Wm.	Middle District	640	2393	31 Jan 1795	3287		83	391	W side of W Fk of Obeys River	yes
Williams, Willoughby	335	Fowler, Burwell heirs	Middle District	640	2394	31 Jan 1795	2716		83	391	W side of W Fk of Obeys River	yes
Williams, Willoughby	34	Betwoods, Samuel heirs	Tennessee	640	1202	10 Nov 1790			74	330	On N side of Cumberland	
Williams, Willoughby	35	Parrish, Mark heirs	Tennessee	640	1203	10 Nov 1790			74	330	On N side Cumberland River	
Williams, Willoughby	350	Murter, Zedekiah	Middle District	640	2399	30 Jan 1795	2861		84	182	On W side of W Fk of Obeys River	yes
Williams, Willoughby	351	Willis, Josiah heirs	Middle District	640	2400	30 Jan 1795	2964		84	183	On W side of Fork of Obeys River	yes
Williams, Willoughby	353	Stormer, Henry heirs	Middle District	1000	2402	5 Feb 1795	2623		84	184	On E side of W Fk of Obeys River	yes
Williams, Willoughby	354	Miles, Abraham heirs	Middle District	1000	2403	5 Feb 1795			84	184	On E side of W Fk of Obeys River	yes
Williams, Willoughby	355	Peney, Francis heirs	Middle District	1000	2404	5 Feb 1795			84	185	On E side of Fk of Obeys River	yes
Williams, Willoughby	356	Smith, Peter heirs	Middle District	1000	2405	5 Feb 1795	2622		84	185	On E side of W Fk of Obeys River	yes
Williams, Willoughby	452	Jordan, John heirs	Davidson	640	424	5 Sep 1787	1167		63	157	S side of Richland Creek	yes
Williams, Willoughby	453	Nichols, John	Davidson	640	425	15 Sep 1787	1183		63	157	On Turnbulls Clay Lick	yes
Williams, Willoughby	515	Ewell, William	Davidson	404	487	15 Sep 1787	429		63	176	S side of Cumberland River	yes
Williams, Willoughby	540	Guin, Thomas	Davidson	365	512	15 Sep 1787	1111		63	185	S side Cumberland River	yes
Williams, Willoughby	609	Pidgeon, Williams	Davidson	274	581	15 Sep 1787	1121		63	208	S side Cumberland River	yes
Williams, Willoughby	76	Grant, Elisha	Davidson	640	924	18 May 1789	1182		63	318	On S side Cumberland River	yes
Williams, Willoughby	909	Morton, Wm.	Davidson	1000	925	18 May 1789			63	318	On waters of Caney Fork	yes
Williams, Willoughby, Ass.	49		Tennessee	1000	1248	10 Nov 1790	2625	30 Jul 1790	74	347	On N side of Cumberland River	yes
Williams, Zachariah	828	Davis, Joshua	Sumner	640	2308	20 May 1793	2444	19 Nov 1792	81	193	On the Caney Fork	yes
Williams, Zadock	192		Davidson	280	178	7 Sep 1786	704		63	67	On waters of Richland Creek	yes
Williamson, Benjamin	1195	Tyrrell, William	Sumner	1000	2745	20 Jul 1796	2628	— —1796	88	455	On N side of Cumberland River	yes
Williamson, Geo	01	Roberts, J.	Montgomery	640			1554	15 Oct 1790			On McFaddins Creek	yes
Williamson, George	044	Smith, Chas.	Robertson	640			1787	17 Oct 1796			On the waters of Brush Creek	
Williamson, George	1923	Tatum, Howell	Davidson	640	1720	20 May 1793			81	59	On waters of W Harpeth River	
Williamson, George	2453	Tatum, Howell	Davidson	640	3348	6 Dec 1797	1724		98	183	On waters of Overalls Creek &c	yes
Williamson, Hugh	238		Tennessee	4800	1576	27 Apr 1793	1148	11 Aug 1784	81	11	On S side of Cumberland	
Williamson, Hugh	383		Western District	4800	2460	31 Dec 1793			81	430	Abt 6 mi from the Masseppire [sic]	
Williamson, Job	853	Anderson, Daniel	Davidson	640	860	17 Jan 1789	2897		63	300	On waters of Caney Fork	yes
Williamson, John	1192	Donelson, Stockley	Sumner	640	2717	20 Jul 1796	3880	8 Jun 1790	88	448	N of 1st creek E of Pond Lick	yes
Williamson, John	2257	Donelson, Stockley	Davidson	640	2718	20 Jul 1796			88	448	On waters of Mill Creek	yes
Williamson, John	559	Haynes, John	Davidson	228	531	15 Sep 1787	1811		63	191	On waters of Mill Creek	yes
Williamson, Thomas	1545		Green	640	1305	17 Jul 1794	3	24 Feb 1778	81	610	On S side of Nolichuckey	yes
Williamson, Thomas, Ass.	361		Sumner	640	1492	4 Jan 1792	2324	11 Nov 1789	77	373	On S side of Cumberland	
Williamson, Thos.	1304		Green	100	1154	12 Jan 1793	2629	28 Aug 1780	78	397	Beg at a chesnut & gum	
Williamson, William	1441	Thornton, Yancey	Sumner	228	3353	7 Apr 1800	3975	23 Mar 1797	106	438	On waters of Peytons Creek	yes
Willias, Benjamin	631	Whitaker, John	Sumner	640	1914	20 May 1793	3249	19 Jul 1788	81	103	On the dividing ridge &c	yes
Williba, Matthew	87		Hawkins	200	79	13 Feb 1791	2243	22 Nov 1779	74	280	Lying in Powells Valley	
Williby, Andrew, Ass.	553		Sumner	640	1769	20 May 1793	2058	27 Nov 1792	81	75	Drakes Cr waters of Big Barren	yes
Willice, John	429		Western District	2500	428	15 Dec 1790	2195		91	320	On Forked Deer River	
Willice, John	430		Western District	2500	429	15 Dec 1796	2194		91	320	On fork Deer River	
Williford, Robert	826	Sanford, Samuel	Sumner	640	2305	20 May 1793	2401	6 Aug 1792	81	192	On head waters of the first &c	yes
Williford, Joseph	650	Bushnell, Eus & Wm Dobbi	Davidson	640	623	15 Sep 1787	1667		63	221	On waters of Stones River	yes
Willis, Henry	1028		Green	400	1255	29 Jul 1793	228	22 Oct 1783	76	489	S side of Noleychuckey	

Claimant:	File #:	Assignee:	County:	Acres:	Grant:	Grant Date:	Entry:	Entry Date:	Bk:	Pg:	Location by Stream Name:	Military:
Willis, Jacob	1520	Blount, Reading	Davidson	640	1077	26 Nov 1789	2556		74	118	On S waters of Persons Creek	yes
Willis, James	2001	Blount, John Gray & Thom	Davidson	640	1942	20 May 1793	2823		81	110	On S W side of Big Harpeth	yes
Willis, James	336		Green	200	338	20 Sep 1787	924	29 Oct 1783	65	469	Situated on S side Holston River &c	
Willis, Josiah	351	Williams, Willoughby	Middle District	640	2400	30 Jan 1795	2964		84	183	W side of the fork of Obeys River	yes
Willis, Samuel	1015	McNeeley, William	Sumner	400	2484	18 Aug 1795			87	508	On S side of Cumberland River	yes
Willis, Taylor	888	Ford, John	Davidson	640	904	17 Jan 1789	3243		63	312	On N side of Cumberland River	yes
Willis, Witton	1933	Robertson, James	Davidson	640	1752	29 Aug 1793	3279		81	67	Joining the N boundary of Barnabas Boyle	yes
Willman, James	852	Wilson, Davids	Sumner	640	2356	20 May 1793	2699	27 Oct 1792	81	203	On S side of Cumberland	yes
Willobay, John	996		Green	100	1223	29 Jul 1793	763	23 Dec 1778	76	484	Stoney Creek waters of Lick Creek	
Willock, William	355		Green	187	357	20 Sep 1787	927	29 Oct 1783	65	474	On N side of Chuckey River &c	
Willoockson, George	1		Sevier/Green	150							N side French Broad River	
Willoughby, Andrew	086		Sullivan	342			306	14 Mar 1780			On both sides of Sinking Creek	
Willoughby, Matthew	636		Sumner	640	1925	20 May 1793	2141	11 Feb 1786	81	106	E/S Main Middle Fork Bledsoes Cr	yes
Willoughby, Nathan	939	Blount, Reading	Davidson	640	955	18 May 1789	2039	6 Jul 1786	63	325	On E waters of Half Pone Creek	yes
Willoughby, Solomon	035	Baker, Charles	not given	640			2784				S side of Cumberland	yes
Willoughby, William, Ass.	804		Sumner	640	2269	20 May 1793	2053	4 Feb 1786	81	185	On W Fk of Gooses Creek	yes
Wills, George	630	Simmons, Benjamin	Davidson	428	602	15 Sep 1787	672		63	215	On a branch of the Sulphur Fork	yes
Wills, Hayden	703	Jeffres, John	Davidson	274	676		321	8 Dec 1787	63	239	N side of Cumberland River	yes
Wills, Haydon	235	Hickman, Ed	Tennessee	640	449	27 Jun 1793			80	357	N side of Cumberland River	
Wills, Jacob	507		Sullivan	400	525	7 Apr 1790	173	3 Apr 1789	71	288	S E side of N Fork of Holeson R	
Wills, Louis	1328		Washington	200	1252	6 Jun 1797	1488	26 Jul 1779	90	310	On waters of Little Doe &c	
Wills, William	49		Washington	50	339	24 Oct 1482	1437	11 Jun 1779	43	314	On Dry Creek	
Wilson, Agusty	38		Eastern District	640	38	11 Jul 1788	650	27 Apr 1779	67	354	On Bull Run of Clinch River	
Wilson, Alexander	974		Green	100	888	17 Nov 1790	2355	16 Dec 1779	76	134	On Holleys Creek	
Wilson, Augustin	440		Sullivan	200	319	10 Nov 1784	2230	21 May 1783	69	183	On Middle Fk of Horse Creek	
Wilson, David	1		Green	2000	3	19 Nov 1784		18 Oct 1783	56	347	Middle Dist on Coney Spring Creek	
Wilson, David	204	Harris, Thomas heirs	Tennessee	1000	1494	4 Jan 1792	1430	19 Nov 1784	77	374	S side of Cumberland River	
Wilson, James	370		Washington	300	362	13 Oct 1783	2610	12 Mar 1781	52	248	On Camp Creek	
Wilson, James, Jr.	664		Washington	200	478	10 Nov 1784	375	8 Sep 1778	69	96	Upon W side of Big Limestone	
Wilson, John	692	Oneal, Archa	Davidson	640	665	8 Dec 1787	2537		63	235	On mouth of Wartrace Creek	yes
Wilson, John	711	Phillips, Mann	Davidson	640	684	8 Dec 1787	2075		63	241	Beg at a poplar & white oak	yes
Wilson, Robert	190		Washington	239	58	23 Oct 1782	374	9 Sep 1778	47	27	On head of Horse Camp Creek	
Wilson, Robert	383		Washington	20	375	13 Oct 1783	2889	1 Aug 1781	52	253	On Sinking Creek	
Wilson, Samuel	1065		Davidson	640	39	17 Apr 1786	29	29 Dec 1783	66	47	Beg on bank of Stones River	
Wilson, Adam	11		Washington	640	300	24 Oct 1782	247	1 Jul 1778	43	297	On branch of Big Limestone Creek	
Wilson, Adam	246		Washington	200	114	23 Oct 1782	293	4 Aug 1778	47	56	On waters of Lick Creek	
Wilson, Adam	291		Middle District	1500	251	7 Jul 1794	2093	7 Mar 1784	82	199	S/W side Clear Fk Cumberland R	
Wilson, Adam	456		Washington	100	448	13 Oct 1783	1525	13 Aug 1779	52	288	Beg tree E corner &c	
Wilson, Adam, Jr.	423		Washington	200	415	13 Oct 1783	1396	24 May 1779	52	273	On Cedar Branch &c	
Wilson, Adam, Jr.	65		Washington	100	233	23 Oct 1782	246	30 Jun 1778	44	261	On Cedar Creek &c	
Wilson, Alexander	957		Green	100	871	17 Nov 1790	1246	27 Feb 1779	76	128	On Franks Creek	
Wilson, Archibald	359		Middle District	500	298	17 Dec 1794	2280	14 May 1784	84	206	On waters of Harpeth	
Wilson, Augusta	432		Eastern District	300	283	21 Jan 1797	301	10 Mar 1780	91	120	In the Grassey Valley	
Wilson, Benjamin	877		Hawkins	150	647	6 Feb 1795	436	19 Apr 1780	84	134	On waters of Beaver Creek	
Wilson, David	1081	Armstrong, M.	Sumner	160	163	22 Feb 1795			83	430	On head waters of Drakes Creek	yes

Claimant:	Assignee:	File #:	County:	Acres:	Grant:	Grant Date:	Entry:	Entry Date:	Bk:	Pg:	Location by Stream Name:	Military:
Wilson, David		1081	Davidson	640	55	17 Apr 1786	44	31 Dec 1783	66	53	On Indian Creek	
Wilson, David	Anthony, James	2000	Davidson	640	1941	20 May 1793	1003		81	110	On E Fk of Harpeth River	yes
Wilson, David	McCoy, Daniel	2109	Davidson	549	2357	20 May 1793	26		81	203	On E Fork of Harpeth River	yes
Wilson, David		252	Sumner	357	1198	30 Nov 1790	596	5 Jan 1785	74	321	On N side of Cumberland River	yes
Wilson, David		96	Middle District	4096	98	10 Jul 1788	464	25 Oct 1783	67	457	On N side of Duck River &c	
Wilson, David & Jno Dickson		362	Sumner	640	1503	4 Jan 1792	950	21 Oct 1791	77	376	N side o Cumberland	y
Wilson, David & Wm.		448	Middle District	2000	387	17 Dec 1794	1638	14 Apr 1784	84	255	On waters of Harpeth	
Wilson, David, Ass.		359	Sumner	428	1487	4 Jan 1792	2393	1 Apr 1788	77	372	N side of Cumberland River	yes
Wilson, David, Ass.		634	Sumner	640	1923	20 May 1793			81	105	On Station Camp	yes
Wilson, David, Ass.		651	Sumner	166	1958	20 May 1793	3697	20 Sep 1791	81	114	On waters of Station Camp Creek	yes
Wilson, David, Ass.		840	Sumner	274	2342	20 May 1793	3238	21 Oct 1791	81	200	On waters of Peytons Creek	yes
Wilson, David, Ass.		847	Sumner	168	2350	20 May 1793	3584	27 Oct 1792	81	202	On N side of Cumberland River	yes
Wilson, David, Ass.		857	Sumner	200	2043	20 May 1793	3586	27 Oct 1792	81	135	On Indian Creek	yes
Wilson, David, Ass.		857	Sumner	274	2362	20 May 1793	1558	27 Oct 1792	81	204	On S side of Cumberland	yes
Wilson, Davids		852	Sumner	640	2356	20 May 1793	2699	27 Oct 1792	81	203	On S side of Cumberland River	yes
Wilson, George	Boyd, Andrew	215	Sumner	640	1120	26 Nov 1789	3387	18 Mar 1789	74	139	On S side of Cumberland	yes
Wilson, Isaac		88	Washington	350	256	23 Oct 1782	904	31 Dec 1778	44	275	N side of Nolachuckey Creek	
Wilson, Jacob		199	Tennessee	640	1486	4 Jan 1792	2729	30 Sep 1785	77	372	W side of W Fk of Jones Creek	yes
Wilson, James	Finney, Thomas	0129	Sumner	274	2002	26 Nov 1792					On waters of Caney Fork	yes
Wilson, James		262	Washington	100	130	23 Oct 1782	616	23 Nov 1778	47	63	On Mill Fork of Big Limestone	
Wilson, James		412	Washington	249	404	13 Oct 1783	615	23 Nov 1778	52	267	On the Mill Fork of Big Limestone	
Wilson, James		417	Middle District	700	356	17 Dec 1794	1814	23 Apr 1784	84	232	On head of Caney Spring Creek	
Wilson, James, Ass		838	Sumner	640 (633	2336	20 May 1793	3669	6 Oct 1789	81	199	On waters of Station Camp Creek	yes
Wilson, James, Ass.		842	Sumner	282	2345	20 May 1793	3700		81	201	On waters of Sinking Creek	yes
Wilson, James, Ass.		867	Sumner	640	2380	20 May 1793			81	208	On waters of Caney Fork	yes
Wilson, James, Jr.		397	Middle District	1000	336	17 Dec 1794	1823	23 Apr 1784	84	222	On S side of Duck River	
Wilson, Jno.		1118	Davidson	640	95	17 Apr 1786	335	10 Mar 1784	66	173	On Big Harpeth River &c	
Wilson, John		1141	Green	100	984	26 Dec 1791	76	16 Nov 1788	77	276	Beg on a line of Samuel Wilsons	
Wilson, John		134	Middle District	626	136	10 Jul 1788	560	27 Oct 1783	67	474	On Falling Creek	
Wilson, John		1662	Green	300	1365	8 Dec 1795	278		88	285	On Little Chuckey Creek	
Wilson, John		1708	Green	3410	1423	6 Jun 1797	1654	16 Apr 1784	90	312	N side of Elk River	
Wilson, John		1713	Green	100	1428	8 Jun 1797	308	15 May 1788	90	322	S side of Vanpell Great Road	
Wilson, John	Burnes, Barnabas	1949	Davidson	640	1787	20 May 1793	1358		81	76	On Yellow Creek	yes
Wilson, John	King, Enock	2073	Davidson	640	2215	20 May 1793	3088		81	172	On Yellow Creek	yes
Wilson, John		376	Middle District	3000	315	17 Dec 1794	1802	23 Apr 1784	84	213	On Weakleys Creek	
Wilson, John	Turrentine, Alex heirs	456	Davidson	640	428	15 Sep 1787			63	158	N side of Sulphur Fork	yes
Wilson, John	Fogerty, James	595	Davidson	274	567	15 Sep 1787	204		63	203	N side of Cumberland River	yes
Wilson, John, Ass.		407	Sumner	640	418	27 Jun 1793	356	12 Mar 1784	80	347	Both sides Dry Fk of Bledsoes Cr	yes
Wilson, Joseph		304	Green	300	306	20 Sep 1787	157	22 Oct 1783	65	460	On Little Chuckey	
Wilson, Joseph		39	Washington	300	329	24 Oct 1782	791	26 Dec 1778	43	310	On Mill Creek &c	
Wilson, Joseph		415	Washington	148	407	13 Oct 1783	2850	12 May 1781	52	269	Beg at a white oak	
Wilson, Joseph		453	Washington	700	445	13 Oct 1783	2674	19 Nov 1780	52	287	Beg at 2 sourwoods	
Wilson, Joseph		465	Hawkins	200	337	29 Jul 1793	2124	4 Nov 1779	80	259	On S side Clinch River	
Wilson, Robert		0109	Green	450	210		37	4 Jan 1795			On Nine Mile Creek	
Wilson, Robert		275	Eastern District	450	210	4 Jan 1795			84	43	On S side of Holston	

Claimant:	File #:	Assignee:	County:	Acres:	Grant:	Grant Date:	Entry:	Entry Date:	Bk:	Pg:	Location by Stream Name:	Military:
Wilson, Robert	319		Washington	150	186	23 Oct 1782	245	30 Jun 1778	49	220	On Cedar Fk of Big Limestone	
Wilson, Robert	440		Washington	40	432	13 Oct 1783	2888	1 Aug 1781	52	281	On Sinking Creek	
Wilson, Robert	585		Sullivan	200	583	29 Jul 1793	2117	11 Nov 1779	76	474	N side of Holston River	
Wilson, Robert	84		Washington	150	252	23 Oct 1782	244	30 Jun 1778	44	273	Inc a spring	
Wilson, Robert, Ass.	85		Washington	400	253	23 Oct 1782			44	273	On head of Rones Creek	
Wilson, Samuel	900		Sumner	357	2456	31 Dec 1793			81	428	On Hogens Fk of Red River	
Wilson, Samuel	0101		Sullivan	640			13	8 Feb 1780				
Wilson, Samuel	088		Sullivan	200			1130	25 Jan 1779				
Wilson, Samuel	231		Hawkins	300 (350	218	26 Dec 1791	995	4 Jan 1779	77	319	On N side of Holston River	
Wilson, Samuel	25		Hawkins	640	57	7 Apr 1790	100	26 Feb 1778	71	281	Lying on Poor Valley Creek	
Wilson, Samuel	300		Hawkins	300	468	29 Jul 1793	1901	8 Oct 1779	80	293	On Poor Valley Creek	
Wilson, Samuel	337		Sullivan	300	477	10 Jul 1788	616	18 Jun 1780	67	485	On both sides of Big Creek	
Wilson, Samuel	40		Hawkins	513	25	18 May 1789	13	8 Jan 1780	72	246	On N side of Holston River &c	
Wilson, Samuel	441		Middle District	3000	380	17 Dec 1794	1819	23 Apr 1784	84	351	In the Hickory Cove &c	
Wilson, Samuel	461		Hawkins	100	333	29 Jul 1793	139	12 Feb 1780	80	258	On N side of Duck River	
Wilson, Samuel	556		Washington	200	821	11 Jul 1788	1931	15 Oct 1779	64	335	On S Fk of Poor Valley	
Wilson, Samuel	596		Hawkins	640	470	29 Jul 1793	840	8 Apr 1784	80	294	On N side of Holston River	
Wilson, Samuel	603		Hawkins	290	477	29 Jul 1793	1402	17 Jan 1784	80	295	On N side of Clinch Mountain	
Wilson, Samuel	702		Green	300	743	11 Jul 1788	1403	17 Jan 1784	66	475	On S side Clinch Mountain	
Wilson, Samuel	714		Green	150	755	11 Jul 1788	(946) 964	2 Jan 1779	66	480	On S side of Nolichucky River	
Wilson, Samuel, Ass.	596		Hawkins	615	695	10 Nov 1795	1421		89	276	S/S Nilichucky River & Cove Creek	
Wilson, Samuel, heirs of	1394		Sumner	640	3321	6 Dec 1797	189	9 May 1797	97	44	Waters of Big Barren	yes
Wilson, Spencer	1623		Green	100	1344	22 Feb 1795	1067	27 Feb 1778	84	328	On head of Tuckalow Creek	
Wilson, William	1337		Washington	100	1238	25 Oct 1796	1066	5 Apr 1795	91	255	N Fk of Rones Creek	
Wilson, William	1338		Washington	200	1239	25 Oct 1796	4	5 Apr 1795	91	255	On the Lorrell Fk of Holston	
Wilson, William	1532		Green	250	1292	17 Jul 1794	1326	24 Feb 1778	81	606	On waters of Nolichuckey	
Wilson, Willis	1672		Green	200	1377	20 Jul 1796		2 Apr 1779	88	490	Beg on a small hickory	
Wilson, Wm. & Philip Fann	829	McCullock, Benjamin	Sumner	640	2309	20 May 1793	2011	26 Nov 1792	81	193	On ridge bet. Bartons Creek	yes
Wilson,David & Jno Dickson	1533		Green	100	1293	17 Jul 1794			81	607	On S side of Nolichuckey River	yes
Wimer, Casper	362	Blount, Reading	Sumner	640	1503	4 Jan 1792	950	21 Oct 1791	77	376	N side of Cumberland &c	yes
Wimpie, William	955	Donelson, Stockley	Sumner	640	2418	22 Feb 1795	2554	30 Sep 1785	84	305	On main Fk of Obeys River	yes
Winborn, John	05	Shepperd, John	Robertson	640			3044	25 Jul 1796			On waters of Red River	yes
Winborn, John	061	Murphree, Hardy by hr of J	not given	640							On Obeys River	yes
Winburn, Henry	82		Davidson	2560	68	14 Mar 1786	113				On both sides Cedar Creek	yes
Winchester, David, Ass.	208		Davidson	389	194	7 Mar 1786	138		63	28	On waters of Stones River	yes
Winchester, David, Ass.	719		Sumner	640	2101	20 May 1793	3650	7 Jun 1792	63	72	Beg at 2 cedar trees & white oak	
Winchester, Geo. & James	860	Armstrong, Martin	Sumner	640	2367	20 May 1793	3652		81	49	Beg at 3 Sycamores	yes
Winchester, Jas. & Geo.	918	Truett, Peter	Sumner	100	164	9 Jan 1794	3670	23 May 1792	81	205	On N side of Cumberland	
Winchester, Jas. & Geo.	0130	Spann, James	Sumner	640	754				81	443	N side Cumberland River	
Winchester, Jas. & Geo.	781		Davidson	228	171	11 Jul 1788	3116	8 Dec 1789	63	265	On E side of Bledsoes Creek	yes
Winchester, Jas. & Geo.	921	Armstrong, M.	Sumner	200	185	9 Jan 1794			81	445	Beg at an ash tree	yes
Winchester, Jas. & Geo.	926	Armstrong, Martin	Sumner	100	170	9 Jan 1794			81	450	2 miles above mouth Bledsoes Cr	
Winchester, John & George	920	Armstrong, Martin	Sumner	50	156	1 Dec 1794			81	445	On N side of Cumberland River	yes
Winchester, Stephen, Ass.	953	Donelson, Stockley	Sumner	400				8 Dec 1792	83	479	W of the Cumberland Mountain &c	yes
Winday, Absalam	2381		Davidson	365	3109	14 Sep 1797	4256		90	406	On branch of Stones River	yes

Claimant:	File #:	Assignee:	County:	Acres:	Grant:	Grant Date:	Entry:	Entry Date:	Bk:	Pg:	Location by Stream Name:	Military:
Windsor, John	290	Rice, Wm. H.	Western District	1000	279	18 Apr 1789	1259	24 Nov 1783	72	84	On waters of Big Hatcher River	
Wine, James	674	Bud, Samuel	Davidson	640	647	8 Dec 1787	3409		63	229	On W side of Millers Creek	yes
Winegar, Andrew	241		Hawkins	100	228	26 Dec 1791	711	30 Nov 1780	77	323	Joining the plantation he now lives	
Winfree, Thomas	1053	King, William	Sumner	640	2530	10 Dec 1795	3034	8 Aug 1795	88	289	On Lick Creek	yes
Wingfield, Jacob	062	Sheppard, John	not given	640			2966	15 Aug 1792			On Obeys River	yes
Winingham, Jerod	782		Hawkins	100	622	12 Jul 1794	1566	31 Aug 1779	82	220	On N side of Holston River &c	
Winkle, Josiah	1002	Nichols, John	Davidson	640	1019	18 May 1789	2590		63	341	On Barretts Creek	yes
Winnegar, Andrew	305		Sullivan	203	444	9 Aug 1787	323	19 Jan 1780	61	463	On N side of Holston Valley	
Winningham, Jarod	29		Hawkins	100	61	7 Apr 1790	1639	16 Sep 1779	71	285	On both sides of W Fk of Flatt Cr	
Winningham, Thos.	026	Nelson, Robt.	Robertson	200	340	19 Feb 1797		7 Jul 1788			On Red River	
Winningham, Thos.	541	Armstrong, M.	Tennessee	200	340	19 Feb 1797			90	252	On Red River	
Winscott, James	121	Wykoff, William	Tennessee	640	1623	23 Feb 1793	2592	30 Sep 1795	76	323	S side of Cumberland	yes
Winstett, Thomas	1560	Weakley, Robert	Davidson	640	1182	30 Nov 1790	2252		74	315	On S side Cumberland River	yes
Winters, Moses	1219		Davidson	640	183	10 Jul 1788	233	4 Feb 1784	66	407	Lying on Calebs Creek	
Winton, John	267		Eastern District	400	151	4 Feb 1795			83	401	S side French Broad	
Wirech, William	087		Sullivan	50			538	29 Apr 1781			Inc where he now lives	
Wirick, Martin	342		Sullivan	150	489	10 Jul 1788	1254	30 Feb 1779	67	487	Joining Shells line &c	
Wisdom, Larkin	858		Washington	300	867	11 Aug 1789			71	33	On S side of Holston River	
Wise, Absalom	26	Nelson, Robert	Tennessee	274	1189	16 Nov 1790	1867	26 Jun 1785	74	318	On Blooming Grove Creek	yes
Wise, John	989	Lock, Matthew	Davidson	428	1006	18 May 1789	1229		63	338	On N side of E Fk of Stones River	yes
Wistner, Samuel	076	Tyrrell, Wm & James Easto	Davidson	640			4073	12 Jun 1797			E side Harpeth River	yes
Witherington, Joseph	2164	Lewis, William Tyrrell	Davidson	264	3065	19 Jul 1797	3891		90	376	Waters of Leepers Fk	yes
Witherington, William	886	Muffree, Hardy	Sumner	280	2421	7 Jan 1794	1563	23 Aug 1792	81	406	On waters of Drakes Creek	yes
Witherow, James	384		Middle District	3000	323	17 Dec 1794	2279	24 May 1784	84	216	On N side of S Fk of Duck River	
Withers, Jno.	1058		Davidson	640	32	17 Apr 1786	97	14 Jan 1784	66	45	Lying on Station Camp Creek	
Witt, Abner	0140		Green	250			57	2 Aug 1788			S side of Holston	
Witt, Abner	1018		Green	250	1245	29 Jul 1793	56	2 Aug 1788	76	487	S/S Holston Cedar Fk of Sinking Cr	
Witt, Abner	495		Hawkins	200	367	29 Jul 1793			80	268	On S side of Holston River	
Witt, Calop	136		Green	200	118	1 Nov 1786	1540	17 May 1784	60	450	Upon a branch of Long Creek	
Witt, Elijah	36		Green	200	99	1 Nov 1786	234	22 Oct 1783	58	460	Upon N side of Nollichuckie River	
Witt, Elijah	81		Green	200	39	1 Nov 1786	1541	17 Mar 1784	59	400	On branch of Long Creek	
Witt, Joseph	103		Green	160	61	1 Nov 1786	235	22 Oct 1783	59	422	Upon French Broad River	
Witty, James	058	Dillon, William	Sumner	366			66	15 Apr 1791			Joining an entry of John Boyd	yes
Wolf, Abraham	900	Blount, Reading	Davidson	640	916	18 May 1789	2045		63	316	Head branches E Fk of Stones R	yes
Wolf, George	228		Hawkins	200	215	26 Dec 1791	1418	19 Jan 1784	77	318	On E Fk of Swan Pond Creek	
Wolf, Nicholas	642		Sullivan	400 (200	590	27 Jun 1793			80	380	On waters of Fall Creek	
Wolfenden, George	382	Stewart, Chas. Legatee	Western District	3840	2091	20 May 1793	3048		81	147	Abt 14 miles from the Mississippi	
Wolsey, John	420		Green	100	422	20 Sep 1787	2163	6 Nov 1779	65	494	W side of Entry of Nathaniel Davis	
Womack, Jacob	63		Washington	262	231	23 Oct 1782	433	23 Sep 1778	44	260	W side Fains Branch	
Womble, Benjamin	2006	Dixon, John	Davidson	228	1950	20 May 1793	1944		81	112	On E waters of Mill Creek	yes
Womble, Dempsey	13	Smith, Daniel	Sumner	640	770	11 Jul 1788	195	9 Mar 1784	63	270	On head E branches of Drakes Cr	yes
Womble, John	2017		Davidson	640	1981	20 May 1793	3558		81	119	On waters of W Harpeth	yes
Wood, Belford	196	Dunlop, Hugh	Hawkins	250	129	16 Nov 1790	1942	12 Oct 1779	77	193	On S side of Holston River	
Wood, Cather, etal	560		Hawkins	300	433	29 Jul 1793	901		80	285	Lying bet 2nd & 3rd Creek	
Wood, Charles	468	Brewer, Thelford & George	Sumner	1000	1625	27 Apr 1793	31	24 Jan 1786	81	23	On head of creek of Stones River	yes

Earliest Tennessee Land Records

Claimant:	File #:	Assignee:	County:	Acres:	Grant:	Grant Date:	Entry:	Entry Date:	Bk:	Pg:	Location by Stream Name:	Military:
Wood, George	617	Black, Martin	Tennessee	274	3179	14 Sep 1797	3976	23 Nov 1796	90	433	S side Cumberland River	
Wood, Isaiah	578	Sanford, Samuel	Sumner	640	1815	20 May 1793	2399	30 Nov 1792	81	82	On Jining Fk of Round Lick Creek	yes
Wood, James	08		Knox	300 & 100				18 & 21 Aug 1779				
Wood, James	1347		Washington	200	1264	19 Oct 1797	2368	23 Dec 1779	92	43	On a branch of Little Limestone	
Wood, John	729		Sumner	1000	2114	20 May 1793	2026	24 Nov 1792	81	153	On waters of E Fk of Stones River	yes
Wood, John	80		Green	1820	38	1 Nov 1786	505	27 Oct 1783	59	399	N side Holston River	
Wood, Joseph	726	Porter, Rees	Sumner	640	2110	20 May 1793	1735	– Nov 1792	81	152	On Jining Fk	yes
Wood, Mary & others	614		Sullivan	840	567	24 Dec 1793	384	10 Sep 1778	68	490	Long Islands of Holstein River	
Wood, Michael	557		Green	200	237	20 Sep 1787	197	22 Oct 1783	66	153	On S side of Nolichuckey River	
Wood, Nathaniel	1111	Harris, Edward	Sumner	640	2617	4 Jun 1796	2478	1 Jun 1795	88	339	Joining sd Harris survey	yes
Wood, Robert, Ass.	240		Eastern District	600	3	12 Jun 1794			82	228	In the Little Valley	
Wood, Robert, Ass.	460		Eastern District	200	142	4 Feb 1795			84	142	On N side of Holston River	
Wood, Robt.	077	Larrimore, Thos.	not given	400							In the Little Valley	
Wood, Samuel	1271		Washington	146	1209	4 Dec 1795	33	26 Feb 1778	89	329	On waters of Little Limestone	
Wood, Samuel	676		Washington	49.50	490	10 Nov 1784	2431	23 Feb 1780	69	101	On branch of Cherokee Creek	
Wood, Solomon	439	Blount, Reading	Davidson	640	411	15 Sep 1787			63	152	On lower road &c	yes
Wood, Wheley & [blank]	1197		Washington	121	1150	6 Jan 1795	2693	19 Dec 1780	83	178	On waters of Kendricks Creek	
Wood, William	1358		Washington	100	1275	19 Oct 1797	2785	23 Feb 1781	92	50	On head drafts of Cherokee Creek	
Wood, William	1359		Washington	55.50	1276	19 Oct 1797	2754	26 Jan 1781	92	51	Waters of Little Limestone	
Wood, William, Ass.	2355		Davidson	640	3033	10 Apr 1797	3643		90	306	On E Fk of Harpeth River	yes
Wood, Zeb, & F. Mayberry	181		Eastern District	500	136	24 Jun 1793	1532	25Jun 1784	80	188	Joining Henderson & Co survey	
Woodard, Noah	618	Simpson, Samuel	Davidson	640	590	15 Sep 1787	901		63	211	On N Fk of Red River	yes
Woodard, Noah, Ass.	806		Sumner	369	2273	20 May 1793	1233	25 Oct 1786	81	185	On Arringtons Fork of Red River	yes
Woodard, Thomas	404		Sumner	640	415	27 Jun 1797	337	10 Mar 1784	80	346	On N side of Cumberland River	
Woodard, Thomas	589	Smith, Redick	Davidson	640	561	15 Sep 1787	1231		63	201	N side of Red River	yes
Woodley, Thomas	2452	Haywood, John	Davidson	640	3347	6 Dec 1797	3120	31 Jul 1792	98	182	On S side of Cumberland River	yes
Woodliffe, George	688	Bristow, James	Sumner	640	2042	20 May 1793	1200		81	134	On S side of Cumberland River	yes
Woodriff, Jesse	404		Middle District	640	343	17 Dec 1794	2021	3 May 1784	84	225	On S side of Elk River	
Woodrough, John	477	Marshall, John	Davidson	640	449	15 Sep 1787	2284		63	165	On Moneyfork Creek	yes
Woods, Bartholomew	330		Washington	558.25	197	24 Oct 1782	262	2 Jul 1778	49	225	Inc place where Wood now lives	
Woods, Bartholomew, Jr.	436		Washington	200	428	13 Oct 1783			52	279	On waters of Little Nolichuckie R	
Woods, Isham	052	McEween, David	Davidson	274			1868	26 Mar 1791			On waters of Big Harpeth River	
Woods, James	563		Green	300	243	20 Sep 1787	339	20 Oct 1783	66	155	On head of First Creek	
Woods, John	1069		Green	150	912	26 Dec 1791	572		77	246	On Little Nolachuckey River	
Woods, Matthew, Capt.	656	Bushnell & Dobbins	Davidson	1640 (22	629	15 Sep 1787			63	223	On main E Fk of Stones River	yes
Woods, Michael	1137		Green	200	980	26 Dec 1791			77	275	On S side of Tennessee River	
Woods, Michael	168		Eastern District	400	132	14 Jan 1793			79	290	On S side of Tennessee River	
Woods, Michael	555		Green	300	235	20 Sep 1787	830	15 Jul 1784	66	152	On Meadow Creek	
Woods, Michael	564		Green	200	244	20 Sep 1787	35		66	155	On S side of Nolichuckey River	
Woods, Michael	843		Washington	640	657	10 Nov 1784	278	31 Jul 1778	69	153	On N side of Nolichuckey River	
Woods, Richard	30		Green	150	93	1 Nov 1786	652	16 Nov 1784	58	454	On Cedar Creek	
Woods, Samuel	717		Washington	87.50	531	10 Nov 1784	1421	5 Jun 1779	69	115	Upon a branch of Cherokee Creek	
Woods, Thomas	901	Todd, James	Davidson	640	917	18 May 1789	2480		63	316	On waters of Caney Fork	yes
Woodslackey, James	804		Green	300	609	23 Aug 1788			68	265	On S side of Clinch River	
Woodward, Abraham	496		Hawkins	50	368	29 Jul 1793	783	27 May 1781	80	269	S side of Holston River	

Claimant:	File #:	Assignee:	County:	Acres:	Grant:	Grant Date:	Entry:	Entry Date:	Bk:	Pg:	Location by Stream Name:	Military:
Woodward, George	1174	Harris, Edward	Sumner	640	2679	4 Jun 1796	3028	1 Jun 1795	88	360	Joining sd Harris	yes
Woodward, Simon	405		Sumner	640	416	27 Jun 1793	340	10 Mar 1784	80	346	On W side of Cumberland River	yes
Woolard, Benjamin	652	Sugg, Noah	Sumner	640	1962	20 May 1793	2331	29 Nov 1792	81	115	On the Poun(sic) Lick Creek	yes
Woollard, Jesse	2147	Glasgow, James	Davidson	228	2441	18 Mar 1794	1151		81	423	On waters of Stones River	yes
Woolsey, John	1366		Green	100	1221	27 Jan 1793	2163		79	504	Joining entry Nathaniel Davises	
Wooten, Thomas	316	Rice, John	Davidson	640	302	13 Jun 1787	2254		63	113	W Fk of Jones Creek	yes
Wooteon, David	2187	Beck, Geo. Heirs	Davidson	1000	2443	22 Feb 1795	1695		84	318	On both sides of Duck River	yes
Work, Jacob	798		Sullivan	142	741	12 Aug 1797	2909	28 Aug 1781	91	625	Beg on a pine	
Work, Robert	824		Sullivan	192	767	17 Nov 1797	236,-277	31 Mar 1780	94	161	N side Holstein River	
Worley, James	265	Sypret, Thos.	Eastern District	1000	2396	4 Feb 1795	3798		83	399	N Eastwardly side Little Tennessee	yes
Worsley, Bryan	1146	Harris, Edward	Sumner	640	2652	4 Jun 1796	1340	1 Jun 1795	88	351	Joining sd Harris survey	yes
Worsley, John	1167	Harris, Edward	Sumner	640	2673	4 Jun 1796	1888	1 Jun 1795	88	358	Joining sd Harris	yes
Worwick, Wyatt	672	Mann, John	Tennessee	640	3262	6 Dec 1797	1471		98	149	On Barretts Creek &c	yes
Wra, John	605		Hawkins	200	479	29 Jul 1793	149	15 Feb 1780	80	296	S side of Wallings Ridge	
Wray, James	305		Washington	123	172	24 Oct 1782	1131	25 Jan 1779	47	83	On both sides of Cherokee Creek	
Wren, John	953	Winchester, Stephen	Sumner	400	156	1 Dec 1794		8 Dec 1792	83	479	W of Cumberland Mountain	yes
Wren, William	1025	Donelson, S. & John Latha	Hawkins	275	2956	1 Mar 1797			90	221	Beg on a stake corner	yes
Wright, Absolam	2400	Stewart, Duncan	Davidson	1000	2797	6 Jan 1796	4518		91	471	S W side of Big Harpeth River	yes
Wright, Adam	1620	Mebane, James	Davidson	1000	1354	10 Dec 1790	3854		74	383	On Meat Camp	yes
Wright, Edward	297		Green	200	299	20 Sep 1787	863	23 Oct 1783	65	458	On Pigeon Creek	
Wright, Edward	613		Hawkins	150	487	29 Jul 1793	372	26 Dec 1778	80	297	S side Holston River &c	
Wright, Gabriel	573	Sanford, Samuel	Sumner	640	1810	20 May 1793	790	6 Aug 1792	81	81	On head waters &c	yes
Wright, James	1321		Green	100	1171	12 Jan 1793	2400	8 Feb 1781	78	407	On N side of Nolechucky	
Wright, John	071		Washington	100			2762	24 May 1779			On Browns Creek	
Wright, John	312	Rice, John & others	Davidson	640	298	13 Jun 1787	1405		63	111	On Kerns Creek of Sulphur Fk	yes
Wright, John	457		Washington	100	449	13 Oct 1783	2060		52	288	On Brown Creek	
Wright, John, Ass.	498		Sumner	640	1666	20 May 1793	1051	26 Nov 1792	81	45	On S side of Cumberland River	yes
Wright, Peter	1729	McCulloh, Benjamin	Davidson	640	1444	20 Dec 1791	2257		77	362	On Knob Creek waters of Duck River	yes
Wright, Stephen	1291	Coman, James	Sumner	640	3050	8 Jun 1797	4236	5 Apr 1797	90	318	On ridge bet Flynn & Doe Creeks	yes
Wright, Stephen	1292	Coman, James	Sumner	640	3051	8 Jun 1797	4208	5 Apr 1797	90	318	Includes a spring	yes
Wright, Stephen, Ass.	556		Sumner	274	1775	20 May 1793	767	4 Jul 1786	81	73	On head waters of Drakes Creek	yes
Wright, Thomas	675	Goodrich, S. S. Wheaton	Tennessee	640	3289	6 Dec 1797	4557		98	167	On waters of Barretts Creek	yes
Wright, William	775	Hart, Anthony	Sumner	640	2228	20 May 1793	2249	19 Nov 1792	81	175	On the Caney Fork	yes
Wulson, Joseph	465		Washington	100	457	13 Oct 1783	1422	5 Jun 1779	52	292	On Mill Creek	
Wyat, Jonathan	577	Sanford, Samuel	Sumner	640	1814	20 May 1793	2403	6 Aug 1792	81	82	On N side of Cumberland River	yes
Wyatt, James	160		Tennessee	640	1417	20 Dec 1791	1594	21 Feb 1785	77	355	On both sides of Pine River	
Wyatt, Thomas	1470		Green	328	1234	12 Jul 1794	1341	20 Feb 1793	81	572	On a branch of Lick Creek	
Wyatt, William	1486		Green	200	1249	12 Jul 1794			81	578	On Buffelow Branch	
Wyatt, William	527		Green	520	529	20 Sep 1787	140	21 Oct 1783	65	532	On Lick Creek	
Wyatte, Ephraim	928	Buchanan, John	Davidson	640	944	18 May 1789	2479		63	323	On Ceader Lick Creek	yes
Wycoff & Clark	757	Howell, Daniel	Davidson	640	730	11 Jul 1788	1980		63	257	On N side of Cumberland River	Yes
Wycoff & Clark	774	Hopper, William	Davidson	228	747	11 Jul 1788	1688		63	262	Lying on Gises Creek	Yes
Wykoff, Wm & Lardn. Clark	862	Bagwell, Frederick heirs	Davidson	640	876	17 Jan 1789	2110		63	304	Abt 2 or 3 miles S Cumberland R	yes
Wykoff & Clark	787	Thompson, John heirs	Davidson	640	789	11 Jul 1788	2165		63	276	On S side of Cumberland River	yes
Wykof, Wm & Lardn.Clark	121	Hopper, William	Davidson	228	747	11 Jul 1788	1688		63	262	Lying on Gises Creek	yes

Claimant:	File #:	Assignee:	County:	Acres:	Grant:	Grant Date:	Entry:	Entry Date:	Bk:	Pg:	Location by Stream Name:	Military:
Wykoff, Wm & Lardn. Clark	822	Capps, James heirs	Davidson	1000	825	17 Jan 1789	2117		63	291	On S side of Cumberland River	
Wykoff, Wm.	121	Winset, Jas.	Tennessee	640	1623	23 Feb 1793	2592	30 Sep 1785	76	323	S side of Cumberland	yes
Wynn, John	782		Sumner	457	2237	20 May 1793	1409	22 Aug 1785	81	177	On Dry Fk of Bledsoes Creek	
Wynn, Robert, Ass.	1459		Sumner	640	3054	4 Jul 1797	4029	25 Nov 1796	91	599	Waters of Caney Fk	yes
Wyns, John	023	Armstrong & Donelson	Middle District	640			2965					yes
Yancey, George	234	Reed, Jesse	Sumner	640	1139	26 Nov 1789	3509	12 Mar 1788	74	148	On W side of Caney Fk	yes
Yancey, John	086		not given	5000				14 Feb 1793				
Yancey, John	1756	Hays, Robert	Davidson	640	1529	14 Jan 1793			79	264	Both sides of small fk of Stones R	
Yancey, John	664	Roberts, Jesse	Davidson	640	637	15 Nov 1787	1841		63	226	Beg at N side of Cumberland River	yes
Yarborough, Edward	375		Sumner	3840	1554	14 Jan 1793	167	19 Nov 1792	79	270	On S side of Cumberland	yes
Yarborough, Reuben	18		Smith	357	3370	29 Apr 1801	11	3 May 1800	112	387	Waters Goose Creek & Dixons Cr	yes
Yarborough, David	2092	McCulloh, Benjamin	Davidson	640	2302	20 May 1793	2263		81	191	On S side of Cumberland River	yes
Yarby, Joseph	036	Dillenberry, Redmon	Sumner	274			4475	6 Sep 1797			On waters of N Fk of Red River	yes
Yarkins, Benajah	998	Weakley, Robert	Davidson	640	1015	18 May 1789	3397		63	340	On E Fk of Stones River	yes
Yates, John	344	Alston, John McCoy	Tennessee	640	2150	20 Mar 1793	22	17 Oct 1783	81	161	On Red River	yes
Yearby, John	38	Anderson, Daniel	Sumner	640	868	11 Jan 1789	2898	5 Jun 1788	63	302	On waters of Red River	yes
Yearby, Josiah	1029	Sheppard, John	Sumner	640	2566	8 Mar 1796	2971	15 Aug 1792	88	188	On waters of Obeys River	yes
Yell, Moses	041		Hawkins	175							S side Holston River	
Yell, Moses	042		Hawkins	100			387	-- Jun 1784			S side Holston River	
Yell, Moses	1720		Green	128	1399	21 Jan 1797	1267	21 Jan 1784	91	125	Waters of Beaver Creek	
Yells, Moses	052		Hawkins	128				20 Jan 1780			On waters of Beaver Creek	
Yoo-ne-gis-kah	070		Tennessee	640	35			3 Aug 1819			On bank of River Tuckasedge	
York, Will	741	Dixon, Tilghman	Sumner	533	2136	20 May 1793	1402	20 Aug 1782	81	158	On S bank of River Tuckaseedge	yes
Young, Abraham	0131	Dailey, Chas.	Sumner	274			3213	11 Aug 1786			N side of Cumberland River	yes
Young, Charles	922		Washington	200	899	17 Nov 1790	1140	27 Jan 1779	76	144	Beg at a black oak &c	
Young, Charles	979		Washington	240	956	17 Nov 1790	430	14 Feb 1784	76	164	Beg at a stake	
Young, Daniel	2142	Love, David	Davidson	2057	2419	7 Jan 1794	339		81	406	On N side Cumberland River	yes
Young, Elizabeth (in trust &c)	124		Sullivan	500	136	23 Oct 1782	248	2 Mar 1780	43	323	On N side of Holstein River	
Young, Elizabeth, Relict Adm	185		Hawkins	400	118	16 Nov 1790	247	2 Mar 1780	77	190	On N side of Clinch River &c	
Young, Henry	330		Middle District	4000	295	4 Feb 1795	2001	1 May 1784	83	388	On a branch of N E Fk of Elk River	
Young, John	0132	Shackler, Phillip	Sumner	1000			375	27 Mar 1786			Middle Fk of Drakes Creek	yes
Young, John	531		Hawkins	100	404	29 Jul 1793	448	24 Apr 1780	80	278	Near where widow Creeley lives	
Young, John	564		Sullivan	300	547	17 Nov 1790	1900	7 Oct 1779	76	194	On a branch of Reedy Creek	
Young, John	604		Sullivan	350	559	26 Dec 1791	38	8 Feb 1780	77	305	In Carters Valley	
Young, John	637	Stewart, Duncan	Tennessee	228	2792	20 Dec 1796	557		91	468	S side of Cumberland River	yes
Young, John	657	Stewart, Duncan	Tennessee	228	3234	20 Nov 1797	557	11 Aug 1797	94	170	On the Piney Fk	
Young, John	752		Washington	300	566	10 Nov 1784	592	10 Nov 1778	69	128	N W cor place Robt Young lives on	
Young, John	807		Hawkins	100	643	6 Jan 1795	379	3 Apr 1780	83	166	S side Clinch River	
Young, John & John Brisko	927		Hawkins	136	709	2 Dec 1795	216	21 Feb 1780	88	264	On N side of Clinch	
Young, John, Ass.	606		Sumner	365	1858	20 May 1793	1535	3 Feb 1786	81	91	On a branch of Drakes Creek	
Young, John, Ass.	751		Sumner	274	2155	20 May 1793	1803	3 Feb 1786	81	162	On small branch of Drakes Creek	yes
Young, John, Ass.	755		Sumner	1000	2161	20 May 1793	374	8 Oct 1788	81	163	On Middle Fk of Drakes Creek	yes
Young, Joseph	23		Washington	637	313	24 Oct 1782	429	24 Sep 1778	434	303	On S side of Watauga River	yes
Young, Joseph	71		Washington	100	239	23 Oct 1782	1473	16 Jul 1779	44	265	In a gap of Buflow Mountain	
Young, Robert	0141		Green	640			22	20 Oct 1787			E side big Pigeon River	

Claimant:	File #:	Assignee:	County:	Acres:	Grant:	Grant Date:	Entry:	Entry Date:	Bk:	Pg:	Location by Stream Name:	Military:
Young, Robert	036		Montgomery	25			379	31 Mar 1780			On Spring Creek	
Young, Robert	084		Sullivan	640	111	23 Oct 1782	379	3 Apr 1780	43	291	On White Top Creek	
Young, Robert	100		Sullivan	500	346	29 Dec 1796		Martin Armstrong	90	196	On the Grassey Valley	
Young, Robert	1014		Hawkins	110	370	4 Jul 1797		Martin Armstrong	91	592	In the Grassey Valley	
Young, Robert	1084		Hawkins	220			196	21 Feb 1780	43	317	In Carters Valley	
Young, Robert	113		Sullivan	200	124	29 Oct 1782	502	11 Oct 1778	76	481	1st branch that runs into Holston	
Young, Robert	123		Eastern District	640	156	29 Jul 1793	227	31 Jan 1784	66	434	On W Fk of Red River at Junction	
Young, Robert	1312		Davidson	640	278	10 Jul 1788	22	2 Apr 1792	81	590	On E side of Pigeon River	
Young, Robert	1524		Green	640	1285	12 Jul 1794	706	13 Nov 1780	69	165	On N side of Holstein River	
Young, Robert	381		Sullivan	150	260	10 Nov 1784	31 & 1728	— —1783	89	295	On N side Clinch	
Young, Robert	402		Eastern District	1858	244	27 Nov 1795	36	8 Feb 1781	69	174	On N side of Holstein	
Young, Robert	414		Sullivan	300	293	10 Nov 1784	428	25 Sep 1778	69	105	Upon Brush Creek	
Young, Robert	688		Washington	640	502	10 Nov 1784	543	22 Oct 1783	82	223	On N side of Holston River	
Young, Robert	788		Hawkins	100	628	12 Jul 1794	1490	19 Feb 1784	71	383	On N side of Holston	
Young, Robert	823		Green	125	811	26 Nov 1789	Four (?)	24 Apr 1789	88	517	In Powells Valley	
Young, Robert	988		Hawkins	2560	737	10 Sep 1796	8 warrants		88	518	On N side of Clinch	
Young, Robert	989		Hawkins	5000	738	10 Sep 1796	552		88	518	On N side of Clinch River	
Young, Robert	990		Hawkins	5000	739	10 Sep 1796			88	488	In the Grassey Valley	
Young, Robert, Ass	366		Eastern District	300	314	10 Sep 1796	1762	16 Sep 1779	89	291	On N side of Clinch River	
Young, Robert, Ass.	394		Eastern District	640	236	27 Nov 1795	363	21 Sep 1779	89	298	On N side of Clinch	
Young, Robert, Ass.	407		Eastern District	274	249	27 Nov 1795	536	26 Oct 1778	80	203	Beg at 2 black oak saplins	
Young, Robert, Jr.	1096		Washington	640	1046	27 Nov 1792	4292	14 Dec 1796	90	50	On Camp Creek	yes
Young, Robert, Jr.	1247	Blount, John Gray	Sumner	640	2852	21 Jan 1797	132	26 Feb 1778	80	172	Beg at a buckeye & white oak &c	
Young, Robert, Jr.	1443		Green	400	1253	27 Nov 1792	2276	1 Mar 1786			On the Many Fk	
Young, Samuel	0135	Lethis, William	Sumner	640			302	15 Dec 1792	76	316	On N Fork of Red River	yes
Young, Sion	327	Fort, William & Howell Tatu	Sumner	640	1607	23 Feb 1793	418	15 Apr 1780	92	48	Waters of Brush Creek	yes
Young, William	1354		Washington	100	1271	19 Oct 1797	32	13 Aug 1780	88	271	On waters of Lick Creek	
Young, William	1660		Green	50	1364	2 Dec 1795	2285		63	163	On Money Fk Creek	yes
Young, William	473	Marshall, John	Davidson	640	445	15 Sep 1787			63	387	Spencers Creek	Yes
z[name not given]	020	Ross, Sam	Sumner	640	1365	15 Dec 1790			74		No. Cumberland River	Yes
Z[name not given]	473		Montgomery	274			1446	14 Dec 1796			On S side of Cumberland River	yes
Zarlett, James	1510	Ross, Joseph	Davidson	640	1067	26 Nov 1789	3400		74	112	On E Fk of Stones River	yes
Zarlett, Timothy	866	Sherrett, Isidore	Davidson	640	880	17 Jan 1789	3398		63	305	On E Fk of Stones River	yes
Zarlett, Zachariah	854	Sherrett, Isadore	Davidson	640	862	17 Jan 1789			63	300	On waters of Half Pone Creek	yes
Zealot, Nelson	996	Weakley, Robert	Davidson	640	1013	18 May 1789	3396		63	339	On the main Tennessee River	yes
Zealot, Jonathan	750	Lock, James	Davidson	274	723	11 Jul 1788	3234		63	254	On N side of Cumberland River	yes
Zealott, Joshua	860	Fenner, Richard	Davidson	640	871	17 Jan 1789	3395		63	302	On first fk of Big Barren	yes
Zealott, Shadrack	39	Armstrong, Andrew	Sumner	640	870	17 Jan 1789	3394	19 May 1788	63	302	On waters of E Fk of Stones River	yes
Zealott, William	948	Lock, James	Davidson	274	964	18 May 1789	3233		63	328	On waters of Bledsoes Creek	yes
Zeglor, Jacob	1054		Davidson	640	28	17 Apr 1786	218	30 Jan 1784	66	44	On Pearsons Creek	yes
Zutson, John	748	Brock, Joseph	Davidson	640	721	11 Jul 1788	2702		63	253	Round Lick Creek	yes
Zuz(?), Alexander	1411		Sumner	274	3345	6 Dec 1797	3572	21 June 1797	97	60		yes

Assignee:	Claimant:	File #:	Assignee:	Claimant:	File #:	Assignee:	Claimant:	File
[blank] heirs	Ross, William	345	Alexander, Robert	Nash, Joseph	665	Anderson, Daniel	O'Barr, Michael	73
[blank] heirs of	Robertson, James	643	Alexander, Robert	Walker, Aaron	858	Anderson, Daniel	Pipkin, Willis	848
arkins, Benajah heirs	Weakley, Robert	226	Alford, Jno.	Fenner, Richard	11	Anderson, Daniel	Ramsey, Solomon	67
ork(?), Wm.	Flanery, Daniel	1317	Alford, William	Alford, William	03	Anderson, Daniel	Reed, Stephen	216
A(M)errian, John	Armstrong, M. & S. Donelson	993	Alford, William	Butts, William	04	Anderson, Daniel	Smiley, Jonathan	70
A. Jackson & S. Donelson	Reiley, Ezekial	1100	Alford, William	Mitchell, John	02	Anderson, Daniel	Tolar, Danl	836
Abbett, John	Bradley, James	498	Alford, William	Reasons, Thomas	01	Anderson, Daniel	Troublefield, Benjamin	46
Abbott, Isaac	Hays, Rachel	321	Alhead, Vernon hrs.	Cannon, Minos	1530	Anderson, Daniel	Weatherington, Jesse	835
Abbott, Jonathan	Davis, Joshua	799	Allen, Alexander	Moore, Nicholas	649	Anderson, Daniel	Whitakers, Joseph	826
Abbott, Wadington hrs	Douglass, Wm.	545	Allen, Archibald	Brown, John	333	Anderson, Daniel	Williamson, Job	853
Aberrion, Jno.hrs	Armstrong & Donelson	021	Allen, Charles	Bowman, Robert	2121	Anderson, Daniel	Yearby, John	38
Abims, Joseph	Blount, John Gray	1048	Allen, George	Brantley, Jeremiah	532	Anderson, James	Ray, Archibald	1014
Abuck, John hrs.	Bonds, Wright	125	Allen, John	Smith, Daniel	1491	Anderson, John	Blount, John Gray & Thoma	2013
Ackenclass, Absalom	Boyd, John	220	Allen, Jesse	Smith, William	118	Anderson, John	Cobb, Jesse	292
Ackinclass, John	Bowman, William	16	Allen, Mary	Furney, Peter	376	Anderson, John	Handcock, Isham	945
Acock, Robert	Shannon, Samuel	867	Allen, Peggy	Lawless, Matthew	513	Anderson, John's heirs	Nash, William	2298
Act of Assembly	Henderson, Richard & others	858	Allen, Samuel	Jones, John	536	Anderson, Matthew	Seal, Frances	2075
Act of Assembly	Henderson, Richard & others	995	Allen, Sarah	Leavoin, John	019	Anderson, Matthew	Seals, Francis	02
Adair, James	Guion, William	344	Allen, Sarah	Scavrons, John	242	Anderson, Meede	Hendri ks, John	21
Adair, James	Wheeler, Samuel	345	Allen, Thomas Adm. Of	Allen, John	2222	Anderson, William	Rearden, Jeremiah	157
Adams, Arthur	Ore, James	2251	Allen, Thomas heir	Allen, John	1940	Anderson, Wm.	Barry, Redmon Dillon	1277
Adams, Howell	Neville, George	4	Allen, Thomas hrs	Fenner, Richard	328	Andrew,Jessop	Armstrong, Andrew	239
Adams, Jacob	McKinney, Robert	1271	Allen, William	Groves, William	327	Andrews, James	Ray, Archibald	1373
Adams, James	Curry, John	1406	Allentharpe, John hrs	Green, Burwell	2295	Andrews, John	Blount, John Gray & Thoma	322
Adams, James	Allentharpe, John hrs	1406	Allgood, H. heirs	Robertson, James	1666	Andrews, John Cole	Donelson, Stockley	0138
Adcock, George	Blair, Thomas	36	Allison, David	Sheppard, John	01	Andrews, Nathan	Boyd, John	243
Adcock, Joshua	McKadon, William	728	Allison, David	Sheppard, John	2220	Andrews, Thomas	Phillips, Mann	636
Adkins, Benjamin	Blount, John Gray & Thomas	2008	Allison, David	Steed, Jesse	555	Andrews, Watson	Easton, James	1036
Adkison, Michael heirs	Sanders, James	2314	Allison, John	Farrow, William	423	Angel, Thomas	Blount, John	30
Aicuff, Timothy	Evans, Richard	193	Allison, John	Wilkes, Francis	412	Angel, Thos.	Donelson, John	1269
Aims, Thomas	Glasgow, James, Co.	285	Alston, John McCoy	Gatley (Gillalee), Isaac	509	Angels, Benj.	Barton, Samuel	335
Albright, Jas heirs	Hadley, Joshua	534	Alston, John McCoy	Yates, John	344	Anglin, Cornelius	Tyner, Lewis	2285
Albritton, Henry	Cobb, Jesse	420	Amis, John	Glasgow, James	180	Anthony, James	Wilson, David	2000
Aldridge, William	McMahan, Daniel	216	Amus, James	Welbern, Daniel	0124	Appleton, John	McNess, John	791
Alexander, Cameron	Malloy, Thomas	2339	Anderson, Chas heirs	Marley, Robert	341	Applewhite, Jesse	Armstrong & Donelson	020
Alexander, Ebenezer	Matthews, William	1865	Anderson, Daniel	Brewer, Benjamin	916	Applewhite, John hrs	Gamble, Edmond	358
Alexander, George	Brukins, John	2146	Anderson, Daniel	Cobb, William	62	Applewhite,Jess.hrs	Armstrong, M. & S. Donelso	996
Alexander, George	Bruskins, John	893	Anderson, Daniel	Fenner, William	48	Archer, Baker	Murphree, Hardy	148
Alexander, George	Hays, Samuel	773	Anderson, Daniel	Johnston, Archibald	51	Archer, Baker hr of Jesse	Archer, Jesse	225
Alexander, George	Wesley, John	772	Anderson, Daniel	Lanier, Robert	1533	Archer, Demsey hrs.	Brehon, James Gloster	984
Alexander, Joseph heirs	Thompson, Jason	1528	Anderson, Daniel	Lee, Hardy	38	Archer, Jac & Demcey	Brahon, John Gloster	17
Alexander, Robert	Almond, Joshua	664	Anderson, Daniel	Myham, William	64	Archer, Laticia heiress	Manly, Mark	254
Alexander, Robert	Brooks, Robert	786	Anderson, Daniel	Norwood, William	831	Archer, Thomas	Haston, Daniel	201

Assignee:	Claimant:	File #:
Arman, Pain	Barton, Samuel	06
Armstong, Henry Joab	Barry, Redmond D.	2382
Armstrong & Donelson	Aberrion, John	021
Armstrong & Donelson	Applewhite, Jesse	020
Armstrong & Donelson	Brantley, Marmaduke	025
Armstrong & Donelson	Fulks, Garret	017
Armstrong & Donelson	Hinton, John	031
Armstrong & Donelson	Jefferson, Joel	016
Armstrong & Donelson	Sheppard, Valentine	019
Armstrong & Donelson	Truebuck, George	024
Armstrong & Donelson	Watson, William	018
Armstrong & Donelson	Whitaker, Josiah	015
Armstrong & Donelson	Williams, Solomon	040
Armstrong & Donelson	Wyns, John	023
Armstrong, Andrew	Conner, Christopher	857
Armstrong, Andrew	Flord, Augustine	246
Armstrong, Andrew	Flowers, Charles	334
Armstrong, Andrew	Hair, David	830
Armstrong, Andrew	Harrison, Jonathan	335
Armstrong, Andrew	Jessop, Andrew	239
Armstrong, Andrew	Langford, Peter	850
Armstrong, Andrew	Tate, Thomas	825
Armstrong, Andrew	Zealott, Shadrack	39
Armstrong, Crutcher, Smith	Roper, Richard	190
Armstrong, James	Mills, William	1041
Armstrong, John	Boyce, Jesse	027
Armstrong, John	Craddock, John	1471
Armstrong, John	Moslander, Abel	026
Armstrong, M,	Robertson, James	1710
Armstrong, M.	Alston, John McCoy	430
Armstrong, M.	Alston, John McCoy	431
Armstrong, M.	Baker, Joshua	1744
Armstrong, M.	Barton, Samuel	1742
Armstrong, M.	Beaty, David	2359
Armstrong, M.	Blackmore, Geo. D.	1010
Armstrong, M.	Blair, James, Senr	1010
Armstrong, M.	Boren, Bazel	448
Armstrong, M.	Boren, Bazil	475
Armstrong, M.	Boren, William	474
Armstrong, M.	Borin, John	427
Armstrong, M.	Bosley, James	10
Armstrong, M.	Bosley, James	11
Armstrong, M.	Bosley, James	13
Armstrong, M.	Bosley, James	14

Assignee:	Claimant:	File #:
Armstrong, M.	Bosley, James	1746
Armstrong, M.	Bosley, James	369
Armstrong, M.	Bosley, James	370
Armstrong, M.	Bosley, James	372
Armstrong, M.	Bosley, James	373
Armstrong, M.	Brigance, Wm.	1220
Armstrong, M.	Brigance, Wm.	1222
Armstrong, M.	Brigance, Wm.	392
Armstrong, M.	Brock, Joseph	1407
Armstrong, M.	Brock, Joseph	1410
Armstrong, M.	Brown, Morgan	553
Armstrong, M.	Bryant, Morgan	1550
Armstrong, M.	Buchanan, John	2126
Armstrong, M.	Buchanon, John	1569
Armstrong, M.	Buckanan, Samuel	339
Armstrong, M.	Buckannan, John	1549
Armstrong, M.	Cage, Wm.	1024
Armstrong, M.	Clark, Lardner	1387
Armstrong, M.	Clark, Lardner	1398
Armstrong, M.	Clark, Lardner	1409
Armstrong, M.	Clark, Lardner	1548
Armstrong, M.	Clark, Lardner	391
Armstrong, M.	Clark, Thos.	454
Armstrong, M.	Cox, John	23
Armstrong, M.	Crockett, Andrew	1413
Armstrong, M.	Crumstock, Thomas	1419
Armstrong, M.	Crutcher, Wm.	1401
Armstrong, M.	Davis, John	452
Armstrong, M.	Davis, John	2316
Armstrong, M.	Davis, John	2396
Armstrong, M.	Dayton, John	2397
Armstrong, M.	Dickson,Jno & H. Wells	1184
Armstrong, M.	Dillard, Wm.	252
Armstrong, M.	Diska, Joseph	1023
Armstrong, M.	Dobbins, Wm.	1009
Armstrong, M.	Dobbins, Wm.	924
Armstrong, M.	Donelson, John	925
Armstrong, M.	Donelson, John	2307
Armstrong, M.	Donelson, Stockley	917
Armstrong, M.	Douglas, Wm.	05
Armstrong, M.	Douglass, James	1217
Armstrong, M.	Douglass, John	191
Armstrong, M.	Douglass, Wm.	580
Armstrong, M.	Douglass, Wm.	1218

Assignee:	Claimant:	File
Armstrong, M.	Drake, John	1404
Armstrong, M.	Ewing, Robert	1892
Armstrong, M.	Ferrell, William	0133
Armstrong, M.	Foster, Anthony	1008
Armstrong, M.	Foster, Anthony	455
Armstrong, M.	Gambill, Bradley	1581
Armstrong, M.	Glasgow, James	1436
Armstrong, M.	Gower, Elijah	1890
Armstrong, M.	Gower, Robert	2179
Armstrong, M.	Gragg, Samuel	1006
Armstrong, M.	Grammer, John	1406
Armstrong, M.	Handley, Samuel	1397
Armstrong, M.	Hays, Robert	1775
Armstrong, M.	Hays, Robert	1776
Armstrong, M.	Hays, Robert	222
Armstrong, M.	Hays, Robert	457
Armstrong, M.	Hays, Robert	487
Armstrong, M.	Hoggatt, James	1570
Armstrong, M.	Hoggt, James	1743
Armstrong, M.	Hoggett, James	1408
Armstrong, M.	Morthrell, John	2324
Armstrong, M.	Nash, William	2198
Armstrong, M.	Nelson, Robert	1391
Armstrong, M.	Nelson, Robert	1391
Armstrong, M.	Nelson, Robert	1392
Armstrong, M.	Nelson, Robert	1394
Armstrong, M.	Nelson, Robert	1395
Armstrong, M.	Nelson, Robert	1396
Armstrong, M.	Nelson, Robert	1568
Armstrong, M.	Nelson, Robert	446
Armstrong, M.	Nelson, Robert	456
Armstrong, M.	Noble, Mark	1423
Armstrong, M.	Noble, Mark	364
Armstrong, M.	Payne, Josiah	1607
Armstrong, M.	Peyton, Ephraim	1018
Armstrong, M.	Peyton, John	0105
Armstrong, M.	Peyton, John & Ephraim	1223
Armstrong, M.	Ramsey, Josiah	361
Armstrong, M.	Ramsey, Josiah	363
Armstrong, M.	Read, Alexander	1542
Armstrong, M.	Read, Alexander	1543
Armstrong, M.	Read, Alexander	1544
Armstrong, M.	Read, Alexander	1545
Armstrong, M.	Reavis, Dabiel [sic]	2323

Assignee:	Claimant:	File #:	Assignee:	Claimant:	File #:	Assignee:	Claimant:	File
Armstrong, M.	Reed, Alexander	1551	Armstrong, Martin	Surcy, Robert	1711	Armstrong, Martin	Henderson, Samuel	321
Armstrong, M.	Reed, Alexander	2243	Armstrong, Martin	Tatum, Howell	2417	Armstrong, Martin	Henry, William	1080
Armstrong, M.	Reed, Alexander	2243	Armstrong, Martin	Thompson, Jason	1487	Armstrong, Martin	Hickman, Thomas	1793
Armstrong, M.	Reed, Alexander	364	Armstrong, Martin	Thompson, Robert	9	Armstrong, Martin	Hill, Green	2293
Armstrong, M.	Reed, Alexander	479	Armstrong, Martin	Walker, Geo.	1025	Armstrong, Martin	Ireson, James	1628
Armstrong, M.	Reed, Wm.	390	Armstrong, Martin	Walker, George	1893	Armstrong, Martin	Lyttle, Wm, Jr.	012
Armstrong, M.	Rhodes, Christian, Ass.	884	Armstrong, Martin	Walker, George	2197	Armstrong, Martin	Messar, Benjamin	1472
Armstrong, M.	Rhodes, Christian, Ass.	888	Armstrong, Martin	Walker, George	251	Armstrong, Martin	Montgomery, Jas.	1219
Armstrong, M.	Rhodes, Christian, Ass.	889	Armstrong, Martin	Walker, George	453	Armstrong, Martin	Padgett, Thomas	377
Armstrong, M.	Rice, John	1629	Armstrong, Martin	Walker, John	1625	Armstrong, Martin	Parker, Charles	1792
Armstrong, M.	Rice, John	871	Armstrong, Martin	Weakley, Robert	1748	Armstrong, Martin	Rothwall, David	514
Armstrong, M.	Roberts, Obed	1388	Armstrong, Martin	Weakley, Robert	2392	Armstrong, Martin	Ryan, Cornelius	454
Armstrong, M.	Robertson, James	020	Armstrong, Martin	Weakley, Robert	362	Armstrong, Martin	Scott, Joshua & John Payto	1007
Armstrong, M.	Robertson, James	08	Armstrong, Martin	Weakley, Robt	078	Armstrong, Martin	Seers, John	0120
Armstrong, M.	Robertson, James	1708	Armstrong, Martin	Wells, Hayden	586	Armstrong, Martin	Sheldon, David	1011
Armstrong, M.	Robertson, James	367	Armstrong, Martin	Wells, Haydon	587	Armstrong, Martin	Smith, John	508
Armstrong, M.	Rolston, David	1609	Armstrong, Martin	White, Henry	079	Armstrong, Martin	Tatum, Ho & Henry Wiggins	1370
Armstrong, M.	Russel, James	1415	Armstrong, Martin	White, James	2122	Armstrong, Martin	Tatum. Howell	2418
Armstrong, M.	Russel, Jas.	075	Armstrong, Martin	White, James	2178	Armstrong, Martin	Trammell, Phillip	1221
Armstrong, M.	Russell, Jas.	554	Armstrong, Martin	White, James, Ass.	2306	Armstrong, Martin	Ward, John, Ass.	887
Armstrong, M.	Russle, Thomas	1741	Armstrong, Martin	White, James, Ass.	533	Armstrong, Martin	Wikoff, Wm. & Lardner Clar	1606
Armstrong, M.	Rutherford, Henry	76	Armstrong, Martin	White, Solomon	1426	Armstrong, Martin	Williams, Oliver	1891
Armstrong, M.	Sanders, James	1414	Armstrong, Martin	Wikoff, William	1745	Armstrong, Martin	Williams, Sampson	883
Armstrong, M.	Sanders, James	1537	Armstrong, Martin	Wikoff, Wm. & Lardner	1546	Armstrong, Martin	Williams, Sampson	884
Armstrong, M.	Sanders, Jas.	193	Armstrong, Martin	Williams, Curtice	1427	Armstrong, Martin	Winchester, Geo. & James	918
Armstrong, M.	Saunders, James	076	Armstrong, Martin	Williams, Curtice	1605	Armstrong, Martin	Winchester, Jas. & Geo.	926
Armstrong, M.	Saunders, Jas. & I. Bledsoe	1011	Armstrong, Martin	Williams, Daniel	1027	Armstrong, Martin	Winchester, John & George	920
Armstrong, M.	Shannon, Robert	2361	Armstrong, Martin	Wilson, David	1081	Armstrong, R.	Thompson, Robert	1429
Armstrong, M.	Shaw, Robert	1216	Armstrong, M.	Winchester, Jas. & Geo.	921	Armstrong, Richard	Igley, Samuel	128
Armstrong, M.	Shelby, David	2185	Armstrong, R.	Winningham, Thos.	541	Armstrong, Thomas	Towler, Absolam	178
Armstrong, M.	Sherkey's Patrick	077	Armstrong, Richard	Ford, John	455	Armstrong, Thomas & Ja	Williams, Harbert	1026
Armstrong, M.	Sides, Peter	434	Armstrong, Thomas	Price, Jonathan	472	Arnold, David	Darden, John	021
Armstrong, M.	Smith, Daniel	189	Armstrong, Thomas & Ja	Brown, John	2157	Arthur, Stephan hrs	Barbour, Richard	1343
Armstrong, M.	Standiford, Wm.	032	Armstrong, M. & A. Crutch	Bryant, Thomas	879	Ash, Stephan heirs	Hughlett, William	044
Armstrong, M.	Steele, Nancy Nesfield	2124	Armstrong, M. heirs	Cash, John	1473	Ashe, Charles	Robertson, James Randolph	1684
Armstrong, M.	Stewart, Duncan	651	Arnold, David	Clark & Wykoff	1422	Askers, Chas.	Donelson, John	683
Armstrong, M.	Stewart, John	585	Arthur, Stephan hrs	Crutcher, Anthony	1587	Askew, Chas.	Biggett, Jesse	1261
Armstrong, M.	Stump, Fred	2330	Ash, Stephan heirs	Crutcher, William	2154	Askin, William	Shannon, Samuel	1577
Armstrong, M.	Stump, Frederick	1400	Ashe, Charles	Daugharty, Wm& CorMc	1588	Asobrow, Wm. Jno.	Reed, Jesse	270
Armstrong, M.	Stump, Frederick	1402	Askers, Chas.	Gillespie, James	029	Aspey, William	Gibson, James	0595
Armstrong, M.	Stump, Frederick	1403	Askew, William	Harris, Peter	467	Aspey, John	Davis, Thomas	162
Armstrong, M.	Stump, Frederick	2193	Askin, William	Hay, David	2308	Atkinson, Charlton	Johnston, Benjamin	666
Armstrong, M.	Stump, Frederick	2329	Asobrow, Wm. Jno.	Hays, Robert	223	Atkinson, Jno & Robt Nels	Edkins, John	102
Armstrong, M.	Stump, Frederick etal	2329	Atkinson, John	Hays, Robert	450	Atkinson, John	Nelson, Robert	102

Assignee:	Claimant:	File #
Atway, Hardy	Isbell, Thomas	512
Austin, Thomas	Tatum, Harrall etal	2440
Averall, William	Halsted, Jollef	2141
Avery, Estridge	Mulherrin, James	2139
Avery, Estridge heirs	Mulherrin, James	926
Avery, Jas.	Harris, Edward	1178
Awell, Jas.	Ellison, Jos.	17
B(P)llips, Thos.	Barry, Redmon Dillon	1288
Backhonham, John	Reed, Jesse	231
Bagley, Isaac	Harris, Edward	1133
Bagley, John heirs	McConnell, Robert	?
Bagley, John heirs	McConnell, Robert	2409
Bagley, Matthias hrs.	Barton, Samuel	1384
Bagwell, Frederick heirs	Wycoff, Wm & Lardn. Clark	862
Bagwell, Jesse	Blount, Reading	937
Baileon, Maon	Hart, Anthony	745
Bailes, Barnabas	Petty, John	1015
Bailey, Ethelred heirs	Banner, Joseph	1009
Bailey, Ethelred heirs	Mulharren, James	2140
Bailey, John	Mulherrin, James	24
Bailey, Lewis	Dickson, Edward	2113
Bailey, Morris	Blount, John Gray & Thomas	863
Bailey, Robert	Hart, Anthony	018
Bailey, Robert heirs	Johnson, Wm.	538
Bailey, Thomas	Johnson, William	279
Bailey, Thomas	Brittain, Philip	158
Bailey, Wm. Heirs	Medlin, Elisha	1489
Bailey, Wm. Henry heirs	Donelson, John	060
Baird, Joseph heirs	Mebane, Chas.	2344
Baker, Amos hrs	Malloy, Thomas	1881
Baker, Charles	Bond, John	2046
Baker, Charles	Matthews, John	035
Baker, John	Willoughby, Solomon	776
Baker, John	Bush, Aaron	09
Baker, John	Devonshire, Joshua	809
Baker, John	Gray, Andrew	742
Baker, John	Hargrove, William	644
Baker, John	Jacobs. Ambrose	832
Baker, John	Lath, Abner	221
Baker, John	McAndrews, Andrew	240
Baker, John	Nelson, Collins	637
Baker, John	Thomas, Zebulon	109
Baker, Jos.	Robertson, Chas.	865
Baker, Obediah	Truet, Stephen	314
Baker, Peter	McCulloh, Benj.	
Baker, Peter	McCulloh, Benjamin	1719
Baker, Simon	Davis, Joshua	788
Balew, Thomas	Harrison, Robert	712
Ballard, Burwell	Breckon, James G.	1578
Ballard, Burwell hrs	Breker, James Glouster	015
Ballard, Frances	Pennington, Jacob	1344
Ballard, Francis	Rice, John	1443
Ballard, James heirs	Sheppard, Nancy	721
Ballard, Joab	Brakey, Andrew	304
Ballard, Peter	Person, Thomas	97
Ballards, Jethro hrs	Blount, John Gray	011
Ballentine, Maltise	Hunt, James	038
Balmore, John	Hays, Robert	1761
Bandy, James heirs	Searcey, Robert	2387
Banks, Gilbert	Banks, Robt	1273
Banks, Richard hrs.	Blackface, Wm.	565
Banks, Robert	Matthew, Gilbert	1273
Banner, Joseph	Saunders, John	875
Barber, James	McCulloh, Benjamin	2025
Barber, Joseph	Nicklas, Issac	027
Barber, Joshua	Long, Nicholas	2048
Barbey, John	Ivey, David	448
Barbour, Richard	Arthur, Stephen	1343
Barbour, Richard	Davis, Frederick	431
Barbour, Richard	Harrison, William	1345
Barbour, Richard	Lippencut, William	430
Barbour, Richard	Terrell, Nimrod	1344
Barco, John	Noble, Mark	024
Bardner, James heirs of	McCrory, Thomas	418
Barfield, Marmaduke	Glasgow, James	403
Baringer, John	Boyd, John	328
Barker, Levy	Rice, John	307
Barker, Lewis	Griffis, Samuel	034
Barker, Nicholas	McCulloh, Benjamin	1717
Barker, Thomas	Howard, Solomon	511
Barkley, Wm. Heirs	Donohoe, John, Ass	563
Barlow, George heirs	Marley, Robert	343
Barnes, Burwell heir of Tho	Robertson, James	1908
Barnes, Henry	Lewis, Joshua	1397
Barnes, Moses	Barton, Samuel	496
Barnes, William heirs	Walker, Geo & Seth Lewi	2078
Barnes, Wm. Heirs	Dickson, James	751
Barnet, Robert	Garrison, Stephen	1772
Barnet, Robert	Pervin, John	467
Barnet, Sion	Borin, John	380
Barnet, Jas.	Benton, Jesse	280
Barnett, Henry	Phillips, P & M. Campbell	1618
Baron, Samuel	Jones, Stephen	352
Barron, Sherrod	Davis, Archibald	890
Barrow, Betsy	Parker, Isom	306
Barrow, Henry	Pursley, John	1638
Barrow, Henry	Wiggins, Charter	901
Barrow, James	Hammond, Feston	902
Barrow, James	Stone, John	305
Barrow, Jas.	Fort, Elias	807
Barrow, Matthew	Underwood, James	307
Barrow, Sherrod	Hansell, Charles	1637
Barrow, Sherrod	Joyner/ Joiner/, Freeman	891
Barrow, Sherrod	Purcell, Barnet	304
Barry, Redmon Dillon	Saunders, Thomas	1284
Barry, Redmon Dillon	Whood, William	1286
Barry, Redmond D.	Armstrong, Henry Joab	2382
Barry, Redmond D.	Bradley, Nimrod	1350
Barry, Redmond D.	Dearman, Michael	1351
Barry, Redmond D.	Dodd, Thomas	1354
Barry, Redmond D.	Gilbert, Abraham	2384
Barry, Redmond D.	Morgan, William	1355
Barry, Redmond D.	Nicolas, Richard	1352
Barry, Redmond D.	Odum, Dickerson	2383
Barry, Redmond Dillin	Wharton, James	1280
Barry, Redmond Dillion	Mehon, James	1287
Barry, Redmond Dillion	Meredith, Benjamin	1285
Barry, Redmond Dillion	Mohon, James	1287
Barry, Redmond Dillion	Monk, Israel	1283
Barry, Redmond Dillion	Anderson, William	1277
Barry, Redmond Dillion	Billups, Thomas	1288
Bartee, John	Gillaspie, William	1910
Bartie, John heirs	McDowell, Joseph	1517
Barton, Gabriel	Cooper, Henry	1396
Barton, Joseph	Marshall, Emanuel	3
Barton, Robert, P of A	Bartons, James McAnge*	3
Barton, Sam.	Elliot, John	1447
Barton, Saml.	Hooks, William	1913
Barton, Samuel	Anglen, Benjamin	335
Barton, Samuel	Bagbey, Matthias	1384
Barton, Samuel	Barnes, Moses	496
Barton, Samuel	Bates [or Boles], Matthias	1687
Barton, Samuel	Beaks, Ignatious	499

Assignee:	Claimant:	File #:	Assignee:	Claimant:	File #:	Assignee:	Claimant:	File:
Barton, Samuel	Butts, Peter	04	Batts, Simon	Price, Jonathan	012	Benjamin McCulloh	Jetts, Jeremiah	1718
Barton, Samuel	Campbell, Charles	1209	Batts, Simon	Price, Jonathan	480	Bennet, Henry	Hays, Robert	466
Barton, Samuel	Campbell, Charles	1211	Baxter, Samuel	Sheppard, William	988	Bennet, Joel	Curtis, George	243
Barton, Samuel	Carter, Joseph	299	Baxter, Thomas	Williams, Sampson	2097	Bennet, William	McCrory, Thomas	733
Barton, Samuel	Crunch, John Watts	1427	Bayd, John	Chance, David	1214	Bennett, Joseph	Sheppard, Nancy	693
Barton, Samuel	Drakes, Benjamin	481	Bayler, John	Barry, Redmon Dillen	049	Bennett, Peter heirs	Robertson, Jas.	1670
Barton, Samuel	Duffy, John	531	Bayles, John	Dillonberry, Redmon	049	Bennett, William	Blair, John	410
Barton, Samuel	Farmer, Peter	593	Beabey, Abraham heirs	McCrory, Thomas	760	Bennett, William's hrs.	Jones, Ambrose	868
Barton, Samuel	Giddy, Thomas	497	Beach, Robert heirs	Brock, Joseph	841	Benson(?), John hrs.	Fenner, Richard	291
Barton, Samuel	Hering, Burwell	349	Beach, Robt.	Donelson, Stockley	09	Benford, James heirs	Williams, Willoughby	329
Barton, Samuel	Herking, Burwell	349	Beaird, J. & Wm. Tyrrell	Edwards, Robert	261	Bentley, John	Nelson, John & Alex	246
Barton, Samuel	Howell, John	134	Beaird, Joseph	Modlin, Ezekial	656	Bently, Isaac	McCulloh, Benjamin	308
Barton, Samuel	Jenkins, Burwell	336	Beaird, Joseph	Morgan, Hardy	188	Benton, Jesse	Barnet, James	280
Barton, Samuel	Jones, Stephen	032	Beaird, Joseph	Morris, James	189	Benton, Jesse	Muckleroy, John	616
Barton, Samuel	Jordan, River	1208	Beaks,Ignatious hrs	Barton, Samuel	499	Benton, Juliah heirs	Smith, Abraham	574
Barton, Samuel	Jordan, River	1210	Bean(?), Robert	Coonrad, Nicholas	397	Benton, Kedar	Davis, Joshua	690
Barton, Samuel	McCollister, James	05	Bean, Henry	King, Robert	675	Benton, Sol	Irwin, Joseph	2421
Barton, Samuel	McKinsey, Hugh	501	Bean, Jesse	Cameron, Alexander	939	Berk, Meradeth heirs	Sugg, Aquilla	910
Barton, Samuel	Pain, Arme	06	Bean, William	King, Robert	511	Berkley, Wm. Heirs	Donahoe, John	563
Barton, Samuel	Pain, John	07	Bear, Jesse	Lanier, James	763	Berry, John	Pasmore, David	952
Barton, Samuel	Pooram, John	1206	Beard, John Lewis	Kidwell, Elijah	241	Berry, John heirs	Hughlett, Wm.	045
Barton, Samuel	Pooram, John	1212	Beard, John Lewis	Marr, John, Jr.	242	Berry, Thomas	Conner, John	665
Barton, Samuel	Ramsey, Henry	08	Beard, John's hr James	Nelson, Robert	673	Berry, Thomas	Meafee, Azariah	667
Barton, Samuel	Reynolds, William	581	Beard, Joseph	Cannon, Sampson	681	Berry, Thomas	Morgan, William	666
Barton, Samuel	Roberts, Thomas W.	1428	Beard, Joseph	English, Joseph	187	Besall, Elisha	Reed, Jesse	591
Barton, Samuel	Rodes, Lewis	376	Beard, Joseph	Rush, William	185	Best, John	Shaw, Williams	1010
Barton, Samuel	Ross, Nicholas	03	Beard, Lewis	Gray, Henry	1356	Betts, Archibald	Campbell, Laughlin	031
Barton, Samuel	Sers, James	293	Beard, Lewis	Smith, James	2366	Betts, Jonathan	Sheppard, Benjamin	379
Barton, Samuel	Skinner, Samuel	528	Beasley, John	Gloster, Thos	40	Betts, William	Cantrell, John	577
Barton, Samuel	Smith, Thomas	1382	Beates, John	Williams, Willoughby	2172	Betts, William	Hicks, Hansel	034
Barton, Samuel	Thow, Thomas	339	Beavears, John	Marshall, John	98	Betwoods, Samuel heirs	Williams, Willoughby	34
Baryer, George Henry	Artist, John	841	Beaver, John	Bushnell, Eusebrus & D	661	Bibby, Edmond heirs	Easten, James	1096
Baryer, George Henry	Clark, Ozburn	850	Beck, Geo. Heirs	Wooteon, David	2187	Biggett, Jesse	Askew, Wm.	1261
Basamore(?), Robt.	Blount, Reading	931	Beck, William	Row, George	255	Biggs, Nath	Hays, Robert	2398
Basded, Jacob	Sheppard, Benjamin	398	Beck, Williams	Pierson, Samuel	140	Biggs, Robt.	Williams, Etheldred	539
Basmore(?),Michl hrs	Blount, Reading	976	Bedwell, Zadock	Dixon, Jos.	302	Biggs, Silas	Blount, John Gray & Thoma	379
Bass, Briton	Donelson, John	600	Beeman, Francis hrs	Gilmoure, Charles	564	Bigworth, Stephen	Donelson, Stockley	027
Bass, Jonathan	Reed, Jesse	214	Belch, James hrs	Clark, William	1601	Billego, John	Reed, Jesse	212
Batchelor, George	Montflorence, James Cole	852	Bell, Elias heirs	Gordon, George	335	Binion, John	Bledsoe, Isaac,	768
Batchelor, George heirs	Montflorence, James Cole	852	Bell, Robert	Brown, James	1572	Bird, John heirs	Stewart, Charles	626
Bateman, Wm. Heirs	Stewart, Duncan	645	Bell, Robert	Jackson, James	1604	Bizzell, David hr.Enoch	Bizzle, Enos	160
Bates(Boles ?), Matt	Barton, Samuel	1687	Bellews, Charles	King, Robt & John Thom	1023	Bizzell, David hr.Enos	Bizzell, David hr.	160
Bates, Luke	Felts, Archibald	604	Belwood, Sam'l.	Oneill, Thomas	1889	Black, Martin	Wood, George	617
Batts, Sampson heirs	Sheppard, Benjamin	392	Benford, Isaac heirs	Sugg, George A.	970	Black, Peter heirs	Robertson, Elijah	814

Assignee Index

Assignee:	Claimant:	File #:	Assignee:	Claimant:	File #:	Assignee:	Claimant:	File
Blackamore, Geo.	Douglass, Elmore	068	Blount, Jno.G. & Thos	Harper, Frederick	2039	Blount, John Gray & Thom	Gardner, George	2107
Blackburn, Randolph	Blount, John Gray	56	Blount, Jno.G & Thos.	Lanier, James	32	Blount, John Gray & Thom	Sweat, David	1996
Blackface William	Turner, Andrew	568	Blount, Jno.G. & Thos.	Dosher, Christopher	377	Blount, John Gray & Thom	Willis, James	2001
Blackface, William	Banks, Richard	565	Blount, Jno. G. & Thos.	Guist, Thomas	2066	Blount, John Gray & Thos.	Rogers, Elisha	2104
Blackface, William	Hammond, Edmund	567	Blount, Jno.Gray &Thos.	Anderson, John	2013	Blount, John Grey	McGound, Thomas	1244
Blackface, William	Minshaw, Micajah	566	Blount, Jno.Gray &Thos.	Andrews, John	322	Blount, John Gray & Thom	Crow, William	2021
Blackface, William	Rothwell, William	2348	Blount, JnoGray & Thos	Collins, Joseph	2058	Blount, Reading	Bagworth, Jesse	937
Blackmore, Geo. D.	Lytle, Archibald	783	Blount, John	Angel, Thomas	30	Blount, Reading	Bazemore, Robert	931
Blacknell, John heirs	Sugg, Aquilla	902	Blount, John G. & Thomas	Rogers, Elisha	037	Blount, Reading	Bosmore, Michael	976
Bladsby, Joel	Blount, John Gray	012	Blount, John G. & Thos.	Meeks, Robt	1976	Blount, Reading	Bowler, James	968
Blair, James	Harrison, Gilbert	2032	Blount, John G. & Thos.	Parish, Henry	1998	Blount, Reading	Burden, Jacob	938
Blair, James	Watkins, Watter	1965	Blount, John G. & Thos.	Parish, Nicholas	618	Blount, Reading	Church, Christopher	937
Blair, John	Bennett, William	410	Blount, John G. & Thos.	Patton, John	440	Blount, Reading	Corne, Thomas	029
Blair, John	Elliot, Simon	271	Blount, John Gray	Abims [Abrams], Joseph	1048	Blount, Reading	Hardy, John	028
Blair, John	Pettigrew, Hara(?)	416	Blount, John Gray	Ballard, Jethro	011	Blount, Reading	Harrison, Henry	433
Blair, John	Ridden, John	1615	Blount, John Gray	Blackborn, Randolph	56	Blount, Reading	Miller, James	707
Blair, Thos.	Adcock, George	036	Blount, John Gray	Bodsby, Joel	012	Blount, Reading	Murdock, McCloud	898
Blake, John	Donoho, Thomas	065	Blount, John Gray	Bricklea, Thomas	592	Blount, Reading	Oglesby, Richard	432
Blamer, John heirs	Tatum, Howell	2436	Blount, John Gray	Browenen, John	013	Blount, Reading	Persythe, Joseph	033
Blan(?), Robt.	Davis, Joshua	792	Blount, John Gray	Craig, John	89	Blount, Reading	Raymore, Daniel	431
Blanchard, John	Walton, William	1748	Blount, John Gray	Dawson, Levi	667	Blount, Reading	Rever, James	434
Blaning, Peter hr John	Cloud, Joseph	1883	Blount, John Gray	Dillon, Benjamin	1035	Blount, Reading	Richards, Clement	936
Blanset, Frederick	Rice, John	22	Blount, John Gray	Dugald, John	151	Blount, Reading	Shaffer, Henry	437
Bledsoe, Abram & Henry	Bledsoe, Thos., Issac & Jno.	266	Blount, John Gray	Dunkinson, John	1947	Blount, Reading	Simons, Peter	827
Bledsoe, Anthony	Dean, Starling	675	Blount, John Gray	Hennis, Benbury	37	Blount, Reading	Siven, Joseph	987
Bledsoe, Anthony	Estis, Abraham	482	Blount, John Gray	McDaniel, John	44	Blount, Reading	Smith, Joel	435
Bledsoe, Anthony	Jacobs, Abraham	701	Blount, John Gray	McDaniels, Allen	08	Blount, Reading	Strand, John	708
Bledsoe, Anthony	Legars, James	704	Blount, John Gray	McNeese, John	1034	Blount, Reading	Tallafarrow, James	436
Bledsoe, Anthony	Lemare, Lewis	835	Blount, John Gray	McNess, John	013	Blount, Reading	Thompson, David	899
Bledsoe, Anthony	Peters, Daniel	502	Blount, John Gray	Province, John	1250	Blount, Reading	Thust, Edward	940
Bledsoe, Anthony	Stedmore, George	329	Blount, John Gray	Steadham, Tobias	07	Blount, Reading	Tripp, John	979
Bledsoe, Anthony	Steedmore, Peter	670	Blount, John Gray	Tyrrell, William	2289	Blount, Reading	Wallace, Brown	032
Bledsoe, Anthony	White, Jacob, Jr.	010	Blount, John Gray	Wheeler, Benjamin	06	Blount, Reading	Welch, William	438
Bledsoe, Isaac	Binion, John	768	Blount, John Gray	Williams, Thomas	45	Blount, Reading	Willis, John	711
Bledsoe, Isaac	Bristow, Philemon	012	Blount, John Gray	Young, Robert, Jr.	1247	Blount, Reading	Willis, Jacob	1520
Bledsoe, Isaac	Harris, Sherwood	721	Blount, John Gray & Thom	Adkins, Benjamin	2008	Blount, Reading	Willoughby, Nathan	939
Bledsoe, Isaac	Harris, Thompson	218	Blount, John Gray & Thom	Bliss, Silas	379	Blount, Reading	Wimer, Casper	955
Bledsoe, Isaac	Hicks, Robert	647	Blount, John Gray & Thom	Byrd, Moses	2103	Blount, Reading	Wolf, Abraham	900
Bledsoe, Isaac	McCann, Michael	614	Blount, John Gray & Thom	Capps, William	33	Blount, Reading	Wood, Solomon	439
Bledsoe, Isaac	McColl, Archibald	760	Blount, John Gray & Thom	Carpenter, William	1980	Blount, Redding	Williams, James	2221
Bledsoe, Isaac	Obarr, Daniel	011	Blount, John Gray & Thom	Darden, John	2106	Blount, Thomas	Ellison, Peter	010
Bledsoe, Isaac	Taylor, Isaac	566	Blount, John Gray & Thom	Dill, George	2031	Blount, Thomas	Howard, Benjamin	1950
Blough, Benjamin	McCullough, Benjamin	2055	Blount, John Gray & Thom	Dupont, Jesse	381	Blount, Thomas	Warwick, Shadrack	05
Blount, Jno. Gray	Hance, Job	1243	Blount, John Gray & Thom	Dupont, Joseph	276	Blount, William	Hooks, Ephraim	291

Assignee Index

Assignee:	Claimant:	File #
Bud, Samuel	Sumner, Jacob	681
Bud, Samuel	Wine, James	674
Bude, Samuel	Kenedy, Anthony	100
Buel, Ambrose (heir)	Moran, John	810
Buell, Samuel	Phillips, P & M. Campbell	1700
Bullard, Joab	Glasgow, James	045
Bullard, Waker(?)	Williams, Willoughby	324
Bullock, Drury	Bonner, John & James	771
Bullock, John	Tyrrell, William	075
Bullock, Lemuel hrs of	Casey, John	2272
Bunnett, John heirs	Hughlett, William	046
Bunnington, Wm.	Thompson, John	1522
Bunton, James	Williams, Willoughby	325
Burden, Archibald	Tuton, William	827
Burden, James' heirs	Nelson, Robert	2423
Burden, Thomas	McConnel, Robert	2413
Burden,Tim,hr of Jacob	Blount, Reading	938
Burgess, George	Harvey, Selby & Ant. Bledsoe	703
Burgess, William	Bray, Cornelious	558
Burgess, William	Gallop, Isaac	764
Burgess, William	Mains, William	761
Burgess, William	Sanderlin, Leevi	552
Burke, Charles	Wikoff & Clark	621
Burn, Andrew	Hays, John	87
Burnes, Barnabas	Wilson, John	1949
Burnes, James	Rowlan, Samuel	268
Burnham, Isaac	Tyrrell, William & Wm. Lytle	2320
Burnsides, David	Kirkpatrick, Michael;	1859
Burrington, Demcey	Hickman, Edwin	369
Burton, Jacob	Douglass, Edward	1514
Burton, John	Murphree, Hardy	57
Burton, Robert	Johnston, Briton	322
Bush, Aaron	Baker, John	776
Bushnell & Dobbins	Goodwin, Peter	847
Bushnell & Dobbins	Lyles, Benjamin	655
Bushnell & Dobbins	Woods, Matthew, Capt.	656
Bushnell & Dobbs	Hayse, William	660
Bushnell & Dobbs	Hill, Isaac	658
Bushnell & Dobbs	Jacobs, Daniel	651
Bushnell, E. & Dobbs	Beaver, John	661
Bushnell, E. & W. Dobbin	Dickey, Jacob	663
Bushnell, E. & W. Dobbin	Cole, Henry	657
Bushnell, E. & Wm. Dobbin	Dykes, John	662
Bushnell, E. & Wm. Dobbin	Simmons, Allason	659

Assignee:	Claimant:	File #
Bushnell, E. & Wm. Dobbi	Ward, John	654
Bushnell, E. & Wm. Dobbi	Davis, William	653
Bushnell, E. & Wm. Dobbi	Rollen, Henry	037
Bushnell, Eus & Wm Dobb	Williford, Joseph	650
Bushnell, Eusebius	Wikoff, William, Ass. [?]	080
Bushop, Colden	Trebell, Speller	2151
Bushop, Wm.	Sheppard, Wm. Etal	1675
Butler, Edward	Hays, Robert	671
Butler, Nathan	Brekon, James G	1724
Butler, Nathan hrs	Brehon, James G.	2465
Butts, Peter	Barton, Samuel	04
Butts, Wm.	Alford, Wm.	04
Butworth, James heirs	Williams, Willoughby	075
Buxton, William	Lilly, John	347
Buxton, Wm.	Teer, William	125
Byenom, Drury	Fort, Elias	273
Bynum, Eb.	Hinds, Levy	35
Byrd, Moses	Blount, John Gray & Tho	2103
Byrn, James	English, John	503
Cabbert, Richard	Nash, William	920
Cahoon, Joseph	Bosley, James Robert	1678
Caldwell, Lemuel heirs	Robertson, Elijah	810
Caldwell, Wm.	Robertson, Elijah	796
Cale, Geo. C. heirs	Comon, James	543
Callahan, John	Bowman, William	234
Callison, William	Smith, Oliver	155
Campbell, Andrew	Dillonberry, Redmon	051
Cameron, Alexander, hrs o	Molloy, James	08
Cameron, Alexr.	Bean, Jesse	939
Campbell, Andrew	Barry, Redmon Dillen	051
Campbell, Chas.	Barton, Samuel	1209
Campbell, Daniel	Hickman, Edwin	535
Campbell, James	Howard, Thomas	687
Campbell, Jas.	Robertson, Jas.	110
Campbell, Laughlan	Butts, Archibald	031
Campbell, M. & Phillip Phill	McKinns, Timothy	1697
Campbell, Michael	Phillips, Phillip	275
Campbell, Michael & P. Phi	Ewell, Samuel	1700
Campbell, Patrick	Gillespie, Wm.	846
Campbell, Patrick	Stewart, Duncan	599
Campbell, Wm.	Sullivan, Michael	193
Canady, James	Peters, Thomas	336
Cane, William heirs	Whitsett, John	949
Caney, Andrew	Hickman, Thomas	085

Assignee:	Claimant:	File
Cannady, Dav.	Easton, James	1098
Cannon, Edward heirs	Stewart, Duncan	2241
Cannon, Minos	Allhead, Vernon	1530
Cannon, Sampson	Donelson, S. & Jos. Beard	681
Cannon, Thos. Hrs.	Clark, Lardner	016
Cantrell, John	Betts, Wm.	577
Cantrell, Stephen	George, Britton	510
Cantrell, Stephen	Johnston, John	1402
Cantrell, Stephen	Weaver, Moses	1003
Cantwell, Stephen	Mackleway, John	942
Capehart, John	Williams, Willoughby	2171
Capps, James heirs	Wykoff, Wm & Lardn.Clark	822
Capps, William	Blount, John Gray & Thoma	33
Capton, John	Greer, Alex & Jas Robertso	1674
Carbar, Jas.	Donelson, S. & Jno. Latham	423
Card, Joseph heirs	Harget, Frederick	2229
Caree, John	Donelson, S. & Wm. Tyrrell	461
Carey, Wm. Heirs	Easten, Jas.	1093
Carleton, John hrs	Coghlin, James	2269
Carleton, John hrs	Drake, Jonathan	1022
Carmack, Joseph	Hobbs, Joel	036
Carnahan, Andrew	McKinley, Daniel	706
Carney, Arthur	Donelson, John	1492
Carpenter, William	Blount, John Gray & Thoma	1980
Carraway, Thomas	Sheppard, Nancy	719
Carrick, Zach heirs	Nelson, Robert	589
Carroll, William	Sheppard, Nancy	2044
Carroll, Douglas	Hill, Bennett	1614
Carroll, Harwell	Marshall, John	488
Carron, James	Hickman, Thomas	785
Carson, James	Oneal, Matthias	2049
Carson, James	O'Neil, Matthew	035
Carson, John	Sheppard, Wm. Etal	1676
Carter, Anthony heirs	Buckman, Samuel	338
Carter, Charles	McLaughlin, Neill	1207
Carter, David	Dean, James	1932
Carter, George	Gilston, David	2282
Carter, George hrs.	Brock, Joseph	842
Carter, Henry hrs	Fenner, Richard	332
Carter, Humphrey	Kilgore, Thomas	2310
Carter, Isaac heirs	Wheaton, Daniel	2449
Carter, Jno & Landon	Calloway, Richard	06
Carter, John	Dennis, William	1443
Carter, John	Sullivant, Lucas	673

Assignee:	Claimant:	File #:	Assignee:	Claimant:	File #:	Assignee:	Claimant:	File
Carter, Jos	Barton, Samuel.	299	Charlescraft, Jas.	McCall, Alex.	056	Clark, Lardner	Styron, Samuel	670
Carter, Landon	Clinton, John	1682	Chas Carlson & Baker	Givins, James & others	138	Clark, Lardner	Taddis, Andrew	613
Carter, Landon	Coffey, Cheslie	07	Chase, Philemon	Cobb, Jesse	382	Clark, Lardner	Tetner, Henry	668
Carter, Robert	Murphrey, Hardy	229	Chason, Joshua	Tatom, Howell	1679	Clark, Lardner & Wycoff	Farmer, William	119
Carter, Saml.	Harris, Edward	1152	Cheek, William	Cheek, John	2	Clark, Lardner, Esq.	Cannon, Thomas	016
Cartwright, Robert	Ferrell, Enoch	855	Chermey, Robert	Guille M. Devereax	114	Clark, Neil heirs	Stewart, Duncan	602
Cartwright, Robert	Lewellen, Thomas	1726	Cherry, Job heirs	Fenner, Richard	331	Clark, Osborn	Baryer, George Henry	850
Carver, Robt & Wm.	Braswell, Richd	01415	Cherry, Jonathan	Sugg, Aquilla	891	Clark, Vachell	Hearn, George	543
Casbol, Robert	Lomack, William	2296	Cherry, Willie	Hicks, James	1	Clark, William	Belch, James	1501
Casey, John	Bullock, Lemuel	2272	Cherry, Jess hr of Jno.	Breaky, Andrew	305	Clark, William	Marshall, John	483
Casey, John	McCullock, Alex	2271	Chesnut, Jas.	Harris, Edward	1129	Clark, William	Phillips, Mann	678
Cash, John	Armstrong, Martin	1473	Chesson, James	Donelson, S. & Wm. Tyr	1081	Clayton, Miles heirs	Donelson, Srock & W.Tyrrell	1080
Casleman, Benjamin	Cole, Burwell	942	Chester, David	Spencer, Thomas	188	Clendening, John	Devining, James	946
Cason, William	James, Daniel	089	Chester, Robert	Sheppard, Nancy	2102	Clendennin, John	Hambleton, William	1147
Cason, William	James, Daniel	892	Childers, John hrs.	Keagey, John	571	Clifton, Absalom hrs	Galloway, Charles	972
Casselman, Andrew	Stobotle, James	334	Childers, Robert hrs	Lenear, James	704	Clifton, Daniel	Hamilton, Thomas	0134
Casselman, Jacob	McKeel, Joshua	286	Chisum, Ignatius	Donelson, John	2275	Clifton, Richard heirs	Donelson, Stockley	1187
Cassliman, Benjamin	Cloyd, John	269	Christee, John	Brown, John	453	Clifton, Richd.	Hays, Sarah	141
Cassleman, Benjamin	Phillips, George	340	Christian, James	Drake, Jonathan	194	Clinton, John	Carter, Landon	1682
Castendree, Metre	Donelson, Stockley	965	Christmas, John	Hogan, Humphrey	201	Cloud, Daniel	Ray, Wm.	638
Castle, Thomas	Sheppard, William	507	Chunney, John	Johnston, William	200	Cloud, Joseph	Blaning, John	1883
Castleman, Jacob	Price, William	604	Church, Christo. Hrs.	Blount, Reading	937	Cloud, Peter	Johnston, Daniel	172
Castleton, Pearce	Cockrell, John	234	Church, Christopher	Peyton, Thomas	0106	Clower, Wm.	Robertson, Michael	0110
Caswell, Richard	Sevier, Jno.	549	Clark, Abraham heirs	Donelson, Wood & McC	192	Cloyd, John	Cassliman, Benj.	269
Caswell, Richard, heir of W	Wilcock, David	646	Clark, Abraham heirs	Williams, Eliza	578	Coast, John	Totevine, Winder	081
Caswell, William	Hudler, Joseph	210	Clark, Benj. Heirs	Stewart, Duncan	601	Cobb, Anthony heirs	Mulherin, James	913
Caswell, William	Hudler, Lemuel	669	Clark, Daniel Howell heirs	Wikcoff,Wm & Lardin. Cl	757	Cobb, Jesse	Albritton, Henry	420
Caswell, Wm hr Wm.	Hudder, John	647	Clark, Jas. & Wm.	Robeson, Edward	350	Cobb, Jesse	Anderson, John	292
Cat-ch, John hrs.	Brock, Joseph	834	Clark, Jno heir of Josiah	Sheppard, Nancy	2095	Cobb, Jesse	Chance, Philemon	382
Cates, Benj.	Robertson, James	1022	Clark, Lardner	Duglas, William	240	Cobb, Jesse	Cooper, Nathaniel	383
Cates, Joshua	Huse, Samuel	023	Clark, Lardner	Guthrop, John	038	Cobb, Jesse	Gray, Samuel	1995
Cates, Mathew	Thompson, Robert	189	Clark, Lardner	Holdman, Mordeca	675	Cobb, Jesse	Hale, Josiah	419
Cates, Wm.	Newman, Isaac	1608	Clark, Lardner	Holf—?, Mordice	675	Cobb, Jesse	Hopkins, Jonathan	422
Cates, Zachariah	Fulkison, Abraham	01	Clark, Lardner	Huddleston, William	1680	Cobb, Jesse	Lane, John	0141
Cathey, Richard	Weaver, William	1000	Clark, Lardner	Jackson, Job	2305	Cobb, Jesse	Lane, Thomas	691
Cathey, William	Deal, John	1921	Clark, Lardner	Jones, Thomas	106	Cobb, Jesse	Rayford, John	414
Cathey, William	Garrett, William	1011	Clark, Lardner	Lewis, Charles	669	Cobb, Jesse	Regans, John	421
Cator, John	Sheppard, Benjamin	382	Clark, Lardner	Liskow, Thomas	182	Cobb, Jesse	Rogers, Joseph	293
Chadwick, Benjamin	Glasgow, James	2217	Clark, Lardner	Martin, John	262	Cobb, Jesse	Shilks, Lewis	423
Chamberlain, Henry heirs	Williams, Willoughby	326	Clark, Lardner	Parker, Jeptha	1601	Cobb, Jesse	Stafford, Josiah	291
Chano(?), David	Boyd, John	1214	Clark, Lardner	Patterson, Hardy	1574	Cobb, Jesse	Stradley, James	2009
Chapman, Samuel	Bonner, John	759	Clark, Lardner	Ramsey, Mills	1681	Cobb, Jesse	Taylor, Jeffrey	667
Chappel, Edward	Oneill, Thomas	055	Clark, Lardner	Robertson, Jesse	820	Cobb, Jesse	Warren, William	303
Chappelle, Wm. Heirs	Oneill, Thomas	140	Clark, Lardner	Smithwick, James	114	Cobb, Jessie	Jones, Wm.	085

Assignee Index

Assignee:	Claimant:	File #	Assignee:	Claimant:	File #	Assignee:	Claimant:	File
Cobb, Jos, Duke, & McDaniel	McCoy, Roger	048	Colton, Thos.	Hafler, Thomas	737	Cooper, Solomon hrs	Fenner, Richard	329
Cobb, Peter heirs	Mountflorence, James Cole	327	Colvin, John heirs	Easten, James	1091	Cooper, Thomas	Donelson, S. & Jos. Beard	680
Cobb, Shadrack hrs	Drake, Benjamin	1515	Colvin, Obed	Hart, Anthony	739	Copeland, Joab	Malloy, Thomas	2338
Cobb, Wm.	Anderson, Danl	62	Colwell, John	Fort, Elias	294	Copeland, Kedar	Long, Nicholas	358
Cobb, Zebb heirs	Malloy, Thomas	558	Coman, James	Foster, William	541	Copeland, Replay	Devers, John	039
Cobbs, Anthony	Mulherrin, James	2138	Coman, James	Galders, George	540	Copeland, Richard	Brown, John	1603
Cochran, Jas. Hrs	Cochran, Wm.	31	Coman, James	Gale, George C.	543	Copeland, Stephen heir	Mayfield, Sutterline	117
Cochran, William	Mays, John	30	Coman, James	Gilkey, Samuel	2357	Corben, Francis hrs	Buckanen, John	2276
Cockran, William	Murdock, Allen	28	Coman, James	Swearingham, Zan or Va	1290	Corbin, Francis	Donelson, Stockley	672
Cockran, William	Nickelson, James	31	Coman, James	White, Jacob	534	Corbin, James heirs	Donelson, Stockley	193
Coffee, Henry	Buckle, Thomas	1768	Coman, James	Wright, Stephen	1291	Corbin, James heirs	Williams, Eliza	577
Coffery, John	Holley, John	06	Coman, James	Wright, Stephen	1292	Corderey, John	Danges, Jacob	783
Coffery, John	Thompson, Lawrance	2303	Combs, William	Sitgreaves, Joseph	041	Cormack, John	Pearson, James	2080
Coffery, John	Thompson, Laurence	2088	Comon, James	East, Sampson	535	Cornelius, Elijah heirs	Philips, Isaac	426
Coffield, Benj.	Tyrrell, Wm.	477	Conester, John heirs	Thompson, Jason	828	Coryer, Stephen	Dorris, Joseph	031
Coghill, James	Peney, Francis	2268	Conner, Chris.hrs.	Armstrong, Andrew	857	Cosman, James	Empson, John	2356
Coghlin, James	Carleton, John	843	Conner, Davey	Robertson, Jas.	1668	Cothram, John	Lee, James,	2224
Coghlin, James	Gafford, William	2270	Conner, John	Berry, Thomas	665	Cotten, Thomas	Smith, James	260
Coit, Farwell	Collins, Matthew	493	Conner, Wm.	Barry, Redmon Dillen	052	Cotton, Ephraim	Sheppard, Nancy	2093
Coit, Farwell	Speight, Joseph	494	Conner, Wm.	Dillonberry, Redmon	052	Cotton, John	Thompson, Thos & Saml.	31
Colanch, Peter heirs	Thompson, Jason	1540	Conners, James	Phillips, P & M. Campbell	1699	Cotton, Thomas	Smith, James, heir of Josep	086
Colbert, Laurence	Hart, Anthony	843	Conrad, Nichollas	Harris, Thomas	941	Cotton, Thomas	Smith, Joseph	2313
Colbey, John	Stewart, Duncan	2377	Conrod, Nicholas	Phelps, Garrett	371	Council(?), Arthur	Council, James	170
Colby, Absalmon	Sheppard, Benjamin	380	Conrod, Nicholas	Rowland, James	2186	Cowenan, Benjamin	Sheppard, Benjamin	387
Colden, Phillip	Williams, Sampson	1504	Conway, Joseph	McCafferty, James, Ass	679	Cowan, James	Williams, Willoughby	2173
Cole, Burwell	Caseleman, Benm.	942	Cook, Frederick heirs	Tyrrell, William	2266	Cowan, John	Donelson, Stockley	02
Cole, Henry	Bushnell, Eusebrus & Dobbins	657	Cook, Isaac	Davis, Joshua	465	Cowan, Joseph	Tatum, Howell	2437
Cole, Jas or Edward heirs	Nichols, John	425	Cook, Jonah	Sanford, Samuel	1961	Coward, Peter	Ford, John	882
Cole, Jesse	Taylor, Thomas	150	Cook, Richard	Faybourne, Joel	658	Cowin, Absolim	Hickman, Thomas	086
Cole, Martin	Nichols, John	409	Cook, Richard	Harrold, John	1376	Cox, Charles	Johnson, Thomas	1575
Cole, William Pample	Johnston, John	145	Cook, Richard	Smith, William	1375	Cox, Phenix	Duffy, Peter	038
Coleman, Spilley	Toney, Anthony	602	Cook, Richard	Weaken, Stephen	1466	Cox, Thomas	Newman, Anthony	2120
Collet, John heirs	McConnel, Robert,	2414	Cooke, Richard	Hays, Thomas	1374	Cox, Thomas	Tatum, Howell	47
Collier, Josiah	Nichols, John	735	Cooker, John heirs	Nichols, John	422	Coyard, David	Whitard, Wm.	241
Collins, Brittain hrs.	Brock, Joseph	35	Cooley, Samuel	Montflorence	92	Crab, Richard	Sheppard, Nancy	2098
Collins, Burwell	Harris, Edward	1155	Cooley, Samuel	Montflorence, James Col	92	Crabb, Benjamin	Weakley, Robert	1887
Collins, Dillard	Harris, Edward	1154	Coon, Conrod	White, Daniel	8	Crabtree, James	Douglas, Ed. & Wm. Montg.	1228
Collins, George heirs	Donelson, Stockley	968	Coonrod, Nicholas	Bean, Robert	397	Crabtree, John	Farmer, Thomas	1102
Collins, John	West, Eli	914	Coonrod, Nicholas	Holland, William	526	Crabtree, Jos.	Eackart, David	2302
Collins, Joseph	Blount, John Gray & Thomas	2058	Coons, Thos. Hrs.	Blount, Reading	029	Craddock, John	Dove, William	1526
Collins, Matt	Coit, Farwell	493	Coonurod [sic], Nicholas	Bateman, Navey	668	Craddock, John	Roberts, Hardy	1538
Collins, Samuel heirs	Mountflorence, James Cole	326	Cooper, Jacob heir of Nat.	Sheppard, Nancy	695	Craddock, John	Wiggins, Thomas	1534
Collins, William	Gise(?), Jonathan	557	Cooper, Nath.	Cobb, Jesse	383	Craddocks,Jno.	Armstrong, John	1471
Colson, Isaac	Wells, Daniel	592	Cooper, Robert	Robertson, Jesse	458	Crafford, Hugh	Kuykendall, Samuel	907

Assignee:	Claimant:	File #:
Dean, Starling	Bledsoe, Anthony	675
Decern, Francis	Kirby, Edmund;	2119
Dedrick, Geo. Michael	Harris, Job	2428
Dedrick, Jacob	Weakley, Robert	993
Defnel(?), Wm.	Donelson, John & Samuel	2060
Delaney, A. J. hrs	Easton, James	1038
Delaney, John	Hogg, Thomas	740
Delaney, Michael	Harris, Edward	1149
Delivay, George	Reed, Jesse	460
Dellenberry, Redmond	Bayler, John	049
Demcey, David	Weakley, Robert	1927
Dennet, William	Lytle, Archibald	093
Denning, Jas.	Robertson, Jas.	642
Dennis, William	Brock, Joseph	95
Denton & Baldridge	Stuart, David, Jno. McNabb &	99
Derden, Joseph	Barry, Redman Dillen	057
Dever, John	Howard, Edward	284
Devers, John	Copeland, Repley	039
Devers, John	Dillard, Osborn	021
Devonshire, Joshua	Baker, John	09
Dew, John	Rogers, Abraham	302
Dickerson, Henry	Totevine, Wm.	182
Dickey, Jacob hrs	Bushnell, Eusebrus & Dobbins	663
Dickey, Thomas	Eller, Joseph	268
Dickey, Thomas	McDaniel, Alexander	251
Dickner, David	King, Robert	683
Dickson, Edward	Bailey, John	24
Dickson, Edward	Mott, Daniel	209
Dickson, James	Lamb, Glibbs	188
Dickson, James	Morrow, Thomas	207
Dickson, James	Pitnor, John	214
Dickson, Joel	Shackler, Phillip	042
Dickson, John	Dillar, John	020
Dickson, John	Griffin, Joseph	183
Dickson, John	Hair, James	206
Dickson, John	Harris, Nathan	190
Dickson, John	Merrit, William	191
Dickson, John	Wilkins, Elisha	163
Dickson, John	Wilson, Jacob	199
Dickson, Joseph	Barnes, William	751
Diggs, Anthony	Bonner, John & James	522
Diggs, William heirs	Robertson, Elijah	812
Dilenberry, Redmon	Malone, Jacob	039
Dill, George	Blount, John Gray & Thomas	2031

Assignee:	Claimant:	File #:
Dillan, Benj.	Blount, John Gray	1035
Dillard, John	Robertson, James	1911
Dillard, Osburn	Devers, John	021
Dillard, Peter	Fenner, Richard	325
Dillard, Sampson	Fort, Elias	805
Dillard, William	Harrison, Patrick	998
Dillonbarry, Redmon	Hoggard, William	1278
Dilebo, Andrew heirs	Williams, Daniel	2389
Dillenberry, Redman	Sherlock, Demsey	025
Dillenberry, Redmod	Phelps, John	034
Dillenberry, Redmon	Bond, Charles	054
Dillenberry, Redmon	Conner, William	052
Dillenberry, Redmon	Derden, Joseph	057
Dillenberry, Redmon	Dillon, Thomas	047
Dillenberry, Redmon	Earpe, John	056
Dillenberry, Redmon	Faulkner, Francis	055
Dillenberry, Redmon	Garner, Gregory	048
Dillenberry, Redmon	Greer, John Gee	044
Dillenberry, Redmon	Ham, John	028
Dillenberry, Redmon	Howard, John	045
Dillenberry, Redmon	Letchmore, Watson	040
Dillenberry, Redmon	Reynolds, Silvester	035
Dillenberry, Redmon	Shaw, Harmon	024
Dillenberry, Redmon	Start, Henry	038
Dillenberry, Redmon	Stowbridge, John	027
Dillenberry, Redmon	Strong, George	026
Dillenberry, Redmon	Whitfield, Wilson	023
Dillenberry, Redmon	Yarby, Joseph	036
Dillenberry, Redmon [sic]	Mintore, John	041
Dillenberry, Redmond	Campbell, Andrew	051
Dillenberry, Redmond	Jordan, Ptolomy	022
Dillenberry, Redmond	Nicholson, Isaac	043
Dillenberry, Redmond	Nowland, Jesse	042
Dillenberry, Redmond	O'Conner, Sullivan	037
Dillenberry, Redmond	Oggden, Dempsey	031
Dillenberry, Redmond	Oglesby, Nehemiah	032
Dillenberry, Redmond	Ouss, Jonathan	2385
Dillenberry, Redmond	Owen, John	033
Dillenberry, Redmond	Seasever, John	050
Dillenberry, Redmond [sic]	Bigby, James	053
Diller, John heirs	Dickson, John	020
Dillon Barry, Redmond	Lucas, Matthew	1281
Dillon Barry, Remond	Lewton, Leonard	1279

Assignee:	Claimant:	File
Dillon, Benj.	Blount, John Gray	1237
Dillon, Thomas	Dillonberry, Redmon	047
Dillon, Thos.	Barry, Redman Dillen	047
Dillon, William	Witty, James	058
Dillonberry, Redmon	Hood, Archibald	30
Dillonberry, Redmon	Hughes, Bartley	029
Dillonbarry, Redmon	Lewis, Thomas	1282
Dillonberry, Remon	Donelson, John	310
Dillum, Jas.	Hudson, George	247
Dix, William	Robertson, James	1935
Dix,(Dees?) Abraham	Gunter, Joel	954
Dixon, Charles	Gubbins, William	360
Dixon, Henry hrs.	Womble, Benjamin	2006
Dixon, John	Badwell, Zadock	302
Dixon, Joseph	Lambert, Aron	385
Dixon, Thomas	Obarr, Michael	457
Dixon, Tilghman	Obarr, Robert	596
Dixon, Tilghman	Southerland, William	2050
Dixon, Tilghman	York, Will	741
Dixon, Tilghman	Roberts, Venson	956
Dixon, Tilman	Jackson, Thomas	478
Dixon, Tilmon	Jacobs, Peter	2051
Dixon, Tilmon	King, James	059
Dixon, Tilmon	Vaughan, James	1641
Dobbins, William	Hadley, Joshua	516
Dobbins, William	Hadley, Joshua	576
Dobbins, Wm.	Armtrong, John	46
Dobbs & Bushnell	Gwinn, Jacob	652
Dobson, Elias	Johnson, Henry	07
Dodd, Jesse	King, Robert	419
Dodd, Thomas	Barry, Redmon D.	1354
Dodson, Charles	Donelson, S. & James Latha	1021
Dodson, John	Stump, Christopher	2144
Doly, James heirs	Mulherin, James	933
Dominas, Domina heirs	Rice, Jno.,Elisha &Abra Rist	313
Donahoe, John	Berkley, William	563
Donald, William	Boyd, Thomas	855
Donaldson, John	Ryal, Joseph	151
Donelly, James	Howard, Isaac	355
Donelson & Armstrong	Harrell, Holland	034
Donelson & Armstrong	Poe, John	035
Donelson & Terrell	Pike, Samuel	062
Donelson & Tyrrell	Newberry, William	463
Donelson S.	Bruce, George	1089

Assignee:	Claimant:	File #:	Assignee:	Claimant:	File #:	Assignee:	Claimant:	File
Donelson, Jesse	Donelson, Stockley	2261	Donelson, S. & Wm. Tyrrel	Vance, John	018	Donelson, Stockley	Myres, Jacob	2259
Donelson, John	Angel, Thomas	1269	Donelson, S., Robt Wood	Clark, Abraham	192	Donelson, Stockley	Nelson, Jesse	040
Donelson, John	Ashers, Charles	683	Donelson, Stockley	Andrews, John Cole	0138	Donelson, Stockley	Parker, Hillary	2255
Donelson, John	Bailey, William	1489	Donelson, Stockley	Beach, Robert	9	Donelson, Stockley	Pope, Samuel	1151
Donelson, John	Chisum, Ignatius	2275	Donelson, Stockley	Bigworth, Stephen	027	Donelson, Stockley	Pratt, James	2379
Donelson, John	Crowell, Rowland	040	Donelson, Stockley	Boxley, John	1246	Donelson, Stockley	Reed, Joseph	1085
Donelson, John	Daughty, Samuel	2115	Donelson, Stockley	Clifton, Richard	1187	Donelson, Stockley	Roberts, John	476
Donelson, John	Dillum, James	310	Donelson, Stockley	Corbin, James	193	Donelson, Stockley	Robertson, Hooker	676
Donelson, John	Elkins, Joseph	2274	Donelson, Stockley	Craigge, Archibald	1194	Donelson, Stockley	Rogers, James	1076
Donelson, John	Freeman, John	966	Donelson, Stockley	Crockley, Allen	041	Donelson, Stockley	Saunders, Peter	043
Donelson, John	Freeman, William	2195	Donelson, Stockley	Daget, James	2254	Donelson, Stockley	Smith, Thomas	2264
Donelson, John	Gale, Daniel	746	Donelson, Stockley	Davis, Ralph	1310	Donelson, Stockley	Stillwell, Jeremiah	1260
Donelson, John	Gay, William	682	Donelson, Stockley	Donelson, Jesse	2261	Donelson, Stockley	Stringer, Lineage	2263
Donelson, John	Griffin, James	745	Donelson, Stockley	Dugan, Jesse	283	Donelson, Stockley	Stringer, Simon	063
Donelson, John	Groves, Nicholas	1972	Donelson, Stockley	Elmore, Morgan	1239	Donelson, Stockley	Thomas, Jeremiah	017
Donelson, John	Hartley, John	2024	Donelson, Stockley	Garrett, William	014	Donelson, Stockley	Todd, Josiah	015
Donelson, John	Kerney, Arthur	1492	Donelson, Stockley	Garris, Stephen	1193	Donelson, Stockley	Vickory, John	016
Donelson, John	Lamb, Nathan	1969	Donelson, Stockley	Gideon, Richard	039	Donelson, Stockley	Whitfield, Jesse	186
Donelson, John	Laughlin, Cornelius	1389	Donelson, Stockley	Gowan, David	040	Donelson, Stockley	Williamson, John	1192
Donelson, John	Lenoir, Charles	1387	Donelson, Stockley	Gray, Peter	967	Donelson, Stockley	Williamson, John	2257
Donelson, John	McCabe, Peter	1642	Donelson, Stockley	Gunter, Samuel	1309	Donelson, Stockley	Wimple, William	05
Donelson, John	Mitchell, John	681	Donelson, Stockley	Hammett, John	964	Donelson, Stockley	Winday, Absalam	2381
Donelson, John	Norton, Jeremiah	2386	Donelson, Stockley	Hay, Abraham	2262	Donelson, Stockley & Willi	Whitney, James	2228
Donelson, John	Ruth, John	1388	Donelson, Stockley	Henry, Jonathan	041	Donelson, Stockley	Castendre, Metre [sic]	965
Donelson, John	Simmons, Malia	060	Donelson, Stokley	Hodgin, Holder	943	Donelson, Stokley	Collins, George	968
Donelson, John	Smith, Benjamin	2273	Donelson, Stokley	Holloway, John	1188	Donelson, Stokley	Crawley, William	961
Donelson, John	Templeton, Thomas	2325	Donelson, Stockley	Hudgins, James	1238	Donelson, Stokley	Ingrim, George	963
Donelson, John	Webb, Joshua	1197	Donelson, Stockley	Hughs, Burwell	2258	Donelson, Stokley	James, Charles	08
Donelson, John & Samuel	Deferel, William	2060	Donelson, Stockley	Hy, Abraham	2262	Donelson, Stokley	Tucker, William	960
Donelson, S & Joseph Bear	Croker, Thomas	680	Donelson, Stockley	Jessop, Isaac	2227	Donelson, Stokley	Smart, Thomas	540
Donelson, S & W. Tyrrel	Perry, William	1084	Donelson, William	Jones, Peter	491	Donelson, William	Blake, William	068
Donelson, S & W. Tyrrel	Perry, William	1087	Donoho, (sic) Thomas	King, Edward	2260	Donoho, Thomas	Hicks, Reubin	1229
Donelson, S.	Bailey, Morris	023	Donoho, Thomas	Kites, William	596	Donohoe, Thomas	Blake, John	065
Donelson, S.	Mardera, James	464	Donohoe, William	Laine, Thomas	061	Donohoe, William	Sanders, James	770
Donelson, S. & Jas. Latham	Dodson, Charles	1021	Donstan, James	Magby, Robert	594		Bowman, William	26
Donelson, S. & Jas. Latham	Tilley, Lewis	1020	Dooston, Abraham	Matchett, Edward	1248		Isbell, Thomas	762
Donelson, S. & John Latha	Canbon, James	423	Dorman, West	McCumber, Humphrey	2380		Reed, Jesse	233
Donelson, S. & John Latha	Proudford, James	1024	Dorris, Joseph	McDaniel, Alexander	1186		Coryer, Stephen	031
Donelson, S. & John Latha	Wren, William	1025	Dosher, Chris	McMurty, William	2		Blount, John Gray & thomas	377
Donelson, S. & Joseph Bea	Stevenson, Peter	684	Doty, James	McNulty, John	1189		Mulherin, James	2137
Donelson, S. & Robt. Youg	Mason, Phillip	414	Douglas & Wm. Montgom	Melory, Thomas	064		Crabtree, James	1228
Donelson, S. & W. Terrell	Dillon, Benjamin	022	Douglas, David	Mills, Elijah	2256		Farmer, John	1616
Donelson, S. & Wm. Terrel	McCoy, James	2226	Douglas, Edward	Mills, William	026		Ellis, Underhill	1226
Donelson, S. & Wm. Tyrrell	Caree, John	461	Douglas, Edward	Morris, Richard	674		Seymore, William	851

Assignee:	Claimant:	File #:	Assignee:	Claimant:	File #:	Assignee:	Claimant:	File
Douglas, James	Hays, John	069	Duggin, John	Harris, Edward	1121	Easton, James	Jordan, Jones	1097
Douglas, John	Guttery, Henry	1049	Duggin, William	Walker, George	2053	Easton, James	McAdoe, James	1039
Douglas, Jonathan	Stuart, David etal	560	Duglas, Wm.	Clark, Lardner	240	Easton, James	Mccoy, Dugald	1044
Douglas, Reubin	Howell, John	523	Duke, Green heirs	Gamble, Edmond	357	Easton, James	Moore, Davis John	1041
Douglass & Sharp	Harris, Claibourn	520	Duke, Plea. McDaniel, & C	Duke, Plea	048	Easton, James	Orme, James (sic)	1092
Douglass, Edward	Burton, Jacob	1514	Duke, Sherod	Sanders, William	489	Easton, James	Parnel, Joshua	1094
Douglass, Edward	Miller, James	545	Dukes, Arthur hrs	Fenner, Richard	330	Easton, James	Reed, Walson	1040
Douglass, Edward	Mills, Jacob	997	Dukes, Elisha	Sheppard, Benjamin	696	Easton, James	Tyson, Grisham	1037
Douglass, Edward	Ross, John	067	Dunbar, Dun(?)	Fort, Elias	271	Easton, James	Weaver, John	1045
Douglass, Elmore	Blackmore, George	068	Dunbar, Isaac heirs	Robertson, Elijah	813	Easton, James	Whitfield, Jesse	071
Douglass, John	Armstrong, Martin	580	Duncan, Jesse	Robertson, Charles	1728	Easton, Samuel Wistner	Tyrrell, Wm. & James	076
Douglass, Reuben	Howell, John	523	Duncan, Martin	Cubbins, William	013	Eaton, James	Goodwin, William	1042
Douglass, William	Abbott, Waddington	545	Duncan, William	Marshall, John	486	Eaton, John	Luter, Andrew	22
Douglass, William	Brewer, Henry	547	Dundelow, Benj.	McKey, Alex	096	Eaton, John	Spear, Seth	1513
Dove, William	Craddock, John	1526	Dundels, Hugh heirs	Sheppard, John	070	Eaton, John	Eaton, John	2393
Dowd, Cornelius	McDonald, Colin	036	Dunham, Daniel	McLean, Ephraim;	1332	Eaton, Pinkerton	McCulloh, Benjamin	2026
Dowde, John	Williams, Daniel	1997	Dunkinson, John	Blount, John Gray	1947	Echols, Abner	McCulloh, Benjamin	343
Dowden, Samuel	Nelson, Robert	1732	Dunlap, Thomas heirs	Mann, John	2434	Edens, John	Sutton, Bailey	619
Dowell, James	Hall, David	082	Dunlop, Hugh	Wood, Cather, etal	560	Edge, Jno.	Robertson, James	632
Dowell, James	Murphree, Archibald	648	Dunn, Thomas heirs	McCulloch, Benj.	034	Edge, Jos. Heirs	Stewart, Duncan	600
Downing, George	Wikoff, William	094	Dunnick, Peter	Tyrrell, Wm.	584	Edge, Thos heirs	Robertson, James	1664
Drahorn, John	Glasgow, James	2218	Dunning, James	Robertson, James	057	Edmonds, Abel	Weeks, Theophilus	1576
Drake, Benj.	Byrnes, James	1903	Duplicate Warrants	Copenhafer, Thomas	0101	Edmunson, Thomas	Godfrey, Clement	5
Drake, Benjamin	Cobb, Shadrack	1515	Dupont, Jesse	Blount, John Gray & Tho	381	Edward Harris	Jewell, Samuel	1156
Drake, Jonathan	Carlton, John	1022	Dupont, Joseph	Blount, John Gray & Tho	276	Edward Harris	Johnson, Richard	115
Drake, Jonathan	Christian, James	194	Dupree, Meal	Brown, Chas.	034	Edwards, David	Pearce, Thomas	127
Drake, Jonathan	Elliott, Thomas	1915	Dupree, Meal hrs	Brown, Charles	084	Edwards, David	Ray, Stephen	213
Drake, Jonathan	Ellis, Robt.	522	Durham, Jachariah hrs	Donelson, Stockley, Ass.	1088	Edwards, Robert	Beaird, Jos. & Wm.Terrell	261
Drake, Jonathan	Evans, Joseph	997	Duroy, Timothy	Boyd, John	1405	Edwick, Edwd.	Elliot, John, heirs of	1872
Drake, Jonathan	Laton, William	224	Dyer, Joel	Hyde, Andrew	420	Ekols, Wm.	Bonner, John & James	629
Drake, Jonathan	Sanders, Peter	979	Dykes, John	Bushnell, Eusebrus & D	662	Elijah Robertson	Gole, Stephen	816
Drew, John	Lewis, Matthew	249	Ea(?)man, Benjamin	Davis, Elisha	122	Elijah Robertson	Harrell, Thomas	811
Drew, John	Minory, George	1557	Earpe, John	Barry, Redmon Dillen	056	Eliza Williams	Harrell, Holland	580
Drew, John	Welsh, Thomas	1556	Easins, Thos.	Tatum, Howell	83	Elkins, Jos. Heirs	Donelson, John	2274
Driskiel, David	Hill, Green	222	Eason, Mason heirs	Lewis, William Tyrrell	561	Eiler, Jno, heir of Jos.	Dickey, Thomas	268
Ducanna, James	McCulloh, Benjamin	2015	East, Sampson hrs	Comon, James	535	Elliot, John	Boren, Stephen	488
Dudley, Bennet	Robertson, Patsey	801	Easten, James	Bibby, Edmond	1096	Elliot, John	Shaw, Robert	1905
Dudley, Matthias	Robertson, Elijah	798	Easten, James	Cannady, David	1098	Elliot, Wm heir of Joseph	Williams, Turner	978
Duffey, John	Barton, Samuel	531	Easten, James	Carey, William	1093	Elliott, James	Bryan, James	458
Duffnel, David	Lewis, Seth & Geo Walker	271	Easten, James	Etheredge, Edward	1095	Elliott, John	Edwick, Edwd.	1872
Duffy, Peter	Cox, Phenix	038	Easter, Moses	Wikoff, Wm.	347	Elliott, John	Englin, Cornelius	033
Dugald, John	Blount, John Gray	151	Easton, James	Andrews, Watson	1036	Elliott, John	Grant, Rubin	2069
Dugan, Jesse	Donelson, Stockley	283	Easton, James	Colvin, John	1091	Elliott, John	McCarty, Jacob	489
Duggan, Jesse heirs	Williams, Eliza	582	Easton, James	Delainey, A. J.	1038	Elliott, John	McVey, John	1598

Assignee:	Claimant:	File #:	Assignee:	Claimant:	File #:	Assignee:	Claimant:	File
Elliott, John	Williams, Sampson etal	0126	Faddis, Andrew hrs	Clark, Lardner	613	Fenner, Richard	Howell, Peter	048
Elliott, John	Drake, Jonathan	1915	Faddis, Jno hr of James	Fifer, Caleb	264	Fenner, Richard	Langston, Josiah	32
Elliott, John hr of Thos	Robertson, James	029	Faigan, George heirs	McDowell, Joseph	1529	Fenner, Richard	Reyley, John	518
Elliott, Samuel	Hadley, West	980	Faircloth, William	Ford, John	881	Fenner, Richard	Richardson, James	289
Ellis, James	Drake, Jonathan	522	Faircloth, Wm.	Ford, John	042	Fenner, Richard	Steel, Joseph	42
Ellis, Robert	Douglas, Edward	1226	Faircloth, Wm.	Williams, Etheldred	537	Fenner, Richard	Zealott, Joshua	860
Ellis, Underhill	Haywood, John	409	Fairfax, Frederick	Sheppard, Benjamin	700	Fenner, Robert	Hadley, Joshua	080
Ellison, A.	Orell, James	072	Fairfax, William heirs	Sheppard, Benjamin	399	Fenner, Wm.	Anderson, Daniel	48
Ellison, Joseph	Blount, Thos.	010	Faison, Jas.	Kemp, Joseph	613	Fenwick, Nathaniel	Hickman, Thos.	1302
Ellison, Peter	Donelson, Stockley	1239	Faithe, William	Fuller, John	786	Ferebe, David heirs	Weakley, Robert	1931
Elmore, Morgan	Holderson, William	744	Faithfull, William	Robertson, James	1926	Ferrell, enoch	Cartwright, Robert	855
Emory, John	Elliott, John	033	Fardin, Joseph hrs.	Franmer (?), Phillip	712	Ferrell, Jacob heirs	Rice, Jno. Etal	319
Englin, Henry Cornel.	Byrn, James	503	Farmer, John	Douglas, David	1616	Ferrell, James	Herndon, Benjamin	1884
English, John	Beaird, Joseph	187	Farmer, Peter hrs	Barton, Samuel	593	Ferrell, Wm.	Rice, John	79
English, Jos. Hrs.	Fenner, Richd	025	Farmer, Thomas	Brokens, Thomas	749	Fetner,Geo.hr.Henry	Clark, Lardner	668
English, Joshua	Jones, Absolom	050	Farmer, Thomas	Crabtree, John	1102	Few, David hr Arthur	Hollis, James	199
Enjamin /sic/ McCulloch	Glasgow, James	906	Farmer, Thomas	Teuton, Caleb	1103	Fifer, Caleb	Faddis, James	264
Eools, William	Cosman (?), James	2356	Farmer, Thomas	Truett, Franklin	1101	Filgena, Wm heirs	Sheppard, John	062
Epsom, John hrs	Newby, Matthew	342	Farmer, William	Clark, Lardner & Wycoff	119	Finley, Abraham heirs	Mann, John	670
Ervin, John	Settleworth, Andrew	179	Farrow, Wm.	Allison, John	423	Finley, Abraham heirs	Sheppard, John	057
Erwin, Andrew	Brinkley, Josiah	2420	Faulke(?), James	Elliott, John	1584	Finney, Thomas	Wilson, James	0129
Erwin, Joseph	Jordan, Fountain	1634	Faulkner, Francis	Barry, Redmon Dillen	055	Fishburn, Phillip	Parker, Joseph	848
Erwin, Robert	Orr, Nathan	1633	Faybourne, Joel	Cook, Richard	658	Fisher, Frederick	Paker, William	042
Espic, William	Attogan [O'Hagen], Charles	2422	Fell, Watson	Pender, Thomas	1275	Fisher, Joel	McCulloch, Benjamin	316
Esteridge, Thomas heirs	Robeson, James	1918	Felts, Archibald	Bates, Luke	604	Fist, Samuel heirs	Nichols, John	430
Estis, Abraham	Bledsoe, Anthony	482	Fenner, Richard	Alford, John	11	Fitzworth, Isaac	Stewart, John	1446
Estridge, Thomas	Laurence, Adam	2057	Fenner, Richard	Allen, Thomas	328	Flanagan, Geo. Heirs	Brock, Joseph	839
Eth(?) Wm. Heirs	Johnson, Henry, Jr.	536	Fenner, Richard	Barker, Samuel	9	Flatt, John	Mitchell, John	197
Etheridge, Edward hrs	Easten, Jas.	1095	Fenner, Richard	Benson, John	291	Fleming, William	Rice, John	622
Etherington, Margaret	Taylor, Elijah	1017	Fenner, Richard	Broomfield, Moses	846	Flemings, William	Privet, Rosana	450
Evans, Joseph hrs	Drake, Jonathan	997	Fenner, Richard	Burns, Isum	10	Flesher, Robert	Johnson, Henry, Jr., Ass	020
Evans, Richard	Alcuff, Timothy	193	Fenner, Richard	Carter, Henry	332	Fletcher, Benjamin	Spencer, Thomas Sharpe	1448
Evans, Thomas	Gary, James	1636	Fenner, Richard	Cherry, Job	331	Fletcher, Joseph heirs	Mullet, Theodore	20
Evans, Thomas	Weeks, Cornelius	870	Fenner, Richard	Cooper, Solomon	329	Flimin, Samuel	Sugg, Geo. A.	069
Evans, Wm.	Hart, Anthoy	495	Fenner, Richard	Crook, Hillary	52	Flood, Elisha	McCulloh, Benjamin	2081
Everitt, Thomas hrs	Lanier, James	764	Fenner, Richard	Dillard, Peter	325	Flood, Frederick	Lytle, Archibald	092
Ewell(?), Stephen	Bonner, James	285	Fenner, Richard	Dukes, Arthur	330	Flood, Zachariah	Sheppard, Benjamin	562
Ewell, William	Williams, Willoughby	515	Fenner, Richard	English, Joshua	025	Flory, Frances	McCulloh, Benjamin	311
Ewing, Alex.	Davis, Leonard	686	Fenner, Richard	Fenner, Richard	780	Flower, Chas.hrs	Armstrong, Andrew	334
Ewing, Alexander	Bond, James	312	Fenner, Richard	Green, Randel	292	Flowers, William	Hill, William	594
Ewing, Alexander	Brewington, Benjamin	893	Fenner, Richard	Griffen, Jacob	290	Floyd, Charles heirs	Sanders, William	365
Ewing, Alexander	Manning, John	541	Fenner, Richard	Heel, Joseph	073	Floyd, Joseph	Sheppard, Nancy	2101
Ewing, Robert	Price, Jonathan	028	Fenner, Richard	Hickman, Charles	773	Floyd,Augustine	Armstrong, Andrew	246
Exum, Etheldred	Tuton, William	977	Fenner, Richard	Holton, James	780	Fluellen, Isaac	Brandon, Wm.	869

Assignee:	Claimant:	File #:
Fogerty, James	Wilson, John	595
Folk, Chris heirs	Robeson, James	467
Ford, Elias	Grant, Ephraim	941
Ford, James	Anderson, John	026
Ford, John	Armstrong, Martin & Anthony	455
Ford, John	Bond, James	885
Ford, John	Coward, Peter	882
Ford, John	Daffin, John	884
Ford, John	Faircloth, William	042
Ford, John	Faircloth, William	881
Ford, John	Griffen, William	463
Ford, John	Grimes, Andrew	1599
Ford, John	Hagins, James	619
Ford, John	King, Edmund	1989
Ford, John	Lewis, Jonathan	861
Ford, John	Middleton, Solomon	883
Ford, John	Phew, Richard	47
Ford, John	Willis, Taylor	888
Ford, Thomas	Perry, John	1736
Forgey, Jas	King, Robert	699
Forgey, Jas.	King, Robert	699
Fork, William	Gilkison, James	483
Forrest, Matthew	Reed, Jesse	235
Fort, Elias	Barrow, James	807
Fort, Elias	Byanom, Drury	273
Fort, Elias	Colwell, John	294
Fort, Elias	Dillard, Sampson	805
Fort, Elias	Dunbar, Dun	271
Fort, Elias	Mannin, Timothy	862
Fort, Elias	Overton, Edward	372
Fort, William & Howell Tatu	Young, Sion	327
Foster, Anthony	Hathcock, Fred	108
Foster, Anthony	More, Benjamin	043
Foster, Anthony	Morris, John	326
Foster, Anthony	Morriss, John	326
Foster, Anthony	Price, Thomas	024
Foster, Anthony	Stallions, James	1920
Foster, Anto. & W. T. Lewis	Smith, Henry	1657
Foster, Thomas	McRea, Saml	620
Foster, William hrs.	Comon, James	541
Foster, Abraham	Mann, John	673
Fowler, Absolom	Armstrong, Thomas	178
Fowler, Burwell heirs	Williams, Willoughby	335
Fowler, David	Brewer, Reese	077
Fowler, David	Lucas, Ball	076
Fowler, Joshua heirs	Sugg, Aquila	904
Fox, Francis	Kerr, Joseph	713
Fragments of papers	Tennessee papers,	00–
Fragments of papers	Tennessee papers,	130
Franklin, James	Maxwell, Jesse	1442
Frazer, George	Morgan, Griffin	1525
Frazier, John	Dickman, Edwin	596
Frazier, John	Taylor, Thomas	2287
Frazier, Simon	Brown, John	1929
Freelers, John	Nichold, John	932
Freeman, David heirs	Nelson, John	036
Freeman, John	Donelson, John	966
Freeman, Nathan	Hughlet, William	443
Freeman, Richd.	Hargatt, Frederick	92
Freeman, Wm. Hrs.	Donelson, John	2195
Frost, William	Whitfield, Bryant	1977
Fry, Buell	Overton, John	514
Fryer, Josiah	Williams, Willoughby	323
Fryer, Wm.	Williams, Willoughby	076
Fulcher, James	Nelson, Robert	421
Fulkison, Abraham	Cates, Zachariah	1
Fulks, Garret hrs.	Armstrong, M. & S. Done	958
Fuller, John	Faith, William	786
Fuller, Wm.	Hague, John	304
Fuller, Garret hrs	Armstrong & Donelson	017
Fussell(?)	Simpson, Smith	668
Gafford, William	Hamilton, Thos.	692
Gafford, Wm. Hrs	Brock, Joseph	858
Gains, Geoffrey	Coghlin, James	2270
Galders, Geo. Hrs	Boyd, John	375
Gale, Daniel	Comon, James	540
Gale, Stephen heirs	Donelson, John	746
Gallop, Isaac	Robertson, Elijah	876(816
Galloway, James	Burgess, Wm.	764
Galloway, John	Clifton, Absolem	972
Galloway, Richard	Hays, Robert	221
Gambill, Bradley	Sheppard, Benjamin	389
Gamble, Edmond	Granston, George	1619
Gamble, Edmond	Applewhite, John	358
Gamble, Edmond	Duke, Green	357
Gamble, Edmund	Nelson, Robert	26
Gamble, Edmund	McCarty, Flourane	175
Gambling, James	Neville, George	187
Gambrill, Bradley	Jones, Jacob	280
Ganthrop, John	Clark, Lardner	289
Gardner, Demsey	Hadley, Joshua	464
Gardner, Geo. Hrs.	Blount, John Gray & Thoma	2107
Garner, Gregory	Barry, Redmon Dillen	048
Garner, Gregory	Dillonberry, Redmon	048
Garner, Gregory	Buchanan, John	1566
Garner, Nathan	King, Robert	525
Garner, Thomas heirs	Sheppard, John	068
Garrett, Jesse heirs	Donelson, Stockley	014
Garrett, Wm.	Cathey, William	1011
Garrett, Wm. Heirs	Donelson, Stockley	1193
Garris, Stephen	Barnet, Robert	1772
Garrison, John	Robertson, Elijah	802
Garrison, William	Stewart, Duncan	2367
Garvey, Matthew heirs	Evans, Thos.	1636
Gary, Joseph	Holliman, Kinchen	735
Gatlin, John	Sheppard, John	620
Gatlin, John	Sheppard, John	620
Gatling, John	Mullen, William	044
Gay, Wm.	Donelson, John	682
Gaylord, Aaron	Sheppard, Benjamin	561
Gaylord, Thomas	Wilkins, William	1051
Gee, Capt. James heirs	Tyrrell, William	2354
Geo. Walker & Seth Lewis	Barnes, William	2078
George Walker & S. Lewis	Armstrong, Thomas	550
George, John	Robeson, Charles	737
Gerard, Charles	Matthews, Joseph	272
Gerard, Charles	Moore, Moses	353
Gerard, Charles	Somerland, James	270
Gerard, Charles	Spain, Eps.	749
Gerard, Charles	Spain, William	757
German, Benj.	Ray, William	0109
Gerris, Joshua heirs	Williams, Willoughby	327
Gibbs, Joel	Gibbs, Raybon	044
Gibson, Charles	King, Robert	526
Gibson, Fuller	Brigriance, William	715
Gibson, Jno.	Foster, Anthony	1705
Gibson, John	Fort, Wm.	253
Gibson, John	Trousdale, John	54
Gibson, William	Walker, George	2153
Gideon Pillow	Luchars, Richard	1435
Gideon, Richard	Donelson, Stockley	039
Gifford, James	Tate, William	539

Assignee:	Claimant:	File #:	Assignee:	Claimant:	File #:	Assignee:	Claimant:	File
Green, Randel heirs	Fenner, Richard	292	Gunter, Samuel	Donelson, Stockley	1309	Hadley, Joshua	Rogers, Austin	1412
Green, Theophilus heirs	Stewart, Duncan	2239	Gurley, James	Logue, John	955	Hadley, Joshua	Ryan, Jeffrey	1411
Green, Thomas hrs.	Gubbins, William	627	Guthrop, John	Clark, Lardner	038	Hadley, Joshua	Spence, Job	512
Green, William	Potter, Daniel	7	Guttery, Henry	Douglass, John	1049	Hadley, Joshua	Storm, Andrew	2406
Greer, A. & J. Robertson	Valentine, Thomas	1677	Gwin, Edward	Jenkins, Levi	181	Hadley, Joshua	Terrel, William	264
Greer, Alex. & J. Robertson	Capton, John	1674	Gwin, Edward	Price, William	289	Hadley, Joshua	Thompson, Ned	251
Greer, Andrew	Bonner, William	35	Gwin, John	Hooker, John	1385	Hadlow, Joseph heirs	Mann, John	2432
Greer, Ann	Foys, Patrick	147	Gwin, John	Jones, Elisha	1434	Hafler, Thomas	Colton, Thomas	737
Greer, Ann	Prowford, John	152	Gwin, William	Strider, George	1386	Hagins, James	Ford, John	619
Greer, John G.	Dillonberry, Redmon	044	Gwinn, Edward	King, Anthony	309	Hague, John	Fuller, William	304
Greer, John Gee	Barry, Redmon Dillen	1673	Gwinn, Jacob heirs	Bushneal, Eus.& Wm Do	652	Hains, Phillip	Bostian, Jacob	1909
Greer, Jos.& Jas Robertson	McCay, John	44	H. Tatum & Henry Wiggins	Austin, Thomas	2440	Hains, William	Hord, John	1973
Gressum, Robert heirs	Stewart, Duncan	609	Hacket, John	Hart, William	866	Hair, David hrs	Armstrong, Andrew	830
Griffen, James	Robertson, Jonathan F.	2388	Hackner, Daniel	King, Thomas & others	789	Hair, James	Dickson, John	206
Griffin, Edward heirs	Mountflorence, James Cole	1499	Haddock, Admiral	McCutchin, John	944	Hair, John	Howell, Tatum & Wiggins	2438
Griffin, Jacob	Fenner, Richard	290	Haddock, Andrew	Brooks, Thomas	108	Hair, John	Smith, Oliver	166
Griffin, Jas.	Donelson, John	745	Haddock, Andrew	Nickols, John	107	Hair, William	Wiggins, Henry & Ho Tatum	2438
Griffin, Jos.	Dickson, John	183	Haddock, Josiah	Robinson, James	1936	Halcolm, William heirs	Smith, Oliver	149
Griffin, Joshua heirs	Hart, Anthony	195	Haddock, Peter	Pyette, Peter	104	Halcom, Phillip	Sugg, Aquilla	875
Griffin, Samuel heirs	Rice, Jno. Etal	311	Haddock, Wm. Heirs	King, Robert	565	Hale, Josiah	Lewis, Wm. T.	051
Griffin, Wm.	Ford, John	463	Hadley, James	Albright, James	534	Hall, David	Cobb, Jesse	419
Griffis, Saml.	Barker, Lewis	034	Hadley, Joshua	Caps, Oliver	1419	Hall, John	Dowell, James	082
Griffis, Saml.	Barker, Lewis	652	Hadley, Joshua	Carnahan, Dennis	1416	Halley, Jollef	Harget, Fredrk & Jas Carne	640
Griffis, Samuel	Mountflorence, James C	864	Hadley, Joshua	Coffery, Nimrod	1414	Halsted, Jollef	Coffery, John	06
Griffith Rutherford	Jinkins, William	1023	Hadley, Joshua	Covinton, John	1050	Halten, James	Averall, William	2141
Griffin, Lamon	Sheppard, Benjamin	385	Hadley, Joshua	Craddock, Shadrack	1417	Ham, John	Fenner, Richard	780
Grimes, Ant hr or And.	Ford, John	1599	Hadley, Joshua	Crow, Millford	1422	Hamilton, Elijah	Barry, Redmon Dillen	028
Grinder, John	Hays, Robert	1754	Hadley, Joshua	Dobbins, William	516	Hamilton, George	Rhone, John	424
Grogan, Jacob	Sanford, Samuel	1963	Hadley, Joshua	Fenner, Richard	080	Hamilton, Hance	Walker, John	083
Grogan, John	Sheppard, Benjamin	697	Hadley, Joshua	Gardner, Dempsey	464	Hamilton, James	Hamilton, Thomas	1958
Groves, Nicholas	Donelson, John	1972	Hadley, Joshua	Gervis, John	548	Hamilton, Jno	Kervin, Thomas	121
Groves, Wm.	Allen, William	327	Hadley, Joshua	Gower, Russell	1418	Hamilton, John heirs	Morris, William	2471
Guatney, Joshua	Sheppard, Benjamin	393	Hadley, Joshua	Green, Samuel	258	Hamilton, Thomas	Crutcher, Arthur	607
Gubbins, William	Dixon, Henry	360	Hadley, Joshua	Hill, James	46	Hamilton, Thomas	Clifton, Daniel	0134
Gubbins, William	Green, Thomas	627	Hadley, Joshua	Hunter, Elisha	45	Hamilton, Thomas	Cunningham, James	537
Guice, Christopher	Cherney, Robert	114	Hadley, Joshua	Jarvis, Lewis	1415	Hamilton, Thomas	Farrell, Clement	53
Guin, Daniel	Davis, Joshua	814	Hadley, Joshua	Jones, Oliver	1358	Hamilton, Thomas	Hamelton, Hance	1958
Guin, Thomas	Williams, Willoughby	540	Hadley, Joshua	Joyner, Lewis	126	Hamilton, Thomas	McClain, Jeremiah	528
Guion, Samuel	White, James	1930	Hadley, Joshua	Lindsay, Isaac	1352	Hamilton, William	Russel, James	692
Guist, Thomas	Blount, John Gray & Thomas	2066	Hadley, Joshua	McDonald, William	524	Hammett, John	Cross, Anthony	2236
Gunn, Abraham heirs	Weakley, Robert	995	Hadley, Joshua	McFarlin, John	1420	Hammon, Tiston	Donelson, Stockley	964
Gunn, Alexander	Rutherford, Griffith	280	Hadley, Joshua	McKinsey, William	165	Hammond	Barrow, James	902
Gunn, John	Walker, George	366	Hadley, Joshua	McRace, Roger	081	Hammond	Graham, Joseph (Matilda)	101
Gunter, Joel	Dixon, Charles	954	Hadley, Joshua	Nicholson, Isaac	1421	Hammonds, John	Brown, John	278

Assignee:	Claimant:	File #:	Assignee:	Claimant:	File #:	Assignee:	Claimant:	File
Hammonds, Ralph	Reed, Jesse	209	Harney, Selby	Jennings, Thomas	084	Harris, Edward	Hadson, Joel	1110
Hammonds, Abraham	Sheppard, Benjamin	391	Harney, Selby & A. Bledso	Gilbert, John	702	Harris, Edward	Hammonds, Willis	1125
Hamond, Ed heirs	Blackface, Wm.	567	Harper, Fred	Lewis, James M.	079	Harris, Edward	Harper, Johnston	1164
Hampton, Andrew	Marshall, Charles	767	Harper, Wm. Heirs	Mann, John	674	Harris, Edward	Hind, Anthony	1145
Hampton, George	McCulloh, Benjamin	342	Harper/Hayes? Robt hr	Gilmore, Charles	637	Harris, Edward	Howard, Edmes /sic/	1142
Hance, Job	Blount, John Gray	1243	Harps, John	Dillonberry, Redmon	056	Harris, Edward	Hubberts, Anthony	1120
Hancock, Ann	Oneill, Thomas	187	Harrell, Benj.	McNairy, John	662	Harris, Edward	Ivey, Elisha	1119
Hankins, Edward	Sypert, Robert	685	Harrell, Ephraim heirs	Williams, Willoughby	320	Harris, Edward	Jermany, Thomas	1168
Hannah, John	Wigbey, Samuel	171	Harrell, Holland heirs	Williams, Eliza	580	Harris, Edward	Johnston, Harmon	1108
Hanner, Rody	Darnold, Thomas	630	Harrell, Holland hrs	Armstrong, M. & S. Done	991	Harris, Edward	Jordan, Joseph	1165
Hannock, Samuel hrs	Blount, Reading	030	Harrell, Holland hrs	Donelson & Armstrong	034	Harris, Edward	Kelly, Dugald	1151
Hansel, Charles	Barrow, Sherrod	1637	Harrell, James	Phillips, P & M. Campbel	91	Harris, Edward	Killingsworth, John	1465
Harver, James hrs.	Brock, Joseph	845	Harrell, Thomas	Robertson, Elijah	811	Harris, Edward	King, Andrew	1160
Hardcock, Isham	Anderson, John	945	Harrewood, Thomas heirs	Sheppard, John	066	Harris, Edward	Lewis, David	1141
Harden, Benj.	Kuykendall, Adam	1867	Harrington, Henry Wm.	Covington, John	781	Harris, Edward	Locust, Thomas	1137
Harden, Moses	Coston, Henry	1372	Harrington, James	Brock, Joseph	838	Harris, Edward	March, Febreas /sic/	1109
Hardick, Richard	Tatum, Howell	2321	Harrington, Richard	Robertson, James etal	148	Harris, Edward	McFoy, Morrie	1123
Hardin, John	McRee, John	1371a	Harrington, Samuel	Nash, William	0103	Harris, Edward	McNeill, John	1126
Hardy, John hrs	Blount, Reading	028	Harris, Abraham	Buckannon, John	1561	Harris, Edward	Morgan, Richard	1143
Hardy, John hrs.	Blount, Reading	967	Harris, Coburn heirs	Douglass, Edward	520	Harris, Edward	Moveal, Henry	1176
Harget & Randall	Robeson, Charles	190	Harris, Ed	Coon, Conrad	2474	Harris, Edward	Moys, John	1180
Harget & Randal	Robeson, Charles	1914	Harris, Edward	Amis [Avery?], Thomas	1144	Harris, Edward	Nervear, David	1116
Harget & Randal	Robeson, Charles	192	Harris, Edward	Avery, James	1178	Harris, Edward	Peters, Titus	1127
Harget & Randal	Robeson, Charles	193	Harris, Edward	Bagley, Isaac	1133	Harris, Edward	Powell, Peter	1112
Harget & Randall	Sevier, Charles	196	Harris, Edward	Boyan, Richard	1143	Harris, Edward	Powers, Robert	1138
Harget, F. & J. Carney	White, Thomas	640	Harris, Edward	Carter, Samuel	1152	Harris, Edward	Praton, Joshua	1148
Harget, Fred	Freeman, Richard	92	Harris, Edward	Cavernor, Timothy	1173	Harris, Edward	Purton, Elexana	1117
Harget, Frederick	Bradsher, John	1955	Harris, Edward	Chesnut, Joseph	1129	Harris, Edward	Ray, Wm.	282
Harget, Frederick	Broadbent, Richard	2237	Harris, Edward	Collins, Burwell	1155	Harris, Edward	Roberts, Sampson	1140
Harget, Frederick	Card, Joseph	2229	Harris, Edward	Collins, Dillard	1154	Harris, Edward	Robertson, Isaac	1115
Harget, Frederick	Jones, James	588	Harris, Edward	Delaney, Michael	1149	Harris, Edward	Roe, Dempsey	1166
Harget, Frederick	Morris, Philamon	1954	Harris, Edward	Duggin, John	1121	Harris, Edward	Rogers, Absolom	1134
Harget, Frederick	Simmon, Felix	1964	Harris, Edward	Dunbar, John	1107	Harris, Edward	Scutchings, Meredy	1124
Harget, Frederick	Skipper, Joseph	1948	Harris, Edward	Emmory, Stephen	1153	Harris, Edward	Shafferd, John	1179
Harget, Frederick	Skipper, Nathan	587	Harris, Edward	Evans, Philip	1128	Harris, Edward	Skipper, Hardy	1122
Harget, Frederick	Tatom, William	589	Harris, Edward	Evans, Richard	1163	Harris, Edward	Smith, Charles	1169
Harget & Randel	Robenson, Charles	238	Harris, Edward	Fletcher, John	1135	Harris, Edward	Sneed, Elbet	1136
Hargett, Frederick	Brown, James	274	Harris, Edward	Frazier, Jeremiah	1132	Harris, Edward	Stanley, Hancock	1170
Hargrove, Wm.	Baker, John	742	Harris, Edward	Garris, Seth	1175	Harris, Edward	Steedman, John	1171
Harnett, Ephraim heirs	Williams, Willoughby	321	Harris, Edward	George, Thomas	1139	Harris, Edward	Stephens, John	1162
Harney & Bledsoe	Jackson, Robert	710	Harris, Edward	Grant, Gilbert	1158	Harris, Edward	Talton, Thomas	1106
Harney & Bledsoe	Jackson, Thomas	707	Harris, Edward	Green, Samuel	1130	Harris, Edward	Thomas, Caleb	1177
Harney, S. & A. Bledsoe	Crisp, William	833	Harris, Edward	Griffith, Henry	1118	Harris, Edward	Thurrill, Abraham	1159
Harney, S. & A. Bledsoe	Mann, Thomas	706	Harris, Edward	Gun, Hardy	1147	Harris, Edward	Tyner, Arthur	1131

Assignee:	Claimant:	File #:	Assignee:	Claimant:	File #:	Assignee:	Claimant:	File
Harris, Edward	Venus, Patrick	1113	Hart, Anthony	Bailey, Morris	863	Hay, Abraham	Donelson, Stockley	2262
Harris, Edward	Walker, Green	1114	Hart, Anthony	Burk, Abraham	601	Hay, Abraham	Roberts, Elijah	262
Harris, Edward	Warren, Richard	1161	Hart, Anthony	Colbert, Laurence	843	Hay, Archibald	Coonrod, Nicholas	668
Harris, Edward	Wells, Zebulon	1172	Hart, Anthony	Colvin, Obed	739	Hay, David	Shelby, David	1901
Harris, Edward	White, Robert	1157	Hart, Anthony	Cross, Randal	045	Hay, David	Williams, Oliver	2304
Harris, Edward	Wood, Nathaniel	1111	Hart, Anthony	Daughtry, Lewis	69	Hay, David	Williams, Oliver	027
Harris, Edward	Woodward, George	1174	Hart, Anthony	Eastwood, John	204	Hay, Joseph	Buchanan, John	2037
Harris, Edward	Worsley, Bryan	1146	Hart, Anthony	Evans, William	495	Haycraft, Mark	Good, John	3
Harris, Edward	Worsley, John	1167	Hart, Anthony	Griffin, Joshua	195	Hayden Wells	Wheaton, Daniel	676
Harris, Elisha	Goodloe, Robert	046	Hart, Anthony	Hammon, James	200	Hayes, James	Hacksaw, James	371
Harris, George	Davis, Joshua	530	Hart, Anthony	Holder, Isaac	654	Hayes, Robert	Jones, Theophilus	368
Harris, Gilbert	Blair, James	2032	Hart, Anthony	King, Richard	202	Hayes, Robert	Setgreaves, John	2353
Harris, Goldman	Briston, James	268	Hart, Anthony	Lassiter, Samuel	600	Hayes, Robert	Williams, William	1758
Harris, Hardy heirs	Hughlett, William	037	Hart, Anthony	Madry, Moses	743	Hayes, Thomas	Henderson, Abrahm	131
Harris, Joab heirs	Sheppard, Jno.	061	Hart, Anthony	Matthews, Gilbert	201	Haynes, James	Story, Jonah	035
Harris, Job	Dedrick, Geo. Michael	2428	Hart, Anthony	Miller, John	840	Haynes, John	Williamson, John	559
Harris, John	Murphree, Hardy	183	Hart, Anthony	Morgan, Lewis	203	Hays, Isaac	Ivey, Clabein /sic/	150
Harris, John	Sheppard, John	067	Hart, Anthony	Nobles, William	157	Hays, James	Humphries, David	633
Harris, Nathan	Dickson, John	190	Hart, Anthony	Reddick, Isaac	602	Hays, John	Burn, Andrew	87
Harris, Peter	Armstrong, Martin	467	Hart, Anthony	Rivers, William	702	Hays, John	Douglas, James	069
Harris, Richard	Bond, John	1866	Hart, Anthony	Sellers, John	705	Hays, John	Mundine, Zebulon	57
Harris, Samuel	Marshall, John	480	Hart, Anthony	West, Cyprian	1506	Hays, John	Munding, Richard	621
Harris, Sherwood	Bledsoe, Isaac	721	Hart, Anthony	Wright, William	775	Hays, John	Nolby, Anderson	360
Harris, Thomas heirs	Willson, David	204	Hart, David	Elmore, George	28	Hays, John heirs	Hays, Robt	028
Harris, Thompson	Bledsoe, Joshua	218	Hart, Hardy	McCulloh, Benjamin	295	Hays, Narcissa	Gray, Jonathan	678
Harris, William heirs	Rice, Jno. Etal	310	Hart, Hardy	Buchanan, John	019	Hays, Patty Thompson	Berry, Francis	687
Harrison, Aug.	Davis, Joshua	791	Hart, Joseph heirs	Brock, Joseph	36	Hays, R. & Edmond Jining	Sumner, Francis	370
Harrison, Dan hr Henry	Blount, Reading	433	Hart, Wm.	Hackett, John	866	Hays, Rachel	Abbott, Isaac	321
Harrison, Geo.	Tatum, Howell	58	Hartley, John	Donelson, John	2024	Hays, Robert	Ballard, Drury	379
Harrison, James	Crump, Abraham	899	Harts, Joseph	Tyrrell, Wm. & Wm. T. L	017	Hays, Robert	Balmore, John	1761
Harrison, John Axley	Todd, James	1957	Hasten, Oliver heir	May, John;	2038	Hays, Robert	Bennett, Henry	466
Harrison, John heirs	Davis, Joshua	688	Hasten, Willis	Foster, Anthony	108	Hays, Robert	Biggs, Nathaniel	2398
Harrison, Patrick	Dillard, Wm.	998	Haston, Daniel	Davis, Joshua	367	Hays, Robert	Briant, William	811
Harrison, Robt.	Balew, Thos.	712	Haun, John	Malloy, Thos.	550	Hays, Robert	Brittle, Benjamin	1774
Harrison, Thos.	Bonner, John & James	698	Hatchcock, Amos heirs	Archer, Thomas	201	Hays, Robert	Brownguary, Gasper	1763
Harrison, Wm.	Barbour, Richard	1325	Hatches, David heirs	Tatum, Howell	112	Hays, Robert	Butler, Edward	671
Harrison,Fran.hr of Jas	Glasgow, James	716	Hathcock, Fred.	Marshall, John	582	Hays, Robert	Galloway, John	221
Harrison,Jona.hrs	Armstrong, Andrew	335	Hathcock, John heirs	Weakley, Polly	106	Hays, Robert	Gray, Henry	2072
Harrold, James	Robeson, James	2291	Haughton, Levi heirs	Davis, Joshua	367	Hays, Robert	Grinder, John	1754
Harrold, Jas.	Robertson, James	080	Hawkins, Joseph heirs	Dillonberry, Redmon	028	Hays, Robert	Hall, James	374
Harrold, Jno. Heirs	Cooke, Richard	1376	Hawkins,Phillips & Campb	Mountflorence, James C	295	Hays, Robert	Herrington, Drury	372
Hart	Tyrrell, William	075	Hawley, Caleb	Simmons, Islar	135	Hays, Robert	Holley, Nathaniel	380
Hart, Anthony	Applewhite, Abraham	199	Hawley, Joseph	McCulloh, Benjamin	2030	Hays, Robert	James, William	672
Hart, Anthony	Bailey, Macon	745	Hawley, Wm.	Person, Thomas	408	Hays, Robert	McCoy, Morris	373
				Ross, Joseph	1523			

Assignee Index

Assignee:	Claimant:	File #
Hays, Robert	Mears, Willis	821
Hays, Robert	Mills, Daniel	367
Hays, Robert	Murral, Matthew	369
Hays, Robert	Parks, Samuel	465
Hays, Robert	Pollock, Benjamin	1759
Hays, Robert	Powell, Stephen	1773
Hays, Robert	Reed, William	046
Hays, Robert	Reed, William	315
Hays, Robert	Ricks, Lewis	1757
Hays, Robert	Rivell, John	1760
Hays, Robert	Roach, Moses	382
Hays, Robert	Robins, John	383
Hays, Robert	Robins, John	383
Hays, Robert	Sampson, Joab	366
Hays, Robert	Smalley, James	1764
Hays, Robert	Tanner, John	028
Hays, Robert	Thomas, John	1765
Hays, Robert	Totevine, Winder	782
Hays, Robert	Vinson, Chatline	365
Hays, Robert	Wilkins, Benjamin	1766
Hays, Robert	Williams, Theophilus	381
Hays, Robert	Yancey, John	1756
Hays, Samuel	Alexander, Geo.	773
Hays, Stockley	Robbins, James	812
Hays, Stokeley	Ward, Isaac	658
Hays, Thomas	Murray, Joshua	115
Hays, Thomas	Smith, Micajah	81
Hays, Thos.	Cook, Richard [?]	1374
Hayse, William	Bushnell, Eusebrus & Dobbins	660
Haywood, James	Sugg, Aquilla	915
Haywood, John	Clay, Jeremiah	245
Haywood, John	Ellison, Ackiss	409
Haywood, John	Medlin, Mills	410
Haywood, John	Medlin, Zeland	411
Haywood, John	Woodley, Thomas	2452
Heakes(?), Robt.	Bledsoe, Isaac	647
Hean(?), Geo.	Clark, Vachel	543
Heaton, Amos	Nelson, Robert	074
Hedgepeth, Marmaduke	Wikoff, Wm. & Lardner Clark	552
Hedgepeth, John	Shelby, Evan	538
Hedspeth, Steph	Boyd, John, Jr.	1379
Heel, Joseph	Fenner, Richard	073
heir of Aaron (?)	Bledsoe, Jacob	798
Heir of Miles	McIlhekee, Jno. Russell	331
Henderson, Abra. Hrs	Hayes, Thomas	131
Henderson, Andrew	Stewart, Duncan	2372
Henderson, James	Williams, Sampson	1521
Henderson, Nathaniel	King, Robt & Walter	784
Henderson, Robert	White, William	071
Hendricks, Jeremiah	Simmons, Holden	1403
Hendricks, Joseph	Anderson, Meeds [?]	1294
Hendricks, Joseph	Robeson, Joel	734
Hendrix, John	McCoy, Ananias	483
Hendry, William	Gore, Jonathan	621
Hendry, William	Hickman, Ed	622
Hendry, William	Hickman, John	623
Henley, John	Hills, Joseph	212
Hennes, Benbury	Blount, John Gray	37
Henry, John	Hill, Green	166
Henry, John	Robertson, Elijah	807
Henry, Jonathan	Donelson, Stockley	041
Henry, Thomas	Seagroves, John	2223
Henry, William	Radley, Ichabod	013
Henry, William	Tyrrell, William	028
Hering, Burrell	Barton, Samuel.	349
Hern, Drury	Brown, John	472
Herndon, Benjamin	Ferrell, James	1884
Herndon, Benjamin	Watson, Lett	1983
Herring, Henry	White, James S.	2427
Herring, Jacob heirs	Sheppard, Nancy	2084
Hester, John	McCrory, James	2096
Hewet, Ebenezer	McConnell, Robt.	049
Hickman, Charles hrs	Fenner, Richard	773
Hickman, Ed	Hendrey, Wm.	622
Hickman, Ed	Wills, Haydon	235
Hickman, Edwin	Burrington, Demsey	369
Hickman, Edwin	Campbell, Daniel	535
Hickman, Edwin	Candler, Joseph	796
Hickman, Edwin	Frazier, John	596
Hickman, Edwin	Freysher, Hugh	578
Hickman, Edwin	Norman, Thomas	784
Hickman, Edwin	Pridgen, Ezekiah	680
Hickman, Edwin	Pulley, Jessey	795
Hickman, Edwin	Stevens, John	2077
Hickman, John Marr	Phillips, Michael	863
Hickman, Thomas	Alexander, Thomas	1335
Hickman, Thomas	Cameron, Abel	1299
Hickman, Thomas	Carney, Andrew	331
Hickman, Thomas	Carrom, James	785
Hickman, Thomas	Christian, William	1298
Hickman, Thomas	Corbin, Francis	1357
Hickman, Thomas	Corbin, Richard	1300
Hickman, Thomas	Cowan, Absolim	086
Hickman, Thomas	Cross, Frederick	769
Hickman, Thomas	Davis, James	771
Hickman, Thomas	Davis, Leonard	1297
Hickman, Thomas	Dickenson, Henry	7
Hickman, Thomas	Dodd, David	1333
Hickman, Thomas	Fenwick, Nathaniel	1302
Hickman, Thomas	Hatfield, Andrew	1334b
Hickman, Thomas	Henderson, Simon	1313
Hickman, Thomas	Lumblyer, Simon	1328
Hickman, Thomas	Madison, John	1329
Hickman, Thomas	McCauley, John	1301
Hickman, Thomas	McCoy, Alexander	1304
Hickman, Thomas	McKenny, Alexander	330
Hickman, Thomas	Morris, James	1263
Hickman, Thomas	Morris, John & James	087
Hickman, Thomas	Ouster, Ferryman	1332
Hickman, Thomas	Pope, William	1390
Hickman, Thomas	Read, William	54
Hickman, Thomas	Reed, William	1303
Hickman, Thomas	Roberson, Cornelius	259
Hickman, Thomas	Robertson, James	1306
Hickman, Thomas	Slaughter, Constantine	1265
Hickman, Thomas	Smith, Nehemiah	766
Hickman, Thomas	Spain, Thomas	533
Hickman, Thomas	Turner, Simon	1317
Hickman, Thomas	Whiteman, William	526
Hickman, Thomas	Whitfield, Jesse	1264
Hickman, Thomas	Williams, Robert	1330
Hickman, Thomas	Bowen, Stephen	198
Hicks, Daniel	Easton, Jas.	1090
Hicks, Henry heirs	Betts, Wm.	034
Hicks, Howell	Cherry, Willis	1
Hicks, James	Sheppard, John	064
Hicks, John	Donoho, Thomas	1229
Hicks, Reubin	Saunders, James	219
Hicks, Wm heir of Henry	Sheppard, John	063
Hicks, Wm.	Carroll, Douglas	1614
Hill, Bennett	Langston, Samuel	1307
Hill, Daniel	Driskel, David	222
Hill, Green		085

Assignee Index

Assignee:	Claimant:	File #:	Assignee:	Claimant:	File #:	Assignee:	Claimant:	File
Hill, Green	Henry, John	166	Hogan, Jas.	Heaton, Robt	218	Hooks, Wm. Hrs	Barton, Samuel	1913
Hill, Green	Humphries, Randolph	180	Hogan, John	McMullin, Michael	469	Hooks, Wm. Hrs	Barton, Samuel	513
Hill, Green	McCoy, John	198	Hogan, Roger	McNary, John	660	Hoover, Abraham	Saunders, Jacob	582
Hill, Green	Randall, Andrew	195	Hogan, William	Proctor, William	1181	Hoover, Henry	Elliot, Simon	270
Hill, Green	Walker, William	243	Hogan, Wm.	Hogan, John	1463	Hoover, Henry henry	Lenear, James	684
Hill, Hardy	Mann, John	671	Hogan, Lemuel hr of Jas	Hogan, James	69	Hopewell, George heirs	Williams, Willoughby	33
Hill, Henry	Kirkendall, John	030	Hogg, Thomas	Delaney, John	740	Hopkins, Isaac	McCall, Alex.	055
Hill, Henry	Kirkendall, John	1071	Hogg, Thomas	Lucas, Benjamin	026	Hopkins, John	Lenear, James	753
Hill, Henry	Laremore, Marmaduke	031	Hogg, Thomas	Lucas, Benjamin	1585	Hopkins, Jonathan	Cobb, Jesse	422
Hill, Henry	Larrimore, Marmaduke	1070	Hogg, Thomas	Mann, Robert	55	Hopkins, Joseph	McKinnie, William	86
Hill, Henry	Parker, Thomas	032	Hogg, Thomas	Norris, George	78	Hopkins, Joseph	Wheaton, Charles	458
Hill, Henry	Parker, Thomas	1072	Hoggard, Wm.	Barry, Redmon Dillon	1278	Hopper, William	Wykoff & Clark	774
Hill, Isaac	Bushnell, Eusebrus & Dobbins	658	Hoggett, James	Spence, James	517	Hopper, William	Wykoff, Wm & Lardn.Clark	121
Hill, Jas.	Hadley, Joshua	46	Hohamer, Phillip	Welburn, Daniel	02	Hord, John	Hains, William	1973
Hill, Joseph heirs	Henley, John	212	Holbrook, John	Graham, Joseph	281	Horseford, James heirs	Mayberry, Francis	410
Hill, Roberson	McCulloh, Benj.	317	Holderness, William	Bryant, Ambrose	206	Horter, Thomas	Truett, Solomon	973
Hill, William	Flowers, William	594	Holderness, William	Emory, John	744	Horton, James	Murphree, Hardy	184
Hill, William	Ward, John	324	Holt—?, Mordice	Clark, Lardner	675	Houston, Daniel	Ker, Joseph	950
Hilton, Wm.	Hilton, Daniel	119	Holingsworth, Thomas	Robertson, Elijah	805	Howard, Benjamin	Blount, Thos.	1950
Himnock, Saml. Hrs.	Blount, Reading	982	Holladay, Hathcock	Sheppard, Nancy	718	Howard, Ed	Dever, John	284
Hinds, John	Alexander, Reuben	1316	Holland, Charles	Lewis, Wm. T. & Wn., Ty	050	Howard, Isaac	Donnelly, James	354
Hinds, John	Hicks, Harris	1339	Holland, Charles hrs	Brock, Joseph	829	Howard, John	Dillenberry, Redmon	045
Hinds, John	Hicks, Isaac	1341	Holland, Daniel	Rowland, John	010	Howard, John	Dillonberry, Redmon	045
Hinds, John	Lumblyes, David	1318	Holland, Josiah	Holland, Joseph	47	Howard, Joshua	Marchant, Caleb	129
Hinds, John	Norwester, John	1340	Holland, William	Coonrod, Nicholas	526	Howard, Solomon	Barker, Thomas	511
Hinds, John	Norwood, Theophillus	1311	Holley, Henry	McAdams, John	2087	Howard, Thos.	Campbell, Jas.	487
Hinds, John	Smith, Thomas	920	Holley, John heirs	Coffery, John	564	Howard, William	Lanier, James	406
Hines, Simon & others	Hinds, Levi, Sylvanus & John	182	Holley, Nathaniel	Stone, Littleberry	345	Howard, William	Lanier, James;	406
Hinton, Jno.hrs	Armstrong & Donelson	031	Holliman, Kinchen	Gatlin, John	735	Howell, Ebenezer	McConnell, Robert	2415
Hinton, John hrs	Armstrong, M & S.Donelson	940	Hollis, Henry	Branks, Robert	1328	Howell, John	Alford, Wm.	03
Hitchcock, Wm heirs	Hunter, James	1493	Hollis, James	Pew, Arthur	199	Howell, John	Howel, John	03
Hobbs, Isaac heirs	Sheppard, John	064	Hollis, Jas.	Varner, Samuel	1345	Howell, Taliefarro	McConnell, Robert	033
Hobbs, Isaac heirs	Tyrrell, William	2267	Hollis, Wm.	Crafford, Wm.	105	Howell, Daniel	Clark & Wycoff	757
Hobbs, Joel	Carmack, Joseph	036	Hollomon, Aaron	Ross, William	062	Howell, Daniel	Wycoff & Clark	757
Hobbs, Moses heirs	Shepard, John	058	Holloway, John	Donelson, Stockley	1188	Howell, Frederick	Good, William - Heir of	2454
Hockamer, Philip	Wilburn, Daniel	678	Holmes, Andrew	McCulloh, Benjamin	2016	Howell, Henry	Smith, John	2349
Hocks, John	McCulloh, Benjamin	1731	Holmes, Shadrack	Murphree, Hardy	159	Howell, James	McNees, John	1593
Hodges, Benja.	Parsons, Harrison	1622	Homer, Charles	Tyner, Nicholas	027	Howell, Jesse	Looney, David	815
Hodges, Hardy	Nash, William	0104	Hood, Archibald	Barry, Redmon Dillen	030	Howell, John	Barton, Samuel	336
Hodges, Hardy heirs	Malloy, Thomas	546	Hood, Archibald	Dillonberry, Redmon	030	Howell, John	Ester, William	353
Hodges, Jno.	Glasgow, James	402	Hood, Charles	Rice, John	2150	Howell, John	Tryall, Christopher	343
Hodgin, Holder heirs	Donelson, Stockley	943	Hood, William	Love, Robert	2059	Howell, John heirs	Douglass, Reubin	523
Hodgin, Humphrey	Christmas, John	201	Hooker, John	Gwin, John	1385	Howell, John hrs.	Barton, Saml	134
Hogan, James heir	Hogan, Samuel	69	Hooks, Ephraim	Blount, William	291	Howell, Peter	Fenner, Richard	048

Left panel

Assignee:	Claimant:	File #
Howell, Talliferro heirs	McConnell, Robert	2410
Hubbard, James	Thomas, Wm.	877
Hubbart, Zebulon	Keay, Jonathan	573
Hubbart, Zebulon	Keay, Jonathan	573
Hubberts, Anthony	Harris, Edward	1120
Huck, Thomas	Hunter, Elisha	1722
Hudder, John	McCulloh, Benjamin	647
Huddleston, Robert	Caswell, Wm hr Wm.	1683
Huddleston, Wm. Hrs	Overton, John	1680
Hudler, John	Clark, Lardner	647
Hudler, Jos.	Caswell, William, heir of Wm.	210
Hudler, Lemuel	Caswell, Wm.	669
Hudson, Chamberlain	Smith, Robert	1960
Hudson, George	Dix, William	247
Hudson, Miles	Robertson, James	1669
Hughes, Bartley	Barry, Redmon Dillen	029
Hughes, Bartley	Dillonberry, Redmon	029
Hughes, George	Sheppard, John	064
Hughlett, William	Freeman, Nathan	443
Hughlett, William	Lambrick, James hrs.	52
Hughlett, William	Lynch, George hrs.	051
Hughlett, William	Ash, Stephen heirs	044
Hughlett, William	Indian Lands	046
Hughlett, William	Barrett, John	45
Hughlett, William	Berry, John	45
Hughlett, William	Berry, John heirs	925
Hughlett, William	Boone, Jacob heirs	046
Hughlett, William	Burnett, John heirs	037
Hughlett, William	Harris, Hardy	052
Hughlett, William	Lambrick, James	043
Hughlett, William	Long, James	47
Hughlett, William	Merrell, Henry heirs	042
Hughlett, William	Mott, Abraham heirs	047
Hughlett, William	Murrell, Henry	579
Hughlett, William	Vaughan, Abraham	579
Hughlett, William	Vaughn, Abraham	2258
Hughs, Burwell heirs	Donelson, Stockley	354
Hughs, David	Thomas, Martin	065
Hughs, George	Sheppard, John	272
Hughs, Jesse	Weakley, Robert	2118
Humphrey, Joseph heirs	Weakley, Robert	872
Humphries, David	Tilman, John	871
Humphries, David	Jackson, Philip heirs	633
Humphries, Elijah	Laster, James	886
Humphries, Elijah	Reaves, David	
Humphries, Henry heirs	Sugg, George Agustus	

Middle panel

Assignee:	Claimant:	File #
Humphries, Randolph	Hill, Green	180
Humphries, Wm.	Hannah, Rody	626
Hunneycut, A.	Cobb, Wm.	081
Hunt, James	Ballentine, Maltine	38
Hunt, Memucan	Glaze, Samuel	145
Hunter, Elisha	Hadley, Joshua	45
Hunter, James	Hitchcock, William	1493
Hunter, Sol.	Jones, Seburn	66
Hunter, Timothy	Sheppard, John	067
Huse, Samuel	Cates, Joshua	23
Hutchings, Edward	Bright, Simon	983
Hutchings, Thomas	Sutherland, George	459
Hutchins, James	Buchanan, John	1563
Hutchins, Robert	Mountflorence, James C	301
Hutsen, Chamberlain	McFarland, Walter	355
Hutson, Chamberlin	Hart, Adam	1404
Hutson, Isaac heirs	Nichols, John	1001
Hutson, John	Marshall, John	48
Hutson, John heirs	Marshall, John	481
Hyde, Andrew	Dyer, Joel	420
Hynes, Hardy	Sheppard, Nancy	724
Hynes, Hardy heirs	Sheppard, Nancy	695
Indian Lands	Amacher [sic]	47
Ingrim, George hrs	Donelson, Stockley	963
Inman(?), George	Person, Thomas	407
Inman, William	Deaderick, John	2390
Irwin, Joseph	Benton, Solomon	2421
Isbell, Thomas	Atway, Hardy	512
Isbell, Thomas	Duoston, Abraham	762
Isbell, Thomas	Smith, Arthur	758
Isley, Saml. Hrs.	Armstrong, Richard	128
Ivey, Claborn	Hays, Isaac	150
Ivey, David	Barbey, John	448
Jackson, A. & S. Donelson	Driver, Charles	1099
Jackson, Andrew	Tatom, Howell	333
Jackson, Fra. Heirs	Robertson, James	1661
Jackson, James	Bell, Robert	1604
Jackson, Jeremiah heirs	Sheppard, Martin Gardn	778
Jackson, Job	Clark, Lardner	2305
Jackson, John	Weakley, William	267
Jackson, Josiah	Twinbull, William	676
Jackson, Philip heirs	Robertson, Elijah	136
Jackson, Philip heirs	Robertson, Elijah	1689
Jackson, Roberson heirs	Sheppard, Benjamin	400

Right panel

Claimant:	Assignee:	File
Harney, Selby & Ant. Bledso	Jackson, Robert	710
Dixon, Tilmon	Jackson, Thos.	478
Bledsoe, Anthony H.	Jacobs, Abraham	701
Baker, John	Jacobs, Ambrose	644
McCawley, Matthew	Jacobs, Benjamin	18
Bushnell, Eusebrus	Jacobs, Daniel	651
Dixon, Tilghman	Jacobs, Peter	2051
Stewart, Duncan	Jacobs, William heirs	2369
Gogun, John	James, Coman	542
Glover, John	James, Sanders	1236
Brock, Joseph	James, Charles hrs	824
Donelson, Stockley	James, Chas.	08
Cason, William	James, Daniel	089
Cason, William	James, Daniel	892
Gillingham, James	James, Miles hrs.	2347
Barrow, Sherrod	James, Truman	891
Hays, Robert	James, William	672
Copeland, John	Jamison, William	709
Stewart, Duncan	Jarrett, Jacob heirs	2371
MacKary, John	Jarvis, Joel	2297
Robertson, James	Jay, Simon heirs	633
Armstrong, M. & S. Donelso	Jefferson, Joel	984
Armstrong & Donelson	Jefferson, Joel hrs	016
Wills, Hayden	Jeffres, John	703
Tiffin, Thomas	Jeffreys, Thomas	1621
Marshall, John	Jeffries, John heirs	623
Breckon, Jas. G.	Jenkins, Josiah	41
Gwin, Edward	Jenkins, Levi	181
Sheppard, Benjamin	Jennett, Lewis	699
Harney, Selby & Anthony	Jennings, Thomas	084
Allen, George	Jerem.Brantley hrs.	532
Phillips, Mann	Jermigan, Gardner	71
Jones, William	Jesse Cobb	1994
Broom, Mason	Jesse Cobb & Ezekial Smi	1939
Lane, James	Jesse Reed	211
Donelson, Stockley	Jessop, Isaac heirs	2227
Sugg, George Augustus	Jetth, Fenner heirs	878
Reed, Alexander	Jimmerson, Thomas	238
Martin, Samuel	Jinkins, Abraham	639
Rutherford, Griffith	Jinkins, William heirs	1023
McCulloh, Benjamin	Jitts, Jeremiah	1718
McCullock, Benjamin	Jitts, Peter heirs	31
Allen, Samuel	Jno.Jones heirs	536
Goldsberry, William	John Ford	873

Assignee Index

Assignee:	Claimant:	File #	Assignee:	Claimant:	File #	Assignee:	Claimant:	File
John Gray & Thomas Bloun	Lewis, William	378	Jones, Ambrose	Johnston, Rice	370	Jordon, River	Barton, Samuel	1210
John Lee	Low, Jonathan	1051	Jones, Ambrose	Newsom, Aaron	1436	Joslin, Benj.	Robertson, James R.	437
John Marshall	Glover, Jonathan	475	Jones, Ambrose	Ray, Daniel	788	Joslin, Daniel	Cromwell, Rowlen	2280
John McNairy	Harrell, Benjamin	662	Jones, Benjamin	Linton, Hezekiah	635	Jourdon, Ptolemy	Dillenberry, Redmon	022
John Rice	Lane, Jesse	306	Jones, Benjamin	Taylor, Thomas	708	Joyner, Joel	Nichols, John	1864
John Rice	Lane, Jesse	869	Jones, Binford	Smith, John	2351	Joyner, Thomas	Brekon, James	919
John Rice &c	Borough, Joel	056	Jones, Brinson	Jones, Abraham	048	Joynes, Lewis	Hadley, Joshua	126
John Sheppard	Lawrence, Josiah	069	Jones, Brittain	Tatum, Ho & Henry Wig	2444	Judge, Thomas	McClurd, Thomas	384
Johnson, Arthur	Boyd, John, Jr.	1378	Jones, David	Ausgood, Thomas	3	Kanady, Abraham	Laurey, Daniel	947
Johnson, Henry	Dobson, Elias	07	Jones, David & D Stewart	Etheredge, Daniel	1367	Keagey, John	Childers, John	571
Johnson, Henry J.	Etheredge, William	536	Jones, Elisha	Gwin, John	1434	Kearr, Robert	Crocker, Abraham	727
Johnson, Henry, Jr.	Flesher, Robert	020	Jones, Henry	Pratt, Peter	167	Keay, Jonathan	Hubbart, Zebulon	573
Johnson, Ptolemy	Barry, Redmon Dillen	022	Jones, Hezekiah	Davis, Joshua	691	Kelley, Thomas	Brown, William	2152
Johnson, S. hr of Richard	Edwards, David	115	Jones, James	Harget, Fred	588	Kelley, William heirs	Tatum, Ho & Henry Wiggins	2441
Johnson, Thomas	Cox, Charles	1575	Jones, Jas.	Fort, Spear	027	Kelly, Charles	Pasmore, David	1496
Johnson, Thomas	McGloskins, Alexander	1686	Jones, John	Allen, Samuel	536	Kelly, Dugald	Harris, Edward	1151
Johnson, Thos.	Boren, Bazel	037	Jones, John	Thompson, Samuel	849	Kelly, John	Long, Nicholas	364
Johnson, William	Bailey, Bazel	18	Jones, Joshua	Tuton, Oliver	348	Kelly, John heirs	King, Robert	682
Johnson, William	Boyd, Francis	4	Jones, Josiah	Brickell, James	1721	Kemp, David heirs	King, Robt.	078
Johnston, Archib.	Anderson, Danl	51	Jones, Josiah	Davis, Joshua	800	Kemp, Joseph	Faison, James	613
Johnston, Briton hrs	Burton, Robert	322	Jones, Nathaniel (heir)	Jones, Samuel	72	Kenady, Anthony	Buds, Samuel	100
Johnston, Daniel	Cloud, Peter	172	Jones, Oliver	Hadley, Joshua	1358	Kenner, Thomas, decd	Kenner, Hawson	41
Johnston, Hardy	Sheppard, Nancy	720	Jones, Peter	Donelson, Stockley	491	Kent, Thomas	Sanders, William	593
Johnston, John	Cantrell, Stephen	1402	Jones, Phillip	Williams, Eliza	583	Kerkandoll, Jane	Lawson, John	377
Johnston, John	Cole, Pemple, William [sic - ?]	145	Jones, Richard	Wilburn, Daniel	0125	Kerkendall, Jane	Ford, Simon	612
Johnston, John	Rowell, Andrew	146	Jones, Samuel	Jones, Nathaniel	72	Kerkendall, Matthew	Carr, Abner	346
Johnston, John	Whitfield, Bryant	269	Jones, Samuel	Tuton, William	351	Kerkendoll, Matthew	Weatherspoon, William	610
Johnston, Lancelot	Padon, Thomas	346	Jones, Seburn	Hunter, Solomon	66	Kerr, John	Malloy, Thomas	2343
Johnston, Peter	Phillips, Phillip	1519	Jones, Seburn	Leary, Luke	36	Kerr, Joseph	Fox, Francis	713
Johnston, Rice	Jones, Ambrose	370	Jones, Seburn	Searcey (Learcey), Luke	36	Kerr, Joseph	Houston, Daniel	950
Johnston, Robert	Ross, Abram	701	Jones, Stephen	Barton, Samuel	352	Kervin, Thomas	Hamilton, James	121
Johnston, Thomas	McGlouren, Alexander	2089	Jones, Stephen	Barton, Samuel	032	Kidwell, Elijah	Beard, John Lewis	241
Johnston, Thomas	Smith, Owen	356	Jones, Taylor	Nelson, Robert	1562	Kilgore, Thomas	Carter, Humphrey	2310
Johnston, Thomas	Willard, James	376	Jones, Thomas	Clark, Lardner	106	Kilgore, Thomas	Malloy, Thomas	1342
Johnston, Walter	Elliott, Simon	269	Jones, Underhill heirs	Malloy, Thos.	549	Killgoworth, John (?)	Harris, Edward	1465
Johnston, William	Cheeney, John	200	Jones, William	Cobb, Jesse	1994	Killoer, Andrew	Province, John	1803
Johnston, Wm.	Brehow, James G.	934	Jones, Wm.	Cobb, Jesse	085	Kincannon, Mathew	McCoy, Eli	463
Johnston,Ben.hrs	Atkinson, Charleton	666	Jones, Wm.	Cobb, Jesse	640	Kincannon, Matthew	Darby, Patrick	731
Joiner, Stephen heirs	Thompson, Robert	1531	Jones, Wm. Hr of Jno.	Cobb, Jesse	0141	Kindle, George	Snyder, George etal	1264
Joines, John	Rice, John	200	Jordan, Fountain	Irwin, Robert	1634	King, Andrew	Harris, Edward	1160
Jones, Absalom	McCulloch, Benj.	050	Jordan, John heirs	Williams, Willoughby	452	King, Anthony	Guinn, Edward	309
Jones, Allen (hr of David)	Wheeeller, David (heir)	787	Jordan, Thos.	McCulloh, Benjamin	298	King, Edmund	Ford, John	1989
Jones, Ambrose	Bennet, William	868	Jordon, Jones hrs	Easton, James	1097	King, Edward	Donelson, Stockley	2260
Jones, Ambrose	Hickman, Corbin	31a	Jordon, River	Barton, Samuel	1208	King, Enoch	McCulloh, Benjamin	320

Assignee:	Claimant:	File #	Assignee:	Claimant:	File #	Assignee:	Claimant:	File
King, Enock	Wilson, John	2073	King, William	Modlin, Ezekial	090	Lane, Jesse	Rice, John	306
King, Jacob	Stewart, Duncan	2374	King, William	Sawyer, Willis	911	Lane, Jesse	Rice, John	869
King, James	Dixon, Tilmon	059	King, William	Winfree, Thomas	1053	Lane, Thomas	Cobb, Jesse	691
King, James	Cock, William	1704	King. Martin	Overall, William	1247	Langford, Peter	Armstrong, Andrew	850
King, John	Robertson, James	061	Kirby, Edmund	Decern, Francis	2119	Langston, David	McFashion, Caleb	470
King, Joseph	Ward, Ennis	447	Kirkland, John heir of Wm	Sheppard, Nancy	2099	Langston, Josiah hrs	Fenner, Richard	32
King, Robert	Bean, Henry	675	Kirkpatrick, Alexander	Rogers, Mark	195	Lanier, Alexander	Trapp, Martin	607
King, Robert	Bean, William	511	Kirkpatrick, John	Boyd, John	1855	Lanier, Edward	McCulloh, Benjamin	2086
King, Robert	Dickner, David	683	Kirkpatrick, Michael	Burnsides, David	1859	Lanier, James	Bear, Jesse	763
King, Robert	Dodd, Jesse	419	Kirkpatrick, Michael	Gillespie, David	1882	Lanier, James	Blount, John Gray & Thoma	32
King, Robert	Garner, Thomas	525	Kirkpatrick, Michael	McDonald, Arthur	1858	Lanier, James	Everett, Thos.	764
King, Robert	Gibson, Charles	526	Kite, William	Sheppard, John	059	Lanier, James	Howard, William	406
King, Robert	Haddock, William	565	Kites, Chas.	Donelson, S. & Wm. Tyr	596	Lanier, James	Leek, Henry	572
King, Robert	Hord, William	636	Kits, Demsey heirs	Davis, James	1393	Lanier, James	Oats, Daniel	1012
King, Robert	Kelley, John	682	Kitt, Solomon	Stokes, John	314	Lanier, James	Rhodes, Jacob	730
King, Robert	Kemp, David	078	Kittrell, Isaac	Tatom, Barnard	1310	Lanier, James	Sally, Thomas	417
King, Robert	McCallister, John	347	Knight, Jesse	Swaggerty, Abraham	2363	Lanier, James	Smart, John	742
King, Robert	Miles, Jacob	364	Knight, Miles	McAustine, John	618	Lanier, James	Starn, Peter	576
King, Robert	Parry, Francis	1039	Knight, Samuel	Mathews, Mussenden /si	462	Lanier, James	Wiggle, Demsey	324
King, Robert	Prescote, Isaac	1040	Krauss, Gotlob	Redy, Jacob	1555	Lanier, Peter	Sugg, Aquilla	877
King, Robert	Swann, Thomas	563	Kuykendall, Adam	Hardon, Benj., Sr.	1867	Lanier, Robt.hrs.	Anderson, Daniel	1533
King, Robert & Joseph Cob	Stevenson, Jonathan	031	Kuykendall, John hrs	Hill, Henry	030	Laremore, Marmaduke	Hill, Henry	031
King, Robert (heir)	King, George	123	Kuykendall, Saml.	Crafford, Hugh	907	Larkin, John (heir)	McDaniel, Hugh	567
King, Robert M.	McCoy, Patrick	536	Lacey, Hopkins	Lively, Matthew	301	Larremore, William heirs	Wheaton, Charles	677
King, Robt & Chas & Coop	Hackner, Daniel	789	Lackey, James W.	Rhea, Jno., Annanias Mc	286	Larrimore, T.	Saunders, John	797
King, Robt & Jno Thompso	Bellers, Chas.	1023	Lackey, John heirs	Ross, William	344	Larrimore, Thos.	Wood, Robt.	077
King, Robt & John Latham	Phillips, Richard	422	Lacy, Hopkins & T. Malloy	Scarbrough, Nathan	266	Lash, Christian	Bryan, John	1505
King, Robt,R. Muir, J. Berry	Thompson, Samuel	1019	Laine, Thomas	Donelson, Stockley	061	Lassiter, Jacob	Nelson, Robert	1559
King, Robt.	Tiers, Jas.	1546	Lamb, Gibbs	Dickson, Jas.	188	Lassiter, Jas.	Stewart, Duncan	610
King, Thomas	Henderson, Nathaniel	292	Lamb, Nathan	Donelson, John	1969	Lassiter, Saml heirs	Hart, Anthony	600
King, Thomas	Maples, Marmaduke	678	Lambert, Aaron	Davis, Archibald	468	Laster, Josiah	Sheppard, John	068
King, Thomas	Nobles. John	677	Lambert, Aaron	Quinn, Michael	205	Lath, Alner(?)	Baker, John	832
King, Thomas	Owens, William	903	Lambert, Aron	Dixon, Thomas	385	Latham, John	Reaves, Samuel	1022
King, Walter	Newhouse, Lewis	1016	Lambert, Henry	Sheppard, Nancy	723	Laton, William	Drake, Jonathan	224
King, Walter	Newhouse, Lewis	1019	Lamore, Lewis	Bledsoe, Anthony	835	Laughlin, Cornelius	Donelson, John	1389
King, William	Bailey, Robert	1056	Lanbrick, James hrs.	Hughlet, William	052	Laurence, Adam	Basco, Lemon	267
King, William	Benson, Bailey	1050	Lancaster, John	Boone, Aaron	374	Laurence, Adam	Estridge, Thomas	2057
King, William	Boyce, Seth	1054	Lancaster, John	Payne, Peter	562	Laurey, Daniel	Kanday, Abraham	947
King, William	Daughtry, John	1062	Lancaster, John	Reedpeth, John	274	Law, Abraham	Mabene, James.; Admin:	53
King, William	Deal, Edward	1064	Lancaster, John	Renn, Aaron	802	Lawless, Matt.	Allen, Peggy	513
King, William	Dunnagen, John	1063	Lancaster, John	Ring, William	778	Lawrence, Adam	Harwood, Howell	1600
King, William	Hudgen, Holder	1061	Lancaster, John	Surles, Joseph	375	Lawrence, Josiah	Sheppard, John	069
King, William	King, James	1069	Lane, James	Reed, Jesse	211	Lawson, William heirs	Mountflorence, James Cole	299
King, William	Mays, Majr /sic/	1065	Lane, Jesse	Rice, John	1592	Lawton, Leonard	Barry, Redmon Dillon	1279

Assignee:	Claimant:	File #	Assignee:	Claimant:	File #	Assignee:	Claimant:	File
L-den, John hrs of	Carveat, Alexander	2362	Lewis, Simpson W. heirs	Murfree, Hardy	2117	Locust, Arthur hrs	Gorham, James C	607
Lea, James	Buckanan, John	1905	Lewis, Thos.	Barry, Redmon Dillon	1282	Locust, Francis hrs	Gorham, John	606
Leader, John	Murfree, Hardy	1991	Lewis, W. T.	Eason, Thomas	561	Logan, James	Bledsoe, Anthony	704
Leamon, Peter	Larkins, Stephen	1430	Lewis, W. T. & W. Tyrell	Thomas, Ross	528	Logue, John	Gurley, James	955
Leanon, Peter	Hartsfield, John	1429	Lewis, W. T. & Wm. Tyrrell	McDonald, John	016	Lomack, William	Casbol, Robert	2296
Learvin, Jno.	Allen, Sarah	019 [?]	Lewis, W. T. & Wm. Tyrrell	Sugg, John	028	Long, Heywood heirs	Smith, Oliver	2105
Leary, Luke	Jones, Seburn	36	Lewis, Watt heirs	Drew, John	249	Long, James heirs	Hughlett, William	043
Lee, Hardy	Anderson, Daniel	38	Lewis, William T.	Mosuire, Francis	817	Long, Nicholas	Barber, Joshua	2048
Lee, Henry	Lanier, James	572	Lewis, William T.	Williams, Jesse	1688	Long, Nicholas	Copeland, Kedar	358
Lee, James	Cockran, John	029	Lewis, William Terrel	Morrison, Joel	2054	Long, Nicholas	Glandon, Major	363
Lee, James	Cothran, John	2224	Lewis, William Terrel	Pitts, Matthew	2056	Long, Nicholas	Kelley, John	364
Lee, James	Eastes, Bartlet	1052	Lewis, William Tyrrell	Witherington, Joseph	2164	Long, Nicholas	Luey, Burrel	351
Lee, James	Martin, Richard	29	Lewis, Wm.	Blount, John Gray & Tho	378	Long, Nicholas	Richardson, William	285
Lee, Peter	Sheppard, Benjamin	384	Lewis, Wm. T.	Halcom, Phillips	051	Long, Nicholas	Swanson, John	329
Lee, Timothy	Brekon, Jas.	88	Lewis, Wm. T.	Waters, William	139	Long, Nicholas	Symmony, James	352
Legget, Elias heirs	Weakley, Robert	1928	Lewis, Wm. T. & Wm.	Locklove, Jonathan	053	Long, Nicholas	Underdue, Demsey	354
Leidmore, Watson	Dillonberry, Redmon	040	Lewis, Wm. T. & Wm. Tyrr	Tarrant, Manlove	052	Long, Nicholas	Wilkeson, John	290
Lenear, James	Childers, Robert	704	Lewis, Wm. T. heir Macaja	Lewis, Micajah	645	Long, Nichols	Thomas, Lemuel	286
Lenear, James	Hoover, Henry	684	Lewis, Wm. Terrel	Williams, Nathan	2041	Long, William	Shelton, David	1589
Lenear, James	Hoover, Henry heirs	684	Lewis, Wm. Terrell	Holland, Chas.	050	Looney, David	Cole, Thomas	23
Lenear, James	Hopkins, John	753	Lewis, Wm. Tyrell	Outlaw, Alexander	362	Looney, David	Duffield, Thomas	457
Lenear, James	Hopkins, John	753	Lewis, Wm. Tyrell	Parmely, Ephraim	694	Looney, David	Howell, Jesse	815
Lenier, James	Mann, Francis	779	Lewis, Joshua hrs	Barnes, Henry	1397	Looney, Moses heirs	Robertson, James	628
Lennon, Eph heirs	Stewart, Duncan	612	Libbincutt, John	Sugg, Geo. A.	068	Losson, John	McCulloch, Benj.	035
Lenoir(?), Chas.	Donelson, John	1387	Lilly, Sarah hr of John	Buxton, William	347	Lott, George	Dixon, Tilmon	454
Letches, William	Marshall, John	484	Lindsay, Isaac	Clayton, Leward	951	Love, David	Young, Daniel	2142
Letchmore, Watson	Barry, Redmon Dillen	040	Lindsay, Isaac	Hadley, Joshua	1352	Love, Josiah	Davis, Bartley	248
Lethis, William	Young, Samuel	0135	Linton, Hezekiah	Jones, Benjamin	635	Love, Josiah	Martin, Nicholas	207
Lett, James	McDowd, Josiah	141	Linton, Hezekiah , hr. Jess	Linton, Jesse	581	Love, Robert	Hood, William	2059
Lewellen, Thomas	Cartwright, Robert	1726	Linton, Jesse heirs	Linton, Hezekiah	581	Love, Thomas	Brooks, Giles	1873
Lewis & Tyrrell	Parr, Josiah	029	Linton, Jesse heirs	Barbour, Richard	724	Lovell, John heirs	McNairy, John	661
Lewis, Amos	Punch, John	2281	Lippencut, Wm.	Clark, Lardner	430	Lowe, Marvel	Stancel, Peter	1336
Lewis, Amos	Terrill, William	351	Liskow, Thomas	Edwards, Robert	182	Lowe, Obediah	Rice, Jno. Etal	309
Lewis, Amos	Tyrrell, William	074	Little, Archibald	Watson, John	613	Lowell, Jas.	Breckon, Jas. G.	43
Lewis, Charles	Clark, Lardner	669	Little, George	Watson, John	0123	Lowell, Zadock	Glasgow, James	472
Lewis, James M.	Harper, Fred	079	Little, Jonas	Zealott, Jonathan	0122	Lucas, Ball(?)	Fowler, David	076
Lewis, Joel	Rainey, James	257	Lock, James	Zealott, William	750	Lucas, Benj.	Hogg, Thos	026
Lewis, John	Hadley, Joshua	495	Lock, James	Davenport, Jos	948	Lucas, Benjamin	Hogg, Thomas	1585
Lewis, John	Nichols, John	419	Lock, Matthew	Rayford, Maurice	1877	Lucas, Matthew	Barry, Redmon Dillon	1281
Lewis, Jonathan	Ford, John	861	Lock, Matthew	Wise, John	990	Lucy, Burrell	Long, Nicholas	351
Lewis, Joshua	Buchanan, John	405	Lock, William	Tatum, Bainard	989	Ludwell, Richard	Tuton, William	353
Lewis, Macajah Green	Green, Micajah	81	Lock, William	Ward, Solomon	2061	Luellen, Daniel	Totevine, Wm.	189
Lewis, Richard heirs	Stewart, Charles	2403	Lockart, John	Lewis, Wm. T. & Wm. T.	641	Lyles, Benjamin	Bushnell, Eusebrus & Dobbi	655
Lewis, Seth & Geo. Walker	Duffney, David	271	Locklove, Jonathan	Lewis, Wm. T. & Wm. T.	53 /?/	Lynch, George hrs.	Hughlet, William	051

Assignee:	Claimant:	File #:	Assignee:	Claimant:	File #:	Assignee:	Claimant:	File
Lynn, Jonathan heirs	Wells, Haydon & John Owens	05	Malloy, John	Donelson, John	1196	Mannifee, Jones	Barton, Saml	1440
Lytle, Andrew	Lyttle, William	2022	Malloy, Thomas	Baird, Joseph	2344	Mannin, Tymothy	Fort, Elias	862
Lytle, Arch.	Blackmore, Geo.D. & Jno.Pay.	783	Malloy, Thomas	Bosten, Andrew	2337	Manning, John heirs	Ewing, Alexander	541
Lytle, Archaibald	Brannon, James	094	Malloy, Thomas	Bradley, Zion	2340	Mansher, George	Gilmour, Charles	1535
Lytle, Archibald	Demmet, William	093	Malloy, Thomas	Brown, Jennings	288	Manson, John	Buchanan, John	2279
Lytle, Archibald	Dennet, William	093	Malloy, Thomas	Cameron, Alexander	239	Manyr, John hrs	Beard, John Lewis	242
Lytle, Archibald	Flood, Frederick	092	Malloy, Thomas	Cobb, Zebulon	558	Maples, Marmaduke	King, Thomas	678
Lytle, Archibald	Johnston, Benjamin	650	Malloy, Thomas	Copeland, Joab	2338	Marchant, McCaleb	Howard, Joshua	129
Lytle, Archibald	Lain, John	504	Malloy, Thomas	Cullifer, James	548	Mardera, James heirs	Donelson, Stockley	464
Lytle, Archibald	Matton, William	722	Malloy, Thomas	Curry, Thomas	556	Marion, F.	Overton, John	518
Lytle, Archibald	Roberson, John	420	Malloy, Thomas	Fain, Melchior	2346	Marion, Frederick	Overton, John	515
Lytle, Archibald	Stephenson, Peter	091	Malloy, Thomas	Hodges, Hardy	546	Marley, Robert	Anderson, Charles	341
Lytle, William	Blount, Thomas	655	Malloy, Thomas	Jones, Underhill	549	Marley, Robert	Barlow, George	343
Lytle, William	Lyttle, Andrew	2022	Malloy, Thomas	Karr, Robert	540	Marley, Robert	Murry, James	340
Lytle, William	Pearce, Theophilus	930	Malloy, Thomas	Ker, John	2343	Martin, John	Ewing, Robert	2300
Lytle, William	Rich, James	1423	Malloy, Thomas	Morris, Phillip	2345	Marr, John	Griffin, Isaac	816
Lytle, William	Rillom, John	1424	Malloy, Thomas	Richy, Thomas	545	Marr, John Sr.	Roberson, James	608
Lytle, William	Stevenson, William	758	Malloy, Thomas	Ruth, Edward	2341	Marret, Wm.	Dickson, John	191
Lytle, William	Towel, Stephen	1425	Malloy, Thomas	Weathers, Benjamin	1270	Mars, Timothy heirs	Mountflorence, James Cole	296
Lytle, Archibald	McVey, Eli	713	Malloy, Thos	Bracken, Joseph	2335	Marsgall, John	Letches, William	484
Lytle, William	Mosley, Joseph	1426	Malloy, Thos.	Pendergrass, William	2336	Marshall, Charles	Hampton, Andrew	767
Lytle, William	Welch, William	306	Malloy, Thos.	Perkins, James	2342	Marshall, Geo.	McCarty, Jacob	1502
M. Armstrong & D.Shelby	Gorley, Ayeres	975	Malloy, Thos.	Williams, Thomas	2334	Marshall, John	Allen, William	206
Mabbey, Wm.	Buchanan, John	2079	Malone, Jacob	Barry, Redmon Dillen	039	Marshall, John	Baltrip, James	223
Mabene, James, Admr.	Law, Abraham*	053	Malone, Jacob	Dillonberry, Redmon	039	Marshall, John	Beavers, James	228
MacCollum, Isaac	Curtis, Thomas	290	Maltrie	Hunt, James	591	Marshall, John	Beavers, John	098
Mackey, Alexander	Dundelow, Benjamin	096	Man, John heirs	Nelson, Robert	424	Marshall, John	Bevearis, John	098
Maclemore, John	Stewart, Duncan	2399	Manly, Solomon	Murfree, Hardy	113	Marshall, John	Carrol, Daniel	229
Maclin, William	Stewart, George	122	Manly, William	Robertson, James	1665	Marshall, John	Carroll, Harwell	488
Macon, John	Person, Thomas	95	Mann, Arnold	White, James	1685	Marshall, John	Curk, William	483
Madison, Jno.	Hickman, Thomas	1329	Mann, Francis	Lanier, James	779	Marshall, John	Denson, William	222
Madry, John	Mulherin, James	055	Mann, John	Brayboy, John	021	Marshall, John	Duncan, William	486
Madry, Moses	Hart, Anthony	743	Mann, John	Dunlop, Thomas	2434	Marshall, John	Harris, John	224
Magley, Robt heirs	Donelson, Stockley	594	Mann, John	Finly, Abraham	670	Marshall, John	Harris, Samuel	480
Mahley, Solomon	Murphree, Hardy	113	Mann, John	Fowler, Abraham	673	Marshall, John	Hatches, David	582
Mahon, James	Barry, Redmon Dillen	1287	Mann, John	Harper, William	674	Marshall, John	Hunt, David	208
Mahon, James	Dillonberry, Redmon	1287	Mann, John	Hill, Hardy	671	Marshall, John	Hutson, John	481
Mains (sic)	Burgess, Wm.	761	Mann, John	Hudlow, Joseph	2432	Marshall, John	Jeffreys, John	623
Malden, James	Kuykendall, Joseph	1256	Mann, John	McFarson, Roger	2431	Marshall, John	Matthews, Richard	487
Mallebey, James	Weakley, Robert	357	Mann, John	Mullen, Michael	2435	Marshall, John	Morris, William	097
Mallet, Theodore	Fletcher, Joseph	20	Mann, John	Pickle, Jonas	2433	Marshall, John	Rigens, Joel	479
Malley, Thomas	Meares, Abraham	544	Mann, John	Worwick, Wyatt	672	Marshall, John	Rogers, Arthur	225
Malley, Thomas	Nelson, Giles	547	Mann, Robert	Hogg, Thomas	55	Marshall, John	Savage, Ransom	478
Mallica, Dan	Gloster, Thomas	999	Mann, Thomas	Harney, Selby & Ant. Bie	706	Marshall, John	Shaw, Zacharias	230

Assignee:	Claimant:	File #:	Assignee:	Claimant:	File #:	Assignee:	Claimant:	File
Marshall, John	Towning, James	226	McAdoe, James hrs	Easton, James	1039	McConnel, Robert	Collet, John	2414
Marshall, John	Valentine, Peter	476	McAfee, Azariah	Berry, Thomas	667	McConnel, Robert	Crozier, Arthur	1319
Marshall, John	Ward, Benjamin	482	McAllister, John	King, Robert	347	McConnel, Robert	Dodson, Belitha	1324
Marshall, John	West, Francis	474	McAllister, John	Shields, John etal	1115	McConnel, Robert	Parker, James	1321
Marshall, John	White, George	485	McAndrews, Andrew	Baker, John	221	McConnel, Robert	Potter, Francis	2411
Marshall, John	Woodrough, John	477	McAustin, John	Knight, Miles	618	McConnel, Robert	Sherkley, Robert	1323
Marshall, John	Young, William	473	McBride, James	Robertson, Elijah	029	McConnel, Robert	Simpson, Jack	1326
Marshall,Emanuel hrs	Barton, Joseph	3	McBride, James heirs	Robertson, Elijah	809	McConnel, Peter	Brunfield, Peter	2408
Marson, Samuel	Crockley, Allen	887	McCabe, Peter heirs	Donaldson, John	1642	McConnell, Peter	Bayley, John	2409
Martial, Solomon heirs	Tatum, Ho & Henry Wiggins	2284	McCafferty, James	Conway, Joseph	679	McConnell, Robert	Crossey, Anthony	2412
Martin, George	Madry, Darling	452	McCain, James	Shute, William	095	McConnell, Robert	Hewet, Ebenezer	049
Martin, Henry	Williams, Willoughby	284	McCall, Alex	Charlescraft, James	056	McConnell, Robert	Howel, Ebenezer	2415
Martin, Isaac	Robertson, James	060	McCall, Alex	Gary, George	048	McConnell, Robert	Howel, Talliafarro	033
Martin, John	Ewing, Robert	2299	McCall, Alex	Moore, James	049	McConnell, Robert	Howell, Talliferro	2410
Martin, John heirs	Rice, Jno. Etal	315	McCall, Alex	Perkins, Isaac	053	McConnell, Robert	Jamison, Roger	1312
Martin, Joseph	McVey, Ei	1597	McCall, Alex.	Ready, Hezekiah	054	McConnell, Robert	Onsley, John	1327
Martin, Joshua	Porter, John	227	McCall, Alex.	Gray, Sylvanus	050	McConnon & Balch	Bradshaw, James	17
Martin, Patrick	Sugg, Aquila	876	McCall, Alex.	Hopkins, Isaac	055	McConough, Dougald heir	Rice, Jno. Etal	308
Martin, Robert	Clark, Lardner	262	McCall, Archibald	Bledsoe, Isaac	760	McCormack & Rowan	Parker, Charles	1123
Martin, Thomas	Glasgow, James Col.	287	McCallum, Isaac	Upchurch, Charles	2294	McCormick, John heirs	Tyrrell, William	2265
Martin, William	Williams, Willoughby	283	McCarnon, Isaac	Barnes, Hezekiah	1437	McCormin, James	Hendrix, John	022
Mason, Aquilla	Moore, William	2064	McCarm, Hugh	Newman, Anthony	1771	McCoy, Anan.	Darron, Benjamin	482
Mason, John	O'Bryan, Laurence	61	McCarty, Florence	Gamble, Edmund	175	McCoy, Anan.	Darrow, Benjamin	486
Massey, Reubin heir	Massey, James	1879	McCarty, Jacob	Marshall, George	1502	McCoy, Anan.	Robinson, Henry	485
Massey, Thomas heir	Massey, James	1884	McCawley, Matthew	Jacobs, Benjamin	18	McCoy, Ananias	Darrow, Benjamin	483
Massey, Zebulon heirs	Williams, Etheldred	538	McCay, John	Greer, Jos & Jas Robert	1673	McCoy, Ananias	Robinson, Henry	028
Mathews, Joseph	Gerard, Charles	272	McCay, John	Robertson, James etal	1673	McCoy, Andn.	Bolic, John	484
Mathews, Charles heirs	Stewart, Duncan	2375	McClain, Jeremiah	Hamilton, Thomas	528	McCoy, Anon	Hendrix, John	483
Matthews, John	Baker, Charles	2046	McClane, Michael	Robertson, Elijah	797	McCoy, Daniel	Wilson, David	2109
Matthews, Musserdan	Knight, Samuel	462	McCleland, James	Nelson, Robert	266	McCoy, Dugald heirs	Easton, Jas.	1044
Matthews, Richard	Marshall, John	487	McCloud, Danl.	Ray, Wm.	898	McCoy, Eli	Kincannon, Matthew	463
Matthews, W.	Alexander, Ebenezer	1865	McClure, Thomas	Judge, Thomas	384	McCoy, James	Donelson, S. & Wm. Tyrrell	2226
Mattock, Nicholas	Barren, Willis	1213	McClure, Hardyman	McNary, John	659	McCoy, James	Terrel, Wm & S Donelson	1570
Mauldin, Ambrose	Devenport, Thomas	695	McCofferty, Thomas	Prescott, Austin	2472	McCoy, James heirs	Donelson, S. & Wm. Tyrrell	1075
May, Abraham heirs	Welburn, Daniel	569	McCollister, James	Barton, Samuel	05	McCoy, James heirs	Robertson, James	629
May, John	Hasten, Oliver	2038	McColloch, Benj.	Hampton, George	342	McCoy, John	Hill, Green	198
May, Thomas	Nelson, John	137	McColloch, Benjamin	Pratt, Zebulon	790	McCoy, John	Williams, Willoughby	2169
Mayberry, Frances	Hynds, Jno.	219	McConn, James	Overton, John	519	McCoy, Patrick N.	King, Robert	536
Mayberry, Francis	Horseford, James	410	McConnel, Robert	O'Carrill, Henry	1322	McCoy, Roger heirs	Duke, McDaniel & Cobb	048
Maybury, Francis	Dyer, Hopkins	092	McConnel, Robert	Bibble, David	1320	McCoy, Spence	Edwards, Jesse	834
Mayfield, Sutterline	Copeland, Joseph	117	McConnel, Robert	Bristoe, Charles	1314	McCraw, Samuel	Bryner, William	687
Mayfield, Sutterline	Morrison, Robert	256	McConnel, Robert	Brook, Zedikiah	1325	McCrery, Thomas	Gardner, James	418
Mayo, Gardner	Breakly, Andrew	303	McConnel, Robert	Burden, Thomas	2413	McCrory, James	Davidson, Thomas	2019
McAdams, John	Holley, Henry	2087	McConnel, Robert	Cameron, Sampson	1315	McCrory, James	Hester, John	2096

Assignee:	Claimant:	File #:
McCrory, Thomas	Bennell, William	733
McCrory, Thomas	Moore, James	2005
McCrory, Thomas	Reaby, Abraham	760
McCubbins, Isaac hrs	Duncan, Martin	588
McCuistian, James	Pyatt, Peter	267
McCullah, Benjamin	Grandall, John	312
McCulloch, Benj.	Haily, Robert	793
McCulloch, Benj.	Holmes, Andrew	2016
McCulloch, Benjamin	Fannon, Thomas	789
McCulloch, Benjamin	Hart, Hardy	295
McCulloch, Benjamin	Head, Luke	813
McCulloch, Benjamin	Hill, Roberson	317
McCulloch, Benjamin	Joperton, Taylor	1715
McCulloch, Benjamin	Jordan, Thomas	298
McCulloch, Benjamin	Losson, John	035
McCulloch, Benjamin	Seymore, Edward	051
McCulloch, Robert hr Jos.	McCulloch, Joseph	1497
McCullock, Alex	Casey, John	2271
McCullock, Benj.	Dunn, Thomas	034
McCullock, Benj.	Hall, Edward	822
McCullock, Benj.	Jett, Peter	031
McCullock, Benjamin	Wilson, Willis	829
McCulloh, Benj	Fisher, Joel	316
McCulloh, Benj	Hawley, Caleb	2030
McCulloh, Benj.	Hooks, John	1731
McCulloh, Benj.	Steell, Hardy	323
McCulloh, Benjamin	Parker, Arthur	2023
McCulloh, Benjamin	Baker, Peter	1719
McCulloh, Benjamin	Barber, James	2025
McCulloh, Benjamin	Barber, Elias	296
McCulloh, Benjamin	Barker, Nicholas	1717
McCulloh, Benjamin	Barker, Alex	2028
McCulloh, Benjamin	Bass [or Brass?], Moses	308
McCulloh, Benjamin	Bentley, Isaac	2055
McCulloh, Benjamin	Blough, Benjamin	2083
McCulloh, Benjamin	Bowman, Jesse	1727
McCulloh, Benjamin	Bracken, Matthew	1716
McCulloh, Benjamin	Curles, Thomas	1730
McCulloh, Benjamin	Davis, James	660
McCulloh, Benjamin	Deal, Lewis	2015
McCulloh, Benjamin	Ducawn [?], James	2026
McCulloh, Benjamin	Echolcis [?], Abner	343
McCulloh, Benjamin	Edens, John	2081
McCulloh, Benjamin	Flood, Elisha	311
McCulloh, Benjamin	Floyd, Francis	
McCulloch, Benjamin	Fowler, Frances	656
McCulloch, Benjamin	Jones, Martin	685
McCulloch, Benjamin	King, Enoch	320
McCulloch, Benjamin	McFascon, Henry	313
McCulloch, Benjamin	Medlin, Elisha	319
McCulloch, Benjamin	Nobles, Robert	2028
McCulloch, Benjamin	Nunnery, Androwson	864
McCulloch, Benjamin	Pool, John	2116
McCulloch, Benjamin	Ralford, John	310
McCulloch, Benjamin	Richardson, James	2027
McCulloch, Benjamin	Shanks, James	297
McCulloch, Benjamin	Shorte, Abraham	315
McCulloch, Benjamin	Spauldin, Edward	659
McCulloch, Benjamin	Taylor, Benjmain	300
McCulloch, Benjamin	Thomas, Jeremiah	2024a
McCulloch, Benjamin	Thomas, Thomas	2091
McCulloch, Benjamin	Thornbell, John	318
McCulloch, Benjamin	Thompson, Joshua	309
McCulloch, Benjamin	Toomer, Joseph	307
McCulloch, Benjamin	Tucker, Willey	368
McCulloch, Benjamin	Tucker, Willey	2195a
McCulloch, Benjamin	Wilborn, John	1720
McCulloch, Benjamin	Wright, Peter	1729
McCulloch, Benjamin	Yarbrough, David	2092
McCullough, Benj.	Huck, Thomas	1722
McCullough, Benjamin	Gannon, Robert	789
McCullough, Benjamin	Lanier, Edward	2086
McCumber, Humphrey	Donelson, Stockley	2380
McCurty, James	Rhodes, Christian etal	885
McCutchin, John	Haddock, Admiral	944
McDaniel, Alex	Donelson, Stockley	1186
McDaniel, Allen hrs	Blount, John Gray	08
McDaniel, Hugh	Larkin, John	567
McDaniel, I., Cobb, & P. D	Cobb, Jos	048
McDaniel, I., Cobb, & P. D	McDaniel, I.	48
McDaniel, Jno.	Blount, John Gray	44
McDaniel, Larkin heirs	Rice, John	037
McDaniel, Thos.	Ross, Henry	290
McDaniel, Thos.	Ross, Henry	623
McDaniel, Jane heir of Alex	Dickey, Thomas	251
McDash, John	Thompson, Jason	1959
McDelton, Joseph	Boyd, John, Senr	2012
McDillon, Jos.	Boyd, John, Jr.	399
McDonald, Arthur	Kirkpatrick, Michael;	1858
McDonald, Colin	Doud, Cornelius	986
McDonald, Colin hrs	Doud, Cornelius, Ass	986
McDonald, Colin hrs	Dowd, Cornelius	036
McDonald, John	Tyrell, Wm & W. T. Lewis	1547
McDonald, John	Tyrrell, Wm. & Wm. T. Lewi	016
McDonald, William	Rice, John	344
McDonald, Wm. Hrs	Hadley, Joshua	524
McDowd, Josiah	Lett, James	141
McDowell, Joseph	Bartles, John	1517
McDowell, Joseph	Brown, John	47
McDowell, Joseph	Faigan, George	1529
McDowell, Joseph	Buchanan, John	2034
McDuel, Willis	Bowman, William	24
McDugald, Archibald	Woods, Isham	052
McEween, David	Hutsen, Chamberlain	355
McFarland, Walter	McFarlin, Alexander	1532
McFarlin, John heir	Crain, John	071
McFarling, Jas.	McCulloh, Benjamin	313
McFascon, Henry	Mann, John	2431
McFurson, Roger	Johnston, Thomas	2089
McGloskey, Alexander	Johnson, Thomas	1686
McGloskins, Alex	Blount, John Gray	1244
McGound, Thomas	Davidson, John	1383
McGueston, John	Cantwell, Stephen	942
Mcileway, John hr of	Braiden, Charles	1588
Mcilykia, John	McDaniel, Hugh	874
McIver, Alexander	Adcock, Joshua	728
McKadon, William	Hardin, John	1371
McKee, Jno.	Casselman, Jacob	286
McKeel, Joshua	Russel, Samuel	192
McKenney, Charles	Boyd, John, Sr	1380
McKenney, Danl.	Rice, John & Harriot	341
McKinis, John	Adams, Jacob	1271
McKinney, Ro.	Hopkins, Jos.	86
McKinnie, Wm.	Campbell, Michael &P. Phillip	1697
McKinns, Timothy	Barton, Samuel	507
McKinsey, Hugh	Hadley, Joshua	165
McKinsey, Wm.	Phillips, P & M. Campbell	1697
McKirns, Timothy	Blackmore, Aaron	785
McKissack, Daniel	McNairy, John	663
McKnight, Pat	White, Robert	054
McKnight, Wm.	Smith, Daniel	274
McLaughlen, Samuel	Carter, Charles	1207
McLaughlin, Neill	Guffy, John	023
McLemore, Robert		

Assignee:	Claimant:	File #	Assignee:	Claimant:	File #	Assignee:	Claimant:	File
McMahan, Daniel	Aldridge, William	216	McWilliams, Jesse	McNeese, John	792	Mills (no other name given	Ramsey, John	39
McMoran, Domin[-?-]	Standley, James	2011	Meadows, Abraham	Shackler, Phillip	417	Mills, Elijah heirs	Donelson, Stockley	2256
McMullen, Isaac	Donelson, S. & Wm. Tyrrell	1086	Mears, Alexander	Nash, John	754	Mills, Jacob	Douglass, Edward	997
McMullin, Michael	Hogan, John	469	Mears, Timothy	McNeese, John	135	Mills, John heirs	Hart, Anthony	840
McMurray, Samuel	Porter, Samuel	030	Measles, Micajah	Nichols, John	411	Mills, Wm.	Armstrong, James	1041
McMurtree, John	Robertson, Elijah	795	Mebane, Chs.	Bailey, William Henry	060	Minoeys, Geo heirs	Drew, John	1557
McNairy, John	Lovell, John	661	Mebane, James	Wright, Adam	1620	Minshaw, Mica. Heirs	Blackface, William	566
McNairy, John	McKnight, Patrick	663	Mebane, Wm heir of Robt.	Mebane, Robert	27	Minshew, Wm. Heirs	Robertson, David	2466
McNairy, John	Pendergrass, John	494	Medearin, John	Mullis, James	06	Minters, John	Barry, Redmon Dillen	041
McNary & Nelson	Oneal,(?) Isham	305	Medearis, John	Herndon, George	07	Minters, John	Dillonberry, Redmon	041
McNary, John	Hogan, Roger	660	Medlin (?) Elisha	Bailey, Thomas	158	Miridith,Benj.hrs	Barry, Redmon Dillon	1285
McNary, John	Jarvis, Joel	2297	Medlin, Elijah	McCulloh, Benjamin	319	Mitchel, Abraham	Person, Thomas	2067
McNary, John	McClure, Hardyman	659	Medlin, Mills	Haywood, John	410	Mitchell, Jacob	Nelson, Robert	408
McNeal, Archibald heirs	Maxwell, George	368	Medlin, Zeland	Haywood, John	411	Mitchell, John	Alford, William	02
McNeel, Absalom	Shackley, Philip	0115	Meeks, Robt.	Blount, John Gray & Tho	1976	Mitchell, John	Donelson, John	681
McNeeley, William	Wells, Samuel	032	Meere, Abraham heirs	Malloy, Thos.	544	Mitchell, John	Platt, John	197
McNeeley, William	White, Walter	521	Melborn, David	Boyd, John	127	Mitchell, Samuel	Moore, Daniel	0100
McNeeley, William	Willis, Samuel	1015	Melbourne, Solomon	Phillips, P & M. Campbel	1698	Modlin, Ezekial	Beaird, Joseph	656
McNees, John	Appleton, John	791	Melchior, Fain	Malloy, Thomas	2346	Modlin, Ezekiel	King, William	090
McNees, John	Blount, John Gray	013	Meloy, Thomas	Donelson, Stockley	064	Moore, Marmaduke	Moore, Marmaduke	2230
McNees, John	Mott, Edge	793	Melton, John heirs	Robeson, James	2233	Molloy, Thomas	Alexander, Cameron	8
McNees, John	Price, Micajah	1590	Melvin, George	Hill, John	617	Molloy, Thomas	Davidson, James	2326
McNees, John	Reaves, Benjamin	1591	Mences, James	Spierpoint, Joseph	1853	Molloy, Thomas	Haughton, Levi	550
McNees, John	Stewart, Andrew	794	Menifee, John	Roads, Christian etal	267	Molloy, Thomas	Kinney, Robert	054
McNees, John	Whealey, Isum	790	Meres, John	Brown, James heirs	398	Molloy, Thomas	Spencer, William	1025
McNeese, John	Blount, John Gray	1034	Merrell, Henry heirs	Hughlett, William	047	Molloy, Thomas	White, Henry	22
McNeese, John	McWilliams, Jesse	792	Merritt, Stephen heir	Mennett, Benjamin	571	Monhouse, Daniel heirs	Mountflorence, James	293
McNeill, Zebulon heirs	Mears, Timothy	135	Messer, Benj.	Armstrong, Martin	1472	Monk, Isaac hrs.	Barry, Redmon Dillon	1283
McNeill, Zebulon heirs	Tyrrell, Wm. & Robt King	2309	Messingale, Solomon	Lamb, John	469	Monk, Notingham	Ryan, Thomas	2070
McNess, James	Nowell, James	1593	Metts, Willis heirs	Sheppard, Nancy	722	Montflorence, J. C.	Lawson, William	299
McNutty, John	Donelson, Stockley	1189	Mewshaw, John	Sheppard, Nancy	2045	Montflorence, James Cole	Sims, Thomas	294
McPherson, Abel	Wheaton, Daniel	559	Michael,------	Bledsoe, Isaac	614	Montflorence, Jas. C.	Gough, William	6
McPherson, Duncan heirs	McPherson, John	558	Mickelray, John	Benton, Jesse, dec'd	616	Montgomery, Alexander	Wiggins, Noah	673
McPherson, John	McFerson, Duncan	558	Middleton, Isaac	Dillonberry, Redmon	043	Montgomery, Michael	Bryant, William	12
McQuillin, Wm. (heirs)	Perkins, Lewis	614	Middleton, Solomon	Ford, John	883	Montgomery, Michael	Relph, Lewis	4
McRace, Robert	Hadley, Joshua	081	Midget, Jacob	Sheppard, Benjamin	388	Montgomery, William	Jimmerson, William	622
McRae, David	Prim, Abraham	1594	Miles, Abraham heirs	Williams, Willoughby	354	Montgomery, William	McLaughlin, Neil	1227
McRae, Reuben hrs.	Brewer, Sterling	1305	Miles, Jacob heirs	King, Robert	564	Moor, William	Owens, Don & Fran	0101
McRee, Samuel	Foster, Thomas	620	Miller, Adam	Roberts, Richard	099	Moore, B. heirs	Foster, Anthony	107
McRory, James	Williams, John	560	Miller, Jacob hr of Jas.	Douglass, Edward	545	Moore, Daniel	Mitchel, Samuel	0100
McRory, James (heir)	McRory, Thomas	48	Miller, James heirs	Blount, Reading	707	Moore, Elijah	Moore, Wm.	159
McRory, John	Brown, David	682	Miller, Randal	Stradley, Edward	1398	Moore, Freeman, heirs	Robertson, James	634
McVey, Eli	Martin, Joseph	1597	Miller, Rich'd	Ramsey, Allen	699	Moore, James	McCrory, Thomas	2005
McVey, John	Elliott, John	1598	Miller, Sol.	Robertson, Jas.	263	Moore, James	Thompson, Robt. Etal	314

Assignee:	Claimant:	File #:	Assignee:	Claimant:	File #:	Assignee:	Claimant:	File
Moore, James Lt. Assn.	McCall, Alex. Ass;	049	Morrow, Samuel	Bowman, William	761	Mountflorence, JC & R.Fe	Nelms, Charles	242
Moore, Jno. Davis hrs	Easton, James	1041	Morrow. Thomas	Dickson, James	207	Movey, Eli	Phillips P & M. Campbell	82
Moore, John	Templeton, Thomas	425	Morton, Jonas	White, James	1656	Moye(?), George	Bonner, John & James	606
Moore, Joseph	Elliott, James	219	Morton, Wm.	Williams, Willoughby	909	Moye?, John	Harris, Edward	1180
Moore, Marmaduke	Molley, Thomas;	2230	Mosier, Francis heirs	Sanders, James	1537	Mulford, Pertie heirs	Nelson, Robert	413
Moore, Morris	Weakley, Robert	1856	Mosier, Samuel heirs	Smith, Daniel	586	Mulherin, James	Cobb, Anthony	913
Moore, Moses	Gerard, Charles	353	Mosland, John	Brooks, Stephen	889	Mulherin, James	Doby, James	933
Moore, Phillip	Donelson, S. & Robt. King	414	Moslanders,Abel.hrs	Armstrong, John	02	Mulherin, James	Madry, John	055
Moore, Saml.	Barrow, John	1439	Motheral, John	Jones, Kedar /sic/	886a	Mulherin, James	Roberts, Elijah	929
Moore, Samuel	Rice, John & Harriet S.	1966	Motheral, John	Sampson, George	887	Mulherin, James	Roundtree, Archer	912
Moore, Thomas	Rawls, Gabriel	6	Motheral, Samuel	Williams, Peter	1723	Mulherrin [sic], James	Avery, Estridge	2139
Moore, William	Macomes, Aquilla	2064	Motherall, John	Roberts, Shadrack	265	Mulherrin, James	Bailey, Etheldred	1009
Moore, William	Moore, Elijah	159	Motherall, Joseph	Hector, Lewis	1262	Mulherrin, James	Bailey, Etheldred	2140
Moore, William	Morrison, Alexander	766	Motherell, Samuel	Tutson, Charles	0102	Mulherrin, James	Cobbs, Anthony	2138
Moore, William	Owens, Francis	679	Mott, Abraham heirs	Hughlett, William	042	Mulherrin, James	Doty, James	2137
Moore, Wm.	Gerrard, Charles	68	Mott, Benj.	Toomer, Henry	615	Mulherrin, James	Roberts, Elijah	2135
Moran, John	Standen, John	2062	Mott, Daniel	Dickson, Edward	209	Mulherrin, James	Rountree, Archer	2136
Moran, John hrs	Buel, Ambrose	810	Mott, Edge	McNees, James	793	Mulkerin [sic], James	Avery, Estridge	926
More, Benj.	Foster, Anthony	043	Mountflorence & Fenner	Bartholowmew, John	241	Mulkey, Wm.	Robertson, James etal	153
Morgan, Griffin hrs	Frazer, George	1525	Mountflorence & Fenner	Collins, Samuel	326	Mullen, Michael	Mann, John	2435
Morgan, Humphrey heirs	Robertson, James	2145	Mountflorence, J. C.	Acock, Moses	40	Mullin, Wm.	Gatling, John	044
Morgan, Isaac	Ray, Archibald	839	Mountflorence, J. C.	Acock, William	41	Mullis, James hrs.	Madearis, John	06
Morgan, James	Sheppard, John	070	Mountflorence, J. C.	Fling, Michael	7	Mundine (?), Joshua	Davis, Joshua	823
Morgan, Peter heirs	Phillips, Jonathan	1917	Mountflorence, J. C. & Fen	Howard, Richard	8	Mundine, Zebulon	Hays, John	57
Morgan, Thos. Heir of Jaco	Robertson, Elijah	516	Mountflorence, J. C. & Fen	Cobb, Peter	327	Murbee, Patrick	Tatum, Ho & Henry Wiggins	2442
Morgan, Wm.	Berry, Thomas	666	Mountflorence, James C.	Boone, James	1498	Murdock, Nathaniel	Blount, Reading	898
Morgan, Wm.	Sellers, Matthew	635	Mountflorence, James C.	Bowman, Robert	1500	Murfree, Hardy	Leader, John	1991
Morris, Benj.hrs	Armstrong & Donelson	041	Mountflorence, James C.	Monhouse, Daniel	293	Murfree, Hardy	Manly, Adam	557
Morris, Jas., hrs	Beaird, Jos	189	Mountflorence, James C.	Powell, John	1580	Murfrey, Hardy	Manly, Solomon	113
Morris, Jno heirs	Foster, Anthony	326	Mountflorence, James Cole	Britt, Sherrard	332	Murfree, Hardy	Nichols, William Jr.	583
Morris, John & James	Hickman, Thomas	087	Mountflorence, James Cole	Brown, Jesse	777	Murfree, Hardy	Wiggins, Matthew	519
Morris, Philemon	Harget, Frederick	1954	Mountflorence, James Cole	Mars, Timothy	296	Murfree, Hardy	Witherington, William	886
Morris, Phillip heirs	Malloy, Thomas	2345	Mountflorence, James Cole	Nelson, John	298	Murfrey, Hardy	Powell, Thomas	1182
Morris, Richard	Donelson, Stockley	674	Mountflorence, James Cole	Newhouse, Joseph	295	Murphey, Archibald	Dowell, James	648
Morris, William	Brown, James	138	Mountflorence, James Cole	Nowell, William	300	Murphree, Hardy	Archer, Baker	148
Morris, Wm.	Marshall, John	97	Mountflorence, James Cole	Polk, John	297	Murphree, Hardy	Bryan, William	244
Morris, Wm. Heirs	Hamilton, Jno.	2471	Mountflorence, James Cole	Reaves, Benjamin	859	Murphree, Hardy	Burton, John	57
Morris,Benj. Hrs	Armstrong, M. & S. Donelson	959	Mountflorence, Jas C	Griffin, Edward	1499	Murphree, Hardy	Carter, Robert	229
Morrison, Joel	Lewis, William Terrel	2054	Mountflorence, Jas. C.	Cooley, Samuel	92	Murphree, Hardy	Hare, Lawrence	263
Morrison, Robert	Mayfield, Sutterline	256	Mountflorence, Jas. C.	Griffis, Samuel	864	Murphree, Hardy	Harris, John	183
Morrison, Robt.	Morrison, Thos.	1635	Mountflorence, Jas. C.	Hutchins, Robert	301	Murphree, Hardy	Holmes, Shadrack	159
Morrison, Thos.	Morrison, Robert	1635	Mountflorence, Jas.	Batchelor, George	852	Murphree, Hardy	Horton, James	624
Morrow, John	Adcock, Edward	1391	Mountflorence, Jas. C.	Carr, William	287	Murphree, Hardy	Lewis, Sampson W.	2117
Morrow, John & James	McGuire, Michael	1395	Mountflorence, Jas. C.	Goodness, Richard	34	Murphree, Hardy	Perkins, Adam	248

Assignee:	Claimant:	File #	Assignee:	Claimant:	File #	Assignee:	Claimant:	File
Murphree, Hardy	Powell, William	161	Nelson, Robert	Beard, James	673	Newland, Eli	Rainey, James	342
Murphree, Hardy	Williams, John	184	Nelson, Robert	Browner, John	10	Newman, Anthony	Cox, Thomas	2120
Murphree, Hardy	Williams, Theophilus	168	Nelson, Robert	Browners, John	655	Newman, Anthony	McCann, Hugh	1771
Murphree, Hardy by hr of J	Winborn, John	82	Nelson, Robert	Burden, James	2423	Newnham, Aaron	Whitfield, Bryant	2065
Murphy, Archibald heir	Murphy, Hugh	616	Nelson, Robert	Bykin, Thomas	491	Newton, Estridge	Phillips, P. & M. Campbell	1691
Murray, James heirs	Marley, Robert	340	Nelson, Robert	Carrick, Zachariah	589	Newton, Henry	Turnbull, William	2040
Murray, Joshua hrs	Hays, Thos	115	Nelson, Robert	Dowden, Samuel	1732	Newton, Joseph	Stewart, Duncan	2368
Murray, Samuel heirs	Murray, Thomas	1702	Nelson, Robert	Fulcher, James	421	Nich.Moore heir	Allen, Alexander	649
Murrell, Jacob	Smith, Oliver	2010	Nelson, Robert	Ginn, Henry	412	Nichlet, John hrs	Bud, Samuel	715
Murson, Samuel	Underwood, Howell	890	Nelson, Robert	Green, Dempsey	654	Nicholas, John	Haddock, Andrew	107
Murter, Zedekiah	Williams, Willoughby	350	Nelson, Robert	Green, Demsey	415	Nicholas, Richard	Barry, Redmon Dillen	1352
Muss, John heirs	Donelson, Stockley	959	Nelson, Robert	Hicks, Jacob	09	Nichols, John	Cocken, John	422
Myers, Wm. Heirs	Rabb, Wm.	1392	Nelson, Robert	Jones, Taylor	1562	Nichols, John	Cole, Edward	425
Myres, Jacob	Donelson, Stockley	2259	Nelson, Robert	Lassiter, Jacob	1559	Nichols, John	Cole, Martin	409
Narress, David heirs	Smith, Jacob	580	Nelson, Robert	Man, John	424	Nichols, John	Collins, Josiah	735
Nash, Francis heirs	Sanders, James	524	Nelson, Robert	McCleland, James	266	Nichols, John	Crook, William	428
Nash, Jos.	Alexander, Robt.	665	Nelson, Robert	Mitchel, Jacob	408	Nichols, John	Daniel, Benjamin	752
Nash, Sarah heiress	Nash, Francis	717	Nelson, Robert	Mulford, Portis	413	Nichols, John	Freleer, John	932
Nash, William	Anderson, John	2298	Nelson, Robert	Nelson, James	656	Nichols, John	Hutson, Isaac	1001
Nash, William	Brumley, William	1860	Nelson, Robert	Orrange, William	407	Nichols, John	Joyner, Joel	1864
Nash, William	Cabbert, Richard	921	Nelson, Robert	Pendergrass, John	493	Nichols, John	Lewis, John	419
Nash, William	Colbert, Richard	920	Nelson, Robert	Pulley, George	880	Nichols, John	Meezles, Micajah	411
Nash, William	Herrington, Samuel	0103	Nelson, Robert	Ross, Samuel	2036	Nichols, John	Ridley, Berriman	459
Nash, William	Hodges, Hardy	0104	Nelson, Robert	Sharpe, Joseph	562	Nichols, John	Salter, John	426
Nash, William	Reaves, Foster	923	Nelson, Robert	Shoecraft, Abraham	172	Nichols, John	Smith, Stephen	1579
Nash, William	Rigby, Ezekial	759	Nelson, Robert	Stedham, Isaiah	401	Nichols, John	Spruel, Richard	1474
Nash, William	Saunders, Daniel	1353	Nelson, Robert	Strader, George	414	Nichols, John	Theregood, Francis	153
Nash, William	Simmons, Isaac	922	Nelson, Robert	Stump, Frederick	022	Nichols, John	Venters, William	022
Nash, William	Whitton, Isum	924	Nelson, Robert	Sugg, Michael	169	Nichols, John	Warner, Hezekiah	2467
Nations, John	Tatum, James	677	Nelson, Robert	Tow, Christopher	404	Nichols, John	White, Benjamin	1919
Nelms, Jesse	Rice, John & Harriot	339	Nelson, Robert	Wadsworth, William	1739	Nichols, John	Wiggins, Jacob	427
Nelson, Alex	Curry, John	248	Nelson, Robert	White, Robert	438	Nichols, John	Williams, Willoughby	453
Nelson, Alexander	Ward, Drury	173	Nelson, Robert	Wilkins, Joseph	402	Nichols, John	Winkle, Josiah	1002
Nelson, Collins	Baker, John	240	Nelson, Robert	Wise, Absalom	26	Nichols, Thomas	Patton, Saml, Jr	37
Nelson, Estridge	Robertson, Elijah	804	Nelson, Robt.	Taitt, Wm.	087	Nichols, Wm. Sr.	Murfree, Hardy	583
Nelson, Giles	Malloy, Thos.	547	Nelson, Wm.	Winningham, Thos.	026	Nicholson, Isaac	Barry, Redmon Dillen	043
Nelson, James	Nelson, Robt.	2301	Nelson, Robert	Glasgow, Jas & Robt Kin	946	Nickels, John	Fist, Samuel	430
Nelson, James	Nelson, Robert	656	Never, David	Harris, Edward	1116	Nickols, John	Sparckman, Edward	429
Nelson, Jesse	Donelson, Stockley	040	Neville, George	Adams, Howell	4	Nicoles, Richard	Dillonberry, Redmon	1352
Nelson, John	Freeman, David	036	Neville, George	Gambling, James	187	Nixon, Robert	Robertson, Elijah	815
Nelson, John	May, Thomas	137	Newberry, Wm. Heirs	Donelson, S. & Wm. Tyr	463	Noble, Mark	Barco, John	24
Nelson, John & Alex	Bentley, John	246	Newbran, Francis	Tatom, Howell	1725	Nobles, John heirs	King, Thomas	677
Nelson, John heirs	Mountflorence, James Cole	298	Newby, Robert	Reed, John	927	Nobles, Robert	McCulloh, Benjamin	2028
Nelson, Nathaniel heirs	Rice, Jno. Etal	318	Newell, John	Sheppard, Nancy	2043	Nobles, Wm.	Hart, Anthony	157

Assignee:	Claimant:	File #:	Assignee:	Claimant:	File #:	Assignee:	Claimant:	File:
Pearce, John (heir of Jas)	Pearce, John	202	Peter, Jan—(?)	Brown, Haggard, & Mayfi	1999	Phillips, P. & Michael Cam	Saunders, Isaac	1690
Pearce, John (heir)	Pearce, James	202	Peters, John	Sugg, Geo. A.	905	Phillips, P. & Michael Cam	Saunders, Richard	1694
Pearl, James	Weakley, Robert etal	2468	Peters, Thomas	Carmady, James	336	Phillips, Phil & Michael	Bradley, John	0107
Pearson, James	Cormack, John	2080	Peters, Titus	Harris, Edward	1127	Phillips, Philip & M. Camp	Cockburn, John	281
Pearson, James	Prescote, Thomas	2047	Pettes, Stephen	Love, Thomas	725	Phillips, Philip & M. Camp	Johnston, Peter	1519
Peasy, Joseph	Blount, Reading	971	Pettie, John	Bailes, Barnabus	1015	Phillips, Philip	Outler, Aaron	279
Pendar, Thos. Heirs	Fell, Watson	1275	Pettigrew, Hara (?)	Blair, John	416	Phillips, Phillip	Newtom. Estridge	691
Pendegrass, Jno.	McNairy, John	494	Pervy, Nehemiah	Randolph, Benjamin Fitz	2240	Phillips, Phillip & Campbel	Comers, James	1699
Pendergrass, Job	Robertson, James	205	Peyton, Ephraim	Herrendon, James	565	Phillips, Phillip & M. Camp	Turner, William	1693
Pendergrass, John	Nelson, Robert	493	Peyton, John	Robertson, James	676	Phillips, Phillip & M. Camp	Watson, Everat	1696
Pendergrass, John	Robertson, James	599	Peyton, John	Shermentine, Hezekiah	567	Phillips, Phillip & Mi. Cam	Tate, William	1692
Pendergrass, Wm. Heirs	Malloy, Thomas	2336	Phelps, Garret	Conrod, Nicholas	371	Phillips, Richard	King, Robert & John Latham	422
Peney, Francis heirs	Williams, Willoughby	355	Phelps, Jesse	Barry, Redmon Dillen	034	Phillips, Thos (heir of Bus	Phillips, Thomas	573
Pennington, Isaac	Tyner, Nicholas	250	Phelps, Jessee	Dillonberry, Redmon	034	Phillips, Wm.	Tuton, Oliver	349
Peraythe, Jos hrs.	Blount, Reading	033	Phelps, Wm.	Williams, Willoughby	334	Phillips, Wm.	Tyrrell, Wm. & Wm. Lytle	478
Percy, Francis	Coghlin, James	2268	Phew, Richd	Ford, John	47	Phillips, Zebulon	Overton, John	2003
Perkins, Adam	Cummins, George	1735	Phifer, Caleb	Harrison, Francis	851	Phillips,P. & Campbell. M.	Grace, James	72
Perkins, Adam	Murfree, Hardy	248	Phifer, Caleb	Lynch, John	356	Pickle, John	Scott, John	928
Perkins, Constant	Poor, John	168	Phifer, Martin	Hardon, Rovert	843	Pickle, Jonas	Mann, John	2433
Perkins, Isaac	McCall, Alex	053	Phifer, Martin	Seener, Peter	853	Pickles, Richard	Sheppard, Benjamin	390
Perkins, James	Whitsell, William	1640	Phillips, Isaac	Thrift, Abraham	1377	Pidgeon, Williams	Williams, Willoughby	609
Perkins, Jesse heirs	Malloy, Thomas	2341	Phillips & Campbell	Herrell, James	91	Pierce, Hardy's heir	Pierce, John	2143
Perkins, John	Stephenson, John etal	1371	Phillips & Campbell	Ramsey, Andrew	275	Pierce, Joseph heirs	Weakley, Robert	664
Perrey, Wm. Heirs	Donelson, S. & Wm. Tyrrell	1084	Phillips and Campbell	Orrell, Thomas	1695	Pierce, Wm.	Pierce, Jeremiah	1612
Perry, John	Ford, Thomas	1736	Phillips and Campbell	Ostin, William	298	Pierson, Samuel	Beck, William	140
Perry, Robert	Porterfield, John	340	Phillips, Isaac	Cornelius, Elijah	426	Plinor, John	Dickson, James	214
Perry, Sion	McConial, Patrick	642	Phillips, John	Caseleman, Benj	340	Pipkin, Lewis	McQuillin, William	614
Perry, Sion	Taylor, John	662	Phillips, Jonathan	Morgan, Peter	1917	Pipkin, Phillip	Neal, Whitaker	859
Perry, Wm. Heirs	Donelson, S. & Wm. Tyrrell	405	Phillips, Isaac	Acinclash, Duncan	787	Pipkin, Willis hrs.	Anderson, Daniel	848
Perrymore, James heirs	Williams, Eliza	1087	Phillips, Mann	Andrews, Thomas	636	Pirtle, George	Gardon, Robert	485
Person, Nathan heirs	Williams, Eliza	581	Phillips, Mann	Cox, Edward	1215	Pitman, Ison heirs	Smith, Oliver	2007
Person, Thomas	Ballard, Peter	579	Phillips, Mann	Jernagin, Gardner	71	Pitman, John	Stewart, Duncan	2373
Person, Thomas	Hawley, Benjamin	97	Phillips, Mann	Sweat, William	50	Pitts, Matthew	Lewis, William Terrel	2056
Person, Thomas	Hawley, Joseph	96	Phillips, Mann	Ward, Jesse	825	Plumley, Geo.	Robertson, James	1660
Person, Thomas	Macon, John	408	Phillips, Mann	Wilkins, Jordan	710	Poe, John heirs	Donelson & Armstrong	035
Person, Thomas	Mitchell, Abraham	95	Phillips, Mann	Wilkins, William	661	Poe, John hrs.	Armstrong, M. & S. Donelso	961
Person, Thomas	Tucker, Samuel	2067	Phillips, Mann	Willson, John	711	Polk, Ezekial	Stephens, Thomas	220
Person, Thomas	Williams, George	98	Phillips, Mark hrs	Clark, William	678	Polk, John	Mountflorence, James Cole	297
Persons, Thomas	Duncan, George	94	Phillips, P & Campbell	McVey, Eli	82	Pollard, Matthew heirs	Sugg, Aquilla	917
Persons, Thomas	Thomas, Asa	407	Phillips, P.	Trouter, Thomas	85	Pollock, Benjamin	Hays, Robert	1759
Pervice, James	Brown, John & John Davis	405	Phillips, P. & M. Campbell	Carrier, John	296	Polson, John	Davis, Joshua	824
Pervin, John hrs	Barnet, Robert	1942	Phillips, P. & M. Campbell	Robertson, Joseph	292	Pond, John	Prince, Robert	415
Peter Furney hr.	Allen, Mary	467	Phillips, P. & M. Campbell	Spoolman, William	295	Pool, John	McCulloh, Benjamin	2116
Peter, Daniel	Bledsoe, Anthony	502	Phillips, P. & Michael Cam	Melbourne, Solomon	1698	Poor–(?), John	Barton, Samuel	1212

Assignee Index

Assignee:	Claimant:	File #	Assignee:	Claimant:	File #:	Assignee:	Claimant:	File
Reed, Jesse	Williams, Phillip	237	Rice, John & Harriett	Pasmore, Enoch	1974	Rivear, William	Hart, Antony	7021
Reed, Jesse	Yancey, George	234	Rice, John & others	Ferrill, Jacob	319	Rivell, John	Hays, Robert	1760
Reed, Joseph heirs	Donelson, Stockley	1085	Rice, John & others	Harris, William	310	Roan, David	Robertson, James	1937
Reed, Phelps	Smith, Britton	1440	Rice, John & others	Martin, John	315	Robb, William	Myers, William	1392
Reed, Stephen	Anderson, Daniel	216	Rice, John & others	Nelson, Nathaniel	318	Robb, William	Stolcop, William	544
Reed, Walson	Easten, Jas.	1040	Rice, John & others	Simpson, Moses	320	Robchete(?), Joshua	Donelson, S. & Wm. Tyrrell	462
Reed, William	Hays, Robert	315	Rice, John & others	Stevens, Henry	323	Roberson /sic/, James	Marr, John, Sr.	608
Reed, William	Sanders, James	0112	Rice, John & others	Vintress, John	321	Roberson, Cornelius	Hickman, Thos	259
Reed, Wm.	Hays, Robert	46	Rice, John & others	Wright, John	312	Roberson, Elijah	Shaw, John	1005
Reid, Fran heirs	Johnson, William	539	Rice, John and others	Dominas, Domina	313	Roberson, James	Estridge, Thomas	1918
Reid, James' heir	Reed, Guilford Dudley, heir	2149	Rice, Wm. H.	Windsor, John	290	Roberts, Delilah	Reed, Guilford	1401
Reid, John	Sanders, James	0113	Richard Fenner	Glover, Solomon	837	Roberts, Elijah heirs	Mulherin, James	929
Reiley, Edm. Heirs	Gorham, J. C.	604	Richards, Clement	Blount, Reading	936	Roberts, Elijah heirs	Mulherin, James	2135
Reilly, Thomas	Robertson, Elijah	806	Richards, Jesse	Reed, Jesse	213	Roberts, Hardy heirs	Craddock, John	1537
Rever, James	Blount, Reading	434	Richards, John heirs	Buchanan, John	1013	Roberts, J.	Williamson, Geo	01
Reyley, John	Fenner, Richard	518	Richardson & McCoy	Tatham, William	226	Roberts, Jesse	Yancey, John	664
Reynolds, Silvester	Barry, Redmon Dillen	035	Richardson & McCoy	Tatham, William	227	Roberts, John heirs	Donelson, Stockley	476
Reynolds, Sylvestor	Dillonberry, Redmon	035	Richardson & McCoy	Tatham, William	228	Roberts, Joshua heirs	Wallace, William	1020
Reynolds, Wm. Hrs	Barton, Samuel	581	Richardson & McCoy	Tatham, William	229	Roberts, Kinney	Malloy, Thomas	54
Rhodes, Christian	Ore, James	866	Richardson & McCoy	Tatham, William	230	Roberts, Richard	Miller, Adam	099
Rhodes, Jacob	Lanier, James;	730	Richardson & McCoy	Tatham, William	231	Roberts, Thos. W.	Barton, Samuel	1428
Rhone, John	Hamelton, Elijah	424	Richardson & McCoy	Tatham, William	265	Roberts, Vinson	Dixon, Tilman	956
Rhymes, Jesse	Williams, James	14	Richardson, James	McCulloh, Benjamin	2027	Roberts, Wm.	Thompson, John	994
Rhymes, Jesse	Williams, Joseph	15	Richardson, James hrs.	Fenner, Richard	289	Robertson & Grier	Herrington, Richard	148
Rice, Daniel	Smith, Robert	1952	Richardson, Jesse	Gilliam, Charles	348	Robertson & Shepherd	Lynnes, John	111
Rice, J. A Rista, & Elisha R	Towal, Obediah	309	Richardson, William	Long, Nicholas	285	Robertson, Charles	Baker, Joseph	109
Rice, Jno & Harriett	Grant, Lewis	277	Richeson, Jesse	Gilliam, Charles	014	Robertson, Charles	Drake, Benjamin, Sr.	1482
Rice, Jno. & others	Griffin, Samuel	311	Richeson, Jesse, pt.	Gilliam, Charles	348	Robertson, Charles	Duncan, Jesse	1728
Rice, John	Armstrong, Martin	871	Richey, Thos. Heirs	Malloy, Thos.	545	Robertson, David	Minahaw, Micajah	2466
Rice, John	Barker, Levi	307	Richman, Mark	Orr, James	542	Robertson, David	Minshaw, Micajah	056
Rice, John	Blanset, Frederick	22	Ricks, Lewis	Hays, Robert	1757	Robertson, Elijah	Black, Peter	84
Rice, John	Ferrell, William	79	Ridden, John	Blair, John	1615	Robertson, Elijah	Caldwell, Lemuel	810
Rice, John	Fleming, Wm.	622	Riddick, Issac	Hart, Anthony	602	Robertson, Elijah	Caldwell, William	796
Rice, John	Hood, Charles	2150	Riddick, Joseph heirs	Rose, Thos.	576	Robertson, Elijah	Campbell, Henry	325
Rice, John	James, John	200	Riding, Robert	Capps, Demsey	124	Robertson, Elijah	Diggs, William	812
Rice, John	McDaniel, Larkin	037	Ridley, Berriman	Nichols, John	459	Robertson, Elijah	Dudley, Matthias	798
Rice, John	Ramsey, William	872	Rigbey, Ezekial	Nash, William	759	Robertson, Elijah	Dunbar, Isaac	813
Rice, John	Realy, Ezekial	870	Rigens, Joel	Marshall, John	479	Robertson, Elijah	Garrison, William	802
Rice, John	Stoveall, John	74	Right, Isaac	Pasmore, David	992	Robertson, Elijah	Gordon, Hastin	803
Rice, John	Tracey, James	685	Rigsby, Frederick	Bosley, James	20 (70)	Robertson, Elijah	Henry, John	807
Rice, John	Wooten, Thomas	316	Riley, John	Robertson, James etal	1672	Robertson, Elijah	Hollingsworth, Thomas	805
Rice, John & Harriet	McKenie, John	341	Riley, Samuel heirs	Robertson, Elijah	817	Robertson, Elijah	Jackson, Phillip	1689
Rice, John & Harriet	Nelms, Jesse	339	Riston, Abr. & Elisha Rice	McConough, Dougald	308	Robertson, Elijah	McBride, James	029
Rice, John & Harriett	Moore, Samuel	1966	Riston, Abraham	Straughan, Richard	1024	Robertson, Elijah	McBride, James	809

Assignee:	Claimant:	File #	Assignee:	Claimant:	File #	Assignee:	Claimant:	File
Robertson, Elijah	McClure, Michael	797	Robertson, James	King,John	061	Robeson, Edward	Clark, James & William	350
Robertson, Elijah	McMurtree, John	795	Robertson, James	Looney, Moses	628	Robeson, Isaac	Robeson, James	1778
Robertson, Elijah	Morgan, Jacob	516	Robertson, James	Manley, William	1665	Robeson, James	Nolley, Dixon	2234
Robertson, Elijah	Nelson, Estridge	804	Robertson, James	Martin, Isaac	060	Robeson, James	Robeson, Isaac	1914
Robertson, Elijah	Nixon, Robert	815	Robertson, James	McCoy, James	629	Robeson, Jas.	Harrold, James	2291
Robertson, Elijah	O'Neil, James	039	Robertson, James	Miller, Solomon	263	Robeson, Joel	Hendricks, Joseph	734
Robertson, Elijah	Rains, Charles	057	Robertson, James	Moore, Freeman	634	Robeson, John	Lytle, Archibald	420
Robertson, Elijah	Reiley, Thomas	806	Robertson, James	Morgan, Humphrey	2145	Robinson, Benj.	Sanders, James	1537
Robertson, Elijah	Riley, Samuel	817	Robertson, James	Patterson, Jesse	1659	Robinson, Henry	McCoy, Ananias	481
Robertson, Elijah	Stockley, Alexander	800	Robertson, James	Pendergrass, John	205	Robinson, Henry	McCoy, Ananias	485
Robertson, Elijah	Surlock, Ephraim	137	Robertson, James	Pendergrass, John	599	Robinson, James	Roe, Terry	030
Robertson, Elijah	Thomas, Brittain	625	Robertson, James	Plumley, George	1660	Robt King & Jas. Cooper	Brickel, Nathaniel	942
Robertson, Elijah	Watkins, Evan	808	Robertson, James	Roan, David	1937	Rodes, Lewis	Barton, Samuel	376
Robertson, Elijah	White, William	058	Robertson, James	Robinson, Jesse	1613	Roger, James	Wikoff, Wm. & Lardner Clar	551
Robertson, Elijah	White, William	2318	Robertson, James	Rogers, Michel	1662	Rogers, Abraham	Dew, John	302
Robertson, Elijah	Willard, Stephen	799	Robertson, James	Rogers, Patrick	1667	Rogers, Austin	Hadley, Josh	1412
Robertson, Eliz.	Raines, Simon (Ephraim)	260	Robertson, James	Rollins, Patrick	630	Rogers, Benjamin	West, Joseph	1017
Robertson, Hardy	Sheppard, Nancy	2090	Robertson, James	Rose, Terry	631	Rogers, Elisha	Blount, John G & Thomas	037
Robertson, Henry	O'Bryan, Laurence	60	Robertson, James	Shockley, Isaac	1934	Rogers, Elisha	Blount, John Gray & Thoma	2104
Robertson, Hooker	Donelson, Stockley	676	Robertson, James	Smith, Saml.	190	Rogers, James heirs	Donelson, Stockley	1076
Robertson, J. & Alex Greer	Mulkey, William (or John)	153	Robertson, James	Tipper, John	1663	Rogers, Joseph	Cobb, Jesse	293
Robertson, James	Alligood, Henry	1666	Robertson, James	Trimnal, Dennis	641	Rogers, Michael	Robertson, James	1662
Robertson, James	Barnes, Thomas	1908	Robertson, James	Wade, James	1938	Rogers, Parker	Stewart, Duncan	2376
Robertson, James	Bennett, Solomon	1670	Robertson, James	White, Jacob	228	Rogers, Patrick	Robertson, James	1667
Robertson, James	Boon, David	059	Robertson, James	Willis, Wilton	1933	Rogers, William	Rogers, Mary	187
Robertson, James	Campbell, James	110	Robertson, James R.	Joslin, Benjamin	437	Rollen, Henry	Bushneal, Eus.& Wm Dobbi	037
Robertson, James	Conner, Davy	1668	Robertson, James Randolp	Ashe, Charles	1684	Rollins, James	Buchanan, John	1956
Robertson, James	Cotes, Benjamin	1922	Robertson, Jas & Ben. Josl	Riley, John	1672	Rollins, Patrick heirs	Robertson, James	630
Robertson, James	Daniel, Ephraim	2286	Robertson, Jas of Valentin	Green, Alexander	1677	Rolston, Isaac	Blount, William	29
Robertson, James	Davie, Richard	196	Robertson, Jas.	Harrod, Jas.	080	Roper, Richard	Armstrong & Crutcher	190
Robertson, James	Davis, Moses	549	Robertson, Jas. & Jno. Da	Stanaland, James	1671	Roper, Stephen heirs	Robertson, Patsy	818
Robertson, James	Dean, Abraham	1935	Robertson, Jesse	Clark, Lardner	820	Rose, Abraham	Johnston, Robert	701
Robertson, James	Dial, James	223	Robertson, Jonathan	Griffen, James	2388	Rose, Andrew	White, James, Sr.	2426
Robertson, James	Dillard, John	1911	Robertson, Jonathan	Tew, Alexander	2405	Rose, Samuel	Nelson, Robert	2036
Robertson, James	Dunning, James	057	Robertson, Jonathan F.	Sessums, Abel	2404	Rose, Terry heirs	Robertson, James	631
Robertson, James	Edge, Joseph	632	Robertson, Michael	Clower, William	0110	Rose, Thomas	Riddick, Joseph	576
Robertson, James	Edmonds, Abel	1664	Robertson, Patsey	Dudley, Bennet	801	Rose, William	Walker, George	2033
Robertson, James	Faithfull, William	1926	Robertson, Patsey	Roper, Stephen	818	Ross, Henry	McDaniel, Thomas	290
Robertson, James	Grant, Joel	546	Robertson, Patsey	Steps, Abraham	819	Ross, James	Bond, Elisha	154
Robertson, James	Hadsock, Josiah	1936	Robertson, Willoughby	Sheppard, Benjamin	383	Ross, John	Douglass, Edward	067
Robertson, James	Hudson, Miles	1669	Robeson [sic], James	Bonds, William	2232	Ross, John heirs	Buchanan, John	2278
Robertson, James	Jackson, Fred.	1661	Robeson [sic], James	Folk, Christopher	467	Ross, Joseph	Hawley, William	1523
Robertson, James	Jay, Simon	633	Robeson [sic], James	Melton, John	2233	Ross, Joseph	Zarlett, James	1510
Robertson, James	King, John	061	Robeson, Charles	George, John	737	Ross, Nicholas	Barton, Samuel	03

Assignee Index

Assignee:	Claimant:	File #:	Assignee:	Claimant:	File #:	Assignee:	Claimant:	File
Scott, James	Carlock, George	770	Shane, Morris	Bowen, Wm.	1438	Sheppard, Benjamin	Colby, Absalon	380
Scott, Jas. Heir	Scott, Samuel	1074	Shanks, James	McCulloh, Benjamin, Ass	297	Sheppard, Benjamin	Covenan, Benjamin	387
Scott, Joshua	Parr, George	1201	Shannon, Samuel	Acock, Robert	867	Sheppard, Benjamin	Curganus, Jeremiah	378
Scott, Joshua & H. Crawfor	Crow, William	0114	Shannon, Samuel	Askin, William	1577	Sheppard, Benjamin	Dukes, Elisha	696
Scott, Marmaduke	Seers (?), Robert	590	Sharkin, James heirs	Molloy, Thomas	2333	Sheppard, Benjamin	Fairfax, Frederick	700
Scott, Marmaduke	Thomas, William	144	Sharp, Anthony	Brooks, Asa	492	Sheppard, Benjamin	Flood, Zachariah	562
Scott, Overstreet	Sugg, Geo. A.	066	Sharpe, Benj.	Ross, William	279	Sheppard, Benjamin	Galloway, Richard	389
Scutchins, Samuel	Tuton, William	976	Sharpe, John	Nelson, Robert	562	Sheppard, Benjamin	Gaylord, Aaron	561
Seagroves, John	Henry, Thomas	2223	Sharpe, Jonas heirs	Weakley, Robt	354	Sheppard, Benjamin	Goodin, Enos	386
Seal, Frances	Anderson, Matthew	2075	Shaw, Harmon	Barry, Redmon Dillen	024	Sheppard, Benjamin	Hammons, Abraham	391
Sear(?), Jas.	Barton, Samuel.	293	Shaw, Harmon	Dillenberry, Redmon	024	Sheppard, Benjamin	Jennett, Lewis	699
Searcey, Ben & Geo Walke	Stillwell, Simon	1916	Shaw, John	Robertson, Elijah	1005	Sheppard, Benjamin	Midgett, Jacob	388
Searcey, Richard	Salmon, Vincent	638	Shaw, Robert	Elliot, John	1945	Sheppard, Benjamin	Pickle, Richard	390
Searchnull, Joshua	Taitte, William	356	Shaw, Robert	Hamilton, Thomas	981	Sheppard, Benjamin	Pugh, Frederick	394
Searcy & Bristow	Bledsoe, Isaac	012	Shaw, William	Best, John	1010	Sheppard, Benjamin	Roberson, Willoughby	383
Searcy, Bennet	Cullenver, Samson	888	Shelby, David	Fry, Basel	1205	Sheppard, Benjamin	Saunderlin, Thomas	381
Searcy, Reuben	Spann, Willis	133	Shelby, David	Fulcher, Joel	537	Sheppard, Benjamin	Wilder, Robert	570
Searcy, Robert	Bandy, James	2387	Shelby, David	Goodson, James	1770	Sheppard, James	Hobbs, Isaac	064
Searcy, Ruben	Bledsoe, Isaac	669	Shelby, David	Holley, Nathaniel	1325	Sheppard, Jno.	Allison, David	2220
Sears, Robert	Scott, Marmaduke	590	Shelby, David	Holly, Nathaniel	1325	Sheppard, John	Cross, Joel	1032
Seaserver, John	Barry, Redmon Dillen	050	Shelby, David	Shelby, David	2185	Sheppard, John	Douglas, Benjamin	1031
Seebery, Mary hr Alston	Good, William	2455	Shelby, David	Stokely, John	276	Sheppard, John	Downdy, Bolin [?]	1030
Selby Harney & A. Bledsoe	Burgess, George	703	Shelby, David	Williams, Peter	536	Sheppard, John	Dundels, Hugh	070
Sellers, John	Hart, Anthony	705/704	Shelby, Evan	Hedgpeth, John	538	Sheppard, John	Filgena [?], William	062
Sellers, Matthew	Morgan, William	635	Shelby, Evan	Standley, Robert	1617	Sheppard, John	Finley, Abraham	057
Semple, Robert	Warner, Harden	1276	Shelke, Lewis	Cobb, Jesse	423	Sheppard, John	Fletcher, Jeremiah	1033
Service Rights	Norris, George	06	Shelton, David	Long, William	1589	Sheppard, John	Garrett, Jesse	068
Sessums, Abel, heirs	Robertson, Jonathan Fier	2404	Shelton, David	Reese, John	768	Sheppard, John	Gatlin, John	620
Settleworth, Andrew	Irwin, Andrew	179	Shelton, David	Reese, Roger	350	Sheppard, John	Hardison, Samuel	1028
Sevenson, Peter, pt(?)	Donelson, S. & Jos. Beard	684	Shelton, David	Thompson, Nathan	471	Sheppard, John	Harrewood, Thomas	066
Seymore, Edward	McCulloh, Benjamin	051	Shepard, John	Sorrell, Thomas	059	Sheppard, John	Harris, Joab	061
Seymore, Solomon	Standley, John	554	Shepherd, Benjamin	Lee, Peter	384	Sheppard, John	Harris, John	067
Seymore, Wm.	Douglas, Edward	851	Sheppar, John	Allison, David	01	Sheppard, John	Hughs, George	065
Shackle, Phillip	McNeel, Absalom	115	Sheppard, Benj.	Basdel, Jacob	398	Sheppard, John	Hunter, Timothy	067
Shackler, Philip	Dickson, Joel	042	Sheppard, Benj.	Fairfax, William	399	Sheppard, John	Kite, William	059
Shackler, Philip	Weeks, Silas	297	Sheppard, Benj.	Gitt, Jesse	698	Sheppard, John	Laster, Josiah	068
Shackler, Philip	Westwardhall, Francis	264	Sheppard, Benj.	Griffin, Lemon	385	Sheppard, John	Morgan, James	070
Shackler, Phillip	Gregory, Isaac	263	Sheppard, Benj.	Grogan, John	697	Sheppard, John	Tilton, Richard	066
Shackler, Phillip	Meadows, Abraham	417	Sheppard, Benj.	Gwaltney, Joshua	393	Sheppard, John	Wingfield, Jacob	062
Shackler, Phillip	Young, John	0132	Sheppard, Benj.	Jackson, Robertson	400	Sheppard, John	Yearby, Josiah	1029
Shackley, Philip	Weeks, Benjamin	0116	Sheppard, Benjamin	Batts, Sampson	392	Sheppard, Martin Gard.	Jackson, Jeremiak /sic/	778
Shaffer, Geo hr Henry	Blount, Reading	437	Sheppard, Benjamin	Betts, Jonathan	379	Sheppard, Nancy	Ballard, James	721
Shaffer, Richard	Bean, Edward [Edmon?]	205	Sheppard, Benjamin	Bradley, Sampson	569	Sheppard, Nancy	Bennett, Nehemiah	693
Shafferd, John	Harris, Edward	1179	Sheppard, Benjamin	Cator, John	382	Sheppard, Nancy	Carraway, Thomas	719

Assignee:	Claimant:	File #:	Assignee:	Claimant:	File #:	Assignee:	Claimant:	File
Smith, Oliver	Long, Haywood	2105	Spencer, Thomas	Chester, David	188	Stewart, Charles	Squires, John	625
Smith, Oliver	Murrel, Jacob	2010	Spencer, Whiliiam heirs	Molloy, Thomas	1025	Stewart, Charles	Stone, Arthur	624
Smith, Oliver	Pace, Demcey	1985	Spruel, Richard	Nichols, John	1474	Stewart, Chas. Legatee	Wolfenden, George	382
Smith, Oliver	Pitman, Isom	2007	Squires, John	Stewart, Charles	625	Stewart, Duncan	Bateman, William	602
Smith, Oliver	Ward, David	2018	Stafford, Josiah	Cobb, Jesse	291	Stewart, Duncan	Campbell, Patrick	644
Smith, Owen	Johnston, Thos	356	Stallings, Jas. Hrs	Foster, Anthony	1920	Stewart, Duncan	Cannon, Edward	2241
Smith, Peter heirs	Williams, Willoughby	356	Standen, John	Moran, John	2062	Stewart, Duncan	Clark, Benjamin	601
Smith, Redick	Woodard, Thomas	589	Standley, James	Mcmoren, Domnick	2011	Stewart, Duncan	Clark, Niel	612
Smith, Reuben	Daugherty, George	142	Standley, John	Seymore, Solomon	554	Stewart, Duncan	Colbey, John	2377
Smith, Robert	Hudson, Chamberlain	1960	Standley, Jonathan	Williams, Willoughby	046	Stewart, Duncan	Davis, Benjamin	2378
Smith, Robert	Lennon, Ephraim	1407	Standley, Robert	Shelby, Evan	1617	Stewart, Duncan	Deboyce, Nicholas	1346
Smith, Robert	Rice, Daniel	1952	Stanland, James	Robertson, James etal	1671	Stewart, Duncan	Edge, Thomas	600
Smith, Samuel	Robertson, Jas.	190	Stanley, Robert heirs	Wheaton, Daniel	2450	Stewart, Duncan	Garvey, Matthew	2367
Smith, Stephens heirs	Nichols, John	1579	Stansil, Peter heirs	Lowe, Marvel	1336	Stewart, Duncan	Gay, James	646
Smith, Thomas	Buffington, Samuel	627	Starr, Peter	Lanier, James	576	Stewart, Duncan	Grice, Theophilus	2239
Smith, Thomas	Crutcher, Anthony	33	Start, Henry	Barry, Redmon Dillen	038	Stewart, Duncan	Grissom, Robert	609
Smith, Thomas	Donelson, Stockley	2264	Steadman, Tobias hrs	Blount, John John Gray	07	Stewart, Duncan	Hall, David	1368
Smith, Thomas	Smith, Clement	245	Stedman, Geo.	Bledsoe, Anthony	329	Stewart, Duncan	Hawthorn, William	1349
Smith, William	Allen, John	118	Stedman, Isaiah	Nelson, Robert	401	Stewart, Duncan	Henderson, Andrew	2372
Smith, Wm.	Cooke, Richard	1375	Steed, Jesse	Allison, David	555	Stewart, Duncan	Jacobs, William	2369
Smithly, Thomas	Cummins, George	643	Steed, Jesse	Parker, Simon	748	Stewart, Duncan	Jarratt, Jacob	2371
Smithwick, Edmund heirs	Tatum, Howell	1912	Steedmore, Peter	Bledsoe, Anthony	670	Stewart, Duncan	King, Jacob	2374
Smithwick, Jos.	Clark, Lardner	114	Steel, Joseph hrs	Fenner, Richard	42	Stewart, Duncan	Lassiter, James	610
Sneed, Elbert	Harris, Edward	1136	Steell, Hardy	McCulloh, Benj.	323	Stewart, Duncan	Lennon, Ephraim	636
Snider, Frederick	Cypell, Robert	081	Stephen Brooks	Gloughn, William	894	Stewart, Duncan	Macklemore, John	2399
Somberland, James	Gerard, Charles	270	Stephens, Thomas	Polk, Ezekial	220	Stewart, Duncan	Matthews, Charles	2375
Sooroons,Jno.hrs.	Allin, Sarah	242	Stephenson, Hugh	Phillips, Oswald	1371	Stewart, Duncan	Nelson, Robert	653
Sorrel, Thomas heirs	Shepard, John	059	Stephenson, Hughey	Whitfield, Bryant	1946	Stewart, Duncan	Newton, Joseph	2368
Southerland, John	Boyd, Robt	517	Stephenson, Jonathan	King, Robt & Jas Cobb	031	Stewart, Duncan	Paul, Norris	1348
Southerland, Wm.	Dixon, Tilghman	2050	Stephenson, Peter	Lytle, Archibald	091	Stewart, Duncan	Pitman, John	2373
Sowell, Lewis	Buchanan, John	2277	Stepp, John	Thompson, Thomas	756	Stewart, Duncan	Prescot, Aaron	1
Spain, Wm.	Gerard, Chas.	757	Steps, Abraham heirs	Robertson, Patsey	819	Stewart, Duncan	Prescot, Charles	2370
Spane, Eps	Gerard, Charles	749	Stern, Andrew heirs	Hadley, Joshua	2406	Stewart, Duncan	Pridgeon, Marmaduke	599
Spann, James	Winchester, Jas. & Geo.	781	Stevens, Henry heirs	Rice, Jno. Etal	323	Stewart, Duncan	Reason, John	1347
Spanns, Mills	Searcey, Reuben	133	Stevens, James	Williams, Willoughby	333	Stewart, Duncan	Rogers, Parker	2376
Sparkman, Edward	Nichols, John	429	Stevens, John	Hickman, Edwin	2077	Stewart, Duncan	White, John	611
Sparkman, Wm. Hrs	Brehon, James G.	18	Stevens, Joseph	Paget, Sarah, heiress	334	Stewart, Duncan	White, Stephen	603
Spear Fort	Jones, James	27	Stevenson, James	Thompson, Robert	1019	Stewart, Duncan	Williams, Arthur	645
Spear, Seth	Eaton, John	1513	Stewart & Robertson	Parrot, Benjamin	040	Stewart, Duncan	Williams, James	2416
Speight, Frances	Davis, Joshua	685	Stewart, Andrew	McNees, John	794	Stewart, Duncan	Wright, Absolam	2400
Speight, Jas.	Coit, Farwell	494	Stewart, Charles	Birch, John	626	Stewart, Duncan	Young, John	637
Speirpoint, Joseph	Mences, James	1853	Stewart, Charles	Bradshaw, Ephraim	627	Stewart, Duncan	Young, John	657
Spellice,_rebell [?]	Bishop (Bushop), Colden	2151	Stewart, Charles	Lewis, Richard	2403	Stewart, George heirs	Machie, Wm.	122
Spencer, Jas.	Hogget, Jess	517	Stewart, Charles	Radley, Jonas	2391	Stewart, John	Thompson, James	238

Assignee Index

Assignee:	Claimant:	File #:	Assignee:	Claimant:	File #:	Assignee:	Claimant:	File
Stewart, Robert	Tyson, Aaron	886	Sugg, Geo. A.	Flimin, Samuel	069	Tate, Thomas	Armstrong, Andrew	825
Stewart, William	Weymouth, Corbyn	1624	Sugg, Geo. A.	Libbincutt /sic/, John	068	Tate, William	Gifford, James	539
Stillwell, Jer. Heirs	Donelson, Stockley	1260	Sugg, Geo. A.	Scott, Overstreet	066	Tate, William	Phillips, P & M. Campbell	1692
Stillwell, Simon heirs	Searcy, Bennet, Ass.	1916	Sugg, Geo. A.	Sikes, James	065	Tate, Wm.	Harget, Fred	589
Stinson, John heirs	Sugg, George A.	879	Sugg, Geo. A.	Smith, Joab	067	Tatom, Howell	Short, William	162
Stobbotle, James	Casselman, Andrew, Ass.	334	Sugg, Geo. A.	Weatherby, Isaac	2111	Tatum & Wiggans	Hair, John	2438
Stockley, Alexander Sgt.	Robertson, Elijah	800	Sugg, Geo. Augustus	Humphries, Henry	886	Tatum & Wiggins	Bolton, Thomas	2443
Stokes, John hrs	Kitt, Solomon	314	Sugg, George A.	Sampson, David	1971	Tatum & Wiggins	Jones, Brittain	2444
Stokes, Peter	Breckon, James G.	59	Sugg, George A.	Stinson, John	893	Tatum & Wiggins	Kelley, William	2441
Stolcop, William	Robb, William	544	Sugg, John	Lewis, Wm. T. & Wm. T	028	Tatum and Wiggin	Ouran, Timothy	1363
Stone, Arthur heirs	Stewart, Charles	624	Sugg, Michael	Nelson, Robert	169	Tatum, Barnard	Currin, Elisha	569
Stone, John hrs	Barrow, James	305	Sugg, Noah	Mosley, Demsey	646	Tatum, Barnard	Currin, Hugh	727
Stone, John hrs	Brehon, James Gloster	986	Sugg, Noah	Rowan, Simon	648	Tatum, Barnard	Reese, John	597
Stone, Littleberry	Holley, Nathaniel	345	Sugg, Noah	Wallace, Thomas	671	Tatum, Brainam	Lock, William	2061
Stone, Littleberry	Stone, Littleberry	429	Sugg, Noah	Woolard, Benjamin	652	Tatum, H & Wiggin	Branton, Levi	2439
Stone, Sylvanus hrs	Brenaman, Melcher	578	Sullivan, James heirs	Tatom, Howell	5	Tatum, H. & H. Wiggins	Murbee, Patrick	2442
Stormer, Henry heirs	Williams, Willoughby	353	Sullivan, Michael	Campbell, William	193	Tatum, H. & H. Wiggins	Trayham, John	2445
Story, Caleb	Ramsey, Allen	465	Sullivan, Port heirs	White, James L.	2424	Tatum, H. & Henry Wiggin	Cromlin, Francis	1362
Story, Jonah	Haynes, James	035	Sullivant, Lucas	Carter, John	673	Tatum, Ho & Henry Wiggi	Mangold, Thomas	1364
Stothart, Robert	Hogan, Rogers	023	Summers, Wm.	Dabney, Cornelius	1448	Tatum, Ho & Henry Wiggo	Spedman, Simon	1365
Stothart, Robert	Hooper, Ennis	024	Summer, Jacob hrs	Bud, Samuel	681	Tatum, Ho. & Henry Wiggi	Mattimore, William	1366
Stothart, Robert	Stothart, Robert	1630	Supper, Nathan	Harget, Fred	587	Tatum, Howell	Bennite, Moses	532
Stoveall, John	Rice, John	74	Surles, Joseph	Lancaster, John	375	Tatum, Howell	Blamer, John	2436
Stowbridge, John	Dilenberry, Redmon	023	Sutherland, George	Hutchings, Thomas	459	Tatum, Howell	Brooks, Daniel	538
Strader, George	Nelson, Robert	414	Sutton, Bailey	Edge, John	619	Tatum, Howell	Cheason, Joshua	1679
Stradley, James	Cobb, Jesse	2009	Swaggerty, Abraham	Knight, James	2363	Tatum, Howell	Cowen, Joseph	2437
Strand,Lewis hr Jno.	Blount, Reading	708 (70	Swann, Thomas heirs	King, Robert	563	Tatum, Howell	Cox, Thomas	47
Stratin, Joab	Brehon, James G.	935 (93	Swanson, John	Long, Nicholas	329	Tatum, Howell	Essins, Thomas	83
Straughan, Larker	Riston, Abraham	1024	Swearingham,Zan hrs	Corman, James	1290	Tatum, Howell	Green, Abraham	1924
Strider, George	Gwin, Wm.	1386	Sweet, William	Phillips, Mann	50	Tatum, Howell	Hardick, Richard	2321
Stringer, Lineage	Donelson, Stockley	2263	Swingle, Michael & Jno	Fitzgarrald, Garrett	1196	Tatum, Howell	Harrison, George	58
Stringer, Samuel	Glasgow, James	401	Sykes, Samson	Bond, John	750	Tatum, Howell	Hathcock, Amos	112
Stringer, Simon	Donelson, Stockley	063	Symms, John heirs	Robertson, James etal	111	Tatum, Howell	Newton, Francis	1725
Strong, George	Dilenberry, Redmon	026	Symonny, James	Long, Nicholas	352	Tatum, Howell	Overstreet, John	113
Stuart, Duncan	Stringer, Robert	1331	Sypert, Robert	Hankins, Edward	685	Tatum, Howell	Palmer, Elisha	80
Stump, Christopher	Dobson, John	2144	Sypress, Thomas	Pritchet, Edward	073	Tatum, Howell	Passmore, Joshua	044
Styron, Samuel	Clark, Lardner	670	Sypret, Thos.	Worley, James	265	Tatum, Howell	Powell, Matthew	1361
Suerlock, Eph.	Robertson, Elijah	137	Tait, William	Searchwell, Joshua	356	Tatum, Howell	Richards, Henry	508
Sugg, Acquilla	Halcolm, William	875	Tallafarrow,Jas hr Ric	Blount, Reading	436	Tatum, Howell	Smithwick, Edmond	1912
Sugg, Aquilla	Cherry, Jonathan	891	Talton, James	Sanders, William	499	Tatum, Howell	Sullivan, James	5
Sugg, Aquilla	Haywood, James	915	Tann, Ephraim	Thomas, Micajah	741	Tatum, Howell	Thompson, Thomas	84
Sugg, Aquilla	Lanier, Peter	877	Tann, Joseph	Thomas, Micajah	071	Tatum, Howell	Williams, Jacob	1925
Sugg, Aquilla	Price, Rice	874	Tanner, John	Hays, Robert	1762	Tatum, Howell	Williamson, George	1923
Sugg, Geo Augustus	Jeth, Tanner	878	Tarrent, Manlore	Lewis, Wm. L. & Wm. T	052	Tatum, Howell	Williamson, George	2453

Assignee:	Claimant:	File #:	Assignee:	Claimant:	File #:	Assignee:	Claimant:	File
Tatum, James	Nations, John	677	Thomas, Micajah	Thomas, Jethro	1018	Thompson, William	Porterfield, John	927
Tatum, John	Whitard, Wm.	239	Thomas, Philemon	Lowman, Mark	9	Thompson, Wm.	Hadley, Joshua	250
Tayloe, John	Bryan, John	520	Thomas, Philemon	Scalp, James	8	Thompson,?	Hays, Patty	687
Taylor, Benjamin	McCulloh, Benjamin	300	Thomas, Richard	Dore, Josiah	386	Thornhill, John	McCulloh, Benjamin	318
Taylor, Elijah	Etherington, Margaret	1017	Thomas, Richard	Flood, Joseph	385	Thornton, Yancey	Davis, Cyrus	1442
Taylor, James	Bailey, Charles	475	Thomas, Richard	Grogan, James	384	Thornton, Yancey	Williamson, William	1441
Taylor, James P.	Knight, Morgan	18	Thomas, Richard	Price, Samuel	224	Thos. Buncomb hrs.	Buncomb, Edward	469
Taylor, Jefrey	Cobb, Jesse	667	Thomas, Richard	Vinson, Thomas	313	Thos, Thos (?)	Barton, Samuel.	339
Taylor, John	Bledsoe, Isaac	566	Thomas, Thomas	McCulloh, Benjamin	2091	Threabers, Hugh	Hickman, Edwin	578
Taylor, Jopaton	McCulloh, Benjamin	1715	Thomas, William	Scott, Marmaduke	144	Thurst, Edward	Blount, Reading	940
Taylor, Thomas	Cole, Jesse	150	Thomas, William	Thompson, Thomas	714	Tiffin, Thomas	Jeffreys, Thomas	1621
Taylor, Thomas	Duke, Hardeman	219	Thomas, Zeb	Baker, John	637	Tillet, Andrew	Weakley, Samuel	011
Taylor, Thomas	Jones, Benjamin	709	Thomas, Zock	Nelson, Robert	256	Tillet, Andrew heirs	Weakley, Saml	595
Taylor, Thomas	Spurr, Spencer	338	Thompson, Ahab	Reed, Jesse	598	Tilley, John	Overton, John	520
Taylor, Thomas	Waggoner, James	0119	Thompson, Asabel	Tyrrell, Wm. & Wm. T. L	015	Tilly, John	Hadley, Joshua	077
Taylor, Wm. & John	Mills, Jesse	780	Thompson, George	Blount, Reading	899	Tilly, Lewis	Donelson, S. & James Latha	1020
Tear [?], William	Buxton, William	125	Thompson, James	Stewart, John	238	Tilton, Richard	Sheppard, John	066
Templeton, Thomas	Moore, John	425	Thompson, Jason	Alexander, Joseph	1528	Tippe, Jno.	Robertson, James	1663
Templeton, Thos heirs	Donelson, John	2325	Thompson, Jason	Braner, Joseph	184	Todd, James	Harrison, John Axley	1957
Terrell, Clement	Hamilton, Thomas	53	Thompson, Jason	Brown, Isaac	1488	Todd, James	Woods, Thomas	901
Terrell, Nimrod	Barbour, Richard	1314	Thompson, Jason	Cotanch, Peter	1540	Todd, John heirs	Weakley, Robt	261
Terrell, Obidiah	Bledsoe, Isaac	1225	Thompson, Jason	Davis, Jonathan	1512	Todd, Josiah	Donelson, Stockley	015
Terrell, William	Boxley, Joseph	294	Thompson, Jason	McDaak /sic/, John	1959	Tolar, Danl.	Anderson, Daniel	836
Terrell, William	Coffield, Gresham	045	Thompson, Jason	Pope, Samuel	1951	Tollock, Arthur	Gilmore, Charles	755
Terrell, William	Cook, Frederick	2266	Thompson, Jason	Smith, Alexander	887a	Toney, Anthony	Coleman, Spilley	602
Terrell, Wm.	Payne, John	028	Thompson, Jasson	Ramage, Alexander	226	Tooley, Henry & James	Tuton, Oliver	14
Terrell, Wm.	Payne, John	098	Thompson, John	Bunnington, William	1522	Toomer, Henry	Mott, Benjamin	615
Teuton, Caleb	Farmer, Thomas	1103	Thompson, John & others	Thompson, Rosiah; Sus	2461	Toomer, Joseph	McCulloh, Benjamin	307
Tew, Alexander	Robertson, Jonathan Tier	2405	Thompson, John heirs	Wykoff & Clark	787	Topp, Roger	Topp, John	026
Therogool, Francis	Nichols, John	153	Thompson, Joshua	McCulloh, Benjamin	309	Topp, Roger	Topp, John	1452
Thomas Dillon	Glasgow, Samuel	1454	Thompson, Laurence	Coffey, John	2303	Totevine, William	Dickerson, Henry	182
Thomas Malloy	Glover, Samuel	557	Thompson, Laurence	Coffey, John	2088	Totevine, William	Luellen, William	189
Thomas, Amos heir of Britt.	Robertson, Elijah	625	Thompson, Nathan	Shelton, David	471	Totewind, Winder hrs	Coart, John	081
Thomas, Ann	Person, Thomas	405	Thompson, Ned	Hadley, Joshua	251	Totewine, Winder Hrs.	Hays, Robert	782
Thomas, Isaac	Prewet, Joshua	070	Thompson, Robert	Cates, Mathew	189	Toton, William	Brannor, Michael	350
Thomas, Jeremiah	Donelson, Stockley	17	Thompson, Robert	Joyner /Joiner/, Stephen	1531	Tow, Christoher	Nelson, Robert	404
Thomas, Jeremiah	McCulloh, Benjamin	2024(a)	Thompson, Robert	Smith, William	480	Tracey, James	Rice, John	685
Thomas, Jethro	Thomas, Micajah	1018	Thompson, Robert	Stevenson, James	1019	Tramer [?], Phillip	Farden, Joseph	712
Thomas, John	Good, Wm.	13	Thompson, Robt & Jac Jo	Moore, James	314	Trayham, John heirs	Tatum, Ho & Henry Wiggins	2445
Thomas, John	Good, Wm.	909	Thompson, Samuel	Jones, John	849	Trimnal, Dennis heirs	Robertson, James	641
Thomas, John hrs	Hays, Robert	1765	Thompson, Thomas	Buckhannon, John	149	Tripp, John hrs	Blount, Reading	979
Thomas, Lemuel	Long, Nicholas	286	Thompson, Thomas	Stepp, John	756	Trotter, Thomas	Phillips, Phillip	85
Thomas, Micajah	Tann, Ephraim	741	Thompson, Thomas	Thomas, William	714	Troublefield, Benj.	Anderson, Daniel	46
Thomas, Micajah	Tann, Joseph	071	Thompson, Thos.	Tatum, Howell	84	Trousdale, John	Gibson, John	54

Assignee:	Claimant:	File #:	Assignee:	Claimant:	File #:	Assignee:	Claimant:	File
Truebeck, Geo.hrs	Armstrong & Donelson	024	Tyrrell, William	Bryan, Demsey	1241	Venters, William heirs	Nichols, John	1021
Truebuck, Geo.	Armstrong, M. & S. Donelson	943	Tyrrell, William	Bullock, John	075	Verell, William	Curry, Thompson	025
Truett, Franklin	Farmer, Thomas	1101	Tyrrell, William	Cyprett, Robert	1293	Vickers, Marmaduke	Tyrrell, Wm. & Wm. Lyttle	014
Truett, Peter	Winchester, Jas. & Geo.	0130	Tyrrell, William	Cyprett, Robert	2358	Vickery, Henry	Deaderick, John	554
Trulock, Sutton	White, William	074	Tyrrell, William	Gee, James	2354	Vickery, John	Donelson, Stockley	016
Trust, Steph.	Baker, Obediah	865	Tyrrell, William	Hart, [no other name]	075	Vicory, John	Brock, Joseph	856
Trustees, Davidson Acad.	Craighead, Thomas & others	2183	Tyrrell, William	Johnston, James	012	Vinson, Moses heirs	Sanders, William	584
Tucker, Saml	Person, Thomas	98	Tyrrell, William	Lewis, Amos	074	Vinson, William	Sanders, William	585
Tucker, Wiley	McCulloh, Benj.	368	Tyrrell, William	McRees, John	2289	Vintress, John heirs	Rice, Jno. Etal	321
Tucker, Willey	McCulloh, Benjamin	2195(a)	Tyrrell, William	Proctor, William	479	W. Wykoff & L. Clark	Bagwell, Frederick	862
Tuckers, William hrs	Donelson, Stockley	960	Tyrrell, William	Saunders, Andrew	0121	Wadsworth, William	Nelson, Robert	1739
Tumbull, William	Newton, Henry	2040	Tyrrell, William	West, Levi	074	Waggoner, James	Taylor, Thomas	0119
Turnbull, William	Warren, Thomas	690	Tyrrell, William	Williams, Ralph	013	Wainwright, Obediah	Tyrrell, Wm & Wm. Lytle	2319
Turner, Absalom hrs	Brehon, James G.	987	Tyrrell, William	Williamson, Benjamin	1195	Walker(?) Wm.	Walker, Allen	174
Turner, And. Heirs	Blackface, William	568	Tyrrell, Williams	Dunnick, Peter	584	Walker, Aaron	Alexander, Robert	858
Turner, Benj. Heirs	Redding, Robert	130	Tyrrell, Wm & James East	Wistner, Samuel	076	Walker, Allen	Walker, William	174
Turner, Daniel heirs	Weakley, Robt & Samuel	2363	Tyrrell, Wm.	Coffield, Benjamin	477	Walker, G. & J. Deaderick	Smith, Hezekiah	561
Turner, Wm.	Phillips, P & M. Campbell	1693	Tyrrell, Wm.	McCormickis, John	2265	Walker, George	Duggin, William	2053
Turrentine, Alex heirs	Wilson, John	456	Tyrrell, Wm. & Wm. Lytle	Burnham, Isaac	2320	Walker, George	Gipson, William	2153
Tusson, Charles	Motherill, Samuel	0102	Tyrrell, Wm. & Wm. Lytle	Wainright, Obediah	2319	Walker, George	Gunn, John	366
Tuton, Oliver	Jones, Joshua	348	Tyrrell, Wm. & Wm. Lytle	Vickers, Marmaduke	014	Walker, George	Rose, William	2033
Tuton, Oliver	Phillips, William	349	Tyrrell, Wm. & Wm. T. Le	Thompson, Asabel	015	Walker, Henry	Solomon, Stephen	1400
Tuton, Oliver	Tooley, Henry & James	14	Tyrrell, Wm. T.	Hart, Joseph	017	Walker, John	Cross, Martin	881
Tuton, William	Boyer, Thomas	865	Tyrrell, Wm. T.	Hobbs, Isaac	2267	Walker, John	Hamilton, George	083
Tuton, William	Burden, Archaibald	827	Tyson, Grisham heirs	Easton, Jas.	1037	Walker, Mary estate	Donelson, Stokeley	085
Tuton, William	Carpenter, Job	43	Underdue, Dempsey	Long, Nicholas	354	Walker, Moses	Davee, John	341
Tuton, William	Exum, Etheldred	977	Underhill, Jas.	Ray, Wm.	895	Walker, Richard Shewell	Ray, William	1509
Tuton, William	Jones, Samuel	351	Underwood, Elizabeth etal	Wheeler, Empery	124	Walker, Walter	Reed, Jesse	236
Tuton, William	Ludwell, Richard	353	Underwood, Howell	Murson, Samuel	890	Walker, Wm.	Hill, Green	243
Tuton, William	Powell, Francis	0120	Underwood, Shadrack	Tuton, William	844	Wallace, Brown hrs.	Blount, Reading	032
Tuton, William	Powell, Nicholas	072	Underwood, Jas.hrs	Barrow, Matthew	307	Wallace, Bunn	Blount, Reading	945
Tuton, William	Scutchins, Samuel	976	Upchurch, Charles	McCullum, Isaac	2294	Wallace, William	Roberts, Joshua	1020
Tuton, William	Smith, Benjamin	352	Upton, Willie	Davis, Joshua	657	Wallis, George	Williams, John	221
Twinbull, William	Underwood, Shadrack	844	Valentine, Daniel	Norris, Robert	833	Walls, Daniel (?)	Colson, Isaac	592
Tyhen, Thos	Jackson, Josiah	676	Valentine, P.	Marshall, John	476	Walton, William	Blanchard, John	1738
Tyner, Robert	Nelson, Robert	491	Valentine, Silas	Brekon, Jas. G.	63	Walton, William	Fenton, Thomas	451
Tyner, Lewis	Anglin, Cornelius	2285	Vance, David	White, William	072	Walton, William	Hannah, Jos.	456
Tyner, Nich	Tyner, Nicholas	250	Vance, John	Donelson, S. & Wm. Tyr	018	Walton, William	Sylvester, Luke	461
Tyner, Nich.	Homer, Chas	027	Vanderfield, Wm.	Bowman, William	5	Ward & Turmin	Gilliland, Ramsey & Stewart	685
Tyner, Nicholas	Pennington, Isaac	250	Vandyke, Charles heirs	Williams, Etheldred	073	Ward, Benjamin	Marshall, John	482
Tyrell & Lyttle	Phillips, William	478	Vann, William	Mott, Daniel	363	Ward, David	Smith, Oliver	2018
Tyrrel, Wm. & Robt. King	McNiell, Zebulon	2309	Vaughan, Abraham	Hughlett, William	579	Ward, Drury	Nelson, Alexander	173
Tyrrel & Jas Easton	Pall, Jacob	077	Vaughn, James	Dixon, Tilmon	1641	Ward, Elijah	Brown, James	277
Tyrrel, W. & S. Donelson	McMullen, Isaac	1086	Venters, Arthur	Brehon, James G.	981	Ward, Ennis	King, Joseph	447

Assignee:	Claimant:	File #	Assignee:	Claimant:	File #	Assignee:	Claimant:	File
Ward, George	Black, Martin	617	Weakley, Robert	Winstett, Thomas	1560	West, Eli	Weeks, Levi	359
Ward, Jas.	Robertson, James	1938	Weakley, Robert	Yarkins, Benajah	998	West, Francis heirs	Marshall, John	474
Ward, John	Bushnell, Eusebrus & Dobbins	654	Weakley, Robert	Zealot, Nelson	996	West, Joseph heirs	Rogers, Benjamin	1017
Ward, John	Hill, Wm.	324	Weakley, Robt & Saml	Turner, Daniel	2365	West, Levi	Bonner, Jas	283
Ware, Geo.	Welburn, Daniel	570	Weakley, Robt.	Sharp, Jonas	354	West, Levi	Tyrrell, William	074
Warner, Hardin	Semple, Robert	1276	Weakley, Samuel	Tillet, Andrew	011	Weston, Aquilla	Bradon, Alexander	1409
Warren, Ed	Glasgow, James	2148	Weaks, Benj.	West, Eli	357	Wetherington, Joseph	Lewis, William Tyrrel /sic/	2364
Warren, H. heirs	Nichols, John	2467	Weaks, Levi	West, Eli	359	Weymouth, Corbyn	Stewart, Wm.	1624
Warren, S. heirs	Bradley, James	461	Wears, John	Cobb, Jesse	672	Wharton, James	Barry, Redmon Dillon	1280
Warren, Thomas	Turnbull, William	690	Weatherby, Isaac heirs	Sugg, George A.	2111	Wheaton & Tisdale	Briggs, William	2451
Warren, Wm.	Cobb, Jesse	303	Weatherington,Jac hrs	Brehon, James Gloster	985	Wheaton, Charles	Hopkins, Joseph	458/6
Warwick, Shadrack	Blount, Thos	05	Weatherington,Jess	Anderson, Daniel	835	Wheaton, Daniel	Carter, Isaac	2449
Washington, Dred	Sheppard, John	060	Weaver, John heirs	Easton, Jas.	1045	Wheaton, Daniel	Hayes, James	676
Waters, John	Creesey, Tho & Wm. Murray	033	Weaver, M.	Cantrell, Stephen	1003	Wheaton, Daniel	Larrimore, William	677
Waters, Wm. Heirs	Lewis, Wm. T.	139	Weaver, Wm.	Cathey, Richd	1000	Wheaton, Daniel	McPherson, Abel	559
Watkins, Evan	Robertson, Elijah	808	Webb, Charles	Graves, Francis	2283	Wheaton, Daniel	Pate, William	2448
Watkins, Jno. Heir of Bur.	Sanders, William, Ass.	2225	Webb, Giles	Glasgow, James	588	Wheaton, Daniel	Stanly, Robert	2450
Watkins, Walter	Blair, James	1965	Webb, John	Good, Wm.	1444	Wheeler, Empery	Wheeler, Mourning & Elizab	124
Watson, Everett	Phillips, P & M. Campbell	1696	Webb, John	Nichols, Joshua	74	Wheeler, Mourning (heir)	Wheeler, Empery heirs	124
Watson, Jacob	Gilmore, Charles	1518	Webb, Joshua	Donelson, John	1197	Wheeler, Sam	Adair, James, Ass	345
Watson, John	Little Jonas	0122	Webb, Lewis heirs	Rains, John	666	Whimer, Carter hrs	Blount, Reading	955
Watson, John	Little, George	0123	Webb. John	Good, Wm.	910	Whitaker, John	Buckner, Michael	629
Watson, Wm.	Armstrong & Donelson	994	Weeks, Benj.	Shackley, Philip	0116	Whitaker, John	Willias, Benjamin	631
Watson,Wm.hrs.	Armstrong & Donelson	018	Weeks, Thos.	Edmunson, Thos.	1576	Whitaker, Josiah	Armstrong & Donelson	944
Weakley, Polly	Hathcock, John	106	Welbern, Daniel	Amus, James	0124	Whitaker, Jos.hrs	Armstrong & Donelson	015
Weakley, R. & Thos Bedfor	Pearl, James	2466a	Welborn, Daniel	May, Abraham	569	Whitakers, Jos.hrs.	Anderson, Daniel	826
Weakley, Robert	Crabb, Benjamin	1887	Welborn, Daniel	Ware, George	570	Whitard, William	Coyart, David	241
Weakley, Robert	Crawford, John	359	Welborn, John	McCulloh, Benjamin	1720	Whitard, William	Tatum, John	239
Weakley, Robert	Dedrick, Jacob	993	Welburn, Daniel	Curfes, John	0143	White, Benjamin	Nichols, John	1919
Weakley, Robert	Demcey, David	1927	Welburn, Daniel	Hohamer, Philip	02	White, David	Coon, Conrad	8
Weakley, Robert	Drummon, Joseph	196	Welch, John	Singleton, Henry	103	White, Elijah	Wells, Hayden	04
Weakley, Robert	Furbe, David	1931	Welch, Thos heirs	Drew, John	1556	White, George heirs	Marshall, John	485
Weakley, Robert	Gunn, Abraham	995	Welch, William	Lytle, William	306	White, George heirs	White, George heirs	1038
Weakley, Robert	Humphrey, Joseph	2118	Welch,Geo.hr of Wm.	Blount, Reading	439	White, Henry	Mollay, Thomas;	22
Weakley, Robert	Jackson, John	267	Wells, Hayden	May, Major /sic/	575	White, Jacob	Comon, James	534
Weakley, Robert	Jenkins, John	590	Wells, Hayden	White, Elijah	04	White, Jacob	Robertson, James	228
Weakley, Robert	Legget, Elias	1928	Wells, Haydon	Jeffries, John	703	White, Jacob Jr.	Bledsoe, Anthony	010
Weakley, Robert	Mallabey, James	357	Wells, Haydon & John Giv	Lynn, Jonathan	05	White, James	Guion, Samuel	1930
Weakley, Robert	Moore, Morris	1856	Wells, Lewis	Branton, Brittain	2429	White, James	Mann, Arnold	1685
Weakley, Robert	Pierce, Joseph	664	Wenoah, Jno.	Arnold, James	154	White, James	Morton, Jones	1656
Weakley, Robert	Prescott, Jonathan	042	Wesley, John	Alexander, Geo.	772	White, James L.	Goodson, William	2425
Weakley, Robert	Raynor, Amos	358	West, Cyprian	Hart, Anthony	1506	White, James L.	Herring, Henry	2427
Weakley, Robert	Todd, John	261	West, Eli	Collins, John	914	White, James L.	Rose, Andrew	2426
Weakley, Robert	Wilburn, Robert	323	West, Eli	Weeks, Benjamin	357	White, James L.	Sullivan, Port	2424

Assignee:	Claimant:	File #:	Assignee:	Claimant:	File #	Assignee:	Claimant:	File
Williams, Willoughby	Fryor, Josiah	323	Williams, Josiah heirs	Williams, Willoughby	351	Winday, Absolam	Donelson, Stockley	2381
Williams, Willoughby	Fryor, Willim	076	Willis, Wilton	Robertson, James	1933	Wine(?), James	Bud, Samuel	674
Williams, Willoughby	Garris, Joshua	327	Willis, Wm. Hr of Taylor	Ford, John	888	Wingfield, Jacob	Sheppard, John	062
Williams, Willoughby	Grant, Elisha	908	Willoughby Williams	Harrell, Ephraim	320	Winkle, Josiah heirs	Nichols, John	1002
Williams, Willoughby	Guin, Thomas	540	Willoughby, Matthew	McConnough, Samuel	636	Winningham, Thomas	Nelson, Robert	026
Williams, Willoughby	Harnett, Ephraim	321	Willoughby, Nathan	Blount, Reading	939	Winset, Jas.	Wykoff, Wm.	121
Williams, Willoughby	Jordan, John	452	Willoughby, Solom	Baker, Charles	035	Winstell, Thomas heirs	Weakley, Robert	1560
Williams, Willoughby	Martin, Henry	284	Willoughby, Solomon	Baker, Charles	176	Winton, John	White, Robert	033
Williams, Willoughby	Martin, William	283	Wills, George	Simmons, Benjamin	630	Wise, John	Lock, Matthew	989
Williams, Willoughby	McCoy, John	2169	Wills, James	Blount, John Gray & Tho	2001	Witty, James	Dillon, Wm.	058
Williams, Willoughby	Merer, Abraham	354	Willson, David	Harris, Thomas	204	Wm Bailey Pvt Cont Line	Bailey, Wm.	7
Williams, Willoughby	Morton, William	909	Willson, John	Oneal, Archer	692	Wms.Jas.heir of Herb.	Armstrong, Thomas & Jame	1026
Williams, Willoughby	Murtes, Zedikiah	350	Willson, John	Phillips, Mann	711	Wolf, Abra	Blount, Reading	900
Williams, Willoughby	Nelvin, Robert	49	Wilson, Adam	McNamee, Joseph & Pet	035	Wollard, Jesse	Glasgow, James	2147
Williams, Willoughby	Nichols, John	453	Wilson, David	Alexander, William	847	Womble, Benj.	Dixon, John	2006
Williams, Willoughby	Olliver, Andrew	282	Wilson, David	Anthony, James	2000	Wood, Charles	Brewer, George & Thelford	468
Williams, Willoughby	Pew, Lewis	804	Wilson, David	Cooper, Samuel	857	Wood, Isham	McEuen, David	052
Williams, Willoughby	Phelps, William	334	Wilson, David	Corbin, Arthur	840	Wood, Nath heirs	Harris, Edward	1111
Williams, Willoughby	Pleney, Francis	355	Wilson, David	Hopewell, George	634	Wood, Robt,	Lawrimore, Thos.	077
Williams, Willoughby	Pretor, George	322	Wilson, David	Humphries, James	651	Wood, Titus heirs	Robertson, Elijah	144
Williams, Willoughby	Pridgeon, William	609	Wilson, David	Lock, John	252	Wood, William	Davis, Henry	2355
Williams, Willoughby	Rusters, David	328	Wilson, David	McCoy, Daniel	2109	Wood,Geo hr Solomon	Blount, Reading	439
Williams, Willoughby	Smith, Peter	356	Wilson, David & John Dick	Egnar, Matthias	362	Woodard, Noah	McMullin, Joshua	806
Williams, Willoughby	Standley, Jonathan	046	Wilson, David & John Dick	Row, Jesse	359	Woodard, Noah	Simpson, Samuel	618
Williams, Willoughby	Stevens, James	333	Wilson, Davids	Willman, James	852	Woodard, Thomas	Smith, Redick	589
Williams, Willoughby	Stormer, Henry	353	Wilson, George	Boyd, Andrew	215	Woodley, Thos.	Haywood, John	2452
Williams, Willoughby	Williams, Oliver	352	Wilson, Jacob	Dickson, John	199	Woodliffee, George	Bristow, James	688
Williams, Willoughby	Willis, Josiah	351	Wilson, James	Clyer, James	838	Woodrough, John heirs	Marshall, John	477
Williams, Willoughby	Daws, William	2167	Wilson, James	Finney, Thomas	0129	Woods, Capt. Matt.	Bushnell, Eusebrus & Dobbi	656
Williams, Willoughly	Hays, Robert	1758	Wilson, James	Simmons, Richard	842	Woods, Jno.	Lackey, Jas. W.	1455
Williams, Wm.	Hays, Robt	1758	Wilson, Jno by J. Torrentin	Torrentine, Alexander, he	456	Woods, Thomas heirs	Todd, James, Ass.	901
Williams, Zachariah	Davis, Josh.	828	Wilson, John	Burnes, Barnabas	1949 [?]	Woolam(?), Stephen	Cook, Richard	1466
Williamson, Geo.	Tatum, Howell	2453	Wilson, John	Fogarty, James	595	Wooten, Thomas heirs	Rice, John, Sapington & Co.	316
Williamson, George	Roberts, J.	01	Wilson, John	King, Enock /sic/	2073	Wooten,Wm &Simpkins, J	Goodrich, Solomon P. &	2446
Williamson, George	Smith, Chas.	44	Wilson, John	Terrentine, Alexander	456	Wootson, David	Beck, George	2187
Williamson, George	Tatum, Howell	1923	Wilson, Whitfield	Barry, Redmon Dillen	23	Worley, James	Syfret, Thomas	265
Williamson, John	Donelson, Stockley	1192	Wimpsie, Wm.	Donelson, Stockley	05	Worton, Ed	Davis, Joshua	534
Williamson, John	Donelson, Stockley	2257	Winborn, John	Sheppard, John	061	Worwick, Walter	Mann, John	672
Williamson, John	Haynes, John	559	Winborn, John heirs	Murfree, Hardy	82	Wren, William	Donelson, S. & John Latha	1025
Williamson, Thomas	Wilkins, Joseph	361	Winchester, David	Dozers, James	719	Wright, Abraham heirs	Stewart, Duncan	2400
Williamson,Job hrs	Anderson, Daniel	853	Winchester, David	McCoy, Daniel	860	Wright, Adam	Mebane, James	1620
Williford, Andrew	Randall, John	553	Winchester, James & Geor	Spann, James	781	Wright, John	Rice, John & John Sapingto	312
Williford, Joseph	Bushnell, Eusebrus & Dobbins	650	Winchester, James & Geor	Truett, Peter	0130	Wright, John	Williams, Edward	498
Willis, Jacob	Blount, Reading	1520	Winchester, Stephen	Wren, John	953	Wright, Peter	McCulloh, Benj.	1729

Assignee Index

Assignee:	Claimant:	File #	Assignee:	Claimant:	File #	Assignee:	Claimant:	File
Wright, Stephen	Brithall, James	556	Yancey, George	Reed, Jesse	234	Young, John	Shakler, Philip	755
Wright, Stephen	Coman, Jas.	1292	Yancey, John	Hays, Robert	1756	Young, John	Stewart, Duncan	627
Wright, Stephen hrs	Coman, Jas.	1291	Yancey, John	Roberts, Jesse	664	Young, John	Stewart, Duncan	657
Wright, Thos heirs	Goodrich, Solomon P.	675	Yarbrough, David heirs	McCulloh, Benj. Ass	2092	Young, Robert Jr.	Blount, John Gray	1247
Wyatte, Ephraim	Buchanan, John	928	Yarby, Joseph	Barry, Redmon Dillen	036	Young, Samuel	Lethis, William	0135
Wycoff & Clark	Hopper, William	774	Yarby, Joseph	Dillonberry, Redmon	036	Young, Sion	Fort, Wm. & Howell Tatum	327
Wycoff & Clark	Howell, Daniel	757	Yarlett, James	Ross, Joseph	1510	Young, William heirs	Marshall, John	473
Wycoff & Clark	Thompson, John	787	Yearby, Jno.hrs.	Anderson, Daniel	38	Zarlett, Timothy	Skerrett, Isidore	866
Wycoff, W. & L. Clark	Capps, James	822	Yeates, John	Alston, John McCoy	344	Zarlett, Zachariah	Skerret, Isidore	854
Wycoff, William	Downing, George	094	York, Will	Dixon, Tilghman	741	Zealott, Nelson heirs	Weakley, Robert	996
Whan, Wm.	Anderson, Daniel	64	Young, Abraham	Dailey, Charles	0131	Zealott, Jonathan	Lock, James	750
Wykoff, William	Winscott, James	121	Young, Daniel	Love, David	2142	Zealott, Joshua	Fenner, Richd	860
Wyne, Jno.hrs.	Armstrong & Donelson	023	Young, John	Dixon, Joel	751	Zealott, Shadrach	Armstrong, Andrew	39
Wyne, John hrs	Armstrong, M. & S. Donelson	992	Young, John	Prescote, Willoughby	606	Zealott, William	Lock, James	948
Wynne, Robert	Richards, Joseph	1359	Young, John	Shackler, Philip	0132	Zutson, John hrs.	Brock, Joseph	748

TimeLine

Laws Applicable to Tennessee Land

Legislative acts, passed by Tennessee and North Carolina, pertaining to land in the State of Tennessee, were taken from the following sources:

Walter Clark, ed. *The State Records of North Carolina* Volumes 23, 24 & 25 (Goldsboro, North Carolina: Nash Brothers, 1886-1907.) (Referred to as SRNC: volume and page number.)

Henry D. Whitney *The Land Laws of Tennessee* 2 Vols (Cincinnati: W. H. Anderson & Co., 1893.) (Referred to as Whitney, page number.)
[Note: This book is out of print but it has been microfilmed. The microfilm can be obtained through interlibrary loan or by purchase from the Tennessee State Library & Archives, 403 7th Avenue North, Nashville, Tennessee 37243-0312.]

Cession Acts, etc.

Date	Chapter	Source		Legislative Act
1780	Chapter 3	Whitney	46	An act for the purpose of ceding to the United States of America, certain western lands therein described.
1789	Cession to U. S.	Whitney	49	An act to accept a cession of the claims of the State of North Carolina, to a certain district of Western Territory. A deed of cession having been executed, and in the Senate offered for acceptance to the United States, of the claims of the State of North Carolina, to a district of territory therein described....
1796	Statehood	Whitney	53	An act for the admission of the State of Tennessee into the Union.—Approved June 1, 1796.
1803	Chapter 82	Whitney	54	An act for the appointment of an agent on the part of this State to go to the Legislature of the State of North Carolina for the purpose of finally settling and adjusting the landed business between the two States, and for other purposes.
1803	Chapter 81	Whitney	54	An act concerning the agent from this State to the State of North Carolina.
1804	Chapter 14	Whitney	55	An act ratifying and confirming an act of the General Assembly of the State of North Carolina, entitled, "An act to authorize the State of Tennessee to perfect titles to lands reserved to this State by the cession act."
1806	Chapter 10	Whitney	58	An act to ratify and confirm an act of the Congress of the United States of America, entitled, "An act to authorize the State of Tennessee to issue grants and perfect titles to certain lands therein described, and to settle the claims to the vacant and unappropriated lands within the same."

Year	Chapter	Citation	Description
1715	Chapter 29	SRNC 23:35-36	An act for preventing disputes concerning lands already surveyed.
1715	Chapter 33	SRNC 23:42-44	An act to regulate divers abuses in the taking up of lands, and to ascertain the method to be observed from henceforth, in taking up and surveying lands.
1777	Chapter 1	SRNC 24:43-48	An act for establishing offices for receiving entries of claims for lands in the several counties within this State, for ascertaining the method of obtaining titles to the same, and for other purposes therein mentioned.
1778	Chapter 3	SRNC 24:159-161	An act to amend an act, entitled, "An act for establishing offices for receiving entries of claims for lands in the several counties within this State, for ascertaining the method of obtaining titles to the same, and for other purposes therein mentioned."
1779	Chapter 6	SRNC 24:214-215	An act to amend an act entitled "An act to amend an act for establishing offices for receiving entries of claims for lands in the several counties within this State, for ascertaining the method of obtaining titles to the same and for other purposes therein named."
1779	Chapter 4	SRNC 24:270-271	An act to amend an act entitled "An act for establishing offices for receiving entries of claims for lands in the several counties within this State, and for ascertaining the method of obtaining titles to the same, and for other purposes therein mentioned."
1779	Chapter 29	SRNC 24:300-302	An act for securing the rights of such persons in the County of Washington, as lie between the river Holstein, and the line lately run by the Commissioners of this State, and the State of Virginia, as the dividing line between the said States; and for dividing the said County of Washington into two distinct counties, and for other purposes.
1780	Chapter 11	SRNC 24:328	An act to amend an act, entitled, "An act to amend an act for establishing offices for receiving entries of claims for lands in the several counties within this State, for ascertaining the method of obtaining titles to the same, and for the purpose therein named."
1780	Chapter 25	SRNC 24:337-339	An act for raising men to complete the continental battalions belonging to this State, and for other purposes.
1780	Chapter 7	SRNC 24:333-334	An act for quieting such persons as may suffer in their title and claims of lands, by reason of the extension of the boundary line between this State and the Commonwealth of Virginia.
1781	Chapter 4	SRNC 24:376-378	An act giving further time to surveyors to complete their surveys.
1781	Chapter 12	SRNC 24:383	An act to continue an act, entitled "An act for quieting such persons as may suffer in their titles and claims of land, by reason of the extension of the boundary line between this State and the Commonwealth of Virginia."
1781	Chapter 7	SRNC 24:353-354	An act to regulate and ascertain the several officers' fees therein mentioned.
1781	Chapter 16	SRNC 24:446-447	An act to confirm certain patents therein specified, issued in Virginia, for lands, which on the extension of the boundary line between this State and that, are found to lie within the State of North Carolina.
1783	Chapter 2	SRNC 24:478-482	An act for opening the land office for the redemption of specie and other certificates, and discharging the arrears due the army.
1783	Chapter 52	SRNC 24:540	An act to erect a county adjoining the line of Virginia, including a part of Cumberland River.
1784	Chapter 12	SRNC 24:563-564	An act to prevent doubts as to the right of sovereignty and jurisdiction in and over the territory lying west of the Appalachian Mountains; for shutting the land office, and for indemnifying John Armstrong, Esquire, entry taker, against vexatious suits for his conduct in office.
1784	Chapter 14	SRNC 24:565-566	An act to amend an act, entitled "An act for opening the land office for the redemption of specie and other certificates, and for discharging the arrears due to the army."
1836	Chapter 67	Whitney 91	Provides for the filing and adjudication of J. Armstrong warrants.

Date	Chapter	Source	Legislative Act
1782	Chapter 3	SRNC 24:419-422	An act for the relief of the officers and soldiers in the continental line, and for other purposes therein mentioned.
1783	Chapter 3	SRNC 24:478-482	An act to amend an act entitled "An act for the relief of the officers and soldiers in the continental line, and for other purposes."
1784	Chapter 15	SRNC 24:566-568	An act to amend an act, entitled "An act for the relief of the officers and soldiers of the continental line, and for other purposes."
1784	Chapter 19	SRNC 24:682-683	An act to prevent the issuing of grants for lands on the western waters to such as have paid for the entry thereof in counterfeit certificates, and until the surveyor's fees shall be paid, and making provisions for those who have entered lands previously located by others
1784	Chapter 20	Whitney 97	Permits the great island in Holston to be entered.
1785	Chapter 10	SRNC 24:732	An act to amend an act entitled "An act for opening the land office and other purposes."
1786	Chapter 1	SRNC 24:783-786	An act providing for a protective military force for the western part of the State to be allowed land west of the Cumberland Mountains as a portion of their compensation.
1786	Chapter 20	SRNC 24:811-812	An act to prevent the obtaining of grants for lands lying in the western parts of this State to the prejudice of the first enterers, and entered in the office lately established for receiving entries of claims of such lands, by an act entitled, "An act for opening the land office for the redemption of specie and other certificates, and discharging the arrears due to the army."
1787	Chapter 23	SRNC 24:912	An act to amend the several acts of Assembly heretofore passed for giving further time to surveyors within the different counties to make their surveys, and return plats thereof to the Secretary's office, and for giving a further time for the registration of certain deeds issued from Lord Granville's office, and marriage contracts therein mentioned.
1789	Chapter 29	SRNC 24:31-33	Provides for selling salt licks.
1789	Chapter 69	SRNC 25:62	An act allowing a longer time for surveying lands entered in the office kept by John Armstrong, military warrants and pre-emption rights.
1789	Chapter 3	SRNC 25:4-6	Cession Act.
1791	Chapter 17	Whitney 100-101	An act for repealing the fourth section of an act of Assembly, entitled, "An act to amend an act entitled, an act for opening the land office for the redemption of specie and other certificates, and for discharging the arrears due to the army," passed in the year one thousand seven hundred and eighty-four.
1796	Chapter 9	Whitney 101-103	An act to authorize the Secretary to issue grants for military lands in the manner therein described, and to direct the Secretary and Comptroller to issue warrants in certain cases therein mentioned.
1797	Chapter 16	Whitney 103-105	An act to amend an act, entitled, "An act to remedy certain inconveniences arising under the present land law," passed in December, one thousand seven hundred and ninety-six.
1798	Chapter 4	Whitney 105-106	An act to amend the several acts of Assembly now in force in this State with respect to entering and obtaining titles for land.
1798	Chapter 7	Whitney 106	An act to establish a court with jurisdiction competent to examine the validity of patents in certain cases, and giving jurisdiction to the Superior Courts of law and equity in other or like cases.
1798	Chapter 14	Whitney 106-108	An act to suspend certain parts of the acts of the General Assembly, passed in the year 1783 and 1784, relative to the office of Martin Armstrong, kept in Nashville, and to direct and limit the manner of issuing grants on military land warrants, and warrants issued from the late office of John Armstrong; and to appoint a board of commissioners for the further examination of frauds committed in the Secretary's office.

Year	Chapter	Reference	Description
1799	Chapter 7	Whitney 108-111	An act to perfect the titles of the officers and soldiers of the continental line of this State, and of claims under entries made in the office of John Armstrong.
1800	Chapter 14	Whitney 111-113	An act to amend an act, entitled "An act to perfect the titles of the officers and soldiers of the continental line of this State, and of claimants under entries made in the office of John Armstrong."
1801	Chapter 14	Whitney 113	An act to amend an act, entitled "An act to amend the several acts of Assembly now in force in this State, which respect the entering and obtaining titles for lands," passed in the year one thousand seven hundred and ninety-eight.
1801	Chapter 15	Whitney 113	An act to repeal the fourth section of an act of the General Assembly, entitled "An act to amend an act entitled 'an act to perfect the titles of the officers and soldiers of the continental line of this State, and of claimants under entries made in the office of John Armstrong, and other purposes therein mentioned."
1802	Chapter 13	Whitney 113-114	An act to ascertain in what manner disputed claims to land warrants for lands entered in the office of John Armstrong, and for military lands, shall be tried and determined.

LAWS OF TENNESSEE

Year	Chapter	Reference	Description
1801	Chapter 4	Whitney 114-118	An act to authorize the Governor to procure certain documents therein mentioned.
1801	Chapter 39	Whitney 118	An act to appoint agents to settle the dispute existing between this State and the United States relative to the vacant and unappropriated lands within this State, and to procure the relinquishment of the claim of the United States to the same.
1803	Chapter 19	Whitney 118-119	An act authorizing the Secretary to surrender grants to the owners in cases where only a part of the land is lost.
1806	Chapter 1	Whitney 119-136	An act directing the division of the State into convenient districts, for the appointment of principal surveyors thereof, and for ascertaining the *bona fide* claims against the same, agreeable to an act of Congress, passed the eighteenth day of April, one thousand eight hundred and six, entitled "An act to authorize the State of Tennessee to issue grants and perfect titles to certain lands therein described, and to settle the claims to the vacant and unappropriated lands within the same."
1806	Chapter 3	Whitney 136	Provides for occupants seated and in actual possession of any vacant and unappropriated land at and before the first day of May in the present year shall be entitled to a preference of entering the same....
1806	Chapter 19	Whitney 136	An act to order the transcribing certain entries or documents therein mentioned.
1807	Chapter 1	Whitney 137	An act to suspend certain sections of an act, entitled "An act directing the division of the State into convenient districts, for the appointment of principal surveyors thereof, and for ascertaining the *bona fide* claims against the same," agreeable to an act of Congress, passed the eighteenth day of April, one thousand eight hundred and six, entitled "An act to authorize the State of Tennessee to issue grants and perfect titles to certain lands therein described, and to settle the claims to the vacant and unappropriated lands within the same." passed at Knoxville, the twelfth day of September, one thousand eight hundred and six.
1807	Chapter 2	Whitney 138-166	An act to amend an act, entitled "An act directing the division of the State into convenient districts; for the appointment of principal surveyors thereof, and for ascertaining the *bona fide* claims against the same," agreeable to an act of Congress, passed the eighteenth day of April, one thousand eight hundred and six, entitled "An act to authorize the State of Tennessee to issue grants and perfect titles to certain lands therein in ascertaining the unsatisfied claims, and in perfecting titles on the same.
1807	Chapter 43	Whitney 166	Provides for extinguishment of the Cherokee claim.

Date	Chapter	Source	Legislative Act
1809	Chapter 7	Whitney 166	Gives further time for the adjudication of claims.
1809	Chapter 10	Whitney 166	Directs certain grants to issue.
1809	Chapter 12	Whitney 166	An act for extending further indulgence to occupants.
1809	Chapter 13	Whitney 166-167	An act to authorize the register of the land office of East Tennessee to issue grants in certain cases therein mentioned, and for other purposes.
1809	Chapter 22	Whitney 167	An act to amend an act, entitled, "An act to order the transcribing certain entries or documents therein mentioned," passed at Knoxville, September eleventh, eighteen hundred and six.
1809	Chapter 31	Whitney 167	An act providing for entries having been made in the office of the surveyor of military lands before the third day of December, eighteen hundred and seven, upon warrants which have been adjudged valid, for the surveyor to transfer the entry upon his books to the person or his representatives, to whom the warrant has been assigned, and to make the survey in the name of the assignee.
1809	Chapter 48	Whitney 167-168	An act to establish the dividing line between the surveyors of the Third and Fourth Districts in this State, and for other purposes.
1809	Chapter 13	Whitney 168	An act making provisions for certain grants.
1809	Chapter 86	Whitney 168	An act to amend the thirty-fourth section of the land law passed in the year 1807.
1809	Chapter 95	Whitney 168-170	An act to authorize the division of warrants and certificates issued for land.
1809	Chapter 96	Whitney 170	An act to provide for the adjudication of certain claims.
1809	Chapter 103	Whitney 170-171	An act extending further the right of preference to occupants.
1809	Chapter 117	Whitney 171	An act providing for adjudication, etc., by commissioners.
1809	Chapter 122	Whitney 171	An act extending the relief granted by the laws of this State, in cases where the land called for in any grants is covered by better interfering titles.
1809	Chapter 125	Whitney 172-173	An act to authorize the register of West Tennessee to issue grants in certain cases.
1811	Chapter 22	Whitney 173	Locates office of 3rd District.
1811	Chapter 35	Whitney 173	Locates office of 2nd District at Shelbyville.
1811	Chapter 36	Whitney 173	Adjudication of warrants and appeals.
1811	Chapter 74	Whitney 173	An act authorizing the citizens residing in the First, Second and Third Surveyor's Districts, to have their grants made out and registered by the register of East Tennessee.
1811	Chapter 76	Whitney 174	Provides for the registration and evidence of certain Virginia land claims.
1811	Chapter 77	Whitney 174	Warrants for certain kind of interference.
1811	Chapter 83	Whitney 174	An act for the countersigning certain grants.
1812	Chapter 13	Whitney 174	An act to confirm and made good certain entries made in the land offices of the Second and Third Surveyor's Districts.
1812	Chapter 26	Whitney 175	Claims of warrants for interference.
1812	Chapter 35	Whitney 175	Relates to adjudication.
1812	Chapter 47	Whitney 175	Adjudication and certificates.
1812	Chapter 72	Whitney 175	An act to repeal the thirty-seventh section of an act entitled, "An act directing the division of the State into convenient districts for the appointment of principal surveyors thereof, and for ascertaining the *bona fide* claims against the same, agreeable to an act of Congress, passed the 18th day of April, 1806, entitled, 'An act to authorize the State of Tennessee to issue grants and perfect titles to certain lands therein described, and to settle the claims to vacant and unappropriated land within the same,'" and to point out the mode to be pursued in ascertaining the unsatisfied claims, and in perfecting titles to the same.
1813	Chapter 52	Whitney 175	An act for the relief of the persons that have lost their grants before being registered by the register of the land office.

Year	Chapter	Page	Description
1813	Chapter 84	Whitney 175	An act to prescribe the duties of the different surveyors in this State in particular cases.
1815	Chapter 25	Whitney 176	An act making provisions for certain grants.
1815	Chapter 124	Whitney 176-177	An act for the benefit of those who are or may be assignee or assignees, on the same land warrant.
1815	Chapter 157	Whitney 177	Adjudication and N. Shipley warrants.
1815	Chapter 174	Whitney 177-178	An act to amend an act, entitled, "An act to prescribe the duties of the different surveyors in this State."
1815	Chapter 177	Whitney 178-179	An act to confirm the grants therein named, and secure the claimants under said grants.
1815	Chapter 178	Whitney 179	Surveys and certificates for interference.
1817	Chapter 22	Whitney 179	An act to authorize the Secretary of State to seal and countersign certain grants therein named.
1817	Chapter 52	Whitney 179-182	An act to provide for making entries for lands to which the Indian title has lately been extinguished, and for other purposes.
1817	Chapter 80	Whitney 182-183	An act requiring each principal surveyor of the several districts to ascertain with correctness the several tracts of land laid off, and plats of survey, made on the general plan of maps, for the use of schools.
1817	Chapter 150	Whitney 183	An act to repeal the first, second and third sections of an act, entitled "An act to prevent entries being made, and grants issuing on warrants and certificates therein specified," passed at Nashville, on the 17th November, 1815.
1817	Chapter 158	Whitney 183-184	An act to provide for the further adjudication of land claims.
1819	Chapter 11	Whitney 184	An act to prevent the division of land warrants.
1819	Chapter 21	Whitney 184-185	An act to authorize the register of East or West Tennessee to issue grants in certain cases.
1819	Chapter 39	Whitney 185	An act for the relief of such persons as shall have lost their grants before they were recorded in the register's office.
1819	Chapter 40	Whitney 185	An act concerning plats and certificates.
1819	Chapter 50	Whitney 185-186	An act to confirm and make good all grants issued by the State of North Carolina, on entries and warrants made west of Brown's line.
1819	Chapter 153	Whitney 186	Office of the 6th District.
1819	Chapter 158	Whitney 186-187	An act requiring the principal surveyor of the Third District to extend the eastern and western boundary of his district, to the southern boundary of the State, or north bank of the Tennessee River.
1820	Chapter 128	Whitney 187	Office of Third District.
1821	Chapter 23	Whitney 187	Provides for adjudications, and limits time of entries and grants.
1821	Chapter 60	Whitney 187	An act granting longer time to enterers of land in the surveyor's office of the Second District to complete their surveys, and for other purposes.
1821	Chapter 9	Whitney 187	An act directing the Governor to sign certain grants.
1821	Chapter 39	Whitney 187-188	An act to authorize the register to issue grants in certain cases.
1822	Chapter 56	Whitney 188	An act to amend the law authorizing the transfer of plats and certificates of survey.
1822	Chapter 18	Whitney 188	An act to provide for warrantees under certain circumstances.
1822	Chapter 34	Whitney 188-189	An act authorizing the commissioners to examine certain claims filed in their office.
1823	Chapter 29	Whitney 189-190	An act giving further time for making surveys, returning plats, and obtaining grants, for land lying north and east of the Congressional Reservation Line.
1825	Chapter 2	Whitney 190	An act giving further time for those that have made surveys north and east of the Congressional Reservational Line, to obtain certain grants.
1825	Chapter 18	Whitney 190-191	An act to provide for closing the business belonging to the office of Surveyor General for the Sixth District.
1825	Chapter 47	Whitney 191	An act to authorize the registers north and east of the Congressional boundary to issue grants in certain cases.
1826	Chapter 30	Whitney 191-192	An act to confirm and make good all grants issued by the State of North Carolinas on entries and warrants made west of Brown's line.
1827	Chapter 1	Whitney 192	An act giving further time for those that have made surveys north of the Congressional Reservation Line to obtain their grants.

Date	Chapter	Source	Legislative Act
1827	Chapter 38	Whitney 192-193	An act to provide for closing the business belonging to the office of Surveyor General for the Third District.
1827	Chapter 87	Whitney 193	An act to repeal an act, entitled, "An act to confirm and make good all grants issued by the State of North Carolina on entries and warrants made west of Brown's line, passed December 9, 1826."
1829	Chapter 81	Whitney 193	An act requiring all the books and papers belonging to the offices of the Second and third Surveyors' Districts in this State to be deposited with the Secretary of State, and for other purposes.
1829	Chapter 106	Whitney 194	An act to provide for surveying entries north and east of the Congressional Reservation Line and north of Tennessee River, founded on warrants.
1829	Chapter 243	Whitney 194-197	An act to dispose of certain lands in Hawkins County, commonly called Sims' Big Survey.
1846	Chapter 191	Whitney 197	An act for the relief of certain enterers of land in Hawkins County, in what is commonly called Sims' Big Survey – Passed Feb. 2.

SOUTH AND WEST OF THE CONGRESSIONAL RESERVATION LINE

Date	Chapter	Source	Legislative Act
1811	Chapter 44	Whitney 198	An act to amend an act, entitled "An act directing the division of the State into convenient districts, for the appointment of principal surveyors thereof, and for ascertaining the *bona fide* claims against the same, agreeable to an act of Congress, passed the eighteenth day of April, 1806, entitled 'An act to authorize the State of Tennessee to issue grants and perfect titles to certain lands therein described, and to settle the claims to the vacant and unappropriated lands within the same."
1812	Chapter 86	Whitney 198-200	An act to prevent certain grants issued by North Carolina, being read as evidence in any court of record in this State.
1813	Chapter 60	Whitney 200	An act to protect the improvers of land south and west of the Congressional Reservation Line.
1819	Chapter 1	Whitney 200-221	An act making provisions for the adjudication of North Carolina land claims, and for satisfying the same, by an appropriation of the vacant soil south and west of the Congressional Reservation Line, and for other purposes.
1819	Chapter 55	Whitney 221-222	An act to allow any person or persons who may have obtained from the State of North Carolina, any warrant or warrants since the time of taking the transcripts from the several offices under the compact act, which said warrants have been issued by the authority of the Legislature of North Carolina, to receive a grant from this State.
1820	Chapter 2	Whitney 222	An act authorizing the deputy of either of the registers of this state shall be as good and available as if the same were done by their principals.
1820	Chapter 3	Whitney 222	An act authorizing the surveyors of land south and west of the Congressional Reservation, to lay down certain fractions in the general plan therein named.
1820	Chapter 20	Whitney 222-223	An act for the relief of those who may have claims lying north of the Kentucky line.
1820	Chapter 26	Whitney 223-224	An act to provide for certain land claims.
1820	Chapter 27	Whitney 224-225	An act supplemental to an act, entitled, "An act making provisions for the adjudication of North Carolina land claims, and for satisfying the same, by an appropriation of the vacant soil south and west of the Congressional Reservation Line, and for other purposes," passed at Murfreesboro, on the 23rd day of October, 1819.
1821	Chapter 23	Whitney, 225-227	An act to limit the time for the satisfaction of land warrants and certificates.
1821	Chapter 31	Whitney 227-228	An act to prevent the surveyors south and west of the Congressional Reservation Line in this State from making more than one entry on any one and the same warrant, and for other purposes.
1821	Chapter 40	Whitney 228	An act to authorize the removal of entries in certain cases.

Year	Chapter	Reference	Description
1821	Chapter 48	Whitney 228-229	An act for the benefit of occupants.
1821	Chapter 49	Whitney 229	An act for the relief of certain grantees.
1821	Chapter 53	Whitney 230-231	An act supplemental to an act passed at the present session of the General Assembly, entitled, "An act to limit the time for the satisfaction of land warrants and certificates."
1821	Chapter 137	Whitney 231	An act to authorize the removal of the offices of the Eleventh, Twelfth and Thirteenth Surveyors' Districts.
1822	Chapter 2	Whitney 231-232	An act concerning the board of commissioners for the adjudication of North Carolina land claims.
1822	Chapter 22	Whitney 232	An act for the relief of persons who have made entries in the Seventh Surveyor's District.
1822	Chapter 23	Whitney 232-233	An act for the relief of certain enterers in the offices south and west of the Congressional Reservation Line.
1822	Chapter 26	Whitney 233	An act to amend an act entitled "An act to prevent the surveyors south and west of the Congressional Reservation Line in this State from making more than one entry on one and the same warrant," passed at Murfreesborough, 1821.
1822	Chapter 28	Whitney 233-234	An act concerning the commissioners for the adjudication of North Carolina land claims.
1822	Chapter 157	Whitney 234	An act more effectually prescribing the duties of the register of the land office of West Tennessee.
1822	Chapter 202	Whitney 202	An act requiring the office of the Seventh Surveyor's District to be kept in the town of Lawrenceburg.
1823	Chapter 32	Whitney 234-235	An act to provide for the safe keeping of all records belonging to the commissioner's office.
1823	Chapter 35	Whitney 235-237	An act to extend the time for locating warrants and certificates south and west of the Congressional Reservation Line, and returning surveys thereon to the register's office, and for other purposes.
1824	Chapter 8	Whitney 237	An act for the relief of the settlers south and west of the Congressional Reservation Line.
1824	Chapter 19	Whitney 238-239	An act providing for the adjudication of certain land claims.
1824	Chapter 28	Whitney 239	An act to continue the adjudication of land certificates.
1824	Chapter 53	Whitney 239	An act authorizing the Surveyor General of the Thirteenth District to remove his office to the place of holding court in Gibson County.
1825	Chapter 11	Whitney 239-240	An act to establish a register's office in the town of Jackson, for the Western District.
1825	Chapter 16	Whitney 240	An act allowing longer time for making surveys and returning plats and certificates south and west of the Congressional Reservation Line.
1825	Chapter 20	Whitney 240-241	An act concerning surveyors south and west of the Congressional Reservation Line.
1825	Chapter 77	Whitney 241-243	An act providing for the adjudication of certain land claims.
1826	Chapter 7	Whitney 243-245	An act to further provide for the occupants south and west of the Congressional Line.
1826	Chapter 9	Whitney 245	An act to continue in force the provisions of act passed at the last session of the General Assembly.
1826	Chapter 42	Whitney 245-246	An act for the benefit of persons having fractions of warrants or certificates heretofore filed in the principal surveyor's office for the Sixth District.
1826	Chapter 47	Whitney 246	An act providing further time to make surveys and return plats and certificates.
1826	Chapter 57	Whitney 246	An act directing the register of the western district to issue grants in certain cases.
1826	Resolution 16	Whitney 246	North Carolina Grants Nos. 161, 844, 397, 617 to be referred to the commissioner for adjudication.
1826	Resolution 54	Whitney 246-247	An act authorizing the register to issue a certificate for excess amount on a valid warrant in which any person produced a plat and certificate of survey.
1827	Chapter 29	Whitney 247-249	An act to provide for the transfer or assignments on plats and certificates, on improvements made south and west of the Congressional Reservation Line.
1827	Chapter 65	Whitney 249-250	An act to provide for the transfer or assignments on plats and certificates, on improvements made south and west of the Congressional Reservation Line.
1827	Chapter 80	Whitney 250	An act relative to the adjudication of land claims.

Date	Chapter	Source	Legislative Act
1827	Chapter 19	Whitney 250-251	An Act to extend the time of surveying entries south and west of the Congressional Reservation Line.
1829	Chapter 22	Whitney 251-254	An act for the relief of the occupants south and west of the Congressional Reservation Line, and for other purposes.
1829	Chapter 42	Whitney 254	An act for the relief of the assignees of occupants south and west of the Congressional Reservation Line.
1829	Chapter 69	Whitney 254-255	An act to provide for certain children.
1829	Chapter 84	Whitney 255	An act for the benefit of the locators in the Western District.
1829	Resolution 18	Whitney 255-256	Resolution directing the register of East and West Tennessee to issue certain conditions.
1831	Chapter 64	Whitney 256	An act to extend the time of making surveys on entries south and west of the Congressional Line.
1831	Chapter 65	Whitney 256	An act for the relief of those who may have balances of warrants unappropriated in the offices of the several surveyors south and west of the Congressional Reservation Line.
1831	Chapter 68	Whitney 256-257	An act to prevent the entry or settlement of the lands lying south of Winchester's Line.
1831	Chapter 78	Whitney 257	An act for the relief of the occupants south and west of the Congressional Line, and for other purposes.
1831	Chapter 79	Whitney 257-258	An act to amend an act, entitled "An act for the relief of occupants south and west of the Congressional Reservation Line,
1832	Chapter 18	Whitney 258-259	An act to encourage the manufacture of iron in this State.
1832	Chapter 29	Whitney 259-263	An act for the relief of the occupants south and west of the Congressional Reservation Line, and for other purposes.
1833	Chapter 25	Whitney 263	An act to authorize persons to have land set apart for the erection of mills.
1833	Chapter 84	Whitney 263-264	An act further to provide for occupants south and west of the Congressional Reservation Line, and north of Winchester's Line.
1835	Chapter 37	Whitney 264	An act giving further time of two years for making surveys and obtaining grants on entries made under the act of 1819, chapter 1, and the acts subsequent thereto.
1836	Chapter 45	Whitney 264-268	An act for the relief of occupants south and west of the Congressional Reservation Line and north of Winchester's Line, and for other purposes.
1836	Chapter 46	Whitney 268-269	An act to authorize the issuance of grants in certain cases.
1836	Chapter 48	Whitney 269-272	An act to abolish the present surveyors' offices south and west of the Congressional Reservation Line, and to establish county offices in lieu thereof.
1836	Chapter 82	Whitney 272-273	An act to provide for correcting mistakes in entries or locations of warrants.
1837	Chapter 1	Whitney 273-276	An act to provide for the occupant settlers south and west of the congressional Reservation Line, and for other purposes.
1837	Chapter 42	Whitney 276-277	An act to encourage the making and manufacturing of salt in the State of Tennessee.
1837	Chapter 70	Whitney 277	An act for the relief of a portion of the citizens of Perry County.
1838	Chapter 107	Whitney 277	An act--to aid in the establishment of a system of education.
1838	Chapter 109	Whitney 277-278	An act extending to individuals and corporations who have constructed turnpike roads across the bottoms and swamps in the Western District, the right of occupants on vacant lands through which turnpikes may have been constructed by law.
1838	Chapter 113	Whitney 278	An act to amend the seventh section of an act, entitled, "An act to abolish the present surveyor's office, south and west of the Congressional Reservation Line, etc."
1838	Chapter 119	Whitney 278-279	An act to consolidate the surveyor's and entry taker's office in that part of Maury County south and west of the Congressional Reservation Line.
1838	Chapter 129	Whitney 279	An act to amend the seventh section of an act, passed the 19th day of February, 1836, entitled, "An act to abolish the present surveyors' offices, south and west of the Congressional Reservation Line, and to establish county offices in lieu thereof."
1838	Chapter 136	Whitney 279-280	An act to authorize the several County Courts, south and west of the congressional Reservation Line, to have new maps or general plans of their several counties made, and for other purposes.

1838	Chapter 232	Whitney 280	An act to consolidate the entry taker's offices in the counties divided by the Congressional Reservation Line.
1839	Chapter 37	Whitney 280	An act to amend the law now in force and use in this State in relation to the appointment of deputy surveyors south and west of the Congressional Reservation Line.
1839	Resolution No. 5	Whitney 280	A resolution directory to the register of the Western District.
1840	Chapter 62	Whitney 280–283	An act for the benefit of the occupant settlers south and west of the Congressional Reservation Line.
1840	Chapter 121	Whitney 283	An act to explain an act passed January 17th, 1838, chapter 109.
1840	Resolution No. 6	Whitney 283	A resolution directory to the several entry takers south and west of the Congressional Reservation Line.
1840	Resolution No. 14	Whitney 283	A resolution instructing our Senators and requesting our Representatives in Congress to use their exertions to procure the passage of a law in relation to vacant lands.
1841	Chapter 7	Whitney 283–285	An act to amend an act, entitled, "An act to authorize the State of Tennessee to issue grants and perfect titles to certain lands therein described, and to settle the claims to the vacant and unappropriated lands within the same," passed the eighteenth day of April, one thousand eight hundred and six.
1842	Chapter 34	Whitney 285–293	An act to amend an act, entitled, "An act to authorize the State of Tennessee to issue grants and perfect titles to certain lands therein described, and to settle the claims to the vacant and unappropriated lands within the same," passed the eighteenth day of April, one thousand eight hundred and six.
1842	Chapter 79	Whitney 293	An act for the relief of owners of iron works south and west of the Congressional Reservation Line.
1842	Chapter 84	Whitney 193	An act to extend the provisions of an act passed 11th January, 1840, entitled "An act for the benefit of occupants south and west of the Congressional Reservation Line."
1842	Chapter 102	Whitney 293–294	An act for the relief of a portion of the citizens of Perry County.
1843	Chapter 37	Whitney 294–295	An act to amend an act entitled "An act to carry into effect an act of Congress, passed and approved the 18th day of February, 1841, authorizing the State of Tennessee to perfect titles to the vacant and unappropriated lands south and west of the Congressional Reservation Line in this State."
1844	Chapter 64	Whitney 295	An act to amend and explain an act entitled "An act to carry into effect an act of Congress passed and approved the 18th of February 1841, authorizing the State of Tennessee to perfect titles to the vacant and unappropriated lands south and west of the Congressional Reservation Line in this State."
1844	Chapter 89	Whitney 295–296	An act to amend the act of 1842, Chap. 34, accepting the agency created by the act of Congress of the 18th day of February, 1841, in relation to the vacant and unappropriated lands south and west of the Congressional Reservation Line.
1845	Chapter 8	Whitney 296	An act to provide for the occupant settlers south and west of the Congressional Reservation Line, and for other purposes.
1845	Chapter 18	Whitney 297	An act to make good certain entries and to suppress litigation.
1845	Memorial No. 1	Whitney 298–301	Memorials of the General Assembly of the State of Tennessee, to the Senate and House of Representatives in Congress assembled.
1846	Chapter 92	Whitney 301–303	An act to surrender to the State of Tennessee all title the United States have to lands in Tennessee, south and west of the line commonly called the Congressional Reservation Line, and to release to said State the proceeds of such of said lands as may have been sold by the State of Tennessee, as the agent of the United States.
1846	Chapter 80	Whitney 303	An act to repeal the twenty-sixth section of an act passed the 11th January, 1842, entitled, "An act to carry into effect an act of Congress, passed and approved the 18th day of February, 1841, authorizing the State of Tennessee, to perfect titles to the vacant and unappropriated lands south and west of the Congressional Reservation Line in this State," and for other purposes.
1847	Chapter 20	Whitney 303	An act further to provide for the occupant settlers, south and west of the Congressional Reservation Line, and for other purposes.

Date	Chapter	Source	Legislative Act
1847	Chapter 46	Whitney 304	An act authorizing the County Courts to appoint commissioners to contract for the making of county plans, and for other purposes.
1852	Chapter 119	Whitney 305-306	An act to consolidate the offices of entry taker and register, south and west of the Congressional Reservation Line.
1854	Chapter 148	Whitney 306	An act to repeal so much of the act passed 16th February, 1852, chapter 119, as relates to the county of Dyer.
1858	Chapter 175	Whitney 306-307	An act to make good certain entries south and west of the Congressional Reservation Line, and to prevent litigation.
1869	Chapter 33	Whitney 307	Provides that A. Gattinger may make a full index of all entries and surveys made for the old district of West Tennessee upon military warrants, certificates, etc., and compensation for the same; but this act repealed by Chap. 42, 1871.

NORTH AND EAST OF CONGRESSIONAL RESERVATION LINE

Date	Chapter	Source	Legislative Act
1823	Chapter 49	Whitney 308	An act to establish offices for receiving entries for the vacant lands in several counties in this State, lying north and east of the Congressional Reservation line, and north of Tennessee River.
1823	Chapter 29	Whitney 315	An act giving further time for making surveys, returning plats, and obtaining grants, for land lying north and east, of the Congressional Reservation Line.
1824	Chapter 22	Whitney 315-317	An act supplemental to an act, entitled, "An act to establish offices for receiving entries for the vacant lands in the several counties in this State north and east of the Congressional Reservation Line, and north of Tennessee River.
1824	Chapter 27	Whitney 317	An act that the entry takers north and east of the Congressional Reservation Line, shall, once every month, furnish the surveyor of their respective counties with an abstract of all the entries made in his office, and the amount of money paid into his office.
1824	Chapter 97	Whitney 317	An act to legalize the official acts of the surveyor of Marion County.
1824	Chapter 9	Whitney 317-318	That the surveyors of the several counties north and east of the Congressional Reservation Line and north of Tennessee River, shall be allowed six months for making surveys, instead of three months, as heretofore provided.
1825	Chapter 2	Whitney 318	An act giving further time for those that have made surveys north and east of the Congressional Reservation Line, to obtain their grants.
1825	Chapter 28	Whitney 318	An act concerning the surveying of lands entered in the different entry takers' offices in this State.
1825	Chapter 42	Whitney 318	An act giving further time to make surveys and obtain grants on entries north and east of the Congressional Reservation Line, and under the act of 1823.
1825	Chapter 47	Whitney 318	An act to authorize the registers north and east of the Congressional Boundary Line to issue grants in certain cases.
1825	Chapter 53	Whitney 318-319	An act to amend an act, passed at Murfreesborough, 22nd November, 1823, entitled, "An act to establish offices to receive entries on the vacant land, north and east of the Congressional Reservation Line, and north of the Tennessee River."
1825	Chapter 64	Whitney 319-320	An act supplemental to an act, entitled, "An act to establish offices for receiving entries for the vacant land in the several counties in this State, lying north and east of the Congressional Reservation Line and north of the Tennessee River," passed, the 22nd November, 1823.
1825	Chapter 76	Whitney 320	An act to apportion the moneys arising from the entering of the vacant land north and east of the Congressional Reservation Line.
1825	Chapter 84	Whitney 320-321	An act supplemental to the act to establish offices for receiving entries north and east of the Congressional Reservation Line, and for other purposes.
1826	Chapter 4	Whitney 321	An act supplemental to an act, entitled, "An act to establish offices for receiving entries for the vacant land in the several counties in this State north and east of the Congressional Reservation Line and north of the Tennessee River," passed, 22nd November 1823.
1826	Chapter 21	Whitney 321-322	An act to compel entry takers to pay over moneys, and for other purposes.
1826	Chapter 32	Whitney 322	An act to make lawful grants and entries to lands within five miles of the falls of Caney Fork.

Year	Chapter	Whitney	Description
1827	Chapter 1	Whitney 322	An act giving further time for those that have made surveys north and east of the Congressional Reservation Line to obtain their grants.
1827	Chapter 4	Whitney 322-323	An act to establish a register's office in the town of Sparta for the Mountain District.
1827	Chapter 10	Whitney 323	An act giving further time for surveying lands lying north and east of the Congressional Reservation Line and north of Tennessee River, and For other purposes
1827	Chapter 33	Whitney 323-324	An act to amend the benfit of an act, entitled "An act for the relief of the citizens who entered lands ceded to Kentucky, under the act of 1823, making provisions for entering vacant land at twelve and one-half cents per acre.
1827	Chapter 46	Whitney 324	That the provisions of an act passed on the 16th November, 1825, entitled "An act concerning the surveying lands entered in the different entry takers' offices in this State" shall extend to all entries made heretofore or which may hereafter be made, north and east of the Congressional Reservation Line where the beginning corner is in one county and a part of the survey in another.
1827	Chapter 69	Whitney 324	An act allowing one thousand acres of land to be entered north and east of the Congressional Reservation Line and north of Tennessee River.
1827	Chapter 76	Whitney 324-325	An act for the relief of such persons as hold lands under grants from North Carolina or Tennessee.
1827	Chapter 95	Whitney 325	An act authorizing the surveying of certain entries in Bledsoe and Marion County.
1829	Chapter 2	Whitney 325	An act giving further time for surveying entries and obtaining grants thereon.
1829	Chapter 7	Whitney 325-327	An act to compel entry takers north and east of the Congressional Reservation Line and north of Tennessee River to make settlements in certain cases.
1829	Chapter 49	Whitney 327-328	An act providing for the entry of the unappropriated islands in the Tennessee River, in the counties of Roane and Rhea.
1829	Chapter 85	Whitney 328	An act to authorize the entering and obtaining grants for any quantity of land under five thousand acres, and for other purposes.
1829	Chapter 87	Whitney 328	An act concerning the surveying and correction of entries made under the acts of 1823 and 1825, authorizing the entering of land at 12 ½ cents, and one cent per acre.
1829	Chapter 106	Whitney 329	An act to provide for surveying entries north and east of the Congressional Reservation Line and north of Tennessee River, founded on warrants.
1831	Chapter 63	Whitney 329	An act giving further time for surveying entries and obtaining grants thereon,
1832	Chapter 28	Whitney 329-330	An act referring certain land claims for adjudication.
1833	Chapter 6	Whitney 330	An act giving further time for surveying lands north and east of the Congressional Reservation Line, and north of Tennessee River, and for other purposes.
1833	Chapter 17	Whitney 330-331	An act to compel enterers of land in certain cases to have their entries surveyed.
1833	Chapter 27	Whitney 331	An act giving further time for surveying entries and obtaining grants thereon,.
1833	Chapter 82	Whitney 331-332	An act to appropriate the reserved lands at the Narrows of Harpeth.
1835	Chapter 83	Whitney 332-333	An act giving further time for surveying and obtaining grants on land north and east of the Congressional Reservation Line, and north of Tennessee River.
1836	Chapter 53	Whitney 333	An act to authorize the clerks of the courts of record in this State, to take the probate or acknowledgment of assignment of plats and certificates of survey and locations.
1836	Chapter 78	Whitney 333	An act to amend the several acts prescribing the duties of entry takers.
1838	Chapter 175	Whitney 333-334	An act to amend an act, entitled, "An act for the relief of such persons as hold lands under grants from North Carolina or Tennessee passed 13th day of December 1827."
1838	Chapter 232	Whitney 334	An act to consolidate the entry taker's office in the counties divided by the Congressional Reservation Line.
1839	Chapter 12	Whitney 334	An act giving further time for Surveying entries and obtaining grants.
1840	Chapter 128	Whitney 334-335	An act to prevent frauds in entering and selling lands previously appropriated.

Date	Chapter	Source	Legislative Act
1845	Chapter 38	Whitney 335	An act for the benefit of persons who may find or discover any mine or valuable minerals.
1846	Chapter 196	Whitney 335	An act to repeal the first section of an act, passed 29th January, 1840.
1848	Chapter 92	Whitney 335-336	An act giving further time to perfect certain titles to lands north and east of the Congressional Reservation Line.
1848	Chapter 109	Whitney 336	An act to authorize the sale of a certain piece of land in Anderson, or in Anderson and Roane Counties.
1854	Chapter 67	Whitney 336-337	An act to authorize the register of the Mountain District to transcribe certain grants.
1858	Chapter 48	Whitney 337	An act to authorize the register of East Tennessee to transcribe certain record books, and for other purposes.
1860	Resolution No. 31	Whitney 337	Joint resolution directory to the Attorney General of the State.
1860	Chapter 89	Whitney 338	An act for the benefit of the register of the Mountain District, and others.
1869	Chapter 24	Whitney 338	An act requiring the register of the Mountain District land office to keep his office in the town of Sparta.
1870	Chapter 8	Whitney 338	An act to attach the county of Franklin to the Middle Tennessee Land District.
1889	Chapter 256	Whitney 339	An act to provide for the supplying and transcribing missing and mutilated records of the Mountain District Land Office, and to make certified copies of the same legal evidence.

South of French Broad and Holston

Date	Chapter	Source	Legislative Act
1796	Constitution	Whitney 340	Extract from Art. XI of the first Constitution.
1805	Chapter 72	Whitney 340	An act directing the mode of ascertaining the bounds of improvements and occupant claims south of the rivers French Broad and Holston.
1806	Chapter 2	Whitney 341-352	An act for the appointment of a register of the land office, and providing for the sale of the lands south of Holston and French Broad, agreeably to the Constitution of this State, and the provisions of the act of Congress therein referred to.
1806	Chapter 46	Whitney 352	That in all cases of trial before a jury on the premises, or on an arbitration to be had under the provisions of an act, entitled, "An act providing for the same of lands south of Holston and French Broad, agreeably to the Constitution of this State, and the provisions of the act of Congress…"
1807	Chapter 17	Whitney 352-354	An act supplemental to an act, entitled, "An act for the appointment of a register of the land office, and providing for the sale of lands south of Holston and French Broad, agreeably to the Constitution of this State, and the provisions of the act of Congress therein referred to."
1807	Chapter 67	Whitney 354	An act to amend an act, passed at Knoxville, the sixth of September, in the year eighteen hundred and six, entitled, "An act for the appointment of a register of the land office, and providing for the sale of the lands south of Holston and French Broad, agreeably to the Constitution of this State, and the provisions of the act of Congress therein referred to."
1807	Chapter 104	Whitney 355	An act to provide for the payment of the members, clerks and door-keepers of the present General Assembly, and for other purposes.
1809	Chapter 13	Whitney 355-356	An act to authorize the register of the land office of East Tennessee, to issue grants in certain cases therein mentioned, and for other purposes.
1809	Chapter 32	Whitney 356	An act to facilitate the transfer of land south of French Broad and Holston.
1809	Chapter 34	Whitney 357-359	An act for the relief of the citizens south of French Broad and Holston, and to provide for the collection of the moneys arising on occupant claims.
1809	Chapter 47	Whitney 359-360	An act for the relief of the citizens residing south of French Broad and Holston, between the rivers Big Pigeon and Tennessee.
1809	Chapter 87	Whitney 360	An act to authorize the register of the land office of East Tennessee, to issue grants to the citizens south of French Broad and Holston, and for other purposes.
1809	Chapter 110	Whitney 360-361	An act that so much of the thirteenth section of an act of Assembly, entitled "An act for the appointment of a register of the land office, and

Date	Chapter	Source	Legislative Act
			providing for the sale of the lands south of Holston and French Broad, agreeably to the Constitution of this State, and other purposes…"
1811	Chapter 9	Whitney 361-364	An act to suspend an act, entitled, "An act for the relief of the citizens residing south of French Broad and Holston, between the rivers Big Pigeon and Tennessee."
1811	Chapter 20	Whitney 364-365	An act for the relief of those who have failed to return their plats and certificates for lands south of French Broad and Holston, within the time limited by law.
1811	Chapter 59	Whitney 365	An act to prevent the selling of lands south of French Broad and Holston, held by grant from the State of North Carolina, for taxation.
1812	Chapter 9	Whitney 365	An act to remit the interest on certain installments due on lands south of French Broad and Holston and west of Big Pigeon.
1812	Chapter 11	Whitney 366	An act for the relief of those who have failed to return their plats and certificates for lands south of French Broad and Holston, within the time limited by law.
1812	Chapter 42	Whitney 366	An act to authorize the keeping a certain map at the Register's office in East Tennessee.
1812	Chapter 58	Whitney , 366	An act to authorize the registers of the land offices to issue grants on land warrants issued to Robert Wier, as compensation for his services as surveyor, as on other bona fide claims against the State.
1813	Chapter 33	Whitney 366	An act for the relief of those who have failed to return their plats and certificates for lands south of French Broad and Holston, within the time limited by law.
1813	Chapter 51	Whitney 367	An act granting further indulgence to the citizens south of French Broad and Holston, and other purposes.
1815	Chapter 12	Whitney 367	An act granting further indulgence to the citizens south of French Broad and Holston, and other purposes.
1815	Chapter 33	Whitney 367-368	An act for the relief of those who have failed to return their plats and certificates for lands south of French Broad and Holston within the time limited by law.
1815	Chapter 156	Whitney 368	An act to amend an act, "To encourage the building of iron works," passed November 2, 1809.
1817	Chapter 88	Whitney 368-369	An act to suspend the collection of the money due from occupants south of French Broad and Holston, and west of Big Pigeon Rivers, until the rise of the next stated session of the General Assembly.
1819	Chapter 54	Whitney 369-372	An act to open an office for receiving entries of vacant and unappropriated lands in the district of country south of French Broad and Holston, and between the rivers Big Pigeon and Tennessee.
1819	Chapter 70	Whitney 372	An act allowing citizens residing south of French Broad and Holston, and west of Big Pigeon Rivers, are hereby permitted to make payment to the Treasurer of East Tennessee….
1819	Chapter 97	Whitney 372-373	An act to provide for the payment of interest on moneys due from the citizens residing south of French Broad and Holston, and between the rivers Big Pigeon and Tennessee, and for other purposes.
1819	Chapter 104	Whitney 373-374	An act authorizing plats and certificates to be returned to the register's office in certain cases.
1819	Chapter 145	Whitney 374	An act for the relief of the citizens therein referred to.
1820	Chapter 15	Whitney 374-375	An act giving preference to occupants south of French Broad and Holston Rivers.
1821	Chapter 48	Whitney 375	An act for the benefit of occupants.
1822	Chapter 8	Whitney 375-376	An act to provide for the sales of certain lands.
1822	Chapter 21	Whitney 376	An act for the benefit of certain claimants of land south of French Broad and Holston.
1823	Chapter 30	Whitney 376-381	An act for the relief of the citizens residing in the district of country south of French Broad and Holston, and between the rivers Big Pigeon and Tennessee, and to appropriate the moneys due from said citizens for their lands.
1824	Chapter 140	Whitney 381	An act to prescribe the duties of the Treasurer of East Tennessee in certain cases.
1825	Chapter 73	Whitney 381-382	An act allowing the citizens residing south of French Broad and Holston, to have until the first day of November 1826, to redeem their lands

Date	Chapter	Source	Legislative Act
			that have been sold for the benefit of colleges and academies of this State, by paying interest on the respective sums that may be due.
1826	Chapter 11	Whitney 382	An act to authorize the Treasurer of East Tennessee to receive certain moneys.
1827	Chapter 82	Whitney 382-383	An act for the relief of the citizens south of French Broad and Holston.
1829	Chapter 18	Whitney 383	An act to repeal an act passed at Nashville on the thirteenth of December, 1827, for the relief of the citizens south of French Broad and Holston.
1829	Chapter 47	Whitney 383-385	An act to settle a controversy between the colleges and academies and the citizens south of French Broad and Holston, and west of Big Pigeon Rivers.
1879	Chapter 252	Whitney 385	An act to amend an act passed September 12, 1806, entitled "An act for the appointment of a register of the land office, and providing for the sale of the land south of Holston and French Broad, agreeable to the Constitution of this State, and the provisions of act of Congress therein referred to."

HIWASSEE DISTRICT

Date	Chapter	Source	Legislative Act
1819	Chapter 59	Whitney 386-393	An act to dispose of the lands lying between the rivers Hiwassee and Tennessee, and north of Little Tennessee River.
1819	Chapter 60	Whitney 393-394	An act supplemental to an act passed at this session of the General Assembly, providing for the sale of the lands between the Tennessee and Hiwassee and north of Little Tennessee River.
1819 north	Chapter 229	Whitney 394	An act forbidding the Surveyor General for the Hiwassee District from surveying any occupant claim in the Hiwassee district, which is situated of Little Tennessee River, and claimed by any person or persons as an occupant claim.
1820	Chapter 18	Whitney 394-395	An act to amend and explain an act passed at Murfreesborough November 15, 1819, to dispose of the lands lying between the rivers Hiwassee and Tennessee and north of Little Tennessee River.
1821	Chapter 170	Whitney 395-396	An act requiring the Treasurer of East Tennessee to sell certain lands therein mentioned.
1822	Chapter 24	Whitney 396	An act to amend the eighth section of an act, entitled, "An act to dispose of the lands lying between the rivers Hiwassee and Tennessee, and north of Little Tennessee River."
1822	Chapter 27	Whitney 396-397	An act for the benefit of certain reserves.
1822	Chapter 41	Whitney 397-398	An act to provide for the issue of grants to purchasers in the Hiwassee District.
1823	Chapter 26	Whitney 398-403	An act supplementary to an act to dispose of the lands lying between the rivers Hiwassee and Tennessee, and north of Little Tennessee River.
1823	Chapter 45	Whitney 403	An act to explain an act, entitled, "An act to confirm and make good all grants issued by the State of North Carolina, on entries and warrants made west of Brown's line."
1823	Chapter 59	Whitney 403-404	An act to provide for the sale of the islands in the Hiwassee District.
1823	Chapter 175	Whitney 404	An act to revive an act, entitled, "An act for the benefit of certain reservees."
1824	Chapter 21	Whitney 404	An act supplemental to an act, entitled, "An act to amend the eighth section of an act, entitled, 'An act to dispose of the lands lying between the rivers Hiwassee and Tennessee, and north of Little Tennessee river.'"
1824	Chapter 31	Whitney 404-405	An act to revive an act, entitled, "An act to provide for the sale of the islands in the Hiwassee District."
1825	Chapter 71	Whitney 405	An act to encourage the building of iron works in the Hiwassee District.
1825	Chapter 1	Whitney 405	An act supplementary to an act, passed Nov. 28, 1823, entitled, "An act to provide for the sale of the islands in the Hiwassee District.
1825	Chapter 12	Whitney 405	An act to revive an act, entitled, "An act for the benefit of certain reservees."
1825	Chapter 27	Whitney 405-406	An act to establish a register's office in the Hiwassee District.

Date	Chapter	Source	Legislative Act
1825	Chapter 34	Whitney 406	An act to amend an act, entitled, "An act supplemental to an act to dispose of the lands lying between the rivers Hiwassee and Tennessee, and north of Little Tennessee River."
1825	Chapter 41	Whitney 406-407	An act for the relief of certain purchasers of land in the Hiwassee District.
1825	Chapter 49	Whitney 407-408	An act prescribing the duty of the entry taker of the Hiwassee District in certain cases.
1825	Chapter 55	Whitney 408	An act supplemental to an act entitled, "An act to amend the eighth section of an act, entitled, 'An act to dispose of the lands lying between the rivers Hiwassee and Tennessee and north of the Little Tennessee River."
1825	Chapter 256	Whitney 408	An act directing certain papers to be read in evidence in suits concerning reservations taken under the late treaties with the Cherokee Indians.
1825	Chapter 280	Whitney 409	All land heretofore sold and not granted in the Hiwassee District, shall be granted and recorded by the register of said district....
1825	Resolution No. 21	Whitney 409	Resolution directory to the Register of East Tennessee.
1826	Chapter 10	Whitney 409	An act to repeal an act entitled, "An act to revive an act for the benefit of certain reserves."
1826	Chapter 15	Whitney 409-410	An act to amend an act entitled, "An act to amend an act, entitled, 'An act supplemental to an act to dispose of the lands lying between the rivers Hiwassee and Tennessee, and north of Little Tennessee River.' "
1826	Chapter 20	Whitney 410-411	An act to amend "An act to dispose of the lands lying between the rivers Hiwassee and Tennessee and north of the Little Tennessee."
1826	Chapter 31	Whitney 411	An act explanatory of an act passed at the present session of the General Assembly.
1826	Chapter 33	Whitney 411	An act for the relief of those citizens in the Hiwassee District who are sued by Indian reservees for their land.
1826	Chapter 171	Whitney 411-412	An act to repeal an act entitled, "An act for the relief of certain purchasers of land in the Hiwassee District," and for other purposes.
1827	Chapter 3	Whitney 411-412	An act concerning the Register of the Hiwassee District.
1827	Chapter 22	Whitney 412	An act to extend the provisions of an act passed at Nashville, 1826, entitled, "An act to amend an act to dispose of the lands lying between the rivers Hiwassee and Tennessee and north of Little Tennessee River."
1827	Chapter 46	Whitney 412-413	An act to extend the benefit of an act, entitled, "An act respecting the improvement of land," passed October 18, 1813, to the people of the Hiwassee District.
1827	Chapter 71	Whitney 413	An act to make entries liable to execution in the Hiwassee District.
1829	Chapter 40	Whitney 413-414	Provision for purchasers of land in the Hiwassee country unable to pay amount due within time limited by law....
1829	Chapter 61	Whitney 414-415	An act to provide for the widows and minor heirs of certain purchasers of land in the Hiwassee District.
1829	Chapter 64	Whitney 415	An act to amend an act, entitled, "An act to authorize the Treasurer to receive certain moneys."
1829	Chapter 89	Whitney 415-416	An act to provide for the issuing of grants to the enterers of land in the Hiwassee District.
1829	Chapter 98	Whitney 416-418	An act for the relief of certain improvers of land in the Hiwassee District.
1830	Chapter 159	Whitney 418-419	An act providing for the entry of certain unappropriated land in Rhea County.
1831	Chapter 31	Whitney 419	An act to appropriate the school lands in the Hiwassee District to the use of schools for the instruction of children therein.
1831	Chapter 32	Whitney 419-422	An act providing for the entry of the forfeited lands in the Hiwassee District.
1831	Chapter 33	Whitney 422	An act giving the purchasers and enterers of land in the Hiwassee District further time to obtain their grants.
1831	Chapter 34	Whitney 423	An act supplemental to an act passed at the present session of the General Assembly entitled "An act to appropriate the school lands in the Hiwassee District, to the use of schools for the instruction of children therein."
1831	Chapter 35	Whitney 423	An act to extend the benefits of the first section of an act, chapter 40, passed at Nashville on the 30th December, 1829.
1831	Chapter 36	Whitney 423-424	An act to amend an act entitled, "An act to make entries liable to execution in the Hiwassee District."
1831	Chapter 37	Whitney 424	An act supplemental to an act passed at the present session of the General Assembly, to dispose of the forfeited lands in the Hiwassee District.
1831	Chapter 38	Whitney 424-425	An act concerning Indian Reservations in the Hiwassee District.

Date	Chapter	Source	Legislative Act
1831	Chapter 39	Whitney 425-426	An act to extend the provisions of an act, entitled, "An act concerning the Register of the Hiwassee District."
1833	Chapter 8	Whitney 426	An act giving further time to the enterers and purchasers of land in the Hiwassee District to obtain their grants.
1833	Chapter 298	Whitney 426-427	An act authorizing the entry of land lying north of Tennessee River within the Hiwassee District, in the entry takers' office of Blount County, and for other purposes.
1835	Chapter 32	Whitney 427	An act giving further time to the purchasers and enterers of land in the Hiwassee District to obtain their grants.
1838	Resolution No. 11	Whitney 427	Resolution directory to the surveyor of the Hiwassee District, and to the entry taker of the Ocoee District.
1839	Chapter 46	Whitney 428	An act to authorize the issuance of grants in certain cases.
1840	Chapter 74	Whitney 428	An act giving further time for obtaining grants in the Hiwassee district.
1840	Chapter 130	Whitney 428-430	An act for the relief of certain purchasers and assignees of purchasers of reservations in the Hiwassee District. Passed Jan. 29.
1841	Chapter 7	Whitney 430	An act giving further time for obtaining grants in the Hiwassee and Ocoee District.
1842	Chapter 64	Whitney 430	An act giving further time for obtaining grants in the Hiwassee and Ocoee Districts.
1842	Chapter 127	Whitney 430-431	An act to repeal a resolution directory to the surveyor of the Hiwassee District, and to the entry taker of the Ocoee District. Passed Jan. 20.
1844	Chapter 166	Whitney 431	An act to revive for a limited time, the 40th chapter of the Public Acts of 1829.
1850	Chapter 19	Whitney 431	An act giving further time for obtaining grants in the Hiwassee District.
1850	Chapter 183	Whitney 431-432	An act to abolish the office of entry taker of the Hiwassee District.
1854	Chapter 25	Whitney 432	An act to authorize the entry of any vacant land in the Hiwassee River.
1855	Resolution No. 14	Whitney 432	A Resolution for the relief of the people of the first fractional township, first range east of the meridian, in the Hiwassee District.
1856	Resolution No. 20	Whitney 432-433	Resolution in relation to school lands in the Hiwassee District.
1860	Resolution No. 32	Whitney 433-434	Joint resolutions in regard to school lands.
1871	Chapter 45	Whitney 434	An act for the benefit of persons who have lost their grants or deeds of conveyance to their lands in the Ocoee District.
1875	Chapter 20	Whitney 434	An act to amend an act, entitled, "Act for the benefit of persons who have lost their grants or deeds of conveyance to their lands in the Ocoee District."
1889	Resolution No. 19	Whitney 434-435	Pertaining to the boundary line between the Hiwassee and Ocoee Land Districts.

OCOEE DISTRICT

Date	Chapter	Source	Legislative Act
1836	Chapter 2	Whitney 436-439	An act to provide for the survey of lands ceded to the United States by the Cherokee Nation of Indians within the State of Tennessee, by the treaty of the 23d day of May, 1836.
1837	Chapter 2	Whitney 440-447	An act to dispose of the lands in the Ocoee District.
1837	Chapter 27	Whitney 447	An act to establish a register's office in the Ocoee District.
1838	Chapter 196	Whitney 447-448	An act prescribing certain duties of the entry taker of the Ocoee District.
1838	Chapter 238	Whitney 448-449	An act to dispose of the gold lands in the Ocoee District.
1838	Resolution No. 11	Whitney 449	Resolution directory to the Surveyor of the Hiwassee District, and to the entry taker of the Ocoee District.
1839	Chapter 8	Whitney 449-451	An act to amend an act entitled "An act to dispose of the lands in the Ocoee District, passed 29 Nov 1837."
1840	Chapter 58	Whitney 451-452	An act to provide for the correction of the survey of range 4, west of the basis line in the Ocoee District.
1840	Chapter 71	Whitney 452-453	An act for the relief of such persons as made improvements upon school sections, in the Ocoee District.

Date	Chapter	Source	Legislative Act
1840	Chapter 83	Whitney 453-454	An act to suspend the entry of lands in the Ocoee District.
1840	Chapter 113	Whitney 454-455	An act to encourage the manufacture of iron in the Ocoee District.
1840	Chapter 123	Whitney 455-456	An act to authorize the entry taker of the Ocoee District to correct mistakes and refund money.
1840	Chapter 127	Whitney 456	An act for the relief of certain persons that have entered lands in the Ocoee District that the State cannot make titles to.
1840	Chapter 138	Whitney 456-457	An act to appropriate the school lands in the Ocoee District, in the counties of Meigs, Hamilton and Marion, to the use of schools for the instruction of children therein.
1840	Chapter 153	Whitney 457	An act for the relief of the heirs of the occupants in the Ocoee District.
1841	Chapter 7	Whitney 457	An act giving further time for obtaining grants in the Hiwassee and Ocoee Districts.
1842	Chapter 70	Whitney 457	An act relating to lands in the Ocoee District and the locations of entry for the same.
1842	Chapter 99	Whitney 457-458	An act to amend an act entitled "An act to dispose of the lands in the Ocoee District," passed the 28th of November 1839, chapter 8.
1842	Chapter 170	Whitney 458-459	An act for the correction of certain mistakes in the entry of lands in the Ocoee District, and for other purposes.
1842	Chapter 184	Whitney 459-460	An act to authorize and require the entry taker of the Ocoee District to refund money in certain cases.
1841	Chapter 93	Whitney 460-461	An act to correct mistakes in entering lands in the Ocoee District, and for other purposes.
1844	Chapter 127	Whitney 461	An act to repeal a resolution directory to the Surveyor of the Hiwassee District and to the entry taker of the Ocoee District.
1844	Chapter 138	Whitney 461-462	An act to authorize and require the entry taker of the Ocoee District to refund money in certain cases.
1848	Chapter 211	Whitney 462-463	An act to provide for surveying certain range and section lines in the counties of Obion and Dyer.
1850	Chapter 19	Whitney 464	An act giving further time for obtaining grants in the Hiwassee and Ocoee Districts.
1850	Chapter 183	Whitney 464	An act to abolish the office of entry taker of the Hiwassee District.
1854	Chapter 22	Whitney 464	An act to dispose of any vacant lands in the Ocoee District.
1856	Resolution No. 20	Whitney 464	Resolution in relation to school lands in the Hiwassee District.
1867	Chapter 23	Whitney 464-465	An act for the relief of B. F. Dugger.
1871	Chapter 45	Whitney 465-466	An act for the benefit of persons who have lost their grants or deeds of conveyance to their lands in the Ocoee District.
1875	Chapter 20	Whitney 466	An act to amend an act, entitled, "An act for the benefit of persons who have lost their grants or deeds of conveyance to their lands in the Ocoee District," passed January 14, 1871.
1877	Chapter 127	Whitney 466-467	An act to authorize the citizens or school commissioners, or both, of the third fractional township, north, fifth range, east of the meridian, Ocoee District, Tennessee, to lease the school lands in said township for mining purposes.
1889	Resolution No. 19	Whitney 467	Boundary between Hiwassee and Ocoee Districts.

School Lands

Date	Chapter	Source	Legislative Act
1813	Chapter 106	Whitney 468-469	An act concerning college and academy money.
1813	Chapter 116	Whitney 470-472	An act to provide for the better disposal of school lands in this State, and to repeal an act therein mentioned.
1817	Chapter 125	Whitney 473-474	An act to provide for leasing school lands, and for other purposes.
1817	Chapter 187	Whitney 474-475	An act providing for the laying off school lands in the county of Bledsoe.
1819	Chapter 66	Whitney 475-476	An act making provision for surveying the school lands within the State of Tennessee, and for the issuance of grants thereon.
1819	Chapter 75	Whitney 476	An act to repeal the second section of an act passed the 5th day of November 1817, entitled, "An act appointing additional trustees to Quincy

Earliest Tennessee Land Laws

Date	Chapter	Source	Legislative Act
			Adams Academy, in Warren County, and for other purposes."
1820	Chapter 23	Whitney 476-477	An act to amend an act passed at Knoxville, the 24th day of November, 1817, entitled, "An act to provide for leasing school lands, and for other purposes."
1821	Chapter 67	Whitney 477-478	An act concerning school lands.
1822	Chapter 3	Whitney 480-484	An act concerning certain lands claimed by the Trustees of the University of North Carolina.
1822	Chapter 30	Whitney 484	An act concerning school lands.
1822	Chapter 93	Whitney 485	An act concerning school lands in Marion County.
1823	Chapter 6	Whitney 486	An act concerning schools.
1823	Chapter 30	Whitney 486	An act for the relief of the citizens residing in the district of country south of French Broad and Holston, and between the rivers Big Pigeon and Tennessee, and to appropriate the moneys due from said citizens for their lands.
1825	Chapter 26	Whitney 486-487	An act to authorize the Secretary of State to give transcripts from the general plan now in his office, of the First, Second and Third Surveyprs' Districts.
1825	Chapter 39	Whitney 487-488	An act to settle the claims of North Carolina, and for the benefit of the occupants of the Western District.
1825	Chapter 73	Whitney 492-493	An Act supplemental to an act, entitled, "An act to settle the claims of North Carolina, and for the benefit of the occupants of the Wester District." Passed at the present session of the General Assembly.
1825	Chapter 74	Whitney 493-494	An act directing the disposal of academy moneys, and the funding the same.
1825	Chapter 76	Whitney 494-495	An act to apportion the moneys arising from the entering of the land north and east of the Congressional Line.
1826	Chapter 85	Whitney 495-497	An act to provide for the sale of the lands which have been reserved for use of common schools, and apportion moneys equally amongst the several counties in this State.
1826	Chapter 8	Whitney 496-497	An act directing the collection of academy moneys loaned by the Treasurers.
1826	Chapter 39	Whitney 501	An act for the benefit of common schools.
1826	Chapter 34	Whitney 499	An act to amend an act, entitled "An act supplemental to an act entitled, 'An act to settle the claims of North Carolina, and for the benefit of the occupants of the Western District."
1826	Chapter 35	Whitney 499-501	An act to suspend the sale of the school lands and collect the rents.
1826	Chapter 39	Whitney 500	An act for the benefit of common schools.
1827	Chapter 11	Whitney 501	An act authorizing the Register of East Tennessee to issue copies of Treasurers' certificates for land sold at the Hiwassee land sales.
1827	Chapter 64	Whitney 501-502	An act appropriating a fund for the support of common schools in the State of Tennessee.
1827	Chapter 77	Whitney 503	An act to provide for improvements made upon school lands.
1827	Chapter 82	Whitney 503	An act for the relief of the citizens south of French Broad and Holston.
1829	Chapter 47	Whitney 504	An act to settle a controversy between the colleges and academies and the citizens south of Fren Broad and Holston, and west of Big Pigeon Rivers.
1829	Chapter 54	Whitney 504	An act for the benefit of common schools.
1829	Chapter 67	Whitney 504	An act to make distribution of the academy fund amongst the academies of this State.
1829	Chapter 92	Whitney 505	An act for the benefit of the academies in this State.
1829	Chapter 97	Whitney 505	An act to authorize the Treasurers of East and West Tennessee to adjudicate certain claims.
1831	Chapter 15	Whitney 505-506	An act prviding for the leasing of lands which have been set apart for common schools, and for the keeping of common English schools on the same in Middle Tennessee.

Year	Chapter	Whitney	Description
1831	Chapter 17	Whitney 50	An act supplemental to an act entitled an act. "Providing for the leasing of lands which have been set apart for the use of common schools, and for the keeping of common English school on the same in Middle Tennessee,"
1831	Chapter 34	Whitney 508	An act to appropriate the school lands in the Hiwassee District to the use of schools for the instruction of children therein.
1831	Chapter 34	Whitney 508	An act supplemental to an act passed at the present session of the General Assembly entitled, "An act to appropriate the school lands in the Hiwassee District, to the use of schools for the instruction of children therein.
1833	Chapter 42	Whitney 508	An act to authorize persons to have land set apart for the erection of school houses and meeting houses in the counties named therein.
1834	Chapter 104	Whitney 508-509	An act to authorize the sale of the common school lands in the State of Tennessee, at the wish of the people of the different townships where they may be situated.
1838	Chapter 107	Whitney 509	An act to aid in the establishment of a system of education.
1838	Chapter 196	Whitney 509	An act prescribing certain duties of the entry taker of the Ocoee District.
1840	Chapter 71	Whitney 510	An act for the relief of such persons as made improvements upon school sections in the Ocoee District.
1840	Chapter 183	Whitney 510	An act to appropriate the school lands in the Ocoee District in the counties of Meigs, Hamilton and Marion, to the use of schools for the instruction of children therein.
1845	Chapter 60	Whitney 510	An act to recover the possession of school lands which may be adversely holden in any of the counties in this State.
1846	Chapter 121	Whitney 510-513	An act to amend an act, entitled "An act to authorize the sale of the common school lands in the State of Tennessee, at the wish of the people of the different townships where they may be situated."
1852	Chapter 120	Whitney 513	An act to authorize the sale of escheated lands and vested in common schools in the State of Tennessee, and for other purposes.
1852	Chapter 296	Whitney 514	An act to provide for the fractional townships in Rutherford, Williamson and Marshall Counties, and for other purposes.
1852	Resolution No. 2	Whitney 514	A Resolution for the relief of the people of the Seventeenth District of Monroe and Blount Counties.
1854	Chapter 46	Whitney 514-515	An act for the relief of purchasers of school land, and for other purposes.
1854	Chapter 316	Whitney 515	An act to correct errors in the sale of school lands in this State.
1856	Resolution No. 20	Whitney 515	Resolution in relation to school lands in the Hiwassee District.
1856	Resolution No. 25	Whitney 515	A Resolution in relation to school lands in White and other counties.
1860	Resolution No. 32	Whitney 516	Joint resolutions in regard to school lands.
1865	Chapter 22	Whitney 516	An act accepting on the part of the State of Tennessee a grant of lands made by the United States to the several States and Territories may provide colleges for the benefit of agriculture and the mecanic arts.
1866	Resolution No. 51	Whitney 516-517	Joint resolution directory to our Representatives in Congress.
1868	Chapter 32	Whitney 517-518	An act accepting the donation of lands to Tennessee, for the endowment of Agricultural Colleges.
1869	Chapter 12	Whitney 518	An act to establish the Tennessee Agricultural College.
1870	Chapter 101	Whitney 518	An act to secure the fund arising from the sale of the school land under the acts passed January 15, 1844 and January 23, 1846, entitled, "An act to authorize the sale of the common school lands in the State of Tennessee, at the wish of the people of the different townships where they may be situated, and to perfect titles to the purchasers of the same."
1875	Chapter 131	Whitney 519	An act to authorize the sale of the common school land in the county of Hardin.
1877	Chapter 127	Whitney 519	An act to authorize citizens to authorize citizens or school commissioners, or both, of the third fractional township, north, fifth range, east of the meridian, Ocoee District. Tennessee, to lease the school lands in said township for mining purposes.
1889	Chapter 44	Whitney 518	An act to authorize the lease of certain school lands in the State for mining purposes and to protect the same from waste.

PUBLIC LANDS

Date	Chapter	Source	Legislative Act
1806	Chapter 10	Whitney 521	An act to ratify and confirm an act of the Congress of the United States of America entitled, "An act to authorize the State of Tennessee to issue grants and perfect titles to certain lands therein described, and to settle the claims to the vacant and unappropriated lands within the same."
1818	Chapter 35	Whitney 521-522	An act supplementary to the act, entitled "An act to authorize the State of Tennessee to issue grants and perfect titles to certain lands therein described, and to settle the claims to the vacant and unappropriated land within the same," passed the eighteenth of April, one thousand eight hundred and six.
1838	Resolution No. 1	Whitney 522-530	The Memorial of the General Assembly of the State of Tennessee, to the Senate and House of Representatives of the United States in Congress assembled.
1841	Chapter 7	Whitney 530	An act to amend an act entitled, "An act to authorize the State of Tennessee to issue grants and perfect titles to certain lands therein described, and to settle the claims to the vacant and unappropriated lands within the same," passed the eighteenth day of April, one thousand eight hundred and six.
1841	Resolution No. 36	Whitney 530-531	A Memorial of the Legislature of Tennessee to the Congress of the United States.
1845	Memorial No. 1	Whitney 531	Memorial of the General Assembly of the State of Tennessee, to the Senate and House of Representatives in Congress assembled.
1846	Chapter 92	Whitney 531	An act to surrender to the State of Tennessee all title the United States have to lands in Tennessee, south and west of the line commonly called the Congressional Reservation Line, and to release to said State the proceeds of such lands as may have been sold by the State of Tennessee, as the agent of the United States.
1849	Resolution No. 33	Whitney 531-532	Senators and Representatives in the Congress to procure the passage of a law giving to each commissioned officer and private, who served in the war of 1812, and who served in the Florida war...a land certificate or warrant for one hundred and sixty acres of land, to be at any time located upon any public or unappropriated lands, now or that may hereafter come into the marked.
1850	Chapter 85	Whitney 532-534	An act granting bounty land to certain officers and soldiers who have been engaged in the military service of the United States.
1852	Resolution No. 36	Whitney 534	A resolution instructing our Senators in Congress and requesting our Representatives to use all laudable means to secure the passage of a law making certain disposition of our public lands.
1852	Memorial No. 3	Whitney 534-535	Memorial to the Congress of the United States in relation to bounty lands.
1854	Chapter 114	Whitney 535-536	An act to extend the benefits of an act of Congress, passed on the 28th of September 1850, to the officers and soldiers who have been engaged in the military service of the United States, within the State of Tennessee.
1836	Resolution No. 19	Whitney 536	Joint resolution and memorial on the subject of bounty lands to the volunteers of 1836.
1858	Resolution No. 9	Whitney 536-537	Joint resolution requesting our Senators and Representatives in Congress to aid in the passage of a law giving to the old soldiers in the War of 1812, six hundred and forty acres of the public domain.
1866	Resolution No. 73	Whitney 537	Joint resolution requesting Congress to grant to the State of Tennessee per pro rata of the public lands.
1867	Chapter 44	Whitney 537-538	An act to cede to the United States the jurisdiction over the National Cemeteries in this State, and to protect the same.
1868	Chapter 28	Whitney 538-539	An act to cede to the United States exclusive jurisdiction of all the lands upon which public buildings are erected.
1887	Resolution No. 35	Whitney 539	For the sale of lands belonging [to] the State.

Map from J. W. Powell, *Bureau of American Ethnology Part II, 18th Annual Report* (Washington: Government Printing Office, 1899.)

MAP SHOWING TENNESSEE INDIAN LAND TREATIES

[Map # 3]	18 October 1770	Treaty of Lochabar [not numbered on map]	
[Map # 55]	17 March 1775	Transylvania Purchase [not numbered on map]	
[Map # 64]	28 November 1785	Hopewell Treaty	
	23 July 1805	Treaty held in Chickasaw Country	
	11 September 1807	Treaty held at Chickasaw Old Fields	
	24 October 1801	Treaty held at Chickasaw Bluffs - Lay out road only	
[Map # 57]	17 December 1801	Treaty held at Fort Adams, MS - Lay out road only	
[Map # 64]	25 October 1805	Treaty held at Tellico, Tennessee	
[Map # 8]	7 January 1806	Treaty held at Washington, D. C.	
[Map # 42]	2 July 1791	Treaty held on Holston River near mouth of French Broad	
[Map # 105,	2 October 1798	Treaty held at Tellico, Tennessee	
107, 108, & 109]	25 October 1805	Treaty held at Tellico, Tennessee	

[Map # 58 & 59]	27 October 1805	Treaty held at Tellico, Tennessee
[Map # 65]	7 January 1806	Treaty held at Washington, D. C.
[Map # 80]	30 September 1816	Treaty held at Chickasaw Council House
[Map # 84]	8 July 1817	Treaty held at Cherokee Agency, Tennessee
[Map # 100]	18 October 1818	Treaty held at Old Town, Mississippi
[Map # 178]	20 October 1832	Treaty held at Council House on Pontitock Creek, MS
[Map # 101, 102,	27 February 1819	Treaty held at Washington, D. C.
& 103]		
[Map # 203]	29 December 1835	Treaty held at Echota, Georgia

Earliest Tennessee Land Treaties

Map

Indian Land Cessions Applicable to Tennessee

Treaty of Lochabar [Not numbered on the map]

18 October 1770, held at Lochabar, South Carolina.

It conveyed lands in Virginia, West Virginia, Kentucky, and Tennessee. A portion of the lands included in Tennessee were in the extreme northeastern corner of the state, in what later became Washington and Sullivan Counties. This land and a portion of the Transylvania Purchase overlap.[1]

Transylvania Purchase [Not numbered on the map]

17 March 1775. Richard Henderson and Associates organized as Transylvania Company, purchased all the lands lying between the Kentucky, Ohio, and Cumberland Rivers, and extending eastward along the north bank of the Holston to the point where it intersects the Virginia line; thence westwardly along that line to the western boundary of the Lochabar Purchase, and north along that boundary to its intersection with Powell Mountain. The treaty embraced two deeds--known as the "Path Deed" and the "Great Grant." The legality of this purchase was not admitted by Virginia or North Carolina but the purchase of the Transylvania purchase served to extinguish claims of the Cherokees.[2]

---

[1]William Robertson Garrett and Albert Virgil Goodpasture, *History of Tennessee, Its People and Its Institutions* (Nashville, TN: Brandon Printing Co., 1900), page 131. (Hereafter cited as Garrett and Goodpasture, *History of Tennessee*.)

[2]Garrett and Goodpasture, *History of Tennessee*, page 131.

Earliest Tennessee Land Treaties

Treaty Held at Hopewell [Map 3].

28 Nov 1785, held at Hopewell on Keowee river, South Carolina, with Cherokee..... **Article 4** fixes the following boundary between the hunting grounds of the Cherokee and the lands of the U. S., viz: Beginning at the mouth of Duck river on the Tennessee; thence running NE to the ridge dividing the waters running into Cumberland from those running into the Tennessee; thence eastwardly along the said ridge to a NE line to be run, which shall strike the river Cumberland 40 miles above Nashville; thence along the said line to the river; thence up the said river to the ford where the Kentucky road crosses the river; thence to Campbell's line, near Cumberland Gap; thence to the mouth of Claud's creek on Holstein; thence to the Chimney Top mountain; thence to Camp creek near the mouth of Big Limestone on Nolichuckey; thence a southerly course 6 miles to a mountain; thence S. to the North Carolina line; thence to the South Carolina Indian boundary and along the same SW over the top of the Oconee mountain till it shall strike Tugaloo river; thence a direct line to the top of the Currohee mountain; thence to the head of the S. Fork of Oconee river.[3]

Treaty held in Chickasaw country [Map No. 55]

23 July 1805, held in Chickasaw country....The Chickasaws cede to the U. S. the following tract of country: Beginning on the left bank of the Ohio at the point where the present Indian boundary adjoins the same; thence

---

[3]J. W Powell, *Bureau of American Ethnology* Part II, 18th Annual Report, (Washington: Government Printing Office, 1899), pages 648 and 649.

down the left bank of the Ohio to the Tennessee river; thence up the main channel of the Tennessee river to the mount of Duck river; thence up the left bank of the Duck river to the Columbian highway or road leading from Nashville to Natchez; thence along the said road to the ridge dividing the waters running into Duck river from those running into Buffaloe river; thence eastwardly along said ridge to the great ridge dividing the waters running into the main Tennessee river from those running into Buffaloe river near the main source of Buffaloe river; thence in a direct line to the great Tennessee river near the Chickasaw Old Fields, or eastern point of the Chickasaw claim on that river; thence northwardly to the great ridge dividing the waters running into the Tennessee from those running into Cumberland river, so as to include all the waters running into Elk river; thence along the top of the said great ridge to the place of beginning.[4]

TREATY HELD AT CHICKASAW OLD FIELDS - CHEROKEE [MAP NO. 64]

11 Sep 1807, held at Chickasaw Old Fields....This treaty is explanatory and in elucidation of the cession made by article 1 of the treaty of Jan 7, 1806, and declares that the eastern boundary of said ceded tract shall be limited by a line so to be run from the upper end of the Chickasaw Old Fields, a little above the upper point of an island called Chickasaw island, as will most directly intersect the first waters of Elk river; thence carried to the Great Cumberland mountain in which the waters of Elk river have their source; then along the margin of said mountain until it shall intersect lands heretofore ceded to the U. S., at the said Tennessee ridge.[5]

TREATY HELD AT CHICKASAW BLUFFS, TENNESSEE

24 Oct 1801, held at Chickasaw Bluffs, Tennessee....The Chickasaw nation cedes to the U. S. the right to lay out and open a road through their land between the settlements of Mero district, Tennessee, and those of Natchez, Mississippi, provided that the necessary ferries over streams crossed by said road shall be the property of the Chickasaw nation.[6]

TREATY HELD AT FORT ADAMS, MISSISSIPPI

17 Dec 1801, held at Fort Adams, Mississippi.... The Choctaw nation, cedes to the U. S. the right to lay out and open a wagon road through their lands, commencing at the northern extremity of the settlements of Mississippi territory and from thence by such route as may be selected until it strikes the lands claimed by the Chickasaw nation. The Choctaws and the U. S. mutually agree that the old line of demarcation heretofore established by and between the officers of his Brittanic Majesty and the Choctaw nation, which runs in a parallel direction with the Mississippi river and eastward thereof, shall be retraced and plainly marked, and that the said line shall be the boundary between the settlements of Mississippi territory and the Choctaw nation. And the nation relinquishes to the U. S. all claim to land lying between said line and the Mississippi river bounded S. by the 31 degree of N latitude and N by the Yazoo river where the said line strikes the same.[7]

TREATY HELD AT TELLICO, TENNESSEE - CHEROKEE [MAP NO. 57]

25 Oct 1805, held at Tellico, Tennessee. The Cherokees cede to the U. S. all the land previously claimed by them, lying N of the following boundary line: Beginning at the mouth of Duck river; thence up the same

---

[4]Powell, *Bureau of American Ethnology*, pages 668 and 669.

[5]Powell, *Bureau of American Ethnology*, pages 672 and 673.

[6]Powell, *Bureau of American Ethnology*, pages 660 and 661.

[7]Powell, *Bureau of American Ethnology*, pages 660 and 661.

into the Tennessee; thence up the river Clinch to Campbell's line, and along the same to the top of Cumberland mountain; thence a direct line to the Cum-berland river where the Kentucky road crosses it; thence down the Cumberland river to a point from which a SW line will strike the ridge which divides the waters of Cumberland from those of Duck river, 40 miles above Nashville; thence down said ridge to a point from whence a SW line will strike the mouth of the Duck river.

The Cherokee cede and relinquish to the U. S. All land to the right of the line described and beginning as aforesaid.[10]

TREATY HELD AT TELLICO, TENNESSEE [MAP 42]

2 Oct 1798, held at Tellico, Tennessee....The Cherokee nation cedes to the U. S. all lands within the following boundaries, viz: From a point on the Tennessee river below Tellico Block House, called the Wild-Cat Rock, in a direct line to the Militia spring near the Maryville road leading from Tellico; from the said spring to the Chillhowie mountain by a line so to be run as will leave all the farms on Nine Mile creek to the northward and eastward of it, and to be continued along Chillhowie mountain until it strikes Hawkins's line; thence along the said line to the great Iron mountain; and from the top of which a line to be continued in a southeastwardly course to where the most southwardly branch of Little river crosses the divisional line to Tuggaloe river.

Also from the place of beginning, the Wild Cat Rock, down the N. E. margin of the Tennessee river (not including islands) to a point or place 1 mile above the junction of that river with the Clinch, and from thence by a line to be drawn in a right angle until it intersects Hawkins's line leading from Clinch; thence down from Clinch; thence down the said line to the river Clinch; thence up the said river to its junction with Emmery's river; and thence up Emmery's river to the foot of Cumberland mountain; from

---

[10]Powell, *Bureau of American Ethnology*, pages 660 and 661.

to the junction of the fork at the head of which Fort Nash stood, with the main south fork; thence a direct course to a point on the Tennessee river bank opposite the mouth of Hiwassa river—if the line from Hiwassa should leave out Field's settlement, it is to be marked round his improvement and then continued the straight course; thence up the middle of Tennessee river (but leaving all islands to the Cherokees) to the mouth of Clinch river; thence up Clinch river to the former boundary line agreed upon with the Cherokee.[8]

TREATY HELD AT WASHINGTON, D. C. - CHEROKEE [MAP No. 64]

7 Jan 1806, held at Washington, D. C..... The Cherokees cede to the U. S. all claim to all that tract of country lying to the northward of the river Tennessee and westward of a line to be run from the upper part of the Chickasaw Old Fields, at the upper point of an island called Chickasaw island, on said river to the most easterly head waters of that branch of Tennessee river called Duck river.[9]

TREATY HELD ON HOLSTON RIVER NEAR MOUTH OF FRENCH BROAD [MAP No. 8]

2 July 1791, held on Holston river, near the mouth of French Broad with Cherokee..... **Article 4** provides that the boundary between the U. S. and the Cherokee nation shall begin at the top of the Currahee mountain where the Creek line passes it; thence a direct line to Tugelo river; thence NE to the Ocunna mountain and over the same along the South-Carolina Indian boundary to the North Carolina boundary; thence N to a point from which a line is to be extended to the river Clinch, that shall pass the Holston at the ridge which divides the waters running into Little river from those running

---

[8]Powell, *Bureau of American Ethnology*, pages 672 and 673..

[9]Powell, *Bureau of American Ethnology*, pages 652 and 653.

thence a line to be drawn northeastwardly, along the foot of the mountain, until it intersects with Campbell's line.[11]

TREATY HELD AT TELLICO, TENNESSEE - CHEROKEE [MAP NOS. 105, 107, 108 & 109]

25 Oct 1805, held at Tellico, Tennessee.... From the foregoing cession the Cherokees reserve a small tract lying at and below the mouth of Clinch river and extending from said mouth down the Tennessee river to a notable rock on the N bank of the Tennessee, in view from Southwest Point; thence a course at right angles with the river to the   road; thence eastwardly along the same to the bank of Clinch river, so as to secure the same to the Cherokees ferry landing to the Cherokees up to the first hill, and down the same to the mouth thereof.

The Cherokee also reserve a tract of 1 square mile at the foot of Cumberland mountain, at or near the Turnpike gate.

It is further provided that, whereas, owing to the above described cession and other circumstances, the site of the garrisons at Southwest Point and Tellico have become incon-venient and unsuitable places for the accommodation of the Cherokees, and it may become expedient to remove said garrisons and factory to a more suitable place, that a tract of 3 square miles is reserved for the particular disposal of the U. S. on the N bank of the Tennessee, opposite to and *below* the mouth of Hiwassa.

It is further provided that, in addition to the roads already established, the citizens of the U. S. shall have the free and unmolested use of the two following roads; One to proceed from some convenient place near the head of Stone's river and fall into the Georgia road at a suitable place toward the south-ern frontier of the Cherokees; the other to proceed from the neighborhood of Franklin, on Big Harpath, and, crossing the Tennessee at or near the Muscle-shoals, to pursue the nearest and best

---

[11]Powell, *Bureau of American Ethnology,* pages 670 and 671.

way to the Tombigbee settlements.[12]

TREATY HELD AT TELLICO, TENNESSEE - CHEROKEE [MAP NOS. 58 & 59]

27 Oct 1805, held at Tellico, Tennessee.... The Cherokees cede to the U. S. the section of land at Southwest Point occupied by the U. S. garrison and extending to Kingston, reserving to themselves the ferries.

The Cherokees also cede to the U. S. the first island in Tennessee river above the mouth of Clinch river.

The Cherokees also agree that citizens of the U. S. shall have, so far as it going through their country, the free use of a road leading from Tellico to Tombigbe.

TREATY HELD AT WASHINGTON, D. C. - CHEROKEE [MAP NO. 65]

7 Jan 1806, held at Washington, D. C.....The Cherokees also cede to the U. S. All right or claim to what is called the Long island in Holston river.[13]

TREATY HELD AT CHICKASAW COUNCIL HOUSE - CHICKASAW [MAP NO. 80]

[This cession overlaps the Cherokee cession of Sept 14, 1816.]

30 Sept 1816, held at Chickasaw council house..... The Chickasaw nation cede to the U. S. (with the exception of such reservations as shall hereafter be specified) all right or title to lands on the N side of Tennessee river.

The Chickasaws also relinquish all claim to territory on the S side of Tennessee river and E of a line commencing at the mouth of Caney creek and running up the same to its source; thence a due S course to the Ridge path, commonly called Gaines' road; along said road southwestwardly to

---

[12]Powell, *Bureau of American Ethnology,* pages 670 and 671.

[13]Powell, *Bureau of American Ethnology,* pages 674 and 675.

a point on Tombigby river, called Cotton Gin Port, and down the W bank of the Tombigby to the Choctaw boundary.[14]

Jan 7, 1806.[15]

TREATY HELD AT CHEROKEE AGENCY, TENNESSEE -CHEROKEE [MAP No. 84]

8 July 1817, held at Cherokee agency, Tennessee.....The chiefs, headmen, and warriors of the whole Cherokee nation cede to the U. S. all the lands lying N and E of the following boundaries: Beginning at the High Shoals of the Appalachy river and running thence along the boundary line between the Creek and Cherokee nations westwardly to the Chatahouchy river; thence up the Chatahouchy river to the mouth of Souque creek; thence continuing with the general course of the river until it reaches the Indian boundary line, and should it strike the Turrurar river, thence with its meanders down said river to its mouth in part of the proportion of land in the Cherokee nation east of the Mississippi, to which those now on the Arkansas and those about to remove there are justly entitled.

Said nation also cede to the U. S. All the lands lying N and W of the following boundary lines: Beginning at the Indian boundary line that runs from the N bank of the Tennessee river opposite to the mouth of Hywassee river at a point on the top of Walden's ridge, where it divides the waters of Tennessee river from those of Sequatchie river; thence along said ridge southwardly to the bank of the Tennessee river at a point near to a place called the Negro Sugar Camp, opposite to the upper end of the first island above Running Water Town; thence westwardly a straight line to the mouth of Little Sequatchie river; thence up said river to its main fork; thence up its northernmost fork to its source, and thence due W to the Indian boundary line.

The Cherokee nation also cede to the U. S. all right to the reservations made to Doublehead and others by the treaty made at Washington city,

TREATY HELD AT OLD TOWN, MISSISSIPPI - CHICKASAW - [MAP No. 100]

19 Oct 1818, held at Old Town, Mississippi.....The Chickasaw nation cede to the U. S. (with the exception of the reservations hereinafter described) all claim to land lying N of the S boundary of the State of Tennessee, which is bounded S by the thirty-fifth degree of N. Latitude, and which land hereby ceded lies within the following boundary, viz: Beginning on the Tennessee river, about 35 miles by water below Col. George Colbert's ferry, where the thirty-fifth degree of latitude to where it cuts the Mississippi river at or near the Chickasaw Bluffs; thence up the said Mississippi river to the mouth of the Ohio; thence up the Ohio river to the mouth of Tennessee river; thence up the Tennessee river to the place of beginning.

It is agreed that a tract of land containing 4 miles square, to include a salt lick or springs on or near the river Sandy, a branch of the Tennessee river, and within the land above ceded, be reserved and laid off in a square or oblong so as to include the best timber.

It is agreed that there shall be paid to Oppassantubby, a principal chief of the Chickasaw nation, within 60 days after the ratification of this treaty, the sum of $500 as a full compensation for the reservation of 2 miles square on the N side of Tennessee river, secured to him and his heirs by treaty with the Chickasaw nation, Sept 20, 1816.

It is agreed that the reservations made to George and Levi Colbert by the treaty of Sept 20, 1816, shall inure to the sole use of the said George and Levi Colbert, their heirs and assigns forever, with their butts and bounds as defined by said treaty and agreeable to the marks and boundaries as laid off and marked by the surveyor of the U. S. **[See Map No. 81]**

It is agreed that the reservation secured to John McCleish on the N.

[14]Powell, *Bureau of American Ethnology*, pages 682 and 683.

[15]Powell, *Bureau of American Ethnology*, pages 684 and 685.

Side of Tennessee river by the treaty of Sept 20, 1816, in consequence of his having been raised in the State of Tennessee and marrying a white woman, shall inure to the sole use of said John McCleish, his heirs and assigns, forever.[16]

TREATY HELD AT COUNCIL HOUSE ON PONTITOCK CREEK, CHICKASAW NATION, MISSISSIPPI - CHICKASAW [MAP NO. 178]

20 Oct 1832, held at Council house on Pontitock creek, Chickasaw nation, Mississippi... The Chickasaw nation, finding themselves oppressed in their present situation by being made subject to the laws of the States in which they reside, which laws they can not under-stand, rather than submit to this evil, prefer to seek a home in the West where they may live and be governed by their own laws. Believing they can procure for themselves a home in a country suited to their wants and condition, provided they had the means to pay for the same, they have determined to sell their country and hunt a new home.

Therefore, for the consideration hereinafter expressed, the Chickasaw nation cede to the U. S. all the land which they own on the E. side of the Mississippi river, including all the country where they are present live and occupy.

In order that the Chickasaws by the foregoing cession should not deprive themselves of a comfortable home it is agreed that unless they shall be able to find a suitable home W of the Mississippi, promptly after the ratification of this treaty, they are to select out of the ceded lands reservations for each family as follows: To each single man 21 years of age, 1 section; to each family of 5 or under, 2 sections; to each family over 10, 4 sections; to each family owning 10 or more slaves, 1 section additional, and to each family owning under 10 slaves, one-half section additional.

[16]Powell, *Bureau of American Ethnology*, pages 694 and 795.

It is agreed that the boundary line between the Choctaw and Chickasaw country as formerly owned by them E of the Mississippi, shall be definitely ascertained and established.[17]

TREATY HELD AT WASHINGTON, D. C. - CHEROKEE [MAP NOS. 101, 102 & 103]

27 Feb 1819, held at Washington, D. C.....The Cherokee nation cedes to the U. S. all of their lands lying N. and E. of the following line, viz: Beginning on the Tennessee river at the point where the Cherokee boundary with Madison county, in the Alabama territory, joins the same; thence along the main channel of said river to the mouth of the Highwassee; thence along its main channel to the first hill which closes in on said river, about 2 miles above Highwassee Old Town; thence along the ridge which divides the waters of the Highwassee and Little Tellico to the Tennessee river at Tallassee; thence along the main channel to the junction of the Cowee and Nanteyalee; thence along the ridge in the fork of said river to the top of the Blue Ridge; thence along the Blue Ridge to the Unicoy Turnpike road; thence by a straight line to the nearest main source of the Chestatee; thence along its main channel to the Chatahouchee; and thence to the Creek boundary; it being understood that all the islands in the Chestatee and the parts of the Tennessee and Highwassee (with the exception of Jolly's island in the Tennessee), which constitute a portion of the present boundary, belong to the Cherokees.

[Map No. 104] The Cherokee nation cedes to the U. S. Jolly's island in Tennessee river.

[Map No. 105] Also a small tract lying at and below the mouth of Clinch river, reserved to the former by treaty of Oct 25, 1805.

[Map No. 106] Also in trust, to be sold for the benefit of the Cherokee national school fund, a tract equal to 12 miles square, to be located by

[17]Powell, *Bureau of American Ethnology*, pages 738 and 739.

thence with said line S 50 miles; thence W to the place of beginning, estimated to contain 800,000 acres. But it is expressly understood that if any of the lands assigned the Quapaws shall fall within the aforesaid bounds the same shall be reserved and excepted out of the lands above granted and a pro rata reduction shall be made in the price to be allowed to the U. S. For the same by the Cherokees, which price it is agreed shall be $500,000.

It is agreed that the military reservation at Fort Gibson shall be held by the U. S., but should the U. S. abandon said post and have no further use for the same, it shall revert to the Cherokee nation.

The U. S. agree to extinguish for the benefit of the Cherokees the titles to the reservations within their country made in the Osage treaty of 1825 to certain half breeds.[19]

commencing at the point formed by the intersection of the boundary line of Madison county and the N bank of the Tennessee river; thence along the said line and up the said river 12 miles.

[Map No. 107] Also one section of 1 square mile at the foot of Cumberland mountain, at and near the place where the turnpike gate stands, which was reserved by said nation by treaty of Oct 25, 1805.

[Map No. 108] Also one section of 1 square mile on the N. bank of the Tennessee river, where the Cherokee Talootiske now lives, which was reserved by said nation by treaty of Oct 25, 1805.

[Map No. 109] Also the three other square miles which were reserved by treaty of Oct 25, 1805, for the particular disposal of the U. S. on the N. Bank of the Tennessee, oppo-site to and below the mouth of Hiwassa river.

From the above cession 31 tracts of 640 acres each were reserved for individuals; it was also agreed that every head of an Indian family who would become a citizen of the U. S. should receive 640 acres.[18]

TREATY HELD AT NEW ECHOTA, GEORGIA - CHERO-KEE [MAP NO. 203, SEE ALSO NO. 490]

29 Dec 1835, held at New Echota, Georgia....The Cherokee nation cede to the U. S. All thelands owned, claimed or possessed by them E. Of the Mississippi river, and agree to remove W of that river.

The Cherokees fearing that the land granted to them by the U. S. as described in the treaties of May 6, 1828, and Feb 14, 1833, will prove insufficient for the accommodation of their whole nation, the U. S. therefore agree to convey to the said Indians and their descendants, by patent in fee simple, the following additional tract of land situated between the W line of the state of Missouri and the Osage reservation, beginning at the SE corner of the same and runs N. Along the E line of the Osage lands 50 miles to the NE corner thereof; and thence E to the W line of the state of Missouri;

---

[18]Powell, Bureau of American Ethnology, pages 696 and 697.

[19]Powell, Bureau of American Ethnology, pages 754 and 755.

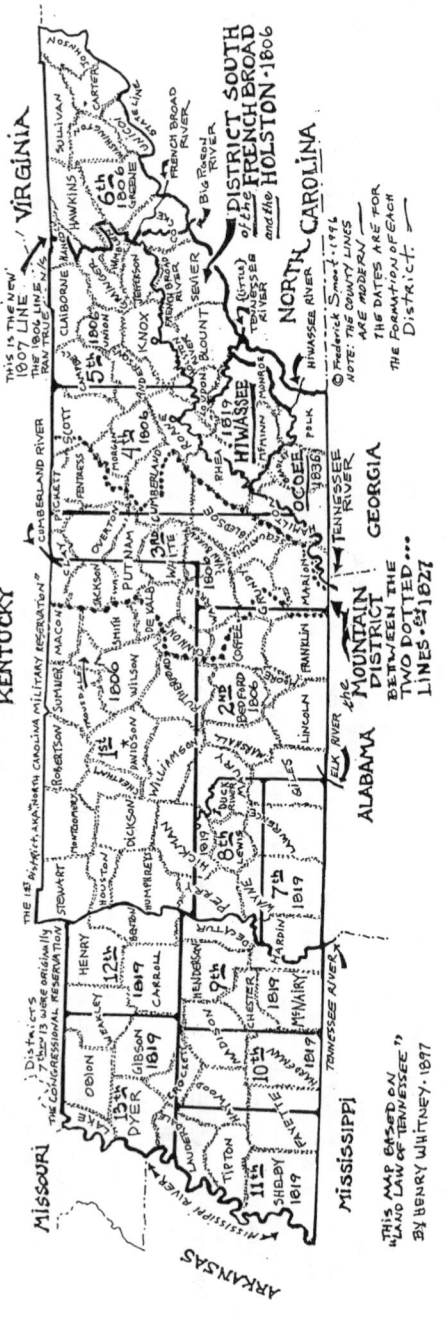

1806, CHAPTER 1, SECTION 3.

The several districts hereinbefore directed to be laid off, shall be bounded and distinguished in the following manner, to wit:

One to be bounded by the lines described in the seventh section of an act of North Carolina, passed on the seventeenth day of May, in the year one thousand seven hundred and eighty-three, entitled, "An act to amend an act, entitled, an act for the relief of the officers and soldiers in the continental line and for other purposes," which shall compose a district, and shall be known and distinguished by the name of the **First District**.

One other district to begin eighteen miles west of the southeast corner of the last mentioned district, to run south according to the true meridian, to the southern boundary of the State, for its eastern boundary, and to be bounded on the west and south by the Congressional Reservation, and on the north and south, by the first district and the boundary of the State; which shall compose one other district, and shall be known and distinguished by the name of the **Second District**.

One other district to begin on the northern boundary of the State, at a point which shall divide by six without a fraction, and which shall be nearest to a point due north of the Flat Rock on the turnpike road, leading from South West Point to Nashville, thence south according to the true meridian to the southern boundary of the State, which shall be its eastern boundary, thence west to be bounded by the two first districts inclusively, which shall compose one other district, and shall be known and distinguished by the name of the **Third District**.

and the three districts as above, shall be attached to the land office of **West Tennessee**.

One other district, to begin at the northeast corner of the last mentioned district, to run east with the north boundary of the State, fifty-four miles, thence south to the southern boundary of the State, or the district south of French Broad and Holston (as the case may be) which inclusively, shall compose one other district, and shall be known and distinguished by the name of the **Fourth District**.

One other district to begin at the northeast corner of the fourth district, to run east with the north boundary of the State forty-eight miles, thence south according to the true meridian, to the district south of French Broad and Holston, which inclusively, shall compose one other district, and shall be known and distinguished by the name of the **Fifth District**.

And one other district, to be bounded by the fifth district on the west, by the Virginia line on the north, and by the district south of French Broad and Holston, and the North Carolina line on the east and southeast, which shall compose one other district, and shall be known and distinguished by the name of the **Sixth District**,

The three last mentioned districts, together with the district south of French Broad and Holston, shall he attached to the land office of East Tennessee.

1819, CHAPTER 1.

AN ACT making provision for the adjudication of North Carolina land claims, and for satisfying the same, by an appropriation of the vacant soil south and west of the Congressional Reservation Line, and for other purposes.

Section 1. Be it enacted, etc., that part of the State usually denominated the Congressional Reservation, shall be divided into seven districts, in each of which one principal surveyor shall be appointed by joint ballot of both houses of the Legislature, whose duty it shall be to engage a sufficient number of skillful surveyors as deputies, who shall be confined to the districts in which they are appointed, and for whose conduct in all points touching his office, the principal surveyor shall be answerable. Each principal shall have authority to frame regulations and instructions for the government of his deputies, to administer the necessary oaths, and to remove them for negligence or misconduct in office; and shall, before he enters upon the duties of his appointment, take and subscribe, before one of the Judges of the Court of Errors and Appeals, or of the Circuit Court, the following oath, to wit:

"I, A, B, do solemnly swear or affirm, that I will faithfully, impartially and justly, perform the duties of my office as principal surveyor, according to law and the best of my skill and judgment SO HELP ME GOD."

And he shall also, before one of the said judges, enter into bond with five sufficient securities, in the sum of fifty thousand dollars, payable to the Governor and his successors in office, for the faithful discharge of the duties imposed on him by law; which bond the said judge shall lodge in the office of the Secretary of State And each deputy shall likewise, before he enters upon the duties of his appointment, take the oath prescribed by his principal, and enter into bond with such security, as his principal shall deem sufficient, for the accurate and faithful discharge of his duty. And each chain carrier shall, before the principal - or deputy surveyor, take an oath, that he will truly and impartially measure every line of which he is a chain carrier, and render a true account thereof to his surveyor.

Section 2. The several districts herein before directed to be laid off, shall be bounded and distinguished in the following manner, to-wit:

one district beginning on the southern boundary line of the State on the Congressional Reservation Line; thence north with the same, to a point equidistant from said southern boundary line, to a point due east from the town of Columbia on said line, and from the point thus ascertained a due west course to the Tennessee River; thence up said river to the southern boundary of the State; thence with the same to the beginning: which shall be called the Seventh District. And the surveyor's office thereof shall be kept at Pulaski. in the County of Giles; Provided, that the Surveyor General s office for the aforesaid district, shall not be opened, nor shall any entry therein be made, for the tract of land granted by the United States, for the town of Pulaski, in Giles County. One other district shall consist of that tract of country, lying south and west of the Congressional Reservation Line, and north of the Seventh District, and east of the Tennessee River; which shall he called the **Eighth District**, and the surveyor's office thereof shall be kept at Columbia in the County of Maury.

One other district to begin thirty-five miles west of the Tennessee River, on the south boundary line of the State; to run north according to the true meridian fifty-five miles for its western boundary; thence east to the Tennessee River; thence up the Tennessee, to the southern boundary of the State, and with said boundary to the beginning; which shall be known and distinguished by the name of the **Ninth District.**

One other district beginning at the southwest corner of the last mentioned, running west with the south boundary line of this State thirty miles; thence north fifty-five miles; thence east to the northwest corner of the aforesaid district; thence south to the beginning, to compose one other district, which shall be known and distinguished by the name of the **Tenth District.**

One other district beginning at the southwest corner of the last mentioned, running thence north fifty-five miles with the west boundary of the last mentioned, to the northwest corner thereof; thence west to the Mississippi; thence down that river to the south boundary of this State; thence east to the beginning, which shall be known and distinguished by the name of the **Eleventh District.**

One other district beginning where, the north boundary line of this State crosses the Tennessee River; thence west with the said north boundary line, thirty-five miles; thence south to the north boundary line of the districts before described; thence east with the said line to the Tennessee River, and down the same to the beginning, which shall be known and distinguished by the name of the **Twelfth District.**

One other district beginning at the southwest corner of the last mentioned; thence running north with the west boundary of the same to the north boundary line of this State; thence west with the same to the Mississippi, thence down said river to the northwest corner of District No. 11; thence east to the beginning; which shall be called and known by the name of the **Thirteenth District.**

All of which districts shall be attached to the **land office of West Tennessee.**